MW01125453

Why Can the Dead Do Such Great Things?

Why Can the Dead Do Such Great Things?

Saints and Worshippers from the Martyrs to the Reformation

Robert Bartlett

PRINCETON UNIVERSITY PRESS
PRINCETON AND OXFORD

Published by Princeton University Press, 41 William Street, Princeton, New Jersey 08540
In the United Kingdom: Princeton University Press,
6 Oxford Street, Woodstock, Oxfordshire OX20 1TW

press.princeton.edu

Jacket Art: Fra Angelico, Fiesole San Domenico Altarpiece, *The Dominican Blessed*:
Outer Left Pilaster Panel, about 1423–24. Egg tempera on wood, 31.8 × 21.9 cm.
National Gallery, London, UK. Photo Credit: © National Gallery, London / Art Resource, NY

ISBN 978-0-691-15913-3

Library of Congress Cataloging-in-Publication Data
Bartlett, Robert, 1950–
Why can the dead do such great things? : saints and worshippers
from the martyrs to the Reformation / Robert Bartlett.
pages cm
Includes bibliographical references and index.
ISBN 978-0-691-15913-3 (alk. paper)
1. Church history—Primitive and early church, ca. 30–600. 2. Church history—Middle Ages, 600–1500. 3. Christian saints—History. 4. Christian martyrs—History. I. Title.
BR162.3.B37 2013
235'.2–dc23 2013019981

British Library Cataloging-in-Publication Data is available

This book has been composed in Garamond Premier Pro

Printed on acid-free paper. ∞

Printed in the United States of America

1 3 5 7 9 10 8 6 4 2

For Gabriel and Rachel

But this she knows, in joys and woes,
That saints will aid if men will call
—Coleridge, *Christabel*

CONTENTS

CONTENTS

ILLUSTRATIONS

FIGURES

COLOUR PLATES (FOLLOWING P. 366)

MAPS

TABLES

PREFACE

This book is in two parts. The first gives a fairly brisk overview of the subject from the beginnings of the Christian cult of the saints in the age of the martyrs to the time of the Protestant Reformation of the sixteenth century. Its purpose is to sketch out the main developments and to give readers some signposts in this vast landscape. The second part, which is by far the longest, deals systematically with the main themes and topics. Examples are drawn eclectically from various times and places, although an attempt has been made to point out regional differences and important chronological changes. The final chapter attempts to step back from the subject and look at it comparatively and theoretically, asking if the Christian cult of the saints has equivalents in other religions and how its dynamics can best be understood.

References are given in the footnotes in abbreviated form; full bibliographical information is in the bibliography.

This book deals with the veneration of the saints in Christian countries in the pre-Reformation period. Byzantium is included to some extent, within the limits of the author's expertise, but the rich culture of saintly cults in the other eastern churches is not, and, while the cult of the saints continues in many branches of Christianity to the present day, to include that history would push the book from being understandably over-ambitious to being absurdly over-ambitious. I hope the book will lead readers to the vast and invigorating literature that has blossomed around the cult of the saints, from the moving account of the deaths of Perpetua and Felicity in the third century to the bubbling world of current scholarship on the subject.

Acknowledgments

Financial support for some of the research underlying this book was provided by the University of St. Andrews, the Royal Society of Edinburgh, and the Alexander von Humboldt Stiftung. I am very grateful for this. The book would not exist without the generosity of the Leverhulme Trust, which awarded me a Major Research Fellowship to write it. This once-in-a-lifetime opportunity is much appreciated. I received welcome advice and help on specific points from Michael Brown, Tim Greenwood, Ruth Macrides, Alexander O'Hara, and Cynthia Robinson. The staff of the University of St. Andrews Library have been consistently helpful, often in difficult circumstances. Alan Thacker was kind enough to offer suggestions on the the text, and I have also benefitted from the careful comments of the anonymous reader for Princeton University Press, who removed his disguise to reveal the learned and encouraging figure of Gábor Klaniczay. Both Alan and Gábor are world-experts in this field, and I appreciate their advice. My friend and colleague John Hudson read the entire text and made numerous helpful suggestions. I owe him a great debt. Nora Bartlett has not only commented on the whole text but has also provided the daily support and encouragement that enabled this somewhat heavily laden barque finally to make harbour. And I would like to mention the undergraduate students who have taken my Special Subject on the cult of the saints over the years. I owe them too a great deal: to teach is to learn.

PART I

Developments

CHAPTER 1

Origins (100–500)

The Martyrs

"Why can the dead do such great things?" Such is a question asked by one of the most important of all Christian thinkers, St. Augustine, as he pondered the miracles worked by the saints.[1] Of all religions, Christianity is the one most concerned with dead bodies. Many religions have the idea of a holy man or woman—a living human being with extraordinary powers derived from special contact with the divine. Medieval Christianity developed to an extreme degree a distinctive form of this concept: the idea that the dead bodies of these holy people should be cherished as enduring sources of supernatural power. There were thousands of shrines in medieval Europe containing the dust, bones, or (an elect group) the undecayed bodies of the holy dead. Men and women came to these places, revered those whose mortal remains lay there, asked them for favours, and, to judge by their accounts, were cured of their ills. The ecclesiastics who guarded these shrines wrote of the lives of those whose bodies they tended, recorded the wonders they performed after death and gave them solemn liturgical commemoration in the churches that often bore their names. These were the saints.

The origins of the cult of the saints lie in the early centuries of Christianity. From at least the second century AD some Christians were regarded as higher, exceptional, in a class of their own. These were the martyrs, a word of Greek origin meaning "witnesses," those who died for their faith, tortured and killed in the elaborate public way typical of imperial Roman civilization. Christians prayed *for* their (ordinary) dead but they prayed *to* the martyrs. Their sufferings were seen as a sacrifice undergone on behalf of other Christians. Even while they were in prison awaiting examination or execution, the martyrs were deemed to have the power of forgiveness of sins. At their tombs, usually located in the cemeteries found outside the walls of Greek and Roman cities, the local Christian community would gather on the anniversary of their deaths to celebrate the Eucharist and perhaps have a commemorative feast. Local churches kept lists of their martyrs, recording the dates of their deaths, and sometimes sent accounts of recent martyrdoms to other churches.

[1] Augustine, *De civitate dei* 22. 9 (2, p. 827).

Persecution of Christians in the Roman Empire was not unremitting. In some periods (notably 260–303), decades passed peacefully, even if Christianity remained technically illegal. But, periodically, major state-sponsored assaults were launched against the religion. The first was under Nero, in AD 64, when the victims probably included St. Peter and St. Paul. In the third century, large-scale persecutions followed the issue of anti-Christian edicts by the emperors Decius, in 250, and Valerian, in 257. The culmination of this policy came in 303, when the emperor Diocletian opened a campaign to wipe out the Church completely. The "holy struggles of the martyrs of God's word" in this "Great Persecution" lasted, in many parts of the empire, until 311.[2] Under Licinius, who ruled only in the eastern half of the empire, persecution was revived for a few years in the early 320s.

The dramatic last days of some of the early Christian martyrs are reported in contemporary accounts. Amongst the earliest of these remarkable records is *The Martyrdom of Polycarp*, which recounts the death of the bishop of Smyrna (in Asia Minor, modern Izmir) at some time in the years 150–80.[3] The aged Polycarp, facing execution, is described praying to God that he may be received "as a sacrifice." When he is brought into the arena and burned at a pyre, there is no stench of burning flesh, but it is rather as if "bread were being baked, or gold or silver purified in a furnace." Afterwards the Christians of Smyrna wish to collect his remains, desiring "to have a share in his holy flesh." Before they are allowed to do so, they have to overcome the objections of pagans and Jews who fear they might worship Polycarp.

> Thus at last, collecting the remains that were dearer to us than precious stones and finer than gold, we buried them in a fitting spot. Gathering here, so far as we can, in joy and gladness, we will be allowed by the Lord to celebrate the anniversary day of his martyrdom, both as a memorial for those who have already fought the contest and for the training and preparation of those who will do so one day.

One of the most moving accounts of a martyr's end is that of Perpetua, much of which was actually composed by the martyr herself while in prison.[4] Perpetua was an inhabitant of Carthage in North Africa, an important early centre of Christianity in the western part of the Roman Empire. She was a married woman in her early twenties, reasonably prosperous and well educated. In the year 203 she was rounded up with other Christians and urged to perform pagan sacrifice. Amongst the other pressures on her was the insistence of her father, who begged her to give way, and worries about her baby, much assuaged when she was permitted to keep the child with her in prison. Perpetua's status as a martyr was already recognized during her imprisonment. She tells how one of her brothers said to her, "Sister, you are now

[2] Eusebius, *Historia ecclesiastica* 8. 2. 3 (3, p. 7).

[3] *Passio Polycarpi*.

[4] *Passio sanctarum Perpetuae et Felicitatis*.

so greatly privileged that you could ask for a vision, to show you whether you will suffer martyrdom or not"; this she asks for and obtains. In a later dream-vision she sees another, deceased brother, suffering after death, but, she says, "I knew that I had the privilege of pleading for him," and by her prayers obtains his release. Intercession is at the heart of the Christian conception of sainthood, and here Perpetua, the living martyr, shows that she possesses the power to intercede, even beyond the grave. It would be left to later theologians to work out doctrines to fit with these experienced realities.

Perpetua and the other Christians with her, including the pregnant slave-girl Felicity, were condemned to be thrown to the wild beasts in the public arena. The day before their execution, Perpetua dreamed that she was brought to the arena to face a villainous-looking Egyptian; handsome young men came up to her to be her seconds in the fight and took off her clothes; she suddenly found that she was transformed into a man; her seconds rubbed her down with oil; in the contest with the Egyptian she was victorious and left the arena through "The Gate of Life," reserved for gladiators whose lives were spared. "Then I woke up," she writes, "and knew that I would not be fighting with beasts but with the Devil; but I knew that victory would be mine." Naturally this is the end of Perpetua's first-hand account, but a contemporary takes up the tale of her martyrdom and that of her companions, including Felicity, who rejoiced that she had given birth in prison and so would be executed with the others and not have her death delayed because she was pregnant. We know the fate of Perpetua and Felicity, but not that of their babies.

Fifty-five years after these dramatic events, another famous martyrdom took place in Carthage, that of its bishop, Cyprian. Although he composed no first-hand account of his sufferings, he left a large body of writings, including 65 letters and a dozen or so treatises. From these it is possible to learn details of the cult of the martyrs in his time and to see the part that martyrdom played in his thinking. He not only faced martyrdom himself but also offers a window on the world of those who venerated the martyrs.

Cyprian was a wealthy and educated inhabitant of Roman Africa, who converted to Christianity in the 240s and was very quickly promoted to the bishopric of Carthage. He thus became head of a growing Christian community in the most important city in Roman Africa. By the time he became bishop he had already established himself as a powerful Christian writer, and the treatises and letters he went on to produce as a bishop have an eloquent and authoritative tone, even when dealing with the vexed and controversial issues that arose during the ten years of his episcopate (248/9–58). One of the main stimuli to such controversies was the renewed persecution of Christians after Decius's edict. This began soon after Cyprian took up office and lasted throughout 250 and into 251. During this persecution Cyprian himself went into hiding and, although he defended this response at length and with apparent sincerity, it may be that the high value he attributed to martyrdom, and the stress he placed on preparation for it, reflect a lingering self-doubt about his own behaviour at this time.

Cyprian's writings represent martyrdom as the highest attainment of a Christian's life.[5] Martyrs are soldiers in Christ's army, fighting in a war against Satan and winning heavenly rewards. The African martyrs Laurentinus and Egnatius, who actually were soldiers in the Roman army, were "in truth spiritual soldiers of God, striking down the Devil by their confession of Christ, earning by their glorious suffering palms and crowns from the Lord."[6] Martyrdom was a "baptism of blood" that sent the martyrs straight to heaven.[7] Hence persecution should be a source of rejoicing: "Because when there are persecutions, then crowns of faith are given, then the soldiers of God are put to the test, then heaven opens to the martyrs."[8]

After their death, martyrs attained an exceptional reward and had powers of intercession. Cyprian believed that, at the Last Judgment, "the merits of the martyrs" would have special weight with God the Judge.[9] But even those who were about to be killed or those who survived imprisonment and torture, to whom Cyprian was also willing to give the name "martyrs," since they too were "witnesses," had, in his view, extraordinary powers and status. They had a right to be ordained without some of the usual formalities.[10] The power of their prayers on behalf of others, especially for "the lapsed," those who had given way under persecution, was great. Some contemporaries even spoke as if martyrs about to die could "remit sin." Although this would not be Cyprian's formulation, he nevertheless gave some weight to the "letters of pardon" that the lapsed sometimes sought from the martyrs.[11]

According to Cyprian, the martyred dead deserved especial reverence. The day of their death should be carefully noted, so that they could be commemorated each year on the anniversary with the celebration of the Eucharist: "We offer sacrifices (that is, the Eucharist) for them whenever we commemorate the sufferings of the martyrs on their anniversary day."[12] These heroes, whose death was commemorated annually and who had special intercessory powers, were the prototype of all subsequent Christian saints.

"The soldier of Christ who has been educated in His commands and admonitions does not shrink fearfully from the fight but is ready for the crown."[13] So wrote Cyprian, and a few years later he had a second chance to demonstrate it, for in 257 the Roman imperial authorities renewed their persecution of Christians. At first exiled, Cyprian was recalled to Carthage the following year and interrogated before

[5] Hummel, *The Concept of Martyrdom According to St. Cyprian*.

[6] *Epistularium* 39. 3. 1 (3B, p. 189).

[7] *Ad Fortunatam*, p. 185; though see his reservation in *Epistularium* 57. 4. 1 (3B, p. 305).

[8] *Epistularium* 58. 3. 1 (3C, p. 323).

[9] *De lapsis* 17, p. 230.

[10] *Epistularium* 38. 1. 1 (3B, p. 183); cf. Hippolytus, *Traditio apostolica* 9, p. 64, on "confessor-martyrs" not requiring laying on of hands to be ordained deacon or priest.

[11] For example, *Epistularium* 15, 27 (3B, pp. 85–89, 127–32); see Dassmann, *Sündenvergebung durch Taufe, Busse und Martyrerfürbitte in den Zeugnissen frühchristlicher Frömmigkeit und Kunst*, pp. 171–78 (pp. 173–74 specifically on Cyprian).

[12] *Epistularium* 39. 3. 1 (3B, p. 189).

[13] Ibid. 58. 11 (3C, p. 335).

the governor of Africa. Faced with the command to participate in pagan religious ceremonies, the bishop replied simply, "I will not do it." On hearing the sentence that he was to be executed, he responded, "Thanks be to God." Cyprian was at once taken outside, followed by a huge crowd, including the Christians of Carthage, and beheaded with a sword.[14] If he had felt any shame over his earlier flight and concealment, he had now made up for it. Within a very short time after his death, other African martyrs were to be comforted by his appearance in dreams and visions, and he was to become one of the most widely revered of the early martyrs.[15]

The Religious Revolution of the Fourth Century

Fifty-five years after Cyprian's martyrdom, an imperial edict granted toleration to Christianity, marking the beginning of a period that was to be one of the most momentous in religious history. At the start of the fourth century Christian worship was illegal; by its end pagan cult had been outlawed. Christianity went from being a persecuted religion to being a state religion, and a major step had been taken toward that identification of the Church and society which was to characterize medieval Europe. After the conversion of the emperor Constantine (306–37), the authority of state and Church became ever more closely intertwined, with bishops and clergy granted legal and fiscal privileges, emperors taking a stand on questions of doctrine, and the organs and institutions of secular and ecclesiastical coercion becoming interdependent. Thus, in the words of Eusebius, Constantine's adviser and the first chronicler of the Church, "a day both bright and radiant, not darkened by a single cloud, shone upon the churches of Christ throughout the world with beams of heavenly light."[16]

Alongside the new relationship with the state, new patterns and habits of worship developed, which it is possible to sum up simply by saying that in this period Christianity became a religion. The Middle Eastern world in which Jesus and his first followers lived had a clear and distinct concept of "religion": the temple cults in which ritual specialists, the priests, represented the people and sought divine favour through sacrifice. In its origin Christianity was a radical revivalist cult that rejected most of these things. By the end of the fourth century they were back again: holy buildings, priestly rituals, the language of sacrifice and mystery. A priest of Baal or of Isis or of Yahweh would certainly have recognized what kind of thing the Christianity of the late fourth century was. It was as part of this immense transformation that the cult of the saints came into new prominence and assumed new forms.

One of the most visible innovations was architectural. The martyrs had originally been buried in the ordinary cemeteries of the Mediterranean world, located along

[14] *Acta proconsularia sancti Cypriani.*

[15] *Passio sanctorum Mariani et Iacobi* 6, p. 202; *Passio sanctorum Montani et Lucii* 11, p. 222.

[16] Eusebius, *Historia ecclesiastica* 10. 1. 8 (3, pp. 78–79).

the roads leading away from the cities. At Rome most were interred in underground cemeteries, the "catacombs," a vast network of tunnels and chambers which lay beneath the funerary areas. Their graves were simple. One that was discovered in the nineteenth century in the catacombs of Bassilla or Hermes bore the plain inscription "Hyacinth, martyr, buried 11 September."[17] And these places could be gloomy, even frightening. St. Jerome describes how, when he was a schoolboy in Rome around the year 360, he used on Sundays "to go around the tombs of the apostles and martyrs and frequently enter the crypts which had been excavated in the depths of the earth and which contain the bodies of those buried there in the walls on either side of those who go in." He remembered how dark these places were and how rarely a beam of light from above "would temper the horror of the shadows." The "blind night" down there brought to his well-educated mind a line of Virgil: "Horror and very silence fill the mind with fear everywhere."[18]

With its new wealth, security and prestige following Constantine's conversion, the Christian Church could establish a public physical presence in the cities of the empire in a way previously impossible. One way was to open up the catacombs by making the burial chambers of the martyrs bigger, building steps and shafts for light, dispelling to some degree "the horror of the shadows" that Jerome felt.[19] Jerome's employer Pope Damasus (366–84) was an enthusiastic promoter of the cult of the martyrs of Rome and enlarged and beautified their burial places in the catacombs, composing elegant Latin epitaphs, inscribed on marble slabs, some of which survive or have been rediscovered. "Look!," begins that for the martyrs Felicissimus and Agapitus, "this tomb contains the heavenly limbs of the saints whom the palace of heaven snatched up."[20] Damasus's epitaph for Sixtus II looks back to the sufferings of the Church in the time of persecutions, "the time when the sword cut the holy entrails of the Mother."[21] Those times were now over, and the Church could embrace public triumphalism.

More striking than the simple elaboration of underground shrines was the building of huge churches over the tombs of the martyrs. Many of these were basilicas—that is, large timber-roofed halls with a central nave, aisles, and a semi-circular apse. Such buildings were common in Roman secular life and often served as courts and throne rooms. In Christian churches it became conventional for the holy end, with the altar, to be at the east, and the public face to be the west. Soon after his conversion, Constantine raised in Rome one of the most important basilican churches in Christian history, St. Peter's on the Vatican hill. This was the traditional site of the tomb of the apostle Peter, in a large cemetery adjacent to Nero's circus, a place

[17] *Inscriptiones Christianae urbis Romae septimo saeculo antiquiores*, n.s. 10, no. 26672; it is illustrated in Bisconti and Mazzoleni, *Alle origini del culto dei martiri*, pl. 7; see BS 10, cols. 1221–23, s.n. "Proto e Giacinto."

[18] Jerome, *In Hiezechielem* 12, on Ezekiel 40:5–13, pp. 556–57 (PL 25: 375).

[19] Nicolai et al., *The Christian Catacombs of Rome*, pp. 37–59.

[20] *Damaso e i martiri di Roma*, pp. 37–38.

[21] Ibid., p. 24.

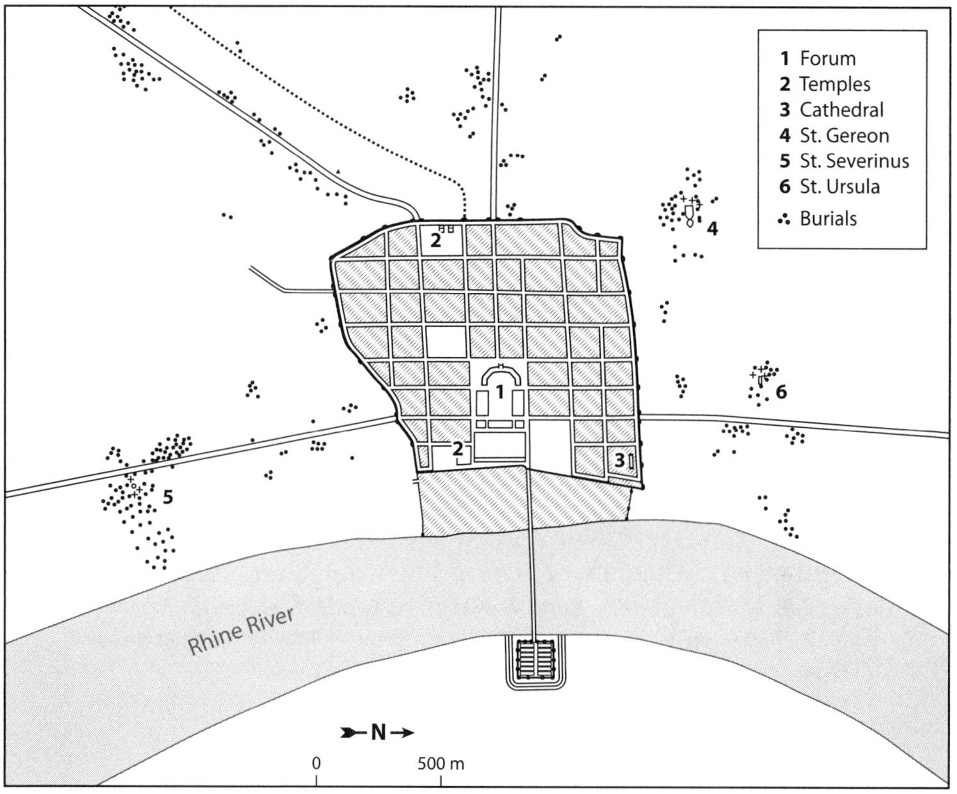

Map 1.

Cologne in the fourth century. Source: *Topographie chrétienne des cités de la Gaule* 12: *Province ecclésiastique de Cologne*, pp. 42–43.

where many Christians had been martyred in AD 64. Because the cemetery was on a hill, an enormous amount of levelling and excavating was necessary to obtain a flat surface for Constantine's huge church. (This also meant that, unusually, the church was aligned to the west, not the east.) It has been calculated that more than 40,000 cubic metres of soil had to be moved. The basilica measured 123 metres (403 feet) in length and 66 metres (216 feet) across the aisles.[22] The building of such monumental martyr churches transformed the setting of the cult. Whereas previously Christians had gathered in cemeteries, above or below ground, to reverence the martyrs at their tombs, they could now assemble in vast and elaborately decorated halls which had these tombs at their heart, a veritable "monumentalization" of the cult of the martyrs.[23]

[22] Brandenburg, *Ancient Churches of Rome*, p. 96.

[23] Saxer, *Morts, martyrs, reliques*, p. 301.

Churches such as those erected over the graves of St. Peter on the Vatican hill or of St. Paul on the Via Ostiense to the south lay outside the city walls—indeed, the church of St. Paul is known as San Paolo *fuori le mura* ("St. Paul's outside the walls"). This was typical, since the martyrs were buried in the cemeteries located outside the walls and the churches were built above their graves. As a result of this development new foci arose in the suburban parts of Greek and Roman cities. In the words of St. Jerome, "the city itself is moving; the people flood past the half-ruined temples and run to the tombs of the martyrs."[24] When Christians assembled at martyr shrines on the feast-days of the saints, they could be described as "pouring out of the city."[25] John Chrysostom spoke enthusiastically about leaving behind "the tumult of affairs and the throng of everyday anxieties" when he went out of the city to the martyr shrine and "enjoyed the company of the saints," later returning refreshed.[26] The ground-plan of fourth-century Cologne shows exactly the new distribution of Christian topography: a cathedral within the walls, near the government buildings, and three new Christian shrines in the cemeteries outside the walls to the north and south (map 1).[27] In some places, Roman if far from Rome, the long-term magnetic attraction of the martyr churches was so great that the settlement itself eventually relocated around them: the English town of St. Albans focuses on the shrine of the martyr Alban, not the nearby Roman town of Verulamium, while in Germany the town which grew up in the cemetery outside of Colonia Ulpia Traiana is even called "By the Saints" (*ad sanctos*)—that is, Xanten.[28]

Translations

Not every church possessed the tomb of a martyr. Within the cities there were basilican churches that were seats of bishops and centres for Christian communities, but not martyr churches. Such churches, built within the cities in the early fourth century, did not incorporate the tombs of the martyrs in the way that the martyr churches in the suburban cemetery areas did. In Rome, as well as building the great shrine-church of St. Peter's (at that time outside the walls), Constantine constructed the church of the Lateran within the walls, to serve for the bishop of Rome. These urban churches lacked saints' remains. But that lack could be remedied. Often this was done by acquiring the bodies of martyrs from elsewhere—the technical term for the ritual relocation of a saint's remains is "translation" (it simply means "transfer").

The earliest certain case of the removal of a martyr's body is the translation of St. Babylas, a bishop of Antioch who had died in prison during the persecution of

[24] Jerome, *Epistula* 107. 1 (5, p. 145) (PL 22: 868).

[25] Basil of Caesarea, *Homilia XVIII in Gordium martyrem* 1, col. 489.

[26] John Chrysostom, *Homilia de sanctis martyribus* 2, col. 649.

[27] *Topographie chrétienne des cités de la Gaule* 12: *Province ecclésiastique de Cologne*, pp. 42–43.

[28] Sharpe, "Martyrs and Local Saints in Late Antique Britain," pp. 75, 82–83, 114–17.

Decius in the mid-third century.[29] Babylas's remains were moved as part of an offensive against the power of the old gods. An hour's stroll outside Antioch was the pleasant and leafy hilltop site of Daphne. Here there was a temple of Apollo. It was also, according to Christian commentators, a scene of "revels and drunkenness."[30] The Christian ruler Gallus, Constantine's nephew (351–54), was inspired to harness the energy of a martyr saint to challenge the pagan cult and wicked practices at Daphne. A martyr church was built there close to Apollo's temple, and Babylas's remains were transferred into it from the cemetery at Antioch. The results were immediate: sobriety and modesty spread, the oracle at Apollo's temple fell silent. However, when Gallus's half-brother Julian became emperor, and initiated a campaign to restore traditional pagan religion, an attempt was made to reverse the process. The pagan oracle at Daphne complained to Julian that it was the presence of dead bodies (that is, Babylas) that had silenced it, and Julian commanded that the saint's body be returned to its original location. But the saint fought back: "he asked God to send forth fire on the temple" and both the roof and the image of the god were destroyed (an event that is well attested).[31] After Julian's death the bishop of Antioch built a big new church across the river from the city to house Babylas's remains. Meanwhile, the empty martyr church at Daphne continued to manifest special powers. "Such is the might of the martyrs . . . such is the might of the saints."[32]

Babylas's remains had been removed from the cemetery at Antioch to the martyr church at Daphne, back to the cemetery, and then into the new martyr church. They had not been brought into the city. This was the next barrier to be broken, and it was breached partly as a result of the hunt for saintly bones that began after the emperors adopted Christianity. Amongst the most renowned of the martyrs revered in the early Church were the apostles, the followers of Jesus who had spread the Christian faith in the decades after his death. The chief of these were Peter and Paul,[33] and there were strong and plausible traditions about where their remains lay. Both appear, in historical reality, to have suffered martyrdom at Rome. For a while their bones seem to have been moved to a common site on the Via Appia, and here graffiti of the third and fourth century show that visiting Christians invoked their aid and intercession.[34] From the fourth century they were venerated at their tombs outside the ancient city walls, at the sites marked by Constantine's St. Peter's and San Paolo *fuori le mura*. Little, however, was known of the fortunes of the other apostles, but before long stories were created about their far-flung missions and their brave deaths. Inventive writers of the third and subsequent centuries told of Thomas's mission to India, John's activities in Ephesus, Andrew's crucifixion at Patras in Greece, and so

[29] John Chrysostom, *De sancto Babyla*; Downey, "The Shrines of St. Babylas at Antioch and Daphne."

[30] John Chrysostom, *De sancto Babyla* 69, p. 182.

[31] Ibid. 93, p. 218; Ammianus Marcellinus, *Res gestae* 22. 13. 1 (3, p. 129).

[32] John Chrysostom, *De sancto Babyla* 127, p. 274.

[33] Although Paul had not been a follower of the living Jesus, he was "the Apostle" par excellence because of his extraordinary missionary work.

[34] Pietri, "L'évolution du culte des saints aux premiers siècles chrétiens," p. 26.

forth. As Christianity underwent the transformation from a minority movement to a majority and public religion, interest was shown in finding the sites of the graves of these other apostles, as also the location of the founding events of the religion. Constantine raised huge churches on the supposed sites of the Nativity in Bethlehem and the Resurrection in Jerusalem, and under his son Constantius apostolic remains were found for the new imperial and Christian capital of Constantinople. In 356 "the relics of the apostle Timothy were brought to Constantinople," and in the following year "the bones of the apostle Andrew and the evangelist Luke were received with wonderful approval by the people of Constantinople."[35] These relics were placed in the Church of the Apostles within the walls. Such supposed discoveries of saintly bones were to have a long future and inspire even the most austere and intellectual Christians, such as St. Augustine, who was an enthusiast for the relics of Stephen, the first martyr, discovered in 415.

The best documented translation of the fourth century took place in 386, when Ambrose, bishop of Milan, moved the remains of the martyrs Gervasius and Protasius, which had been miraculously discovered in one of the suburban cemetery churches, to his own new basilican church:

> At this same time the holy martyrs Protasius and Gervasius revealed themselves to the bishop. For they were situated in the basilica in which there are today the bodies of the martyrs Nabor and Felix. But the holy martyrs Nabor and Felix were well known and visited by great crowds, while the names and burial place of the martyrs Protasius and Gervasius were unknown, so much so that everyone who wished to approach the railings which protected the tombs of the holy martyrs Nabor and Felix from damage walked over the tombs of Protasius and Gervasius. But when the bodies of the holy martyrs had been raised up and placed in shrines, it is well known that many people's ailments were cured.[36]

Here we have a picture of a successful martyr church, where the shrine of the martyrs Nabor and Felix are visited by crowds and marked out by special railings. Inside it, through a miraculous revelation, Ambrose finds new martyrs, whose remains he removes. The new basilica to which they were relocated (today known as the Ambrosian basilica) was to be the site of Ambrose's own burial as well as a martyr church housing the remains of the saints. The physical remains of the previously unknown martyrs Protasius and Gervasius were placed beneath the altar of Ambrose's new building. The church of Milan was no longer so "barren of martyrs."[37]

Such translations of physical remains were rare, however. More usual than the removal or discovery of the bones of a saint was the creation of "contact relics," that is, small objects that had been in physical touch with the saint's tomb: oil from the

[35] Jerome, *Chronicon*, pp. 240–41; Wortley, "The Earliest Relic-Importations to Constantinople."
[36] Paulinus, *Vita Ambrosii* 14, p. 70.
[37] Ambrose, *Epistularum liber decimus*, *Epistula* 77 (22). 7, p. 131 (PL 16: 1021).

lamps that burned there, perhaps, or dust—dust which was regarded as "a treasure."[38] These relics could easily be multiplied. Hence in Christian Africa, for example, there were not only great churches above the tombs of the native martyrs, but also dozens of relics scattered throughout the churches of the region, relics not in the sense of fragments of saints' bones, but tiny jars containing earth, dust, oil, and so on.[39] The multiplication of such relics, along with the occasional translation of physical remains ("corporeal relics"), gave a new fluidity and mobility to the cult of the saints.

Rituals of Commemoration and Invocation

Along with these big changes in the venue and staging of the commemoration of the martyrs came other important developments in the cult of the saints. These were of two types, since members of the Christian community connected with the shrines of the martyrs in two ways: they undertook regular routine rituals to honour them, and they expected extraordinary help from them.

The earliest evidence for the cult of the saints, from the account of Polycarp's martyrdom, mentions the faithful gathering together for an annual commemoration of the martyr's death, and thus indicates routine rituals concentrated on the martyr's feast-day, or "birth-day" as it was known (their birth into heaven).[40] Naturally, for this to happen, a record needed to be kept of the day of martyrdom. Local churches would build up lists of their own native martyrs. The earliest surviving list of martyrs comes from Rome, and was compiled in its present form after persecution ended during the reign of Constantine; it was subsequently incorporated into a chronographical compendium of 354.[41] It contains the names of fifty martyrs, giving the day of their commemoration, that is, the day of their death, and usually adding the site of their burial. For example, under 10 August, the list reads "Lawrence in Tiburtina," that is, the cemetery on the Via Tiburtina, the road leading out of Rome to the north-east. Very occasionally, the year of death is also recorded (and sometimes modern historians can deduce it, as in the case of Pope Sixtus II, who was executed in 258, as other sources reveal). Most of the martyrs in the list are Roman, but a handful of those recorded suffered elsewhere in the empire: "7 March, Perpetua and Felicity, Africa"; "14 September, Cyprian, Africa; commemorated at Rome in the cemetery of St. Callixtus." Some of the saints mentioned, such as Sebastian and

[38] Gregory of Nyssa, *De sancto Theodoro*, p. 63 (PG 46: 740).

[39] See Duval, *Loca sanctorum Africae: le culte des martyrs en Afrique du IVe au VIIe siècle*.

[40] Quando natus sit [Cyprianus], ignoramus; et quia hodie passus est, natalem ejus hodie celebramus. Sed illum diem non celebraremus, etsi nossemus. Illo enim die traxit originale peccatum: isto autem die vicit omne peccatum: Augustine, *Sermo* 310 (PL 38: 1413); Natalem sanctorum . . . nolite putare illum dici, quo nascimur de carne . . . sed de terra in caelum: Petrus Chrysologus, *Collectio sermonum* 129.1 (24B, p. 793) (PL 52: 555).

[41] *Liber Pontificalis* 1, pp. 11–12; *Codice topografico della Città di Roma* 2, pp. 1–28; see the discussion in Thacker, "Rome of the Martyrs," pp. 20–23.

Lawrence, are well known and were to be commemorated on the days given in the list throughout the succeeding centuries, while others are entirely mysterious. No one has been able to say anything further about the last entry: "13 December, Ariston, in Pontus." But, on the whole, this calendar from the fourth century sets out a framework for fixed ceremonies of the Christian year, with some basic elements that would be recognizable a thousand years later: commemorations of Peter and Paul, Perpetua and Felicity, Sebastian and Lawrence—as well as the very earliest mention of Christmas. Long-lasting annual commemoration, which was the essence of martyr cult, really was achieved in these cases. St. Lawrence's day is still 10 August, as it was in Rome 1700 years ago.

Such a list laid down a series of days on which commemorative rituals should take place. The nature of some of these rituals and the controversy that could surround them is clear from a story St. Augustine tells about his mother, Monica, who was visiting him in Milan in 385.[42] Back home in north Africa, she had been accustomed to celebrate the anniversaries of the martyrs by going to their shrines with a basket of pottage, bread, and wine. She would taste a little of these and share them with others visiting the shrines. In Milan, however, Monica found her way to the shrines barred by a door-keeper who told her that Ambrose, bishop of Milan, had prohibited such customs. Monica immediately abandoned her old-fashioned ways, henceforth content that only the Eucharist should be celebrated at the martyrs' shrines. Later in life, Augustine reflected on this issue: "Some people bring banquets to the places of the martyrs but this is not done by the better Christians, and in most parts of the world there is no such custom."[43]

Objections to Monica's practice saw it as too close to traditional paganism, "very similar to the festival in honour of the dead of pagan superstition."[44] Communal commemorative meals at the tomb were indeed a standard feature of Roman memorial practice, and some of the more elaborate burial sites even incorporated stone tables and benches for this purpose, while it was not unusual for the graves themselves to have access tubes down which wine or oil could be poured, so that the dead themselves could join in the meal.[45] Bishops like Ambrose and Augustine, shaping religious practice in the first century of official Christianity, clearly viewed this as a semi-pagan anachronism to be discouraged. In their view, the martyrs were to be commemorated by a Eucharistic celebration, not by such private and picnic-like rituals as Monica had engaged in. The very nature of saintly cult was being hammered out by these debates and prescriptions.

Anyone in the local Christian community could visit the martyrs' shrines and participate in the annual rituals performed there. Much more exceptional was the privilege of being interred close to a martyr's grave, so-called burial "*ad sanctos* (next

[42] Augustine, *Confessiones* 6. 2, p. 74.

[43] Augustine, *De civitate dei* 8. 27 (1, p. 248).

[44] Augustine, *Confessiones* 6. 2, p. 74.

[45] For a summary, see Volp, *Tod und Ritual in den christlichen Gemeinde der Antike*, pp. 77–86; Saxer, *Morts, martyrs, reliques*, is of enduring value.

to the saints)" (like the name of Xanten mentioned earlier). Indeed the inscription on one grave even exults, "Many desire it but few obtain it."[46] The earliest dateable case occurred during the time of persecutions. After the martyrdom of the North African youth Maximilian in 295, a woman called Pompeiana obtained his body and had it interred next to the body of St. Cyprian in Carthage. Thirteen days later she herself died and was buried in the same place, thus in the vicinity of two Christian martyrs.[47] Inscriptions in the Roman catacombs and elsewhere have many examples of such treasured proximity. One, from Spoleto, records an interment in the year 384 with the words, "receive to yourselves, O saints, the brother and worthy minister Tullius."[48] At about the same time Gregory of Nyssa buried his parents near the relics of the Forty Martyrs of Sebaste, "so that at the time of the resurrection they will awake with those bold-tongued helpers."[49] The interment of a Christian as near as possible to a favoured saint was to be a feature of the cult of the saints for centuries to come.

This practice also provides evidence for an important development in the use of the word "saint."[50] When Christianity began, all Christians were "saints." The word "saint" (*hagios* in Greek, *sanctus* in Latin) was applied to every member of the Christian community, not to an elite. St. Paul's epistle to the Philippians, addressed to "all the saints in Christ Jesus which are at Philippi" and concluding "All the saints salute you, chiefly they that are of Caesar's household," shows this inclusive usage. A particularly telling instance, from about the year 260, occurs in a commentary on the Book of Revelation written by a Christian bishop. He distinguishes various classes or categories of saint, explaining that "the fifth category of saints designates negligent people, who do not behave in the world as they should, who are without value in their actions, Christians only in name."[51] Obviously the term "saint" here means simply "Christian," not "perfect or heroic Christian." This wide sense of the word continued even after Christianity became the official religion of the Roman Empire and the number of believers multiplied. In the fifth century Christian writers could still ask, "What is the Church other than the community of all the saints?"[52]

However, even during the period when the phrase "the saints" had as an ordinary meaning "all Christians," there are signs also of a more restricted sense in use. The martyrs were "the saints" in the highest degree. They had earned the title more fully. For instance, when Christians like Pompeiana wanted to be buried as near to the bodies of the martyrs as they could, to be associated with their merits, this practice is described as burial "near the saints" (*ad sanctos, meta ton hagion*). When a grieving

[46] *Inscriptiones Christianae urbis Romae septimo saeculo antiquiores*, n.s. 1, no. 3127.

[47] *Acta Maximiliani* (BHL 5813) 3, p. 248.

[48] Diehl, *Inscriptiones latinae Christianae veteres*, no. 2169.

[49] Gregory of Nyssa, *In XL martyres II*, p. 166 (PG 46: 784).

[50] For a detailed case-study, see Zocca, *Dai "santi" al "santo."*

[51] Victorinus de Poetovio (Ptuj), *In Apocalypsin* 3.1, p. 60.

[52] Nicetas of Remesiana, *De symbolo* 10, p. 48 (PL 52, col. 871); cf. Philippus Presbyter (Pseudo-Jerome), *Commentarii in librum Iob* 26, col. 689: Ecclesia, quae est sanctorum omnium congregatio.

family erected an inscription saying that their dead relative was buried "near the saints" or "in the place of the saints," they meant "near to the bodies of the martyrs." Sometimes they specified the martyr in question: "near Saint Felicity," "near Saint Cornelius." Here one can see fully formed the familiar current practice: the name preceded by the title "saint" to describe a special category of dead Christians.[53]

The saints could be appealed to. As is clear from the case of Perpetua, the martyrs had long been credited with special powers of intercession. In the fourth century it becomes evident just how concrete and how physical their intercession might be. Basil, bishop of Caesarea (370–78), the brother of Gregory of Nyssa, preaching a sermon in honour of the local martyr St. Mamas, addressed

> those who have enjoyed the presence of the martyr in dreams, those who have come here and found his help in prayer, those who have called on his name and been helped in your deeds, who have been brought safely to journey's end, relieved of sickness, had the lives of your children saved or had your life lengthened.[54]

The stress on the healing power of the saint indicates one of the most important facets of the Christian cult of the saints: miraculous healing. When Jesus sent out his apostles, he instructed them to "heal the sick, cleanse the lepers, raise the dead, cast out devils," and the *Acts of the Apostles* in the New Testament record several miraculous cures, including resurrection of the dead, performed by the apostles. Such powers were now attached to the tombs of the saints, as well as associated with living holy men. The expulsion of demons and the grant of physical healing were a new kind of "witness" of the martyrs: "everywhere the holy blood of the blessed martyrs is received and their revered bones are a daily witness, for through them the demons groan and sickness is driven out."[55] The translation of Protasius and Gervasius at Milan, discussed earlier, was vindicated by the fact that at their shrine "many people's ailments were cured." Martyr tombs were no longer simply sites of commemoration; they were also sources of supernatural aid.

Confessor Saints

The end of persecution in the early fourth century meant that new martyrs were no longer being created on a regular basis within the Roman Empire. It is possible that at this point the cult of the saints could have been "sealed," with a finite number of

[53] Delehaye, *Sanctus*, pp. 30–34; for a full discussion of this subject see Duval, *Auprès des saints corps et âme: l'inhumation "ad sanctos" dans la chrétienté d'Orient et d'Occident du IIIe au VIIe siècle*.

[54] Basil of Caesarea, *Homilia XXIII in Mamantem martyrem* 1, col. 589.

[55] Sanctus ubique beatorum martyrum sanguis exceptus est, et veneranda ossa quotidie testimonio sunt: dum in his daemones mugiunt, dum aegritudines depelluntur . . . : Hilary of Poitiers, *Contra Constantium* 8, pp. 182–83 (PL 10: 584). The text dates to 360.

martyr-cults, perhaps refreshed on occasion by discoveries of remains, such as those of Gervasius and Protasius. This did not, in fact, happen, for a new source of Christian saints emerged in the fourth century—not those who had died for their faith but those who had lived for it, in a heroic and resolute way. (They were designated "confessors," as distinct from martyrs.) It is no accident that this important development in the history of sanctity coincided with the rise of a new movement, that of the ascetics, for these ascetics, beginning with the monks and hermits of the Egyptian desert, were committed to extreme forms of religious life: chastity, poverty, solitude, sleeplessness, deprivation of food and drink. They may not have been tortured and executed by hostile pagan authorities, but their life was "a daily martyrdom."[56] Such heroic Christians formed the new style of saint.

The most important of these new model saints were Antony of Egypt (d. 356) and Martin of Tours (d. 397). Antony came from a propertied family of Christians in Egypt, was supposedly a well-behaved boy, but, along with his little sister, was orphaned by the time he was twenty (this would probably be around the year 270).[57] In church one day he was struck by some of the most radical of Jesus' words in the Gospels: "if thou wilt be perfect, go and sell that thou hast, and give to the poor" and "take no thought for the morrow" (Matthew 19:21 and 6:34). He took these commands literally, distributed his property (after making provision for his sister), and began a quest into the solitary religious life. He sought out the hermits who could be found on the edges of the villages of Egypt and modelled himself on them. Over the course of time, he withdrew further and further from human habitation, first living in some tombs, later in an abandoned fort in the desert, finally in the mountains above the Red Sea (where subsequently the Monastery of St. Antony, Deir Mar Antonios, was founded and still stands). He achieved heroic asceticism, "suppressed and enslaved his body more and more," and engaged in constant battle with the demons of the desert.[58] These wicked spirits tried various tactics, attempting to seduce him in the form of a beautiful woman, or, failing that, beating him all over. In fact, like many saints, Antony was more familiar with devils and better informed about them than most Christians. On two recorded occasions Antony left the desert to go to the great Egyptian metropolis of Alexandria, once to give moral support to martyrs during the persecution of 311, and again, after the official acceptance of Christianity, to condemn heretical views. He had the gifts of prophecy and of miraculous healing, and was a wise adviser to those who sought him out—and many did so. He was emulated to such a degree that "the desert became a city of monks."[59]

The monastic way of life, a full-time commitment to poverty and celibacy, which Antony had pioneered, took institutional form and spread throughout the Roman Empire. One of those whom it inspired was Martin, a young man of military

[56] Athanasius, *Vita Antonii* 47. 1, p. 262, and the references given there on p. 263.

[57] For the following, Athanasius, *Vita Antonii*.

[58] Ibid. 7. 4, p. 150.

[59] Ibid. 14. 7, p. 174.

family who, after leaving the army, had come under the patronage of Hilary, bishop of Poitiers (c. 350–367/8), and founded a monastic cell outside that city.[60] Martin was later chosen as bishop of Tours. It was a controversial choice. Previously, bishops had come from the educated, propertied class of the Roman Empire, and had undertaken the rule of their cities in an aristocratic style. Martin cut a very different figure. Several bishops complained that Martin "was a contemptible person, a man unworthy to be a bishop, despicable in appearance, filthy in his clothing, and with an ugly hairstyle."[61] Here the assumptions of the aristocratic bishops of Gaul and those of the eastern ascetics came into apparently irreconcilable conflict. Yet Martin did become bishop of Tours, and thereafter the monk-bishop was to be a common and important figure in the Christian Church and a not unfamiliar type of saint, blending the charisma of personal asceticism with the authority of official position. Martin was, like Antony, a healer and a warrior in the battle against demons. Unlike Antony, he was an active evangelist, bringing the Christian message to the still mainly pagan rural population of Gaul, disrupting their rituals and felling their sacred trees. He was no less strenuous in policing the Christian community, on one occasion suppressing the cult of a supposed martyr, who, when miraculously resurrected by Martin, confessed himself to be in truth a brigand.[62]

Antony and Martin were important not merely because they lived hard lives in the service of God but because those lives were recorded in powerful literary form. The "life" lived by the saint had to be transformed into the Life (Latin *vita*, Greek *bíos*) penned by another, before it could become part of the common heritage of Christians. Antony's Life was written by Athanasius, bishop of Alexandria (328–73), who spent much of his long episcopate in exile because of his vigorous defence of orthodox belief against what he saw as the heresy of Arianism. It was probably during one of these spells of exile, among the monks of the Egyptian desert, that he composed his Life of Antony. Athanasius had known Antony, and had even been bequeathed a sheepskin by the saint, so he had first-hand knowledge of his subject, but he also used the Life to express his own views and attitudes on doctrine and authority. The long central part of the Life, consisting of almost a third of the text, is a supposed speech of Antony, encouraging monks to persevere in their repudiation of the secular world and setting out, in considerable detail, all he knows about the demons and their tricks. Later in the Life, Antony is emphatic in his opposition to Arianism. It is impossible to know how much of the mix in the Life is Antony and how much Athanasius. Perhaps they would not have troubled over the distinction. Athanasius was a bishop but also a champion of monasticism, and may even have been the first to consecrate monks as bishops.[63] Whether the words are his or Antony's, the func-

[60] For the following, Sulpicius Severus, *Vita sancti Martini*.

[61] Ibid. 9. 3 (1, p. 272).

[62] See later, p. 603.

[63] *Lexikon der antiken christlichen Literatur*, p. 58; see Brakke, *Athanasius and the Politics of Asceticism*, pp. 99–110; Rapp, *Holy Bishops in Late Antiquity*, p. 147.

tion of the Life is clear—to convey in writing an exemplary life. As Athanasius says, "For monks, the life of Antony is a sufficient model of the ascetic life."[64]

The author of Martin's Life, Sulpicius Severus, an aristocrat from south-west France, also felt the strong attraction of the ascetic life. Martin's reputation reached him, and he describes his visit to the saint and his questioning of him and his followers. Very unusually for a saint's Life, Sulpicius's Life was written while Martin was still alive, being composed in 396, the year before the saint's death. This is one of the reasons it is often accompanied in the manuscripts by later writings of Sulpicius describing Martin's death. Sulpicius is explicitly writing in the awareness that Martin had enemies and detractors—"people envious of his virtue and his life, who hated in him what they did not see in themselves and what they were not able to imitate."[65] The Martin of the Life, presented as a wonder-worker, evangelist and ascetic, as well as a bishop, is a strong authorial creation designed to lay such objections to rest. If Martin was an inspiration to Sulpicius, Sulpicius was a champion of Martin. The beneficial relationship of saint and hagiographer was explicitly recognized by Sulpicius's friend Paulinus of Nola: Martin was "blessed through his merits, he who deserved by his faith and life such a worthy narrator, he who is consecrated to divine glory by his merits and to human remembrance by your writing."[66]

The Birth of Hagiography

The Lives of Antony and Martin were widely disseminated, serving as models for many later saints' Lives. Works of hagiography could spread a saint's reputation quite separately from the translation of relics. Many people read the Lives of Antony and Martin, and were inspired by them, who had nothing to do with their cult, in the traditional sense of commemoration at a tomb or reverence for relics. Within a few decades of its composition the Life of Antony was being read by imperial officials at Trier in the western Roman Empire, and it was hearing of St. Antony's response to the Gospel injunction, "if thou wilt be perfect, go and sell that thou hast, and give to the poor," that partially inspired Augustine's own conversion in 386.[67]

The two Lives had, however, different fortunes in East and West, and this fact adumbrates an important future development in the history of the cult of the saints, the divergence of East and West. Antony won universal recognition as saint. There are more than 165 Greek manuscripts of Athanasius's Life of Antony, and translations were made into Syriac, Coptic, and, eventually, Old Church Slavonic, this last serving as a model for later Russian hagiography.[68] It was also translated into Latin within a decade or so of its composition. It was thus accessible to the clergy and

[64] Athanasius, *Vita Antonii*, prologue, 3, p. 126.

[65] Sulpicius Severus, *Vita sancti Martini* 26. 3 (1, p. 314).

[66] Paulinus of Nola, *Epistula* 11. 11, p. 70.

[67] Augustine, *Confessiones* 8. 6, 12, pp. 122, 131.

[68] Athanasius, *Vita Antonii*, pp. 77–101 (editorial introduction).

monks of western Europe, who revered Antony as "the Father of Monks," and it enjoyed enormous success there throughout the Middle Ages.[69] Through such media as sermons, pictorial representations, and vernacular translations, its account became widely known even by those who were not literate in Latin or literate at all. In the eleventh century a brotherhood of St. Antony was founded in the south of France at a place that claimed to have his remains, brought from the East. They specialized in care of those suffering from ergotism, or "St. Antony's fire" as it was known, and enjoyed the privilege of feeding their pigs freely—hence the old English name for the smallest pig of a litter, a "tantony [that is, St. Antony] pig." The brethren formed an order of hospitallers with, at their height, over 350 hospitals.[70] The fourth-century Life had thus given birth to a literature and a cult which lasted throughout the Middle Ages in both eastern and western Christendom.

In the West, Martin was an even more prestigious saint than Antony. His cult was taken up by the kings of the Franks, who patronized Martin's cult-centre at Tours, and he was one of the most popular saints in the area of modern France and Germany, over three thousand churches being dedicated to him in France alone. His feast-day on 11 November ("Martinmas" in England, "Martini" in Germany, "la Saint-Martin" in France, and so on) was widely recognized as a turning point in the year, for rent payments, for university terms, for fairs, and for the hiring of servants. Images of Martin in manuscripts, wall-paintings, mosaic, and sculpture run into the hundreds. In the East, the story is different. Although he was recognized by the Eastern Church, Martin was quite insignificant in comparison with the West. There was a Greek version of his Life, and he is virtually the only western saint to have an entry in the Synaxarion of Constantinople, the great collection of readings on the saints put together in the tenth century, but (with one exception) there is no evidence of images, and church dedications are completely lacking.[71] As the Synaxarion shows, there was a gulf between saints of the East and saints of the West. Apart from the apostles and some of the early martyrs, the overlap between those revered in the Latin West and those in the Greek East was very slight. This was a parting of the ways that goes back as far as the time of Martin.

Between 360 and 400 Athanasius and Sulpicius Severus, along with Jerome, who composed Lives of the Egyptian hermit Paul and other ascetics, shaped Christian hagiography for good. The centrality of this first generation of hagiographic Lives is revealed by the comment of Paulinus of Milan at the beginning of his own *Life of St. Ambrose*, written probably in 422, a quarter-century after the saint's death. Paulinus addresses Augustine, bishop of Hippo:

[69] Leclercq, "Saint Antoine dans la tradition monastique médiévale."

[70] Fenelli, *Il tau, il fuoco, il maiale. I canonici regolari di Sant' Antonio abate tra assistenza e devozione.*

[71] *Vita et miracula sancti Martini episcopi* (BHG 1181); *Synaxarium Ecclesiae Constantinopolitanae*, pp. 217–18; the image is in the Menologion of Basil II (Vat. gr. 1613), facs. (*Il menologio di Basilio II*), fol. 176, which shows Martin raising a dead man. Other Byzantine images of "St. Martin" are of the seventh-century pope of that name: *Lexicon der christliche Ikonographie* 7, col. 574.

> Reverend father Augustine, you have encouraged me to write the Life of the blessed Ambrose . . . just as bishop Athanasius wrote the Life of St. Antony the hermit and Jerome wrote the Life of St. Paul the Hermit, just, too, as Severus composed in lucid style the Life of Martin, the reverend bishop of Tours.[72]

By this time, then, there were well-known models for those engaged in the task of writing a saint's Life—it had become a recognized genre. The texts that Paulinus mentions, Athanasius's *Life of Antony*, Jerome's *Life of Paul the Hermit*, and Sulpicius Severus's *Life of Martin*, the great formative saints' lives of the fourth century, served as models and stimuli not just for Paulinus but for hundreds of Christian hagiographers throughout the centuries.

Narratives about holy men and women were not completely new at this time—one has only to think of the historical books of the Old Testament, or the Gospels and Acts of the Apostles in the New. And very early in the history of Christianity the desire to know more about the apostles, especially their eventual fates, had stimulated the writing of the so-called Apocryphal Acts, in which the careers of Peter, Andrew, Thomas, and the others were traced well beyond their New Testament limits, with increasingly romantic elaboration.[73] The impetus was evidently the same as that which makes modern readers wonder "what happened" to the characters in a novel they have read after the closing pages. The Apocryphal Acts have indeed been described as novels.

This was one narrative tradition in the writing about holy people. The other was the record of the sufferings and heroic endurance of the martyrs (narratives often called "Passions," meaning "Sufferings"). Like the Acts of the Apostles, martyr literature too had a historical core and a more or less romantic elaboration. The early Christian martyrs were real people who suffered bravely for something they believed in. Sometimes a fair amount is known about them, even, in a few exceptional cases, like those of Perpetua and Cyprian discussed earlier, through writings from their own hand. However, once the concept of a "martyr" had been born, it developed its own conventions. The model acquired an independent momentum, spurring the elaboration of martyr legends based on pious inference, misidentifications, and pure invention. In the centuries after the conversion of Constantine the number of martyrs diminished, but the number of stories of martyrdom multiplied enormously. For every genuine account from the time of the persecuted Church, there are dozens of ahistorical literary constructions. St. George may well have been a genuine early martyr, but every narrative about him is later fiction.

By the end of the fourth century, then, a Christian literature of the saints had taken shape: the first surviving Christian calendar comes from that century, there were Acts of the Apostles, apocryphal and genuine, Passions of the martyrs, which were in some places read out on their feast-days, and there were the Lives of heroic ascetics as pioneered by Athanasius and Sulpicius Severus. It was a literature that was

[72] Paulinus, *Vita Ambrosii* 1. 1, p. 54.

[73] There is a very convenient compendium of translated material in *The Apocryphal New Testament*.

to swell to ever greater proportions and to become one of the main types of literary activity in the medieval period.

The First Miracle Books

The final major kind of writing to be added to the Christian literature of the saints was the Miracle Book, a collection of miracle accounts. Naturally, miracles had been recorded from the time of the Gospels, and before, but the collective account of miracles first appears as a literary genre in the early fifth century. This development is particularly associated with the discovery in Palestine of the body of St. Stephen, the first Christian martyr.[74] The Acts of the Apostles (chapters 6–7) recount Stephen's trial for blasphemy and his death by stoning, events dateable to c. 35. Thereafter there is no tradition of his burial place until it was revealed miraculously in 415. His relics were then quickly disseminated throughout the Church, and their coming stimulated numerous miracles. Amongst the places most affected was North Africa, where St. Augustine, now in his sixties, was deeply moved. Over the course of time he had become increasingly sympathetic to the idea that the flow of miracles had not dried up after the biblical period but was still powerful and active in the contemporary world. As a young, philosophically inclined, convert, he had been struck by the majestic regularities of God's creation; as an old man he thought more about miraculous healing.[75] One of the things that excited Augustine so much about the discovery of Stephen's relics was the stream of cures that followed when relics of the saint were brought to his native Africa. Augustine encouraged those who had received miraculous healing at the shrines housing the relics to make a written record of the event, a *libellus*, which could then be read out to the congregation.[76] Book Twenty-Two of his own *City of God* (the last book of this huge work) contains a long chapter recounting miraculous cures and other wonders performed through the saints and their relics in his own time and place.[77]

The earliest free-standing collection of miracle stories seems to be that of the miracles of St. Stephen performed in the African city of Uzalis (modern Al 'Aliyah, Tunisia) and written down, at some point in the 420s, at the command of its bishop, Augustine's friend Evodius.[78] This has all the features of the genre as it is found in the following centuries: a prologue communicating the subject of the treatise ("the things that Christ has done for us through our patron Stephen"), avowing

[74] *Revelatio Sancti Stephani.*

[75] De Vooght, "Les miracles dans la vies de saint Augustin"; Brown, *Augustine of Hippo*, pp. 413–18; Lepelley, "Les réticences de saint Augustin face aux légendes hagiographiques."

[76] Augustine, *Sermones* 79, 94, 286, 319–22 (PL 38: 493, 580, 1300, 1442–45).

[77] Augustine, *De civitate dei* 22. 8 (2, pp. 815–27); summary table in Saxer, *Morts, martyrs, reliques*, pp. 255–57.

[78] *Miracula sancti Stephani* (PL 41: 833–54); general analysis in the same volume, and in Saxer, *Morts, martyrs, reliques*, pp. 245–78.

1.1. Trier Ivory, showing entry of relics. Trier Cathedral Treasury. Photo: akg-images.

the truthfulness of the accounts and expressing the author's personal and literary unworthiness; then, in two books, a series of discrete tales, typically beginning with a standardized introduction of the character who benefitted from the miracle: "at the same time a certain barber of the city, called Concordius," "there was a certain noble woman of the city of Carthage called Megetia." Short narrative segments of this type were, over the course of the Middle Ages and beyond, to be one of the most common types of Christian literature; they number in the tens of thousands.

This account of Stephen's miracles at Uzalis starts with the arrival of the relics in the vicinity. They were corporeal relics ("a portion of his body") in a little container (*ampulla*) and were first placed, provisionally, in the church of the martyrs Felix and Gennadius, which was located, like all early martyr churches, outside the city. From there they were taken into the city by bishop Evodius in a triumphal procession. The text describes how "the holy relics were carried in the lap of the holy bishop, sitting in a carriage." Remarkably, this is exactly how the arrival of relics in a city is portrayed in a unique ivory carving of the subject, produced probably in sixth-century Constantinople: two bishops, seated on a carved wagon, hold a box on their laps while a procession heads towards an urban church (figure 1.1). What is even more extraordinary, it is likely that the scene depicted on the ivory is the reception of relics of this same saint, Stephen, in Constantinople in 421, much the same time as relics reached Uzalis.[79]

Once inside the bishop's church in Uzalis, the relics immediately displayed their miraculous healing power. While they were temporarily located on the bishop's throne, covered with a cloth, a blind woman called Hilara, a well-known baker, approached them, touched the cloth to her eyes, and then went home, praying all the

[79] Holum and Vikan, "The Trier Ivory."

while. During the night she went to her door and found that she could recognize the walls and flagstones of the street. When told this, her unsympathetic son responded by asking, "What lies are you telling?" but she persevered: "raising her eyes to the sky, she said, 'Lo, I see also the moon half-full above the theatre!'" She gave thanks to God and next morning went to church and gave a full account of this miraculous happening to all the faithful. "Thus," concludes the author, "there shone forth the first and most well-known work amongst us at the coming of the holy relics."[80]

The *Miracles of St. Stephen* describes twenty or so miraculous events: cures of blindness and paralysis, resurrections, prisoners released from their chains, prophetic dreams, even an incident so mundane as spoiled wine being cleared. On one occasion a woman was tormented with doubt after her husband had been gone on a journey for almost three years: would he return, was he dead, should she remarry? She took her troubles to the shrine of St. Stephen and there heard the words, "Your husband is coming." Soon thereafter the missing spouse came back. More dramatic than this prophetic reassurance was the occasion when, one market day, a huge storm hit Uzalis. Riding on it was a fiery dragon. Everyone sought refuge in the church and prostrated themselves before St. Stephen's shrine. "The lord Stephen's" prayers were, as usual, efficacious in the eyes of God, and the storm and the monster broke up and dispersed.

The text, although quite short, conveys the essential features of saints' shrines as they were to function throughout the medieval centuries and beyond. Pilgrims come to the shrine from some distance, one from Carthage, over 40 miles from Uzalis. They pray before the shrine, seek to get as close to the relics as possible, perhaps spend the night there. When cured, or after obtaining some other favourable outcome, they give thanks and recount the event publicly. The *Miracles* record what may be the earliest mention of an ex-voto, that is, an offering to a saint made in pursuance of a vow. A blind man named Donatianus, from a town about 18 miles from Uzalis, "came to the abode of the most powerful doctor, Stephen," and, on the eighth day, "received his sight through faith." Then, "desiring to fulfil his vow to the holy martyr, he offered a silver candle." The author points out the appropriateness of such a gift for the recovery of sight, but candles were in any case a standard feature of cult by this time.

Twenty years after the composition of the *Miracles of St. Stephen*, which form the earliest Miracle Book, another was put together, this time in Greek, not Latin. This was the *Miracles of Thecla*, an account of 46 miracles, originally composed in the 440s, and subsequently lightly revised and augmented, describing the wonders at her cult centre in Asia Minor.[81] Thecla was a very different saint from Stephen. While the latter was revered as the first martyr, and the account of his trial and death in the Acts of the Apostles entered the canon of the Christian Bible and is generally agreed to be largely historically accurate, Thecla's story is part of the imaginative

[80] *Miracula sancti Stephani* 1. 3, pp. 276–78.

[81] *Miracula Theclae*; see Davis, *The Cult of St. Thecla*; Johnson, *The Life and Miracles of Thekla*.

elaboration of apostolic history that took place in the first Christian centuries. From as early as the second century, Thecla's story was widely known.[82] She is described as a companion of St. Paul, who had spurned the chance of marriage in favour of a life devoted to virginity, and was twice condemned to be executed for her beliefs. On neither occasion did she die, although the texts consistently refer to her as a martyr, or even "protomartyr," that is, "first martyr," thus making her an exact female equivalent to Stephen.[83] There are several unusual features in her story. She baptizes herself, when in the arena, by throwing herself into a tank full of savage seals (it has been suggested that there might be a confusion here with sharks).[84] At one point she dresses as a man. She teaches the word of God, with Paul's approval. And eventually, in the expanded version of her story current by the fifth century, she does not die but sinks alive into the ground.

Aspects of this tale were highlighted by different people for different ends. As early as AD 200, those who wanted "to permit women to teach and baptize" used Thecla as an example.[85] She could also be praised as the chief of virgins.[86] From the point of view of cults, however, the oddest thing was that she was not only a martyr who had not died in the arena, she was a martyr without remains. Interestingly, this proved no obstacle to the development of her cult. This was centred near Seleucia (modern Silifke, in south-east Turkey), at the spot where she supposedly sank into the ground. Pilgrims are recorded here in the 370s and 380s, by which time there was a central church surrounded by the cells of monastic men and women.[87] And, as the text of the *Miracles* shows, this was a centre of supernatural activity.

The 46 miracles recorded in the Miracle Book of the 440s are very diverse. Thecla silences the pagan oracles and replaces their temples with churches, she defends the cities under her protection against marauding raiders, and she takes special care of her "assistant," the bishop, advising him to use oil from the lamps that burned at her shrine as a medicine. She helps in the law courts, prevents shipwreck, heals broken legs, cures scrofula and boils. Towards those who are disrespectful towards her, she can be implacable. A man who lusts after a woman in the congregation during Thecla's feast-day suffers a horrible death, as do two thieves who hold a rowdy party in the saint's precinct. Thecla has a strong physical presence: she appears riding the air in a fiery chariot, she spends the night with one of her devout female followers, holding her tightly in her arms. And she has tastes of her own: she is "a lover of literature" and much appreciates it when her devotees can cite Homer to her.

[82] *Acta Pauli et Theclae*.

[83] *Vita Theclae* (title), p. 167

[84] *Vita Theclae*, p. 251 n. 5: "Les phoques n'ont pas, dans l'antiquité, cette reputation injustifiée d'être des bêtes dangereuses: on le sait joueurs, on les croit en general bénéfiques." It is good to hear such a spirited defence of seals.

[85] Tertullian, *De baptismo* 17. 5, pp. 291–92 (PL 1: 1219).

[86] Methodius, *Symposium* 11.284, p. 308 (her speech in praise of virginity, ibid., 8, pp. 200–258).

[87] Gregory of Nazianzus, *De vita sua*, lines 547–49, col. 1067; Egeria, *Itinerarium Egeriae* 22, p. 66.

Just as the Lives of Antony and Martin in the fourth century stand at the head of an enormous stream of Latin and Greek saints' Lives, so these collections of the miracles of Stephen and Thecla in the fifth century do likewise for Latin and Greek Miracle Books. The cult of the saints had generated a new kind of literature and, in its turn, that literature bolstered and embodied the cult of the saints.

CHAPTER 2

The Early Middle Ages (500–1000)

As Roman imperial power disintegrated in western Europe and was shaken in the East, the Christian cult of the saints already had some of the basic contours that it was to maintain throughout the following centuries: a host of tomb-shrines containing the remains of the especially venerated Christian dead, whose intercession and aid could be sought in every aspect of life, especially in illness, and whose memory was celebrated both in annual liturgy and in literary compositions. The number of the saints was continually augmented by holy men—ascetics and bishops—and a smaller number of women, who joined the apostles and martyrs as intercessors in heaven. Hundreds, and soon thousands, of saints were commemorated and invoked.

The continuities in cult are in contrast with the big changes in political and religious life that took place between the fifth and the eighth centuries. In the 300 years after the abdication of the last western Roman emperor in 476, the geography of the Christian world was changed dramatically, first by the extension of Christianity beyond the old boundaries of the empire, and then, from the early seventh century, by the rise of Islam. Both of these new circumstances had important consequences for the cult of the saints, even if the fundamental features of the cult remained the same. When Christianity spread beyond the Roman world, the cult of the saints spread with it. This involved two things: the import of the existing features of Roman sainthood—the names, feast-days, cult practices, and books—and also the emergence of native saints, Christian holy men of one's own people, in the conversion period or later, whose bodies were treated in the same way as those of earlier Christian saints. From Ireland in the fifth century to Saxony in the ninth to Russia in the tenth and Lithuania in the fourteenth, conversion of areas outside the former Roman Empire incorporated them into a common culture, a culture that included saint, shrine, and miracle.

This process is clear in the case of the Anglo-Saxons. Although they had settled in the former Roman province of Britain, they were pagan and hence required conversion. Pope Gregory I organized a mission that arrived in England in 597, and among the things "necessary for the worship and ministry of the Church" brought by the missionaries were "relics of the holy apostles and martyrs."[1] Within the next century these imported cults were supplemented by native ones, such as those of Cuthbert,

[1] Bede, *Historia ecclesiastica* 1. 29, p. 104.

bishop of Lindisfarne (d. 687); the English evangelist Chad (d. 672), whose shrine provided dust that cured both men and animals; and Oswald, king of Northumbria (d. 642), "who gave the first fruits of sanctity to his people," and was an early example of a type of saint that was to be important in northern and eastern Europe, the king who died a violent death.[2] A bishop like Acca, bishop of Hexham (709–31), whose grandparents must have been pagan, and whose parents may originally also have been so, was an active champion of the cult of the saints: "when he had acquired relics of the blessed apostles and martyrs of Christ from all sides, he set up altars in veneration of them . . . also assembling the stories of their passions."[3] The introduction of relics and hagiography, and the birth of the cults of new native saints, were a central part of the conversion of Europe.

As Christianity and its saints spread slowly through new parts of Europe, it simultaneously suffered a huge unexpected setback in its heartlands. In the period after the formation of the Muslim community in 622, the armies of Islam invaded and conquered the oldest centres of the Christian religion—Palestine, Syria, Egypt—going on to subject to their rule the north Africa where Perpetua, Cyprian and Augustine had lived, and march on into Spain and southern France. Within a century of the birth of Islam, Muslim rule extended from central Asia to Provence. Islam gave explicit toleration to Christianity and Judaism, the "religions of the book," so Christian communities continued in all these areas, but no longer in Christian states. Hence the cult of the saints in the Middle East or North Africa, while continuing to the present day, was always a feature of a subordinate, and eventually minority, religion. By the year 750 the only Christian states of any size were the Byzantine Empire and the Kingdom of the Franks, while smaller Christian political units were limited to Italy, northern Spain, and the British Isles.

These changes in the territorial extent and political fortunes of Christianity were not the only notable religious developments of these centuries. Also highly important for the history of saintly cult was the efflorescence of Christian monasticism. As early as the official acceptance of Christianity in the fourth century, and long before then in many circles, it was recognized that "two ways of life have been instituted in the Church of Christ." One was "extraordinary and beyond the common behaviour of humanity"; it involved rejection of marriage and property, and total commitment to the service of God. The other way of life was more lowly but more suited to human beings, and involved marriage, children, and other things necessary for life in society.[4]

Monasticism emerged from the Egyptian desert in the time of St. Antony, as described earlier. It had not been an original feature of Christianity, which was a religion based in the urban communities of the Roman Empire and one which, although placing a special value on virginity, presumed that the building blocks of

[2] William of Malmesbury, *Gesta regum Anglorum* 1. 49, p. 74.

[3] Bede, *Historia ecclesiastica* 5. 20, p. 531.

[4] Eusebius of Caesarea, *Demonstratio evangelica* 1. 8, p. 39 (PG 22: 76–77).

the Church (*ecclesia*, meaning "assembly") would be ordinary Christian families. From the fourth century, however, this urban and familial Church was galvanized, reshaped and redirected by the ascetic movement, with its ideal of a new kind of life: without personal property, without sex or family, in obedience, in community. Monasteries spread from Egypt through the East, to Palestine and Syria; by the middle of the century there were numerous monasteries in the imperial capital of Constantinople; great Church Fathers of the fourth century, East and West, such as Basil and Gregory of Nazianzus, Augustine and Jerome, adopted the monastic life; St. Martin established a little wooden cell in the wild country outside his episcopal city of Tours, which formed the nucleus of a group of eighty or so followers who lived without personal property, engaged in writing and prayer and emulated the desert fathers, some even to the extent of wearing camel hair.[5] A new model of religious life had been born, one which was to flourish for a thousand years and more, and which provided a hospitable cradle for the Christian cult of the saints.

The View from the 590s

It is possible to convey some of the characteristics, and some of the diversity, of the cult of the saints in the early Middle Ages, by taking a standpoint in the 590s, and from there surveying what was happening across selected regions of the Christian world, while also allowing our gaze to sweep back and forth a little in time.

Ireland

A Christian heartland of the 590s, the very existence of which would have amazed the great Church Fathers of the fourth century, was Ireland.[6] When St. Jerome, writing at that earlier time, wanted to make a rhetorical point about the most remote ends of the earth, he included references to Britain ("the Briton, who is separated from our world," "men of the whole world, from India to Britain," and so on), but he could scarcely have imagined Christian missionaries from beyond Britain spreading and strengthening the faith in former provinces of the Roman Empire.[7] But by the 590s, two hundred years after Jerome's day, the Irish, although still, in their own words, "the most distant inhabitants of the world," were also "disciples of Saints Peter and Paul."[8] And to be disciples of Peter, that is, to be Christian, meant having saints, not only the ones whose relics and rituals were imported from the Roman

[5] Sulpicius Severus, *Vita sancti Martini* 10. 4–8 (1, p. 274).

[6] For a comprehensive guide to Irish saints who lived before before 1200, see Ó Riain, *A Dictionary of Irish Saints*.

[7] Divisus ab orbe nostro Britannus: Jerome, *Epistula* 46 (2, p. 110); totius orbis homines, ab India usque ad Britanniam: idem, *Epistula* 60 (3, p. 93); cf. *Epistulae* 58, 133 (3, p. 77; 8, p. 63).

[8] Columbanus, *Epistula* 5, p. 38.

world, but also home-grown ones. By the late sixth century the Irish had produced a rich crop.

Columba is the best attested Irish saint active in the 590s.[9] Member of a royal lineage from northern Ireland, but trained from boyhood for the Church, he set out in 563 "wishing to be a pilgrim for Christ."[10] This kind of pilgrim was not a traveller to distant shrines, who then returned home, but someone who left his homeland for good. Columba came to western Britain, to the kingdom of Dalriada, which was ruled by an Irish dynasty, and there established the island monastery of Iona. By the time of Columba's death in 597, Iona had become the mother-house of a group of monasteries in Ireland and Britain, and a mission centre amongst the pagan Picts. (Later it also played an important role in the conversion of the English.)

The reason it is possible to know so much about Columba is that a subsequent abbot of Iona, Adomnán, composed a Life of the saint, drawing on a hundred years of oral tradition and written stories. This Life is organized into three parts, dealing in turn with prophecies, miracles, and apparitions. Although it concludes with an account of Columba's death, it is thus not structured chronologically but thematically. Columba's prophetic powers gave him foreknowledge of matters as great as the outcome of battles and as trivial as the fact that a visitor would upset his inkwell. His miracles include healing, resurrection, calming of storms, encouraging a dissatisfied wife to sleep with her husband, and driving off an early version of the Loch Ness monster. And he was on intimate terms with angels; on one occasion he sent off an angel, who happened to be standing by the door of Columba's writing-hut in Iona, to save a monk from falling from the roof of the monastic buildings being constructed at Durrow in Ireland, a daughter-house of Iona and more than 200 miles distant from the mother-house. The angel arrived "with the speed of lightning."[11]

The *Life of Columba* which Adomnán composed is influenced by earlier models of hagiography, including Sulpicius Severus's *Life of Martin*, but there is a great deal of distinctive material alongside the generalities of the European saint's Life. The importance of cattle in these tales suggests very well the pastoral nature of early medieval Ireland and north Britain, and there are a conspicuous number of references to travelling by boat, although this is not perhaps surprising in the Life of an island saint (or an "island soldier" as he is termed).[12] Columba's conflicts with pagan priests and seers show a world where Christianity was young and still rubbed up against a hostile and distinct religion, and the constant presence of angels is also a characteristic feature of Irish sainthood.

Columba is the Irish saint whose image is transmitted most clearly, but he was only one of many Irish monastic founders of the early Christian period who came to be revered. Ireland has been known as "the isle of saints" from at least the eleventh

[9] Adomnán, *Vita Columbae*; there is a rich and detailed commentary in Adomnan, *Life of St. Columba*, tr. Sharpe; see also Herbert, *Iona, Kells, and Derry*, pp. 134–50.

[10] Adomnán, *Vita Columbae,* second preface, p. 6.

[11] Ibid., 3. 15, p. 202.

[12] Ibid., second preface, p. 6.

century, and that phrase reflects the fact that the Celtic world had more local saints than any other Christian region.[13] These numerous local saints were usually associated with one monastery or church, which was sometimes named after them (such as Tech Munnu, "the house of St. Munnu," now Taghmon in County Wexford) and which then took up the duty of commemorating them and maintaining and increasing their reputation and renown. Amongst these early Irish saints, there are nine or ten whose Lives, it has been argued, were collected in a hagiographical anthology put together by 800.[14] These include figures like Ailbe of Emly, who was fostered by a she-wolf (whom he later saved from hunters) and who could produce a hundred horses from a cloud and walk on the sea; or Luguid or Molua of Clonfertmulloe, whose shoe miraculously cleared the beer which was being served at a royal feast but was making the guests vomit—after Luguid's shoe had been dipped in it, "it made everyone very drunk." Such semi-legendary founders left an imprint on the landscape: crosses marked the spot where Luguid had miraculously kindled fire with his bare hands, while the name of Ailbe was revered at the rock where the wolf had raised him. The monasteries that claimed them as founders were headed by men whose very title was "successor" (*coarb*) of the saint, for example, "*coarb* of Ailbe" or "*coarb* of Columba."

Without a doubt, Ireland's most famous saint today is St. Patrick, the British missionary of the fifth century, associated forever in legend with the shamrock, and celebrated in Ireland and throughout the Irish diaspora on 17 March. Yet, despite this celebrity, a thick fog arises if any attempt is made to discern such basic facts as when and where he lived. He had certainly died at least a hundred years before Columba, but whether he should be placed in the earlier or later fifth century is debated, as also is his relationship with the well-attested mission of Palladius, described as being sent by the pope as "first bishop to the Irish believing in Christ."[15] The confusion here is so deep that some medieval writers (followed by some modern scholars) even sought to clarify things by suggesting that there were two St. Patricks.[16]

In another sense, however, it is possible to know a great deal about Patrick, at least in comparison with other saints of the early Middle Ages, because there survive two genuine writings from his own pen: the *Confession* and the *Letter*.[17] The writings disclose a person who repeatedly calls himself "an uneducated sinner" but is also clear that he has a mission from God: "I live amongst barbarous people, a stranger and an exile for the love of God—He is the witness it is so . . . I am compelled by

[13] Sharpe, *Medieval Irish Saints' Lives*, pp. 3–5.

[14] As identified by Sharpe, ibid., pp. 297–339, who dubs them the "O'Donohue group"; they are edited in *Vitae sanctorum Hiberniae e Codice olim Salmanticensi*, pp. 118–224 (or to p. 233 if the Life of Columba of Terryglass is also included, as Sharpe thinks possible). Criticisms have been made of Sharpe's proposition: Breatnach, "The Significance of the Orthography of Irish Proper Names in the Codex Salmanticensis." In support, Herbert, "Latin and Vernacular Hagiography of Ireland," pp. 336–39.

[15] Prosper, *Epitoma Chronicon*, p. 473.

[16] O'Rahilly, *The Two Patricks*.

[17] Patrick, *Confessio* and *Epistola*.

God's zeal, and Christ's truth has stirred me."[18] He declares his orthodox Christian belief, announces his duty "to spread God's name everywhere without fear and with confidence," and expresses his gratitude "that the Gospel has been preached as far as this place beyond which there is no one."[19] Patrick is personally humble—"I have not led a perfect life," he says[20]—yet bold and certain in his sense of mission.

After his death, Patrick's historically attested identity as a missionary amongst the Irish was embellished and inflated by the church that claimed closest connection with him, Armagh. Several centuries after Patrick's death, Armagh was making a bid for primacy amongst the churches of Ireland, and to do so it promoted an image of Patrick—and it is one that had great success—as "Apostle of the Irish." This is how Patrick was remembered in continental martyrologies (lists of saints arranged according to the calendar-year): "17 March: In Ireland the feast of St. Patrick, bishop and confessor, who first preached the Gospel of Christ there."[21] Armagh writers had to acknowledge one weakness in their case, however. Patrick's remains were not at Armagh but at Dún Lethglaisse (modern Downpatrick). They devised stories that explained why: when Patrick was on his death-bed, an angel had commanded that when he died, his body should be placed on a cart yoked to "two unbroken oxen, and let them go wherever they wish, and wherever they rest, let a church be built in honour of your poor body."[22] Only such a divine injunction could explain why the saint's body did not lie in Armagh.

But, although Armagh suffered the disadvantage of not possessing Patrick's body, writers like Tírechán of Armagh, working at much the same time as Adomnán of Iona, constructed a figure who was responsible for founding virtually all the churches of Ireland, implicitly asserting the widest bounds for the authority of Armagh.[23] It is from this milieu that there comes one of the great surviving documents of early medieval Irish hagiography, the Book of Armagh, written in 807, which contains the two earliest Lives of Patrick, by Muirchú and Tírechán, along with a version of Patrick's own *Confession*. In addition it has a great deal of material supportive of Armagh's claims, and, appropriately, a copy of Sulpicius Severus's *Life of Martin*, the first great confessor-saint of the West (by the tenth century it was even claimed that Patrick and Martin were related through Patrick's mother).[24] The Book of Armagh became one of the insignia of the see of Armagh, legend even claiming that it had belonged to Patrick himself.[25]

[18] *Epistola* 1, ed. Bieler, p. 91; ed. Hood, p. 35.

[19] *Confessio* 4, 14, 34, ed. Bieler, pp. 58–60, 64, 76; ed. Hood, pp. 23–24, 25, 29.

[20] *Confessio* 44, ed. Bieler, p. 83; ed. Hood, p. 31.

[21] Usuard, *Martyrologium*, p. 195 (PL 123: 849); as is standard usage at this time, *Scotia* designates "Ireland."

[22] Muirchú, *Vita sancti Patricii* II. 11 (9), p. 120.

[23] Tírechán, *Collectanea de sancto Patricii*.

[24] *Betha Phatraic*, 1, p. 9.

[25] Insignia quaedam sedis illius, textum scilicet Evangeliorum, qui fuit beati Patricii: Bernard of Clairvaux, *Vita sancti Malachiae* 12. 24, p. 334.

Patrick may be viewed today as the patron saint of Ireland, but in the Middle Ages an Irish saint with a cult of much greater international dissemination was Brigid. It is a situation which teaches a central rule about saintly cult: there is no relation between the historical reality of a saint and the importance of their cult. Unlike Patrick and Columba, who are well-attested figures, in one case with writings from his own pen, in the other with a secure genealogy and a sequence of dated events, Brigid hovers in a legendary mist. Some even argue that she is simply a retouched version of a pagan Irish goddess (see later, pp. 613–14). Nevertheless, her first Life is as early as those of Patrick and Columba (all are late seventh century), and her name came to be known throughout Europe. Her Life can even be found in an eleventh-century collection now in Naples where all other saints are Mediterranean or eastern.[26]

The Irish annals place the death of Brigid in the 520s (although these entries are not contemporary). By the late seventh century, when her first Lives were written, there had been plenty of time for different traditions about the saint to grow. For the author of one of these Lives, Cogitosus, Brigid was especially important as the patron of the great double-monastery of Kildare. He described how she and her ally, the local bishop, were enshrined in the church there:

> The glorious bodies of the two of them lie there, placed in tombs on the right and the left side of a beautiful altar, adorned with skilfully worked gold and silver and precious stones, with gold and silver crowns hanging above them and with various carved and painted images.[27]

Miracles, asserts Cogitosus, continue to occur there, and Kildare is "the head of almost all the churches of the Irish," its bishop even being titled "archbishop."[28]

In contrast to this awe-inspiring enshrined saint, there are traditions of a humbler Brigid.[29] According to these alternative accounts, she was the daughter of a slave-girl, had no especial connection with Kildare, and was a friend to the poor and weak. When asked why she helped common people to conceive and bear children, but seemed unwilling to do the same for the wife of a king, she replied: "For the common people all serve God and call on the Father, but the sons of kings are serpents and sons of blood and death."[30] This friend of the people was deeply involved in the pastoral, beer-drinking society of Ireland, providing food, healing, and advice. Her most attractive miracle (also reported by Cogitosus) was to hang her cloak to dry on a sun-beam.

Brigid's cult spread to Britain early and was taken to the continent by Irish monks. Her Lives were copied in monasteries across Europe throughout the Middle

[26] Poncelet, "Catalogus codicum hagiographicorum latinorum bibliothecarum Neapolitanarum," pp. 154–57 (Naples, Biblioteca Nazionale, VIII. B. 3).

[27] Cogitosus, *Vita sanctae Brigitae* 8. 37, p. 141.

[28] Ibid., prologue, 2, p. 135.

[29] As recorded in the *Vita prima sanctae Brigidae* and the *Bethu Brigte*; a careful analysis of the differences can be found in Charles-Edwards, "Brigit."

[30] *Vita prima sanctae Brigidae* 10. 60, p. 126.

2.1. St. Brigid from Book of Hours, Belgium, perhaps Bruges, ca. 1420.
Pierpont Morgan Library, New York, M. 76, fol. 259v.
Purchased by J. Pierpont Morgan (1837–1913), 1902.

Ages, and her name occurs frequently in Kalendars and martyrologies. She can be found depicted on a twelfth-century altar from a Danish church (Lisjberg) and in a fifteenth-century Dutch prayer-book, holding a cow on a rope (figure 2.1).[31] There was a famous church dedicated to her in Fleet Street in London (St. Brides), and a rather less famous one in Ölling by Henndorf, in the diocese of Salzburg, where the chief church itself possessed relics of Brigid as early as 846.[32]

[31] New York, Pierpont Morgan Library, M. 76, fol. 259v.

[32] Ó Mara, "Die heilige Brigid und ihr Kult im Salzburger Land"; *Monumenta necrologica monasterii sancti Petri Salisburgensis*, p. 16n.

But Cogitosus's picture of Brigid, entombed in glory at the heart of her great abbey church, demonstrates the exception not the rule. Columba, Patrick, and the others were saints of great repute, but, unlike their counterparts in most areas of Christendom, they did not usually become the focus of cults centred upon their tombs. The cult of bodily relics was not as important in Ireland as elsewhere.[33] Even in the twelfth century, an acute, if unfriendly, observer could note a preference for secondary or contact relics rather than bones: "the people and clergy of Ireland, Scotland and Wales greatly reverence the handbells of the saints and their curving staffs, which are covered with gold silver or bronze."[34] Bells, staffs, books (like the Book of Armagh), and other objects associated with the saint in his or her life retained a numinous power, but their bodies did not. Here was a world where the saints were numerous and revered, but their tombs were not the main focus of cult. It was very different in the contemporary Merovingian world.

Merovingian Sainthood

Of all the barbarian kingdoms that arose on the territory of the western Roman Empire, the largest and most powerful was that of the Franks. From the time of Clovis, who died in 511, until the year 751, the Franks were ruled by the Merovingian dynasty, and their territories covered most of Roman Gaul as well as lands of varying extent beyond the old Roman frontier, east of the Rhine. The most important source of information about the cult of the saints in the Merovingian period is the body of writings created by Gregory of Tours, who died in 594, just three years before Columba. Despite this close chronological overlap, the two men belonged to different worlds.

Gregory was from an old aristocratic family, whose members had ruled the cities of Merovingian Gaul for generations, holding lay titles as senators and ecclesiastical titles as bishops. Their ancestry and traditions were Roman, as their choice of names (Florentinus, Georgius, Gregorius, and the like) shows, although they moved in the world of Frankish politics, which could be dangerous—Gregory himself almost fell foul of the violent and suspicious King Chilperic, a grandson of Clovis. When Gregory became bishop of Tours in 573, he was joining a long line of family members, past and present. What distinguished him was that he was a prolific author.

Gregory's most extensive and most well-known literary composition is his *History*, a vital source of information about the sixth-century Merovingian world, but he also composed many hagiographical works: *The Glory of the Martyrs*, *The Passion and Miracles of St. Julian*, *The Miracles of St. Martin* (in four books), *The Life of the Fathers*, and *The Glory of the Confessors*.[35] Some of these books dealt with miracles

[33] Charles-Edwards, *Early Christian Ireland*, p. 348; see also the brief but cogent remarks in Herbert, "Hagiography and Holy Bodies: Observations on Corporeal Relics in Pre-Viking Ireland."

[34] Gerald of Wales, *Topographia hibernica* 3. 33, p. 179; idem, *Itinerarium Kambriae* 1. 2, p. 27.

[35] Gregory of Tours, *Gloria martyrum*; *De passione et virtutibus sancti Iuliani*; *De virtutibus sancti Martini*; *Liber vitae patrum*; *Gloria confessorum*. He may also have been the author of a work on Andrew.

at the shrines of long-dead saints, others with recent and contemporary holy men. *The Glory of the Martyrs* starts with Jesus, Mary, and the apostles, while, on the other hand, *The Life of the Fathers* is almost entirely dedicated to saints of the sixth century, Gregory's own age, many of them in fact being his relatives. A notable example is Gregory's namesake and great-grandfather, Gregory, bishop of Langres, who died in 539 or 540; he was, in the first part of his life, a family man, a senator, and count of Autun, then, on his wife's death, he entered the Church, and became a bishop and a famous exorcist. After his death "he manifested himself by many miracles."[36] Such high-born episcopal saints were characteristic of Merovingian Gaul.

But Gregory of Tours had the closest and most important relationship not with his own family members but with his distant predecessor as bishop of Tours, St. Martin. Martin was, indeed, Gregory's "lord." On one occasion when Gregory was trying to intercede with the king on behalf of some defeated rebels and having little initial success, he then addressed the king, "O king, let your great power listen! I have been sent to you by my lord as a messenger. What answer shall I carry back to him who sent me?" "Who is your lord, who sent you?," the astonished ruler asked. It was of course St. Martin.[37] By presenting himself in such a way, as the mouthpiece of St. Martin, Gregory was enabled to undertake this delicate matter under the cloak of the saint's identity. A claim to represent the long-dead saint was always one important way that the heads of churches, bishops and abbots, could turn stubborn defence of the rights and property of their institution into a heroic principle.

Gregory eagerly collected reports of the miracles performed by "his lord." They are found in several of his writings but most extensively in his four-part book on *The Miracles of St. Martin*. In this work, after going over some of the miracles described by earlier writers, he launches into a series of accounts of the wonders of his own times. He tells of 295 such events, the vast majority (280) being miracles of healing.[38] Martin was "a doctor" who "brought healing medicine."[39] These were not rare occurrences, as Gregory himself notes: "every day we see the kind of miracles we have written about," he writes.[40] The most common ailments cured were blindness, paralysis and other crippling conditions, fever, demonic possession, deaf-mutism, and intestinal and gastric illnesses, and the beneficiaries were predominantly laymen (74 per cent), rather than clerics or women. Typically, they would come to the shrine, pray for varying lengths of time, and receive healing. Frequently contact relics

---

There are English translations of all these works: *Glory of the Martyrs*; *Life of the Fathers*; *Glory of the Confessors*; the works on Julian and Martin in Van Dam, *Saints and Their Miracles in Late Antique Gaul*, pp. 162–95, 199–303. For comment see Van Dam; Goffart, *The Narrators of Barbarian History*, pp. 127–53; see also Giordano, "Sociologia e patologia del miracolo."

[36] *Liber vitae patrum* 7, pp. 686–90, quotation at p. 689 (repr., 1969, pp. 236–40, quotation p. 239).

[37] Gregory of Tours, *Libri historiarum X* 8. 6, p. 375.

[38] Giordano, "Sociologia e patologia del miracolo," contains, along with other insightful comments, statistical analysis of *De virtutibus sancti Martini*, esp. at pp. 171–80.

[39] *De virtutibus sancti Martini* 3, pref., p. 632 (repr., 1969, p. 182).

[40] Cum talia miracula quae scripsimus cotidie cernamus: ibid., 2. 32, p. 620 (repr., 1969, p. 170).

were employed—oil from the lamps that burned at the shrine, dust from the tomb. Sometimes the cures might occur at other places dedicated to Martin. In one village near Bordeaux, which was suffering from an outbreak of disease amongst the horses, the villagers borrowed the key of the church, which was dedicated to St. Martin, and branded their animals with it, thus ensuring the end of the epidemic.[41] Martin's power, writes Gregory, "is shown in the punishments of fools just as in the grace of healing," but he recounts virtually no punishment miracles.[42] For him saintly power meant, essentially, wonders, especially healing miracles, at the shrine. He says explicitly that posthumous miracles are more important than whatever a saint does in life: "the power that comes from the tomb is more praiseworthy than what the living person does in this life."[43]

Naturally, as St. Martin's successor, and bishop of the city that housed his tomb, Gregory had a formal and official relationship with the saint. He was the public representative of the cult. But his attachment to Martin was personal as well as institutional. He carried with him relics of St. Martin, which saved him from drowning and could put out a fire.[44] When going on a journey, he took with him dust from the saint's tomb, so that it could bring its "customary assistance."[45] And this assistance was available for quite mundane problems. On one occasion, for instance, Gregory had a fish-bone stuck in his throat, until, going to Martin's tomb, he touched his throat with the cloth that covered the shrine, and, at once, as if someone had pulled the bone out, he was freed of all discomfort.[46]

Gregory of Tours was not familiar with, or sympathetic to, the city of Paris, but he does record some facts about it, including the burial in the church of St. Peter there of the matriarch of the Merovingian dynasty, Clotilda. To this piece of information he adds the comment, "Saint Geneviève is also buried there."[47] Alongside the reverence for episcopal saints like Martin, and Gregory's own aristocratic and patriarchal relatives, the Merovingian kingdoms also witnessed the growth and efflorescence of the cult of numerous female saints, and Geneviève was one of the earliest and most renowned. She was eventually to give her name to the church in which she was buried (it is now the Panthéon) and to become the patron saint of Paris.

Born into the disintegrating world of the late Roman Empire, Geneviève lived through the invasion of Gaul by Attila's Huns in 451 and the take-over of the Paris region by the Franks in the later fifth century. While she organized prayer-vigils in

[41] Ibid., 3. 33, p. 640 (repr., 1969, p. 190).

[42] Gregory of Tours, *Libri historiarum X* 5. 6, p. 203; the story here is of an archdeacon punished by a relapse for consulting Jewish doctors. Punishments also befell those swearing falsely at a church dedicated to St. Martin (ibid., 8. 16, pp. 383–84).

[43] Gregory of Tours, *Liber vitae patrum* 2. 2, pp. 669–70 (repr., 1969, pp. 219–20).

[44] Gregory of Tours, *Libri historiarum X* 8. 14, p. 380; idem, *Gloria martyrum* 10, p. 495 (repr., 1969, p. 45).

[45] Gregory of Tours, *De virtutibus sancti Martini* 3. 60, p. 647 (repr., 1969, p. 197).

[46] Ibid., 3. 1, p. 632 (repr., 1969, p. 182).

[47] Gregory of Tours, *Libri historiarum X* 4. 1, p. 135.

response to Attila's invasion and was credited with keeping the Huns from Paris by this means, she established a personal relationship with the Frankish kings Childeric (d. 481/2) and Clovis (d. 511), often interceding for their captives.[48] It was Clovis who began construction of the church in which she was buried. Geneviève's sanctity, as conveyed in the Life written 18 years after her death,[49] consisted in her vow of perpetual virginity; her continual prayer, fasting, and weeping; her miracles of healing and—a speciality—rekindling candles that had gone out; and a certain kind of religious perspicacity: "she declared most openly to many people living in the world the inner secrets of their mind."[50] By encouraging the building of a basilica outside Paris for the relics of St. Denis, by visiting Martin's shrine at Tours, and by receiving the greetings of the contemporary eastern saint Simeon Stylites, she demonstrated that she was part of a wider world of saintly cult, both past and present.

Geneviève was the first female saint to be the object of an important cult in Gaul. Traces of the cult of female martyrs there are slight (although there were several important male martyrs), and Gregory of Tours lists only seven female figures amongst his confessor-saints.[51] This fact is probably to be linked to the absence in this early period of organized monastic life for women—Geneviève herself was a consecrated virgin but, unlike later Merovingian female saints, she was not an abbess, heading a community of nuns whose continued corporate existence would provide both means and motives for a continuing cult. In the late sixth and seventh centuries such powerful abbesses would be the predominant type of female saint: Radegund of Poitiers (d. 587) and Gertrude of Nivelles (d. 659) are prominent examples, the former having been a queen before entering monastic life, the latter the daughter of the ancestor of the Carolingian dynasty.

Slowly, between the fourth and the eighth century, the Frankish kingdoms thus built up a rich repertoire of saints: early martyrs, both historical and invented, including one of the most famous, St. Denis, supposed bishop of Paris executed with his companions on "martyrs' hill" (Montmartre);[52] the great confessor-saint of the early Middle Ages, Martin, whose miraculous cape was guarded by clerics in the service of the Merovingian dynasty, giving rise to the new terms "chapel" and "chaplain"; the aristocratic bishop-saints that Gregory of Tours wrote about; and the new female saints like Geneviève or the high-born abbesses like Radegund and Gertrude.[53]

[48] *Vita Genovefae virginis Parisiensis* 12–13, 26, 56, pp. 219–20, 226, 237.

[49] There has been considerable controversy over the dating of the Life: see Heinzelmann and Poulin, *Les vies anciennes de Saint Geneviève*, who accept the authenticity of the author's claim to have written 18 years after the saint's death.

[50] *Vita Genovefae virginis Parisiensis* 10, p. 218.

[51] Beaujard, *Le culte des saints en Gaule*, pp. 295–300.

[52] In colle qui antea mons Mercurii, quoniam inibi idolum ipsius principaliter colebatur a Gallis, nunc vero mons Martyrum vocatur: Hilduin of St.-Denis, *Passio sanctissimi Dionysii* 36, col. 50.

[53] On this process, see the meticulous study of Beaujard, *Le culte des saints en Gaule*.

Byzantium

At the same time as Columba was confronting monsters in Scotland and Gregory of Tours was commemorating his saintly predecessors in Gaul, a figure of far less exalted ancestry was building up a reputation as a saint in the dusty heart of Anatolia. This was Theodore of Sykeon, son of a prostitute and an acrobat, born in a tavern in a small town in Galatia (modern central Turkey) around the middle of the sixth century.[54] Despite this apparently unpromising beginning, dreams and prophecies marked him out as a saint. And, from an early age, Theodore had a special relationship with St. George (who was believed to have come from the neighbouring province of Cappadocia). George appeared in a vision to Theodore's mother, commanding her to give up her plans to seek a secular career for her son, and he appeared to Theodore himself, throughout his life, protecting him and guiding him. Theodore reciprocated by expanding the nearby church of St. George into a flourishing monastery, and by seeking out relics of St. George, which he then placed in the monastery; even the demons recognized that Theodore and "George of Cappadocia" were effective partners.[55]

Theodore's sainthood was based on a fierce asceticism: he fasted, he spent years enclosed in a cave, he passed months in an iron cage. The fruits of his sainthood were the ability to heal, to exorcise demons, to protect crops from locusts, to bring rain in times of drought, to have friendly and peaceful relations with wild animals. The battle with demons was especially intense. Even when he was a boy, Theodore was tempted by a demon who appeared in the shape of one of his playmates and threw himself down a cliff, suggesting that he could do likewise; only the appearance of St. George saved him from this temptation to suicidal vainglory.[56] Much later in his life, when some villagers were quarrying stone for the construction of a bridge, they unwittingly released "a throng of unclean spirits," some in the shape of flies or hares or mice, and these possessed the villagers and beset local travellers. Only when Theodore was summoned was this crisis ended, as he cast the devils out and forced them back into the hole from which they had come, having it sealed behind them.[57] And bad magic of various kinds was all around: a jealous sorcerer (*pharmakos*) sent his attendant demons to attack Theodore, and also tried poisoning his food; the lid of an ancient pagan sarcophagus, re-used as a drinking trough, provided a gateway for the demons to infest both men and beasts. Of course Theodore overcame these challenges. The sorcerer repented and burned his books, the sarcophagus lid

[54] *Vita Theodori Syceotae*. For an attempt to identify Sykeon, see Barchard, "Sykeon Rediscovered?" For discussion of the world presented in the Life, see Mitchell, *Anatolia* 2, pp. 122–50; Wickham, *Framing the Early Middle Ages*, pp. 406–11.

[55] Festugière, the editor, summarizes the incidents involving St. George in his commentary (*Vita Theodori Syceotae*, vol. 2, p. 173).

[56] *Vita Theodori Syceotae* 11, pp. 9–10.

[57] Ibid., 43, pp. 38–39.

was cleansed and allowed to retain its useful function—"it is there to this day," commented the author of Theodore's Life.[58]

While Theodore sometimes appears as the champion or patron of the local peasantry, protecting their crops, curing their illnesses, and freeing them from demonic infestations, he also had an official position. Ordained a priest at the early (and uncanonical) age of eighteen, he was appointed—supposedly unwillingly—bishop of the nearby regional centre, Anastasioupolis, in which office he continued for eleven years before being allowed to return to the monastic life he craved, but even as an abbot he had contact with the powerful. At one point the victorious general Maurice, passing through Galatia, visited the holy man and heard from him the prophecy that, if he were assiduous in his prayers to St. George, he would become emperor, but that when he did so he must always remember the poor.[59] The prophecy was fulfilled when Maurice acquired the imperial throne in 582. The new emperor may have continued to be mindful of the poor but was also mindful of this saintly encouragement, and granted both revenues and privileges to Theodore's monastery. Nor were Theodore's horizons limited to his provincial homeland. He made three devotional trips to the Holy Land and visited the imperial capital Constantinople for prolonged periods, not only continuing his unassuming work of providing medical advice, reconciling spouses and litigants, and moral exhortation, but also meeting emperors and patriarchs. Theodore died in 613. He is a perfect example of the local holy man, a protector, patron, and mediator, who was also a widely travelled confidante of the highest powers and authorities.

Amongst Theodore's followers was one who went on to become a stylite, a very distinctive type of eastern saint, an ascetic who spent years on top of a pillar or column (*stylos*).[60] The founder of this new mode of self-mortification was St. Simeon Stylites (d. 459), the same saint who sent greetings to St. Geneviève in distant Gaul (see earlier, p. 38). He took up permanent residence on top of a column near the Syrian monastery of Telanissus around the year 423, and, over the next three and a half decades, remained "mid-way between heaven and earthly things,"[61] the only changes being his transfer to ever higher columns. The last was over 15 metres (fifty feet or so) tall; the space at the top has been estimated at between a metre and two metres (three feet and six feet) square.[62]

Simeon won a wide reputation for his harsh behaviour to his own body—fasting, wakefulness, and endless repetitive prayer—but he was also an active participant in the society around him. People came to his column to hear him preach, to receive his blessing, to beg for miraculous healing, and to have their disputes resolved. He had an especial following among the nomadic Arab tribes. On one occasion two

[58] Ibid., 37–38, 118, pp. 32–34, 94–95.

[59] Ibid., 54, pp. 46–47.

[60] Delehaye, *Les saints stylites*.

[61] Evagrius, *Historia ecclestiastica* 1. 13, p. 158.

[62] Theodoret of Cyrrhus, *Historia Religiosa* 26. 12 (2, p. 184 and n.); Peña et al., *Les stylites syriens*, pp. 40–42.

rival groups turned up, both asking for his blessing on their chief and urging him not to bless the enemy chief. Eventually they fell on each other and were separated only after Simeon had threatened them and called them dogs.[63] His withdrawal from the world involved him in it.[64] Simeon's role as "rural patron" is stressed in a contemporary Life: "How many oppressed were delivered from their oppressors at his word. How many bonds were torn up through the efforts of the saint. How many afflicted were relieved from their coercers. How many slaves were freed."[65]

Simeon Stylites on his pillar was the first of a long tradition, characteristic especially of eastern Christianity. An isolated case of a stylite saint is known from western Europe, but it shows how, in some sense, the practice went against the grain there. Some time around the middle of the sixth century the deacon Ulfilaic, a Lombard from Italy, came to the Middle Meuse region, in the hills of the Ardennes, and there set himself upon a column. He ate nothing but bread, water, and herbs. During the winter his beard froze and his toe-nails repeatedly fell off. Although he drew crowds, the local bishops were unhappy. "This path you are following is not reasonable," they said, "nor will an ignoble person like you be able to be compared with Simeon of Antioch, who sat on a column. But nor does the position of the place allow you to sustain this torment—come down, rather." Reluctantly Ulfilaic obeyed and, while he was away, workmen with hammers destroyed his column.[66] The attempt to transplant this extravagant feature of eastern asceticism to the west had been swiftly crushed by the authoritarian action of the bishops, assisted by the north European weather.

In the East it was different. There the names of around one hundred stylite saints are recorded from the Middle Ages, and the tradition lingered on, with the last examples in nineteenth-century Russia and Rumania.[67] One at least was a woman.[68] Their lives were painful and could be perilous—one was hurled from his column into the sea by an earthquake[69]—but they were revered and consulted by many, including bishops and emperors, and, after their deaths, their relics were the centres of pilgrimage and healing cults.

Alongside the living holy men like Theodore of Sykeon or the stylites, we find in Byzantium the same kind of healing shrines that dominate the pages of Gregory of Tours in the West. A very good example is provided by the cult of the twin saints Cosmas and Damian, who were believed to be early martyrs. One of the chief centres of their cult was the so-called Cosmidion, a church founded in the fifth century just

[63] Theodoret of Cyrrhus, *Historia Religiosa* 26. 15 (2, pp. 192–94).

[64] See especially Brown, "The Rise and Function of the Holy Man"; there is criticism as well as tribute in Howard-Johnston and Hayward, eds., *The Cult of Saints in Late Antiquity and the Middle Ages: Essays on the Contribution of Peter Brown.*

[65] *The Syriac Life of St. Symeon Stylites* 77, p. 159 (see also editorial introduction, pp. 18–23); "rural patron": Brown, "The Rise and Function of the Holy Man," p. 87.

[66] Gregory of Tours, *Libri historiarum X* 8. 15, pp. 380–83; despite his unhappy experience as a stylite, Ulfilaic became the centre of a local cult under the name St. Walfroy.

[67] There is a list (not limited to Syrian saints) in Peña et al., *Les stylites syriens*, pp. 80–90.

[68] Ibid., p. 88 (Maia).

[69] Ibid., p. 87 (989).

outside the walls of Constantinople, to which, at some point prior to 518, a monastery was attached. Although its position outside the defences made it vulnerable, the foundation survived throughout the Middle Ages; the emperor Michael VIII spent the night here in 1261, before he entered the city, which had just been reconquered from the Latins.[70] Forty-eight miracle accounts survive from this healing shrine, of various dates, but a series of twenty-six can be assigned to the period prior to the early seventh century, and hence are roughly contemporary with Columba and Gregory of Tours.[71]

Many saints provided healing, but Cosmas and Damian are the most unmistakably medical of them all. The twins are "glorious and awe-inspiring doctors," their church is "the surgery of the saints," and the two of them even "go on their rounds."[72] Sometimes they turned up with basin, sponge, and bandages.[73] But they were doctors of a very unusual kind. They asked for no fees. The saints were revered as "wondrous doctors, who cure without charging."[74] This gave them their epithet, Anargyres, from the Greek "without silver (αργυρος)."

From these stories Cosmas and Damian come through as strong and vivid characters, with a jocular side. Like Thecla, discussed earlier (see p. 25), they were very physical saints, carrying one disgruntled suppliant on his litter, on another occasion appearing in the form of a bath attendant to help a paralyzed priest have a very vigorous—and healing—bath.[75] They are rather tricky saints. They advise one poor suppliant to take a pubic hair from Cosmas, burn it, place it in water, and drink the result. This bemuses the sick man, until he realizes that Cosmas is also the name of a pet sheep kept in the church![76] At other times their sense of humour had a more malicious side. They tell a Jewess suffering from cancer that she must eat pork. After much resistance and distress, she is just about to do this, when the cancer leaps miraculously from her body into the piece of pork. As a consequence she converts.[77]

The saints' broad sense of humour is most evident in a miracle that occurred when a paralyzed man and a mute woman were amongst those spending the night in their church hoping for miracle cures.[78] Appearing to the paralytic in a dream-vision, Cosmas and Damian said that, if he wished to be cured, he should sleep with the dumb woman. The man dismissed this as wicked nonsense, but the saints appeared twice

[70] For various opinions on the origins of the church, see Janin, *La géographie ecclésiastique de l'Empire byzantin*, pp. 297–98; *Saint Thècle, Saints Côme et Damien, Saints Cyr et Jean (extraits), Saint Georges*, p. 87; Mango, "On the Cult of Saints Cosmas and Damian at Constantinople." For the emperor Michael's visit, Akropolites, *The History* 88, p. 383.

[71] *Miracula Cosmae et Damiani.*

[72] For example, ibid., 5, 9, pp. 108, 114.

[73] Ibid., 17, p. 143.

[74] Ibid., 10, p. 121.

[75] Ibid., 1, 14, p. 99–100, 134–37.

[76] Ibid., 3, pp. 104–7.

[77] Ibid., 2, pp. 101–4.

[78] Ibid., 24, pp. 162–64.

more with the same advice. Finally convinced, the man crawled slowly and painfully towards the woman. As he reached her bed, she awoke and cried out, whereupon her attendants came running, and the paralyzed man dashed off. In this way, "the paralyzed man taught the dumb woman to speak, the dumb woman taught the paralyzed man to run." The story ends with the man and the woman getting happily married.

The robust double-act of Cosmas and Damian was not uncharacteristic of Byzantine healing shrines. Already in the fifth century, as noted earlier, St. Thecla was vividly physical and present at her shrine in Anatolia, appearing in a chariot, appreciating study of Homer. Across the Mediterranean from the Cosmidion at Constantinople was the shrine of St. John and St. Cyrus, just outside Alexandria. Here, around the year 610, a collection of seventy of the saints' miracles was recorded. Like Cosmas and Damian, they seem to have had a slapstick sense of humour, on one occasion insisting that an unbeliever be led around their sanctuary by a bridle, with the pack-saddle of an ass on his back and a bell around his neck, repeating, "I am stupid."[79]

It is only hypothesis, but perhaps it was this flamboyant physical aspect to the posthumous cults of early Byzantine saints that explains a curious contemporary reaction among some Byzantine theologians, that is, the belief that the saints could not appear in their bodies, that they slept disembodied until the Last Day, and that their apparent manifestations were just that—apparent, not real. To some sensibilities, there might be something ridiculous or unseemly about saints who made jokes about pubic hair, pretended to be bath attendants, or played ridiculous pranks. Better that these antics should be undertaken by emanations, while the saints themselves rested in dignified powerlessness in heaven—saved, of course, but "inactive."[80] (The issue is discussed at greater length later, on pp. 589–90.)

Gregory the Great

By the 590s western and eastern Christendom were beginning to drift apart. It was a tendency which deepened in the seventh and eighth centuries. Personal contact at high level became rarer: the visit of Constans II to Rome in 663 was the last by an eastern Roman emperor for over 700 years, while the visit of Pope Constantine to Constantinople in 710 was the last by a pope until 1979.[81] The last Greek speaker to be pope was Zacharias (741–52). Pope Gregory I (590–604), known as "Gregory the Great," the incumbent in the 590s, is often seen as the first pope to turn decisively to the West. Although this scarcely takes into account his continuing whole-hearted recognition of the suzerainty of the emperor in Constantinople, nevertheless, his independent activities and undertakings in western Europe, notably the launch of

[79] Sophronius of Jerusalem, *Miracula Cyri et Ioannis* 30. 8–11, pp. 304–5.

[80] *Anenergētoi*: Eustratius of Constantinople, *De statu animarum*, line 54, p. 5.

[81] The next visit of an eastern emperor to Rome after that of Constans was that of John V in 1369.

the mission to England, laid the foundations for a later papacy that was to ally with Germanic dynasties in the West and eventually break its ties with the emperor in the East.

Gregory was part of a wide web of saintly contacts and hagiographic activity. He received a letter from Columbanus, himself a disciple of St. Columba, in which the Irish monk praised Gregory's book *The Pastoral Rule* as "sweeter than honey" and asked the pope to send him some of his works of biblical exegesis.[82] Gregory of Tours, the great hagiographer of sixth-century Gaul, was interested in Pope Gregory and includes an entire sermon of his in his *History*.[83] Born into a wealthy and prestigious Roman family, Gregory was proudly aware of the great store of relics that Rome possessed and, when pope, often sent gifts of contact relics along with his letters (letters which survive in their hundreds).[84] These relics were usually keys containing filings from St. Peter's chains, which had healing powers. Amongst the recipients of such gifts were churchmen and high officials of the eastern empire, as well as kings of the barbarian kingdoms of the west, like Childebert II, the Frankish king, to whom Gregory sent some keys for the king to hang around his neck as a protection against all evil.[85] Amongst the most remarkable of Gregory's gifts of contact relics was that to the Lombard queen, Theodolinda: oil from the lamps that burned at the shrines of more than sixty Roman saints, contained in little ampullae (flasks) and individually labelled. Remarkably, many of these ampullae and their papyrus labels survive, along with a contemporary list of the relics, in the treasury of the cathedral at Monza, to which Theodolinda bequeathed them.[86]

But despite his ready use of contact relics as instruments of diplomacy, Gregory was unshakeable when approached for corporeal relics. In a celebrated letter to the empress, who had requested that the head of St. Paul, or some other part of his body, be sent to her for the church of St. Paul in Constantinople, the pope replied, "I cannot nor do I dare to." He explained the awe-inspiring and terrifying nature of the bodies of the saints, and recounted stories of the sudden deaths of those who had approached them rashly. He also contrasted western and eastern practice in this matter:

> In the Roman lands and in the whole of the West it is utterly intolerable sacrilege for anyone to wish to touch the bodies of the saints. If they should presume to do so, it is certain that their boldness will in no way remain unpun-

[82] Columbanus, *Epistola* 1, pp. 2–12.

[83] Gregory of Tours, *Libri historiarum X* 10. 1, pp. 479–81.

[84] See McCulloh, "The Cult of Relics in the Letters and Dialogues of Pope Gregory the Great: A Lexicographical Study" (which is more than a lexicographical study).

[85] Gregory I, *Registrum epistolarum* 6. 6 (1, pp. 373–74); for a full list of such gifts, Richards, *Consul of God*, p. 270 n. 73.

[86] *Chartae latinae antiquiores: Facsimile-Edition of the Latin Charters Prior to the Ninth Century 29: Italy X*, no. 863, pp. 5–11.

> ished. This is why we are totally amazed and can scarcely believe the custom of the Greeks, who say that they raise up the bones of the saints.

As some kind of consolation, he offered the empress filings from St. Paul's chains.[87]

At the same time that Gregory of Tours was composing his accounts of the lives and miracles of the martyrs and bishops of Gaul, far to the south his namesake Pope Gregory was also putting together similar accounts of the saints of Italy, a work known as the *Dialogues*, written in 593, in the early years of Gregory's pontificate.[88] The subject of the *Dialogues* is the miracles performed by the saints of Italy, as Gregory had learned them "from the accounts of venerable men."[89] He frequently cites his sources:

> There was a man of venerable life, named Boniface, who held the office of bishop in the city called Ferento and discharged it virtuously. The priest Gaudentius, who is still living, tells of the many miracles of this man. He was raised in his service, so he can relate things about him so much the more truthfully, as he was present at them.[90]

Seventy figures are discussed in the pope's text: saintly bishops and monks; martyrs suffering under the persecution of pagan barbarians or heretics; a perspicacious hermit; a pure-minded priest with healing powers (and the ability to kill snakes by making the sign of the cross). But the dominant figure by far, the subject of an entire book of the four that make up the *Dialogues*, is St. Benedict, the formative figure of western monasticism.

Gregory was the first monk to become pope and it is not surprising that he was so interested in this great abbot, who was the author of the monastic Rule that was to govern the lives of tens of thousands of monks in the centuries to come. The second book of the *Dialogues* is virtually a Life of Benedict, and creates a powerful and enduring image of the author of "a Rule for monks, remarkable for its discernment and brilliant in its style."[91] Benedict died around 560 (or earlier), so more than thirty years before Gregory wrote his *Dialogues*, but the pope had four informants for his life, including two of Benedict's successors as abbots of Monte Cassino, the monastery which he had founded and where he was buried.

Benedict was from a wealthy family in Umbria in central Italy and turned to the religious life early, rejecting plans for a secular education, taking up the way of life of a hermit, clad in animal skins, and dealing with an attack of sexual temptation

[87] Gregory I, *Registrum epistularum* 4. 30 (1, pp. 248–50).

[88] See Boesch Gajano, *Gregorio Magno: Alle origini del Medioevo*, part 2, pp. 149–305.

[89] Gregory I, *Dialogi* 1. prologue, 10 (2, p. 16); see Dal Santo, *Debating the Saints' Cults in the Age of Gregory the Great*. Doubts about Gregory's authorship do not seem to be well grounded.

[90] Ibid., 1. 9 (2, p. 76); Ferento is an abandoned site north of Viterbo.

[91] Ibid., 2. 36 (2, p. 242).

by rolling naked in thorns and nettles, after which he never felt such a thing again. He later attracted followers, became a founder of monasteries, and wrote his Rule. One thing that Gregory's Life of Benedict stresses is the questions of authority and discipline that the saint encountered. For instance, very early in his life as an abbot, his first community of monks became so unhappy with the rigour of his Rule that they tried to poison him. Benedict therefore left them, and Gregory spends some time justifying this decision to relinquish his charge. Later, when Benedict had established several flourishing monasteries, he was called to one of them to deal with the problem of a monk who refused to join in community prayers, but instead wandered around doing various trivial tasks during prayer time. The saint came to the monastery and immediately perceived that at prayer time "a little black boy dragged this monk out by the fringe of his clothes." After a few days, as the monk continued in his lax behaviour, "the man of God came out from prayers and, finding the monk standing outside, hit him with his staff for the blindness of his heart." Thereafter the monk was assiduous in his prayers.[92] On another occasion some of Benedict's monks went out on a task. It was the practice that when they did, they should not eat or drink anything outside the monastery, but, being kept out late, they went into the house of a religious woman and had a meal. On their return Benedict confronted them: "Where did you eat?" When they denied what they had done, he asked, "Why are you lying in this way? Did you not go into the house of such a woman? Did you not accept such and such food? Did you not drink so many cupfuls?" The astonished monks confessed, were forgiven and told they should never do this again.[93]

In Benedict's Rule, the central figure is the abbot. He is "the representative of Christ in the monastery," who will be judged at the Last Judgment for his teaching and for the obedience of his followers, although if he has struggled hard against difficult and disobedient monks, they, not he, will be punished.[94] The picture of the Benedictine abbot presented in the Rule, a "blend of biblical patriarch and Roman paterfamilias," as he has been described,[95] makes sense when set alongside the picture of Benedict in Gregory's *Dialogues*. Authority and obedience are fundamental concerns.

Gregory's *Dialogues* were an enormous success, surviving in numerous manuscript copies and also being translated into Greek, which earned the pope the epithet "Gregory Dialogos" in the Greek hagiographic tradition.[96] In the West, book two, the Life of Benedict, often circulated separately, or sometimes, appropriately enough, together with Benedict's Rule. The image of Benedict and the provisions of the Rule together shaped the form of monasticism which was to dominate the West for centuries to come.

[92] Ibid., 2. 4 (2, pp. 150–52).
[93] Ibid., 2. 12 (2, pp. 174–75).
[94] *Regula Benedicti* 2, pp. 20–26.
[95] Richards, *Consul of God*, p. 35.
[96] Gregory I, *Vita Benedicti*, tr. Zacharias.

The Benedictine Centuries

The phrase "the Benedictine centuries," employed, perhaps for the first time, by Cardinal Newman,[97] has been applied in various ways, but at its core is the idea that western European religious life was deeply coloured by Benedictine monasticism in the long period between the lifetime of Benedict and the rise of new religious orders in the twelfth and thirteenth centuries. The phrase perhaps underestimates the gradual way that the Benedictine Rule spread, for there were alternative models of monasticism, notably the Irish-inspired version of Columbanus, and it was only really with the endorsement of Benedictinism by the newly established Carolingian dynasty, which came to power in 751, that it won a hegemonic position. Nevertheless, from the point of view of the cult of the saints, the period 600–1200 was characterized by the vital role of Benedictine monks both in transmitting hagiographic literature and also in providing one of the most common types of new saint, the saintly abbot and founder.

Odilo of Cluny, abbot of the most important monastery in Europe at his time, conveys the Benedictine conception of this history clearly and explicitly.[98] He is writing around the year 1033 about a previous saintly abbot of Cluny, Maïeul, who had died in 994; he places his life in a long perspective:

> After the holy, divine and saving teaching of the apostles and evangelists, and the most victorious and unconquerable glorious struggles of the martyrs, in third place, so to speak, divine grace provided new comforts for His church, namely lamps burning with love and bright with the power of speech. . . . Through their honest labour the acts of the apostles are explained and commended to the faithful. Through their devoted study the triumph of the blessed martyrs and their merit are commended to the Holy Church.

So the history of salvation runs from the biblical heroes to the martyrs, and then to the Fathers of the Church, the "lamps burning with love," who transmit and interpret the traditions of these holy pioneers. Then comes the fourth stage: "After the heavenly court received these great men . . . the divine judgment wished to provide for the little ones of the Church in the fourth place. . . . Then the monastic order began to spread." Odilo traces the roots of monasticism to Elijah, the Hebrew prophet, and John the Baptist, the precursor of Christ. Monks are those who have taken seriously Christ's counsel of perfection, "If thou wilt be perfect, go and sell that thou hast" (Matthew 19:21). Amongst the early monks, for this Benedictine abbot, there is one who stands out: "Amongst the most intent listeners and most energetic followers of this saving command, our most blessed father Benedict shone like a bright star of

[97] "We pass from the Benedictine centuries to the Dominican which followed. . . . The writers of the Benedictine centuries are supposed to have the barbarism, without the science of the Dominican period.": Newman, "The Benedictine Schools," p. 470.

[98] Odilo of Cluny, *Vita beati Maioli abbatis*, cols. 943–47.

heaven." After referring to Gregory the Great's account of Benedict, Odilo goes on to the subsequent history of Benedictine monasticism: a period of dissemination and success, followed by a time of decline, halted only with the foundation of Odilo's own monastery of Cluny, by William, duke of Aquitaine (this took place in 909). A list of the abbots of Cluny then leads him to his main subject, the life of Maïeul. Odilo's chronology is thus a sequence, running from apostolic Christianity, through the age of the martyrs and the age of the Fathers, to the foundation of the monastic tradition of the West by Benedict (as described by Gregory) and its revival, after a period of decline, by Cluny.

This account of Christian history takes Benedict and his Rule as its central thread through the early Middle Ages, and the story is not without foundation in reality. In the seventh century, that following the one in which Benedict had lived, his Rule was adopted by many monasteries in Gaul, where it was often combined with the Rule of Columbanus, to create a so-called mixed Rule. In England, St. Wilfrid (c. 634–709/10) claimed to be the first person to have introduced "the life of monks according to the rule of father Benedict."[99] In 787 Charlemagne asked the abbot of Monte Cassino, Benedict's own monastery, for a copy of the Rule, and in the early years of the reign of his son, Louis the Pious, it was made obligatory for all the monasteries of the Frankish empire, with, at the same time, Benedict's feast-day being declared a special solemnity.[100] In the tenth century the foundation of Cluny marked a new beginning, and an efflorescence of Benedictine monasticism was also visible in England under the patronage of King Edgar (957–75) and the leadership of three dynamic bishop-abbots, Dunstan, Æthelwold, and Oswald, all of whom were subsequently regarded as saints.

The great monasteries of the early Middle Ages were not only communities of ascetics, engaged in endless liturgical ritual, but also homes of shrines and cradles of hagiography. In Anglo-Saxon England monasticism and the cult of the saints arrived together. In 601, four years after the arrival of missionary-monks from Rome, Pope Gregory the Great sent "relics of the holy apostles and martyrs" for "the new church of the English."[101] And the new church of the English soon found a great native monastic historian to record its triumphs and celebrate its saints. In his *Ecclesiastical History*, the monk Bede (d. 735) wrote of the founding figures of Christianity amongst his people: Pope Gregory the Great; Augustine, first archbishop of Canterbury; the Irish missionary Aidan; the convert-kings and martyrs Edwin and Oswald; the great royal and noble abbess-saints, like Etheldreda of Ely or Ethelburga of Barking; and, with especial interest, Cuthbert, the most important saint of Northumbria, Bede's own homeland, to whom he also dedicated not one but two Lives, in verse and in prose. Bede's *History* and his prose *Life of Cuthbert* were widely read

[99] Stephen of Ripon (Eddius Stephanus), *Vita Wilfridi episcopi* 47, p. 98.

[100] Paul the Deacon, *Epistolae variorum* 13; *Capitularia regum Francorum* 1, no. 170, pp. 344, 346 (*Capitulare monasticum* cl. 1–3, 46).

[101] Bede, *Historia ecclesiastica* 1. 29, p. 104.

works and spread knowledge of these English saints across the continent of Europe. Bede was also the author of a martyrology—a list of saints (originally martyrs, but subsequently including confessors) according to the calendar of the year, with notes of their origin and fate—which he himself describes as "a martyrology of the feast-days of the holy martyrs, in which I strove to note down with care all whom I could find, and not only the day but also with what kind of struggle and under which judge they conquered this world."[102]

In Bede's martyrology, alongside the early Christian martyrs, one finds record of saints of his own country. Thus, under 20 March, we find:

> In Britain the feast-day of St. Cuthbert, who became bishop of the church of Lindisfarne after being a hermit and who from childhood to old age led a life remarkable for its miracles. When his body had lain buried for eleven years, it was found incorrupt, as if he had died that moment, along with the shroud in which he was wrapped.[103]

Bede's martyrology was used by the Carolingian martyrologists of the following century, so some of his entries can be traced down the years and across Europe. For example, both the martyrology of Hrabanus Maurus, which was composed in the period 840–54, and that of Usuard, a monk of St.-Germain-des-Prés outside Paris, composed in the 850s and 860s, contain entries for Cuthbert on 20 March unmistakably derived from Bede.[104] In this way texts spread from monastery to monastery.

Benedictine monasticism not only transmitted texts about the saints; it also fostered new saints and their cults. Fulda, one of the most important Benedictine abbeys in Germany, provides a good example. St. Boniface, writing in 751, describes the establishment of the house:

> There is a wooded place in a vast and lonely wilderness, in the midst of the peoples to whom we are preaching, where we have built a monastery and established monks living under the Rule of the holy father Benedict, men of strict abstinence, without meat or wine, without mead or slaves, content with the labour of their own hands.[105]

Three years after the date of this letter, Boniface was himself killed by pagan Frisians and his body was brought for interment to the church at Fulda, where it became the centre of healing miracles. He was accorded the status of a martyr, and in 819 his relics were translated, that is, moved to a position of greater honour, in a great ceremony attended by prelates and aristocrats.[106] Hrabanus Maurus, who was abbot of Fulda 822–42, included several references to him in his martyrology, noting his martyrdom, along with his companions, on 5 June, the anniversary of his ordination

[102] Ibid., 5. 24, p. 570; on Bede's martyrology, see Thacker, "Bede and his Martyrology."

[103] Bede, *Martyrologium*, p. 52 (PL 94: 863).

[104] Hrabanus Maurus, *Martyrologium*, p. 30; Usuard, *Martyrologium*, p. 197 (PL 123: 859).

[105] Boniface, *Epistula* 86, p. 290.

[106] Bruno Candidus, *Vita Eigilis abbatis Fuldensis* 15, MGH, SS 15/1, p. 230.

2.2. St. Boniface's martyrdom in the Fulda Sacramentary of c. 975.
Göttingen, Universitätsbibliothek, MS Theol. 231, fol. 87. Photo: akg-images.

on 1 December, and that of the translation of 819 on 1 November: "On this day in the monastery of Fulda the dedication of the church of St. Boniface the martyr and the translation of the body of that holy martyr."[107] Hrabanus was also the author of verse inscriptions recording the relics in the church of Fulda, including Boniface's.[108] In the following century there is a memorable depiction of Boniface's missionary activity and his martyrdom in the Fulda Sacramentary of c. 975 (figure 2.2).[109] In such ways, through inscriptions, texts, images, and relics, a cult was nursed and publicized.

The tenth century saw an efflorescence of Benedictine sanctity. Successive, and long-lived, abbots of Cluny won a reputation as saints: Odo (927–42), Maïeul (965–94), Odilo (994–1049), and Hugh (1049–1109). Lives of these four were sometimes copied together as a group.[110] In England the reforming trio of Dunstan, Æthelwold and Oswald transformed some of the English cathedrals into monastic communities, drew up new guidelines for the monastic life (the *Regularis Concordia*), sponsored elaborate translation ceremonies of English saints, and oversaw an artistic and literary revival. Shortly after their deaths (in 988, 984, and 992, respectively) they became the subject of lively cult: liturgical commemoration and miracles began, Lives were written, translations were undertaken.

All western monks looked back to Benedict, "the founder," "the legislator of monks," but they were not all agreed where his relics lay.[111] His own monastery of

[107] Hrabanus Maurus, *Martyrologium*, pp. 54, 123, 111.

[108] Hrabanus Maurus, *Carmina* 41. 1–14, pp. 205–8.

[109] Göttingen, Universitätsbibliothek, MS Theol. 231, fol. 87.

[110] For example, Cambridge, Corpus Christi College, MS 161, fols. 75v–108v (English collection of saints' Lives, c. 1200).

[111] Paris, BnF, lat. 17626, fol. 85v: "de vita vel miracula venerabilis Benedicti conditoris vel abbatis," which is an alternative reading for the heading of the capitula of Gregory I, *Dialogi* 2 (2, p. 126); *Miracula*

Monte Cassino had been devastated and abandoned not long after his death in the later sixth century, and, although it was refounded in the early eighth century, the hiatus had, according to the monks of Fleury in France, allowed them to remove the body of both Benedict and his sister Scholastica to their monastery on the Loire. There thus began a long and enduring dispute between the two monasteries about possession of the founder's relics. Monte Cassino was not willing to let its own claims go by default, and the monks there insisted that the tombs of Benedict and Scholastica still lay within their abbey church and recorded miracles performed there, as well as producing the spectacular illustrated Codex Benedictus, containing readings for the feasts of Benedict, Scholastica, and Maurus, Benedict's first disciple.[112] But it was at Fleury that the most remarkable record of the saint's miraculous activity was produced, for monastic authors at Fleury compiled a record of the miracles of St. Benedict which they sustained, fairly continuously, from the ninth century to the twelfth.[113] Here the record of the saint's activities in defending the rights and property of his monks blends at times into a general history of the monastery and the locality. This is understandable: the cult-centre, with its shrine, relics, pilgrims, and hagiography, formed part of a monastic institution with wide traditions, liturgical, historical, and—importantly—proprietorial.

The great Benedictine monasteries were natural centres of the cult of the saints in western Europe. Their library catalogues indicate the rich hagiographic resources they had. For example, that dating to 1122/3 from the Benedictine cathedral-monastery of Rochester includes works of such variety as Jerome's Lives of Paul the Hermit, Hilarion, and Malchus; Athanasius's Life of Antony, in Latin translation; Bede's martyrology; Lives of Dunstan and Alphege, archbishops of Canterbury, by Osbern of Canterbury; a four-volume set of saints' Lives; books of sermons for saints' days; and a volume of miracles of the Virgin Mary.[114] The hagiographical works in the Rochester library thus range in date from the fourth to the eleventh century and include most of the main genres—Lives, miracle-collections, martyrologies, sermons. A later catalogue shows that the monks kept their hagiography up-to-date, acquiring in the course of the twelfth century Lives of Malachy of Armagh, who died in 1148, of Bernard, who died in 1153, and a book of the miracles of Thomas Becket, which date to the 1170s, as well as several copies of the miracles of their own local saint, Ithamar, composed at Rochester after 1125.[115]

And, in addition to the evidence of catalogues like this, and despite the destructiveness of Reformation and Revolution, of fire and war and flood and mice, there

---

sancti Benedicti 8. 10, p. 287.

[112] Desiderius of Monte Cassino, *Dialogi de miraculis sancti Benedicti*; Peter the Deacon, *Historica relatio de corpore sancti Benedicti*; the Codex Benedictus is BAV, Vat. lat. 1202; there is a full-colour facsimile edition: *The Codex Benedictus: An Eleventh-century Lectionary from Monte Cassino*.

[113] *Miracula sancti Benedicti*; see Rollason, "The Miracles of St. Benedict"; the longest hiatus occurs in the tenth century.

[114] *English Benedictine Libraries: The Shorter Catalogues*, pp. 469–92.

[115] *English Benedictine Libraries: The Shorter Catalogues*, pp. 510, 515, 517, 527.

are also the surviving manuscripts themselves. From Fleury there is a manuscript, now in Orleans, which can be dated very closely to the years 1002–4 and contains a copy of the martyrology of Usuard adapted to Fleury's needs, with especial attention to the feasts of Benedict and Scholastica, notes on the altars of Fleury saints and, in a slightly later hand, marginal notes referring to the hagiographic works in Fleury's library. The book was used for reading at the Chapter, that is, the daily assembly of the monks.[116] And, more rarely, besides the books, there are the surviving shrines and images of the saints. The cult of St. Foy at Conques has left not only a huge collection of her dramatic miracles, preserved in the dependent priory of Sélestat (Schlettstadt) in Alsace, but also, still in the monastery of Conques itself, the gleaming hieratic image of St. Foy (shown later in figure 12.1).[117]

New Christendoms: Eastern and Northern Europe

At the same time as the cult of the saints was elaborated in the churches of western Europe, it was also being exported to new areas, as Christendom expanded north and east.[118] Eventually Bohemia, Poland, and Hungary were fully integrated into the world of western, that is, Latin and Catholic Christianity, while Russia and Bulgaria adopted the Greek Byzantine version. In Scandinavia, too, a Catholic hierarchy was established between the tenth and twelfth centuries. The century centred on the year 1000 was especially remarkable for the extension of Christianity and, with it, the cult of the saints. In eastern Europe, the Polish ruler Mieszko was baptized in 966, Géza, ruler of the Magyars, soon thereafter (c. 972), and the ruler of Kiev, Vladimir, around 988. Within little more than twenty years, therefore, a huge area of eastern Europe had seen its rulers adopt Christianity. This was not the same thing as deeply rooted conversion, but it was a prerequisite for it. Similar developments occurred in the north. Three bishops were appointed for mainland Denmark (Jutland) in 948, and the Danish king Harald Bluetooth, who died around 987, claimed that he "had made the Danes Christian."[119] Olav Tryggvason, who ruled Norway from 995–1000, and Olav Haraldsson, who ruled there from 1015–28, both had reputations as active, not to say brutal, missionary kings, and at this same period there is evidence of Christianity in Sweden, where the first recorded Christian king is Olof Skötkonung, who died in 1022. The Scandinavians who settled in England, Ireland, and France also adopted Christianity in the tenth and eleventh centuries. Vikings had been predators on the churches of western Europe but now "the very great and

[116] Mostert, *The Library of Fleury*, p. 175; the MS is Orleans, BM 322 (273).

[117] Bernard of Angers, *Liber miraculorum sancte Fidis*; later, p. 482, on the image.

[118] Cormack, *The Saints in Iceland*; Antonsson, "Saints and Relics in Early Christian Scandinavia"; Berend, ed., *Christianization and the Rise of Christian Monarchy; Sanctity in the North: Saints Lives and Cults in Medieval Scandinavia*; Antonsson and Garipzanov, eds., *Saints and their Lives on the Periphery*.

[119] Sawyer, *The Viking-Age Rune-Stones*, pp. 158–59 (the Jelling stone).

prolonged assault of the pagans" came to an end, and the Northmen sought saints and relics of their own.[120]

The author of the first piece of hagiographic writing to be produced in Scandinavia, around 1095, recognized that "although, throughout the churches of the whole world, it is fitting for every Christian people to celebrate the feast-days of the saints," nevertheless in each individual place there were those who were "worthy to be honoured with special reverence." These special local saints were marked out either by the presence of their relics or by being "familiar fellow inhabitants" of the worshippers.[121] Both could be found in Scandinavia by this time. The importation of relics was a normal part of evangelization, but the first local saints marked a deeper stage in the process of Christianization.

Northern and eastern Europe produced their own saints quite quickly. The earliest native saints were actually from a part of eastern Europe that had been Christian far longer than the rest, that is, Bohemia (which corresponds, roughly, to the modern Czech Republic), where the new religion had been introduced in the ninth century, and they represent a type of saint, the ruler who suffered a violent death, that was to be a distinctive feature of both eastern Europe and Scandinavia. These first Czech saints were St. Ludmila, murdered in 921, and her grandson St. Wenceslas (Václav in Czech), who ruled Bohemia from 921 until his murder by his brother in 935.[122] Several hagiographic accounts of Ludmila and Wenceslas were produced in the century after their deaths, both in Latin and in Slavonic. One of the most interesting, although also the most controversial, is the so-called *Legend of Christian* (*Legenda Christiani*), a work that, if genuine, dates to 992–94, was composed by the monk Christian, of an aristocratic Czech family, and provides a window into the mentality of early Bohemian Christianity (some scholars would see the work as a compilation of later centuries on the basis of earlier material).[123]

The author was well aware that Bohemia was undeveloped terrain for the cult of the saints. He writes in honour of those "new stars" Ludmila and Wenceslas and explicitly contrasts the cult they receive in Bohemia with the situation in the old Christian lands of the Carolingian west:

> If the mortal clay of such outstanding saints and acceptable witnesses of Christ were situated in the lands of the Lotharingians or Carolingians (*in partibus Lutheringorum seu Carlingorum*) or other Christian peoples, flourishing with remarkable miracles, they would long ago have painted these deeds with (so to say) golden letters, they would have adorned a canticle of responses with

[120] Nimiam atque diutinam paganorum infestationem: *Recueil des actes de Charles III le Simple*, no. 53, pp. 114–16.

[121] *Passio sancti Kanuti regis et martiris* 1, p. 62.

[122] The date of 935 is now preferred to the earlier commonly given 929.

[123] Christian, *Vita et passio sancti Wenceslai et sancte Ludmile*. There is an English translation, along with a thorough discussion of the scholarly controversies on the subject of the text, in *The Origins of Christianity in Bohemia*, pp. 3–46, 163–203.

> antiphons, along with sermons, with the walls of many monasteries, even though they are proud to possess the venerable relics of many similar holy martyrs, confessors, virgins and other saints.

Christian is thus aware of the richness of the cult of the saints in western Europe and points out the elaborate forms of veneration that were to be found there: hagiographic writing, liturgical commemoration, and (if that is what is meant by "the walls of many monasteries") churches housing shrines or dedicated to the saints. In contrast, the Bohemians have only these two saints: "we lack all these, having, after God, only these."

Christian begins his story with the mission of Cyril and Methodius to the Moravians in the ninth century, explaining how the former had "devised new letters or script" for the Slavic language and translated biblical and other texts into Slavonic. He then moves on to the first Christian ruler of Bohemia and the foundation of the first church in that country, dedicated to the Roman martyr St. Clement, soon followed by another, dedicated to the Virgin Mary; other early dedications in Bohemia mentioned in the text include George and Peter. Focus then shifts to Ludmila, widow of this first Christian ruler, her virtues, and the hostility she encountered from her daughter-in-law, the wife of the new ruler, a hostility that culminated in Ludmila being strangled by her daughter-in-law's henchmen. Her sanctity soon became evident: a sweet smell came from her tomb and mysterious lights glowed there at night. The reaction of her murderer, the daughter-in-law, was curious: she ordered a church to be raised over Ludmila's tomb, dedicated to St. Michael, "so that if any miracle should happen there in the future, it would be attributed not to the merits of the holy martyr [that is, Ludmila], but to those of the saints whose relics were contained there." It is impossible to say if this unusual and ingenious piece of planning has any basis in reality, but it is certainly in the text and so has to count as something that could be imagined in the Middle Ages.[124]

Christian's portrayal of Wenceslas as ruler emphasizes his personal piety and his attempts to build up the new religion. Wearing a hair-shirt next to his skin, "like a monk," he went barefoot in Lent, and made the wine and bread for the Eucharist with his own hands. He arranged the translation of his grandmother's body to a church in the castle at Prague and was delighted to find it incorrupt (or almost so); he built the church of St. Vitus in his capital; and south German clergy swarmed into Bohemia, bringing relics and books. But the devil and certain "evil people" stirred up against him his younger brother Boleslav, who hatched a plot to murder him. Wenceslas was invited to a celebration at Boleslav's stronghold on 27 September, the feast-day of Sts. Cosmas and Damian—ironically enough, considering that these

[124]The statement is also found in the expanded version of the Passion of Ludmila known as *Fuit in provincia Boemorum*: *The Origins of Christianity in Bohemia*, p. 159. Exactly similar motivation is ascribed by Cosmas of Prague in explaining the translation of Wenceslas by his brother and murderer Boleslav into St. Vitus's church in Prague: "quatenus, si que Deus mira suis ostenderet ad gloriam sanctis, non eius fratris, sed sancti Viti martiris asscriberetur meritis": Cosmas of Prague, *Chronica Boemorum* 1. 19, p. 38.

saints were renowned as loving and cooperative brothers—but the plotters were inhibited from carrying out their plan that day. Christian observes, "God the governor prevented them from accomplishing it, perhaps because He chose to sanctify the following day, which had no feast on it." This is a rather remarkable picture of the deity planning the saintly calendar in this way. In any event, the murder took place the following day, 28 September, and Wenceslas was launched on his career as martyr and patron of Bohemia. Three years after his death his body was translated to the church of St. Vitus he had built, which is now the huge Gothic cathedral of St. Vitus, St. Wenceslas, and St. Adalbert. The murdered Bohemian ruler became renowned from Russia, where he entered the calendar of saints, to Britain, where he inspired one of the most popular Christmas carols.

Wenceslas is only one example of the many rulers of northern and eastern Europe who came to be revered as saints after suffering a violent death. Later in the tenth century there is similar case of bloodshed caused by factionalism within a ruling dynasty, in the murder of Edward, king of England, in 978. Edward's brother Ethelred succeeded him. Unlike Wenceslas's brother, he was not the instigator of the murder, and actually furthered the cult of his murdered brother, initiating a grand translation ceremony in 1001 and referring to him as "Christ's saint, my brother Edward, whom, sprinkled with his own blood, the Lord has deigned to glorify through many miracles in our time."[125] Interestingly, Boleslav had also promoted Wenceslas as a saint. Perhaps a guilty conscience was at work, or perhaps the new rulers saw espousal of their murdered predecessors as a way of healing rifts and repairing a damaged solidarity. The eleventh and twelfth centuries saw more of these murdered princes. Boris and Gleb, sons of Prince Vladimir of Kiev, the ruler who converted Russia, were murdered after his death in 1015, according to their later hagiography by their half-brother Sviatopolk; their relics enshrined at Vyshgorod became a major pilgrimage centre. King Olav of Norway, who was killed in battle in 1030, trying to reclaim his kingdom, was the centre of one of the most important cults in the Nordic world. The chronicler Adam of Bremen, writing in the1070s, describes his end and then goes on:

> So Olav, king and martyr as we believe, met such an end. His body was buried with fitting honour in the great city of his kingdom, Trondheim, where today, through many miracles and cures that are performed by him, the Lord deigns to show of how much merit he is in heaven, who had such honour on earth. His feast-day on 29 July is commemorated in perpetuity by all the peoples of the northern ocean, the Norse, Swedes, Götar, Samlanders, Danes and Slavs.[126]

Subsequent slaughtered Scandinavian ruler-saints include King Canute IV of Denmark (d. 1086), Earl Magnus of Orkney (d. 1116), Duke Canute Laward of

[125] *Passio sancti Eadwardi regis et martyris*, pp. 12–13; Sawyer, *Anglo-Saxon Charters*, no. 899.
[126] Adam of Bremen, *Gesta Hammaburgensis ecclesiae pontificum* 2. 61, pp. 300–302.

Schleswig (d. 1131), and, although the evidence in his case is mainly late, King Erik of Sweden (d. c. 1160).

Such a roll-call naturally raises questions, about the distinctive geographical distribution of these murdered ruler-saints; about the relationship between their rulership, their bloody end, and their sanctity; and about the possible links with the tradition of murdered Anglo-Saxon royalty which was already old when Wenceslas died—one thinks of Oswald of Northumbria (d. 642) and Edmund of East Anglia (d. 869). These are topics that will be discussed later (see pp. 212–15).

CHAPTER 3

The High and Later Middle Ages (1000–1500)

Papal Canonization

In the early Middle Ages saints' cults arose spontaneously and such official enquiry or scrutiny as existed was in the hands of local bishops. Amongst those who could declare someone a saint were the popes (who were also, of course, bishops) and the earliest certain record of a papal canonization is that of Ulric of Augsburg in 993.[1] But although popes could canonize, they did not claim that they were the only ones who could do so. The shift to this more radical position, in the late twelfth and early thirteenth centuries, marked a new stage in the history of the cult of the saints and also in the history of the papacy.[2]

The monarchical papacy was (and is) one of the most important features of the western Catholic Church. In the medieval period it marked it off sharply from the eastern Orthodox Church, for, whereas both these branches of Christianity recognized the high authority of the bishop and the necessity of hierarchy, the western model placed at the apex of the episcopal hierarchy one bishop who was superior to all others, who could judge all others but be judged by none. Papal claims and papal authority have a long history, but were pushed to ever greater heights in the period 1050–1300, and one of the consequences was a new interpretation of the role of the pope in defining sanctity: "you may not revere [anyone] as a saint without the permission of the Roman Church."[3] This is a formulation completely foreign to the early Middle Ages, or to the eastern tradition, but it has formed the basis of the Catholic view of sanctity to the present day.

The crystallization of the papal claim to a monopoly of canonization occurred in the years around 1200, and thus fits centrally into a period when popes were

[1] Although Wolf, "Die Kanonisationsbulle von 993 für den Hl. Oudalrich von Augsburg," noting that the first mention of Ulric's canonization dates to a century after the event, and that the text of the canonization bull is found only in a printed book of 1595, thinks it permissible to have "not entirely groundless doubt" whether this is "really the first extant evidence of papal canonization."

[2] On canonization, see Kemp, *Canonization and Authority*; Vauchez, *Sainthood*; *Procès de canonisation*, ed. Klaniczay; Wetzstein, *Heilige vor Gericht. Das Kanonisationsverfahren im europäischen Spätmittelalter*; Krafft, *Papsturkunde und Heiligsprechung*; Roberto Paciocco, *Canonizzazioni e culto dei santi*; Finucane, *Contested Canonizations*.

[3] *Decretales Gregorii IX*, 3. 45. 1, *Audivimus*, col. 650.

expanding their claims and their powers to an unprecedented degree. A pioneer in this process was Gregory VII (1073–85), who asserted the following: "that all rulers should kiss the feet of the pope alone," "that his name alone should be recited in churches," "that this name is unique in the world," "that he may depose emperors," "that he may be judged by no one."[4] The spirit is echoed in Boniface VIII's claims in the bull *Unam sanctam* of 1302:

> there is one holy catholic and apostolic church, outside of which there is neither salvation nor the remission of sins . . . of this one and only church there is one body and one head: Christ and the vicar of Christ, St. Peter, and the successor of St. Peter . . . we declare, announce and define that it is altogether necessary for every human creature to be subject to the bishop of Rome.[5]

In the two and a quarter centuries between these extravagant claims of Gregory VII and Boniface VIII, the popes also made concrete additions to their power: they imposed an income tax on the clergy; they reserved to themselves many of the most important ecclesiastical appointments throughout Europe; they legislated and held great councils. This process of centralization and bureaucratization extended to the cult of the saints.

In a letter written to the king of Sweden in 1171–72, Pope Alexander III expressed both reservations about a specific case and a general rule about canonization:

> We have heard that some among you, deceived by a devilish fraud, are, in the manner of unbelievers, venerating as a saint a certain man who was killed in drinking and drunkenness, although the Church scarcely allows prayers to be said for such people killed in drunkenness. For the Apostle says, "drunkards will not possess the kingdom of heaven" (1 Cor. 6:10). Therefore henceforth you should not presume to render him any cult, since, even if miracles are performed through him, it is not permitted to you to venerate him as a saint without the authority of the Roman Church.[6]

This ruling, known as *Audivimus* from its opening word, passed into the canonical collections of the later twelfth and early thirteenth centuries and was included in the first great piece of codified papal legislation, the Decretals of 1234.

There has been debate about *Audivimus*, not only regarding which king it was directed to and which saint it meant (perhaps Erik), but also, a matter of more general significance, whether it is best seen as "a specific decision in a peculiar case" or as Pope Alexander's "expression of what he believed to be the law . . . about the papacy

[4]Gregory VII, *Registrum* 2. 55a (1, pp. 201–8) (*Dictatus papae*).

[5]*Extravagantes communes* 1. 8. 1, cols. 1245–46.

[6]*Decretales Gregorii IX,* 3. 45. 1, *Audivimus*, col. 650; full text PL 200: 1259–61, reprinted from *Diplomatarium suecanum* 1, ed. J. G. Liljegren (Stockholm, 1829) 61, which edits it from the late-medieval cartulary of Linköping, Registrum ecclesie Lincopensis (Stockholm, Riksarkivet A 9).

and canonization."[7] It is actually hard to imagine that the pope is here making a statement that applies only to Swedes or drunkards, but, regardless of the import of this specific ruling at the time it was first issued, there is no doubt that it was soon being interpreted as a claim to a papal monopoly of canonization. Two canon law collections from around the year 1200 include *Audivimus*, along with a bull of Alexander III canonizing Thomas Becket, under the heading "that the authority of the Roman bishop is necessary for anyone to be regarded as a saint."[8] In the bull in which Innocent III announced the canonization of the German empress Cunigunda in 1200, the pope noted the request of the German clergy "that we should deign to inscribe the empress in the catalogue of saints, ruling that her memory should henceforth be celebrated among the saints by all the faithful, since this highest judgment pertains to him alone who is the successor of St. Peter and the vicar of Jesus Christ."[9]

In this way, the popes of the late twelfth century proclaimed their unique rights in cases of canonization. By the mid-thirteenth century Innocent IV was able to make the lapidary statement: "only the pope can canonize saints."[10] The habits of a millennium were not to be changed by a few papal pronouncements. Throughout the later Middle Ages, hundreds of new saints were recognized in the traditional manner. But the lawyer popes of the twelfth and thirteenth centuries had created new rules about canonization, and the papally canonized were henceforth in a different category from other saints. Powerful and influential protagonists would wish to see their own candidates for sanctity accorded this new and higher honour.

As a consequence of this development, the history of papal canonization in the Middle Ages can be divided into three phases. Before 993, when Pope John XV canonized Ulric, bishop of Augsburg, there are no reliable accounts of such canonizations at all. There then follows a period when the popes were pronouncing canonizations, but made no claims to have a monopoly of the right. Eventually, at the end of the twelfth century, they did come to insist on this claim, and henceforth maintained it (as they do to this day). Numbers involved were not large. Between the canonization of Ulric of Augsburg in 993 and the accession of Innocent III in 1198 about 38 papal canonizations are recorded. (The exact number is uncertain because of inadequacies in the sources, especially in the eleventh century.) Between 1198 and 1500 there were another 40, bringing the total of medieval canonizations

[7] On the issue of which king it was addressed to, Knut Eriksson or his rival Kol, which saint it meant, and the political implications of each position, see Line, *Kingship and State Formation in Sweden,* pp. 370–72. "A specific decision": Kuttner, "La réserve papale du droit de canonisation," p. 195. "Expression of what he believed": Kemp, *Canonization and Authority*, p. 104. See also Vauchez, *Sainthood*, pp. 24–27.

[8] Kuttner, "La réserve papale du droit de canonisation," pp. 197–98.

[9] Kuttner, "La réserve papale du droit de canonisation," p. 228. There is a critical edition in Petersohn, "Die Litterae Papst Innocenz' III. zur Heiligsprechung der Kaiserin Kunigunde," pp. 20–25 (quote at p. 24); Petersohn argues that Innocent is here simply citing the words of the petitioners' own letter, but, even if this is the case, he must be endorsing them. See the comments of Vauchez, *Sainthood*, pp. 27–28 n. 24.

[10] Innocent IV, *Apparatus super V libros decretalium*, ad X. 3. 45. 1, *Audivimus*.

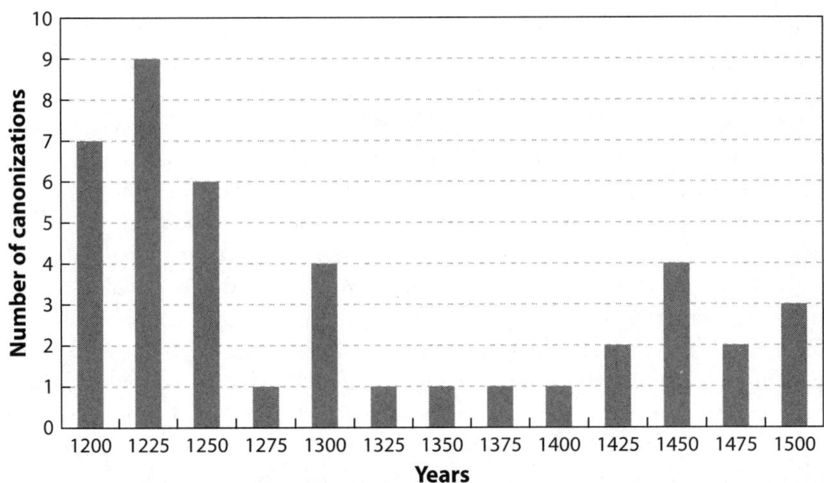

3.1. Number of canonizations, 1200–1525.

to 78 (figure 3.1). The relative smallness of this total is shown by the fact that it is outstripped by the number of canonizations under a single modern pope, John Paul II (1978–2005), who canonized 482 saints in 52 ceremonies (some were large groups, like the 103 Korean martyrs canonized in 1984).[11] The "age of canonization" is not to be sought in the Middle Ages at all, but in the late twentieth century.

One of the reasons that the number of papal canonizations was small was that canonization was a slow and costly process. A remarkable example is that of Osmund, bishop of Salisbury, who died in 1099. The clergy of Salisbury undertook canonization attempts in 1228, 1387, 1406, 1416, 1442, and 1452, the last finally leading to his canonization in 1457, more than three and a half centuries after Osmund's death. The cost of the 1450s attempt is known and, at just over £713, is equivalent to the average annual income of an English baron of that time.[12] Osmund's case is extreme in its duration, but canonizations were major enterprises and took time. They have indeed been described as "the world's longest and most complicated judicial process."[13] Moreover, the amount of time increased over the course of the later Middle Ages: under Innocent III, in the early thirteenth century, successful canonizations required an average of two years, but a hundred years later they needed twenty, and under the Avignon popes (1309–78) more than thirty years (these figures exclude, of course, the unsuccessful cases).[14]

The canonization process underwent various developments in form, especially in the first half of the thirteenth century, but it is possible to draw a fairly accurate

[11] Figures from the Vatican website.

[12] Kemp, *Canonization and Authority*, pp. 138–40; *The Canonization of St. Osmund*; for average baronial income, see Gray, "Incomes from Land in England in 1436," p. 619.

[13] Howe, "Saintly Statistics," p. 82.

[14] Vauchez, *Sainthood*, p. 64.

general picture of the mature process of the later Middle Ages. It began with a postulation, that is, a petition. Popes virtually never initiated canonizations themselves; they responded to requests. Hence for a canonization process to begin, there had to be a sufficiently strong and influential body of opinion, somewhere in Christendom, that a dead person was a saint, and that it was worth seeking the most public and prestigious recognition of that fact. It was also accepted that the request to the papacy had to be "frequently repeated and insistent."[15] Common practices included form letters circulated to bishops and other high figures, which were then sent to the papacy, or the appointment of a representative at the papal court to pursue the matter full time.

If the pope were eventually convinced, commissioners were then appointed to hold hearings in the region where the candidate-saint had been active (the inquest "in partibus"). These commissioners were usually three in number, including both local ecclesiastical dignitaries and other high-ranking churchmen known to the pope, and were often distinguished by their legal and administrative expertise. For instance, in 1219 Pope Honorius III entrusted the inquest into the sanctity of Hugh of Lincoln to Stephen Langton, archbishop of Canterbury; William of Cornhill, bishop of Coventry; and John, abbot of Fountains.[16] Langton was a cardinal, a famous theologian with a reputation throughout Christendom (and responsible for the present system of dividing the Bible into chapters) as well as one of the moving spirits behind Magna Carta; William of Cornhill had served as a royal judge and tax collector, had also been involved in the negotiations leading to Magna Carta, and had been present at the great Fourth Lateran Council of 1215; while abbot John was well regarded enough to be appointed to the bishopric of Ely immediately after the canonization hearings. Although the bishop of Coventry was not, in fact, able to participate, having already gone off on crusade, the two other experienced churchmen went on to conduct the inquest, which was followed by Hugh's canonization in 1220.

Although all the commissioners in the case of Hugh of Lincoln's process were English, they were not from Hugh's diocese or Order (Hugh was a Carthusian, John of Fountains a Cistercian), and this balance of local knowledge and impartiality seems to have been the ideal sought for.[17] The commissioners in the case of the saintly Breton priest Yves of Tréguier in 1330 were the bishops of Limoges and Angoulême and the abbot of Troarn, from the kingdom of France but not from Brittany.[18] Angoulême is about 250 miles from Tréguier, and Limoges a little farther, while Troarn, although much nearer, was still in the neighbouring Normandy, not

[15] "Pluries et instanter": Hostiensis, *Lectura siue Apparatus super quinque libris Decretalium*, ad X. 3. 45. 1, *Audivimus*; followed by Johannes Andreae, *Novella Commentaria in quinque Decretalium libros*, ad X. 3. 45. 1, *Audivimus*; cf. the phrase "sepe et instanter" used to describe the campaign for the canonization of Birgit of Sweden, *Acta et processus canonizacionis Beate Birgitte*, p. 4.

[16] *The Canonization of St. Hugh of Lincoln*, pp. 90–93.

[17] See the comments of Vauchez, *Sainthood*, p. 43.

[18] *Processus de vita et miraculis sancti Yvonis*.

in Brittany. Although such a clear separation between candidate and commissioner was not invariable, especially in the thirteenth century, it did eventually become the general rule.[19]

The other vital figure in these local inquests was the proctor, who represented the petitioners in the case and was responsible for identifying relevant witnesses. He was also usually in charge of drafting the articles of the questionnaire which would shape the inquest, although in the case of the inquest into the sanctity of Thomas de Cantilupe, bishop of Hereford, in 1307, it was actually the papal commissioners who undertook this task. The requirements they drew up for the interrogation of witnesses were detailed.[20] Witnesses had to state "if they were literate or illiterate, noble or commoner, rich or poor and if they were of Thomas's kindred or household, and what their age was." The questions to be asked were grouped under three headings: Bishop Thomas's life and his virtues during life; his reputation; and his miracles. Under the first heading, the topics included biographical details, ranging from his birthplace, parentage, and place of baptism, to his age at death and the place and manner of his death; his qualities during the distinct phases of his life, as student and as bishop; and general questions about his virtues:

> if he was by nature discreet and prudent, humble, gentle and mild, patient and benevolent, sober, modest and chaste; if he was diligent in prayer, devotion, and contemplation or meditation; if he was just, God-fearing, and merciful and peaceable; if he had suffered persecution or adversity in his life, and of what type and for what cause.

The second heading addressed the general question "whether it was public knowledge and general report and opinion or belief of the people that the said lord Thomas was a saint," then probing into who had been heard asserting this, when and where and by what kind of person, and then, even more searchingly, what the witness understood by the phrase "public knowledge." The final heading was the most elaborate, with fifteen separate sections on the alleged miracles.

Such a demanding questionnaire set the framework for an interrogation that was both thorough and systematic. Reticent witnesses could be pushed to search their minds for details, while the loquacity of garrulous witnesses could be channelled and directed, although sometimes the questions might be challenging or confusing: in particular, the exact meaning of "public knowledge" provoked some head-scratching among the witnesses. These proceedings were an "Inquisition," just like the inquisitions against heretics taking place at the same time and with many of the same procedures. Witnesses gave evidence on oath and could be cross-examined by the commissioners, and their evidence was written down by notaries, scribes authorized to produce official records. A local inquest into sanctity was sometimes termed a

[19] For exceptions, see Vauchez, *Sainthood*, p. 43 nn. 44–45.

[20] BAV, Vat. lat. 4015, fols. 3v–5.

"process" (*processus*), and, although this did not have a technical meaning, it is significant that this was also a word frequently applied to legal proceedings.

The number of witnesses called to give testimony varied enormously, but it could be very large. Several processes involved more than 200 witnesses, and that of Peter of Morone (Celestine V) over 320, while in the hearings held in the Italian Marche in 1325 during the canonization process of Nicholas of Tolentino 371 witnesses were heard, 196 men and 175 women.[21] Since the proceedings were written down in Latin, and the commissioners might well speak a language different from the witnesses, interpreters were necessary. In the canonization hearings for Thomas de Cantilupe, only 61 per cent of the clergy were able to give their evidence in Latin, while for laymen the figure was far lower—17 per cent for town-dwellers, 7 per cent for countrymen; none of the female witnesses deposed in Latin; and the linguistic situation was further complicated in this case by monoglot Welsh speakers, for whom some bilingual friars had to be rustled up from Hereford friary.[22] With depositions in Latin, English, French (the upper-class language in England at this time), and Welsh, as well as two commissioners from southern France, who are unlikely to have understood the French spoken in England, and a record produced in Latin, in the third person rather than as direct speech, the hearings must have sounded like Babel, but they were organized Babel, eventually producing lengthy, ordered records that testify to the administrative skills of the high medieval Church.

Witnesses were questioned about the life and virtues of the candidates for sanctity, about the miracles they had performed in their lifetime or after their death, and about the general reputation for sanctity that they enjoyed (*fama*). The balance between virtue in life and miraculous powers is a subject to be discussed later. The enquiries about reputation bring out an important point. If there was evidence that someone was being regarded as a saint, this strengthened the case. The canonization process thus *required* evidence that the candidate was being treated as a saint: invocation, miracles, *fama*, and so on. It did not seek to ban these *until* it had issued a verdict. Hence pre-canonization cult was not only licit, but essential.

After the hearings in the localities, there came the "curial phase," when the documents would be sent to the papal court, there to be sifted, sorted and organized by chaplains, before being entrusted to a committee of three cardinals for evaluation. Sometimes the cardinals who undertook this task were already experienced in the winding paths of the canonization process. William de Testa, entrusted with examining the evidence for the sanctity of Thomas Aquinas in 1318, had served eleven years earlier as a commissioner in the canonization hearings of Thomas de Cantilupe, and was in action again in 1319 reviewing the case for the canonization of

[21] Vauchez, *Sainthood*, pp. 500, 563 n. 22 (cf. Toynbee, *St Louis of Toulouse and the Process of Canonization in the Fourteenth Century*, p. 171 n. 2); *Il processo per la canonizzazione di S. Nicola da Tolentino*, p. XXI.

[22] Richter, *Sprache und Gesellschaft im Mittelalter*, pp. 171–217.

Clare of Montefalco.[23] The bulk of such material could be immense: it was reported that the enquiries into the sanctity of Louis IX produced "more written material than one ass could carry."[24] This partly explains the long periods that often ensued between the local inquest and canonization, 14 years in the case of Louis IX, but as long as 89 years in the unusual case of Nicholas of Tolentino (inquests took place in 1325 and 1357, but he was canonized only in 1446). This final examination at the papal court often involved sophisticated analysis of claims about miracles.

The canonization process of the later Middle Ages was a demanding scrutiny and these hard new criteria were noticed at the time. "If the merits of the holy fathers of old had been boiled down by an examination or purgation in this way," said one commissioner involved in a canonization process in the 1240s, "scarcely one of them would have come to the high dignity of canonization."[25] Not all requests led to an inquest, and not all inquests led to canonization—the success rate was 50 per cent. But eventually, a small select group emerged, the papally canonized. After final deliberations between pope and cardinals, they were publicly recognized by an elaborate liturgical ceremony, where the pope himself presided. In a brilliantly lit church, amid a great crowd of brightly clothed clergy and laity, and after the chanting of the hymn *Veni creator*, the pope announced the canonization and celebrated the Mass of the new saint, specifying his or her feast-day and promising an indulgence to those who should visit the shrine—this was a partial release from the temporal punishment of sin. The new saint was publicized not only by this liturgy but also by the promulgation of a canonization bull, that is, an authoritative papal proclamation informing believers that he or she had been "inscribed in the catalogue of the saints."[26]

This ceremony occurred on average only every seven or eight years in the later Middle Ages. "The canonization of new saints," noted one fifteenth-century liturgical writer, "is rare."[27] In contrast to this small and elite group, however, new, uncanonized saints continued to be revered in great numbers. It has been calculated, for example, that over 500 people who lived in the thirteenth century came to be venerated as saints immediately after their death.[28] The ratio between canonized and non-canonized saints in that century is approximately 1:21, and this is a period when canonizations were more frequent than in following centuries. It is thus clear that, however important papal canonization was, and however grateful we must be for the donkey-loads of material it generated, the great stream of the cult of the saints flowed on in the later Middle Ages without being too strongly influenced by it.

[23] BAV, Vat. lat. 4015, *passim*; *Fontes vitae sancti Thome Aquinatis* 4, p. 270; ASV, Riti, Processus 2929, fol. 655v.

[24] Boniface VIII, *Sermones et bulla de canonisatione sancti Ludovici*, pp. 151–52.

[25] Albert Suerbeer (archbishop of Armagh), *Historia canonizationis et translationis sancti Edmundi archiepiscopi et confessoris*, col. 1851.

[26] See Schimmelpfennig, *Die Zeremonienbücher der römischen Kurie*.

[27] BL, Lansdowne 451, fol. 136v.

[28] Goodich, *Vita perfecta*, p. 15, with list on pp. 213–41.

Mendicant Saints

In the later Middle Ages (1200–1500) Europe became more urban, the laity assumed a greater role in religious life, and there was a small but unmistakable expansion in the sphere of activity for women. All these tendencies are reflected in the history of the cult of the saints. The most dramatic new development in religious life, however, was the rise of the mendicant Orders (that is, the friars), and, with them, the mendicant saints.

The long tradition of Benedictine monasticism was always throwing up new reformist groups. These claimed their inspiration from Benedict's rule and the model of the early monks, but it was often the case that such claims cloaked innovation, in patterns of piety and in institutional arrangements. The Cluniacs of the tenth, eleventh, and twelfth centuries devised their own distinctive liturgy and elaborated novel forms of subordination and association between Cluniac monasteries, while the Cistercians of the twelfth and thirteenth centuries aimed at a series of dramatic changes, including a stress on simplicity and uniformity, symbolized by their white habits, the cessation of the practice of recruiting monks as children, and a distinctive international organization of mother-houses and daughter-houses, with a central authority. It was characteristic of this uniform and international outlook that no Cistercian monastic churches were dedicated to local saints but all were under the patronage of the Virgin Mary.

At the beginning of the thirteenth century there arose a yet more radical innovation than that represented by the Cluniacs or Cistercians: the friars. While monks of the Benedictine tradition were committed to stay within the monastery where they had taken their vows, and lived off the corporate resources of their monastery, the friars were launched as wandering mendicants, travelling from place to place and begging their bread. Francis, the inspiration of the Order of friars customarily named after him, the Franciscans (although their official name is "The Order of Lesser Brothers"), expressed his commitment to poverty in a dramatic gesture, stripping off all his clothes before the bishop of Assisi, his home town, who, recognizing him as "a man of God," embraced him and covered him with his own cloak.[29] This took place in 1206, when Francis was twenty-five. Subsequent events show the extraordinary appeal of this model of apostolic life, that is, a life of wandering evangelism without any private property. Francis received verbal approval for his project from Pope Innocent III in 1209 and soon thereafter sent out his brethren (the literal meaning of "friars") on preaching missions which reached France, Spain, and Germany in 1217, England in 1224, and eventually established Franciscan convents throughout western Christendom—at a rate of 14 a year in the first century of the Order. A papally approved Rule was drawn up in 1223, three years before Francis's death in 1226.

Despite the radical eccentricities of his style of life, Francis always stressed the importance of orthodox belief and respect for the authorities of the Church, and he had

[29] Thomas of Celano, *Vita prima sancti Francisci* 1. 6. 14–15, p. 14.

patrons in high places. As soon as he was dead, and posthumous miracles began, "the bishop of Rome, leader of the Christians and lord of the world, rejoiced that in his own time he saw the Church of God renewed."[30] The pope at this time, Gregory IX, had been a supporter of the Franciscans for many years, and he acted at once to have Francis's sanctity proclaimed to the world. After declaring the need for "a special church in which his body should be enclosed" and commissioning a Life of Francis from the Franciscan Thomas of Celano, the pope organized a speedy investigation of the miracles which culminated in canonization in July 1228.[31]

Thomas of Celano undertook his task with matching speed and his Life of Francis (known as the *First Life* or *Vita prima*, as Thomas later wrote another) was ready for papal approval by the spring of 1229. It is the earliest hagiographic portrait of one of the most important saints of the Middle Ages. Among the things that makes the *Vita prima* compelling, and indeed convincing, is the strange ambiguity and incoherence of Francis's early spiritual development as described in the first part of Thomas of Celano's work. Francis is, like all Christian children, "brought up in arrogance and according to the vanity of the world" and indulges in pranks, gossip, and fine clothes. It is a serious illness when Francis was about 20 that makes him start to reflect and to begin to despise himself as much as he had previously admired himself. He had a special friend with whom he discussed these things. One day Francis went into a crypt outside Assisi and had such an intense religious experience there that when he emerged he seemed like "another person."[32]

Then follows the clash with his father, something which has been of particular interest in the Freudian age. Francis took some of his father's expensive cloth to a nearby town, sold it and then set off back to Assisi with the profit. On the way he found it intolerable to carry the money for a moment longer and offered it to the priest of the decayed church of St. Damian, a kilometre or so outside Assisi. The priest, significantly, refused it for fear of Francis's family, but let him stay in the church. Soon Francis's father found out where he was, and set off to find his son. At this point the remarkable fact emerges that Francis had already prepared a hiding place for himself in a friend's house in Assisi. It is described as "a pit," and Francis lived in it for a month, scarcely daring to come out to meet the needs of nature. His boldness in taking his father's property was thus balanced by the fact that he was terrified of him. Eventually he emerged from the pit, endured the mockery of his neighbours and a brutal imprisonment by his father, but was in the end freed by his more emollient mother. It is at this point that he responded to his father's summons to appear before the bishop by coming before them and taking off all his clothes in an act which combined dramatic religious symbolism with filial defiance.[33]

[30] Ibid., 3. 121, p. 96.

[31] The original of the bull (*Recolentes qualiter*) is reproduced in Brooke, *The Image of St. Francis*, p. 54, pl. 8; Thomas of Celano, *Vita prima sancti Francisci* 3. 119–26, pp. 94–103.

[32] Thomas of Celano, *Vita prima sancti Francisci* 1. 1–3, pp. 5–10.

[33] Ibid., 1. 4–6, pp. 11–14.

Francis was now committed to a full-time religious life, first as a hermit, helping to repair derelict churches, then, inspired by the Gospel injunctions, as a penniless preacher of repentance. He wanted to fulfil the Gospel commandments "to the letter" and hence even abandoned shoes in accordance with Christ's instructions in Matthew 10:10. Instead of a belt he wore a cord (the French word for a Franciscan is *Cordelier*) and insisted that his followers never even touch money. The years between the approval of his way of life by Innocent III in 1209 and his death in 1226 were marked by dramatic and memorable events: preaching to the birds (and to the flowers); the amazing missionary trip to the Sultan of Egypt; the building of the first crèche, with ox and ass and hay; and, most remarkable of all, reception of the stigmata, that is the marks of Christ's wounds, on his own body.[34] The claim that Francis had received the stigmata was unprecedented and controversial, but, naturally, one that his Order cherished; in the mid-fourteenth century the Franciscans even instituted a liturgical feast-day to celebrate the reception of the stigmata.[35]

Unsurprisingly, after the death of the saint, some thought that the success of the Franciscans as an institution had involved a sacrifice of their ideals. One group reacted by calling for a return to the original principles. They eventually formed a dissident movement—the Spirituals—and some of them even perished in the Inquisitors' flames. Their stress was on the absolute poverty that Francis had embraced—"most holy poverty." Francis himself seems to have been afraid of a compromise on this issue, for in his Testament, composed in his last days, he extols the poverty of the early friars, warns the brethren against receiving churches or seeking privileges, and orders them to preserve the Testament along with the Rule, never seeking to interpret or construe it other than literally. This attempt to shape the Order after his death was in vain. In 1230 Pope Gregory IX himself declared that the Testament had no binding authority; much later, the Spirituals even claimed that the superiors of the Order "in the Marche and in many other places had strictly commanded that the Testament of St. Francis be confiscated from everyone and burned."[36] Even if this was simply partisan propaganda, there is no question that, looking back on their founder 40 years after his death, the Franciscans had to recognize that several features of Francis's life and sayings did not fit comfortably with the Order as it had come to be in their own day, with its great churches, papal privileges, and friars in positions of power and authority.

At this point the leaders of the Order decided that, rather than adapt the present to the ideals of the past, they would change the past to fit the present. In the 1260s an ambitious attempt was made to rewrite the early history of the Order. The Minister-General, Bonaventure, composed his own *Life of St. Francis* and, at the Franciscan Chapter-General of 1266, it was decreed that this should be the only account of the

[34] Ibid., 1. 8–9, 20–21, 29–30; 2. 3, pp. 16–19, 42–47, 59–60, 63–65, 72–74; on the meeting with the Sultan, see Tolan, *Saint Francis and the Sultan*; on the stigmata, see also p. 376 later.

[35] Vauchez, "The Stigmata of St. Francis"; *Chronica XXIV Generalium Ordinis Minorum*, p. 528; *Francis of Assisi: Early Documents* 3, pp. 659–70.

[36] Ubertino da Casale, *Declaratio contra falsitates datas per fratrem Raymundum*, p. 168.

saint. All other earlier Lives of Francis, including those of Thomas of Celano, were to be destroyed. If copies of these earlier Lives had come into the hands of those outside the Order, the friars should strive to get hold of them.[37] This attempt at suppression was—given medieval circumstances—remarkably successful. There exist today a mere handful of manuscripts of Thomas of Celano's works which can be shown to have Franciscan origins, while even those from outside the Order are not numerous in comparison with the hundred of more manuscripts of Bonaventure's Life. This rewriting of Francis's history continued to shape knowledge of the saint even in the age of print. Bonaventure's Life was first printed in 1509, Thomas of Celano's *Vita prima* in 1768. For the intervening 250 years the Francis whom the interested public saw was an image produced by that selection and suppression of 1266. Hagiography has been called "an exercise in persuasion," and the Order was here deciding how and to what end it was undertaking this process of persuasion.[38]

The other great Order of friars, the Dominicans (the Order of Preachers), had a less turbulent history. Their origins were rather different from the Franciscans, but they gradually converged with them in many respects. Dominic, their founder, was, unlike Francis, a regular cleric, that is, he had taken vows of poverty, chastity, and obedience, before he embarked on his life of wandering preaching. It was the spread of heresy in southern France that induced him to take this step, and the Dominicans were always deeply involved in the fight for orthodoxy, sometimes with the tongue, sometimes with the pen, and sometimes with crueller instruments—they provided the main staff of the papal inquisition established by Gregory IX. Dominic had clear targets, sending out his friars to the chief academic centres of Europe, Bologna, and Paris, and thus initiating a tradition of Dominican scholarship which reached its heights with Albertus Magnus and Thomas Aquinas. The Franciscans eventually imitated their example in this respect, just as the Dominicans adopted the Franciscan attitude to property (although avoiding the controversies of the other Order). Dominic was canonized in 1234, six years after Francis.

The friars were conscious that they represented something new, as is well illustrated by this story from Gerard de Frachet's *Lives of the Brethren of the Order of Preachers* of 1260. The earlier, Benedictine view of the Christian tradition, as expressed by abbot Odilo of Cluny, has already been cited. He traced a line from the apostles and martyrs, through the Fathers of the Church, to the monastic movement as shaped by St. Benedict. The view of the Dominican friar Gerard de Frachet,

[37] The decision to compile "one good Legend from all of them" was taken in 1257: *Sources of the Modern Roman Liturgy* 2, p. 417; for the order to destroy all except Bonaventure's, see Fonzo, "L'Anonimo Perugino," p. 247; Little, "Decrees of the General Chapters of the Friars Minor, 1260 to 1282," p. 705, from Bodl. MS Lat. th. d. 22, olim Phillipps 9479 (lot 207) (repr. *Archivum Franciscanum Historicum* 7 [1914], p. 678); on surviving manuscripts and printings, see *Analecta Franciscana* 10, pp. XVII, LXXIII, LXXVII. Discussions of the contrast between Bonaventure's and earlier Lives include Moorman, *A History of the Franciscan Order*, p. 287; Cook, "Fraternal and Lay Images of St Francis," pp. 266–69; see also Brooke, *The Image of St Francis*, pp. 242–46.

[38] Kleinberg, "Proving Sanctity," p. 185.

two centuries later, offers an interesting variation. He pictured Christ talking to his mother, lamenting the hard-heartedness of the human race:

> Mother mine, what further can I or should I do for the world? I sent patriarchs and prophets for their salvation and they reformed themselves scarcely at all. I myself came to them and I sent apostles, and they wickedly killed me and them. I sent many martyrs, doctors and confessors but they did not accept them. But since it is not right that I should deny you anything, I will give them my Preachers, through whom they may be enlightened and cleansed.[39]

Here the monks have silently slipped out of the long story of Christ's efforts to save humanity, and the friars, in the form of the Dominicans, have assumed the central culminating role.

Such self-congratulation was not totally without reason. The rapid expansion of the friars, their deep penetration into European society and the formative role they had in shaping late medieval spirituality indicate how important they were as a part of the religious landscape, especially in the newly mushrooming towns. Francis, the wool merchant's son, had when young had a dream in which he saw with surprise that his family home was full of arms and armour, "for he had not been accustomed to see such things in his house, but rather bundles of cloth for sale."[40] In the previous century his class had been deemed far from salvation: "What hope do merchants have? Little; for they acquire almost all that they have through cheating, perjury and unlawful gain."[41] Francis reacted with an almost pathological hatred of money, but the Franciscans, and the other mendicant Orders, could not be imagined without the urban and commercial environment in which they existed. They undertook to evangelize the godless masses of the growing towns, but also, rejecting the fixed agricultural endowments of the older Benedictine monasticism, they needed the fluid capital of this world.

The friars were very well represented amongst the saints of the later Middle Ages, both those who were officially canonized and those who were not. In the century after the canonization of St. Francis, the first mendicant saint, in 1228, almost 40 per cent of canonization processes were of friars. These included the two swiftest canonizations of the Middle Ages, of Antony of Padua and Peter Martyr, both canonized within twelve months of their deaths, one each, very tactfully, from the Franciscans and the Dominicans. The favourable position the mendicants enjoyed in this respect was clear to contemporaries. During the prolonged attempt to secure the canonization of Osmund of Salisbury, who was not a friar but a long-dead bishop, a canny cardinal commented, "If this Osmund had belonged to a mendicant order he would have been canonized long ago."[42]

[39] Gerard de Fracheto, *Vitae fratrum Ordinis Praedicatorum* 1. 1. 2, p. 7; taken up by Jacobus de Voragine, *Legenda aurea* 109 (2, p. 723).

[40] Thomas of Celano, *Vita prima sancti Francisci* 1. 2. 5, pp. 8–9.

[41] Honorius Augustodunensis, *Elucidarium* 2. 18, col. 1148.

[42] *The Canonization of St Osmund*, p. 14; see Kemp, *Canonization and Authority*, p. 140.

Saintly friars of the later Middle Ages were of a variety of types, not all of them close to the model of Francis. There were learned academics like Bonaventure or Thomas Aquinas, charismatic preachers like Bernardino of Siena (d. 1444), and "martyrs," victims either of heretics, like Peter Martyr, or in the mission field beyond Europe. Italy was especially fertile in mendicant saints, sometimes closely associated with their native towns. Francis of Fabriano (d. 1322) assembled an impressive theological library for the Franciscan convent in his home town in central Italy, and was revered as a saint there after his death; "Look kindly on your home town of Fabriano," runs one hymn to the saint.[43] The early Franciscan Andrew Caccioli of Spello in Umbria was buried in the Franciscan church in Spello, where, at least from the early modern period, worshippers prayed to him for good weather.[44]

The last Dominican friar to be canonized in the Middle Ages was Vincent Ferrer, and he exemplifies many of the features that gave the mendicant Orders their distinctive character and left such a deep mark on late medieval spirituality. Born in Valencia to a well-off urban family—a typical background for the friars—he entered the Order in 1367 and received a comprehensive education in logic and theology at various Dominican centres in Catalonia and southern France. Such schooling and such itineration were familiar for the Dominicans: Thomas Aquinas, from southern Italy, studied at Cologne and Paris before entering on his career as a teacher. Vincent had close ties with the royal house of Aragon, and was often involved in the affairs of the kingdom, serving, for example, as one of the members of the arbitration council that sought to end the Aragonese succession crisis of 1410–12.

Most of Vincent's adult life coincided with the Great Schism (1378–1417), that period when two rival lines of popes, one based in Avignon, one in Rome, struggled to assert their legitimacy and win the allegiance of Christendom. From 1394 the Avignonese line was represented by Benedict XIII, a Catalan like Vincent, who championed his cause and served as his confessor. Involvement in the high politics of the Church was quite usual for the friars; what was less usual was that, in the midst of his deep entanglement with papal power struggles, Vincent experienced a transformative vision. As he himself described it, writing in the third person,

> When this friar was seriously ill and was praying wholeheartedly that he might be cured, so that he could preach God's word . . . there appeared to him, as it were in his sleep, the two saints, Dominic and Francis, praying at Christ's feet . . . and at length Christ came down and, with them at his side, came to the friar lying sick in his bed and stroked his cheek, and he gave a clear mental command to that sick friar that he should go through the world preaching like an apostle, just as those two saints had done, and that He would mercifully

[43] BS 5, cols. 1155–56; AASS Aprilis 3 (1675): 991 (Hymnvs ad II Vesperas).

[44] *Commentarius historicus de beato Andrea Hispellate*; BS 1, cols. 1155–56; Menestò, ed., *Il beato Andrea Caccioli da Spello*.

> await his preaching, for the conversion and correction of mankind, before the coming of Antichrist.[45]

This vision, which Vincent experienced in Avignon in 1398, changed the course of his life. Miraculously returned to health, he quitted papal service and began an endless round of revivalist preaching throughout western Europe, which ended only with his death. He was now "Christ's legate," charged with preaching urgently to the world. The Last days were near—"the time of Antichrist and the end of the world will be soon, and very soon, and indeed shortly to come."[46] At the time of the canonization hearings, some 35 years after his death, the power of Vincent's sermons could still be vividly recalled: "although he seemed to be like a weak old man when he turned up on his donkey, when he prayed and gave the people his blessing he seemed like a young man of thirty or so."[47] He had stirred many people to penitential flagellation. They would put on the white clothing of penitents and then whip themselves on the shoulders, sometimes with scourges of iron, until the blood flowed. "And this mode of discipline spread much more widely than before through the preaching of Master Vincent."[48] In the diverse religious world of southern France and Spain, his preaching also involved him with other faiths. While he did not believe that the conversion of the Jews should be achieved by violence or intimidation, he nevertheless deemed it highly desirable and supported the idea that Jews should be forced to attend Christian sermons. He also espoused residential and other forms of segregation between Jews and Christians, and was of the opinion that "we have no greater enemies."[49]

Vincent was one of the more remarkable of the Dominican saints of the Middle Ages. He was an academic, but also a charismatic preacher; a man intimately involved with royal and ecclesiastical politics, but also powered by an apocalyptic vision; and his legacy included confraternities of flagellants and anti-Jewish legislation, as well as collections of sermons, spiritual treatises, and technical works of logic. He exemplifies in a strong and individual form the mendicant saints who were such important figures in the cult of the saints in the later Middle Ages.

Lay Female Saints

Since the earliest days of Christianity, some women had made solemn promises to live a life of chastity and devotion. For many centuries, they had been taken their vows in communities following a Rule, the Benedictine, or, from the twelfth century,

[45] *Notes et documents de l'histoire de Saint Vincent Ferrier*, pp. 220–21.

[46] Ibid., p. 220.

[47] Ibid., p. 331.

[48] Ibid., p. 283.

[49] Vincent Ferrer, *Sermons* 3, no. 56, p. 14.

some other variant of the life of the nun. In the thirteenth century, this pattern began to loosen and diversify. Alongside the Poor Clares and Dominican nuns, female equivalents of the friars, the last centuries of the Middle Ages saw a less spectacular but nevertheless noticeable rise in the number female saints who did not belong to a religious order. This was a period of experimentation in the religious life of the laity, and women were conspicuous in their pursuit of new forms and new experiences, both individual and collective. These included private devotional practices such as the use of Books of Hours, small personal prayer-books; the pursuit of more intense and more subjective mystical experience, often focussing on the Virgin Mary and the sufferings of Christ; and, with the beguines, the development of a kind of ordered, religious life accessible to women still "living in the world." Beguines were pious women who lived in communities without taking vows, often supporting themselves by handicrafts. They engaged in charitable works and devotional practices, and were frequently guided and supported by neighbouring friars. The Low Countries was amongst the earliest regions to see an important beguine movement and it also produced the first beguine saint, Mary of Oignies (d. 1213), member of a well-off family from Brabant who convinced her husband to live in a chaste marriage and devoted herself to the care of lepers, living a life marked by extreme asceticism, manual labour, and meditation upon the Passion. She was held up as a model example of those "holy women, serving the Lord devoutly within marriage."[50]

The female lay saint also appears in canonization processes. The numbers involved in official papal canonization were always small, but there is a clear pattern. Between 1200 and 1500 fourteen women were the subject of canonization processes; of these ten were lay people, not nuns.[51] Hence, although women were a minority amongst those considered for canonization, almost three-quarters of these women were lay. Examples range from queens to servant-girls. There is also a general increase in non-canonized female lay saints.

Amongst the most famous and remarkable of the female lay saints of the later Middle Ages was Elizabeth of Thuringia. Elizabeth was a Hungarian princess who married Ludwig IV, Landgrave of Thuringia (1217–27), while in her teens.[52] She bore him three children but seems to have pined for something other than the world of the great princely dynasty. One story tells of how she was lying in bed one night with her husband, when she sketched out what would, for her, be the good life: "I would wish us to have just enough land for one plough and 200 sheep, and you

[50] Jacques de Vitry, *Vita Mariae Oigniacensis*, prologue, p. 637.

[51] Vauchez, *Sainthood*, pp. 268–69 n. 21, 369: the discrepancy between these two lists arises from the inadvertent omission of Hedwig of Silesia from the former.

[52] Many important sources were edited in *Quellenstudien zur Geschichte der heiligen Elisabeth*; much is translated in Wolf, *The Life and Afterlife of St. Elizabeth of Hungary: Testimony from Her Canonization Hearings*; there are two important collections associated with exhibitions: *Sankt Elisabeth: Fürstin, Dienerin, Heilige*; Blume and Werner, ed., *Elisabeth von Thüringen—eine europäische Heilige*; see also Bertelsmeier-Kierst, ed., *Elisabeth von Thüringen und die neue Frömmigkeit in Europa*.

would cultivate the land with your own hands and I would milk the sheep."[53] This vision of the simple life inspired attempts to be more like a common person than a princess. She insisted her servants address her by the informal singular form (*tu* in Latin, *du* in Middle High German) rather than the more deferential plural (*vos, ir*).[54] With her own hands she spun wool for the clothing of the poor and the friars. She visited the sick, making their beds for them. Rather sadly, given her milkmaid ambitions, she was unsuccessful in her attempt to milk a cow for a poor woman who wanted some milk.[55]

Elizabeth had as her spiritual adviser Conrad of Marburg, renowned in his day as preacher and inquisitor. His reputation was that of "a most famous preacher, the sharpest critic of vice, the terror of tyrants and heretics."[56] Conrad seems to have taken as hard a line with the young princess as he did with the heretics he persecuted. When she missed one of his sermons, she and her maidservant, whom Conrad also deemed guilty, were stripped to their underclothes and soundly beaten by him.[57] Conrad also had his companion Gerhard beat Elizabeth and her servants "with a long stout rod," while he stood by singing "*Misere mei Deus* (God, have mercy on me)" (figure 3.2). The marks were still visible on Elizabeth's body three weeks later.[58] Beating was obviously an important part of the saint's pursuit of self-humiliation. Even when her husband was still alive and she was Landgravine of Thuringia, Elizabeth had encouraged her servants to beat her.[59] After her husband's death in 1227, Conrad often beat and slapped her "with great zeal."[60]

Elizabeth never entered a religious order, although she took personal vows and had close links with the Franciscans. She wore a grey tunic, like the Franciscans (Greyfriars), and founded a hospital dedicated to St. Francis in Marburg (the first dedication to Francis in Germany). Like Francis, she idolized poverty. This meant not only care for the poor but also imitation of them. She distributed clothes to the poor but also fantasized about begging herself.[61] When other ladies went to church for the first time after childbirth (a ceremony known as "churching" in English), they would go "glorying in a great company and in their most expensive clothes," but Elizabeth came dressed in wool, with bare feet and (something apparently worth pointing out) "holding her child in her own arms."[62] After her husband's death, she wished to beg door-to-door, but Conrad refused permission. He did, however, cut her household down to three persons, a lay-brother to take charge of practical affairs,

[53] Caesarius of Heisterbach, *Vita sancte Elyzabeth lantgravie* 5, p. 354.
[54] *Libellus de dictis quatuor ancillarum*, p. 136.
[55] Ibid., p. 118.
[56] Caesarius of Heisterbach, *Vita sancte Elyzabeth lantgravie* 4, p. 351.
[57] *Libellus de dictis quatuor ancillarum*, pp. 118–19.
[58] Ibid., p. 136.
[59] Ibid., p. 117.
[60] Ibid., p. 127.
[61] Ibid., p. 120.
[62] Ibid., p. 117.

3.2. St. Elizabeth of Thuringia beaten by Conrad of Marburg, thirteenth-century Psalter.
Paris, Bibliothèque Sainte-Geneviève, MS 2689, fol. 12.
Photo: akg-images/Jean-Claude Varga.

a devout maidservant, and a deaf widow. She and the servant took turns at cooking and washing up.[63]

A particular feature of Elizabeth's spirituality was her immersion in the more repellent side of physical illness. She kept a paralyzed orphan with a bloody flux in her bed at night, carrying him to the toilet and washing his soiled clothing. After this boy's death she took in a leprous girl and, later, a scabby boy.[64] Such extreme self-abnegation was a powerful ideal for Elizabeth and others—later in the century An-

[63] Conrad of Marburg, *Epistola de vita beate Elyzabet*, pp. 157–58.
[64] Ibid., pp. 158–59.

gela da Foligno would wash the feet and hands of the poor and lepers and then drink the water.[65] However, there is record of a fascinating exchange which shows that it was by no means universally accepted as the model life. This is recorded by Irmingard, Elizabeth's companion, and one who followed her in adopting vows and the grey tunic. Irmingard attested to such of Elizabeth's practices as carrying the scabby boy to the toilet, bathing the sick, and touching lepers. One day the saint had said to her, "How good this is for us, that we bathe and touch Our Lord in this way." "It is good for us," asked Irmingard, "when we do this kind of thing? I do not know if others would think so."[66] This is doubly interesting, as not only reflecting a quite understandable variety of opinion about the value of such behaviour but also showing that even those who participated in it, like Irmingard, might be aware of the dissentient views of others. The Hungarian count who was sent to bring Elizabeth back to the Hungarian court after the Landgrave's death and found her spinning wool would be one of these "others": "never has a king's daughter been seen spinning wool before," he commented (needless to say she did not return with him).[67]

Elizabeth died in 1231 at the age of twenty-four and was buried in the hospital of St. Francis which she had founded at Marburg. The following year Conrad of Marburg helped launch the campaign for her canonization and was one of the commissioners appointed by the pope to inquire into her miracles. He associated Elizabeth's sanctity and his campaign against heresy, urging her canonization "as an aid to the universal Church and confutation of the wickedness of the heretics."[68] Early in 1233 the commissioners sent a list of over one hundred miracles to the pope. Official canonization followed in 1235, but Conrad did not live to see it. His killing spree in the Rhineland, in which the flimsiest charges had been sufficient to bring hundreds of so-called heretics to the flames, enraged important people and, in the summer of 1233 Conrad, along with Gerhard his companion, was murdered by enemies. Even after Conrad's death, however, Elizabeth did not escape his supervision. He was buried next to her in the church at Marburg.

Elizabeth's cult flourished, taken up by the Teutonic Knights, who received possession of the hospital in Marburg and built over her shrine the first Gothic church in Germany (and one of the most beautiful). Her relics were placed there in an elaborate golden reliquary carved with representations of her life and acts. The written hagiographic record is also rich, with Lives written by both Franciscan and Dominican authors and inclusion of versions of her Life in the great collections of saints' Lives produced in the later Middle Ages; she is, for example, the only contemporary female saint in the most successful of these collections, the *Golden Legend*.[69] She

[65] *Il "Liber" della beata Angela da Foligno*, p. 43.

[66] *Libellus de dictis quatuor ancillarum*, p. 128.

[67] Ibid., p. 130; there is a nice fourteenth-century illustration of her and her ladies spinning, reproduced in Klaniczay, *Holy Rulers and Blessed Princesses*, p. 221.

[68] *Hessisches Urkundenbuch* 1. 1, no. 28, p. 29.

[69] Jacobus de Voragine, *Legenda aurea* 164 (2, pp. 1156–79); there is a succinct discussion of the hagiography in Klaniczay, *Holy Rulers and Blessed Princesses*, pp. 419–23.

represents a dramatic intersection of the high-born female saint familiar from the early Middle Ages onwards with the ethos of humility and self-abasement fostered by the friars.

A late medieval female saint of a different type was Francesca Romana (1384–1440), a member of a noble Roman family, the subject of a Life in Italian, written by Giovanni Mattioti, the parish priest of Santa Maria in Trastevere, who was Francesca's confessor at the end of her life.[70] There is also a great deal of information about her in the three canonization hearings which took place in the 1440s and 1450s (she was eventually canonized only in 1608).[71]

Something that emerges at once from these accounts is Francesca's apprehensiveness about sex. From childhood she could not bear to be touched, even by her own father; when married at the age of twelve (not unusual in fifteenth-century Italy) she immediately fell ill; after, in obedience to the directives of her spiritual father, she had sex, she would vomit, sometimes bringing up blood. This attitude was generalized, for she had great disdain for men, even her son, and did not let men touch her until she had covered her hand with a towel. It is not entirely surprising that, after her husband was wounded and, later, exiled "she did not care about tribulations of their kind." But even the deaths of her children "gave her joy not sorrow."

Her asceticism was so extreme that her spiritual advisers had to insist she give up such practices as self-laceration and burning herself with hot wax, but she continued with a general abstemiousness, being mainly vegetarian, drinking water not wine, and giving up sugar. She slept very little, partly because she was tormented by demons at night. She dressed simply, with no jewellery, and encouraged other ladies to give up such vanities too, and to avoid dancing, singing, and wedding parties. She studied the scriptures in Italian, and wept terribly when thinking of the Lord's Passion.

Her cousin Vannoza was her spiritual companion and soul-mate for thirty-eight years. Sometimes the two of them would go out to parts of the city where they were not known and beg. This pretend mendicancy was balanced by some strange indulgences. On one occasion Vannoza fancied a lobster and one instantly appeared. Another time the two cousins were invited to a neighbour's childbed, "as is the custom of Roman ladies," but when they arrived they preferred to go into the garden, wishing to be like desert saints; here, although it was April, two ripe figs fell on them—"a fact which was reported throughout the entire city." Not all contemporaries were impressed by their spirituality: one priest wondered why rich married women should want to receive holy communion so often.

One of Francesca's especial saintly merits was "her superinfused grace of recognizing the faults of others." She grieved because she saw "many weak in spirit who do

[70] Giovanni Mattioti, *Vita di S. Francesca Romana*; see in general Bartolomei Romagnoli, ed., *Francesca Romana: La santa, il monastero e la città alla fine del Medioevo*; on her fifteenth-century iconography, see Böse, *Gemalte Heiligkeit*, pp. 15–89.

[71] *I processi inediti per Francesca Bussa dei Ponziani (Santa Francesca Romana).*

not resist the vices and temptations of this world"; she could see evil spirits hovering over people indicating their particular vice; and once, seeing a priest looking like a leper, she realized he must have a concubine. Her accompanying angel revealed to her not only her own vileness but also that of her neighbours. Her young son also had prophetic powers, and pointed out that his father would receive a serious wound in the wars. This boy, who always said he wanted to be with the angels, died aged nine, but a year later revisited his mother. When she asked if he thought of her in heaven, he replied he was now in such glory that he had no care for her; he had in fact come for his five-year-old sister, who duly died too.

Francesca's visionary life was intense. She constantly saw devils, sometimes in animal form, sometimes in the guise of angels or men. Only she, not her confessor, Giovanni, could see her accompanying angel, and she had to indicate how tall the angel was by putting her hand on its head, while the priest saw nothing. Likewise, when she had a vision of cradling the Christ child in her arms, the poor priest was unable to see Him "not having brought his spectacles."

In 1425 Francesca became a founder member of the *Oblati*, a group of continent women, living in their own homes, but attached to a local monastery. They acquired their own premises in 1433, and Francesca joined them there three years later, after her husband's death. Within a year she was in charge, and could give free rein to her special grace: "she seemed not a woman but a lion in correcting faults."

While there are some features that Francesca and Elizabeth of Thuringia have in common, such as their romanticism about the mendicant life, their asceticism, and their abstemiousness, the contrast in the personal dynamics of their sanctity is more obvious. Although Elizabeth came from a great dynasty, far above the level of Francesca's urban patricians, she nevertheless was in a dependent and vulnerable relationship to her male relatives and her male confessor. Francesca, despite the limitations imposed by having to marry and having to have sex, was more in charge of her life. Her confessor, fumbling for his glasses and asking innocently about the stature of angels, was no Conrad of Marburg. With her eagle-eye for others' failings, her complicated semi-detachment from her own family, and her companionable cousin with a fondness for shellfish and a willingness to play-act sanctity, Francesca is a far less pathetic figure than Elizabeth, although not a more attractive one.

New Devotions

Mendicant saints, like Francis and Vincent Ferrer, and lay female saints, like Elizabeth of Thuringia and Francesca Romana, formed part of a large number of new saints who lived and were venerated in the thirteenth, fourteenth, and fifteenth centuries. Some were influential figures in the religious life of the period. Clare of Assisi (d. 1253) was inspired by the ideals of Francis, founded the Order of female Franciscans known as the Poor Clares, and was officially canonized in 1255. Other saints emerged from among the tertiaries, lay people associated with the religious orders (friars were the first order, nuns the second order, and lay people the third order, hence "tertiary"). One of the most notable saints of the later Middle Ages, Catherine of Siena, was a Dominican tertiary. But there were also new saints at this time of an older stamp, like Thomas de Cantilupe, bishop of Hereford, a prelate who defended his rights with determination and litigious fervour and was canonized in 1320, or suffering rulers, like prince Ferdinand of Portugal, who died in a Muslim prison in 1443, and Henry VI of England, murdered in 1471, and the subject of canonization attempts up to the eve of the Reformation.[72]

It was thus clearly true, as Jacques de Vitry put it in his Life of Mary of Oignies, that "in our days God works in modern saints [*in sanctis modernis*]."[73] But, alongside these contemporary saints, there were also shifts in fashion in the cults of the ancient inherited saints. The most popular saint remained one of the oldest, the Virgin Mary, and her cult continued to develop and diversify in the later Middle Ages. Ever more elaborate collections were made of accounts of her miraculous interventions. The famous *Cantigas de Santa Maria*, produced at the court of Alfonso X of Castile (1252–84), contain, in their fullest form, more than 400 poems recording the miracles and singing the praises of Mary. They are accompanied by music and hundreds of miniature illustrations. New festivals of Mary arose and spread. The feast of the Visitation of the Virgin Mary on 2 July was prescribed as a universal feast-day by Pope Urban VI in 1389, while the local Roman festival of Our Lady of the Snows on 5 August, commemorating the miraculous foundation of the Church of Santa Maria Maggiore, first occurs in liturgical books north of the Alps around the middle of the fourteenth century and became a popular dedication in Germany at the very end of the Middle Ages.[74] Many great churches added chapels dedicated to the Virgin Mary, like the Lady Chapels found in English cathedrals, while the personal name Mary became more common (for further discussion of the Marian cult, see later, pp. 151–62).

The elaboration of the cult of the Virgin Mary in later medieval Europe was paralleled by the rise of other female saints of New Testament times, notably Mary's mother, Anne.[75] Anne is not mentioned in the Bible, but occurs in the apocryphal Gospels of the second century, and her cult developed quite extensively in eastern

[72] Jancey, ed., *St Thomas Cantilupe*; BS 5, cols. 622–23; *Henrici VI Angliae regis miracula postuma*.

[73] Jacques de Vitry, *Vita Mariae Oigniacensis*, prologue, 9, p. 638.

[74] Later, pp. 156–57, on the Visitation; the legend of Our Lady of the Snows is mentioned in the indulgences granted to Santa Maria Maggiore by Pope Nicholas IV in 1288: ASV, Reg. Vat. 44, fols. 100–100v, printed in part, *Les Régistres de Nicholas IV*, pp. 127–28, nos. 630–35; New York, Pierpont Morgan Library, M. 75 (France 1350–74), fol. 462v, shows the dream of John the Patrician in the Office for Mary of the Snows; the first mention of the feast in Bruges is 1368–71: Brown, *Civic Ceremony*, p. 106; the Carmelites introduced the feast in 1393: *Fontes liturgiae Carmelitanae*, p. 44; on late medieval Germany, see *Marienlexicon* 6, pp. 40–42, s.v. "Schnee."

[75] Kleinschmidt, *Die heilige Anna*; Ashley and Sheingorn, eds., *Interpreting Cultural Symbols: Saint Anne in Late Medieval Society*; Dörfler-Dierken, *Die Verehrung der heiligen Anna in Spätmittelalter und früher Neuzeit*; Nixon, *Mary's Mother: Saint Anne in Late Medieval Europe*.

Christianity. In the West, however, she is relatively unimportant in the early Middle Ages, not occurring, for instance, in any liturgical Kalendar from Anglo-Saxon England, or in any Kalendar or litany from the Rhineland prior to the late twelfth century.[76] After 1200 this comparative neglect changed notably, with the foundation of chapels, altars, and guilds dedicated to her, the addition of her name to Kalendars, and the proliferation of images of her, alone or as part of a group with the Virgin Mary and Jesus, the most famous of which are the sketch and painting by Leonardo da Vinci. In the 1330s the Teutonic Knights raised the feast of Anne to a higher level of liturgical solemnity and organized the composition of a special Office for her.[77] The cult of Mary Magdalene also blossomed in the later medieval period (Magdalen College, Oxford, was founded in 1458).

The emphasis on Mary and other New Testament saints is consistent with the Christocentric nature of late medieval piety, which was preoccupied with the suffering and the blood of Jesus. The feast of Corpus Christi ("Christ's body") was prescribed for the entire Church by Pope Urban IV in 1264 (although its acceptance was in fact gradual). There was an efflorescence of miracles in which the Eucharistic bread shed blood, or turned into the figure of Christ, and relics of Christ's blood became the centre of new cults, notably at Wilsnack in Germany.[78] In the later Middle Ages new wonder-working places tended to be associated with blood miracles, or with visions and images of the Virgin Mary, rather than with traditional tomb-shrines. For instance, in the fifteenth century, thirty-four new pilgrimage sites arose in the diocese of Strassburg, but only four of these were saints' graves.[79]

Alongside the new emphases in the objects of cult went new institutional forms, notably the confraternity. Everywhere there were guilds and confraternities dedicated to a particular saint, often with a chapel or an altar where members assembled to sing praises, light candles, and remember their dead. Sometimes these associations were purely devotional, sometimes they also had economic purposes, and always there was a social and convivial side—indeed, one definition of guilds was "assemblies of drinkers."[80] They also ranged very widely in composition, a few being entirely clerical, many entirely lay, with others having a mixed membership, and could be extremely socially exclusive, at one extreme, or include only the poor, at the other. They were numerous and growing more so. Partial records survive from a survey of confraternities in England undertaken in 1388–89 and they give details of 507 confraternities, many of recent origin.[81] It has been estimated that there were around

[76] Rushforth, *Saints in English Kalendars*; Littger, *Studien zum Auftreten der Heiligennamen im Rheinland*, p. 159.

[77] *Die Statuten des deutschen Ordens*, p. 148.

[78] See Bynum, *Wonderful Blood*.

[79] Angenendt, *Heilige und Reliquien*, pp. 136–37.

[80] Gerald of Wales, *Vita Galfridi archiepiscopi Eboracensis* 2. 8, p. 404.

[81] Westlake, *The Parish Guilds of Mediaeval England*, p. 38, with a summary of the returns on pp. 137–238.

5,000 confraternity members in early-fifteenth-century Bologna, a figure equivalent to 10 to 20 per cent of the adult population.[82]

More of these confraternities were dedicated to the Virgin Mary than to any other saint. She was the patron of one-fifth of the guilds in Cambridgeshire and over a third of those in Yorkshire.[83] In Zamora in Castile fourteen of the forty-one late-medieval confraternities were dedicated to her, in various guises, sometimes drawing on local geography ("Our Lady of Val de Mora"), sometimes on aspects of her cult ("Our Lady of the Annunciation").[84] But alongside these guilds dedicated to Mary, the most universal of the saints, or the Christ-centred guilds, like the Corpus Christi confraternities, were others with a more local coloration. At March in the English Fenland there was a guild "in honour of St. Wyndred the Virgin," whose members provided candles to burn at the shrine of this irrecoverably obscure Anglo-Saxon saint.[85]

The activities of these confraternities can be explored through some examples from Venice, a city which had dozens of small-scale devotional confraternities (*scuole piccole*) alongside the great trade and craft guilds, although sometimes in association with them. Four or five are recorded in the thirteenth century, a further thirty in the fourteenth, and then a wave of foundations followed in the fifteenth and subsequent centuries—a comprehensive survey lists 925 in all.[86] They usually drew up regulations and kept a membership list, and some of these survive, sometimes with an elaborate opening illustration. Their activities were both liturgical and charitable. The fraternity of St. Anne, for instance, whose ordinances were drawn up in 1351 and which met in the monastic church of St. Anne in the parish of San Pietro di Castello, required its members to attend a monthly Mass, holding a lighted candle in their hand between the reading of the Gospel and the elevation of the host, to visit sick members and to participate in a Mass for dead members to be held at an altar in the church. They also possessed painted images with the story of St. Anne. The fact that there was a matriculation list of the lady-members shows that the fraternity included both men and women.[87] The confraternity of San Biagio, founded in 1360, likewise included men and women, with a minimum age for membership of sixteen. It provided lights for the church of San Biagio and contributed to the building works there. Its members had to help the sick, recite Our Father and Hail Mary for dead members, be present at their funerals, and attend communion once a year.[88] The confraternity of San Sebastian, mentioned in 1436, was closely linked with the guild

[82] Terpstra, *Lay Confraternities and Civic Religion in Renaissance Bologna*, p. 83 and n.

[83] Bainbridge, *Gilds in the Medieval Countryside*, pp. 63–64; Crouch, *Piety, Fraternity, and Power: Religious Gilds in Late Medieval Yorkshire*, pp. 99–100.

[84] Flynn, *Sacred Charity: Confraternities and Social Welfare in Spain, 1400–1700*, pp. 16, 27.

[85] Westlake, *The Parish Guilds of Mediaeval England*, p. 145; on the saint see Blair, "A Handlist of Anglo-Saxon Saints," p. 562.

[86] Vio, *Le scuole piccole nella Venezia dei dogi*.

[87] Ibid., p. 56.

[88] Ibid., p. 84.

of glassworkers. Its membership seems to have been around 40, and members were expected to attend a monthly Mass, members' funerals, and a twice-yearly meeting of the confraternity, where the ordinances were read out. They had their own chapel in the church of San Polo and their own banner.[89]

Such groups had many functions, but commemoration of their saint was one of the more important ways that confraternities created their identity. The name, the celebration of the feast, perhaps images of the saint, helped shape their distinctive culture. Some also took their saints out into the streets and public squares through drama, for the later Middle Ages sees the birth of the so-called saint play, a staged representation of scenes from saints' lives, and, although such plays were patronized and performed by groups of many different kinds, confraternities were particularly involved. Thus the confraternity of St. Didier in Langres commissioned a Play of St. Didier, which they performed in 1482.[90] All the paraphernalia of true dramatic performance was involved in these productions. There are texts with stage directions, as in the Play of St. Geneviève, probably performed by the Confraternity of the Passion of Paris and certainly with a set of the French capital: "Then let her stop in front of Paris a little downstage, and there let there be a small altar on which is an image of Our Lady and in front of the altar a small bench where she can say her prayers." In the Play of St. Margaret there is a fearsome dragon, whose opening lines are, "See my sharp pointed teeth."[91] The fourteenth-century confraternity of St. Dominic in Perugia built up a collection of props, including cardinals' hats, a white mantle for the Play of St. John, and a big face, probably for a beheading scene.[92]

Participation in confraternities and attendance at a saint play were ways in which lay people could become more actively involved in the cult of the saints, and this lay involvement intensified over the course of the later medieval period. While, at the top of the lay hierarchy, princes could build up collections of relics, some numbering in the thousands, there were ways for the lower classes too to become engaged. Possession of images of the saints by lay people, including the less wealthy, was made easier by the development of the wood-block print, which made such pictures cheaply reproducible. Corresponding to the increased general visibility of lay people in late medieval religious life was a vast expansion in the use of the vernacular for religious literature, and hagiography began to be written regularly in the everyday language (like the Life of Francesca Romana). A survey of late medieval manuscripts containing hagiography in Italian lists more than 1,100.[93] The first complete manuscript in the Hungarian language, from c. 1440, contains the story of St. Francis and his companions.[94]

[89] Ibid., p. 345.

[90] Muir, "The Saint Play in Medieval France," p. 140.

[91] Ibid., pp. 133–35, 148.

[92] Flavey, "The Italian Saint Play: The Example of Perugia," p. 189.

[93] *Biblioteca agiografica italiana*.

[94] Klaniczay and Madas, "La Hongrie," p. 141.

The multiplication of books and the wider dissemination of literacy, helped by use of the cheaper medium of paper rather than parchment, meant that private or household devotional reading of saints' Lives became much more common. Printing can be seen as the natural culmination in this growth of literacy. As writing became a more everyday activity, books a more common sight, and the scribble of the pen increasingly part of the life of the laity, there came a point where the preconditions were in place for a radical step forward in the technology of script. The use of the written word was so widespread that a mechanical means of reproducing it was conceivable, desirable, and, in Germany in 1455, attainable. Hagiography, although an ancient genre, embraced the new technology at once. The French version of the *Golden Legend* printed in 1476 was the first book printed in French, and between that event and 1550, sixty-five different saints' Lives in the French vernacular appeared in print.[95] William Caxton, the first English printer, published an English version of the same work, the *Golden Legend*, at Westminster in 1483.

The cult of the saints was not made redundant by changes in technology and society, but adapted and expanded. It was fully part of the urban and lay world of the late Middle Ages. Although the plague killed half the population of Europe in 1348–50, the result was not a reversion to a rural or significantly less urban society. Many towns were smaller, but they retained their urban character and functions, and slowly increased again in size. Despite the Black Death, the urbanization of Europe was irreversible, and this new urban population, like the old rural population, could give meaning and structure to its life through the cult of the saints.

The sacral density of the late medieval town is well illustrated by Cologne.[96] A major river port, a centre of industry, and a place of great political importance, it had grown to be one of the largest cities in Europe. Some parts of its religious geography were ancient. The cathedral, dedicated to St. Peter, probably has Roman origins. It possessed the saint's staff and part of his chains, and, in 1164, had also acquired relics of the Three Kings or Magi, which, enshrined in a magnificent surviving reliquary of gold, became a centre of pilgrimage from across Europe. The present High Gothic cathedral building was begun in 1248. In addition to its cathedral, Cologne had ten collegiate churches and two Benedictine monasteries of early medieval, or even Roman, origins, dedicated to Andrew, the Apostles, Cecilia, George, Gereon, Kunibert, Martin, Mary (two examples), Pantaleon, Severinus, and Ursula. Some of these saints were local. Severinus and Kunibert were early bishops of Cologne, buried in the churches which eventually took their name (they had earlier been dedicated to Sts. Cornelius and Cyprian and to St. Clement, respectively), while Gereon and Ursula were venerated as local Roman martyrs. Besides these thirteen foundations, there were parish churches dedicated to Alban, Brigid, Christopher, Columba (not the Irish saint, but the female martyr of Sens), James, John the Baptist, John

[95] Bledniak, "L'hagiographie imprimée: oeuvres en français, 1476–1550."

[96] For the following see Hegel, *Das mittelalterliche Pfarrsystem und seine kirchliche Infrastruktur in Köln um 1500*; Legner, *Kölner Heilige und Heiligtümer*; Kracht and Torsy, *Reliquiarium Coloniense*.

the Evangelist, Lawrence, Lupus, Martin, Mary (three examples), Maurice (this also housed Benedictine nuns), Paul, and Peter.

Building on this already extensive base, the new Orders and new styles of devotion of the later Middle Ages made their own mark. The Hospitallers had a church in Cologne from the middle of the thirteenth century, dedicated jointly to St. John, their patron, and St. Cordula, the latter supposedly a companion of St. Ursula whose bones were discovered in Cologne and translated into the church by the great Dominican scholar Albertus Magnus.[97] All the main branches of the friars were represented in the city. The Franciscans had their church dedicated to St. Francis, the Augustinian Hermits theirs dedicated to St. Augustine. The Dominican church was dedicated to the Holy Cross. The Poor Clares had their church of St. Clare by 1304. Cologne was also an important centre for beguines. These pious women, although living according to rules of piety, were not vowed to an Order, but if their communities endured they might be drawn into the existing Orders. In this way, the beguines or recluses attached to the chapel of St. Gertrude in Cologne joined the Order of Dominican nuns in the 1280s, while another group, founded in 1267, adopted the Augustinian Rule in the fifteenth century as the Penitents of Mary Magdalene. The Cell-brothers or Alexians (*Alexianer* or *Celliten* in German), a confraternity devoted to charitable works, who were particularly prominent in Cologne, adopted the Augustinian Rule in the late fifteenth century. Their female branch had churches or chapels in Cologne dedicated to Augustine; Augustine and Mary Magdalene jointly; Elizabeth; Ursula; and the Holy Trinity. One community, which began as a group of beguines in 1307, joined the female branch of the Augustinian Alexians in 1474, and had the designation "the cloister of the Blessed Virgin Mary in Little Nazareth."

Just as in Venice, lay confraternities proliferated in the fifteenth and sixteenth centuries, with more than 120 being mentioned in Cologne in the period up to 1563, half of them first occurring in the fifteenth century.[98] The newly fashionable saints of the later Middle Ages were well represented. A confraternity of St. Mary Magdalene was founded in St. Lawrence's church in 1444, another in 1505 in the church of the Augustinian nuns dedicated to the saint. It may have been no coincidence that this latter group was formed by the workers in white leather, since the nuns were known as the White Ladies from the colour of their robes.

And images of the saints were created in great numbers, for both private and public display. The wealthy Cologne citizen Thonis Berthold, who died in 1519, had "a Deposition and small image of the Virgin in the parlour, a panel showing the Apostles in the hall, an Annunciation on canvas and a St. Christopher in the 'room with four beds,' and a carved Virgin and St. Anne in the master bedroom."[99] The confraternity of St. Mary Salve Regina, founded in 1450, had two pictures of their patron, the Virgin Mary, on and behind their altar in the collegiate church of

[97] *Inventio sanctae Cordulae virginis et martyris.*

[98] *Quellen zur Geschichte der Kölner Laienbruderschaften* 3, pp. XVII–XVIII.

[99] Corley, *Painting and Patronage in Cologne*, p. 267 n. 15.

3.3. The *Dombild* of Cologne. Cologne Cathedral.
Photo: akg-images/Erich Lessing

St. Martin.[100] For the chapel of the town hall, built in the 1420s on the site of the synagogue that had been abandoned when Cologne expelled its Jewish population, the councillors of Cologne commissioned a large altarpiece depicting the Adoration of the Magi (whose shrine stood in the cathedral), flanked by Cologne's other patron saints: Ursula on one side, Gereon on the other.[101] The central panel is 238 centimetres high and 263 centimetres wide (roughly 8 feet by 8 ½ feet), so when the wings are open it is twice that width. It was thus an enormous and public celebration of the saintly guardians of "Holy Cologne" (figure 3.3).

Cologne exemplifies the rich and many-textured saintly culture of a prosperous German town at the end of the Middle Ages. The priests, friars, nuns, and confraternity members who invoked the saints, revered their images, and knelt before their relics had little intimation that it was from the heart of this world that a challenge was about to arise, a challenge which would destroy the cult of the saints across half of Europe.

[100] *Quellen zur Geschichte der Kölner Laienbruderschaften* 2, p. 1056.

[101] The painting is now in the cathedral and known as the *Dombild*; attribution to Stefan Lochner is disputed: Corley, *Painting and Patronage in Cologne*, pp. 147–54.

CHAPTER 4

The Protestant Reformation

The traditional birthdate of the Protestant Reformation is 31 October 1517, when the German friar Martin Luther nailed up his ninety-five theses on the church door at Wittenberg. These theses were propositions about the Church's use of indulgences, that is, remission of the penalties of sin, including the punishment the soul might undergo in purgatory after death. Luther opposed the sale of indulgences and questioned the doctrine of purgatory. Although the ninety-five theses say nothing explicitly about the cult of the saints, the promise of indulgences was one of the most common ways of encouraging pilgrims to visit a particular shrine, and Luther's opposition to indulgences had a consequence in his view of pilgrimage. He was quite clear, in his treatise *To the Christian Nobility of the German Nation*, written a few years after the ninety-five theses, that the grant of an indulgence for visiting a particular pilgrimage church was absurd, attempting to make "a big distinction between Christians who have the same baptism, Word, belief, Christ, God and all things," and that such practices were usually motivated simply by a desire for money. Christians had all they needed in their parish church: baptism and the Gospel.[1]

There is no early sign in Luther's life that he was inspired by any particular objection to the cult of the saints. It was indeed a vow to St. Anne that had led him to become a friar. But certain aspects of the cult, especially anything that suggested that spiritual merit could be attained through it, came under his critical scrutiny and his withering rhetoric. The last two saints to be canonized by the pope before the Reformation finally split the western Church apart were Antoninus of Florence and Benno of Meissen, two bishops of earlier times, who were declared saints by Pope Hadrian VI in 1523.[2] It was to be a lifetime—another sixty-five years—before the next canonization (St. Diego in 1588). The case for Benno had been pushed by one of Luther's political opponents, George, duke of Saxony, and supported by one of his most bitter-tongued intellectual antagonists, Hieronymus Emser. It also concerned a local Saxon saint. Luther's response to the translation of Benno in 1524, which followed the canonization, was the polemic entitled *Against the New Idol*.[3] While

[1] Luther, *An den christlichen Adel deutscher Nation*, pp. 447–50.

[2] Pietschmann, "Ablauf und Dimensionen der Heiligsprechung des Antoninus von Florenz"; Volkmar, *Die Heiligenerhebung Bennos von Meißen*; Finucane, *Contested Canonizations*, pp. 167–240.

[3] Luther, *Widder den newen Abgott*; there is discussion of the text in Volkmar, *Die Heiligenerhebung Bennos von Meißen*, pp. 164–69.

he began by claiming that he was not judging "the dead bishop Benno," for "he has his judge," he nevertheless did not hold back his characteristically personal and vituperative assault on the long-dead Saxon bishop. He also questioned and mocked the miracles that had been described in the papal bull of canonization. "Who would not laugh to hear that the bell blessed by Benno drove off bad weather?," he wrote, and went on to raise the possibility that Benno's miracles might have been false or diabolical. Moreover, he asked, how could the pope be certain that he does not err in cases of canonization—a topic of prolonged debate on the Catholic side too. Luther pointed out that he had not made a special target of the cult of the saints, and that he would be quite happy to regard Elizabeth of Thuringia, Augustine, Jerome, Ambrose, Bernard, and Francis as saints, although he would not "die for it," but he was opposed (naturally) to papal canonization and regarded the opulent translation of Benno's relics as trumpery, trickery, and foolery (*gauckelspiel, affenspiel, narrenspiel*). The expenditure could be put to better use: "All the finery, all the expense and effort, all the reverence and service, and whatever they do there at Meissen, that is not so good nor so pleasing to God as if you fed or clothed one poor Christian." This is an argument that had been advanced long before by critics of the cult of the saints: money spent on images, elaborate rituals and pilgrimages could be better spent helping the poor (see later, p. 596). But Luther's fundamental objection was not the squandering of resources but the lack of scriptural authority: "My belief should be certain and have certain foundation in Scripture . . . they have no Scriptural argument [*keyne schrifft*] that one should invoke saints and have them as mediators, but Scripture makes Christ alone mediator and intercessor." In 1530 this view was incorporated into the first official statement of Protestant belief, which stated explicitly that Scripture did not support the invocation of saints. Saints might be taken as fruitful examples for our life, but there was only one intercessor—Christ.[4]

Luther's arguments could be taken out onto the streets. While the holy bones of Benno were being translated in Meissen, the inhabitants of another Saxon town, Buchholz, were parodying the ritual with a carnival procession featuring a mock bishop who extracted the jawbone of a cow from a barrow of dung and held it up, saying to the crowd, "Dear worshippers, see, this is the holy arse-bone of the beloved St. Benno."[5] This public, popular and subversive aspect of the Reformation worried many of the Protestant leaders and theorists, encouraging them to stress order, or to argue for more moderate positions. In response to an outbreak of image-smashing in Wittenberg in the winter of 1521–22, Luther made the case that images were neither good nor bad in themselves. "We can have them or not have them," he said, arguing that these purely external things cannot influence inner belief, and citing the

[4] Augsburg Confession c. 21: Sed Scriptura non docet invocare sanctos, seu petere auxilium a sanctis, quia unum Christum nobis proponit mediatorem . . . (available on-line).

[5] Volkmar, *Die Heiligenerhebung Bennos von Meißen*, p. 176; discussed by Scribner, *Popular Culture and Popular Movements in Reformation Germany*, pp. 74–75; Finucane, *Contested Canonizations*, pp. 207–8.

example of St. Paul against violent destruction of images. He also admitted the positive value that images could have for some people.[6] The Zurich reformer Huldrych Zwingli expressed his disappointment at this part of Luther's thinking. "You would have cleansed the Augean stable if you had had the images removed," he wrote to him, although it is clear that when Zwingli's Zurich removed all religious images, it had attempted to do this in an orderly and understanding way, "without abuse, practical jokes or insults that might upset anyone."[7] No cow's jawbones there.

In England the break with Rome, which was in origin political and institutional, led to an attack on the cult of the saints which became more extreme over time. In 1536 Thomas Cromwell, the architect of the English Reformation, issued injunctions to the clergy forbidding them to "set forth or extol any images, relics or miracles," and two years later commanded them to remove any images that were "abused with pilgrimages or offerings," also prohibiting the burning of candles before images.[8] Cromwell also organized the removal of images from the monasteries that he closed. Some of them were stored in his house in London, where, in the autumn of 1538, the image of Our Lady of Ipswich nestled alongside that of St. Anne of Buxton and St. Modwenna of Burton, "with her red cow and her staff, which women labouring of child in those parts were very desirous to have with them."[9] A centralizing state bent on religious revolution was depriving the local population of its ancient consolations from the saints.

A particularly dramatic fate befell England's most famous saint, Thomas Becket. Henry VIII became convinced not only that Thomas could be, like any saint, the cause for superstitious practices, but also that the historical archbishop had been a subversive rebel. In 1538 a royal proclamation was issued, explaining that Becket was not a saint but "a rebel and traitor to his prince." It excused his murderers, commanded that "from henceforth the said Thomas Becket shall not be esteemed, named, reputed, nor called a saint, but Bishop Becket," and ordered that his images should be removed, his liturgical commemoration discontinued, and his name erased from service books.[10] Dozens of surviving medieval books with excisions and scrubbed out entries show that this erasure actually took place. The shrine itself was demolished, the bones disappeared, and all the rich offerings and ornaments passed into the king's broad hands.

Under Henry VIII's son and successor, Edward VI, a yet more radical Reformation was attempted. After an initial attempt to remove those images that had been "abused with pilgrimages, offerings or censing [that is, suffusion with incense]," much in the spirit of Thomas Cromwell's injunctions, the Privy Council governing on behalf of the young king determined in 1548 on a more thorough approach,

[6] Luther, *Predigten des Jahres 1522*, pp. 26–36 (sermons of March 1522).
[7] Potter, ed., *Huldrych Zwingli*, pp. 100, 27–28.
[8] Cromwell, Thomas, *Life and Letters* 2, pp. 28, 153 (spelling modernized).
[9] *Letters and Papers, Foreign and Domestic, of the Reign of Henry VIII* 13/2, no. 256, p. 101.
[10] *Tudor Royal Proclamations* 1, no. 186, pp. 275–76.

ordering that "all the images remaining in any church or chapel . . . be removed and taken away." They referred to the only partial success of their earlier attempts, with some places retaining images, and others restoring them again after they had been removed. "Almost in every place," they bemoaned, "is contention for images." Their conclusion was that "in no places of this realm is any sure quietness, but where all images be wholly taken away and pulled down already."[11]

Perhaps one of the most vulnerable aspects of the cult of the saints, and one which had its critics in the medieval period, was the elaboration of relic veneration. Protestant leaders targeted it with zeal. Calvin's *Treatise on Relics* of 1543 went through six editions in French and was translated into Latin, German, and English.[12] It is a vigorous piece of Protestant polemic addressed to a central feature of the medieval cult of the saints. Much of it consists of mockery of easy targets: the claims of more than one church to possess the relics of a saint, so that "each apostle would have more than four bodies, and each saint at least two or three," and the vast quantities of such things as the milk of the Virgin Mary: "if the holy Virgin had been a cow and nursed her whole life, she would have had great difficulty producing such an amount."[13] Calvin has a strong historical sense and cannot believe that relics of Christ and other New Testament figures could have survived for hundreds of years before the first claims about their possession were made, and he notes that the churchmen who maintain they possess the Virgin's wedding or engagement ring assume that wedding customs were the same in New Testament times as they were in his time.[14] He observes that St. Peter's slipper preserved at Poitiers is incongruously "made of satin embroidered with gold." "See," he adds, "how they make him stylish after his death as a compensation for the poverty which he had during his lifetime."[15] His tone is often sarcastic in this way. Commenting on John the Baptist's shoe in the church of the Carthusians in Paris, he remarks: "It was stolen twelve or thirteen years ago but they immediately found another one. Indeed, there will never be a shortage of such relics as long as the race of shoemakers endures."[16] And Calvin can strike a low blow: the supposed arm of St. Antony, previously venerated in Geneva, and kissed and adored in its reliquary, turned out on inspection to be a stag's penis.[17]

But if Calvin devotes considerable space to the argument that many relics cannot be genuine, this is hardly the fundamental point he wishes to make. Early in the *Treatise* he gives his basic objection: "the greedy desire to have relics is scarcely ever without superstition, and, what is worse, it is the mother of idolatry."[18] So this kind

[11] Cranmer, *Miscellaneous Writings and Letters*, p. 510.

[12] Calvin, *Traité des reliques*.

[13] Ibid., pp. 53, 75.

[14] Ibid., p. 76.

[15] Ibid., p. 82

[16] Ibid., p. 81.

[17] Ibid., p. 53.

[18] Ibid., p. 50.

of worship is superstitious, that is, fatuous and foolish, and it is idolatrous, turning us away from God to inappropriate objects. Hence it does not matter whether a relic is genuine: "it is execrable idolatry to adore any relic, whatever it is, true or false." The only solution is complete suppression of the practice: "to abolish amongst us Christians this pagan practice of canonizing relics, of Jesus or his saints, to make them idols."[19] This idea, that relic cult was essentially pagan, had a long future, amongst secular critics as well as Protestants (see later, pp. 609–18).

The Protestant assault on the cult of the saints extended as far as naming patterns. It was not uncommon for children to be given saints' names (see later, pp. 459–70), and this was a link with the old religion that reformers sometimes sought to sever. In Calvin's Geneva, for example, there was an official ban on giving children the names of the local saints Martin and Claude. Parents, especially those named Martin and Claude, were outraged, and riots sometimes broke out at baptisms. Calvin suggested at one point that it might be necessary to post guards at baptisms.[20] Even if this never happened, it indicates that reformation was not simply a matter of written polemic and peaceful change; it could be imposed—and resisted—by force.

The image-smashing that had taken place in Wittenberg in 1521–22 was the first drop in a torrent of Protestant iconoclasm that marked the religious conflicts of the sixteenth and seventeenth centuries.[21] Sometimes the destruction and removal of images of the saints was undertaken by governments, sometimes by violent crowds, sometimes in the course of civil wars. Iconoclasm had its own geography and chronology. A wave of iconoclastic violence swept around the coasts of the Baltic Sea in the late 1520s, while the destruction in Münster when it was under the control of the Anabaptists in 1534 or the so-called *beeldenstorm* ("storming of the images") in the Netherlands in summer 1566 became legendary moments of triumph or disaster, depending on one's position. In France the 1560s, 1570s, and 1580s saw the pillaging of thousands of churches and monasteries by the Huguenots, determined to destroy the visible symbols of Roman Catholic worship, altars, crucifixes and images of the saints.

Scotland's iconoclastic year came a little earlier. After the radical Protestant leader John Knox preached a sermon in St. Andrews in 1559, there followed a ferocious assault on the images there:

> The sermon was scarcely done when they fell to work to purge the kirk and break down the altars and images and all kinds of idolatry; they passed to the Friars Black and Grey . . . before the sun was down there was never an inch

[19] Ibid., p. 94.

[20] Naphy, "Baptisms, Church Riots and Social Unrest in Calvin's Geneva."

[21] There is a huge bibliography. See, for example, Eire, *War against the Idols: The Reformation of Worship from Erasmus to Calvin*; Aston, *England's Iconoclasts 1: Laws against Images*; Christin, *Une révolution symbolique: l'iconoclasme huguenot et la reconstruction catholique*; Michalski, *The Reformation and the Visual Arts*; Blickle et al., eds., *Macht und Ohnmacht der Bilder: reformatorischer Bildersturm im Kontext der europäischen Geschichte*.

> standing but bare walls; the idols that were in the abbey were brought to the north part of the said abbey and there they burned the whole idols.[22]

So in one day the images of the saints in the parish church, the two friaries, and the cathedral priory were all swept away, with "bare walls" as a permanent reminder of the storm that had occurred. Similar ferocity broke out elsewhere in the kingdom.

This violence and intransigence made halfway houses and moderate reform more difficult. In Cologne, archbishop Hermann von Wied sought to make changes in a direction similar to that advocated by the Protestants. His reform proposals published in 1543 condemned prayer to the saints and misuse of images.[23] But the middle ground was already disappearing. Hermann von Wied was excommunicated by the pope in 1546 and resigned his office the following year. Cologne remained Catholic, preserving its rich heritage of images, processions and confraternities, and developing them further as the Jesuits and other Catholic reformers became active.

The eventual result of the struggle over reformation was the outbreak of open war—in Germany in 1546, in France in 1562, in the Netherlands in 1568. Some of these conflicts lasted decades, and led seamlessly into the wars of the following century. A division of Europe took place in the sixteenth century that marks its culture to this day. The territorial pattern was far from stable but, to speak approximately, what emerged was a north-south split, with Britain and Scandinavia Protestant, Spain and Italy Catholic, and France, Germany and most of eastern Europe mixed. These patterns were then exported as the European powers established their rule across the non-European world. It is unclear what explains this pattern. It may be that prior social and religious characteristics of the various regions are significant, or perhaps the crucial determining factor is the reach of the power of Spain, the most important Catholic state and one prepared to use vigorous and brutal repression. In any case, the cult of the saints virtually disappeared from Protestant Europe. Pilgrimages, relics, liturgies of the saints, and most of the images had gone. There were a few vestiges. It was impossible, for example, for Protestants to deny that the apostles and early martyrs were holy men, or that the miracles recorded in the New Testament as performed by Peter and others had truly occurred. But even these saints were only to be honoured, not invoked, and their physical remains were irrelevant to the life of the Christian. Protestants circulated stirring stories of their martyrs, such as Jean Crespin's work first published in 1554 and constantly augmented, which declares its purpose very clearly in its title: *Collected accounts of several people who endured*

[22] *A Historie of the Estate of Scotland from July 1558 to April 1560*, p. 60 (spelling modernized). For the general context, see Kirk, "Iconoclasm and Reform."

[23] Wied, *Einfaltigs bedencken, etc.*, fols. 9v, 13v, 62v–66; the corresponding passages in the Latin translation published two years later are: *Simplex ac pia deliberatio, etc.*, fols. 7, 10v, 51v–56v. Strikingly, the commandment against graven images is called the first commandment (*das erste gebott*, fol. 66) in the German but the second commandment (*secundo . . . capite decalogi*, fol. 55v) in the Latin, thus showing the adoption of the system of numbering of the commandments more hostile to images, as employed by Jews, Orthodox, and Reformed Protestants, rather than the less emphatic system of Catholics and Lutherans. Reformers were active contributors to the texts published under the archbishop's name.

death with constancy for the name of Our Lord Jesus Christ.[24] It begins with Wycliffe and Hus in the late fourteenth and early fifteenth centuries and thus argues for a prehistory of Protestantism in a way that became standard. The Latin translation, which appeared two years later, was even more explicit: *Acts of the martyrs, namely those who in our times in France, Germany, England, Flanders and Italy gave their steadfast name to the Gospel and sealed it with their blood, from Wycliffe and Hus to our own day.*[25] Foxe's *Book of Martyrs* is an English equivalent. But these "martyrs" were heroes who had died for the Gospel, not souls in heaven who could be asked for favours.

The Reformation involved issues far beyond the cult of the saints—doctrine, ritual, authority, the fate of souls, and the shape of communities. But attitudes to the holy dead, and all that went with them in the way of belief and practice, were a simple and easily ascertained boundary between the confessions. In France the Roman Catholic counter-attack to Protestant iconoclasm sometimes took the form of setting up public images of the Virgin Mary, to which passers-by were required to show reverence.[26] The nature of Roman Catholicism after the Reformation was defined by the decisions made at the Council of Trent, an assembly of leading ecclesiastics which met (on and off) in the Alpine town of Trent from 1545 to 1563. In its very final session the Council addressed the issue of the cult of the saints. Although also warning against superstitions and abuses connected with the cult, it approved the invocation of saints and the veneration of their relics and images.[27] The same year, 1563, the Church of England defined its own position on saints in Article 22 of the thirty-nine articles which were approved as its official doctrine: "The Romish doctrine concerning Purgatory, Pardons, worshipping and adoration as well of Images as of Relics, and also Invocation of Saints, is a fond thing vainly invented, and grounded upon no warranty of Scripture; but rather repugnant to the word of God." The division of Christendom was complete and was to be enduring. It found one of its most visible and most emotive expressions in attitudes to the saints. In 1588 Pope Sixtus V created the Congregation of Rites to deal with canonizations, and that same year the first canonization for sixty-five years took place, that of St. Diego of Alcalá.[28] It marks a new phase in the history of the cult of the saints, when the common heritage of Christians was split by hostile denominational allegiances. Henceforth the living cult of the saints was only a memory in the Protestant world.

[24] Crespin, *Recueil de plusieurs personnes qui ont constamment enduré la mort pour le Nom de nostre Seigneur Iesus-Christ.*

[25] Crespin, *Acta Martyrum, eorum videlicet, qui hoc seculo in Gallia, Germania, Anglia, Flandria, Italia, constans dederunt nomen Euangelio, idque sanguine suo obsignarunt: ab Wicleffo & Husso ad hunc vsque diem.*

[26] Christin, *Une révolution symbolique: l'iconoclasme huguenot et la reconstruction catholique*, p. 29.

[27] *Decrees of the Ecumenical Councils*, 2, pp. 774–76 (session 25, 3–4 December 1563).

[28] Diego's cause was already so advanced that it was not subject to the new regime, the first cause dealt with by the Congregation of Rites being in 1589: Papa, *Le cause di canonizzazione nel primo periodo della Congregazione dei Riti*, pp. 33–35

PART II

Dynamics

CHAPTER 5

The Nature of Cult

Name, Body, Text

A saint was not a person of a particular type but a person who was treated in a particular way. That "way" can be summed up by the word "cult," and its three key elements were public recognition of the name and the day of the saint; special treatment of the saint's bodily remains; and celebration of the saint in writing.

In its very earliest and simplest form in the cult of the martyrs, the commemoration of a saint involved, as a minimum, the recording of a name and a day—the date of the martyr's death, his or her "birthday" into heaven. The Roman funerary inscription "Hyacinth, martyr, buried 11 September," mentioned earlier (on p. 8), or the earliest list of martyrs (see p. 13) are of this type. Clearly the name was necessary, since it is hard to invoke anonymous saints, while the day of their transition to the heavenly kingdom was a natural time for Christians to remember them.

Invocation means uttering a name, and the name itself has power. Both Christianity and other traditions stress the Holy Name, since it is important to know which supernatural power one is addressing. One of the things that Moses has to ask of God, when confronted with him at the burning bush, is his name. What, he asks, should he say when he tells the Hebrew slaves that God has sent him and they demand to know "What is his name?" (Exodus 3:13). The name unlocked supernatural energy. Jesus promised "whatsoever ye shall ask in my name, that will I do" (John 14:13). Similarly, to invoke the saints was to summon up their power through the utterance of their name. "Wherever St. Foy is named, there also is her power," wrote the author of her *Miracles*.[1] St. Francis's biographer, Thomas of Celano, described how the saint's miraculous help could be procured "simply at the invocation of his name."[2]

But more than one saint might have the same name. One eleventh-century German, instructed in a dream to seek out a cure for his ailments at the shrine of St. Maximinus, went first to the shrine of St. Maximinus of Trier, then to the only approximately appropriate shrine of St. Maximus at Chinon, before finally hitting

[1] Bernard of Angers, *Liber miraculorum sancte Fidis* 1. 33, p. 143.

[2] Thomas of Celano, *Vita prima sancti Francisci* 3. 120, p. 96.

the right spot in Micy near Orleans, where the monks of the monastery of St. Maximinus (St. Mesmin) recorded his miraculous cure.[3] And there are instances of medieval writers and artists getting their saints mixed up. A fifteenth-century Spanish breviary confuses two saints called Dominic.[4] In one edition of the *Golden Legend*, the Life of the thirteenth-century Elizabeth of Thuringia is introduced by an illustration showing an incident in the life of her namesake, the biblical St. Elizabeth, mother of John the Baptist, while in another version of the same work her Life has a heading "Here begins the Life of St. Elizabeth, mother of John the Baptist."[5] In the first case the illustrator had become confused, or been given misleading instructions; in the second the rubricator responsible for the headings had obviously not read very far into the text.

The need to be exact about names is emphasized by a curious moment in the canonization process of Thomas de Cantilupe in 1307. One witness claimed that "St. Thomas" had appeared to him in a vision when he was in prison, promising that he would not die on the scaffold. The papal commissioners immediately launched into cross-examination. The witness had presumed the saint was Thomas de Cantilupe but there were other saints called Thomas, such as Thomas the apostle and Thomas Becket. They wanted to know how the witness could be sure that the visionary figure was Thomas de Cantilupe rather than some other Thomas.[6]

But sometimes such ambiguities were disregarded. The monk who recorded the miracles of St. Margaret of Scotland at her shrine in Dunfermline did not mind that many humble folk gathered there on the feast-day of St. Margaret the virgin martyr, for "perhaps they believed our Margaret to be the precious martyr of the same name." This "identity of name" had led them into "a devout error" but not deprived them of grace and reward. "There is no disunity between those who reign jointly in the kingdom of heaven," he remarked. Although the two Margarets differed "in essence," they were similar "in mind and work."[7] A more rigorous attempt to identify the saint in question can be found in a rather different situation. When St. Martin's relics had found a temporary home in the church of St. Germanus in Auxerre, a dispute arose about which saint was responsible for the miraculous cures that were occurring—Martin or Germanus. To resolve these doubts, an empirical test was devised: a leper was placed overnight between the shrines of Martin and Germanus. In the morning only that half of the diseased man adjacent to Martin's tomb was found to be cured.[8]

The place of burial and the day of death are what the great hagiographical scholar Hippolyte Delehaye called, by analogy with geometry, "the hagiographic coordi-

[3]Head, "I Vow Myself to Be Your Servant"; idem, *Hagiography and the Cult of the Saints: The Diocese of Orleans, 800–1200*, pp. 12–13, 169–71.

[4]Lappin, *The Medieval Cult of Saint Dominic of Silos*, p. 380.

[5]Bertelsmeier-Kierst, ed., *Elisabeth von Thüringen und die neue Frömmigkeit in Europa*, p. 274 and n. 57.

[6]BAV, Vat. lat. 4015, fol. 221.

[7]*Miracula sancte Margarite Scotorum regine* 8, p. 90.

[8]*De reversione beati Martini a Burgundia* 5–6, cols. 827–29.

nates," that is, those two pieces of information, which together give a unique identification.[9] These coordinates helped define a saint. As a consequence, there are many people of the late antique and medieval period whose day of death is known, but whose year of death is uncertain, since contemporaries were concerned to record which day they died, for commemorative purposes, but did not have the same concern with the much less highly charged fact of the calendar year. Specification of a saint's day allows saints with the same name to be distinguished: when St. Thomas, for example, is commemorated on 21 December, this must be the apostle; if on the 29 December, it is Thomas Becket, the murdered archbishop of Canterbury. The names of the saints had an impact on the naming choices of worshippers (see later), while the commemoration of their feast-days flowered into a major aspect of Christian liturgy (also discussed later), with special services for the main saints and careful recording of feast-days in ecclesiastical Kalendars.

Saints' days made their mark on secular life as well as on the round of church services. In the lands north of the Alps, dating for many purposes, economic and legal as well as ecclesiastical, turned on saints' days.[10] For example, of the 209 agreements drawn up in the court of Richard I of England during the ninth year of his reign (1197–98), although three are so damaged it is not possible to be sure of their dating convention, of the remaining 206, no fewer than 204 are dated by reference to a saint's day or major church feast (of the two that are not so dated, one has no day at all, one has a date of the familiar modern form "19 January"). The most common feast-days of the 36 referred to are St. Matthew (26 cases), St. Luke (22), Easter (19) and the Conversion of St. Paul (13), and there are several singular occurrences (including the English saints Botulph, Swithun, and Bertholin). For the English royal judges of this period, their proceedings were signposted by the saints.[11]

Dating by church festivals was by no means the only method. There were other ways of dating documents, notably the Roman system, which was based on reference to three fixed points in the month (Kalends, Nones, and Ides), and the continuous form (1 August, 2 August, 3 August) used in the modern world, and these were preferred in some times and places and by particular authorities. The popes and the Holy Roman emperors of the High Middle Ages, for example, dated their official documents according to the Roman system, as did many other rulers, while the modern system, always common in Italy, became increasingly important throughout western Europe at the end of the Middle Ages. It was the thirteenth century,

[9] Delehaye, *Cinq leçons sur la méthode hagiographique*, pp. 13–14.

[10] For the use of saints' days for dating documents, see Sachse, *Das Aufkommen der Datierungen nach dem Festkalender*; Bresslau, *Handbuch der Urkundenlehre* 2, pp. 393–478, "Die Datierung der Urkunden"; Lorcin, "Le temps chez les humbles: passé, présent et futur dans les testaments foréziens"; Cheney, *A Handbook of Dates for Students of British History*, pp. 59–95; Rück, "Zur Verbreitung der Festdatierung im 13. Jahrhundert," with a survey of the bibliography and historiography at pp. 145–49; Mitterauer, *Ahnen und Heilige*, p. 472 n. 328.

[11] *Feet of Fines of the ninth year of the reign of King Richard I.*

in the lands north of the Alps, that saw, alongside an increasing precision in dating documents, a move towards dating by church feasts. For example, the number of Genevan documents dated to the day was around 40 per cent at the beginning of the thirteenth century, but around 95 per cent at the end of that century. The first Genevan document dated by a church feast occurs in 1201, and, by 1265, 60 per cent of documents dated to the day are dated in this way. The Roman and the continuous modern forms of dating are also found, and the latter takes over by the middle of the fourteenth century.[12] An interesting phrase in a Bavarian charter of 1226 suggests that the Roman system was considered less familiar to lay people than the system of church feasts: it is a grant dated "the second day before the Nones of May, which is known to lay people as the feast of St. John before the Latin Gate."[13] The chroniclers and historians of the Middle Ages, who were frequently monks or clerics, also turned naturally to feast-days to date events, although they were often eclectic in their dating conventions.

Some saints' days had a wide significance in everyday life, like St. Michael's day (29 September), which coincided roughly with the end of harvest and the growing season, and was one of the commonest terms for paying rent in more than one part of Europe—in the twelfth century the tenants of the abbey of Santo Domingo de Silos in Castile paid their rent half at Easter and half on St. Michael's Day, while payments from the burgh of Elgin, more than a thousand miles from Santo Domingo, were made to the bishop of Moray in Scotland at exactly these same two terms.[14] St. Martin's day (11 November, "Martinmas" as it was called in English from at least the tenth century) likewise made a natural break in the agricultural year, after the spring-sown grains had been harvested and the autumn-sown grains sown.[15] When the archbishop of Magdeburg built up a new village in the eastern part of his diocese, he granted the settlers freedom from rent and tolls for five years, "starting on the feast-day of St. Martin in the year of the Lord's incarnation 1159."[16] St. Remigius's (St. Remi's) day (1 October) had a similar significance in northern France. For instance, when Henry II endowed prayers for his father, Geoffrey of Anjou, from his income from Le Mans, the payments were to be made in four instalments: Easter, St. John's day, St. Remi's day, and Christmas.[17]

Fairs and markets were also linked to saints' days (modern German *Messe*, "fair," comes from *missa*, "Mass"). The burgesses of Hamburg were granted the right to hold a big market twice a year, "on the Assumption of St. Mary and on the feast-day

[12] Rück, "Zur Verbreitung der Festdatierung im 13. Jahrhundert," pp. 169–70.

[13] *Monumenta Boica* 8, p. 324 (for Bernried).

[14] *Documentación del monasterio de Santo Domingo de Silos (954–1254)*, no. 47, p. 61; *Acts of William I, King of Scots, 1165–1214* no. 360, p. 355.

[15] "Martines mæssan": *Anglo-Saxon Chronicle*, s.a. 913, pp. 96–97.

[16] Helbig and Weinrich, eds., *Urkunden und erzählende Quellen zur deutschen Ostsiedlung* 1, p. 76, no. 12.

[17] *Recueil des actes de Henri II* 1, p. 494, no. 354.

of St. Vitus," giving them a nicely spaced pattern of an August and a March fair.[18] St. Giles's fair, outside Winchester, was originally held annually "for three whole days, that is, the day before the feast, the feast, and the day after the feast" (31 August–2 September).[19] In Sweden there was "St. Botvid's market" (St. Botvid's day was 28 July).[20] In this way, saints' days marked the course of the year and could even give their names to the products of the earth that became ripe at their season. The cultivated hazel nut known as the filbert derives its name from the fact that in Normandy it becomes ripe near St. Philibert's day (22 August), and hence entered Norman dialect as "Philibert-nut."[21]

"What's a saint?" ask the devils in Cardinal Newman's poem *The Dream of Gerontius*, and answer with glee, "A bundle of bones, which fools adore." One of the fundamental features of the cult of the saints was the positive role of dead bodies. They even had therapeutic power—"the dead body heals living bodies," as the hagiographer of St. Francis put it.[22] It was also one of the most notorious aspects of Christianity in the eyes of its opponents (a subject to be discussed later). The cult of the saints began in the cemetery and ended, not only by bringing the dead into the city (unthinkable in the ancient world), but by making them a focus of devotion inside the place of worship itself. As mentioned earlier (p. 10), Jerome noted that "the city itself is moving; the people flood past the half-ruined temples and run to the tombs of the martyrs," and this attractive pull of the tomb became one of the defining characteristics of medieval culture. People ran to the tombs, the bones of the saints were brought into the city, human remains were prized, given and stolen. The corpse was a source not of pollution but of supernatural power. When Elizabeth of Thuringia's body was laid out after her death in 1231, crowds assembled and cut away portions not only of her clothing, but also of her hair, her nails, even her nipples, which "they preserved for themselves as relics."[23]

Saints' bodies were treated differently from other bodies, for "no fleshly substance is more noble than the flesh of the saints."[24] This had been true from earliest times, and the building of martyr churches above the martyrs' graves from the fourth century was a spectacularly visible example of such distinction. When, in the early medieval period, Christian burial within churches became more common, the saints were still marked out by the treatment of their tomb, adorned with lights, precious cloths, and the like. The elaborate carved, jewelled shrines of the great saints were the culmination of this treasuring of dead bodies. Papal canonization only formalized the process. When the pope canonized Thomas Becket in 1173, he not only ordered

18 Helbig and Weinrich, eds., *Urkunden und erzählende Quellen zur deutschen Ostsiedlung* 1, p. 134, no. 28.

19 *Regesta regum Anglo-Normannorum* 1, no. 377, p. 96.

20 *Acta et processus canonizacionis Beate Birgitte*, p. 149.

21 *Anglo-Norman Dictionary*, p. 523, s.v. "philbert."

22 Thomas of Celano, *Vita prima sancti Francisci* 3. 121, p. 96.

23 *Libellus de dictis quatuor ancillarum*, p. 139.

24 Thiofrid of Echternach, *Flores epytaphii sanctorum* 1. 3, p. 16.

that the monks of Canterbury should celebrate the day of Becket's death "each year with fitting reverence," but also that they, "devoutly and reverently, in solemn procession, with clergy and people assembled," should place his body in an altar or in an elevated shrine.[25]

Although they were treated with special reverence, saints' bodies could decay just like the bodies of any other human. Incorruptibility of the flesh was a rare gift, dependent on "divine miracles," according to Paul the Deacon.[26] It was certainly not a requirement for sanctity. Most long-dead saints had become just dust. When the remains of St. Æbbe were uncovered, more than 400 years after her death, the monk recording the event made no effort to conceal the utter decay of the saint's body—what was found was "dust," which soon dissolved, and bones, which turned to dust.[27] Even William of Malmesbury, writing in the 1120s, who claimed that the English had more incorrupt saints than any other people, actually knew of only five (Etheldreda, Werburga, Edmund, Alphege, and Cuthbert); and even this small tally was, he said, a special mark of divine favour.[28]

Sometimes, the dissolution of the saint's body was actually planned as part of the treatment of the dead. When St. Birgit of Sweden died in Italy in 1373, it was decided that her body should be boiled, to soak off the flesh and enable the bones to be transported to Sweden. The water was already heating, and razors and swords were ready to carve off the flesh, when the temporary tomb was opened and, to everyone's amazement, "they found that all the flesh had decayed and the bones were bare and without flesh, just as if she had been buried for ten years (except for the head in which there was still a little of the brains)."[29] Here is a reversal of the usual miracle of the uncorrupted body: Birgit has considerately, and miraculously, decomposed, in order to help out the process of the repatriation of her bones. There could scarcely be a more telling demonstration that incorruptibility is *not* an essential feature of sanctity than physical decay being regarded as a miracle.

Nor was the decay of an incorrupt body necessarily something to be worried about. The hagiographer of St. Euthymius of Sardis (d. 831), a victim of iconoclast persecution, noted with pride that the saint's body was still whole and life-like forty days after his death. He thought that it was a particular grace that the more nauseating aspects of decomposition had been avoided: "Even if he becomes dust, like other saints, and dissolves over time, he suffered neither the onset nor the consequence of decay, namely swelling and liquefaction in stinking fluid."[30] The passage implies that Euthymius's body might eventually disintegrate, but in a clean and tolerable manner.

[25] *Materials for the History of Thomas Becket* 7, p. 546, no. 784 (Alexander III, 12 March 1173, *Gaudendum est*).

[26] Paul the Deacon, *Historia Langobardorum* 6. 2, p. 165; on incorruptibility, see Angenendt, *Corpus Incorruptum*.

[27] *Vita et miracula sancte Ebbe virginis*, p. 24.

[28] William of Malmesbury, *Gesta regum Anglorum* 2. 207, p. 386.

[29] *Acta et processus canonizacionis Beate Birgitte*, p. 507.

[30] *Vita Euthymii Sardensis* 43, pp. 81–83.

But if incorruptibility was not a requirement for sanctity, when it occurred it was taken as a strong presumption that the dead person was a saint. When the body of Theobald, archbishop of Canterbury, was found "whole and solid" in 1180, during removal of his tomb, "the rumour resounded among the people and he was immediately called 'saint Theobald' by many, because of the unusual integrity of his body" (although his cult did not last long).[31] And incorruptibility was viewed as a sign of purity of life. When the body of Gregory of Langres was uncovered, prior to being moved to a more honourable place in his cathedral,

> Lo! His blessed face appeared so intact and unharmed that you would think him not dead but sleeping, nor was there any damage to the clothes he had been buried in. It was right that he should appear so glorious after death, since his body had not been stained by any sexual sin. Great is wholeness of body and heart, bringing grace in the present life and life eternal in the future.[32]

It is worth noting that Gregory of Langres was not a virgin (he was the great-grandfather of Gregory of Tours), so that his "wholeness" consisted in sexual fidelity, not abstinence. "Virginity of the heart" could be praised as well as virginity of the body.[33]

But the view that real saints should be incorrupt was not unknown. The great thirteenth-century canonist Hostiensis reported that lay people believed this: "For if they see bare bones, they take it as an occasion for disparagement and blasphemy, saying, 'this is mere trickery, for if he were a saint, he would not be decayed in this way.'"[34] And a concrete example of such a belief is recorded in ninth-century Spain. Eulogius of Cordoba, defending the claim that certain Christians killed by the authorities in Muslim Spain were truly martyrs, had to face objections from his fellow-Christians that the bodies of the dead had decayed. Obviously they believed that incorruptibility was a requirement for sanctity, however much Eulogius might object "that this temporal corruption of the body takes away nothing from the souls of the saints."[35] There is even a case of incorruptibility transmitted through contact: when the tomb of St. Odilia's wet-nurse was opened, eighty years after her death, in order to place another burial in it, it was found that the nurse's body had completely decayed, except for the right breast, with which she had suckled the saint.[36]

[31] Gervase of Canterbury, *Chronica*, pp. 25–26.

[32] Gregory of Tours, *Liber vitae patrum* 7, p. 690 (repr., 1969, p. 240).

[33] "*Virginitas cordis et corporis*" was a common phrase from patristic times onwards. Hagiographers used it frequently, for example, Milo, *Vita Amandi episcopi* 6, p. 475; Garinus, *Vita Margaritae Hungaricae (Legenda minor)* 4. 25, p. 903.

[34] Nam et ex hoc sumunt materiam detrahendi et blasphemandi, videntes enim ossa nuda dicunt, trufe sunt, si esset sanctus, non esset sic consumptus: Hostiensis, *Lectura siue Apparatus super quinque libris Decretalium*, ad X. 3. 45. 2, *Quum ex eo*.

[35] Eulogius, *Memoriale sanctorum* 1. 26, pp. 389–90 (PL 115: 759).

[36] *Vita Odiliae abbatissae Hohenburgensis* 10, p. 43.

It was not long before body parts, as well as whole bodies, began to be revered. Reverence at a tomb is a feature of some strands of pre-Christian religion as well as of several non-Christian religions of the present day, but a concentration on body parts, detachable and moveable, is a distinctive feature of the Christian cult of the saints. And it was always emphasized that the power of these bodily fragments was just as great as that of the whole body. When welcoming the arrival of saintly relics in the 390s, bishop Victricius of Rouen set out to show that "the whole can be in a part," and, especially, that "healing power is no less in the parts than it is in the whole."[37] Not long afterwards, around the year 400, bishop Gaudentius of Brescia preached a sermon at the dedication of his basilica. He explained how he had acquired some of the relics of the Forty Martyrs of Sebaste for the church and went on:

> We took a portion of the relics, and we have confidence that we would possess nothing less if we were embracing and honouring the ashes of all forty . . . that part, which we have deserved to have, is completeness.[38]

This sense of the part being as powerful as the whole lies behind the acquisition of often tiny fragments of saint's bones or other relics, although it should be noted that Victricius and Gaudentius seem to have felt the need to emphasize and argue the point.

The public commemoration of saints and the special treatment of saints' bodies marked them out from the rest of the Christian dead. This individual recognition was strengthened and enriched by the composition, recitation, and reading of literary works recounting their lives and miraculous deeds, including both those they performed during their life and those that occurred after death. The literature of the saints grew to enormous proportions and took many forms: the individual Life or *vita*, collections of such Lives in Legendaries and Passionaries, Miracle Books, accounts of translations of relics, and so on This literature is discussed in more detail later.

These three components, the name and day, the body, and the literary commemoration, were the foundations of a saint's cult. Sometimes one or two were lacking: there are cases of saints whose names were known but whose remains were lost or forgotten, cases too of tombs where miracles took place but whose occupant could only be identified after a visionary revelation. Given the inventiveness of the medieval imagination when it came to tradition, it is no surprise that these lacks could be made good. A name, the bones, and a story were what was needed, and they could be provided.

A common situation was of a saint known by repute but whose burial place was unidentified. This was then revealed or discovered. Such a discovery was termed an "invention," not anything fraudulent, but from the Latin word *inventio*, meaning "finding." The most famous "invention" and among the earliest was the discovery of

[37] Victricius of Rouen, *De laude sanctorum* 10, 11, pp. 85, 86 (PL 20: 452–53).

[38] Gaudentius of Brescia, *Tractatus* 17, p. 150 (PL 20: 970).

the tomb of St. Stephen in the Holy Land in 415. His name and the story of his life and death had long been familiar from the Bible; now his physical remains could provide a concrete stimulus to his cult. Conversely, the absence of hagiographic writings was a disadvantage to a cult even when it had a focus in the tomb of the saint. Gregory of Tours tells the story of the shrine of the martyr Patroclus at Troyes in Champagne. It was extremely modest, consisting of a small oratory served by a single cleric. Gregory explains this neglect in significant terms:

> For the people of that place showed little respect to the martyr, because there was no account of his Passion available. For it was the custom of rustic people to venerate more attentively the saints of God whose martyrdoms they read.[39]

Needless to say, eventually an account of Patroclus's Passion turned up.

Patronage and Invocation: The Mutual Relationship

Intercession and Invocation

The name and day, the physical remains, and a written account of some kind were thus core elements of the cult of the saints. But what moved and motivated worshippers? The Miracles of Thecla (discussed earlier, p. 24) contain a concise but vivid description of what saints were, why they were needed, and what they did:

> Since it is not an easy or simple thing for all men to attain to God, for his power is of the highest . . . while the race of men is always drawn towards danger, forever pierced with many and varied pains and troubles, God, because he loves human beings, . . . sowed the earth with saints, as if he were dividing up the world between some wonderful doctors, so that they could easily work wonders, being nearer to those in need, able to hear them at once and bring healing, and through God's grace and power to perform those great things which especially need his help, being ambassadors, intercessors, mediators, for nations, cities, races and peoples against plague, famine, war, drought, earthquake.[40]

God is great but not easily accessible; human life is full of dangers; the saints are "sown" across the land by a loving God to act as the bridge between desperate human beings and his divine power. These were to be the fundamental ideas of the cult of the saints throughout its history.

The saint was a powerful, if usually invisible, patron—"an invisible friend"—who could provide direct help and also access to yet higher levels in the cosmic hierarchy.[41] Any society that knew the patron-client relationships of the ancient world, or

[39] Gregory of Tours, *Gloria martyrum* 63, p. 531 (repr., 1969, p. 81).

[40] *Miracula Theclae* 4, pp. 294–96 (abbreviated).

[41] Gregory of Nyssa, *De sancto Theodoro*, p. 70 (PG 46: 748).

the significance of lordship in the medieval one, would find the dynamics of invocation and saintly intercession self-explanatory. Saints were intercessors, intermediaries between needy human beings and the Almighty. The world of patronage and favours extended beyond this earthly life. A telling simile was that having a saint on your side was a bit like winning over the bodyguard of a great king to give you access to him.[42] And, just as suppliants sought out powerful helpers, so too the honour of those helpers was increased by the requests made to them. To have clients and to be able to help them was a mark of power. This double aspect is made clear by Jacobus de Voragine, author of the *Golden Legend*, the most successful collection of saints' Lives ever put together, who explains at one point the reasons for praying to the saints:

> The first reason is our need, . . . so that where our own merits are insufficient, we may receive the help of the merits of others; and . . . so that, we, who cannot receive the highest light in ourselves, should at least be able to see it in the saints; . . . for many an imperfect man feels more moved by one of the saints than even by God. The second reason is the glory of the saints. For God wishes us to invoke the saints, so that, while we beg for what we seek through their help, we glorify them and praise them more nobly.[43]

The practice of invoking the saints implied that the dead cared about what was happening in the world of the living. This was not an entirely uncontroversial belief. "Can it be that a dead man brings help to a living man?," wondered one pagan.[44] Augustine thought that, in the normal and natural course of events, the dead could have no involvement in the affairs of the living, and that saintly intervention was "marvellous," not "natural": "the martyrs are involved in the affairs of the living through the divine power, for the dead cannot be involved in the affairs of the living through their intrinsic nature."[45] Jacobus de Voragine insisted that "the saints are able to know the requests of suppliants."[46] Critics of the cults of the saints often argued that the dead could not hear or heed the living (later, pp. 589, 592).

"Let your requests be addressed to the martyrs," Basil of Caesarea advised his flock in the later fourth century, and then drew a word-picture for them of a pious woman praying for her children, or for a husband who was away on a journey or sick.[47] These are moving scenes. Gregory the Great provides evidence, however, that some requests made at the tombs of the saints were more materialistic or could even be viewed as wicked:

[42] Ibid., pp. 63–64 (PG 46: 740).
[43] Jacobus de Voragine, *Legenda aurea* 76 ("De letania maiori et minori") (1, pp. 477–78).
[44] Paul the Deacon, *Historia Langobardorum* 4. 16, p. 151.
[45] Augustine, *De cura pro mortuis gerenda* 16. 19, p. 653 (PL 40: 607).
[46] Jacobus de Voragine, *Legenda aurea* 76 ("De letania maiori et minori") (1, p. 477).
[47] Basil of Caesarea, *Homilia XIX in sanctos quadraginta martyres* 8, col. 523.

> We see, dear brethren, how many of you gather for the martyr's feast-day, kneel, beat your breast, utter prayers and confessions, water your face with tears. But think, I beseech you, about what you request. One prays for a wife, another requests a nice house, another demands clothing, another prays that he should be given food. And, indeed, when these are lacking, they should be sought from God. But another demands the death of an enemy, and pursues him in prayer, whom he cannot pursue with the sword. God commands that we should love our enemy, but nevertheless God is presented with a request that he should kill our enemy.[48]

The idea of a Christian going to the tomb of a saint to pray that God would kill his enemy, while very much in the tradition of the Psalmist, shocked the great pope. It is not surprising that the literature that records the requests of the faithful, particularly the Miracle Books, is dominated by prayers for healing: perhaps the prayers for the death of enemies were more numerous than this type of source reveals.

A request to a saint, delivered with conviction, was expected to produce results. "Know," wrote Gregory of Tours in his account of Martin's miracles, "how quickly he will appear to deal with that for which he is invoked, if he is asked with faith."[49] Sometimes, however, the saint might first have to be woken up: when the monks of Gigny in the Jura went to the relics of St. Taurin that they possessed, "they stirred him up by their continuous prayers and unceasing orations like a sleeping man."[50]

Invocation was a personal address, and the practice of visiting saints' shrines shows that many people thought that such appeals were best made in the presence of the physical remains. Saints were imagined as having a bodily location and a site that could be visited. But there was debate and discussion about the value of invocation at the tomb versus invocation at a distance, since there was always some tension between the belief that the saint was in some sense "in" his or her shrine, and the idea that a saint could be appealed to anywhere. Sometimes there is clear evidence of a belief that saints could only operate close to their shrine. A knight who invoked St. Eutropius to regain his lost horse was mocked by his acquaintances. "Do you think St. Eutropius, whom you continually invoke, can restore your lost horse? The saint is ten leagues away!"[51]

The devotees and guardians of any particular shrine faced a dilemma between a simple desire to get people to the shrine, which could best be done by emphasizing the miracles that occurred in that very place, and a more general desire to glorify their saint, which might well lead to the claim that the saint's power was ubiquitous and could be summoned up anywhere. The author of the Miracles of Thecla says

[48] Gregory I, *Homiliae in Evangelia* 27. 7 (2, p. 176) (PL 76: 1208–9). Citation abbreviated. A theory about the context of the passage is advanced by Leyser, "The Temptations of Cult: Roman Martyr Piety in the Age of Gregory the Great," pp. 303–5.

[49] Gregory of Tours, *De virtutibus sancti Martini* 2. 16, p. 614 (repr., 1969, p. 164).

[50] *CircumvectioTaurini episcopi* 1. 2, p. 650.

[51] *Miracula Eutropii episcopi Santonensis* 4. 35, p. 743.

that "those who are not able to be present and attain to her shrine, if they make their invocations in the place where they are, readily obtain her aid in this way, since she is present and hears them."[52] Medieval authors might argue that the saints' powers were strong not only at the spot where they were buried but also in churches or even at altars dedicated to them. Or they might assert that the power of a saint could be invoked anywhere:

> The saints are perceived to make their appearance not only where they are seen to be present temporally in their ashes and remains, but they are believed to be of assistance to the faithful wherever they are invoked in faith, through him who is present everywhere, by the power and majesty of the creator rewarding their merits, in every place of his dominion.[53]

The data gathered by André Vauchez show a definite tendency, over the course of the later Middle Ages, for the miracles recorded in canonization processes to take place less often at the tomb of the saint and more frequently at a distance. A particular disjuncture seems to occur around the middle of the thirteenth century.[54]

There was even the, apparently paradoxical, argument that the saints exercised greater power in the absence of their physical remains. In his *Dialogues*, Pope Gregory the Great has his interlocutor ask him to explain the fact that the martyrs "do not manifest such great benefits through their bodies as they do by their other relics." Gregory replies,

> there is no doubt that the holy martyrs perform innumerable miracles where they lie in their bodies . . . but since weak minds may doubt whether they are present to hear them in places where they do not lie in their bodies, it is necessary that they perform greater miracles there.[55]

Reciprocity

"Bring me gifts! Ask my help!," saints demanded.[56] The gifts and the help were two sides of the relationship. Suppliants brought offerings of candles, wax, money, and other things, and gave gifts at the shrine to express their thanks for cures; but they expected help, and were sometimes vociferous when it did not appear to be forthcoming.

In 1376 a rich and powerful woman of Naples, named Alfarana, pregnant for the seventh or eighth time, was extremely worried, for all her earlier pregnancies had ended in stillbirths. She made a promise to St. Birgit of Sweden that if God granted,

[52] *Miracula Theclae* 10, p. 310.

[53] Angsar, *Miracula Willehadi*, preface, p. 847.

[54] Vauchez, *Sainthood*, p. 447, table 40; see also Krötzl, "Miracles au tombeau—miracles à distance."

[55] Gregory I, *Dialogi* 2. 38. 2–3 (2, p. 246).

[56] Arcoid, *Miracula sancti Erkenwaldi* 10, p. 142 (the words are spoken in mockery by a blasphemer parodying the saint).

through the merits of the saint, that she give birth to a live child, "she would send to Rome, to the tomb of St. Birgit, a silver image in the shape of a little child." Happily, she bore a healthy son, and fulfilled her vow.[57] This is a classic example of an ex-voto, an offering made in thanks after a promise.[58] Alfarana had been quite specific about what she wanted, which saint she expected it from, and what she would give in return. And the idea of giving something of an appropriate shape was extremely common, although in her case the preciousness of the material marked her out as a wealthy suppliant.

Offerings to the saint, large or small, were an essential sign of reverence and devotion. Kings could make regal gifts, and did so from the early days of the cult of the saints. Around 400 a Scythian king sent his golden crown and breastplate to St. Phocas of Amasea in Asia Minor as a votive offering.[59] Reccared I, king of the Visigoths (586–601), offered a golden crown at the tomb of the martyr Felix in Gerona, an object which was presumably similar to the surviving Visigothic votive crowns in the Musée de Cluny in Paris and the National Archaeological Museum of Spain in Madrid.[60] Grants of land were often made, not simply to the church or clergy that housed and served the shrine of a saint, but to the saint himself or herself. Thus, when William the Conqueror granted land to the bishop of Durham, he declared that he was giving it "to God Almighty and the most holy confessor Cuthbert and to William, bishop of Durham."[61] More modest gifts were made, down to the level of the single candle or small coin. Nor was the offering of a cheese to be spurned.[62]

As in the case of Alfarana of Naples, it was common to give as a thank-offering a model or image, often in the shape of an affected body-part, or some other item associated with a miraculous cure. This was a practice that continued throughout the medieval period, and beyond. It is attested as early as the first half of the fifth century, when Theodoret of Cyrrhus mentions model eyes, feet, and hands donated by grateful pilgrims.[63] Papal commissioners, investigating the tomb of Vincent Ferrer at Vannes (Brittany) a thousand years later, in 1453, found a profusion of such mimetic objects:

> We indeed saw wax offerings there, namely, many ships, wax images of bodies, heads, eyes, hands, arms, shin-bones, feet, and various other members, many sheets, wax breasts, crutches, and very many wooden crosses and some biers

[57] *Acta et processus canonizacionis Beate Birgitte*, pp. 282–83, 340–41, 410–11.

[58] On ex-votos, see Bautier, "Typologie des ex-votos"; Sigal, *L'homme et le miracle*, pp. 86–107; Trombetta, "L'ex-voto au Moyen-Age"; Sigal "L'ex-voto au Moyen-Age."

[59] Asterius of Amasea, Homily 9. 12, p. 127.

[60] Julian of Toledo, *Historia Wambae* 26, p. 522; *El tesoro visigodo de Guarrazar*, pp. 35–40 (pls. 1–6), 20–22 (plates 53–54), 322–32, 349–54; for crown offerings, see *Le liber ordinum en usage dans l'église wisigothique et mozarabe d'Espagne*, col. 165, section 59, with n. 2, and col. 545.

[61] *Durham Liber Vitae* 1, p. 158 (fol. 54v).

[62] For example, *Miracula beati Domitiani*, p. 703.

[63] Theodoret of Cyrrhus, *Graecorum affectionum curatio* 8. 64 (2, p. 333).

> from dead people who, as they say, were brought back to life; there were so many that it would not be possible to enumerate them in many days.[64]

The commissioners in the case of Thomas de Cantilupe at Hereford in 1307 were less easily daunted, and undertook a meticulous enumeration of the ex-votos at his shrine: 170 silver ships, 41 wax ships, 129 silver images of the complete body or limbs, 436 wax images of the complete body, 988 wax images of parts of the body, 77 images of horses, animals and birds, and so on.[65] Offerings such as these were in the care of the custodian of the shrine. One thirteenth-century account from Siena mentions an incident that occurred "when the custodian of the saint's tomb was arranging above the tomb the wax images which had been offered in his honour and declared the truth of his sanctity through miracles."[66] Some rare surviving wax ex-votos, dating to the fifteenth century, were discovered in Exeter cathedral when repairs were being made after air-raids in World War II. They include fragments of arms, legs, and heads, as well as the complete figure of a woman 20 centimetres (8 inches) high.[67]

Neither Vincent Ferrer's nor Thomas de Cantilupe's shrine seems to have been adorned with a kind of ex-voto consisting of a picture of the saint, something that is mentioned in several Italian sources of the thirteenth and fourteenth centuries. For instance, in Apulia in the 1230s, a woman suffering from a lengthy illness vowed "that if she were freed by the merits of St. Benvenuto, she would have his picture painted and place it before his tomb in memory of him."[68] Likewise, a chaplain of the church of Sant'Angelo Magno in Ascoli Piceno vowed that, if St. Peter Martyr freed him from his ailment, "he would have his image painted."[69] A young woman of Pavia, who had become secretly engaged to a man who seemed unwilling to proceed to a public wedding, prayed to St. Thomas Aquinas that he would bring it about, promising to make a priestly vestment with her own hands, to perform a hundred genuflexions before the saint's altar, to visit his chapel every year, and "to have him painted in the church of the friars." Another Pavian lady also promised to have St. Thomas painted if he cured her of an ailment of the heart.[70] In 1323 a woman testified that the recently deceased Simon of Todi, buried in Bologna, had cured her little daughter of epilepsy, after she had vowed to have an image of Simon painted.[71] There seems to be a pattern here: in every case the saint in question is an Italian friar, and in all cases bar one the devotee making the promise is a woman. Pious women commissioning pictures of saintly friars thus form one small tributary to the great river of

[64] *Notes et documents de l'histoire de Saint Vincent Ferrier*, p. 399.
[65] BAV, Vat. lat. 4015, fols. 74–74v.
[66] *Vita Andreae de Galleranis* 3. 30, p. 57.
[67] Radford, "The Wax Images Found in Exeter Cathedral."
[68] *Dialogus de gestis sanctorum Fratrum Minorum* 2. 8, p. 91.
[69] Ambrogio Taegio, *Vita sancti Petri martyris* 9. 72, p. 708.
[70] *Miracula sancti Thomae de Aquino* 22, p. 724.
[71] *Miracula Simonis Tudertini* 6. 60, p. 828.

late medieval Italian painting. In the fifteenth century such ex-votos are common—a dozen are recorded in the miracle accounts of St. Bernardino from the mid-century.[72]

A vow could involve a service as well as an object. One notary, who had been employed in writing letters to promote the canonization of Nicholas of Tolentino, promised that, if Nicholas healed his wounded hand, he would not only bring a wax hand to the saint's shrine and fast every year on the vigil of his feast but would also "write constantly in service of your canonization, without any pay and whenever required."[73]

The worshippers thus had duties: to respect and revere the saint, to bring offerings, to participate in celebrations on feast-days. But the saint had duties too. He or she was expected to provide help, and it was unquestionably the worshipper's right to reproach saints who failed to help. On one occasion, for example, Adomnán, abbot of Iona, and the successor and hagiographer of St. Columba, had to "accuse" his patron saint. He was supervising the transport of timber by sea when a contrary wind sprang up. He records that,

> We complained about how unwelcome it was that the wind was against us in this way, and we began to make a kind of accusation against our Columba, saying, "Does this set-back that we are suffering please you, O saint? Until now we have hoped to obtain from you, with God's aid, some encouraging help in our efforts, considering that you were someone of high honour with God."

Naturally enough, this imputation of low heavenly status stirred Columba to immediate action, and the wind changed.[74] In a similar vein, dissatisfied adherents might imply that their saint was dozing. When the Vikings attacked Tours in 903, the clergy ran to "the tomb of their defender"—St. Martin—and reproached him for his apparent negligence in letting the pagans reach their doors: "Martin, God's saint, why have you been sleeping so deeply?"[75] A disappointed suppliant at the shrine of St. Berengar in the church of St.-Papoul in the south of France beat the saint's tomb with his stick, shouted out, "So you are a saint? You never were nor will be a saint, nor have you ever done any miracles!," and stormed out. He was then rewarded with a cure.[76]

If a simple rebuke were not enough, then the saint might be threatened with counter-measures. When St. Columba (in this case not the Irish saint but the female

[72] Jansen, "Un exemple de sainteté thaumaturgique," p. 151, table III; the earliest surviving examples are fifteenth-century: Ciarrochi and Mori, *Le tavolette votive italiane*, pp. 7–8, pls. I–XII; see also Antoine, "Images de miracles," and the general comments in Freedberg, *The Power of Images*, pp. 136–60 ("The Votive Image").

[73] *Il processo per la canonizzazione di S. Nicola da Tolentino*, p. 465.

[74] Adomnán, *Vita Columbae* 2. 45, p. 174.

[75] "Sancte Dei Martine, quare tam graviter obdormisti?": Radbod of Utrecht, *Libellus de miraculo sancti Martini* 5, p. 1243 (the text was written 903–17). St. Martin's body must have been brought inside the walled area from its suburban basilica at the time of the attack. For discussion, see Farmer, *Communities of Saint Martin*, pp. 31–34.

[76] Flavius Anselmus, *Vita Berengarii* 9, p. 449.

martyr of Sens) was careless enough to let thieves get away from her church in Paris with some precious vessels, she was addressed sternly by bishop Eligius of Noyon:

> Listen, Saint Columba, to what I say. My redeemer knows that, unless you quickly get back the vessels stolen from the shrine, truly I will bring thorns and block up this door, so that never will any veneration be offered to you in this place from this day on.[77]

This blackmail worked. In a like mood, the mother of a sick girl, who had waited for ten days at a saint's tomb, praying for her daughter without any effect, eventually threatened the disappointing saint with public exposure: "I will turn everyone away from visiting your tomb because you have not heeded me." This naturally got an immediate result.[78] Another woman, whose daughter had been carried off by a wolf, went to a statue of the Virgin Mary and grabbed away from her the figure of the Christ child she was holding. "Lady," she said, "you will never get your child back unless you restore my child to me unharmed!" When her daughter was restored to her, through the Virgin's power, she replaced the image of the Christ child on Mary's lap.[79]

Expectations about the patronage owed by a saint were unmistakably based on that owed by an earthly lord, and the parallel is sometimes made explicit. One sick man, entreating saintly aid from St. John the Baptist, St. Artemios, and St. Febronia in their joint cult-centre in Constantinople, was quite clear about their failure in this respect:

> He broke out into a heartfelt lament, wetting his mattress with his tears and accusing the saints, saying, "Indeed, St. John and St. Artemios and St. Febronia, have I served you from the age of ten up to the present, in order that I should become maimed in old age? If I had attached myself to some man on earth, I would have been thought worthy of support and care and provision. See what satisfaction I have attained!"[80]

This shaming of the saints is recorded by hagiographers of many times and places without any sense that it is incongruous or lacking in respect. Just as, in Old Irish law, dissatisfied plaintiffs dealing with higher-class defendants could bring moral pressure to bear on them by fasting outside their door, so the devotees of a saint could try the tactic of public reproach of their heavenly lord.[81] Saints had duties to their followers.

The most public and physical embodiment of this pressurizing of the saint was the ritual known as "humiliation of relics"—literal humiliation, in the original sense

[77] *Vita Eligii* 1. 30, p. 686.
[78] *Miracula sancte Elyzabet* 3, p. 164.
[79] Caesarius of Heisterbach, *Dialogus miraculorum* 7. 45 (2, pp. 63–64).
[80] *Miracula sancti Artemii* 22, p. 132.
[81] Kelly, *A Guide to Early Irish Law*, pp. 182–83.

of "placing on the ground (*humus*)."[82] The customs of Farfa, from around 1030, describe how, when there is need, a cry should be raised to God, with the crucifix, Gospels and relics of the saints placed on a piece of sacking on the ground before the altar, while the monks lie prostrate reciting the psalm beginning, "O God, why hast thou cast us off for ever?"[83] When the abbot of Burton upon Trent, in the English Midlands, became involved in a violent dispute with a neighbouring noble, he had recourse to this tactic, going straight to the virgin saint enshrined in his church: "he and the monks entered the church, barefoot and groaning greatly, and placed the shrine of the blessed virgin, where her most holy bones lay, upon the ground. All together called out to the Lord with their whole heart."[84] A similar episode is recorded during a dispute between the canons of St. Osyth's in Essex and the bishop of London in the early twelfth century, when the canons decided "to take their complaint to God and to their lady, St. Osyth, whom they had served so well." They first took her image outside the church and then covered her shrine with a piece of coarse sacking. They were reminding her that "she ought to defend them against their enemies," and reproaching her for tolerating the wrongs they were suffering. The device worked. At the very hour that the canons were humiliating her image, the hostile bishop was struck with paralysis.[85]

Humiliation—placing the relics or images low—could be combined with another common ritual of punishment, the use of thorns. A ritual book of Tours from the thirteenth-century describes the procedure: after recitation of the seven penitential psalms and the litany, the silver crucifix and the all the moveable reliquaries are placed on the ground and covered with thorns, while the great shrine of St. Martin is also covered and surrounded with thorns, and the wooden crucifix is treated likewise in the body of the nave and all the doors are semi-blocked.[86] A case of such a procedure is recorded from the same period. In 1260, during the course of a long dispute between the abbey of Senones in the Vosges and the noble house of Salm, the monks, seeing that they had "no true defender," took the images of Christ and their local saint, Simeon, from their usual locations in the church and "placed them on the ground on top of thorns, crying out to the Lord with tears and saying, "We have maintained peace, and it has not come; we have sought the good, and behold turbulence!"[87]

[82] Geary, "La coercition des saints"; idem, "L'humiliation des saints"; Little, *Benedictine Maledictions*, pp. 26–30, 131–34, 139–43.

[83] Ibid., p. 262; the Psalm is 73 in the Vulgate and 74 in the King James Bible.

[84] Geoffrey of Burton, *Vita sancte Modvenne virginis* 47, pp. 192–94.

[85] *La Vie seinte Osith, virge e martire*, lines 1484–1525, pp. 426–30 (*envili* is the word used for humiliation); see Zatta, "The 'Vie Seinte Osith"; Bethell, "The Lives of St Osyth of Essex and St Osyth of Aylesbury."

[86] Little, *Benedictine Maledictions*, p. 266.

[87] Richer of Senones, *Gesta Senoniensis ecclesiae* 4. 9, p. 335 (Simeon was a supposed early bishop of Metz).

One of the most enlightening passages about the humiliation of saints is, curiously enough, fictional; nor does it concern Christian saints. It occurs in the twelfth-century epic the *Song of Roland*. After a great defeat, the Muslims of Spain retreat to Zaragoza. There they turn on their gods, Apollo, Tervagan, and Muhammad. "O wicked god!," they rail at Apollo in his crypt. "Why have you brought us such shame? . . . You give poor rewards to those who serve you best." They remove Apollo's sceptre and crown, then smash his idol into pieces, going on to humiliate the idols of Tervagan and Muhammad in a similar way. Muhammad is thrown into a ditch for pigs and dogs to bite and trample.[88] The whole incident is, of course, nothing but ignorant Christian fantasy. But fantasies tell us something; and what this one tells us is that Christians assumed that the failures of powerful invisible protectors—be they saints or gods—could and should be punished. Because the passage concerns, not treatment of saints by Christians, but treatment of their so-called idols by Muslims, it is particularly revealing of the medieval assumption that your supernatural patrons could be punished for dereliction of duty.

But to some medieval churchmen, especially the sophisticated intellects of the age of high scholasticism, this berating of the saints had a primitive air about it. At the Second Council of Lyons in 1274, in a clause dealing with suspension of religious services during a dispute, they managed to have their say:

> we strictly forbid that detestable abuse of those people who, in order to aggravate the suspension of services and with horrible lack of devotion, treat images or statues of the cross, the blessed Virgin and other saints with audacious irreverence, placing them on the ground under nettles and thorns.[89]

These are the views of that active reforming party in the Church that had already replaced trial by ordeal with the more rational and centralized judicial procedures of inquisition and torture, and had developed the complex and bureaucratic examinations characteristic of modern canonization. You should not surround an image with thorns; you should simply kneel in front of it and pray. The age of humiliation of the saints was coming to an end.

[88] *Chanson de Roland*, lines 2580–91, p. 76.

[89] *Conciliorum oecumenicorum decreta*, p. 323 (cl. 17).

CHAPTER 6

Saints' Days

Liturgy

The early Christians kept Sunday as a day of Eucharistic worship, and, from at least the second century, they celebrated the great annual feast of Easter—since the date of the latter is based on the phases of the moon, it is "moveable," that is, it falls at different times in different years. Local churches also commemorated their martyrs on the anniversary of their deaths, as is made explicit in the account of the death of Polycarp of Smyrna. This triple pattern, of weekly holy day, annual moveable feasts, and annual fixed feasts, has formed the basic framework of Christian worship to the present, despite enormous elaboration over the centuries, with the introduction of many new feasts, such as Christmas, which is first mentioned in the fourth century. The feasts of the saints, some celebrated universally by all Christians, some only by local churches, had an important place in this complex dance of the liturgical year.[1]

The French theologian William of Auxerre, writing his liturgical handbook in the first decade of the thirteenth century, gave seven reasons why the church celebrates the feasts of the saints:[2]

1. "Because they celebrate feasts for us; for there is joy in heaven amongst the angels of God and the holy souls over one sinner who repents" (an adaptation of Luke 15:10).
2. "Their feast is ours; whence the Apostle says, 'all things are ours, and we are Christ's'" (an adaptation of 1 Corinthians 3:22–23).
3. "So that we should have them as intercessors."
4. "So that we should imitate them."
5. "To support hope, for if mortal men, similar to us, can be raised so high by their merits, we can too."
6. "So that seeing their beauty and purity, a man may be ashamed of his sins and despise earthly things."
7. "The chief and best cause is that in them we honour God alone."

[1] Nilles, *Kalendarium manuale utriusque ecclesiae orientalis et occidentalis*; Kellner, *Heortologie: oder die geschichtliche Entwicklung des Kirchenjahres und der Heiligenfeste*; Dubois and Lemaitre, *Sources et méthodes de l'hagiographie médiévale*, pp. 59–102.

[2] William of Auxerre, *Summa de officiis ecclesiasticis* 4. 1.

This list was taken up and elaborated by later liturgical writers.[3] It contained several key ideas: the saints are intercessors and examples; in honouring them we honour God; and we are, in some sense, in community with them.

The celebration of saints' feast-days was a central part of church ritual—"the cult of the saints is a liturgical fact."[4] Veneration of these heavenly figures was enacted in forms of public worship. The two main types of church service were the Mass and Office, the former involving celebration of the Eucharist, the sacrament of bread and wine, which, according to medieval theologians, turned into the body and blood of Christ, while the latter comprised a series of services, consisting of prayers, Psalms, hymns and readings. In order through the day, the services of the Office were Matins, Lauds, Prime, Terce, Sext, None, and Vespers.

Certain saints were mentioned in every Latin Mass, since their names were recited in two prayers in the Canon of the Mass, the central part of the service.[5] The list of saints mentioned in the first prayer (known as *Communicantes*) includes the apostles and St. Paul, five early popes (Linus, Anacletus, Clement, Sixtus, and Cornelius), and seven early martyrs (Cyprian, Lawrence, Chrysogonus, John and Paul, Cosmas and Damian), while that in the second (*Nobis quoque peccatoribus*) names four New Testament figures (John the Baptist, Stephen, Matthias, and Barnabas), four post-biblical male martyrs (Ignatius, Alexander, Marcellinus, and Peter) and seven female martyrs (Felicity, Perpetua, Agatha, Lucy, Agnes, Cecilia, and Anastasia). These names would thus be familiar, throughout the medieval West, to anyone who attended Mass at all regularly. Some of them were major saints, but others are obscure. The Roman pattern was dominant, but there were variations, since local saints were sometimes added to these lists, and the church of Milan maintained its own distinctive version, with special mention of its own saints, such as Protasius, Gervasius, and Ambrose.[6]

The most elaborate liturgical commemoration of a saint took place on his or her feast-day, both in the Mass and in the Office. Important saints would have prayers and readings dedicated to them in the variable part (Proper) of the Mass. This included, most conspicuously, the priest's prayers of collect, secret, and postcommunion. In addition, there might be a so-called prose or sequence, recited before the Gospel and taking the saint as its direct subject and perhaps with a narrative element. For example, a common sequence at the Mass on the feast-day of Thomas Becket began, "In the hope of reward and the crown, Thomas stood in his last struggle obedient unto death."[7] The texts of Proper Masses, as recorded in medieval Missals, include just these variable parts, since the priest would either know by heart or have

[3] William Durandus, *Rationale divinorum officiorum* 7. 1. 2 (140B, pp. 9–10); Jacobus de Voragine, *Legenda aurea* 158 ("De festivitate omnium sanctorum") (2, pp. 1101–2).

[4] Dubois and Lemaitre, *Sources et méthodes de l'hagiographie médiévale*, p. 60.

[5] Kennedy, *The Saints of the Canon of the Mass*.

[6] *Le sacramentaire grégorien* 1, p. 88 n.; Kennedy, *The Saints of the Canon of the Mass*, pp. 69–80, 204.

[7] Spe mercedis et corone stetit Thomas in agone ad mortem obediens: this was an adaptation of a common hymn for martyrs' feast-days: Chevalier, *Repertorium hymnologicum* 2, p. 588, nos. 19249–50.

a separate text available for the standard invariable part of the Mass that formed a framework for them.

The Office, especially the service of Matins, devoted much more time to the saint being celebrated. Matins was the longest service (it could be two hours in duration) and included readings, which, on saints' days, were usually drawn from accounts of the saint's life or miracles. The recitation of an Office in honour of a saint was indeed one way that the person concerned was recognized as a saint. In 1317, responding to a charge of paying unauthorized cult to a recently deceased friar, a member of the Spiritual branch of the Franciscans offered as a defence: "solemn prayers and Offices have not been and are not celebrated in his honour, nor is his name placed in Kalendar or litany."[8] The implication of this statement is that celebration of an Office was unequivocal acknowledgment as a saint.

To take one example to illustrate the Office of a feast-day, that of St. Andrew the apostle (30 November) unfolded in the greater English churches of the later Middle Ages in the following way.[9] The celebration of an important feast such as this one began on the evening before the feast (the vigil) with celebration of First Vespers (so-called since there would also be Vespers on the feast-day itself). First Vespers included a short hymn to St. Andrew, as well as a prayer, "We beseech thee, Almighty God, that blessed Andrew the apostle should beg your help for us." Matins on the feast-day itself began with an invocation, "Let us adore Christ the most victorious king, who crowned the blessed Andrew the apostle as victor through the trophy of the cross." The service of Matins included six readings from the well-known account of Andrew's martyrdom, much of it consisting of Andrew's speeches to his judge and his address to the cross on which he was to be crucified, and three readings about Jesus' calling of Andrew. These readings were interspersed with Psalms and antiphons (sung responses) and concluded with the choir singing the verse and response, "The Lord loved Andrew" and "for a sweet savour" (a biblical phrase of frequent liturgical occurrence). The shorter services of Lauds, Prime, Terce, Sext, and None were all composed of Psalms and appropriate antiphons based on Andrew's address to the cross, "Hail, precious cross! [*Salve crux pretiosa!*]." Second Vespers, on the evening of the feast-day, which began with those same words, "Hail precious cross!," included Psalms especially appropriate for the apostles and elaborate antiphons and hymns.

In the great churches of the medieval world, the liturgy provided the fundamental structure of daily life. Monks in the abbeys, canons in the cathedrals and collegiate churches, and, in the later Middle Ages, friars in the larger friaries, devoted a major part of their waking hours to Mass and Office, and would be experts in their complex patterns. Variations in the liturgy between regions, Orders, and seasons would be immediately apparent to these specialists. Minute regulation could be undertaken of such details as vestments to be worn, the amount of incense, the presence or absence of certain chants. For instance, the liturgical treatise of the Norman bishop John

[8] Vauchez, *Sainthood*, p. 95 n. 34 (the case concerned Peter John Olivi).

[9] *Breviarium ad usum insignis ecclesiae Sarum* 3 *(Sanctorale)*, cols. 1–19.

of Avranches, written in the 1060s, gives the following directions for the feasts of John the Baptist, Peter and Paul, Andrew, Michael, and Martin (the Octave which he mentions is a subsidiary feast-day celebrated a week after the main festival):

> On these feast-days the bells should be rung two by two. The five psalms at Vespers are to be sung with only one antiphon. Two clergy in copes sing the response and then lead the choir, until they come to "let us bless the Lord." The altar is to be censed with one thurible. The invitatorium at Matins is to be sung by three clergy. They should sing responses two by two. In Nocturns and Lauds a hymn is to be sung. There is no procession. Each day until the Octave, unless a major feast falls then, they should sing about those saints, and the whole of Matins is said. The Octave is celebrated like a Sunday.[10]

Liturgical compositions for these feast-days demanded skill and learning, and, in addition to the texts required, music was needed for the chants of the Office and hymns. And there was a complex interplay between the texts of the liturgy and hagiographic writing, with hagiographic texts sometimes being composed specifically for inclusion in public worship (see later, pp. 506–7). Specialist skill might be acknowledged in this field, as in the case of Eugenius, archbishop of Toledo (646–57), a renowned liturgical expert, who was asked by bishop Protasius of Tarragona to write a Mass of St. Hippolytus.[11]

The effort involved in creating a new Office and Mass is shown by the case of Edmund Lacy, bishop of Exeter 1420–55, who was especially devoted to the cult of the archangel Raphael and applied himself to creating the requisite liturgy for Raphael's feast on 5 October. He "conceived, composed and published"

> a Proper Office of the blessed archangel Raphael, of nine readings, with antiphons, responds, collects and chapters, along with a full Mass with appropriate prayers, to be sung, said and celebrated each year for ever in his cathedral church of Exeter and anywhere else in his diocese, . . . together with fitting plain chant and notation.

This liturgy was examined and approved by a panel of leading theologians, and was introduced not only into Lacy's own diocese of Exeter but also into the diocese he had previously presided over, Hereford, where it was celebrated with "an Office of nine Proper readings, with its own hymns and responses, antiphons, versicles, chapters, collects and invitatory, along with a Proper Mass." The collect (prayer) in the Mass was to be in one form during bishop Edmund's life, and another prescribed form after his death. He must have been gratified to see his new Office and Mass also introduced into the diocese of York in what was to be the last year of his life.[12]

[10] John of Avranches, *Liber de officiis ecclesiasticis*, p. 48 (PL 147: 60–61).

[11] Eugenius of Toledo, *Epistula* 3, p. 287.

[12] *The Register of Edmund Lacy, Bishop of Exeter* 2, pp. 295–99; 3, pp. 340–47, 393–96; *The Register of Thomas Spofford, Bishop of Hereford*, pp. 267–79.

The canonization of a new saint immediately required a Mass and Office for that saint. This could be provided in various ways. The simplest was to adapt or borrow wholesale the liturgy of another saint, as happened in one version of the Mass of Thomas Becket, which was simply that of the early martyr Vincent with the names changed.[13] More creatively, when Pope Innocent III proclaimed the canonization of the German empress Cunigunda in 1200, he also specified, in the canonization bull itself, the prayers (collect, secret, and postcommunion) that should henceforth be said in the Mass in her honour.[14] But the pope could not be expected to do this on every occasion, and alternatives were available, including the commissioning of paid specialists. In the summer of 1298, the year following the canonization of Louis IX of France, the French royal accounts show a considerable outlay for payments to clerics for composing an Office for the new saint.[15] On occasion, Offices were composed for uncanonized saints in the hope and expectation that they would eventually be canonized, like that for Richard Rolle of Hampole, which is titled, "The Office of St. Richard the hermit, after he will have been canonized by the Church, for in the meantime it is not allowed to sing the canonical hours for him in church or celebrate his feast."[16]

Not all saints had a Mass or Office specifically devised for them (their Proper Mass or Office), but there were still forms of Mass and Office that could be used for them, for certain liturgical forms were "common," that is, they could be used for a whole class of persons. Thus, alongside Mass and Office for individual saints, there was the Common of the Saints, subdivided by type of saint: martyr-bishops, martyrs not bishops, confessor-bishops, virgin-martyrs, and so on. The celebration of a less important saint could be conducted by using these forms with the addition of the saint's name at the appropriate point.

The preface to the Martyrology ascribed (wrongly) to St. Jerome asserted that there were hundreds of saints to be commemorated every day.[17] While it was clearly not possible to have Masses and Offices for every saint on his or her day, there were two ways that collective celebrations of saints might take place: at the level of the local church, there was the so-called Feast of the Relics, while, at the level of the universal Church, there was the Feast of All Saints.

The Feast of the Relics was a commemoration of all those saints whose relics the church possessed but who were not distinguished by an individual feast-day (or,

[13] Compare BL, Add 46203, fols. 79v–80v (a late-twelfth-century Cistercian Missal, perhaps from Rievaulx) with the text in the *The Gregorian Sacramentary under Charles the Great*, p. 21 (this contains references to all the variable texts); ironically, the Cistercian manuscript prescribes for the feast of St. Vincent on 22 January "all as on the feast of St. Thomas the martyr" (fol. 83).

[14] Petersohn, "Die Litterae Papst Innocenz' III. zur Heiligsprechung der Kaiserin Kunigunde," p. 25.

[15] Gaposchkin, *The Making of Saint Louis*, p. 78.

[16] *The Officium and Miracula of Richard Rolle of Hampole*, p. 12; see, in general, Vauchez, *Sainthood*, pp. 95–99.

[17] *Martyrologium Hieronymianum*, p. 2.

indeed, who were unidentified). The introduction of such a feast is recorded in the *History of the Church of Abingdon*:

> Richard the Sacristan pondered the fact that many saints' relics were preserved in the church, of whom no commemoration was celebrated at that time, and so, with the consent of the abbot and the whole body of monks, he instituted the Tuesday after the two weeks of Easter as the day on which there should be a commemoration of all the relics of this church.[18]

At Abingdon, the Feast of the Relics, because of its dependence on Easter, would thus fall on a different date each year. Similarly, there would be some variation in the date of the Feast of the Relics in the Sarum Use, the most widespread liturgy of late medieval England, since it fell on the Sunday after the translation of Thomas Becket (which was on 7 July), although it had earlier been on a fixed date, 15 September. At the abbey of St.-Germain-des-Prés outside Paris, it fell on the Sunday before Michaelmas (29 September).[19] In 1400, Pope Boniface IX granted an indulgence to all who visited the Dominican church at Roskilde "on the first Sunday after the feast of the Visitation of the Blessed Virgin Mary (2 July), when the Feast of the Relics there is celebrated each year."[20] Frequently, however, the commemoration was on a fixed date. The Feast of the Relics at the Sainte-Chapelle in Paris was 30 September, that of the cathedral of Notre-Dame, 4 December.[21]

From an early date commemorations were held not only of individual martyrs, but also of all the martyrs collectively.[22] These feasts took place in spring, soon after Easter or Pentecost, as in the present-day Greek Church, which celebrates "All Saints Sunday" on the Sunday after Pentecost. Fourth-century evidence shows that the Syrian and Greek churches held general commemorations of this kind, and there is some trace of a similar spring feast in the West.[23] However, by 800, the feast in the West was being celebrated on 1 November.[24] It has been argued that this new date was due to Irish influence, since 1 November was an important traditional (and pre-Christian) festivity in Ireland.[25] Whatever was actually the cause for the adoption of 1 November, by the twelfth century western liturgical experts had their own story about the origin of the feast. According to this explanatory tale, Pope Boniface IV (608–15) had requested and received from the emperor Phocas the Pantheon in Rome a temple dedicated to all the gods, and had converted it into a church dedi-

[18] *Historia Ecclesie Abbendonensis* 2. 278 (2, p. 290); but see the editor's comment, 2, p. cvi.

[19] BnF, lat. 12043 (Diurnale Guillermi abbatis, 1399), fols. 5, 102.

[20] *Diplomatarium Danicum* 4/7 (1399–1400), no. 444, p. 438–39.

[21] Branner, "The Sainte-Chapelle and the Capella Regis in the Thirteenth Century," p. 21.

[22] On the history of the feast of All Saints, see *Martyrologium Romanum*, pp. 488–89.

[23] Ephraem the Syrian, *Carmina Nisibena* 6. 30 (219 [93], p. 27) (German translation); John Chrysostom, *Homilia in sanctos martyres*; Maximus of Turin, *Sermo* 14, pp. 53–55 (wrongly ascribed to Maximus but found in manuscripts of the seventh and eighth centuries).

[24] Alcuin, *Epistola* 193, p. 321.

[25] Hennig, "The Meaning of All the Saints."

cated to the Virgin Mary and all the martyrs—"for the feasts of confessors were not yet celebrated." The dedication feast of this church was in May, but subsequently, according to this report, Pope Gregory IV (827–44) moved the feast to 1 November because at that time there would be better food supplies for the crowds who came to attend, and, at the same time, he extended the feast to all the saints, confessors as well as martyrs.[26]

This account was woven of various elements. The dedication of the Pantheon by Boniface IV is reported in near-contemporary sources and is likely to be historically accurate; this event was commemorated on 13 May, so it fell in the same general season as the Syrian and Greek feast for all the martyrs.[27] By the Carolingian period (the ninth century), liturgical writers were connecting the dedication of the Pantheon to the newly current feast-day of All Saints of 1 November, asserting that the feast had been on this day ever since the time of Boniface IV, and also that the emperor Louis the Pious (814–40) had decreed that it should be celebrated throughout his realm. Neither claim seems to be historical.[28] Later writers, confronting the coexistence of a feast on 13 May and on 1 November then developed their rationalizing theories about a change from a spring to an autumn feast because of the better food supplies.

This piece of liturgical history shows how medieval authors were often themselves in a fog when it came to the development even of major feast-days. What is clear is that from the ninth century the feast of All Saints on 1 November was an important ceremony in the western Church. It gave worshippers the opportunity to make up for any lack in the respect they had shown to the saints. It had been instituted "so that what human frailty had neglected in the celebrations of the saints throughout the year, can today by their merits be relieved."[29] Because the number of saints is almost infinite and humans are weak and time is short, "the church has reasonably ordained that since we cannot celebrate the feasts of all the saints individually, at least we can honour them all generally at the same time."[30]

The liturgy of All Saints day, as found in late medieval service books, has an elaborate structure.[31] Each of the nine readings at Matins was dedicated to a different group: the Trinity, the Virgin Mary, the angels, prophets and patriarchs, apostles, martyrs, confessors, virgins, and all saints. These texts first told the story of Pope Boniface's dedication of the Pantheon and his institution of the new feast, and went on to praise and glorify its subjects: "this beautiful and famous festival is dedicated with honour to all the saints who have been born on the earth since the beginning

[26] Honorius Augustodunensis, *Speculum ecclesie*, cols. 1021–22; John Beleth, *Summa de ecclesiasticis officiis* 127, pp. 242–43.

[27] *Liber pontificalis* 1, p. 317; Bede, *Chronica maiora*, p. 310.

[28] Ado of Vienne, *Martyrologium*, p. 371 (PL 123: 387); Quentin, *Les martyrologes historiques*, pp. 636–41.

[29] Ut quicquid toto anno humana fragilitas in celebrationibus sanctorum neglexisset, eorum meritis possit hodie relaxari: Honorius Augustodunensis, *Speculum ecclesie*, col. 1022.

[30] Jacobus de Voragine, *Legenda aurea* 158 ("De festivitate omnium sanctorum") (2, p. 1101).

[31] *Breviarium ad usum insignis ecclesiae Sarum* 3 *(Sanctorale)*, cols. 959–82.

of the world"—the twelve apostles, "whom divine providence chose to build the foundations of the new faith and raise up the Church, still young and tender"; the martyrs, "triumphant friends of God"; the confessor-saints "who watered the hearts of the faithful with spiritual showers . . . and, although they did not feel the sword of the persecutors, nevertheless through merit of their life are not deprived of a martyrdom worthy of God, for martyrdom is achieved not only through the shedding of blood but also through abstinence from sin and following God's commandments"; and "the chorus of holy virgins," who were begged "to intercede for us with the Lord." The second Vespers of All Saints was followed immediately by the beginning of the feast of All Souls—those who were prayed *for* succeeding those who were prayed *to*.

The Hierarchy of Feast-days

Not all church festivals were of equal importance, and it was explicitly recognized that some feasts were to be celebrated with a greater degree of solemnity than others—God approved the custom of giving honour to his saints, "but to some more than to others."[32] In the eleventh century, writing of the saints, John of Avranches explained that, "although they enjoy one and the same glory in the kingdom of God, nevertheless we should celebrate their feast-days according to their priority in order and the proximity of their bodies," that is, according to their status and whether their relics were nearby.[33]

Formal systems of grading feast-days developed gradually, varying from region to region and from religious community to religious community. From an early time some feast-days were marked out by vigils, which were a ritual commemoration on the night preceding the festival, or an Octave, the matching celebration a week after the feast. The saints' days dignified in this way were either those of the greater saints or those of local significance (John of Avranches's "priority" and "proximity"). Writing of Octaves, the Carolingian liturgical writer Amalarius of Metz explained this selectivity and variety:

> We have the custom of celebrating the Octaves of the feast-days of some saints, namely, those whose feast is more renowned amongst us, such as is the case with the Octaves of the apostles Peter and Paul, and of other saints whose Octaves the custom of various churches celebrates.[34]

Gregory of Tours preserves a list of those feast-days celebrated with vigils in his own church of Tours. Alongside the major festivals of Christmas, Epiphany, Easter, Ascension Day, and Pentecost (as well as the more unusual celebration of the Resurrection on the fixed date of 27 March), the following saints' days were distinguished in

[32] *Synodicon Hispanum* 4: *Ciudad Rodrigo, Salamanca y Zamora*, p. 43 (Salamanca, 1396).
[33] John of Avranches, *De officiis ecclesiasticis*, p. 46 (PL 147: 59).
[34] Amalarius of Metz, *Liber officialis* 4. 36, pp. 516–17 (PL 105: 1228).

this way: John the Baptist (both his birthday and his death), Peter's Chair, Peter and Paul, Martin (two feast-days), Symphorian, Litorius, Bricius, Hilary.[35] These saints are either great New Testament figures, or saints of central Gaul: the early martyr Symphorian of Autun, the fourth-century bishops Hilary of Poitiers, and Litorius and Martin of Tours, and Martin's successor, Bricius. Hence, to adapt Amalarius's words about Octaves, some are "more renowned" and others celebrated by "the custom of various churches." In the twelfth century the liturgical writer John Beleth noted that only Stephen and Lawrence among martyr-saints and Martin among the confessor-saints have Octaves (he presumably includes such saints as Peter and Paul among apostles rather than martyrs), but says that even when a saint does not have a prescribed Octave, as in the case of Nicholas or Mary Magdalene, it is still permissible for a church dedicated to that saint to celebrate the Octave.[36] Conscientious Christians might fast on the vigil of a major feast-day, and miracles frequently took place in the church during the night of the vigils.

The Octave extended the special commemoration of the saint to a whole week, and could be taken advantage of in various ways. For example, it was possible to grant indulgences for this longer period, as happened in the case of the shrine of St. Bede junior (to be distinguished from the Anglo-Saxon historian) in the church of St. Benignus at Genoa. Pope Innocent IV, who was himself Genoese, issued a bull for the church in 1247. In this he writes,

> desiring that your church, where the body of Bede the priest rests (as you say), should be frequented with fitting honour, we remit forty days of the enjoined penance for all who, truly penitent and confessed, visit the church on the feast-day or up to eight days after the feast.[37]

Miraculous cures were common on the vigils of a feast-day, with its excited night-time atmosphere, and could also occur on an Octave, as in the case of poor crippled girl from the region of Florennes, south-west of Namur. Her parents brought her to the local shrine of St. Gengulph on the feast-day of the saint, but, although they prayed for her and made offerings, she was not cured. They returned home sadly. A week later, on the Octave of the feast, the girl's father was in his house, and uttered an impassioned prayer to Gengulph:

> My lord, St. Gengulph, you are always available for others, you spurn me alone and I know it is because of my sins. I brought my child to your feast-day but it did not please you to cure her. But, lo, now it is your Octave. I believe that if you wish you can bring help now just as well as then.

[35] Gregory of Tours, *Libri historiarum X* 10. 31, p. 530; on the 27 March festival, see Graviers, "L'expression 'dominicae resurrectionis dies' dans les oeuvres de Grégoire de Tours."

[36] John Beleth, *Summa de ecclesiasticis officiis* 145d, 163c, 135c, pp. 281, 321, 261.

[37] AASS Aprilis 1 (1675): 873 (13 December 1247); the letter does not appear to be recorded in the papal registers or in Potthast.

The next thing he heard was his daughter calling out, "Father! Father! Come and see!," for she was suddenly fully healed.[38]

Sometimes there is explicit evidence about how and when an Octave was added to a feast. A handbook to the customs of the great Burgundian monastery of Cluny explained, "the fact that we celebrate the feast-day of St. Martin with an Octave goes back to the first abbot of our place, the lord Odo, who came from Tours and was a child of St. Martin"—that is, a devotee of the most famous saint of Tours.[39] Thirteenth-century tradition ascribed the introduction (or re-introduction) of the Feast of the Octave of the Birth of the Virgin Mary to Pope Innocent IV. The story goes that, after the death of Pope Gregory IX in 1241, the cardinals were unable to agree on a successor. To put pressure on them to make up their minds, they were locked up in unpleasant conditions. After weeks of stifling heat and inadequate food, they vowed that if the Virgin Mary were able to bring them to agreement, they would reinstitute celebration of the Octave of her birth. Soon afterwards they elected Celestine IV, but, since he died a very short time later, it was left to his successor, Innocent IV, to fulfil the promise to the Virgin.[40]

Apart from vigils and Octaves, there were other ways of marking out feasts, such as the number of readings at Matins. Benedictine churches had either three or twelve, most other great churches three or nine, and in both cases the feast of twelve or nine lessons was of greater prestige. Feasts are sometimes recorded as "in cappis," that is, to be celebrated by the clergy in copes. These distinctions grew ever more detailed and systematic, and by the later Middle Ages an elaborate system of grading feast-days had become general.

Lanfranc of Canterbury, in the late eleventh century, distinguished three levels of solemnity: first, "five principal feast-days," namely Christmas, Easter, Pentecost, the Assumption of the Virgin Mary, and the "the feast-day of the house" (presumably of the monastery's patron saint); second, "other feast-days, which are celebrated solemnly but not at the same level," seventeen in number and including both important commemorations of the life of Christ, such as Ascension, and the days of major saints like John the Baptist, or saints of local significance like Augustine of Canterbury; third, "feast-days of the third rank," sixteen of which are named, including mostly commemorations of the apostles.[41] Lanfranc's system is fairly straightforward, but by the later thirteenth century the terminology had become more technical: the great liturgist William Durandus the elder classes feast-days as "wholly double, simply double, semi-double, and simple."[42] "Doubling" refers to the fact that

[38] Gonzo, *Miracula sancti Gengulphi* 3. 28, pp. 653–54 (eleventh century).

[39] Ulric of Cluny, *Antiquiores consuetudines cluniacensis monasterii* 1. 43, col. 689.

[40] Bartholomew of Trent, *Liber epilogorum in gesta sanctorum* 298, pp. 283–84; Jacobus de Voragine, *Legenda aurea* 127 (2, p. 907); in the twelfth century, John Beleth, *Summa de ecclesiasticis officiis* 146, p. 283, says that only the Assumption among the Marian feasts has an Octave.

[41] Lanfranc, *Decreta Lanfranci*, pp. 55–67.

[42] In totum duplex; simpliciter duplex; semiduplex; simplex: William Durandus, *Rationale divinorum officiorum* 7. 1. 31 (140B, p. 22).

TABLE 6.1
Liturgical Systems of St.-Martial of Limoges and St.-Martin of Tulle

St.-Martial of Limoges	St.-Martin of Tulle
First class	12 lessons, in copes, with a procession
In copes	12 lessons, in copes
All in albs	12 lessons, double
Two in albs	12 lessons, in hoods
12 lessons	12 lessons
8 lessons	8 lessons
3 lessons	3 lessons
Commemoration	Commemoration

the antiphon, a short piece of chant, was sung both before and after each Psalm in the service, rather than just afterwards, as was usual.

These terms became common, although with variations according to region and Order. At Wrocław (Breslau) in Silesia feasts were graded "triple, double, of nine lessons, of three lessons, commemoration." The Dominicans adopted a system of "wholly double, double, simple, of three lessons, commemoration."[43] Even neighbouring churches of the same Order might show differences. Table 6.1 compares the grading system of St.-Martial of Limoges and St.-Martin of Tulle, both of them old Benedictine monasteries about forty miles apart, as found in the fourteenth century. The underlying structural similarity co-exists with variations in terminology and practice.[44]

Feasts might be raised in status for particular reasons, as, for example, in Florence, where a vigil was added to the feast of St. Philip and St. James after the city acquired one of Philip's arms in 1215.[45] And sometimes we hear of individuals lobbying for the elevation of a feast, like Ralph of Cornwall, a chaplain of St. Paul's, London, in the early thirteenth century, at whose "devout request" the feasts of St. Catherine and St. Mary Magdalene had been "doubled," that is raised from "simple" to "double."[46] Not all such campaigns bore fruit. Pope Gregory VII supposedly ordained that the feast-days of all martyr-popes should be celebrated

[43]Grotefend, *Zeitrechnung des deutschen Mittelatters und der Neuzeit* 2/1, pp. 23–28: Wroclaw—festum triplex, duplex, novem lectionum, trium lectionum, commemoratio; 2/2, pp. 34–37: Dominicans—totum duplex, duplex, simplex, trium lectionum, memoria.

[44]Dubois and Lemaitre, *Sources et méthodes de l'hagiographie médiévale*, p. 148.

[45]Brand, "The Vigils of Medieval Tuscany" p. 32 n. 38.

[46]*Early Charters of the Cathedral Church of St Paul, London*, no. 306, p. 245.

everywhere with a full Office, but there is no trace of such an ambitious project being implemented.[47]

As mentioned earlier, the ritual year of medieval Christendom was structured by interlocking rhythms: the weekly holy day of Sunday; the great annual Christian feasts celebrating Christ's birth (Christmas) and resurrection (Easter); and the feast-days of the saints. Christmas and saints' days fell on the same date each year but Easter, and the other feast-days dependent on it, such as Whitsun (Pentecost) or the Ascension, were "moveable." The interplay of Sundays, moveable feasts, and fixed feasts made for a complex pattern. Rules were developed about how to deal with an overlap between holy days. When a feast of lesser standing coincided with a feast (or season) of higher standing, it was "overshadowed," and was not celebrated with the solemnity that would otherwise be due to it—"rather as if a friend of the king should come with the king, and not receive such deference as if he came alone, because of the presence of the king."[48]

One way to mark a lesser feast which coincided with a greater, was through a "commemoration," that is, the insertion of part of the service of the lesser feast into the service of the greater feast. The general principle, as stated in the late eleventh century, was that "When two feasts of nine lessons coincide on the same day, both of which should be celebrated with a full Office, we observe the more important of them fully, and the other only with a commemoration.[49] This simple rule might, however, require further elaboration. The following is an example, from a fifteenth-century Italian liturgical hand-book:

> If the feast of St. Mark the Evangelist or another feast falls on a Sunday, one celebrates the Office of the feast, with a commemoration of Sunday. But if these feasts fall on the Sunday of the Octave of Easter, which is called Sunday *in albis*, or within the Octave of Easter, then one does not celebrate the feast but transfers it to the Monday after Sunday *in albis*, unless the church is dedicated to that saint. In that case, if it falls on the Sunday, one celebrates the feast of that saint with commemoration of Sunday at both vespers and matins. And the nine lessons will be read from the Sunday homily.[50]

The situation here involves several things: the fixed saint's day, with St. Mark's (25 April) as a chief example; the moveable feast of Easter and its following week; and the unrelated pattern of Sundays and weekdays. Since the latest date on which Easter can fall is 25 April, it would not be uncommon for St. Mark's day to occur in the following week. Moreover, in this text the dedication of the church is an added complication. The rule here is that St. Mark's day takes precedence over a Sunday, except in

[47] Bernold of Constance, *Micrologus de ecclesiasticis observationibus* 43, col. 1010; on authorship, see Bäumer, "Der Micrologus."

[48] John Beleth, *Summa de ecclesiasticis officiis* 128, p. 244.

[49] Bernold of Constance, *Micrologus de ecclesiasticis observationibus* 42, col. 1009.

[50] BL, Add. 10788, fols. 11–11v.

the week after Easter when the church is not dedicated to St. Mark. One can imagine that such rules could be confusing and require specialist handbooks.

One of the richest sources to inform us of which saints were remembered in any given community is the liturgical Kalendar, a list of the days of the year frequently prefaced to a Psalter and with indication of which saints were commemorated, often showing the grading of feast-days, sometimes by use of gold or red ink (hence the expression "red-letter day"). Hundreds of Kalendars survive from the Middle Ages. While it cannot simply be assumed that a Kalendar reflects the liturgical practice of the religious community that produced it, since Kalendars and entries could be borrowed or become fossilized, it usually bears marks of locality and period.[51] For example, the inclusion in a Kalendar of St. Segolena, virgin, on 24 July; St. Eugenius, bishop, on 6 September; and St. Carissima, virgin, on 7 September, points almost definitively to Albi in southern France.[52] In another Kalendar, the unusual entry of "the Translation of St. Montanus" on 16 May moves the scene to north-east France, and, indeed, the manuscript containing this Kalendar comes from Laon.[53] This Laon book ranks the feast-days by use of red ink, by indicating vigils and Octaves, and by specifying grade: "annual feast" (*festum annuale)*, "double," nine lessons, three lessons, commemoration (some feasts had three lessons usually but nine if on a Sunday). It also frequently specifies where the readings should be drawn from: the Office, the Life, the Passion if a martyr, and sometimes from other sources, such as Paul's epistles or the exposition of the Gospels.

There are a few examples of Kalendars which, unusually, were designed for another use, as a guide to where to find saints' Lives in the library, rather than for any liturgical purpose. A ninth-century Kalendar from the great monastery of St. Gallen notes after each saint's name the volume that contains his or her Life: "in the larger Passionary," "in Ebo's collection," and so on.[54] Another example comes from an unidentified English Cistercian house. The Kalendar is quite normal in form, but after each saints' name there is the shelf mark of the book (for example, "B XXI," "G III") where that saint's Life could be found, as is explained by an inscription in the Kalendar itself: "This Kalendar serves just for finding the Lives or Passions of the saint written in various books."[55]

[51] "The appearance of a saint in a calendar, let alone a litany, is no proof that the person will in fact be honoured on his or her 'day' ": Pfaff, *The Liturgy in Medieval England*, p. 214.

[52] Albi, Médiathèque municipale Pierre Almaric d'Albi, Ms. 5 (olim Bibliothèque municipale 150), fols. 1–6v (consulted on-line); the contents are described in Rivière, "Deux calendriers liturgiques de l'église cathédrale d'Albi," pp. 70–77. Segolena and Carissima were early (and largely legendary) female saints of Albi. Eugenius was a bishop of Carthage who died at Albi in 505; Gregory of Tours records miracles at his tomb there: Gregory of Tours, *Libri historiarum X* 2. 3, p. 44. The celebration of Eugenius's feast-day on 6 September was a local peculiarity: AASS Julii 3 (1723): 497–98. The same saints occur in Cambridge, Corpus Christi College 540, a fourteenth-century Book of Hours from the south of France.

[53] Laon, Bibliothèque municipale 254, fols. 1–6v, a fourteenth-century breviary.

[54] St. Gallen, Stiftsbibliothek, Cod. Sang. 566, pp. 2–21.

[55] Proud, "Collections of Saints' Lives in the Thirteenth and Fourteenth Centuries"; the manuscript is Oxford, Bodleian Library, Rawlinson C 440.

In the later Middle Ages, as Books of Hours for private devotion proliferated, the Kalendar assumed a new function. Prefaced to these private books, it was no longer a guide to collective worship, but a reminder, for the pious individual who owned it, of the saint to be contemplated that day. The Kalendars of some Books of Hours took a particular form, with one saint (and no more) for each day. The choice of saints to be included in these daily lists could vary enormously. For instance, the Kalendars prefixed to two fifteenth-century Books of Hours now in the British Library, one in French, one in Dutch, show much more divergence than similarity, even though they are the same type of book and from the same period.[56] The two Kalendars have in common 153 saints or festivals on the same or adjacent days (representing 42 per cent of the 365 days). This means that well over half of the entries differ (although sometimes the same saint crops up on very different days in the two books). The saints in common are New Testament figures or events (45 in number, so about 12.5 per cent of the total for the year); early martyrs, some historically well attested figures like Agnes, Polycarp, and Vincent, others, such as Catherine, largely legendary; and some of the great names of the early medieval Church, especially those from Merovingian Gaul (Augustine, Martin, Remigius, Gertrude of Nivelles). The only saints in this common core who lived later than the year 1000 are Bernard of Clairvaux, Thomas Becket, Dominic, Elizabeth of Thuringia, and Thomas Aquinas. The Dutch Book of Hours marks 51 feasts in red, while the Kalendar of the French volume has 42 feasts marked in gold. Many of these (32) are the same, but there are also some informative differences: the French Kalendar marks the feast-days of St. Charlemagne and St. Louis, king of France, in gold, while neither of these even appears in the Dutch book; the Dutch book gives its highest ranking to Pontianus, Servatius, Boniface, Odulf, Lebuin, Lambert, and Willibrord, all of them saints connected with Utrecht, of whom only one, Boniface, occurs in the French book. The two books thus illustrate both the deep common roots of late medieval devotion to the saints and also the variety of its exuberant local efflorescence.

Even richer in saints' names than the Kalendar is the litany of the saints.[57] There is a sense in which the litany represents the essence of the cult of the saints—the invocation of a name. It is, indeed, simply a list of names, followed by the repeated entreaty, "Pray for us!" The list could be extremely long. For example, the litany of the saints in the little prayer book probably made for archbishop Arnulf II of Milan (998–1018) contains 454 names (and some of the text is missing).[58] It is clear that there could not be full liturgical celebration of these 454 saints, but the choice of saints in litanies, as in Kalendars, usually gives some indication of local preferences and of changes over time. For instance, the appearance of Samson, bishop of Dol, and Corentinus, bishop of Quimper, in a litany immediately suggests a book made in

[56] BL, Add. 4836, fols. 1–12v; BL, Add. 17354, fols. 2–13v.

[57] Coens, "Anciennes litanies des saints"; *Anglo-Saxon Litanies of the Saints*; Krüger, *Litanei-Handschriften der Karolingerzeit*.

[58] BL, Egerton MS 3763, fols. 126v–136v.

or for Brittany, while the rise of St. Anne, mother of the Virgin Mary, to a new popularity in the west in the later Middle Ages can be tracked by her mention in litanies.[59]

There were a few saints whose feast-day did not fall on the anniversary of their death, the most important being John the Baptist, whose midsummer feast-day (24 June), coinciding with the old summer solstice, marked his birth not his execution (which was commemorated separately on 29 August). The exceptional nature of John's feast-day was very early, being noted by St. Augustine preaching on that day: "The Church celebrates the birthday in the flesh of no prophet, patriarch or apostle; she celebrates only two, this and Christ's."[60] St. John's Day, coinciding as it did with the solstice, was a major secular as well as liturgical feast, celebrated with bonfires and other ceremonies (Augustine was critical of the practice of lighting such bonfires, which he viewed as a diabolical and pagan custom).[61] In Byzantium the fires were used as part of a fortune-telling ritual, at least until the practice was banned by the clergy in the twelfth century.[62] The fifteenth-century English writer John Mirk explains that

> In the worship of Saint John, men wake at even and make three manner of fires: one is clean bones and no wood, and is called a bonfire; another is of clean wood and no bones and is called a wake-fire, for men sit and wake by it; the third is made of bones and wood, and is called St. John's fire.[63]

Medieval liturgical writers also noted that the feast of St. Stephen on 26 December and that of John the evangelist on 27 December were unusual in not commemorating the saint's death, and developed (not very convincing) explanations of why this should be so:

> the Passion of St. Stephen took place on the day in August when the discovery of his relics is celebrated (3 August), and the discovery of his relics took place on the day after Christmas, but, because the feast of the Passion is more significant, it was moved to Christmas time.[64]

[59] For Samson and Corentinus, Geneva, Bibliothèque de Genève, Ms. lat. 33, fol. 112v (consulted online). St. Anne occurs only once in a Carolingian litany (Krüger, *Litanei-Handschriften der Karolingerzeit*, p. 448) and, revealingly, of the three entries for Anne in Michael Lapidge's comprehensive edition, *Anglo-Saxon Litanies of the Saints*, pp. 117, 199, 216, all are post-Conquest additions to the manuscripts.

[60] Augustine, *Sermo* 287 (PL 38: 1301); cf. *Sermo* 292 (PL 38: 1319–20).

[61] Augustine, *Sermones post Maurinos reperti, Sermo* 293B, pp. 227–31, variant in PL 46: 996, "Hesterno die post vesperam putrescentibus flammis antiquitus more daemoniorum tota civitas flagrabat."

[62] For the bonfires, John Beleth, *Summa de ecclesiasticis officiis* 137, p. 267; Petrus Comestor, *Historia scholastica, Evangelica* 73, col. 1574; Ernoul, *Chronique d'Ernoul et de Bernard le Trésorier*, p. 113. For Byzantine custom, Rhalles and Potles, *Syntagma tōn theion kai hierōn kanonōn tōn te hagiōn kai paneuphēmōn Apostolōn* 2, p. 459 (Balsamon's commentary on the canons of the Trullan Council).

[63] Mirk, *Festial* 44 (1, p. 166).

[64] John Beleth, *Summa de ecclesiasticis officiis* 70d, p. 131; cf. ibid. 143, pp. 278–79; Honorius Augustodunensis, *Sacramentarium* 92, col. 797; idem, *Speculum ecclesiae*, col. 832. The evidence for Stephen's post-Christmas feast is early (Gregory of Nyssa, *In Basilium fratrem*, p. 109 [PG 46: 789]), but it was also claimed that 26 December commemorates his translation in 415 (*Revelatio Sancti Stephani*, p. 214).

the dormition of St. John the Evangelist is on the nativity of John the Baptist, but, since it cannot be celebrated then, it is done here.[65]

Other feasts not on the anniversary of the death include feasts commemorating the translation of relics and, in the case of bishops and abbots, the date of ordination. The ordination of Pope Gregory I, for example, on 29 or 30 March occurs in half of surviving Anglo-Saxon Kalendars.[66] The dedication of a church could generate a feast for the saint: St. Michael's feast on 29 September commemorates the dedication on that day of a church of St. Michael in Rome, at some time in the sixth century (it would be awkward to celebrate either the birth or death of an angel). And, as already mentioned, the feast of All Saints was also associated with the dedication of a Roman church.

A feast-day usually, however, commemorated the death of a saint, not something that could be planned to the day, although, as mentioned earlier (p. 55), the hagiographer telling of the murder of St. Wenceslas noted that the assassins had to postpone their attack by a day: "God the governor prevented them from accomplishing it, perhaps because He chose to sanctify the following day, which had no feast on it." But mortal men might also have some choice, and, if there was any chance of controlling the date of a feast, efforts were made to stop it being entangled with the major annual celebrations of the church year. For example, when Innocent IV canonized the murdered Dominican inquisitor Peter Martyr in 1253, he commanded, "since the day of his passion was 6 April, which frequently falls amidst the celebrations for Easter, his feast-day should be celebrated on 29 April."[67]

Sometimes the date of a feast-day was changed. There is an unusually explicit example from late medieval Cornwall, involving not the feast-day of the local saint, St. Dominica, but the day of the dedication of her church. The bishop of Exeter allowed the feast of the dedication to be removed from 30 August to 9 May, because the former date was very inconvenient for the harvest, "being at a time when our parishioners are extremely busy gathering and storing the autumn crops, which have been brought forth by heavenly providence to support human life, since it is the middle of the harvest season."[68] A similar case occurs in the Salisbury Statutes of 1319, which changed the Feast of the Relics from 15 September to the Sunday after the Translation of Thomas Becket (7 July), mentioning as one ground the demands of agricultural labour in September.[69] Such readjustments of the ritual to the farming year are rarely spelt out in this way.

[65] Honorius Augustodunensis, *Sacramentarium* 92, col. 797. The *Notitia de locis sanctorum apostolorum*, p. 2, records "Natale dormitionis sancti Iohannis apostoli et evangelistae in Epheso" on 24 June, while the *Festa apostolorum*, pp. 2–3, gives two variant dates for John on 27 December and 24 June. Both texts were frequently prefixed to the pseudo-Jerome Martyrology.

[66] Rushforth, *Saints in English Kalendars*.

[67] Ambrogio Taegio, *Vita sancti Petri martyris* 6. 45, pp. 700–701.

[68] *The Register of Edmund Lacy, Bishop of Exeter* 2, pp. 336–37.

[69] "Occupatio rerum rusticarum": *Statuta et Consuetudines Ecclesiæ Cathedralis Beatæ Mariæ Virginis Sarisberiensis*, pp. 246–48; *The Registers of Roger Martival, Bishop of Salisbury* 2, pp. 293–94.

Saints' Days and Local Identity

On the feast-day of St. Zenobius, one of the patrons of Florence, all the clergy of the city assembled in the cathedral, which had been carefully cleaned and decorated, and the choir sang to their special protector: "Zenobius, shining so brightly throughout the world, do not spurn the vows of your Florentines"—they were "*your* Florentines."[70] Because different saints were commemorated in different places and at different times, the pattern of saintly cult became a strong expression of local and regional identity. The local variation could be on a small scale, marking out one town or village or parish from another, while, at the broadest level, it distinguished the major Christian traditions, East and West.

In 1166 the Byzantine emperor Manuel Comnenus issued legislation regulating which days of the year meetings of the law-courts might take place.[71] He had been worried by the proliferation of holidays and hence his list of days on which the courts could not meet is intended to limit their number. Even so, it is long. Apart from general prohibitions such as bans on court meetings on Sundays and during the Christmas and Easter seasons (the former containing several important saints' days that consequently the law does not itemize), he lists sixty-five whole holidays and twenty-eight half-holidays. Of the former, six are Marian feasts, and fifty-five relate to New Testament events and figures, mainly the apostles; the remaining four are the feasts of John Chrysostom; Athanasius and Cyril; Gregory the Theologian (that is, Gregory of Nazianzus); and Helen and Constantine. Of the half-holidays, five are Marian or New Testament, two are dedicated to angels, one commemorates the Old Testament prophet Elijah, while the remaining twenty celebrate early Greek martyrs or church leaders. The latest saint in the whole list is Stephen the Younger, a monk executed in 764 or 765 during the Iconoclastic period. Apart from the Virgin Mary, there are few female saints in the list: Anne, the Virgin's mother; the empress Helen; and, amongst the half-holidays, the martyrs Barbara and Euphemia.

The divergences between feast-days celebrated in East and West can be illustrated by comparing this list with that in the Decretals of 1234, the first officially sanctioned papal lawbook, which contain a ruling of Pope Gregory IX that law-suits should be suspended on religious feast-days. He then gives a list of these festivals: Christmas, St. Stephen, St. John the Evangelist, Holy Innocents, St. Silvester, Circumcision, Epiphany, Easter (with the weeks before and after), Ascension, Pentecost (with the two following days), the Nativity of John the Baptist, all the feasts of the Virgin Mary and of the twelve apostles (especially Peter and Paul), St. Lawrence, St. Michael, All Saints, and all Sundays. In addition, there are "the other festivals which the individual bishops have determined should be celebrated with solemnities

[70] Brand, "The Vigils of Medieval Tuscany," p. 40.

[71] Macrides, "Justice under Manuel Komnenos," pp. 148–55.

in their dioceses."[72] The pope's text draws on earlier legislation as far back as the ninth century, which specifies an almost identical list of feast-days.[73]

The western list contains a fixed and intense period of feast-days in midwinter, from Christmas on 25 December to the Feast of the Circumcision on 1 January, with Epiphany following on 6 January; also a major spring festival, Easter, which could fall in March or April, with Ascension and Pentecost respectively forty days and fifty days later; and midsummer marked by St. John's day on 24 June, the old summer solstice. These all have some natural as well as ecclesiastical meaning. The other saints' days mentioned are more arbitrary: Peter and Paul on 29 June, Lawrence on 10 August, Michael ("Michaelmas") on 29 September, All Saints on 1 November. The main Marian feasts ranged from February to December.

Christians inherited a common pool of saints—the Apostles, the Virgin Mary, the more prominent of the early martyrs—but there was always a strong countercurrent of localism. Martyrs might have a reputation only in one city or region, and the new saints of the post-Constantinian period were not all known and recognized across the whole of Christendom. An idea of the mixture of universal and particular in the liturgical cycle can be gained from the list of non-moveable commemorations in the Visigothic Church of Spain, as contained in the so-called *Oracional* of c. 700.[74] Of the thirty-six services listed, fifteen relate to biblical figures, such as the apostles, and events of universal significance, like Christmas; eleven concern early martyrs from outside Spain; nine are for early Spanish martyrs; while a solitary feast marked the great confessor-saint of Gaul, Martin. The balance, considered simply numerically, is clearly towards the common heritage of the Church, as expressed in the New Testament and the deeds of the early martyrs, but, on the other hand, the inclusion of nine Spanish martyrs shows that the tradition expressed in this volume was a Spanish one. When we consider the cult of the saints, we almost always see local or regional identity coexisting in this way with a sense of the shared collective identity of the Church as a whole. The replacement of the local liturgy of Spain by the Roman liturgy in the eleventh century was one aspect of the fundamental cultural reorientation that the peninsula underwent at that time.[75]

The written record of saints acknowledged at a particular church might build up new layers over time. Two manuscripts from Exeter cathedral, in south-west England, can illustrate the way that this happened. One of them is an early-twelfth-century martyrology.[76] Its core of entries stems from the Martyrology of Usuard,

[72] *Decretales Gregorii IX* 2. 9. 5, *Conquestus est nobis*, cols. 272–73 (dated 1227–34).

[73] Haito of Basel, *Capitula* 8, p. 212; Burchard, *Decretum* 2. 77, col. 640; Ivo of Chartes, *Decretum* 4. 14, cols. 226–27; Gratian, *Decretum* 3 (de consecratione) 3. 1, col. 1353. Haito and Gregory omit Martin's feast-day, the others include it.

[74] *El Oracional Visigótico*, from Verona, Biblioteca Capitular 89; García Rodríguez, *El culto de los santos en la España romana y visigoda*, p. 53.

[75] There is a detailed study in Walker, *Views of Transition: Liturgy and Illumination in Medieval Spain*.

[76] Exeter Cathedral Library, MS 3518; described in Ker, *Medieval Manuscripts in British Libraries* 2, p. 815; see also Doble, *Some Remarks on the Exeter Martyrology*.

written in the mid-ninth century by a monk of St.-Germain in Paris. The original text in the Exeter manuscript has, as well as the entries from Usuard, notes about saints of interest to an English community. For instance, the entry for 23 June reads as follows:

> The vigil of St. John the Baptist. On the same day, the feast of St. John the priest, whom the wicked Julian ordered to be beheaded unheard, on the old Via Salaria, before an idol of the sun. In Tuscany in the city of Utrina, the feast of St. Felix the priest, whose mouth the prefect Turtius ordered for a long time to be crushed with a stone until he gave up his spirit. In Great Britain in the island called Ely the feast of St. Etheldreda the virgin whose body was found incorrupt when she had been buried for sixteen years. On the same day in Winchester the feast of St. Judoc the confessor.[77]

The first three entries concern a great biblical saint and two Roman martyrs (neither of them very well known). Then follows an entry of interest to English readers, on the early Saxon virgin saint Etheldreda. Most of this entry is in Usuard, so it is not exclusively an English tradition, but the Exeter text adds geographical information: specifying "Great" Britain (to distinguish it from Brittany, an area also of interest to a community in Exeter) and naming the Isle of Ely. The Exeter entry also gives the correct time-span, "sixteen years," for Etheldreda's first inhumation, whereas many continental manuscripts of Usuard give other readings. The final entry, about St. Judoc, is not found in Usuard's text, and is an insertion of local interest: Judoc was a Breton saint whose relics were claimed to be housed in Winchester cathedral. Both the Breton and the Wessex connection might explain the interest in this saint in Exeter.

This martyrology, made up as it already is of different layers of tradition, has also been supplemented by two kinds of additions, entered in the margins or at the end of the original entries. Most numerous are the "obits," records of the day of death of those associated with the cathedral, usually canons but also benefactors and others.[78] But there are also additions relating to the saints. Under 26 July, St. Anne, mother of the Virgin Mary, is added in late medieval handwriting, an addition which fits very well with what is known of the great expansion of her cult in the West in the years after 1200. Under 30 September, there is an addition to the original entry about St. Jerome, noting that he was "a doctor and cardinal of the Roman Church." The pope formally proclaimed Jerome's status as doctor in 1298 (see p. 187), and depictions of him as a cardinal date only from the mid-fourteenth century.[79] Under 4 October there is an entry added in the margin: "On the same day in Assisi, the feast-day of St. Francis the confessor, the founder and first Minister of the Order of Friars Minor." In this way, the list of saints recorded at this English cathedral was updated,

[77] Exeter Cathedral Library, MS 3518, fol. 29v.

[78] These are edited by Lepine and Orme, *Death and Memory in Medieval Exeter*, pp. 250–58.

[79] BS 6, col. 1134; Réau, *Iconographie de l'art chrétien* 3/2, p. 742.

by the addition of newly significant (though ancient) saints, by the incorporation of new legends about ancient saints, and by the inclusion of the new saints of the later Middle Ages.

Likewise, the Kalendar of another Exeter manuscript, prefaced, as was common, to a Psalter, shows evidence of updating.[80] Additions include St. Gabriel (the archangel); St. Francis (as in the martyrology); St. Edmund Rich of Abingdon; and St. Barbara.[81] Francis and Edmund Rich were new saints of the thirteenth century, Barbara one of the legendary early virgin martyrs whose cults blossomed in the later Middle Ages. Gabriel is more unusual, and there is evidence in this case that a particular bishop of Exeter promoted the cult.[82]

A similar local imprint can be seen in the statutes of the collegiate church of St. Aphrodisius (Aphrodise) in Béziers, drawn up in 1307. These specified that the bells should be rung on the following feast-days: All Saints, Christmas, St. Stephen, St. John the Evangelist, Circumcision, Epiphany, Candlemas, Peter's Chair, Annunciation, Easter, Aphrodisius, Ascension, Pentecost, John the Baptist, Peter and Paul, Peter's Chains, Assumption, Nativity of the Virgin Mary, the dedication of the church of St. Aphrodisius, Holy Trinity.[83] The inclusion in this list of the feasts of St. Aphrodisius and the dedication of his church placed these local markers of identity on the same symbolic level as the great feasts of the Incarnation and the major biblical saints. Three years later the canons of St. Aphrodisius added a significant supplement:

> We decree and ordain that two of the great bells shall in future be rung on the feast-days of St. Lawrence, St. Martial, St. Gerald and the Invention of St. Stephen, to whose honour and veneration altars have been specially set up in our church.[84]

Both Martial and Gerald had a strong regional identity in the south of France, and the public bell-ringing was here being brought into conformity with the pattern of piety already represented by the supplementary altars in the church.

[80] Exeter Cathedral Library, MS 3508; described in Ker, *Medieval Manuscripts in British Libraries* 2, p. 815.

[81] 24 March: St. Gabriel (fol. 6); 4 October: St. Francis (fol. 9v); 16 November: St. Edmund Rich of Abingdon (fol. 10); 16 December: St. Barbara (fol. 10v)—although her feast-day is more usually 4 December, she also occurs on this day in an eleventh-century Kalendar from Salisbury, BL, Cotton Vitellius A. xii, fol. 71 (Rushforth, *Saints in English Kalendars*).

[82] Orme, *English Church Dedications*, pp. 37, 205.

[83] *Documents sur l'ancienne province de Languedoc* 1, pp. 163–64, 167. The position of Holy Trinity in this list shows that it was celebrated on the Sunday before Advent, a variant from the more usual Sunday after Pentecost (which was also known as "Trinity in Summer," to distinguish it). Celebration on the Sunday before Advent is recorded, for example, in Auxerre and Reichenau and in Lanfranc's *Constitutions*: *Gesta pontificum Autissiodorensium* 59 (2, p. 253) (PL 138: 339); Berno of Reichenau, *Qualiter adventus Domini celebretur* 3, col. 1084; Lanfranc, *Decreta Lanfranci*, p. 8.

[84] *Documents sur l'ancienne province de Languedoc* 1, p. 167.

Holy Days and Holidays

The clergy might know the complex pattern of the liturgical year, but ordinary lay people needed to be notified about forthcoming feast-days.[85] A liturgical document that represents Roman ecclesiastical practice of the seventh century contains a text to be used in announcing a forthcoming saint's day:

> Most holy brothers, let your devotion know that the anniversary day of the holy martyr *N* is arriving. . . . So, let us praise the Lord, who is wonderful in his saints, so that he, who gave them the crown of victory, may, through their merits, grant us forgiveness of our sins. Therefore in *such a place* or in *such a street* on *such a day*, let us celebrate this feast with customary devotion.[86]

The practice continued throughout the Middle Ages. The parish priest announced forthcoming saints' days ahead of time.[87] After the relics of St. Maurontus had been brought to Douai, it was agreed that his feast-day of 5 May should be celebrated each year, and "when the turning of the year brought that feast around, it was announced by the priests in charge of the people, in church on the preceding Sunday, and all servile work was prohibited."[88] The monks of Ely denounced a wicked priest who refused to make this announcement in the case of their local saints Withburga and Sexburga: "he was quite unwilling to proclaim to the people the feasts of saints Withburga and Sexburga, which were coming up in the same week, on the preceding Sunday, nor did he make any mention of them." Supposedly his congregation murmured their confusion and dissatisfaction.[89] The priest could be reminded to make such announcements by having a written record of feast-days. In 1311 the clergy of the province of Ravenna were ordered to announce the feast-days of the patron saints of Ravenna, and, "so that they should not be able to make any mistake in this matter, they should have these feasts written down in their Kalendars."[90]

Saints' days were "holy days," and "holy days" might mean "holidays." Pious lay people might keep the feast-day with devotion, perhaps fasting on the vigil if required, but for many the important point would be that it was a day off work.[91] Not that every solemn feast demanded abstention from work. At a synod held in the diocese of Avila in 1481, the local clergy attempted to draw up an agreed list of feast-days, distinguishing those which should be celebrated solemnly in church but did not require cessation from labour, and those which did.[92] In addition to Sundays,

[85] Cabrol, "L'annonce des fêtes"; Klauser, "Festankündigung," cols. 779–85.

[86] *Liber Sacramentorum Romanae Aeclesiae ordinis anni circuli* 2. 1, p. 129.

[87] Burchard, *Decretum* 2. 77, col. 640; Gratian, *Decretum* 3 (de consecratione) 3. 1, col. 1353.

[88] *Miracula Rictrudis* 2. 3. 34, p. 106.

[89] *Liber Eliensis* 3. 121, pp. 370–71.

[90] Mansi, 25, cols. 455–56 (Rubric 10).

[91] Rodgers, *Discussion of Holidays in the Later Middle Ages*; d'Avray, "Popular and Elite Religion: Feastdays and Preaching."

[92] *Synodicon Hispanum 6: Avila y Segovia*, pp. 60–61.

they listed thirty-two days on which work was prohibited (although for one feast, that of the Avilan martyrs Vincent, Sabina and Cristeta on 27 October, this was limited to the city only). On another fifteen days there should be a solemn celebration in church but there was no need to abstain from work. Taking into account Sundays, work was thus prohibited on a total of eighty-four days in the year (and a feast might well coincide with a Sunday, thus lowering this number). These were spread fairly evenly through the year, usually numbering only one, two, or three a month, although the vagaries of the moveable feasts meant that, if Easter was very late, then, very rarely, June might have a total of eleven days when the Church frowned on manual work (and June was a time when work in the fields was important).

Similar concerns preoccupied the clergy of Meaux. At a synod in 1493 they bemoaned the lack of respect shown for feast-days in modern times, but recognized that one of the problems might be an excessive multiplication of feasts and the economic damage done to the poor if they scrupulously abstained from work on every prescribed holiday. In an effort to avoid these difficulties, a reform of the schedule of feast-days was proposed. Some recently introduced feast-days were exempted from the ban on work, as were all the feasts categorized as "manual or of the arms [*manualia seu brachiorum*]," "in which that prohibition for the whole day extends only to those works and activities which can be done without a horse and cart." The new schedule of feast-days now included only thirty-seven with a compulsory ban on work (excluding Sundays), while another twenty were recommended but not compulsory.[93] Presumably the "manual" feasts had previously banned such work as digging. It was not uncommon for the Church to specify the kinds of work that might be allowed on feast-days. Sometimes work with the plough was allowed, sometimes only "women's work" was banned.[94]

The church courts were busy trying to enforce respect for saints' days. Records from the diocese of Durham in the mid-fifteenth century, for example, show repeated attempts to punish those who did not come to church or worked on the main feast-days:[95]

> October 1441: John Huchonson of South Sherburn worked with three carts on the day of the Decollation of St. John the Baptist.
>
> 3 October 1443: Beatrice Atkynson and Margaret Domyll. It is charged that they harvested on the feast-day of the dedication of St. Oswald's church. They must clear themselves with the oath of six honest women neighbours.
>
> 28 July 1451: Isabella Hunter and Katerina Pykryng. It is charged that they washed linen on the feast-day of Mary Magdalene. They confess and should be beaten twice (around the church) with a bundle of linen.

[93] Du Plessis, *Histoire de l'église de Meaux* 2, pp. 541–43.

[94] Cheney, "Rules for the Observance of Feast-days in Medieval England," pp. 135–40, 144; Harvey, "Work and 'Festa Ferianda' in Medieval England," pp. 291–92.

[95] *Depositions and Other Ecclesiastical Proceedings from the Courts of Durham*, pp. 28–32; cf. Coulton, *Medieval Panorama*, pp. 183–84.

> 25 November 1451: Thomas Kirkham, John Hunter. It is charged that they reaped on the feast-day of St. Oswald. They confess it and as punishment they must be beaten four times, having in their hand a bundle of hay.

Despite this evidence of indifference amongst the country dwellers of the north of England, the atmosphere on saints' days was generally a heightened one. These were times when large numbers of people gathered. On St. Denis's feast-day at his abbey outside Paris, the crowd was supposedly so packed "that the women ran to the altar on the heads of the men, as if on a pavement."[96] Given such a mood, it is not surprising that feast-days stimulated miracles. Almost half of the miracles recorded at the shrine of St. Martin in Tours in the sixth century took place on one of his two feast-days—one miracle is recorded as taking place at the shrine on the saint's feast-day in 579, as the lector read from the saint's Life—while, of the 102 miracles recorded at the shrine of St. Gibrien at Rheims in 1145, almost 40 per cent (39) took place either on a Sunday or on a feast-day (Abbot Suger of St.-Denis noted that Sunday night was a time "when the divine hand worked most powerfully").[97] The mood on the feast-day also encouraged people to loosen their purse strings. Records of offerings at St. Lawrence's church in Nuremberg in the fifteenth century show that almost 15 per cent of the annual offerings were made on St. Lawrence's day.[98] Offerings on the feast-day were about 44 times higher than what could be expected if there were a uniform distribution of offerings every day.

The feast-day combined the devotional and the festive. The aristocratic poet Sidonius Apollinaris describes the festival of St. Justus at Lyons in the 460s:

> we came to the tomb of St. Justus; the procession was before daybreak on the solemn anniversary; there was a huge crowd of people of both sexes, which the large basilica could not hold even with all its surrounding galleries. After the observance of vigils, which the monks and the clergy celebrated together, charming the ear with the singing of psalms in turn, we each went our own way, but not too far, since we had to be ready for the third hour, when the divine service would be celebrated with the priests.

In this interval the worshippers gave themselves up to ball-games, board-games, and even dice.[99] In the following century Gregory of Tours describes a feast following the

[96] Suger, *Gesta Suggerii abbatis* 2. 2 (1, p. 112) (PL 186: 1227, as cap. 25).

[97] Pietri, *La ville de Tours du IVe au VIe siècle*, p. 573; Gregory of Tours, *De virtutibus sancti Martini* 2. 49, p. 626 (repr., 1969, p. 176); cf. ibid. 2. 29, p. 620 (repr., 1969, p. 170); Van Dam, *Saints and Their Miracles*, p. 253; Heinzelmann, "Une source de base," for chronology; Sigal, *L'homme et le miracle*, p. 194, summarizing his "Maladie, pèlerinage et guérison," p. 1529; Suger, *Gesta Suggerii abbatis* 26 (1, p. 100) (PL 186: 1224, as cap. 20).

[98] Weilandt, "Heiligen-Konjunktur: Reliquienpräsentation, Reliquienverehrung und wirtschaftliche Situation an der Nürnberger Lorenzkirche im Spätmittelalter," pp. 190–92.

[99] Sidonius Apollinaris, *Epistula* 5. 17, pp. 201–5.

Mass in honour of St. Vincent in a village in the Vendée, indicating the festive nature of the occasion.[100]

It is clear from the critics that saints' days could be celebrated in ways less than devout or solemn. A chorus of disapproval rings down the centuries. As early as the fourth century there were protests that people went straight from the service commemorating a martyr to the pub, and likewise in sixth-century Gaul the complaint was raised, "There are some people who desire to come together on the feast-days of the saints for this reason only, so that they can damn themselves and others by getting drunk, dancing, and singing disgraceful songs."[101] Augustine criticized drunkenness and dancing at the shrines of the martyrs.[102] The indiscriminate association of the sexes was something that always aroused the suspicions of puritanical observers, and the fact that it was sometimes at religious ceremonies and observances that men and women mingled did not make such critics any the less hostile. During his great revivalist sermons in the early fifteenth century, which drew audiences of hundreds, Vincent Ferrer insisted that a thick rope separate the male and female listeners.[103] The fifth-century Syrian hermit Maris was praised for having preserved his virginity even though, as an attractive young man, he had served as cantor "in the many festivals celebrated for the martyrs."[104] The implication has to be that such occasions provided a good opportunity for losing one's virginity. Six centuries later similar concern was echoed in the standard canon-law collection, Gratian's *Decretum*, which decried the "immodest gambolling" and unseemly singing that "the common people [*vulgus*]" engaged in on saints' feast-days.[105] In one English parish at the end of the twelfth century, the people who had gathered outside the church spent all night singing love songs, with the result that next day at Mass the priest, who could not get the words out of his mind, instead of the standard liturgical greeting "The Lord be with you," chanted the chorus of one of the songs: "Lover, be merciful."[106] Saints' days could be an excuse for a party.

[100] Gregory of Tours, *Gloria martyrum* 89, p. 547 (repr., 1969, p. 97).

[101] John Chrysostom, *Homilia in martyrem Pelagiam* 3, col. 582; Caesarius of Arles, *Sermo* 55. 2 (2, p. 468); Brown, "Enjoying the Saints in Late Antiquity," pp. 2–3.

[102] Augustine, "Nouveaux sermons de S. Augustin. IV–VII. 'De martyribus,' " p. 4.

[103] *Procès de la canonisation de Saint Vincent Ferrier*, pp. 39, 41, 64, 70, 330.

[104] Theodoret of Cyrrhus, *Historia Religiosa* 20. 2 (2, p. 66).

[105] Gratian, *Decretum* 3 (de consecratione) 3. 2, col. 1353 (from the Council of Toledo of 589).

[106] Gerald of Wales, *Gemma ecclesiastica* 1. 43, p. 120.

CHAPTER 7

Types of Saint

Counting Saints

There is not, and cannot be, a definitive list of Christian saints. This is because sanctity is not an objectively identifiable feature but an attribute: saints are people who are treated as saints. Hence someone might be a saint in one time and place and not in another, a saint for some people but not for others. However, to the simple question, "how many people at one time or another in the pre-Reformation period have been treated as saints?," it is clear that the answer is in the thousands. They range from very well known historical individuals, such as Thomas Becket, to entirely imaginary ones, like St. Catherine; from queens, such as Margaret of Scotland, to serving girls, like Zita; they include heroic early Christian martyrs, aristocratic bishops, wandering holy men, female visionaries, and little boys supposedly killed by the Jews.

The most complete scholarly list of saints is that in the *Bibliotheca sanctorum*, in twelve volumes, published in Italy from 1961–69 (followed by subsequent index and supplementary volumes). This covers saints of all periods and includes around 20,000 entries. It would be a laborious task to calculate how many of these are pre-Reformation, but the average per century is 1,000, so, if saints should happen to be distributed evenly in time, there would be 15,000 from the early Christian and medieval period. The perspective of the work is avowedly Catholic and this determines its scope (although two subsequent volumes address the "eastern" churches and contain another 2,200 entries).[1]

The late 1970s and early 1980s were a boom time for counting saints. American scholars, in particular, flung themselves into large-scale statistical analyses of Christian sanctity (just as they were doing in other fields of historical inquiry).[2] In an article published in 1978 Jane Tibbetts Schulenburg summarized the results of a determined trawl through the *Bibliotheca sanctorum* looking for saints from the early medieval period (500–1200), but excluding saints "whose existence appeared to be highly improbable or undatable" and those from Ireland or the Iberian peninsula.

[1] BS; *Bibliotheca sanctorum orientalium*; see Boesch Gajano, "La 'Bibliotheca sanctorum.' Problemi di agiografia medievale," for an evaluation, which also gives the figure of 20,000 entries (at p. 140).

[2] For description (and criticism), Stone, "The Revival of Narrative," esp. pp. 10–13.

Her total was 2,680 over seven centuries, that is, 383 per century.[3] David Herlihy, in an article published in 1985, used a different set of data, basing himself not on a biographical encyclopaedia but on a bibliographical one, the *Bibliotheca hagiographica latina*, which attempts to list all Latin hagiographical writings of the early Christian and medieval period.[4] Herlihy worked his way through this list to create what he called a "census of medieval saints," even though it actually embraces Christian saints of the entire pre-Reformation period, including those of the Roman empire. His total was 3,276 over fifteen centuries, that is, 218 per century. It is not surprising that his list, although longer, is thinner than Schulenburg's, since he was counting only saints whose lives were recorded in Latin literary works while she listed all saints for whom there is evidence (albeit with a more restricted geographical scope than Herlihy).

The difficulties of counting saints can be illustrated by the contrast between two rather different attempts to undertake this tricky task, one by Donald Weinstein and Rudolph Bell, the other by Michael Goodich, both published in 1982.[5] Despite their twentieth-century sociological perspective, both studies relied on the work of the religious orders for their raw material. Weinstein and Bell, writing one of the most systematic statistical analyses of medieval sanctity, based their study on 864 cases, which were drawn from a list in Pierre Delooz, *Sociologie et canonisations* (Liège, 1969), who in turn relied upon Jules Baudot and Léon Chaussin, *Les vies des saints* (13 vols., Paris, 1935–59).[6] The selection was thus fundamentally the work of the last authors, French Benedictines who were both born in the nineteenth century (Baudot in fact died in 1929, prior to publication).[7] Weinstein and Bell took all officially canonized and beatified saints from the list, and then every second name of the remaining saints. It is possible to deduce that the total they were selecting from must have been 1,458. They chose to deal with saints from the period 1000–1700, thus omitting the late Roman era and the early Middle Ages but including almost two centuries of post-Reformation history (hence such otherwise surprising conclusions as "a large majority of British saints were martyrs").[8] Michael Goodich set himself a narrower but more intensive task, studying the saints only of the thirteenth century, but all of them. He worked his way through the volumes of the *Acta sanctorum*, the immense, but incomplete, assemblage of hagiography produced by the Bollandists, a branch of the Jesuits dedicated to this task, and identified 518 people from the

[3] Schulenburg, "Sexism and the Celestial Gynecaeum"; the quotation is from her summary of method in her later book, *Forgetful of Their Sex*, pp. 11–12.

[4] Herlihy, "Did Women Have a Renaissance?."

[5] Weinstein and Bell, *Saints and Society*; Goodich, *Vita perfecta*; for incisive commentary, see the review article by Howe, "Saintly Statistics," where the two books are discussed alongside the classic work by Vauchez, *La sainteté en Occident*; Kleinberg, *Prophets in Their Own Country: Living Saints and the Making of Sainthood in the Late Middle Ages*, pp. 13–16, is penetrating in his criticisms of Weinstein and Bell but perhaps too harsh.

[6] *Vies des saints et des bienheureux*.

[7] Baudot lived 1857–1929, Chaussin 1891–1945.

[8] Weinstein and Bell, *Saints and Society*, p. 179.

period "whose immediate post mortem veneration is attested to by at least two contemporary or nearly contemporary sources."[9]

Weinstein and Bell, as mentioned, based themselves on the list in Delooz, *Sociologie et canonisations*. His list includes 1,300 saints from the period 1000–1600, thus averaging 217 per century. This is less than half the figure that Goodich was working with for the thirteenth century. From the *Bibliotheca Sanctorum*, the analyses of Schulenburg and Herlihy, and the works of Delooz, Weinstein and Bell, and Goodich, we thus get figures ranging from 217 to 1,000 per century, hardly precise but at least establishing parameters. It is possible to be more exact and meticulous if one limits consideration to a particular category. For example, André Vauchez's ground-breaking book on late medieval sanctity owes some of its strength to the fact that its core is a study of a small but well-defined group of saints, those who were the object of a papal canonization inquest in the period 1198–1431. They number only 71.[10] Analysis of large sets of data presents several methodological problems, some of which are discussed later, and Vauchez's restricted but clear sample avoids these, but, of course, cannot be used as the basis of large-scale generalization.

Chronology of Sanctity

The purpose of even considering the attempt to obtain large global figures of this type is not simply to conclude "there have been such or such a number of saints," but to use them for further statistical investigations into such issues as chronological developments, geographical patterns and the relative proportions of male and female saints.

Turning to the first of these topics, the longest run of data, covering the whole of the pre-Reformation period, is presented by Herlihy. Like all the other scholars of this subject, he sorted saints chronologically by year of death. Since he divided up his list of saints not by century, but by significant historical periods, it is not possible to make exact comparisons with the results of other scholars, but one can calculate an average number of saints per year for each of his periods, as shown in Table 7.1.

There are two peaks in this profile, one in the early years of the Church, which is not surprising given that all the New Testament saints and early martyrs belong to this period of persecution, and a second in the 275 years after the fall of the Roman Empire in the West, a period corresponding to the rule of the Merovingian dynasty in continental western Europe. These figures have been used to support the claim that "more new saints were created in the sixth and seventh centuries than in any other comparable period of the post-Constantinian Church" (although the figures themselves suggest that the reservation "post-Constantinian" is unnecessary).[11]

[9] Goodich, *Vita perfecta*, p. 15.

[10] For the comparable post-Reformation numbers, see Congregatio de causis sanctorum, *Index ac status causarum*, pp. 547–96, which lists canonizations 1594–1999.

[11] Fouracre and Gerberding, *Late Merovingian France*, p. 44. The footnote leads to a slightly different claim: "more saints' lives were written in the period c. 450–750 A.D. than in any comparable period in

TABLE 7.1
Herlihy's Figures for Numbers of Saints per Period

Period	No. of saints	No. per year
1–313	925	3
313–475	378	2.3
476–750	866	3.2
751–850	115	1.2
851–999	133	0.9
1000–1150	235	1.6
1151–1347	324	1.7
1348–1500	87	0.6

Schulenburg's figures would support this proposition (although she does not deal with the early Church). Of her half-century periods from 500 to 1200, only six produced more than 200 saints, and five of these periods fall into the continuous chronological stretch 500–750. Coincident results like this from analyses of different bodies of evidence strengthen their plausibility, and Schulenburg omits Irish saints, who were particularly numerous in the sixth and seventh centuries, so their inclusion would make the "bulge" in saints at that time even more pronounced. The term "the age of saints" is a widely used label when talking of the Celtic countries in the fifth to seventh centuries, and perhaps it really was.[12]

Moving into the second half of the Middle Ages, Weinstein and Bell's 630 saints from the years 1000–1500 are distributed unevenly but not dramatically so:

11th century: 20.3 per cent
12th century: 24.3 per cent
13th century: 25.2 per cent
14th century: 17.0 per cent
15th century: 13.2 per cent

These figures, like Herlihy's, suggest a decline in the number of saints in the later Middle Ages, although it is not quite clear what exactly that would mean. It could point to a saturation of the field, since there were now enough saints to meet believers' needs, it could mean that certain saints of long standing, like the Virgin Mary,

the post-Constantinian church": Fouracre, "Merovingian History and Merovingian Hagiography," p. 9, citing Herlihy in support.

[12]For example, Chadwick, *The Age of the Saints in the Early Celtic Church.*

were eclipsing all others, or it might also point to a shift towards various forms of devotion not focussed on the saints, such as Eucharistic cult or study of scripture.

These statistical analyses are not without interest but neither are they entirely satisfactory in their methodology. They assign the saints to chronological periods according to when they lived, but the problem with any system of counting based on the date of the saint's life is that this fails to show the rise of old saints to new importance, or their decline in importance. St. Anne, the mother of the Virgin Mary, who was an important saint in the eastern Church from early days, only rose to prominence in the West in the later Middle Ages. Simply categorizing her as "first century" obscures this important fact. The real life of saints, as saints, is when their cult is active, not when they themselves trod the earth. For example, the Anglo-Saxon abbess Æbbe of Coldingham lived in the seventh century and details of her life are reported in several trustworthy contemporary sources. There is no hint in this material that she was regarded as a saint. After her death, there is a silence of some 400 years. Then, basing themselves largely on the information from those early sources, the monks of Coldingham concocted a cult for her. She is, in any meaningful sense, a saint of the twelfth century (and subsequent centuries), not a saint of the seventh.[13]

One way of escaping this particular methodological problem is by concentrating on the saints venerated at one time and place. Thus it has been established that there is evidence of the cult of 164 saints in late-sixth-century Gaul.[14] Something like 650 saints are mentioned in the surviving Kalendars from Anglo-Saxon England.[15] These figures reveal the number of saints venerated, not the number of saints who lived in the given period. But it is then possible to undertake a chronological analysis of the list of saints venerated, to ask what are the dates of the saints venerated in sixth-century Gaul or Anglo-Saxon England. For instance, a text from late Anglo-Saxon England with the heading "God's saints who rest in England" lists eighty-nine saints, the latest of whom died in the 990s.[16] Of these, seventy-nine can be given a reasonably assured, even if often approximate, date. The pattern is striking. No fewer than forty-two of these saints died in the period 600–750—that is, 53 per cent of the dateable and 47 per cent of the total. Half of England's early saints are from that 150-year period, which is often labelled "the age of conversion" but is also "the age of saints" (and also "the age of Bede," the historian who recorded many of them). In this respect, this medieval list supports the view of twentieth-century scholars that the years between the fall of the Roman Empire in the West and the rise of the Carolingian dynasty were particularly fertile in generating saints. By contrast the

[13] *The Miracles of St. Æbbe of Coldingham and St. Margaret of Scotland*, pp. xii–xxii.

[14] Beaujard, *Le culte des saints en Gaule*, p. 200.

[15] Rushforth, *Saints in English Kalendars*.

[16] "*Secgan be þam Godes sanctum þe on Engla lande ærost reston*": *Die Heiligen Englands*; for comment, see Rollason, "Lists of Saints' Resting-Places in Anglo-Saxon England"; Blair, "A Saint for Every Minster?."

Carolingian period, rich as it was in hagiographic writing about earlier saints, saw a "dearth of the living holy."[17]

Geography of Sanctity

Turning from chronology to geography, and starting with Vauchez's small but precisely defined sample, his analysis shows that, of papally canonized saints in the period he covers (1198–1431), 75 per cent were from France, Italy, and England, and about 25 per cent from southern Germany, Scandinavia, and eastern Europe. The Iberian peninsula, northern Germany and the Low Countries produced none. Papal canonization is a very special case in two senses, one of which helps the study of sanctity, and one of which does not. Helpfully, canonization was a procedure that generated an enormous amount of written record. Papal government was the most bureaucratic and literate of the Middle Ages, and its continuity ensured that much of the parchment and paper that its procedures produced has been preserved. Unhelpfully, however, the papally canonized are a small and unrepresentative sample. Even in the thirteenth century, which saw more canonizations than any other in the medieval period, those who were the subject of a canonization inquest (including unsuccessful ones) only numbered 47, while Michael Goodich, as mentioned, was able to unearth evidence for 518 new saints venerated in that century. If less than 10 per cent of new saints came under the scrutiny of the papacy, it would be unwise to generalize from them to the saints as a whole. A case brought by a powerful lobby to the central organs of the Church is unlikely to be typical of local sanctity in remote regions.

Vauchez's figures can be compared with those of Weinstein and Bell. Their overall percentages for the period 1000–1500 (using their geographical categories and rounding the figures) are shown in table 7.2.[18]

The peripheral regions of Europe geographically thus also appear peripheral when saints are counted. The explanation for this pattern is most likely a combination of real social differences and imbalances in documentation and scholarship. Countries like Sweden and Bohemia were poorer and less densely populated than Italy or France and supported a much smaller ecclesiastical establishment. They produced saints, some of them of significance, like Birgit of Sweden, but it is unlikely she would have had the impact she did if she had not spent the last twenty-four years of her life in Italy (or on pilgrimage). The dense networks of cathedrals, monasteries, and (from the later Middle Ages) friaries to be found in Italy and France preserved and transmitted the memories of many local saints. These imbalances were reinforced by subsequent history, as the Protestant Reformation marked a sharp break with medieval traditions of sanctity, while the religious Orders of the Counter-Reformation cherished and promoted the cult of the saints, preserving the memory of even very

[17] Smith, "The Problem of Female Sanctity in Carolingian Europe," p. 4.
[18] Weinstein and Bell, *Saints and Society*, p. 167, table 6.

Table 7.2
Weinstein and Bell's Figures for Saints per Geographical Area

Italy	42.4
France	16.2
Holy Roman Empire	14.6
British Isles	8.4
Iberian peninsula	7.6
Low Countries	4.4
Eastern Europe	3.2
Scandinavia	2.2

local or obscure figures. As has been mentioned, the statistical analyses of the later twentieth century, secular in their inspiration, still rely for their tools on the Jesuits and Benedictines of earlier, sometimes much earlier, generations.

A few features of this apparent pattern are worth comment: the dominant position of Italy, the perhaps surprisingly low place of Spain and Portugal, and the distinctive geographical and chronological profile of Germany.

Italy was, for much of the Middle Ages, the home of the papacy, but this can hardly explain the large number of non-canonized saints—indeed, it might have been expected to inhibit the profusion of such cults. Weinstein and Bell point to the fact that Italy's rise to dominance in saintly statistics is largely a late medieval phenomenon: "In the eleventh and twelfth centuries every part of Europe contributed its saints in numbers roughly comparable to geographical extent. . . . But most saints who lived and died between the early thirteenth and the mid-sixteenth centuries were Italian."[19] They point to the unusual degree of fusion between "popular piety and civic patriotism" in the powerful and wealthy cities of Italy as part of the explanation for this efflorescence.[20] Later medieval sanctity existed in a world that was more urban, lay and literate, a world with important new Orders of friars and a world with new kinds of female spirituality, and all these features were at their most intense in Italy.

Spain and Portugal embraced the Counter-Reformation with such baroque fervour that it is hard to imagine them as lands poor in saints in the Middle Ages, but the impression given by the figures of Weinstein and Bell is reinforced by Goodich's analysis of thirteenth-century sanctity. He found evidence (some of it slight) for a total of 15 saints or groups of saints either born in or venerated in Portugal;

[19] Ibid., p. 167.
[20] Ibid., p. 176.

his Italian saints number 254.[21] The disparity is enormous. The Portuguese figure of 15 saints in a century compares much more closely to that for England, which generated 20 new saints in the period 1075–1225.[22] There was no "Mediterranean" pattern, to be found in Iberia and Italy but not north of the Alps. Historians are always saying "Italy is different" and, as far as late medieval sanctity is concerned, that statement may be true. The land of St. Francis was generating new saints in a way that other regions did not. Possibly relevant, too, is the density of the episcopal network: in the later Middle Ages, Italy had almost 300 bishoprics, the Iberian peninsula 41, England 17.

Up to the thirteenth century Germany had a fairly typical cast of saints: early martyrs from the Roman cities of the Rhineland, powerful bishops of the Ottonian and Salian periods (919–1125), a smattering of royal saints, like Matilda, wife of Henry I, and the emperor Henry II. From the 990s onwards several of these received the additional accolade of papal canonization; indeed, the earliest recorded canonization is that of a German bishop, Ulric of Augsburg, in 993. But then this all changed. Between 1250 and 1400 no saints from the German-speaking lands were canonized, nor were there even any unsuccessful canonization inquests; there is, indeed, evidence of only two requests for such proceedings to be initiated.[23] Even as early as the 1180s, a supercilious Roman cardinal could express scepticism that Germans could be saints. To a delegation seeking the canonization of Anno of Cologne, he remarked, "It is usually fighters who come from your country. How remarkable that there can be saints there!"[24] It is hard to find an explanation for this sterile era. In any event, the fifteenth century saw a revival of activity in the canonization of German saints. In 1404 a process was initiated for the Prussian holy woman Dorothea of Montau, who had died ten years earlier, and, although this did not have a successful outcome, there were canonizations of German saints in 1425 (Sebald of Nuremburg), 1485 (Leopold of Austria), and 1523 (Benno of Meissen).[25] Even if none of these was a contemporary, and hence Germany was not generating new saints at this time, nevertheless requests for canonizations from Germany were being made and heard. The canonization of Benno was, indeed, the occasion for the first attack of Lutherans on Catholic sainthood (earlier, p. 85).

The absence of new saints cannot be taken as an indication that spiritual or devotional life is moribund. Vauchez comments on the strange fact that the Low Countries, which saw "the most modern forms of beguine and mystical sanctity" in the later Middle Ages, produced no canonized saint nor even an unsuccessful attempt

[21] Goodich, *Vita perfecta*, Portuguese figures calculated from the list of saints, pp. 218–41, Italian total given on p. 74.

[22] Bartlett, *England under the Norman and Angevin Kings*, pp. 461–63.

[23] Vauchez, *Sainthood*, pp. 72–73, 252–55, tables 4 and 9 (the two cases are Jutta of Sangerhausen in 1275 and Burchard of Magdeburg in the 1320s).

[24] *Translatio sancti Annonis archiepiscopi* 3, p. 516.

[25] *Die Akten des Kanonisationsprozesses Dorotheas von Montau*; Wetzstein, *Heilige vor Gericht. Das Kanonisationsverfahren im europäischen Spätmittelalter*; Finucane, *Contested Canonizations*.

at canonization in that period.[26] The history of sanctity and the history of religious life are not synonyms. Yet it is clear that something about Christian history is revealed by these chronological and geographical patterns. Saints were generated in high numbers in the centuries of persecution under the Roman Empire, in the sixth and seventh centuries, both in Merovingian Europe and the British Isles, at a time of missionary activity and monastic foundations, and in late medieval Italy. There were ages of saints, even if the saints in each of those ages were very different.

Male and Female Saints

The difficulties that arise in counting saints, sometimes from the simple problem of inadequacies in the surviving sources, but also from the very conceptualization of sanctity, as in the case of people who are regarded as saints in one place or time but not in another, become acute when considering the distribution of male and female saints in the Middle Ages. Particularly awkward is the question of how one is to weigh the significance of different saints, for while there is no doubt at all that most saints, either canonized or non-canonized, were male, the most popular and indeed ubiquitous saint was female—the Virgin Mary. Medieval Christendom generated far fewer female saints than male saints, but revered one female saint at a level far beyond any male saint.

In terms of numbers, male saints considerably outweighed female saints throughout the early Christian and medieval period. Women form just under 16 per cent of Herlihy's figures, while Schulenburg's statistics for the years 500–1200 suggest that a little over 14 per cent of saints in that period were women. In Byzantium the predominance of male saints was also marked. The Synaxarion of Constantinople, compiled in the tenth century, which gives readings for saints' feast-days throughout the year, lists only eighty-one female saints, the majority of them early martyrs. Female saints of the eighth and ninth centuries in the Synaxarion are outnumbered by male saints of the same period eight to one (64:8), so female saints in this category form a bare 11 per cent of the total.[27] This imbalance continues into the later centuries of the Middle Ages. In Byzantium, there are no female saints in the last centuries (1261–1453).[28] In the West, Weinstein and Bell's figures for the period 1000–1500 show that 17.9 per cent of saints were female. This is remarkably close to Vauchez's figure of 18.3 per cent.

Although the number of female saints is always smaller than that of male saints, there are significant changes over time (again, based on a system of sorting saints by year of death) (figures 7.1 and 7.2). Schulenburg's analysis indicates that certain centuries of the early Middle Ages were more productive of female sanctity than others, notably the seventh, eighth, and tenth. In the eighth century the percentage

[26] Vauchez, *Sainthood*, p. 271.
[27] *Holy Women of Byzantium*, pp. x–xi.
[28] Talbot, "Old Wine in New Bottles," p. 16.

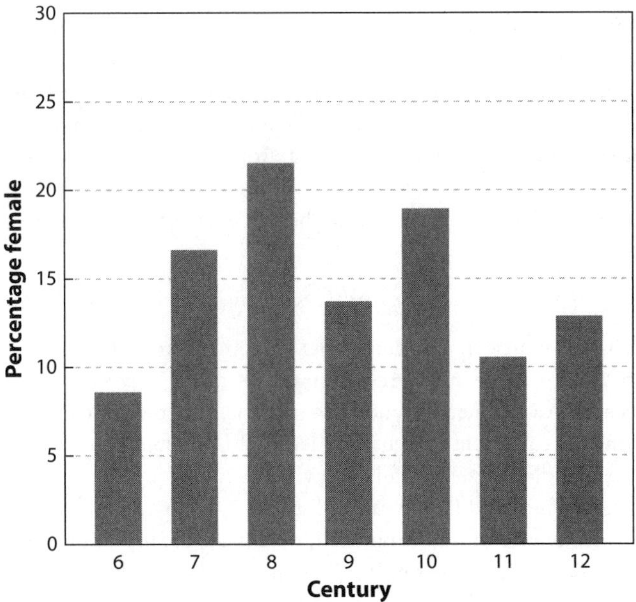

7.1. Percentage of female saints according to Schulenberg.

is as high as 21.5, over a fifth. Weinstein and Bell's figures show that, over the period 1000–1500, the percentage of female saints rose from around 9 per cent of the total to almost 28 per cent. Women are always and everywhere a small minority among medieval saints, but they are less of a minority in 1500 than in 1000. Vauchez's study of canonized saints shows a similar pattern. Of the seventy-one candidates for canonization between 1198 and 1431, only thirteen were women, but there is a slight increase in the percentage of female saints, especially lay saints, over time. So Vauchez's pattern is the same as Weinstein and Bell's: women are a minority, but less of a minority as the Middle Ages proceed. Vauchez even uses the phrase "feminization of lay sainthood," although given the overall numbers the term "feminization" may seem overblown.[29]

Since the calculations of Herlihy, Schulenburg, and Weinstein and Bell do not cover exactly the same chronological period and do not always employ the same chronological units, it is not possible to compare them directly and systematically. Nevertheless, there are important agreements. For example, to take the period 1000–1500, which is covered by Weinstein and Bell in century-long units, by Herlihy in three phases (1000–1150, 1151–1347, 1348–1500) and for which Schulenburg, while dealing primarily with the early Middle Ages, gives summary statistics in a footnote, a common trend emerges, as shown in table 7.3.

[29] Vauchez, *Sainthood*, pp. 267–69.

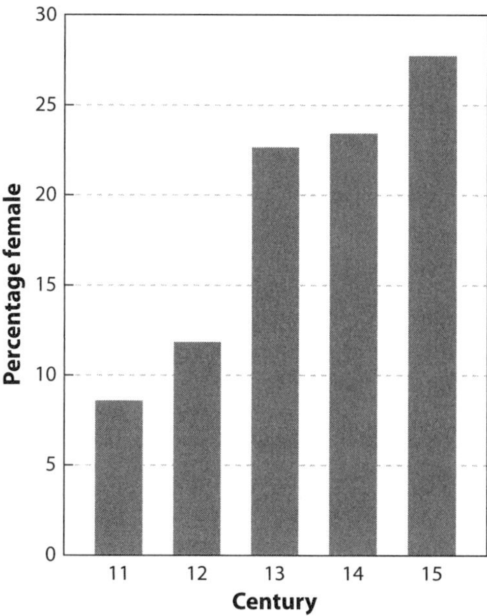

7.2. Percentage of female saints according to Weinstein and Bell.

The picture of a major change in the first half of the thirteenth century, when the proportion of female saints began to move from figures of 10 to 15 per cent towards 20 per cent and above, is clear, and the more persuasive since the authors were using three different sources for their data.

The picture in the early Middle Ages is less well defined, partly because there are only two sets of figures, and partly because Herlihy's periodization is so different from Schulenburg's. If one takes their overall figures for the early Middle Ages (476/500–1000), Herlihy reckoned that female saints made up 13 per cent of the total, while Schulenburg gave a figure of 15.2 per cent, near enough to be convincing. This suggests that female sanctity at this time was more important than in the eleventh and twelfth centuries, but did not approach the significance of that of the later Middle Ages.

Measuring new saints is only one way of approaching this issue. Clearly it was possible for there to be lively cults of long-dead female saints. England provides a good example of the way a distinction can be drawn between cults of inherited female saints and the genesis of new female saints. In the conversion period of 600–750 numerous female saints came to be revered, many of them royal abbesses like Etheldreda of Ely or Hilda of Whitby. Later in the Anglo-Saxon period other female saints occur, some of them of this same type, royal abbesses or nuns, such as Edith of Wilton or Edburga of Winchester. After 1000, however, England produced no new

TABLE 7.3

Percentages of Female Saints (by date of death)

Period	Weinstein and Bell	Herlihy	Schulenburg
1000–1100	8.6		10.5
1000–1150		7.7	
1100–1200	11.8		12.8
1151–1347		21.3	
1200–1250			15
1200–1300	22.6		
1250–1300			24
1300–1350			23
1300–1400	23.4		
1348–1500		27.6	
1350–1400			28.6
1400–1450			29.7
1400–1500	27.7		
1450–1500			21.8

female saints.[30] Nevertheless, the inherited native saints, the virgin martyrs such as Catherine and Margaret, and, above all, the Virgin Mary herself, provided numerous female saints for devotees, even in a society which, for some reason, was no longer producing female saints of its own. In England in the period 1000–1500 female saints were thus revered but not created. It was not that there were no female objects of veneration, but that the society was not generating new ones.

[30] The evidence for the cult of Christina of Markyate is slight and elusive. In their entries on Christina, both Farmer, in *The Oxford Dictionary of Saints*, and Alfonso M. Zimmerman, in BS 4, col. 339, mention liturgical evidence: "some Parisian calendars" and "due messali parigini del sec. XIV," respectively. Farmer also refers to a rood screen at Gately (Norfolk) with an image of "puella de Ridibourne," perhaps Redbourn (Hertfordshire), where Christina was freed from her marriage vows and which was, later, the site of a priory of St. Albans which possessed the only surviving copy of her Life: *The Life of Christina of Markyate*, pp. 1–2, 112–13 with note. The fact that the Life was added to John of Tynemouth's fourteenth-century *Sanctilogium* would also suggest that someone at that time thought Christina was a saint. In general see Koopmans, "The Conclusion of Christina of Markyate's *Vita*."

7.3. Statue of Mary Magdalene from the church of St.-Pierre, Montluçon.
Photo: Peter Willi/The Bridgeman Art Library.

And there is also the more fundamental question of what did the femininity of female saints mean? It is likely to have meant many different things. Men and women surely responded to female saints in different ways. The Virgin Mary, most universal of the female saints, was a maiden and a mother, a paradoxical combination that offered two completely different aspects of the female image. The fascinating figure of Mary Magdalene, who, before she met Jesus, was a wealthy noblewoman given over to the pleasures of the body, offered the painters and sculptors of the later Middle Ages the chance to depict an erotic femininity, as in the stone sculpture 138 centimetres (54 ½ inches) high in the church of St.-Pierre, Montluçon, dating to the 1490s, which endows the saint with almond eyes, an hour-glass figure, trailing hair, and elegant, embroidered robes (figure 7.3).[31] Even if the laborious task of counting medieval saints can be achieved, there still remain the difficult issues of their cultural and emotional meaning.

Categorizing Saints

So, the saints number in the thousands. It is worth investigating the patterns in this great ocean of sanctity. Although saints were not people of a particular type, but people treated in a particular way, it is still possible to look at the list of saints and see whether it is possible to sort them into groups. The Church itself devised a typology. Saints in the litany were organized into categories: first the Virgin Mary, then angels, apostles, martyrs, confessors and virgins. These classifications could be used to distinguish synonymous saints. The saintly Edward the Confessor has that title because an earlier Anglo-Saxon king with the same name was regarded as a martyr on account of his violent and innocent death, and hence the two Edwards were distinguished as Edward the Martyr and Edward the Confessor. Another reason it was important to know to which category a saint belonged, was that the Church specified generic liturgical services for saints who did not have an individual (Proper) Mass or Office. Hence there were prescribed forms of the Mass and Office for saints belonging to a general category. This was one reason Kalendars usually specify the category to which a saint belongs. Because there were overlaps between the categories—a martyr might also be a virgin—as well as distinctions within them—a confessor might or might not be a bishop—the number of appropriate liturgical forms of the generic type multiplied. The common forms in one medieval service-book include Offices for one apostle, several apostles, the evangelists, one martyr, several martyrs, a confessor-bishop, a confessor-doctor, a confessor not a bishop (also used for an abbot), several confessors, a virgin martyr, a virgin not a martyr, and a married woman.[32]

Variant schemes of classification existed. The thirteenth-century Cistercian monk Caesarius of Heisterbach, for example, referred to the four "orders of the Church," meaning martyrs, virgins, confessors, and widows, explaining that the apostles and married saints are subsumed under the martyrs, "because almost all of them were married and crowned with martyrdom."[33] And there might be fanciful correspondences between categories of saints and other patterns of order:

> Note that there is a fourfold classification of the saints of the New Testament whom we celebrate through the cycle of the year . . . apostles, martyrs, confes-

[31] *Kings, Queens, and Courtiers: Art in Early Renaissance France*, fig. 65, p. 134.

[32] *The Monastic Breviary of Hyde Abbey* 5, fols. 410–42.

[33] Caesarius of Heisterbach, *Sermo de translatione beate Elyzabeth*, p. 388.

> sors, and virgins . . . these are signified by the four parts of the world, apostles by the east, martyrs by the south, confessors by the north, virgins by the west.[34]

Vincent Ferrer, in one of his sermons, adopted the magic number of seven for his classes: apostles, martyrs, doctors, confessors, virgins, the continent, the penitent.[35]

The Queen of Heaven

Mary, mother of Jesus, was a saint of a unique type.[36] Honoured as "Mother of God," she had, according to her legend, been taken up bodily into heaven, and hence, like Jesus, she left no corporeal remains. Such physical traces as there were comprised hair, clothing, or milk. Even without a body (or perhaps because of that lack) her cult was of a quite different order from that of other saints. "We deem her to be superior to all created things, visible or invisible," wrote one Byzantine patriarch.[37] The scholastic theologians of the West even invented a special term, *hyperdulia*, to describe the veneration owed to her, which was distinct from and superior to the *dulia* owed to the rest of the saints, thus making her a kind of super-saint.[38] Just as Christ was "Our Lord," so Mary was "Our Lady."

Her appearances in the New Testament are few, and the story of her birth and childhood had to be devised in the early Christian centuries, in the same inventive spirit that gave rise to the Apocryphal Acts of the Apostles—Christians were eager for background stories, prequels and sequels to what they could read in the canonical books of scripture. The so-called *Protevangelium of James* of the second century, written in Greek, fills in the tale of Mary's parents, Joachim and Anne, their longing for a child, the miraculous conception of Mary and her upbringing in the Temple, before moving on to Mary's relations with Joseph, the Nativity and the slaughter of the Innocents.[39] Most of this material was then incorporated into a later Latin apocryphal work, the Gospel of Pseudo-Matthew, which had a very wide

[34] Jacobus de Voragine, *Legenda aurea* 158 ("All Saints"), (2, p. 1105); the text attributes the suggested signification to Hrabanus, but such a source is not identified by the editor and it has not proved possible to trace it.

[35] Vincent Ferrer, *Sermones de sanctis*, fol. 51 (St. Benedict).

[36] The bibliography is endless. A few orientations: *Lexikon des Mittelalters* 6, cols. 243–75 ("Maria, hl."); Warner, *Alone of All Her Sex*; Rubin, *Mother of God*; Clayton, *The Cult of the Virgin Mary in Anglo-Saxon England*, also contains excellent summaries of general developments in Marian cult; *Marienlexikon*. There are two useful volumes of selections from original sources by Luigi Gambero: *Mary and the Fathers of the Church*; *Mary in the Middle Ages*.

[37] Germanus of Constantinople, Letter to John of Synada, ed. Thümmel, *Die Frühgeschichte der ostkirchlichen Bilderlehre*, p. 376 (PG 98: 160).

[38] It is often said that the term was first used by Bonaventure, *In tertium librum Sententiarum* 9. 1. 3, p. 206, although Bonaventure himself writes, "this honour is accustomed to be called hyperdulia by the masters (*Hic autem honor consuevit a magistris hyperdulia vocari*)," suggesting that the term needed explanation but also that he had read it elsewhere; there are no references in *A Patristic Greek Lexikon*.

[39] *Protevangelium Jacobi.*

dissemination, surviving in 130 manuscripts.[40] This was in turn adapted into the vernacular, for example, in the form of an Old English translation, probably made in the eleventh century, and a thirteenth-century Old French poem of more than 2,000 lines, *The Infancy Gospel*, whose author commended his tale as more profitable and more truthful than the stories of King Arthur and the Round Table.[41]

Early Christian discussion of the Virgin Mary shaped, and was shaped by, theological questions about the nature of Christ. As the Jesus of the Gospels was refracted through the prism of Greek philosophical thinking, divided opinions arose on such issues as the relationship of Christ to God the Father, and precisely how the human and the divine were combined in him. The orthodox position, as enshrined in early creeds and councils, tried to establish a middle way. It sought to avoid, on the one hand, a hostility to the world of matter and consequent exclusive emphasis on Christ's spiritual nature. Jesus was a man, not an angel or pure spirit, the creeds asserted. But, on the other hand, if Jesus was human, some people wondered how a little Jewish baby could unequivocally be said to be God. Christ was a human, the creeds proclaimed, but not only human—he was at once perfect God and perfect Man. And Mary was the mother, not of half this being, the human half, but of the God-Man. The Council of Ephesus in 431 pronounced that Mary was *Theotokos*, that is, "the one who brought forth God," and anathemized anyone who denied this.[42]

Although there were no early feast-days specifically dedicated to the Virgin Mary, over the course of time she came to have the richest cycle of liturgical commemoration of any saint. At the end of the Middle Ages, Vincent Ferrer classed the feast-days of the Church into three groups in ascending order of importance—the saints, the Virgin Mary, and Christ—thus giving her a category all of her own.[43] But the first Christians celebrated only Easter and Pentecost (Whitsun), and neither had a prominent place for the Virgin Mary, although she was present at the Resurrection and the first Pentecost, and did feature in the scriptural readings for those occasions. By the fourth century Christmas had been added to the list of major feast-days, and here Mary's role is obviously far more central. The natural consequence of adopting a day for Christ's birth was the ability to calculate a day for his conception, nine months earlier, and so, as 25 December became generally accepted as the date of Christmas, 25 March rose into prominence too, and, just as Christmas had the added significance of being the old winter solstice, so 25 March was the old vernal equinox, and was regarded as the beginning of the year in some calendrical systems. This feast was linked with the passage in the Gospels (Luke 1:26–38) in which the angel Gabriel announces to Mary that she will bear Jesus. The Annunciation ("Lady Day" in later English usage) became an important feast and the angel's message a

[40] *Pseudo-Matthaei Evangelium*; Gijsel, *Die unmittelbare Textüberlieferung des sog. Pseudo-Matthäus.*

[41] Clayton, *The Cult of the Virgin Mary in Anglo-Saxon England*, pp. 248–53; eadem, *The Apocryphal Gospels of Mary in Anglo-Saxon England*; *The Old French Evangile de l'enfance.*

[42] *Conciliorum oecumenicorum decreta*, pp. 58–59.

[43] Vincent Ferrer, *Sermones de sanctis*, fol. 37v (Purification of the Virgin Mary).

favourite subject for illustration. His words to Mary, "Hail, full of grace!" were the basis for a whole genre of Greek hymns as well as one of the most popular Latin prayers, the *Ave Maria*. Ingenious western churchmen noticed that *Ave* (Hail!) was *Eva* (Eve) reversed: "Receiving that *Ave* from Gabriel's mouth, she transformed the name of Eve."[44] Since Jewish law prescribed that a mother and her newly born male child should come to the Temple forty days after the birth for rites of purification (Leviticus 12), this was another date that could be calculated once Christmas had been fixed at 25 December. The feast of the Purification of the Virgin, which was also the feast of the Presentation of the Christ child, thus occurs on 2 February. It was marked by a procession with lights, and hence it is known in English as Candlemas, in German as *Lichtmesse*, in French as *la Chandeleur*, and so on.

It is a delicate matter to distinguish these feasts of the Virgin Mary from feasts of Christ. The Annunciation and Nativity commemorate events that obviously involved them both, while the feast of 2 February can even have different names depending on which perspective is adopted: it is both the Presentation of the Christ child in the Temple and the Purification of the Virgin Mary. There also arose, however, feasts that focussed exclusively on Mary's Life: her conception (8 or 9 December), birth (8 September), presentation as a child in the Temple (21 November), and her passing (15 August).

The centuries between 400 and 700 were crucial for the formation of the cycle of Marian feasts. The earliest evidence for feasts commemorating Mary comes from Palestine. Already by the late fourth century, the feast of the Presentation of Christ/Purification of the Virgin was celebrated there. The pilgrim Egeria describes the solemn procession in the church of the Resurrection and the use of the *Nunc dimittis*, the famous canticle that the elderly Simeon had uttered when he saw the Christ child in the Temple.[45] According to a writer of the sixth century, it was the wealthy widow Ikelia who, when she founded a church dedicated to the Virgin between Jerusalem and Bethlehem in the 450s, had introduced the custom of carrying candles during this feast.[46] Another feast of the Virgin Mary was celebrated on 15 August in Jerusalem in the first half of the fifth century. It is not clear if it originally had any special connotations, but this day eventually became associated with Mary's passing, her Dormition or Assumption as it was known, when she "fell asleep" and was then received into heaven.[47] The imperial capital also had an early festival, for a feast of the Virgin Mary was celebrated in Constantinople by 430, as is attested by a

[44] The second verse of the hymn *Ave maris stella*.

[45] Egeria, *Itinerarium Egeriae* 26, p. 72. At this time the church in Palestine celebrated Christmas on 6 January and hence the Presentation/Purification 40 days later on 14 February: Avner, "The Initial Traditions of the Theotokos at the Kathisma," pp. 22–24.

[46] Cyril of Scythopolis, *Vita Theodosii*, p. 236.

[47] *Le codex arménien Jérusalem 121*, 36/2, pp. 354–57 (no. 64). Experts believe that this Armenian evidence reflects early Jerusalem usage. In general, see Mimouni, *Dormition et assomption de Marie*; Shoemaker, *Ancient Traditions of the Virgin Mary's Dormition and Assumption*; for other early feasts in Palestine, see *Le calendrier palestino-géorgien du Sinaiticus* 34.

famous homily of Proclus of Constantinople, although the exact day on which it fell is not certain; 26 December is most likely (a day later celebrated as the feast of St. Stephen).[48]

The earliest evidence for the feast of the Annunciation on 25 March is a Greek sermon preached in the period 530–53.[49] It was clearly an innovation at that time, and it did indeed present some liturgical problems, for it almost always fell in the penitential season of Lent (or, much more rarely, during Easter). The Church in Spain acknowledged that the feast of the Annunciation on 25 March would constantly become entangled either with Lent or with Easter, and, in the year 656, ordered it moved to 18 December.[50] It was celebrated on this date until the Spanish Mozarab liturgy was replaced by the Roman at the end of the eleventh century.[51] The so-called Council in Trullo, held at Constantinople in 692, also recognized that the Annunciation would often fall in Lent, but allowed it to be an exceptional case which could be celebrated with a full liturgy.[52]

The early history of the feast of the Nativity of the Virgin Mary is obscure, but it seems to have been kept in the East by the first half of the seventh century, and was certainly well established by the eighth century, when Andrew of Crete, composer of famous liturgical hymns, wrote a series of sermons for the occasion.[53] The choice of 8 September for the feast is unexplained.

Sometimes the Byzantine state threw its weight behind certain Marian feasts. The emperor Justinian (527–65) sought to enforce uniform celebration of the Annunciation on 25 March and the Presentation of Christ/Purification of the Virgin on 2 February, while a late medieval Byzantine historian, who may, however, had had access to earlier and now lost material, says that the emperor Maurice (582–602) prescribed 15 August as the feast-day of the Dormition.[54]

In Byzantium there was thus a full and well-established sequence of feasts of the Virgin Mary. These feasts then spread west. Liturgical evidence shows that the four main feasts of the Virgin Mary—the Purification, Annunciation, Assumption, and the Nativity of the Virgin—were introduced into Rome during the course of the seventh century, eclipsing an earlier Marian Mass on 1 January.[55] Pope Sergius (687–701) is credited with instituting extra prayers and processions for these feasts.[56] They

[48] Proclus of Constantinople, Homily 1, "On the Holy Virgin Theotokos."

[49] Abraham of Ephesus, *Oratio in Annuntiationem beatissimae Mariae virginis*.

[50] *Concilios visigóticos et hispano-romanos*, pp. 309–10 (Tenth Council of Toledo, cl. 1) (PL 84: 441).

[51] *Le liber ordinum en usage dans l'église wisigothique et mozarabe d'Espagne*, pp. 491–92; there are texts for the Mass of this feast in *Le liber mozarabicus sacramentorum*, cols. 50–53.

[52] *Conciliorum oecumenicorum generaliumque decreta* 1, p. 265 (canon 52).

[53] The assumption of observance in the East is deduced from its arrival in the West (see later); Andrew of Crete, *Orationes in nativitatem sanctissimae Deiparae I–IV*.

[54] Van Esbroek, "La lettre de l'empereur Justinien sur l'Annociation et la Noël"; Theophanes, *Chronographia*, s.a. 6034, p. 222; ibid., s.a. 6028, p. 216; Nikephoros Kallistos, *Historia Ecclesiastica* 17. 28, PG 147: 292.

[55] Chavasse, *Le sacramentaire gélasien*, pp. 375–402.

[56] *Liber pontificalis* 1, p. 376; see Ó Carragáin, *Ritual and the Rood*, pp. 237–47.

are still the only four Marian feasts to be found in the Kalendar of the papal court of 1260, or to be given entries in the *Golden Legend*, composed just at that time.[57] A comparison with the law of the Byzantine emperor Manuel II of 1166, listing the most important feast-days on which the law courts should not sit, shows that in this period there were six major feasts of the Virgin in the East, compared with the four in the West: the Nativity, Presentation, Conception, Purification, Annunciation, Assumption.[58]

The feasts of the Conception and Presentation were thus accepted in the East long before the West. Just as the date of Christmas determined the date of the Annunciation, so the celebration of the Virgin's birth on 8 September implied a conception nine months earlier. It was celebrated on 9 December in Byzantium, and 8 December when introduced to the West.[59] Both the feast of the Conception and the feast of the Presentation were introduced into England in the eleventh century, probably through influence, direct or indirect, from Byzantium, but they were not celebrated everywhere in the country and they did not spread quickly to other parts of the West.[60] The feast of the Conception was indeed controversial. St. Bernard of Clairvaux protested against "this new feast, which is unknown to the rituals of the Church, and is neither supported by reason, nor approved by ancient tradition."[61] Later in the twelfth century the French liturgical authority John Beleth recognized that the feast had sometimes been celebrated and that some people might still celebrate it, but, he argued, "it is not authorized but, rather, it appears it is prohibited, for she was conceived in sin."[62] His comment makes it clear that, although there is no logical connection between celebration of Mary's conception and the doctrine that she was conceived without sin (the Immaculate Conception), contemporaries believed that one implied the other. (Bernard makes the same point.) Beleth's contemporary, the Oxford theologian Alexander Nequam, was so convinced that the feast should not be celebrated that he always planned to lecture then as usual. Only when he noticed that he always fell sick that day did he realize that he was being given a lesson.[63]

The feast of Mary's Presentation in the Temple (21 November) commemorates a legendary event in her life, namely, the moment when, at the age of three, she was placed in the Temple by her parents, to be brought up there until she reached

[57] *Sources of the Modern Roman Liturgy* 2, pp. 365–76; Jacobus de Voragine, *Legenda aurea* 37, 50, 115, 127 (1, pp. 238–51, 326–34; 2, pp. 779–810, 900–917).

[58] Macrides, "Justice under Manuel Komnenos," pp. 148–55.

[59] *Synaxarium Ecclesiae Constantinopolitanae*, p. 289; Nilles, *Kalendarium manuale utriusque ecclesiae orientalis et occidentalis* 1, pp. 348–50.

[60] Clayton, *The Cult of the Virgin Mary in Anglo-Saxon England*, pp. 42–51, 82–87.

[61] Bernard of Clairvaux, *Epistola* 174 (7, p. 388).

[62] John Beleth, *Summa de ecclesiasticis officiis* 146e, p. 284.

[63] Hunt, *The Schools and the Cloister: The Life and Writings of Alexander Nequam*, p. 8 and n. 36.

puberty.[64] The first certain evidence for the feast seems to be from the early eighth century, when Patriarch Germanus of Constantinople (715–30) wrote two sermons on the Presentation, both of which refer to "the feast" on which they are preached.[65] Thereafter, evidence for the feast in Byzantium is reasonably common. The feast, like that of the Conception, was introduced into England in the eleventh century, but it was rare in the West until the later Middle Ages, when it found a devoted champion in the person of the French knight Philip de Mézières, who, in 1372, undertook what has been called a "campaign" to win papal approval of the feast of the Presentation of the Virgin. He was aware that he was bringing an essentially eastern custom to the West:

> Let us sing a new song to the Queen of Heaven, and let us proclaim to all our Christian brothers living in the west, south and north, the ancient praises of the presentation of Mary in the Temple that shine anew from the east.[66]

Philip's campaign was successful. Pope Gregory XI authorized the feast, and it was celebrated in the Franciscan church at Avignon on 21 November 1372. It spread to France and other regions and, in 1472, exactly a century after Philip's first victory, Pope Sixtus IV introduced the feast of the Presentation into the Roman Breviary.

The feast of the Visitation, the last major Marian feast to develop in the Middle Ages, marked the encounter between the Virgin Mary and her cousin Elizabeth, mother of John the Baptist, when the former was three months and the latter was six months pregnant. It is a scene described in Luke's Gospel and was the occasion for the Virgin's song, the Magnificat, which was a central part of the liturgy. It became increasingly popular during the later Middle Ages and it won the approval of Pope Urban VI in 1389, although, since this was at the period of the papal Schism, it was not adopted universally for some time.[67] The evidence of liturgical manuscripts reflects the late and slow development of this feast. The late-thirteenth-century Coldingham Breviary, for example, has a Kalendar in which both the Feast of the Visitation and the Octave of the Visitation are additions made in the following

[64] Kishpaugh, *The Feast of the Presentation of the Virgin Mary in the Temple*; for the feast in England, including observance prior to the time of Philip de Mézières, see Pfaff, *New Liturgical Feasts in Later Medieval England*, pp. 103–15, "The Presentation of the Virgin."

[65] Germanus of Constantinople, *In praesentationem sanctae Deiparae* 1–2, col. 309.

[66] *Philippe de Mézières' Campaign for the Feast of Mary's Presentation*, p. 42.

[67] Boniface IX's bull of 9 November 1389, *Superni benignitas conditoris*, confirms the decision of his predecessor Urban VI, who had died before he could send out official letters prescribing the feast: *Bullarium diplomatum et privilegiorum sanctorum romanorum pontificum Taurinensis editio* 4, pp. 602–4; AASS Julii 1 (1719): 295–99. The claim that the Franciscans introduced the feasts of the Conception and Visitation in 1263, advanced by the seventeenth-century Irish Franciscan Luke Wadding, is unsubstantiated: *Sources of the Modern Roman Liturgy* 1, p. 127 n. 1; for Adam Easton's Office for the Visitation, see *Analecta hymnica medii aevi* 24, pp. 93–94; 52, pp. 47–51, nos. 42–44; there is a full discussion in Polc, *De origine festi visitationis B.M.V.*

centuries.[68] Other late-medieval breviaries actually head their entries for the Office of the Visitation "the new feast" and even include descriptions of its introduction, sometimes with the complete text of the papal bull of 1389.[69]

In such ways, the liturgical commemoration of the Virgin Mary became ever richer and fuller. And, in addition to her annual feasts, Saturdays were dedicated to her, and in many places her Mass and Office were recited daily. The never-ceasing evolution and diversification of the cult of the Virgin Mary is also mirrored in the growth of the cult of her mother, known by the name of Anne in the apocryphal Gospels (but not mentioned in the New Testament).

It has been pointed out that the New Testament gives such a bare and colourless picture of Mary that subsequent generations of worshippers could fill her out with almost any of the qualities they required. She could be hieratic and imperial; tender and suffering; virginal; motherly. Her very status as a virgin mother enshrined some of this complexity and paradox. It has occasionally been suggested that Mary appealed particularly to women, but the evidence for this is not convincing. Men as well as women are interested in mothers, and possibly more interested in virgins. Countless examples of stern, autocratic, masculine figures, like Bernard of Clairvaux, who were devotees of the Virgin (even if not, in his case, of the feast of her Conception), could be cited to show that devotion to Mary is by no means "feminine."

The image of the Virgin Mary, in painting, mosaic, or sculpture, was one of the most widely distributed and well known in Christendom. Her images were so common in church that there was even a special liturgy for blessing them. The prayer on this occasion requested that the image might ward off thunder and lightning, fire and flood, civil war and attacks by pagans, diseases of men and beasts, and bring peace and plenty.[70]

Proclus's hymn on the feast of the Virgin celebrated "the perfection of womankind and the glory of the female."[71] But womankind is many-sided. Mary was a maiden, a mother, and a queen, and she is depicted in word and picture in all these roles. Representations of the Annunciation have her demure, indoors, often with a book. As a mother, in the scenes of the Nativity, or holding and sometimes nursing

[68] BL, Harley 4664, fol. 129; for the slow dissemination of the feast in the later Middle Ages and for its history in England, see Pfaff, *New Liturgical Feasts in Later Medieval England*, pp. 40–61, "The Feast of the Visitation."

[69] For example, Dublin, Trinity College 89 (an Italian Franciscan Breviary of the late fourteenth or fifteenth century), fols. 280 (rubric "In festo nove sollempnitatis visitationis beate Marie"), 280–84 (an account of the introduction of the feast, including a bull of Boniface IX, which forms readings 2–6 of the Office and the reading for the Octave); Sitten, Kapitelsarchiv 58 (fifteenth century), fols. 119v–123 (Bull of Boniface IX, 9 Nov. 1389, *Superni benignitas conditoris*), described by Leisibach, *Die liturgischen Handschriften des Kapitelsarchiv in Sitten*, p. 241. The Carmelites introduced the feast in 1393: *Fontes liturgiae Carmelitanae*, p. 44.

[70] For example, Cambridge, Corpus Christi College 44 (English Pontifical; eleventh century), pp. 139–40; Cambridge, Corpus Christi College 79 (English Pontifical; fifteenth century), fols. 216–216v.

[71] Proclus of Constantinople, Homily 1, "On the Holy Virgin Theotokos," p. 136.

her child, she is one of the most common subjects of illustration, from the catacombs of ancient Rome to the painters of the Renaissance, and well beyond. Her milk was treasured at shrines, such as the Sainte-Chapelle in Paris, and might be taken into battle as a talisman.[72] She even appeared to St. Bernard to squirt some of her milk into his mouth, clearly not bothered by his views on the Conception.[73]

She is a nurturing but also a suffering mother. Her grief as she stands at the foot of the cross is depicted in thousands of representations and gave birth to one of the most well-known hymns of the Middle Ages, the Stabat mater:

> Stabat mater dolorosa
> juxta crucem lacrimosa,
> dum pendebat filius.
>
> Cuius animam gementem,
> contristatam et dolentem
> pertransivit gladius.
> [The sorrowful mother stood tearfully by the cross, as her son hung there. A sword pierced her groaning, grieving, sorrowing heart.]

The shy maiden and the sorrowing mother was also a queen. A scene in the story of Mary that became an enormously popular subject for illustration in the later Middle Ages was the Coronation of the Virgin, when Christ (or God the Father or the Trinity) places a crown on the Virgin's head in heaven. This image emerged in the twelfth century.[74] An early example can be found in a Psalter from northern France, dating to around 1175 (figure 7.4).[75]

A particularly magnificent example of the scene of Jesus and Mary sitting enthroned, and him crowning her, is the mosaic in the apse of the church of Santa Maria Maggiore in Rome, which, appropriately, was the earliest building in the city to be dedicated to the Virgin Mary, in the fifth century.[76] The mosaic was commissioned by Pope Nicholas IV (1288–92), who had a special devotion to the Virgin Mary, and executed by the artist Jacopo Torriti, who proudly signed his name in it. It shows Christ and Mary on a throne, surrounded by the sun, moon, and stars, and ranks of angels, with Christ holding a book inscribed,"Come my chosen one and I will place you on my throne." Below, on the Virgin's side, stand Peter, Paul, and Fran-

[72] *Le trésor de la Sainte-Chapelle*, p. 78; for an example of her milk taken into battle, see p. 323 later.

[73] The earliest image is from Catalonia c. 1290, the earliest textual reference from France c. 1330; Dewez and van Iterson, "La lactation de saint Bernard"; Dupreux, "La lactation de saint Bernard de Clairvaux."

[74] Earlier, the more common literary metaphor had been that Mary crowned Christ by giving him flesh. There are earlier images of crowned Virgins and, in the late-tenth-century Benedictional of St. Ethelwold, the scene of the Virgin's passing shows God's hand descending from heaven holding a crown (fol. 102v). These are not the same scene, however, as the actual crowning by Christ.

[75] New York, Pierpont Morgan Library, M. 44, fol. 16.

[76] Gardner, "Pope Nicholas IV and the Decoration of Santa Maria Maggiore"; Tomei, *Iacobus Torriti pictor*, pp. 99–125, with colour plates XVIII–XXX.

7.4. Coronation of the Virgin from Miniatures of the Life of Christ, France, perhaps Corbie, ca. 1175. Pierpont Morgan Library, New York, MS M. 44, fol. 16. Purchased by J. Pierpont Morgan (1837–1913) in 1902.

cis, with the pope himself kneeling before them, and on the other side there are John the Baptist, John the Evangelist, and Antony of Padua, along with Giacomo Colonna, the co-patron of the work, kneeling. The inclusion of the two earliest Franciscan saints, Francis and Antony, is not a surprising choice for Nicholas, who was the first Franciscan to become pope. The palace adjoining Santa Maria Maggiore was one of his favourite residences, the church itself the place of his burial.

The cult of the Virgin Mary continued to expand and deepen down to the Reformation (and, in non-Protestant areas, well beyond). The Cistercian Order, founded in 1098, dedicated all its churches to her. When the Christians conquered the cities of Muslim Spain, they turned the chief mosques into cathedrals under her patronage. The Teutonic Knights, as they established themselves along the east Baltic coasts in the thirteenth and fourteenth centuries, claimed her as their special protector and named their chief fortress after her: Marienburg. From early in the twelfth century, large collections of her miracles were assembled, not connected with any shrine but demonstrating her intercessory powers always and everywhere. It was in twelfth-century England that collections of miracles of the Virgin Mary were first made, but they soon spread.[77] Early in the thirteenth century, the French abbot and poet Gauthier de Coincy produced *The Miracles of Our Lady*, 30,000 lines dedicated "To the praise and to the glory, in remembrance and in memory, of the queen and the lady, to whom I commit my body and my soul," while one of the most celebrated literary and musical works of the Middle Ages is the *Cantigas de Santa Maria*, an elaborate, illustrated cycle of her miracles in the Galician tongue fashionable at the court of Castile.[78]

Mary was a universal saint, but she also put down deep local roots. Constantinople was especially "the city of the Mother of God [*Theotokoupolis*]."[79] The Virgin had several great churches in Constantinople, such as the Blachernae and the Chalkoprateia, each claiming a relic of her clothing, and the Hodegetria with its miraculous icon, as well as 120 other churches dedicated to her in Constantinople and its European suburbs.[80] She was credited with saving the city from attack on several occasions, notably during an Avar attack in 626. In the West, there were Marian shrines of varying levels of importance everywhere. From the shrine of Our Lady of Rocamadour, deep in central France, there is a record of 126 miracles, composed in 1172–73.[81] At Chartres the chemise that she wore when giving birth to Jesus was a valued relic, and the author of a collection of her miracles, which was written there around 1210, described Chartres as "the place she loved particularly and es-

[77] Southern, "The English Origins of the 'Miracles of the Virgin'"; Ward, *Miracles and the Medieval Mind*, pp. 132–65 ("The Miracles of the Virgin").

[78] Gautier de Coinci, *Les miracles de Nostre Dame* 1, lines 1–4 (1, p. 1); *Cantigas de Santa Maria*.

[79] A term from Mango, "Constantinople as Theotokoupolis"; see also Cameron, "The Theotokos in Sixth-Century Constantinople."

[80] Janin, *La géographie ecclésiastique de l'Empire byzantin*, pp. 156–244.

[81] *The Miracles of Our Lady of Rocamadour*; see, in general, Rocacher, *Rocamadour et son pèlerinage*.

pecially" and the cathedral as "the special dwelling she had chosen upon earth."[82] Aachen might dispute this claim. The church dedicated to Mary in that city possessed the Virgin's dress, which, amongst other relics, was displayed to public view every seven years during the later Middle Ages, drawing crowds of thousands.[83]

New shrines of Mary multiplied in the later Middle Ages in all parts of Christendom. At St. Mary's church in Zaragoza, for example, there was a column or pillar upon which the Virgin Mary had miraculously appeared. First recorded in 1299, the chapel of Santa Maria del Pilar (St. Mary of the Column) became a centre of pilgrimage, and, at the end of the fourteenth century, Pope Benedict XIII gave his approval to the cult: the chapel of the column, dedicated to "the queen of heaven, the virgin mother of God . . . the mother of mercy, friend of devoutness, comforter of the human race," received the gift of indulgences for all who visited on the Marian feasts of the Nativity, Annunciation, Purification, and Assumption, as well as those of the local saints and St. Anne. The pope was recognizing the "great and frequent miracles" that occurred there, and "the multitude that flocked there from different parts of the world."[84] Women in the Spanish-speaking world are still called Pilar, or Maria Pilar, in honour of the Virgin of the Pillar.

Many of the new shrines focussed on miraculous images. According to the legend of the shrine at Santa Maria de Guadalupe in Extremadura, an image of the Virgin had been hidden in the time of the Muslim conquests, but was revealed, after many centuries, to a poor herdsman, and a small chapel was then built for it. This became the centre of miraculous cures and pilgrimage, and eventually an imposing Jeronimite monastery backed by royal patronage. The earliest definite evidence of the shrine is an indulgence granted in 1326.[85] The fifteenth century also saw an explosion in the number of Marian sanctuaries in central Italy, many of them associated with images, just as the late Byzantine empire was "dotted with pilgrimage icons" of the Virgin.[86] At Częstochowa in southern Poland an image of the Virgin reputedly painted by St. Luke drew crowds of pilgrims from the 1420s (and still does today).[87]

In later medieval England the most important new Marian shrine was that at Walsingham. The legend of its origin, as told in the fifteenth century, was that the Virgin Mary had appeared to a pious widow in the last days of Anglo-Saxon England, and instructed her to build a replica of the family home in Nazareth. By the middle of the thirteenth century there was a famous image of the Virgin and Child

[82] *Miracula beatae Marie virginis in Carnotensi ecclesia facta* 1, p. 509.

[83] Lermen and Wynands, *Die Aachenfahrt in Geschichte und Literatur*; the event is first recorded in 1312 (ibid., p. 16).

[84] Fita, "El templo del Pilar y san Braulio de Zaragoza: Documentos anteriores al siglo XVI," pp. 457–60 (no. 11).

[85] Linehan, "The Beginnings of Santa María de Guadalupe."

[86] Caroli, "Dalla reliquia all'immagine: percorsi nell'area ravennate"; Carr, "Icons and the Object of Pilgrimage in Middle Byzantine Constantinople," p. 90.

[87] Maniura, *Pilgrimage to Images in the Fifteenth Century: The Origins of the Cult of Our Lady of Częstochowa*.

at Walsingham, for which Henry III commissioned a golden crown.[88] Miracles and pilgrims multiplied. Because it is the site of Walsingham (and long before Blake wrote of building Jerusalem in England's green and pleasant land) the country could rejoice that "this our New Nazareth here should stand."[89] But England's New Nazareth had serious competition from Loreto in Italy. While Walsingham had a replica of the Virgin's home, the Italian shrine claimed to possess the "Holy House" itself, miraculously transported there from Palestine. After the Muslim conquest of the Holy Land, angels had carried it away from Nazareth, but had some difficulty finding a suitable new location. First they transported it to the land of the Slavs, but it received insufficient veneration among them, then they tried a wooded spot in Italy, but this was made unsafe by brigands. Another site became unsuitable because of quarrels among the proprietors. Finally the angels put the house down in the public street, where it stayed. Since it had no foundations, the local people surrounded it with a stone wall, and, in order to ensure that it was genuine, a delegation went to Nazareth and ascertained that the foundations on the spot where the Virgin's house had been were an exact match in size and shape to the one angelically delivered to Italy. There is evidence of pilgrimage to Loreto from the fourteenth century and the huge present church was begun in 1468.[90]

The Protestant assault on Marian veneration thus did not encounter a dwindling or dubious cult that it mopped up, but rather set itself in opposition to a vast and swelling tidal wave of devotion. Mary was the most widely and, if one can judge, the most deeply revered of the saints. And, as the raptures of the theologians and the fervent acclamations of the liturgy attest, her devotees loved to address her directly. The Akathistos hymn, composed in the sixth or perhaps even fifth century and the most familiar liturgical celebration of the Virgin in the Orthodox Church, contains a hypnotic listing of her epithets:

> Hail, you, through whom joy will shine forth!
> Hail, you, through whom the curse will cease!
> Hail, restoration of the fallen Adam!
> Hail, redemption of the tears of Eve!
> Hail, height that cannot be reached by human reasoning!
> Hail, depth that cannot be penetrated even by the eyes of angels![91]

During the disputes over the status of the Virgin Mary in the 420s, the patriarch Nestorius (later condemned as a heretic) warned, "do not make the Virgin a goddess."[92] It was not an unfounded worry.

88 Dickinson, *The Shrine of Our Lady of Walsingham*, p. 19.

89 Ibid., p. 126 (the Pynson Ballad).

90 *Translatio miraculosa ecclesie beate virginis Marie de Loreto*; see Grimaldi, *La chiesa di Santa Maria di Loreto nei documentia des seculi XII–XV*; idem, *La historia della Chiesa di Santa Maria de Loreto*; *Marienlexikon* 4, pp. 151–54, s.v. "Loreto."

91 PG 92: 1337.

92 *Nestoriana. Die Fragmente des Nestorius*, p. 353, no. III.

Angels

As early as the Epistle to the Hebrews (before AD 70), it had been necessary to warn believers against placing angels on the same level as Christ, and the Epistle to the Colossians also disparages "the cult of angels."[93] This continued to be a delicate subject. In the first half of the third century, the great Alexandrian theologian Origen, argued, defensively, that it would not be reasonable to invoke angels, while, in the mid-fourth century the Council of Laodicea in Phrygia ruled that "Christians must not abandon the Church of God and invoke angels."[94] A hundred years later, Bishop Theodoret of Cyrrhus (d. c. 466) was aware of the Council's prohibition but noted its ineffectiveness; there were many oratories of St. Michael in Phrygia and Pisidia in his day.[95] Already in fourth-century Egypt richly decorated shrines dedicated to the archangels Michael and Gabriel could be found "not only in the towns but also in private lanes, houses, and fields," drawing devotees from far and wide.[96] And the imperial capital itself was not immune from this questionable aspect of Christian cult. There was a church dedicated to the archangel Michael (the Michaelion of Anaplous) at Constantinople certainly by c. 440, and eventually the city and its suburbs had more than twenty.[97] The existence of angel-saints shows how flexible the concept of sanctity could be. No one could expect to take Michael or Raphael or Gabriel as an example for living their life; they had no graves or physical remains; yet they clearly counted as saints, with feast-days, dedications and pilgrimage sites.

Only two angels are named in the Hebrew Bible, Gabriel and Michael, both of them mentioned in the book of Daniel (chapters 8–10), while a third, Raphael, occurs in the Book of Tobit (or Tobias), which is part of the Greek and Latin Old Testament and is accepted as canonical by the Orthodox and Roman Catholics but not by Jews or Protestants. These three, Michael, Gabriel, and Raphael, were regarded as archangels in the Middle Ages and are the three named angels invoked in the litany of the saints. A fourth, Uriel, appears in apocryphal literature. Medieval liturgical writers explained that these four were the only angels to have individual personal names and that these names had not been bestowed by God or by the angels themselves, but by men, although it was not known by whom; all other angels are named simply by their order—cherubim, seraphim, and so on.[98]

[93] Hebrews 1–2; Colossians 2:18—a phrase rendered in St. Jerome's Vulgate version as *religio angelorum*.

[94] Origen, *Contra Celsum* 5. 6, SC 147, p. 24 (PG 11: 1185); *Discipline générale antique 1/ii: Les canons des synodes particuliers*, pp. 144–45 (canon 35) (Mansi 2, col. 570).

[95] Theodoret of Cyrrhus, *Interpretatio Epistolae ad Colossenses* 2: 18, 3: 17, cols. 613, 620.

[96] Didymus of Alexandria, *De trinitate* 2. 7. 8. 10, p. 236 (PG 39: 589); see also Papaconstantinou, *Le culte des saints en Egypte*, pp. 68–69, 154–59.

[97] Sozomen, *Historia ecclesiastica* 2. 3. 8 (1, pp. 240–42) (he attributes the construction to Constantine); Janin, *La géographie ecclésiastique de l'Empire byzantin*, pp. 337–50.

[98] John Beleth, *Summa de ecclesiasticis officiis* 154, p. 295; William Durandus, *Rationale divinorum officiorum* 4. 33. 20 (140, p. 406).

Even after the invocation of angels had become common practice, prayer to non-biblical angels was regarded with great suspicion, although they sometimes crept in, for instance in an eighth-century litany from Soissons, which, after calling on Michael, Gabriel, and Raphael, goes on to appeal to Orihel (Uriel), Raguhel, and Tobihel.[99] The funeral crypt of abbot Mellebaudis at Poitiers, from about the same period, contains a bas-relief of the archangel Raguel as well as Raphael.[100] There is some, possibly dubious, evidence of a chapel of Uriel, along with chapels of Michael, Raphael and Gabriel, at Milan.[101] England also provides evidence of the invocation of extra-canonical angels. The ninth-century Book of Cerne contains prayers not only to Gabriel, Michael, and Raphael, but also to Urihel, Rumihel, and Phannihel, while the archangel Panchiel, "who is over all the fruits of the earth and over seed," is invoked in a tenth-century Durham manuscript to protect the fields and crops.[102]

The misgivings that such aberrant figures aroused are revealed at a papal synod in 745, which uttered a fierce condemnation of a prayer formula reading: "I pray you and I conjure you and I kneel down before you, angel Uriel, angel Raguel, angel Tubuel, angel Michael, angel Adinus, angel Tubuas, angel Sabaoc, angel Simiel." The assembled clergy decreed that this prayer be burned and its author excommunicated. Except for Michael, they said, these were the names of demons not angels. "As we are taught by you, holy pope, and as divine authority has handed down, we acknowledge the names of only three angels, namely, Michael, Gabriel, and Raphael. This has introduced the names of demons under the pretext of angels."[103] Charlemagne's ecclesiastical legislation of 789, the *Admonitio generalis*, cited the prohibition of the Council of Laodicea, and ruled "that unknown names of angels should not be feigned nor named, except those which have authority, namely Michael, Gabriel, and Raphael."[104] Later in the reign, bishop Haito of Basel put it in similar form: "They should not revere the false names of angels but those only that are taught by the writings of the prophets and the evangelists, namely Michael, Gabriel, Raphael."[105] The canonists of the eleventh and twelfth century took up this wording.[106]

[99] Coens, "Anciennes litanies des saints," p. 284 (from Montpellier, Bibliothèque de la Faculté de Médicine H 409); see Ewig, *Spätantikes und fränkisches Gallien* 2, pp. 230, 254; Krüger, *Litanei-Handschriften der Karolingerzeit*, pp. 347–49; ibid., pp. 440–536, for an alphabetical list of all saints in the Carolingian litanies, including angels. Raguhel and Tobihel occur only in the Montpellier manuscript, but there is one other invocation of Uriel: *Liber sacramentorum Augustodunensis* 537, p. 66.

[100] Salin, *La civilisation mérovingienne d'après les sépultures, les textes et le laboratoire* 2, p. 47.

[101] The ultimate evidence for a chapel of St. Uriel in Milan appears to be a seventeenth-century plan, but its authenticity has been disputed; see Verzone, "Les églises du haut Moyen Age et le culte des anges," p. 74 and plate 9, which reproduces the plan.

[102] *The Prayer Book of Aedeluald the Bishop, Commonly Called the Book of Cerne*, p. 153, no. 54; *The Durham Ritual*, fols. 66–66v; see Jolly, "Prayers from the Field."

[103] Boniface, *Epistulae*, pp. 408–10 (MGH, *Epistolae selectae* 1, p. 117).

[104] *Capitularia regum Francorum* 1, no. 22, p. 55 (cl. 16).

[105] Haito of Basel, *Capitula* 19, p. 216.

[106] Burchard, *Decretum* 3. 198, col. 712; Ivo of Chartres, *Decretum* 3. 250, col. 256.

The vigorous campaigning of the authorities ensured that the non-biblical angels did not win a permanent place in the worship of the Church. It seems that only in the Ethiopian Church did the liturgical commemoration of these non-scriptural angels become permanent, with feast-days for Raguel, Phanuel, Souriel, and Uriel, as well as Michael, Gabriel, and Raphael.[107]

Michael was by far the most important of the angels, and he was recognized as "Saint Michael" throughout Christendom.[108] Yet, although he was a popular saint, St. Michael was extremely unusual. He was not, like all other saints, a dead human being who had gone to heaven, but an angel, created before the human race had come into existence. And he was a warrior. The Book of Revelation (12:7) tells how "there was war in heaven: Michael and his angels fought against the dragon." He was "St. Michael, appointed to lead the armies of the bodiless."[109] And it was Michael who had inflicted the plagues on Egypt and parted the Red Sea; and he was also "master of paradise and guardian of souls."[110]

As was customary for all angels, Michael was represented as winged and beardless. He was sometimes shown in the robes of an imperial official, but also, and increasingly commonly, in armour, as his military role gradually eclipsed other aspects of his cult.[111] The Byzantines regarded him as their special protector—"he guards the Roman state, arms the emperor against barbarians and brings victory to the Christians"—and called him "field marshal [*archistratigos*]."[112] He is often depicted carrying a banner or a spear: angels are called "spear-bearing" or "guardian" in the fourth century and images of Michael spearing a dragon or the devil are numerous.[113] The German army carried an angel standard into battle against the pagan Magyars in the tenth century.[114] Michael's role as knight and champion was also evident in late medieval France, where, in 1469, Louis XI created the Order of St. Michael the Archangel, in honour of Michael, "the first knight," who had always protected his shrine at Mont-St.-Michel from falling into the hands of the enemies of the kingdom (that is, the English). Its membership was intended to comprise thirty-six companions of royal or aristocratic status, meeting annually at Mont-St.-Michel on Michael's feast-day, 29 September, although these intentions were not realized in practice.[115]

[107] Zanetti, "Fêtes des anges dans les calendriers et synaxaires orientaux," pp. 347–48.

[108] Peers, *Subtle Bodies: Representing Angels in Byzantium*, chapter 5, "Apprehending the Archangel Michael"; Johnson, *Saint Michael the Archangel in Medieval English Legend*; *Pellegrinaggi e santuari di San Michele nell'Occidente medievale/Pèlerinages et sanctuaires de Saint-Michel dans l'Occident médiéval.*

[109] Didymus of Alexandria, *De trinitate* 2. 7. 8. 9, p. 234 (PG 39: 589).

[110] John Beleth, *Summa de ecclesiasticis officiis* 154, pp. 295–96; William Durandus, *Rationale divinorum officiorum* 7. 12. 4 (140B, p. 52).

[111] Rohland, *Der Erzengel Michael, Arzt und Feldherr.*

[112] Pantaleon Diaconus, *Encomium in maximum et gloriosissimum Michaelem*, col. 1265; "archangeli Michahelis, qui Grece archistratigos apellatur": Liudprand of Cremona, *Antapodosis* 1. 10, p. 256.

[113] Didymus of Alexandria, *De trinitate* 2. 7. 8. 3, p. 226 (PG 39: 584).

[114] Widukind of Corvey, *Res gestae saxonicae* 1. 38, 3. 44, pp. 76, 152.

[115] Boulton, *The Knights of the Crown*, pp. 432, 440, 443.

In western Europe, alongside Michael the warrior, a new image of Michael emerged: weigher of souls.[116] He is depicted quite literally, holding a pair of scales, with a human soul on one side, while often the devil, with his intrinsic sense of unfairness, is trying to pull down the other. Possibly the oldest depiction of the scene is found in Ireland, a carving on the eastern side of Muiredach's Cross in Monasterboice, dating to the ninth or tenth century.[117] From the twelfth century it is common in both carving and painting, culminating in such large and magnificent examples as Roger van der Weyden's *Last Judgment*, where the archangel stands centrally, scales in hand, confronting the viewer. (See plate 1.) Joan of Arc was asked at her trial whether St. Michael had been carrying scales when he appeared to her (she replied that she did not know).[118]

Because Michael was a judge of the dead as well as a heavenly warrior, he could be found as a patron of cemeteries and places of the dead. At the German monastery of Fulda in 822, for example, a circular chapel was dedicated for the burial of the monks; it was under the patronage of St. Michael.[119]

The great shrines of St. Michael were located in dramatic and unusual landscapes, and were associated not with corporeal relics, but with stories of apparitions.[120] At Chonae in Anatolia (modern Honaz, Turkey) Michael appeared and split open the rocks with his spear, diverting a flood of water; at Monte Gargano in southern Italy his shrine was located in a mountain-top cavern where the archangel had appeared and dedicated his own church; on the borders of Normandy and Brittany, he was venerated at the offshore outcrop of Mont-St.-Michel, likewise the site of an apparition of the saint.[121] Michael, it was thought, "rejoices in high mountain peaks."[122] At San Michele della Chiusa (la Sacra di San Michele), his church stands on a rocky spur high above the Piedmont plain, at an altitude of more than 900 metres (3,000 feet). Even in cities, he might be revered on high points, as in Rome, where the church of the archangel on top of the Castell Sant' Angelo was nicknamed "the church of the holy angel up to heaven."[123]

The different cult centres had different feast-days associated with them: 8 May commemorated the appearance of the archangel on Monte Gargano, 6 September that at Chonae, 16 October that at Mont-St.-Michel. But by far the most important feast in the West was 29 September, "a day dedicated in the name of the archangel

[116] Kretzenbacher, *Die Seelenwaage*, pp. 65–182; on one particular development of this motif, Scheller, *Die Seelenwägung und das Kelchwunder Kaiser Heinrichs II.*

[117] Harbison, *The High Crosses of Ireland* 1, pp. 141, 300–301; 3, fig. 941.

[118] *Procès de condamnation de Jeanne d'Arc* 1, p. 87.

[119] Bruno Candidus, *Vita Eigilis abbatis Fuldensis* 17–18, MGH, SS 15/1, pp. 230–31.

[120] *Millénaire monastique du Mont-Saint-Michel* 3: *Culte de saint Michel et pèlerinage au Mont*; *Culte et pèlerinages à Saint Michel en Occident*; *Culto e santuari di san Michele nell'Europa medievale.*

[121] Chonae: *Narratio de miraculo a Michaele Archangelo patrato*, pp. 1–19; Monte Gargano: *De apparitione sancti Michaelis* (BHL 5948) (repr., with Eng. tr., Johnson, *Saint Michael the Archangel in Medieval English Legend*, pp. 110–15); Mont-St.-Michel: *De apparitione sancti Michaelis* (BHL 5951).

[122] *Chronica Monasterii Sancti Michaelis Clusini* 2, p. 961.

[123] Liudprand of Cremona, *Antapodosis* 3. 45, p. 390.

Michael which has a bright fame for all Christians throughout the world."[124] In England this feast-day was known as "Michaelmas," and it gave its name to a university and legal term. Elsewhere it was also frequently stipulated as a term for financial and legal purposes.

Michael was more important than the other archangels, but dedications to him were often accompanied by those to the others or to "all angels." At the abbey of St.-Riquier (Centula) in the Somme valley, the west door had an altar dedicated to Michael, the south door one dedicated to Gabriel, and the north door one dedicated to Raphael; these were consecrated in the time of abbot Angilbert (c. 790–814).[125] While liturgical commemoration of the other archangels was much rarer than of Michael, there are signs that it was increasing in significance at the end of the Middle Ages.[126] The creation of a liturgy for Raphael in the dioceses of Exeter and Hereford in the fifteenth century is mentioned earlier (p. 116). There is a similar increase in liturgical interest in Gabriel, exemplified, for example, by the addition of his Office to several Spanish breviaries in the fifteenth century.[127] Gabriel was the angel of the Annunciation, and hence his image would be familiar throughout Christendom at every level. And the gradual adoption of the names of the archangels in late medieval Italy also points to a new significance for these angelic saints. The name Michael was common in Byzantium and that of Gabriel not unusual in the eastern churches, but they were rare in western Europe until the end of the Middle Ages—it is fitting that two of the greatest artists of the Italian Renaissance are Raphael and Michelangelo.

Apostles and Evangelists

Of human saints, the Virgin was pre-eminent. After her came the apostles: "After the Virgin, the greatest saints and the most spiritual and the most filled with the Holy Spirit were the holy apostles. After them the holy martyrs and then the holy confessors."[128]

The New Testament offers three lists of Jesus' twelve disciples (Matthew 10:2–4; Mark 3:16–19; Luke 6:13–16). Differences between the lists are slight, although the figure known variously as Thaddaeus, Lebbaeus, and Judas (or Jude), son of James, has provoked some debate and confusion. The other eleven are Simon Peter and his brother Andrew; James son of Zebedee, and his brother John; Philip and Bartholomew; Thomas and Matthew; James son of Alphaeus; Simon the Canaanite or the Zealot; and Judas Iscariot, who was replaced after the crucifixion by Matthias.

[124] Rainer, *Miracula sancti Gisleni* 2, p. 581.

[125] Angilbert, *De ecclesia Centulensi libellus*, p. 175; Hariulf, *Chronicon Centulense* 2. 8, p. 60.

[126] *Enciclopedia cattolica* 10, col. 471, for examples of new attention to Raphael.

[127] See Janini and Serrano, *Manuscritos litúrgicos de la Biblioteca Nacional*, under relevant entries for Madrid, Biblioteca Nacional MSS 6086 (Seville Breviary; fourteenth century), fol. 403v; 6326 (Dominican Psalter, etc.; fifteenth century), fol. 177; 8902 (Breviary; fifteenth century), fol. 328v; Res. 186 (Roman Breviary with supplement for Jeronimites; 1463), fol. 432.

[128] Vincent Ferrer, *Sermones de sanctis*, fol. 61v.

7.5. The apostles from a twelfth-century altar frontal from La Seu d'Urgell in Catalonia. Barcelona, Museu Nacional de Arte de Catalunya. © SuperStock/Alamy.

These twelve, including Matthias but not Judas Iscariot, formed a distinct group among the saints and were sometimes commemorated together in literary compositions like the so-called Pseudo-Abdias, a collection of Lives of the apostles probably dating to the sixth century (see later, p. 547). They were also often depicted together in paintings and sculpture, notably in the scene of the Last Supper (here including Judas) but also in many other contexts, such as on the coffin of St. Cuthbert or on a twelfth-century altar frontal from La Seu d'Urgell in Catalonia (figure 7.5).[129] The Anglo-Saxon church at Wearmouth had panel paintings of the twelve apostles in the nave.[130]

Sometimes the apostles were celebrated liturgically as a group. The eastern Church had a feast-day of the apostles on 30 June, and western liturgical writers believed that there had originally been a common feast-day for them on 1 May.[131] In Constantinople there was a famous Church of the Apostles, founded by the emperor Constantine, who was himself buried there and hailed as "equal to the apostles."[132]

[129] Battiscombe, ed., *The Relics of Saint Cuthbert*; Cronyn and Horie, *St Cuthbert's Coffin*; idem, "The Anglo-Saxon Coffin"; Barcelona, Museu Nacional de Arte de Catalunya, no. 015803-000.

[130] Bede, *Historia abbatum* 6, p. 369.

[131] Nilles, *Kalendarium manuale utriusque ecclesiae orientalis et occidentalis* 1, pp. 196–97; *Synaxarium Ecclesiae Constantinopolitanae*, p. 779; Macrides, "Justice under Manuel Komnenos," p. 150; John Beleth, *Summa de ecclesiasticis officiis* 124, pp. 237–38; Honorius Augustodunensis, *Gemma animae* 3. 140, col. 681.

[132] Janin, *La géographie ecclésiastique de l'Empire byzantin*, pp. 41–50.

Table 7.4
Feast-days and Burial Places of the Apostles in Western Tradition

1 May. Philip: Hierapolis in Asia (later also of James the Less).

29 June. Peter and Paul: Rome.

25 July. James the brother of John ("James the Great"): Jerusalem.

24 August. Bartholomew: India.

21 September. Matthew: Persia or Ethiopia.

28 October. Simon and Jude: Persia.

30 November. Andrew: Patras in Greece.

21 December. Thomas: India (with subsequent translation to Edessa).

27 December. James the brother of the Lord ("James the Less") and John.

The fates and fortunes of the apostles were of natural interest to early Christians, and quite soon stories were told about them and the place and manner of their death. Some of these tales were elaborate and sensational, such as the *Acts of Thomas*, which begin with the apostle travelling to the court of an Indian king on the day that the monarch is to give his daughter, his only child, in marriage. Here Thomas encounters a Jewish flute-girl who seems much smitten by him. A surly cup-bearer hits Thomas, but is then eaten by a lion when he goes to get water, a black dog finding his severed hand and bringing it back to the wedding banquet. After this, Thomas preaches to the bride and groom and converts them to chastity. All this happens in the first chapter, and there are a dozen more. It is not surprising that the Acts have been termed a "romance."[133]

By the early Middle Ages, all the apostles had been given their own feast-days, along with mention of the place of their martyrdom. Because this process took place at a time when the western and eastern Churches were drifting apart, there are considerable differences between the feast-days of the apostles in the Latin and Greek liturgical cycles.[134] One early standard version in the West is shown in Table 7.4.[135]

The feast-days on this list were not at first all celebrated liturgically in every church, but some were important: the feast of Peter and Paul was a major occasion,

[133] *Acta apostolorum apocrypha* 2/2, pp. 98–288; other versions are listed in *Lexikon der antiken christlichen Literatur*, p. 604, s.v. "Thomas-Literatur"; there is an English translation in *The Apocryphal New Testament*, pp. 364–438, whose editor regularly uses the term "romances" for these apocryphal Acts (for example, at p. 364).

[134] For the apostolic feast-days in Byzantium, see Macrides, "Justice under Manuel Komnenos," pp. 148–55; the feast of John on 27 December is not mentioned because it is subsumed in Christmastide.

[135] *Notitia de locis sanctorum apostolorum*, p. 2; *Festa apostolorum*, pp. 2–3, both commonly prefixed to the Pseudo-Hieronymian Martyrology.

St. Andrew's day came to mark the beginning of the liturgical year, and the late December feasts of Thomas and John (James tended to be dropped from 27 December) were celebrated as part of Christmastide. These feasts of Peter and Paul, Andrew, and John (along with that of Bartholomew) are the only apostolic feast-days common to the western and Byzantine world. In Sarum Use, the most common liturgical pattern in late medieval England, the apostolic feasts were classed as follows: Peter and Paul on 29 June and John on 27 December had the high grading of "lesser double [*minus duplex*]," while Philip and James on 1 May, James on 25 July, Bartholomew on 24 August, Matthew on 21 September, Simon and Jude on 28 October, Andrew on 30 November, and Thomas on 21 December had the next grade down, "lower double [*inferius duplex*]."[136] Matthias, the late-comer among the apostles, was celebrated on 24 February. For obvious reasons, there was a long history of confusion between him and Matthew (they are Matthias and Mattheus in Latin).

Two or three other saints often supplemented the cast of the twelve apostles. Of the four evangelists, Matthew and John were also among the twelve apostles, but the two others, Mark and Luke, were not. Nevertheless, the grouping "apostles and evangelists" was a common one, and naturally included Mark and Luke as well as the twelve. The emblems of the four evangelists, Matthew's winged man or angel, Mark's lion, Luke's ox, and John's eagle, were amongst the most widespread symbols of saints. In addition, although he had never seen Jesus in the flesh, Paul was "the Apostle" par excellence. In the Middle Ages, references to "the Apostle" without further specification always imply Paul. As hero of the Acts of the Apostles, missionary, and early martyr at Rome, he is usually paired with Peter.

Peter, the fisherman, the leader of the disciples, "the rock" on which the Church would be built, holder of the keys of heaven, was the most celebrated and revered of Jesus' followers: he was "the Prince of the Apostles." Peter's grave in the Vatican cemetery was a focus of Christian devotion from the time of his martyrdom, probably in AD 64, and the emperor Constantine immortalized the site by building a huge basilican church above it, which is still today the heart of the Roman Catholic world. Peter's cult spread early and wide. In a sermon preached on the feast-day of Peter and Paul, St. Augustine used the language of the Psalms to praise the two apostles: "Their sound hath gone forth into all the earth: and their words unto the ends of the world."[137] Peter stands for the whole Church; "among the apostles, Peter is first"; so, concludes Augustine, referring to both Peter and Paul, "we are celebrating their feast-day, consecrated for us by the blood of the apostles; let us love their faith, life, labours, sufferings, confessions of faith and preaching."

As keeper of the keys of heaven, Peter had a special role in the conversion of pagan peoples. The first monastery constructed at Canterbury after the conversion of Kent in 597 was dedicated to Peter and Paul, and of the church dedications re-

[136] *Breviarium ad usum insignis ecclesiae Sarum* 3 *(Sanctorale)*, pp. iii–xiv (Kalendar), app., pp. xl–xliv (*Tabula festorum*).

[137] Augustine, *Sermo* 295 (PL 38: 1348–52); Ps. 18:5 (Douai-Rheims translation) (= KJV 19: 4).

corded in England prior to 800, 37 per cent are to Peter (sometimes with Paul), making him just more popular than the Virgin Mary herself.[138] Boniface, the Anglo-Saxon missionary to Germany, after cutting down a great oak sacred to Thor, used the timber to build a church dedicated to St. Peter.[139] Bede tells a famous story of a debate amongst the newly converted Northumbrians about the correct date of Easter: should they follow Roman or Irish practice? The issue was decided when the champions of Roman practice invoked the name of Peter, holder of the keys of heaven. "Since he is the doorkeeper," decided the Northumbrian king, "I am unwilling to go against him . . . in case there is no one to open the gates of the kingdom of heaven when I arrive there."[140]

Peter had feast-days in addition to the one he shared with Paul on 29 June. The feast of St. Peter's Chains, kept on 1 August in the West and 16 January in the East, refers to the relics of the bonds that the apostle wore during his periods of captivity, some of which are preserved in a reliquary in the church of San Pietro in Vincoli in Rome, while the feast of St. Peter's Chair on 22 February commemorates his elevation as bishop, "for he had the office of prelate over the whole Church."[141]

The presence of the bodies of Peter and Paul in Rome was well established, and is credited by most scholars today. The fate of the other apostles rests on a less secure basis, but claims that an apostle had preached in one's region, or that the bones of an apostle had been found there, enhanced the sacred history of one's land, and such claims multiplied. In the ninth century, the tomb of the apostle James was identified in Spain, and, at some point in the eighth or ninth century, the bones of St. Andrew turned up in Scotland. The adoption of a new place name at the sites of these discoveries—Santiago (that is, "Saint James") and St. Andrews—underlines the new holy geography that was being created. The story that St. Thomas preached in India, as recounted in his extravagant *Acts*, was ancient and well known, but it was also claimed that his relics had been subsequently translated to Edessa in Syria, where the pilgrim Egeria visited his shrine in the late fourth century.[142] An alternative tradition maintained that the saint's bones were still in India and, in the thirteenth century, Marco Polo reported that pilgrims (both Christian and Muslim) came to Thomas's shrine on the Coromandel Coast.[143] The so-called Thomas Christians of south-west India maintain this link.

[138] Bede, *Historia ecclesiastica* 1. 33, p. 114; Orme, *English Church Dedications*, p. 17 (Levison's figures for 597–800 tabulated).

[139] Willibald, *Vita Bonifatii* 6, p. 494.

[140] Bede, *Historia ecclesiastica* 3. 25, p. 306.

[141] Jacobus de Voragine, *Legenda aurea* 44 (1, p. 273).

[142] Gregory of Nazianzus, *Oratio* 33, *contra Arianos* 11, p. 180 (PG 36: 228) mentions the link between Thomas and India; Gregory of Tours, *Gloria martyrum* 31, p. 507 (repr., 1969, p. 57), reports Thomas's martyrdom in India and translation to Edessa; Egeria, *Itinerarium Egeriae* 17, p. 58.

[143] Marco Polo, *Le devisement du monde* 170 (6, p. 36, with notes, ibid., pp. 143–46).

These invented apostolic traditions could generate their own sub-legends.[144] In the fifteenth century the Portuguese clergy began to claim that the first bishop of Braga was a certain Peter, a disciple of James the apostle.[145] By this time James had been linked with the Iberian peninsula for centuries, and now this well-established apostolic connection could be developed for the benefit of a local see.

Since the apostles were recognized as "the greater saints," it is not surprising that claims to apostolic status were sometimes raised on behalf of other, non-biblical, saints by their champions and devotees, in order to inflate their prestige. The Aquitainian monk Ademar of Chabannes undertook a determined and devious campaign to establish the apostolicity of the local saint, Martial of Limoges.[146] According to Gregory of Tours, writing in the sixth century, seven bishops had been sent to Gaul in the third century, and one of these was Martial, who became bishop of Limoges, lived a holy life, made many converts, and died a confessor-saint.[147] This was not enough for Ademar. He championed, and elaborated, a quite different Martial, who had been a member of the tribe of Benjamin and a direct disciple of Jesus himself—present at the raising of Lazarus, the Last Supper, the Ascension and Pentecost. This apostolic Martial had received his authority directly from Christ, and, after preaching in Greece and accompanying his relative St. Peter to Rome, had come to Limoges. Ademar pursued his efforts to establish this alternative picture of St. Martial through forgery and liturgical innovation, but encountered serious opposition and public setbacks. At one point, while he was reciting the litany and included Martial's name among the apostles, he was interrupted by a hostile monk, who then shouted out Martial's name in the section of the litany dedicated to confessor-saints.[148] But the campaign had some success: Martial is listed among the apostles in ten litanies from eleventh-century England and at least two from twelfth-century Flanders.[149]

Another famous case concerns St. Denis (Dionysius).[150] The great royal abbey of St.-Denis, just outside Paris, housed the bones of St. Denis, but there was some disagreement about who this Denis was. Gregory of Tours tells of a Denis, a contemporary of Martial of Limoges, who was sent to evangelize Gaul in the third century, and was bishop of Paris and a martyr.[151] Another Denis (Dionysius the Areopagite) is referred to in the Bible, as one of St. Paul's converts at Athens (Acts 17:34). In the late fifth or early sixth century a Christian Neoplatonic writer, author of works on

[144] For a case-study, Herrick, "Studying Apostolic Hagiography: The Case of Fronto of Périgueux, Disciple of Christ."

[145] BS 10: 672–73, s.n. "Pietro."

[146] Landes, *Relics, Apocalypse, and the Deceits of History: Ademar of Chabannes, 989–1034.*

[147] Gregory of Tours, *Libri historiarum X* 1. 30, p. 23.

[148] Ademar of Chabannes, *Epistola de Apostolatu Martialis*, col. 109.

[149] *Anglo-Saxon Litanies of the Saints*, pp. 93, 123, 142, 158, 174, 244, 252, 270, 277, 296 (in one fifteenth–century addition to an earlier manuscript, he is listed separately as *discipulus* rather than *apostolus*, p. 214; the index entry to p. 290 actually leads to an entry as a martyr); Coens, "Anciennes litanies des saints," pp. 265 (no. 18B) and 269 (no. 18C).

[150] Luscombe, "Denis the Pseudo-Areopagite in the Middle Ages."

[151] Gregory of Tours, *Libri historiarum X* 1. 30, p. 23.

angels and arcane theology, passed off his compositions as those of Dionysius the Areopagite. A spectacular fusion was now engineered between the martyred bishop of Paris, the Athenian convert, and the Neoplatonic author. They were, argued the monks of St.-Denis, all the same person. This gave them the relics of both a famous theologian and an apostolic figure at one blow. Hilduin, abbot of St.-Denis (814–40), sent a long letter to the emperor Louis the Pious, explaining how "our lord and patron" Denis "was ordained apostle of the whole of Gaul."[152] The apostolic status of the abbey's patron saint was generally accepted thereafter, despite occasional doubts, such as those raised by the combative and excessively self-confident theologian, Peter Abelard, while he was himself a monk at St.-Denis. His scepticism about the identification of the patron of the abbey with Denis the Areopagite and his unwillingness to accept Hilduin's authority drove the monks to such a fury that he had to flee the monastery.[153] To doubt the apostolicity of the saint of this wealthy royal abbey, who was acclaimed as "patron and defender of the kings of the French," was indeed a perilous business.[154]

The title of apostle was also extended to those saints who were the first missionaries or initiators of mission to pagan peoples, often in the form of "Apostle of . . ." followed by the name of the convert nation. Saint Gregory the Illuminator won the soubriquet "Apostle to the Armenians," after he baptized King Tiridates III of Armenia early in the fourth century; Remigius or Remi, who baptized Clovis two centuries later was "Apostle of the Franks"; St. Patrick, partly through the enthusiastic backing of Armagh, was awarded the title "Apostle of the Irish"; the English monk Bede hailed Pope Gregory the Great as "our apostle," and in the eleventh century Gregory's feast was counted as a greater feast in England "because he is the Apostle of the English people"; Otto of Bamberg, who led missions to the pagan Pomeranians on the southern Baltic coast in the 1120s, was revered as "Apostle of the Pomeranians."[155]

The extension of the term "apostle" to these post-biblical saints, as well as the controversial claims to apostolic status of such as Martial and Denis, is explained by the fact that the title was a source of power and authority. As the first followers of Jesus and the founding fathers of the Church, the apostles represented the true and original Christianity. Many, very different, parties, appealed to apostolic authority, from the radical heretics of the twelfth and thirteenth centuries who claimed to be following the apostolic life to the pope himself, holder of the apostolic see—in Old French, the word for pope is simply *l'Apostoile*.

[152] Hilduin of St.-Denis, *Epistolae variorum* 20, pp. 328, 332.

[153] Peter Abelard, *Historia calamitatum*, pp. 89–91; Clanchy, *Abelard*, pp. 232–37.

[154] On this aspect of Denis's cult, see later, pp. 232–33.

[155] Terian, *Patriotism and Piety in Armenian Christianity*, pp. 18, 25, etc.; Hincmar of Rheims, *Vita Remigii episcopi Remensis*, preface, p. 253; *Vita secunda sancti Patricii*, preface, p. 47; Jocelin of Furness, *Vita Patricii*, prologue, p. 540; Bede, *Historia ecclesiastica* 2. 1, p. 122; Lanfranc, *Decreta Lanfranci*, p. 61; Petersohn, "Apostolus Pomeranorum.."

CHAPTER 7

Martyrs

Christianity began with a slow and painful execution by the Roman state, and such horrific public killings continued to be defining events for the new religion. The first Christian saints were martyrs, witnesses for the faith. Their deaths were not presented as tragedies but as triumphs. As early as 200 it was claimed that "the more you mow us down, the more we multiply: the blood of Christians is seed."[156] And martyrs' blood was precious. When Cyprian of Carthage was beheaded, the Christians spread linen cloths and towels in front of him, to soak up the blood.[157] And there was a lot of martyr blood. The victims were numerous. One medieval story told how a census of the martyrs had been carried out in the reign of Constantine with remarkable results: "every day of the year more than five thousand feasts of the saints occur together."[158] If this statistic—something approaching two million martyrs—is, in fact, impossible, there were certainly hundreds and perhaps thousands. They laid the bedrock of Christian sainthood.

The imagery of martyrdom was drawn from athletic contests. St. Paul encouraged the first Christians to keep in training, like athletes preparing for a race, with their eyes on the prize—specifically "the prize in the games"; victorious contestants in the public games receive a crown, he writes, but theirs is corruptible, while the crown won by Christians is incorruptible.[159] The races, the struggles, the stadia, the prizes, and the crowns became standard features of Christian rhetoric. The account of the persecution of Christians at Lyons in 177, after describing the horrible tortures that the martyrs suffered, bursts out, "it was indeed fitting that the noble athletes, having undergone this elaborate contest and having triumphed mightily, should attain the great crown of incorruptibility."[160] When, in 259, the Spanish bishop Fructuosus was led out to be burned alive, "he went to an imperishable crown rather than to punishment."[161] A martyr shrine was "the august and beautiful stadium of the martyrs."[162] In the ancient world a palm leaf was awarded to victors in contests of all kinds, as a sign of victory, and Christian writers took this up metaphorically, "the palm of martyrdom" or "the martyr's palm" becoming one of the most common phrases in accounts of the sufferings of the saints. As early as the Book of Revelation (7:9) the saints are described standing before the Lamb, clothed in white and with palms in their hands. Cyprian of Carthage writes that a martyr "has received the palm that he merited."[163] In the medieval iconography of the saints, martyrs can be identified by the palms they hold.

[156] Tertullian, *Apologeticum* 50. 13, p. 171.
[157] *Acta proconsularia sancti Cypriani*, p. 174.
[158] John Beleth, *Summa de ecclesiasticis officiis* 154 *Be*, p. 296.
[159] I Corinthians 9:24–25; "prize" is βραβειον, latinized as *bravium*.
[160] Eusebius, *Historia ecclesiastica* 5. 1. 36 (2, p. 15).
[161] *Passio sanctorum martyrum Fructuosi episcopi, Auguri et Eulogi diaconorum*, p. 180.
[162] Basil of Caesarea, *Homilia XVIII in Gordium martyrem* 1, col. 489.
[163] Cyprian of Carthage, *Epistularium* 10. 4. 3 (3B, p. 53)

The acceptance of Christianity as, first a legal, and then an official, religion in the fourth century meant that the Roman state stopped executing people simply for being Christians, so one main stream of martyrs ceased at that time. But that did not mean that there were to be no future martyr-saints. Apart from such episodes as the pagan reaction under the emperor Julian the Apostate (361–63), there were periods of persecution outside the empire, notably in Persia under Shapur II, where many Christians were executed in the middle decades of the fourth century. (Their relics were later enshrined in the town of Martyropolis on the Roman-Persian border.) And anywhere missionaries moved into pagan lands, there was the possibility of a violent death for the faith. Victims of heretical regimes, such as the Arian Vandals or the iconoclast Byzantine emperors of the eighth and ninth centuries, could also earn the crown, while from the twelfth century the myth of Jewish ritual murder generated the cult of many child martyrs. Eventually, too, the category of "martyr" was extended to those who died at the hands not of unbelievers, but of wicked Christians, especially tyrants attacking the rights of the Church—Thomas Becket, the most prominent new martyr of the High Middle Ages, was of this sort.

It would thus be wrong to regard the cast of martyrs celebrated by medieval Christians as simply the creation of Roman persecution in the early Christian centuries.[164] Moreover, in addition to the martyrs created later, in various circumstances, cults of supposedly early martyrs were continually being spontaneously generated in succeeding generations. A name on a list, the chance discovery of a grave, or a dream—all might lead to the "invention," that is, the discovery, of an ancient martyr. In fact, many important "Roman" martyrs were created long after the disappearance of the Western Roman Empire.

Martyrdom always remained an ideal, the highest form of sanctity in most people's eyes. The desire for martyrdom animated many saints. St. Patrick fantasized about it:

> If I have ever given the appearance of any good on account of my God, whom I love, I ask him to grant this to me, that I should pour out my blood for his name among the converts and captives, even if I should lack burial or my corpse should be wretchedly torn to pieces by dogs or fierce beasts or if the birds of the air should eat it.[165]

St. Francis is recorded as "burning intensely with desire for holy martyrdom" and did the best he could to obtain it by going to Muslim lands to preach.[166]

The idea of non-literal martyrdom was also widespread. "There can be martyrdom even without evident suffering," wrote Pope Gregory I, while Isidore of Seville's great encyclopaedia of the early Middle Ages, *Etymologies*, asserts, "There are two

[164] For later medieval martyrs, Rubin, "Choosing Death? Experiences of Martyrdom in Late Medieval Europe."

[165] Patrick, *Confessio* 59, ed. Bieler, p. 89; ed. Hood, p. 34.

[166] Thomas of Celano, *Vita prima sancti Francisci* 1. 20. 55–57, pp. 42–44.

kinds of martyrdom, one in open suffering, the other in the secret powers of the spirit."[167] Confessors, who had not been able to die for the faith, could make up for it by a hypothetical willingness to endure martyrdom and by an asceticism that could stand as a substitute for it: "but if the times do not offer the chance of martyrdom, nevertheless they do not lack the glory of martyrs, for both in intention and in power they could be martyrs and wished to be so."[168] In this way Bertila, abbess of Chelles near Paris in the late seventh century, "would willingly have submitted her neck to martyrdom with great desire, had the right hand of the persecutor not been lacking," but, failing to find anyone to chop off her head, she "fulfilled the martyrdom of her own blood by mortifying her limbs."[169]

The early Irish monks theorized that there were three kinds of martyrdom: white, green, and red.

> This is the white martyrdom to man, when he separates for sake of God from everything he loves, although he suffer fasting or labour thereat. This is the green martyrdom to him, when by means of them (fasting and labour) he separates from his desires, or suffers toil in penance and repentance. This is the red martyrdom to him, endurance of a cross or destruction for Christ's sake.[170]

The distinction between the first two, virtual, forms of martyrdom is not entirely clear but may be between monks and penitents.

Liturgical commentators also discussed kinds of martyrdom, noticing that the three days after Christmas were dedicated to martyrs: 26 December to St. Stephen the protomartyr, 27 December to John the Evangelist (although his attempted execution, by boiling oil, had not succeeded, and the feast of 27 December celebrates his "Dormition," or "falling asleep"), and 28 December to the Holy Innocents, that is, the children whom Herod had killed in his pre-emptive attempt to destroy the threat that he thought Christ posed. These three cases prompted reflections on the various types of martyrdom:

> There are three kinds of martyrdom: the first willed and effected, the second willed but not effected, and the third effected but not willed: St. Stephen is an example of the first, St. John of the second, the Innocents of the third.[171]

Stephen had been willing to die for Christ and had done so, John had been willing but had not done so, while the Innocents had died but were too little to have willed their martyrdom—the Innocents "confessed Christ not by speaking but by dying."[172]

[167] Quia enim esse possit et sine aperta passione martyrium . . . : Gregory I, *Dialogi* 3. 26. 8 (2, p. 370, with rich annotation); Isidore, *Etymologiae* 7. 11 (PL 82: 290).

[168] *Acta synodi Atrebatensis* 11, col. 1301.

[169] *Vita Bertilae abbatissae Calensis* 8, p. 108.

[170] *Thesaurus palaeohibernicus* 2, pp. 246–47 ("the Cambrai Homily"); see the discussion by Stancliffe, "Red, White and Blue Martyrdom" (who obviously thinks "blue" a better translation than "green").

[171] Jacobus de Voragine, *Legenda aurea* 8 (1, p. 86).

[172] *Le sacramentaire grégorien* 1, pp. 110, 578.

One kind of martyr's death which continued throughout the Middle Ages (and well beyond) was murder in the mission field. The Roman Empire may have been officially converted in the fourth century, but, as Christianity spread outside the old imperial boundaries, those preaching the word often encountered violent opposition from armed and hostile pagans. In 754 the English missionary Boniface was cut down, with his companions, while evangelizing the pagan Frisians. His first hagiographer, Willibald, has no doubt about his status: in the introduction to his Life he refers to "the fame of St. Boniface the martyr," later mentions "the glorious witness of his martyrdom," and, in the passage describing the death of Boniface and his companions, employs the terms "martyr" and "martyrdom" eight times; he eventually concludes the Life by giving the date on which the saint "went to the Lord, rewarded with the triumph of martyrdom" and telling a story of how a spring was miraculously discovered on the spot "where the precious blood of the holy martyr had been shed."[173]

In 997 Adalbert, bishop of Prague, was likewise cut down in the mission field. His hagiographers explain that he had already shown that he was "all aflame with the desire for martyrdom" on an earlier occasion and in very different circumstances, namely when protecting a woman caught in adultery in Prague. The wronged husband and his supporters, pursuing her, had crashed into the bishop's court. "If you are looking for me," Adalbert said, "here I am." He was inwardly preparing himself for martyrdom. "He heard the sound of weapons and the insolent threats with delight, and, pondering silently if he might now, through God's mercy, undergo the martyrdom he had always desired, he waited in doubt and joy." According to one account, the bloodthirsty mob were well aware of the bishop's thinking: "your hope for martyrdom is in vain," one of them supposedly mocked, and threatened revenge on Adalbert's family unless he surrendered the guilty woman. In the event, the bishop was not killed and the posse caught and beheaded the woman. What is clear from the Lives is that death in these circumstances could be seen as a genuine martyrdom, even though all parties were Christian and the woman was actually guilty. It is Adalbert's readiness that is being stressed, a readiness that was finally satisfied when the pagan Prussians he was seeking to convert cut down "the most holy and glorious martyr of Christ."[174]

From the early seventh century, Christianity faced a new and expansive rival in Islam. Muslims conquered Jerusalem in 638, Constantinople in 1453, and, in the eight centuries between these two traumatic moments, the opposing religions encountered each other in a hostile proximity that stretched over three continents. It was the normal practice of Muslims to tolerate Christians and Jews within their own states, but warfare on the borders between the land of Islam and Christendom was incessant, and those who fell or were killed on both sides were sometimes regarded

[173] Willibald, *Vita Bonifatii* preface, 4, 8–9, pp. 456, 476, 514, 516, 518, 522.

[174] *Vita et passio sancti Adalberti* 19, 30, pp. 28–68, at pp. 50–52, 68; Bruno of Querfurt, *Passio sancti Adalberti* 16, pp. 88–90.

as martyrs. An unusual and celebrated case occurred after Muslim armies captured the important Byzantine city of Amorion in 838 and reserved forty-two high-status Byzantine prisoners for special treatment. After being kept imprisoned for several years, they were faced with the choice of conversion to Islam or death. They chose to remain true to their faith and were all publicly executed in 845. Several hagiographical accounts were written soon after the event and they are listed as "martyrs" in the Synaxarion of the church of Constantinople.[175]

Although close in time and number, the forty-eight martyrs executed at Cordoba in the 850s were of a completely different type. The martyrs of Amorion were prisoners-of-war being threatened in order to make them convert to Islam (a highly unusual situation), but most of the Cordoban martyrs, living in a society ruled by Muslims but which tolerated Christianity, went out of their way to provoke martyrdom, by offensive references to Muhammad and public preaching. The chronicler and champion of these voluntary martyrs was the priest Eulogius. He had to face a great deal of doubt and opposition among his own Christian community. Critics objected that "those who are not dragged violently to martyrdom, but come of their own free will, are not to be treated as martyrs."[176] Christians were always clear that to be ready for martyrdom was a virtue, but were often wary of those who sought it out. And Eulogius himself had to admit that these martyrs did not perform any miracles, and he needed quite subtle arguments to explain this lack.[177] In 859 Eulogius himself joined the list of martyrs, and twenty-four years later his remains were translated to Oviedo in Christian Spain. Public preaching of Christianity, especially combined with insulting remarks about the Prophet or the Koran, was an almost certain way of provoking violent reaction among Muslims. For instance, the five Franciscan missionaries who were executed in Marrakesh in 1220, and were venerated as "the five protomartyrs of the Minorite Order," had denounced in their preaching "the iniquities of Muhammad and his religion."[178] These protomartyrs were indeed the first of a small but steady stream of Franciscans killed in Muslim lands.

Before the eleventh century, the title of "martyr" was rarely given to those who died fighting in battle, even against non-Christians. Oswald of Northumbria, killed in battle against pagans in 642, is only an apparent exception, for he was not treated as a martyr until c. 1000.[179] This appears to be the turning point. In 1030 Olav of

[175] Kolia-Dermitzaki, "The Execution of the Forty-two Martyrs of Amorion"; *Synaxarium Ecclesiae Constantinopolitanae*, p. 516.

[176] Eulogius, *Memoriale sanctorum* 1. 21, p. 385 (PL 115: 754).

[177] See Wolf, *Christian Martyrs in Muslim Spain*, chapter 6, "Martyrdom without Miracles."

[178] *Legenda sanctorum martirum quinque fratrum minorum*.

[179] Gunn, "Bede and the Martyrdom of St Oswald." Although Hroswitha of Gandersheim says that Oswald "submitted to death for the name of Christ" (Hrotsvit, *Opera omnia*, p. 279 [*Gesta Ottonis*, lines 95–97]), the earliest evidence for the title "martyr" seems to be a late-tenth-century Kalendar: Paris, BnF, lat. 7299, fol. 7: *Osuualdi regis et martiris*. See Rushforth, *Saints in English Kalendars*, under 5 August. He is also "king and martyr" for Ælfric, writing in the 990s: Ælfric, *Lives of Saints* 2, p. 124 (no. 26). By the twelfth century Oswald's status as a martyr was well established: Reginald of Durham, *Vita sancti Oswaldi regis et martyris*.

Norway was killed while trying to reclaim his throne, and he is styled "king and martyr," and his death "martyrdom," in the chronicle of Adam of Bremen, writing thirty or so years later.[180] This is Olav 's standard style in medieval liturgies. Later in the century, the fallen leader of a Genoese raid on the north African city of Mahdia in 1087 was acclaimed as "a beautiful martyr, in Jesus' service."[181] With the First Crusade of 1096–99 the term becomes common.[182] The crusaders who died at Nicaea, during the first siege of the campaign, "received martyrdom" and "triumphantly carried into heaven the robes of martyrdom."[183] These "were the first happily to receive martyrdom for the name of Christ."[184] If they were the first to earn martyrdom in crusading battle, they were not the last. In 1218, those who fell in the assault on Damietta "were crowned as martyrs," while any previous faults committed by the French nobles killed in the fighting at Mansurah in 1250 "were cut away by the scythe of martyrdom."[185] Since the crusade was a spiritually meritorious form of warfare, those who died in its course went straight to heaven.

The novelty of a martyr dying sword in hand was recognized at the time, not always without a sense of its strangeness: "It is a new kind of martyrdom, to want to kill someone!"[186] And cults of such fallen heroes were rare. The use of the term "martyr" for crusaders did not lead to any significant crusader-saints, and martyr-saints who died in battle, like Oswald and Olav, are the exception. The typical martyr was executed or murdered without putting up resistance. It may indeed be a feature of Christian martyrdom that aligns it with Jewish martyrdom and contrasts it with some forms of Muslim martyrdom (both discussed later, pp. 633–34).

A small but significant group of "martyrs" are the children supposedly killed by the Jews. The earliest case is from England, and concerns William of Norwich, a young apprentice whose body was found in a wood outside the trading town of Norwich in 1144.[187] Thomas of Monmouth, the local monk who took up William's case, blamed the Jews of Norwich for the death, and saw it as part of an international Jewish plot: "it was an ancient custom of theirs that every year they must sacrifice a Christian in some part of the world to the most high God in scorn and contempt of Christ."[188] Thomas was a vigorous champion of William's sanctity, but something of

[180] Adam of Bremen, *Gesta Hammaburgensis ecclesiae pontificum* 2. 60–61, 77; 3. 13, pp. 298, 300, 318, 340.

[181] *Carmen in victoriam Pisanorum*, p. 27.

[182] Riley-Smith, *The First Crusade and the Idea of Crusading*, pp. 114–19, 151–52; Morris, "Martyrs on the Field of Battle before and during the First Crusade."

[183] *Gesta Francorum* 2. 8, p. 17.

[184] Peter Tudebode, *Historia de Hierosolymitano itinere*, p. 36 (PL 155, col. 765).

[185] Jacques de Vitry, *Epistula* 4, p. 105; Cole, *The Preaching of the Crusades to the Holy Land*, p. 238 (sermon of Odo of Châteauroux).

[186] *Insignis liber de poenitentia et tentationibus religiosorum* 27, col. 893; Riley-Smith, "Death on the First Crusade," pp. 20–22.

[187] Ward, *Miracles and the Medieval Mind*, pp. 68–76; Langmuir, "Thomas of Monmouth"; Yarrow, *Saints and Their Communities*, pp. 122–67.

[188] Thomas of Monmouth, *Vita sancti Willelmi Norwicensis* 2. 9, p. 93.

a solitary voice. He recorded many miracles and managed to get William translated to an honourable position in the monastic church at Norwich, but the cult remained a minor one, although offerings were made at the shrine down to the time of the Reformation.[189]

However, once the idea of the ritual murder of a Christian boy by Jews, the so-called blood libel," had been launched, it proved enduring.[190] Dozens of cases are recorded in the Middle Ages, and many more in modern times. By no means all of them produced a new saint, but there are several examples where the report of miracles and the writing of hagiography suggest, as in the case of William of Norwich, that at least the basic elements of a cult were present. In 1303, for example, at Weißensee in Thuringia, according to a chronicler from nearby Erfurt,

> the wicked Jews, following the footsteps of their fathers, seized the son of the castellan of Weißensee and subjected him to a wretched and secret death, then hanged him with his own belt in a hut in a vineyard near the town, as if he had strangled himself with his own hands. He was found there after three days and brought into the city, where he was distinguished by many miracles; on account of this all the Jews in that city, and in others, were killed.[191]

This would also have been the fate of the Jews of Erfurt, concludes the chronicler wistfully, if they had not bribed the city councillors. The dead boy, Konrad of Weißensee, became the focus of a minor but tenacious cult. An early-fourteenth-century Passion of "the most holy boy and martyr Konrad" records numerous miracles, while in the early sixteenth century there was even an attempt at formal canonization, backed by the duke of Saxony and furthered by the printing of a new Life.[192] The cults of these child-martyrs were numerous, especially in the German-speaking lands, and some of them were important. Werner of Bacharach or Oberwesel (d. 1287) was the subject of (unsuccessful) canonization hearings in 1428–29, and the cult of Simon of Trent (d. 1475) won papal approval in 1588.[193]

There is a sense in which all saints, being embodiments of community identity or social ideologies, are "political," but a particular group of them have been given the label "political saints" or "political martyrs."[194] These are the aristocratic vic-

[189] Nilson, *Cathedral Shrines of Medieval England*, pp. 156–57.

[190] Erb, ed., *Die Legende vom Ritualmord*; Wasyliw, *Martyrdom, Murder, and Magic: Child Saints and Their Cults*, pp. 107–36.

[191] *Cronica sancti Petri Erfordernis moderna*, p. 323.

[192] Fischer, *Katalog der Handschriften der Universitätsbibliothek Erlangen* 1: *Die Lateinischen Pergamenthandschriften*, pp. 506–7 (Erlangen, Universitätsbibliothek 423, fols. 106–125v); Möncke "Der Gute Konrad von Weissensee."

[193] *Processus Bacheracensis de vita, martyrio et miraculis beati Wernheri*; BS 11, col. 1186; Hsia, *Trent 1475: Stories of a Ritual Murder Trial.*

[194] Walker, "Political Saints in Later Medieval England"; Piroyansky, *Martyrs in the Making: Political Martyrdom in Late Medieval England.* The martyred kings Edward II and Henry VI are also often included in this group; see brief comment later, p. 216. An earlier example is Earl Waltheof, executed in 1076.

tims of the political violence of late medieval England, notably Simon de Montfort (d. 1265), Thomas of Lancaster (d. 1322), Richard fitzAlan (d. 1397), and archbishop Richard Scrope (d. 1405). These all met violent deaths as rebels or opponents of English kings.

Simon de Montfort was killed in battle at Evesham and buried in the abbey there. Soon after his death miracles began to be reported. The cult was clearly seen as subversive, for, once the royal government had re-established its authority, in 1266, it was ruled that Simon de Montfort "should be deemed a saint by no one . . . and the empty and foolish wonders that some people have related about him shall not ever be uttered by any lips."[195] Despite this prohibition, almost two hundred miracles are attributed to his intervention, though it is noticeable that virtually none of them involve the sick going to his tomb.[196] In most cases the sufferers either invoke Simon while at home, sometimes then sending a candle or a wax image as an ex-voto to Evesham, or they seek out the water from the miraculous fountain that sprang up on the site of the battle (or, in one case, earth from the site). Such open-air cult sites are much harder to police than a tomb in a church (although on one occasion royal soldiers apprehended a servant girl carrying water away from the spring in a jug—it miraculously turned into beer to give her an alibi).

The liturgical evidence for the cult includes hymns, one of which sees Simon, "the new martyr," being welcomed into heaven by Thomas Becket, another saint renowned for crushing "false laws" through his martyrdom, and the following prayer:

> O God, who fortified with the power of constancy your martyr, the blessed Simon, in his last agony, and who united with him brave knights, in order to renew the kingdom of Britain, grant that we may be helped by the prayers of him who merited the consummation of a famous martyrdom.[197]

Miracles also began to occur at the tomb of Thomas, earl of Lancaster, soon after he was beheaded during the political upheavals of the 1320s:

> And soon after the good earl Thomas of Lancaster was martyred, a priest that long time had been blind, dreamed in his sleeping that he should go unto the hill there that the good earl Thomas of Lancaster was done unto death, and he should have his sight again.[198]

Thomas was hailed by some as a "holy martyr," and the site of his execution, and an image of the earl in St. Paul's cathedral, London, were also the scene of

[195] Stubbs, ed., *Select Charters*, p. 409 (Dictum de Kenilworth, c. 8).

[196] *Miracula Simonis de Montfort*; for analysis, see Heffernan, "'God hathe schewed for him many grete miracules': Political Canonization and the *Miracula* of Simon de Montfort," pp. 186–91; Valente, "Simon de Montfort, Earl of Leicester, and the Utility of Sanctity"; on one aristocratic pilgrim, Maddicott, "Follower, Leader, Pilgrim, Saint: Robert de Vere, Earl of Oxford, at the Shrine of Simon de Montfort."

[197] Prothero, *The Life of Simon de Montfort*, app. 4, pp. 388–91.

[198] *The Brut or The Chronicles of England*, pp. 228, 229 (modernized).

miraculous cures. As in the case of Simon de Montfort, the royal government immediately placed a ban on anyone going to the place of his execution or his tomb, enforcing this with armed guards.[199] The Despensers, who virtually controlled the government at this time, were particularly hostile; one of their messengers even excreted on the site of Thomas's execution.[200] But politics change quickly. Within five years of the earl's death, the Despensers had been hanged, drawn and quartered, and a new regime installed, under Edward III, that was highly favourable to earl Thomas. A move was made to have him officially canonized. This never happened, but the cult remained active until the Reformation, being well enough developed to have pilgrim badges showing the earl's execution and the ascent of his soul to heaven.[201]

Richard fitzAlan, earl of Arundel, was executed under Richard II, when the king was clearing a backlog of vengeance. After he was beheaded, his body was buried in the Augustinian church in London, where it immediately became the focus of an incipient cult. The "common people" revered him as a martyr, made "pilgrimages" to his tomb, and passed on the tale that his head had been miraculously rejoined to his body. In response, the king ordered him to be reburied in an unmarked grave beneath the church floor.[202] Likewise, in the next reign, after the execution of Richard Scrope, archbishop of York, on a charge of rebellion, wonderful signs followed: the field where he had been beheaded yielded a magnificent crop of corn; the king, who had ordered his execution, was struck by leprosy; and the dead archbishop himself appeared in the night to an old man, ordering him to remove the logs that had been placed on his tomb to prevent offerings being made there.[203] Eventually an enduring, if small-scale, cult developed, rooted in the city of York and with official backing from the Yorkist dynasty: in 1471 Edward IV even claimed that it was "for the right of our ancestry" that Scrope had "died and suffered death and martyrdom."[204]

These "political saints" were political in a special sense. Other cults rarely witnessed government guards, official prohibitions, and, what is also telling, a dramatic shift in their fortunes paralleling a change of regime. These "martyrs" had led controversial lives, defied their kings and suffered violent death as a consequence. To regard them as saints—as martyrs—was an implicit political statement.

But martyrdom could also have a radically depoliticising effect, with the blood of murdered kings, princes, and bishops offering a unifying centre, around which former enemies could muster. A spectacular example of the way a bloody death could instantaneously transform a difficult and divisive figure into a saintly martyr is provided by Thomas Becket, archbishop of Canterbury, murdered by four knights in

[199] *Flores historiarum* 3, pp. 206–7, 213–14; *The Brut or The Chronicles of England*, pp. 228–31; *The Anonimalle Chronicle 1307 to 1334*, pp. 108, 112, 114.

[200] *The Brut or The Chronicles of England*, p. 230.

[201] *Age of Chivalry*, p. 223, no. 80.

[202] Walsingham, *Historia Anglicana* 2, p. 226.

[203] *Martyrium Ricardi archiepiscopi*.

[204] *Calendar of the Close Rolls, Edward IV* 2, p. 189; on the cult, see Norton, "Richard Scrope and York Minster"; Piroyansky, *Martyrs in the Making: Political Martyrdom in Late Medieval England*, pp. 49–73.

his own cathedral on 29 December 1170. Becket had long presented himself as a champion of the rights of the Church against the king, Henry II, and, while the four knights had not received explicit instructions or approval from Henry, they certainly regarded themselves as acting on his behalf against an enemy. Hence Becket could reasonably be regarded as dying for a cause. He was thus "a new martyr."[205] Becket's status as a martyr was recognized quickly and widely. In the year 1200, for instance, one of the parties in a lawsuit could refer to her tenure of a piece of land "from the time when St. Thomas, archbishop of Canterbury, suffered martyrdom."[206] This had nothing to do with the substance of the case but was a natural landmark, and was cited even though tenure from 1198 would have been sufficient in law. When Becket's remains were translated in 1220, the occasion was a great celebration of national unity and harmony between Church and State.

Just at this time, there is a case of a murdered archbishop whose chief hagiographer adopted an interestingly different line. This is Engelbert, archbishop of Cologne, murdered in 1225 during what was basically an aristocratic feud. His tomb, like Becket's, immediately became the site of miraculous healing. Engelbert's hagiographer is unusually frank about him: "the sanctity that was lacking in his life, was supplied by his precious death, and, if he was less than perfect in his behaviour, nevertheless he was made a saint by his passion."[207] But this was definitely a minority position: more common was a rewriting of the martyr's earlier life to conform to saintly standards, as happened in the case of Becket.

The year 1253 saw the canonization of two martyrs, Stanislaus of Cracow and Peter Martyr. They were very different cases. Stanislaus was a bishop who had been cut down at the command of the Polish king in 1079, so almost two centuries before the canonization. Peter Martyr was a Dominican inquisitor murdered by heretics only a year before he was canonized. Church lawyers recognized that, in cases of martyrdom, the cumbersome procedures of official canonization need not be followed to the letter, and, in these circumstances everything could be done "more easily and lightly," but, while Peter Martyr's canonization was one of the quickest recorded, the canonization of Stanislaus was contentious, and encountered stubborn opposition from one of the cardinals, who thought the case too ancient. It required the appearance of Stanislaus himself in a vision before the canonization proceeded.[208]

These were to be the last martyrs canonized in the Middle Ages.

[205] Gerald of Wales, *Vita sancti Remigii episcopi Lincolniensis* 27, p. 52.

[206] *Curia Regis Rolls* 1, p. 320.

[207] "Sanctitatem, que vite defuit, mors pretiosa supplevit, et si minus perfectus erat in conversatione, sanctus tamen effectus est in passione": Caesarius of Heisterbach, *Vita, passio et miracula sancti Engelberti* 1. 1, p. 236; see Jung, "From Jericho to Jerusalem: The Violent Transformation of Archbishop Engelbert of Cologne."

[208] On Peter Martyr, see Prudlo, *The Martyred Inquisitor: The Life and Cult of Peter of Verona*; Vincent, *Vita (major) sancti Stanislai Cracoviensis episcopi* 55, pp. 434–36; "facilius et levius": Hostiensis, *Lectura siue Apparatus super quinque libris Decretalium*, ad X. 3. 45. 1, *Audivimus*; followed by Johannes Andreae, *Novella Commentaria in quinque Decretalium libros*, ad X. 3. 45. 1, *Audivimus*.

Although martyrs were recognized as an elite within the saints, it is not clear that their cults were any different from those of other saints. There were successful and unsuccessful martyr cults, just as there were successful and unsuccessful confessor cults. The cures that the martyrs offered were of the same type as the cures the confessors offered. It was in their story, and their image, that they stood out, with their sufferings and their bloody end, not in their function as saints.

A phrase of Augustine's was frequently invoked to clarify the nature of martyrdom: "it is not the suffering but the cause" that makes a martyr.[209] Persecution, torment, or a violent death were not enough in themselves; the cause for which one suffered must be right and just. The debates that might arise on this issue can be illustrated by a conversation that took place between Lanfranc, the first archbishop of Canterbury after the Norman conquest of England in 1066, and his protégé (and eventual successor) Anselm. They were talking about one of the saints venerated in Canterbury, Alphege or Ælfheah, an earlier archbishop who had been killed by marauding Danes in 1012, after he refused to raise a ransom to secure his release. Lanfranc wondered whether Alphege could properly be regarded as a martyr. "These English amongst whom we live," he said to Anselm, "have set up for themselves certain people whom they revere as saints. . . . I cannot help having doubts about the merit of their sanctity." He was particularly concerned about the designation of Alphege as a martyr, since all agreed that he had been killed, not for refusing to deny Christ, but for refusing to impose upon his people the crippling cost of a ransom. Anselm reassured him, with a complex piece of argument: someone who would die rather than commit a small sin would obviously die rather than commit a greater sin; it is a greater sin to deny Christ than to impose the burden of a ransom; since Alphege died rather than impose the burden of a ransom, he would clearly have been willing to die if he had been asked to deny Christ. Alphege, Anselm asserted, had died for justice, just as John the Baptist (who had not been asked to deny Christ) died for truth. Christ is truth and justice. Alphege was as much a martyr as John the Baptist. Whatever one might think of this reasoning, it satisfied Lanfranc, who thereafter encouraged the cult of his martyred predecessor.[210]

Since papal canonization required a Mass and Office for a new saint, a decision had to be made about whether the liturgy was to be for a martyr or confessor. Thus, when the pope canonized Thomas Becket, he decreed "that he should be numbered in the college of holy martyrs," whereas when, a century and a half later, Louis, bishop of Toulouse, was canonized, the day of his death, 19 August, was proclaimed as "the feast-day of that bishop and confessor" in the bull of canonization.[211] Sometimes this decision was unpopular. Joinville was exasperated that his old master, king Louis of France, who had suffered on crusade, and died during one, was not numbered among

[209] Augustine, *Enarrationes in Psalmos* 34. 2. 1, p. 312 (PL 36: 333); idem, *Sermo* 275. 1 (PL 38: 1254).

[210] Eadmer, *Vita Anselmi* 1. 30, pp. 50–54.

[211] *Materials for the History of Thomas Becket* 7, p. 546, no. 784 (Alexander III, 12 March 1173, *Gaudendum est*, Jaffé, *Regesta* no. 12201); *Processus canonizationis sancti Ludovici episcopi Tolosani*, p. 399 (John XXII, 7 April 1317, *Sol oriens*).

the martyrs: "For if God died on the cross, so did he: for he was signed with the cross when he died at Tunis."[212] The campaign to have king Louis canonized had stressed, as early as 1275, twenty-two years before the canonization, that the king deserved "the palm of martyrdom," and one version of his liturgical Office hailed Louis as "a martyr by desire," but the papacy was not willing to recognize this virtual martyrdom as a literal one.[213]

The most unusual martyr of the Middle Ages was a dog. This was St. Guinefort, a greyhound that had been wrongly killed by its owner on suspicion of taking the life of a baby, when in fact it had bravely protected the child. The site where the dog was buried, at a castle north of Lyons, quickly became a shrine: "the country people, seeing the dog's noble deed and how it was killed although innocent, visited the place and honoured the dog as a martyr, invoking its help in illness and need." The outraged Dominican Stephen de Bourbon eventually had the dog's bones dug up and burned.[214] The essence of martyrdom, a brave and innocent death, here transcended the line between species, at least in the eyes of the local people.

If it was not common for a dog to be revered as a martyr, there was, nonetheless, a diversity of type amongst those venerated in this way. Death because one refused to renounce one's faith, which was the original form of martyrdom, became less common after the conversion of the Roman Empire, and, although a missionary's violent death at the hands of pagans or Muslims was a fairly clear-cut situation, what of the case of Adalbert of Prague, envisaging martyrdom for protecting an adulterous wife, or Alphege's refusal to have a ransom paid, and what exactly was the cause for which Thomas of Lancaster died? St. Augustine might have stressed that "it is not the suffering but the cause that makes a martyr," but it seems to have been the flow of innocent blood that was the most fruitful seed of martyr cult.

Confessors

The first great distinction to arise historically between types of saint was between martyrs and confessors, a distinction that was a consequence of the emergence of the Church from persecution in the fourth century. It was, indeed, a fundamental turning point in the history of Christian sanctity that the veneration previously given only to martyrs was extended to holy men and women who did not suffer a violent death. It was not an inevitable development, and the status of the confessor-saint needed constant reaffirmation. As late as the thirteenth century, it had to be pointed

[212]Jean de Joinville, *Vie de saint Louis* 5, p. 4; on this passage, see Smith, "Martyrdom and Crusading in the Thirteenth Century: Remembering the Dead of Louis IX's Crusades," esp. p. 191 and n. 15.

[213]Gaposchkin, *The Making of Saint Louis*, pp. 32–33, 173–75.

[214]Stephen de Bourbon, *Tractatus de diversis materiis praedicabilibus* 4. 7. 370, pp. 325–28; see Schmitt, *Le saint lévrier*.

out that "Although the order of martyrs is superior in dignity to the order of confessors, nevertheless some confessors are far superior in merit to some martyrs."[215]

Confessor-saints were extraordinarily numerous, and can be categorized in various ways. One approach is to take the Church's own categories: doctors, bishops, abbots, virgins.

DOCTORS OF THE CHURCH

Around the year 500, or shortly thereafter, a list was drawn up of "the works of the holy fathers which are received in the Catholic Church."[216] Although composed in the West, the list includes the great figures of both eastern and western Christianity: Gregory of Nazianzus, Basil, Athanasius, John Chrysostom, Cyril of Alexandria, and (the less renowned) Theophilus of Alexandria amongst those writing in Greek; Cyprian, Hilary, Ambrose, Augustine, Jerome, Prosper of Aquitaine, and Leo I amongst those writing in Latin. There is no hint that these writers had a special cult or were marked out in the liturgy, but they are distinguished as "holy fathers" and explicitly endorsed. They are virtually all confessors rather than martyrs, and it is their role as shapers of Christian thought and doctrine that distinguishes this small special group among the confessor saints.

The list of Fathers or Doctors of the Church continued to be augmented later in the Middle Ages. An example is provided by Lawrence, prior of Durham (d. 1154), who included a section on "Doctors" in his verse epic *Hypognosticon*.[217] He catalogues twenty names: Jerome; John (presumably Chrysostom); Gregory; Augustine; Lactantius; Ambrose; Bede; Rufinus; Eusebius; Orosius; Basil; Caesarius; Hilary; Prosper; Leo I; Hrabanus Maurus; Haimo; Anselm; Ivo; Hildebert. Of these twenty figures, twelve belong to the patristic period of the fourth and fifth centuries; these are followed chronologically by Caesarius of Arles (d. 542), who left numerous sermons and guides to monastic life, by Pope Gregory the Great (d. 604), and by the exegete and historian Bede (d. 735); there are two Carolingian scholars, Hrabanus Maurus and Haimo (Haimo's identity and corpus of works are both subject to discussion and debate); and finally three figures who had died during Lawrence's lifetime. The list thus suggests that the "doctors" are not just a group of distant, long-dead heroes, a closed club of founding fathers, but, rather, are still active in the contemporary world. The three near-contemporary figures are Anselm, an Italian by birth, who was abbot of the Norman abbey of Bec before becoming archbishop of Canterbury; Ivo, a famous canon lawyer and bishop of Chartres; and Hildebert, bishop of Le Mans and then archbishop of Tours, who left an influential body of prose and poetry (Lawrence calls him "first of them all, renowned in prose and verse"). These three died between 1109 and 1133.

[215] Caesarius of Heisterbach, *Dialogus miraculorum* 8. 71 (2, p. 141); cf. William Durandus, *Rationale divinorum officiorum* 7. 42. 2 (140B, pp. 107–8).

[216] *Decretum Gelasianum de libris recipiendis et non recipiendis*, p. 36.

[217] Lawrence of Durham, *Hypognosticon* 9, lines 491–506, pp. 245–46.

The overlap between Lawrence's list of doctors and later ones is far from complete. Only nine of Lawrence's doctors are deemed "Doctors of the Church" by the modern Roman Catholic Church. Moreover, of the ten doctors in his list who are not so regarded by modern Catholics, only one or two have any evidence of saintly cult. Thus being a "doctor"—a learned man whose writing buttressed the Church—did not necessarily mean being a saint; some doctors were saints, some were not.

Of the western Fathers, four stand out in the written and pictorial record: Ambrose, Jerome, Augustine, and Gregory, formative Christian leaders of the fourth, fifth, and sixth centuries. Their Lives are sometimes grouped together in hagiographic collections, they can be found together in litanies and they are depicted together in locations as diverse as prefaces to Carolingian bibles and late medieval altarpieces.[218] In 1260 the Franciscans ordered that the feasts of the four should be "semi-doubles," and in 1298 the pope decreed that "Mother Church" ordained special honours for certain saints: the apostles and evangelists, and also "the outstanding doctors of the Church," named as Ambrose, Augustine, Jerome, and Gregory the Great.[219] These four formative figures thus received precise recognition at this time, with special liturgical commemoration on the same level as the apostles and evangelists.

In the Byzantine Church there was an equivalent group of learned founding fathers: Basil (d. 378), John Chrysostom (d. 407), and Gregory of Nazianzus (d. 389). Between them, they had produced a huge quantity of sermons, biblical commentary, and theological writing, which formed the foundation of later Greek Christian culture. They had their own feast-days, but also a shared celebration on 30 January. The late medieval Greek Synaxaria give an account of the origin of this joint feast-day.[220] During the reign of Alexius I (1081–1118), according to this story, there was a debate among the scholars of Constantinople about the relative merits of Basil, John, and Gregory. It became so acute that they even formed parties: Basilites, Johnites, and Gregorites. At this point, the three ancient saints appeared in a vision to the aged, holy, and eloquent John, bishop of Euchaita. "We are one before God," they said to him, "as you see, and there is no opposition or quarrel between us . . . there is no 'first' or 'second' among us." They commanded him to institute a common feast for the three of them. John obeyed their commands, choosing 30 January since all three had feast-days in January, and composing the necessary liturgical chants and prayers. An oration he preached on this occasion survives.[221] Like the Four Doctors of the western Church, the Three Holy Hierarchs, as Basil, John, and Gregory were

[218] Philippart, *Les légendiers latins*, p. 93; *Reclams Lexikon der Heiligen und der biblischen Gestalten*, p. 356, s.v. "Kirchenväter."

[219] *Sources of the Modern Roman Liturgy* 2, p. 419; *Liber Sextus* 3. 22, cols. 1059–60.

[220] *Historia institutionis (communis festi)*; see Agapitos, "Teachers, Pupils and Imperial Power in Eleventh-Century Byzantium," pp. 188–91; for some problems of attribution and dating, Hussey, "The Canons of John Mauropous," pp. 72–73.

[221] *Iohannis Euchaitorum Metropolitae quae in codice Vaticano graeco 676 supersunt*, pp. 106–19, no. 178; Papadopoulou-Kerameos, *Hierosolymitikē Bibliothēkē* 2, p. 250.

known, were frequently depicted together, in icons and illustrated manuscripts, such as the Theodore Psalter of 1066, where they stand side by side, gazing out at the reader, with their haloes, vestments, and books, looking very much as if there was no opposition or quarrel between them.[222]

BISHOPS

Bishops formed the backbone of the Christian Church throughout the late antique and medieval period. Each city of the Roman empire had a bishop, whose authority, from the time of Constantine, was supported by the state. He supervised the other clergy, had legal and financial privileges, and met with his fellow bishops to decide dogmatic and disciplinary matters. After the fall of Rome, the role of bishops increased in importance. Chosen mainly from the aristocracy, these natural rulers formed a government more literate and more stable than that of the warrior kings whom they might advise. There were important ecclesiastical functions that could only be fulfilled by a bishop, including the ordination of priests, the dedication of churches and the rite of confirmation.

Bishops had their own retinues, including men of letters, and these clerical disciples sometimes produced Lives of their episcopal masters. Since several early martyrs were also bishops, there are accounts of them, but the first Lives of non-martyr bishops were written around the year 400: Sulpicius Severus's *Life of Martin*, bishop of Tours, composed in 396 (supplemented by *Letters* and *Dialogues* dealing with Martin, 397–404), and Paulinus's *Life of Ambrose of Milan*, of either 412–13 or 422.[223] In some dioceses, a genre of serial biography developed. Agnellus of Ravenna, in the first half of the ninth century, wrote his *Book of the Pontiffs of the Church of Ravenna*, "in order to recall to memory the holy fathers, the bishops of the church of Ravenna who have gone before, and what each of them did in his time."[224] On occasion, these serial biographies were maintained and extended over many generations. The first version of the *Deeds of the Bishops of Auxerre*, for example, was composed in the 870s, and covered the bishops from Roman times to the date of composition, and was then periodically continued, finally reaching as late as the seventeenth century.[225]

It is not surprising that a number of these leaders of the Christian community were regarded as saints.[226] If the anniversary of a bishop's death was marked liturgically, there was the seed from which a feast-day might grow. In the middle of the fourth century, Cyril of Jerusalem explained the liturgical distinction between two groups of names that were mentioned in the Mass: first, the patriarchs, prophets,

[222] Der Nersessian, *L'Illustration des psautiers grecs du Moyen Age* 2, p. 26, fig. 60, from BL, Add. 19352, fol. 35v.

[223] Moorhead, *Ambrose*, p. 10 on dating, with further references.

[224] Agnellus of Ravenna, *Liber pontificalis ecclesiae Ravennatis*, prologue, at p. 278.

[225] *Gesta pontificum Autissiodorensium*; on the genre in general, Sot, *Gesta episcoporum, gesta abbatum*; on the first version of this particular text, Bouchard, "Episcopal *Gesta*."

[226] Wünsch, "Der Heilige Bischof."

apostles, and martyrs, who were invoked in the hope of having the support of their prayer and intercession; second, the deceased holy fathers and bishops, and other faithful, for whom the congregation prays.[227] Cyril is stressing the distinction between saints, the first group, *to whom* one prays, and the ordinary Christian dead, the second group, *for whom* one prays, but it was possible for a deceased bishop to make the transition from the second to the first group, and for the local congregation to go beyond revering his memory and to begin to treat him as a saint. The writing of Lives and the translation of relics might follow.[228] The bishops of early medieval Italy and Gaul, defending their cities against barbarian attack, offering charity to the poor and mercy to captives, came easily to be idealized as patrons of their cities.[229] The poet Venantius Fortunatus, writing in the 560s, claimed that Metz, protected as it was by its walls and the river Moselle, was yet more strongly secured "by the merit of its bishop."[230]

Bishop-saints were not uncommon in the early and High Middle Ages. Gregory of Tours, writing his accounts of the saints in the sixth-century Merovingian kingdoms, recorded the virtues and miracles of dozens of recent or contemporary bishops, as well as earlier saintly patrons like Severinus, bishop of Bordeaux, whose tomb offered the citizens his protection whenever "disease came upon them or an enemy besieged them or disputes struck."[231] In Byzantium between the eighth and the eleventh centuries, some twenty Lives of contemporary bishop-saints were written, while, in that same period, one in five of the saints represented in French hagiographic booklets is a bishop.[232] Of the 20 new saints who lived and were revered in England in the period 1075–1225, 8 were bishops.[233] And this figure, equivalent to 40 per cent, is very close to that provided by André Vauchez: 38 per cent of those subject to a canonization process in the years 1198–1431 were bishops (27 of 71).[234]

A church might venerate its early bishops as saints, as in the case of Trier, which included in its litany the names of fourteen early bishops of the see.[235] Sometimes an entire series of bishops was viewed as saintly. Just as Gregory VII claimed that every pope "is, without a doubt, made a saint," so bishops in Germany or France might

[227] Cyril of Jerusalem, *Catacheses mystagogicae* 5. 9, pp. 158–59.

[228] Classically studied by Picard, *Le souvenir des évêques*, pp. 679–711. For discussion of particular cases in the shadowy landscape between episcopal biography and hagiography, see Coué, *Hagiographie im Kontext: Schreibanlass und Funktion von Bischofsviten*; Haarländer, *Vitae episcoporum. Eine Quellengattung zwischen Hagiographie und Historiographie.*

[229] Orselli, *L'idea e il culto del santo patrono cittadino*, pp. 97–119.

[230] Venantius Fortunatus, *Carmina* 3. 13, lines 15–16 (1, pp. 109–10) (MGH, AA 4/1, p. 66).

[231] Gregory of Tours, *Gloria confessorum* 44, p. 775 (repr., 1969, p. 325).

[232] Moulet, *Évêques, pouvoir et société à Byzance*, p. 21; Poulin, "Les *libelli* dans l'édition hagiographique," p. 53.

[233] Bartlett, *England under the Norman and Angevin Kings*, pp. 461–63.

[234] Vauchez, *Sainthood*, p. 257.

[235] Coens, "Anciennes litanies des saints," pp. 205–6 (no. 9).

claim that every incumbent of their see was a saint.[236] The *Deeds of the Bishops of Verdun* were written "to perpetuate among us the memory of those whose names, as we believe, are written in heaven forever."[237] Even if this is not taken as an explicit claim to sanctity, there can be no doubt about the evidence of John of Avranches, listing the feast-days to be celebrated in his church, who gives a long list of names, starting with the Virgin Mary and concluding with "all the holy bishops who have presided over this church."[238]

One conventional qualification for becoming a bishop was *not* to desire the office, an attitude that is sometimes summed up in the phrase "I am unwilling to become a bishop [*nolo episcopari*]," the answer supposedly expected of potential pontiffs. Although there seems to be no evidence that these words were actually used, the assumption was there, and sometimes quite explicit. The sixth-century Justinianic Code states,

> A bishop should be ordained through prayers not money. He should be so far from any unlawful canvassing that he should obtain the office only when forced; if he is asked, he should withdraw, if he is invited, he should run away . . . he is unworthy of episcopal office unless he is ordained unwillingly.[239]

Examples of this unwillingness are numerous. In 374, the local population of Milan were eager that their governor, Ambrose, accept the bishopric. His stratagems to avoid this were ingenious. First, exercising his authority as governor, he ordered various people to be tortured. Since the Church forbade the ordination of "those who impose torture as part of legal proceedings," he thought this might offer an escape from episcopal office. But the crowd called out, "your sin be on our head!" Foiled in this way, Ambrose next tried inviting all the prostitutes of the town to his house, thinking perhaps that this presumably unepiscopal behaviour might dissuade the Christians of Milan. "Your sin be on our head!" they called out again. Even a nocturnal flight from the city was in vain, for God returned him to Milan in the morning. Eventually, truly "unwillingly" (at least according to his hagiographer), he was ordained bishop.[240]

Over a thousand years later, in 1446, when the distinguished Dominican Antoninus heard that the pope intended to appoint him archbishop of Florence, his first thought was to run away to Sardinia and live incognito. After he was hauled back to Florence, he still "strove in every way he could to avoid this dignity." Only the pope's unyielding stance eventually forced him to give way.[241] These two examples, a millen-

[236] Gregory VII, *Registrum* 2. 55a, (1, p. 207); but Ullmann argued that "sanctus" refers to the pope's Petrine powers, not individual sanctity: "Romanus Pontifex indubitanter efficitur sanctus: Dictatus Papae 23 in Retrospect and Prospect."

[237] *Gesta episcoporum Viridunensium*, p. 37.

[238] John of Avranches, *De officiis ecclesiasticis*, pp. 46–49 (PL 147: 59–61).

[239] *Codex Iustinianus* 1. 3. 30, p. 37.

[240] Paulinus, *Vita Ambrosii* 6–9, pp. 60–64.

[241] Castiglione, *Vita Antonini archiepiscopi Florentini* 5–7, p. 315.

nium apart, illustrate the enduring power of this ideal: only those who did not want to be bishops were worthy to be bishops. And the ideal only makes sense because many people did want to be bishops, because bishops had power, prestige and the opportunity to become rich. The passage of laws against bribing your way to a bishopric was just as enduring a feature of Church history as the dream of *nolo episcopari*, the former recognizing a reality, the latter envisaging an ideal.

Saintly bishops might be held up as models and provide a standard against which other bishops could be judged, and usually deemed to have failed. Antoninus shunned luxury in food and clothing, had no vessels of gold and silver, and kept no horse or hounds, "as many bishops do."[242] The monk-bishops and the friar-bishops were particularly striking examples of the tension between the ascetic ideal and the bishop's role as lord, leader and judge. These dilemmas had been explicit from the time of St. Martin, bishop of Tours, who was despised by the aristocratic bishops of Gaul for his unkempt appearance. St. Hugh of Lincoln, who went from being a prior in the rigorist Carthusian Order to bishop of England's largest diocese, supposedly envisaged his new appointment with the same feelings as a sailor catching sight of threatening clouds or a knight seeing his enemies approaching. His biographer praised him for the care he took in his duties as bishop. When he confirmed children on his journeys, he always dismounted from his horse to do so, unlike "a certain young and healthy bishop," who simply sprinkled them with chrism while on horseback—"not like our Hugh." Hugh had a special devotion for St. Martin and, "for him, as for his patron St. Martin, real glory was always in the monastic Order." He withdrew to his former Carthusian house once or twice a year to live, for a while, a life of simplicity and manual labour.[243] Hugh was an ideal bishop partly because he had other ideals.

But there were different kinds of ideal bishop and not all of them were based on an ascetic or unworldly model. An enlightening picture of the saintly bishop as perceived by an elite royal official emerges from the testimony of a witness in the canonization process of Thomas de Cantilupe. Thomas had been bishop of Hereford from 1275 to 1282 and a long campaign finally led to canonization hearings in 1307. The first witness was the elderly Ralph Hengham, the chief justice of the common bench, who had known Thomas for many years. He also remembered that Thomas's father was "a knight and baron having a thousand pounds sterling in income." Ralph praised the bishop for the following characteristics: he was rumoured to wear a hairshirt; he was conscientious in his duties as bishop and a great preacher; he did not speak badly of the archbishop of Canterbury, even when the archbishop had persecuted him; he was just, God-fearing, and merciful; he had opposed the promotion of a Jewish convert to a judicial position; he had challenged the earl of Gloucester over the earl's usurpations of hunting rights in his woods, even though the earl was

[242] Ibid., 9, p. 317.

[243] Adam of Eynsham, *Magna vita sancti Hugonis* 3. 4, 13; 4. 9–10 (1, pp. 99, 128; 2, pp. 43–44, 49–51).

the richest and most powerful man in England. Ralph Hengham had not seen any of Thomas's miracles himself, but he had heard of them. This testimony shows a very slight interest in asceticism (the rumour of a hair-shirt), a fuller appreciation of Thomas's fulfilment of the duties of his office, such as preaching, and an enthusiastic and empathetic approval of the bishop's vigorous defence of his rights.[244]

ABBOTS

The special goal of the monastic communities that sprang up in late antiquity and the early Middle Ages was a full-time Christian life, in pursuit of the perfection that Jesus had described. Like "St. Antony Abbot," as Antony of Egypt was often styled, they were moved by Christ's words, "if thou wilt be perfect, go and sell that thou hast, and give to the poor" (earlier, p. 17). Communities of ascetics arose in Egypt, Palestine, and Syria, then throughout the Middle East and the eastern Mediterranean, reaching western Europe in the later fourth century and becoming firmly established there in the fifth. They aimed to be "a choir of angels, a populace of athletes, a city of the pious," as the followers of St. Sabas in the Judean desert were described.[245]

Since monks not only aimed at perfection but also dominated the world of letters and liturgy, it is not surprising that they were well represented among the saints. Of the twenty new saints who lived and were revered in England in the period 1075–1225, half were monks or monk-bishops.[246] The seventy-one papal canonization processes between 1198 and 1431 include twenty-one (36.6 per cent) that concerned monks or friars (and this figure does not take account of monks and friars who were also bishops).[247] Byzantine sanctity was even more marked by a monastic predominance: of the ninety Byzantine saints living in the period from the seventh to the fifteenth century, at least seventy-five were monks.[248]

Monastic communities were headed by an abbot, who had a semi-monarchical position. If this arrangement might produce enmity and conflict, it could also generate favourable conditions for a cult. The abbot's friends and admirers would keep his memory fresh, might listen encouragingly to rumours of miracles, and had the literary skills to commemorate him, while the monastery, as an enduring corporate body, offered a guarantee of undying continuity and perpetual veneration. Abbot-saints are numerous, from the time of St. Antony onwards. They include the heads of the desert monasteries of the East, like Sabas; the great Irish abbot-saints, such as Columba; many Benedictines, like the Cluniacs discussed earlier (p. 47); and such dominant figures of the twelfth century as St. Bernard. In the later centuries of the Middle Ages they are not so prominent, their place being taken by the mendicant

[244] BAV, Vat. lat. 4015, fols. 5–7v.

[245] Cyril of Scythopolis, *Vita Sabae* 16, p. 100.

[246] Bartlett, *England under the Norman and Angevin Kings*, pp. 461–63.

[247] Vauchez, *Sainthood*, pp. 261–62.

[248] Charanis, "The Monk as an Element of Byzantine Society," p. 61; the figure of 90 is calculated from BHG.

saints, who were less tied to one foundation because of their mobility (they did not take a vow of "stability" like monks).

Some of the standard tropes, and some of the vicissitudes, of an abbot's life can be found in the near-contemporary account of St. Dominic, abbot of Silos 1040–73.[249] The author states at the outset that Dominic was born, in the Rioja, "from a noble and religious father" but says he mentions his noble ancestry not to boast but because, "if it is perfect for someone of servile condition to turn to the religious life, it is more perfect for someone of noble family to do so." During his boyhood, Dominic avoided childish follies and shunned secular literature. Later he had charge of flocks of sheep, like Abel the Just in the Old Testament. He preserved his virginity and would have been willing to endure martyrdom "if there had been a persecutor." Instead, he fought against demons.

Then, after a period as a hermit, devoted to vigils, fasting and prayer, he entered the great monastery of San Millán. Here, to test his obedience, he was sent to the run-down dependency of St. Mary in Cañas, his home town, which he restored by his care and providence. As a consequence he was appointed prior of San Millán. So far, the profile is uneventful: Dominic is a well-born, chaste, ascetic figure with a gift for running monastic establishments efficiently. This smooth course is suddenly disrupted, however, by a violent confrontation with the king, Garcia III of Navarre (1035–54). Significantly, it is about property.

One day the king comes to the monastery with his retinue and demands supplies. Dominic refuses and Garcia explodes: "it seems unjust and wrong to me, and to all right-thinking people, that I should be deprived of the property of my father and my ancestors, and that I should not possess what my predecessors possessed." Dominic explains that the property *used to be* his, but "it ceased to be yours when it was granted to the king of heaven and to St. Millán for the needs of his servants." It is contrary to ecclesiastical law, he adds, "for lay people to usurp things given to the Church." Garcia, understandably annoyed at being called a "lay person" and an appropriator rather than a benefactor, threatens him with blinding and death but Dominic holds firm. The king then gets the abbot, who is secretly jealous of Dominic, to dismiss him as prior and send him off to another dependency of the monastery. Even after this event, Garcia continues to make demands on him and Dominic eventually leaves Garcia's realm and goes to Ferdinand of Leon, "inspired and led by the Lord."

This conflict between saint and king, in the middle of the eleventh century, which was a crucial period for the transformation of relations between secular rulers and their churchmen, hinges on two divergent views of ownership. King Garcia does not think that giving land or other goods to a monastery—or, more precisely, to God and St. Millán—means that the gift is no longer, in some sense, still his. Dominic has a sharper and more juridical view: ownership has been transferred to the Church,

[249] Grimaldus, *Vita Dominici Siliensis*; for detailed discussion of the composition and manuscripts of the text, see Lappin, *The Medieval Cult of Saint Dominic of Silos*, pp. 3–30.

and cannot now ever be taken away. Garcia's view was challenged by the ecclesiastical reformers of this period, but it continued to have some vitality. Well over a century after the clash between Dominic and Garcia, king Henry II of England, annoyed at a dispute within the Gilbertine Order, threatened to "take back all the demesnes and possessions he had conferred."[250] And at the Reformation such resumptions altered the property map of northern Europe forever.

Dominic found a more understanding royal patron in Ferdinand of Leon. Perhaps aware of the saint's record as a restorer of run-down monasteries, the king appointed him as abbot of the decayed monastery of Silos. Here he looked after the monastic property well, even leading a posse to recapture the abbey's Muslim slaves, who had run away but were not able to hide from the saint's penetrating vision, guided as he was by the Holy Spirit. King Ferdinand proved a loyal friend, sending supplies to Silos during a famine. The renewal of the abbey was one of Dominic's great achievements: in a dream-vision he was promised three crowns, one for leaving the world, one for preserving his virginity and one for restoring Silos.

Dominic died on 20 December 1073, already, at least according to his biographer, with a reputation for miracles. His cult was to become an important one, famous for miraculous healing and liberations, but the Life shows something else, a man with an unsullied sexual reputation, a gift for administration and management, and a willingness to stand up to kings but also to accept their patronage.

The Life of Dominic of Silos has much more to say about his relations with his kings than with his monks, but abbots were in charge of large communities, and how the superior handled the community was vital, both for the daily experience of the members and also for the chances of an abbatial cult. A successful abbot not only protected the property of his abbey but also steered its members through the sea of doubt and moral turmoil that could afflict even (or especially) those permanently committed to the religious life. For instance, monasteries included not only mature monks, but also young men in their novitiate or, in the case of the Benedictine Order, until at least the twelfth century, very young boys, and this was recognized as a source of temptation for the older monks. St. Sabas would allow no one into his monastery until he had a full beard, because of "the traps of the Evil One."[251] One eleventh-century set of regulations for monks forbade any of them from making any sign to the monastery's children or even smiling at them.[252]

A rigorous abbot might produce more than one reaction. William of Æbelholt, the French-born abbot of a Danish religious house, who died in 1203, won praise from his hagiographer for his rectitude:

> He was a tireless follower of the holy religious life, a wonderful guardian of the Order and the holy rules, a powerful extirpator of vice, a true lover of virtue.... He was severe in reproof, assiduous in correction, sweet and humble

[250] *The Book of St Gilbert*, p. 82.
[251] Cyril of Scythopolis, *Vita Sabae* 29, pp. 113–14.
[252] Lanfranc, *Decreta Lanfranci*, p. 117.

> in exhortation. . . . Inspired by zeal for the Order, sometimes he was harsh towards the proud and arrogant and forced transgressors of the Order to undergo corrective punishment.[253]

William had been brought to Denmark to clean up the monastery, which had become famous for long lunches and generous hospitality to relatives (both male and female), and, although he was canonized in 1224, during his lifetime William's flock did not always appreciate him. Some of them spent their time plotting to kill him, although they found it hard to decide whether to drown him in a sack, stab him with knives, sell him into slavery, or axe him in the head. Violence against reforming abbots was, in fact, not unknown, with examples going back to St. Benedict himself, whose monks had tried to poison him.[254]

A less abrasive picture of a great abbot emerges from the Life of William's contemporary, the Cistercian Aelred of Rievaulx. One thing that saintly abbots had to deal with was doubting or runaway monks. A fair amount of Aelred's time was taken up with one particular individual, a cleric who wished to enter the monastery of Rievaulx.[255] He first arrived at a time when Aelred was not yet abbot but serving as novice-master. The cleric was notably unstable: "he was very unsteady in his mind, frequently staggering from one thing to another, now here, now there, like a reed borne about by the breeze of the changing will." Aelred, "that man of mercy" was moved by his state, and prayed to God, "Give to me his soul." Nevertheless, and despite Aelred's counsel, the cleric left Rievaulx. However, by a divine miracle, he found that, after wandering all day, he was back in the monastery. Aelred concealed this absence without leave from the abbot, "fearing the holy father's severity." Later, when Aelred became abbot of Rievaulx's daughter-house of Revesby, the unstable monk, who had evidently also transferred to that house, expressed his disgust with the rigours of monastic life and his intention to leave. Aelred said he would not eat until the monk returned. Again a divine miracle prevented the monk's departure: when he came to the abbey gates, he felt the air "like an iron wall." Some years later, after Aelred's election as abbot of Rievaulx, the monk died there, clothed in his monastic habit, in Aelred's arms.

William of Æbelholt and Aelred of Rievaulx, although contemporaries, present different models of the saintly abbot, one harder, one softer. It is perhaps significant that among William's writings there is a polemical treatise attacking certain "enemies of religion and honesty," while the most famous work of Aelred is *On Spiritual Friendship*.[256]

[253] *Vita et miracula sancti Willelmi abbatis Ebelholtensis* 17, pp. 328–29.

[254] Gregory I, *Dialogi* 2. 3. 3–4 (2, pp. 140–42).

[255] Walter Daniel, *Vita Ailredi* 15, 22, 28, pp. 24–25, 30–32, 35–36.

[256] William of Æbelholt, *Tractatus de revelatione capitis et corporis beate Genovefe*; Aelred of Rievaulx, *De spiritali amicitia*.

CHAPTER 7

HERMITS

Although they were not usually acknowledged as a distinct liturgical category, hermits formed a recognizable group amongst the confessor-saints—Gregory of Tours sorts the saints in his *Life of the Fathers* into bishops, abbots, and hermits.[257] Calling on biblical prototypes like Elijah and John the Baptist, but with a definite continuous tradition from the third century, Christian hermits exemplified unreserved commitment to the religious life: "the hermit life, the holy life, the angelic life, the blessed life."[258] The Egyptian and Syrian holy men who had sought out the desert, in order to embrace self-denial, prayer, and contemplation, were the founding heroes of that tradition. Their stories and sayings were retold in the *Lives of the Fathers*, a compendium that provided a stock of instructive anecdotes and pithy maxims throughout the Middle Ages and beyond. It circulated in various forms, but everywhere it could be found it presented such views as, "A man fleeing men is like a ripe grape, a man dealing with men like a sour grape."[259]

The flight from human society was the core of the hermit life, at least in theory. The desert fathers provided the model. Going into the wilderness, they sought to escape the company of their fellow humans. The wilderness was not, however, without inhabitants. Here the demons flocked, and the arrival of holy men brought them buzzing like wasps to honey. The devils were affronted by this intrusion into what they regarded as their own domain. "Keep away from our dwellings!" they warned St. Antony, "What have you got to do with the desert?"[260] The wilderness was home to the demons, whom the hermit has to fight and defeat. In order to clear the mountain of Kastellion of demons, St. Sabas spent the whole of Lent there in prayer, and eventually the demons were forced to flee, in the form of a great flock of ravens, crying out, "What force is in you, Sabas!"[261]

In the wet and windy north of Europe, uninhabited forest and bog took the place of the sandy desert. The marshy wilderness that St. Guthlac chose as the site of his life of heroic asceticism in the English Fens had previously defeated any effort at human settlement: "many people attempting to live there had rejected it, on account of the strange monsters of the wilderness and terrors of varying shapes."[262] The hermit endured horror and pain during his epic struggles with these "crowds of unclean spirits." With hideous shrieks, they swarmed into his hermitage through gaps in the walls and cracks in the door, and dragged him into "the muddy waters of the black marsh," then pulled him through the brambles, lacerating his limbs and com-

[257] Gregory of Tours, *Liber vitae patrum, capitula*, pp. 661–62 (repr., 1969, pp. 211–12); see Monaci Castagno "Il vescovo, l'abate e l'eremita: tipologia della santità nel Liber Vitae Patrum di Gregorio di Tours."

[258] Peter Damian, *Epistola* 28 (*Liber qui appellatur Dominus vobiscum*) (1, p. 277).

[259] *Verba seniorum* 2. 10, col. 859.

[260] Athanasius, *Vita Antonii* 13. 2, p. 170.

[261] Cyril of Scythopolis, *Vita Sabae* 27, pp. 110–11.

[262] Felix, *Vita sancti Guthlaci* 25, p. 88.

manding him to leave their wilderness. Guthlac endured all this "with an unchanged mind and sturdy faith." Eventually, after ever-increasing threats and torments, St. Bartholomew appeared and came to his rescue; the evil spirits had to restore Guthlac to his hermitage and then vanished like smoke.[263]

Rough clothing or no clothes at all characterized the hermit. John the Baptist, one of the prototypes of the Christian hermit, is described in the Gospels as wearing clothing of camel hair (Mark 1:6), and some hermit-saints wore no clothes at all, but were covered only by their own exuberant hair. The early Egyptian hermit Onuphrius, who had gone into the desert inspired by the example of the prophet Elijah, wore a loin-cloth of leaves but was otherwise clothed only in his own long hair. His story was told in both Greek and Latin, and images of him, as an aged man swathed in hair, can be found in the rock churches of Cappadocia, among the mosaics of Monreale in Sicily and on the panel paintings of the later Middle Ages, as exemplified by a remarkable altarpiece now in the Fitzwilliam Museum in Cambridge (with Onuphrius holding an anachronistic rosary) (figure 7.6).[264] The German humanist Sebastian Brant was a devotee and named his eldest son after the saint.[265]

Some of the standard features of the hermit life are brought out in the account of the ninth-century saint, Meginrat, who, after serving as a monk and a schoolmaster at a monastery in south-west Germany, was drawn to live as a solitary.[266] He first felt the attraction of this way of life when he took some of his pupils to the lake to fish and was struck by the lonely wilderness, which looked out on the mountains: "he was fired by great love of that solitary spot." Although "solitary," it was also not too far from a village, and here Meginrat opened his heart to a pious woman who had given him and his students hospitality. He explained that he wished to live in that quiet place and devote himself to prayer, "if I could find someone who would be willing to minister to my needs." The woman took the hint and promised to help him, and soon thereafter he left the monastery and his school, and built himself a little hut in the empty countryside, not far from the woman's village, and devoted himself to prayer and fasting, receiving the necessities of life "from this woman and from other men of religion." After seven years, he found that too many people were coming to visit him, and he removed himself to "a level place among the mountains, four miles from the shore of the lake and difficult of access." This search for ever more remote spots is common in the hermit story. So too was the assault of demons. On one occasion such a flock of them surrounded Meginrat that they blocked out the light of day, and they were only dispersed by an angel coming from the east in a blaze of light, in answer to his prayers. The Life gives tiny glimpses of the hermit's daily routines. In his second hermitage Meginrat was supported by unnamed "men of religion" and especially by a nearby abbess, but he also kept hens. As a priest, he could supply the

[263] Felix, *Vita sancti Guthlaci* 31–33, pp. 100–108.

[264] Brodbeck, *Les saints de la Cathédrale de Monreale*, pp. 632–35; Cambridge, Fitzwilliam Museum: *Virgin and Child between Saint John the Baptist and Saint Onuphrius*, Neapolitan School, c. 1507.

[265] Stieglecker, *Die Renaissance eines Heiligen: Sebastian Brant und Onuphrius eremita.*

[266] *Vita sancti Meginrati.*

7.6. St. Onuphrius from *Virgin and Child between Saint John the Baptist and Saint Onuphrius*, altarpiece of c. 1507, Neapolitan School. Fitzwilliam Museum, University of Cambridge, UK/The Bridgeman Art Library.

Eucharist himself, and he had relics of the saints in his little chapel. And a visiting monk once saw him receive heavenly visitors, a common enough story in the case of hermit saints: it reflects the social reality of the visits they received and also provides a narrative explanation of how their private supernatural experiences could be made public—they would not be expected to broadcast these signs of grace themselves, so the visiting monk is a necessary device. Meginrat's story ends unusually, with his murder by thieves, but otherwise it is typical enough.

The wilderness was the home, not only of demons, but also of animals, whom the hermit might command, tame, or heal. In his remote hermitage St. Giles lived off the milk of a female deer, which he protected from the huntsmen's hounds.[267] Likewise, hounds hunting their prey suddenly stopped paralysed when they came to the leafy retreat of St. Mansuetus of Toul.[268] Hermits might even protect wolves from hunters, as in the case of the Italian hermit John the Good (d. 1249), who saved a she-wolf, carrying its young in its mouth, from the men and dogs pursuing it and sent it on its way safely.[269] The story of the saint protecting hunted animals is so common that it has been called the "Hermit and Hunter" topos.[270] There is further discussion of saints and wild animals later (pp. 390–98).

People living alone often appreciate the companionship of an animal. It was, however, a disputed question whether hermits and solitaries were allowed a pet. "No cat, no chicken, no little animal, no irrational creature, should live with you; fleeting time should not be wasted," wrote Goscelin of St.-Bertin in his book of advice and criticism addressed to the anchoress Eve, but the Middle English *Anchoresses' Guide* of a century and half later was more lenient, explicitly allowing a cat.[271] One of the temptations to which hermits were subject was indeed to love their cats too much. The *Golden Legend* transmits two stories about this failing. In each case an unnamed hermit receives a divine rebuke. The section on St. Basil records that

> a hermit saw Basil proceeding in his episcopal robes and looked down on him, judging him in his heart as someone who delighted in such pomp. But lo! A voice was heard saying to him: "You take more delight in stroking the tail of your cat than Basil does in his vestments."[272]

A remarkably similar story is told in the section on St. Gregory. A hermit pridefully contrasted in his mind his own poverty with the wealth of Pope Gregory I, but was rebuked in the night by the voice of the Lord:

> It is not possession of wealth that makes a wealthy man but desire for it. Why do you dare to contrast your poverty with Gregory's wealth, when it is clear that you love that cat which you stroke every day more than he loves such great riches? [273]

[267] *Vita Aegidii abbatis* 2. 11–12, p. 301.

[268] Adso of Montier-en-Der, *Vita sancti Mansueti primi Leucorum urbis pontificis* 1. 6, col. 625.

[269] *Processus apostolici beatae Joannis Boni* 15, p. 775.

[270] Golding, "The Hermit and the Hunter"; Alexander, *Saints and Animals in the Middle Ages*, chapter 6, "The Hermit and the Hunter."

[271] Goscelin of St.-Bertin, *Liber confortatorius* 3, p. 80; *Ancrene Wisse* 8. 11, p. 157.

[272] Jacobus de Voragine, *Legenda aurea* 26 (1, p. 181).

[273] Jacobus de Voragine, *Legenda aurea* 46 (1, pp. 294–95); the immediate source of the story is Vincent of Beauvais, *Speculum historiale* 22. 19, p. 867, but it certainly existed earlier: Gerald of Wales, *De principis instructione* 1. 20, pp. 121–22.

Remarkably enough, there is evidence from the pen of an early medieval hermit himself for this love of cats:

> I and Pangur Bán, each of us two at his special art:
> his mind is at hunting mice, my own mind is my special craft.
> I love to rest—better than any fame—at my booklet with diligent science:
> not envious of me is Pangur Bán: he himself loves his childish art . . .
> He is joyous with speedy going where a mouse sticks in his sharp claw:
> I too am joyous, where I understand a difficult dear question.
> Though we are thus always, neither hinders the other:
> each of us two likes his art, amuses himself alone . . . [274]

The hermit life might be permanent but could also be a phase in a saint's life. St. Cuthbert, for example, spent many years as a recluse on Inner Farne, a rocky island in the North Sea, between a long period as a monk and a later, shorter period as a bishop. Others took up the hermit life after a career in the world. A striking example is Nicholas of Flüe (d. 1487), sometimes regarded as patron saint of Switzerland. He was a married layman with ten children, who served the Swiss Confederation as a soldier and political leader before, at the age of fifty, leaving all this and settling in a remote spot, where he experienced visions and lived only on the Eucharist. Despite his life as a hermit, he continued to have political influence, and was instrumental in the agreement at Stans on 22 December 1481 which expanded the Confederation and laid out its future constitutional shape.[275]

Such political involvement was not unknown amongst recluses. Several received visits from rulers or high born exiles, who clearly sought them out for advice or prophetic insight. Guthlac in his Fenland retreat was visited by the exiled Mercian prince Ethelbald and encouraged him with a prophecy of his future success: "I have asked the Lord to help you in your misery, and he has heard me and has granted you lordship over your people." When this prophecy was fulfilled, after Guthlac's death, Ethelbald returned the favour by erecting an ornate shrine over the saint's tomb.[276] On his way to war in Spain, the Frankish king Childebert I (511–58) also visited a hermit, Eusicius, in the place where the old man lived "amongst dense thorns, far from men." Eusicius declined the king's offer of gold but gave him a promising prediction: "Go and you will obtain victory and get what you want."[277] It sounds very much as if the king had come to the saint for just such guidance and encouragement.

Two famous early saints came to symbolize the hermit state: Paul the First Hermit and, perhaps more surprisingly, St. Jerome. They have two links, in that Jerome wrote an influential Life of Paul, and that both had, or came or have, a lion or lions as an attribute. Paul supposedly lived for a hundred years in the Egyptian desert,

[274] *Thesaurus palaeohibernicus* 2, pp. 293–94.

[275] Vasella, "Flüe, Niklaus von"; Huber, *Bruder Klaus*—an anthology of sources in modern German; Collins, *Reforming Saints: Saints' Lives and Their Authors in Germany, 1470–1530*, pp. 99–122.

[276] Felix, *Vita sancti Guthlaci* 49, 51, pp. 148–50, 162.

[277] Gregory of Tours, *Gloria confessorum* 81, pp. 799–800 (repr., 1969, pp. 349–50).

7.7. St. Jerome in the Desert, from Prayer Book, Tours, France, c. 1500. Pierpont Morgan Library, New York, MS M. 292, fol. 27v. Purchased by J. Pierpont Morgan (1837–1913) in 1907.

and at the end of his life met with St. Antony, that other desert-saint, who arranged to have him buried, with the help of the lions. Jerome, in contrast to Paul, is a well-attested historical figure, although the subject of much legendary elaboration. By the eleventh century he had acquired his lion, which served loyally after the saint had healed its foot, and also a (radically anachronistic) cardinal's hat.[278] Although Jerome's time living in seclusion in the Syrian desert was in fact only a short part of his life, he also served as a model hermit for some of the religious reformers and activists of the fourteenth and fifteenth centuries: the Order of St. Jerome (Jeronimites) was

[278] Both the lion and his appointment as cardinal are mentioned in *Vita divi Hieronymi* (BHL 3870), of which there are eleventh-century manuscripts (listed on the Bollandist website).

influential in Spain, with its members combining solitary living and communal worship, while Italy produced the Hermits of St. Jerome. The Jerome that inspired them was the one depicted in numerous late medieval paintings, an emaciated and solitary figure in the wilderness, beating himself with a rock (figure 7.7).[279] St. Jerome was one of the most important saints of the later Middle Ages, and, while he was significant as Doctor of the Church, translator of the Bible, cardinal and leophile, he was also a powerful emblem of the saintly hermit.

Virgins

In the Parable of the Sower, Jesus talked of those who receive the Word of God: some reap a thirtyfold fruit, some a sixtyfold, some a hundredfold.[280] It seems to have been the fourth-century Church Father Jerome who first interpreted these three classes of increasing merit as chaste spouses, widows, and virgins.[281] Thereafter it was a commonplace of ecclesiastical preachers and writers: marriage could be good, but widowhood was better, and virginity was best of all.

Like incorruptibility, virginity was not an official requirement for sanctity but was sometimes spoken of as if it were. One bricklayer in the Prussian city of Marienburg doubted the sanctity of Dorothea of Montau and forbade his wife from visiting her tomb, saying in challenge, "Do you really think this Dorothea was a saint, when she was married and bore many children?"[282] Likewise, some people were amazed that Elizabeth of Thuringia performed so many posthumous miracles, "when she was not a virgin in the body but a widow and had known a man." Her champions replied "the merit and the prize does not consist in integrity of the body but in charity," and took the offensive, with the claim that, if Elizabeth had been a virgin and then performed such miracles, foolish people might think this was "more from the merit of her virginity than of her charity." They also argued that the intention to preserve virginity was more important than the mere physical fact: a virgin who intended to marry but died before she did so did not earn the golden crown of glory, but a virgin who intended to remain so but was in fact raped still earned the crown.[283]

This high evaluation of virginity had become part of Christianity in its early centuries, and it always mattered more in the case of women. In the litany the category "virgins" always means "female virgins." There are cases of male saints praised for maintaining their virginity, but they did not form a large, identifiable category in the way that female virgins did. Important male examples include two saint-kings of the eleventh century, Henry II of Germany (d. 1024) and Edward the Confessor of England (d. 1066), who both had a posthumous reputation for remaining virgins

[279] BS 6, cols. 1132–33; Russo, *Saint Jérôme en Italie*, esp. pp. 201–51.

[280] Matthew 13:23; Mark 4:8.

[281] Jerome, *Commentariorum in Matheum libri IV* 2, p. 106 (PL 26: 89).

[282] *Miracula beatae Dorotheae* 5. 18, p. 565.

[283] Caesarius of Heisterbach, *Sermo de translatione beate Elyzabeth*, p. 390; idem, *Vita sancte Elyzabeth lantgravie* 9, p. 358.

throughout their lives, despite being married. Within a century of his death, it was being explained that an aspect of Henry's sanctity was his chaste marriage to the empress Cunigunda (herself also a saint):

> He is said to have lived so very chastely that, on the point of death, in the presence of all the bishops, he summoned the relatives of Cunigunda, his wife, and returned her to them, with the words, it is said, "Receive your virgin whom you handed to me."[284]

Edward the Confessor's childlessness was also converted into a reputation for saintly virginity. The author of the earliest version of his Life, which was not originally hagiographic and was actually begun in the king's lifetime, has a few hints that could be interpreted in this sense, such as references to the relations between Edward and his wife as being like those between father and daughter.[285] Writing in 1125, almost 60 years after the king's death, William of Malmesbury reports that it was commonly said that Edward had died a virgin, although he does not advance this as a proof of sanctity.[286] In contrast, the campaign to have Edward canonized, which culminated successfully in the winter of 1160–61, made much of the fact that "throughout the whole course of his life, he remained a virgin."[287] Henry II of Germany had already been canonized by this time, the canonization bull of 1146 mentioning that, "having entered a legitimate marriage, he preserved the integrity of chastity until the end of his life."[288]

In these cases it seems likely that the two kings' virginity was deduced from the fact of their childlessness. But this raised the question whether their espousal of virginity might not have indicated a certain irresponsibility about royal succession. Both kings were reputed to have left this matter to God. In a vision recorded in his contemporary Life, after Edward is promised by St. Peter an unmarried or celibate life, he asks who will succeed him. Peter replies "The kingdom of the English is God's and he will provide a king after you according to his will."[289] With more deliberation, Henry II "chose to have the Lord his heir."[290] Henry was in fact succeeded peacefully by a distant cousin. Edward's succession was more troubled.

But it was female saints who were understood to form the group "virgin saints" and one of the most common types of virgin saint was the female virgin martyr. A typical list of early virgin martyrs occurs in the work of Lawrence of Durham, an

[284] *Chronica monasterii Casinensis* 2. 46, p. 254.

[285] There is also a vision in which the king is promised an "unmarried life" (the Latin *celebs* means "unmarried" but could perhaps have prompted a retrospective reading as "without sex"): *Vita Ædwardi regis* 1. 1; 2. 1, 11, pp. 14, 90, 122; on the whole question, see Barlow's introduction, pp. lxxiii–lxxviii.

[286] William of Malmesbury, *Gesta regum Anglorum* 2. 197, pp. 352–54.

[287] See the letters edited by Barlow, *Edward the Confessor*, app. D, pp. 309–24 (quote from p. 314).

[288] Eugenius III, *Epistola* 93, cols. 118–19 (Jaffé, *Regesta* no. 8882).

[289] *Vita Ædwardi regis* 1. 1, p. 14.

[290] Ekkehard of Aura, *Chronica*, p. 192 (the author is now identified as Frutolf of the Michelsberg, Bamberg).

author discussed earlier (p. 186) for his parallel list of "doctors." This Benedictine monk, writing in the 1130s or 1140s, named Faith, Thecla, Agatha, Margaret, Lucy, Cecilia, and Agnes.[291] All were supposedly martyr-saints of the Roman period. Their degree of historicity varies. Early mentions in the lists of martyrs suggest that Agatha, Lucy, and Agnes were probably real people who suffered for their faith. In some ways, however, this is irrelevant, for all the virgin martyrs, those with a named historical person behind them and those entirely fictional, were subject to the same literary elaboration. They are personae in a narrative. As such, they are discussed in more detail later in the section "The Literature of Sanctity" (pp. 535–41.).

Some of the most celebrated virgin martyrs of the later medieval period seem to have been entirely legendary constructions. St. Barbara, for example, who was supposedly martyred at Nicomedia (modern Izmit in Turkey), is not mentioned in any early lists of martyrs. Amongst the earliest accounts of Barbara is a sermon by John of Damascus, who died around the middle of the eighth century, and Lives in Greek and Latin survive from the ninth century.[292] These tell how her father shut her in a tower (which became her attribute in later pictorial representations) and subsequently handed her over to the Roman authorities, who had her tortured and eventually condemned to death. She was a popular saint in the East earlier than the West, with several churches or chapels in Constantinople, and her feast-day occurs in the official list issued by the Byzantine emperor Manuel Comnenus in the twelfth century.[293] In the West, her Life was copied fairly frequently (there are at least a dozen copies from the twelfth century), but she does not appear in the original edition of the *Golden Legend*, although she was added in later versions.[294] Her rising popularity in the later Middle Ages can be traced in numerous ways: the addition of her feast-day to Kalendars, the growing popularity of the name Barbara, the multiplication of images. When the Teutonic Knights acquired Barbara's head, they naturally gave her a higher liturgical profile, raising her feast to a "semi-double" in the 1330s and commissioning an Office for her, although it was an effort for them to explain how they had gained possession of this valuable relic (four different versions are recorded).[295] Barbara was popular in the German lands. In the fifteenth century the Franciscans of Cologne had a volume with a section of almost eighty folios dedicated just to her: her Passion, translation and miracles.[296] One of Tilman Riemenschneider's lime-

[291] Lawrence of Durham, *Hypognosticon* 9, lines 507–16, "De virginibus," p. 246.

[292] John of Damascus, *Laudatio sanctae martyris Barbarae*; the next oldest appear to be BHG 215i (John of Sardis); 213–14 (anon.); 216 (PG 116: 301–16: Symeon Metaphrastes); the Latin Life BHL 913 is extant in a manuscript from the second half of the ninth century.

[293] Janin, *La géographie ecclésiastique de l'Empire byzantin*, pp. 56–57; Macrides, "Justice under Manuel Komnenos," p. 152.

[294] The Bollandist website lists 54 manuscripts of BHL 913, with twelve certainly and several others possibly of twelfth-century date.

[295] *Die Statuten des deutschen Ordens*, p. 148; Peter of Dusburg, *Chronica terre Prussie* 3. 36, pp. 138–40; *Qualiter caput beate Barbare processu temporis in Pomeraniam pervenit.*

[296] Coens, "Catalogus codicum hagiographicorum latinorum archivi historici civitatis Coloniensis," pp. 190–91 (Codex G. B. octav. 3).

wood masterpieces is his carving of St. Barbara, 132 centimetres (52 inches) high, probably made around 1510 and now in the Bavarian National Museum. Created on the eve of the Reformation, its compelling presence epitomizes the continuing fascination of the figure of the virgin saint.

Old Testament Saints

The twelfth-century liturgical writer John Beleth noted that "the feast-days of the saints of the Old Testament, such as Abraham, Isaac and Jacob, and David and Daniel and others, are celebrated throughout Greece and Venice and they have churches there," but, in contrast, "the western church celebrates the feast of no saint of the Old Testament."[297] His point was broadly true. In the West, although the patriarchs and prophets of the Old Testament were often invoked as a group, and they were frequently depicted in carvings and paintings, very few of them had either a liturgical commemoration or churches dedicated to them. And Venice, with churches dedicated to Daniel, Jeremiah, Isaiah, Samuel, Zacharias, Job, and Moses, clearly belonged to the eastern tradition.[298]

One reason that Old Testament saints were more prominent in the East than in the West is that their tombs and relics were located there. The Gaulish or Spanish pilgrim Egeria visited the tomb of Job on her tour of the Holy Land in the later fourth century, and new discoveries of the relics of prophets were continually made in Palestine: Micah and Habakkuk between 379 and 395, Zacharias in 415.[299] Churches were often built above the tombs of these patriarchs and prophets, sometimes christianizing earlier Jewish cult sites, as seems to have been the case with the tomb of Moses on Mount Nebo.[300] Palestine and Syria were dotted with these sanctuaries; in Egypt, by contrast, the cult of Old Testament saints was unimportant.[301]

Relics of several Old Testament figures were translated to Constantinople in the fifth century, encouraging their cult in the imperial capital.[302] Those of the prophet Samuel arrived in 406 and those of the patriarch Joseph (along with those of Zachary, father of John the Baptist) in 416.[303] This was part of the great city's special prestige. An English chronicler of the twelfth century noted, among all the wonderful relics in Constantinople, the bodies of "the prophets Elijah, Samuel, Daniel,

[297] John Beleth, *Summa de ecclesiasticis officiis* 128b, 142c, pp. 244, 278.

[298] Nieri, "Culto dei santi dell'antico testamento."

[299] Egeria, *Itinerarium Egeriae* 13, p. 54; Sozomen, *Historia ecclesiastica* 7. 29; 9. 17 (4, pp. 216–18, 444–48); put in context by Maraval, *Lieux saints et pèlerinages d'Orient*, pp. 41–42.

[300] Maraval, *Lieux saints et pèlerinages d'Orient*, pp. 282–83.

[301] For sites in Syria and Palestine, see Maraval, *Lieux saints et pèlerinages d'Orient*, pp. 268, 269–71, 276, 286, 289, 290, 335, 340, 341; for their absence in Egypt, Papaconstantinou, *Le culte des saints en Egypte*, pp. 230–31.

[302] Wortley, "Iconoclasm and Leipsanoclasm," p. 263.

[303] Jerome, *Contra Vigilantium* 5, pp. 12–13 (PL 23: 343); *Chronicon paschale*, cols. 784, 788; Marcellinus Comes, *Chronicon*, pp. 72.

and many others."[304] Constantinople had several churches dedicated to the prophets Elijah and Elisha.[305] The cult centre of the prophet Isaiah was in the church of St. Lawrence near the Blachernae palace and there is record of a series of healing miracles that took place here, perhaps datable to the tenth century.[306] The Synaxaria of the eastern Churches, which record details of the saints in calendar order, include many patriarchs and prophets, such as Isaiah on 9 May and Elijah on 20 July.[307] The legislation of Manuel Comnenus specified St. Elijah's feast-day as one on which courts were forbidden to meet (see earlier, p. 129.). In Byzantium the Old Testament prophets were thus integrated with the Christian saints in a way that was unfamiliar in the West.

In the West, Old Testament figures are not usually named individually in litanies, although there are exceptions, especially in the early Middle Ages, when more than a quarter of Carolingian litanies include them.[308] A prayer, titled "The Prayer of St. Gregory the Pope," which was composed prior to the ninth century, probably in Ireland, and then spread to England and the continent, is in the form of a litany, addressed to Old Testament figures as well as New. They appear in what was, in western terms, a strange guise: St. Enoch, St. Noah, the faithful Abraham, the just Isaac, St. Abel the first martyr, Jacob the blessed, St. Moses, St. David, St. Elijah, St. Elisha, St. Isaiah, the blessed Jeremiah, St. Ezekiel, Daniel the chosen one, as well as the three children freed from the burning fiery furnace and the twelve minor prophets.[309]

Despite these hints, the liturgical cult of Old Testament figures did not take off in the West. It was not common to speak or write about "St. Noah," "St. Moses," and so on as "The Prayer of St. Gregory the Pope" did. A small but significant indication of the distinction drawn in the West between Old Testament and New Testament figures is found in a prayer book written in England around 800 for (and possibly by) a female owner.[310] The litany begins with invocation of David, Elijah, and Moses, before moving on to the apostles, martyrs, and virgins, but, while all the New Testament saints and early martyrs are addressed in the form "St. Peter, I beseech you," "St. Paul, I beseech you," for the three Old Testament figures the wording is reversed, "David the holy, I beseech you," and so on. It is only the difference between "David sancte" and "Sancte Petre," but it is a difference, and a consistent one, pointing to underlying assumptions and habits.

[304] William of Malmesbury, *Gesta regum Anglorum* 4. 356, p. 626.

[305] Janin, *La géographie ecclésiastique de l'Empire byzantin*, pp. 110–11, 136–38.

[306] *Synaxarium et miracula sancti Isaiae prophetae*; for dating, see Efthymiadis, "Greek Byzantine Collections of Miracles," pp. 204–5; see also Janin, *La géographie ecclésiastique de l'Empire byzantin*, pp. 139–40.

[307] For example, Nilles, *Kalendarium manuale utriusque ecclesiae orientalis et occidentalis* 1, pp. 156, 218; *Le Synaxaire arménien de Ter Israël*, pp. 427, 748–51.

[308] Krüger, *Litanei-Handschriften der Karolingerzeit*, pp. 394–403, "Heilige des Alten Testaments in Litaneien."

[309] *The Prayer Book of Aedeluald the Bishop, Commonly Called the Book of Cerne*, pp. 103–6, no. 15; other copies discussed by Lapidge, "A New Hiberno-Latin Hymn on St. Martin," pp. 241–42.

[310] *Anglo-Saxon Litanies of the Saints*, pp. 210–11, no. 25 (from BL, Harley 7653).

Martyrologies, which consist of extensive lists of saints, sometimes include Old Testament figures amongst the hundreds they list.[311] Bede's martyrology, for example, has Ezekiel on 10 April, Jeremiah on 1 May, Elisha on 14 June, Isaiah on 6 July, Daniel on 21 July, Samuel on 20 August, and Zacharias the prophet on 6 September.[312] Of these, Jeremiah, Elisha, Samuel, and Zacharias fall on the same (or adjacent) dates in the Synaxarion of Constantinople. The Martyrology of Usuard, with more than a thousand names, can find room for many Old Testament figures.[313] But references in martyrologies do not indicate a liturgical cult. Mentions in Kalendars, which list far fewer saints and can often be linked to individual churches, are more significant indications of real interest (even if they are not certain evidence of feast-days actually celebrated), and there are some Old Testament figures who crop up occasionally in these texts. For example, the prophets Elisha and Abdias are commemorated on 14 June and the prophet Isaiah on 6 July in an eleventh-century German Kalendar, while the Kalendar of the sumptuous "Elizabeth Psalter" of the early thirteenth century lists Amos on 31 March and Elisha on 14 June.[314] More regularly present are the three Hebrew children saved from the burning fiery furnace (as in Daniel 3). They occur, usually under their Hebrew names Ananias, Azarias, and Misael, rather than the Babylonian versions of Shadrach, Meshach, and Abednego, in several Kalendars and martyrologies on 24 April or 16 December.[315]

The evidence of dedications and relics underlines the point, that Old Testament and New Testament figures were treated differently in the western Church. In western Europe there was no tradition of dedicating churches to the patriarchs and prophets, although rare exceptions can be found, such as the church of Saint Isaiah at Bologna, and even minor dedications are extremely unusual, although not unknown—in the late Middle Ages the cathedral at Siena had an altar to "Saint Daniel," who is likely to be the prophet.[316] The distribution of relics shows the same pattern. Amongst the hundreds of relics which are mentioned in English relic lists of the medieval period, only a tiny proportion have any link with Old Testament figures: a dozen churches had relics of Moses, either part of his rod or of the burning bush; eleven claimed relics associated with Abraham, such as parts of the tree he had sat under when visited by God; eight had pieces of Aaron's rod; five had relics of Isaac and the same number had relics of Jacob; and relics of the clay from which Adam was made, of Daniel and the three children in the burning fiery furnace, of

[311] Marrou, "Les saints de l'ancien testament au martyrologe romain."

[312] Quentin, *Les martyrologes historiques*, p. 586; Bede, *Martyrologium*, pp. 59, 77, 107, 120, 132, 153, 164 (PL 94: 876, 895, 945–46, 967, 980–81, 1011, 1034).

[313] Usuard, *Martyrologium*, "index sanctorum," pp. 366–416.

[314] Munich, Bayerische Staatsbibliothek, clm 14569, fols. 9v, 10; Cividale del Friuli, Museo Archeologico Nazionale, Cod. CXXXVII ("Elizabeth Psalter"), fols. 2v, 4, reproduced in *Salterio di Santa Elisabetta. Facsimile*; Amos appears on 31 March in Usuard, *Martyrologium*, p. 204 (PL 123: 891).

[315] For example, *The Calendar of St. Willibrord*, fol. 36 and p. 28; BL, Add. 17354 (a fifteenth-century Dutch Book of Hours), fol. 5v; Quentin, *Les martyrologes historiques*, pp. 349, 450, 483, 587.

[316] Aronow, "A Description of the Altars in Siena Cathedral."

Elisha, of the Maccabees and of the prophet Zacharias were each claimed by two churches. Glastonbury, always notorious for the extent of its pretensions, also had fragments of the tombs of Isaiah and Rachel.[317] In comparison with relics of Jesus, the apostles, the martyrs and the confessor-saints of the Middle Ages, this is an insignificant tally, and points to a few Holy Land souvenirs rather than saintly cult. Elsewhere in western Europe, similarly slight evidence can be found: in the twelfth century the church of Vézelay had "some of the clothing of the three boys, Shadrach, Meshach and Abednego," while the Aberdeen relic collection of 1436 included bones of "Isaac the patriarch."[318] Relics of the patriarchs were also brought back by visitors to the East, like Count Rudolf of Pfullendorf, who went on pilgrimage to the Holy Land in 1180, and sent back to the monastery of St. Gallen relics of Abraham, Isaac, and Jacob, which the monks enshrined in the altar of St. Gallen, along with their own relics.[319]

A particular interest was shown in some of the prophets, such as Elisha. He was commemorated on 14 June in both the Eastern and Western Church and, in the later Middle Ages, he had a particular veneration among the Carmelites. The late medieval Carmelite Kalendar indeed lists him under 14 June as "Elisha the prophet, originator of the Carmelites."[320] A remarkable story was told of the discovery of his relics in Italy. According to the Franciscan chronicler Thomas Tuscus, writing in 1278–79, the emperor Frederick II had held a great council at Ravenna almost fifty years earlier, in 1231. Amongst those who had attended in the entourage of the German princes was "a knight called Richard, who was Oliver's shield-bearer in the time of Charlemagne." The emperor asked this aged figure, who must have been more than four hundred years old, if he had ever been in Ravenna in the time of Charlemagne and if he had any secrets to show him, to confirm his story. Richard had, and was willing to show Frederick the hidden site of the three tombs of the emperor Theodosius, his wife, and the prophet Elisha. Frederick had the tomb of Theodosius opened, but left the others intact. Later, according to Thomas Tuscus, Bonaventure, minister-general of the Franciscans, asked the new archbishop of Ravenna, Philip, to translate Elisha's body, which he did, giving Bonaventure a tooth of the prophet.[321]

[317] Thomas, "The Cult of Saints' Relics," pp. 354–46, 385, 393, 413–14, 426, 437, 451, 477.

[318] "De vestimentis preterea trium puerorum, Sidrac, Misac, et Abdenago": Hugo Pictavinus, *Historia Vezeliacensis* 4, p. 567 (PL 194: 1660); *Registrum episcopatus aberdonensis* 2, p. 143.

[319] St. Gallen, Stiftsbibliothek, Cod. Sang. 453, fol. 235 (annals added to a twelfth-century Chapter book).

[320] *Le codex arménien Jérusalem 121*, 36/2, pp. 346–49 (no. 60); *Synaxarium Ecclesiae Constantinopolitanae*, p. 747; Quentin, *Les martyrologes historiques*, pp. 52, 304–5, 482; Bede, *Martyrologium*, p. 107 (PL 94: 945–46); for the Carmelites, Grotefend, *Zeitrechnung des deutschen Mittelatters und der Neuzeit* 2/2, p. 15; Elisha is commonly found in Carmelite Kalendars, for example, Trinity College Dublin 82, fol. 3v, Trinity College Dublin 86, fol. 117v, an Irish Carmelite Missal and Breviary, respectively, both from the second half of the fifteenth century: Colker, *Trinity College Library Dublin: Descriptive Catalogue of the Mediaeval and Renaissance Latin Manuscripts* 1, pp. 144, 155; see also *Fontes liturgiae Carmelitanae*, index, p. 366, s.v. "Eliseus proph."

[321] Thomae Tuscus, *Gesta imperatorum et pontificum*, pp. 512–13 (Philip was archbishop 1250–70).

Another Franciscan historian, the famous Salimbene, takes up the story at this point. Archbishop Philip, he writes, preferred war to the relics of the saints, and had freely given the relics of Elisha to Salimbene himself, who had placed them in the high altar of the Franciscan church at Parma. The head, however, was lacking, since a rival Order had already illicitly carried this off.[322]

All this evidence shows only an occasional and sporadic place for the prophets and patriarchs in the liturgical life of the western Church. For those who died before Christ, the western Church usually celebrated three feast-days only: for the Maccabees, the heroic defenders of the Jewish faith in pre-Christian times; the Holy Innocents, the children slaughtered by Herod; and John the Baptist. These exceptions were sometimes the source of perplexity. Doubt about whether it was right for Christians to celebrate the feast-day of the Maccabees went back to the time of the Church Fathers.[323] In the twelfth century St. Bernard had to write a long letter in response to someone who had asked why it had been decided that, "of all the righteous men of old, the Maccabees alone by a special privilege should enjoy a solemn annual celebration in the Church equal to those of our martyrs."[324] His reasoning in this letter is so complicated and abstruse that one feels he almost needs to convince himself. Bartholomew of Trent explained that the Church celebrated the feast of the Maccabees, not only to stir up zeal for the faith among Christians, when they witnessed such zeal for the Old Law, but also "to endorse the idea that the fathers of the Old Testament are worthy of celebration."[325] He explained why there was no annual commemoration of the Old Testament patriarchs and prophets, apart from the representative figures of the Maccabees: partly because they, like all people who lived before Christ, had descended into hell, and partly because "so many new figures have been introduced." The implication is that the flood of Christian saints, heroes of the faith who had gone straight to heaven on their deaths, had crowded out these earlier heroes.

The Holy Innocents and John the Baptist, the cousin and precursor of Christ, had a curiously complicated position. Although they are New Testament not Old Testament figures, found in the Christian not the Hebrew Bible, they had died before Christ and hence, according to later Christian theologians, they had gone down to hell, not directly to heaven like the saints who died after Christ. At least one litany lists John the Baptist at the end of its roll-call of Old Testament prophets, rather than giving him his own separate invocation, as was usual.[326] The Innocents and John the Baptist were amongst those whom Christ had led out of hell ("The Harrowing of

[322] Salimbene, *Cronica*, p. 400; the rival Order is named as the *Heremitani*, which usually means Austin Hermits, but the Carmelites also had a special devotion to Elisha; BS 4, col. 1131, s.n. "Eliseo, profeta," says the church of S. Apollinare Nuovo in Ravenna claims his head.

[323] Braulik, "Verweigert die Westkirche den Heiligen des Alten Testaments die liturgische Verehrung?," pp. 7–10.

[324] Bernard of Clairvaux, *Epistola* 98 (7, pp. 248–53).

[325] Bartholomew of Trent, *Liber epilogorum in gesta sanctorum* 252, p. 203.

[326] Leroquais, *Les psautiers manuscrits* 1, p. 21 (no. 12) (Angers BM 18 [14] of the eleventh century).

Hell" as it was known in medieval England) when he descended there between his death and resurrection.[327]

Liturgists sometimes got into a tangle about these unusual saints. One monastic writer boldly asserted that, "the Passion of the Holy Innocents is celebrated less festively than that of other saints, because, although they were crowned with martyrdom, they descended to the pains of hell and not yet to glory," but he classifies the feast-day of John the Baptist, who is also reckoned to have descended into hell, as "a most distinguished feast."[328] He was right, however, that the feast-day of the Innocents was celebrated "less festively," since the so-called joyful canticles, that is, the *Gloria* and *Alleluia*, were omitted from Mass on that day.[329]

This discrepancy was noticed in the Middle Ages. William Durandus wrote, "One may ask why, in the Mass on the feast-day of the Innocents, the *Gloria in excelsis* and *Alleluia* and other canticles of joy are not sung." He knew what earlier writers had to say—"The masters say that it is because they died before the Passion of the Lord and so descended into hell"—but he pointed out that exactly the same reasoning applied to the feast-day of John the Baptist. He concluded that the real reason for the omission of these joyful chants on the day of the Holy Innocents was that the author of their liturgy "wished to join us on this feast-day with the spirits of the pious women who lamented and grieved the death of the Innocents."[330] He has moved the interpretation from a theological point to an expression of human sympathy.

Lay Saints

While it is possible to categorize saints in the way that the medieval Church did, into martyrs, confessors, virgins, and so on, it is also reasonable to classify them in other ways, such as by status, class, or nationality. The Church did not provide any special liturgy for lay saints, as it did for martyrs and confessors (who could be lay or clerical), but they form a natural and recognisable group—men and women who were neither clergy, nor monks or nuns.

A good example is provided by Homobonus of Cremona, an Italian layman canonized by Pope Innocent III in 1199. He was a small-scale trader in clothing, and also had his own vineyard where he would often work. A married man, with many children, he managed to pursue a life of piety and practical virtue alongside his family obligations, although not without some tensions—his family considered that his alms-giving was excessive, perhaps believing that charity begins at home. Besides offering gifts to the poor, Homobonus also visited the sick and prisoners. He was regular in his attendance at church, went to confession every week, and prayed constantly. He undertook a programme of self-mortification through fasting, beating

[327] See Tamburr, *The Harrowing of Hell in Medieval England.*

[328] Bernold of Constance, *Micrologus de ecclesiasticis observationibus* 36, 62, cols. 1006, 1022.

[329] Amalarius of Metz, *Liber officialis* 1. 41, pp. 192–93 (PL 105: 1074); John Beleth, *Summa de ecclesiasticis officiis* 70h, p. 132.

[330] William Durandus, *Rationale divinorum officiorum* 7. 42. 11 (140B, pp. 110–11).

himself, and secretly wearing a rough belt beneath his clothes. Especially when he was working at his vineyard, he suffered the attacks of evil spirits, until St. Michael appeared and gave him a special staff that would keep them off.[331] Pope Innocent's canonization bull, while mentioning the works of charity and perpetual prayer, also stresses that "the perversity of heretics is especially confounded when they see miracles multiplying at the tombs of Catholics" and mentions Homobonus's contempt for the heretics, who were numerous in his home town of Cremona.[332] A pious and orthodox layman in a north Italian town at this time would provide a model of good Catholic behaviour in a world where the allure of heresy and anti-clericalism might, the pope feared, be overwhelming. Another lay saint, also characteristically from Italy, was the Tuscan serving-girl, Zita, who died in 1272 after a lifetime of service to a wealthy family of Lucca. She was assiduous in her duties, kind to the poor and needy, sparing in her food and drink, and devoted herself to prayer and contemplation of the Passion of Christ. On one occasion she was so rapt in prayer that she forgot she had been supposed to bake bread for the household, but, running back to the house, she found the bread all ready for the oven, prepared by no human hands. She preserved her virginity, even scratching the face of a fellow servant who made advances, and died—or "went to the heavenly nuptials of the Lamb"—at the age of sixty. Miracles immediately followed.[333]

Lay people could, of course, be married, and the thin but continuous thread of married saints can be traced from Perpetua, nursing her baby in prison while awaiting martyrdom, to the martyr-king, Henry VI of England, murdered, and some said martyred, in 1471. More than a thousand years separate them, as does their sex, rank, land of birth, language, importance as a saint, and, obviously, the reasons for their death, but they show that fertile marriage was no absolute barrier to becoming a saint. But lay saints, and married saints, were always a minority.

Royal Saints

Although it is easier for a camel to go through the eye of a needle than for a rich man to enter into the kingdom of God, this did not stop the wealthy and powerful trying, and, judging by the number of high-born saints, they had considerable success. Studies have demonstrated that the top levels of society were disproportionately represented among both canonized and uncanonized saints.[334] Some contemporaries thought this only natural. One Spanish noble of the thirteenth century even declared, "I wholeheartedly believe that the son of a ruler or of some great man can become a saint, but utterly disbelieve that any labourer or peasant can."[335]

[331] *Quoniam historiae* (Life of Homobonus).

[332] Innocent III, *Die Register Innocenz' III* 1, pp. 761–64.

[333] *Vita sanctae Zitae virginis.*

[334] Weinstein and Bell, *Saints and Society*, pp. 194–219; Vauchez, *Sainthood*, pp. 279–83.

[335] *Vita et miracula Isidori agricolae* 13, p. 118 (AASS Maii 3: 518); see the comments of Wolf, "The Life and Afterlife of San Isidro Labrador."

Most remarkable of all was the fusion of royalty and sanctity. Since medieval kings were primarily war-leaders, and their aim and duty was to perpetuate their dynasty, violence and sex were inherent in their lives, so it might be thought they would be unlikely candidates for sainthood. Yet a fair number were regarded as saints, and some of their cults were major ones. In his studies of this subject Robert Folz discusses twenty-eight kings and twelve queens who were the object of saintly cult between the sixth and the thirteenth centuries (although this figure includes nine Anglo-Saxon kings of the seventh and eight centuries for whom evidence of cult is slight).[336] These forty kings and queens fall naturally into groups. Exactly half of them (including all the obscure Anglo-Saxon kings) are early, that is, prior to the year 800, and are Burgundian, Frankish, or Anglo-Saxon. These early cases divide again into two groups, the Burgundian and Frankish examples of the sixth and seventh centuries (seven cases) and the Anglo-Saxon ones of the seventh and eight centuries (thirteen cases).

This early stage is followed by something of a hiatus. On the continent, there is a period of almost 300 years after the death of Balthildis (around 680) during which there is not a single contemporary trace of any new cult of a king or queen, while in England there is a solitary ninth-century example (Edmund of East Anglia).[337] In the tenth and eleventh century, cases again multiply, in Germany (queen Matilda, the empresses Adelheid and Cunigunda [although evidence for her cult is late], the emperor Henry II), eastern Europe (Wenceslas, Stephen and Ladislas of Hungary), Scandinavia (Olav of Norway, Canute of Denmark), England (Edward the Martyr, Edward the Confessor), and Scotland (Margaret). The twelfth century sees only one addition to Folz's catalogue, Canute Laward of Denmark (although it was also the century that witnessed the canonization of Charlemagne).

There is a striking pattern to the geography of both the initial phase (500–800) and the second phase (900–1100) of regal saints. The first is restricted to the Frankish, Burgundian, and Anglo-Saxon kingdoms, while the second can be delimited by a line drawn along the English Channel and the Rhine: south and west of this boundary there are no cases, north and east of it they are quite numerous. These saint-rulers are all Germanic, except for the three east European examples (who were under strong German influence). This leads naturally to the question of the significance of this Germanic pattern.

It has been suggested that royal sainthood was a Christian version of an old sacral kingship found among the Germanic peoples.[338] It is a suggestion that has also been vigorously denied.[339] There is no doubt that early medieval kings had a sacral aura

[336] Folz, *Les saints rois du moyen*; idem, *Les saintes reines du Moyen Age*.

[337] Richardis, wife of Charles the Fat, lived in the later ninth century, but the evidence for her cult begins only in the eleventh, with her translation in 1049: *Annalista Saxo*, p. 688.

[338] For example, Chaney, *The Cult of Kingship in Anglo–Saxon England*; Hoffmann, *Die heiligen Könige bei den Angelsachsen und den skandinavistischen Völkern*, esp. pp. 50–55.

[339] For example, Graus, *Volk, Herrscher und Heiliger im Reich der Merowinger*, pp. 390–433; Nelson, "Royal Saints and Early Medieval Kingship." See also the comments of Ridyard, *The Royal Saints of Anglo-*

quite apart from any claim to Christian sanctity. This aura was not limited to the Germanic world. Seventh-century texts from Ireland, in both Latin and Irish, link the uprightness of the king with good weather and the fertility of the land. The author of the tract *On the Twelve Abuses of the World* lists the horrible consequences of an unjust king:

> The peace of the people is often broken, obstacles arise concerning the kingdom, the fruits of the land also decrease . . . the deaths of dear ones and children brings sorrow, attacks of the enemy devastate the provinces on every side, wild beasts rip apart the flocks and the herds, storms of the air and disturbances in the heavens hold back the fertility of the soil and commerce by sea, and sometimes lightning burns up the fruits and flowers of trees and the young shoots.[340]

Conversely, a just king brings peace, health, good weather, and fertility. A contemporary Old Irish tract on kingship describes how "it is through the justice of the ruler that milk-yields of great cattle are maintained . . . that abundance of fish swim in streams . . . that fair children are well begotten."[341]

In a long letter of spiritual advice to Ethelred, king of the Northumbrians, in 793, the Anglo-Saxon scholar and cleric Alcuin advanced a classic definition of this link between the fortune of the king and the land:

> We read that the goodness of the king is the prosperity of the whole people, the victory of the army, the pleasantness of the air, the abundance of the soil, the blessing of sons, the health of the populace. It is a great thing to rule a whole people.[342]

Alcuin proceeds to give this idea a Christian elaboration: a good king will earn from God the reward of a heavenly kingdom, and he should devote himself to prayer and vigils.

And this idea, that the fertility of the land depended on the king, was not simply the view of educated clerics. When the emperor Henry IV died in 1106, eager crowds attempted to touch his funeral bier, "believing that they sanctified themselves by doing so," while others sought fertility for their crops:

> Many people scraped up the earth from his grave with their nails and scattered it on their own fields and homes as a blessing; others placed last year's corn on

Saxon England, pp. 74–95, and the thoughtful historiographical analysis in Klaniczay, *Holy Rulers and Blessed Princesses*, esp. pp. 2–18, 64–67, 78–79.

340 Pseudo-Cyprianus, *De XII abusivis saeculi*, p. 52.

341 *Audacht Morainn* 12–21, p. 7.

342 Alcuin, *Epistola* 18, p. 51; he is indebted to the earlier Irish *De XII abusivis saeculi*: Wallach, *Alcuin and Charlemagne*, pp. 8–9.

> his bier and, mixing it with new seed, sowed it, hoping in this way to secure for themselves an abundant harvest.[343]

In medieval Scandinavia, women would press forward their babies to be touched by the king to obtain for them "a happier natural growth" and peasants would think that if he scattered grain "it would grow better."[344]

Underlying such beliefs and practices is a conception of the channels of blessedness different from the story of salvation preached by the clergy. Good kings are not those who pursue their own individual salvation, but those who, by fulfilling their role correctly, bring natural abundance, peace and prosperity. It is not that good kingship of this type is defined by inherited or intrinsic qualities, while Christian sanctity involves virtues or merits that are attained, for the sacral king can be just or unjust. It is rather that the qualities of successful sacral kings and royal saints, and also the blessings they bring, are different.

In the late eleventh century, the radical reforming pope, Gregory VII, tried to make a sharp distinction between kings, even good ones, and saints, especially monastic saints.[345] "Has any emperor or king shone with miracles like St. Martin, St. Antony, or St. Benedict?" he asked. "Which emperor or king has raised the dead, healed lepers, or given sight to the blind?" Even good and pious rulers, the pope argued, like Constantine and Charlemagne, did not perform miracles. Nor were churches or altars dedicated to them, or Masses celebrated in their honour. These were tendentious claims. By Gregory's time, cults of royal saints could be found in northern and eastern Europe; Constantine might not be regarded as a saint in the West, but the Eastern Church celebrated his feast-day; and Charlemagne was to be formally canonized in 1166, even if by a pope later regarded as illegitimate. A more plausible clerical position was to recognize that some kings could be saints but deny any inherent sacrality in their status. The monastic historian William of Malmesbury criticized those who claimed that Edward the Confessor's healing powers "stemmed not from sanctity but hereditarily from royal stock."[346] He was willing to recognize a saint king but not sacral monarchy.

The complexity of the figure of the royal saint is illustrated by the earliest example, Sigismund, king of the Burgundians, who was executed by his enemies in 523. Although he had won a favourable reputation in the eyes of the Catholic Church by embracing Catholicism, rather than the Arian heresy which the Burgundians had adopted, and by his patronage of the shrine of St. Maurice at Agaunum, he had also murdered his son with his own hands. It was his remorse at this act that made him a suitable candidate for sanctity. Writing at the end of the sixth century, Gregory of Tours includes Sigismund in his *Glory of the Martyrs*: "The Lord often crushes the arrogance of a wicked mind with the rod of correction, in order to restore it to

[343] Sigebert of Gembloux, *Chronica*, pp. 371–72, variant d.

[344] Saxo Grammaticus, *Gesta Danorum* 14. 28. 13 (2, p. 306).

[345] Gregory VII, *Registrum* 8. 21 (2, p. 559).

[346] William of Malmesbury, *Gesta regum Anglorum* 2. 222, pp. 406–8.

reverence for his worship." He then describes the king's penitence and his death, and goes on to explain why he can be regarded as a member of "the company of saints":

> At the present day, if those who are suffering from a chill fever celebrate a Mass devoutly in his honour, and make an offering to God for his repose, they are immediately restored to health, the shaking ceases and the fever is extinguished.[347]

So Sigismund's power as a posthumous healer confirmed the efficacy of his repentance in his lifetime. Later a *Passion of St. Sigismund, King and Martyr* was composed.[348]

Gregory treats of Sigismund in his book on martyrs, and one of the remarkable things about these royal saints is how many of the saintly kings died violent deaths—sixteen of Folz's catalogue of twenty-eight, that is, 57 per cent. If one broadens the definition to include members of ruling families who were not technically sovereigns, such as princes or dukes, the numbers can be increased. Charles, count of Flanders, murdered in 1127, was performing miracles even before his body was buried.[349] And cults of murdered royal saints continue into the later Middle Ages, into a period not covered in Folz's studies. Nor does Folz discuss the murdered princes of Russia, such as Boris and Gleb, whose stories have a similar shape to those in the West.

There is thus an important group of royal saints whose passage to sanctity was via a bloody death, from Sigismund in the sixth century to Henry VI of England in the fifteenth, and from Kiev to Herefordshire. The great historian of sainthood André Vauchez has even postulated a model of "the suffering chief" as characteristic of the sanctity of non-Mediterranean Europe.[350] The dynamics of these cults has been much discussed. On the one hand, there is plenty of evidence that veneration of these slaughtered saints represents "a spontaneous popular cult resulting from the attribution of sacred powers to the victims of sudden and violent death."[351] But, while most of them were labelled martyrs, it is clear that many of these murdered kings and rulers were the victims of political conflict in which only material interests were at stake. The idea that they were "martyrs," dying for a higher cause, had to be devised by followers and partisans, and then established by the hagiographers who gave literary life to their cult and the clerics who furthered it. As so often in the cult of the saints, the spontaneous and popular, on the one hand, and the learned, on the other, acted together.

In the later medieval period there continued to be royal saints of the early medieval type. Folz's total of forty royal saints between the sixth and thirteenth century

[347] Gregory of Tours, *Gloria martyrum* 74, p. 537 (repr., 1969, p. 87).

[348] *Passio sancti Sigismundi regis.*

[349] Walther of Therouanne, *Vita Karoli comitis Flandriae* 30, p. 551; Galbert of Bruges, *De multro . . . Karoli comitis Flandriarum* 22, p. 55; for subsequent cult see BS 3, cols. 794–97, s.n. "Carlo il buono."

[350] "La souffrance du chef," Vauchez, *Sainteté*, p. 186, translated as "the suffering leader" in *Sainthood*, p. 158.

[351] Cubitt, "Sites and Sanctity: Revisiting the Cult of Murdered and Martyred Anglo-Saxon Royal Saints," p. 79.

(five per century) can be compared with Weinstein and Bell's figures, which overlap chronologically to some extent. They included 39 royal saints from the period 1000–1500 in their sample, that is, eight per century, and that is explicitly not a complete figure.[352] A complicating factor is that Folz deals only with ruling monarchs and their spouses.[353] He thus excludes saints who were the children of monarchs, such as Edburga, daughter of King Edward the Elder of Wessex; Emeric, son of St. Stephen of Hungary; or Margaret, daughter of Bela IV of Hungary (d. 1270). They are "royal saints" in some sense. Given Folz's narrower definition, the figures do not suggest that royal saints were more characteristic of the early Middle Ages than the later Middle Ages. Numerous prominent cases can be found in the later centuries. Louis IX of France (St. Louis) was canonized in 1297, his great-nephew Louis of Toulouse, son of king Charles II of Naples, in 1317. Although they were never canonized, two English kings of the fourteenth and fifteenth centuries, Edward II (d. 1327) and Henry VI (d. 1471) had significant cults. And there was an official enquiry into the miracles of queen Isabella (or Elizabeth) of Portugal (d. 1336), daughter of Peter III of Aragon and wife of King Dinis of Portugal.[354]

The veneration of some royal saints spread well beyond their native lands. Oswald is an Anglo-Saxon saint-king with a surprisingly wide continental cult.[355] Edmund, king and martyr, crops up in Italy. Quite remarkably, the name of "St. Ferdinand, king of Spain," that is, Ferdinand III of Castile and Leon (d. 1252), was added to the Kalendar in the Psalter owned by John de Grandison, bishop of Exeter (d. 1369).[356] Grandison was a highly educated and cosmopolitan man, with a deep interest in the cult of the saints, but the appearance here of this Spanish royal saint is still a rarity.

FEMALE ROYAL SAINTS

Placing female royal saints in the same category as male royal saints rests purely on the formal criterion of royal birth. They do not suffer bloody deaths, they rarely rule in their own right, and a large number of them gained their reputation for piety in the nunnery rather than in the court. Radegund of Poitiers (d. 587) was the daughter of a Thuringian king and the wife of a Frankish one, but what her Life emphasizes is her long years of renunciation of the world, first during her husband's lifetime, then, after his death in 561, in her nunnery at Poitiers.[357] Etheldreda (d. 679), daugh-

352 Weinstein and Bell, *Saints and Society*, p. 197.

353 Although not all of them bore the title "king" or "queen." Those without the title were Wenceslas, Canute Laward, Elizabeth of Thuringia, and Hedwig of Silesia.

354 Azevedo, "Inquiração de 1336 sobre os milagres da Rainha D. Isabel"; there is an early Life: *Vita Elisabethae reginae Portugalliae* (Latin translation of Portuguese original); see McCleery, "Isabel of Aragon."

355 Clemoes, *The Cult of St Oswald on the Continent*; Ó Riain-Raedel, "Edith, Judith, Matilda: The Role of Royal Ladies in the Propagation of the Continental Cult"; Jansen, "The Development of the St Oswald Legends on the Continent."

356 BL, Add. 21926 ("Grandison Psalter"), fol. 5.

357 Venantius Fortunatus, *Vita sanctae Radegundis*; Baudonivia, *Vita sanctae Radegundis*.

ter of the king of the East Angles, married twice, the second time to a king of Northumbria, but preserved her virginity throughout these marriages, and eventually became abbess of the nunnery she founded at Ely.[358]

In contrast, the later tenth and eleventh centuries see a group of female royal saints who combined their sanctity very easily with secular authority and dignity. Matilda, wife of Henry I of Germany, who lived in royal widowhood for 32 years, was celebrated in a Life written less than a decade after her death. This recounts at some length Matilda's descent from the great Saxon hero Widukind, who fought against Charlemagne until forced to submit and convert, and describes the young Matilda as "the future hope of her people." Her marriage is happy and brings her "secular power," although she puts God's service ahead of "the glory of the world"; her children attain "the highest honour"; it is recognized that she is one of those "who preside over an earthly kingdom."[359] She is not only "most holy" (*sanctissima*) but also "a ruler" (*domina*).[360] Matilda's daughter-in-law, the empress Adelheid, was likewise the subject of a hagiographic work shortly after her death. It celebrated her "royal and religious lineage" and declared that "through her the state was strong."[361] The monks of Selz, where she was buried, kept a record of her miracles, which included powerful acts in defence of the monastic property, and, in the course of time, her reputation as a wonder-worker was enough to convince Pope Urban II to canonize her, probably in 1097. He chose an entirely appropriate verb to express this: "we have enthroned Adelheid."[362] Royal saints remained tenaciously royal. Other empresses, Richardis and Cunigunda, were also the subjects of cult in the eleventh and twelfth century. Queen Margaret of Scotland (d. 1093), although she ruled a kingdom far from the empire, was of this same type, and may even have had family connections with the imperial ladies, since her father grew up in exile on the continent and, according to some sources, was married to a relative of "the emperor Henry."[363] Margaret was a severe matriarch, insistent on royal dignity, as well as a charitable giver and patron of monks.[364]

The tone changes somewhat after these great saint-empresses and saint-queens, as Latin Christendom moved into an age of increasing papal authority and the blossoming of the new orders. The thirteenth century saw a remarkable cluster of saintly princesses in east-central Europe, linked by ties of blood and marriage (figure 7.8).[365] They were wives and daughters of the ruling dynasties, the Arpads of Hungary,

[358] Bede, *Historia ecclesiastica* 4. 19, pp. 390–96.

[359] *Vita Mathildis reginae antiquior* 1, 2, 3, 4, 9, pp. 113–14, 115, 118, 119, 130.

[360] See the acute comments on the significance of this word by Sean Gilsdorf in his translation: *Queenship and Sanctity: The Lives of Mathilda and the Epitaph of Adelheid*, p. 66.

[361] Odilo of Cluny, *Epitaphium domne Adalheide auguste*, preface and 1 (II), pp. 27, 29 (PL 142: 970).

[362] *Miracula Adelheidis reginae*; Loewenfeld, ed., *Epistolae pontificum romanorum ineditae*, no. 135, p. 65; on both Matilda and Adelheid, see Corbet, *Les saints ottoniens*.

[363] John of Worcester, *Chronicle* 2, pp. 502–4; *Anglo-Saxon Chronicle* D, s.a 1057, p. 188.

[364] Turgot, *Vita sanctae Margaretae Scotorum reginae*, *passim*.

[365] Klaniczay, *Holy Rulers and Blessed Princesses*, pp. 195–294.

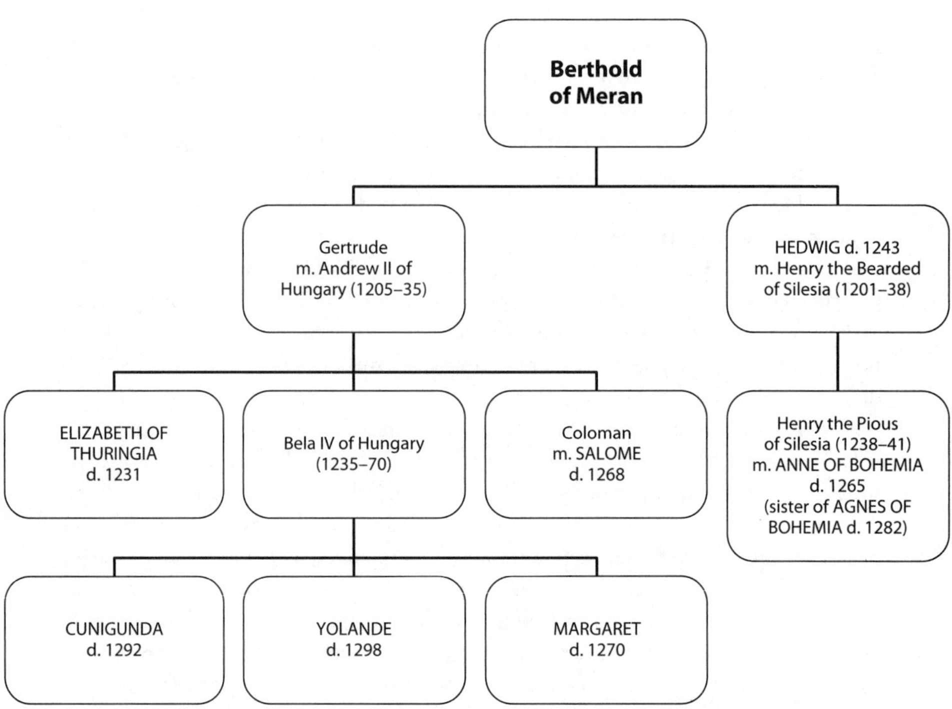

7.8. Saintly princesses of east-central Europe. (Saints' names are in capitals.)

Přemyslids of Bohemia and Piasts of Poland. The earliest, and most important as a saint, was Elizabeth of Thuringia (d. 1231), followed both in time and significance by her aunt Hedwig of Silesia (d. 1243). The tradition continued with Elizabeth's sister-in-law, nieces, and cousins. The lives of these women covered the whole thirteenth century. Only two of them (Margaret of Hungary and Agnes of Bohemia) remained unmarried, but another two (Cunigunda and Salome) supposedly insisted on chaste marriage, and Hedwig and her husband took vows of chastity after she had borne him seven children. So, although four of these eight princesses were mothers, they still, as a group, recognized the high value of sexual renunciation.

They were closely involved with the new religious Orders, especially the Poor Clares, the female branch of the Franciscans. Agnes of Bohemia corresponded with Clare herself, and founded the first convent of Poor Clares in central Europe, at Prague in 1234, of which she became the abbess.[366] She turned down an offer of marriage from the emperor Frederick II in order to do so, and the pope, locked in mortal struggle with Frederick at this time, was wild in his enthusiasm:

[366] Mueller, ed., *Clare's Letters to Agnes*.

> Agnes, the handmaid of Christ, the virgin daughter of the king of Bohemia, in whose youth we are discovering exceptional signs of a heavenly way of life, so much that, fleeing the desirable heights of imperial eminence like poisonous reptiles, and, naked, taking up the standard of the triumphal cross, she is now on the way to meet her spouse, with lighted lamps and accompanied by a choir of holy virgins.[367]

Like Agnes, Salome, Cunigunda, Yolanda and Anne, Agnes's sister, all eventually founded houses of Poor Clares, where they ended their days. The Franciscan ideal was one of poverty, but the female branch of the Order, being enclosed, needed housing and a church, and, in the eyes of many, a proper endowment of property, and the fathers, brothers, and cousins of these pious ladies were willing to provide that. Only Elizabeth and Hedwig were canonized in the medieval period, but all the members of this the interlinking web of devout and high-born women left a mark on the saintly landscape of east central Europe.

The study of royal saints makes it clear, not only that sainthood could vary in its nature and forms but also that the secular world had powerful positive ideals of its own. It has been argued, very convincingly, that "there was surely a model of good queenship that need not have anything at all to do with sainthood."[368] And the same is true of kingship. There were, in fact, several ways in which the idea of a saint king might appear to be self-contradictory. Kings were proud and warlike dynasts. They were brought up to believe that their blood was better than other people's and they were trained in the use of deadly weapons. Some of the Christian virtues, such as humility, might not seem to fit easily with this kind of education. It is clear that contemporaries felt the discord of values. In order to illustrate the virtues of King Oswin of Deira, Bede reports how the saintly Aidan praised the king for a gesture of self-abasement he had made. "Never before this" says Aidan, "have I seen a humble king."[369] Many people said that Sebbi, king of Essex (d. 693/4), who was devoted to God and spent much time in prayer and alms-giving, was more suited to being a bishop than a king.[370]

There was tension too between the dynastic duties of a ruler and the high evaluation of chastity and virginity that shaped conceptions of sainthood. It was a king's obligation to secure the succession, by fathering sons. Sexual renunciation in these circumstances could be seen as a dereliction of duty: a virgin nun was one thing, a virgin king another. The Lives of Ethelbert, king and martyr, contain a passage in which the saintly king's yearning for sexual renunciation encounters the solid rock of the insistence of his nobles that he should marry:

[367] ASV, Reg. Vat. 18, fols. 41v–42 (Register of Gregory IX); *Iesus filius Sirach*, 7 June 1235, Po. 9933, to Beatrice, queen of Castile.

[368] McCleery, "Isabel of Aragon," p. 675.

[369] Bede, *Historia ecclesiastica* 3. 14, p. 258.

[370] Ibid., 4. 11, p. 364.

He was admonished to lead his life according to the manner and custom of his ancestors and select some noble virgin, outstanding for her looks and the elegance of her body, to join to him in the bond of marriage and from whom he could raise up an heir for his kingdom; they added that it was not fitting for a king to be without children.

Ethelbert, "although virgin innocence pleased him more than married chastity or the union of wedlock," bowed to their advice (although things did not work out well).[371] Saintly queens were usually excused virginity on the grounds of dynastic duty. There were virgin married queens, like Etheldreda and Cunigunda, but most queens who were recognized as saints were mothers, and some, such as Matilda of Germany and Margaret of Scotland, were dynastic matriarchs. (Some modern historians even use the term "Margaretsons" to describe the Scots rulers of the twelfth and thirteenth centuries.)

Saintly queens were praised for their charitable works, for their devotions, and for running a pious and well-ordered household. The chamber of queen Margaret of Scotland was full of noblewomen, "of sound morality," who spent their time sewing vestments for the clergy; men could enter only when the queen was there, and there was to be no intimacy or frivolity with them.[372] Queen Isabella of Portugal (d. 1336) gave alms to the poor, fasted, treated wanderers and the oppressed with mercy, and recited the canonical hours from the breviary; she also strung onions on strings, and forced her ladies in waiting also to engage in manual tasks of this kind.[373]

Pious widowhood or entry into the nunnery offered hagiographers the chance to stress the contrast between the ladies' royal status and the life of humble service which they adopted. "Once a queen, then a handmaid of the poor and the servants of God," wrote the author of the Life of Clotilda, queen of the Franks (d. 544), describing her life of good works and piety during her widowhood.[374] After queen Balthildis had been widowed and retired to the nunnery of Chelles, she undertook lowly tasks gladly, even cleaning the toilets: "Who would believe that a majesty of such power would take care of such a vile business?" asked her hagiographer.[375] Agnes of Bohemia made her gesture of renunciation in public, before her brother king Wenceslas I and the assembled clergy and nobility of the kingdom of Bohemia, "rejecting the exalted rank of the kingdom and despising all earthly glory. She flew like an innocent dove from the Flood of this wicked world to the Ark of holy religion." Entering the

[371] Osbert of Clare, *Vita Ethelberti regis*, Gotha, Forschungsbibliothek Memb. I 81, fols. 30–39, at fol. 31v; most of Osbert's Life was incorporated into Richard of Cirencester's *Speculum historiale* 1, pp. 262–94, with this quote at p. 266; comparable passages are found in an earlier Life and in a later version by Gerald of Wales: James, "Two Lives of Ethelbert, King and Martyr," pp. 224 (Gerald), 237 (earlier anonymous Life).

[372] Turgot, *Vita sanctae Margaretae Scotorum reginae* 4, p. 239.

[373] *Vita Elisabethae reginae Portugalliæ* 3. 16, p. 176.

[374] *Vita sanctae Chrothildis* 14, p. 347.

[375] *Vita sanctae Balthildis* 11, p. 497.

nunnery of Poor Clares that she had founded, she had her hair cropped, took off her "royal vestments," and began a life of service to the sick.[376]

Sometimes the hagiographers of saintly queens had a difficult task reconciling discordant ideals. Turgot, author of the Life of Margaret of Scotland, explained how she had made the ceremonial and etiquette of the Scottish court more magnificent, introducing more expensive and colourful fashions, increasing the size of the royal retinue, decorating the royal hall with bright hangings, and having gold and silver vessels for the use of the king and his nobles.[377] Turgot's tone at first seems celebratory: "this most noble jewel of royal stock made the magnificence of the royal honour much more magnificent for the king." But he then puts on the brakes: Margaret did all this, "not because she delighted in worldly honour but because she was forced to perform what the royal dignity demanded of her." She is a victim of her social role, which hides her true self: "although she went out dressed in precious garments, as befitted a queen, she trampled on all ornamentation in her mind, like a second Esther; under the jewels and gold, she considered herself nothing but dust and ashes." There could scarcely be a more grating conjunction of the contradictory values of royal dignity and saintly self-abnegation.

Saints as Patrons

Saints and Their Churches

Although Christians recognized the heroic virtues of all the saints, it was natural that some were more vivid than others, more familiar and more important to them. Special reverence was directed to local saints, those whose tombs or relics were close at hand. Writing around the year 400, bishop Maximus of Turin declared, "All the martyrs are to be venerated with the greatest devotion, but we should pay special reverence to those whose relics we possess . . . we have a kind of friendship with them."[378] "He is to be venerated generally by the whole world," wrote one of the clergy at the shrine of St. Verolus in Burgundy, "but he is to be specially honoured by us, who enjoy the presence of his most holy body."[379]

The first and most natural community of a saint was the body of clergy or monks whose church housed the relics. They tended the shrine and composed the hagiographic writings that publicized the powers of the saint. The lands of the big monasteries and churches were regarded as the property of their patron saint. Thus "the land of St. Cuthbert" was the designation for the concentration of estates in the

[376] *Vita illustrissime uirginis sororis Agnetis ordinis Sancte Clare de Praga* 3, ed. Seton, p. 80; ed. Vyskočil, p. 107.

[377] Turgot, *Vita sanctae Margaretae Scotorum reginae* 7, pp. 241–42.

[378] Maximus of Turin, *Sermo* 12, p. 41 (an alternative dating of Maximus places him much later in the fifth century).

[379] *Miracula sancti Veroli* 1. 1, p. 382.

north of England belonging to the church of Durham (it could also go by the Old English name *Haliwerfolc*, "the people of the saint"), while the compact block of monastic property centred on Monte Cassino, St. Benedict's monastery in central Italy, was "the land of St. Benedict."[380] The fact that the saints embodied enduring property claims in this way explains why they have been called "Undying Landlords."[381] Donations were often seen as gifts to the saint rather than just to the church or community. When King Ferdinand of Leon broke a wine-glass during a visit to the monastery of Sahagún, which was dedicated to the martyrs Facundus and Primitivus, he gave in amends a golden goblet, with the words, "in place of the one I broke, I give this vessel to the holy martyrs." He had been careless with something that belonged, not to the monks, but to the saints.[382]

This sense of "the saint as owner" comes out from the wording of various surveys and grants.[383] Domesday Book, which records the great survey of England carried out in 1086, mentions Robert of Mortain, William the Conqueror's half-brother and a great landowner, holding land in Cornwall "from St. Petroc," and, lower down the social scale, peasant tenants "who could not be separated from the saint," again referring to St. Petroc.[384] Robert could have been described as holding land from St. Petroc's church at Bodmin, and the lesser men as permanent tenants of the same church, but the wording chosen presents them in a relationship with the saint rather than with an ecclesiastical institution. A grant to the monastery of St. Peter's outside Vienne in 1057 was made "to God and St. Peter and the other apostles and saints who rest there and to the monks who serve God in that place," thus encompassing the deity and the saints in the grant, which would, nevertheless, be enjoyed in literal and physical terms by the monks of Vienne.[385] In this way the saint embodied the continuing corporate existence of the church, its community and its property.

The body of clergy or monks who tended a shrine always formed the main champion and beneficiary of a saint's prestige, but the saint could serve as a patron to a wider group too. The lay people of the vicinity formed a potential clientele as long as they were not hostile to the church that housed the saint, and "the vicinity" could be interpreted in quite a wide sense. Saints took Orders, cities, guilds, nations and kingdoms under their wing, and were constantly celebrated by their protagonists for appealing to and unifying the high and the low, of both sexes, from far and wide, even if this was sometimes a wish rather than a fact.

[380] *Terra sancti Cuthberti*: for example, Richard of Hexham, *Historia*, p. 178; Lapsley, *County Palatine Of Durham*, pp. 21–24; *terra sancti Benedicti*: for example, *Chronica monasterii Casinensis* 1. 12; 4. 52, 75, 82, 96, 98, 108, pp. 47, 518, 541, 546, 556, 560, 570; Richard of San Germano, *Chronica*, pp. 22, 81, 110, 153, 190.

[381] Rollason, *Saints and Relics in Anglo-Saxon England*, p. 196, title to chapter 8.

[382] *Historia Silense* 104, p. 206.

[383] The phrase cited is from Pollock and Maitland, *The History of English Law* 1, p. 499.

[384] *Domesday Book* 1, fol. 121 (Cornwall 4. 6–17); for discussion of the Domesday estates of this saint, Jankulak, *The Medieval Cult of St Petroc*, pp. 124–30.

[385] *Diplomata regum Burgundiae e stirpe Rudolfina*, no. 143, p. 324.

The concentric circles that might revere a saint are nicely illustrated in the closing part of the Life of Stanislaus of Cracow:

> So let Poland celebrate, that has deserved to have such a happy offspring and such a holy and blessed parent. Let Cracow rejoice, and especially the cathedral church endowed with the holy body. And let mother Church with all the faithful be happy.[386]

Here there is the church that houses the body, the city that houses the church, the country that houses the city, and, beyond all, the Church universal.

But loyalty to a saint could divide as well as unite. "Every Order of monks wishes to have the most saints," claimed one early Protestant.[387] The monks and friars of the religious Orders had a strong sense of their own identities and loyalties, and members of one Order were not always enthusiastic about celebrating the saints of another Order. In 1255 the pope had to write, in a somewhat exasperated tone, to the General Chapter of the Cistercians, reminding them that, although the great Dominican saints, Dominic and Peter Martyr, had been canonized and hence their feasts should be celebrated universally, "you do not celebrate them, seizing on the pretext that it has not been specially demanded of you." He commanded them to so, and they complied, instituting feasts of twelve lessons for each of these Dominican saints, although even then maintaining a touch of truculence. Peter Martyr's feast-day was 29 April, but, they ruled, "since the Office of our blessed father Robert, first abbot of Cîteaux, falls on that day, let the feast of St. Peter Martyr be on the preceding day."[388]

The Cistercians could, however, be more accommodating than this. In 1259, the Franciscans asked them to upgrade the feast of St. Francis, which the Cistercians had celebrated as a simple commemoration since 1228, to a fully fledged feast of twelve lessons and a Mass, and this request was granted. Perhaps it was a grateful response when, in the following year, the Franciscans ruled that the feast of the most important Cistercian saint, Bernard of Clairvaux, could be celebrated on the day it actually fell (20 August), even though this was within the Octave of the feast of the Assumption of the Virgin Mary, when feast-days were usually postponed.[389]

The two chief Orders of friars were often on bad terms. According to one account, during the proceedings that led up to the canonization of the great Dominican theologian Thomas Aquinas, the Franciscans were deeply envious. One of them, "a man of great learning and authority," distinguished himself by his opposition to the canonization. When it was finally approved, on the eve of the formal ceremony,

[386] Vincent, *Vita (major) sancti Stanislai Cracoviensis episcopi* 57, p. 438.

[387] *Gesprechbiechlin neüw Karsthans*, p. 432 (the tract dates to 1521; the authorship is not certain).

[388] Alexander IV, *Licet apostolica sedes*, 21 July 1255, Po. 15940: Martène and Durand, *Thesaurus novus anecdotorum* 1, col. 1063; *Statuta capitulorum generalium ordinis Cisterciensis* 2, p. 410 no. 4.

[389] *Statuta capitulorum generalium ordinis Cisterciensis* 2, p. 65, no. 2 (1228), p. 450, no. 9 (1259); *Sources of the Modern Roman Liturgy* 1, pp. 128–30; 2, p. 419 (Chapter general of Narbonne, 1260); this exception was cancelled at the Chapter general of Lyons in 1272, ibid., 2, p. 443.

this man "said that he never wished to see the day on which such a man would be canonized." He had his wish. By "a stupendous and terrifying miracle of God and the saintly man," he was found dead next morning.[390]

Sometimes the Orders fought over the same saint. St. Augustine was not only the shared founding father of Latin Christendom but also the special saint of two groups, the Augustinian canons and the Augustinian Hermits (who were in fact friars). The Hermits developed their association with the saint vigorously. Augustine's relics were believed to be in Pavia, at the church of San Pietro in Ciel d'Oro, which was in the hands of the Augustinian canons, but the Hermits pressed for, and in 1327 received, permission to share responsibility for the shrine and build an adjacent convent. From then on, the canons and the friars fought a prolonged guerrilla war at close quarters in the church. Another ferocious dispute broke out at nearby Milan in 1474, when a decision was made to erect a statue of St. Augustine on the roof of the cathedral. The Augustinian canons insisted that the saint should be dressed as a canon, the Hermits that he should be dressed as a Hermit. Learned men on both sides published their views, the duke of Milan became involved, the repercussions spread far beyond Italy and even the pope's prohibition on any further discussion of the topic, issued in 1484, ten years after the dispute began, was ineffective.[391] The question was too deep for easy settlement: which Order owned this great saint?

Saints and the City

"A martyr's country is the place where he suffered," wrote Gregory of Nyssa, invoking St. Theodore the Recruit, whose shrine lay in the Pontus region, south of the Black Sea. "Be an ambassador for your country," he begged the saint. "As a soldier, fight for us . . . ask for peace."[392] Gregory was seeking protection against threatened Scythian raids, and he appealed to the saint's local patriotism to get it. Theodore had a "country" and should look after it. The idea of patronage could thus be extended beyond an individual city church. In his poem in praise of the three martyr-saints of Tarragona, Prudentius writes that "all we people of the Pyrenean lands are protected by their guardianship."[393] Saints could be patrons of regions, states or peoples. In the city-based society of the Roman empire, saints were "city protectors."[394]

The Italian cities of the high and later Middle Ages, which were richer, more independent and more strongly conscious of their identities than cities elsewhere, developed deep attachments to their local saints. They hailed them as defenders, patrons,

[390] Grabmann, "Hagiographische Texte in einer Handschrift des kirchenhistorischen Seminars der Universität Muenchen," p. 382.

[391] Elm, "Augustinus canonicus–Augustinus hermita"; Warr, "Hermits, Habits and History."

[392] Gregory of Nyssa, *De sancto Theodoro*, p. 70 (PG 46: 748).

[393] Prudentius, *Peristefanon* 6, lines 146–47, p. 319.

[394] Theodoret of Cyrrhus, *Historia Religiosa* 21. 20 (2, p. 102, and p. 103 n. 20).

and protectors.[395] Dante calls Florence "the sheepfold of St. John," after its patron saint, John the Baptist.[396] The feast-day of the patron or patrons was celebrated with processions, game and races. St. John's day in Florence provided a famous spectacle, while Siena still has its annual horse race through the streets, the *Palio*.[397] At Bologna, where the cathedral was dedicated to St. Peter, every year on St. Peter's day there was a horse race from one of the city bridges to one of the gates, with the winner receiving a prize of precious cloth and the runner-up a chicken. The inhabitants of the houses along the route had to keep the course clear and a list of runners was drawn up.[398] Everyone would know when it was St. Peter's day.

The patron saint was a symbol of the identity of the city but also of its authority, and, as the Italian cities extended their power into the surrounding countryside, subduing local lords and communities, they insisted that these subjects come to the city on the feast-day of their patron, bringing gifts and expressing their recognition of the supremacy of the larger power.[399] As the authorities of Bologna put it, at the end of the fourteenth century, "by this action is demonstrated the fealty and obedience that the said communes and officials hold to the commune of Bologna."[400] Wider political relationships could be symbolized in the same way. In 1364, after a decisive defeat in battle against the Florentines, the Pisans had to promise to pay reparations of 100,000 golden florins, at the rate of 10,000 a year; these annual payments were to be made "in Florence on the vigil of the nativity of St. John the Baptist."[401] The payments would thus be made when the city was full of crowds celebrating Florence's patron saint, and Pisa's reluctant tribute-bearers would have felt the full triumph of their old enemy.

The Italian cities were notoriously faction-ridden, and their saints could be equally partisan. The victorious Guelf party in Florence celebrated two victories it had won over neighbouring hostile towns, both coincidentally on St. Barnabas's day, by revering the saint not only as protector of Florence but also as champion of the Guelfs.[402] And internal victories over dissidents were marked in the same way: in 1382, the patrician faction in Florence met to plan a coup on St. Sebastian's day, and carried it out on St. Antony's day, and subsequently both days were celebrated as holidays.[403] As in the case of the Pisan tribute money, here the celebration of the saints of the victors underlined their victory.

[395] Golinelli, *Città e culto dei santi nel medioevo italiano*; Webb, *Patrons and Defenders*, pp. 103–5; short but useful bibliography in the edited collection of sources, Webb, *Saints and Cities in Medieval Italy*, pp. 257–58; see also *Patriotische Heilige*, pp. 179–323 ("Städte").

[396] Dante, *Paradiso* 16. 25.

[397] On St. John's day at Florence, see Trexler, *Public Life in Renaissance Florence*, pp. 240–78, and also later, p. 302.

[398] *Statuti di Bologna dell'anno 1288* 12. 25 (2, p. 220–21).

[399] Webb, *Patrons and Defenders*, p. 81.

[400] Ghirardacci, *Della historia di Bologna. Parte seconda*, p. 467.

[401] Matteo Villani, *Cronica* 11. 102 (Filippo Villani) (2, p. 504).

[402] Webb, *Patrons and Defenders*, p. 152.

[403] Trexler, *Public Life in Renaissance Florence*, pp. 222–23.

Venice was under the special protection of St. Mark. Ever since his body had, according to tradition, been brought to the city from Egypt in the ninth century, he had been the most important saint in the city, and his church, San Marco, the most famous and elaborate building.[404] Both the Venetian coinage and the seal of the Doge showed St. Mark giving the standard of office to the Doge.[405] Treaties and capitulations were made not with "Venice" but with "St. Mark and the Doge."[406] St. Mark's symbol, the winged lion, was adopted as the symbol of Venice, and his banner led them to victory. When the Venetians attacked Constantinople during the Fourth Crusade, it was the banner of St. Mark that led the way:

> The Doge of Venice, who was an old man and could see nothing at all, was fully armed at the prow of his galley, and had the banner of Saint Mark before him. And he cried to his men to put it on land . . . and they jumped out and carried the banner of St. Mark before him to land. And when the Venetians saw the banner of St. Mark on land, and their lord's galley touching land before them, every one held himself dishonoured, and all went to land.[407]

Just as Caesar's legions had followed their eagle on to the British shore, so the Venetians followed St. Mark to conquest in the East.

Bishops and despots could take advantage of the cults of the city-saints of Italy, but these cults could also be symbols of a corporate identity that did not rely on a prince or dynasty, and it is significant that, on the extinction of the direct line of the Visconti dynasty, rulers of Milan, in 1447, a republic was established in the city styling itself the "Ambrosian Republic." St. Ambrose embodied Milan, not the dynasty. And when the city of Como freed itself briefly from the overlordship of Milan in that same year, it declared an "Abbondian Republic" (*Respublica Abbondiana*), named after its local saint, Abbondius, who appeared on the coins of the republic.[408] Neither of these republics lasted long, but their choices about the name of their state and the imagery of their coins shows the role that saints could take, as embodiments of an organization that was civic and public but not dynastic.

One area of urban life, outside Italy as well as within it, in which a link between saints and particular occupations can be frequently seen is the world of guilds and their patrons. In Bruges, one of the leading cities of northern Europe, there were more than 200 fraternities in the later Middle Ages, deeply involved in both economic activity and public devotion.[409] Most had at least an altar in one of the town's churches, and the wealthier and more successful guilds had their own chapels and

[404] Zettler, "Die politischen Dimensionen des Markuskults."

[405] Maurizio, *"Sigillum Sancti Marci." Bolle e sigilli di Venezia*, with numerous illustrations; Stahl, *Zecca*, pp. 302–12, on legends, style, and images of Venetian coins.

[406] For example, Tafel and Thomas, *Urkunden zur älteren Handels—und Staatsgeschichte der Republik Venedig* 1, pp. 90, 105 (nos. 41, 48).

[407] Geoffrey de Villehardouin, *La conquête de Constantinople* 173–74 (1, pp. 174–76).

[408] *Corpus Nummorum Italicorum* 4, p. 187, and plate XIV 21.

[409] For the following, Brown, *Civic Ceremony*, esp. pp. 133–55 and app. 5.

almshouse. This was a period when devotion to Mary and Christ, in the form of the Holy Blood, Corpus Christi, and the Holy Name, was increasingly important, but many of the older saints were recognized as appropriate patrons of the guilds: the smiths had the metal-worker, St. Eligius (Eloi), the archers had St. Sebastian (who had been martyred by being shot full of arrows), and the barber-surgeons the doctor-saints, Cosmas and Damian. Some of the guilds fostered important cult-centres. The archers guild, which had more than 350 members, acquired a relic of St. Sebastian's skull in 1428 for its chapel in the Franciscan friary, and papal indulgences for all who prayed there on the saint's feast-day. The smiths ran a hospital alongside their free-standing chapel of St. Eligius and, in 1449, secured the right to be buried in the chapel. In these ways, the merchants and craftsmen of the late medieval city defined themselves and their group identities through the medium of the saints. It might not be quite true, as one thirteenth-century critic had it, that "If there were a saint for every guild, there would soon be more saints than there are days!," but the number was close.[410]

National Saints

Saints could be the patrons of dynasties, kingdoms, and peoples.[411] It might even be suspected that the saints had national prejudices. One Slav living in the neighbourhood of some relics of the saint-emperor Henry II, considered it pointless to seek healing at the shrine of a German saint: "Since this Henry is a German, he offers the help of his grace only to Germans."[412] Needless to say, after being talked around, the man was healed, and the Slavs thereafter became enthusiastic devotees of St. Henry, but his statement points to an assumption that would be credible to readers and listeners, that a saint might well prefer his own people and be unresponsive to aliens.

Dynastic or community identity could be expressed through the adoption of a particular saint. In the early Middle Ages, St. Martin and St. Denis were closely associated with the Frankish ruling dynasty as their "special patron"[413] Royal saints (already discussed) were a natural focus for such loyalties. When the Holy Roman Emperor, Frederick Barbarossa, recognized the elevation of Vladislav, duke of Bohemia, to the status of king, he granted him the right to wear his crown formally on the great feasts of Christmas, Easter and Pentecost, just as Frederick himself did, but then added that the newly recognized king could also wear his crown "on the feast-days of St. Wenceslas and St. Adalbert, because the whole of Bohemia observes those solemnities of their patrons with greater reverence and celebration."[414] An echo of this tradition can be found in the dating clauses of some late medieval Bohemian

[410] Thomas of Celano, *Tractatus de miraculis beati Francisci* 102, p. 307.

[411] Borst, "Patron Saints in Medieval Society"; *Patriotische Heilige*.

[412] Iste Heinricus Teutonicus cum sit, solis Teutonicis gratie sue prestat subsidium: *Miracula sancti Heinrici*, p. 816 (PL 140: 137).

[413] Guillot, "Les saints des peuples et des nations"; Thacker, "Peculiaris patronus noster."

[414] *Diplomata Friderici I.* 1, no. 201, pp. 335–37.

charters, which mention the feast-days of Wenceslas as well as other saints popular in Bohemia, like Vitus and Procopius.[415] The tenth-century Bohemian ruler thus became embedded in the rituals and remembrance of his dynasty and people.

Royal saints could indeed be revered as undying champions of their dynasty or their country. By the third quarter of the twelfth century St. Olav (d. 1030) is being called "perpetual king of Norway," and the ruling Norwegian king recognizes that he is only the "representative and tenant" of the saint, holding the kingdom, which is "the possession of the glorious martyr," just as a knight holds from a lord.[416] Norway's enemies had their supernatural protectors too. When Haakon IV of Norway attacked Scotland in 1263, he faced not only the forces of the Scottish king but also the power of St. Margaret, the queen of Scots who had died 170 years earlier. She was seen rushing from the church where she was enshrined to the scene of battle, explaining, "I am hurrying to bring victory over that tyrant who is attempting to subject my kingdom to his power. For I have accepted this kingdom from God, and it is entrusted to me and my heirs for ever."[417] The heart of the cult of royal saints tended to lie in their own lands, but it was possible for royal saints to be adopted by a nation other than their own. After relics of St. Sigismund, the early medieval king of the Burgundians, were deposited in Prague cathedral in 1365, healing miracles began to occur at his shrine. This was no threat to the well-established native saint, Wenceslas: "Who could doubt that our patron, the most holy Wenceslas, had obtained St. Sigismund as a companion for himself before God? Rejoice, happy Bohemia, that you have multiplied your intercessors to the Lord when troubled."[418] The chapel of St. Sigismund north of the choir in Prague cathedral now balanced the chapel of St. Wenceslas to the south.[419]

Ruling dynasties prided themselves on having saints in their lineage. The French were particularly insistent on this gratifying self-image: "the illustrious house of the kings of France, in which there were many resplendent with miracles and venerated as saints in the church."[420] Lives of these dynastic saints were sometimes dedicated to their descendants and successors. The earliest Life of Matilda, wife of Henry I of Germany, was dedicated to her grandson Otto II; that of Margaret of Scotland to her daughter, queen Edith/Matilda of England; Joinville's *Life of St. Louis* was addressed to Louis's great-grandson and namesake (later Louis X), and composed at the request of Louis's mother.[421] When the Cistercian monk Jocelin of Furness wrote a

[415] Hlaváček, "Die heimischen und lokalen Heiligen in den urkundlichen Datierungen," pp. 244–45.

[416] *Historia Norwegie* 15, p. 86; Magnus Erlingsson's *Privilegiebrev*, cited ibid., p. 209.

[417] *Miracula sancte Margarite Scotorum regine* 7, p. 88.

[418] *Miracula sancti Sigismondi martyris, per ipsum in sanctam Pragensem ecclesiam manifeste demonstrata*, p. 463.

[419] Crossley, "The Politics of Presentation: The Architecture of Charles IV of Bohemia," pp. 101 (plan), 160.

[420] Vauchez, *Sainthood*, p. 182 n. 83, citing an unpublished part of the canonization process of Charles of Blois.

[421] *Vita Mathildis reginae antiquior*, prologue, p. 110; Turgot, *Vita sanctae Margaretae Scotorum reginae*, prologue, p. 234; Jean de Joinville, *Vie de saint Louis* 1–2, p. 2.

Life of Waltheof of Melrose, who was related (somewhat indirectly) to the Scottish royal house, he dedicated it to members of the Scottish royal family and told them they had a cause for exultation in "the common stock and descent you share."[422] And it was a source of exultation that relatives of a saint might take up. Sophie, duchess of Brabant (1224–75), the daughter of Elizabeth of Thuringia, proudly styled herself just that—"daughter of St. Elizabeth"—on her seal and in her documents.[423]

England provides an interesting example of how national saints could change over the course of time. In the Anglo-Saxon period there were saints whose cults transcended regional boundaries, or who came to transcend them. The Church tried hard to promote the cults of Pope Gregory the Great and Augustine of Canterbury, who had initiated the Christian mission to the Anglo-Saxons, and in 747 a council headed by the archbishop of Canterbury ruled that "the feast-day of the blessed Pope Gregory and also the day of burial of St. Augustine the archbishop should be celebrated with honour by all, as is fitting."[424] These ecclesiastical saints, however, did not win a wide popular following. Gregory's cult remained "primarily a liturgical cult fostered by a clerical elite."[425]

The saints who gained the most prominent following in later Anglo-Saxon England included two of those murdered kings who made up a distinctive feature of the sanctity of eastern and northern Europe: Edmund, King of the East Angles, killed by Vikings in 869, and Edward "the Martyr," King of England, murdered, probably as a result of a dynastic dispute, in 978. Their Englishness could be stressed. When he translated Abbo's Latin account of the martyrdom of Edmund into Old English, Ælfric of Eynsham added the following passage to the text: "The English people is not deprived of the Lord's saints, when such saints as this holy king lie in England . . . there are also many other saints among the English who perform many miracles."[426] Ælfric was one of the earliest writers to use the vernacular term "England." Their cults received official backing. Early in the eleventh century the royal council decided that the feast of Edward, king and Martyr, should be celebrated on 18 March "over all England."[427] After the Norman Conquest of England in 1066, the last ruler of the house of Wessex, Edward "the Confessor," joined this list of national saints. His reign was romanticized as a time of good rule—in 1100 Henry I promised his subjects "the law of King Edward"—and in 1161 Edward became the first English saint to be canonized.[428]

[422] Jocelin of Furness, *Vita sancti Walthenis*, prologue, pp. 248–49.

[423] Fleith and Backes, "Eine Heilige für alle?," p. 270 n. 47.

[424] *Councils and Ecclesiastical Documents*, ed. Haddan and Stubbs, 3, p. 368.

[425] Thacker, "*Peculiaris patronus noster*," p. 19.

[426] Ælfric, *Lives of Saints* 2, pp. 332–34 (no. 32).

[427] Liebermann, *Die Gesetze der Angelsachsen* 1, pp. 240–41, 298–99 (V Aethelred 16; 1 Canute 17. 1).

[428] Liebermann, *Die Gesetze der Angelsachsen* 1, p. 522 (Henry I's Coronation Charter, cl. 13); Barlow, *Edward the Confessor*, pp. 256–85.

Throughout the years 1100–1400 these English royal saints continued to be an expression of both royal and national identity. When English crusaders helped to capture the Egyptian city of Damietta in 1219, a mosque in the town was converted, in their honour, into a church dedicated to St. Edmund the Martyr.[429] Depictions of Edward and Edmund in paintings, illuminated manuscripts and other media were common. Their Englishness was no bar to their veneration by Norman and Angevin rulers whose horizons and ancestry were largely French. Henry III of England (1216–72), whose four grandparents had all been born in France, nevertheless had a deep devotion to St. Edward the Confessor, rebuilding the abbey church of Westminster around his shrine, translating his bones to a grand new shrine and naming his eldest son Edward (and his second son Edmund). In this way these Anglo-Saxon personal names, which had been eclipsed after the Norman Conquest, re-entered the lexicon of high-status names.

England thus had revered and long-established native saints. What is rather remarkable is that a new and definitely non-native saint eclipsed them in the later Middle Ages and early modern period.[430] An entirely fictional account of George, a martyr saint, was composed in the eastern Mediterranean region in the fifth century, the story of whose sufferings was so fantastical (he is executed and miraculously resurrected three times) that it was included in the earliest papal condemnation of apocryphal literature. Yet by the later Middle Ages he was widely regarded as "special protector and advocate of the kingdom of England" (see later, p. 231). Unlike many things attributed to the influence of the crusades, the rise of the cult of St. George really does seem to be explained by western crusaders encountering this very popular eastern saint and making him their own patron. It was Edward I, the last English king to go on crusade, who first decreed that his troops should wear the red cross of St. George as their uniform.[431]

The fourteenth century was a transitional period in the history of England's national saints, symbolized by the fact that when Edward III of England repulsed a French attack on Calais in 1349, he enheartened his men with the calls "Ha Sant Edward! Ha Sant George!," invoking both the older and the newer heavenly patron.[432] When this same king founded the Order of the Garter, its patrons included both Edward the Confessor and George, although the latter grew to overshadow the former. The king possessed "a little pendant vessel of silver with relics of St. George."[433] At the battle of Poitiers in 1356 the English war-cry was "St. George!," the French "St. Denis!."[434] Despite this, there is still some parity between the old saints and the new in the reign of Edward III's grandson, Richard II. The most famous artistic

[429] Walter of Coventry, *Memoriale* 2, p. 242.

[430] Bengtson, "St George and the Formation of English Nationalism"; Summerson, "George"; Good, *The Cult of St George in Medieval England.*

[431] Good, *The Cult of St George in Medieval England*, p. 53, citing PRO (TNA) E 101/3/15.

[432] Walsingham, *Historia Anglicana* 1, p. 274.

[433] *Antient Kalendars and Inventories of the Treasury of His Majesty's Exchequer* 3, p. 207, no. 9.

[434] Geoffrey le Baker, *Chronicon*, p. 149.

product from Richard's reign, the Wilton Diptych, shows the young king kneeling before the Virgin Mary, with his saintly sponsors behind him. They are Edmund, King and Martyr, Edward the Confessor, and John the Baptist. Yet the Ordinances of War that were drawn up for Richard's Scottish campaign of 1385 prescribe that every soldier in his army "should bear a large badge of arms of St. George, before and behind" and that any enemy soldiers wearing such a badge, presumably to disguise themselves, were to be killed.[435] (Curiously enough, it was for this very campaign that the Scottish army was ordered, for the first time recorded, to wear "a white cross of St. Andrew.")[436] In that same year the guild of St. George was formed in Norwich, an organization that, by the middle of the fifteenth century, had merged with the city government and included such distinguished members as the Earl of Suffolk and the bishop.[437] These deep local roots complemented George's standing as a dynastic and national saint.

Eventually St. George's position became undisputed. The great English victory of Agincourt in 1415 was won under the invocation of the names of Jesus, Mary, and George.[438] In January 1416 the archbishop of Canterbury decreed that the feast of St. George, who is described as "special patron and protector of the English nation," be celebrated at a higher level of solemnity throughout the province of Canterbury.[439] Thereafter George's position as the national saint of England was assured, so that it was an expected scenario when a late-fifteenth-century writer portrays "an Englishman" swearing by St. George.[440] Even beyond the chasm of the Reformation Elizabethan playgoers could thrill to the war-cry in Shakespeare's *Henry V*: "God for Harry, England, and St. George!"

England's earlier national saints, Edmund, King and Martyr, and Edward, King and Martyr, were rulers who had suffered an innocent death, while Edward the Confessor was revered for his perpetual virginity. None had a reputation as a winner in war. This is perhaps what St. George provided. Although technically a martyr, George was uniformly portrayed as a knight, fighting dragons and saving maidens. That is what the martial classes of later medieval England seem to have wanted.

A similar story can be told about Scotland, with a long-term shift from native saints to a universal saint who was adopted as a national saint. St. Columba (discussed earlier, p. 30), sometimes regarded as the "apostle" of the Scots, also helped them in battle.[441] In 1211 or thereabouts custody of Columba's reliquary,

[435] *Monumenta Juridica: The Black Book of the Admiralty* 1, p. 456.

[436] *Acts of the Parliaments of Scotland* 1, p. 191 (it should be noticed that, if the solider were wearing white, the background to the cross was to be black, not blue).

[437] Westlake, *The Parish Guilds of Mediaeval England*, pp. 116–19.

[438] *Gesta Henrici quinti* 12, p. 84.

[439] Patrono et protectore dicte [scil. anglicane] nacionis speciali: *The Register of Henry Chichele* 3, pp. 8–10; George's feast was elevated to a "major double (*magis duplex*)"; cf. *Gesta Henrici quinti* 18, p. 132.

[440] Commynes, *Mémoires* 4. 11, p. 302.

[441] *Early Sources of Scottish History* 1, p. 407 (from Dualtach Mac Firbhisigh).

known as the Brecbennach, was granted to Arbroath abbey, along with land to support it; the monks had the duty of bringing it when the royal army went on campaign.[442] Columba was thus clearly regarded as a patron of the Scots and their kings, even if his own monastery of Iona no longer served as a royal mausoleum by this time. But another saint was already of great significance in Scotland, namely the apostle Andrew, whose bones were, according to legend, brought to the country in the eighth or ninth century and had, by the eleventh century at the latest, become a centre of pilgrimage at the place that drew its name from the saint, St. Andrews in Fife.[443] When a regency government was established in Scotland in 1286 under a group of Guardians, their seal showed St. Andrew, with a motto reading, "Andrew, be the leader of the compatriot Scots."[444] In the absence of a king and with the nobles ready to cut each other's throats, the saint was an abstract and uncontentious symbol of unity. By the fifteenth century St. Andrew could be described, easily and naturally, as "patron of the kingdom of Scotland."[445] Just as in England, an imported Mediterranean saint had come to symbolize people and kingdom.

Like George, St. Denis was the saint of both king and nation. The conjunction of the two in this way should not be taken for granted. In the French case, unlike the English, the cult was helped by the backing of an important monastic body, for the monks of St.-Denis outside Paris were strident champions of the idea that their saint, Denis, was patron of both the kings and the kingdom of the French.[446] Suger, abbot of the monastery and chronicler of the reign of Louis VI, describes the king coming to the shrine in 1124, to seek the help of "the blessed Denis, the special patron and, after God, the singular protector of the kingdom."[447] Writing around 1200, a monk of St.-Denis could refer to the saint as "the most blessed Denis, patron and defender of the kings of the French."[448] A century later, another monk of the abbey recounts how Louis IX was saved from a perilous illness by St. Denis and the other saints of the abbey: "the king placed his hope in them as advocates and protectors of him and his kingdom."[449] The same writer envisages an even more capacious aura of protection, when he writes of Denis as "defender of the Gallic people."[450] Denis could defend the French people as well as the French king. "Through his patronage the whole realm rejoices and the power of the kingdom stands firm," as the words of the Mass

[442] *Acts of William I, King of Scots, 1165–1214,* no. 499, pp. 453–54; they later delegated this duty, along with a grant of the lands attached, to the family of Monymusk: *Liber sancti Thome de Aberbrothoc* 1, pp. 296–97, no. 340 (28 February 1315). There seems no firm evidence that the reliquary was carried at the battle of Bannockburn in the preceding summer.

[443] Ash and Broun, "The Adoption of St Andrew as Patron Saint of Scotland"; Hall, *St Andrew and Scotland.*

[444] *Andreas dux esto Scotis compatriotis*: Birch, *History of Scottish Seals* 1, pp. 31–33 and pl. 14.

[445] *Liber cartarum prioratus sancti Andree*, p. 406 (1424).

[446] See Spiegel, "The Cult of Saint Denis and Capetian Kingship."

[447] Suger, *Vita Ludovici Grossi regis* 28, ed. Henri Waquet (Paris, 1929), p. 220.

[448] Rigord, *Gesta Philippi Augusti* 3, p. 124.

[449] William of Nangis, *Gesta sancti Ludovici*, p. 344.

[450] William of Nangis, *Gesta Philippi tertii regis Franciae*, p. 468.

for St. Denis put it.[451] At the battle of Sluys in 1340, the French fleet had a big ship called *St. Denis*, yet the fact that they also had a ship called *St. George* shows that the saints had not been corralled into strict national enclaves.[452]

Saints and Individuals

Saints could be patrons of religious Orders, cities and kingdoms; there was also, however, the simple but intense relationship between an individual and a saint. There are countless cases where someone is said to have "a special devotion" to a saint. The seventh-century Egyptian church administrator Christodorus, for example, was a special devotee of St. Theodore (he is described as *philotheodoros*, "lover of Theodore") and, in return, the saint listened to his requests, "as if to a friend."[453] The emperor Henry II (d. 1024) was "a special devotee of the martyr George."[454] The German knight Gerard of Hollenbach

> loved St. Thomas the Apostle so ardently, honoured him so particularly above other saints, that he could deny alms to no poor person who begged them in his name. He used to devote to him many private services, such as prayers, fasts and the celebration of masses.[455]

In the Cistercian monastery of Clairvaux in the early thirteenth century there was a young monk called John, "an amazing devotee of St. John the Baptist," on whose day he had been born and after whom he had been named: "he loved him more than the other saints and whenever anything was sung that pertained to him, such as the canticle of his father Zachary, he did not spare his voice at all."[456] Zachary's canticle is the Benedictus, a regular part of the Christian liturgy, and John had obviously been noticed belting it out. Even devotion to the Virgin Mary, that most universal of the saints, could take an individual coloration, as she put down roots at local shrines. "Of all Our Ladies," says a character evoked in one of Thomas More's Dialogues, "I love best Our Lady of Walsingham." "And I," replies another, "Our Lady of Ipswich."[457]

It is not usually possible to know why someone might select a particular saint as their special patron and protector, but sometimes there are descriptions of how such a choice was made. Since there were hundreds of saints, it was necessary to make a choice among them when seeking supernatural help. This must have presented some vexing questions. Which saint offered the surest help? To which one was it advisable to bring gifts? How did one choose among the heavenly host? A simple way of choosing a saint was to cast lots, although a preliminary selection was even then

[451] William of Nangis, *Gesta sancti Ludovici*, p. 344, from a sequence of Denis's Mass.

[452] Knighton, *Chronicon*, p. 28.

[453] Sophronius of Jerusalem, *Miracula Cyri et Ioannis* 8. 10–11, pp. 255–56.

[454] *Sancti Georgii martyris singularis cultor*: *Miracula Adelheidis reginae* 5, p. 49 (MGH, SS 4, p. 647).

[455] Caesarius of Heisterbach, *Dialogus miraculorum* 8. 59 (2, p. 131).

[456] Ibid., 8. 49 (2, p. 120).

[457] Thomas More, *A Dialogue Concerning Heresies* 1. 17, p. 99.

necessary. In 1375, after a man called Olav, living in the diocese of Uppsala, went insane, his relatives gathered together "and cast lots for three saints, Olav, Theobald, and the lady Birgit, and the lot fell on the lady Birgit." They promised to visit her shrine with an offering and Olav was immediately cured.[458] A pilgrimage to the shrine of Nicholas of Linköping in 1408 was the outcome of a similar procedure.[459] The Scandinavian world was familiar with the casting of lots for various purposes, and it is not surprising that it was a technique used here to choose between the saints. It could also be used to decide whether to seek the help of a saint or undertake some other pious deed, as in the *Orkneyinga Saga*, which describes two cases of a lottery to determine the exact votive act that was to be undertaken on behalf of a sufferer: should it be a pilgrimage south, the emancipation of a slave, or an offering at St. Magnus's shrine.[460]

Another form of lottery involved candles. In the 860s a woman from a hamlet near Rheims was suffering from fever, and wished to know which of the local saints to invoke:

> she made three candles of the same size, one for St. Theoderic, one for St. Rigobert, one for St. Theodulf. She lit them at the same moment and let them burn down until she saw which of them lasted longest, wishing to learn in this way, as the common people are accustomed to do, to which of these saints she should make her vow most efficaciously.[461]

The phrasing suggest a widespread practice of the lower-classes, but a similar story concerns a nobleman, living in southern England in the later eleventh century, who was struck by leprosy. He turned to the saints, first narrowing his choice down by selecting only those saints famed for the fact that their bodies were incorrupt: Cuthbert of Durham, Edmund of Bury, and Etheldreda of Ely. He dedicated a candle to each and lit them. He would visit the shrine of that saint whose candle burned down, not last, but first. Cuthbert won, because, as our source (not surprisingly, a Durham monk) points out, although all three saints were incorrupt, only Cuthbert was actually still flexible. The "gift of flexibility" made him a leader even among the incorrupt.[462] This same source recounts another similar story, but set a century later, and here lots are cast among a significantly different trio: Cuthbert, Edmund, and Thomas of Canterbury, the newcomer who overshadowed the saintly world after 1170.[463] When the Byzantine emperor Andronicus II was choosing a name for his

458 *Acta et processus canonizacionis Beate Birgitte*, p. 70; the significance, and indeed identity, of Theobald is unclear, but Dr. Haki Antonsson helpfully pointed out to me that the feast-day of Theobald of Marly, abbot of Vaux-de-Cernay, on 27 July is very close to that of Olav (29 July) and Birgit (23 July), and this may be relevant.

459 Krötzl, "Fama sanctitatis," p. 233.

460 *Orkneyinga Saga* 57, pp. 106–7.

461 *Vita Rigoberti episcopi Remensis* 25, pp. 75–76.

462 Reginald of Durham, *Libellus de admirandis beati Cuthberti virtutibus* 19, pp. 38–39.

463 Ibid., 115, p. 260.

baby daughter, he employed the same technique, lighting a candle in front of images of each of the twelve apostles and then giving the child the name of the saint whose candle burned longest. She was called Simonis and later became queen of Serbia.[464]

But such lotteries can hardly explain most cases of special devotion, which must have depended upon other things: family tradition, locality, persuasive monks or clergy, perhaps even some individual circumstance.

One of the most detailed and intimate accounts of a relationship between an individual and the saints in the Middle Ages is found in the trial records of Joan of Arc, although the picture that emerges is far from typical (as perhaps with all aspects of Joan of Arc). At her examination in 1431, Joan explained that she had, from her teenage years, been guided by "voices."[465] It was only after several days of cross-examination, and after being asked bluntly whether the voice she heard was that of an angel, a saint, or God himself, that Joan identified her voices as St. Catherine and St. Margaret.[466] It may be that she made this identification only under the pressure of the interrogation, but it seems that these two saints were not chosen at random, for she said on a later occasion in her trial that she had often placed garlands of flowers on images of Catherine and Margaret in church.[467] St. Michael had also appeared to her when she was 13 years old or thereabouts, bringing her great comfort. "He did not come to France," Joan added, "except at God's command."[468] Catherine, Margaret, and Michael were saints of widespread importance in later medieval Europe, as well as having plenty of local associations in Joan's vicinity.[469] Joan's relations with Catherine and Margaret were concrete—she kneeled before them and embraced them—and they spoke to her sweetly and beautifully in French (Joan was irate at the suggestion that St. Margaret might speak English: "How should she speak English when she was not of the English party?")[470]

However, the interrogators at Joan's trial also turned up evidence about the "Tree of the Fairies" in her home village, a huge beech with a healing fountain nearby. The local girls sang and danced here and hung garlands on the branches. Some people (but not Joan) claimed to have seen the fairy ladies.[471] Joan's descriptions of these rural practices and beliefs gave her judges a weapon. It suggested the charge that "in her youth Joan was not brought up or instructed in belief or in the rudiments of the faith, but was habituated and imbued by some old women to use fortune-telling, divination and the works of superstition and magic arts."[472] And it gave her enemies

[464] Pachymeres, *Romaike historia* 3. 32 (3, p. 305); curiously, this is a way of choosing a child's name that John Chrysostom had criticized as pagan a thousand years earlier: *De inani gloria* 48, p. 146; *In epistulam I ad Corinthios* 12. 7, col. 105.

[465] See *Procès de condamnation de Jeanne d'Arc* 3, pp. 296–307, analytical index, s.v. "Voix."

[466] Ibid., 1, p. 71.

[467] Ibid., 1, p. 177.

[468] Ibid., 1, p. 73.

[469] Ibid., 3, pp. 95–96.

[470] Ibid., 1, pp. 177–78, 84.

[471] Ibid., 1, pp. 65–67, 198–99.

[472] Ibid., 1, p. 196.

the chance to ask some sceptical questions about the saints she claimed had conversed with her. Joan's inquisitors asked her if St. Catherine and St. Margaret had spoken with her under the Tree of the Fairies or by the healing well. Joan answered that they had spoken with her by the well. She was asked if the garlands hung in that tree had been placed in honour of the two saints and Joan replied no. The court tried further to elide the distinction between Joan's saints and fairies by talking of her two "Counsellors of the Fountain."[473]

A trial record of a peasant girl hounded by ecclesiastical lawyers who were determined to have her imprisoned or burned is not a cool or impartial report on the beliefs of fifteenth-century France, but it does uncover some things that other sources do not. Joan's subjective experience is of a childhood in which fairy trees, healing wells and the saints of the Church all had a place, and her intense inner life focussed on voices that guided her, even to extraordinary deeds. Her enemies wanted to squeeze her experience into certain channels: they knew, or thought they did, the difference between saints and fairies. The parties in the trial would have been speaking at cross-purposes even without the added poison of misogyny and the urge to convict.[474]

An altogether more conventional picture emerges if we turn to another famous military leader of the fifteenth century, Richard of Gloucester, briefly Richard III (1483–85). In 1478, five years before he became king, Richard established a collegiate church at Middleham, an important property of his in Yorkshire.[475] The church was dedicated to the obscure virgin saint Alkyld but she figured not at all in Richard's plans.[476] He planned for a dean and six priests, who occupied stalls named after the saints. In order of precedence, these were: the Virgin Mary, St. George, St. Catherine, St. Ninian, St. Cuthbert, St. Antony, St. Barbara. He also specified that the feast-days of "such saints as that I have devotion unto" should be celebrated as "doubles," whether or not this was their general ranking. These saints were quite numerous, thirty-nine in all: John the Baptist; John the Evangelist; Peter; Paul; Simon; Jude; Michael; Anne; Elizabeth; Fabian; Sebastian; Antony; Christopher; Denis; Blaise; Thomas; Alban; Giles; Eustace; Erasmus; Eligius (Eloi); Leonard; Martin; William of York; Wilfrid of Ripon; Catherine; Margaret; Barbara; Martha; Wenefrid; Ursula; Dorothea; Radegund; Agnes; Agatha; Apollonia; Zita (Cithe); Clare; Mary Magdalene. In addition, Richard expressed his wish that four feast-days—St. George (23 April), St. Ninian (16 September), St. Cuthbert (20 March), and St. Antony (17 January)—be observed "as principal feasts" (the implication is that the St. Antony whose feast was celebrated as a double was a different saint). Ninian and George are also given a special place in the regular liturgy, and "an anthem of St. Ninian" is to be sung in future on the day of Richard's death.

[473] Ibid., 1, pp. 85, 178, 264.

[474] See the discussion in Sullivan, "I do not name to you the voice of St. Michael."

[475] *The Statutes ordained by Richard Duke of Gloucester for the College of Middleham.*

[476] She remains unidentified: Blair, "A Handlist of Anglo-Saxon Saints," p. 511.

The thirty-nine saints "that I have devotion unto" and the four others who had stalls named after them and feasts celebrated as principal thus total forty-three (excluding the Virgin Mary, in a category of her own). Of these forty-three, sixteen are female, twenty-seven male. The majority (twenty-eight) are either biblical saints or early martyrs. The most recent amongst them are three saints from thirteenth-century Italy: Antony of Padua (if, as is likely, this is the second Antony in the list), Clare, and Zita. Some, like Alban, Ninian, Wenefrid, and Thomas (almost certainly Becket), are British or have an association with England by this time, as in the case of George. Richard's power was based in the north of England and several of his special saints were northern, such as Cuthbert and Wilfrid, both of them early Anglo-Saxon bishops and missionaries, enshrined at Durham and Ripon respectively, and William, the thirteenth-century archbishop of York.

A peculiar distinction is reserved for Ninian, reputed founder of the see of Whithorn in Galloway and apostle of the southern Picts. At Middleham he has a stall named after him, his anthem is to be sung on the anniversary of Richard's death, and his feast is a principal one. Moreover, a special prayer to St. Ninian was written into Richard's own prayer book ("The Hours of Richard III").[477] By the later Middle Ages Ninian was associated with Scotland—the Scots merchants in Bruges had a chapel dedicated to the saint—but even this did not preclude an English Plantagenet prince from adopting Ninian as his own special patron.[478]

Apart from their northern English connections, the grounds for the attachment of Richard of Gloucester to St. Ninian are not clear. Indeed, in most cases it is only possible to speculate about how personal bonds between saint and worshipper were formed. The young Joan of Arc had placed garlands on images of St. Catherine and St. Margaret, and perhaps these distinctive statues, and also painted images of the saints on the walls of churches, were among the more important influences creating special devotions amongst individual worshippers. They provided life-like and often life-size representations of the human figure with which it would be possible to imagine a personal relationship. Naming patterns sometimes express attachment to a particular saint (see later, pp. 459–70) and the saint who you swear by obviously has some kind of significance: Commynes reports the Duke of Burgundy swearing by St. George, the saint of chivalry.[479]

To choose to be buried near the saint or the saint's image was a powerful way of expressing a special devotion. Arnulf of Carinthia, king of the East Franks (d. 899), had a special devotion to St. Emmeram, and was buried near to the relics of the saint in his monastery at Regensburg. Subsequently, the monks gloried in this connection:

> Hoping that God would be favourable to him, he chose St. Emmeram as patron of his life and kingdom . . . and he had full experience of this patronage in difficult dealings and many battles . . . he commanded a tomb to be prepared

[477] Sutton and Visser-Fuchs, *The Hours of Richard III*, pp. 41–44.

[478] Brown, *Civic Ceremony*, p. 324; Clancy, "Scottish Saints and National Identities," p. 404.

[479] Commynes, *Mémoires* 4. 8, p. 278.

> for him at St. Emmeram's, so that when he died he would have as a kindly patron in heaven the one whom he had desired to have on earth when he was alive.[480]

The evidence of wills, which survive in increasing numbers in the last centuries of the Middle Ages, often reveals an individual's favourite saint. Approaching their last moments, people could be quite explicit and many, like king Arnulf, had a natural desire to be buried as close as possible to their favourite saint or to the image of that saint. In the summer of 1348, as the Black Death swept through Europe, a goldsmith from Sarzana, north of Lucca, made his will, asking to be buried in St. Andrew's church, Sarzana, "against the wall with the image of St. Lucy," while in 1487 Richard Robart of Faversham requested burial in his local church before "the great image of St. Catherine."[481] And the testament of the wealthy ecclesiastic Jacques de Clerval reveals a network of saints who were on his mind as he lay dying in his house in Besançon in 1481.[482] He appeals for help on the day of his death from "the glorious ever-virgin Mary, St. Peter and St. Paul, both St. John the Baptist and St. John the Evangelist, St. Stephen the Protomartyr, and St. James, with whose name we have been designated" (Jacques is the French for James); he asks to be buried alongside his dear uncle in St. Agapitus's chapel in St. Stephen's church, Besançon; he funds memorial masses in the chapel of St. James in the collegiate church of Mary Magdalene in Besancon, where his father and many ancestors are buried; he leaves money to four shrines, hoping to benefit from the indulgences associated with them: the Holy Spirit and St. Antidius at Besançon, St. Bernard of Montjoux (or Aosta) at the Great St. Bernard Pass, and St. Antony at Vienne; and he is worried about the state of some other shrines, especially the thumb of the arm-reliquary of St. Stephen, and leaves money for gilding, adorning and repairing them. It might not be flippant to describe him as spreading his bets.

[480] Arnold of St Emmeram, *Libri de sancto Emmerammo* 1. 5, p. 551.

[481] Bacci, *Pro remedio animae: immagini sacre e pratiche devozionali in Italia centrale*, pp. 267–68; Lewis, *The Cult of St Katherine*, p. 120.

[482] *Testaments de l'officialité de Besançon, 1265–1500*, 2, pp. 192–99, no. 219.

CHAPTER 8

Relics and Shrines

Body Parts

The cult of the saints began with the veneration of the dead bodies of the martyrs. The Christians of Smyrna buried the ashes of their martyred bishop Polycarp and then looked forward in hope that "gathering here, so far as we can, in joy and gladness, we will be allowed by the Lord to celebrate the anniversary day of his martyrdom."[1] Relics were "remains" (Latin *reliquiae*, Greek *leipsana*), that is, the physical remains of the martyr.[2] Throughout the medieval period, there were shrines that consisted simply of the entombed entire remains of the saint. A list from later Anglo-Saxon England names more than eighty such whole-body shrines.[3] But from early times, such corporeal (that is, bodily) remains might become fragmented, and body parts then went into circulation. In the sixth century, for example, Aemilianus, bishop of Germia in central Asia Minor, possessed "a piece of the head, one finger of the hand, one of the teeth, and another piece" of St. George.[4] Moreover, while the usual image of saint's relics is of this kind—the physical remains of the body, especially the bones—relics could be of a different type. Objects that had been in contact with the saint during his or her lifetime, and objects that had been in contact with the saint's tomb, were treated as relics, and given the same reverence and credited with the same power as corporeal relics. Such non-corporeal or contact relics were extremely common. Indeed, the most probing analysis of the cult of the saints in north Africa between the end of the persecutions in the fourth century and the Muslim conquest in the seventh, concluded that in that region portable relics (as distinct from entombed martyrs) were *never* parts of the body of a saint.[5]

While the tombs of the saints were centres of veneration throughout Christendom, the most important tomb for Christians was an empty one, the sepulchre of

[1] Earlier, p. 4.

[2] On relics in general, see Rollason, *Saints and Relics in Anglo-Saxon England*; Legner, *Reliquien in Kunst und Kult*; Bozóky and Helvétius, ed., *Les reliques: objets, cultes, symboles*; Bozóky, *La politique des reliques*; Deuffic, ed., *Reliques et sainteté.*

[3] *Die Heiligen Englands.*

[4] *Vita Theodori Syceotae* 100, p. 80.

[5] Duval, *Loca sanctorum Africae: le culte des martyrs en Afrique du IVe au VIIe siècle*, p. 549; the exception of Stephen's relics (earlier, on p. 23) should be noted.

Jesus in Jerusalem, a grave whose very emptiness bore witness for them to the Resurrection and which drew pilgrims throughout the Middle Ages. And it is worth pointing out that, although Jesus left no corporeal relics in the sense of a whole body or bones, this did not mean that there could be no cult of his relics. First, there were contact relics of various types: earth on which he had stood, pieces of his clothing, stone from his tomb. Then there were the portions of his body that might reasonably be assumed to have been left on earth: his foreskin, milk teeth, sweat, and—an increasingly powerful and magnetic substance—his blood. Analysis of relic cult must place such relics alongside those of the saints, for that was often their context. Earth from the Holy Land was being exported to other Christian countries and revered there by the 350s, and, already by that date, the cross on which Jesus was crucified had supposedly been found in Jerusalem, and fragments of the wood from this cross were soon spread throughout Christendom.[6] They, and other relics from the Holy Land, formed part of the relic collections of many churches, and the cult of the Holy Blood was one of the major devotional features of the later Middle Ages.

Over the course of time, despite laws prohibiting the disturbance of graves, corporeal relics became mobile. The simplest way for this to happen was through the translation (that is, ritual relocation) of the whole body. Instances occur from the mid-fourth century (discussed earlier, on p. 10). Especially notable are the cases where the bodies of the saints were brought within the city, into the bishop's church or into basilicas built especially for them. Translations of whole-body relics continued throughout the medieval period, for many different reasons, and this is a topic analyzed later (p. 282). A further step was the fragmentation of the bodily remains, with pieces of bone being separated and sent to different locations. The earliest known instance of a fragmentary corporeal relic appears to be the bone possessed by the wealthy lady Lucilla in Carthage around 300.[7] She had the habit of kissing it before taking communion and, when reprimanded for this by the local archdeacon, stormed out of the church. It should be noted, however, that the account of this incident is not a neutral piece of reporting but a late and polemical account, written in the 360s by an opponent of the church faction to which Lucilla belonged (the Donatists). This is clear from its tone: "before the spiritual food and drink (the Eucharist), she was said to kiss the bone of some martyr or other—if indeed it was a martyr's." Both the writer who records the story, the north African bishop Optatus, and the archdeacon who is a protagonist in it, obviously thought that such a private devotion was to be discouraged in church. Whether this is simply anti-Donatist propaganda intended to smear an important founding figure in the sect, or a true, even if hostile, report, it is impossible to say. In any case, as early as the fourth century, there is evidence that corporeal relics were being bought and sold. A Roman imperial law of

[6] Hunt, *Holy Land Pilgrimage in the Later Roman Empire*, pp. 38–39, 129–30; Egeria, *Itinerarium Egeriae* 37, 48, pp. 80–81, 89.

[7] Os nescio cuius martyris: Optatus of Milevis, *De schismate Donatistarum* 1. 16 (1, pp. 206–8); Optatus records that the incident took place immediately before the beginning of persecution in 303.

386 ruled that "no one should divide up or trade in a martyr," while, writing slightly later, around 401, Augustine criticized insincere monks who "offer for sale pieces of the martyrs."[8] Fragments of martyrs' remains were thus in circulation by this time, just as in the case of Lucilla. Sometimes the physical remains of the martyrs could be dispersed because of the manner of their execution. The Forty Martyrs of Sebaste, whose bodies were burned after death, provided a large store of ashes which came to be distributed amongst many churches. Much later, Oswald, king of Northumbria, whose head and arms were hacked off after his defeat in battle in 642, owed the early success of his cult in large part to the availability of these ready-made relics.[9]

The severed head was particularly potent. Of all body parts, the human head has the most complex significance, as the locus of all five senses, the most easily identifiable marker of personal identity, and often, indeed, the only visible part of a clothed individual. It is not surprising that head relics were especially revered. As early as c. 400 the Romans were supposedly trying to get the severed head of St. Phocas from Asia Minor.[10]

The most famous detached head in Christian tradition is that of John the Baptist, the precursor of Christ, whose beheading is recorded in the Gospels. The existence of multiple supposed heads of this saint in the medieval period was one of the more notorious scandals concerning relics, cited both by medieval critics and Protestant reformers. As is the case with many relics of New Testament figures, there is a long silence between the time of John's earthly life in the first century and the earliest mention of the supposed discovery of remains, or "invention" as it was termed. The Greek historian Sozomen, writing around 450, describes how the head of John the Baptist had been discovered almost a hundred years earlier. He reports that the emperor Valens (364–78) commanded it to be brought to Constantinople, but, miraculously, it was unable to be carried beyond a village on the Asiatic side of the Bosporus, where it remained until the emperor Theodosius I (378–95) was able to bring it across the straits, to be enshrined in the church of St. John the Baptist at the Hebdomon, an important political and military site seven miles from the city.[11] A completely different account of the travels of John's head emerges in the sixth century. According to this, the head had been revealed to two eastern monks at Jerusalem and had then come by devious means to the Syrian city of Emesa (Homs), where it had been hidden in a cave. Here it was rediscovered in the year 453.[12] The later tradition at Constantinople was that the head had been removed from Emesa during the Arab invasions, had been kept secretly for many years, and then had been translated to the

[8] *Codex Theodosianus* 9. 17. 7 (386), p. 466; Augustine, *De opere monachorum* 28. 36, p. 585 (PL 40: 575).

[9] See especially Thacker, "Membra disiecta."

[10] Asterius of Amasea, Homily 9. 10, p. 123.

[11] Sozomen, *Historia ecclesiastica* 7. 21 (4, pp. 178–82).

[12] Marcellinus Comes, *Chronicon*, pp. 84–85; Dionysius Exiguus, *De inventione capitis Johannis Baptistae.*

imperial chapel in Constantinople around the year 850.[13] This obviously contradicts the account given in Sozomen. Both stories, however, bring the head to Constantinople, and this is where it is recorded in subsequent centuries. The western crusaders who sacked the city in 1204 report that it was still in the palace chapel then.[14]

Constantinople's claim was not without a western rival, however. According to the eleventh-century chronicler Ademar of Chabannes, king Pippin of Aquitaine, who died in 838, had founded the monastery of St.-Jean- d'Angély. The same author mentions the discovery there of the head of John the Baptist during the rule of duke William V of Aquitaine (995–1030).[15] Ademar is doubtful about the authenticity of the relic—"by whom, at what time, and whence, it was brought here, and if it is the precursor of the Lord, can scarcely be established with certainty"—and he is scathing about the legend that described how the head had been brought from Alexandria at the time of Pippin, and had given him victory over an army of Vandal invaders.[16] It is to Ademar's credit as a historian that he points out that Pippin and the Vandals were not contemporaries, although it must also be remembered that the head of John the Baptist at Angély would compete with his own favoured saint, Martial, at Limoges (a few days' journey away), for whom Ademar produced a string of forgeries.[17] Despite Ademar's views, the head at Angély became an important pilgrimage centre, well placed as it was on the route from the north towards Santiago de Compostella, one of Europe's major shrines. Early in the twelfth century the thoughtful critic Guibert de Nogent expressed dismay over the rival claims of Constantinople and St.-Jean-d'Angély—"there were not two John the Baptists, nor one with two heads!"[18]

Beheading was a neat and immediate way of producing body fragments, but more usual in medieval circumstances was the deliberate dismemberment of a saint's body in order to procure relics. The Anglo-Norman monk Orderic Vitalis provides a few examples, which followed on the acquisition of the body of St. Nicholas by the Italian town of Bari in 1087.[19] One of the people present at the translation of the saint's body "kept for himself a rib up his sleeve"; he later became a monk at Venosa in southern Italy (about 55 miles [90 km] from Bari), and deposited St. Nicholas's rib there. Soon afterwards those same monks obtained another relic of St. Nicholas. A

[13] *Sermo de capitis Johannis Baptistae inventionibus* (an anonymous account); however, Theophanes, writing c. 814, asserts that John's head was revered at his church in Emesa in his own day: *Chronographia*, s.a. 6252, p. 431; in their translation of Theophanes (pp. 596–97), Mango and Scott insist that the discovery in the cave was in 452 not 453. (The date in the account translated by Dionysius Exiguus [as in previous note] is given according to the Seleucid era.)

[14] Robert of Clari, *La conquête de Constantinople* 82, p. 82.

[15] Ademar of Chabannes, *Chronicon* 3. 16, 56, pp. 133, 175–77; there dated 1016.

[16] As reported in *De revelatione capitis beati Joannis Baptistae tractatus*; the earliest manuscripts seem to be eleventh century.

[17] See earlier, p. 172.

[18] Guibert de Nogent, *Dei gesta per Francos* 1. 5, p. 103; cf. idem, *De sanctis et eorum pigneribus*, pp. 102–3.

[19] Orderic Vitalis, *Historia ecclesiastica* 7. 12–13 (4, pp. 68–72).

French cleric stole an arm relic of the saint, encased in silver, from the shrine at Bari, but, hunted down by the men of Bari, had to take refuge at Venosa, where he sold the silver casing. When the Venosa monks got to hear of this, they extorted the relic from the cleric and placed it in the abbey church. At around the same period, a Norman knight, William Pantulf, made his way to southern Italy in search of relics of St. Nicholas, and was able to acquire a tooth and two marble fragments from Nicholas's original tomb. These he brought back to the church he had founded at Noron, south-west of Bayeux, where they were received joyfully by the local clergy, enshrined in a silver box and proved to have healing powers. In these typical ways, Nicholas's rib, arm, and tooth became the centres of devotion distant from his "whole-body" shrine at Bari.

The catalogues of relics that the big churches drew up often specify which fragments they possessed, as at York Minster c. 1200, which had, amongst many other items, a finger of St. Pancras, a rib of St. Cassian, and a jawbone of St. Susanna.[20] And the dismemberment is sometimes even depicted. A manuscript from early-twelfth-century Italy has a lively illustration of a bishop with a knife, removing the head and right arm of a saint who was enshrined in his cathedral, in order to give them as a gift to his father, a great nobleman (figure 8.1).[21]

Less orderly than the careful dissection by such a local authority was the tactic resorted to by bishop Hugh of Lincoln, who, after asking to be allowed to revere the arm of Mary Magdalene at the abbey of Fécamp, bit off two fragments from the relic with his teeth—"first his incisors, then his molars." He immediately handed them to his chaplain with the words, "Look after these for me with especial care."[22]

But the results of such vigorous dismemberment could be disconcerting. When the Holy Roman Emperor Charles IV visited the nunnery of the Poor Clares in Prague in 1353, and was offered a finger of St. Nicholas to venerate, "he snatched up a knife and cut off a portion of the finger, wishing to retain it for himself out of devotion." The emperor was horrified to see that the knife bore the marks of fresh blood. Dissuaded from his original intention, he restored the portion he had cut off to the finger, "with fear and reverence"; "it adhered to it as if it had never been cut off," leaving only the slightest trace of a scar.[23]

The medieval geography of the holy thus included hundreds of whole-body shrines and thousands of bodily fragments. Nowhere was far from one of the former, while the big churches had huge collections of the latter.

[20] *The Historians of the Church of York* 3, pp. 106–10.

[21] BAV, Vat. lat. 4922, fol. 19; there is a facsimile edition: *Vita der Mathilde von Canossa*; the relevant text is p. 76 in the edition accompanying the facsimile and also MGH, SS 12, p. 360, with facsimile opposite p. 350. The text is Donizo's *Vita Mathildis*, the bishop Gotefredus of Brescia, the saint Apollonius, and the recipient count Atto, ancestor of the margraves of Canossa.

[22] Adam of Eynsham, *Magna vita sancti Hugonis* 5. 14 (2, p. 169).

[23] Beneš Krabice of Weitmile, *Cronica ecclesiae Pragensis* 4, p. 521.

8.1. Dismemberment to obtain relics, early-twelfth-century Italy. Donizo, *Vita Mathildis*, early twelfth-century Italy. Biblioteca Apostolica Vaticana, Vat. lat. 4922, fol. 19r. ©2013 Biblioteca Apostolica Vaticana. Reproduced by permission with all rights reserved.

Contact Relics

In his treatise on relics, composed in or around 1103, the German monk Thiofrid explains that "the divine power works through things that have been consecrated by use and contact with the hands" of the saints.[24] The idea that objects that had been in contact with holy men could acquire some of their healing virtue is found as early as the New Testament: "God wrought special miracles by the hands of Paul: So that

[24] Thiofrid of Echternach, *Flores epytaphii sanctorum* 3. 3, p. 64.

from his body were brought unto the sick handkerchiefs or aprons, and the diseases departed from them" (Acts 19:11–12). And contact relics could be obtained from the tombs of the saints as well as from living holy men: dust, or oil from the lamps that burned on the tombs. Pilgrims at the tomb of St. Nicetius in Lyons around 590 were allowed to carry away wax, dust, and threads from the tomb-covering.[25]

The most intimate of the things it was possible to separate from a saint—dead or alive—were hair and clothes. During St. Bernard's preaching tour in Milan in 1135, the crowds "plucked hairs from his clothes if they could, and pulled off pieces of the hems of his garments as remedies for sickness."[26] A dead saint was even more vulnerable to such plucking and pulling. After the death of Caesarius of Arles in 542, the mourning congregation tore off his clothes in a kind of "devout violence" and the local clergy had to struggle to get them back.[27] When St. Nikon lay dead in Sparta, at some time in the late tenth century, a crowd gathered "like a swarm of bees," and some of them took locks from his head, others hairs from his beard, others pieces of his old cloak and shaggy goatskin.[28] Hair is technically a corporeal relic, but, containing no blood and being easily separable from the body, it shares some of the features of inanimate contact relics like clothing.

All sorts of items of clothing became holy relics. A list of relics taken to Ghent in the year 944 has entries for ninety-seven individual saints, as well as two groups of saints (the Holy Innocents and the Seven Sleepers), and relics of Christ. Of these ninety-seven entries for named saints, most do not specify the nature of the relic, but no fewer than nineteen of them mention clothing: tunics, cloaks, belts, ecclesiastical vestments, and a brooch. The chief Gallic saint in the list, St. Wandregisilus (Wandrille), is represented by his chasuble, hood, a boot, and sandals, in addition to his basket and part of his crozier.[29] Even an object as humble as a shoe could absorb miraculous power through its regular and close contact with a holy man. Libertinus, prior of the Italian monastery of Fondi around the middle of the sixth century, used to carry with him the shoe of his revered, recently deceased, abbot, Honoratus. One day he encountered a woman clutching her dead baby; she believed he had the power to bring the child back to life. Struggling between humility and pity, Libertinus eventually prayed for the child, then placed Honoratus's shoe upon its chest, and "at his prayers the soul of the child returned to the body."[30]

Garments such as tunics and capes were more common relics than shoes. When the monks of Iona were faced with a serious spring drought, they had recourse to the tunic which St. Columba, their founder, was wearing when he died, and also to some books that he had copied out with his own hand. Some of the older monks carried

[25] Gregory of Tours, *Liber vitae patrum* 8. 6, p. 696 (repr., 1969, p. 246).

[26] *Vita prima sancti Bernardi* 2. 2. 9, col. 274.

[27] *Vita Caesarii episcopi Arelatensis* 2. 49, p. 344 (MGH, SRM 3, p. 500).

[28] *Vita Niconis* 47, pp. 162–64.

[29] *Sermo de adventu sanctorum Wandregisili, Ansberti et Vulframni in Blandinium*, pp. 30–37; also in *Translationis sanctorum Wandregisili et Ansberti quae supersunt*, pp. 817–18.

[30] Gregory I, *Dialogi* 1. 2. 6 (2, p. 28).

these relics around the newly ploughed fields, then held up the tunic and shook it three times, and read out passages from the books. Sweet spring rain immediately fell.[31] The cape (*cappa*) of St. Martin, which was preserved by the Merovingian kings, even gave rise to the word "chapel" (*cappella*)—"so called on account of St. Martin's cape."[32] Famous relics of the tunic of the Virgin Mary were revered at the church of Blachernae in Constantinople, and at Chartres and Aachen.

Items that could be put around the body, like belts, or that could enclose it, like cloaks, seem to have been seen as particularly appropriate for help in childbirth. For instance, the iron belt that Peter Hieremia of Palermo (d. 1452) had worn during his lifetime as a penitential discipline was preserved after his death, and "God performed many miracles through his iron belt, which was brought to the sick or to women in child-bed."[33] The belt of St. Foillan preserved as a relic at Fosses-la-Ville (in modern Belgium) was also a customary recourse in difficult childbirths:

> If it happened at any time that a pregnant woman was having a painful labour, and, as time passed, despaired of the life of the child, the holy pontiff's belt was taken reverently from its silver shrine by the hands of a priest and was brought to her, so that, when the woman was girded with it, her womanly nature might be dissolved and the pain of that intimate suffering diminished.[34]

Likewise, the cloak of St. Gerard of Monza was preserved in the hospital which he had founded in that city, and was carried to women labouring dangerously in child-bed. One citizen of Monza remembered how, around the year 1554, his own wife had been helped by the relic:

> When Helen my wife was giving birth and was in labour for a whole day and two nights, because only half of the baby's head was coming out, I arranged for this cloak to be brought to her, by the reverend priest John Peter of Arsago, and as soon as my wife touched it and was wrapped in it, the baby came out whole.[35]

The pregnant ladies of the ruling classes sometimes sought out clothing from the female saints of their own dynasty, like the Scottish queens in the later Middle Ages who used St. Margaret of Scotland's "sark," or chemise, during childbirth. In 1451, for instance, payment was made to ship this relic across the Firth of Forth from Dunfermline, where it was usually kept, "to our lady queen in child-bed," while, in a subsequent generation, on 10 March 1512, Luke of the Wardrobe was paid eight shillings "to fetch St. Margaret's sark to the queen." The future James V was born exactly a month later.[36] The descendants of St. Elizabeth of Thuringia used her cloak

[31] Adomnán, *Vita Columbae* 2. 44, p. 172.
[32] Notker Balbulus, *Gesta Karoli magni imperatoris* 1. 4, p. 5.
[33] *Vita Petri Heremiae*, p. 297.
[34] Hillinus, *Miracula sancti Foillani* 2. 12, p. 420.
[35] *Acta ex processu Gerardi tinctorii* 3. 22, p. 774.
[36] *Exchequer Rolls of Scotland* 5, pp. 447, 512; *Accounts of the Lord High Treasurer of Scotland* 4, p. 334.

or mantle in a similar fashion. In 1490 the prior of the Teutonic Knights carried St. Elizabeth's cloak from Marburg to Cleves, where the teenage Mechtilde, daughter of Landgrave Henry III of Hesse-Marburg and wife of John II of Cleves, was pregnant with her first child.[37] She thus not only had the comfort of the enveloping and enclosing relic but also the knowledge that her saintly ancestress, who had herself gone through the pain of child-birth, was there to help her. The Landgrave of Thuringia at this time, William III (1445–82), who was related to St. Elizabeth, although not a direct descendant, also possessed relics of the saint, including her belt, and lent them out on at least twelve occasions to his daughters and nieces during their pregnancies.[38] Likewise in the East, two late Byzantine empresses, the successive wives of Andronicus II (1282–1328), were cured of barrenness by wearing a belt made of threads from the coffin of St. Euphrosyna.[39]

In his discussion of contact relics, Thiofrid mentions "beds endowed with the glory of the highest holiness," which never rot; straw and splinters from these miraculous beds heal toothache and fever.[40] Examples of bed-relics are not hard to find. The inhabitants of Narni in Umbria pointed out the bed of St. Juvenal, an early Christian bishop of their city, in one of the towers in the town walls.[41] "Many miracles were performed" in places where Austrigisilus, bishop of Bourges, had lived, "and in the bed in which he had lain." Devotees flocked to the bed in one of his episcopal estates:

> Many sick people, when they lifted up some of that bed, or carried it, or touched themselves with it, were cured of various sicknesses. One sick person came there and placed a candle that he had promised before the bed, to burn all night. When he left, he found a spark from that candle in the bed, yet could discover no sign of burning in the bedding.[42]

These beds commonly possessed miraculous powers of survival of this kind. The bed in which St. Geneviève died was preserved in a nunnery near Paris and, during flooding of the Seine, remained miraculously dry and unharmed.[43] In the monastery of Les Châtelliers,[44] founded by the saintly Gerald de Salles (d. 1120), there was "a wooden bed, with straw and coverings, in which, as they say, Gerald died, which God preserved unharmed and unburned in the midst of flames, through the merits of his servant."[45] Bed-relics could also be divided up. Fragments of St. Martin's bed had healing powers.[46] The bed that St. Gertrude died in (in 659) was preserved at

[37] Küch, "Zur Geschichte der Reliquien der Heiligen Elisabeth," p. 204 and n. 5.

[38] Krüger, "Elisabeth von Thüringen und Maria Magdalena. Reliquien als Geburtshelfer," pp. 76–79.

[39] *Vita sanctae Euphrosynae* 38–39, pp. 875–76; Efthymiadis, "Late Byzantine Collections of Miracles and Their Implications," p. 247.

[40] Thiofrid of Echternach, *Flores epytaphii sanctorum* 3. 7, p. 77.

[41] *Vita Iuvenalis episcopus Narniensis* 3, p. 388.

[42] *Vita et miracula Austrigisili episcopi Biturigi* 2. 4, p. 202.

[43] *Miracula sanctae Genovefae post mortem* 8, p. 148.

[44] Canton de Ménigoute (Deux-Sèvres).

[45] *Vita beati Giraldi de Salis* 4. 38, p. 265.

[46] Gregory of Tours, *De virtutibus sancti Martini* 1. 35, p. 605 (repr., 1969, p. 155).

Nivelles; in 691/2 a portion of it was given to the newly founded nunnery of Andenne.[47] In old age St. Erkenwald, bishop of London (675–93), had to be carried around in a horse-drawn bed-litter, and after his death this was preserved as a source of miraculous healing, and "even splinters broken off from it and brought to the sick obtained quick healing for them."[48]

Beds are, in some ways, ideal contact relics. The saint touches them for prolonged periods and over almost every part of his or her body. Yet they are also rather cumbersome, larger and heavier than most other forms of contact relics. Perhaps, also, they lack the heroic quality: saints were often praised for their all night vigils and the austerity of sleeping on bare or hard surfaces, and the usual associations of a bed scarcely fit naturally with this kind of asceticism. As far as one can see, bed relics are chiefly a feature of the early Middle Ages, so possibly their popularity tailed off over time.

Other objects associated with saints were also preserved as relics. Veneration of books, bells and crosiers was an especially prominent part of the cult of the saints in Ireland, where the role of these contact relics was more widespread and significant than any cult of tomb-shrines. St. Patrick's Bell, the Book of Durrow, and the Book of Moling are surviving examples of such treasured non-corporeal relics. And humbler items were also elevated to the status of relics, with special protective powers. When St. Darerca, abbess of Killevy in northern Ireland, died in 517, she left her sheepskin garments and her hoe as victory talismans to the local tribe: "if you carry them with you against enemies who come to devastate your land, have no doubt that you will obtain victory through them." She warned them, however, against aggressive war—these relics were defensive weapons.[49]

A contact relic of a different kind was the water which had been touched either by the living or the dead saint. The water that Gerald of Aurillac used for washing his hands had healing power, especially for restoring sight to the blind, although because of the saint's humility, this water had to be acquired surreptiously from his servants.[50] Curative properties might be transmitted by the very water in which a saint's corpse had been washed. After St. Cuthbert's death, the water he had been washed in was poured away outside the church. Earth and stones that were taken from the site effected "many works of healing," and the site was marked out and protected by a wooden fence.[51] This case demonstrates how a chain of contact could be established to transmit miraculous power: from Cuthbert's body to the water used for washing it to the earth where the water was poured, without any diminution of intensity.

The same is true of things in contact with the saint's tomb. Gregory of Tours wrote of the miraculous cures at Martin's shrine:

[47] *De virtutibus quae facta sunt post discessum beate Geretrudis abbatisse* 10, p. 469.

[48] *Vita sancti Erkenwaldi*, p. 88.

[49] *Vita sanctae Darercae seu Moninnae abbatissae* 30, p. 94.

[50] Odo of Cluny, *Vita sancti Geraldi Auriliacensis* 2. 10–13, 20, 23–24, 33, pp. 210–14, 222–24, 226–30, 238–40 (AASS Octobris 6, pp. 317–18, 320, 321–22, 323).

[51] *Vita sancti Cuthberti auctore anonymo* 15, pp. 132–34; Bede, *Vita sancti Cuthberti* 41, pp. 288–90.

> Many people were cured when they consumed dust scraped from the saint's tomb, a great number were freed from disease after being anointed with the oil that is found there, and the water used for washing the tomb before Easter was a cure for not a few.[52]

Dust from a saint's tomb is one of the earliest attested forms of contact relic, mentioned as "a treasure" in the later fourth century (see earlier, p. 13). It was also one of the most readily available kinds. The son of a Scottish noble was cured when a pilgrim happened to turn up, who had in his possession dust he had scraped off the tomb of St. Margaret of Scotland; after drinking some of this in water, the boy was healed.[53] There were occasional curious variations in the pattern. Just as in the case of many saints, particles from the tomb of the holy empress Cunigunda in the cathedral at Bamberg had healing properties. But something unusual happened to this dust "that was scraped away from the tomb of the most holy empress by the hands of the sick for healing." Once the cure had been effected, it turned into corn![54]

The oil that served as a contact relic was usually taken from the lamps burning at the tomb-shrine, but it was also sometimes obtained by pouring it through a hole in the top of the saint's tomb or reliquary and collecting it from another hole at the side or bottom. It had thus been in direct contact with the relics.[55] Oil flowing directly from the body of the saint was a much less common phenomenon. Caesarius of Heisterbach noted that healing oil flowed from the body of St. Elizabeth of Thuringia, and explained that this was a very rare privilege. He thought only three other saints, Demetrius, Catherine and Nicholas, exuded such oil. He had heard that in Greece almost every house had a little of the oil of St. Demetrius, as a remedy for ailments.[56] The westerners who occupied Greece after the Fourth Crusade noted that so much oil flowed from the holy body of "my lord Saint Demetrius" in Thessalonica, that "it was a fine marvel."[57] Caesarius underestimated the number of oil-exuding saints, but he was right that they were rare, and he was also right to give as his examples saints with Mediterranean and southern locations. The Greek term *myroblytos*, meaning "giving forth oil or myrrh," was a title of honour for saints of this type.

It was, naturally enough, in the oil producing regions that healing oil was to be found, either emanating from shrines or simply taken from lamps, but even more plentiful, and available everywhere, was water that had been used to wash the shrine. It could be multiplied indefinitely. In 1042, Richard, the saintly abbot of St.-Vanne

[52] Gregory of Tours, *De virtutibus sancti Martini* 2. 51, p. 626 (repr., 1969, p. 176).

[53] *Miracula sancte Margarite Scotorum regine* 21, p. 116.

[54] *Miracula varia Cunegundi imperatricis* 7, p. 279.

[55] There is a good example in *Treasures of Heaven: Saints, Relics, and Devotion in Medieval Europe*, p. 32, no. 4; see also Yasin, *Saints and Church Spaces in the Late Antique Mediterranean*, pp. 165–69; Comte, *Les reliquaires du Proche-Orient et de Chypre*, pp. 68–71.

[56] Caesarius of Heisterbach, *Sermo de translatione beate Elyzabeth*, p. 388.

[57] Robert of Clari, *La conquête de Constantinople* 116, p. 108.

in Verdun, provided a large quantity of healing liquid of this kind during an epidemic of ergotism ("St. Antony's fire").

> You could see the great father's monastery full of crowds of those suffering from St. Antony's fire. He sprinkled holy water over the relics of the saints and washed them in wine, mixed with that wine some dust that he had scraped from the stone of the Lord's sepulchre [during a pilgrimage to the Holy Land] and gave it to those poor people to drink, in this way restoring them to health.[58]

Small pieces of cloth which had been placed on the saint's tomb were among the most common types of contact relic. They acquired so much of the nature of the saint's body itself that they might even bleed when cut.[59] There was sometimes a breathtaking physicality in the supernatural power inhering in these relics. Gregory of Tours tells how small pieces of cloth would be weighed before being lowered onto the tomb of St. Peter in the Vatican. When brought up again, the cloth "will be so soaked with divine power that it will weigh much more than it weighed previously."[60] Similarly, in another of Gregory's stories, the ambassadors of a barbarian king came to the shrine of St. Martin at Tours and "placed a piece of a silk cloth, which they had weighed, on the holy tomb, saying, 'If we find favour before the patron we have invoked, what we have placed here will subsequently weigh more.' " Next morning they weighed the piece of silk and found that "so much of the grace of the holy man had poured into it" that it sent a bronze weight shooting up.[61] In these instances, miraculous power actually registers on the scales.

The Shrine in the Church

The cult of the saints began at the tombs of the martyrs in the cemeteries outside the walls of the Greco-Roman cities, where Christians visited them, especially on the anniversary of their death. Hostile emperors attempted to ban them from the cemeteries, but after the end of the persecutions, Constantine restored to the Christian Church "those place which are honoured by the bodies of the martyrs and which stand as memorials of their glorious departure."[62] Over the course of time, these tombs came to be marked out by special commemorative structures, culminating in the martyr churches, some of huge dimensions, to be found garlanding the cities of late antiquity, from Spain to Syria, from Africa to Britain, where St. Albans provides

[58] Hugh of Flavigny, *Chronicon* 2. 30, p. 403.

[59] Gregory I, *Registrum epistularum* 4. 30 (1, p. 249); for later versions of the story, see McCulloh, "The Cult of Relics in the Letters and Dialogues of Pope Gregory the Great: A Lexicographical Study," pp. 167 n. 88, and 183–84.

[60] Gregory of Tours, *Gloria martyrum* 27, p. 504 (repr., 1969, p. 54).

[61] Gregory of Tours, *De virtutibus sancti Martini* 1. 11, p. 595 (repr., 1969, p. 145).

[62] Eusebius, *Vita Constantini* 2. 40, p. 65.

a clear, if rare, surviving example. Tomb-shrines were always significant. Because ancient legislation forbade the disturbance of human remains, the martyr churches of the late antique period were raised above the tombs of the saints, leaving them in their original position. St. Peter's, Rome, is a striking example, since a vast amount of earth had to be moved, and the preferred eastern orientation disregarded, in order to erect the church above what was held to be (and may well be) St. Peter's resting place. In St. Peter's, as in several other martyr-churches, the main altar was placed directly above the saint's tomb. "Behold," wrote Paulinus of Nola, describing such an arrangement, "beneath the well-lit altar, a marble slab of royal purple covers the bones of the holy men."[63] Outside the walls of Carthage lay two churches dedicated to Cyprian, one at the site of his martyrdom, the other above his tomb.[64] Preaching on St. Cyprian's day, St. Augustine wrote, "we adorn the holy body of this victorious soul with the high honour of a divine altar in this place."[65]

Since the cult of the saints had begun as a form of special reverence for the tombs of the honoured dead, it made sense to go down to their shrines. While early Christian martyr churches were often built above graves and, in the sixth and seventh centuries, underground churches were even excavated around the tombs of Roman martyrs in the catacombs, later the tradition continued artificially, by the excavation of space below ground level, where the saint's remains could be placed. St. Artemios, a supposed martyr of the fourth century, was interred in a lead coffin below the main altar of the church of St. John the Baptist in the Oxeia district of Constantinople, and, on certain occasions, suppliants were permitted to go down to the coffin, and even to touch it or spread themselves upon it.[66] Such a chamber was often called a crypt (Latin *crypta*, Greek *kryptê*), a word originally meaning "secret place." Later it came to mean a vaulted space (even if above ground). Moving a body into a crypt was a recognition of its importance, as in the case of St. Remigius of Rheims, whose "most holy body was translated into a crypt behind the altar" after it had been responsible for "many amazing miracles" in the place of its first interment.[67] A particularly important type was the so-called ring-crypt of the kind Gregory the Great built in St. Peter's. Pilgrims could descend steps and follow a semi-circular corridor around the tomb of the saint, re-emerging by another set of steps. It was an arrangement designed to secure a smooth circulation of devotees, and was taken up by many other churches that housed important tomb-shrines.[68]

[63] Paulinus of Nola, *Epistula* 32. 17, p. 292.

[64] Victor of Vita, *Historia persecutionis Africanae provinciae* 1. 5 (16), p. 5; Saxer, *Morts, martyrs, reliques*, pp. 182–85.

[65] Augustine, *Sermo* 313 (PL 38: 1424–25).

[66] *Miracula sancti Artemii* 17, 21, 24, 33–34, pp. 108–10, 126–28, 140, 174, 178.

[67] Hincmar of Rheims, *Vita Remigii episcopi Remensis* 25, p. 321; this passage found its way into the *Golden Legend*: Jacobus de Voragine, *Legenda aurea* 143 (2, p. 1012, there traced to the intermediate text of Flodoard of Rheims).

[68] A clear summary in Crook, *The Architectural Setting of the Cult of the Saints*, pp. 80–82.

The Carolingian period saw the continued creation of crypts to house saintly bodies. In the 830s one was constructed at the abbey of Farfa to house the relics of the martyrs Valentine, Hilarius and Alexander; it was two metres or so (6 feet 6 inches) beneath the floor of the main church, and was entered down a flight of eight to ten steps leading to a corridor 1.3 metres (4 feet 4 inches) wide, which was decorated with paintings of the deeds of the saints housed there.[69] The crypt at St.-Germain-d'Auxerre, built in the middle years of the ninth century for the shrine of the abbey's major saint, Germanus, is described by the monk Heiric of Auxerre:

> Once the work had been completed and everything that might conduce to its beauty had been put in place, the most holy body of St. Germanus, venerable throughout the entire world, was translated into the crypt, which was indeed worthy of such a great treasure.[70]

This ceremony took place in January 859, and dendrochronological investigations at the site have shown that the timber-work comes from trees felled in the period 820–55.[71] There are traces of wall-paintings showing the story of St. Stephen.[72]

A classic example of a Carolingian ring-crypt was excavated at San Vincenzo al Volturno in central Italy in the last decades of the twentieth century. The crypt is partly underground, entered by steps from the east end of the church, and comprises a curving corridor following the line of the central apse, covered in a barrel vault. Off it, in line with the main axis of the church, is another, straight, corridor, also barrel-vaulted, terminating in a cruciform chamber directly below the main-altar, with a niche for the relics of St. Vincent, flanked by four niches probably with other relics. As at St.-Germain, traces of wall-painting remain.[73] (See plate 2.)

When the body of St. Nicholas was brought from its original resting place in Anatolia to the southern Italian city of Bari, a crypt was constructed to house it. This was consecrated by Pope Urban II in 1089 and the remains of the saint still lie there, beneath an altar, under the huge basilica which was built above in the late eleventh and twelfth centuries.[74]

Another common position for the chief shrine in a large church was east of the main altar, sometimes immediately behind it, sometimes in an apse, that is, a semi-circular or polygonal recess at the end of the church. When Perpetuus, bishop of Tours in the late fifth century, built a grand new church for the remains of his prede-

[69] Crook, *The Architectural Setting of the Cult of the Saints*, p. 88.

[70] Heiric of Auxerre, *Miracula sancti Germani episcopi Antissiodorensis* 2. 2 (96), cols. 1252–53.

[71] *Archéologie et architecture d'un site monastique*, pp. 237–56 (p. 255 for the dendrochronological dating).

[72] Rollier-Hanselmann, "D'Auxerre à Cluny: technique de la peinture murale entre le VIIIe et le XIIe s. en Bourgogne," pp. 68–69.

[73] Hodges, *Light in the Dark Ages: The Rise and Fall of San Vincenzo al Volturno*, pp. 88–94, with photo and plan.

[74] Cioffari, *Storia della Basilica di S. Nicola di Bari* 1, pp. 61–76; Belli D'Elia, *La Basilica di S. Nicola a Bari*, pp. 11–125.

cessor, St. Martin, the saint's "blessed body" was placed in its apse.[75] Likewise, in the following century, when bishop Tetricus of Langres wished to remove the body of his saintly predecessor (and earthly father) Gregory from the "corner" where it had been interred, since the flock of pilgrims made its location awkward, he opened up a new apse at the east end of the church and placed the remains there.[76] The inconvenience of access was often cited as grounds for such relocation. Illidius, saintly bishop of Clermont in the fourth century, was first buried in a crypt, but because this was "narrow and difficult of access," a subsequent bishop, Avitus (c. 572–94), had his remains re-interred in a shrine in a new circular apse at a higher level and filled in the crypt.[77] Later, in the high Middle Ages, several of the English cathedrals—Ely, Winchester, Durham, London, and Lichfield—had major shrines east of the main altar, and shrine-chapels east of the main altar were constructed for Thomas Becket at Canterbury in the late twelfth century, for St. Margaret at Dunfermline in the 1240s and for Edward the Confessor in Westminster Abbey after its rebuilding under Henry III.[78]

Whether the saint's body was placed in a crypt or east of the main altar, both such positions marked it out. The orientation of Christian churches meant that the west end was less holy and freer of access, so movement toward the east end was movement towards the more holy and less accessible. Transit past the main altar, or under it, intensified this sense of approach to a numinous and extraordinary site. These fixed tomb-shrines, in their crypts or behind the main altar, had a deep influence on the architecture of the churches which housed them, and on patterns of behaviour within them, shaping both liturgy and pilgrim behaviour. The attempt to allow a smooth flow of pilgrims without disrupting church services led to the plan of the so-called pilgrimage churches, with an ambulatory around the east end, so devotees could approach the shrine or shrines at the far east end without entering the choir, where the monks or canons maintained their perpetual round of prayer and chant. In some churches, complete new chapels were erected beyond the east end in order to house a saint's shrine. Such an extension was undertaken at Canterbury in the years after the canonization of Thomas Becket in 1173, and the saint's remains were moved there in a grand ceremony in 1220. This eastern extension, the Trinity Chapel, is horseshoe-shaped, with the saint's tomb in the centre, and culminates, at the extreme east end of the cathedral, in a small circular chapel where the top of Becket's head, which had been sliced off during his murder, was enshrined separately. This was known as the Corona ("crown").

The shrine of a saint was distinguished from ordinary burials by obvious visible signs, notably precious fabrics and special lighting. It was recognized that when the burial place of a holy body was discovered, the proper thing to do was "to cover

[75] Gregory of Tours, *Libri historiarum X* 10. 31, p. 529.

[76] Gregory of Tours, *Liber vitae patrum* 7. 4, pp. 689–90 (repr., 1969, pp. 239–40).

[77] Ibid., 2. 4, p. 671 (repr., 1969, p. 221).

[78] Nilson, *Cathedral Shrines of Medieval England*, p. 67; Binski, *Becket's Crown*, pp. 3–27; Yeoman, "Saint Margaret's Shrine at Dunfermline Abbey"; Binski, *Westminster Abbey and the Plantagenets*, pp. 90–101.

it with cloths, light a lamp, and give the cult it is owed."[79] The coverings of tomb-shrines were often elaborate and expensive, such as that on the "holy tomb" of St. Denis outside Paris, which was covered with "a silken cloth adorned with gold and jewels." [80] These coverings had some of the same healing power as the bones of the saints themselves. People possessed by demons were exorcized by being wrapped in the tomb-covering of St. Julian of Brioude.[81] The linen cloth covering the tomb of St. Melanius of Rennes miraculously survived a fire.[82] Pieces of such coverings could have the same miraculous power as the relics of the saint and were treasured as relics.

Burning lights at the saint's tomb was one of the earliest recorded practices in the cult of the saints: Jerome mentions women who light candles at the tombs of the martyrs—"they do this in honour of the martyrs," he explains.[83] A seventh-century injunction orders the newly converted English to revere the relics of the saints, and adds, "if possible a candle should burn there every night."[84] When Bishop Heribald of Auxerre brought relics of St. Alexander and St. Crisantius from Rome in the middle of the ninth century, he took care to grant a small property "to provide perpetual lighting for the relics of those saints."[85] An eleventh-century visitor to Rome describes the catacombs "where lamps always burn."[86] Later in the Middle Ages, the financial accounts that survive from some shrines always include a large sum for wax for candles.[87] This conjunction of candles and cloths at the tomb of the saint could actually be dangerous. Numerous miracle stories describe how the precious coverings of a shrine were miraculously saved or restored when a candle fell on them from a nearby candle-holder.

There were other ways of honouring the shrine. The area might be strewn with herbs, like the sage "that had been scattered in the crypt in honour of the martyrs" around the tombs of St. Ferreolus and St. Ferrucio at Besançon.[88] Decorated hangings around the shrine were common.[89] It might be marked out by a canopy, like the "canopy adorned with various metals" that was raised above the tomb of Hugh of Rouen in the abbey of Jumièges after his death in 730, to express the monks' love for him and their reverence for his sanctity.[90] A tomb-shrine could also be elevated

[79] Gregory of Tours, *Gloria confessorum* 21, p. 761 (repr., 1969, p. 311).

[80] Gregory of Tours, *Gloria martyrum* 71, pp. 535–36 (repr., 1969, pp. 85–86).

[81] Gregory of Tours, *De passione et virtutuibus sancti Iuliani* 43, p. 581 (repr., 1969, p. 131).

[82] Gregory of Tours, *Gloria confessorum* 54, pp. 779–80 (repr., 1969, pp. 329–30).

[83] Jerome, *Contra Vigilantium* 7, p. 16 (PL 23: 345).

[84] *Die Canones Theodori*, pp. 243, 268, 275, 312.

[85] *Gesta pontificum Autissiodorensium* 36 (1, p. 151).

[86] *Chronicon Sancti Michaelis in pago Virdunensi* 16, p. 19 (MGH, SS 4, p. 83).

[87] Nilson, *Cathedral Shrines of Medieval England*, pp. 136–37.

[88] Gregory of Tours, *Gloria martyrum* 70, p. 535 (repr., 1969, p. 85); cf. idem, *Liber vitae patrum* 8. 6, p. 696 (repr., 1969, p. 246); Heiric of Auxerre, *Miracula sancti Germani episcopi Antissiodorensis* 2. 1 (87), col. 1248.

[89] For example, Hermann the Archdeacon, *Liber de miraculis sancti Edmundi* 18, p. 50; *Miracula sancte Elyzabet* 76, p. 218.

[90] *Gesta sanctorum patrum Fontanellensis coenobii* 4. 3, p. 42 (MGH, SRG 28, p. 28).

on columns, providing a space beneath, where suppliants might place themselves. An example is the tomb of St. Rosendo at Celanova in Galicia. A cripple came to his tomb and "lay between the columns of the monument," and, when cured, "he arose and held onto the columns of the tomb." Later a blind woman came to the church and "touched with her hands the columns which supported St. Rosendo's tomb."[91] The twelfth-century tomb-shrine of St. Magnentia at Ste.-Magnance in Burgundy consists of a house-shaped container, showing scenes from her life, resting on four columns with carved capitals. Much later, a panel from an altarpiece by Gentile da Fabriano, painted in 1425, shows the shrine-tomb of St. Nicholas at Bari, supported on columns so high that pilgrims have to raise their arms above their heads to touch it. One woman, who is sick or fainting and supported by a friend, is completely underneath it. A man hobbles towards the tomb on his crutch while another, healed, strides away from it with his crutch now over his shoulder. (See plate 3.)

A feature that seems to have been especially favoured in English shrine-tombs was an aperture or series of openings in the side of the monument, allowing closer access to the actual coffin or sarcophagus within. An early example is the seventh-century tomb of St. Chad, "a wooden tomb in the shape of a little house, having a hole in the side." Pilgrims could put their hands in this hole to gather healing dust.[92] Examples from the twelfth and thirteenth centuries are common, and contemporary illustrations show shrines with these openings. The tomb in which St. Thomas Becket was buried in the period 1171–1220 had such apertures:

> A wall of large hewn stones was erected around the marble tomb, strengthened most securely with mortar and iron and lead, with two apertures on each side, through which those who came there could put their heads in order to kiss the tomb.[93]

This tomb is illustrated in the stained glass of Canterbury Cathedral (figure 8.2).

A woman spending the night at the tomb of St. Hugh of Lincoln in 1208 fell asleep "with her head in a circular aperture in the marble tomb."[94] In 1287 a man suffering from a disfiguring growth on the back of his neck went to the shrine of Thomas de Cantilupe in Hereford cathedral, offered a penny, and then

> placed his head within a stone opening that adjoined the tomb, and when he had held his head in that opening for as long as it takes to say the Lord's Prayer and *Ave Maria* three times, he withdrew his head and felt himself cured of that swelling.[95]

[91] *Miracula Rudesindi*, pp. 218, 224 (AASS Martii 1, pp. 116, 117); see Sánchez Ameijeiras, "Imagery and Interactivity," p. 29, with p. 30 fig. 8.

[92] Bede, *Historia ecclesiastica* 4. 3, p. 346.

[93] Benedict of Peterborough, *Miracula sancti Thomae* 2. 29, p. 81.

[94] Gerald of Wales, *Vita sancti Hugonis Lincolniensis episcopi* 3. 3, p. 140.

[95] BAV, Vat. lat. 4015, fol. 183 (AASS Octobris 1 (1765): 625).

8.2. Thomas Becket's tomb from stained glass in Canterbury Cathedral.
© Peter Barritt/Alamy.

These "porthole-style" tombs may well have been inspired by the Holy Sepulchre in Jerusalem, with its three round apertures, but it is difficult to explain why they are hard to find outside England.[96]

A shrine can thus be regarded as an especially honoured grave. The process of the transformation of a grave into a shrine could, however, be a protracted—and disputed—process. The case of William of Norwich, a boy supposedly martyred by Jews in 1144, provides a well documented example. In 1144 William's body was interred in the cemetery outside the cathedral church of Norwich, but six years later,

[96]Crook, *English Medieval Shrines*, pp. 191–204, 240–44; St. Leopold of Austria's tomb had apertures: Finucane, *Contested Canonizations*, p. 84.

after an insistent struggle by Thomas of Monmouth, a monk in the cathedral community, it was taken into the chapter-house. Here, according to Thomas, the tomb miraculously protruded above the level of the floor, despite the best efforts of the masons to make it flush, thus proclaiming its own importance. Thomas now continued his efforts to assert William's sanctity: "I covered his tomb with a decorated cloth and placed at its head a large lighted candle." The prior of Norwich was outraged at this presumption, and ordered both covering and candle to be removed, an insult to the saint that, Thomas says, could well be connected to the prior's death later that year. His successor wisely restored the covering. Eventually William was translated into the church itself, but these early struggles show how such visible honours were clearly interpreted as a claim to sanctity.[97]

Large fixed shrines were almost part of the architecture of the church. Rudolf, a monk of Fulda, describes the emplacement of newly acquired relics by his abbot, Hrabanus Maurus, in 838.[98] Hrabanus first brought to a newly built church the relics (both bones and clothing) of several female saints, and "raised above them a wooden construction, which he adorned with gold and silver"; the names of the saints were written on the sides of this structure. Later that day, "he translated the bones of St. Leoba and placed them in the crypt of that same church behind the altar of St. Mary and the virgin saints, in a stone container, which he had enclosed with wood and decorated with gold and silver." Next day he placed relics of numerous saints in St. Boniface's church:

> He built a stone tower behind the altar, on top of which he placed the relics of the saints, enclosed in a stone container, on top of which he raised a wooden structure on four columns, decorated with gold and silver; within this he placed a four-sided rectangular container, which he had decorated with gold and silver and jewels, and adorned with images of the saints.

Such constructions were large permanent features of the church.

A surviving example of a stone shrine of large size is located in the church of St. Vincent in Avila.[99] Dating to the late twelfth century, it is actually a cenotaph rather than a tomb, since Vincent's relics had been removed from Avila by that period. It is covered with relief sculpture depicting the martyrdom of St. Vincent and his sisters, the visit of the Three Kings, and Christ in majesty. Restoration in the early twenty-first century gave back to the shrine its original gaudy polychrome. From the second half of the thirteenth century, some of the more notable saints in Italy were also given huge monumental stone tombs. The earliest was that for St. Dominic, the Ark of St. Dominic, which was created in the 1260s by the famous sculptor Nicola

[97] Thomas of Monmouth, *Vita sancti Willelmi Norwicensis* 1. 19; 3. 1, 3; 4. 1, 8; 5. 1; 6. 1, pp. 54, 123–24, 127, 165–66, 173, 186, 221.

[98] Rudolf of Fulda, *Miracula sanctorum in ecclesias Fuldenses translatorum* 14, pp. 339–40; see Lübeck, "Die Reliquienerwerbungen des Abtes Rabanus Maurus"; he calls Hrabanus "der zweifellos größte ostfränkische Reliquiensammler seiner Zeit" (p. 131).

[99] Rico Camps, "A Shrine in Its Setting: San Vicente de Ávila."

8.3. Tomb-shrine of St. Peter Martyr, Sant'Eustorgio, Milan.
© 2013. Photo Scala, Florence.

Pisano.[100] It is a large free-standing ensemble, which, in its original form, was at least 2 metres (approximately 6 ½ feet) high, and supported by carved figures representing archangels, virtues and clerical acolytes. On the corners of the tomb itself are figures of the Church Fathers, while around it run narrative reliefs showing incidents in the life of Dominic, such as the pope's approval of the Order and several of his miracles. Dominic's relics were translated into this grand new sepulchre in 1267. It proved to be an influential model. When the Dominicans commissioned a tomb-shrine for St. Peter Martyr in 1335, it is described as "in form and material similar in every respect to the tomb of our father St. Dominic."[101] This tomb, bearing the date of completion 1338, stands in the church of Sant'Eustorgio in Milan (figure 8.3). Not long afterwards a monumental tomb with elaborate reliefs and an effigy of the saint was erected for the remains of St. Augustine in the church of San Pietro in Ciel d'Oro, Pavia; this bears a date of 1362. These large stone monuments of the thirteenth and fourteenth centuries, which honoured the saints and recorded their deeds, provided models for the non-saintly tombs and monuments of the princes and popes of the later Middle Ages.

Running a Shrine

The daily routine of running a shrine is described in detail in the so-called Customary of the shrine of Thomas Becket, which dates to 1428.[102] It is eleven folios long and was drawn up by the feretrars (*feretrarii*, meaning custodians of the *feretrum* or shrine) to remove all future doubts and ambiguities about the "practices, payments and other obligations of the feretrars." There were two feretrars, a spiritual, who served as chaplain, and a temporal, and both spent the night in the shrine, recited the canonical hours there and celebrated the Mass of St. Thomas. The temporal feretrar had the duty of opening the doors in the morning, "announcing by ringing the bell three times that it was time to gather for the Mass of St. Thomas, and inviting and summoning to it any pilgrims and travellers there might be."

One of the feretrars was always to be present, except during dinner-time. Then it was important to lock up the shrine, but, before that, one of the clerks

> should make a careful search with an offensive or defensive weapon in all the dark places and suspect corners in which some wicked and cunning person could hide in order to commit robbery (which God forbid!) or in which some stray or mad dog might be lurking.

[100] Moskowitz, *Nicola Pisano's Arca di San Domenico*; for other examples and general discussion, Garms, "Gräber von Heiligen und Seligen."

[101] The Dominican General Chapter of 1335 describes it as "in forma et materia simile per omnia sepulcro beati dominici, patris nostri": *Acta capitulorum generalium ordinis praedicatorum* 2, p. 233.

[102] BL, Add. 59616, fols. 1–11v; discussed in Turner, "The Customary of the Shrine of St Thomas Becket."

The duties and services for the different days of the week are meticulously described. Tuesday was a day of special veneration for St. Thomas, since seven remarkable things had happened to him on that day: birth, confrontation with the king at Northampton, exile, hearing a voice from heaven during his exile, returning to England, martyrdom, and the great translation of 1220. There were several high points in the liturgical year, including the feast of Thomas's Passion (29 December) and Translation (7 July). At the Passion, which was in the middle of winter, the feretrars were provided with bread, cheese and beer for the pilgrims, and with coals to warm them. The crowd were admitted to hear "the course of life of the glorious martyr Thomas, which is accustomed to be read there clearly in the mother tongue." On the feast of the Translation the cover of the shrine was removed and a beautiful woven canopy placed over it: this had been the gift of Joan, countess of Kent, wife of the Black Prince.

The duties of the temporal feretrar included drawing up weekly accounts of the receipts of the shrine and making necessary payments. In the first week of Lent there was a stocktaking of all the vestments, ornaments, and jewels, and everything was to be cleaned before the feast of the Translation. There are detailed instructions about relations between the feretrars and other members of the community, notably the *coronarius*, the guardian of the shrine of Becket's crown (the detached part of his head), while rulings about wax and candles approach the obsessive. On chief feasts eight candles are to be lit at the shrine and four at the altar; on the day of Becket's return from exile seven candles of 7 pounds weight are to be lit before the relics of the church to commemorate his seven years of exile; the twelve big square candles on the beam near the shrine are to be renewed every Maundy Thursday, with the assistance of the candle-maker; every fourth year the feretrars are to renew the twelve painted candles, each weighing 3 pounds, that burn on special occasions—these are alternately red and green and painted with roses and other flowers. Naturally, supply of wax is also important. It was bought in bulk in London, taken by water to Faversham, and then carted the last nine miles to the cathedral. A spectacular supplementary source of light was provided by the barons of the town of Dover, who were obliged, every third year, to supply a candle the length of the circuit of their town: what is envisaged is a long wax taper coiled up into the shape of a wheel.[103]

The Customary of Becket's shrine ends on a melancholy note. It had been their practice, the feretrars record, to pay a large sum annually to the cellarer, but this was no longer possible, "because in modern times (which we say in sorrow) the number of people coming here has declined and their devotion has chilled and grown lukewarm." Hence that charge had been placed instead on the general income from the cathedral estates, until, they add hopefully, "the dayspring from on high visits the devotion of the people and increases it, through the fullness of its piety and the merits of the martyr." Their hope has not yet been realized, although their pessimistic

[103] A comparable taper, the length of their ramparts, was offered by the inhabitants of Montpellier in 1348: Sigal "L'ex-voto au Moyen-Age," p. 19.

view of the decline of shrine income at the end of the Middle Ages is endorsed by the most careful modern research.[104]

The need for custodians to guard a shrine, and, in particular, to prevent thefts of offerings or precious objects from it, is well borne out by incidental anecdotes, although stray and mad dogs are not mentioned in other sources. One story tells of a woman who used to come to the shrine of St. Edmund at Bury and, under the pretext of kissing it, would lick up the gold and silver offered there and carry it off in her mouth.[105] When the building work on the church of St. Leonard at Inchenhofen in Bavaria was being completed in 1310, one of the builders took a coin from St. Leonard's altar to buy some fruit, but his hand adhered to his mouth when he ate it.[106] An even less respectful attitude was shown by a heretic who took two coins from the shrine of St. Peter Martyr in Milan, saying it would be good to use the money to buy a drink. He immediately began to shake all over and became rooted to the spot until he put the money back, subsequently abandoning his heretical beliefs.[107]

Access to shrines was sometimes restricted, especially if they were housed in monasteries, where lay people, particularly lay women, were not welcome.[108] The dilemma was recognized early. One saintly monk of the fifth century, admitting that, although "unworthy and not deserving of it," he possessed healing powers, requested that he be buried, not in a monastery, "where women are not allowed to enter," but in a place where crowds could come for miraculous cures.[109] This demand for lay and female access sometimes resulted in special arrangements being made for the display of relics, as happened, for instance, when abbot Boso of Fleury brought new relics to his abbey on the Loire in the 820s.[110] A huge crowd of men and women gathered, inspired by talk of miracles. They were keen to accompany the relics and were unwilling to stop at the church door, even though "it was absolutely forbidden for women to pass the outer doors of the monastery." They begged to be allowed to enter the church where the relics had been deposited, to pray and fulfil their vows. The monastic authorities rejected this idea as "contrary to monastic practice," but, when some nobles added their voice to the requests of the people, a compromise was found. The abbot and monks agreed to erect a tent in a woody spot outside the monastery gates and to bring the shrines of the saints there, to be available to everyone for twenty-four hours, from Saturday evening to Sunday evening, under the careful eyes of monastic and clerical guardians. Crowds came from far and wide, and the short summer night (it was 21 June) and long summer day were filled with the cries of the sick being healed and the shrieks of demons being expelled.

[104]Nilson, *Cathedral Shrines of Medieval England*, caps. 6–7, with data on pp. 211–42, including a "model graph" on p. 241.

[105]Gerald of Wales, *Itinerarium Kambriae* 1. 2, p. 24.

[106]Eberhard of Fürstenfeld, *Exordium et miracula sancti Leonhardi in Inchenhofen*, p. 185.

[107]Ambrogio Taegio, *Vita sancti Petri martyris* 8. 59, p. 705.

[108]For the early Middle Ages, see Smith, "Women at the Tomb."

[109]Gregory of Tours, *Liber vitae patrum* 1. 6, pp. 667–68 (repr., 1969, pp. 217–18).

[110]For the following, *Miracula sancti Benedicti* 1. 28, pp. 64–65.

Exceptional access to the shrine-church was sometimes granted, either for favoured individuals or, sometimes, whole classes of women on special occasions. Adela, countess of Flanders, who suffered from frequent illnesses, was desperate to be allowed to pray at the altar of St. Bertin in the monastery where the saint lay.[111] She clearly had influence, for eventually, after securing the backing of two local bishops, she was permitted to enter "where never yet was it allowed to any woman to enter," and, on Easter Monday 938, the bishops led her into the church, "not without great trembling." She showed her appreciation by donating many ornaments to the church, while her husband the count added a gift of the reversion of a rich estate. Pope Alexander IV granted a more general dispensation in 1255, when he authorized English women to enter the abbey of Pontigny to visit the relics of St. Edmund there, notwithstanding the contrary custom of the Cistercian Order (although they were not allowed to eat or sleep within the monastic precincts).[112]

A longer period of grace could also be granted. When the shrine of St. Philibert was brought from the island monastery of Noirmoutier to the church of Deas in 836, in order to escape the attacks of the Vikings, enthusiastic crowds "of every sex, status and age" gathered there.[113] The monks wondered whether women should be admitted along with the other worshippers, but eventually "wiser counsel" prevailed, and female devotees were given access for a year, from the saint's feast-day (20 August) until its next occurrence twelve months' later. During this period many women came to the shrine and were cured of their ills. But, after the twelve months, "access of women was prohibited," and a cross was erected beyond the outer door of the monastery to mark how close they might come in future. According to the monastic author reporting all this, "a huge number of the female sex was present, rejoicing in such a great patron but grieving that they were denied access."

A saint with a particular reputation for animosity towards women was Cuthbert, whose tomb-shrine lay in the cathedral church at Durham from 995. What is remarkable about Cuthbert's misogyny, however, is that it was in no way an original feature of the living saint's personality, and nor is there any evidence of it in his cult for centuries after his death. The earliest written record of a hostile attitude towards women is in fact in a work of Symeon of Durham, writing between 1104 and 1115 (although Symeon attributes it to an incident during the saint's life).[114] Later in the twelfth century a story presents Cuthbert going so far as to appear in a vision to his sacristan when a woman sneaked into Durham cathedral with instructions to

[111] Folcwin, *Gesta abbatum sancti Bertini Sithiensium* 106 (with phrase from 103), pp. 627–28.

[112] Alexander IV, *Ut illibata permaneant*, 22 April 1255, Po. 15818: Martène and Durand, *Thesaurus novus anecdotorum* 3, cols. 1924–25; Lawrence, *The Life of St Edmund by Matthew Paris*, p. 99, gives the date of 13 April, the date of the letter of John, cardinal of St Lawrence in Lucina, which the pope is confirming.

[113] For the following, see Ermentarius, *De translationibus et miraculis sancti Filiberti* 1. 29, 68, 71, pp. 35, 48, 49: comment by Cartron, *Les pérégrinations de Saint-Philibert*, pp. 32–35, on the move to Deas, pp. 24–26, on the source.

[114] Symeon of Durham, *Libellus de exordio atque procursu istius hoc est Dunhelmensis ecclesie* 2. 7–9, pp. 104–10; see Tudor, "The Misogyny of St Cuthbert."

"throw that bitch out."[115] Cuthbert's newly discovered distaste for women is likely to be a consequence of the introduction of monks into the church of Durham in 1083. It was at this time that it became necessary for the new monastic community to erect a barrier against the casual arrival of female pilgrims and devotees seeking out the saint's body in the midst of their church. The nearby cult of Godric of Finchale, in contrast, shows a predominance of female pilgrims at this time, and it has been argued that, Godric filled the gap left by Cuthbert, providing for that local female clientele.[116] Certainly, women were aware that they needed to seek alternatives: on one occasion, in 1148, a young noblewoman took advantage of the arrival of some relics that were temporarily located in St. Nicholas's church in Durham, in order to obtain a cure, knowing that "the cathedral church did not allow the entry of women."[117] In the later twelfth century the desires of female worshippers in Durham were met in a different way, by the erection of the Galilee chapel at the far west end of Durham cathedral, "in which women were allowed to enter, so that those who did not have physical access to the more secret parts of the holy places, should have some comfort from contemplation of them."[118]

Reliquaries

Although the starting point for saint's cults was the tomb, practices such as the repositioning of saint's bones, the fragmentation of relics, and the development of secondary or contact relics, meant that the physical location and housing of saintly relics could be of many and varied types, from a massive and elaborate shrine placed in the nave or choir of the church to a phylactery hung around the neck.[119] Relics were prized objects, and those who could afford to do so, such as the great churches or rulers, often commissioned elaborate and expensive reliquaries to contain them. The bare bones of long-dead human beings might thus become enshrined in awe-inspiring casings of gold and jewels.

The terminology of shrines and reliquaries gives an insight into how they were viewed.[120] As the etymology of "shrine" and related words suggests, the core idea of a reliquary was that of a box or container. The modern English word "shrine," like the Irish *scrín*, comes from the Latin *scrinium*, originally meaning a box for books or papers. In the later Roman Empire there were public *scrinia*, where doc-

[115] Reginald of Durham, *Libellus de admirandis beati Cuthberti virtutibus* 74, pp. 151–54.

[116] Ward, *Miracles and the Medieval Mind*, p. 81; Finucane, *Miracles and Pilgrims*, p. 167.

[117] *Translatio cum miraculis beati Guthlaci anachorite*, p. 726.

[118] Geoffrey of Coldingham, *De statu ecclesiae Dunelmensis* 7, p. 11.

[119] On reliquaries see Braun, *Die Reliquiare des christlichen Kultes und ihre Entwicklung*; Ó Floinn, *Irish Shrines and Reliquaries of the Middle Ages*; Legner, *Reliquien in Kunst und Kult*; Van Os, *Der Weg zum Himmel: Reliquienverehrung im Mittelalter*; Legner, *Kölner Heilige und Heiligtümer*; Noga-Banai, *The Trophies of the Martyrs*; *Treasures of Heaven: Saints, Relics and Devotion in Medieval Europe*; Comte, *Les reliquaires du Proche-Orient et de Chypre*.

[120] Braun, *Die Reliquiare des christlichen Kultes und ihre Entwicklung*, pp. 15–79.

uments of state were kept (and like all parts of the Roman state they might thus be described as "sacred"). Throughout the Middle Ages, the word kept its general meaning of "box," rather than having a specialized sense of "box containing relics" (and in the modern Romance languages words deriving from *scrinium*, like French *écrin* or Spanish *escriño*, still have this general meaning). Hence in medieval Latin it was necessary to specify "box of relics" (*scrinium reliquiarum*) when this specific sense was required.[121] Greek *thēcē*, meaning "case" or "coffer," and also "coffin," was another standard term for the shrine of a saint, and passed into Latin as *theca*. John Chrysostom urged worshippers to embrace the "*thēcais* of the martyrs."[122] *Capsa* was another Latin word with the general meaning of "box" or "coffer" and was frequently employed for reliquaries, again often with an additional explanatory term: "coffer of the holy relics" or, with reference to an individual saint, "the coffer which had contained the holy relics of the blessed martyr," or "the coffer of St. Aubert the bishop."[123] *Capsa* gave rise to the Old French word for "reliquary," *chasse* (modern French *châsse*). Reliquaries were thus primarily identified as boxes or containers for mortal remains. Perhaps surprisingly, the word for reliquary rarely implies its sacred nature. One of the few languages in which it does is German. When Isolde swears her deliberately ambiguous oath in Gottfried von Strassburg's version of *Tristan*, it is a "holy thing' (*heiltuom*) she swears upon.[124] The familiar modern word "reliquary" in its various Latin and vernacular forms only becomes common in the later Middle Ages. In English "reliquary" is attested only from 1550, although the word "relics" is recorded in the early thirteenth century.[125]

Another term that was frequently used for a saint's shrine was *memoria*, that is, "a memory," a word that expresses unambiguously the relationship between the physical structure housing the bones and the practice of commemoration. St. Eligius or Eloi, the famous goldsmith of the seventh century, was praised for his renovation and decoration of saints' shrines: "at Soissons he brought the holy martyrs Crispin and Crispian up from a crypt and adorned them wonderfully and decorated their shrine [*memoriam*] with exquisite ornament . . . and he lavished the greatest care on

[121] For example, *Chronicon Sancti Huberti Andaginensis* 44 (56), p. 592; Gilbert of Limerick, *De statu ecclesie*, col. 1002; *Chronica Monasterii Casinensis* 3. 21, p. 388.

[122] John Chrysostom, *Oratio in sanctas Bernicen et Prosdocen* 7, col. 640.

[123] *Capsa sanctarum reliquiarum*: Goscelin, *Vita sanctae Wulfhildae* 3, p. 423; *capsa quae sacras beati martyris reliquias continebat*: Einhard, *Translatio et miracula sanctorum Marcellini et Petri* 4. 2, p. 256; *capsa sancti Auberti episcopi*: Robert of Torigni, *Chronica*, p. 199.

[124] Gottfried von Strassburg, *Tristan*, lines 15672–81, (2, p. 183).

[125] The OED, s.v. "reliquary," cites Middle French *reliquaire* (also *reliquiaire, reliquiere*; French *reliquaire*) from 1328; Latin *reliquiarium* (from fourteenth century in continental sources; earlier [Vetus Latina] in the sense "remnant, heritage"), *reliquiare* (thirteenth century in a British source; fifteenth century in a continental source); Old Occitan *reliquari* (fourteenth century), Spanish *relicario* (fifteenth century; earlier *reliquiario* [thirteenth century]), Portuguese *relicário* (fourteenth century), also Catalan *reliquiari* (fourteenth century), Italian *reliquiario* (sixteenth century as *reliquiere*). "Relikes" occurs in the *Ancrene Wisse* 1. 2, p. 8.

other shrines of the saints [*memoriis sanctorum*]."[126] When referring to a saint, the phrases "at his tomb" and "at his *memoria*" were synonyms: sick pilgrims coming to the shrine of St. Conrad, bishop of Constance, and placing themselves before it could be described indifferently as being "before the *memoria* of the blessed man" or "at the tomb of the most holy man."[127]

One of the most common words for a shrine in medieval Latin is *feretrum*, originally meaning a litter or funeral bier (something on which a body is carried, still the meaning of modern Spanish *féretro*), but soon also taking on its more specialized meaning as the place where the mortal remains of a saint were preserved. The word went into French as *fietre*. In late medieval England, as at Canterbury, the word *feretrar* or *feretrarius* was used for a shrine-keeper. At Westminster abbey the duties of the *feretrarius* included dealing with the offerings on the feast of the translation of St. Edward.[128] The term is also found in Middle English: in his will, dated 1463 and proved in 1467, John Baret of Bury St. Edmunds left, among numerous bequests, a valuable coin and an elaborate piece of jewellery "to Seynt Edmond and his schryne," these gifts to be fastened upon the shrine "by the avys of my executours wher they and the ffertrerys thynke and fynde a place moost convenient."[129]

Beroul's poem *Tristan*, composed in the twelfth century, has a passage which includes a wide sample of the French terms for reliquaries. All the relics of Cornwall have been brought to the scene of queen Isolde's trial, and to convey a sense of the complete ransacking of the relics of the county on this occasion, the poet reaches as far as he can into the terminology of reliquaries: "There was not a relic left in Cornwall, in treasury or phylactery, in aumbries or other biers, in feretories or shrines or coffers."[130] Here we have a list of seven different terms for places where relics might be contained.

Medieval terminology does not usually distinguish the large fixed shrines from smaller portable ones. Reliquaries containing fragmentary corporeal relics and contact relics could be tiny, but even whole-body reliquaries need not be large. Indeed, after the decay of the flesh, human remains can be squeezed into a fairly small space, constrained only by the length of the thigh bone (rarely more than 51 centimetres or 20 inches), and the size of the skull. A box 51 by 30.5 by 30.5 centimetres (20 by 12 by 12 inches) could thus easily contain a person's complete remains. Reliquary-caskets of this size are not uncommon. A shrine measuring 172 by 51 by 136 centimetres (67 ⅔ by 20 by 53 ½ inches) can be classified as "in the class of large reliquary-chests."[131] Shrines of these dimensions could be moved by one person, placed on an altar, or stored easily in cupboards. The coffin of St. Cuthbert into which his

[126] *Vita Eligii* 2. 7, p. 700.

[127] *Vita altera Chounradi episcopi Constantiensis, De signis* 5, 7, p. 441.

[128] Flete, *The History of Westminster Abbey*, p. 131.

[129] *Wills and Inventories from the Registers of the Commissary of Bury St Edmund's*, p. 35.

[130] *En tresor ne en filatieres, / En aumaires n'en autres bieres, / En fiertes n'en escrinz n'en chases*, Beroul, *Tristan*, lines 4130–33, p. 214.

[131] *Medieval Reliquary Shrines and Precious Metalwork*, p. 29.

remains were placed in 698, eleven years after his death, is one of the oldest surviving wooden shrines, possibly the oldest. It is made of oak, measures 169 centimetres (66 ½ inches) in length, and is decorated with incised figures of the apostles, Christ and the symbols of the evangelists, Virgin and Child, and the archangels.[132] It is described as a *theca* in the earliest sources, and we know for certain that it was portable, since it was carried all over northern England and southern Scotland between its departure from Lindisfarne in 875 and its arrival at Durham 120 years later.[133]

Some of the earliest surviving portable reliquaries are in the form of small silver containers, several of them shaped like miniature tombs, others oval or polygonal.[134] They range in size from 18.5 by 18.5 by 17.5 centimetres (7 ⅓ by 7 ⅓ by 7 inches) to 4.5 by 3 by 2.9 centimetres (1 ⅘ by 1 ⅕ by 1 inches) (although the reliquary function of this tiny box has been doubted). The former is from the church of San Nazaro in Milan and has been dated to c. 380, about the time that St. Ambrose was building new basilicas in the city and undertaking his celebrated translation of the relics of Protasius and Gervasius. It is decorated with biblical scenes, such as the Adoration of the Magi and the Three Children in the Burning Fiery Furnace. An oval silver box from the cathedral at Grado, the dimensions of which are 11.4 by 6.8 by 8.9 centimetres (4 ½ by 2 ¾ by 3 ½ inches), may date from c. 500. It has images of five saints, identified by inscriptions as Cantius, Cantianus, Cantianilla, Quirinus, and Latinus, the first three being saints of Aquileia (whose see was transferred to Grado), the other two bishops from north Italy and the Balkans. A further inscription identifies the donors of this box, the nobles Lawrence, John and Nikephoros. It is assumed, fairly logically, that the box contained relics of local martyrs. Portable silver reliquaries of this type continued to be made for the Christian elite down the centuries. A particularly impressive example is the reliquary of St. Demetrius made by John Autoreianos for the Byzantine emperor Constantine Ducas (1059–67) and his wife Eudocia. It is an octagonal container, 15 centimetres (about 6 inches) high, with images of the imperial couple and the soldier saints Nestor and Lupus. It probably originally held a small box with an image of St. Demetrius and containing some of the blood or myrrh of the saint.[135]

In the early Middle Ages, reliquaries were frequently in the shape of purses or small houses. A famous example is the Enger purse reliquary.[136] It is 16 centimetres (6 ⅓ inches) high, made of gold and silver gilt embedded with gems and enamel, and has images of Christ, the Virgin Mary and saints on the reverse, and crouching lions on the top. Since the late nineteenth century both scholarly and popular works have often associated the reliquary with Widukind, leader of the Saxon resis-

[132] Battiscombe, ed., *The Relics of Saint Cuthbert*; Cronyn and Horie, *St Cuthbert's Coffin*; idem, "The Anglo-Saxon Coffin."

[133] *Theca*: Bede, *Vita sancti Cuthberti* 42, p. 294; idem, *Historia ecclesiastica* 4. 30, p. 444; on Cuthbert's wanderings, Rollason, "The Wanderings of St Cuthbert"; *Historia de Sancto Cuthberto.*

[134] Noga-Banai, *The Trophies of the Martyrs.*

[135] *The Glory of Byzantium*, pp. 77–78 (no. 36).

[136] Lasko, *Ars Sacra*, pp. 6–7.

tance to Charlemagne until his conversion in 785, and, although this is unproven, it is to roughly to this period that the reliquary dates.[137] House-shaped reliquaries need be no bigger than purse-shaped ones. The Emly Shrine, of the seventh or eighth century, for example, is an Irish house-shaped reliquary, measuring 9.2 by 4.1 by 10.5 centimetres (approximately 3 ½ by 1 ½ by 4 inches), made of enamel on bronze over yew wood, with gilt bronze mouldings and inlay of lead-tin alloy.[138] As mentioned earlier, however, in Ireland relics were as often bells, staffs and books as they were corporeal remains, and these objects were themselves frequently enshrined. A celebrated example of an Irish bell shrine is St. Patrick's Bell, an iron bell 20 centimetres (about 8 inches) high, of uncertain date, housed in an elaborate shrine 26 centimetres (10 ⅕ inches) high. The shrine was made at the instigation of Domnall Ua Lochlainn (O'Lochlainn), king of Cenél nEógain, who died in 1121, and, while the bell is plain to the point of starkness, the shrine is an elaborate riot of interlace and pattern in bronze and gold.[139]

The simple box-form continued to be common throughout the Middle Ages. At Limoges, a famous centre of enamel work, reliquary caskets were mass produced from the twelfth century.[140] Fifty-two examples of just one type, showing the martyrdom of Thomas Becket, survive, with their medieval owners ranging from Italy to Sweden.[141]

A notable development of the later Middle Ages was the increased use of transparent reliquaries, in which a window of crystal or glass allowed direct sight of the relic. This paralleled the simultaneous use of transparent receptacles to display the consecrated host. From the fourteenth and fifteenth centuries the new term "monstrance," which means "something used for showing or exhibiting a thing," was applied to both kinds of vessel. The relics of St. Wenceslas preserved at Karlstein castle in Bohemia in the early fifteenth century were in "a crystal monstrance," and an inventory of the treasures of York Cathedral from the early years of the sixteenth century mentions "a monstrance with the bones of St. Peter in beryl, with a crucifix on top and an image of the blessed Mary."[142] Rock crystal, clear colourless quartz, was used for many reliquaries, like that now in Cologne Cathedral, dating to the first half of the thirteenth century, and containing relics of Andrew, Lawrence, George, Cosmas and Damian, and Walburga.[143] The heart of this reliquary is a hollowed out

[137] See the discussion, with sources and citations, in Rosenberg, "Ersten Zellenschmelz nördlich der Alpen," pp. 29–33.

[138] Now in the Museum of Fine Arts, Boston (the source of this description); image available on-line. Reproduced in *Treasures of Early Irish Art*, no. 31, commentary on p. 137 (Liam de Paor).

[139] Reproduced in Ó Floinn, *Irish Shrines and Reliquaries of the Middle Ages*, pp. 18–19, pl. 2 (a) and (b); *Treasures of Early Irish Art*, no. 61, commentary on pp. 213–14 (Roger Stalley). The bell and shrine are now in the National Museum of Ireland.

[140] *Enamels of Limoges 1100–1350*, nos. 9, 10, 17, 20–22, 24, 27– 31, 39–41, 44, 45, 55, 75, 76, 83–85, 112, 114, 115, 118, 141.

[141] Caudron, "Les châsses reliquaires de Thomas Becket."

[142] AASS Septembris 7, p. 809; *Fabric Rolls of York Minster*, p. 222.

[143] Van Os, *Der Weg zum Himmel: Reliquienverehrung im Mittelalter*, pp. 148–50, and figs. 175–77.

crystal in the shape of a house or roofed box, decorated with engraved arches and curlicues. It is set in a gilt silver container, studded with precious stones, and stands on legs that end in animal claws. The crystal is 9.52 by 4.6 by 6.7 centimetres high (3 ¾ by 1 ⅘ by 2 ⅔ inches). Sometimes transparent media, such as crystal or glass, were added to existing reliquaries to obtain the desired visibility. A piece of the bread from the Last Supper, which had been found in a box of silver and gold in Sens in 1095, was enshrined in a small container of silver and crystal around the middle of the thirteenth century, "so that it could be shown to the faithful people."[144]

A common form for both Eucharistic monstrances and reliquaries of the later Middle Ages was a container placed on an upright stand. A good example is the gilt silver reliquary of the hand of St. Martha from the convent of St. Martha in Venice, made by Giovanni Leon in the early 1470s and now in the Louvre. It is 71 centimetres (28 inches) high and the metalwork encloses a central glass receptacle for the relic.[145] A variant of this basic form is exemplified by a reliquary now in the Metropolitan Museum in New York. It is a monstrance centred on an egg-shaped crystal containing a tooth of Mary Magdalene, placed between two gilt silver architectural features, with figures of saints and angels, standing on an elaborately decorated upright column with a wide base. It is 55.8 centimetres (22 inches) high.[146] (See plate 4.)

Another development of the late medieval reliquary was the use of small statuettes of the saints to hold the relic, like the gilt silver image of St. Lawrence on his gridiron, holding a tiny, finger-shaped container for a relic of his finger. This reliquary, now in the Louvre, measures 19.5 by 7.5 by 7.5 centimetres (7 ¾ by 3 by 3 inches).[147]

Body-part Reliquaries

An especially striking kind of reliquary was that in the shape of a human body-part.[148] It was perhaps natural for churches that possessed an identifiable part of a saint's body to place it in a reliquary of the same shape as that part, as the canons of Alnwick did upon coming into possession of a foot of Simon de Montfort, who was regarded by many people as a saint after his gory death in 1265: "they made for the incorrupt foot a shoe of purest silver."[149] Separate enshrinement of the head is recorded as early as the sixth century, for, during his pilgrimage to the Holy Land around 570, a pilgrim from Piacenza saw in the church of Holy Sion in Jerusalem "a human head enshrined in a golden reliquary decorated with jewels, which they

[144] Geoffroy de Courlon, *Le livre des reliques de l'abbaye de Saint-Pierre-le-Vif*, p. 18.

[145] Louvre OA 5641.

[146] Van Os, *Der Weg zum Himmel: Reliquienverehrung im Mittelalter*, fig. 181.

[147] Ibid., fig. 7.

[148] Falk, "Bildnisreliquiare"; Bynum and Gerson, eds., *Body-Part Reliquaries*; Junghans, *Die Armreliquiare in Deutschland*; Wittekind, "Caput et corpus. Die Bedeutung der Sockel von Kopfreliquiaren"; Reudenbach, "Visualizing Holy Bodies: Observations on Body-Part Reliquaries."

[149] *Chronica de Mailros*, p. 204.

say is St. Theodota the martyr."[150] Whether the shrine itself was head-shaped is not clear. The earliest example of a head-shrine known in the West is from the later ninth century. The epitaph of Boso, King of Provence 879–87, records that "he enclosed the head of St. Maurice in gold, adorned it with glittering gems above, and placed on it a crown gleaming with gold and precious stones."[151] This head reliquary no longer survives, but a description and drawings made in the early seventeenth century by Nicolas-Claude Fabri de Peiresc do.[152]

Later in the Middle Ages reliquaries that mimic the shape of the body-part within become common. An Irish example, containing St. Lachtin's arm, is dated by an inscription to 1118–21; it consists of a wooden core covered with bronze inlaid with silver, and is 38.5 centimetres (15 ⅕ inches) long.[153] The head reliquary of St. Alexander, which was commissioned by abbot Wibald of Stavelot and completed in 1145, is now in the Royal Museums of Fine Arts of Belgium. It is made of silver, close to life size and stands on a box mounted on dragons.[154] In 1306 Philip IV of France acquired the head of his saintly grandfather, St. Louis, from the monks of St.-Denis, and had it enshrined in a head-reliquary in the Sainte-Chapelle.[155]

A head reliquary of St. Juliana from the nunnery at Perugia dedicated to the saint, and now in the Cloisters Museum in New York, turned out, on examination, to have an interesting history.[156] It is a reworking of an earlier head, which was actually that of a male. The craftsman responsible for modifying it, "Master William," had used thick layers of gesso (plaster of Paris) and pink and cream paint to turn it into a representation of the female martyr. The reliquary is hollow, to house the relic, which arrived at the nunnery in 1376, and originally had an elaborate surrounding tabernacle, which is now in the Galleria nazionale dell'Umbria, Perugia. The head stands 29.8 centimetres (11 ¾ inches) high, so it is life size. The gilt silver bust reliquary of St. Lambert, made by the renowned goldsmith Hans von Reutlingen in the early sixteenth century, and now in the treasury of Liège cathedral, is even larger for a reliquary of this type: 159 high by 107 by 79 centimetres (approximately 62 ½ by 42 by 31 inches).[157]

When churches possessed the whole body of a saint, it was not uncommon for the head, as the most precious part, to be detached and placed in a separate reliquary. When the head of Elizabeth of Thuringia was separated from her body in this way

[150] *Antonini Placentini Itinerarium* 23, p. 141 (the work is pseudonymous).

[151] *Epitaphium Bosonis regis*; Kovács, "Le chef de Saint Maurice a la cathedrale de Vienne."

[152] Hubert and Hubert, "Piété chrétienne ou paganisme? Les statues-reliquaires de l'Europe carolingienne," p. 239 n. 7, and plate 2.

[153] Now in the National Museum of Ireland, Dublin; reproduced in Ó Floinn, *Irish Shrines and Reliquaries of the Middle Ages*, p. 26, pl. 10; *Treasures of Early Irish Art*, no. 62, commentary on p. 214 (Roger Stalley).

[154] Lasko, *Ars Sacra,* p. 193 (with full page colour plate at p. 191, ill. 263).

[155] Gaposchkin, *The Making of Saint Louis*, pp. 74–76.

[156] Hoving, "The Face of St. Juliana: The Transformation of a Fourteenth Century Reliquary."

[157] Grimme, *Hans von Reutlingen*, pp. 33–48.

during the solemn translation of her remains in 1236, care was taken that it should make an easy transition from decaying flesh to glorious relic.

> The head of the blessed Elizabeth had previously been separated from her body, and, to ensure that the sight of it should not strike horror into the onlookers, the brethren separated the flesh, with the skin and hair, from the skull, with a little knife. The Emperor (Frederick II) placed a golden crown with precious gems on the head.[158]

Head-reliquaries could then be placed in a location in the church different from that of the main shrine, and might have their own altar and receive visits and donations from pilgrims in their own right. The head of St. Martial in Limoges had its own altar, and a woman might promise to bring a candle "before that holy head . . . and a similar candle before the body of the saint."[159] This would clearly involve definite, if not extensive, movement between two holy sites in the church.

Another example of the separation of the head and its enshrinement in a part of the church different from the remaining body-relics occurred on 1 December 1323, when the skull of St. Martin of Tours was removed from the saint's shrine and placed in its own reliquary.[160] The king of France himself had suggested the move, but the monks of Tours were unwilling to undertake such a major relocation without the authority of the pope. This they received, along with the pope's instructions that henceforth the head should be exhibited to the people twice a year, namely on 1 December, the anniversary of the translation of the head, and on another day of their choice. The monks choose 4 July, long established as the feast of the translation of St. Martin, as the second day. The pope also authorized an indulgence of three years and three forty-day periods for those visiting the church on the feast of the translation of the head. After receiving the papal authorization, the king commissioned a glorious golden reliquary for the head from the goldsmiths of Paris. We know that it was made by the famous goldsmith Jean de le Mote.[161] So, on the appointed day, the king and queen, along with many great nobles and bishops, came to St. Martin's church before dawn, and, when the common people had been excluded, proceeded to the opening of Martin's tomb-shrine. Inside was a silver casket, which enclosed a wooden coffin containing the saint's body, along with a label, "Here is the body of the most blessed Martin, archbishop of Tours." The bishop of Chartres removed the head and offered it to the king, but he, "unwilling to presume to touch the holy head," instructed the bishop to place it in the new reliquary. Before he did so,

[158] Caesarius of Heisterbach, *Sermo de translatione beate Elyzabeth*, p. 387.

[159] *Miracula sancti Martialis anno 1388 patrata*, miracles 4, 41, pp. 417, 430.

[160] *Translatio capitis sancti Martini*, from BnF, lat. 9732, fols. 128–31 (fifteenth century); there is an illustration of the scene in Farmer, *Communities of St. Martin*, p. 300, pl. 12, and *Treasures of Heaven: Saints, Relics and Devotion in Medieval Europe*, p. 169, fig. 68, both from Tours, Bibliothèque Municipale 1023, fol. 101.

[161] Rouse and Rouse, "The Goldsmith and the Peacocks: Jean de la Mote in the Household of Simon de Lille," pp. 286–89.

the clergy begged the bishop to exhibit the head to them, and this he did, proclaiming, "dearly beloved, behold, know for certain that I hold the head of the blessed confessor our patron." The following day, after enshrinement, the people were admitted to visit the new shrine, which was placed on the high altar, amongst the ringing of bells and the glitter of candles. (See plate 5.)

A head reliquary or bust reliquary, as a three dimensional likeness, can be regarded as a statue of the saint. It offered a focus for devotion that was human in form, not a box or a coffin. The worshipper looked at the saint, and the saint looked back.

"Boxes of Gold and Silver Full of Dead Men's Bones"

A twelfth-century description of the shrine of St. Giles in Provence gives some idea of the elaborate and sumptuous monuments that could be found in the great churches at this time.[162] The shrine was "a huge golden box" located behind the altar, decorated with carved scenes of some iconographic complexity. The front showed God in a golden circle, with the signs of the four evangelists and the symbolic letters alpha and omega, all surrounded with circles of jewels. On the sides of the shrine were the apostles, signs of the zodiac, and golden flowers, with the twenty-four elders of the Book of Revelation above. The back showed a complex and detailed Ascension scene. The lid had a fish-scale pattern and was decorated with rock crystals, one of them in the shape of a huge fish. None of this imagery refers directly to the saint whose bones lay within, whence perhaps the need for the inscription carved above the heads of the Elders: "this wonderful vessel, adorned with gold and jewels, contains the relics of St. Giles."

The shrine of St. Giles has long disappeared, a victim of time.[163] Fortunately, some shrines of comparable splendour do survive from the Middle Ages. One of the earliest, dating probably to 1063, is the shrine of St. Isidore of Seville in Leon. It is made of silver, measures 80 by 45 by 33 centimetres (31 ½ by 17 ¾ by 13 inches), and is decorated with scenes from the story of Adam and Eve.[164] During the following century, and into the early thirteenth century, a series of large shrines of precious metal was produced in the Rhineland (see table 8.1).

There were clearly expert goldsmiths available, and stylistic similarities between these shrines suggest that the same individuals worked on several shrines or that workshops developed their own styles.[165] The shrine of the Three Kings at Cologne was made after their relics were brought to the city from Italy in 1164 and, at 220

[162] *The Pilgrim's Guide to Santiago* 2, pp. 36–40 (*Codex Calixtinus* 5. 8); see Hamann, *Die Abteikirche von St. Gilles und ihre künstlerische Nachfolge*, Textband, pp. 299–319.

[163] For discussion of its fate, see Girault, "La châsse et les reliques de saint Gilles au Moyen Age," pp. 195–97.

[164] *The Art of Medieval Spain: A.D. 500–1200*, pp. 239–44, no. 110; Bredekamp and Seehausen, "Das Reliquiar als Staatsform. Das Reliquiar Isidors von Sevilla und der Beginn der Hofkunst in Léon."

[165] Ciresi, "Of Offerings and Kings: The Shrine of the Three Kings of Cologne and the Aachen Karlschrein and Marienschrein in Coronation Ritual," p. 182 n. 10.

TABLE 8.1
Shrines of the Rhine-Moselle Area

Saint	Place	Date	Base size (cm)
Victor	Xanten	c. 1130	61 × 142
Heribert	Deutz	1150–60	68 × 153
Servatius	Maastricht	1160–70	74 × 175
Maurinus	Cologne	1165–70	60 × 130
Aetherius	Cologne	1170	60 × 94
Three Kings	Cologne	1181–1230	220 × 110
Charlemagne	Aachen	1182–1215	94 × 204
Alban	Cologne	1186	153 × 50
Mary	Tournai	1205	90 × 126
Mary	Aachen	1215–37	95 × 184

by 110 by 153 centimetres (86 ½ by 43 ⅓ by 60 ⅕ inches), it is the largest surviving non-monumental medieval shrine. It weighs an amazing 515 kilogrammes (more than half a ton).[166] Dotted all over the golden surfaces are ancient gems and cameos, numbering 304 in the present state of the shrine, carved with figures. Most are Roman, but others are Greek, and their subjects include emperors, pagan gods and mythical beasts. These images of Nero, Mars, and Venus, engraved on cornelian, amethyst, and other precious materials, have been wrenched from their original historical context and thrust into the service of the Christian cult of the saints.[167]

The great golden shrines made later in the thirteenth century, such as that of Elizabeth of Thuringia at Marburg and Remaclus at Stavelot, continued this tradition. These are "the boxes of gold and silver full of dead men's bones" that worldly secular officials eyed with greed.[168] Occasionally contracts between churchmen and goldsmiths survive, like that of 11 April 1312 between the prior of San Cugat del Vallès, near Barcelona, and Arnold of Camprodon and John of Genoa, two craftsmen of Perpignan, in which they agree to make, "as best we can and know how," a silver shrine (*caxia*) for St. Cugat. The monks were to provide the silver, and the craftsmen were to receive 30 shillings for every mark of silver that they worked on, as well as expenses, including those incurred travelling between Perpignan and the monastery (a journey of about 190 kilometres, or 118 miles).[169] This reliquary is still in existence.

[166] Lauer, *Der Schrein der Heiligen Drei Könige*, inside back cover.
[167] Zwierlein-Diehl, *Die Gemmen und Kameen des Dreikönigenschreines*.
[168] William of Malmesbury, *Gesta regum Anglorum* 4. 318, p. 562.
[169] Torra, "El arca de Sant Cugat," pp. 560–61.

There is another surviving contract from 65 years later. In 1377 the queen of Hungary, Elizabeth, commissioned a shrine for St. Simeon, whose relics were preserved in the Dalmatian town of Zadar (Zara).[170] The contract specified that the artist, Francis of Milan, was to depict on the shrine the saint's miracles and also the presentation of the baby Jesus in the Temple, when the aged Simeon had taken him in his arms and uttered the words that were to become part of the liturgy—"Lord, now lettest thou thy servant depart in peace" (*Nunc dimittis*). A model of the shrine had been made of strong paper and the artist was to use this as a template. Queen Elizabeth donated a thousand marks of silver for the purpose. The surviving shrine, still in Zadar, is 192 by 62.5 by 71 centimetres (high) (approximately 75 ½ by 24 ½ by 28 inches) and has a large image of the reclining saint, with the narrative scenes on the sides. An inscription records that work was completed in 1380. Reclining images were common on the tombs of the rich and powerful but less characteristic of saints' shrines, although there are other examples, such as the fifteenth-century stone sculpture of St. Monica on her tomb in the church of Sant'Agostino in Rome.[171]

Reliquaries could form part of an ensemble of precious items, some of which might be used by benefactors to memorialize their gift and their name. At St.-Sernin of Toulouse, for example, an inventory of 1489 records that the body of St. Giles, which had at some point come to Toulouse from its earlier shrine at St.-Gilles, was in a wooden chest, the size of which has been calculated as 81 by 55 by 36 centimetres (32 by 21 ¾ by 14 ⅕ inches); it was covered with silver at the front and surmounted by a silver image of the saint with four other bishops and covered with precious stones. Before the reliquary stood a silver lamp with the arms of abbot Lawrence Alamandus and, nearby, a silver bowl with the arms of the duke of Bourbon. Abbot Lawrence's gift was recent, but the bowl had been given by Louis de Bourbon as long ago as 1336, together with lamps to burn before the relics of St. Sernin and St. Giles, and a candle of three pounds weight to burn before St. Giles from Friday to Sunday, all this secured by rental income. The inventory shows that Louis de Bourbon's gift of 1336 was still bearing public witness to his piety and (through his coat of arms) his descent, a century and a half after his donation. Moreover, this great prince had stimulated lesser men by his example, for in 1340, four years after the duke's gift, a rich gardener of Toulouse made a bequest to help supply the lamps and the candle for St. Giles,

> moved by a long devotion to St. Sernin, St. Exupery and St. Giles . . . considering that the most noble and excellent prince, the lord Louis, duke of Bourbon . . . placed a bowl of silver and two lamps of silver in the monastery in the oratory of St. Giles.[172]

[170] Vidas, "Elizabeth of Bosnia, Queen of Hungary, and the Tomb-Shrine of St Simeon in Zadar."

[171] BS 9, cols. 561–62 (photo).

[172] *Documents sur l'ancienne province de Languedoc* 2/1, pp. 99, 100, 494–95.

A touch of heraldic pride and a note of social deference mingled with devotion to a saint in this little history. Nine hundred miles to the north, in the cathedral at St. Andrews in eastern Scotland, a similar dynasticism hung around the statue of the Virgin Mary donated by the earls of Douglas: it was known locally as "the Douglas Lady."[173]

The love of gold and gems, as proper adornments of the saints, comes out vividly in abbot Suger's own account of his activities at St.-Denis, notably in his presentation of the translation of the church's relics that he undertook in the 1140s:

> We therefore gave thought to the translation of our lords, the most holy martyrs, and other saints, who were revered in various oratories at different places in the church. We resolved that the most holy shrines, especially of our lords, should be decorated, and the place where they were transferred to be made illustrious by the refined skill of the goldsmiths and a mass of gold and precious stones.[174]

It is an impulse that would have been comprehensible, three centuries earlier, to Bishop Angilbert of Milan (824–59), the patron responsible for the earliest surviving piece of elaborate goldsmith work dedicated to the saints. This, the Paliotto or Golden Altar of St. Ambrose, stands in the church built by St. Ambrose himself.[175] It is 85 centimetres high and 220 centimetres wide (33 ½ inches by 86 ½ inches), gold on the front and gilt silver on the other sides, and shows a series of pictures, from the life of Christ on the front and from the life of St. Ambrose on the back. The scenes from Ambrose's life are grouped into six on the right and six on the left, and in between these two sets of images there is a large central panel, showing the archangels Michael and Gabriel above and bishop Angilbert and the goldsmith Wolvinius below; the bishop is handing the altar to St. Ambrose, Wolvinius is being crowned by the saint. It is an early example of a named craftsman being depicted on his work and an expression of workmanly pride and confidence.

The central panel of the Golden Altar makes up a hinged pair of doors, which opened to give access to the saintly tomb below. Here, in a sarcophagus of porphyry, lay enshrined not only Ambrose but also Gervasius and Protasius, the martyr saints who Ambrose, on a famous occasion, had discovered and brought to the church. The remains of the three saints were still there when the sarcophagus was opened in the 1860s. The sarcophagus is a re-used ancient tomb, perhaps, because of its valuable material, even an imperial tomb, and it illustrates the point that not all reliquaries were originally made for the purpose of housing relics. Objects with quite different origins and functions could be adapted. Many rock crystal vessels from the Islamic world, which had a long tradition of the craft of shaping and decorating this mate-

[173] *Liber cartarum prioratus sancti Andree*, p. 406 (1424).

[174] Suger, *Scriptum consecrationis ecclesiae sancti Dionysii* 10 (1, p. 32) (PL 186: 1248).

[175] Lasko, *Ars Sacra*, pp. 42–46; *L'Altare d'Oro di Sant'Ambrogio*.

rial, were refashioned for use as reliquaries by Christian owners.[176] An example now in the Victoria and Albert Museum in London served originally as a fish-shaped perfume bottle in Fatimid Egypt, but was adapted around 1300 by being given a silver mount and rings for hanging it. Its dimensions are 6.2 centimetres high by 2.5 centimetres wide (about 2 ½ inches by 1 inch). It is possibly the same object as that described in an inventory of Margaret, duchess of Burgundy (d. 1405): "a little vessel of crystal in the shape of a fish, mounted in silver, for holding relics."[177]

A most remarkable example of the re-use of an Islamic object is the coffer-reliquary of Sts. Nunilo and Alodia in the Navarrese monastery of Leyre. This elaborately carved ivory box, 38.4 by 23.7 by 23.6 centimetres (approximately 15 by 9 ⅓ by 9 ⅓ inches), was originally made in the Caliphate of Cordoba in the early eleventh century to celebrate the victories of the Muslim general Abd al-Malik al-Muzaffar over the Christian armies. To add to the irony, Nunilo and Alodia were martyr-saints who had been executed by the Muslims in the ninth century. Perhaps the monks of Leyre thought it appropriate that their remains should now rest in a box covered with Arabic inscriptions.[178] Exoticism was also an attraction, something that might explain the occasional use of coconut shells as reliquaries, like the one at Angers cathedral in 1255, with a silver foot and lid.[179]

If the fragments were small enough, relics could enter private possession and be carried around the neck, or elsewhere, as a talisman. They might be worn in a pectoral cross. Gregory of Tours had a gold cross that he bore around his neck, inside of which were relics of the Virgin Mary, the apostles and St. Martin.[180] He possessed other portable relics, which had previously belonged to his father and then his mother.[181] According to his father, these had been a wonderful source of protection for him in his travels, often enabling him to escape "the violence of brigands and the risks of rivers, the wickedness of turbulent men and the attacks of swords," while his mother had quelled a fire with these relics, which she wore around her neck. Thomas Aquinas recognized the legitimacy of carrying relics around one's neck, although warning against any supplementary superstitions, such as the belief that the container had to be triangular.[182] Many reliquary pendants survive from the later Middle Ages, and others are described in inventories.[183]

[176] Shalem, *Islam Christianized: Islamic Portable Objects in the Medieval Church Treasuries of the Latin West.*

[177] Lightbown, *Mediaeval European Jewellery*, pp. 223, 500–501 (no. 33), 469 (pl. 127); he discusses many other reliquary pendants, pp. 221–28.

[178] The box is now in the Museo de Navarra, Pamplona; *Al-Andalus: The Art of Islamic Spain*, pp. 198–201, no. 4; Harris, "Muslim Ivories in Christian Hands: The Leire Casket in Context"; BHL 6252–53 for the hagiography of the martyrdom and translation to Leyre.

[179] De Farcy, "L'ancien trésor de la cathédrale d'Angers," p. 188.

[180] Gregory of Tours, *Gloria martyrum* 10, p. 495 (repr., 1969, p. 45).

[181] Ibid. 83, pp. 544–45 (repr., 1969, pp. 94–95).

[182] Thomas Aquinas, *Summa Theologiae* IIa–IIae q. 96 a. 4 arg. 3 and ad 3 (40, pp. 80–84).

[183] Examples in Lightbown, *Mediaeval European Jewellery*, pp. 221–28.

Placing the saint's relics in a small and portable container could also be a practical move, as was the case for the monks of St.-Riquier, suffering Viking attacks in the mid-ninth century:

> When the country was devastated by the attacks of the barbarians, and the brethren were forced to flee, they made a wooden reliquary in which they place the blessed head of St. Riquier, so that they might carry it with them easily and lightly, wherever they wished.[184]

It has been suggested that the silver box from Grado, mentioned earlier, was brought from Aquileia along with other treasures of that church when its clergy fled from the Lombard assault.[185]

Boxes of gold and silver, encrusted with jewels, made a tempting target. Some were plundered by enemies, some by rulers who wanted to turn their frozen capital into wages for soldiers. In 1336 king John of Bohemia carried off the images of the twelve apostles that adorned the tomb of St. Wenceslas in Prague, although he was punished for this by going completely blind.[186] It is not surprising that many golden shrines have disappeared. Those that survive, however, give an unforgettable impression of the glittering glory that shone out into a world unaccustomed to such brilliance.

Relic Collections

Throughout the Middle Ages the hunt for relics went on. Italy continued to be the great reservoir of saintly bones, supplying the undernourished churches north of the Alps. In the early 970s the high-born bishop of Metz, Dietrich (Theoderich), took advantage of an expedition to Italy in the service of his cousin, the emperor Otto I, to acquire relics for the church of St. Vincent he had just founded in his episcopal city. A contemporary account describes the process.[187] Altogether, relics of nineteen saints were obtained from the dilapidated churches and cemeteries of central Italy. The anonymous author of the account gives due credit to the bishop's clerks who undertook most of the demanding work involved, and he gives details of how the precious booty was acquired and on what day. Some of the saints are truly obscure.[188] Others were well known, but associated with sites other than the ones where the German clergy found them. A convoluted explanation is necessary to explain why

[184]Hariulf, *Chronicon Centulense* 3. 11, p. 120.

[185]Noga-Banai, *The Trophies of the Martyrs*, p. 97.

[186]Beneš Krabice of Weitmile, *Cronica ecclesiae Pragensis* 3, pp. 488–89.

[187]Sigebert of Gembloux, *Vita Deoderici episcopi Mettensis*, pp. 473–76 (a participant account incorporated by Sigebert); summarized in Sigebert, *Chronica*, p. 351; discussed by Wagner, "Collection de reliques et pouvoir épiscopal au Xe siècle."

[188]As even the Bollandists admitted: "At obscurum est, quis sit ille Elpidius," AASS Septembris 1 (1746), p. 211.

St. Lucy's relics were found in the ruins of Cortona, rather than in Syracuse, where tradition located them:

> We were told that a certain Faroald, duke of Spoleto, had translated her to this place. The bishop of the place himself, with his hand on the holy gospels, confirmed that she was the one from Syracuse, about whom responses and antiphons are everywhere sung during Mass.

Sometimes the German relic-hunters were beaten to their prey by the emperor Otto himself. And sometimes the hagiographic record was unsatisfactory. After finding the relics of St. Asclepiodates in some ruins in the neighbourhood of Perugia, where the emperor had gone to enjoy the autumn hunting, "we learned from the locals that his feast-day is 24 October, for we were not able to wring a saint's Life for him from the bishop." The relics they found, the author stresses, were often neglected, a fact that justified the Germans taking them to a home where they would have greater honour. And throughout there is the emphasis that these were genuine, if not well known, saintly relics. In this way, returning home after three years, bishop Dietrich was able to bring his large haul of bones to Metz "to be venerated more fully with cult and honour worthy of them."

One consequence of the bustling circulation of relics was the accumulation of vast assemblages of relics and reliquaries, sometimes numbering in hundreds or thousands. The great churches built up large collections. An inventory of the treasures of the church of St.-Riquier in 830 mentions thirty "relic chests adorned with gold and silver or ivory."[189] On St. Michael's day (29 September), 1015, bishop Bernward of Hildesheim consecrated the crypt of the new monastery he had founded in his episcopal city, in honour of Jesus, Mary, Michael, the whole hierarchy of angels "and of the sixty-six relics deposited there."[190]

The plan of the east end of St. Augustine's abbey, Canterbury, drawn around 1410 by the monk Thomas of Elmham, gives a vivid picture of the arrangement of the numerous portable shrines in this important English monastic church.[191] Above the high altar are two beams or shelves. On the lower one there is the shrine of St. Ethelbert, first Christian king of Kent, placed centrally, with on either side two arm-shaped reliquaries and the books brought by Augustine of Canterbury, "the apostle of the English." The upper beam has the shrine of St. Letard, who was a Christian bishop serving Ethelbert's foreign queen, and a box labelled simply "relics," along with images of Christ and angels. Access to the space behind the altar is through two doors, "the north door to the bodies of the saints" and "the south door to the bodies of the saints." At the far east end of the church is the shrine of St. Augustine, and ranged on either side, between the high altar and his shrine, are twelve others, of early archbishops and abbots, along with the local female saint Mildred.

[189] Hariulf, *Chronicon Centulense* 3. 3, p. 87.
[190] Thangmar, *Vita Bernwardi* 47, p. 778.
[191] *Local Maps and Plans from Medieval England*, pp. 107–26 (Cambridge, Trinity Hall MS 1, fol. 77).

Some of the shrines are on altars and all are represented in the drawing as identical house-shaped coffers. These saints are from the seventh and eighth centuries and thus represent the abbey's ancient saintly inheritance.

The great churches sometimes drew up lists of the relics they owned, partly as a celebration of the glories they possessed, partly as a precautionary inventory, "lest perhaps by the passage of time they should be deprived of the honour they are owed."[192] The surviving lists illuminate the cultural horizons of the church where the relics were housed, pointing to the geographical range and historical roots of its traditions. For instance, in 1517, an inventory was drawn up of the relics of the cathedral of Stavanger in Norway, and it reveals a striking mix of the local and the universal.[193] Most of the relics were labelled but some had lost their labels and so the saints could not be identified, although the clergy undertaking the inventory noted piously, "their names still stand in the Book of Life in heaven." There are some 36 individual items, mostly bones but also cloth soaked in blood. The cathedral possessed relics of Christ and the Virgin Mary, but the first on the list is the arm of St. Swithun, the Anglo-Saxon saint to whom the church is dedicated. This reflects the importance of England in establishing organized Christianity in Norway in the eleventh and twelfth centuries. Other English relics were the blood-stained clothes of Edmund, king and martyr, and of Thomas Becket, as well as a bone of Willehad, a ninth-century English missionary in north Germany who had become first bishop of Bremen. The other relics fall into two main groups, those with a specifically Scandinavian connection, on the one hand, and early martyrs, on the other. The former include the female saint Sunniva, legendary patron of Bergen, Olav, the "perpetual king of Norway," and Canute IV, king of Denmark and martyr, the latter two classic examples of the slaughtered ruler saint so typical of Scandinavia in the eleventh and twelfth centuries. Early martyrs include Lawrence, Valentine, Stephen, Clement, Juliana and Agatha, as well as the recently acquired relics of Andrew, Barbara, Cosmas and George ("part of the banner of the knight St. George"). The collection is thus unmistakably Scandinavian and yet predominantly composed of the universal saints of the Church.

The Stavanger relic list does distinguish relics that had been acquired by the bishop who made the inventory from those already in the church, which is why we know which ones were recent additions, but for the most part we have no idea how the relics came to the cathedral. In some cases, however, it is possible to know more. One of the most extensive and fascinating accounts of the relics of an individual church is that drawn up by Geoffrey de Courlon, monk of the abbey of St.-Pierre-le-Vif in Sens, in 1293.[194] Far from being a simple list, his account explains when and

[192] De Gaiffier, "Les reliques de l'abbaye de San Millán," p. 93.

[193] Jørgensen and Saletnich, *Letters to the Pope: Norwegian Relations to the Holy See in the Late Middle Ages*, chapter 4, "Let us open St. Swithun's shrine," analyzing *Diplomatarium Norvegicum* 4, no. 1074 (many thanks to Professor Jørgensen for a copy of the book).

[194] *Libellus super reliquiis sanctorum et sanctarum que in monasterio sancti Petri Vivi Senon' continentur*, Paris, BnF, nouv. acq. lat. 311; Geoffroy de Courlon, *Le livre des reliques de l'abbaye de Saint-Pierre-le-Vif.*

where a relic was acquired, and gives its history since it came to the church, detailing such things as translations and the making of new reliquaries.

The list begins with relics of Christ, such as pieces of the bread from the Last Supper, Christ's tunic, the cross, the sponge and lance, then moves on to clothes, hair and milk of the Virgin Mary, before listing relics of more than thirty saints or groups of saints, organized in the categories apostles and evangelists, martyrs, confessors, and virgins. Universal saints, like John the Baptist, Christopher and Mary Magdalene, are found alongside the important local saints: Savinianus, identified as one of the seventy-two apostles who Christ sent out according to the Gospel of Luke, who built the first church in Sens and was its earliest martyr; Potencianus, another of the seventy-two, martyred a year to the day after Savinianus; and Theodechild, reputed daughter of the Frankish king Clovis, and foundress of the monastery of St.-Pierre.

Geoffrey is explicit about the provenance of many of these relics. Some are ancient possessions of the abbey, like the

> relics of many apostles, evangelists and martyrs in a silver and bronze reliquary which St. Theodechild, the daughter of Clovis, most Christian king of the Franks, foundress of the monastery of St.-Pierre-le-Vif, obtained by means of a solemn embassy from the blessed Felix, chief bishop of the see of Rome.[195]

The priceless remains of Savinianus and his companions were the gift of the "praiseworthy" archbishop Wenilo of Sens (d. 865).[196] Other donations are more recent. The bodies of St. Felix and St. Aubert had been brought from Langres by abbot Gebert (d. 1078).[197] Geoffrey notes that written records of their Life and translation are preserved in the monastery. In 1120 Alexander, the priest of St.-Loup-de-Naud, where there was a dependent priory of St.-Pierre, had given half a tooth of St. Nicholas, relics of St. George, a fragment of the Holy Sepulchre and a portion of the cross. The last three items he had acquired in the Holy Land when count Stephen of Blois, whose overseas chaplain he was, had been allowed a free run amongst the relic collection of king Baldwin I of Jerusalem (1100–1118); Alexander had purchased the tooth of Nicholas himself separately, at great expense.[198] Abbot Walter (d. 1202) had also been overseas, and seized the chance to bring back some relics.[199]

Geoffrey specifies in detail the various translations and enshrinements the relics have undergone. Those of the founding saint, Savinianus, had been translated in 847 from his tomb to the high altar, then later hidden "through fear of the pagans," and raised up again in the early eleventh century.[200] The saint's body had also been taken to one of the great Peace of God assemblies in 1024, and shortly afterwards

[195] Ibid., p. 4. The chronology fits pope Felix IV (526–30) (sometimes known as Felix III); cf. ibid., pp. 40, 73–74.

[196] Ibid., pp. 4–5; cf. pp. 35, 52, 94.

[197] Ibid., pp. 5, 58.

[198] Ibid., pp. 5, 7, 20, 24, 60, 67; *Chronicon Sancti Petri Vivi Senonensis*, pp. 184–86.

[199] Geoffroy de Courlon, *Le livre des reliques de l'abbaye de Saint-Pierre-le-Vif*, p. 82.

[200] Ibid., pp. 5, 35–36, 52–53, 77, 94.

King Robert and Queen Constance of France had an expensive reliquary made for it.[201] The half-tooth of St. Nicholas, the gift of the priest Alexander, had been placed in a phylactery of crystal, along with a tooth of St. Marius, which had been donated by "our fellow monks in the Auvergne," that is, from the dependent priory of Mauriac.[202] The monastic treasurer had arranged this double enshrinement in 1292, just a year before Geoffrey drew up his list. A moment of importance for the cult of relics at St.-Pierre-le-Vif had been the opening of the head-reliquary of St. Gregory the Great in 1095. It transpired that the relics of many other saints had been enshrined with Gregory's head: John the Baptist, Peter, Hilary, Martin, Columba (of Sens), Benedict, as well as bread from the Last Supper, one portion of Christ's cross, and garments and hair of the Virgin Mary. These were then given their own housing.[203]

Geoffrey pays a special tribute to the recently deceased abbot, his namesake and uncle Geoffrey (1240–81), who seems to have been exceptionally active in the renovation of the abbey's reliquaries. Abbot Geoffrey is credited with renewing the silver shrine containing St. Gregory's head, adorning St. Savinianus's shrine, and enshrining the relics of Felix and Aubert, Ebbo, Ursicinus, the bread from the Last Supper, the piece of Christ's tunic and winding sheet and a fragment from his tomb, as well as the clothes of John the Baptist and clothes and milk of the Virgin Mary. He translated the body of St. Theodechild and placed her head in a silver head-reliquary. He commissioned a silver crown with images of the apostles, attached to a silver tabernacle with an image of the Virgin Mary. His admiring nephew adds accounts of his successful lawsuits and acquisitions, his building work and his fierce defence of his abbey's privileges, to develop a picture of the very model of a modern abbot.[204]

Geoffrey de Courlon's account of the relics of St.-Pierre-le-Vif, although not arranged chronologically, is historical. He looks back to the apostolic beginnings of Christianity in Sens and its martyr-heroes, then on to the patronage of the Merovingians, sketching out the fate and fortunes of the relics of these foundational figures. The devastations of the barbarians are mentioned, but also the slow accumulation of relics, their enshrinement, the powerful patrons the monastery had, the long list of abbots, mostly good, some remiss. With the gifts of the relics of St. George, St. Nicholas, the Sepulchre, and the cross, we see a new influx from the East, stimulated by the crusades. Geoffrey's list of relics is followed in his manuscript by a chronological account of the abbots of his house, and lists of the archbishops of Sens and the kings of France, from Priam to Philip the Fair. It is not surprising that Geoffrey,

[201] Ibid., p. 80; the Peace assembly "in Autissiodorensi pago" during the abbacy of abbot Ingo alias Hugh (d. 1025) was presumably that at Héry in 1024; cf. *Gesta pontificum Autissiodorensium* 49 (1, p. 251): "concilium . . . in pago Autissiodorense apud Airiacum."

[202] Geoffroy de Courlon, *Le livre des reliques de l'abbaye de Saint-Pierre-le-Vif*, pp. 7, 67; on St. Marius, *Vita sancti Marii solitarii*.

[203] Geoffroy de Courlon, *Le livre des reliques de l'abbaye de Saint-Pierre-le-Vif*, pp. 18, 20, 28, 43, 53, 62, 63, 68, 70.

[204] Ibid., pp. 6, 18, 22, 23–24, 28, 38, 58–59, 62, 64–65, 75, 83–87.

immediately after completing his book of the relics of St.-Pierre, went on to write a chronicle, covering the period from the Incarnation to his own time.[205] The traditions of his community could be embodied both in holy objects and in historical texts.

The survival of princely and governmental records from the late Middle Ages throws light on the rich collections of relics to be found in the secular courts of the time. It is entirely possible that rulers had such collections in earlier centuries, but the surviving evidence from that period mainly concerns the great churches. In the fourteenth and fifteenth centuries, however, inventories like those of the house of Valois illustrate how princes were building up collections of precious reliquaries that counted as part of their treasure.[206] The inventories show that elaborate reliquaries, magical jewels and other deluxe objects could all be listed together, perhaps suggesting that a reliquary might be prized for its precious materials and fine workmanship as well as the holy bone it contained. The following reliquary of St. Philip was in the possession of the Duke of Berry, who granted it to the church of Notre-Dame in Paris in 1406:

> A reliquary of gold containing the head of our lord St. Philip, with shoulders of gold, and a necklace around the shoulders with two shields with the arms of the Duke of Berry at each end; and there are four sapphires, four rubies, and eighteen great pearls; at the end of the arms are two more great pearls and two more in their midst; at the tip of the beard there is a collar decorated with a great sapphire, three rubies and three great pearls. The base, which is of silver, is supported by five bears and five children, holding little chains to which the bears are tied. Around the foot are three images, Our Lady holding her child on the left, and the child holding a little mill, with a little pearl above, and on the right Our Lady holding a brooch of one great pearl and four smaller ones. And above the base there are two angels supporting the head, and under their hands are two columns that descend to the base. And all around the base are the arms of the lord. And on the base, in the middle at the back, there is a swan holding a little roll and small chain with the arms of the lord.[207]

One can imagine favoured visitors being given the chance to admire this elaborate object and to be impressed by its precious materials and the skill exhibited in its manufacture. It is hard to be sure they would all be moved by the fact that it contained St. Philip's head.

One of greatest of these princely collectors of the later Middle Ages was Charles IV, king of Bohemia and Holy Roman Emperor (d. 1378).[208] Some of the

[205] Geoffroy de Courlon, *Chronique de l'abbaye de Saint-Pierre-le-Vif de Sens*.

[206] Bozóky, "Private Reliquaries and Other Prophylactic Jewels."

[207] Delaborde, "Le procès du chef de Saint Denis," p. 300, from an inventory of the treasury of Notre-Dame in 1416.

[208] Machilek, "Privatfrömmigkeit und Staatsfrömmigkeit"; Schmid, "Vom Rheinland nach Böhmen. Studien zur Reliquienpolitik Kaiser Karls IV."

relics he acquired were given to Prague cathedral, and to other churches, but most went to his castle at Karlstein, which housed a priceless collection of relics of Christ's Passion, and has even been called a "reliquary stronghold."[209] In the Chapel of the Holy Cross in the Great Tower of Karlstein there were 130 panel paintings of saints, by Master Theodoric, the first Bohemian artist known by name, and each painting had relics inserted into its frame.[210] Some of the German relic collections of the later Middle Ages were so enormous that catalogues were drawn up devoted solely to the collection.[211] In 1509 a printed catalogue was published of the relics in the Wittenberg Castle Church, with a title page showing the two princes of the house of Wettin who had assembled them.[212] It listed 134 reliquaries, and was adorned with woodcut illustrations by the great German craftsman Lucas Cranach. There can have been no expectation that any individual reliquary in this collection would be the focus of regular devotion or daily cult. These collections of thousands of reliquaries, usually small precious objects, were to be admired for their beauty and number. That is why printed catalogues of them circulated—one might be tempted to call them "exhibition catalogues."[213] These relics and reliquaries are on the cusp of becoming objets d'art for the admiration of connoisseurs. The path towards museums was clear.

Relics in Movement

Translation

"Translation" means the ritual relocation of a saint's relics.[214] The logistics and significance of the ceremony could vary enormously. A translation might involve the movement of bones over hundreds of miles, into areas where there were few relics or, in the case of mission areas, none. But translation was often over a shorter distance, from the original burial site in a cemetery outside the walls to a basilica within the city. The earliest example of this kind in Rome seems to be that undertaken by Pope Theodore (642–49), who translated the bodies of the martyrs Primus and Felicianus from the cemetery on the Via Nomentana to the church of Santo Stefano Rotundo within the city of Rome, where he commissioned a spectacular apse mosaic depicting the two martyrs on either side of Christ's cross.[215] Thereafter, in the later seventh, eighth, and ninth centuries, such translations became common. However, transla-

[209] Crossley, "The Politics of Presentation: The Architecture of Charles IV of Bohemia," p. 139.

[210] Horníčková, "Memory, Politics and Holy Relics," p. 140; Fajt, *Magister Theodoricus, Court Painter to Emperor Charles IV*; idem, *Court Chapels of the High and Late Middle Ages and their Artistic Decoration.*

[211] Kühne, *Ostensio Reliquiarum*, pp. 34–50.

[212] *Dye zaigung des hochlobwirdigen hailigthums der Stifft kirchen aller hailigen zu Wittenburg.*

[213] Cárdenas, *Friedrich der Weise und das Wittenberger Heiltumsbuch*, p. 120.

[214] Dubois and Lemaitre, *Sources et méthodes de l'hagiographie médiévale*, pp. 280–86; Heinzelmann, *Translationsberichte*; Sigal, "Le déroulement des translations de reliques"; Caroli, "Bringing Saints to Cities and Monasteries"; Vocino, "Le traslazioni di reliquie in età carolingia."

[215] *Liber Pontificalis* 1, p. 332; Brandenburg, *Ancient Churches of Rome*, p. 213.

tion could also signify simply movement of relics from one place to another within a church, to give them greater honour in a more exalted position or in a new shrine, perhaps to mark canonization. For instance, when St. Cuthbert's remains were translated in 698, eleven years after his death, the monks of his monastery planned "to enclose them in a light coffer and place them in the same spot, but above the floor, for the sake of more worthy veneration."[216] This was the simplest form of "elevation"—"raising up" the body, marking it out by a tomb above the ground or floor level. In general, it was thought "unjust and ungrateful" that a holy man with a reputation for miracle-working "should still lie in the bosom of the damp earth."[217]

As mentioned earlier (p. 10), the first recorded translations took place around the middle of the fourth century. From that date they were a common feature of the cult of the saints. Holy bones were constantly being found, identified and moved. Some of the earliest of these "discoveries" involved the remains of biblical figures, of both the Old and New Testament. The relics of the prophet Samuel were brought to Constantinople in 406, and nine years later an especially significant discovery was the remains of St. Stephen, the first Christian martyr.[218] The Latin term for such an inspired rediscovery of the tomb of a holy person in this way was *inventio*, "a finding," and it came to be applied both to the literary genre describing such events and the feast-day commemorating them. Gregory of Tours provides a classic account of such an "invention" in the sixth century:

> Benignus, witness of the name of the Lord, was martyred at the fortress of Dijon. Because he was placed in a large tomb after his martyrdom, the men of our time, and particularly the blessed Gregory, the bishop, thought that it was a pagan who had been laid there. The country people made requests there and they quickly received what they asked for. Someone, who had received many benefits, brought a wax taper to the saint's tomb . . . a little boy went down to the tomb . . . to take away the taper . . . but behold a huge serpent came from the other direction and encircled the taper . . . this, and other similar occurrences, were reported to the bishop, but he did not believe and ordered even more strongly that no-one should worship there. At length the martyr . . . revealed himself to the bishop.

The indignant martyr asked the bishop what he thought he was doing and ordered a covering for his tomb. The bishop, thunderstruck, begged the saint's pardon and built a crypt for his relics, into which they were translated.[219]

Gregory's account traces the steps from the tomb of the unknown pagan to the creation of an important martyr-shrine very clearly. The process began with "the

[216] Bede, *Vita sancti Cuthberti* 42, p. 292; cf. idem, *Historia ecclesiastica* 4. 30, p. 442.

[217] Hariulf, *Vita sancti Arnulfi episcopi Suessionensis* 3, preface, col. 1427 (a letter of Lisiard, bishop of Soissons, regarding his predecessor Arnulf); cf. Kemp, *Canonization and Authority*, p. 72.

[218] *Chronicon paschale*, col. 784; Jerome, *Contra Vigilantium* 5, pp. 12–13 (PL 23: 343); for Stephen see earlier, p. 22.

[219] Gregory of Tours, *Gloria martyrum* 50, pp. 522–23 (repr., 1969, pp. 72–73).

country people," who treated the tomb as a source of power, sought help there, and brought gifts of thanksgiving, notably candles, that almost universal marker of a saintly shrine. The curious incident of the serpent protecting the candle adds an element of mystery but was clearly not the kind of event that could convince a bishop. It needed a vision of the martyr himself before the bishop was willing to endorse, and embody in stone, what was already an active cult. The country people initiated this cult, with their requests at the tomb (although we do not know what name they used in their invocations), and with their gifts and candles, but the official ecclesiastical authorities accepted it only after a visionary vindication.

Revelation of new saints like Benignus, and discovery of the remains of well known but previously hidden saints, such as Stephen, were common motives for translations. Equally important were the planned relocations of saints to new shrines or new locations. These could be major public occasions. When, in 1220, the body of Thomas Becket was moved into the new chapel that had been especially built for it, the assembled dignitaries included not only the king and chief barons and bishops of England, and Berengaria, the queen-mother, but also an archbishop from Hungary and "many of the great men of France," counts and bishops, including the archbishop of Rouen. The English did them the courtesy of taking lodgings outside Canterbury, so the foreign visitors could stay in the town itself. It was decreed that the day of the translation should henceforth be celebrated as a feast-day throughout England.[220]

Translations of saintly relics were not to be undertaken lightly, for they were dangerous objects, and a disturbance of the holy tomb, even with the best of intentions, was a kind of violation (one abbot undertaking an elevation of his local saint is termed a "pious violator").[221] And saints' bodies could be lethal. In the 580s, during the restoration of the church of St. Lawrence in Rome, those who accidentally uncovered the saint's tomb all died within ten days.[222] One arrogant young Anglo-Saxon aristocrat went insane after he had insisted on viewing the body of St. Edmund King and Martyr.[223] The bishop of Prague, prior to the translation of the body of St. Adalbert from Gniezno in 1039, expressed the fear "that we may be struck with mental stupor or blindness or some weakness of our limbs if we presume to do this too boldly."[224] To purify themselves, the participants in the translation might devote themselves to fasting and prayer before the ceremony (as the bishop recommended in this case). The monks of Hautmont, as they got ready to open the shrine of St. Marcellus, around the year 1068, were commanded to fast and pray, "lest they

[220] *Histoire des ducs de Normandie et des rois d'Angleterre*, pp. 208–9; Walter of Coventry, *Memoriale* 2, pp. 245–46. In general, see Eales, "The Political Setting of the Becket Translation."

[221] *Miracula sancti Faronis* 1, p. 616.

[222] Gregory I, *Registrum epistularum* 4. 30 (1, pp. 248–49); Gregory dates the event to the time of his predecessor, that is, Pelagius II (579–90).

[223] Abbo of Fleury, *Passio sancti Eadmundi* 16, p. 85.

[224] Cosmas of Prague, *Chronica Boemorum* 2. 4, p. 84.

approach such a treasure unprepared."[225] When St. Margaret of Scotland was moved from her tomb to a new shrine in 1180, the monks of Dunfermline, where her body was buried, lay prostrate on the floor of the choir reciting the seven penitential psalms and the litany, "not without fear and trembling."[226]

It was also wise to get the approval of both earthly and heavenly powers before actually undertaking the ceremony. The former might be bishops or kings, the latter God and the saint. One of the provisions of the Council of Mainz in 813 was: "Henceforth no one should presume to move the bodies of the saints from one place to another without the advice of the ruler and permission of the bishops and the holy synod."[227] Before undertaking the translation of the relics of St. Edmund at Bury St. Edmunds in the 1090s, the abbot of Bury, Baldwin, sought the permission of the king, William Rufus.[228] But it was not only earthly powers who had to give their consent. It was clear that the saint too had to approve of his or her translation for it to have a chance of taking place. Many initial attempts to move a saint failed. Some saints expressed their disfavour at some aspects of the translation by becoming immoveable. Margaret of Scotland could not be moved until her husband, King Malcolm, was also brought from his tomb to join her in the new chapel dedicated to her.[229]

During a translation the relics were unusually accessible, which meant they could be displayed, as in 1164, when the body of St. Rotrudis was translated at the north French monastery of Andres, and the presiding bishop took the opportunity to exhibit her head to the assembled people.[230] Crowds would try to get as close as possible on such occasions. Translation also offered opportunities to acquire relics, as the tomb was opened and the remains of the saint were within reach. When, in the later eleventh century, abbot Garcia of San Pedro de Arlanza translated the bodies of Sts. Vincent, Sabina and Cristeta from Avila, where they had been "treated with neglect," a huge crowd of clerics, nobles, and people gathered for the ceremony. After the service, the bishops and abbots asked for relics, which Garcia gave them.[231]

If translation involved movement of the relics to a distant city, the entry of the holy objects into the city that was to be their new home was celebrated with some of the ceremony and expression of public joy that characterized the formal arrival of a ruler.[232] It is a parallel made explicit in the sermon given by Victricius, bishop of Rouen, on the occasion of the arrival of relics of the apostles and martyrs in his city in the 390s:

[225] Ursio of Hautmont, *Acta Marcelli papae* 2. 2. 5, p. 13.

[226] *Miracula sancte Margarite Scotorum regine* 9, p. 92.

[227] *Concilia aevi Karolini* 1/1, p. 272, no. 36, cl. 51.

[228] Hermann the Archdeacon, *Liber de miraculis sancti Edmundi* 44, p. 85.

[229] Bower, *Scotichronicon* 10. 3 (5, pp. 296–98).

[230] William of Andres, *Chronica Andrensis* 54, p. 707.

[231] Grimaldus, *Vita Dominici Siliensis* 1. 8, p. 246.

[232] MacCormack, *Tradition and Ceremony in Late Antiquity*; McCormick, *Eternal Victory: Triumphal Rulership in Late Antiquity, Byzantium and the Early Medieval West.*

> In these relics there is perfect grace and perfect power . . . the apostles and martyrs are coming . . . if some secular ruler was visiting our city, instantly every space would be smiling, garlanded with flowers, mothers would crowd onto the roofs, the gates would pour out a wave of people. . . . O blessed people, when the triumph of the martyrs and the parade of their powers marches below our roofs, why should we not dissolve into joy?[233]

A famous ivory carving from fifth- or sixth-century Constantinople shows the arrival of a saint's relics, perhaps the arm of St. Stephen in 421 (figure 1.1).[234] The relics are in a chest borne by two bishops, who are seated in a richly carved carriage, and are preceded by a procession headed by the emperor himself. They are welcomed at a newly built church (workmen are still on the roof) by the empress, while from upper windows a row of onlookers sing and swing incense-burners. It is quite possible that this ivory carving itself formed one side of a box containing these relics. The chronicler Theophanes gives accounts of just such a ceremony. In 550, when the relics of Andrew, Luke, and Timothy were redeposited after building work, the patriarch of Constantinople "processed with the holy relics, seated in the imperial jewel-encrusted golden carriage, holding the three reliquaries of the holy apostles on his knees." Next year the patriarch was again involved in the translation of relics, accompanied by his colleague, the patriarch of Alexandria: "they both sat in the imperial carriage, holding the holy relics on their knees."[235]

The arrival of relics could generate jubilation and exalted feelings. When, in the 820s, Einhard was bringing relics of St. Marcellinus from Aachen to their final resting place at Seligenstadt, their passage stimulated heightened emotion and encouraged the local population to forgive debts and end feuds.[236] One man, who was owed half a pound of silver, told his debtor, "For love and honour of this saint, I absolve you of the debt." Another, even more dramatically, dragged his enemy to the relics and said:

> You killed my father and hence we have been enemies. But now, for love and honour of God and this saint, I wish to establish a sincere agreement with you, so that our friendship will endure forever. Let this saint be the witness of our mutual love and the avenger of whoever tries to disrupt this peace.

"The arrival of such patrons," wrote one enthusiastic German cleric about the reception of newly acquired relics, "is rightly a source of joy, for through them, and the Lord's help, famine, pestilence, disease, sedition and war are all laid to rest."[237]

[233] Victricius of Rouen, *De laude sanctorum* 11–12, pp. 86–89 (PL 20: 454–55).

[234] Holum and Vikan, "The Trier Ivory." The ivory is now in the cathedral treasury at Trier.

[235] Theophanes, *Chronographia*, s.a. 6042, 6044, pp. 227, 228; cf. John Malalas, *Chronographia* 18. 109, 113, pp. 412, 414–15.

[236] Einhard, *Translatio et miracula sanctorum Marcellini et Petri* 2. 8, p. 247.

[237] *Gesta episcoporum Halberstadensium*, p. 120.

Some of the most long-distance translations were those into newly converted regions. As Christianity spread, so too the cult of the saints spread, and this required the translation of relics into the mission areas. In the century after Charlemagne's subjection of Saxony (775–804), which was accompanied by the imposition of the Christian religion by force, there were fifty or so translations of relics into the newly conquered area.[238] Their missionary function was sometimes made explicit. The relics of the Roman martyr Alexander were brought to Saxony in the mid-ninth century in order that the Saxons "might be converted from pagan rites and superstitions to the true religion by their miracles and wonders."[239] Warin, abbot of the newly founded Saxon monastery of Corvey, himself of mixed Saxon and Frankish descent, sought out relics from back in the Frankish heartlands "to strengthen the faith of his people."[240]

The thinking behind such importation of relics is evident in the account of the translation of St. Liborius, which took place in 836. Badurad, the second bishop of Paderborn, was obviously frustrated with his newly converted flock:

> Since the populace, especially the common people, still unformed in the ways of the faith, could only be turned away completely from pagan error with difficulty, as they secretly gave themselves up to the cultivation of their ancestral superstitions, the man of great wisdom understood that, if the mass of the people began to venerate the body of some famous saint which had been brought there, persuaded by the display of miracles (as is accustomed to happen), and the grace of healing, and growing used to seeing his patronage, nothing could recall them more easily from disbelief.[241]

As well as being moved into newly converted lands, relics were also translated out of areas conquered by non-Christians. The bones of St. Augustine, the great bishop of the north African city of Hippo, who died in 430, were subsequently removed to Sardinia "on account of the ravagings of the barbarians," and then later, around the year 720, when Sardinia was threatened by Muslim raiders, brought to Pavia in northern Italy.[242] Here they were enshrined in honour in the basilica of San Pietro in Ciel d'Oro. The huge marble "Ark of St. Augustine," produced in the fourteenth century for the basilica, contains carvings showing the saint's life and miracles, as

[238] Röckelein, *Reliquientranslationen nach Sachsen im 9. Jahrundert* (list at pp. 374–76); see also Zender and Fellenberg gen. Reinold, "Reliquientranslationen zwischen 600 und 1200"; Vocino, "Le traslazioni di reliquie in età carolingia," pp. 231–36.

[239] Rudolf and Meginhard of Fulda, *Translatio sancti Alexandri* 4, p. 427 (MGH, SS 2, p. 676).

[240] *Translatio sancti Viti martyris* 5, p. 48 (MGH, SS 2, p. 581); see Van Landschoot, "La translation des reliques de saint Vit."

[241] *Translatio sancti Liborii* 7, p. 51 (MGH, SS 4, p. 151).

[242] Bede, *Chronica maiora*, p. 321. There is debate about whether these "barbarians" were Vandals, Berbers or Muslims: Rowland, "The Sojourn of the Body of St Augustine in Sardinia"; Hallenbeck, *The Transferal of the Relics of St Augustine.*

8.4. "Ark of St. Augustine," detail showing the saint's translation to Pavia, San Pietro in Ciel d'Oro, Pavia, fourteenth century. © 2013. Photo Scala, Florence.

well as the translation to Pavia itself (although Augustine's remains were not placed in the Ark until modern times) (figure 8.4).[243]

Another famous case of translation from the realm of Islam was that of Mark the Evangelist, whose body was smuggled out of Egypt in the 820s, reportedly hidden under a consignment of pork, to discourage the Muslim port officials in Alexandria from investigating too closely. The saint's remains came to Venice, and the long and ardent association of the city with St. Mark began.[244]

After the Muslims conquered most of the Iberian peninsula in the eighth century, there were several attempts by those Christians who were not within Islamic power, either in northern Spain or beyond the Pyrenees, to obtain relics from Muslim

[243] Bourdua, "Entombing the Founder."
[244] *Translatio sancti Marci*, p. 257.

Spain and bring them into the Christian world. In 858, for example, the monks of St.-Germain-des-Prés outside Paris sent a delegation to Muslim Spain, to hunt out and retrieve relics of the saints there.[245] According to the twelfth-century bishop Pelayo of Oviedo, Silo, king of Asturias (774–83), had taken a huge army to Merida and removed the remains of St. Eulalia from her tomb, along with part of her cradle, which was also regarded as a relic, and then, placing the bones in a silver shrine, he had brought them back to Asturias.[246] There were relics of Eulalia in Pelayo's cathedral in his lifetime, but, since he was a famous forger and fabricator, perhaps the story of King Silo's expedition should be seen as a plausible legend rather than literal truth.

A notable example of the transfer of saintly relics from Muslim to Christian lands is the translation of St. Isidore from Seville to Leon in December 1063.[247] This took place at a time when Christian rulers in the north of the peninsula had established a temporary ascendancy over the fragmented Muslim kingdoms of the south. Under pressure from Ferdinand I of Leon and Castile, the Muslim ruler of Seville agreed to surrender to him the remains of the early Christian martyr, St. Justa. A delegation of bishops and knights set out for Seville, but there they were told that they would have to look for the relics themselves. The head of the delegation, the bishop of Leon, suggested they undergo a three-day period of fasting and prayer. During this time he had a vision in his sleep of a venerable bishop, who told him that St. Justa was to remain in Seville but that "my body has been granted to you," and, when asked who he was, identified himself:"I am the teacher of all the Spains, Isidore, bishop of this city." The saint offering himself in this way was the famous early medieval scholar Isidore of Seville (d. 636). His tomb, when discovered, gave off a perfume that suffused the hair and beards of the Christian delegation. The relics were placed in a portable wooden chest, covered by a silken cloth which the Muslim ruler of Seville himself offered, and received a royal welcome in Leon, where they were enshrined in the newly built church of St. John the Baptist (which later came to be known as St. Isidore's). The shrine still exists (see earlier, p. 271). Thereafter the feast of the translation was observed, and the shrine became the centre of "so many and so great miracles . . . that if anyone should write them down, he would have to compose no few volumes."[248]

This account of the transfer of Isidore's remains shows many features that are commonplace in such narratives: the visionary appearance, the odour of sanctity,

[245] Aimoin of St.-Germain-des-Prés, *De translatione sanctorum martyrum Georgii monachi, Aurelii et Nathaliae.*

[246] Pelayo of Oviedo, *Historia de arcae sanctae translatione*, pp. 354–55; Fernández Conde, *El libro de los testamentos de la catedral de Oviedo*, pp. 57, 116–17, on this passage, which he regards as an interpolation by bishop Pelayo in an earlier chronicle (Madrid, BN 1513, fols. 47v–48).

[247] *Acta translationis corporis sancti Isidori*; the text was largely incorporated into the *Historia Silense* 95–102, pp. 198–204, with editorial comment on pp. 45–49. There is a later, elaborated and extended, version: *Historia translationis sancti Isidori*. See Henriet, "*Rex, lex, plebs*. Les miracles d'Isidore de Séville."

[248] For the uncertainty about the date of the feast (21, 22, or 23 December) see PL 81: 955 note; *Historia Silense*, p. 203 n. 250.

the honourable reception. There is little attempt to underline the fact that the relics were leaving territory under Muslim rule and being relocated in a Christian kingdom. The Muslim king himself recognizes Isidore's sanctity: "although an infidel," this "king of the Saracens" laments, "If I bestow Isidore on you, with whom do I remain here?" His gift of the silken cloth reinforces the impression that even the Muslims acknowledge the value of such a holy man. The point of the story is how great a saint the "royal city" of Leon is acquiring; it is not an anti-Muslim or proto-crusading narrative.

Saints were sometimes described as giving death-bed instructions about the future fate of their bodies. Severinus of Noricum, who died in 482, supposedly foresaw that the place of his burial would be devastated and abandoned, and, citing Joseph's words in Genesis, commanded, "ye shall carry up my bones from hence."[249] His body was indeed translated to Italy. Two centuries later, as St. Cuthbert lay dying on his island off the Northumbrian coast, he calmly planned the site of his shrine and then advised his monks,

> Know and remember, that if necessity forces you to choose one of two evils, I would much rather that you should depart from here, digging up my bones from the tomb and carrying them with you, and live wherever God should provide, than that you should ever agree to the wickedness of schism.[250]

In these instances, it is natural to assume that a hagiographer of a later generation, knowing that the saint's bones were indeed moved, has given a retrospective justification by attributing such an attitude to the saint. In the case of Cuthbert, however, this is difficult to argue, since his words are recorded in a work that long pre-dates the actual removal of his bones. It seems either that Cuthbert himself or his hagiographers envisaged a "schism" over the two divergent ways of calculating the date of Easter, a controversial and divisive issue in his time. In fact, what eventually led, over two centuries later, to the departure of the saint's remains from its tomb was Viking raiding. The monks of Durham, where Cuthbert's body was finally enshrined, naturally interpreted his words as a premonition of this disturbance.[251]

Viking raids were in fact a major cause of (involuntary) translations. One of the recurrent features of the Viking age was the destruction of churches and the flight of relics in the face of the threat from Norse or Danish raiders. This story of destruction and flight began with the attacks on Cuthbert's monastery of Lindisfarne in 793 and the Irish monastery of *Rechru* (either Lambay off the coast of County Dublin, or Rathlin Island off the Antrim coast) in 795. There followed a long period when the rich shrines of western Europe became the target of Viking greed and violence. Iona was another early victim. St. Columba had been praised as an "island soldier" for his life of strenuous holiness on the sea-washed retreat (earlier, p. 30), but

[249] Eugippius, *Vita Severini* 40. 5, pp. 274–76 (MGH, SRG, p. 48), with reference to Genesis 50:25.

[250] Bede, *Vita sancti Cuthberti* 39, p. 284.

[251] Symeon of Durham (attrib.), *De miraculis et translationibus sancti Cuthberti* 2 (1, pp. 234–35); Reginald of Durham, *Libellus de admirandis beati Cuthberti virtutibus* 12, pp. 16–17.

sometimes the soldiering became more literal. In 825 Vikings landed on Iona (not for the first time), and this "pagan gang of Danes" was seeking loot, especially "the precious metals within which the bones of St. Columba lay." The Irish monk Blathmac bravely refused to reveal the spot where the shrine had been hidden for safety and quickly earned the title of martyr.[252] In subsequent years there is record of Columba's relics being taken from Iona to various sites in Ireland and Scotland, and in 878 a definitive statement in the *Annals of Ulster*: "The shrine of Colum Cille (Columba) and his other relics arrived in Ireland, having been taken in flight to escape the foreigners."[253]

Monastic shrines situated on islands off the coast, like Iona, were especially vulnerable. At the island monasteries of Lindisfarne and Noirmoutier, the monks took up their precious relics (of Cuthbert and Philibert, respectively) and, after extended periods of wandering, eventually found safer inland homes, at Chester-le-Street and Tournus.[254] But the Vikings could penetrate up the rivers as well as raid the coasts, and many riverine monasteries discovered their vulnerability. Rivers like the Seine and the Loire led into the heart of Carolingian Europe. In 859 St.-Denis, on the outskirts of Paris, was affected: "the bones of the blessed martyrs Denis, Rusticus and Eleutherius, for fear of those Danes, were taken to Nogent, a town under their jurisdiction, and carefully placed in shrines."[255] Nogent is 80 kilometres (50 miles) upstream from St.-Denis. During these same Viking assaults on Paris in the mid-ninth century, the relics of St. Geneviève were likewise taken for safety from the abbey church outside the walls where they were housed to monastic estates further away from the threatened city. In 857 they were taken temporarily about 20 kilometres (12 miles) up the Seine, but subsequently they spent five whole years (858–63) at an estate in Picardy almost 80 kilometres (50 miles) from Paris.[256] They were back in Paris in time to be carried in procession to ward off the Vikings during the siege of 885–86.[257] The Rhine was another entry point. In 881 Vikings burned Cologne and Bonn and "whoever could escape from there, canons or nuns, fled to Mainz, carrying with them the treasures of the churches and the bodies of the saints." [258] The following year a threatened Viking raid on Rheims induced the ailing archbishop

[252] Walafrid Strabo, *Versus de beati Blaithmaic vita et fine*; *Annals of Ulster* s.a. 825, p. 283.

[253] *Annals of Ulster* s.a. 829, 831, 849, 878, pp. 287, 288, 309, 335. The theory of a planned division and dispersal of the relics in 849 rests on the coincidence in time between the *Annals of Ulster* statement and the claim in the so-called Scottish Chronicle that, in the very same year, Kenneth Macalpine "transferred relics of St Columba to a church he built," the latter identified with Dunkeld: Anderson, *Kings and Kingship in Early Scotland*, p. 250; *Early Sources of Scottish History* 1, pp. 279–80 n. 4; Broun and Clancy, *Spes Scotorum*, pp. 73, 105 n. 40.

[254] *Historia de Sancto Cuthberto*; Symeon of Durham, *Libellus de exordio atque procursu istius hoc est Dunhelmensis ecclesie* 2. 6, 10–13, pp. 94–104, 110–26; *Monuments de l'histoire des abbayes de Saint-Philibert* (Paris, 1905); Cartron, *Les pérégrinations de Saint-Philibert*.

[255] *Annales Bertiniani* s.a. 859, p. 52.

[256] *Miracula sanctae Genovefae post mortem*.

[257] Abbo, *Bella Parisiacae urbis* 2, line 247, p. 105.

[258] *Annales Fuldenses* s.a. 881, p. 97.

Hincmar to flee in a litter, along with "the body of St. Remigius and the ornaments of the church of Rheims," stopping only 24 kilometres (15 miles) away at Epernay on the far side of the Marne.[259]

For monastic and clerical writers of later centuries, the ravages of the Vikings and the flight of relics became "a fashionable literary theme."[260] The fury of the Northmen was a recognizable stereotype to be invoked, often to explain a gap in the recorded traditions, even if this was not due to Viking destruction. There is, however, also no doubt of the reality of the disruption caused, with many well-attested cases of the destruction of shrines or their desperate removal to safer places.[261] Many of these displacements of relics were only temporary but others proved permanent, and then often led to complex and sometime competitive relations between the site of the old shrine and the new.

Translation could also be an assertion of the possession of relics. Opening the shrine or reliquary was sometimes a response to doubters, as in 1091, for example, when the abbot of Corvey in Saxony inspected the relics of the local saint, Vitus, "since it was being doubted whether the body of the precious martyr Vitus was in our possession."[262] Exactly the same motive inspired the translation of the relics of St. Cuthbert at Durham in 1104, since some people thought that Cuthbert's relics had been removed long before.[263] Likewise, when, early in the thirteenth century, the abbot of Sens arranged for a grand public translation of the relics of St. Potencianus into a silver shrine, it was clearly the purpose of the ceremony to vindicate the monks' claim to possess the relics. Maximum publicity was achieved. The archbishop of Sens presided, in the presence of the bishop of Troyes "and a multitude of priests, clerics, monks and people of both sexes."

> And the body of St. Potencianus was exhibited above the gate of the abbey and in the church, with letters which were completely trustworthy. For the nuns of Jouarre said that it was preserved in their monastery, but on that day the contrary was proved.

The reality of the saint's presence in Sens was reinforced by the grant of an indulgence to any who came to the monastery on the day of the translation or in the following week.[264]

[259] *Annales Bertiniani* s.a. 882, p. 154.

[260] Haenens, *Les invasions normandes en Belgique*, p. 162.

[261] Felice Lifshitz, in particular, has criticized "the thesis that there was a haemorrhage of relics and clerics out of Neustria (northern France) in the face of invading Viking hordes": "The Migration of Neustrian Relics in the Viking Age," p. 176. However, even when specific dubious cases have been discounted, there remain many well-attested examples; see the cases listed by the (otherwise sceptical) Haenens, *Les invasions normandes en Belgique*, pp. 126–27, with references to his further analysis of the source material later in the volume, and the balanced discussion in Potts, "When the Saints Go Marching: Religious Connections and the Political Culture of Early Normandy."

[262] *Annales Corbeienses maiores*, p. 38 (MGH, SS 3, p. 7).

[263] Symeon of Durham (attrib.), *De miraculis et translationibus sancti Cuthberti* 7 (1, p. 248).

[264] Geoffroy de Courlon, *Le livre des reliques de l'abbaye de Saint-Pierre-le-Vif*, p. 53–54, 82.

Saints could be translated more than once. A rather extreme case is that of St. William of Norwich, whose body was moved four times in ten years: from the wood where he was found to the monks' cemetery in 1144, from the cemetery to the Chapter House in 1150, from the Chapter House to the south side of the high altar in 1151 and from there to its own chapel in 1154.[265] There are many other cases of multiple translations on a more leisurely scale. There are well documented translations of St. Bavo of Ghent in 1010 and 1058, apart from a less clearly attested migration during the time of the Viking invasions. In 1010 the reliquary was opened by a smith and the relics were then paraded around the vicinity, bringing miraculous healing; exactly the same procedure was followed in 1058, although on this occasion the bishop was also present; both translations were stimulated by doubts that some had expressed that Bavo's relics were actually in the reliquary.[266] The rebuilding of a church was also a frequent stimulus to translations, while the fragmentation of saintly bodies and the possibility of contact relics meant that translations of the same saint could occur in many different places.

Important translations were often given an annual liturgical commemoration, just like the day of a saint's death. Some of these were celebrated widely, such as the translations of St. Nicholas (9 May), St. Martin (4 July), or St. Benedict (11 July), while others were associated primarily with a particular region or a local church: Autun commemorated the translation of Rocho or Racho, a Merovingian bishop of that city, and the monastery of St.-Memmie in Châlons-sur-Marne the translation of Memmie or Memmius, its titular saint.[267] This liturgical practice had one specific attraction. While the day of a saint's death could scarcely be controlled, the day of his or her translation could. On occasion the saint's feast-day, that is, the day of his or her death, was chosen also as the day of the translation. When, in 698, the bishop of Lindisfarne was approached for permission for the translation of the body of St. Cuthbert, who had died eleven years earlier, he gave his consent and "ordered that this should be done on the day of his burial, that is, 20 March."[268] The translation of the relics of the Roman martyrs Chrysantus and Daria, brought to Münstereifel in 844, was celebrated on "25 October, that is, the day of their Passion."[269]

There are also not a few cases where a saint's feast-day in the inconvenient winter season was supplemented by a translation feast arranged for a more clement time of year. Cuthbert again provides an example, for, while his translation of 698 coincided with the day of his death, his subsequent translation fell on 4 September in a

[265] Thomas of Monmouth, *Vita sancti Willelmi Norwicensis* 1. 18–19; 3. 1; 5. 1; 6. 1, pp. 50–55, 116–25, 185–86, 220–22.

[266] *Translatio prima sancti Bavonis*; *Translatio secunda sancti Bavonis*.

[267] Leroquais, *Les bréviaires manuscrits des bibliothèques publiques de France* 1, pp. 121 (from Beaune, Bibliothèque municipale 26, a thirteenth-century Breviary from Autun), 248–49 (from Châlons-sur-Marne, Bibliothèque municipale 5 (6), a fifteenth-century Breviary from St.-Memmie).

[268] Bede, *Vita sancti Cuthberti* 42, p. 292.

[269] *Translatio Chrysanti et Dariae*, p. 375; other examples in Heinzelmann, *Translationsberichte*, p. 112 and n. 13.

warmer part of the year. Most big English churches marked this translation feast.[270] The feast-day of Margaret of Scotland was 16 November but her translation of 1250 was on 19 June; the feast of Thomas Becket was 29 December, his translation feast 7 July. The feast-day of the saintly Swedish bishop Brynolf was on 6 February, deep in the gloom of the Scandinavian winter; the celebration of his translation, which took place in 1492, was arranged for the more cheerful date of 16 August.[271]

If there were two feast-days of this kind, they would be carefully distinguished as "in summer" or "in winter." Rent might be payable "at the feast-day of St. Benedict in summer," that is, on 11 July, not the day of Benedict's death on 21 March.[272] Likewise, when reference was made to "the feast-day of the protomartyr Stephen that is celebrated in summertime," this was to distinguish the feast commemorating the discovery of the saint's bones (on 3 or 4 August) from that of his winter feast of 26 December.[273] The feast-day of St. Martin on 11 November was sometimes called "the feast-day of St. Martin in winter" or, in English and Scots, "Martinmas in winter," to distinguish it from the translation feast of 4 July, which could be correspondingly distinguished as "St. Martin's day in summer."[274] Clearly what stayed in people's minds was the season in which the feast-day was celebrated, not the technicalities of whether it commemorated a death or a translation.

The liturgy for translation feasts mirrored that for feast-days marking the saint's death and required the same kind of texts and chants, although adapted for the specific purpose of celebrating the translation. The Carolingian archbishop Hincmar of Rheims divided his Life of St. Remigius in two distinct ways: first, he indicated which parts were for public reading and which were more suited for study by the educated, marking the former passages with an asterisk; then the readings were classed into a group of nine for reading on the saint's feast-day, and a group of six for the feast of Remigius's translation (the number of readings on this occasion would be made up to nine by three homilies on the Gospels). The readings on the feast-day were to cover Remigius's life on earth, those on the feast of his translation would deal with posthumous miracles.[275]

270 Rushforth, *Saints in English Kalendars*; Wormald, ed., *English Benedictine Kalendars after A.D. 1100*; it is not clear which translation the feast of 4 September celebrated; the final move to Durham seems to be excluded by the presence of the feast in the late-ninth-century manuscript Bodleian Digby 63; David Rollason kindly provided advice on this matter.

271 Fröjmark, "The Canonization Process of Brynolf Algotsson," p. 99.

272 Stenton, "St. Benet of Holme and the Norman Conquest," p. 235; West, ed., *St. Benet of Holme* 1, p. 78, no. 137 (charter of Abbot Anselm of St. Benet at Hulme 1134–1140).

273 In festivitate itaque protomartyris Stephani, quae aestivo tempore celebratur: *Miracula sancti Girardi monachi Andegavensis* 23, p. 504.

274 "A festo S. Martini hiemalis": William of Chartres, *Vita et miracula sancti Ludovici regis Francorum* 48, p. 568; for "Martinmas in winter," see OED, s.v. "Martinmas" 1b, with examples from 1389 onwards, mostly Scottish; Grotefend, *Zeitrechnung des deutschen Mittelatters und der Neuzeit* 1, p. 119, with examples from 1293 and 1302 of "sent Martynsdach in die somer" and "sente Martinusdach die compt in den somer."

275 Hincmar of Rheims, *Vita Remigii episcopi Remensis*, proem, pp. 258–59.

A very full account of a translation, illustrating many aspects of the ritual, occurs in the *Deeds of the Abbots of St.-Trond*.[276] St.-Trond (Sint-Truiden) was an important abbey, 35 kilometres (21 miles) north-west of Liège, and its abbot in the middle of the twelfth century was the energetic Wiricius. He had been saving up money to finance the expedition to Italy that he had been commanded to undertake in support of the emperor Frederick Barbarossa in his war with the Italian cities, but the collapse of Frederick's campaign in 1167 meant he did not go and could spend the money in a "better and more noble" way, reconstructing the chapel that sheltered the tombs of St. Trond and St. Eucherius, the abbey's chief saints. As the foundations were being dug, an unexpected tomb turned up. This was interpreted as the grave of the martyr Libertus, who, according to "ancient opinion," was buried in the area. Large amounts of blood in the tomb confirmed this identification, and the surviving remains (a few of the larger bones, ashes, the brain) were reverently enshrined, while the bells rang and crowds assembled. Continuing their excavations, after turning up another unsuspected martyr, the monks and their workmen eventually found the bones of Trond and Eucherius, in separate shrines but in a single tomb. As word spread, crowds gathered and talk began about how the remains should be translated. Abbot Wiricus, who had originally intended to adorn the graves of Trond and Eucherius more elaborately rather than move them, consulted Rudolf, bishop of Liège, and his chief clergy, who rejoiced "that God had predestined the translation of such great fathers for their own time."

On the day of the translation ceremony, the bishop came to the abbey, where a huge crowd of high clergy, nobles and "an innumerable multitude of people of both sexes" had assembled, and reverently raised the remains of the two saints, placing them in a reliquary of gold and silver, "in the middle of the monastery, for the people to look at." He then celebrated the Mass of the two saints, and commanded that the day of their translation be henceforth celebrated by the local people. On a subsequent day, the relics were taken in procession around the town, in the especial hope that they would protect it against the fires that had done great damage in the region that year. Once the work on the new chapel was completed, the relics were solemnly enshrined there, but in the meantime they were accessible in the middle of the monastery to crowds coming there "from far and wide." Amongst them was a Norman knight, who wore an iron band around his arm as a penance. Coming to the shrine, he prayed to be released. One of the priests in the church saw the bright figure of a venerable cleric appear in the church and strike the iron band with his staff. It immediately broke in two and fell to the ground. The crowds rejoiced, the bells rang, and the monks sang the *Te Deum*. This miracle is the final ingredient in this very typical translation story, with its trajectory from the semi-archaeological investigations of the tombs to the great public ceremonies, its stress on the crowds and the noisy rejoicing, and the parts played, in different ways, by the bishop, the liturgical commemorations and the gold and silver of the reliquaries.

[276] *Gesta abbatum Trudonensium*, pp. 351–54.

8.5. An impression of a relic procession: the Children of Israel leaving Egypt (Psalm 113), English, c. 1130. St. Albans Psalter. Dombibliothek Hildesheim, HS St. God 1 (Property of the Basilica of St. Godehard, Hildesheim).

Relic Processions

When relics became portable, this meant that they could be taken out of the church that normally housed them, either as part of a regular ritual or in response to a sudden emergency or necessity. Typically this involved a procession, in which clergy and often the local populace participated (figure 8.5).

The saint's feast-day was a natural occasion for the relics to be borne in procession. A woman seeking a cure from St. Bertilia, the local saint of Maroeuil in Artois, "was present on the solemn day of St. Bertilia's passing," and took advantage of the chance to kiss her shrine "when the holy body of St. Bertilia was carried in solemn procession, as is the custom."[277] The annual procession was such a common practice that general rules were made about how it should be conducted. The Third Council of Braga in 675 approved the old custom that "on feast-days deacons, not bishops, bear on their shoulders the ark of the Lord with the relics," although conceding that, if the bishop insisted on carrying them, he should proceed on foot.[278] Hungarian legislation ruled that relics should only be carried on such occasions "by a good and religious clerk."[279]

A fourteenth-century account from the town of Temse (in modern Belgium, on the river Scheldt) conveys the noise, the crowds and some of the fun of such annual processions:

> It has been the custom since ancient times every year on the Wednesday after Pentecost to carry the shrine of the holy virgin Amalberga, with her relics and those of other saints, around the boundaries of the town of Temse. All the clergy and nobles of the town, along with the common people of the town and neighbouring towns, the citizens of Temse barefoot and fasting, go in a circuit around the town with reverence and great devotion, following the bearers of the holy shrine. Also present are clowns and other jesters, actors, musicians, trumpeters, drummers, fiddlers, harpers, and many others who praiseworthily desire to play every kind of musical instrument to the praise and glory of the blessed virgin Amalberga.[280]

The custom at Temse was evidently a form of the "beating of the bounds" familiar in England as a regular assertion of the parish boundaries. The procession also brought together all levels of society in a festive atmosphere, and, being on the Wednesday after Pentecost, coincided with one of the so-called Ember Days, which the Church prescribed for prayer and fasting. The ceremony would always fall in the period 13 May to 16 June, so good weather was more likely, and blossom, green shoots and newborn animals would form a cheerful backdrop.

These were predictable annual processions, but it was also the case that relics might be taken out "when some necessity urged it."[281] In 959, when a strange and frightening disease threatened the people of Artois, they sought the shrines of their "great patrons," St. Omer and St. Bertin, which were located in two sister churches about half a mile (0.8 km) apart.[282] Their bishop declared a day of prayer and fast-

[277] *Miracula sanctae Bertiliæ* 3. 21, p. 1118.
[278] *Concilios visigóticos e hispano-romanos*, no. 30, p. 8 (cl. 5) (PL 84: 589).
[279] *The Laws of the Medieval Kingdom of Hungary* 1, p. 30 (Laws of Coloman 69).
[280] *Miracula Amelbergae virginis* 2, p. 105.
[281] Ulric of Cluny, *Antiquiores consuetudines Cluniacensis monasterii* 3. 15, col. 758.
[282] Folcwin, *Gesta abbatum S. Bertini Sithiensium* 109, p. 632.

ing for 22 January, and on that day "a countless number of people" assembled. The bishop raised up the shrine of St. Omer and carried it, accompanied by the weeping crowds, to the church of St. Bertin, where, after prayers, he then raised up the shrine of St. Bertin, "that devout protector of his people in need," along with the reliquaries of the other saints whose relics were in the church, Riquier and Valery. Bearing the shrines of all four saints, the bishop and people then set out back to the church of St. Omer. Along the way, the bishop preached, and the local castellan was moved to grant one of his estates to St. Bertin, while his wife offered two pieces of her golden jewellery. Coming to the church of St. Omer, the four shrines were placed on a shelf above the entrance and the people filed in beneath them. There they spent the night, before, next day, all the shrines were returned to their original locations. The itinerary had not been a long one, but it had provided the setting for group action, expression of emotion, generous and spontaneous gifts to the saint, and ultimately, it appears, security from danger.

The purposes of such relic processions could be very various. They were undertaken in response to Viking invasion: a law of Ethelred the Unready, issued "when the great army came to the country," orders penitential assemblies in church, then "all shall go out with the relics."[283] While William of Normandy was awaiting a favourable wind for his invasion of England in 1066, he had the body of the local saint, Valery, brought out of the church: "he fought with holy prayers, even bringing the body of Valery, the confessor most acceptable to God, outside the church, against an unfavourable and for a favourable wind."[284] The reliquary of St. Oswald of Worcester showed especial versatility: it was taken out to defend against enemy attack, fire and drought; in 1390 it was "carried out in time of great dryness" and in 1437 as a remedy against "continual rain."[285]

An excursion of the relics outside the church was also necessary when ecclesiastical communities brought their reliquaries together for practical and ritual purposes. Assemblies of relics in this way might mark the dedication of a major church. An example is provided by the dedication of the monastic church of Hasnon in northern France in 1070.[286] On this occasion the relics of 26 saints were brought together from the surrounding abbeys (see map 2).

A total of twenty-one religious communities participated in this great assembly of the saints (several brought relics of more than one saint). Most were within 30 miles of Hasnon, but a few, like Bruges, Bergues and St.-Omer, were more than 50 miles distant, and the journey must have been a weighty undertaking. Participants came from several dioceses and from both sides of the political boundary dividing the kingdom of France from the Holy Roman Empire. The saints represented were

[283] Liebermann, *Die Gesetze der Angelsachsen* 1, p. 262: *gan ealle út mid halidome* (VII Aethelred 2. 1); the exact year cannot be ascertained.

[284] William of Poitiers, *Gesta Guillelmi ducis Normannorum* 2. 6, p. 110.

[285] Nilson, *Cathedral Shrines of Medieval England*, p. 42.

[286] Sigebert of Gembloux, *Chronica: Auctarium Hasnoniense*; Tomellus, *Historia monasterii Hasnoniensis*, p. 157; Bozóky, "La politique des reliques des premiers comtes de Flandre," p. 273.

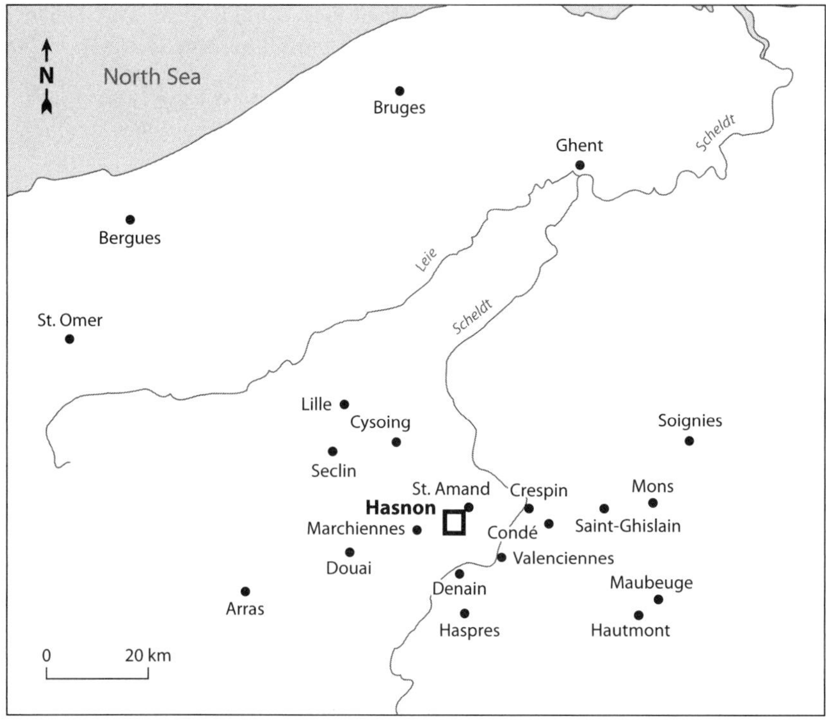

MAP 2.

Assembly of relics at the dedication of Hasnon, 1070; dots indicate churches that sent their relics for this occasion.

overwhelmingly abbots and bishops of the Merovingian period, such as Vedast, bishop of Arras (d. c. 540), Amand (d. c. 680), founder of the monastery subsequently named after him, or Winnoc (d. c. 717), whose relics had been brought to Bergues in 900 by Baldwin II of Flanders as part of his programme of territorial expansion, but there were also a few early martyrs. Six of the twenty-six were female, all of them seventh-century abbesses and nuns. On this occasion the procession of dozens of reliquaries, with the accompanying monks in their vestments, would have been a vivid visual embodiment of the rich pattern of local sanctity in Flanders, Hainault and Artois.

One of the more dramatic settings in which relics were brought together was provided by the councils of the so-called Peace of God movement, large gatherings dedicated to establishing protection for the Church and the defenceless through oaths and ecclesiastical sanctions.[287] These councils began in the south of France in the

[287] Hoffmann, *Gottesfriede und Treuga Dei* (esp. index s.v. "Reliquien"); Cowdrey, "The Peace and Truce of God in the Eleventh Century"; Landes and Head, eds., *The Peace of God*.

late tenth century, and then spread throughout France and beyond. The monastic chronicler Raoul Glaber provides a classic description, under the year 1033:

> At that time there first began in Aquitaine gatherings of councils, assembled from the whole people by the bishops, abbots and other devout men of monastic life; to these many bodies of the saints were also brought, and countless containers of holy relics . . . it was proclaimed throughout all the dioceses that councils should be celebrated in appointed places by the bishops and nobles of the whole country, to deal with renewing peace and instituting the holy faith. When all the people heard this, they came happily, high, middling and low, ready to obey whatever the pastors of the Church commanded . . . all of them burned with such ardour that, as the bishops raised their croziers to heaven, they spread out their hands to God and cried with one voice, "Peace! Peace! Peace!"[288]

The presence of relics was meant to have an intimidating effect on wrongdoers. At the Peace councils held in Burgundy in the early 1020s "innumerable relics of the saints from almost the whole region" were brought together.[289] At one of these, in Héry in 1024, held as a response to "the greedy plundering of the horsemen," the leading churchmen assembled with their relics,

> so that if the lovers of wickedness were not willing to be pacified through the coercion of earthly powers, they might at least accept the establishment of peace through fear of God and his saints, whom they could see present and in some sense awaiting them.[290]

At Bourges in 1038 an oath was taken to oppose plunderers and looters, and this was sworn on the relics of St. Stephen.[291] The relics of the saints thus played a central part in this important movement.

One purpose for which relics were taken on tour was to raise money.[292] A French prior observed "as often as a church suffers some terrible affliction, that community takes its relics on a tour, so that it may recover from that distress through the gifts and offerings of the faithful."[293] Such "relic-quests" are recorded in some numbers from the mid-eleventh century, although they are not without distant precedents. In the 550s a miraculous image of Christ was carried "on a circular progress through the cities" to raise funds for rebuilding the church of Diyabudin (probably in the

[288] Rodulfus Glaber, *Historiarum libri quinque* 4. 5. 14–16, pp. 194–96.

[289] *Gesta pontificum Autissiodorensium* 49 (1, p. 251).

[290] *Miracula sancti Veroli* 2. 6, p. 385.

[291] *Miracula sancti Benedicti* 5. 2, p. 194.

[292] Héliot and Chastang, "Quêtes et voyages des reliques"; Hermann-Mascard, *Les reliques des saints*, pp. 296–312; Sigal, "Les voyages de reliques"; Kaiser, "Quêtes itinérantes avec des reliques pour financer la construction des églises."

[293] *Miracula Marculphi anno MCI facta Peronæ*, p. 534.

Pontus south of the Black Sea).[294] This purpose—collecting for a building fund—was the most common reason for taking relics from their usual home and undertaking a journey, long or short, with them. The itinerary might be limited to the local dioceses, but it could be far more ambitious: the monks of Laon took their relics as far as Cornwall, a trip of over 750 kilometres (466 miles), although they then found themselves embroiled with the locals when they expressed doubt that King Arthur was still alive.[295] The link between fund-raising for building work and the relic tour could be quite explicit. In 1165 a shrine of the Virgin Mary was taken out of the church of Cambrai "since there was a shortage of money for the various workers repairing the church."[296] Indeed, the possibility of a fund-raising tour was so accepted that it might even find a place in the written rules of the church. "If it should so happen that the reliquary has to be carried to remote parts of the diocese to obtain offerings" begins one of the twelfth-century statutes of Lichfield cathedral.[297]

In 1488 the relics from the collection in St. Stephen's, Dijon, were inventoried prior to being taken out on a fund-raising tour.[298] This had been made a pressing necessity by the collapse of the bell-tower, bringing down with it much of the roof and walls of the church. To remedy this "mournful ruin," the church's collection, including arm-reliquaries, head-reliquaries, silver images and dozens of small relics, was entrusted to two "special representatives and exhibitors," whose task was to raise contributions to the building fund from the faithful. The display of the relics was a crucial psychological tactic. Its purpose was clear:

> so that the faithful might be eager to give and bestow their offerings more fervently and freely for such a pious and saving task and stretch out helping hands, when they feel that they can be helped by the patronage and prayers of so many and such great saints, whose holy relics they can see with their own eyes.

The monks or clergy who went out with their relics in this way regarded the journey as a triumphant procession. Reporting the relic tour of the monks of Lobbes in the spring of 1060, one of their number expressed this sense of power and renewal.[299] War and neglect, he explained, had ravaged the church of Lobbes and its estates. Now, with the blessing of both the secular rulers and the local bishop, the monks took up the bones of their saint, Ursmar, "to redeem his own and ward off the downfall of his property." His power was many sided: "No attack of demons could

[294] *The Syriac Chronicle known as that of Zachariah of Mitylene* 12. 4, pp. 320–21.

[295] Hermann of Laon, *De miraculis sanctae Mariae Laudunensis* 2. 15–16, col. 983.

[296] Lambert of Wattrelos, *Annales Cameracenses*, p. 537, s.a. 1165.

[297] Si contingat quod feretrum debeat per aliquas partes remotas diocesis ad elemosinas colligendas deportari: "Lichfield Statutes," in *Statutes of Lincoln Cathedral* 2, pp. 11–25, at p. 22.

[298] Durnecker, "Les reliques de Saint-Etienne de Dijon," pp. 454–56 (annexe 2, from Archives départmentales de la Cote-d'Or, G 169, no. 14).

[299] *Historia miraculorum sancti Ursmari in circumlatione per Flandriam* (extensive excerpts in MGH, SS 15/2, pp. 837–42); on the monks' peacemaking, see Koziol, "Monks, Feuds, and the Making of Peace in Eleventh-Century Flanders."

succeed in his presence, no dispute among adversaries could reign unchecked, no painful disease could prevail." A pestilence affecting the population stopped at once "wherever the holy confessor passed among them on his progress." The people of Lille erected a cross on the spot outside their town where the holy body had rested, and this later proved to have acquired healing powers of its own. Ursmar protected a beautiful girl from her wicked step-mother ("a type of woman usually very bad"), pacified or punished the feuding knights of Flanders, brought rain to parched fields, and healed a monk of toothache. Finally, after a circuit of hundreds of miles, the monks returned to their monastery of Lobbes, and the body of St. Ursmar "was put back in his place."

One of the more inventive relic quests took place in Paris in 1445, when the reliquary of St. Quentin was carried around the churches of the city, where those in charge of the relics would set up a large weighing-beam and then weigh people on it, reciting the names of saints, and those who were weighed would then ransom themselves with corn or money.[300] It was noted that the "questers" obtained a fine haul of money on this occasion.

Even if they did not form the main focus of a procession, relics might still be a significant part of it. The grand processions characteristic of the great cities of later medieval Italy saw troops of clergy, guildsmen, elaborate floats and displays and dramatic enactments, but also relics being marched past. The enthusiastic abbot, Augustine di Portico, visiting Florence on the occasion of its most important public procession, St. John's day, in 1452 or 1453, wrote how crowded the streets were, what fine clothes he saw ("especially on the ladies"), and reported on the groups in the parade, the members of the hospitals with their crosses, banners and relics, Franciscan tertiaries with their beautiful vestments and relics, the Camoldolensian Order (of which Augustine was a member) with their banner, vestments and relics, as well as the amazing tableaux vivants of biblical scenes.[301] Clearly the relics were not the main attraction for the starry-eyed visitor, but they were worthy of note, and gave a distinctive identity to the groups passing by.

Relics might also be moved a much shorter distance, perhaps only to another part of the church, in order to display them to pilgrims and devotees. In 1388, for example, the monks of Limoges took the head of St. Martial out of its reliquary "so that it should be exposed uncovered to all pilgrims."[302] Sometimes there was a regular exhibition of relics at a festival especially for that purpose.[303] The visiting Metz burgess, Philippe de Vigneulles, gives a lively account of such a festival at Maastricht in 1510. He describes arriving at

> Maastricht in Germany, which is one of the most beautiful and finest big towns one could find, where they exhibit the treasures to be described. First

[300] *Journal d'un bourgeois de Paris*, p. 424.
[301] Delcorno Branca, "Un camaldolese alla festa di S. Giovanni," pp. 9–11.
[302] *Miracula sancti Martialis anno 1388 patrata*, miracle 60, p. 438.
[303] Hermann-Mascard, *Les reliques des saints*, pp. 206–16; Kühne, *Ostensio Reliquiarum*.

> they exhibit the head of St. Servatius, his pilgrim staff, his cross, his chalice and his paten, and two or three worthy cloths, that is, a cloth which the angels brought from heaven, with others, a second cross that St. Luke gave to Our Lady and which she bore between her breasts for many years, and the arm of St. Thomas and his key, which was sent to him from heaven, as they say, and a drinking vessel that was sent to him from heaven, and one does not know what stone it is made of and it is of many colours. We arrived at the town just as they exhibited these treasures, for they exhibit them only once a day during the time of indulgence, and they exhibit them on walkways with openings above the choir of the great church in the manner and way they do at Aachen, and they preach before each treasure they exhibit. And there in the great square below, behind the choir, there were so many people it was marvellous, and then they rang the bells, the town servants blew their trumpets near to the treasures and relics and all the people blew their horns, which is a marvellous thing to hear and see, and there was scarcely anyone who did not have tears come to their eyes.[304]

Philippe's account is particularly valuable since it comes from a visiting layman, and hence his enthusiastic tone is independent of the clergy of Maastricht, who would naturally wish to stress the power and attractiveness of their relics.

In the later Middle Ages the use of woodcuts offered a new way of advertising these periodic exhibitions. A single sheet from the early sixteenth century, beginning with the words, "These relics are exhibited in the church of Tongres every seven years," has illustrations of eighteen reliquaries containing prestigious relics: the arm of St. Maternus, first bishop of Tongres, in an arm-shaped reliquary, and his pastoral staff; the arm of St. Lawrence, also in an arm-shaped reliquary; relics of St. Ursula in a cylindrical reliquary, and the heads of two of her companions in head-shaped reliquaries; some of the bones of St. Sebastian, in a reliquary in the shape of the saint tied to a column and shot with arrows; the veil and belt of Elizabeth of Thuringia; the arm of St. Christopher inside a statue of the saint carrying the Christ child; milk of the Virgin Mary inside a statue of the Virgin and child; her veil in a rectangular reliquary; the finger of John the Baptist inside a statue of the saint; two teeth of St. Peter inside a statue of the saint; relics of Andrew, Stephen, and Servatius inside a monstrance; the jaw of St. Matthias inside a statue of the saint; a cross containing drops of Jesus' blood; part of the True Cross in a rectangular reliquary; a cross containing manna, a thorn from the crown of thorns, and a fragment of Christ's robe.[305] The accompanying text explains when the relics are exhibited and the extent of the indulgences that can be gained.

[304] Vigneulles, *Mémoires*, p. 173. On the Maastricht exhibition of relics, see Kühne, *Ostensio Reliquiarum*, pp. 208–27.

[305] BL, C. 18. E. 2. (118): "Iste reliquie ostenduntur in ecclesia Tungrensi."

CHAPTER 8

Gift, Sale, and Theft

Relics were goods—moveable property—and might circulate, through gift, sale, or theft.[306] To give a relic, a powerful and precious object, was an act of friendship. It could seal an alliance, signify a relationship, or even be a call for help, as in the 920s, when Charles the Simple, king of the West Franks (roughly, France), was imprisoned by his own nobles. Seeking the aid of Henry I, king of the East Franks (roughly, Germany), Charles managed to send to him an envoy, who spoke effusively of Charles's admiration for Henry. As a token of his good faith, he produced from his cloak the hand of St. Denis, encrusted with jewels. "Have this token of perpetual alliance," he said, "and of a distant love."[307] Henry never, in fact, came riding to Charles's rescue, but offering the jewelled hand was a recognizable gesture in the exchanges between the rulers of Christendom. The Byzantines, who were accomplished diplomats, used relic gifts constantly as an instrument in their diplomacy, although in their case it was relics of Christ, notably fragments of the Cross, that were the most prized of their gifts, rather than relics of the saints.[308]

Local loyalties also played a part in the acquisition and dissemination of relics. During the First Crusade the eastern Christians gave to Ilger Bigod, a Norman knight, twelve hairs of the Virgin Mary. On his return to France, he divided these among several churches to which he felt a devotion: two to the church of Rouen, two to the monastery of St.-Ouen, two to the monastery of Bec, and so on. A kinsman of his at Chartres and his friend Anselm, archbishop of Canterbury, also obtained two. Ilger explained to Anselm:

> I should not have dared to take these hairs, had I not been moved to do so by love of this my native land where I was born and brought up. I hoped some day to come back here and with these to glorify my country.[309]

The links established between Normandy and southern Italy in the eleventh century, as Normans created their own lordships in this fragmented political landscape, bore fruit in the transmission of relics, like the tooth of St. Nicholas mentioned earlier (p. 243), brought by the Norman knight William Pantulf from Bari to his priory of Noron near Falaise.[310]

Relics that were personal property could be bequeathed. In his will, drawn up in 1218, the Holy Roman Emperor Otto IV bequeathed "all the relics which our father had and we have" to the cathedral church of Brunswick, his chief town, except for a tooth of John the Baptist that belonged with the imperial insignia, and should be

[306] Geary, "Sacred Commodities."

[307] Widukind of Corvey, *Res gestae saxonicae* 1. 33, p. 64.

[308] Klein, "Eastern Objects and Western Desires: Relics and Reliquaries between Byzantium and the West."

[309] Eadmer, *Historia novorum*, pp. 179–81; Orderic Vitalis, *Historia ecclesiastica* 9. 15 (5, p. 170).

[310] Orderic Vitalis, *Historia ecclesiastica* 5. 16, 7. 13 (3, p. 162; 4, p. 72); for general comment, Chibnall, "The Translation of the Relics of St Nicholas and Norman Historical Tradition."

transmitted to the next emperor.[311] William Haute of Bishopsbourne, an important landowner in Kent, who died in 1462, bequeathed several relics in his will: his parish church received a piece of the stone on which Gabriel had stood when announcing the birth of Jesus to the Virgin Mary, which was, appropriately, to be used as the base of a statue of the Virgin; nearby Waltham church received bones of St. Bartholomew; while the Austin friars of Canterbury, in whose church William desired to be buried, received a piece of St. Catherine's hair shirt and one of St. Nicholas's bones, along with the reversionary right to all the rest of William's relics after his eldest son's death.[312]

Gifts of relics were meant to be freely given. Buying and selling relics was often disapproved of, or even legislated against. Roman imperial legislation of the 380s asserted unambiguously "let no one put up for sale or purchase a martyr."[313] Not long after that, St. Augustine condemned those who "offer for sale pieces of the martyrs."[314] Clearly, already by this time, "the relic had become an article of commerce."[315] The Roman Law prohibition was echoed by the Norman kings of Sicily in the twelfth century: "we permit no one to sell or buy relics of the martyrs or of any of the saints."[316] The Fourth Lateran Council of 1215 decreed that relics "should not be exposed for sale," and this ruling passed into the general law of the Church.[317]

Despite this legislation, relics clearly were bought and sold. A good example of both the buying and selling of relics, and their donation as gifts, is provided by the activities of the Anglo-Saxon king Athelstan (924–39). Soon after his accession he is reported to have set about assembling a relic collection:

> He then sent honest, discerning men over the sea, and they travelled as widely as they could travel, and with his treasure they purchased the most precious treasures which might ever yet be purchased on this earth, which was the greatest of relic-collections, gathered far and wide from every place.[318]

Having purchased these relics, the king was now ready to give some of them away to favoured churches. One third went to Exeter. Relics of St. Samson were given to the king's new foundation of Milton Abbas. Westminster also claimed that many of its relics had come from Athelstan. Athelstan's taste for relics was well known. Seeking his favour and support, the prior of Dol sent to the king the relics of several saints, "which we know are dearer to you than any worldly wealth." Amongst them were relics of Paternus of Avranches, which Athelstan then donated in turn to the abbey

[311] *Constitutiones et acta publica imperatorum et regum* 2, no. 42, p. 52.

[312] *The History of Parliament: The House of Commons 1386–1421* 3, p. 327 (L. S. Woodger).

[313] Humatum corpus nemo ad alterum locum transferat; nemo martyrem distrahat, nemo mercetur: *Codex Theodosianus* 9. 17. 7 (386), p. 466.

[314] Augustine, *De opere monachorum* 28. 36, p. 585 (PL 40: 575).

[315] Saxer, *Morts, martyrs, reliques*, p. 244.

[316] Monti, "Il testo e la storia esterna delle assisse normanne," p. 119 (Assises attributed to Roger II, 5).

[317] *Conciliorum oecumenicorum decreta*, p. 263 (cl. 62); *Decretales Gregorii IX*, 3. 45. 2, *Quum ex eo*, col. 650.

[318] Conner, *Anglo-Saxon Exeter*, p. 177, from the Old English Exeter relic list (text, p. 176).

of Malmesbury, commissioning a gilded shrine for them. When Hugh the Great, duke of the Franks, sent an embassy to request the hand of Athelstan's sister, he was sure to include spectacular relics amongst the gifts the envoys brought. Athelstan was even accompanied to the grave by "the relics of the saints that he had purchased from Brittany."[319]

Since relics were valuable and portable, they could be stolen.[320] An example occurs as early as the 370s, when the body of St. Hilarion, who had died and been buried in Cyprus, was stolen by one of the monks from his old monastery of Majuma near Gaza and re-enshrined there. This was a risky business. The monk had to invent a story to throw off suspicion and even then "was in great danger of his life." Years later there was still "amazing contention between the people of Palestine and the people of Cyprus" over Hilarion's legacy.[321] Interminable disputes of this kind, and the stealing of saintly remains that lay behind them, were recurrent features of the cult of the saints. Some famous thefts, like those of the bones of St. Mark, taken from Alexandria to Venice, or those of St. Nicholas, brought from Myra to Bari, involved bringing the saint from Muslim to Christian lands, but the majority were thefts by Christians from Christians. They were genuinely clandestine operations, often undertaken at night. In the tenth century a nocturnal raid on the tomb of St. Wenceslas, in which the saint's own sister was involved, secured his jawbone for the thieves.[322] In 1070, while returning from Rome to Germany, archbishop Anno of Cologne stopped at St.-Maurice-en-Valais, bribed the custodian of the church, and, "in the secret of the night," entered it with a few companions and removed the body of St. Innocent and the head of St. Vitalis, two martyred companions of St. Maurice. Then, "with Christ guiding his steps," he made his way back to Cologne and enshrined the relics in his favourite monastery of Siegburg.[323] The monks of Conques, eager to obtain the body of St. Foy from the clergy of Agen, even planted a "sleeper" in Agen, a secret agent who did his job so well that he was even appointed custodian of the church, something that obviously made his job of stealing the relics much easier.[324]

Theft of relics was not impious but pious. One ninth-century abbot of Figeac in Aquitaine was praised because "always his custom was to take away the bodies of the saints, from whatever place, through secret deceits, and to bring them to the places over which he presided." Desiring to obtain the body of St. Bibianus (or Vivianus) from nearby Saintes, "he sent out scouts and took away the holy body of the great

[319] William of Malmesbury, *Gesta pontificum Anglorum* 2. 85; 5. 247–49, pp. 292, 594–98; idem, *Gesta regum Anglorum* 2. 135, 140, pp. 218–20, 228; Flete, *The History of Westminster Abbey*, pp. 69, 70, 72 (not entirely consistent with p. 52). Abingdon also claimed to have received relics from Athelstan: *Historia Ecclesie Abbendonensis* 1, p. 282.

[320] Hermann-Mascard, *Les reliques des saints*, pp. 364–402; Geary, *Furta sacra*.

[321] Jerome, *Vita Hilarionis* 32. 6–7, p. 296 (PL 23: 52–54).

[322] Christian, *Vita et passio sancti Wenceslai et sancte Ludmile* 10, pp. 96–98.

[323] *Vita Annonis* 1. 33, pp. 480–81.

[324] *Translatio altera sanctae Fidis*.

bishop by a clandestine trick." These men went armed with metal wedges to open up the tomb and one of them simulated demonic possession in order to enter the church without arousing suspicion.[325] None of this trickery was concealed by the monk of Figeac recording these events, but, instead, emphasized. Stealing relics in such a way could be called "a praiseworthy theft," or even "a happy sacrilege."[326]

The monks and clerics who wrote about relic thefts were interested in justifying their own church's possession of the stolen relics. One way of doing this was to claim that the saint was not receiving due honour in his or her previous location. The saint might attest to this neglect in person, as in the (probably much later) account of how the great Saxon noblewoman Gertrude of Brunswick stole the relics of St. Auctor from Trier and placed them in the church of St. Giles she founded at Brunswick in 1115. The story begins with the saint himself appearing to Gertrude.[327] He explained who he was and complained that "little or no reverence and honour is shown to me" in Trier. He had decided that his body, "buried at Trier with so little care shown to it," should be brought to Brunswick. Calming Gertrude's doubts, Auctor explained that the God who guided the Magi by a star could certainly help her find his tomb in Trier, but he assisted by describing its position in the monastic church where it was located. Next day, after taking counsel with her advisors, Gertrude assembled her retinue—"an impressive company of knights and an entourage of beautiful ladies-in-waiting"—and set off for Trier. She arrived at the monastery where Auctor was buried when the monks were just getting ready for their midday meal. The guardian was doing the rounds of the church to make sure no thief was lurking there, just as the Customary of Becket's Shrine advised (p. 259, earlier), but he had no suspicions about "that noble crowd of unexpected thieves," Gertrude and her train.

After she had prayed in the church, she went on a tour with the guardian, who pointed out to her the tombs of the saints, including that of Auctor, which allowed Gertrude not only to identify the tomb but also to ask the date of his feast-day (it was 20 August). As the dinner bell rang insistently, Gertrude was at last able to persuade the guardian to go off to the refectory, leaving her and her followers alone in the church. The moment he left, they barred the door, took out the tools they had been carrying and raised the stone lid of Auctor's tomb. There they found not only Auctor's remains, but also the relics of many other saints. Quickly loading these on their horses, they pushed back the lid of the coffin into its original position, removed all the handbells and the clappers from the big bells, so that the monks could not sound the alarm, and rode off "swifter than eagles." Pursuit was in vain. Auctor ended up in Brunswick, as he had wished. There is still an "Auctor Street" in the town—parallel to "Gertrude Street."

One of the more unusual accounts of a relic theft is that describing how St. Petroc's relics were stolen in 1177. It is unusual because it is written not by the thieves

[325] *Translatio et miracula sancti Viviani*, pp. 258–59.

[326] Furto laudabili: Rather of Verona, *Translatio sancti Metronis* 3, p. 14 (PL 136, col. 455); felix sacrilegium: *Translatio altera sanctae Fidis* 2. 16, p. 298.

[327] *Translatio sancti Auctoris episcopi Trevirensis.*

but by the victims. Normally it was the triumphant new possessors who described how they had come by their relics, but, in this case, it was the angry canons of Bodmin, Cornwall, where Petroc's remains lay, who recounted with indignation the theft of the relics of the saint and their efforts, eventually successful, to recover them.[328] The thief was one of their own, a canon of Bodmin named Martin, who had a grudge because he had first been put in charge of one of the manors belonging to the canons (Newton St. Petrock in Devon) but then later been recalled. Taking Petroc's remains from their reliquary, Martin made his way to Brittany and came to the abbey of St.-Méen, west of Rennes. Here he received hospitality, but, while he was at dinner, the serving boys found Petroc's bones in his bag and played around with them. Immediately their hands swelled up and their arms became rigid. When the monks of St.-Méen were alerted to this, Martin had to confess what was in the bag. The abbot of St.-Méen responded not to the theft but to the presence of these holy relics: "he ordered a festive procession, with hymns and canticles, to bring the relics solemnly from the guest rooms to the church."

The presence of the relics was now public knowledge. News of their arrival in Brittany spread, as Martin tried to get the support of Roland of Dinan, the representative of Henry II of England, overlord of Brittany, and miracles occurred at St.-Méen, including the cure of the paralyzed serving boys. But this also alerted the canons of Bodmin to their loss; they opened the reliquary and found it empty; and immediately launched a vigorous campaign to recover the relics. One of the canons was sent to Brittany, and the help was enlisted of some influential men: the bishop of Exeter (in whose diocese Bodmin lay), the Justiciar, and the Keeper of the King's Seal. Henry II responded to this powerful lobbying, issued letters commanding the return of the relics and sent an envoy to accompany the prior of Bodmin to Brittany to recover them. The Keeper of the King's Seal acquired a beautiful ivory box to house them (this still exists).[329] In Brittany, the prior met up with many important protagonists, including the canon who had been sent earlier, Roland of Dinan and a helpful relative of the Keeper of the Seal, and recovered the relics, which fitted perfectly into the ivory box. On their return journey through England, Henry II himself took the opportunity to revere the relics, and, tactfully, arranged for three joints and a rib to be sent to St.-Méen as a friendly gesture. Finally, the relics were brought back to Bodmin in triumphal procession. The bishop of Exeter took the bones out, one by one, to show them to the assembled crowds, then enshrined the head in the ivory box and the remaining relics in a gilt box, and granted an indulgence for all who came to revere them at that time or at future anniversaries of these transactions.

[328] Robert of Tawton, *De reliquiarum furto*; for comment, Jankulak, *The Medieval Cult of St Petroc*, pp. 153–201. Another account of this type, describing the recovery of stolen relics, is edited and discussed in Dolbeau, "Un vol de reliques."

[329] Pinder-Wilson and Brooke, "The Reliquary of St Petroc."

The Year 1204

The most breath-taking relic theft of the Middle Ages concerns not a single saint or a single church but an entire city. In 1204 Constantinople, capital of the Byzantine Empire, was seized and sacked by an army of western Crusaders, who had been diverted from their initial goal, Muslim Egypt, partly by the ambitions of the Venetians, who provided their shipping, and at first with the pretext of supporting a Byzantine claimant to the imperial throne. Eventually the crusaders and Venetians seized the city for themselves, plundered it, and set up a Latin, that is, western Catholic, empire, which lasted until 1261. Constantinople had been acquiring relics ever since the fourth century, and this treasury of holy objects now became the prey of pious and greedy western clergy and nobles.

The most vivid portrait of an excitable western relic hunter during the sack of Constantinople comes from the pen of the German Cistercian monk, Gunther of Pairis, who describes how his abbot, Martin, came to the church of Christ Pantocrator, and bullied a Greek priest there into revealing where the relics were kept. When the relic chest was opened, Martin thrust in both hands and grabbed what he could, piling up the booty in the folds of his habit, and then quickly made his way back to his ship. On the way other crusaders asked him how he had done. "We have done well," he replied. And he had. The relics that he eventually brought back with him to his monastery of Pairis in Alsace comprised some of Christ's blood, a portion of the cross on which he was crucified, milk of the Virgin Mary, and some fifty or so other relics. These included many relics of eastern saints, either early martyrs, like Christopher, George, Theodore, Cosmas, and Damian, and Demetrius, or great figures of the Byzantine church, such as John Chrysostom and John the Almsgiver. Significantly, abbot Martin also acquired relics of the patriarchs Abraham, Isaac, and Jacob, for the cult of such Old Testament figures was far more important in the East than in the West. Relics of eight virgin martyrs were also part of his spoil.[330]

The fortunes of the relics of Constantinople in the aftermath of 1204 were traced by count Paul Riant in an encyclopaedic work published in the 1870s.[331] He assembled the evidence of narrative sources, charters, letters, and liturgical texts, including Kalendars recording the feast-days of translations of relics from the East. The majority of the relics looted from the Byzantines were relics of Christ (which take up three pages in Riant's index), but the remains of many saints also found their way to the churches of western Europe.

One of the crusaders rampaging through the church of Hagia Sophia in 1204 was the German knight Henry von Ulmen. There he acquired a tooth of John the Baptist. He later had it enshrined in a specially constructed oratory in his castle in the Eifel mountains, but subsequently presented it to the Cistercians of Heisterbach,

[330] Gunther of Pairis, *Hystoria Constantinopolitana* 19, 24, pp. 158–61, 175–77; Janin, *La géographie ecclésiastique de l'Empire byzantin*, pp. 515–23, on the church of Christ Pantocrator.

[331] *Exuviae sacrae Constantinopolitanae.*

in return for their prayers.[332] Another church benefitting from his holy plunder was St. Pantaleon in Cologne. In 1208, "coming from Greece," he donated to it the skull of its very own patron, Pantaleon.[333] Conrad, bishop of Halberstadt, also participated in the capture of Constantinople, and later went on to the Holy Land. He brought back a rich haul of relics to his home diocese, including some of Christ's blood, wood from his cross, a piece of his tomb, portions of the Crown of Thorns, some of the hair and clothing of the Virgin Mary, part of the skull of John the Baptist, along with some of his hair, clothing, and a finger, and relics of the apostles, St. Stephen, and numerous other saints, many of them distinctly eastern, such as Cosmas and Damian, George, Procopius, Theodore, Demetrius, "Abel the Just," John Chrysostom, John the Almsgiver, Gregory of Nazianzus, and Basil, as well as the female martyrs Euphemia, Lucy, Margaret, Catherine, and Barbara.[334]

French churches had their share of the loot. The head of St. Mammas was brought to Langres by a cleric from that diocese, who begged it from the central depository of plundered relics that the papal legate on the crusade had established in Constantinople.[335] The relics coming to the West included the face of John the Baptist, to be kept in Amiens and a perpetual irritant to the clergy of St.-Jean-d'Angély, who claimed they had the head, and a second body of St. Denis for the monks of St.-Denis: Pope Innocent III explained that there was doubt about whether the Denis the Areopagite converted by St. Paul was the same as the Denis who was the first bishop of Paris (as the monks maintained) so, "not wishing to prejudge either opinion," the pope urged the monks to accept the body from Greece, to be on the safe side, since "when you have both sets of relics, there will be no doubt that the relics of St. Denis the Areopagite are possessed by your monastery."[336]

The renowned French abbey of Cluny acquired from Constantinople the head of St. Clement, which the monks enshrined in a silver reliquary and celebrated by especially composed hymns.[337] Quite remarkably, the Burgundian knight who brought the relic to Cluny has left a detailed first-hand account of how he managed to steal it.[338] This happened in the months after the capture of the city, when simple plundering had ceased. The knight, Dalmase de Sercy, had made a promise to go on to the Holy Land, but contrary winds prevented this, and he found himself stranded in the city for weeks with diminishing funds. He was then inspired by the thought that a good substitute for the trip to the Holy Land would be attained "if I could bring overseas some of the relics that are there in such abundance, since they are treated so

[332] Caesarius of Heisterbach, *Dialogus miraculorum* 8. 54 (2, p. 127).

[333] *Exuviae sacrae Constantinopolitanae* 2, pp. 87–88; cf. ibid. 2, pp. 175, 185.

[334] *Gesta episcoporum Halberstadensium*, pp. 120–21; *Exuviae sacrae Constantinopolitanae* 2, pp. 83–87.

[335] *Historia translationum sancti Mamantis* 3. 14–22, pp. 444–46 (PL 217: 132–33).

[336] Innocent III, *Utrum gloriosus martyr*, 4 Jan. 1215, Po. 5043 (PL 217: 241).

[337] Rostang of Cluny, *Translatio capitis sancti Clementis Cluniacum*; *Exuviae sacrae Constantinopolitanae* 2, p. 46, "Cerula freti iubilant."

[338] It is incorporated in the history of the translation by Rostang of Cluny: *Exuviae sacrae Constantinopolitanae* 1, pp. 133–40 (PL 209: 910–14).

disrespectfully." He consulted the ecclesiastical leaders of the crusade, who encouraged him in this ambition, although they cited the Roman Law prohibition on the selling and buying of relics, thus giving him implicit approval for a pious theft.

Sitting at dinner in Constantinople with his friend, the knight Ponce de Bussière, and a French priest they had met, and the talk turning to relics, Dalmase was delighted to hear that the priest had seen St. Clement's head, properly labelled in Greek, at the monastery of Theotokos Peribleptos in the south-west of the city.[339] The French party then set out for the monastery and requested permission to venerate the relics. This was granted, and a Greek cleric assigned to guide them and keep an eye on them. While Dalmase distracted this man's attention, asking him about the icons and "talking to him about many other things," the French priest seized his chance and took St. Clement's jawbones. When the relic raiders assembled outside the monastery, Dalmase expressed himself very unsatisfied with this partial haul. "You have done nothing," he said to the priest. "I and my companion Ponce will see what we can do." So, pretending to have left his gloves behind, Dalmase returned to the monastery, along with Ponce, who was deputed to seek out the rest of the saint's skull. He had luck, finding the monastic guardian asleep, and obtained the relic from a cupboard behind the altar. "And so," writes Dalmase, "we mounted our horses with joy and rode away from the monastery with speed." This was not the end of their adventures, which included a return visit to the monastery in disguise, but they now had their "holy plunder," and eventually brought it back to their homeland, to be joyfully received by the monks of Cluny on 27 July 1206.

This unusual first-person narrative illustrates some of the underlying thoughts of these relic thieves. Constantinople was a matchless treasury of relics, but their possessors did not properly revere them. Dalmase states this explicitly, and the account of the acquisition of the face of John the Baptist stresses the fact that it was in a neglected spot. The theft was pious in nature, and enhanced the prestige of the saints concerned: "the further their relics are brought, the more brightly their glory and praise shrine." The events of 1204 still embitter the feelings of Orthodox Christians, but for western Christians they meant an exceptional windfall of holy objects, to be distributed with pride among the churches of their homelands.

Relics in Law and War

When Godfrey, bishop of Bath, granted an estate to the monks of Bath in 1135, the donation ceremony involved his placing his charter on the altar of their church, "humbly imploring the patronage of the holy apostles and the relics that were present before our eyes, as an aid and as vengeance on those who dare to violate this."[340]

[339] See Janin, *La géographie ecclésiastique de l'Empire byzantin*, pp. 218–22, on this monastery; it was also called Triakontaphyllos.

[340] *English Episcopal Acta 10: Bath and Wells 1061–1205*, no. 7, p. 5.

The gift was thus to be protected by the power of the relics that were, physically and literally, witnesses to it. The transaction illustrates the important role that relics played in legal proceedings.

One of the most pervasive of these legal functions was the buttressing of an oath.[341] In fact, the modern Irish word for "oath," *mionn*, derives from the term *mind*, meaning "relic."[342] The holiness of the oath had been recognized from ancient times. Jewish law prescribed "Thou shalt fear the Lord thy God, and serve him, and shalt swear by his name" (Deuteronomy 6:13), Greeks swore by Zeus and other gods, and the Latin for "oath," *sacramentum*, means literally "securing by a religious sanction." Christians adopted the practice, despite Jesus' injunction in the Gospels, "Swear not at all" (Matthew 5:34), which radical and dissident groups throughout Christian history have cited in support of their refusal to swear oaths. But such groups were a minority, and the solemn oath became a cornerstone of medieval Christian society, just as it had been in the ancient world. The Rule of St. Benedict prescribed that every Benedictine monk make his vows before the community "in the name of the saints whose relics are there."[343]

The oath involved a declaration or a promise backed by the invocation of some divine or holy power. This power did not have to be a relic, and in eastern Christendom it appears that oaths were sworn only on the Gospels or the cross.[344] The emperor Justinian frequently specified forms of oaths on the Gospels in his legislation, as in the case of the oath of office for magistrates:

> I swear by Almighty God and his only begotten son our Lord Jesus Christ and the Holy Spirit and the holy and glorious mother of God, the ever-virgin Mary, and the four gospels, which I am holding in my hand, and St. Michael and St. Gabriel the archangels.[345]

In the West, however, the physical remains of the saints were also enlisted for this purpose, and there is evidence of the shrines of saints playing a part in legal procedures as early as the time of St. Augustine. When a dispute between two members of his community could not be resolved, he suggested that they be sent to the shrine of St. Felix at Nola in Italy, "where the dreadful works of God open up the guilty conscience and compel it to confess by punishment or fear." He cited the example of Milan, where a thief had gone to a saintly shrine, "in order to deceive by a false oath," but had been compelled to confess.[346] In the following centuries oaths on the tombs

[341] Hofmeister, *Die christlichen Eidesformen*; Hermann-Mascard, *Les reliques des saints*, pp. 235–70.

[342] Lucas, "The Social Role of Relics and Reliquaries in Ancient Ireland," p. 6; Kelly, *A Guide to Early Irish Law*, p. 199.

[343] *Regula Benedicti* 58, p. 188.

[344] Oikonomidès, *Documents et études sur les institutions de Byzance* (London, 1976), no. III, p. 112; in the four mentions of oaths in Psellos, they are sworn only on "holy things": *Chronographia* 3. 21; 5. 4, 44; 6. 121 (1, pp. 47, 87, 112; 2, p. 28). See also Lerou, "L'usage des reliques du Christ par les empereurs," pp. 172–75.

[345] *Corpus Iuris Civilis 3: Novellae*, p. 89 (Justinian, Novel 8, *iusiurandum*).

[346] Augustine, *Epistula* 78, pp. 84–86 (PL 33: 268–69).

of the saints became common. In 596, for example, during a dispute concerning the church of Ravenna, Pope Gregory I required an oath of the senior clergy: "Let them come before the body of St. Apollinaris and let them swear while touching his tomb."[347] Popes, emperors and others swore at St. Peter's tomb. A famous example is the mutual oath sworn by Charlemagne and Pope Hadrian I in 774 "at the body of St. Peter."[348]

Oaths could be of various kinds, including oaths of loyalty or fidelity, in which a party swears allegiance or support to a superior or ally; oaths of office, to perform a function faithfully; and oaths in the context of lawsuits, to tell the truth, or to establish or refute a claim or charge. In western Christendom, relics played a part in oaths of all these kinds. In the sixth century, for instance, an oath of loyalty could be sworn on St. Martin's tomb in Tours and "the cloth on St. Martin's tomb" invoked as a guarantor.[349] The Frankish kings made use of the oath of loyalty sworn on relics, and Charlemagne extended the requirement for such an oath to all his subjects. Its wording included an explicit reference to the relics:

> I promise on oath that from this day forth I will be faithful to lord Charles, the most devout emperor . . . just as a man ought to be to his lord. So help me God and these relics of the saints that are in this place.[350]

The oath of allegiance to Charlemagne's grandson Charles the Bald taken by his magnates in 876 concluded with the same words, "So help me God, and these relics of the saints."[351] This was a standard phrasing found in later canon law treatises.[352]

But it was important that when reliquaries were produced, the relics were inside them. During the lethal factional squabbles of the late seventh century the Frankish leader Martin, assured of his safety by his victorious enemies, was deceived in this way: "they swore to him deceitfully and falsely, on empty reliquaries," and hence had no compunction in putting him to death when he was in their hands.[353] This scheme was a nasty trick, but, more than three centuries later, this same part of the world saw an identical deception being practised, not as a Machiavellian device, but as a "pious fraud."[354] According to his biographer Helgaud, King Robert of France (996–1031) was so committed to truth and justice that he had a beautiful reliquary made of crystal and gold, which was to be used when his nobles had to swear him an oath. The distinctive thing about this reliquary was that it contained no relics, although

[347] Gregory I, *Registrum epistolarum* 6. 31 (1, p. 404).

[348] *Liber pontificalis* 1, p. 497.

[349] Gregory of Tours, *Libri historiarum X* 5. 48, p. 258.

[350] *Capitularia regum Francorum* 1, no. 34, p. 101 (appendix to *Capitularia missorum specialia* of 802); see in general Ganshof, "Charlemagne's Use of the Oath"; Becher, *Eid und Herrschaft: Untersuchungen zum Herrscherethos Karls des Grossen*.

[351] Sic me Deus adiuvet et ista sanctorum patrocinia: *Capitularia regum Francorum* 2, no. 220, p. 100.

[352] For example, Burchard, *Decretum* 1. 92, 7. 25, cols. 573, 784; Gratian, *Decretum* 2. 35. 6. 5, 7, col. 1279.

[353] *Liber historiae Francorum* 46, p. 320.

[354] For the following, Helgaud, *Epitoma vite regis Rotberti pii* 12, pp. 76–78.

8.6. Harold swearing an oath on relics, Bayeux Tapestry.
The Art Archive/Musée de la Tapisserie Bayeux/Gianni Dagli Orti.

the aristocrats were unaware of this. The king also had another reliquary made, this one of silver, on which the common people were to swear their oaths. Like the other, it did not contain relics, but, in this case, it was not empty. Inside was an ostrich egg.

It is difficult to know what to make of this story, or indeed to decide if there is any truth in it. As Helgaud presents it, the king was concerned to avoid lying and adhere to the truth "in heart and mouth." It is unclear exactly how having his followers swear their oaths on empty reliquaries fulfilled these admirable desires. Perhaps he thought this way they would avoid perjury, since, if they broke their oaths, these had not actually been sworn on holy relics.[355] But Helgaud praises the king as one who "speaketh the truth in his heart," quoting Psalm 14:13 (15:2), not as one who helped others avoid the consequences of lying.

A few decades after king Robert's death, northern France saw another famous oath supposedly sworn on relics. Earl Harold, the most powerful man in England and a strong contender to succeed to the throne, found himself (exactly how and why is not clear) at the court of William, duke of Normandy, who himself had his eye on the English crown. According to the Norman version of events, Harold swore

[355] This is how Helgaud's editors interpret the passage, choosing as their chapter summary, "Ruse du roi pour éviter les faux serments sur les reliques" (p. 164).

an oath on this occasion, to support William's succession rather than pursue his own. This was a very important part of the Norman propaganda case during and after William's conquest of England in 1066 and the scene is portrayed on the Bayeux Tapestry, that unique pictorial record of the Conquest (figure 8.6). Harold stands before duke William, who is seated in a position of authority, and puts his fingers, not on one, but on two reliquaries, doubtless brought there for the occasion (one of them has carrying handles). The caption above the scene is quite cryptic, reading simply, "where Harold swears an oath to duke William," but informed viewers would know exactly what was being depicted: perjury. Five scenes later Harold is crowned king.

Oaths of loyalty and fidelity continued to be sworn on relics. Those sworn by the great men of Catalonia to count Raymond Berengar I of Barcelona (1035–76) invoked "God and these holy things," "God and these holy relics," "God and these his saints" or, on one occasion, "God and this altar consecrated to St. Just."[356] In 1138 Sobeslav I of Bohemia wished to secure recognition of the succession of his son from the German king Conrad III, and the ritual involved the king handing a banner of investiture to the son, "in confirmation of which, in the presence of the king, all the chief men of Bohemia swore an oath on the relics of the saints."[357] Oaths could be taken by the lords and rulers as well as to them. When the new count of Flanders, William Clito, came to Bruges, one of the chief cities of the county, in 1127, in the company of king Louis VI, the canons of St. Donatian brought out the relics of their saints; the count and the king swore on the relics that they would observe the rights and privileges of the canons and the citizens of Bruges, and the citizens then swore fidelity.[358] In 1189 Richard the Lionheart swore his coronation oath "in front of the altar in the presence of the holy gospels and the relics of many saints."[359]

Probative oaths were an essential part of lawsuits. Accusers would swear to the truth of their accusation, defendants to their innocence, and witnesses to the accuracy of their testimony. Early Germanic laws, like the Frankish, Lombard and Visigothic Laws, are full of reference to such oaths, but say little about the formalities involved in swearing. Here, as in the case of the oath of loyalty mentioned earlier, Charlemagne was more forthright. In an addition to, or clarification of, Frankish law, Charlemagne insisted that "every oath shall be sworn in a church or on relics."[360] The version of Frisian Law that was probably drawn up at his court is also explicit about the role of relics in oath-swearing: if a slave is accused of stealing an object of value, his lord should swear for him "on relics of the saints"; heavy fines should be inflicted on "any man who swears a false oath on the relics of the saints"; if a group of men are accused of killing in a melée, the individual responsible shall be ascertained by lots, "and the lots shall be cast upon the altar, or, if it is not possible to

[356] Zimmermann, "Aux origines de la Catalogne féodale," p. 115.

[357] *Canonici Wissegradensis continuatio Cosmae*, p. 229.

[358] Galbert of Bruges, *De multro . . . Karoli comitis Flandriarum* 55, pp. 103–5.

[359] Roger of Howden, *Chronica* 3, p. 10.

[360] *Capitularia regum Francorum* 1, no. 41, p. 118 (*Capitulare legi ribuariae additum*, cl. 11).

get to a church, on relics of the saints"; in a case of homicide, an accuser "has to swear on relics of the saints" that he will only charge genuine suspects.[361]

This central role of relics in the legal system can be traced in the centuries after Charlemagne, at every social level. When, in 861, a group of tenants of the abbey of St.-Denis in the village of Mitry claimed that they were free men and opposed the servile labour being demanded of them, even taking the case before the king at his palace of Compiègne, the abbey officials produced an opposing group of men from Mitry, who recognized that all the men of the village were serfs, "and affirmed this on holy relics."[362] In 1081 Pope Gregory VII had a French bishop clear himself "by an oath on the most holy body of St. Peter, prince of the apostles" in the confidence that no one would risk perjuring themselves so drastically, while, in the following century, when the emperor Frederick Barbarossa was attempting to restrain the destructiveness of the wars and feuds between his nobles, he issued a constitution forbidding wanton arson, adding that, if one of a lord's followers committed arson during a raid, then that lord had to swear on relics that he had not consented to it.[363] Sometimes miracle stories recount the immediate punishment of a perjurer, as in the case of a trader who falsely claimed to have paid his partner, and swore an oath before the church where St. Benedict's relics had rested: "By this Saint Benedict, I have given those coins to him." At once he froze into the position he had taken for the oath, with his hand outstretched, and was only released when he had confessed his fault before the tomb in the church.[364]

The wide use of oaths upon relics is illustrated (in both senses of the word) in the *Sachsenspiegel*, the German lawbook of the thirteenth century to which pictures were added in the fourteenth. The text has more than twenty references to swearing "on the saints" (*op den hilgen*).[365] Issues in which such oaths were used include inheritance disputes, claims to land, relations between lord and vassal, exculpation from charges of assault and plundering, appraisal of the value of stolen hawks and hounds, disagreements about status, and servants' suits for arrears of pay. The fourteenth-century illustrated manuscripts, of which four survive, provide many illustrations of this procedure.[366] The relics are usually in a golden box with a pointed lid, and are placed on a stand or small column. The person swearing the oath stands, usually with one hand on the relics and the other raised. The images often depict the legal issue

[361] *Lex Frisionum* 3. 6; 10; 12. 1; 14. 1, 3, pp. 44, 52, 54, 56, 58.

[362] *Recueil des actes de Charles II le Chauve* 2, no. 228, pp. 7–9.

[363] Gregory VII, *Registrum* 9. 16 (2, p. 516); *Constitutiones et acta publica imperatorum et regum* 1, no. 318, p. 451 (c. 11).

[364] *Miracula sancti Benedicti* 1. 35, pp. 77–78.

[365] *Sachsenspiegel: Landrecht* 1. 13, 20, 22, 63; 2. 4, 17, 19, 34, 41, 62, 65, 72; 3. 32, 41, 47, 48, 78; *Lehnrecht* 24. 6, 29. 4, 47. 1, 51, 59. 4, 64. 2, 66. 2 (1, pp. 81, 85, 87, 122, 132, 148 [bis], 159, 166, 181, 184, 193, 213, 222, 234, 235, 262; 2, pp. 44, 52, 66, 70, 79, 82, 90).

[366] The illustrated versions are the Heidelberg, Oldenburg, Dresden, and Wolfenbüttel manuscripts. Facsimiles of all four have been published: *Der Oldenburger Sachsenspiegel*; *Sachsenspiegel: Die Wolfenbütteler Bilderhandschrift*; *Die Heidelberger Bilderhandschrift des Sachsenspiegels*; *Die Dresdener Bilderhandschrift des Sachsenspiegels*. There are also on-line versions.

8.7. Swearing an oath on relics that one killed a dog or bear in self-defence. *Sachsenspiegel, Landrecht* 2.62, ed. K. A. Eckhardt (1955–56), p. 181; Wolfenbüttel Sachsenspiegel, fol. 40v. © 2013. Photo Scala, Florence/BPK, Bildagentur fuer Kunst, Kultur und Geschichte, Berlin.

as well as the swearing of the oath, as, for example, in the case of the illustrations to the passage dealing with dangerous pets, such as fierce dogs, tame wolves and bears. If someone kills such a dog or bear in self-defence, he need pay the owner nothing, if he clears himself by an oath on relics. The vigorous clubbing of a dog and a bear (apparently in alliance) depicted in the illustration is followed by the oath-swearing scene before a judge (figure 8.7).

It seems to be the case that the significance of relics on oaths diminished over the course of the Middle Ages, as more reliance was placed on the Gospels as a guarantor of honesty.[367] For example, the oaths sworn by royal officials and advocates in the kingdom of Sicily in the thirteenth century were simply on the Gospels.[368] A particularly telling development can be observed in Bordeaux, where, in the early thirteenth century, the urban magistrates swore their oath of office on the relics of St. Severinus (Seurin), the great local saint, but by 1261 they were swearing the oath "on God's holy gospels and on the relics," and by 1340 or so the oath on relics had been discontinued, and the officials now swore just on the Gospels.[369] The peace treaties and agreements of the Hundred Years War were sworn, not on saints' relics, but on the Gospels (perhaps in the form of Gospel texts in the missal), on portions of the cross, and sometimes on the consecrated host, as in the case of the Treaty of Brétigny of 1360.[370] As in other areas of life, strong local attachments were being affected by an increasingly powerful universal culture, as common Christian models overshadowed regional distinctiveness. In the modern period only traces of the oath on relics survived, such as the invocation of the saints in the oaths sworn in Catholic

[367] Kolmer, *Promissorische Eide im Mittelalter*, pp. 234–39.

[368] *Die Konstitutionen Friedrichs II. für das Königreich Sizilien* 1. 62, 84, pp. 228, 258.

[369] Hermann-Mascard, *Les reliques des saints*, p. 254.

[370] Offenstadt, *Faire la paix au Moyen Age*, pp. 270–73; Knighton, *Chronicon*, p. 182.

Germany down to the end of the eighteenth century, or the use of relics for oaths in Ireland as late as the nineteenth.[371]

Until the later Middle Ages, however, relics were central to lawsuits as guarantors of oaths. But they played another significant role in litigation, as symbolic representatives of one of the parties. The monks and clergy of a large medieval church saw themselves as communities belonging to the particular saint who was their patron. They had to defend the interest of their saint and, reciprocally, he or she had to defend theirs. These interests were, of course, identical: the property and prestige of their church. And one dramatic procedure that ecclesiastics involved in struggles over lands or rights might pursue was to take the relics of their saint from their resting place in the church, and bring them into court to confront their opponents or judges. In 929, for example, the monks of Bobbio took the shrine of St. Columbanus to the royal capital of Pavia, in order to force those who had appropriated their property to return it.[372] Some years later, in 944, during a meeting of the court of Otto I at Duisburg, the canons of Maastricht "brought there the body of St. Servatius, on account of the many wrongs that count Immo had inflicted on them."[373] Similarly, in the reign of Henry I of England (1100–1135), the canons of Bodmin in Cornwall brought the shrine, staff and ivory horn of their local saint, Petroc, to court, and placed them before the king to induce him to remit unjust exactions.[374] Henry marvelled at the relics and "understood that it was something big that had led the canons to undertake the labour of such a journey."

One of the fullest and most vivid accounts of this tactic comes from the eleventh century. In 1071 the monks of Stavelot (about 20 miles south of Liège) were in dispute with Anno, archbishop of Cologne, about their rights over their sister-monastery of Malmedy, which, they claimed, the archbishop, with royal support, had wrongly taken away from them.[375] The case had dragged on for years and was not going well, and they decided on drastic action. They knew that the king was holding a great Easter court at Liège, and they determined "to carry to that court the body of St. Remaclus our protector." It was not the first time they had brought the relics of their chief saint to court, but on this occasion they were to achieve a dramatic success. They set out for Liège early in May and on the way the bearers of the shrine felt they were being rushed along by a kind of "divine propulsion." This urgency could be seen as an expression of the saint's own desire: the patron saint of Liège was Lambert, and the monks were convinced "that St. Remaclus wanted to

[371] Schaab, "Eide und andere Treuegelöbnisse in Territorien und Gemeinden Südwestdeutschlands," pp. 24–25; Ó Floinn, *Irish Shrines and Reliquaries of the Middle Ages*, p. 12.

[372] *Miracula sancti Columbani* 8–26, pp. 1001–13.

[373] *Continuatio Reginonis* s.a., p. 162.

[374] *Miracula sancti Petroci* 3, pp. 172–73.

[375] For the following see *Triumphus sancti Remacli de Malmundariensi coenobio*; discussions include Jenal, *Erzbischof Anno II. von Köln* 1, p. 56–109, "Die Affaire Malmedy," with a chronological guide to events in the *Triumphus* on pp. 86–90; Vogtherr, *Der König und der Heilige*; Legner, *Reliquien in Kunst und Kult*, pp. 37–40.

visit St. Lambert." Between Stavelot and Liège they also picked up the relics of St. Symmetrius, usually housed in one of their dependent churches, which they brought to Liège along with the body of Remaclus.

The arrival of the relics in Liège caused some consternation. The bishop of Liège, apprehensive about the reaction of his superior, the archbishop of Cologne, at first refused to give them a ceremonial welcome, but was talked around by his own clergy. The young king Henry IV, just twenty at this time, began to have his doubts whether the monks of Stavelot had been justly treated, and one of the episcopal colleagues of archbishop Anno urged him to return Malmedy. Anno's response was brusque: "Even if this person they call a saint were himself to assume bodily form and come and ask, he would not get his way with my consent."

The monks placed the reliquary of St. Remaclus on the Trinity altar in Liège cathedral, but evidently grew restless while their abbot went off to plead his case. "It occurred to us all," writes the anonymous monk of Stavelot who describes these events, "that the best advice would be to beseech God our helper." So, standing in front of the Trinity altar, the Stavelot monks sang the hymn *Veni creator spiritus*, followed by the seven penitential psalms. Then they took the relics of Remaclus in procession around the cathedral, first to St. Lambert in the crypt, then to the shrine of the Virgin Mary, then back to the altar of the Holy Trinity, all the time singing and praying. "Our supplication was not slight, or, rather our fear, because, seeing that reverence for our great Confessor had turned into contempt, we feared that this place would in future be destroyed." At this point God gave a clear sign: with a sudden sound, the reliquary of St. Remaclus rose into the air. Encouraged by this, the monks decided to go and find the king at once and state their case. They found him at dinner in an orchard. They urged him to recognize what he had done "against God's saint."

The king, bemused, looked to the archbishop of Cologne, who was dining with him, "as if to learn from him what he should do." The archbishop harshly rejected the monks' demands, while one of the bishops present suggested that the case be heard on the following day. At this point the monks had recourse to their most powerful weapon—the body of the saint: "By common consent we deemed it necessary at this very moment to bring up the body of our patron, which, without warning, we placed on the royal table." The board full of dishes and food that the king and bishops had been enjoying was now dominated, incongruously, by the casket containing the bones of the angry saint. A scene of commotion followed, as the archbishop urged the young king not to listen any further to "these impudent monks" and guided him back to the royal palace. The monks pursued him, but the king's door-keepers "repelled the saint," and Remaclus's body was returned to the royal table, which promptly collapsed. At the king's command some of the door-keepers attempted to remove it, but it suddenly became as heavy as a rock. The archbishop of Cologne, regarding these reports as "fantastic lies," sent more men to remove the saint's body, but they too were unable to do so, and returned, supposedly saying, "the loyal monks of that saint will not be coerced by any power." By this time crowds had filled the orchard, healing miracles were occurring at the shrine, and the monks, resisting all threats and entreaties, remained with it amongst the royal fruit trees all that night.

The next day saw a resolution. The monks agreed to return the reliquary to the cathedral. There, around midday, they again heard a sound, "like that of a spirit arriving," and the shrine of Remaclus again rose several feet into the air. An answering sound came from the crypt where St. Lambert was enshrined. A thick cloud filled the crypt, and was then followed by a blazing light, in the middle of which the glowing figures of St. Remaclus and St. Lambert appeared. A stream of healing miracles began, both at the shrine of Remaclus and that of Lambert, and the bells of the cathedral rang out of their own accord. Messenger after messenger ran to the palace, reporting all these events. Finally one of his bishops spoke frankly to the king:

> My lord king, there is no use your just sitting there . . . those two knights of the heavenly emperor have a serious quarrel with you . . . if you do not wish to perish, restore to the saint without delay what you have taken away.

King Henry was convinced. He went to the cathedral, and there, placing a staff symbolically on Remaclus's remains, restored Malmedy to the jurisdiction of Stavelot. Next day the monks departed in triumphal procession from Liège and made their way back to their own monastery, where "the victorious bones of our glorious patron were put back in their place."

The story throws light on many aspects of the politics of the Holy Roman Empire at this time: the powerful position of Anno of Cologne, and his influence over the young king (the archbishop had actually kidnapped Henry when he was a boy of eleven); the tensions between the secular princes backing either party, which are described in some detail; the role of bishops, the queen (whose tearful intervention is reported), and even the populace. But the guiding voice is that of a monk of Stavelot completely committed to his monastery as embodied (literally) in his saint. The author of the account is willing to criticize his own abbot if he thinks he is failing the cause. And the body of the saint is a weapon in the fight. Earlier in the dispute, years before the confrontation at Liège, the monks had taken Remaclus's relics from their usual position and placed them on the floor of the church. In this way the saint would be more closely identified with the monks' complaint: "supplication would thus be more urgent, with him to whom the injustice had been done." This happened at a time when their abbot was away, and, when he returned, he persuaded them to return the relics to their usual place, since it seemed to him that Remaclus "would not help us any less on that account." At a hearing of the case in Aachen in 1065 the monks had unanimously decided to take Remaclus's remains to the city, hoping "that, with him present, our opponents would be struck with remorse and would fear to hang on to his property unjustly." So, when they thumped down the reliquary onto the king's table in Liège in 1071, they already had years of experience of moving it strategically in pursuit of their claims. The disquiet and confusion it produced on that occasion was part of the strategy. A hearing deferred to the following day, with the powerful archbishop arguing his case before the young king, was unpromising, but the arrival of a saint's body on the king's table raised the stakes and demanded an instant response. The surviving shrine of St. Remaclus, still in Stavelot, dates from two centuries after the events at Liège, but its large, elaborate and precious form is a reminder of the triumphs of the saint as patron and protector.

Relics were not only of value in the ritualized disputes of the law but also in more tangible struggles. The arrival of the saints in person to help in battle will be discussed (pp. 378–83), but their remains, or the contact relics associated them, also played a part in war. Relics were imagined as a concrete defence. The relics of St. Andrew and St. Timothy, transported to Constantinople in the fourth century, provided the city with "twin towers."[376] The inhabitants of Antioch (unwalled at the time) regarded the relics of St. Simeon Stylites as their wall.[377] When besieged by the Franks in 541, the inhabitants of Zaragoza made a penitential circuit of the walls, carrying with them the tunic of St. Vincent. Not only did this protect them successfully, but the Frankish kings were apparently so impressed that they sought and received relics of the saint from the bishop of Zaragoza, enshrining them in a new church outside Paris on their return.[378] Similarly, when Autun was attacked during an aristocratic feud in 676, the defenders went around the circuit of the walls "with the sign of the cross and the relics of the saints."[379]

Saints' relics were not only static defences but could be taken into battle as talismans.[380] A famous example was St. Martin's cape, which was carried to war by the kings of the Franks, and even gave birth to new words, "chaplains" and "chapel": "chaplains (*cappellani*) take their name from St. Martin's cape (*cappa*), which the kings of the Franks used to have with them in battle to help them to victory."[381] In the mid-eighth century a church council held in Germany prohibited clergy from bearing weapons or going to war, except for those who had been specially delegated either to celebrate Mass for the soldiers or "to carry the relics of the saints"; significantly, the word used for relics in this context was *patrocinia*, literally "defences" or "protections."[382] Preparations for a campaign would thus include appointing clergy to carry the relics. In the same way, Columba's reliquary was taken to war by the clergy of Scotland (earlier, pp. 231–32). Or relics might be sought out for a particular campaign, as in the 580s, when the Byzantine general Philippicus requested relics of St. Simeon Stylites to be sent from Antioch to his army on the Persian frontier.[383] And relics were not only communal talismans for an army but could be carried by

[376] Paulinus of Nola, *Carmen* 19, lines 337–38, p. 130.

[377] *Syrische Lebensbeschreibung des hl. Symeon* 136, p. 179 (German trans.); see also Evagrius, *Historia ecclestiastica* 1. 13, pp. 164–66.

[378] Gregory of Tours, *Libri historiarum X* 3. 29, pp. 133–34; *Liber historiae Francorum* 26, pp. 283–84; the church is now St.-Germain-des-Prés.

[379] *Passio Leudegarii I* 22, p. 304.

[380] Gaier, "Le rôle militaire des reliques et de l'étendard de saint Lambert."

[381] Walafrid Strabo, *De exordiis et incrementis quarundam in observationibus ecclesiasticis rerum* 32, p. 515.

[382] *Concilia aevi Karolini* 1/1, p. 3, no. 1 (Concilium Germanicum, 742), cl. 2.

[383] Evagrius, *Historia ecclestiastica* 1. 13, p. 166.

individuals as well. The hero Roland had in the pommel of his sword a tooth of St. Peter, blood of St. Basil, hairs of "my lord" St. Denis, and portions of the clothes of the Virgin Mary.[384]

The Battle of Hastings between Duke William of Normandy and King Harold of England saw a particularly appropriate deployment of relics in battle, for, when he was preparing for the day's fight, William hung around his neck the relics on which Harold had earlier sworn his oath to him, thus calling up the power of the saints against the man he viewed as a perjurer.[385] When the Scots invaded the north of England in 1138, the archbishop of York, Thurstan, summoned all able-bodied men to resist the invaders. They were to march out "from every parish, with their priests before them bearing the cross and banners and relics of the saints."[386] Thurstan thus not only envisaged mobilization by parish but also saw the holy remains of the saints playing somewhat the part of regimental colours. A similar combination of relics and banner buttressed the spirits of the troops from Würzburg in a local war in 1266:

> On the day of St. Cyriacus the martyr [8 August] at Kitzingen, the army of Würzburg, with the holy relics and the banner of St. Kilian, attacked count Hermann of Henneberg and his men with confidence, and the fight was fought bitterly that morning.[387]

The Würzburgers were successful, and thenceforth celebrated St. Cyriacus's day as a festival. Remarkably, the banner of St. Kilian still survives, now in the keeping of the Fürstenbaumuseum. It is 5 by 3 metres (almost 16½ by 10 feet) in size and shows Kilian with his episcopal staff in one hand and a large sword in the other.[388]

In the Byzantine Empire, where the cult of icons was as important as the cult of relics, holy images were likewise carried into battle. When Heraclius, sailing from Africa to Constantinople, overthrew the emperor Phocas in 610, he did so with the aid of a "helping image " of the Virgin Mary.[389] Basil II, confronting a powerful rebel in 989, went forward at the head of his troops with a sword in one hand and, in the other, an icon of the Virgin Mary, "making this the surest defence against the other's tremendous assault," while on the Aleppo campaign of 1030 the Byzantine forces brought the icon of Mary "which the Roman [that is, Byzantine] emperors customarily bring with them in war, as a leader and guard of all the army."[390] But the Byzantines also took relics to war, for amongst the booty captured by the Bulgars when they defeated the emperor Isaac in 1190 or 1191, was a reliquary containing a

[384] *Chanson de Roland*, lines 2345–48, ed. F. Whitehead (Oxford, 1942), p. 69.

[385] William of Poitiers, *Gesta Guillelmi ducis Normannorum* 2. 14, p. 124.

[386] Aelred of Rievaulx, *Relatio de standardo*, p. 182.

[387] *Chronica Minor Minoritae Erphordensis*, *Continuatio* I, p. 672.

[388] *Franconia sacra*, p. 31 and pl. 7; Zimmermann, "Die Cyriakus-Schlacht bei Kitzingen," pp. 422–24.

[389] George of Pisidia, *Heraclias* 2, line 14, p. 252; by the time of Theophanes, the story was that he had reliquaries (*kibōtia*) as well: *Chronographia*, s.a. 6102, p. 298.

[390] Psellos, *Chronographia* 1. 16, 3. 10 (1, pp. 10, 39).

fragment of the True Cross, relics of the martyrs, and some of the milk and the girdle of the Virgin Mary.[391]

In the campaign of the bishop of Liège against the stronghold of Bouillon in 1141 the relics of St. Lambert, the chief saint of Liège, had a central role, which is brought out clearly in a contemporary account.[392] The bishop claimed that he had been wrongly dispossessed of the castle by the count of Bar, and began a siege. Bouillon is on a rocky site in the Ardennes about 100 kilometres (60 miles) south of Liège. The bishop's knights were outnumbered by the garrison they were besieging, and also short of supplies in this remote spot, while they feared that the count of Bar, whose two sons were leading the defence, might arrive with relieving forces. The bishop gave them a pep talk, stressing the wickedness of the count, comparing them with the heroes of the Old Testament and urging them to wear the sign of the cross, confess their sins and be confident of God's help. The bishop's men, however, wanted something more concrete and local than this crusading posture he had offered: they wanted the relics of St. Lambert, the martyr-saint of Liège. They thought that victory would be secured, "if the martyr we are fighting for came to our camp."

The bishop was uncertain if this could be done, but promised to summon all his subjects, "from the city, the towns and villages," to come with arms and supplies. The knights insisted, however, and finally the bishop agreed that the relics should be brought from Liège to the siege. He sent one of his archdeacons back to the city carrying his orders: the leaders of the clergy and people should set out to reinforce the troops at Bouillon, bringing with them "the most holy shrine of our blessed patron." Again, there was some doubt and hesitation about this, but the common people of Liège bluntly refused to go on the expedition "unless the blessed martyr was at their head." Hence the relics were taken from their location and placed in the middle of the church, amongst enthusiastic crowds, and on the following day they were carried in procession down to the river Meuse—much of the journey to Bouillon could be done by boat. The wives and children of the departing soldiers lined the streets, wishing them well. They watched the boat with the relics until it disappeared from view, then returned, "as if they had been to the funeral of some dear friend."

The reinforcements, along with the relics, made their way south, miracles occurring along the way, until they reached the embattled forces at Bouillon. There, "our knights came to meet the relics of the blessed martyr, prostrating themselves to the ground," and carried them on their shoulders, while the clergy sang hymns of praise. The arrival of the relics had an immediate effect. The garrison of Bouillon lost heart, and Hugh, the eldest son of the count of Bar and head of the defenders, fainted. When recovered, he suggested immediately that the garrison surrender. The garrison raised some objections to this suggestion, and it might well be that there was both

[391] Akropolites, *The History* 11, p. 133.

[392] *Triumphus sancti Lamberti de castro Bullonio*; Gaier, "Le rôle militaire des reliques et de l'étendard de saint Lambert"; Bachrach, *Religion and the Conduct of War*, pp. 172–81.

disagreement in the besieged castle and some wishful thinking on the part of the besiegers.

What is clear is the place of the relics of St. Lambert in this combat. They were placed in a little tent at one of the crucial spots in the fight, guarded by the clergy of Liège, who were housed in their own huts and sang the services throughout the day. The levies from Liège camped around them. At this point, the narrative of the siege becomes complex and occasionally hard to follow—this is indeed one of the things that makes its credible as a contemporary account of a military operation (as Fabrizio, the hero of Stendhal's *Charterhouse of Parma* reflects, "Was what he had seen been a real battle? And, if so, was that battle Waterloo?"). Morale goes up and down, and there are skirmishes, rumours, and attacks by the besiegers, in which their low level of casualties are ascribed to "the patronage of the martyr." The crisis comes when it is clear that the count of Bar will not turn up with his relieving forces, while his son Hugh, inside the castle of Bouillon, is now seriously ill. Eventually the defenders agree to surrender the castle, the ailing Hugh is brought down to the shrine of St. Lambert and promises never again to usurp the saint's property, and Lambert's relics are carried into the disputed stronghold: "the blessed martyr, the glorious victor, was carried into the castle." And, after establishing his proprietary rights so decisively, Lambert was finally put on a cart and taken home to Liège.

The siege of Bouillon in 1141 is a perfect example of the life of relics, the way that these dead bones could play an active part in the conflicts waged by the powers of medieval Europe. Begged for by the knights and levies, sent on their way by the worried families of Liège, powerful enough to paralyze a great aristocratic enemy, these dry remains were also "famous and triumphant." Human remains, so mute and so poignant when contemplated by bereaved families, were fearful and enduring sources of military and political power.

Relics in Dispute

Quarrels over Relics

Some of the most rancorous prose of the Middle Ages was produced by churchmen defending their claims to have the true relics of a saint against the contentions of rivals. A monk of St.-Wandrille in Normandy, describing the discovery there of the relics of St. Wulfram in the early eleventh century, seized the opportunity to launch such a diatribe:

> Whoever claims to have the body of St. Wulfram, or thinks it rests elsewhere, must be believed to be acting very foolishly, or, rather, to be insane, since they think their opinion to be right, although it rests on no authority.

He goes on to list the supporting evidence for the claims of St.-Wandrille: the tomb itself, an inscription found alongside it, the known historical details of the site and its fortunes over time. Others who claim to have the body may be inspired by devotion, but there can be no compromise with their error.

> But we, to whom such a great treasure has been granted and reserved by God, let us render fitting service . . . so that we may deserve to enjoy the protection of the one at whose presence we rejoice.[393]

The monks of St. Peter's, Ghent, who also claimed the body, would have disagreed.[394]

A dispute between the churches of Dorchester-on-Thames and Winchester cathedral in the early thirteenth century illustrates some of the intricacies of such struggles. At issue was the location of the relics of St. Birinus, a seventh-century missionary, who, all agreed, had established the first episcopal see at Dorchester, and had been buried there. The great English historian Bede, writing a generation or two after Birinus's death, was not only the source of his activities at Dorchester but also reported that, "many years later," Birinus's body had been translated to Winchester.[395] Thereafter there is an almost complete silence about Birinus's cult until the late tenth and eleventh centuries, when evidence can be found of attention to the saint at Winchester: a translation within the cathedral, with its own feast, liturgical commemoration, and a Life composed perhaps in the 1090s.[396]

The canons of Dorchester had not forgotten Birinus, however. In 1224 they petitioned Pope Honorius III to allow them to transfer the body of Birinus to a more honourable position. Understandably, they made no mention of Winchester or Bede's report of a translation to that city. Perhaps aware of some uncertainty, Honorius wrote to Stephen Langton, archbishop of Canterbury, on 9 March 1224, asking his opinion: "having complete confidence in your judgment, we instruct you to grant permission, by our authority, if you find the case to be so."[397] Finding "the case to be so" presumably encompassed ascertaining whether Birinus's body was actually in the monastery of Dorchester, and the archbishop commissioned his officials to make enquiries and hear sworn testimony on the matter.

The community of Dorchester did not have a strong hand, but they played it as best they could.[398] One of the canons swore on oath that he had often heard another canon (presumably deceased, since he did not give his own testimony) say that he had been instructed in a vision that the body of Birinus could be found before the altar of the Holy Cross. When they had excavated at this spot, they had found the body of a bishop, buried with his stole and chasuble, pectoral cross and chalice. Soon

393 *Inventio et miracula sancti Vulfranni* 21, pp. 39–40; see, in general, Howe, "The Hagiography of Saint-Wandrille."

394 *Sermo de adventu sanctorum Wandregisili, Ansberti et Vulframni in Blandinium*, pp. CXXI–CXXV; Van Houts, "Historiography and Hagiography at St-Wandrille."

395 Bede, *Historia ecclesiastica* 3. 7, p. 232.

396 On both Life and cult, see *Three Eleventh-century Anglo-Latin Saints' Lives*, pp. xlix–lxxxviii.

397 ASV, Reg. Vat. 12, fol. 173, 9 March 1224 (*Regesta Honorii papae III*, no. 4847); *Nova legenda Anglie* 1, p. 119 (with minor verbal differences).

398 For the following, *Nova legenda Anglie* 1, pp. 120–21.

afterwards miracles began to occur at the tomb. A blind man recovered his sight, a man who was dumb was given the power of speech, first in English, then, when a canon pointed out that this was hardly a polite language, in French. Unfortunately, the abbot of Dorchester had to admit to the commissioners from Canterbury, no writing had been found with the body. The tomb was then reopened. The abbot made another bid. "I am certain," he said, "that this is the body of St. Birinus, for I heard last night a voice like that of some great person saying in Latin, 'Have no doubt about finding the body of St. Birinus; you will find the whole body, although reduced to dust.' "

At this point the awkward testimony of Bede was brought up: had not Birinus's body been translated to Winchester long ago? Well, said the abbot, Bede had indeed written that, but chroniclers write down many things that are just hearsay. He agreed that the body of a bishop had been taken from a cramped corner behind the door of the church of Dorchester to Winchester, but the body of so great a saint as Birinus would not have been buried in so undistinguished a spot. Moreover, a holy hermit had heard a voice saying, "Birinus in the church floor, Bertinus behind the door," making it clear that it was this Bertinus, not Birinus, who had been buried in the dark corner. Moreover, many miracles had taken place at Dorchester, but none at Winchester.

The Canterbury commissioners sent their report to the pope, explaining that, although the miracles occurring at Dorchester and the evidence of the burial there meant "it was very probable that that the body of the saint lay in that place," they were still concerned about Bede's statement about the translation to Winchester. Honorius wrote to them on 13 August 1225, commanding them to go to Winchester and find out if miracles "equal to or greater than" those at Dorchester had occurred there at invocation of the name of Birinus. If not, clearly either Bede had been reporting only hearsay, or else he had been referring to Bertinus, but had been taken to mean Birinus, through scribal error.[399] In that case permission to proceed with the translation could then be given.[400] Detailed evidence of these proceedings dries up at this point, but there is no doubt that the canons of Dorchester kept their nerve. In the fourteenth century, it was reported that they were still saying, "it was another body than St. Birinus's that was translated," and hence they had had no qualms in erecting "a shrine of wonderful workmanship" on the site of his burial.[401] "The offeringe to Seynt Berren" at Dorchester was still worth five pounds a year on the eve of the Reformation.[402] The case exemplifies very clearly the armoury that churchmen had at their disposal in their attempts to win such disputes: visionary validation, the

[399] *Nomine scriptorum negligentia viciato.*

[400] ASV, Reg. Vat. 13, fol. 78v, 13 August 1225 (*Regesta Honorii Papae III* 2, pp. 359–60, no. 5601); *Nova legenda Anglie* 1, pp. 121–22. For suggestions about this Bertinus, *Three Eleventh-century Anglo-Latin Saints' Lives*, p. lxxiii.

[401] Ranulph Higden, *Polychronicon* 5. 15 (6, p. 4).

[402] *Valor ecclesiasticus* 2, p. 170.

evidence of corporeal remains, written record (which might have to be explained away), and, perhaps above all, miracles.

The great churches were dogged defenders of their claims. In the early years of the fifteenth century, a dispute about relics between the monks of St.-Denis and the canons of Notre-Dame de Paris became so heated and controversial that it eventually came before the Parlement de Paris, the highest royal court in France.[403] The canons claimed to possess the crown of the skull of St. Denis, while the monks held that they possessed the head entire. The representatives of both parties energetically hunted through the evidence of old chronicles and of depictions of the saint's martyrdom. The canons pointed out that many of the chronicles that the monks produced to support their case had actually been written by members of the monastery of St.-Denis, not to mention the interpolations and false attributions of which the monks were guilty. Much turned on whether Denis had been beheaded cleanly through the neck or whether the top of his head had been sliced off (in the manner of Thomas Becket, whose "crown" had its own shrine in Canterbury cathedral). The canons claimed "Monseigneur St. Denis had his head sliced through the middle, as is depicted on the left portal of the church of Paris, on the St. Denis gate of the city of Paris, and in many other places and ancient paintings," although they recognized that the executioner might then have chopped the head off at the neck. They even attempted an art-historical hypothesis: images showing Denis with his head chopped off at the neck were recent innovations by those who wished to stress Denis's role as first bishop of Paris, and hence wanted to depict him with the episcopal mitre, which would be difficult if they showed the crown of his head sliced off. In any case, the images that supported the canons' case were ancient and public stone images, not manuscript illuminations that the monks had cooked up in their own monastery. The monks, of course, had their counter-arguments. The Parlement was not able to bring the affair to a conclusion because of the rising civil disorder in France, and the disagreement between the two churches continued and was alive still in the eighteenth century.

Testing Relics

The relic was "a trusty pledge."[404] It was a token of power, a sign of the faith and a pointer to the resurrection. But the trusty pledge itself needed to be trusted. Writing around 401, Augustine criticized insincere monks who "offer for sale pieces of the martyrs (if indeed they are martyrs)."[405] His reservation clearly implies that he thought it possible that there could be false relics. It is an early indication of something that was to be a feature of the cult of the saints throughout the Middle Ages. A fifth-century Christian prelate in Egypt condemned as "drunk with pseudo-

[403] Delaborde, "Le procès du chef de Saint Denis."

[404] Prudentius, *Peristefanon* 6, line 135, p. 319.

[405] Augustine, *De opere monachorum* 28. 36, p. 585 (PL 40: 575).

knowledge" those who claimed that "martyrs have appeared to us and taught us where their bones are." He thought that "numerous people have been tricked by demons in this way."[406] It is clear from his words that he doubts the composure and level-headedness of these people rather than their sincerity—they really have been fooled by demons—but there were also charlatans and swindlers, who undertook conscious deceptions in hope of gain. Around 450 a wandering monk (or apparent monk) in Carthage claimed to be able to heal ailments by means of oil that had been in contact with a certain bone, but the cures were illusory and temporary.[407] The highest authorities of the Church recognized that these deceptions were taking place. The cardinal and canonist Hostiensis mentioned those who passed off "the rib of a sinful man or of an ass" as saints' relics, or who faked tears flowing from an image by cunning use of oil.[408] Some people made a living from the trade. One huckster of this kind was active in France and Italy in the 1020s: "He used to dig up bones from the graves of the recently dead, place them in reliquaries and sell them as the relics of holy martyrs and confessors."[409] Bishops and high nobles were among the people fooled by this charlatan. False relics might bring the whole cult into disrepute and doubt. One of the objections that heretics raised against the cult of the saints in the thirteenth century was the existence of "false relics, which some people carry around through the villages, and with which they fool people in the taverns, like the milk of the Virgin Mary."[410]

The suspicion that false relics were being cynically exploited emerges strongly in the satirical writing of the later Middle Ages. Pardoners, who were licensed to travel around selling indulgences, were a particular target. Chaucer's pardoner in the *Canterbury Tales* is portrayed as an avaricious, sexually ambiguous charlatan. He carries around with him "pigges bones" and other false relics, including a pillow-case, which he claims is the veil of the Virgin Mary, and part of the sail from St. Peter's boat, while he was still a fisherman, and with these gains more money in a day than an honest parson can in a year, making the clergy and the people "his apes."[411] The pardoner in Sir David Lindsay's *Satire of the Three Estates* of 1540 is presented in exactly the same way: the pardoner's servant comes and tells him that, in accordance with his master's orders, he has found a horse's bone upon a dung-heap that can be passed off to the local women ("wyfis") as a bone of St. Brigid's cow, good for curing the fever: "All the wyfis will both kiss and kneel, / Betwixt this and Dumbarton."[412]

There is a rather different tone in the account of a deception found in the works of the Cistercian monk, Caesarius of Heisterbach, writing in the 1220s. He tells the

[406] Lefort, "La chasse aux reliques des martyrs en Egypte," p. 227 (a fragment of Shenouda the Archimandrite).

[407] Quodvultdeus, *Liber promissionum*, "Dimidium temporis," 6. 11 (2, pp. 608–10).

[408] Hostiensis, *Lectura siue Apparatus super quinque libris Decretalium*, ad X. 3. 45. 2, *Quum ex eo*.

[409] Rodulfus Glaber, *Historiarum libri quinque* 4. 3. 6, p. 180.

[410] *Quellen zur Geschichte der Waldenser*, p. 99 (the Passau Anonymous).

[411] Geoffrey Chaucer, *Canterbury Tales*, General Prologue, lines 669–714, p. 34.

[412] Lindsay, *Ane Satyre of the Thrie Estaits*, p. 75.

story of a dishonest priest, who sold a set of horse's reins to a pious knight, falsely claiming that they had often been used by St. Thomas Becket. The knight revered them as a relic and they did indeed perform miracles. Eventually he built a church to house them. "In my judgment," wrote Caesarius, "ignorance in such cases excuses any fault; devotion deserves grace . . . sometimes the Lord works miracles through false relics to honour the saints to whom they are ascribed and through the faith of those who honour them."[413] Several clerical and monastic writers expressed this idea, that it was the believer's intention that mattered, not the real identity of the relic. The canons of Notre-Dame de Paris, engaged in their dispute over relics in 1410, piously asserted that it was the practice of the Church to tolerate identical relics being venerated in two different churches, and that it was better for the two churches to publicize the positive evidence for their own relics than to attack their rivals.[414]

If there was any doubt about the identity or genuineness of relics, there were various ways to resolve the issue. Some relied on seeking a sign from God, others on more mundane and practical forms of validation. When the travelling relic salesman Felix turned up in Bavaria in the 830s, claiming to have the body of St. Bartholomew, one of the local bishops was "uncertain whether this was credible or not" and initiated a three-day fast to see if God would give some indication.[415] Just a few years later, Archbishop Amolo of Lyons was disturbed when he heard, sometime in the early 840s, from his suffragan, the bishop of Langres, who described how two men claiming to be monks had brought to his city the bones of some saint whose name they said they had forgotten. The relics produced extremely unusual miracles: they did not heal, but knocked women about the church, striking them to the ground. Amolo thought that the bishop was wise to be circumspect about "relics of this kind, which lacked any authority and whose very name was unknown." He reminded him of the story in the Life of Martin, when the saint had miraculously revealed that a supposed holy shrine was in fact the burial place of a robber. He raised the possibility of human or diabolical deceit and trickery, and encouraged the bishop to take steps to close down this disruptive and suspicious cult.[416]

Bones and dust do not bear a name. As the German poet Walther von der Vogelweide put it, "Who can tell the lord from the serf if he found only their mere bones?"[417] Hence corporeal relics need some form of identification. Their context and meaning are not intrinsic but have to be declared in some way, and therefore there was a need to link name and relics. There were various ways that the identity and genuineness of relics could be ascertained, even though human remains, after a little time, are such anonymous objects.

[413] Caesarius of Heisterbach, *Dialogus miraculorum* 8. 69–70 (2, p. 140).

[414] Delaborde, "Le procès du chef de Saint Denis," p. 392.

[415] Erchanbert of Freising, *Epistolae variorum* 23, p. 338.

[416] Amulo of Lyons, *Epistola* 1, pp. 363–68; comment in West, "Unauthorised Miracles in Mid-Ninth-Century Dijon."

[417] Wer kan den hêrren von dem knechte gescheiden / swer ir gebeine blôzez fünde . . . : Walther von der Vogelweide, "Swer âne vorhte, hêrre got," lines 11–12 (Lachmann 22, 12–13), *Spruchlyrik*, p. 242.

A common form of proof in medieval disputes, at least until the thirteenth century, was trial by ordeal, in which a hazardous test, such as carrying hot iron or being thrown into a pool of water, was undergone, and guilt or innocence determined by the outcome: a hand healing cleanly denoted innocence, an infected burn guilt, while a body that sank was being received by the pure element of water, but one that floated was being rejected as guilty. It was a natural extension of this procedure to use it to test the authenticity of relics: the holy objects would be cast into a blazing fire, with the expectation that genuine ones would survive unscathed. There are some examples from early in the Middle Ages. In the aftermath of the conversion of the Visigothic rulers from Arianism to Catholicism at the end of the sixth century, the Catholic bishops ruled that relics from Arian churches "should be tested by fire."[418] A curious variant of this type of test is found in a report that the authenticity of the relics of St. Helen, brought from Rome to the land of the Franks in the ninth century, had to be proved by the monk who brought them walking naked through hot water.[419]

Trial of relics by fire is particularly frequent in the tenth, eleventh and twelfth centuries.[420] In 1100, for example, during the dedication of a church by the bishop of Prague, one of the relics brought to him for the service was a piece of cloth from the veil of Ludmila, the Czech princess murdered in 921 whom many regarded as a saint.[421] The bishop was clearly not one of them. "Don't talk about her sanctity," he said. "Let the old woman rest in peace." Faced with an indignant response, the bishop decided to test the relic:

> at the bishop's command, a great pan was brought, full of burning coals, and, after invoking the name of the Holy Trinity, the bishop threw the cloth onto the fiery coals. A wonderful thing, the smoke and flames darted around the cloth but did not harm it. And this made the miracle even greater, that for a long time it was impossible to take the cloth from the flames because of the intense heat, and, when at length it was taken out, it was as undamaged and strong as if it had been woven that very day.

A ritual from the church of Rheims describes the liturgical formula that could be used in such tests, including the following prayer:

> Lord God Jesus Christ, who is king of kings and lord of lords, and lover of all who believe in you, who is a just judge, strong and powerful, who has revealed your holy mysteries to your priests, and who tempered the flames of the fire for the three children, grant to us, your unworthy servants, and hear our prayer, so

[418] *Concilios visigóticos e hispano-romanos*, no. 15, pp. 1–2 (sic), Second Council of Zaragoza, 592, cl. 2 (PL 84: 317).

[419] Notker of Hautvilliers, *De translatione sanctae Helenæ imperatricis*, p. 603.

[420] See especially Head, "Saints, Heretics, and Fire: Finding Meaning through the Ordeal"; idem, "The Genesis of the Ordeal of Relics by Fire."

[421] Cosmas of Prague, *Chronica Boemorum* 3. 11, p. 171.

> that this cloth, or thread, in which the bodies of the saints have been wound, if they are not true, may be burned by this fire, and if they are true, they may escape that.[422]

Although authenticity could be established in this way, as well as through visionary revelations, the simplest way to link bones and name was to label them, with pieces of parchment or other material bearing the name of the saint to whose relics they were attached.[423] There are numerous references to this practice. For example, the Byzantine emperor Alexius Comnenus sent Henry IV of Germany gifts, including "a gilded reliquary containing portions of various saints, each identified by a small label fastened to them."[424] When the shrine of St. Helen, kept at the monastery of Hautvilliers near Rheims, was opened in the year 1095, a label was found inside, reading "the body of St. Helen the queen, mother of Constantine, without the head."[425] And, when the relics of Acca of Hexham were moved in 1154, the participants took special care over this, and, "lest in future times the name and merit of the saint should be lost to memory because of the lack of a label, they wrote them on parchment and inscribed them on lead sheets and then placed these with the relics ."[426]

If the relic and label became separated, the history and value of the isolated human remains were in a void. This is when one might need a seer. One of the indications of the holy and visionary powers of Mary of Oignies, the beguine saint of the early thirteenth century, was her ability to discern the identity of a relic that had lost its label. While she prayed about this question, a saint appeared to her in a vision and spelt out the opening letters of his name, AIOL: "Then she clearly knew that these relics were those of St. Aiolis."[427] Here, the visionary solution is a fall-back when the more straightforward means has failed.

A large number of relic labels survive from the nunnery of Chelles, east of Paris. They were discovered in 1983 and those earlier than the ninth century—some 139—have been published.[428] Although they are just tiny slips of parchment, some no larger than 26 by 6 millimetres (1 by ¼ inch), they are a rare survival from the period 650–800, and have been described as "a crucial source for the Merovingian liturgy and the scale and nature of the cult of the saints."[429] Several of them record

[422] *Oratio ad probandas reliquias*, PL 71: 1185–86.

[423] Hermann-Mascard, *Les reliques des saints*, pp. 120–26; Heinzelmann, *Translationsberichte*, pp. 83–88; Bertrand, "Authentiques de reliques: authentiques ou reliques?"

[424] Anna Comnena, *Alexiad* 3. 10. 5 (1, p. 135).

[425] Notker of Hautvilliers, *De translatione sanctae Helenae imperatricis*, p. 609.

[426] Aelred of Rievaulx, *De sanctis ecclesiae Haugustaldensis* 11, p. 195.

[427] Jacques de Vitry, *Vita Mariae Oigniacensis* 2. 10. 91, pp. 660–61; the saint in question is described as "honoured at Provins in Champagne" and can thus be identified as Aigulph, abbot of Lérins (d. c. 676, feast-day 3 September), one of whose cult centres was St.-Ayoul de Provins; see Godefroy, "L'histoire du Prieuré de Saint-Ayoul de Provins."

[428] *Chartae latinae antiquiores 18: France VI*, no. 669, pp. 84–108. On the Chelles labels, see Ganz and Goffart, "Charters Earlier than 800," pp. 928–32 ("The Relic Labels"); Hen, *Culture and Religion in Merovingian Gaul*, pp. 92–96.

[429] Ganz and Goffart "Charters Earlier than 800," p. 928.

early martyrs, such as Stephen, Sebastian and Victor, while many refer to the bishops and abbots of Merovingian Gaul: Amand, Medard, Ouen. Geneviève of Paris appears prominently. Great saints, like the Virgin Mary and John the Baptist, can be found along with the totally obscure—who, one wonders, was "Uurgonezlus"? There are royal saints, both Frankish and foreign (Radegund, Sigismund, Oswald), and a piece of the beard of the Anglo-Saxon missionary Boniface, martyred in 754. Sometimes the labels specify the saint's day. Along with the relic labels, fragments of precious cloth have also survived, pieces of exotic Byzantine or Persian silk used to wrap the holy bones.[430]

Remarkably, in the aftermath of the bomb damage of World War II, a complete labelled collection of relics was discovered in the high altar of St. Kunibert's church in Cologne.[431] It was contained in a leaden box measuring 8.8 by 29.5 by 10 centimetres (about 3 ½ by 11 ½ by 4 inches) and was full of small relics and other items, including pieces of St. Kunibert's stole, St. Antony's beard, and fragments of Spanish silk. More than fifty saints are represented. In addition to the relic labels, the box contained a piece of parchment explaining the origin and purpose of the collection: "I, Constantine, humble priest and canon of this church, have gathered these relics, so that they may lead me to eternal rest on the Last Day and a pure life in this world." Dateable to the first half of the thirteenth century, this modest box is evidence of the ultimate impulses of the collector as well as the more prosaic matter of the labelling practices of relic cult. (See plate 6.)

[430] Laporte, *Le trésor des saints de Chelles*, pp. 133–50, plates IX–XI.

[431] *Ornamenta Ecclesiae* 2, pp. 79–83, Cat. Nr. D 61.

CHAPTER 9

Miracles

The Meaning of Miracle

One of the most distinctive things about the saints was the fact that they are reported to have performed thousands of miracles, both in life and after death.[1] For some modern scholars, confronted with this abundance of miraculous events, the question "what really happened?" is too grossly literal.[2] They argue that, if these accounts have a meaning for the person recording them, they make sense in the thought-world of the time, and they serve comprehensible polemical or apologetic purposes, and "what really happened?" is a bone-headed response to such riches of meaning. Yet it is not an illegitimate question, and it is one that can, at times, be answered. Sometimes the events recounted as a miracle seem not to have been out of the ordinary at all. To take one example, the story is told of a young student at the cathedral school of Angers, early in the eleventh century, who mislaid his Psalter while travelling through a wood near the city.[3] When he discovered his loss, he was advised to promise a candle to St. Foy and return next day to the place where he had lost the book. He did this, and as he entered the wood, called out, "at the divine command," "St. Foy, give me back my Psalter!" Hearing his call, a shepherd emerged from the trees and asked him what was the matter, and, upon being told, indicated that someone had found the book, and the student recovered it and returned rejoicing. What happened here is quite clear, and susceptible of an entirely naturalistic explanation. It is the construal of the sequence of events as a miracle that needs further elucidation. The person recounting the story (who happened to be the student's teacher) also felt the need to explain this. "This event" he writes, " is to be explained by reference to the power of St. Foy rather than to chance, since the shepherd could not have

[1] Finucane, *Miracles and Pilgrims*; Ward, *Miracles and the Medieval Mind*; *Miracles, prodiges et merveilles au Moyen Age*; Goodich, *Violence and Miracle in the Fourteenth Century*; *Miracle et karāma*; Goodich, *Lives and Miracles of the Saints*; Goodich, *Miracles and Wonders*; Signori, *Wunder*; Wittmer-Butsch and Rendtel, *Miracula: Wunderheilungen im Mittelalter*; Kleine, *Gesta, fama, scripta: Rheinische Mirakel des Hochmittelalters*.

[2] See the acute comments of Andrić, *The Miracles of St John Capistran*, pp. 351–63, and Justice, "Did the Middle Ages Believe in Their Miracles?."

[3] Bernard of Angers, *Liber miraculorum sancte Fidis* 2. 15, pp. 179–80; also discussed by Sigal, *L'homme et le miracle*, pp. 211–12.

been elsewhere nor did he (the student) utter a similar cry there." This argument insists that the event was ordained, not fortuitous. What made the student see it in that light was the prior invocation of St. Foy. If he had gone back into the wood and recovered his book without involving the saint, this would have been understood as a perfectly natural event.

Miraculous power had been part of the Christian conception of sanctity from the earliest days. When Jesus sent out his disciples to preach, he commanded them, "Heal the sick, cleanse the lepers, raise the dead, cast out devils" (Matthew 10:8). Miraculous healing and the ability to expel demons were thus part of the powers of these biblical saints, and they continued to be the surest markers of Christian sanctity.

The Greek Bible refers to miracles, sometimes by the general term "works," but also as "wonders," "powers," and "signs."[4] These three terms convey three different aspects of the miraculous: the subjective response of beholders to a miracle—wonder; the force behind the miraculous event—power; and its meaning—it is a sign. All three aspects were important.

Miracles are amazing. Although the term "miracles" (*miracula*) does not occur in the Latin New Testament, it became the most common way of referring to saintly miracles in Latin, and, like its Greek equivalent, *thaumata*, it means things that are a cause of wonder.[5] This stress on the response of the beholder could lead to complications. On the one hand, there were clearly marvels in the natural world. The Latin terms for "miracle" and "marvel" both come from the word for "wonder," and it was necessary to discuss the line between miracles and marvels: "all miracles are wonders but not all wonders are miracles."[6] And wasn't the great world we live in more wonderful than anything? The Jewish philosopher Philo, a contemporary of Jesus, had listed various cosmic phenomena, such as "the creation of the heaven, and the revolutions of the planets and fixed stars, and the shining of light," and commented

> All these things, though they are in truth really wonderful, are despised by us by reason of our familiarity with them. But the things to which we are not

[4] εργα; τερατα; δυναμεις; σημεια. For some discussion of the New Testament terminology of miracle, see Moule, "The Vocabulary of Miracle"; more generally, Grégoire, *Manuale di agiologia* 4/1, pp. 293–308.

[5] The Latin Vulgate translation uses the word *miraculum* a few times in the Old Testament, but it does not occur in the New. Here the preferred term is *signum*, "sign." The equivalent for the Greek "wonders" is *prodigia*. Hence, in St. Peter's speech at Pentecost, the reference to Jesus Christ being approved and confirmed δυναμεσιν και τερασιν και σημειοις becomes *virtutibus et prodigiis et signis* (Acts 2:22). In the earliest Miracle Book, the *Miracles of St Stephen*, the word "miracle" occurs 17 times, while *signum*, in the sense of "miracle," is found only once, in a biblical citation. The word *virtus* is more common in this work, sometimes in association with *miraculum*: the subject of the book is the *virtutum miracula*, "the miracles of power" (which became a common phrase), while the miracles (*miracula*) are seen as including "powers—or mighty deeds—of healing" (*virtutes sanitatum*) (*Miracula sancti Stephani* 1. prol., 2. 5, pp. 268, 346).

[6] *Omnia miracula sint mirabilia tamen non omnia mirabilia sunt miracula*: Collationes of Clement VI, cited by Goodich, *Miracles and Wonders*, p. 44 n. 81.

> accustomed, even though they may be unimportant, still make an impression upon us from our love of novelty.[7]

The idea was taken up by Augustine, who taught that God's government of the universe was a greater miracle than such things as turning water into wine or even raising the dead. These events were contrary to the usual course of nature and hence excited human wonder, which sleepily forgets the "daily miracles" of birth and growth—"the wonderful and astounding works of God in every seed of grain."[8]

In the Middle Ages, definitions of miracle were elaborated. The Church lawyers required that the miracles in canonization processes be demonstrated to be "beyond the forces and power of nature."[9] They specified that the saint's miracles should be: "from God and not from some skill"; "contrary to nature"; "not from the force of the words but from the merit of the person"; and "tending to strengthen the faith."[10] These criteria were sometimes cited explicitly in canonization documents themselves.[11] The standard monastic understanding of miracle, while expressed less technically, was not that different: "We call a miracle that which is done contrary to the usual course of nature and amazes us . . . the author of miracles is God."[12]

There was a great deal of high-level discussion of miracles during the scholastic period, but it rarely had much to do with the common everyday healing miracles that took place at the shrines of the saints. The questions asked in Thomas Aquinas's *Questions about Power* illustrate the kinds of problem that were engaging the subtle intellects of thirteenth-century scholastic theologians:

> Whether God can perform something in created things that transcends natural causes or is against nature or the course of nature.
> Whether everything that God does against the course of nature can be called a miracle.
> Whether spiritual creatures can perform miracles by their natural powers.
> Whether good angels and men can perform miracles through some gift of grace.
> Whether the performance of a miracle should be attributed to faith.
> Whether demons are forced by means of sensible and corporeal things, deeds or words to perform those miracles which appear to be accomplished through magic.[13]

[7] Philo of Alexandria, *De vita Mosis* 1. 212–13, pp. 128–30.

[8] These views are expressed particularly clearly in Augustine, *In Johannis Evangelium tractatus CXXIV* 8. 1; 9. 1; 24. 1, pp. 81–82, 90–91, 244 (PL 35: 1450–51, 1458, 1593–93).

[9] Innocent IV, *Apparatus super V libros decretalium*, ad X. 3. 45. 1, *Audivimus*.

[10] Hostiensis, *Summa super titulis decretalium* 3, "De reliquiis et veneratione sanctorum"; followed by Johannes Andreae, *Novella Commentaria in quinque Decretalium libros*, ad X. 3. 45. 1, *Audivimus*.

[11] *Acta et processus canonizacionis Beate Birgitte*, p. 605; see also the summary in *The Register of John Morton, Archbishop of Canterbury, 1486–1500* 1, pp. 49–50, item 181.

[12] Caesarius of Heisterbach, *Dialogus miraculorum* 10. 1 (2, p. 217).

[13] Thomas Aquinas, *Quaestiones disputatae de potentia* 6 pr., p. 230.

This wide range of complex questions shows how reflection on miracles led to ever more demanding issues, such as distinctions between God and nature, or the line between miracle and magic. But it was clearly Biblical rather than contemporary miracles that inspired these debates.

A point that careful theologians re-emphasized was that God was the author of miracles, not the saints themselves. They were merely agents and intercessors. Standard phrasing in descriptions of miracles was "many miracles were performed through God's efforts," "the holy remains were resplendent with many miracles through God's efforts ," "the wonderful works of God that the Lord worked in her and through her," all of them stressing God's working through the saints, rather than the saints acting autonomously. When the Carolingian bishop and polemicist Agobard of Lyons was refuting the idea that storms could be summoned up by human beings, which he regarded as a superstitious belief, he had to make an exception for the saints. He recognized that there had been cases when holy men, by their prayers, had brought welcome rain, but, he insisted, this had happened not by their own intrinsic power or by any power contrary to God's will, but by the will of the creator.[14]

There was clearly an influential line of thought in the Middle Ages arguing that miracles demonstrated sanctity. There was also a persistent body of opinion that they did not, but the first view was the more widely held, and was a commonplace of hagiographic literature. As Thomas of Monmouth, champion of the supposed boy-martyr William of Norwich, put it, "That he ought to be called—no, that he *is*—a saint, the divine grace proclaims publicly, by the miracles that occur every day around his tomb."[15] When, after the murder of Thomas Becket, opinion was divided whether he was a traitor or a martyr, "Christ resolved the dispute, since he glorified him with many great miracles."[16] Becket's miracles were, in fact, more conclusive even than papal canonization, for one priest, confronted with a spectacular miracle of this new saint, burst out, "Why are we waiting for the pope's command? I will wait no more, but will begin a solemn service for Thomas, the glorious friend of God, as for a most precious martyr!"[17]

This probative understanding of miracles comes out strongly in a story told about events at the French Cistercian monastery of Signy, after a monk with a reputation for holiness was buried in the monastic precinct. His tomb attracted crowds seeking cures. The abbot and monks, disturbed and distracted, went solemnly to the grave and addressed their departed brother:

> What is this, brother? We do not doubt the sanctity of your life and conduct. Why then these miracles? Do you not see that laymen coming to your tomb disturb the quiet of the monastery? In the name of our lord Jesus Christ, we

[14] Agobard of Lyons, *De grandine et tonitruis* 9, p. 10.
[15] Thomas of Monmouth, *Vita sancti Willelmi Norwicensis* 2. 2, p. 65.
[16] Caesarius of Heisterbach, *Dialogus miraculorum* 8. 69 (2, p. 139).
[17] Benedict of Peterborough, *Miracula sancti Thomae* 4. 2, p. 180.

order you to stop performing miracles. Otherwise, we will bury your body outside the monastery.

The threat was effective and miracles ceased.[18] The story shows how clearly these monks thought of miracles as proofs of sanctity much more than as marvellous help for the sick. They did not doubt the holiness of their departed brother. Why, then, did he need to perform miracles?

The development of papal canonization did not lead to any decline in the importance attached to miracles. Papal canonization bulls stressed that both miracles and virtues were necessary for official recognition as a saint. In practice, canonization processes paid much more attention to miracles. In those of the thirteenth and fourteenth centuries more than three-quarters of the witnesses gave evidence about the saint's miracles rather than his or her virtues and behaviour, and in the fifteenth century this proportion rose to almost 90 per cent.[19] The powerful cardinal Giacomo Colonna, deeply engaged in a canonization process, expressed the belief that "miracles performed after death are the particular evidence of a good end and a holy life."[20] Miracles required proof but also provided it.

A different emphasis was earlier struck by Gregory the Great, who insisted that, while "miracles sometimes demonstrate sanctity, they do not constitute it."[21] In the same vein, the Cistercian monk Caesarius of Heisterbach wrote that "Miracles are not the substance of sanctity but a kind of indication of sanctity," although this did not prevent him recording more miracles than perhaps any other single medieval author.[22] These views were not literally incompatible with the idea of probative miracles, but they suggest a difference of outlook. And other propositions also might lead to a less celebratory view of contemporary miracles: evil people can perform miracles too; virtue is better than supernatural power; and, in any case, the age of miracles has passed.

The Bible showed, and medieval theorists agreed, that even evil people might have the power to produce wonders. Pharaoh's magicians in the Exodus story had been able to change their rods into serpents, and, although Aaron's rod also turned into a serpent and then swallowed them up, there was no doubt that the Egyptian

[18] *Chronique de l'abbaye de Signy*, p. 649.

[19] Vauchez, *Sainthood*, p. 500, table 33; Vauchez argued, on the basis of the number of witnesses reporting on the life and on the miracles, that there was a shift from an interest in miracles in the thirteenth century to an emphasis on the life in the fourteenth and early fifteenth, but his interpretation is not strongly supported by his statistics; in the processes of 1223–66, almost 20 per cent of depositions were on the life, in those of 1307–1417, 24 per cent. For the fifteenth-century figures, see Wetzstein, "*Virtus morum et virtus signorum*? Zur Bedeutung der Mirakel in den Kanonisationsprozessen des 15. Jahrhunderts," p. 356.

[20] "S. Pierre Célestin et ses premiers biographes," p. 476.

[21] Gregory I, *Homiliae in Evangelia* 29. 4 (2, p. 206) (PL 76: 1216).

[22] Signa enim non sunt de substantia sanctitatis sed quedam indicia sanctitatis: Caesarius of Heisterbach, *Vita, passio et miracula sancti Engelberti* 3, prologue, p. 282; he repeated the phrase, with *miracula* instead of *signa*, in his *Sermo de translatione beate Elyzabeth*, p. 390.

sorcerers had actually achieved this amazing transformation. Many orthodox thinkers of the Middle Ages also accepted the possibility of "natural magic," which produced wondrous results by exploiting the occult forces of the physical world. In the high Middle Ages, popes stressed repeatedly that miracles were no sure indicator of sanctity, for even the devil could assume the form of an angel of light. Canonization bulls, and canon lawyers, reiterated that both miracles and virtue were necessary for sainthood because it was agreed that the supernatural was not monopolized by the saintly: "some do good works, as it seems to men, and some are resplendent with miracles, whose lives are nevertheless wicked."[23] The ascetic and reformer Peter Damian, who was an earnest critic of simony (the buying and selling of church office) and clerical marriage, had to admit that the bishop of Fiesole, who was notorious for having bought his office and for living with a woman as his wife, was nevertheless a wonder-worker: "through a man of this type many miracles are reported to have been performed."[24] Even miracles at the tomb might be no guide to true sanctity, and the great canon lawyer Hostiensis, writing in the thirteenth century, and discussing claims to sainthood, reported that "there are some people who say that, if the case is illusory, then miracles can scarcely continue beyond forty days," although he adds that he himself was uncertain about this.[25]

Augustine agreed that wicked people could perform miracles, but thought there was a purpose here:

> Even wicked men can perform some miracles that the saints cannot, but that does not mean that they should be deemed to have better standing with God. For the magicians of Egypt were not more acceptable to God than the people of Israel because the people could not do what they did. . . . The reason these things are not granted to all saints, is that weak minds should not be deceived into thinking that they are greater gifts than the works of justice.[26]

The consideration of the subject found in a popular Byzantine collection sums up the main points and examples used in discussions of this kind. Wicked people and unbelievers can perform miracles and can prophesy. Pharaoh's magicians were able to turn their staffs into serpents, while Balaam in the Old Testament (Numbers 22–24) and Caiaphas in the New (John 11:49–52) made accurate prophecies, although they were wicked unbelievers. Foreknowledge, in particular, can be imparted by demons, who have subtle senses able to read the signs of forthcoming events. Miraculous powers do not, in themselves, demonstrate personal sanctity. John the Baptist is

[23] Innocent III's canonization of Homobonus: Innocent III, *Die Register Innocenz' III* 1, pp. 761–64; other canonization bulls of Innocent's are similar; see Paciocco, *Canonizzazioni e culto dei santi*, pp. 36–38.

[24] Peter Damian, *Epistola* 40 (1, p. 439).

[25] Hostiensis, *Lectura siue Apparatus super quinque libris Decretalium*, ad X. 3. 45. 1, *Audivimus*; followed by Johannes Andreae, *Novella Commentaria in quinque Decretalium libros*, ad X. 3. 45. 1, *Audivimus*.

[26] Augustine, *De diversis quaestionibus octoginta tribus* 79. 3, p. 228 (PL 40: 92).

not reported to have performed any miracles, but Judas was sent out with the other disciples, to raise the dead and heal lepers. "You should not acknowledge a believer as a saint because of miracles and prophecies," the text concludes, "but because of his way of life."[27]

Augustine and the Byzantine writer, who could not have read each other, make an identical point: how a saint lives matters much more than his or her extraordinary powers. Many agreed that virtue was better than supernatural gifts.[28] The fifth-century cleric Verus, author of a Life of Eutropius, bishop of Orange, after recounting the saint's miracles (expelling demons, quelling fires), becomes reflective: "But why are we spending time on his miracles?" he asks, "It is better to tell of the things that will stir, instruct and edify listeners through his example." Verus then turns to Eutropius's active works of charity.[29] The virtuous way of life of Eutropius's contemporary, bishop Honoratus, was described as "a kind of perpetual miracle," while a hagiographer of the twelfth century could write that his saintly subject died "perfected in the grace of virtue, which is a greater thing than if he had shone with the glory of miracles."[30] And to reach out to others through the Word could be seen as better, and a more profound kind of connection, than spectacular wonders. As Alcuin put it, "there is no doubt that the office of preaching is greater than any manifestation of miraculous powers."[31]

Moreover, while thousands of miracles were recorded in the Middle Ages, there is also the countervailing fact that medieval writers often expressed the view that "the age of miracles" was over.[32] This position had deep roots and a long history. An important passage in St. Paul's First Letter to the Corinthians (14:22) deals with the "gift of tongues," that is, the divinely inspired ability to speak in foreign and unknown languages, as manifested by the apostles at Pentecost. This miraculous gift, St. Paul says, "is a sign not to believers but to unbelievers." He means that its purpose is to convince non-Christians and it is of little significance for the believers themselves. In saying this, he was attempting to shift the emphasis away from a spectacular, but rather self-centred, display of charismatic spirituality towards the fruitful teaching and preaching which the Christian community did require. Outsiders might be impressed by the uncanny show of speaking in tongues, but the Christian community had a greater need for "edification and exhortation." Paul's term "sign," which was rendered in the Latin Vulgate as *signum*, was one medieval word for a

[27] Anastasius of Sinai (attrib.), *Quaestiones et responsiones* 20, cols. 517–32; this collection is found in manuscripts of the eleventh century and later; the text takes as its starting point a genuine question of Anastasius of Sinai, writing in the late seventh century, but then elaborates it extensively. See Anastasius of Sinai, *Quaestiones et responsiones* 62, pp. 112–13, and the editorial discussion there on pp. XXI–XXII.

[28] See the discussion in Demm, "Zur Rolle des Wunders."

[29] Verus, *Vita Eutropii*, p. 61.

[30] Hilary of Arles, *Vita Honorati*, pp. 169–70; Sigebert of Gembloux, *Vita Wicberti* 17, col. 675.

[31] Alcuin, *Vita Richarii* 9, p. 120 (MGH, SRM 4, p. 394).

[32] See Van Uytfanghe, "La controverse biblique et patristique autour du miracle."

miracle, and a condensed version of his words, "miracles are not for believers but for unbelievers" (*signa non fidelibus, sed infidelibus*), became proverbial.

A natural development of this kind of thinking was the idea that, once the Church had established itself and come to dominate society, miracles were no longer needed. Augustine wrote that Christ's "visible miracles" were a kind of baby food, which enabled faith to grow; but faith, he argued, "was the stronger, the more it did not seek this kind of thing."[33] Once the Church had spread throughout the world and had been established, he argues, miracles could dry up.[34] He later changed his view on this subject, but it was an attitude that endured as a subsidiary stream in Christian thinking. In the century after Augustine's death, Pope Gregory I addressed people who wondered why they did not see in the Church of their own day miracles such as those described in the New Testament. In the early days of the Church, he wrote, miracles were necessary to ensure its growth, rather as one waters a newly planted shrub until it is well established.[35] He explained that the Church had needed such a support in the time of persecution but nowadays only good works were required, citing St. Paul's comment from I Corinthians and concluding, "Why should it be surprising if, now that the faith has spread, miracles do not happen frequently?"[36] Taking his text from Jesus's words, "Heal the sick, cleanse the lepers, raise the dead, cast out devils," Pope Gregory argued that such miracles were necessary in the missionary days of the early church, but not in his own time, when "the number of the faithful has increased":

> Miracles were granted to the holy preachers for this reason, so that the power they displayed might make their words credible, and those who preached new things might perform new things . . . who would believe that there was another life or prefer invisible things to visible things? But when the sick returned to health, when the dead rose again to life, when lepers received purity of the flesh, when those possessed were snatched from the power of demons, who would not believe what they heard about invisible things?

Nowadays, he says, there are many faithful Christians who excel in virtue but do not have the power of performing miracles.[37] Such a position could be found repeatedly throughout the Middle Ages, amongst Christians of very different types. The thirteenth-century scholastic theologian who wrote, "Since the faith is much stronger nowadays than earlier, it is right that greater miracles were done in former times," would have had no disagreement, in principle, with the fifteenth-century her-

[33] Augustine, *De peccatorum meritis et remissione* 2. 32. 52, p. 122 (PL 44: 182).

[34] Augustine, *De vera religione* 25. 47, pp. 216–17 (PL 34: 142).

[35] Gregory I, *Homiliae in Evangelia* 29. 4 (2, pp. 204–6) (PL 76: 1215–16).

[36] Gregory I, *Moralia in Iob* 27. 18 (143B, p. 1359) (PL 76: 420).

[37] Gregory I, *Homiliae in Evangelia* 4. 3 (1, p. 156) (PL 76: 1091); for discussion of Gregory's views on this topic, see McCready, *Signs of Sanctity: Miracles in the Thought of Gregory the Great*, pp. 7–32 ("Miracles Past and Present").

etic who asserted, "now, when the faith of God is established in Christendom, the word of God suffices to man's salvation, without such miracles."[38]

The argument that the age of miracles has passed generally presumed that earlier, unbelieving periods needed a convincing demonstration of Christian supernatural powers, but it could also take a slightly different, more pessimistic form, painting the modern world as cold and weak in belief. "Now is that time in which love grows cold," wrote the twelfth-century monk Orderic Vitalis. "Miracles, the indications of sanctity, cease." He saw the coming "time of Antichrist" as preceded by "a dearth of miracles."[39] His contemporary, William of Malmesbury, stressed, not the absence of miracles, but modern doubts. Recording the wonderful posthumous miracles of Wulfstan of Worcester, William noted indignantly,

> And indeed, if the ready belief of the men of old had been here to help, he would long ago have been elevated on high and recognized as a saint. But the lack of belief of men of our own time, which adorns itself with the pretext of caution, does not wish to believe in miracles, even if seen with the eye and touched with the finger.[40]

Sometimes the two ideas, that the age of miracles had passed and that virtue was more important than miracles, were combined, with apologetic purpose. Alpert of Metz, describing how the saintly Bishop Ansfried of Utrecht (995–1010) carefully tended a leper, raises a question that the reader might ask: why did this holy man not simply cure the leper? He devotes a special chapter to this subject, with the title, "Why Ansfried did not cure the sick." After citing the verse from Corinthians that asserts "miracles are not for believers but for unbelievers," Alpert uses words borrowed from Gregory the Great to explain that miracles were necessary for the early days of the Church. In modern times, he continues, when the whole world is filled with the name of Christ, what need does the Church have of miracles? Ansfried was not interested in the applause of men but in a good conscience; and the leper might have benefited from his disease, since it prevented him from committing some sins; and Ansfried's spiritual powers were, in any case, recognized by the demons. "I have treated this matter briefly," Alpert concludes,

> lest anyone judge in his heart that it was because of some defect in his excellent life that our Lord Jesus Christ was unwilling to grant to his servant the power of miracles, he who granted him something that is greater and far more blessed than these, that is, eternal life in the heavenly kingdom.[41]

[38] Alexander of Hales, *Glossa in quatuor libros Sententiarum Petri Lombardi* 2. 18. 5 (2, p. 159); Hudson, ed., *Two Wycliffite Texts*, p. 61 (William Thorpe, 1407, modernized).

[39] Orderic Vitalis, *Historia ecclesiastica* 5. 1 (3, p. 8).

[40] William of Malmesbury, *Gesta pontificum Anglorum* 4. 149, p. 438.

[41] Alpert of Metz, *De diversitate temporum* 1. 14–15, pp. 30–34 (MGH, SS 4, pp. 707–8).

So, there are no more miracles, and, in any case, they are not the most important thing. Perhaps Alpert would have had an easier task as a hagiographer if he had been able to record dozens of Ansfried's miraculous cures.

Patterns of Miracles

Just as the late 1970s and early 1980s were a boom time for counting saints (earlier, pp. 137ff.), so they were for counting miracles. Ronald Finucane studied 2,363 miracles from England and France in the twelfth and thirteenth centuries, Pierre-André Sigal 4,756 from eleventh- and twelfth-century France, and André Vauchez more than 1,743 from canonization processes between the late twelfth and the early fifteenth centuries.[42] The 2,447 miracles recorded for Bernardino of Siena (d. 1444) were given a summary analysis in 1984.[43] Several other studies, some from this period, some later, dealing with samples of several hundred miracles, have added to the overall picture, although variations in systems of classification and presentation of data mean it is not always easy to synthesize their findings.[44] Despite all the reservations one might have about these figures, they do constitute at least the beginnings of an attempt to chart the patterns of miraculous activity in the Middle Ages, even if one must remember that the trends they reveal have to be analysed as changes in what was recorded, and, by inference, what was valued, in the activities of those viewed as saints, before it is possible to ask about changes in actual behaviour.

The most extensive and detailed statistical analysis of medieval miracles was that undertaken by Sigal, published in 1985. His overall figures break down as shown in tables 9.1 and 9.2 (I give the raw data so that others can employ them as they will).[45] In Sigal's enormous collection of data, the ratio of posthumous miracles to those accomplished in the saint's lifetime is 3:1—many more miracles are performed from the tomb than by a living holy man or woman. The same imbalance is found in the miracles recorded in the canonization processes of the thirteenth, fourteenth, and fifteenth centuries analysed by Vauchez. In almost all cases, the posthumous miracles that are described in these processes outnumber the miracles performed in the saint's lifetime by 3:1 or more, sometimes constituting 90 or even 100 per cent of the total.[46]

[42] Finucane, *Miracles and Pilgrims*, p. 143; Sigal, *L'homme et le miracle*, p. 289; Vauchez, *Sainthood*, p. 503, table 34, lists 1,743 miracles, but these are only a sample.

[43] Jansen, "Un exemple de sainteté thaumaturgique," p. 150, tables I and II.

[44] For example, Gonthier and Le Bas, "Analyse socio-économique de quelques recueils de miracles dans la Normandie"; Giordano, "Sociologia e patologia del miracolo"; Rouche, "Miracles, maladies et psychologie de la foi"; Dalarun, *La sainte et la cité*; Krötzl, *Pilger, Mirakel und Alltag*; Goetz, "Heiligenkult und Geschlecht"; Andrić, *The Miracles of St John Capistran*; Goetz, "Wunderberichte im 9. Jahrhundert."

[45] Calculated from the figures in *L'homme et le miracle*, pp. 289, 294, 297, 300–301.

[46] Vauchez, *Sainthood*, p. 503, table 34; the preponderance of posthumous miracles in the cults of the new saints of the Middle Byzantine period (eighth to tenth century) is less marked, at 53 per cent: Talbot, "Pilgrimage to Healing Shrines," p. 169.

TABLE 9.1
Sigal's Figures for Typology of Healing Miracles

	Posthumous miracles	In vita miracles	Total
Paralysis	697	234	931
Blindness and eye affections	305	170	475
Deafness and dumbness	201	101	302
Mental illness	197	44	241
Unspecified illness	143	21	164
Tumours and ulcers	110	14	124
Fevers and infections	88	24	112
Wounds	91	13	104
Ergotism	60	0	60
Resurrection	53	7	60
Neural problems	40	13	53
Digestive ailments	30	6	36
Various	15	3	18
Skin disease	9	7	16
Urinary ailments	11	1	12
TOTAL	2,050	658	2,708

An explicit declaration that posthumous miracles have special significance is found in the works of Gregory of Tours. He is describing a local saint of an earlier generation, who was credited with only one miracle in his lifetime. This is no objection to his sanctity, Gregory says, for he performed many miracles after his death, and "the power that comes from the tomb is more praiseworthy than what the living person does in this life, for that can be stained by the continual bother of worldly business, while the former is clearly free of all stain."[47] Gregory may have been especially appreciative of this saint's posthumous powers since he himself was one of the beneficiaries of his healing miracles. The preponderance of miracles from the tomb was an enduring feature of the medieval cult of the saints. Abbot Desiderius of Monte Cassino explained,

[47] Gregory of Tours, *Liber vitae patrum* 2. 2, pp. 669–70 (repr., 1969, pp. 219–20).

TABLE 9.2
Sigal's Figures for Typology of Non-healing Miracles

	Posthumous miracles	In vita miracles	Total
Visions	387	188	575
Punishments	421	49	470
Favourable interventions	241	106	347
Protection from danger	197	38	235
Deliverance from prison	154	5	159
Glorification of saint	122	29	151
Prophetic vision	6	77	83
Obtaining children	16	12	28
TOTAL	1,544	504	2,048

> Almighty God often acts in such a way that he does not allow to be concealed the merit of those who strive to serve him devoutly, although they show no sign of sanctity when still in the flesh; nevertheless, after death, when their bodies are destroyed, they are perceived so to glisten with miracles, that human minds are enflamed more sharply in his service.[48]

A Franciscan author, writing in the 1240s, also noted that saints often performed far more posthumous miracles than miracles in their lifetime; he explained this partly because it discouraged adulation of the living saint and the consequent temptation to self-pride, but more emphatically because it demonstrated the truth of the doctrine of the resurrection: "It builds up faith in the glory of the resurrection in feeble minds when contact with the holy remains, which the carnal intellect considers worthless and destroyed, bestows various cures and sometimes even bodily life itself."[49]

Despite this emphasis on the importance of posthumous miracles, it is worth pointing out that some of the major saints of the Middle Ages did not have significant careers as posthumous miracle workers. St. Bernard of Clairvaux, a dominant figure in the Church in the twelfth century, performed numerous miracles during his life on earth, but scarcely any thereafter. St. Francis, whose image was of enormous

[48] Desiderius of Monte Cassino, *Dialogi de miraculis sancti Benedicti* 2. 3, p. 1129.

[49] *Dialogus de gestis sanctorum Fratrum Minorum*, p. 120 ("De fratre Benevenuto de Eugubio" 31).

importance to subsequent generations as a model and inspiration, did not have a shrine-cult involving miracles; in fact his body was buried away under tons of concrete that made it impossible to get anywhere near the saint.[50] Bernard and Francis were great leaders and innovators in the full-time religious life, and it is not accidental that their cults show a certain distrust of posthumous tomb miracles, for, even though miracles might bring pilgrims and profit, they also disturbed the quiet of monastic life and the rhythm of daily services that formed its core.

Tensions between healing cult and monastic ideals can be found on more than one occasion.[51] The case of the monks of Signy has already been mentioned (p. 336) but there were many more incidents of that kind. When the Byzantine monastic saint, Paul, abbot of Latros near Miletus, died in 955, a miracle occurred at his tomb almost immediately. A monk who was unknowingly possessed by evil spirits began to leap about and utter loud nonsense; the presence of the saintly body quickly cured him, but the monastic service had been disrupted. Paul's successor Simeon went to the saint's tomb and spoke "as if to a living man." Did this spectacular miracle, he demanded, show the contempt for human glory that Paul had advocated while alive? When word of it spread, the church would be full of crowds of men, women and children. "What then," he asked, "of our freedom, what then of a quiet life free of tumult?" If the saint wished to help his own monks, he should do so secretly; otherwise Simeon would have to move his body. Paul immediately stopped healing those possessed by demons (although Simeon moved him into a specially constructed oratory anyway).[52]

In the West, it was the Cistercians who had the greatest reservations about healing shrines in their churches. When crowds of sick people began to flock to the tomb of Waltheof, the recently deceased abbot of Melrose in the Scottish borders, the new abbot "ordered all those sick people who turned up to be barred from going to or from the saint's tomb." The avowed reason for this ban was "so that the monks of the Cistercian Order should be spared the excessive crush of crowds," although Waltheof's hagiographer was sceptical of abbot William's motives and happy to report that he was soon dismissed from office.[53] Cistercians showed this reticence even in the case of their revered saint, Bernard, one of the greatest thaumaturges of the twelfth century:

> The abbot of Cîteaux, who had come to the funeral of the man of God, along with many other abbots of his Order, pondering the rude insistence of the tumultuous crowd of common people, and deducing the future from the present, began to be deeply afraid that, as miracles multiplied, such an intolerable

[50] Brooke, *The Image of St Francis*, pp. 454–71.

[51] See Sigal, *L'homme et le miracle*, pp. 223–25, for several examples from the eleventh and twelfth centuries; also Demm, "Zur Rolle des Wunders," pp. 308–9.

[52] *Vita sancti Pauli Iunioris* 45, pp. 165–67; also in Wiegand, *Milet* . . . 3/1: *Der Latmos*, p. 131.

[53] Jocelin of Furness, *Vita sancti Walthenis* 9. 120, p. 274; on this work, see Birkett, *The Saints' Lives of Jocelin of Furness*, pp. 115–38, 201–25.

> throng of common people would flock together that the discipline of the Order would succumb to their wickedness and the fervour of holy religion in that place would grow cool. So, after taking advice, he went reverently and prohibited him from performing any more miracles, under obedience . . . the holy and truly humble spirit of our father was obedient to mortal man even after the death of the flesh. For the miracles that had, at that time, begun to shine forth ceased, so that, from that day on, never was he seen to perform any miracles in public, although he could not fail certain of the faithful, especially the brethren of his Order, who have invoked him for various misfortunes, up to the present day. For it is clear that the abbot of Cîteaux only wished those miracles to stop which might threaten the discipline of the Order through crowds of common people coming together.[54]

It is worth noting that, despite their very different worlds, the French Cistercian of the twelfth century, like the Byzantine monk of the tenth, was expected to continue to help his monastic fellows secretly. It was crowds of lay people around the shrine that might bother the more austere communities. Exactly the same concern about disruption is reported about a living saint in the Life and Miracles of the sixteenth-century Spanish Franciscan Salvador de Horta, who was told with some irritation, "if these miracles of yours stop, the crowds of people will also stop," but it was the healing tomb that represented the most commonly perceived intrusion.[55]

Statistical analysis of thousands of miracles can illuminate many different aspects of saintly cult. One simple question that can usually be answered is the proportion of male and female beneficiaries of the saint's powers (even when the pilgrim is anonymous, the Latin language distinguishes through its word endings). Large-scale studies of miracles in the high and late Middle Ages reach a striking agreement that the usual ratio of those cured was roughly 60 per cent male and 40 per cent female.[56] Characteristically, the sex ratio in the miracle collections from Normandy in the period 1050–1300 is 59:41.[57] Similar proportions are found in later medieval Byzantium: of seventy-seven miracles recorded in five late Byzantine collections, 58 per cent benefitted males and 42 per cent females.[58] It is not possible to be certain whether this represents the reality of the situation or a bias in the reporting, but since there were greater inhibitions on women's travel than on men's, it may well be that male pilgrims did predominate slightly.

[54] Conrad of Eberbach, *Exordium magnum Cisterciense* 2. 20, pp. 97–98 (PL 185: 448); see Bredero, *Bernard of Clairvaux: Between Cult and History*, pp. 65–73.

[55] Serpi, *Vita Saluatoris de Horta* 11 (14). 106, pp. 684–85.

[56] Sigal, *L'homme et le miracle*, p. 300 (healing miracles among the "classes populaires"; his overall proportions of 75:25 are affected by the inclusion of many miracle stories from *exempla* collections); Finucane, *Miracles and Pilgrims*, p. 143; Sargent, "Saints' Cults and Naming Patterns in Bavaria," pp. 676–77 n. 11.

[57] Gonthier and Le Bas, "Analyse socio-économique de quelques recueils de miracles dans la Normandie," p. 27 (excluding "non precisé").

[58] Efthymiadis, "Late Byzantine Collections of Miracles and Their Implications," p. 246.

The evidence earlier in the Middle Ages is less clear-cut but, in general, is comparable. A study of 477 miracles of the Carolingian and immediately following period in the region between the Loire and the Rhine established that 73.5 per cent (351) were healing miracles, and the division between the sexes in these healing miracles was 57 per cent male to 43 per cent female (200:151).[59] A sample of 724 miracles from the sixth to ninth centuries showed the proportion of males at 53 per cent.[60] These are lower than the figures for later periods but not significantly so. More striking is the pattern in the sixth-century miracles of St. Martin of Tours. Of 280 people cured or helped by the saint, 230 (82 per cent) were male, only 50 (18 per cent) female.[61] It would be rash to see this as characteristic of its time rather than the idiosyncrasy of a particular cult, since it is clear that individual cults had their distinctive features, including the pattern of division between the sexes. Like St. Martin, Thomas Aquinas bestowed his favours unequally. Of 124 people healed by the saint, 78 per cent were male, 22 per cent female.[62] The opposite imbalance is also found. The miracles of St. Æbbe, for example, at a minor cult centre in southern Scotland in the late twelfth and thirteenth centuries, benefitted 42 individuals, 26 (62 per cent) of them female, only 16 (38 per cent) male.[63] There clearly were saints and shrines that were particularly attractive to women. Contemporaries sometimes noticed such special "constituencies." Werburga, the local saint of Chester, for example, particularly answered the prayers of women and children.[64]

Both Æbbe and Werburga were female, and a question that arises very naturally is whether the cult-followers, the pilgrims and others who revered a particular saint, in some way reflected the kind of saint involved. For example, one of the simplest questions of this type that one might ask is whether more men went to male saints and more women to female saints. The study just mentioned of 724 miracles recorded in the Frankish lands from the sixth to the ninth centuries (the great majority from the ninth century) showed a slight tendency for male saints to cure males and female saints to cure females; those cured by male saints were 56.4 per cent male, those by female saints 58.3 per cent female. The total number cured breaks down into 382 male and 342 female, so there is only a small preponderance of males (52.8:47.2).[65] Evidence from Byzantium in the ninth and tenth centuries also supports the idea that "men were somewhat more likely to be healed by the relics of male saints and women by female saints."[66]

[59] Rouche, "Miracles, maladies et psychologie de la foi," p. 336, table I.

[60] *Goetz,* "Heiligenkult und Geschlecht," p. 96.

[61] Giordano, "Sociologia e patologia del miracolo," p. 172; not dissimilar figures in Pietri, *La ville de Tours du IVe au VIe siècle,* p. 558.

[62] William de Tocco, *Ystoria sancti Thome de Aquino,* p. 54 (editorial introduction).

[63] *The Miracles of St Æbbe of Coldingham and St Margaret of Scotland*, p. xxiii.

[64] William of Malmesbury, *Gesta pontificum Anglorum* 4. 172, p. 468.

[65] Goetz, "Heiligenkult und Geschlecht."

[66] Talbot, "Pilgrimage to Healing Shrines," p. 163.

Miracles were more frequent in some times and places than others. As early as the age of Augustine, the uneven incidence of miraculous activity was noticed. "God is everywhere," wrote the saint, "but who can grasp his counsel, why these miracles occur in some places and not in others?"[67] Nor was miraculous activity at any given shrine constant and regular. When it is possible to trace the origins of those who came to the shrine and to date their journey, it becomes clear that, over the course of time, suppliants seeking cures came from further and further away as the fame of the healing sanctuary spread (if it prospered). The locals, often lower-class and/or female, were joined by a higher-class and more masculine clientele from further afield.[68] Often miracles would start during spring, have a boom period and then trail off; sometimes 40 per cent of all miracles recorded at a shrine would take place in the first month.[69] This initial surge, and subsequent diminuendo, was noted at the time in the case of the cult of Enrico or Rigo of Bolzano, whose death in 1315 was followed by a wave of enthusiasm: "The throng of people lasted about a year, but it was at its greatest in the first three months."[70] In Byzantium too many healing cults were "of relatively short duration."[71] There was no steady state. Just as raindrops, when they begin to fall on the surface of a pond, splash, ripple out in a circle and then disappear, to be succeeded by others, so shrines were always bursting into activity, fading away and being challenged or replaced by new ones. As one saint declined in popularity, others would arise. Contemporaries might even envisage them spurring each other on, like cocks crowing at dawn.[72]

A story from the miracles of Thomas Becket pictures the old saints retiring and letting the new saint have his turn. The son of a priest near Dieppe has fallen ill and his father has invoked Our Lady of Rocamadour and other saints:

> but they did not heed the invocation of their name, for their time of glory was past and they wished the martyr of modern days to have his own time of mercy. Formerly they ran as fast as they could and as they ought, flashing bright with signs and wonders, but now it was the time for the new martyr to run, so that he might be deemed wonderful in the catalogue of the saints. God determines what ought to be done, by whom and at what time. He [that is, St. Thomas] now runs and traverses great spaces, while the other saints have the leisure of veterans and old soldiers.[73]

[67] Augustine, *Epistola* 78. 3, p. 85 (PL 33: 269).

[68] Finucane, *Miracles and Pilgrims*, pp. 181–88; Sigal, *L'homme et le miracle*, pp. 304–9; Andrić, *The Miracles of St John Capistran*, pp. 320–22, 333–34; Lappin, *The Medieval Cult of Saint Dominic of Silos*, p. 97.

[69] Sigal, *L'homme et le miracle*, pp. 188–96.

[70] Peter, bishop of Treviso, *Vita Henrici Baucenensis* 2. 23, p. 374.

[71] Talbot, "Pilgrimage to Healing Shrines," p. 157.

[72] Paschasius Radbertus, *Epitaphium Arsenii* 2. 1, col. 1608.

[73] William of Canterbury, *Miracula sancti Thomae* 3. 33, p. 290.

Healing Miracles

Miraculous Cures

Most miracles are miracles of healing and hence the study of the cult of the saints also involves study of the history of medicine and concepts of cure. Hagiography is, indeed, one of the more important sources of the history of medieval medicine. For many centuries, when there are no detailed case studies of illness, and even later, in the periods when there are plenty of medical treatises, these stories of saintly cures provide the most elaborate and detailed accounts of individual ailments. The modern editors of the rich and extensive canonization hearings for St. Nicholas of Tolentino, held in the Marche in 1305, thought it worthwhile to index some hundred references to medical doctors in the text, as well as producing a special index of medical terms to be found there.[74]

The saints were themselves seen as doctors. Cosmas and Damian, those "glorious and awe-inspiring doctors," are a famous example (see earlier, p. 42), while, writing of the miracles of St. Martin, Gregory of Tours thanked God, "who deigned to give us such a doctor."[75] St. Cyrus and St. John became irate when one of the ushers in their sanctuary invited a real human doctor in to deal with a disturbed pilgrim who had cut his own throat After healing the man, they rebuked the usher: "Don't you know that our house is the surgery of the whole world; don't you know that Christ has given us to believers as their doctors?"[76] A healing miracle could be celebrated by a direct simile: "The saint, a helper in troubles, restored her to pristine health, like a true doctor."[77] Sometimes saints, particularly, it seems, those of Constantinople, actually prescribed natural medicinal remedies. Cosmas and Damian recommended a rather unpalatable drink of cedar oil, while Artemios advised a treatment of vinegar and salt.[78] In the mid-fifth century the Constantinopolitan lawyer Aquilinus was cured after "a divine power" appeared to him at the church of St. Michael of Anaplous and recommended a potion of honey, wine, and pepper.[79] Some saints might even boast about their medical skill. After one of his cures, Thomas Becket says, "Ho! Aren't I a good physician!"[80]

Writers of miracle accounts were aware that the greatest rivals of the saints were doctors, and they revelled in describing their failures. Of the eighty-two miracles recorded in the canonization hearing of Ambrose of Massa in 1240, twenty—so

[74] *Il processo per la canonizzazione di S. Nicola da Tolentino*, pp. 679, 665–77 (the indexes were produced by editors after the death of Occhioni, editor of the text itself).

[75] *Talem medicum*: Gregory of Tours, *De virtutibus sancti Martini* 3, pref., p. 632 (repr., 1969, p. 182).

[76] Sophronius of Jerusalem, *Miracula Cyri et Ioannis* 67. 10, p. 389.

[77] *Miracula sancti Sigismondi martyris, per ipsum in sanctam Pragensem ecclesiam manifeste demonstrata*, p. 464.

[78] *Miracula Cosmae et Damiani* 11, pp. 122–28; *Miracula sancti Artemii* 20, p. 124.

[79] Sozomen, *Historia ecclesiastica* 2. 3. 10–11 (1, pp. 242–44).

[80] William of Canterbury, *Miracula sancti Thomae* 2. 7, p. 164.

almost a quarter—involve failed recourse to doctors before the cure.[81] In one case, a citizen of Orvieto had such a severe abscess that "all the doctors said that he was dying of that ailment and it was incurable," but his faithful wife invoked Ambrose and he was immediately cured.[82] After the failure of medical remedies a suppliant might appear at a shrine "blaming himself, because he had sought out the doctors before the saints."[83] Sometimes it was a condition of a miraculous cure that people should *not* seek medical help. One suppliant to Lawrence of Subiaco "vowed to God and the blessed brother Lawrence that he would never again take any medicine . . . as soon as he had made this vow sincerely, he began to get better."[84] A more drastic case concerned William, sacristan of Norwich cathedral in the mid-twelfth century, who suffered from a long illness. St. William of Norwich appeared in a dream to two people, giving instructions about how the sacristan should seek healing from one of the saint's relics, adding, "But I wish him first to promise to me that he will henceforth take no medicine except this of mine." The sacristan followed the instructions, made the vow and was cured, but later, when his illness recurred, "the doctors persuaded him and he sought refuge in the deceits of medicine." Needless to say, he was dead within a few days, leaving the hagiographer to reflect, "how carefully the commands of the saints are to be kept."[85]

In the canonization processes of the later Middle Ages medical doctors were occasionally called as witnesses or to give expert advice.[86] In 1304, for example, a bone doctor reported on the case of Massus of Città di Castello (near Arezzo), who had broken his arm falling from a horse. The arm had healed very badly and Massus could scarcely move it. All of the doctor's efforts had been in vain, until the bystanders had invoked St. Rainier of Arezzo and the arm cracked back into its proper shape.[87] Medical opinion was by no means a requirement in the examination of miraculous cures, but, when it is given, it is there to demonstrate the limits of the doctor's powers. The purpose of the medical evidence in these canonization hearings was to underline the failure of ordinary healing techniques and hence the miraculous nature of the cure. As one (non-medical) witness put it,

> It truly seems to be a miracle when the sickness was so severe and lasted such a long time and such experienced doctors found no cure, but, rather, one had

[81] *Processus canonizationis beati Ambrosii Massani*; Galletti, "'Infirmitas' e terapia sacra in una città medievale," p. 23. On the difficulties of this process, see Pellegrini, "*Negotium imperfectum*: il processo per la canonizzazione di Ambrogio da Massa."

[82] *Processus canonizationis beati Ambrosii Massani*, p. 592.

[83] Sophronius of Jerusalem, *Miracula Cyri et Ioannis* 3. 2, p. 248.

[84] *Inquisitio de vita et miraculis Laurentii Sublacensis*, miracle 32, p. 86.

[85] Thomas of Monmouth, *Vita sancti Willelmi Norwicensis* 4. 9, pp. 174–77.

[86] Ziegler, "Practitioners and Saints."

[87] *Relatio miraculorum quæ facta sunt meritis beati Rainerii* 41, p. 398; Ziegler, "Practitioners and Saints," p. 197.

> said that he had given up all hope, and the sickness, which seemed to get worse every day, was so suddenly cured.[88]

On some occasions doctors were themselves cured by the saints, as in the case of Michael Berruti, physician to the Duke of Savoy in the late fifteenth century, who was plagued with stomach pains for seven years and more, until he invoked St. Goslinus: "The human doctor ran to seek the help of the heavenly doctor."[89]

Accounts of miraculous healing, while often being vague on the subject of the illness or ailment ("a very serious disease," "desperately sick," and so on), can sometimes be more precise. It is not uncommon for miracle accounts to describe symptoms and even to give a technical medical name for an ailment, as in the case of a sick boy seeking a cure in Angers around about the year 1100, "whose throat and mouth were so seriously swollen by the disease that is called *anguina* by the doctors, that he was unable to utter a word or swallow food."[90] The illness here is clearly an inflammation of the throat, which was often termed *angina* (of which *anguina* must be a variant) in the Middle Ages and later. The monks or clergy recording the miracles would sometimes themselves have had medical training or experience, and this shows through in their vocabulary. A notable example is William of Canterbury, collector of the miracles of Thomas Becket at Canterbury in the 1170s, whose narratives are full of medical terms.[91]

A particularly full description of an ailment occurs in the account of a posthumous miracle of St. Cuthbert, curing a poor peasant boy in Scotland:

> He was burning and labouring with a most serious illness, for he had sustained a "good boil" above the thighs next to the groin. This pestilential disease had taken hold of the young man where the belly joins the thigh, at the angle of leg and groin, so that he could expect nothing except the release of death. For it had grown bigger than a man's head and this great tumour had pulled away almost the whole surface of the skin. It was red as a flame coming from a fire or like a red-hot coal burning in the heat of a fire. But, underneath, the matter was so discoloured with blackness from accumulated dirt, that it appeared to onlookers, not to have the redness of flesh or the heat of fire, but to be the filthy mess of putrefaction. Within, there arose sharp stabbing pains that seemed to pierce his heart and bore into his inmost organs with inexpressible suffering. His agony was unspeakable and all who saw him judged that there was no hope of healing or recovery.[92]

88 *Processus canonizationis sancti Ludovici episcopi Tolosani* 115, p. 186.

89 *Historia inventionis corporis et miraculorvm sancti Goslini* 2. 1, p. 633; Ziegler, "Practitioners and Saints," p. 207.

90 *Vita sancti Girardi confessoris* 2. 15, p. 497.

91 Koopmans, *Wonderful to Relate*, pp. 183–98.

92 Reginald of Durham, *Libellus de admirandis beati Cuthberti virtutibus* 101, p. 224.

Clearly the term "good boil" (*bonum malagnum*) is technical (it occurs elsewhere as a synonym for "carbuncle," or malignant boil), but the description in any case leaves little doubt about the nature of the disease—or the suffering.[93]

The categories of illness used by Sigal and others who have analysed miracle accounts are obviously modern, but most of them fit quite easily with the medieval terminology. Definitions are general—paralysis, blindness, and so on—and do not aspire to diagnostic exactitude. And the picture that emerges, the world of cripples, blind people, people with chronic neural and digestive illnesses, is not surprising. The Middle Ages was a time of malnutrition, unsanitary conditions and medical care that was minimal or more dangerous than the disease.

The existence of large-scale analyses of miracles like those of Sigal, Vauchez, and Finucane not only means that their figures can be compared (with due attention to the different times, places and purposes which generated the records) but also allows individual cults to be compared with these general patterns, to see what is typical and what distinctive about them. This has been done, for example, in the case of the miracles of Peter Martyr, the Italian Dominican murdered in 1252.[94] Taking Vauchez's figures as the general model for comparison, the analysis shows that Peter was not as active as other saints in healing the blind and the lame, but took a special interest in problems of childbirth and fertility. Interestingly, he was also particularly energetic in inflicting miraculous punishment, perhaps appropriately for a man who had been an Inquisitor in life.

Sigal's figures, because they constitute such a large sample, are an especially useful yardstick, and can be compared with those from other times and places. For instance, paralysis, blindness and deaf-mutism comprise 63.1 per cent of the ailments mentioned in the miracle cures he studied.[95] This predominance, of the order of 60–70 per cent, is common in several other samples too.[96] For the same groups of ailments, however, Vauchez gives a figure of 45.7 per cent for the thirteenth century and, for the fourteenth century, the significantly lower figure of 30.5 per cent.[97] Vauchez argues that the decline in these ailments corresponds to an increase in the practice of

[93] "Carbunculus, quod malum Franci per antiphrasim bonum malannum vocant": Goscelin of St.-Bertin, *Historia translationis sancti Augustini episcopi* 1. 19, col. 22.

[94] Prudlo, *The Martyred Inquisitor*, pp. 144–48.

[95] Sigal, *L'homme et le miracle*, p. 256.

[96] Gonthier and Le Bas, "Analyse socio-économique de quelques recueils de miracles dans la Normandie," p. 22, table II; Rouche, "Miracles, maladies et psychologie de la foi," p. 337, table II; Krötzl, *Pilger, Mirakel und Alltag*, p. 188 ("Reliquienmirakel" only); Goetz, "Heiligenkult und Geschlecht," p. 98. Goetz, "Wunderberichte im 9. Jahrhundert," p. 208, table 6, gives 73.4 per cent. Fifty-six per cent of the healing miracles of St. Dominic of Silos from the late eleventh and early twelfth century concern paralysis, blindness, and deaf-mutism: Lappin, *The Medieval Cult of Saint Dominic of Silos*, p. 110. They seem, however, to represent only 44.6 per cent of the healing miracles of St. Martin recorded in the sixth century: Giordano, "Sociologia e patologia del miracolo," p. 196, although the total here is 258, less than the total of 280 referred to elsewhere in the article.

[97] These are as a percentage of cures, not of all miracles, and are adjusted appropriately from the figures in Vauchez, *Sainthood*, p. 468, table 31.

invocation and cure at a distance from the shrine, but the logic would seem to be the opposite: paralysed and blind people would find it easier to obtain a cure if they did not need to go to the shrine in person. Moreover, the evidence from the huge miracle collection of St. Bernardino does not fit with this hypothesis, since here again, in a collection made in the middle of the fifteenth century, paralysis, blindness, and deaf-mutism constitute two-thirds of the ailments cured.[98] It is certainly not surprising, in a world of malnutrition, poor sanitation and ineffective medicine, to find a large population suffering from crippling ailments, eye disease, and problems with hearing and speech.

Other patterns are also discernible. Resurrection, the most spectacular kind of cure, represents only 2.2 per cent of the healing miracles in Sigal's sample and 2.4 in Vauchez's thirteenth-century sample, but rises to 12.9 per cent in his fourteenth-century figures.[99] This increase in resurrections is also found in the analysis of the miracles of Peter Martyr. His thirteenth-century miracles, 83 in number, include only two resurrections, while his fourteenth-century miracles, numbering 68, have 12, a rise from 2.4 per cent of the total (including both cures and other types of miracle) to 17.7 per cent.[100] Of this group of fourteen resurrections ascribed to St. Peter Martyr, one of the deaths involves drowning, one is a suicide by hanging, two are stillbirths and five involve infants.[101] This is significant. Many cases of miraculous resurrection occur after drowning or hanging, and the survival of apparently dead victims in such cases is well known, while the rise in the number of children helped by the saints is a common feature of later medieval miracle collections. Sometimes the two features coincide: a sample of 156 miracles in which the saints helped children involved in accidents showed that just over half of these were cases of drowning.[102]

A common feature of modern dictionaries and encyclopaedias of saints is the list of the saints' patronages or specialities. Thus, Apollonia is the saint to seek in case of toothache, St. Blaise helps those with illnesses of the throat, and so on. This practice of linking individual saints with a specific ailment was not unknown in the Middle Ages, but it was by no means a general or defining feature of the cult of the saints.

The practice of assigning specialities to the saints is described critically by one of the characters in Thomas More's *Dialogue Concerning Heresies*, which was published in 1531:

> We do them little worship while we set every saint to his office and assign him a craft such as pleaseth us. St. Eloi we make a horseleech and must let our horse rather run unshod and mar his hoof than to shoe him on his day. . . .

[98] Jansen, "Un exemple de sainteté thaumaturgique," p. 150, table I.

[99] These are as a percentage of cures, not of all miracles, and are adjusted appropriately from the figures in Vauchez, *Sainthood*, p. 468, table 31.

[100] Prudlo, *The Martyred Inquisitor*, pp. 144–48.

[101] Ambrogio Taegio, *Vita sancti Petri martyris* 10. 73–81, pp. 708–10.

[102] Finucane, *The Rescue of the Innocents*, p. 143; see also Goodich, *Miracles and Wonders*, pp. 93–99.

> St. Apollonia we make a tooth drawer and may speak to her of nothing but of sore teeth. St. Osyth women set to seek their keys. St. Roche we set to see to the great sickness because he had a sore.[103]

This link between saint and specialism is thus sometimes through earthly occupation: Eloi (Eligius) was a metal-worker, hence his association with horse-shoes (although one can imagine that the belief might have developed in reverse—that you *should* shoe your horse on his feast-day). Sometimes, in the case of martyrs, the link was with the form or instrument of torture: Apollonia had her teeth knocked out. And, in the case of St. Roche, he is a fellow-sufferer, for his sore is a sign of the plague ("the great sickness").

A very early example of a saintly medical speciality is St. Artemios attention to sufferers from hernia. This is explained by the fact that "he suffered in those parts."[104] Another clear example of medical specialization occurs in the cult of St. Fiacre, as revealed by the following story. A group of unruly pilgrims, returning from the shrine of St. Denis near Paris, were encouraged to take a detour to visit Fiacre's shrine near Meaux. They responded, "we don't have haemorrhoids, and the only people who need to go him are sufferers from haemorrhoids. He has no pilgrims except sufferers from haemorrhoids."[105] In the thirteenth century, a German lay-brother suffering from a fistula (a narrow, pipe-shaped, suppurating ulcer) heard that St. Quirinus at Neuß "was specially privileged by God in cure of that ailment."[106] St. Margaret of Antioch was frequently invoked in childbirth, as, for example, by Eleanor of Provence, queen of England, in 1240.[107] This special patronage might be explained directly, by the fact that, before her martyrdom, Margaret had prayed that in the homes of her devotees "no child should be born lame or blind or dumb."[108] On a slightly more symbolic plane, it might also be relevant that she had been swallowed by a dragon but had burst forth from it unharmed. And the use of the chemise of St. Margaret of Scotland as a protective relic for the pregnant queens of Scotland might well be explained through similarity of name (see p. 246).

There are thus certain cases where a saint and a particular ailment or medical predicament are linked, but they are not common. As miracle accounts reveal, most saints dealt with the common sicknesses and ailments of suffering humanity.

[103] Thomas More, *A Dialogue Concerning Heresies* 1. 17, pp. 226–27 (modernized).

[104] *Miracula sancti Artemii* 24, p. 144.

[105] *Vita et miracula sancti Fiacrii*, p. 110 (AASS Augusti 6: 610).

[106] Caesarius of Heisterbach, *Libri miraculorum* 1. 18, pp. 40–41.

[107] Matthew Paris, *Chronica majora* 4, p. 48.

[108] *Vita sancte Margarete virginis et martyris*, p. 140 (p. 46 for the Middle English; also in *Seinte Margarete*, p. 78); cf. Jacobus de Voragine, *Legenda aurea* 89 (1, p. 619).

The Rituals

The appeal for saintly help began with a vow or a ritual, intended to alert the saint and to link saint and suppliant. While it was a universal practice to offer a coin at the shrine of a saint, a custom found mainly, or perhaps only, in England was the bending in half of a silver penny in order to dedicate a sick person, or other suppliant, to the saint whose help was being sought.[109] Bending an object in order to make it useless for its normal purpose and to show that it was votive was an ancient tradition—swords bent in half have been found in Bronze Age deposits. Treating a coin in this way was thus clearly explicable as an invocatory gesture. Examples can be found in the twelfth, thirteenth, fourteenth and fifteenth centuries.

An account written in the 1160s or 1170s tells of a monk of Durham, who injured his testicles in a riding accident, and decided to seek help at the shrine of St. Cuthbert on Farne Island: "drawing a penny from his purse, he vowed to carry it with him to St. Cuthbert on Farne Island, and he bent it in half, so that he should recognize it by that sign." On arrival at the church on Farne, "he offered that bent penny" and immediately began to recover.[110] A penny bent in honour of St. Wulfstan and tied around the neck of a struggling woman in the grip of insanity calmed her and prepared her for cure.[111] A generation or two later, after a woman in Sussex had brought forth what seemed to be a still-born baby, which was "better suited to be covered by the earth of the grave than laid in a cradle," both she and her husband appealed to St. Richard of Chichester (d. 1253), the man saying, "O blessed Richard, if you infuse the vital spirit into this boy through your merits, I will bring a wax image of this boy, along with the boy, to your tomb." He then made the sign of the cross on the boy's forehead, and "bent a penny over the boy, to confirm the vow and honour the saint." Immediately the child showed signs of life.[112] In the canonization proceedings of Thomas de Cantilupe in 1307, there are numerous examples: a falcon belonging to the Worcestershire knight Geoffrey d'Abitot was brought back to life by having a penny bent over it, and it was even possible to put out a dangerous fire by praying to the saint and bending a penny in the direction of the flames.[113] At the very end of the Middle Ages, such votive coin-bending is frequently mentioned in the miracles of Henry VI.[114] Cantilupe's canonization hearings explicitly describe the practice of bending a penny over the sick person as "the custom of England," and, while examples may be turned up from continental cults, none have yet done so.[115]

[109] Finucane, *Miracles and Pilgrims*, pp. 94–95.

[110] Reginald of Durham, *Libellus de admirandis beati Cuthberti virtutibus* 103, p. 231.

[111] *Miracula sanctissimi Wlstani* 1. 21, p. 128.

[112] Ralph Bocking, *Vita sancti Ricardi episcopi Cycestrensis* 2. 4, pp. 141–42 (AASS Aprilis 1, p. 309).

[113] BAV, Vat. lat. 4015, fols. 256v–257, 257v–258 (AASS Octobris 1 [1765]: pp. 654, 669); Geoffrey d'Abitot is described as *Ralph* d'Abitot, ibid., p. 662.

[114] *Henrici VI Angliae regis miracula postuma*, pp. 108*–111*.

[115] BAV, Vat. lat. 4015, fol. 221 (AASS Octobris 1 [1765], p. 634); Finucane, *Miracles and Pilgrims*, pp. 94–95.

Perhaps the fine silver pennies so characteristic of the English currency system were ideal for bending.

Another distinctive and noteworthy method of creating a bond with the saint was the measuring of a sick person.[116] The thread used for this purpose would then be incorporated into the healing ritual, usually by providing the wick for a votive candle, or at least serving as a guide for its dimensions. A characteristic example can be found in the account of a miracle attributed to Godehard, bishop of Hildesheim (d. 1038). Folcward, a priest in charge of the administration of the estates of the bishopric of Hildesheim, was making a tour of the manors under his authority and, coming to the village of Eschershausen, was offered hospitality by a poor woman. He found that the woman's child was lying sick in bed and was generally thought to be at death's door. Folcward suggested that she have recourse to the help of the saintly Godehard, who had died only recently and whose body lay in the cathedral church:

> He persuaded the weeping mother to promise candles of the same dimensions as the boy at the tomb of the holy bishop . . . but because the poor woman did not have the wax for such a thing, he himself ordered a wick from flax to be prepared and had the boy measured along every limb, so that he might take away an accurate measurement with him, and offer at the saint's shrine candles, made from wax he had himself procured, on behalf of the sick child.[117]

The boy was cured even before the woman and the priest had finished their meal.

The origins of the custom of "measuring to a saint" are not clear. An early example of such a mimetic practice playing a part in the process of a saintly cure can be found in the *Miracles of Thecla*, which were written in the 440s. A boy is suffering from scrofula. St. Thecla appears to the child's grandmother and instructs her to spin wool to the length of the standing child, then burn it, mix the ashes with medicine and apply it. This produces the desired cure.[118] But while Thecla's remedy does involve thread to the height of the patient, the usual procedure was not to burn the thread and use the ashes in this way, but rather to make a candle with it.

A closer similarity to the usual pattern can be found in the Life of St. Radegund (d. 587):

> Goda, a secular girl who later became a nun serving God, who had lain weeping in her bed for a long time and, having spent a great deal on medicine, continued to be ill, made a candle of her own height, by the Lord's mercy, in the name of the holy woman. At the time when she expected her chill to come, she lit it and held it, and by its benefit the chills were banished before the candle was burnt up.[119]

[116] Finucane, *Miracles and Pilgrims*, pp. 95–96; Sigal, *L'homme et le miracle*, pp. 88–89.

[117] Wolfhere, *Vita sancti Godehardi episcopi posterior* 39, pp. 217–18; Folcward later became bishop of Brandenburg, at some period in the years 1063–68.

[118] *Miracula Theclae* 11, pp. 312–14.

[119] Venantius Fortunatus, *Vita sanctae Radegundis* 1. 32, p. 374.

Here the candle is specifically dedicated to the saint; it is "made in her name." The ritual, however, appears to have taken place in private space, and also, unusually, during Radegund's lifetime. Gregory of Tours, a contemporary of Radegund's, also tells of a woman who was cured after spending all night in prayer holding a candle of her own height, although he makes no explicit mention of a vow to a saint.[120]

The standard procedure, as it is revealed in the story about Folcward and St. Godehard, was to measure the sick person "to the saint," and to promise to bring to the saint's shrine a candle of that length. Many examples can be found from the ninth to the fifteenth century, in most parts of Christendom. The earliest case appears to be from the 880s. In 883 the relics of St. Prudentius were translated to the Burgundian monastery of Bèze and a wave of miraculous cures followed. On 23 August in the following year a woman came to the shrine telling how the saint had appeared to her in a vision at night, instructing her, "Arise and quickly bring to where I lie a candle of your own height."[121] Another early instance is the cure of Stephen, bishop of Liège, in 919. Although originally joyful that the relics of St. Eugenius of Toledo had been brought to the abbey of Brogne in his diocese, he was persuaded by some of his clergy that "it was not right that he should allow an unknown saint to be venerated in his diocese." When terrible intestinal pains struck him, bishop Stephen interpreted this as a punishment by the saint, and commanded that two candles should be made "of the length and the breadth of my body." Once these had been burned before Eugenius's relics, he recovered.[122]

In the following centuries the custom is recorded on many occasions. In Italy, a sick child was healed by the intervention of St. Peter Martyr (d. 1252) after he had been "commended to the holy martyr by the mother's vow and reverently measured according to the custom of the country."[123] In the late 1220s a young man called Atto in San Severino in the Marche was suffering from leprosy, and lay swollen and bedridden. His father suggested that his son vow himself to St. Francis and

> had paper brought to him, and measured his son's stature in length and girth. "Get up, my son," he said, "and vow yourself to St. Francis, and, after you have been granted relief, bring a candle of your length, every year of your life."[124]

This shows a variation on the usual custom of measuring with a thread, and incidentally illustrates the early availability in Italy of paper, a material which would not be readily at hand in northern or eastern Europe at this time. The vow was also a

[120] Gregory of Tours, *Gloria martyrum* 15, p. 498 (repr., 1969, p. 48); see also idem, *De virtutibus sancti Martini* 1. 18, p. 598 (repr., 1969, p. 148).

[121] Theobald of Bèze, *Acta, Translationes et Miracula sancti Prudentii Martyris* 2. 1, pp. 57–58; for the date, see the commentary, AASS Octobris 3, pp. 338–40, and also *Chronicon Besuensis abbatiae*, p. 269.

[122] *Miracula sancti Eugenii Broniensia* 1. 8, pp. 263–64.

[123] Ambrogio Taegio, *Vita sancti Petri martyris* 11. 87, p. 712; in his translation, Prudlo, *The Martyred Inquisitor*, p. 248, marks this as a genuine passage by Thomas Agni de Lentino of c. 1270 but fails to translate *mensuratus*.

[124] Thomas of Celano, *Vita prima sancti Francisci* 3. 146 (mir. 5), pp. 112–13.

perpetual one, rather than a promise to bring one gift. Rather less usual was a promise to offer "an image or painted figure" of the saint the same size as the devotee.[125] Images of the saint were promised as ex-votos in late-medieval Italy (earlier, p. 108), but specifying the dimensions in this way seems unparalleled.

Measuring could be employed for animals as well as humans. After a peacock had become miraculously paralysed because it had flown onto an altar, its owner "commanded a flaxen wick to be made, to the measurements of the peacock, from the tip of its beak to the end of its tail, and then to be encased in wax." Once the candle was burned before the altar, the bird was free and healthy again. This story comes from eleventh-century France.[126] Larger animals could also be measured, like the ox bought by Henry, prior of Hereford, in the early part of the thirteenth century. His purchase was being admired and praised when the beast fell to the ground and began swelling. Perhaps this was a case, someone pointed out, that confirmed the popular saying: "it was bewitched by the words of praise." Henry should measure the ox to St. Wulfstan of Worcester. This was done, the creature recovered, and next day was part of the plough-team, while prior Henry brought the candle from Hereford to Worcester himself.[127] The biggest commitment of this kind on record seems to be that offered by the wife of a knight whose horse was so wild it could not be bridled. She made a promise to St. Raymond of Peñaforte that she would give "a candle as big as the horse if he tamed its ferocity and wickedness." As soon as she made this vow, the horse became tame.[128] The subsequent delivery of the candle can only be imagined.

There are cases where the measuring is not of the sufferer but of the miraculous object itself. In the sixth century there is record of the Column of the Flagellation in Jerusalem being used in this way: "a measurement is taken of it, for all illnesses; people hang it around their necks and are cured."[129] And a similar practice could be employed with images of the saints. The Byzantine empress Zoe, grieving over her childlessness, came to a miraculous icon of the Virgin Mary housed in the Pege church, and measured it with a thread. She then girded herself with this thread, and soon conceived, giving birth to the future emperor Constantine Porphyrogenitus, in 905.[130] Here the principle of the replication of dimensions is still at work, as with the candles, but in a reverse direction: the mimesis goes from holy object to sufferer, not the other way round.

Measuring to a saint was thus widespread in place and time, and also in terms of the social position of those who employed it. It certainly cannot be categorized as "popular," meaning characteristic of the lower classes. It was used, as we have seen, by bishops, priors, and members of knightly families. A case in 1446 involved Vit-

[125] *Il processo per la canonizzazione di S. Nicola da Tolentino*, p. 299.

[126] *Miracula sancti Benedicti* 8. 5, pp. 281–82.

[127] *Miracula sanctissimi Wlstani* 2. 4, p. 151.

[128] BAV, Vat. lat. 6059, fol. 46v.

[129] *Antonini Placentini Itinerarium* 23, p. 140 (the work is pseudonymous).

[130] *Miracula Deiparae ad Fontem* 26, p. 885; on the text see Talbot, "Two Accounts of Miracles at the Pege Shrine," esp. pp. 607–9; eadem, "The Anonymous Miracula of the Pege Shrine."

toria Colonna, a member of one the most important families of Rome and a niece of Pope Martin V.[131] The encounter between Folcward and the poor woman is a very clear case of a practice being suggested by cathedral clergy to local villagers. If one does wish to use the distinction between "clerical culture" and "folkloric traditions" when analyzing medieval culture, Folcward might be seen as a representative of clerical culture shaping folkloric traditions—it was he who took the initiative in recommending this practice.

Incubation, the practice of sleeping overnight at a shrine, was a further way of seeking a miracle.[132] An early example is reported in north Africa in the 420s.[133] A paralyzed man named Restitutus, a blacksmith from the region of Hippo Diarrhytus (modern Bizerte in Tunisia), was carried to the shrine of St. Stephen in Uzalis. One night, after he had lain there in silent prayer for twenty days, a beautiful young man appeared to him in a dream and told him to approach the shrine on his own two feet. This was the beginning of his cure. There is also evidence of incubation being practised at the Michaelion in Constantinople by c. 440, and the miracles of St. Thecla, which date from the same period, have several mentions of those who spent the night in her sanctuary, like the grammarian Alypios, who judged that his illness was beyond human help and came to Thecla's church, where "she came to him at night, as it is her custom always to do with sick people."[134] Those seeking healing from St. Artemios, who specialized in dealing with hernias, would sleep in the church of St. John the Baptist in Oxeia in Constantinople, where the saint's shrine was located, bringing with them their mattresses. Sometimes they might be there for months. Large crowds gathered on a Saturday night for the all-night vigil.[135] There were particularly elaborate and extensive rituals for those sleeping at the shrine of St. Cyrus and St. John outside Alexandria, where incubation was combined with bathing and the saints might appear in a dream-vision to offer a prescription.[136]

The practice was not limited to these churches of the late antique and early Byzantine period, but could be found throughout the Middle Ages, in the West as well as the East. Of the 45 miracles recorded at the shrine of St. Margaret of Scotland in the thirteenth century, 30 involved incubation, and one night a week was set aside especially for the sick to spend in her church.[137]

An account of the miracles of St. Wulfstan of Worcester, written in the thirteenth century, has numerous cases of incubation: a paralysed woman, "carried to the tomb of the saint, slept a little; awaking, she found that she was cured"; a boy

[131] *Il processo di canonizzazione di Bernardino da Siena*, pp. 403, 427–28.

[132] Mallardo, "L'incubazione nella cristianità medievale napoletana"; Fernádez Marcos, *Los Thaumata de Sofronio: Contribución al estudio de la incubatio cristiana*; Wacht, "Inkubation"; Beaujard, *Le culte des saints en Gaule*, pp. 326–29; Klaniczay, "Dreams and Visions in Medieval Miracle Accounts."

[133] *Miracula sancti Stephani* 1. 11, pp. 294–96 (PL 41: 839–40).

[134] Sozomen, *Historia ecclesiastica* 2. 3. 10–11 (1, pp. 242–44); *Miracula Theclae* 38, pp. 390–92.

[135] *Miracula sancti Artemii.*

[136] Sophronius of Jerusalem, *Miracula Cyri et Ioannis.*

[137] *Miracula sancte Margarite Scotorum regine* 1, p. 74; editorial comment, p. l.

who had lost his tongue slept at the tomb and, "awakening around the middle of the night, recovered his tongue and the power of speech"; a young shepherd, mute from birth, came to Wulfstan's tomb "and slept in a deep slumber, like someone tired from a journey"; during the night he was visited in a dream-vision by a bishop who placed his hand on his lips and said, "speak"; a woman was healed of a suppurating sore after she had come to Worcester "to visit St. Wulfstan" and sought help "for three days and the same number of nights."[138]

There were certain practicalities associated with incubation. For poor pilgrims who had come a long way, sleeping at the shrine obviously solved an accommodation problem. And it was a meritorious deed to distribute bread to the poor people keeping vigil around the saint's tomb.[139] It was necessary to get permission to spend the night in a church, perhaps from the sacristans in charge of vessels and relics. A little boy with an infected foot was carried by his aunt to the church of St. Maximinus at Micy to seek a cure and spent eight days there, unable to sleep because of the pain. Eventually one of the monks advised the aunt "to ask the sacristans to let her boy spend one night inside the church." During the night, after the arrival of a miraculous white dove, the boy was completely cured.[140] In 1080 a pilgrim came to the shrine of St. Cuthbert in Durham cathedral and "asked from the custodians of the monastery that, according to the custom of the country, he might be granted permission to spend the night there, for he had vowed this to God."[141] The pilgrim turned out to be a cunning thief, but that does not rob the passage of its value as evidence for "the custom of the country." And the ritual of incubation sometimes allowed the usual patterns of segregation and seclusion to be relaxed. For example, women were allowed to spend the night at the shrine of St. Edmund within the male monastery of Bury St. Edmunds.[142] But those seeking permission to pass the night in a church had to behave themselves. One woman was barred from the church of Worcester and had to sleep outside because she was "noisy and rude to the doorkeepers" (she was cured nonetheless).[143]

Delay and Disappointment

As Ronald Finucane put it, very cogently, "Since about nine-tenths of . . . miracles were cures, by asking what the pilgrims meant by 'cure' we are also asking what the majority of them meant by 'miracle.' " And he notes that "cures" could be temporary, partial or very long in the coming.[144]

[138] *Miracula sanctissimi Wlstani* 1. 2, 4, 19, 35, pp. 117, 118, 126–27, 136; other examples listed in the index, p. 204.

[139] *Miracula sanctissimi Wlstani* 2. 18, p. 177.

[140] Letaldus of Micy, *Miracula sancti Maximini* 52, col. 821.

[141] Symeon of Durham (attrib.), *De miraculis et translationibus sancti Cuthberti* 8 (2, p. 334).

[142] For example, Hermann the Archdeacon, *Liber de miraculis sancti Edmundi* 18–19, pp. 49–52.

[143] *Translatio sancti Wlstani,* p. 186.

[144] Finucane, *Miracles and Pilgrims*, pp. 69, 71–82.

Hagiographers sometimes stressed the speed of the cure, as in the record of miracles at St. Agilus's fountain, which includes the story of a bedridden man, who ordered water from the fountain to be brought to him: "as he drank, there was no gap in time, but he received the water and the cure at the same moment."[145] Some medieval theologians even thought that instantaneous effect was part of the definition of miracle: "a true miracles requires . . . that it is accomplished, not slowly and gradually like a work of nature, but instantaneously and at once."[146] One of the cardinals investigating the miracles of Celestine V obviously shared this view, for, when he came across the written account of how the saint had blessed a blind child, "and then" (*et tunc*) the child had recovered its sight, he concluded: "if 'and then' means 'immediately' this is a miracle, otherwise not."[147] The author of the earliest Life of Bernard of Clairvaux took advantage of the opportunity of rewriting the work a few years later to remove several phrases that indicated a gradual cure, presumably thinking that the saint's reputation would be enhanced by quick and immediate cures.[148] Of the large number of posthumous healing miracles studied by Sigal, 87 per cent took place after the suppliant had spent less than a week at the shrine.[149]

If one takes this view of miracle, then many saintly cures would not qualify. Miracle Books are, unsurprisingly, largely devoted to the successful cures and the happiness of the fortunate beneficiaries, like the woman who said she felt as if she could fly after being healed.[150] But they are also full of accounts of suppliants who waited at shrines for days or months or even years, or who wandered from shrine to shrine without receiving the miraculous help they sought. Some cures were gradual, like the case of the man, miraculously recovering his sight, who could at first only see "windows, and men looking like walking trees."[151] These stories almost always end with the sufferer finally obtaining a cure, or finally approaching the right saint, but nevertheless they indicate a world of disappointment that has to be taken into account when we ponder the nature of miraculous healing.

It was often the case that the suppliants at shrines had been suffering from chronic complaints. A man called Malulfus, of the diocese of Tours, was bedridden for five years before he had himself carried to Martin's tomb, where he was cured.[152] A sample of 454 miraculous cures drawn from late medieval canonization processes found that over 46 per cent involved ailments that had lasted more than a year.[153] But even when the sufferers arrived at the saint's tomb, there might still be a long wait. Of

[145] *Miracula sancti Agili* (BHL 149) 2. 2. 14, p. 594.

[146] Albertus Magnus, *Summa theologica* 2. 8. 30, ed. A. Borgnet, *Opera omnia* 32 (Paris, 1895), p. 322.

[147] "S. Pierre Célestin et ses premiers biographes," p. 478; he clearly did not have access to the text printed ibid., p. 438, which says the cure occurred "at once (*statim*)."

[148] Sigal, *L'homme et le miracle*, pp. 73–74.

[149] Ibid., p. 69.

[150] Benedict of Peterborough, *Miracula sancti Thomae* 2. 24, p. 74.

[151] Fenestras vidit et *homines* quasi *arbores ambulantes*: John of Jentzenstein (Jenstein), *Miracula beate Marie visitacionis*, BAV, Vat. lat. 1122, fols. 157–61v, at fols. 159v–60 (drawing on Mark 8:24).

[152] Gregory of Tours, *De virtutibus sancti Martini* 3. 44, p. 543 (repr., 1969, p. 193).

[153] Wittmer-Butsch and Rendtel, *Miracula: Wunderheilungen im Mittelalter*, p. 100.

the 2,050 posthumous healing miracles studied by Sigal, 1,102 were recorded with some indication of time: in 13 per cent of these cases there was a delay of a week or more between invocation of the saint, or arrival at the shrine, and the cure.[154] This was obviously considered a reasonable wait, for two women, giving testimony in 1375 during hearings about Micheline of Pesaro, said that they had vowed to make a gift to the saint "if she freed them from infirmity within eight days."[155] But the wait could be longer. An Italian cripple called Richard was carried to the church of St. Aigulph at Provins, site of one of the important fairs of Champagne, where he was given shelter beneath the tables of the money-changers. "When he had stayed there patiently from the first of November to the first of August, in winter and in summer," he finally decided to try another church, but Aigulph immediately appeared to him telling him that this was his jurisdiction. Richard was eventually cured at Aigulph's shrine and became a porter in the service of his church, strong enough "to carry the burden of a strong animal." He had, however, had to wait more than nine months for a cure.[156]

There might be general reasons for these delays. It was occasionally argued that the saints appreciated a little persistence: "Those people are foolish who throw down their offerings and then immediately leave, since it is pleasing to the saints that their help should be sought with waiting and perseverance."[157] And sometimes the hagiographer recording these long waits implies a fault on the part of the suppliant that might account for the delay. A recalcitrant serf, for example, whose thumb had been dislocated as a divine punishment, had to wait four months at the tomb before being healed.[158] Particularly complex is the web of blame and obligation in an account of a miracle of St. Wulfstan of Worcester.[159] An inhabitant of the village of Stoke Prior, which was an ancient possession of the church of Worcester, was struck with sciatica so severely that he could not walk. Carried to Wulfstan's shrine in a cart, he passed three weeks there, begging the saint for a cure. The monk of Worcester recording all this then goes on: "but he did not merit to obtain any remedy. The man was one of those singers who lead public choruses in the streets, and he had engaged in this levity for many years." There is nothing explicit here except the juxtaposition—was it his light-hearted merriness that had postponed his cure? The sufferer himself did not think so. Instead, he felt that Wulfstan owed him, as "someone born and brought up on the land of your church," special regard. "My lord, St. Wulfstan," he complained, "surely I am your serf by birth? . . . Why is it that you spurn me? You cure foreigners and strangers every day in my sight, and you do not deign to regard me, your special servant?" This was enough to spur the saint into

[154] Sigal, *L'homme et le miracle*, p. 69.
[155] Dalarun, *La sainte et la cite*, p. 218.
[156] *Miracula sancti Aigulphi* 19–20, pp. 762–63.
[157] *Miracula sancte Elyzabet anno 1235 comprobata (Ordo I)* 15, p. 254.
[158] *Miracula sancti Benedicti* 5. 8, p. 206.
[159] *Miracula sanctissimi Wlstani* 1. 33, p. 135.

action. The sin of choral singing (if that is what it was) was balanced by being one of Wulfstan's dependants.

A particular record of disappointment is provided by the sufferers who went from shrine to shrine. One of the earliest such account dates to the 420s. Paul of Caesarea in Cappadocia had visited the shrines of Lawrence at Ravenna and Stephen at Ancona and Uzalis in Africa before finally being cured at the shrine of Stephen in Hippo. He explains the failure of the other shrines in a way that was to be a pious commonplace: "I could not be cured elsewhere for I was being kept for this place by divine predestination."[160] There is always a purpose in these failed requests for healing. A lame young woman from Norway visited the shrines of many saints before being cured at that of St. William of Æbelholt in Denmark. "God deferred giving her a cure through the others, so that there should be a cause of praise and glory for his saint William," wrote the happy author recording William's miracles.[161]

One particular twist to the stories of such failed requests for healing is the common motif of saints recommending other saints. St. George told one blind Russian suppliant at his church, "Why are you crying thus to me? If you wish to see, go to the holy Boris and Gleb, and they will give you sight. For to them has God given the grace of healing in this land."[162] A paralysed man who had himself carried to the shrine of San Gennaro (Ianuarius) in Naples received clear instructions from the saint:

> Why do you press me with your tears, night and day? You will not be cured here, nor will you receive peace through my merits. If you go to the tomb of my beloved friend Agrippinus, it is there that you will obtain what you wish.[163]

A woman possessed by a demon was brought to the shrine of St. Bernardino but the saint "was unwilling to cure her," wishing "to bring honour" to another saint, John Bassando, at whose tomb she was indeed cured.[164] These stories usually try to preserve the standing of both the older or inactive saint and the new active one.

The clergy associated with a saint's shrine had a natural interest in giving creditable accounts of why a miraculous cure had not been forthcoming. One of the wardens at the shrine of St. Artemios in Constantinople in the seventh century explained that pilgrims who came to the church and sought healing without any success were visited by the saint after they had returned to their distant homes in Alexandria, Africa, and Rhodes.[165] This unverifiable claim accounted for the apparent failures of the saints to provide the cure that suppliants requested.

[160] Augustine, *Sermo* 322b (PL 38: 1444); the miracle is also described in Augustine, *De civitate dei* 22. 8 (2, pp. 825–27).

[161] *Vita et miracula sancti Willelmi abbatis Ebelholtensis* 59, p. 364.

[162] Nestor, *Lesson on the Life and Murder of the Blessed Passion-Sufferers Boris and Gleb*, p. 30.

[163] *Miracula sancti Agrippini* 10, p. 124.

[164] *Vita Johannis Bassandi* 9. 89, p. 891.

[165] *Miracula sancti Artemii* 44, pp. 220–21.

Explanations of the failure to obtain a miracle more often stress the spiritual state of the beneficiaries, since miracles require faith in the suppliant. Bede has a particularly ingenious passage on this issue. After the abbess of Whitby and one of her nuns had been cured by St. Cuthbert's belt, the belt miraculously disappeared. Bede explained the cause:

> One should understand that this happened through divine providence, so that through these two miracles of healing the sanctity of the father, beloved of God, should be revealed to believers, and that then thereafter any occasion for doubting his sanctity should be taken away from unbelievers. For if that belt had been permanently there, the sick would have always wanted to come to it, and when one of them might happen not to deserve healing from his or her illness, that person would criticise the failure to cure, although they were in fact unworthy of a cure. So, by the careful providence of the holy power above, after the faith of believers had been strengthened, soon any opportunity for criticism from the malicious envy of unbelievers was removed.[166]

Bede here has an answer to the problem of failed miracles—the suppliant obviously did not deserve to be cured—but also clearly preferred the situation not even to arise.

Even apparently desperate cases could be given an interpretation that preserved the saint's reputation. A woman in the region of Ferentino had a son who never grew or walked or talked. This was a source of constant grief. When the boy was seven years old, his mother took him to the tomb of the saintly Celestine V in Ferentino, and prayed: "Lord God, I beseech you to liberate me from these continual troubles, through the merits of this saintly man who lies here; either deliver this my son or receive him to you." The account concludes quickly: "After this, she lifted up her son and returned home. As soon as she reached the house, the boy died, and she was released from that sadness."[167] A tragic family situation, the appeal to the saint, the death of the child—all this turned into a miracle that could be recorded in a collection of the saint's wondrous deeds.

The spiritual disposition of participants is also relevant in a small but revealing class of miracle accounts, namely, those first-person accounts that say some people, or a few people, witnessed a miracle, but that the writer himself did not. The authors of miracle accounts are, by their nature, committed to the truth and verifiability of their stories, and a first-hand account would seem to be the strongest possible circumstance to back this up, but, every so often, there are these unusual incidents. Gregory of Tours records a tale of how the vessel containing the bread for the Eucharist, brought into church by an adulterous deacon, floated away from the man's grasp, "because he was polluted in his conscience." He adds,

[166] Bede, *Vita sancti Cuthberti* 23, pp. 232–34.

[167] "S. Pierre Célestin et ses premiers biographes," p. 454.

> It was allowed to only one priest and to three women, one of whom was my mother, to see this; the others did not see it. I myself was present at this feast-day, I must confess, but I was not worthy to see this.[168]

Gregory knows the miracle took place, because his mother tells him so, but he cannot honestly say that he himself witnessed it.

Usually the account of a suppliant's unsuccessful prayers is only a prelude to a successful approach to a favoured saint, but sometimes the poor sufferer was told frankly that he was not to be cured, as in the case of two boys, one crippled and one blind, who came to the shrine of Thomas Becket. "Why are you lying on me?," asked the saint of the first boy, who had rested his head on the saint's tomb, "You will not have healing; go away; I will do nothing for you." Even the monk recording Becket's miracles had to admit his sorrow at these cases.[169]

Miracles of Provision

Just as Jesus had fed five thousand from a few loaves and fishes, so the saints were able to supply miraculous provisions. The early Irish saints seem to have been particularly generous, but such miracles of provision are found throughout the centuries in all parts of Christendom, performed both in the saint's lifetime and after death.[170] Some, just like Jesus' feeding of the five thousand, involved the miraculous multiplication of what was already present; others entailed the transformation of a substance into something more appetizing—also with a biblical precedent, in Jesus turning water into wine; yet others concerned the discovery of supplies unexpectedly.

On one occasion, when Antoninus of Florence was being shaved by a barber-surgeon, there was a knock on the door and a poor man appeared begging bread. Although there were only three loaves in the house, the saint instructed his servant to give one to the beggar. Soon thereafter another poor man came by, then a third, and each was given a loaf. When the saint and the barber sat down to eat, the servant, wondering what food there was in the house, went to the cupboard and found it full of bread.[171] This is a perfect example, not only of the miraculous multiplication of matter, but also of the maxim, "Give and it shall be given unto thee" (Luke 6:38). A similar concern for the poor and indigent was shown by Margaret Fontana of Modena (d. 1513), a member of the Dominican Third Order, who doled out the entire contents of a barrel of wine to the needy. The complication here was that the wine had been set aside for a celebration, because Margaret's sister-in-law was expecting a child. After the birth, the barrel was found to be empty and her

[168] Gregory of Tours, *Gloria martyrum* 85, p. 546 (repr., 1969, p. 96).

[169] Benedict of Peterborough, *Miracula sancti Thomae* 2. 16–17, pp. 67–68.

[170] For such miracles in early Ireland see Bray, *A List of Motifs in the Lives of the Early Irish Saints*, pp. 105–6, s.v. "Miraculous Provision."

[171] *Summarium processuum impressum Antonini archiepiscopi Florentini* 3. 21, p. 340.

relatives were understandably enraged with her, but Margaret suggested that they check the barrel again, since a demon might have deluded them into thinking it was empty, in order to stir up domestic strife. They looked, and the barrel was full of wonderful wine.[172] The poor had been provided for, but the family party could still go ahead.

The transformation of water into wine was one of the most frequent miracles of provision, clearly recalling Jesus' first miracle at Cana (John 2:1–11).[173] Although saints were sometimes praised for their abstemiousness in drinking only water, like St. David of Wales, who was called "David of the Watery Life," most of them were happy to provide alcoholic drinks for others, or even for themselves: St. Francis, one of the most famously austere of the saints, once asked for wine while ill, and, there being none, turned some water into "the finest wine."[174] A particular variant of this miracle occurs in the story of St. Hedwig, duchess of Silesia, who was reproached by her husband for drinking only water. He thought this both ostentatious and unhealthy. One day, as she was dining, he seized the cup she had on the table before her and quaffed down the drink inside. He was amazed to find that it tasted of excellent wine. Obviously a choleric type, the duke said, "Your eyes ought to be torn out for all your lying!" The servants, who had poured out the drink, and Hedwig's noble companions, who tasted it, could both attest to the miraculous transformation.[175] It is an ambiguous incident, since it obviously left Hedwig vulnerable, in her husband's eyes at least, to a charge of hypocrisy, yet it is recorded as a sign of Hedwig's sanctity.

Jesus, as a Mediterranean man, had turned water into wine, but in the cooler northern and western parts of Europe other beverages might be more suitable. When the body of St. Arnulf of Metz was being carried to his episcopal city for burial, one of the nobles in the entourage invited his companions to spend the night at his manor house. He had to admit, however, that all there was to drink was "a little beer." But he had faith in the saint whose body they were carrying. "Now," he said to the funeral escort, "let the blessed lord Arnulf provide for you tonight! Whatever you lack can be supplied through his intercession." The beer immediately multiplied, so that there was enough for all, and plenty still left in the morning.[176] The saintly John of Beverley, bishop of York, was more solicitous of his guests' tastes, and, when inviting the king and his following to a feast, ordered three large jugs to be filled, respectively, with wine, mead, and beer. He blessed them, and the cup-bearers then began to pass the drink around, but, however much was drunk, the jugs remained full to the brim. The hagiographer telling this story underlines the Gospel parallels: "In the power of this drink to multiply, recall the wedding feast at Cana in Galilee . . .

[172] *Vita Margaritae Fontanae* 2. 10, p. 137.

[173] There is an entire page of references to miracles of this type in Loomis, *White Magic*, p. 188.

[174] Rhygyfarch, *Vita sancti David* 2, p. 108; Thomas of Celano, *Vita prima sancti Francisci* 21. 61, p. 47; idem, *Tractatus de miraculis beati Francisci* 3. 17, p. 280.

[175] *Vita beate Hedwigis (maior legenda)* 4, p. 84 (AASS Octobris 8: 231); the scene is illustrated in the Hedwig Codex: see the facsimile, ibid., vol. 1, fol. 30v.

[176] *Vita sancti Arnulfi* 25, p. 444.

Plate 1. St. Michael weighing souls in Roger van der Weyden's *Last Judgment*. Musée de l'Hôtel-Dieu, Beaune. Photo: akg-images / François Guénet.

Plate 2. Ring-crypt at San Vincenzo al Volturno. Richard Hodges, *Light in the Dark Ages: The Rise and Fall of San Vincenzo al Volturno* (London, 1997). Photo: Richard Hodges.

Plate 3. Gentile da Fabriano, Italian, c. 1370–1427, *The Crippled and Sick Cured at the Tomb of Saint Nicholas*, 1425, tempera on panel, painted surface: 35.5 x 35.5 cm (14 x 14 in.). Washington, DC, National Gallery of Art, Samuel H. Kress Collection, 1939.1.268 Photo: NGA Images.

Plate 4. Fifteenth-century Italian reliquary with tooth of Mary Magdalene. New York, Metropolitan Museum of Art, accession no. 17.190.504. © 2013 The Metropolitan Museum of Art / Art Resource / Scala, Florence.

Plate 5. Translation of St. Martin's head, 1323. © Bibliothèque municipale de Tours, MS 1023, fol. 101. © CNRS-IRHT.

Plate 6. Sepulchrum containing relics found in the high altar of St. Kunibert's, Cologne. Photo © Rheinisches Bildarchiv Köln, c003979.

Plate 7. Painting of St. Roche dressed as a pilgrim. Bari, Pinacoteca Provinciale "Corrado Giaquinto," inv. 1993, n. 101, reproduced in *Romei e Giubilei*, p. 375, no. 160.

Plate 8. Meo da Siena, altarpiece for Santa Maria di Valdiponte at Montelabate, c. 1320. Perugia, Galleria nazionale dell'Umbria. © 2013 Photo Scala, Florence. Courtesy of the Ministero Beni e Att. Culturali.

Plate 9. Scenes from the Life of St. Gerard (Gellert) of Csanád, from The Angevin Magyar Legendary, Bibioteca Apostolica Vaticana. Vat. lat. 8541, fol. 69v.

Plate 10. Fra Angelico, Dominican blessed from the predella of the altar of San Domenico, Fiesole, 1420s. London, National Gallery, NG663.4. © 2013 The National Gallery, London / Scala, Florence.

remember the Lord's feeding of the five thousand."[177] But the saints had no special brief for beer. St. Stanislaus, the bishop of Cracow murdered in 1079, refused to allow water from his holy lake to be used for brewing, fixing to the spot those who tried to take it away for this purpose: "by these and many other miracles St. Stanislaus wished to honour the water of the lake into which his dismembered body had once been thrown."[178]

Several of the different types of miraculous provision are exemplified in the miracles of St. Richard, bishop of Chichester (1244–53).[179] On one occasion, when unexpectedly large crowds of the poor had come to him seeking alms, he blessed the bread that had been set aside for them, and what was scarcely sufficient for a hundred fed almost three thousand. Another time, when bread ran out and beans were being cooked to give to the poor, he blessed the beans, and, again, what had been deemed adequate only for a third of those seeking charity, proved to be enough for all, and with some to spare. When staying with his old boyhood friend, John, prior of Selborne, Richard was invited to go down to the fish-pond and see if they could catch a fish, but the nets were so tangled that they could catch nothing. At this point one of the bishop's household suggested that he give a blessing. He did so, and immediately, "behold, there was a pike—three feet long or more—dragged and enticed out of the water by the holy man's blessing." Another fishy story sees the bishop crossing the bridge at Lewes and encountering some fishermen, who are having no luck and ask his blessing. As soon as this is given, they catch "four beautiful fish, that are called 'mullet' in the vernacular." The hagiographer telling this tale explains that there is something improbable about it, because mullet are marine rather than river fish, but he has a theological explanation:

> It ought not to be incredible, that the creator of the waters, who by his blessing produced every creature that lives and moves in the water according to its kind, should, at the invocation of his name and through the benediction of his servant, produce fish of whatever type, and wherever, he wished.

St. Richard had spent a long period at the beginning of his episcopate staying with the rector of Tarring in Sussex, since he was out of favour with the king and could not yet get possession of his own estates. While there he did a little gardening, grafting a cutting onto a tree, which then immediately flourished and flowered "beyond the course of nature." Nor was he a burden to his host, for, at the end of his long stay, the rector's barns and storehouses and cellars were fuller than ever—another "indication of the sanctity" of the bishop.

The multiplication of bread and beans, the blessed catch of fish and the sprouting branch all have biblical echoes, which Richard's hagiographer repeatedly underlines.

[177] Folcard, *Vita sancti Iohannis episcopi Eboracensis* 9, pp. 254–55.

[178] Jan Długosz, *Vita et miracula Stanislai episcopi Cracoviensis* 3. 5 (51), p. 270 (a miracle of the mid-fifteenth century).

[179] Ralph Bocking, *Vita sancti Ricardi episcopi Cycestrensi* 1. 21, 31–33, 35; *Littere eius canonizationis*, pp. 106, 125–28, 155 (AASS Aprilis 1, pp. 293, 303–4, 316).

A biblical precedent was also often stressed in descriptions of a saint's power to bring rain, an indirect rather than a direct miracle of provision. In the Bible (1 Kings 17–18) the prophet Elijah ends many years of drought by his prayers, after a dramatic confrontation with the priests of Baal. It is a reference that comes naturally to the author of an account of the translation of the relics of the martyrs Claudius, Lupercus and Victoricus in the city of Leon in 1173, when he describes how rain began to fall, after a long drought, on the very day of the translation:

> He who, in days gone by, at the prayers of his servant Elijah, had opened the heavens, that had withheld their rains, now pours forth heavy showers through the great merits of his martyrs, without the violence of winds or the terror of lightning or the rumbling of thunder, so that the earth might recover and bristle with crops and flowers and bring back hope to its cultivator.[180]

Such wondrous control of the weather was something that a predominantly agricultural society would naturally dream of, and love to hear about. Just as saints offered healing in a world of sickness and suffering, so they could bring fruitfulness and plenty in a world of scarcity.

Visions, Prophecy, and Rapture

Saints could see things other people could not. Sometimes these were events that were taking place far away, sometimes things that were to happen in the future. As has already been mentioned, they were able to perceive demons, even in disguise or, imperceptible to others, inside possessed human beings. And also saints might have visions of Christ, the Virgin Mary or other wonders of the faith.

Some saints, like Hildegard of Bingen or Birgit of Sweden, left lengthy written accounts of their visions, which often had a public or political aspect, while others were simply famous in their own institutions for the intensity and frequency of their visionary experiences. An example is Flora of Beaulieu (d. 1347), a sister of the Order of St. John, who was repeatedly seized by raptures during which she had visions: Jesus, pierced with his wounds; an angel bearing a sword, the hilt of which she grasped as a protection against demons; the marriage of St. Cecilia with her heavenly bridegroom and Cecilia's entry into the palace of the heavenly king; and a splendid and sweet-smelling throne that was reserved for Flora herself in heaven.[181]

Sometimes the wondrous visions that the saints experience are clearly designed to demonstrate the truth of the Christian faith, or some part of it. Eucharistic miracles are a perfect example.[182] One of the most difficult doctrines of medieval Christian-

[180] *Miracula sanctorum martyrum Claudii, Luperci et Victori in translatione* 3, p. 294.

[181] *Vida e miracles de sancta Flor* 1. 4, 6, 7, 13, pp. 17–19, 22–23 (AASS Iunii 6, pp. 106, 108, 110 [Latin translation of the Occitain]).

[182] Browe, *Die eucharistischen Wunder*; Ward, *Miracles and the Medieval Mind*, pp. 13–18.

ity was its teaching that the bread and wine of the Eucharist really became the body and blood of Christ. There are innumerable references to people doubting this, even people of devout life and theological training, like the English scholar Richard Albericanus, who taught in Paris in the late twelfth century, and who was unable to swallow the Eucharist on his death-bed, confessing that "this had happened to him by God's just judgment, because he had never been able to hold this first article of the faith."[183] He could not swallow the Eucharist literally because he could not swallow it metaphorically. Miraculous support for this challenging belief was provided by stories of the consecrated host bleeding, or being visible in the form of a child, stories that were so common that Thomas Aquinas devoted a section of his great theological compendium to them.[184]

One such event is described at some length in the eighth-century Miracles of St. Ninian.[185] Ninian was buried in the church he had founded at Whithorn (now south-west Scotland) and an English bishopric was established there at some point. The story tells, in its own words, "How a priest celebrating Mass at the body of the man of God saw, at his own request, Christ, the son of God, sitting in the paten in the form of a most beautiful infant." The priest, named as Plecgils, who was in the custom of celebrating Mass at Ninian's tomb, prayed earnestly to God and the saint that he might be permitted to see the consecrated host in the physical form of Christ's body, "not because he was doubtful about the body," but because he desired this special privilege. Eventually his wish was granted: "he saw the blessed boy sitting in the paten." An angelic messenger encouraged him: "if you wish to see Christ, whom you have always been accustomed to sanctify hidden in the cover of gleaming bread, now look, and remember to touch him with your hands." Plecgils embraced the Christ child and kissed his lips. Then, after the body had returned to the form of "white bread," the priest "was found worthy to eat the holy sacrifice." The author of this account stressed Plecgils's piety and devotion, but the fact that the story is contained in the Miracles of St. Ninian implies that there was a role too for the saint over whose body the Mass was being celebrated.

Although it is expressly stated that Plecgils was not inspired by any doubt that the bread of communion truly became the body of Christ, it is noteworthy that the issue of doubt is raised at all. Yet more remarkable is a retelling of this story by the Carolingian theologian Paschasius Radbertus, who writes that Plecgils sought this special privilege, "from piety of mind, not, as is customary, from lack of faith."[186] He includes the story in his work on the Eucharist, in a chapter devoted to such literal, physical appearances. "No one," he writes,

> who reads the Lives of the saints can be ignorant that often this mystical sacrament of body and blood is displayed in the visible form of a lamb or with

[183] Gerald of Wales, *Gemma ecclesiastica* 1. 9, p. 33.

[184] Thomas Aquinas, *Summa Theologiae* III q. 76. 8 (58, pp. 118–22).

[185] *Miracula Nynie Episcopi* 13, pp. 957–59.

[186] Paschasius Radbertus, *De corpore et sanguine Domini* 14, p. 89 (PL 120: 1319–20).

> the colour of flesh and blood, either on account of doubters or on account of those who love Christ more ardently.[187]

He goes on to give some examples from the Fathers, before turning to the Ninian story.

Later medieval saints, especially women, also experienced such Eucharistic miracles.[188] Mary of Maillé, a pious widow associated with the Franciscans, saw, as the priest elevated the host, "the Lord Jesus Christ in the form of a little infant, shedding blood from various parts of the body, with wounds in his side, hands and feet, so that blood flowed in great amounts."[189] A story that became enormously popular in the later Middle Ages concerned St. Gregory (Pope Gregory I) and a miraculous vision he had experienced. It is known as "St. Gregory's Mass" and involves the appearance of Christ himself, in the battered form of the Man of Sorrows, on the altar as the pope celebrates the Eucharist. Images of this event are extremely numerous (figure 9.1). Some show the blood pouring from Christ's wounds into the chalice, and it is understandable that the legend has been called "the quintessential Eucharistic tale."[190]

Saints not only experienced visions but also appeared in them, both during their lifetime and, more frequently, after their death and ascent to heaven. For instance, of the 45 miracles described in the Miracles of St. Margaret of Scotland, which were written in the thirteenth century, 29 involve a visionary appearance of the saint. This number, constituting almost two-thirds of the miracles, is distinctively high. In these accounts, the usual pattern is for the saint—"a woman clothed in snow-white garments," "shining with inexpressible splendour"—to appear while the pilgrim is asleep in her church, identify herself ("I am Margaret, queen of the Scots"), and then, perhaps by touching, cure the suppliant.[191] The frequency of visionary appearances is clearly related to the frequency of such overnight cures.

Saints who appear in visions are often recognized because they look just as they do in their painted images (see later, p. 493), but identification is not always so simple. Saints might appear in forms other than their own. This seems especially true of early Byzantine saints. The capers of Cosmas and Damian have been discussed earlier (p. 42), while St. Artemios, whose miracles were recorded in the seventh century, turned up in the form of a doctor, a noble, an official in charge of the Imperial Granaries, a butcher, a sea-captain, a senator, or a friend or relative of the suppliant.[192] Even if they are not in such disguises, saints sometimes need to identify themselves

[187] Ibid., pp. 85–86 (PL 120: 1316).

[188] See the reflections of Kieckhefer, *Unquiet Souls*, pp. 171–73.

[189] *Processus informativus pro canonizatione Mariæ de Maillye* 5. 54, p. 758 (she is also known as Jeanne Marie and Jane Mary).

[190] Rubin, *Corpus Christi*, p. 308. A rather different interpretation of the significance of this legend is advanced in Bynum, "Seeing and Beyond: The Mass of St Gregory in the Fifteenth Century"; the article also provides further bibliography.

[191] *Miracula sancte Margarite Scotorum regine* 4, 11, pp. 80, 98, with editorial comment on pp. l–li.

[192] *Miracula sancti Artemii*, pp. xiii–xiv.

9.1. Simon Bening, *Mass of St. Gregory*, c. 1535–40, tempera colors, gold paint and ink on parchment, leaf 13.7 × 10 cm (5 3/8 × 3 5/16 in.), Bruges, Belgium. J. Paul Getty Museum, Los Angeles, MS 3, leaf IV.

to the pilgrim or suppliant, as Margaret of Scotland characteristically did. In the ninth century, when Muslims raided the southern Italian monastery of Monte Massico, where the bones of the holy hermit Martin were revered, the saint appeared to his monks, calling out "know that I am Martin, whose praises you repeat everyday," and then leading them to victory.[193] A paralyzed woman in Trondheim was visited at night by a venerable lady who said, "I am Birgit of Vadstena and now I will cure you of your incurable illness." She said this not only to reassure, but to make it clear where the credit for the cure should be given, since, once healed, the woman had to go to Birgit's shrine, "to confess publicly the grace you have been given."[194]

Sometimes the physical location and position of the saint is described in such a way that the scene has nothing "visionary" in the loose modern sense of the word. For example, when Pope Leo IX (1049–54) was a baby in his cradle, he was bitten in the neck by some toads, which had crept in through a hole in the wall. His tearful nurse had then invoked St. Benedict. The response was immediate:

> The frightened child, roused from sleep, saw the most blessed father Benedict coming to him through the window, who came and cured the boy visibly. For such a great benefit, he sang the seven canonical hours in honour of that father Benedict.[195]

Benedict does not just "appear"; he comes through the window. Just as the horrible toads had gained access through a literal, physical aperture in the wall, so the saint does not materialize or pass through solid objects, but comes through the window. And this is no dream, not even a dream-vision, for the baby has just been "roused from sleep."

A saintly vision could provide authorization and sanction for behaviour that might otherwise be difficult or even objectionable, as in the case of a woman from Laleham in Middlesex, to whom St. Thomas Becket appeared in a vision at night, instructing her to reprimand her fellow-parishioners, including the parish priest, for their failings. He named names: a woman called Joheta did good works but had fallen into the vainglorious vice of seeking praise; then there was Adelicia, who breast-fed her baby during Mass. The saint seemed almost as well informed about the neighbours' bad behaviour as the woman doubtless was herself. He sealed their pact by giving her a ring.[196]

Saints appeared in visions to help or to admonish, and they might also come to give instructions. If there were doubts about the identity of newly discovered bones, a visionary appearance by the saint could resolve them, and saints also appeared to suggest or approve a translation of their bones. One such case involved a deeply obscure saint called Bernard, who appeared in a dream-vision to a man of Rocca d'Arce,

[193] Peter the Deacon, *Vita, translatio et miracula sancti Martini abbatis* 2. 7–8, pp. 837–38.

[194] *Acta et processus canonizacionis Beate Birgitte*, p. 117.

[195] Peter the Deacon, *Historica relatio de corpore sancti Benedicti*, pp. 288–89.

[196] William of Canterbury, *Miracula sancti Thomae* 2. 38, pp. 198–99.

saying, "Friend, do not be afraid, I am Bernard, whose body is buried near the church of St. John on the road from Rocca d'Arce to Arpino." He explained that he wishes to be translated to Rocca d'Arce.[197] These two places are in Lazio and about 7 kilometres (4 ⅓ miles) apart. Bernard had to be precise about his location, presumably because there was no pre-existing cult, and also had to be insistent, returning to repeat his request. Eventually a small local cult was established.

Dead saints could communicate with the living through visions and dream-visions. Living saints were able to speak directly, and one of the things they sometimes imparted was the privileged information that they had, for saints had knowledge of hidden things and future things. The saints' spirit of prophecy told them many things: the fate of kingdoms and of individuals; hidden sins; distant disasters; the date of their own and others' death. Some were especially renowned for their spirit of prophecy. St. Columba, for instance, was famous for his pronouncements on distant and future events, which came out almost compulsively—"now let us pray to the Lord with fervour for king Aedán and this people, because they are joining battle at this very hour"; "this one will outlive all his brothers and be a very famous king"; "your son will die at the end of seven days, on the Friday, and will be buried here on the eighth day, the Saturday"; "a terrible vengeance has befallen a remote part of the world . . . at this very hour sulphurous flames have been poured out over a city in Italy"; "you will not die in war, nor at sea, but a travelling companion you do not suspect will be the cause of your death."[198]

It was also known that St. Cuthbert had "the spirit of prophecy." The abbess Ælfflaed, who was the sister of Ecgfrith, king of Northumbria, insistently asked him how long her brother would reign, and who would succeed him, questions of vital importance not only for the royal family but for anyone living in a dynastic monarchy. Cuthbert's replies were allusive rather than direct and literal, but conveyed without much doubt that Ecgfrith would not live long and that his half-brother Aldfrith, then in exile, would succeed him. Within the year Ecgfrith was killed in the battle of Nechtansmere and Aldfrith was king. Cuthbert happened to be in Carlisle on the very day of the battle:

> suddenly he was troubled in spirit, so that he leaned on his staff and turned a sad face to the ground, then, straightening up and raising his eyes to heaven, he groaned deeply and said in a quiet voice, "perhaps now the battle is being decided."

Cuthbert warned the queen to seek a secure refuge. When a survivor from the battle turned up, it was learned that the king had been cut down at the very hour that Cuthbert had made his pronouncement.[199]

[197] *Acta et miracula Bernardi confessoris*; see BS 3, cols. 61–63.

[198] Adomnán, *Vita Columbae* 1. 8, 10, 16, 28, 47, pp. 32, 34, 40, 54, 84.

[199] Bede, *Vita sancti Cuthberti* 24, 27, pp. 234–38, 242–48.

The outcome of a nearby battle was obviously valuable knowledge, and other examples can be cited of saints who followed the course of fighting in this way. For instance, the saintly beguine Gertrude of Delft knew the outcome of the naval battle of Zwartewaal, which was fought at the mouth of the river Meuse, not far from Hook of Holland, in 1351, during a civil war in Holland.

> This devout Gertrude had the gift of prophecy, as experience demonstrated. Through God's grace she knew what was happening in secret at the present time; she also knew what was happening far away and what was to happen. Her knowledge of what was happening in the present but far away was demonstrated in the year 1351, when there was a battle on the Meuse. During the battle Gertrude was in the parish church with the other beguines, when she suddenly knew in the spirit the danger that was imminent and cast down her body in prayer, humbly urging the beguines to pray devoutly to our Lord, and she said to the beguines, "Sisters, now is the time for prayer, and great need, for at such time there is battle on the waters of the Meuse." A short time later, the battle being over, and Gertrude knowing this in spirit, she said to the praying beguines, "Sisters, praise the Lord, for our side has won."[200]

The other concern that Ælfflaed brought up with Cuthbert, the succession, was also a perpetual cause of anxiety in the medieval world. A story was told of Henry, count of Portugal, coming to the saintly John Cirita, and begging him to beseech from God that he be granted a son to inherit his county. "Have confidence, my lord," John said, "for you will have a son, who will be famous for his exploits both in war and peace, and he will obtain a great name among the princes of the earth, and will be a terror to the infidels and a scourge to the pagans."[201] The son was Alfonso I (1139–85), founder of the Portuguese monarchy and conqueror of Lisbon from the Muslims.

A saint whose prophetic powers were linked to an active life as a transformative influence in the religious history of Europe was Bernard of Clairvaux, the great Cistercian leader. He was not only a famous preacher, healer and exorcist, but also endowed with the gift of prophecy. This enabled him to monitor the Cistercian Order at a distance, for, even after monks of the Order had spread throughout western Europe, Bernard was supernaturally aware of their situation:

> Often, without any disclosure through flesh and blood, divine influence brought to the attention of his paternal care what was happening to them when they were far away: if they needed anything, if anything in them should be corrected, their temptations and wrong-doings, their illnesses and deaths, and the pressure of worldly troubles. For he often indicated to the brethren around him what they should pray for on behalf of the absent brethren.[202]

[200] *Vita Gertrudis ab Oosten* 5. 22, p. 352.
[201] *Vita Joannis Ciritae* 2, col. 1663 (the Life is late and legendary).
[202] *Vita prima sancti Bernardi* 1. 13. 63, cols. 261–62.

Bernard's powerfully attuned radar might have been more than a way of gathering information. A story that raises another interesting psychological possibility is told of Bernard's meeting with a young nephew of the bishop of Noyon, Hervey de Beaugency. The night after being introduced to him, the saint saw a vision of Christ, who gave a kiss of peace to an angel during Mass, a kiss that the angel then passed on to Hervey. Bernard took this as a clear sign that Hervey would become a monk, and his view was such public knowledge that Hervey himself later admitted that "it was impossible, after a promise of this kind from the saint, to remain in secular dress." Hervey ended up as abbot of the Cistercian abbey of Ourscamp.[203] In these circumstances, the line between prophecy and persuasion is hard to draw. If Bernard wanted this promising young man to join his Order, then a prophetic vision of this type, especially if made public (necessarily by Bernard) would be a useful means of presenting that wish as the choice of destiny.

Of all the miracles recorded of a saint in his or her lifetime, levitation and the reception of the stigmata are the most astonishing. Healing miracles, when looked at closely, often seem to be less surprising and more susceptible of a natural explanation than their categorization as "miracles" might suggest. The same cannot be said about miracles of levitation, when the saint floated in the air, or about the imprint of Christ's wounds on the saint's flesh. Either these miracles truly took place or the witnesses who reported them were deeply misled by their own senses.

These extraordinary cases seem to be much more common in the later Middle Ages, when ecstatic and extreme forms of sanctity flourished, but there are earlier examples. In the eleventh century a saintly abbess of St. Peter's Benevento supposedly levitated "three cubits" on her death-bed (a cubit is about 50 centimetres, or 20 inches).[204] Thomas Aquinas (d. 1274) was seen to rise "two cubits" into the air when praying at the high altar in the Dominican church at Salerno; this was taken as an indication of his "elevation of mind and subjugation of the body."[205] In the later Middle Ages numerous cases are reported. During one Pentecost service, Flora of Beaulieu was seen by all the other sisters in the church to rise "more than two cubits from the ground." [206] In the canonization hearing of St. Birgit of Sweden, it was reported that "the blessed Birgit was seen by some people to be miraculously raised in the air from the ground to a great height."[207] Catherine of Siena herself claimed that, as a pious little girl, she had been raised in the air while praying, and that later, as an adult, she was raised into the air after having receiving holy communion. It was an all-embracing experience: "as a fish enters the water and water enters it, so her soul entered into God and God into it."[208]

[203] *Vita prima sancti Bernardi* 4. 2. 9, col. 326.

[204] Desiderius of Monte Cassino, *Dialogi de miraculis sancti Benedicti* 3. 10, p. 1150.

[205] William de Tocco, *Ystoria sancti Thome de Aquino* 33, pp. 160–61 (cf. ibid. 34, 52, pp. 161–62, 189) (AASS Martii 1, pp. 670–71, 675–76).

[206] *Vida e miracles de sancta Flor* 1. 17, p. 25 (AASS Iunii 6, p. 111 [Latin translation of the Occitain]).

[207] *Acta et processus canonizacionis Beate Birgitte*, pp. 24, 190, 203, 589.

[208] Raymond of Capua, *Vita Catharinae Senensis* 33, 192, pp. 46, 270 (AASS Aprilis 3, pp. 861, 901).

This form of ecstasy was not limited to women, as the case of Aquinas demonstrates. There are further examples from the later Middle Ages. Robert of Salle, an Italian monk who died in 1341, was praying in church one day when "he began to be raised from earthly things by love of divine things to such a degree that he began to be raised towards heaven in his body also." Observers saw him "more than a cubit" in the air.[209] During the canonization hearings of Antoninus of Florence, which took place in 1516, fifty-seven years after the saint's death, several elderly men were recruited to give evidence that on more than one occasion Antoninus had risen into the air while praying in his chamber. One of them, aged seventy-five, said that his father had told him he had seen the saint raised into the air during prayer; others aged forty-two, sixty-six, and seventy, had heard this from Antoninus's servants.[210]

Levitation is not uncommon as a sign of holiness in many religions. In the profile of Christian sainthood, however, it is relatively rare, and occurs mainly in the ecstatic saints of the later Middle Ages. In this respect it parallels another spectacular, and controversial, manifestation of sanctity, the reception of the stigmata, that is, the imprint of Christ's wounds on the hands, feet and side. The most famous, and the first widely publicized, case of the stigmata was that of St. Francis.[211] While he was spending time at the mountain hermitage of La Verna, two years before his death, Francis had a vision of a six-winged seraph fixed to a cross and, as he pondered this, the marks of Christ's nails appeared on his hands and feet and a bloody scar on his right side. But "the crucified servant of the crucified Lord" concealed this as much as was possible.[212] It became public knowledge only after his death and, even then, was not mentioned in the canonization bull of 1228.

Francis's reception of the stigmata was not acclaimed universally.[213] In the course of the thirteenth century four popes had to issue bulls condemning those who denied the authenticity of Francis's stigmata, while, at the Franciscan General-Chapter of 1254, a companion of Francis was called to bear witness to their reality, "for many people throughout the world had doubts about them."[214] Some of the opposition was deep-seated and based on principle, and outrage at the audacity of the Franciscan claim. The bishop of Olomouc in Moravia commanded that "neither St. Francis nor any saint should be depicted in church with the stigmata, and that no credit should be given to anyone preaching the contrary."[215] Some people were so hostile to the idea of Francis's stigmata that they made attempts to obliterate depictions of them on images of the saint. One enraged sceptic, a member of another Order of

[209] *Vita Roberti Salentini* 4. 41, p. 503.
[210] *Summarium processuum impressum Antonini archiepiscopi Florentini* 1. 4, p. 335.
[211] See Frugoni, *Francesco e l'invenzione delle stimmate.*
[212] Thomas of Celano, *Vita prima sancti Francisci* 2. 3, pp. 72–73.
[213] Vauchez, "The Stigmata of St. Francis."
[214] Thomas of Eccleston, *De adventu fratrum minorum in Angliam* 13, p. 74.
[215] ASV, Reg. Vat. 18, fol. 275v (Gregory IX, *Usque ad terminos*, 12 April 1237, Po. 10308).

friars, supposedly cried out, "These Franciscans want to make their saint like Christ!," before pulling out a knife and attempting to dig out the painted stigmata.[216]

But another response to the new supernatural manifestation was imitation. Francis is not unique, but stands at the head of a long, and continuing, line of saints who have been marked out by reception of the stigmata. Some of these were Cistercians, or associated with the Cistercians. The abbot of Clairvaux, who was visiting the area where the saint lived, described the stigmata of Elizabeth of Spalbeek in 1267: "this girl bears in her body the stigmata of our Lord Jesus Christ most manifestly."[217] He was also amazed at the way the young girl, who was an invalid, nevertheless acted out the Passion of Christ during church services. Elizabeth was later consulted because of her prophetic reputation. Whether she was ever a Cistercian nun is debated, but she moved in Cistercian circles. More clear-cut is the case of the Cistercian nun Lukardis of Oberweimar (d. 1309), who was also imprinted with the marks of Christ's wounds; a fearful vision of Christ himself vouched for their genuineness against doubters.[218]

But it was the Dominicans who, as the other main Order of friars, were most interested in having something to match their Franciscan rivals. They emphasized the claims of members of their Order, especially women. The earliest case, if the hagiographic record is trustworthy, would be the Dominican nun Helena of Hungary, who died in 1240.[219] She had the stigmata in an unusual form, as her fellow nuns testified:

> She had scars on both hands and both feet and on her breast. The first scar was made on her right hand, on the night of the feast of St. Francis, while she resisted and said, "Lord, let this not be, Lord, let this not be!" We heard her voice but did not see to whom she was speaking. Another scar was made on the feast-day of the apostles Peter and Paul, at noon. A golden thread grew in the scar in her right hand . . . we saw a lily grow with the most beautiful flowers . . . which she dug out of her hand, so that others should not see them. We had these flowers for a long time after her death.[220]

A younger contemporary of Helena, the royal Dominican nun, Margaret of Hungary (d. 1270), was later credited with the stigmata and is depicted in many paintings

[216] *Chronica XXIV Generalium Ordinis Minorum*, p. 279; Vauchez, "The Stigmata of St. Francis," pp. 68–69; *Actus beati Francisci et sociorum eius* 40, pp. 130–32; Doelle, "De institutione festi SS. Stigmatum."

[217] Philip of Clairvaux, *Vita Elizabeth Sanctimonialis in Erkenrode* 3, p. 363. There has been considerable interest in her case: see, for example, Caciola, *Discerning Spirits*, pp. 113–24; Njus, "The Politics of Mysticism." On the general milieu of Elizabeth and other female saints with Cistercian connections, see Roisin, *L'hagiographie Cistercienne dans le diocèse de Liège*.

[218] *Vita venerabilis Lukardis* 10, 63, pp. 315–16, 347.

[219] The earliest copies of her Life are from the early fifteenth century; see the *Commentarius praevius* to her Life, AASS Novembris 4, pp. 267–72.

[220] *Vita beatae Helenae Ungarae*, p. 272.

of the later fourteenth and fifteenth century bearing them.[221] Catherine of Siena, a member of the Dominican Third Order, received the stigmata but invisibly.[222] In later tradition the story of her stigmata was elaborated and emphasized, but also became a fiercely controversial issue between Dominicans and Franciscans.[223] Images of Catherine receiving the stigmata are sometimes closely modelled on those of Francis at La Verna.[224] Reception of the stigmata remains, to the present day, one of the rarest marks of sainthood, and something highly controversial, prized by the devotees of stigmatic saints but viewed with distrust and doubt by many.

While no claim was made that she had received the stigmata, St. Birgit of Sweden is a classic example of a late medieval female saint endowed with gifts of prophecy and rapture. The articles in her canonization inquiry stress these features of her sanctity and constitute a kind of check-list of them. During hearings at Spoleto in 1380, for example, the articles mention her visions and revelations, the fact that "she was endowed by God supernaturally with the gift of the holy spirit of prophecy," her inspired knowledge of the secrets in the hearts of men, the guidance God gave her about what advice to give to popes and princes, how she saw the secrets of God while completely rapt from her senses, the fact that she saw Christ incarnate in the Eucharist, her levitation and the way her face shone like the sun.[225] In this world of late medieval sanctity, which was increasingly full of rapture, visions, and extreme physical manifestations, like levitation and stigmata, it is possible to glimpse, more and more clearly, the contours of Counter-Reformation and Baroque sainthood.

Saints in War

One situation in which the help of a powerful supernatural patron would be most valuable was battle, and saints sometimes appeared to give victory in war.[226] As early as 380 an apparition of St. Theodore the Recruit was credited with repulsing a Scythian attack in Asia Minor.[227] When Arnulf, king of the East Franks, was fighting the Moravians in the 890s, the enemy observed that Arnulf's battle-line "was defended by unknown and most beautiful men, who were the saints whose patronage he had invoked on setting out."[228] During the crucial battle of the First Crusade, outside

[221] Klaniczay, *Holy Rulers and Blessed Princesses*, pp. 376–84.

[222] Raymond of Capua, *Vita Catharinae Senensis* 193–95, pp. 272–74 (AASS Aprilis 3, pp. 901–2).

[223] Vauchez, "The Stigmata of St. Francis," pp. 76–77; Giunta, "La questione delle stimmate alle origini della iconografia cateriniana e la fortuna del tema nel corso dei secoli"; Lemeneva, "The Borders and Borderlines of Sainthood: On the Stigmata of St. Catherine of Siena"; Warr, "Visualizing Stigmata"; Giunta, "The Iconography of Catherine of Siena's Stigmata."

[224] For example, that by Giovanni di Paolo in the Metropolitan Museum, New York, of the mid-fifteenth century: acc. no. 1975.1.34.

[225] *Acta et processus canonizacionis Beate Birgitte*, pp. 201–3 (similar articles occur elsewhere).

[226] *Graus,* "Der Heilige als *Schlachtenhelfer.*"

[227] Gregory of Nyssa, *De sancto Theodoro*, pp. 61–62 (PG 46: 737).

[228] Arnold of St. Emmeram, *Libri de sancto Emmerammo* 1. 5, p. 551.

Antioch on 28 June 1098, the crusaders, threatened with encirclement, were saved by the sudden appearance of a huge army, mounted on white horses and bearing white banners. Three famous soldier-saints, George, Mercurius and Demetrius, led these miraculous allies.[229] St. Andrea Corsini, a fourteenth-century bishop of Fiesole, outside Florence, appeared at the battle of Anghiari in 1440, dressed in white, mounted, and carrying a staff in his hand, to encourage his fellow-country men to victory over the Milanese.[230]

A good example of the way that local saints could be mustered to help in time of war is provided by events during a Scots raid on Hexham (probably in 1079). The most important saint associated with Hexham was St. Wilfrid, although he was not actually buried there, being interred in Ripon, some sixty miles to the south. This did not stop him coming to the rescue of his devotees, however. Appearing in a vision, he explained

> I am called Wilfrid and lo here with me is Saint Cuthbert, whom I brought with me when I passed through Durham, so that together we might come to our brothers who lie in this church and together protect this place and people.

The Scots king, recognizing the presence of these powerful saints, abandoned the attack: "let us leave this place, for these saints are at home."[231]

It was natural that saints who were themselves soldiers might be especially sought out in time of war. Some saints were soldiers in their lifetime. St. Martin is a famous example of a Roman soldier who turned his back on warfare and the army, but many of the martyrs (both real and legendary) died as soldiers. The Forty Martyrs of Sebaste were soldiers in the famous Twelfth Legion and were among the last martyrs to suffer under Roman imperial persecution. Refusing to abandon their Christian faith, they were exposed naked on a frozen lake overnight, while a warm bath was prepared at the edge of the lake to tempt them to apostatize and warm themselves. One of them gave way, but his place was taken by one of the sentries, inspired by their example and by a heavenly vision. Next day their bodies were burned, but the Christians were able to obtain some of their ashes, which were regarded as precious relics and eventually spread to many parts of the Christian world. There are numerous images of the Forty Martyrs, including a spectacular tenth-century ivory relief from Constantinople, only 17.6 centimetres by 12.8 centimetres (approximately 7 by 5 inches) in size, but which succeeds in conveying both the group identity and the individuality of the forty.[232] They stand in a compact mass, more or less in ranks, and some embrace or seem aware of each other. It is a group martyrdom and they are soldiers, used to acting together, and since the martyrdom is slow, they are fully

[229] *Gesta Francorum* 9. 29, p. 69.

[230] Petrus Andreas de Castaneis, *Vita Andreae Corsini* 34, p. 1070; see the discussion in Ciappelli, "Edificazione e politica nella nascita (tardiva) di un culto. La *Vita* di S. Andrea Corsini."

[231] Aelred of Rievaulx, *De sanctis ecclesiae Haugustaldensis* 2, p. 179.

[232] *Meisterwerke aus Elfenbein der Staatlichen Museen zu Berlin*, no. 9, pp. 40–41, with colour reproduction (Museum für Spätantike und Byzantinische Kunst, Inv. 574).

conscious of their shared danger and suffering, and their shared endurance. Yet they are also individualized by hair—some are bearded, some not—and by posture, as some pray, some droop and many hug themselves in the cold.

The Forty Martyrs, although remembered as soldiers, were not depicted in military costume, but, in accordance with the nature of their martyrdom, naked except for loin-cloths. Most military saints were, naturally, portrayed in armour. The warrior saints most revered in Byzantium, such as George and Theodore, are typically shown bearing lance, sword and shield, and wearing a breastplate and military boots.[233] George was "the trophy-bringer" (*Tropaiophoros*), who brought the spoils of war, as he is described, for example, on an eleventh-century enamel now in St. Mark's, Venice.[234] Demetrius presents the interesting case of a saint who was not originally described as a soldier but joined the ranks of military saints some centuries after his death.[235] In the earliest accounts he is a martyred deacon, but he soon assumed the role of defender of the city of Thessalonica, where he was enshrined, and then developed into a fully fledged soldier saint, often depicted alongside St. George with identical arms and armour. Demetrius took a very direct approach to the task of protecting his city, obviously believing that attack was the best means of defence. When Slav raiders were climbing up the siege ladders that they had placed against the fortifications of Thessalonica, Demetrius appeared on the walls and speared the first man up, killing him and causing him to bring down the rest in his fall.[236] Centuries later, as Johannitzes (Kalojan), ruler of the Bulgars and Vlach, was besieging Thessalonica in 1207, he also encountered the wrath of St. Demetrius, "who would never allow the city to be taken by force." The saint came upon him while he was in his tent "and struck him through the body with a lance, and killed him."[237] The special place of these military saints in the Byzantine empire is reflected in the imperial rituals for Christmas, when banners were paraded bearing images of Michael, "the field marshal," and the soldier saints George, Demetrius, Procopius, and the two Theodores (Theodore "the General [*Stratelates*]" and Theodore "the Recruit [*Tiron*]").[238]

A soldier saint of great importance in the West, but not in the East, was Maurice, who, according to his hagiography, was chief officer of the Theban Legion in the time of Diocletian. Because of their Christianity, every member of the legion was martyred, at a site to the south-east of Lake Geneva, called at that time Agaunum and now known as St.-Maurice-en-Valais. Maurice's aid was highly valued by the rulers of early medieval Europe. Charlemagne supposedly carried "the banner of

[233]Walter, *The Warrior Saints in Byzantine Art and Tradition*; Grotowski, *Arms and Armour of the Warrior Saints*.

[234]*La Pala d'Oro*, p. 63 (no. 142); colour pls. XLV, LVI.

[235]Walter, *The Warrior Saints in Byzantine Art and Tradition*, pp. 67–93; Grotowski, *Arms and Armour of the Warrior Saints*, pp. 62 n. 17, 112–17.

[236]*Miracula sancti Demetrii* 1. 13, p. 135.

[237]Robert of Clari, *La conquête de Constantinople* 116, p. 108.

[238]Pseudo-Kodinos, *Traité des offices*, pp. 195–96.

the most blessed martyr Maurice" in his wars in Spain.[239] Maurice was also a favourite saint of the Ottonian dynasty, who founded a church dedicated to the saint at their power-centre of Magdeburg on the Elbe, and his military help was repeatedly invoked for the dynasty and the kingdom. The chronicler Thietmar of Merseburg refers to the generosity of Otto I "to God and his knight, Maurice", talks of how Maurice's relics were preserved at Magdeburg "for the security of the whole country" and calls the saint God's "invincible general" and "Christ's knight."[240] In 1007, as another chronicler relates, a Polish attack directed against Magdeburg was turned back "by the opposition of St. Maurice, knight of the highest king."[241] As a soldier saint, Maurice was frequently depicted armed with sword and shield. One of the more arresting images is the coloured stone statue, 110 centimetres (43 inches) high, in Magdeburg cathedral, which shows Maurice as a black African in thirteenth-century armour. (The Theban Legion was from Egypt and the name Maurice is related to the Latin *maurus*, meaning "black.")

With the rise of chivalry, soldier saints could be interpreted, simply, as "knights." The poet Simund de Freine introduces St. George in his French Life with the words, "He was a knight [*chivaler*], and had undertaken to gain a reputation through his prowess," while a later French prose version has George declaring himself "a knight of God" (*chevallier Dieu*).[242] The Sienese, who honoured George as one of their patrons, called him "the knight of knights."[243] The German *Saxon World Chronicle* of the thirteenth century talks of the martyrdom of "the good knight Sebastian" (*de gude riddere Sebastianus*).[244] A fifteenth-century Dutch Kalendar has entries for *Jorijs ridder*—"the knight George" and *Longijn ridder*—"the knight Longinus" on 23 April and 2 December.[245]

It was not only soldier saints who brought miraculous help in battle. Female saints too offered their patronage. The "blessed martyr" Eulalia provided protection for her city of Merida against the Germanic invaders of the fifth century. Theodoric II of the Visigoths was scared off by her threatening manifestations, while the Suevic leader Hermigar drowned in the stormy waters of the river Guadiana after "he had shown disrespect to Merida, offending the holy martyr Eulalia."[246] One version of the Life of Brigid of Ireland has her promising "victory in every battle" to

[239] William of Malmesbury, *Gesta regum Anglorum* 2. 135, p. 218.

[240] Thietmar of Merseburg, *Chronicon* 2. 11, 17, 30; 7. 16, pp. 46, 52, 66, 370.

[241] *Annales Quedlinburgenses*, p. 524.

[242] Simund de Freine, *Vie de saint Georges*, lines 83–84, p. 64; Matzke, "Contributions to the History of the Legend of Saint George," p. 106.

[243] *Constituti Comunis Senarum* 1. 123, 126, pp. 54–55.

[244] *Sächsische Weltchronik*, p. 114.

[245] BL, Add. 17354, Kalendar at fols. 2–13v. 2 December is a rare date for Longinus. The Bollandists mention an Anchin MS that has this as a feast of Longinus, AASS Martii 2 (1668): 386, while the Kalendar in an Italian Missal of the 1460s sold at Christies on 12 November 2008 (Lot 36 / Sale 7548) has, as an addition, the sale catalogue reports, "the finding of the relics of Longinus (2 December), which occurred at Mantua in 1304."

[246] Hydatius, *Continuatio chronicorum Hieronymianorum*, pp. 21, 30.

an Irish king, who then instructs his men to call on her when they engage in war. As soon as they have done so, "the king saw St. Brigid going before him with a staff in her right had and a column of fire burned from her head up to heaven. Then the enemy turned in flight." The king was victorious in all his battles, and after his death his warriors still had such faith in him that they placed his dead body in a chariot in their midst when going to war, for "St. Brigid's divine gift persisted in the king."[247]

A saint with no military traditions in his earthly life but who became a leading warrior was James the Apostle, whose shrine was at Santiago de Compostella.[248] The *Chronicle of Alfonso the Emperor*, which was composed around 1148, describes several campaigns in which the Castilians invoked St. James in battle against Muslims. Facing a large Muslim army, the men of Avila and Segovia "called out in prayer to the God of heaven and earth and to St. Mary and to St. James"; when the Toledan troops on a raid in Muslim territory heard their opponents sounding their trumpets and drums and supposedly invoking Muhammad, "they called with all their heart on the Lord God and St. Mary and St. James"; and the prayer of the army led by Munio Alfonso, governor of Toledo, in 1143 was, "St. James, apostle of Christ, defend us in battle, so that we do not perish in this fearful trial with the Muslims."[249] In 1158 Ferdinand II of Leon termed himself "standard-bearer of St. James."[250] The close association between St. James and war against the Muslims was institutionalized when the Order of Santiago was founded in 1170. Its members were vowed not only to poverty, chastity and obedience, but also to holy war. They were "vassals and knights of the most blessed James the Apostle, going to fight under Christ and under the banner of St. James, for the honour of his Church and the expansion of the faith."[251] In the late Middle Ages James even acquired the nickname *matamoros*, "the Moor-killer," and in the post-medieval period he continued to be an emblem of militant Spanish Catholicism.

Just as the Castilians turned to St. James for aid in battle, so the Bohemians appealed to St. Wenceslas. He was a native saint, and had been duke of Bohemia, so the bonds between him and his devotees were strong. He repeatedly appeared in battle to help his followers.[252] In 1126, for example, when the Bohemians were confronted by an invading German army, and the Bohemian clergy accompanying their troops had massed around St. Wenceslas's lance, which they carried into battle as a talisman, one of the chaplains suddenly called out: "Companions and brethren, hold firm, for I see, above the point of the lance, St. Wenceslas sitting on a white horse and dressed in white, fighting for us." Although the others could not see this vision, they were

[247] *Vita prima sanctae Brigidae* 14, p. 131.

[248] Herbers, "Politik und Heiligenverehrung auf der Iberischen Halbinsel."

[249] *Chronica Adefonsi imperatoris* 2. 22, 26, 69, pp. 205, 207, 227.

[250] "*Beati Iacobi vexillifer*": *Regesta de Fernando II*, p. 350.

[251] *Bullarium Equestris Ordinis Sancti Iacobi de Spatha* (Madrid, 1719), p. 5 (a document of Peter, archbishop of Santiago, of 1171); Lomax, *La Orden de Santiago*, p. 5, gives the manuscript reference.

[252] *Graus,* "Der Heilige als *Schlachtenhelfer," pp. 341–45;* Klaniczay, *Holy Rulers and Blessed Princesses*, pp. 163–66.

inspired by it nevertheless, and inflicted a crushing defeat on the Germans.[253] Wenceslas continued to support the Bohemians in war down to the end of the Middle Ages, even being invoked by the Hussites.

The saints could be present in battle in more or less visible forms. Sometimes they were simply invoked by the combatants, and the name of a favoured saint might then function as a war-cry, as when the English called on St. George and the French on St. Denis at the battle of Poitiers (earlier, p. 230). This kind of invocation was not uncommon. Once, for example, when a French noble who was sympathetic to the monks of St. Benedict at Fleury (and eventually became one himself) was in a tight corner, confronting superior enemy forces, he instructed his men "to call on father Benedict as one man, to bellow out 'Benedict!' "[254] The Venetian war-cry was "Viva San Marco!" down to the extinction of the Republic in 1797.[255]

But the saints might also appear visibly and join the fight, as the examples already cited show. And these miraculous interventions could be remembered and have long-term consequences. At the beginning of the ninth century the inhabitants of Patras were besieged by the Slavs who had settled in the Peloponnese. With their backs to the wall, they decided on a sortie and were astonished to see that St. Andrew the Apostle, who had been martyred at Patras, led the attack and routed the Slavs. Andrew was mounted and is described as an invincible soldier and general. Rather ironically, the defeated Slavs took refuge in St. Andrews church. When the emperor heard reports of all these events, he decided that the captives, along with their families and lands, should be given in perpetuity to the church of St. Andrew in Patras. There they formed a service group, responsible for the feeding and provision of imperial officials and foreign envoys.[256] The story is clearly a foundation legend, explaining the origins and duties of these Slavic dependants of the church, as well as a story glorifying Andrew as a patron saint willing to fight for his own people.

Saints and Demons

"The air is as full of demons and evil spirits as a sunbeam is of tiny specks."[257] Christian theologians taught that many of the angels had fallen into sin, rebelling against God and waging a tireless war against humanity. It was their leader, Satan, the devil, "the prince of this world," who deceived Eve, tempted Christ, and presided over hell. Evil spirits retained some of the powers they had as angels: special knowledge, the

[253] *Canonici Wissegradensis continuatio Cosmae*, p. 204.

[254] *Miracula sancti Benedicti* 5. 15, pp. 212–13.

[255] Peyer, *Stadt und Stadtpatron im mittelalterlichen Italien*, p. 24.

[256] Constantine Porphyrogenitus, *De administrando imperio* 49, pp. 228–32.

[257] Haimo of Halberstadt (*recte* of Auxerre), *In Epistolam ad Ephesios* 6: 12, col. 732; on saints and demons, see *Santi e demoni*; Caciola, *Discerning Spirits*; for an enlightening case-study, Sigal, "La possession démoniaque dans la région de Florence au XVe siècle d'apres les miracles de saint Jean Gualbert."

ability to transform objects (even if only in appearance), invisibility, and celestial speed. It was the demons who were behind magic and pagan religion.

These evil creatures, who, if we believe the hagiographers, were encountered much more frequently than angels, were a major terror of the world, and one of their most fearful aspects was that they could enter into humans: "since spirits are subtle and not to be apprehended, they penetrate the bodies of human beings and work secretly in their entrails, undermining strength, exciting sickness, terrifying the mind with dreams and shaking the understanding with frenzy."[258] Amongst the earliest tasks of the saints, as recorded in the Gospels, was the expulsion of demons (Matthew 10:8), and it continued to be a defining activity. The demons, indeed, were witnesses to the power of the saints in this respect. When a possessed man came to the shrine of Isidore of Seville, after a few days "the sick man—or something inside him—called out, again and again, 'Isidore is casting me out!'" As everyone gathered around, the demon left the man with a great sound.[259] On one occasion a bishop of Hamburg cured a possessed man with a fragment from the shrine of St. Winnoc, and forced the demon inside him to acknowledge whose relic it was and to admit the saint's fearful power: "none of us," said the demon, "not even our prince, can resist him."[260]

Demons resent the interference of the saints and often insult them. When one evil spirit was expelled at the shrine of St. Gebhard of Constance, he came back at night to the woman he had possessed, whispering in her ear like a jealous lover:

> Oh, my beloved vessel, why have you behaved so wickedly towards me, spurning me, your ancient inhabitant, and breaking the faith that you have long kept with me, for that seducer Gebhard, who has expelled me from you? Come back, I beseech you, come back to me, for it is not right that you should receive another in your vessel instead of me; I ask you not to refuse me the long, and so loving, cohabitation I had with you.

Fortified by the support of religious women and signed with the cross and the Gospels, the woman resisted his sinister entreaties.[261] "That seducer Gebhard" had beaten his rival.

Saints expelled demons both during their lifetime and from their tomb.[262] Living saints sometimes simply commanded the demon to leave, but they also often made use of the established rituals of exorcism. Caesarius of Arles stopped a poltergeist who had the habit of throwing showers of rocks by sprinkling the affected house with holy water.[263] When exorcizing a possessed nun, St. Ursmar read the service of exorcism from a book held above her head, and anointed her eyes, nose and mouth with holy oil; although the demon was expelled, the nun was still fearful, so Ursmar

[258] Lactantius, *Divinae institutiones* 2. 14 (1, p. 188) (PL 6: 333).
[259] *Historia translationis sancti Isidori* 6. 1, p. 174.
[260] Drogo, *Liber miraculorum sancti Winnoci* 23, p. 282.
[261] *Vita Gebehardi episcopi Constantiensis* 2. 5, pp. 592–3.
[262] See especially Chave-Mahir, *L'exorcisme des possédés*.
[263] *Vita Caesarii episcopi Arelatensis* 1. 41, p. 313 (MGH, SRM 3, p. 473).

called for salt and water, blessed it, and ordered it to be sprinkled throughout the nunnery, "and thus, straightaway, all fear, and its author the devil, went away."[264] In these cases it is hard to draw a line between the effects of routine ceremonies of exorcism and the special power of the saints.

Demoniacs who were brought to the shrines of the saints often had to be forced to come, sometimes being bound, and frequently with the demon inside them protesting. When people possessed by evil spirits were brought to the shrine of St. Severus, "it happened that, when they were not yet a mile from his monastery, the unclean spirit would break out in loud complaints and insults against St. Severus."[265] A woman demoniac was being dragged by force to the shrine of St. Bernward of Hildesheim, when the demon inside her "shouted that he would not enter Bernward's house, because he was a bitter enemy of his master." The woman writhed out of the hands of her escort and threw herself into a nearby swamp, but was rescued and healed.[266]

Variations in the proportions of exorcisms recorded in medieval Lives and Miracle Books suggest that some saints specialized in driving out evil spirits. In Sigal's large sample of miracles, from the eleventh and twelfth centuries, about 6.2 per cent of the cures are exorcisms.[267] However, the healing miracles of St. Dominic of Silos, which date from the same period that Sigal studied, show a much higher proportion of exorcisms (over 27 per cent).[268] In Byzantine miracle accounts of the ninth and tenth centuries about one-third of all maladies involve demonic possession, so they are five times as common as in Sigal's sample.[269] A characteristic example of these Byzantine cases would be the posthumous exorcisms at the tomb of St. Elias Spelæotes (d. 960).[270] A pious monk found that his niece was being troubled by a wicked spirit; she was shy about going to the tomb of St. Elias but her uncle disguised her as a man and she came there, spent the night and fell asleep; during her sleep the saint appeared to her, took "a little crooked thing" out of her mouth and killed it; and when she awoke she was cured. One of the saint's godsons was married to a woman who was likewise troubled by an evil spirit; his father took the woman to the saint's tomb and the very moment that they both "made their salutations with fear and faith at the tomb aperture," the evil spirit left her. A man called George had a son vexed by a demon, who made him fling himself about and utter indecencies; after being brought to the saint's tomb, he was freed from this affliction. Another evil spirit so vexed a priest that he even lost the power of speech and was afraid that he

[264] Anso, *Vita Ursmari episcopi et abbatis Lobbiensis* 4, pp. 458–59.

[265] *Miracula sancti Severi martyris*, p. 233.

[266] *Historia canonizationis et translationis sancti Bernwardi episcopi* 3. 24, p. 1031.

[267] Sigal, *L'homme et le miracle*, p. 236; he groups together demonic possession and madness under the category "affections mentales" but notes that "about 70 per cent" of the 241 instances in this category involve demonic possession.

[268] Lappin, *The Medieval Cult of Saint Dominic of Silos*, pp. 110, 148.

[269] Talbot, "Pilgrimage to Healing Shrines," p. 158.

[270] *Vita Eliae Spelæote* 12. 82–85, pp. 881–82 (there are other cases later in the text).

might be demoted from his office, but, after he had visited the saint's tomb, "washing it with his tears and kissing it with his trusting lips," he was cured. A relative of his was also freed from an evil demon in a similar way. This handful of miracles shows a busy shrine at which men, women and children, priests and lay people, were being exorcized, alongside many other suppliants who came for more mundane ailments, such as toothache.

In some collections of miracles the number of women being exorcised is significantly greater than the number of men. Of thirteen exorcisms in the posthumous miracles of Nicholas of Tolentino recorded in the canonization proceedings of 1325, ten concern women and only three men, while, of twenty-six exorcisms in the posthumous miracles of St. Dominic of Silos recorded before 1120, nineteen concern women and seven men.[271] Such ratios of approximately 3:1 are significant, even if they cannot be generalized to all miracle collections.[272] Just as some shrines seem to have drawn more cases of possession, so some drew more female demoniacs. Possessed women, like possessed men, could behave outrageously, like the Polish woman (eventually to be cured by St. Hedwig) who spat whenever the saint was named or the cross was offered to her.[273] Such responses to the emblems of Christianity are common among those possessed. And possessed women might express themselves in other shocking ways. Three Cistercian nuns of the convent of Santa Lucia in San Ginesio, who were possessed by evil spirits around 1320, threw off all restraint, and one of them, Sister Antonia, sang "really dirty songs," while another, Sister Philippucia, uttered "reprehensible words" that even a prostitute would be ashamed to say.[274] But demons not only unleashed blasphemy and libidinousness, they could also use their superior powers of observation and insight to point out sinners, as in the case of the Danish woman, possessed by a demon, who, when the local deacon turned up to exorcize her, shouted at him,

> "Deacon, what are you coming here for? Stay out! You are not worthy to enter under my roof. I know well who you are, and your deeds, having knowledge of your ways. You are the one who stole a poor woman's chicken."

Conscious of his guilt, the deacon left.[275] Since one of the signs of demonic possession was the abandonment of usual social and moral constraints, it could be expressed both by lasciviousness and by frank rebukes.

[271] Lett, *Un procès de canonisation au Moyen Âge*, p. 105; Lappin, *The Medieval Cult of Saint Dominic of Silos*, p. 110.

[272] Sigal, *L'homme et le miracle*, p. 237, records that 62 per cent of the miracles in his category of "affections mentales" involve males; since about 70 per cent of these "affections mentales" are demonic possession, it is extremely unlikely that females predominated in cases of possession.

[273] *Vita beate Hedwigis (maior legenda)* 10. 14. 4, p. 142 (AASS Octobris 8: 257).

[274] *Il processo per la canonizzazione di S. Nicola da Tolentino*, pp. 323, 324, 327.

[275] *Vita et miracula sancti Willelmi abbatis Ebelholtensis* 33, p. 346.

The demons frequently appeared in the form of animals—lions, vultures, black dogs—or black Africans.[276] They might come out as a huge flock of bats, darkening the sun.[277] They often make the sounds of various beasts: "the roaring of lions, the bleating of the flocks, the braying of asses, the hissing of snakes, the squealing of pigs and mice."[278] On one occasion the devil tried repeatedly to distract St. Dunstan from his nightly devotions, first by appearing "shaggy and bristling, in the form of a bear," then as a savage dog and finally turning into "a foul fox, in order, with his twitching tail and running about, to turn the attention of God's servant away from God." Dunstan simply laughed and made the devil disappear with the sign of the cross.[279] Dunstan knew how to handle the devil. One story tells how he seized the devil by the face with red-hot tongs when the evil spirit, chatting in human form, was trying to turn the subject to "women's names" and "acts of lust."[280]

St. Colette, who reformed the Poor Clares, the female branch of the Franciscan Order, in the fifteenth century, was, like Dunstan, subject to the attentions of demons trying to distract her from her devotions, although they seem to have taken their task more seriously. Starting simply with disturbing noises, they later beat her with rods, leaving welts, and then began to appear in various animal and monstrous shapes: foxes, red men, giants, dragons, serpents. At Besançon, the first nunnery she reformed, she found her cell full of foul toads, which vanished when she appealed to God. She disapproved of ants, because they store up food and plan for the future, contrary to the Franciscan spirit, but came across thousands of them crawling over her books. In the south of France it was flies that particularly persecuted her. She hated snails but discovered them all over her oratory and on her bed. Her biographer thought that no saint had ever been persecuted to such a degree in this way. In one demonic tour de force, the evil spirits brought corpses from the gallows to Colette's oratory so she found them as she entered, although at her command the demons had to put them back where they had found them.[281]

But demons could also appear in other, more pleasing, forms, to trick and deceive. They might even pretend to be Christ himself. The Life of St. Martin describes a visitation of this kind, when the devil appeared crowned, with royal vestments, and a serene expression, and said to Martin, "Martin, why do you hesitate to believe. I am Christ." The saint was not fooled: "the Lord Jesus did not predict that he would come again in imperial purple and with a glistening crown; I will not believe that Christ has come until I see him in the form in which he suffered, bearing the marks

[276] Loomis, *White Magic*, p. 74, gives numerous references.

[277] *Historia translationis sancti Vedasti Bellovacum dein Atrebatvm* 2. 12, p. 811.

[278] Gregory I, *Dialogi* 3. 4. 2 (2, p. 270).

[279] "B.," *Vita sancti Dunstani* 16, pp. 54–56.

[280] Osbern of Canterbury, *Vita et miracula sancti Dunstani*, *Vita* 14, pp. 84–85.

[281] Pierre de Vaux, *Vie de sainte Colette* 16. 153–58, pp. 131–36 (AASS Martii 1: 572–74 [Latin translation of the French]).

of the cross."[282] These devious stratagems were as much part of the demonic armoury as the more direct assaults in the shape of fierce animals or slimy creatures.

One of the things demons do is engage in conversation. Sometimes they do so willingly, sometimes compelled by the saint, but these chats suggest that demons and saints understand each other in a way that not all fellow humans do. A good example is the conversation between St. Parthenius, a fourth-century bishop of Lampasacus, and a demon that had possessed a man without anyone's knowing.[283] When the man greeted Parthenius, the saint refused to answer. The man, or rather the demon inside him, said that, since he had desired to see Parthenius and had greeted him, why had he not returned the greeting? Parthenius replied curtly, "So you see me; what then?" This rudeness is obviously predicated on the fact that the saint could perceive, beyond the human appearance of the man, the evil spirit within. "Yes indeed," responded the demon, "I have seen you and known you." "If you have truly seen and known me," said Parthenius, "then come out of that image of God." The demon begged him not to expel him "after such a time," and the saint then inquired how long he had inhabited the man. The demon answered that he had been in the man since childhood. Negotiations followed about where the demon would be expelled to. The saint said he would give him a new place, the demon presumed he would be sent into pigs—he obviously knew the Gospels well—but the saint offered him a man instead. The demon worried that this was just a trick but Parthenius insisted he was sincere, and the demon accepted these terms. The saint then opened his mouth and said, "Lo! I am the man. Come in and inhabit me." At this, the demon cried out as if he has been burned, confessed that he could not enter such a "house of God," and, muttering that you cannot believe a word that the Christians say, left the possessed man and went off to the desert.

The story shows the wonderful power and perspicacity of the saint, but it could have done this without anywhere near the amount of conversation that it gives. Parthenius's question about how long the demon has been in the man is not necessary, nor is the evil spirit's reference to being sent into pigs. The former has almost the ring of the saint showing a polite interest, while the latter could be comic. The human victim, the possessed man, says not a word in the story, and is a silent bystander while the really engaged protagonists, the saint and the demon, conduct their own verbal sparring. And demons sometimes make announcements about the saints that suggest a privileged knowledge. Just before the death of Daniel the Stylite in 493, a man possessed by an evil spirit announced that Daniel was about to go to heaven and that the man himself would be freed of the demon. Here the demon is a presumably unwilling spokesman of truth, and Daniel's sanctity is endorsed by such recognition from the world of spiritual beings, albeit wicked ones.[284]

[282] Sulpicius Severus, *Vita sancti Martini* 24. 4–8 (1, pp. 306–8).

[283] *Vita sancti Parthenii*, col. 1352.

[284] *Vita sancti Danielis stylitae* 97, pp. 90–91.

People, including saints, are curious about the demons. Parthenius wished to know how long the demon had been in the possessed man, and demons are often asked to tell their names. These names are sometimes generic—"I am the demon of pride," admitted one evil spirit, caught in the form of a little black boy by a holy abbot in the Egyptian desert; sometimes their names are mock Hebrew, and probably influenced by such biblical names as Beelzebub, like Belcephas, the demon who possessed a gambler and was expelled at the tomb of St. Peter Martyr; and they are sometimes simply the ordinary names of the time and place, like the Frankish demon Wiggo.[285] An unusual case is the demon who said he was Salmanasar, the ancient Assyrian king mentioned in the bible.[286] Demons are meant to be fallen angels, not wicked dead humans, but, of course, he could have been lying.

Demons have great linguistic abilities. The gift of tongues was granted to the apostles at Pentecost, but was very rarely one of the things that medieval saints exhibited; it was not part of the normal medieval repertoire of miracles. There are some examples, like St. David, who was given the gift of tongues when he made the pilgrimage from Wales to Jerusalem, so that he needed no interpreter, but it seems that, overall, the demons are better linguists than the saints.[287]

A passage from Jerome's Life of Hilarion of Gaza illustrates the point.[288] A powerful German in the service of the Roman empire had suffered since childhood from demonic possession, which made him moan and gnash his teeth at night. Hearing of the miraculous powers of Hilarion, he sought out the saint. The people of Gaza were terrified that he was on a mission from the emperor and led him nervously to Hilarion. The saint blessed the people and dismissed them, then turned his attention to the possessed man, "for he knew from his eyes why he had come." The devil inside the man sensed the challenge and raised him up on the tips of his feet and got him roaring. To Hilarion's questions, which were in Syriac, he responded in the same language, although the German himself knew not a word of it, being able to speak only his own native tongue and Latin: "you would hear, from the mouth of this barbarian, pure Syriac, lacking nothing of the emphasis, aspiration and accent of the dialect of Palestine." In order to make things clear to the German's interpreter, who spoke only Latin and Greek, Hilarion then questioned the devil in Greek, and got replies from the demon in the same language. The evil spirit explained many of his tricks, including how he had entered the poor German in the first place, but Hilarion was brusque: "I don't care how you got in—but I command you, in the name of our Lord Jesus Christ, to get out!"

The story is a wonderful window into the linguistic complexity of the late Roman empire: a German who speaks German and Latin has an interpreter who speaks Latin and Greek, who converses with a Palestinian holy man who knows Greek and

[285] *Vitae patrum sive historiae eremiticae libri decem*, PL 73, col. 1155; Ambrogio Taegio, *Vita sancti Petri martyris* 14. 112, p. 718; Einhard, *Translatio et miracula sanctorum Marcellini et Petri* 3. 14, p. 253.

[286] *Vita et miracula sancti Willelmi abbatis Ebelholtensis* 14, p. 325.

[287] Rhygyfarch, *Vita sancti David* 45, p. 140.

[288] Jerome, *Vita Hilarionis* 13, pp. 248–52 (PL 23: 39–40).

Syriac. We thus get from German to Syriac in three steps. But the point of the story is not to illustrate linguistic sociology; it shows the skill of the devil, and summons up the chilling picture of a man speaking a language he does not know, because a wicked spirit inside him is using him as a ventriloquist's puppet.

Similar linguistic aptitude was demonstrated by a demon who had entered a girl living in Nivelles, on the linguistic borderland between the Germanic and Romance language groups. When confronted by St. Norbert (d. 1134), "in order to show off," the evil spirit recited the Song of Songs from the Bible first in Latin, then in French and German.[289] In multilingual Prague in the fourteenth century a demon possessed a woman and "answered questions in various tongues."[290] One teenage girl in Carolingian Germany, who knew no Latin, was able to communicate fluently in that language when possessed, but "she was unable to speak Latin once the demon had been expelled."[291]

Demons might boast about their knowledge of languages. A loose-living servant of one of the canons of Beauvais was possessed by a horde of demons. They mocked the bishop's efforts at exorcism:

> "Why do you labour in vain? Do you not know what power and might we have? For I am the one who, when asked by the Lord Jesus, as you read in the gospels, what was my name, answered 'Legion.' For I am legion. For we are many collected in one. My power is multiple and spread though all the peoples and all their languages are known to me."

The demons suggested that some Jews should be summoned to test this claim, "since they know many languages."[292]

Invisible, sometimes inside a human being, or visible in frightening forms, and endowed with deep knowledge of the world and its ways, the demons were terrifying enemies of the human race. Saintly power was a treasured defence against them.

Saints and Animals

"If someone serves the Creator of all creatures faithfully and wholeheartedly, it is no wonder that every creature should serve his commands and desires."[293] So wrote Bede, describing the way that the birds, and even the tides of the sea, provided for the needs of St. Cuthbert. In another vignette, he portrays a scene in which two otters warmed and dried Cuthbert's feet after he had spent the night immersed in

[289] *Vita Norberti* 10, p. 478 (MGH, SS 12, p. 680).

[290] *Miracula sancti Sigismondi martyris, per ipsum in sanctam Pragensem ecclesiam manifeste demonstrata*, p. 464.

[291] Einhard, *Translatio et miracula sanctorum Marcellini et Petri* 3. 14, pp. 253–54.

[292] *Historia translationis sancti Vedasti Bellovacum dein Atrebatvm*, 2. 8–10, pp. 810–11.

[293] Bede, *Vita sancti Cuthberti* 21, p. 224.

the sea as an ascetic exercise.[294] The animals here are on the side of the saints. Saintly power over animals recalled the idyllic harmony of the Garden of Eden. St. Launomar, a Merovingian abbot, was so holy "that savage wild beasts obeyed when he commanded, as a man who imitated the angelic life, just like the first created humans still living in the sweetness of paradise."[295]

Many saints had a special relationship with animals.[296] They could control savage beasts, and win the trust of timid ones. Often animals brought food or fed the saint. The biblical model for this was I Kings 17, where the prophet Elijah is fed by ravens, and one of the earliest accounts of a Christian saint being sustained by wild creatures involves a raven bringing food to St. Paul the Hermit. Usually it brought half a loaf every day, but, on the occasion when St. Antony visited Paul, it knew to bring a whole loaf.[297] And other needs could also be met through their ministration. Ravens brought St. Cuthbert lard to grease his shoes.[298] Crocodiles carried St. Pachomius across the Nile.[299] And when the Breton saint Leonorius (Lunaire) and his companions needed to plough the land they had settled, twelve stags appeared and were readily yoked to the ploughs, then ploughed back and forth at the same pace without any guidance, working during the day (except on Sundays) and returning each morning, for a period of more than five weeks.[300] Animals could also perform a last service: two lions dug the grave for Paul the Hermit.[301]

Saints often had exceptional compassion for animals. Wild animals thronged to St. Blaise and, if they suffered some ailment, would not leave him until they had received his blessing.[302] The early medieval monastic saint, Marianus of Auxerre, was credited, in his later hagiography, with a special affinity for wild creatures. While serving in a remote spot as the monastery's cowherd, he would feed the birds from his hand, on one occasion he saved a wild boar from hunters, and on another dealt with a she-bear that had threatened his herd and that the other monks wished to catch and kill, simply by rebuking it: "What are you up to, she-bear? What are you doing here, you wretched creature? Rise up quickly and leave off these secret attacks."

[294] Ibid. 10, pp. 188–90.

[295] *Vita sancti Launomari* 12, p. 337 (2nd ed., p. 319).

[296] Amongst the titles on this subject: Zoepf, *Das Heiligen-Leben im 10 Jht.*, chapter 9 (pp. 218–29), "Das Naturgefühl im Heiligen-Leben"; Glacken, *Traces on the Rhodian Shore*, pp. 213–15, 288–318; Klingender, *Animals in Art and Thought*, pp. 344–50; Anti, *Santi e animali nell'Italia Padana*; Salter, *Holy and Noble Beasts*; Sensi, "Mondo rurale e micro santuari per la terapia degli animali"; Alexander, *Saints and Animals in the Middle Ages*.

[297] Jerome, *Vita beati Pauli monachi Thebaei* 10, p. 166 (PL 23: 25).

[298] *Vita sancti Cuthberti auctore anonymo* 3. 5, pp. 100–102; Bede, *Vita sancti Cuthberti* 20, pp. 222–24.

[299] *Vita altera sancti Pachomii* 20, p. 186.

[300] *Vita Leonorii episcopi et confessoris* 1. 2–3, p. 121; on this text, see Poulin, *L'hagiographie bretonne du haut Moyen Âge*, pp. 134–36.

[301] Jerome, *Vita beati Pauli monachi Thebaei* 16, pp. 176–78 (PL 23: 27–28).

[302] *Prima acta sancti Blasii* 2, p. 337.

The bear bowed its head and left "humbly and gently"; it was never seen again.[303] The special power of the saints over dangerous animals of this type was revealed in their friendly contacts with them. A she-wolf used to attend St. Martin during dinner, waiting patiently until the meal was finished, when the saint would give her the left over bread and the wolf would lick Martin's hand.[304] A wild ox, "forgetful of all savagery," used to visit St. Carileph, and the saint would stroke it and scratch the bristles on its head.[305]

When a blackbird laid its eggs in the hands of St. Kevin, which were outstretched in prayer, "he pitied it with such great patience and gentleness" that he continued holding his hands in this position until the eggs hatched.[306] Similarly, when St. Malo found that a wren had laid an egg on his cape, which he had left on the ground, he did not disturb it until the egg hatched, and miraculously, no rain ever fell on the cape.[307] Just as now, feeding the birds was one way of expressing fellowship with other creatures. The birds used to come at fixed meal times to feed from the hands of St. Baldomarus, an early medieval saint of Lyons.[308] St. Matilda, wife of Henry I of Germany, had her servants scatter breadcrumbs under the trees, so that the birds "might find alms there, in the name of the Creator," while the saintly bishop Ansfried of Utrecht (d. 1010) "had sheaves placed in the trees to feed the little birds in winter."[309]

The Life of Aventinus of Troyes, an early medieval hermit, contains a series of events in which the saint shows his concern for animals: feeding the birds from his hands, protecting a deer from hunters, allowing a snake to lay its eggs in his fireplace, throwing back into the river the live fish that were brought to him to eat. One of the most dramatically described of these events involves the visit of a bear:

> Once, in the dead of night, there came to the holy man's cave a terrifying beast, a savage woodland bear, which sought to break into the cave, roaring and growling all around in a furious rage. The holy man was disturbed and astonished, and saw death before his eyes. "Alas! Alas!," he cried to the Lord. When he had persevered in prayer and the sky began to lighten, the holy man opened the door of his cell and the beast entered. Tired out and mild, it lay its head and ears on the ground, reclining by the holy man's feet, which it began to lick. It stretched out its front paw, which was wounded where a huge splinter of wood had pierced it, and still stuck there. The blessed man grasped the wounded paw and drew out the splinter, eased it with lukewarm water, blessed the creature, and anointed and bandaged the opening. When the

303 *Vita sancti Mariani*, p. 760; the saint is also known as Marcianus; see BS 8, cols. 686–87.

304 Sulpicius Severus, *Dialogi* 1. 14, pp. 156–60 (PL 20: 193).

305 *Vita Carilefi presbyteri* 2. 14, p. 93.

306 Gerald of Wales, *Topographia hibernica* 2. 28, p. 116.

307 Sigebert of Gembloux, *Vita sancti Maclovii sive Machutii episcopi* 15, col. 739.

308 *Vitae Baldomeri epitome*, p. 684; the saint is also known as Galmier; see BS 2, cols. 725–26.

309 *Vita Mathildis reginae posterior* 17, p. 179; Thietmar of Merseburg, *Chronicon* 1. 21; 4. 36, pp. 24, 152.

> bear saw this perfect treatment, it at once returned to the vast solitude of the woods and never appeared again.[310]

Certain stock themes recur to illustrate the saint's concern with the animal world. The "Hermit and the Hunter" motif, in which the hermit shelters a hunted animal, has been mentioned (earlier, p. 199f.), and the story is told of saints other than hermits, too, like St. Marculph, abbot of Nanteuil, who came between the huntsmen of king Childebert I and their prey, a frightened hare, which took shelter under his robe. The hounds suddenly froze in their tracks, and Marculph sent the hare on its way, while one of the huntsmen, who had threatened the saint—"Clerk, how do you dare to interfere with the king's hunting?"—fell from his horse half-dead, and was only cured because the saint "was readier to have mercy than take revenge."[311] It was very rare for saints to be on the side of the human hunters rather than the hunted beast, although occasional examples occur, as in the case of some Flemish fishermen, who had harpooned a whale, but had great difficulty finishing it off, as it "spouted waters up to the sky, or plunged into the deep or, resurfacing, smashed the ship's tackle," and could only capture the poor creature after invoking St. Arnulf of Soissons and promising him a "part of the fish."[312] Perhaps a vast sea creature evoked less pity than a frightened hare.

The fierce animal with the thorn or splinter that the saint removes, as in the story if Aventinus and the bear, is an enduring theme. An early version of the story tells how the aged abbot St. Gerasimus, walking by the banks of the Jordan, had removed the sharp point of a reed from the paw of an injured lion. In its gratitude, the lion had refused to leave the old man but had followed him "like a dear pupil." Gerasimus looked after the lion, giving him the name "Jordan," feeding him on bread and pottage and allotting him the task of accompanying the ass that went down to the Jordan to fetch water for the monks. One day an Arab camel-driver stole the ass, and, when the lion returned without it, Gerasimus had feared that he had reverted to his leonine ways and eaten it. Henceforth the lion had to carry the panniers with the water-jugs himself. Later, however, the lion encountered the camel-driver with the ass, scared him off and brought the animal back to Gerasimus. When Gerasimus died, the lion grieved at his grave, and then expired himself. This all happened, not because the lion had a rational soul, but so that God could demonstrate "what subjection the animals had towards Adam before his disobedience and expulsion from the joys of paradise."[313] The story was later applied to St. Jerome, who, from the twelfth century onwards, is commonly shown in illustrations with a lion.

310 *Vita Aventini*, pp. 476–77 (the translation is slightly shortened); the Life is preserved in an eleventh-century manuscript: BnF, lat. 5572, fols. 102–5 (*Catalogus codicum hagiographicorum latinorum . . . in Bibliotheca Nationali Parisiensi* 2, pp. 480–81). It is unclear what the connection is between this saint and the one of the same name mentioned in Gregory of Tours, *Gloria confessorum* 67, pp. 787–88 (repr., 1969, pp. 337–38); see BS 2, cols. 640–43.

311 *Vita Marculphi abbatis* I 3. 18–19, p. 74; *Vita Marculphi abbatis* II 4. 18, p. 78.

312 *Vita sancti Arnulfi episcopi Suessonensis* 3. 8, p. 550.

313 John Moscus, *Pratum spirituale* 107, cols. 2965–69.

Animals were also beneficiaries of the saints' miraculous healing powers. Living saints, like St. William of Æbelholt, "healed not only men but also animals," and this healing power extended beyond the death of the saint, and the same routine rituals of measuring and offering wax images were employed to enlist posthumous help as in the case of human sufferers.[314] In 1286, for instance, Edward I of England had a wax image of one of his sick falcons sent to the shrine of Thomas Becket at Canterbury.[315] Cases of a peacock, an ox and a horse being "measured to a saint" are cited earlier (p. 358). There were also techniques that were thought appropriate for animals that were not employed for people, notably branding. The collegiate church of Ripon in Yorkshire received payments from local people who wished to have their livestock branded with "the iron of St. Wilfrid called *Seintwilfrideburningeyron*" to protect them from sickness.[316] This is rather similar to the branding of sick animals by the key to St. Martin's church mentioned earlier (p. 37).

Placing one's animals under the protection of a local saint through a vow and a prayer could guard them from harm. The following story is told of a woman on the estates of the monastery of St.-Wandrille in Normandy, where the relics of St. Wulfram were preserved:

> There was a woman on the estates of St.-Wandrille, who sent out her few little sheep to pasture in the morning, as she generally did, but, when she went to collect them at the usual time, she could not find them, and was very afraid that wolves had snatched them away. She invoked the protection of her patron, St. Wulfram, to restore to her the sheep that she had lost, making a vow and praying with faith. Her neighbours, who had likewise lost their sheep on the same day, sought them far and wide and discovered some of them eaten by wolves and others killed by the birds of the air. Only the sheep of this poor little woman were found, after six whole days, alive, with not one missing, all in one place and unharmed. The savagery of those animals had not been able to dare anything against them, since the woman's devotion had committed them to such a guardian.[317]

Francis of Assisi is the saint best known for his love of animals, "contemplating in creatures the wisdom, power and goodness of the Creator." This affection extended to even the humblest animals—"he burned with great love for worms"—and to inanimate nature, for he preached to the flowers, "and invited them to praise the Lord." This especially struck his first biographer: "he certainly seemed to be a new man and from some other time (or world)."[318] Bonaventure, Francis's official biographer and head of the Franciscan Order also stressed this feature of Francis's view of the world:

[314] *Vita et miracula sancti Willelmi abbatis Ebelholtensis* 31, p. 344; Aitchison, "Holy Cow!: The Miraculous Cures of Animals in Late Medieval England."

[315] Taylor, "Edward I and the Shrine of St. Thomas of Canterbury," p. 26 n. 22.

[316] *Memorials of the Church of SS. Peter and Wilfrid Ripon* 3, p. 167 (dating to 1503–4).

[317] *Miracula varia sancti Vulfranni* 2. 18, p. 156.

[318] Thomas of Celano, *Vita prima sancti Francisci* 1. 29, pp. 59–61 (*novus certe homo et alterius saeculi*).

> Just as a man loves a dog with a sort of natural dutiful kindness, because he sees that the dog obeys him, so also, as things were in their original condition, man was born to love and nurture the other beasts and irrational creatures naturally out of dutiful kindness. Therefore, the more a man is changed for the better and brought back to the state of innocence, the more these types of creature become tame for him, and the more he is moved by compassion for them. Just as we read of St. Francis, that he overflowed with great compassion towards creatures of this type, because, in a certain way, he had already recovered innocence. As a sign of this, irrational creatures obeyed him.[319]

This Edenic state was exemplified not only in the obedience of the animals but also in the love and concern that the innocent human showed for them. For some reason, Francis had a special love of larks. When considering the special obligation of charity at Christmas, he is reported to have said that,

> If I speak to the emperor in the future, I will beg that a general law be passed, that everyone who can should scatter grain and seed on the streets, so that on such a solemn feast-day there should be plenty for the birds, especially our sister larks.[320]

But relations between saints and animals were not all full of harmony and understanding. Sometimes peaceful co-existence was not possible. As well as encountering demons in the form of animals (as discussed earlier, p. 387), the saints also faced real dangerous beasts. Especially when searching for remote and secluded spots, they would encounter wild animals, and often had to expel them before they could establish their settlements. The Life of the two brothers, St. Julius and St. Julianus, describes how they preached and built churches in Italy during the late Roman period. Julius, seeing a little island in a lake, determined to found a church there, but the place, rocky and overgrown with thorns, was "full of serpents." Not deterred, Julius sailed to the island on his cloak, made a rough cross from the brambles and summoned the serpents to him: "You have possessed this harsh rock for a long time," he said. "But now, in the name of the Father and the Son and the Holy Spirit, I command you to leave this place and give it to me, Christ's servant, to inhabit, and build a church of the Twelve Apostles." They immediately obeyed.[321]

The removal of serpents was a common miracle of the saints, and one of the most celebrated examples is St. Patrick's expulsion of the snakes from Ireland. It is an exploit that is only attributed to the saint more than five hundred years after his death, in Jocelin of Furness's Life of Patrick, written in the 1180s or 1190s.[322] According to this work, Ireland was plagued from ancient times by three things: innumerable

[319] Bonaventure, *In tertium librum Sententiarum* 3. 28. 1, conclusion, p. 622.

[320] Thomas of Celano, *Vita secunda sancti Francisci* 151, p. 244.

[321] *Vita Iulii et Iuliani* 3. 8–9, p. 1103; the island is Isola San Giulio in Lake Orta, Piedmont.

[322] Jocelin of Furness, *Vita Patricii* 17. 147–48, p. 574; on this work, see Birkett, *The Saints' Lives of Jocelin of Furness*, pp. 25–57, 141–70.

poisonous creatures, the oppressions of visible demons, and many sorcerers. Patrick turned his mind to eliminating this "triple plague." He dealt first with the poisonous creatures, wielding the Staff of Jesus (an important relic which was preserved in Ireland down to the time of the Reformation) and summoning all these beasts from every part of Ireland to the high peak subsequently known as Croagh Patrick, overlooking the Atlantic Ocean. At his command, the poisonous animals flung themselves into the Ocean and were drowned.

Several saints had a reputation for defeating dragons.[323] Front, bishop of Périgueux, killed one huge dragon simply by telling it to submit to him, and ejected another marine reptilian monster by sending it down the river Dordogne to the sea.[324] Gerard of Anjou (d. 1123) once saved a peasant who was threatened by a dragon that had emerged from a nearby thicket; the saint made the sign of the cross and commanded the creature to go, and "the serpent, fierce in appearance and of unusual size," returned to the dense woods, never to be seen again.[325] Some of the soldier saints were dragon-slayers, starting with St. Michael the archangel, who fought the dragon in the Book of Revelation. The two namesakes, St. Theodore the General and St. Theodore the Recruit, both soldier saints, are credited with killing dragons, and Byzantine and other eastern images frequently depict them, armed and mounted, spearing these monsters.[326] St. George did not originally have a dragon but, certainly by the eleventh century, had acquired one, and this eventually became an indispensable character in his tale, represented in hundreds of images from Nubia to Prussia, in frescoes, panel paintings, illuminated manuscripts and pub signs.

So we encounter saints curing animals, taming them, providing for them and being provided for by them, and dealing with the more dangerous of them, but, although saints had a special relationship with animals, and could control them in a way ordinary people could not, there is little of the truly fantastic in saints' Lives when they deal with this subject. There are very few talking animals, and metamorphosis, the transformation of humans into animals, is rare.

It is the Lives of the early Irish saints that have the most "fairy-tale" treatments of animals.[327] Sometimes this takes the form of blatant anthropomorphism. When St. Ciarán of Saigir established his remote hermitage, his "first disciple" was a wild boar, which cut down sticks and grass with its teeth to help build the saint's cell. Later he was joined by a fox, a badger, a wolf and a deer, who all obeyed Ciarán "like monks." One day, however, the fox, "which was craftier than the other animals," stole "his abbot's" shoes. Ciarán sent the badger after him, "to bring his brother back." The badger, "since he was very skilled in the woods," soon tracked down the fox, bit off

[323] Rauer, *Beowulf and the Dragon*, with a list of examples at pp. 174–93.

[324] *Vita sancti Frontonis episcopi Petragoricensis* 2. 12, 17, pp. 411, 412.

[325] *Vita sancti Girardi confessoris* 1. 8, p. 495.

[326] For example, Walter, *The Warrior Saints in Byzantine Art and Tradition*, pls. 25, 27, 28; Grotowski, *Arms and Armour of the Warrior Saints*, figs. 47, 60, 86.

[327] Examples are assembled in Plummer, *Vitae sanctorum Hiberniae* 1, pp. cxli–cxlvii; Bray, *A List of Motifs in the Lives of the Early Irish Saints*, pp. 88–90, s.v. "Animals."

his ears and tail, and brought him back to the saint. "Brother," said Ciaran, "why have you done this wicked thing, which it is not right for monks to do?" The fox begged forgiveness, and did penance by fasting (although there is no record of his recovering his ears or tail).[328]

One of the very rare miracles of metamorphosis in hagiography occurs when St. Patrick turns the tyrannical British king Coroticus into a fox. Patrick had written to him, rebuking him for his actions, but Coroticus had scoffed at this, and Patrick then prayed to God "to expel this perfidious man from the present and the future life." Soon afterwards, the king heard his men singing that he would depart from the royal seat.

> Then, as he was in the midst of his court, he suddenly assumed the form of a wretched fox, and set off, in the presence of all his men, never to be seen again from that day and that hour, passing away like flowing water.[329]

Another tradition relates that Patrick and his followers avoided an ambush by appearing in the shape of deer.[330]

Both these tales are told in sources written in the seventh to ninth centuries. A comparable metamorphosis features in a story set in the years 876–83 concerning St. Cuthbert, not an Irish saint but one with strong Irish connections. This strange event takes place in the period after the Viking invasions of the ninth century, when Cuthbert's body was removed for safety from Lindisfarne, where he had first been buried, and carried from place to place by a small band of loyal devotees. It was a time of famine, and their provisions were soon reduced to a salted horse's head and a fresh cheese, stored in Cuthbert's casket. When they went to fetch the cheese, however, it had gone. One of the companions had secreted it, for private consumption. The response of the others was unusual: they prayed to St. Cuthbert that the thief might be turned into a fox. Immediately there appeared a little vixen, running around Cuthbert's shrine with a fresh cheese in its mouth. It was also noticed that one of the companions, Eilaf, was nowhere to be found. The conclusion was obvious: Eilaf had been turned into a fox. After repeated prayers to Cuthbert for clemency, Eilaf was restored to his proper form and begged forgiveness. And, adds the hagiographer, "his whole family line bears the surname Tod, which means 'fox.' "[331]

These early medieval stories, from Ireland and the north of England, are very rare examples of human-animal metamorphosis in hagiographic writing. Such tales could be found in classical literature; they are reasonably frequent in the Old Norse legends and sagas, as in the Volsunga Saga; and medieval romances not infrequently included werewolves. Yet in hagiographical narratives, which recount literally thousands of miraculous events, such transformations are virtually unknown. The

[328] *Vita sancti Ciarani de Saigir* 5–6, pp. 219–20.
[329] Muirchú, *Vita sancti Patricii* I. 29 (28), p. 100.
[330] *Betha Phatraic* 1, p. 47.
[331] Reginald of Durham, *Libellus de admirandis beati Cuthberti virtutibus* 15, pp. 22–28.

supernatural imagination of the Middle Ages was not uniform. Some extraordinary events were usual in a given context, others were unusual. Resurrections were not uncommon in hagiography, and demonic apparitions frequent, but readers did not expect to encounter human-animal metamorphosis.

Liberation

One common sound at the shrines of the saints was the clink of chains and the ringing note of iron on stone. Some of the most noticeable amongst the crowds of pilgrims would be those penitents who had been commanded to bear iron bonds or wear mail coats in atonement for their sins, and one sign of the merciful miraculous power of the saints was the sudden bursting and breaking of these harsh exterior signs of punishment. In the church of Burton upon Trent, around the year 1090, the monks were amazed to hear "a great clang" as the iron band around the arm of a praying penitent sprang off and landed at their feet.[332]

A vivid example of the same thing can be found in the story told of a German named Conrad, a notorious sinner who was punished by a hideous affliction that made him stink like a corpse. He eventually repented and sought remittance of his sins from the pope himself, Gregory VII (1073–85). Gregory imposed upon him the penance of wearing a mail-coat, bound with five bands of iron, and of carrying around with him a parchment listing his sins:

> he should travel around all the places where the saints rest, and this would be the sign of divine visitation, when divine grace would visit him through the intercession of the saints, namely when the chains would break, the mail coat fall apart and the parchment be found blank.

After much wandering, which took him as far as Jerusalem, Conrad found release at the tomb of Prince Emeric of Hungary in Székesvehérvár (Stuhlweißenburg). The chains broke and the mail-coat fell apart, startling the people in the church with the noise of shattering iron. Upon inspection, the parchment that Conrad carried was found to be blank. The report of this miracle led directly to the translation of Emeric's body and the start of a successful cult.[333]

Saints were also able to free prisoners from captivity.[334] One hagiographer reports that a crusader, who had been captured by the Muslims and shut in a box, was miraculously transported by St. Eutropius back to France, to his church in Saintonge, and adds that "the box, with its strong chain attached, still remains hung up in that church, for visiting pilgrims to view as a confirmation of this deed."[335] In the late

[332] Geoffrey of Burton, *Vita sancte Modvenne virginis* 46, pp. 188–90.

[333] *Legenda sancti Emerici ducis* 7, pp. 457–60.

[334] Graus, "Die Gewalt bei den Anfängen des Feudalismus und die 'Gefangenenbefreiungen' der merowingischen Hagiographie."

[335] *Miracula Eutropii episcopi Santonensis* 2. 10–11, p. 738.

sixth century, Gregory of Tours had seen the broken chains hanging in the church of St. Medard at Soissons "as proof" of such miracles:

> We have see the broken and shattered shackles and chains of prisoners lying at his holy tomb, where they are kept to this day as proof of his power.[336]

Certain saints acquired a reputation for freeing prisoners. Gregory of Tours writes, "The renowned martyr Victor is praised at Milan because he often releases those who lie fettered in prison and allows captives to go away in freedom."[337] It is clear from Gregory's words that in his time the saint had a special reputation for freeing prisoners, but it is not clear why. Nor does it seem to have been an enduring feature of Victor's cult (although, ironically, one of the churches dedicated to him in Milan is now the site of a prison, San Vittore al Carcere). In the eleventh century St. Foy was "specially famous and well known" for this kind of miracle.[338] St. Leonard was also recognized as "the special patron of prisoners" by the twelfth century.[339] When the crusader prince Bohemond was captured by his Muslim enemies in 1100, he placed his hope in St. Leonard: "St. Leonard is a special refuge in captivity. By the power of St. Leonard solid iron melts away like wax before a fire."[340] Nor was he deceived. After several visionary appearances of the saint, Bohemond was released (although a large ransom might also have played a part) and, in due course, came to St. Leonard's shrine in France to offer him the chains of his captivity. This was the saint "powerful in loosing bonds."[341]

Saints did not exert their powers simply to save the innocent, for the guilty were freed too. St. Foy of Conques, as mentioned, had a reputation for freeing prisoners, and it was expressly noted that "it makes no difference whether they are imprisoned justly or unjustly."[342] St. Dominic of Silos freed one of the prisoners of king Alfonso VI of Castile and Leon, even though the king had imprisoned the man "justly enough" for attacking his Muslim tributaries.[343] In the early Middle Ages, the people who were miraculously revived after hanging tended to be guilty rather than wrongly punished innocents.[344] To free the guilty was to show the saint's free, untrammelled, independent power—not righting wrongs or re-establishing the moral order, but bringing undeserved and unhoped for salvation out of the blue.

Miracles of liberation are to be found throughout Christendom, but the violent and shifting frontier between Christians and Muslims in the Iberian peninsula was

[336] Gregory of Tours, *Libri historiarum X* 4. 19, p. 152; cf. idem, *Gloria confessorum* 93, p. 807 (repr., 1969, p. 357).

[337] Gregory of Tours, *Gloria martyrum* 44, p. 518 (repr., 1969, p. 68).

[338] Bernard of Angers, *Liber miraculorum sancte Fidis* 1. 31, p. 136.

[339] Robert of St.-Marianus of Auxerre, *Chronicon*, p. 228.

[340] Waleran of Naumburg, *Miraculum de Bohemundo*, p. 163.

[341] William of Malmesbury, *Gesta regum Anglorum* 4. 387, p. 692.

[342] Bernard of Angers, *Liber miraculorum sancte Fidis* 1. 31, p. 137.

[343] Grimaldus, *Vita Dominici Siliensis* 2. 26, pp. 376–78; the incident is dated to 1088–91 by Lappin, *The Medieval Cult of Saint Dominic of Silos*, p. 8.

[344] Lotter, "Heiliger und Gehenkter."

a place where they had special meaning. Cross-border raiding led to enslavements on both sides. Here captives were a large, unhappy class and the captivity was given a hard and distinctive edge by being at the hands of men of another religion. Some saints became specialists in freeing these wretches. One was St. Dominic of Silos, discussed earlier, who died in 1073. His posthumous miracles include cross-frontier liberations, such as one that can be dated exactly to 1088, involving a man called Servando of Coscorrita, who was captured by Muslims and carried off to Medinaceli, where he was placed in a deep dark dungeon with shackles on his feet. He prayed to God for release, and, one night, St. Dominic appeared to him in a blaze of light and called him by name, explaining that God had sent him to Servando "to snatch you away from this horrible and stinking den and restore you to your homeland and family." The saint's supernatural help involved throwing Servando a little wooden hammer, which miraculously broke his chains, and then casting him a rope by which he pulled him out of the dungeon. The happy captive made his way to Silos to place his fetters on the saint's tomb, arriving there during the ceremony of dedication of the church (which is how we know the exact date of this event).[345] Dominic's posthumous career as a liberator continued into the thirteenth century, when a vernacular account of his miracles records 66 escapes from Muslim captivity, most of them dating to the 1270s and 1280s, along with five escapes from Christians, and six miracles of other kinds.[346]

There was a similarly dangerous and uncertain landscape in France during the Hundred Years War. A collection of the miracles of St. Martial of Limoges from 1388 recounts numerous cases of English garrisons and mercenaries capturing and imprisoning members of the local population, who then need Martial's help to escape.[347] An English garrison in the region seized a group of pilgrims on their way to Martial's shrine and flung them into a dark dungeon, saying that they would only be freed in exchange for some Englishmen held prisoner in Poitiers. One of the pilgrims, working on the assumption that the English captives they were to be exchanged for had already been killed by the Poitevins, turned instead to St. Martial, promising to walk naked from the gate of Limoges to the saint's shrine if he and his companions were freed. As soon as his prayer was finished, the captain of the garrison sent for the captives, freed them, and promised that no harm would come to any pilgrims in future.[348] Others captured by the English included a man who had forgotten or lost his safe-conduct, a man thrown into chains in one of the little English forts that bristled throughout the area, and the son of a smith, who could not afford the ransom the English demanded.[349] One man was freed from the English by an unknown but terrifying squire, who then vanished; a villager with two cows and a pack-animal,

[345] Grimaldus, *Vita Dominici Siliensis* 2. 21, pp. 356–60.

[346] Lappin, *The Medieval Cult of Saint Dominic of Silos*, p. 275; García de la Borbolla, "Hagiografía de frontera."

[347] *Miracula sancti Martialis anno 1388 patrata.*

[348] Ibid., miracle 4, pp. 416–17

[349] Ibid., miracles 13–14, 19, pp. 420–21, 422–23.

who promised three animals made of wax to Martial's shrine if the saint protected them "when the English came running through the parish," found that the plunderers were unable to drive off his livestock.[350] Another, transporting a valuable consignment of wine, had the bad luck to encounter some English, who, tying his legs under the belly of a horse and his hands behind his back, were leading him off to captivity when he, "seeing the loss of all his property and his own imminent destruction," called out on St. Martial. Suddenly a French force turned up, the English fled, and the man recovered his wine and his liberty.[351] Examples could be further multiplied. Martial can save Englishmen too, although they have to turn over a new leaf, like the squire whose girth gave way when fording a river during a plundering raid and who was saved from drowning once he had promised to take a gift of wax to St. Martial and "never henceforth to bear arms against any Christian."[352]

There would be such looting and imprisonment for ransom in any region where fighting was prevalent, especially of the small-scale raiding and plundering kind. And, in the absence of a powerful state force to impose its own order, it was natural that victims would turn to the saints, like Martial, who had a reputation as liberators. Martial's hagiographer exults in his hero's miraculous deeds:

> So many shackles shattered through the merits of the patron, so many people, accused and on the point of death, who, by presuming upon the fatherly care of Martial, are freed from their chains, snatched from prison, released from iron bonds, liberated from long misery and torture of their limbs; many too, for whom human help could do nothing, taken from the tyrannical grasp of captivity, so that they escaped not only death but even any loss of their goods.[353]

Punitive Miracles

Saints could use their supernatural powers to hurt as well as to heal.[354] As Gregory of Tours put it, speaking of St. Martin, "his power is shown in the punishment of the foolish just as in the grace of healing."[355] Sudden and immediate death is the most dramatic punishment the saints inflict, but wounds, illness, blindness and demonic possession are also part of their repertoire. A woman who had acted as a guide to some pilgrims to the shrine of St. Paulinus at Trier, but had then secretly pocketed the money they left as an offering, "had not yet reached the threshold of the monastery when, suddenly calling out mad things, she began to repeat 'alas!' over and over

[350] Ibid., miracles 22, 25, pp. 423–24.
[351] Ibid., miracles 36, p. 428.
[352] Ibid., miracle 1, p. 415.
[353] Ibid., preface, p. 413.
[354] Klaniczay, "Miracoli di punizione e *maleficia*."
[355] Gregory of Tours, *Libri historiarum X* 5. 6, p. 203.

again and ran through the street, no one knowing when this sudden insanity had come upon her."[356] A man who swore falsely by St. Cuthbert was immediately struck blind.[357] And, while one of the commonest ailments that saints cured was paralysis, they could also inflict it as a punishment. Rooting someone to the spot showed the power of a saint to freeze time and space. A sceptic who derided Simon de Montfort, the English baron killed in battle in 1265, whose adherents regarded him as saint, "lost the power of speech and was unable to move a hand or a foot but sat like a dead person." Only the prayers of others present enabled him to breathe a little. Eventually he recovered after promising never to say anything bad about de Montfort again.[358] Thieves who stole the property of the saints or their devotees might become confused and wander in circles, like those who stole cows from St. Modwenna's monastery in Ireland and, after wandering all night, found they were back where they had started, at the monastery.[359] Likewise, after a man whose cattle had been stolen prayed at the shrine of St. Marianus at Bourges, the thief "lost his way and, like someone out of his mind, returned to the place from which he had set out."[360]

Some saints inflicted punishments during their lifetime. St. Bertrand, bishop of Comminges in the early twelfth century, discovered that one of his deacons had become completely infatuated with a beautiful woman: "this man was imprisoned and no one released his bonds, he was held tied without hope of release, and he had shamelessly abandoned the lily of chastity."[361] Bertrand reproved the deacon, who repented and recognized his fault, and then he turned on the woman, demanding why she had ensnared his minister and invoking God's anger. The woman was defiant, but vengeance immediately befell her:

> Then the evil woman, despising the holy bishop's warnings, poured out wicked words. And while she was speaking such foolishness, there came down on her a terrible rod, sent by God, and soon, in the sight of all around, she was gravely troubled by a demon and straightaway died, losing her life and her soul together. After this, all who were present were filled with great fear and mighty wonder.

This was not the only one of Bertrand's miraculous punishments. After a knight had kidnapped a man under Bertrand's protection, and refused to free him at the bishop's command, the malefactor "felt an affliction in his eyes, sent from heaven, as if the mark of Cain were imprinted on his eye-lids, making them move continually; unwillingly, he released the man." A priest who refused to correct his sexual behaviour after the bishop had warned him, saw his house collapse when Bertrand

[356] *Vita sancti Paulini Trevirensis* 22–23, p. 679.

[357] Reginald of Durham, *Libellus de admirandis beati Cuthberti virtutibus* 24, p. 55.

[358] *Miracula Simonis de Montfort*, p. 89.

[359] Geoffrey of Burton, *Vita sancte Modvenne virginis* 8, pp. 22–24.

[360] Gregory of Tours, *Gloria confessorum* 80, p. 799 (repr., 1969, p. 349).

[361] For the following, Vitalis, *Vita sancti Bertrandi episcopi Convenensis* 2. 13–14, 17, 24–26, pp. 1177–80.

cursed it, and, after Bertrand excommunicated a man for building on the land set aside for a burial ground, "he immediately, although unwillingly, had to change his mind through the merits of the saint, and fell into a perpetual illness." A woman who swore a false oath before him, that she was innocent of adultery, saw her hand wither and dry up.

Bertrand's miracles reflect his rights and duties as a bishop, enforcing proper sexual behaviour on his clergy and his lay flock, fulfilling his role as a lord and protector and defending land set aside for pious uses. The punishments that are inflicted are described as "sent from heaven" or "divinely" and are often dramatic, although sometimes characterized only vaguely: the "terrible rod," the "perpetual illness."

Bertrand used both the precise and legal form of excommunication and the more general curse or malediction. A saint's curse was a dangerous thing and might endure for generations. In the middle of the twelfth century, for instance, St. Malachy of Armagh "imposed a weighty sentence" on Robert de Bruce, lord of Annandale, who had promised to spare the life of a robber at the saint's request but then deceived him and hanged the man anyway. Robert soon "died a wretched death" and three of his heirs in succession "were snatched away in the first flower of their age." More than a century after the initial curse, Robert's descendant and namesake, Robert de Bruce, went to Malachy's tomb and offered him a landed endowment to pay for lights to burn at his tomb forever. He thus "made perpetual peace with the saint," died in his seventies (and was grandfather of the later King of Scots).[362]

Nicholas of Fara, author of a Life of the fifteenth-century Franciscan saint John of Capistrano, actually devoted a special section to demonstrate "how great a vengeance the Lord inflicted on those who spoke wickedly about the integrity of his servant."[363] John warned a high-born man who doubted the miracles of St. Bernardino, the most famous saint of John's own branch of the Franciscans, to beware the judgment of God, but the scoffer disregarded him and a few days later died of a fall from his horse. On another occasion, in Regensburg, he condemned a priest who was addicted to gambling, and a wanton woman who indulged in such female vanities as false hair, but they both scorned his criticisms. The next night they both died at the same moment. Filled with fear, the local population organized a public bonfire of gaming boards and "shameless female enticements." Nicholas gives other examples of this kind, but perhaps the most striking is a story from another part of the Life, relating how John joined the Franciscan Order:

> When he first undertook this great change, he sought to persuade his betrothed to enter the religious life too, threatening that the terrible scourge of God would fall on her unless she consecrated her virginity to the Lord through a perpetual vow and was united to an immortal spouse. She was not

[362] *Chronicon de Lanercost*, pp. 160–61; the charter granting the endowment is printed in PL 185: 1759–60.

[363] Nicholas of Fara, *Vita clarissimi viri fratris Joannis de Capistrano* 76, p. 463; see Andrić, *The Miracles of St John Capistran*, pp. 198–203.

> persuaded by the exhortation of her holy fiancé, and at length married a mortal spouse and was struck by a horrific leprosy.[364]

The living saint thus had impressive vindictive power, but punishment by the dead saint was more common. Of the 470 punitive miracles studied by Sigal (earlier, p. 344), 421, that is, almost 90 per cent, are posthumous. The saint was generally enshrined in a particular church, and took care of his own: the monks, canons or other clergy of that church, and their property. Book Two of the *Miracles of St. Bavo*, describing the wonders of the saint enshrined at Ghent, is almost entirely devoted to "the miracles of the saint avenging wrongs done to him."[365] Some concern failure to pay rent or dues to the monastery, others relate the punishment of those who had usurped or damaged the property of the abbey, or describe how the saint protects his own dependants, and several involve enforcement of respect for the saint's feast-day. These stories are often crisp in presentation:

> A knight chasing a young hare trampled the growing crops. A servant of the saint grieved at this and said, "Alas, St. Bavo, why do you not defend your field?" As soon as he said this, the knight fell and broke his hip. The young hare stumbled and broke its neck.[366]

St. Remigius, bishop of Rheims, was renowned as "a frequent avenger against intruders." On one occasion, a man who had usurped a rich field that had been granted to Remigius's church and had refused all requests to restore it, was riding home from the city but "the injury he had done to the bishop stopped his efforts": "he fell to the ground covered in blood; his tongue, which had commanded that field to be taken away, was paralysed; the eyes that had desired were closed up; the hands that had grasped now seized up." He gasped out the command that he be taken to Remigius's tomb and that all the gold he had on him should be placed on the tomb, but, on the way, he encountered the pious man who had originally given the field to the saint. "Do not regard his gifts, O saint of God," this man prayed, "and do not be his helper, I pray." Remigius listened, and, despite his gifts of gold, the offender died on his way home.[367]

It is evident from stories of this type that protection of property is one of the main tasks of a saint, and that vulnerable monks and clergy would cherish such stories of how their enemies had been shamed or destroyed by their powerful saintly patrons. A contemporary reflection on punitive miracles shows a clear awareness of this function. Gerald of Wales, after describing several miraculous punishments inflicted by Irish saints, comments that the saints of Ireland have a more vengeful spirit than the saints of other lands, and goes on:

[364] Nicholas of Fara, *Vita clarissimi viri fratris Joannis de Capistrano* 60, p. 459.

[365] *Miracula sancti Bavonis* 2, pp. 298–300, quote at 2. 40, p. 300; see De Gaiffier, "Les revendications de biens dans quelques documents hagiographiques," pp. 130–31.

[366] *Miracula sancti Bavonis* 2. 40, p. 300.

[367] Gregory of Tours, *Gloria confessorum* 78, p. 795 (repr., 1969, p. 345).

> No other reason for this occurs to me than this: that the Irish people, having no castles but many brigands, usually seek protection for themselves and their possessions in the refuge of churches rather than the defences of castles, and this is especially the case with their churchmen. Hence, through divine providence and kindness, there was need for sharp and frequent punishment of the enemies of churches.[368]

This fine piece of sociological insight—saintly protection is particularly important in societies without castles—must, however, be qualified by considering its opposite, for the years in which western Europe became covered with castles, that is, the tenth to twelfth centuries, were also a heyday of punitive miracles. It was, indeed, often the mounted predators in their strongholds who were the targets of these miracles. A stock figure in these accounts is the arrogant knight. A classic example occurs in the *Miracles of St. Benedict*. After plundering the property of the monks of St. Benedict of Fleury, one wicked knight ridiculed the idea that the saints could protect the property of their servants; he boasted that he had often plundered churches and scoffed at the saints—"And the whole world is supposed to be protected by their help!" He was immediately possessed by a demon and thrown from his horse.[369]

Disrespect for the saint, especially the expression of ignorance of, or contempt for, the saint's name or identity, was a sure way of bringing fierce and sudden vengeance. In the sixth century, some Frankish soldiers, attempting to exact a fine for avoidance of military service from the inhabitants of a monastery dedicated to St. Martin, were told by the estate manager there, "These are men of St. Martin." "Your Martin," the soldiers replied, "whom you always bring out so inanely, means nothing to us." As one might expect, one of them fell to the ground in agony and was only cured by recognizing St. Martin's power and calling on his name.[370] In the eleventh century, a German robber-knight, appealed to by his poor victim to restrain himself in the name of St. Adelheid, replied, "I am alive, and tonight will dominate you and yours; Adelheid is dead and is powerless to bring you protection." Needless to say, he was immediately struck with frenzy.[371]

A story of disrespect for a saint that remains curiously unresolved occurs in the twelfth-century *Book of Ely*, written by a monk of Ely, when recounting events after the Norman Conquest of England in 1066. The Conquest was followed by the greatest property upheaval the country has ever known, and the big churches and their saints were frequent victims of the greedy new masters. One of the most notorious of the Norman plunderers was Picot, sheriff of Cambridgeshire, described by the irate monk of Ely as "a hungry lion, a roving wolf, a crafty fox, a filthy pig, a shameless dog." Ely's saint and patron was the Anglo-Saxon royal abbess St. Etheldreda, and many people reproached Picot for seizing her lands. His response was

[368] Gerald of Wales, *Topographia hibernica* 2. 55, p. 137.

[369] *Miracula sancti Benedicti* 5. 10, p. 208.

[370] Gregory of Tours, *Libri historiarum X* 7. 42, p. 364.

[371] *Miracula Adelheidis reginae* 6, p. 50 (MGH, SS 4, p. 647).

contemptuous: "Who is this Etheldreda whose lands you say I have occupied? I do not know Etheldreda and will not give up the lands." The author of the *Book of Ely* rages at this insult and stirs God to action—"Do you hear this, Lord, and keep silent? Arise, therefore, and crush the arm of the sinner!"—but is unable to report a satisfactory punishment. More satisfying must have been the fate of one of Picot's men, who oppressed "the men of St. Etheldreda" and was punished by the saint herself, who appeared to him at night and stabbed him in the heart with her staff. Next morning he lived only long enough to describe what had happened.[372]

Respect for a saint was shown by observing his or her feast-day, and disregard for such days, especially by working on them, was an expression of disrespect and hence a target of punishment. The attempt to prevent work on holy days was one of the most difficult and enduring tasks that the Church set itself, and both legislation and deterrent stories can be found throughout the Middle Ages (and beyond). In the sixth century a man who went to work in his vineyard on St. Avitus's day found that, the moment his hoe struck the ground, his head was twisted round backwards. Only after several days of repentance in St. Avitus's church did it return to its normal position.[373] In the twelfth century, after a general announcement was made in the diocese of London that everyone should stop work and attend church on St. Erkenwald's feast-day, one man continued with his ordinary tasks, carrying his burdens, and, when reproached, burst out into a long anti-clerical diatribe, culminating in a contemptuous dismissal of the cleric who had criticized him: "Go, then! You are welcome to your feast-days and your chants, along with your Erkenwald. Leave the work of strong men to us, you sluggard!" He turned away, stumbled on a half-buried skull, fell on his head and died.[374]

A particularly persistent offender lived in the Dutch town of Gorinchem in the fifteenth century.[375] In the year 1445, the feast-day of St. Apollinaris, whose arm was preserved as a relic in the church of Gorinchem, was proclaimed as a day free from labour, but John Haver, "who lived by the work of his hands," disregarded this, damned "the priests and St. Apollinaris," and went out to harvest his crops (Apollinaris's day is 23 July). However, he struck his foot with his sickle and thus "was forced to observe the feast unwillingly." But he ascribed this to misfortune, "not to God or his saint," and the following year he again went out to harvest. This time he struck himself in the hand. Returning wounded to town, he still insisted that the event had been due to carelessness and chance, but then, as he jumped over a ditch, his dagger slipped from its sheath and pierced him in the thigh. He now finally admitted his offence. Thenceforth, for the rest of his life, he celebrated the feast-day of St. Apollinaris obediently, and was always willing to show his scars to people, to convince them of the importance of this duty.

[372] *Liber Eliensis* 2. 131–32, pp. 210–13.

[373] Gregory of Tours, *Gloria confessorum* 97, pp. 810–11 (repr., 1969, pp. 360–61).

[374] Arcoid, *Miracula sancti Erkenwaldi* 2, pp. 108–14.

[375] *Translationes reliquiarum corporis sancti Apollinaris a Ravenna in Gorinchem* 37–40, p. 384.

In missionary regions, where Christianity was being newly imposed, it was perhaps especially difficult to enforce this new discipline of time. In early-twelfth-century Pomerania, for example, an area where native paganism was strong, when a missionary priest attacked a peasant for working on the Feast of the Assumption of the Virgin (15 August), he received a hostile reply:

> It was a Monday. The peasant said, "Yesterday it was wrong to work because it was Sunday, and again today we are ordered not to work. What is this teaching which commands men not to do what is necessary and good? When, then, are we going to get our crops collected? I think you begrudge us our produce!"[376]

As the narrative requires, the peasant was immediately struck dead and consequently the Pomeranians learned "to treat feast-days with greater reverence."

Sigal's analysis of a sample of punishment miracles from the south of France in the eleventh and twelfth centuries explores a very important point: a chain of events has to be construed as miraculous punishment; there is nothing self-evident about it.[377] He distinguished saintly punishment that was a response to "attacks on goods or persons placed under the protection of the saint" from that responding to "offences against the saint himself or herself." The former offences included seizure of church lands and attacks on clergy or monks, the latter concerned such matters as disrespectful speech about a saint, work on a saint's feast-day and violations of sacred space. Interestingly, these two classes corresponded to another grouping, that between cases where the link between the offence and the punishment was made by the victim, and that where the offender made it. To put it simply, the first class is typified by such cases as a wicked knight usurping church lands or manhandling monks, then suffering a fall or blindness, and the monks then interpreting the misfortune as a saintly punishment, while in the latter type a cynical layman speaks insolently about the saint or works on a feast-day or a lazy cleric or monk fails in his proper duty to the saint and then interprets a subsequent illness or accident as the saint's punishment. Sigal's analysis carefully identifies who does the construing and in what circumstances: the come-uppance of an arrogant usurper is construed by the victims, while the punishment for supercilious arrogance is recognized by the perpetrator.

It has sometimes been suggested that there was a long-term trend away from punitive towards healing miracles, and there are pieces of evidence that might support this view. In a sample of many hundreds of miracles from the Frankish lands recorded from the sixth to the ninth centuries, around 10 per cent were punishment miracles; Sigal's figures for the eleventh and twelfth centuries produce a similar figure of 9.9 per cent; but a study of 545 miracles that were recorded in Normandy in the eleventh, twelfth and thirteenth centuries shows that only 3.85 per cent were punishments, while, of Becket's miracles recorded in the 1170s, a mere 2.8 per cent

[376] Herbord, *Dialogus de vita et operibus beati Ottonis Babenbergensis episcopi* 3. 29, p. 468.
[377] Sigal, "Un aspect du culte des saints"; cf. idem, *L'homme et le miracle*, pp. 276–82.

are punishments.[378] By the late Middle Ages many miracle collections have very few such miracles, or indeed none.[379]

If these statistics are sufficient to reveal a genuine trend, then they demand some explanation. It is possible that the saints had become kinder, but there are other ways of accounting for a decline in the number of recorded miracles of punishment. One way is to stress a change in the nature of the evidence. The miracles of the early Middle Ages are usually recorded by monks and emphasize the amazing powers of the saint enshrined in the monastery: the miracles of Benedict of Fleury and Foy of Conques are famous and much-cited examples. After 1200, however, the largest miracle collections are those put together for canonization processes. It might be argued that those proposing a case to the papacy would wish to stress beneficent miracles, such as healing, rather than the sudden death of enemies. It is indeed the case that the miracles in canonization hearings are rarely miracles of punishment. Vauchez, analysing eight such processes from the thirteenth century, notes that only 3.8 per cent are "religious miracles," a category that includes "punishments for blasphemy or broken vows, visions and apparitions, sacramental miracles, etc."[380] Clearly, the percentage of the punishments in this class must be considerably lower than 3.8. But the decline in the proportion of punitive miracles seems to predate the development of papal canonization. It appears already to have occurred by 1200.

It is also worth stressing that miracles of punishment can be of different types. In Reginald of Durham's collection of the miracles of St. Cuthbert, composed c. 1166–74, the saint is reasonably vindictive. Almost one-fifth of the contemporary miracles Reginald records are miracles of punishment, concerning chastisement of those who showed disrespect for the saint or violated his sanctuary, sanctuary which extended even to the sparrows in the churchyards of his churches.[381] However, one thing that is surprisingly absent from these particular miracles is the saint protecting the lands of the monastery from encroaching neighbours.[382] Just as Vauchez's sample finds "punishments for blasphemy or broken vows," so Reginald's record of punitive miracles reveals insolent knights deriding the veneration of the saint, but not knights plundering the lands of Durham. This contrasts even with a record as recent as the

[378] Goetz, "Heiligenkult und Geschlecht," p. 98 (these statistics are not always easy to interpret, but are supported by Goetz, "Wunderberichte im 9. Jahrhundert," p. 208, table 6); Sigal, *L'homme et le miracle*, p. 289 (rounding is closer to 9.9 than 9.8); Gonthier and Le Bas, "Analyse socio-économique de quelques recueils de miracles dans la Normandie," p. 21; Foreville, "Les 'Miracula S. Thomae Cantuarensis'"," p. 456, tables III and IV.

[379] Vauchez, *Sainthood*, p. 468, table 31; Dalarun, *La sainte et la cite*, p. 44, table III; Jansen, "Un exemple de sainteté thaumaturgique," p. 150, tables I and II; Andrić, *The Miracles of St John Capistran*, p. 301.

[380] Vauchez, *Sainthood*, p. 468, table 31.

[381] Of the 118 twelfth-century miracles in Reginald's collection, 22 are miracles of punishment: Tudor, "The Cult of St. Cuthbert in the Twelfth Century," p. 454 n. 47; for the sparrow, Reginald of Durham, *Libellus de admirandis beati Cuthberti virtutibus* 133, pp. 281–82.

[382] One possible minor exception is Cuthbert helping Furness in a law suit, Reginald of Durham, *Libellus de admirandis beati Cuthberti virtutibus* 55, pp. 112–14.

Book of Ely, which has many cases of aristocratic plunderers of Etheldreda's property. Perhaps it was around the year 1150 that the great churches began to rely on sanctions other than the supernatural power of their saints in order to defend their property interests, even if scoffers and sceptics still needed a reminder that saints demanded respect.

CHAPTER 10

Pilgrimage

Origins and Definitions

> Men undertake pilgrimages to serve God and honour the saints, and, to do this, they leave their families and their native soil, and their wives and their homes and all that they have, and go through alien lands, wearying their bodies and expending their goods in the pursuit of holy places.[1]

Unlike Judaism or Islam, Christianity did not originally have the idea of pilgrimage, that is, a journey to a holy place, a specially sanctioned spot with intrinsic spiritual significance like Jerusalem or Mecca.[2] However, when Christians adopted the features of a traditional religion in the fourth century, the holy place was among them. The Holy Land itself was amongst the first destinations for Christian pilgrims.[3] Christian (and Jewish) Scripture presents not only moral and religious teaching but also a detailed geography. The sites described in the Bible drew Christian visitors from far afield as early as the fourth century, and the trip to Jerusalem, while never obligatory in the sense that the pilgrimage to Mecca is for Muslims, remained a powerful religious ambition throughout the Middle Ages, even when control of the city had passed out of Christian hands. Pilgrimage to Rome is also ancient. The city possessed the graves of many martyrs, most importantly those of the founding fathers of the Church, Peter and Paul; indeed, a pilgrimage to Rome came to be described as a journey to "the threshold of the apostles." The evidence of memorial

[1] *Las siete partidas* 1. 24. pref. (1, p. 497).

[2] There is a huge bibliography on Christian pilgrimage. See, for instance, Kötting, *Peregrinatio religiosa: Wallfahrten in der Antike*; Sigal, *Les marcheurs de Dieu: pèlerinages et pèlerins au Moyen Age*; Sumption, *Pilgrimage*; *Le Pèlerinage* (Cahiers de Fanjeaux 15); *Wallfahrt kennt keine Grenzen*; Maraval, *Lieux saints et pèlerinages d'Orient; Wallfahrt und Alltag in Mittelalter und früher Neuzeit*; Webb, *Medieval European Pilgrimage*; "Pilgrimage in the Byzantine Empire"; *Wallfahrten in der europäischen Kultur*; *Encyclopedia of Medieval Pilgrimage*.

[3] Hunt, *Holy Land Pilgrimage in the Later Roman Empire*; Markus, "How on Earth Could Places Become Holy?"; Walker, *Holy City, Holy Places?*; Yasin, *Saints and Church Spaces in the Late Antique Mediterranean*, pp. 14–45.

structures and graffiti suggests that pious visitors were seeking out the remains of Peter and Paul as early as the second and third centuries.[4]

The concept of pilgrimage was difficult to reconcile with the universal, transcendental and spiritual emphasis of Jesus' teaching and Pauline doctrine and, indeed, voices were raised against the idea of Christian pilgrimage as soon as it arose.[5] The Church Fathers Gregory of Nyssa and Jerome both expressed criticism. Jesus had not mentioned going to Jerusalem as a good act or included it in the Sermon on the Mount, wrote Gregory, while Jerome in his writing was insistent on the spiritual equality of all places: "I do not dare to confine the omnipotence of God to some small territory," he asserted, underlining the point by arguing "the heavenly palace can be reached as easily from Britain as from Jerusalem."[6] This did not stop him from moving to the Holy Land, however. Even though insisting that "it is not praiseworthy to have been in Jerusalem but to have lived well in Jerusalem," Jerome clearly felt the personal pull of the Holy Places.[7] A letter of his disciples Paula and Eustochium describes how a visit to the Holy Sepulchre could stir up powerful visualizations of Christ: "whenever we enter there, we perceive the Saviour lying in his shroud."[8]

It is possible to trace a thin line of principled objection to pilgrimage throughout the Middle Ages. In the Carolingian period, Theodulf of Orleans wrote "God is not to be sought in any particular place. . . . I do not believe that one reaches heaven by the path of the feet but by the path of conduct."[9] An Irish text echoes his view: "It is not by track of feet nor by physical movement that one draws near to God, but by practice of good habit and virtues."[10] The Council of Chalon-sur-Saône, one of a series held in 813, expressed several diverse reservations about pilgrimage: priests were going to Rome or Tours (site of the shrine of the country's most famous saint, Martin) without the permission of their bishop; some people, both clergy and lay folk, thought that such pilgrimages automatically cleared them of their sins, whatever they might be; rich men sometimes used the pretext of a pilgrimage to squeeze money from their poor dependants; poor people went on them to have a better chance of begging. Nevertheless, for those who had properly confessed and been given penance, the desire "to visit the threshold of the apostles or any other saint"

[4]There is a large and controversial bibliography. A summary of the crucial evidence is presented in Bisconti, "Le origini del pellegrinaggio petriano e il culto dei martiri romani."

[5]On criticism of pilgrimage, see Constable, "Opposition to Pilgrimage in the Middle Ages"; Schreiner, " 'Peregrinatio laudabilis' und 'peregrinatio vituperabilis' "; Bitton-Ashkelony, *Encountering the Sacred: The Debate on Christian Pilgrimage in Late Antiquity*.

[6]Gregory of Nyssa, *Epistula* 2, pp. 106–22; Jerome, *Epistula* 58 (3, p. 77).

[7]Non Hierosolymis fuisse, sed Hierosolymis bene vixisse laudandum est: Jerome, *Epistula* 58 (3, p. 75).

[8]Jerome, *Epistula* 46. 5 (2, p. 105) (PL 22: 486).

[9]Quod Deus non loco quaerendus sit. . . . Non via, credo, pedum, sed morum, ducit ad astra: Theodulf of Orleans, *Carmen* 67, p. 557.

[10]*Betha Colum Cille*, pp. 220, 249 (a twelfth-century text).

was entirely praiseworthy.[11] Abuse of pilgrimage, not pilgrimage itself, was under attack here.

St. Bernard was quite clear that the monastic life was of far greater value than any pilgrimage. When he waylaid a visiting English cleric who was intending to go to Jerusalem but ended up becoming a monk at Bernard's own monastery of Clairvaux, he wrote an explanatory letter back to the young man's superior asserting bluntly that "Clairvaux is Jerusalem."[12] One Italian saint, who had proposed to devote himself to a life of perpetual pilgrimage, was rebuked by Jesus himself, who appeared to him saying, "Do not think that I will take special account of pilgrimages and pious activities of that kind on the Day of Judgment, when I will say, 'Come, ye blessed of my father, inherit the Kingdom.' " Instead, he commanded a life devoted to charitable activities in the saint's home town.[13]

But reservations about Christian pilgrimage, although recurrent, were never more than a minor dissentient note in the Middle Ages. The journey to Jerusalem or to Rome remained an aspiration, an ultimate dream, for the devout throughout Christendom. The African monastic writer Fulgentius came to Rome in 500 and "toured the holy places of the martyrs with reverence."[14] The Anglo-Saxons, converted by missionaries from Rome, were enthusiastic pilgrims to the city, as the eighth-century historian Paul the Deacon observed: "Many of the English race, noble and commoner, men and women, leaders and ordinary people, were accustomed to come from Britain to Rome, stirred by divine love."[15] Sometimes we know the names of individuals. A runic inscription in the Catacomb of Commodilla shows that the Anglo-Saxon Eadbald visited the site, probably around 700.[16] The great attraction of Rome lay in the fact that it contained the shrines of the apostles Peter and Paul, but there were also many subsidiary saints and shrines to attract pilgrims: "how full of saints is Rome!," wrote the poet Prudentius.[17] When the English archbishop Sigeric visited the city in 990, he recorded twenty-three churches that he visited.[18]

Journeys to the tombs of saints far from Rome also began in the late Roman period. At the end of the fourth century Prudentius, writing a eulogy of the martyrs of Calahorra in Spain, stressed that they drew visitors from afar: "The inhabitant of the outside world also comes here, for the word has run through all lands that here

[11] *Concilia aevi Karolini* 1/1, pp. 282–83, no. 37, cl. 44–45. Clause 45 passed into later canon law collections: Ivo of Chartres, *Decretum* 15. 65, PL 161: 877.

[12] Bernard of Clairvaux, *Epistola* 64 (7, pp. 157–58).

[13] Neque vero existimes, me peregrinationum ac piorum id genus exercitiorum rationem tempore judicii præcipuam habiturum esse, cum dicam: Venite, benedicti Patris mei; possidete regnum*: Vita Raymundi Palmarii* 3. 11. 29, p. 650. The Life is a translation into Latin of a sixteenth-century Italian translation of a lost Latin original. The biblical reference is Matthew 25:34.

[14] *Vita Fulgentii* 13, col. 130.

[15] Paul the Deacon, *Historia Langobardorum* 6. 37, p. 229.

[16] Carletti, "I graffiti sull'affresco di san Luca nel Cimiterio di Commodilla," p. 132, with table I and fig. 4; see further Insley, "Anglo-Saxons in Rome: The Evidence of the Names."

[17] Prudentius, *Peristefanon* 2, line 542, p. 275.

[18] Ortenberg, "Archbishop Sigeric's Journey to Rome in 990."

are patrons of the world, whom those who pray may resort to."[19] Around the year 400, during the course of a long itinerary around the Mediterranean, Postumianus, a friend of St. Martin's biographer Sulpicius Severus, visited the shrine of the most famous north African martyr: "it pleased my mind to go to Carthage, to visit the places of the saints, and especially to worship at the shrine of the martyr Cyprian."[20] The eastern Mediterranean was particularly rich in important martyr-shrines. Pilgrims to the church of St. Menas on the edge of the Egyptian desert were so numerous by the fifth century that they stimulated, and presumably partly funded, the building of a huge complex of hostels, bath-houses and churches, including the main one, the largest basilica in Egypt. There was also a cemetery, a workshop producing pilgrimage mementoes and a garrison to protect the site.[21]

Christian pilgrimage had thus become a major feature of the religion. However, the definition of a pilgrim or a pilgrimage is not as simple as it might appear. Clearly, a journey and a religious purpose are essential components, but, beyond that, questions might arise. Does a pilgrimage have to be over a certain distance? Does it have to have a specific goal, from which the pilgrim then returns home? A visit to one's parish church is not usually classed as a pilgrimage, although it might be inspired by motives indistinguishable from those behind longer journeys, but it is conventional to apply the terminology only when some distance is involved. These distances need not be great. Chaucer's pilgrims went from London to Canterbury, a distance of only sixty miles, while it would be hard to deny the title "pilgrims" even to the villagers of Varangéville in Lorraine, who assembled to march to the shrine of St. Firmin at Flavigny on the saint's feast-day, with "an energetic man called Walefrid" singing songs about Firmin's miracles at their head, even though the distance from Varangéville to Flavigny is only seven miles.[22] In addition to such groups on clearly focussed excursions, there were the perpetual pilgrims, those who left their homes for good and travelled in foreign lands, perhaps visiting shrines, but perhaps simply undertaking exile "for love of God," like the three Irishmen who arrived at the court of king Alfred of Wessex in 891, determined "to be abroad, they did not care where."[23] Such goal-less wandering was a common feature of early medieval Irish religious life, "almost natural to them" according to one continental observer, although it was not without its critics.[24]

These ambiguities are reflected in the contemporary terminology. The Latin word *peregrinus* is the origin of the current terms for "pilgrim" in many modern European languages: English "pilgrim," French "pèlerin," Spanish "peregrino," Italian "pellegrino," German "Pilger," and so on. However, the meaning of the Latin word

[19] Prudentius, *Peristefanon* 1, lines 10–12, p. 251.

[20] Sulpicius Severus, *Dialogi* 1. 3. 2, p. 112.

[21] Maraval, *Lieux saints et pèlerinages d'Orient*, pp. 319–22.

[22] *Translatio et miracula sancti Firmini Flaviniacensibus*, p. 808; Sigal, *L'homme et le miracle*, p. 118.

[23] *Anglo-Saxon Chronicle*, s.a. 891, p. 82.

[24] Walafrid Strabo, *Vita Galli* 2. 46, p. 336; Hughes, "The Changing Theory and Practice of Irish Pilgrimage."

was broader than its modern derivatives, since it indicated any kind of foreigner or traveller, rather than one on a specifically religious journey. This is its meaning in the Latin Bible, where we find Abraham describing himself as "a stranger and a sojourner" (*advena et peregrinus*), while the third epistle of John contrasts "the brethren" (*fratres*) and "strangers" (*peregrini*).[25] Throughout the Middle Ages, the term *peregrinus* continued to designate travellers and foreigners in a general sense as well as pilgrims, and hence it is sometimes impossible to know whether any given reference is generic or specific. For instance, when Ansgar, archbishop of Hamburg-Bremen (d. 865), is credited with founding hostels "for the care of the poor and the reception of *peregrini*," are these "pilgrims" or "travellers"?[26] The ambiguity of the word was felt at the time, for when, in 796, Charlemagne wrote to king Offa of Mercia offering protection for English pilgrims, he needed to spell out exactly which category of person he meant: "*peregrini*, who wish to travel to the threshold of the blessed apostles, for love of God and the salvation of their souls."[27]

A particular development of the term *peregrinus* can be seen in the history of its use for crusaders. Originally there was no terminological distinction at all between pilgrimage and crusade.[28] Crusaders were pilgrims, even if armed pilgrims—"pilgrim knights of the Holy Sepulchre."[29] The military expedition that modern historians term the Third Crusade of 1189–92 was, for contemporaries "the journey of pilgrimage," or "the pilgrimage of Richard, king of England, and Philip, king of France," while the Holy Roman Emperor Frederick Barbarossa also "assumed the insignia of holy pilgrimage" at this time and was, in fact, the first to fulfil "the vow of pilgrimage."[30] Terms expressly for crusade and crusaders developed late, and the link between the practice of pilgrimage and crusade can be seen in the fact that some of the rituals and rights of crusaders developed directly from those for pilgrims.[31]

A more specialized terminology for "pilgrim," beyond the generic and ambiguous term *peregrinus*, also evolved. From the twelfth century onwards there is evidence that the word "palmer" was employed, originally designating those who had been to the Holy Land and acquired a memorial palm there. It soon extended its meaning, however, to pilgrims in general. The twelfth-century French epic *The Crowning of Louis* has a character who swears "by the apostle whom palmers go to visit," clearly indicating St. Peter and Rome.[32] Versions of the word occur in Latin, French, Italian, Portuguese and English, and it was also adopted as a name. For those who went to Rome, the term "Rome-seeker" (*Romipeta*) was also used from at least the

[25] Genesis 23:4; 3 John 1:5.

[26] Adam of Bremen, *Gesta Hammaburgensis ecclesiae pontificum* 1. 30, p. 202; interestingly, Adam's source, the Life of Ansgar by Rimbert, refers only to a *hospitalem pauperum*: *Vita Anskarii* 35, p. 112.

[27] Alcuin, *Epistola* 100, p. 145.

[28] Tyerman, "Were There Any Crusades in the Twelfth Century?," pp. 555–71.

[29] Robert the Monk, *Historia Iherosolimitana* 2. 14, p. 746.

[30] *Itinerarium peregrinorum et gesta regis Ricardi* 1. 17–19, pp. 32, 34, 43.

[31] Brundage, "Cruce Signari: The Rite for Taking the Cross."

[32] *Li coronemenz Looïs*, line 1180, p. 37.

early twelfth century. The First Lateran Council of 1123 extended its protection to "those who travel to Rome [*Romipetas*] and *peregrini* visiting the threshold of the apostles and the oratories of other saints."[33] Since those who had been as far as Rome were obviously good sources of news and gossip, they could be labelled alliteratively "rumour-spreading Rome-farers" (*Romipete rumigeruli*).[34] And, just as Muslims can assume a name like Hajji indicating that they have accomplished the pilgrimage to Mecca, or Haj, so those who made the long journey to Rome might be called "Rome-farer." There was a prominent man in Lincolnshire with the name Romfar or Rumfari in the second half of the twelfth century.[35]

The Life of Gerald of Aurillac, composed around 930, has several references to *romei*, a term designating pilgrims who are on their way to Rome.[36] It was a word that soon became more general in its meaning, for, early in the eleventh century, there is reference to a pilgrim who had visited the shrine of St. Foy in southern France as a *romeus*, "for in that country that is what pilgrims of the saints are called."[37] The customs of the town of St.-Gilles, itself an important pilgrimage destination, mention "pilgrims, whom we call *romevos*, who travel far from their homes in order to pay their vow to God."[38] The disassociation of the word from a specific geographical reference is apparent in the *Cantigas de Santa Maria*, which were produced at the court of Alfonso X of Castile (1252–84) and written in Galician. They have dozens of stories about pilgrims going to many different destinations, and the terms used are consistently those derived from *romeus*. Going to Santiago on pilgrimage is rendered as going to St. James *en romaria*; pilgrims on their way to the Marian shrine at Soissons are described as a "great company of *romeus*"; and there is a story about a woman who refuses to go on pilgrimage (*romaria*) to Rocamadour.[39] Alfonso X himself recognized that any distinction between *romero* and *pelegrino* based on the idea that the former were heading for Rome and the latter elsewhere was quite inconsistent with common usage.[40] The thirteenth-century Spanish Alexander Romance finds it natural that Alexander the Great's visit to the temple of Amon in the Libyan desert

[33] *Conciliorum oecumenicorum decreta*, p. 193 (cl. 14). The occurrence of the term *Romipetis sancti Petri* in a text usually dated to c. 1020 has been interpreted by its editors as a later insertion: *Die "Honorantie civitatis Papie,"* pp. 18–19, 36. However, the existence of the vernacular terms *romeus* for "pilgrim" at precisely this period, the early eleventh century (see later) might make their conclusion less convincing.

[34] Gervase of Canterbury, *Chronica*, p. 431.

[35] *Documents Illustrative of the Social and Economic History of the Danelaw*, pp. 49, 80, 96, 227, 232, 283–84, nos. 74, 122, 146, 302, 308, 379–80 (assuming these references are all to one person); his son rendered account for Lincoln in 1178–79: *The Great Roll of the Pipe for the Twenty-fifth Year of the Reign of King Henry II*, p. 47.

[36] Odo of Cluny, *Vita sancti Geraldi Auriliacensis* 1. 27, 29; 2. 17, 23; 4 (liber miraculorum). 12, pp. 174, 176, 220, 226, 278 (AASS Octobris 6, pp. 309, 310, 320, 321, 331). The etymology of the word is not simple: Montaner Frutos, "Sobre el étimo de rome(r)o 'peregrino.'"

[37] Bernard of Angers, *Liber miraculorum sancte Fidis* 1. 1, p. 78.

[38] *Les coutumes de Saint-Gilles*, p. 80 (cl. 17).

[39] *Cantigas de Santa Maria* 26, 49, 153 (1, pp. 176, 242, 528).

[40] *Las siete partidas* 1. 24. 1 (1, p. 498).

should be called a *romeria*.[41] In modern Spanish *romería* and in modern Portuguese *romaria* still mean "pilgrimage."

The complexity of the terminology for pilgrimage is well illustrated by a passage in Dante's *Vita nuova*, where he refers to a body of pilgrims, and then proceeds to explain:

> "Pilgrims" [*peregrini*] can be understood in two senses, a general one and a more restricted one: in a general sense, anyone away from their homeland is a pilgrim; in the more restricted sense, a pilgrim is someone travelling to or from the house of St. James [that is, Santiago]. However, you should know that there are three particular terms for people journeying in the service of the Most High: those who go overseas and, in many cases, bring back a palm, are called "palmers"; those who go to the house in Galicia are called "pilgrims" [*peregrini*], because the burial place of St. James is further from his homeland than that of any other apostle; those who go to Rome are called *romei*.[42]

The great Italian poet is here employing a double distinction: the general sense of *peregrinus* as "exile" (something that had a special significance for him), versus the specialized meaning of pilgrim to Santiago; then the triple distinction amongst religious pilgrims, based on their goal—the Holy Land, Santiago, or Rome. As is clear from instances already discussed, this was by no means the only system of classification available, but it does highlight the continued coexistence of the general and the specifically religious sense of *peregrinus*, and also the way that the great pilgrim destinations generated their own terminology.

Modern German has a rather distinctive term, *Wallfahrt*, which is commonly used for "pilgrimage." It derives from an Old German word *wallen*, meaning simply "to wander," and, like Latin *peregrinus*, it originally had no religious connotations, but acquired a more specialized sense over time. Also like *peregrinus*, it is not always clear which sense is intended. When, in the early thirteenth century, Walther von der Vogelweide writes of "*waller unde pilgerîne*" is he equating the two terms or distinguishing them, as in "travellers and pilgrims"?[43] The noun *wallevart* or *wallefart*, formed by compounding *walle* with the common word for journey (modern German *Fahrt*), occurs from around 1300. The crusade undertaken by Landgrave Ludwig of Thuringia, the husband of St. Elizabeth of Thuringia, is described in a fourteenth-century German version of Elizabeth's Life as his "*wallefart* over the sea."[44] In the late medieval Alsfeld Passion Play, a blind man begging charity offers to share with anyone who helps him the benefits of his religious exercises: "for his com-

[41] *Libro de Alexandre*, stanza 1167.

[42] Dante Alighieri, *La vita nuova* 40, pp. 238–39.

[43] Walther von der Vogelweide, "Owe, waz êren sich ellendet von tiutschen landen," verse 2, line 4 (Lachmann 13, 15), *Liedlyrik*, p. 464.

[44] *Das Leben der heiligen Elisabeth*, line 5574, p. 220; cf. Ködiz von Salfeld, *Das Leben des heiligen Ludwig*, p. 61.

fort and salvation, a hundred Our Fathers every day, and many a pilgrimage (*walfart*) I have made."[45] In the sixteenth century the word became very common.

Pilgrim Garb and Status

Over the course of time pilgrimage became formalized, assuming some of the characteristics of an institution: distinctive garb developed, so pilgrims could be identified at a glance; pilgrims were recognized as having a special status, and a body of law and custom spelled out the privileges and protections they should enjoy.

At least as early as the eleventh century it was possible to recognize a pilgrim by his "pilgrim dress."[46] The most distinctive aspects of this were the "scrip and staff," that is, the shoulder-bag and stick, explicitly regarded as characteristics of a pilgrim.[47] It was natural to refer to someone "standing with a staff and scrip, as if he were about to go to Rome," while the figure of a pilgrim, holding staff, scrip and palm, is depicted in a fresco of the later eleventh or twelfth century in the church of Tavant south of Tours.[48] Although these are very sensible items for a long journey, they are in some ways surprising, as they are exactly the things that Jesus forbade his disciples to take with them, as recorded in the Gospels of Matthew and Luke—"take nothing for your journey, neither staves, nor scrip." The Vulgate translation even used the word *pera* for scrip, which is exactly the term used of the pilgrim bag in the later Middle Ages. The version in Mark's Gospel is less demanding, allowing a stick, although not a scrip (*pera*).[49]

An interesting light is cast on pilgrim dress by representations, both visual and literary, of Jesus' encounter with the disciples on the road to Emmaus, as told in the Gospel of Luke (24:13–27). In the Latin Vulgate version of the Bible, the disciples, not recognizing the risen Christ, presume he is a *peregrinus*, which must have originally had the sense of "stranger." However, this was a cue for medieval artists and writers to depict him (and sometimes the two disciples he meets) dressed characteristically as a pilgrim. Good examples are provided by three series of pictures of the Emmaus scene in books produced in England in the early twelfth century.[50] They

[45] *The Alsfeld Passion Play*, p. 112 (lines 1435–37).

[46] In peregrino habitu; sacrum peregrini habitum: Bernard of Angers, *Liber miraculorum sancte Fidis* 1. 1, pp. 78, 79. In general, see Belli D'Elia, "Pellegrini e pellegrinaggi nella testimonianza delle imagini."

[47] For example, Eadmer, *Vita Anselmi* 2. 21, p. 97: peram et baculum peregrinantium more coram altari suscepit; Orderic Vitalis, *Historia ecclesiastica* 3 (2, p. 100): sub specie peregrinorum peras et baculos portantes.

[48] *Annales Magdaburgenses*, p. 156; Michel, *Les fresques de Tavant*, pl. XIX; perhaps earlier, a fresco in the lower church of San Clemente in Rome, dated to c. 1090, has a depiction of St. Alexis as a pilgrim with scrip and staff: Demus, *Romanesque Mural Painting*, colour plate at p. 43.

[49] Matthew 10:10; Luke 9:3; Mark 6:8.

[50] Pächt et al., *The St Albans Psalter*, pp. 73–79, with pls. 38–40; Kauffmann, *Romanesque Manuscripts*, pp. 31–32, 74–75 (no. 35), 93–96 (no. 66), with figs. 99, 180; Geddes, *The St Albans Psalter*, pp. 69 (fig. 58), 73–74.

are similar in their imagery and perhaps are all copies of a common source. In the illustration in the St. Albans Psalter, Christ is shown with a furry or rough cape, a long staff, a shoulder-bag marked with the cross, a close-fitting cap likewise marked with the cross, and barefoot. In the Bury Gospels the two disciples are also depicted as pilgrims. They, and Jesus, wear rough capes and are carrying staffs. They all have large hats, two with wide brims and one without but with a curious corrugated surface. The third sequence, now surviving as an isolated sheet in the Victoria and Albert Museum in London, shows the three figures with capes, staffs and wide-brimmed hats. Clearly cape, hat, staff and scrip were by this period the standard imagined, and perhaps actual, pilgrim garb.

Further detail is provided by the stage directions in medieval plays, especially the so-called *Peregrinus* play, which has as its subject the meeting on the road to Emmaus.[51] The Fleury version of this play describes how Jesus is to be represented as a pilgrim: "carrying a scrip and a long palm, fully equipped as a pilgrim, having a cap on his head, dressed in a *hacla* and tunic, with naked feet."[52] No one seems to know what a *hacla* is, but the other features are easily recognisable. In the stage directions for a version of the play found in a thirteenth-century Paduan manuscript, the two disciples are to be "dressed in cloaks and capes, and with staffs, in the manner of pilgrims," while Christ has "a cape, a staff, and a little barrel of wine, in the manner of a pilgrim."[53] Pilgrims are sometimes depicted with flasks, usually, like their scrips, slung around their shoulders, but sometimes tied to their staves.

A formal ecclesiastical blessing for those about to go on pilgrimage to Rome is found in an eleventh-century manuscript of the so-called Romano-German Pontifical. It has the rubric, "a blessing over the scrips and staffs and over those who are about to set out with them for the thresholds of the holy apostles to seek their intercession." It uses *capsella* for scrip rather than *pera*, but there is no doubt that the pilgrim bag is meant. God's blessing is invoked upon the scrips and staffs, which the pilgrims "are to receive as a sign of their pilgrimage." Basing itself on Jesus' words in Mark rather than Matthew or Luke, it has a prayer addressed to Christ, "who commanded your blessed apostles to take only staffs when they went out preaching."[54] The staff was so characteristic of pilgrims that Cathar heretics mockingly referred to pilgrims as "staff-carriers" (*burdonarii*, perhaps with a play also on *burdo*, "mule").[55]

[51] See Ogden, *The Staging of Drama in the Medieval Church*, p. 130; Gibb, "Pilgrims and Prostitutes: Costume and Identity Construction in Twelfth-Century Liturgical Drama," pp. 374–79.

[52] Peram cum longa palma gestans, bene ad modum peregrini paratus, pilleum in capite habens, hacla vestitus et tunica, nudus pedes: Young, *The Drama of the Medieval Church* 1, p. 471.

[53] Induti byrris et sclavinis cum burdonibus ad modum peregrinorum . . . cum sclavina, burdone et barisello vini ad modum peregrini: ibid., p. 482; also in *Lateinische Osterfeiern und Osterspiele* 8, p. 847.

[54] *Le Pontifical romano-germanique du dixième siècle* 212 (2, p. 362); on the dating see Fletcher, *Saint James's Catapult*, pp. 89–90.

[55] Pierre des Vaux-de-Cernay, *Historia Albigensis* 313 (2, p. 13).

According to the Anglo-Norman historian Orderic Vitalis, writing in the 1130s, penitents and pilgrims grew their beards as signs of their status.[56] This is, however, a rather isolated piece of evidence. Pilgrims are often depicted with a beard, but not invariably so, and growing a beard might simply be a convenience on a long-distance journey. On the other hand, hats were a common part of pilgrim garb, and it seems that, over the course of the centuries, a particular style of headgear did come to be associated with pilgrims. In the twelfth-century English illustrations of the Emmaus story, the hats of Christ (in all three cases) and the two disciples (except in the St. Albans Psalter) are extremely prominent features. A hat with a broad flat brim is frequent in thirteenth-century depictions of pilgrims; it is often has a cord, which can be used to hang it on one's back, as in the Emmaus scene in the Lewis Psalter or that painted by Duccio, or in one of the pilgrim images in the Grandison Psalter.[57] Large and broad-brimmed hats continued to be characteristic of pilgrims throughout the later Middle Ages, while one distinctive variant was the hat with the front of the brim turned up. This might also be the place where signs and badges of pilgrimage were displayed (figure 10.1). A classic example of pilgrim garb at the end of the Middle Ages is provided by a life-size painting of St. Roche dressed as a pilgrim, now in the local museum in Bari.[58] He has an iron-tipped staff, a scrip with buckle, and a voluminous cloak. He wears a large hat with a cord, and on its upturned front brim there are scallop shells and crossed keys, symbols of pilgrimage to Santiago and Rome. The rosaries around his neck indicate this is a late medieval image. (See plate 7.)

The church authorities insisted repeatedly that pilgrims should be able to travel unimpeded and unharmed, although the need for such repetition suggests that pilgrimage was in fact a dangerous undertaking. Individual cases of pilgrims robbed or imprisoned can easily be found. In the 1120s the archdeacon of Liège and the abbot of St.-Trond undertook a pilgrimage to Rome and had reached Tuscany when,

> going out one morning they encountered robbers and were led off captive through the by-ways, losing everything necessary for their pilgrimage. Eventually, with great difficulty, effort and fear, they recovered the horses, along with a very few possessions, but nevertheless did not desist from their pilgrimage.[59]

In response to such dangers, protective legislation developed to safeguard pilgrims, giving them a distinctive legal status.[60] Charlemagne commanded his subjects to offer "a roof and a hearth and water" to any *peregrini* "travelling the land through love of God," and in Carolingian Italy the killing of "wayfarers and *peregrini* who hasten to Rome or to other bodies of the saints in the service of God" was punished

[56] Orderic Vitalis, *Historia ecclesiastica* 8. 10 (4, p. 188).

[57] Philadelphia, Free Library, Lewis E 185, fol. 18v; Duccio's depiction of the scene is on the reverse of his Maestà in the Museo dell'Opera del Duomo in Siena; BL, Add. 21926, fol. 12.

[58] Bari, Pinacoteca Provinciale, inv. 1993, n. 101, reproduced in *Romei e Giubilei*, p. 375, no. 160.

[59] *Gesta abbatum Trudonensium*, p. 306.

[60] Garrison, "A propos des pèlerins et de leur condition juridique."

10.1. Pilgrim badges worn on hats, St. Anne altarpiece from the Carmelite church in Frankfurt by an unknown artist around 1500. Historisches Museum, Frankfurt. Photograph: Horst Ziegenfusz.

by huge fines.[61] Letters of safe-conduct for pilgrims from north of the Alps travelling to Rome survive from the seventh and eighth centuries.[62]

Legislation conveying immunities and privileges for pilgrims, issued by both secular and ecclesiastical authorities, can be found throughout the Middle Ages. Pippin, king of the Franks, declared that "*peregrini* who travel to Rome or elsewhere for the sake of God" should be exempt from tolls.[63] Pilgrims were often granted such freedom from tolls, although there was a recurrent worry that unscrupulous merchants might pose as pilgrims to take advantage of such privileges. The property of a pilgrim, while absent on the journey, was under special protection. The English lawbook Glanvill (c. 1188) recognizes absence on pilgrimage as an acceptable excuse for a defendant not to appear in court, allowing a grace period of at least a year if the pilgrimage is to Jerusalem, and leaving it to the king or his judges to decide the grace period if the pilgrimage is elsewhere, "according to the length or brevity of the journey."[64]

[61] *Capitularia regum Francorum* 1, nos. 33 (*Capitulare missorum generale*, cl. 27), 91 (*Pippini Italiae regis capitulare*, cl. 10), pp. 96, 193.

[62] Marculf, *Formulae* 2. 49, pp. 104–5; *Formulae Salicae Bignonianae* 16, p. 234.

[63] *Capitularia regum Francorum* 1, no. 13, p. 32 (*Pippini regis capitulare*, cl. 4).

[64] Glanvill 1. 29, pp. 16–17.

Motives

Pilgrims were stirred to undertake their journey by various motives. Some of these were not strictly spiritual. It was recognized that long-distance pilgrimage could be undertaken simply out of "vanity," to have something to boast about on return home, while a group of aristocratic Germans travelled to Castile in the spring of 1387 not only "for the sake of pilgrimage" but also "so they could see the customs of the land."[65] Erasmus tells the story of a man drinking with companions, who "when the wine had gone to our heads," vowed to go on pilgrimage to Rome and Santiago.[66] For most, however, the pious intention seems to have been uppermost. The *Siete partidas*, the law code issued by Alfonso X of Castile and Leon, distinguishes three ways that pilgrimage could be entered into: some pilgrimages were purely voluntary, some undertaken as a consequence of a vow, and some imposed as a penance.[67]

The most common phrase used in describing a pilgrim's purpose was "for the sake of prayer" (*causa orationis*, or similar). Bishop Haito of Basel (802/3–23) drew up rules for those "who desire to travel to the threshold of the blessed apostles for the sake of prayer (*causa orationis*)."[68] When Ethelwulf, king of Wessex, came to Rome in 855 with his young son Alfred, this was likewise "for the sake of prayer."[69] In 1072 Archbishop Siegfried I of Mainz "set off, for the sake of prayer, to Galicia to St. James" (although he never completed his pilgrimage).[70] St. Clare's pious mother undertook several pilgrimages, including one to the shrine of the archangel Michael on Monte Gargano "for the sake of prayer."[71] Especially in the absence of a standard technical term for "pilgrimage," such phrases made the devotional nature of the journey in question quite clear. An exactly parallel situation existed in the Greek world, where there was no special term for "pilgrim" or "pilgrimage" but pious journeys to shrines could be identified by the appearance of the term "veneration" or "prayer" as a motive.[72]

But pilgrims' purposes might be more specific than general veneration, and more concrete. In the late tenth century, groups came to the tomb of St. Ulric in Augsburg "for the sake of prayer," but among them was a blind man, who miraculously recovered his sight there.[73] The journey in pursuit of miraculous healing, or as thanksgiving for healing already received, is one of the best documented aspects of the cult of the saints (discussed earlier, pp. 342ff.). The shrine of St. Thecla at Seleucia was, in

[65] Rodulfus Glaber, *Historiarum libri quinque* 4. 6. 18, p. 200; Vázquez de Parga et al., *Las peregrinaciones a Santiago* 3, pp. 19–20, app. no. 7 (the vow was subsequently commuted).

[66] Erasmus, *Colloquia familiaria*, pp. 147–49 ("De votis temere susceptis").

[67] *Las siete partidas* 1. 24. 1 (1, p. 498).

[68] Haito of Basel, *Capitula* 18, p. 216.

[69] *Liber Pontificalis* 2, p. 148.

[70] Marianus Scotus, *Chronicon*, p. 560.

[71] Thomas of Celano, *Vita sanctae Clarae* 1, p. 92.

[72] "Pilgrimage in the Byzantine Empire," pp. 60–61.

[73] Gerhard, *Vita et miracula sancti Oudalrici episcopi Augustani* 2. 15, pp. 421–22.

the late Roman period, both "a centre of healing for all and a common mercy-seat for the whole world," where some pilgrims came simply to honour and pray to the saint but others to seek "healing and assistance for the ailments and sufferings that oppressed them," while, much later, prayer and healing were, as its patrons recognized, the two great objectives of those coming to the abbey of Conques, which housed the shrine of St. Foy: the crowds consisted of "pilgrims coming for the sake of prayer or the recovery of their health."[74]

The sick in body thus came to shrines seeking miraculous healing. The sick in soul also came, and might hope to gain some definite and even measurable remedy there, in the form of indulgences. An indulgence was a remission of the penalty due to sin, issued by a bishop or by the pope. Since penance was commonly imposed for a specified term of days or years, indulgences too phrased their remission in such a temporal framework—"forty days" remission was a standard grant.

Pilgrim traffic could be channelled and controlled by the grant of indulgences for visiting a church at a specific time. In the late 1150s Theobald, archbishop of Canterbury, focussed the attention of the faithful in this way on the relics of St. James in Reading abbey:

> It is right and fitting to venerate with especial devotion here on earth those saints, notably God's apostles, whose company it is certain that the angels enjoy in heaven. We believe without a doubt that God's apostle St. James is one of their number, and that by a special grace he deigns to hear the prayers of all who revere him. So, whoever, with pious intention, visits the church of St. Mary, the mother of the Lord, at Reading, where the hand of the glorious apostle is housed, along with many other relics, on the feast-day of the apostle, which is celebrated on 25 July, or in the week following, and takes the apostle as his patron, we remit for him forty days of the penance enjoined on him, trusting in the merits of the apostle and of the other saints whose relics are gloriously housed there.[75]

Such indulgences could be granted for a wide variety of purposes, but the way that archbishop Theobald was using them here, to mark out and exalt a saint's day and reward those who visited the saint's relics, was a common one.

The merit of a pilgrimage could be obtained by paying someone else to go on your behalf. These vicarious pilgrimages crop up especially in testaments, when the dying person leaves money for a pilgrim to visit a shrine. In 1317 a Somerset will had the provision, "I bequeath forty shillings to a man to go on pilgrimage to Santiago and Rocamadour for me."[76] In a will of 1354, a man from Frías in Castile ordered that "a man be sent to Santiago for me and another to Our Lady of Roncesvalles and

[74] *Vita Theclae* 28, p. 280; *Cartulaire de l'abbaye de Conques*, no. 53, p. 53.
[75] Saltman, *Theobald, Archbishop of Canterbury*, p. 436 (doc. 213).
[76] *Bridgwater Borough Archives, 1200–1377*, no. 80, p. 59.

another man to Our Lady of Rocamadour, and I order that another man be sent to Jerusalem."[77] In 1356 a wealthy woman of Pamplona specified in her will that

> my knights should send on pilgrimage a good man on foot to Santiago in Galicia for the soul of my father. And they should send another good man on foot to Our Lady of Rocamadour on pilgrimage for the soul of my mother. And I command that my knights should send a man on horseback to Santiago in Galicia for me on pilgrimage for my soul. And they should send another man on horseback on pilgrimage to Our Lady of Rocamadour for my soul.[78]

Vicarious pilgrimage was a commonplace provision in the wills drawn up in the Umbrian town of Foligno between 1341 and 1413, with forty-seven wills specifying such undertakings, sometimes prescribing more than one pilgrimage, while the Perugian notary Andrea di Pepo, working between 1326 and 1374, drew up seventy-five wills that have survived, and a third of these were either made on the occasion of the testator departing on pilgrimage or specify a vicarious pilgrimage for the testator's soul.[79] The destination of thirteen of these was Rome and of the remaining twelve the shrine of St. Michael at Monte Gargano, the former involving a round trip of at least two weeks and the latter twice that. In one instance, a dying husband requested that "a good person" should go on pilgrimage to Monte Gargano for his soul, and the journey was actually undertaken by his widow the following month.

Pilgrimage could be entered into through a vow, and sometimes after a public liturgical blessing. Such a pilgrim vow might be made in in desperation, as in the case of John de Sutton of Holderness, who, in 1350, requested licence, for himself with eight horses and with his people, to go on pilgrimage to Santiago, which he had vowed to do in peril of death.[80] A curious case of a pilgrim vow taken during pilgrimage involved the Dutch knight Nicholas of Borssele, who, when returning from a pilgrimage to Jerusalem, was in imminent danger of drowning in a shipwreck, until "he vowed, if he were freed from this danger, to visit in person the threshold of St. James the Apostle in Compostella."[81]

Pilgrimage could be demanding, difficult and uncomfortable. It was thus a suitable penance to be imposed on sinners and wrong-doers.[82] Peter Damian, writing to margrave Rainer, one of the most powerful nobles in eleventh-century Italy, recalls, "I have enjoined on you, most noble lord, that, on account of the sins that you have confessed to me, you should take the road to Jerusalem and appease divine justice

[77] Vázquez de Parga et al., *Las peregrinaciones a Santiago* 1, pp. 120–21 n. 3, with other examples.

[78] Leroy, "La mort et la vie chrétienne en Navarre au XIVe siècle," p. 495.

[79] Meloni, "Mobilità di devozione nell'Umbria medievale: due liste di pellegrini," pp. 344 and 346 with nn.; see also Sensi, "Pellegrinaggi votivi e vicari alla fine del Medioevo, l'esempio umbro."

[80] London, Kew, The National Archives, SC 8/246/12267.

[81] Vázquez de Parga et al., *Las peregrinaciones a Santiago* 3, p. 34, app. no. 20.

[82] See, in general, Sumption, *Pilgrimage*, pp. 98–113 ("The Penitential Pilgrimage"); for more recent references, Van Herwaarden, "Obligatory Pilgrimages and the Cult of Santiago de Compostela in the Netherlands."

by the satisfaction of such a long pilgrimage."[83] Jerusalem was the most distant pilgrimage site in Christendom, and presumably the margrave's sins were appropriately grave, but lesser offences could be purged by lesser journeys. In 1300 Sicard de Orto of Réalmont in southern France, confessed that he had shown reverence to a leader of the heretical Cathars. On admitting his fault to a "fat old friar," he had been given the penance of visiting eight shrines in the region.[84] Thirty-two years later a chaplain from Kent who had been found guilty of adultery was ordered to make pilgrimages to Canterbury and Hereford. The former destination would certainly not have involved a major journey, although the monetary offerings he was required to make at the shrines might have brought the punishment home.[85]

Penitential pilgrimage came to be formalized, with set rules and procedures. The church to which the pilgrim was sent issued a certificate, attesting that the pilgrimage had actually been completed. One of the duties of the custodian of the relics at St. Matthias, Trier, alongside showing the relics to pilgrims, was "providing testimonial letters for those who require them."[86] Some letters of this type survive:

> To all Christ's faithful who read these present letters, the humble sacristan of the monastery of St. Giles in Provence sends greetings in the Lord. Know that John de Sacco, a townsman of Bruges, to make amends and peace, has visited the threshold and tomb of the holy confessor Giles, in humility and devotion. In witness whereof we have caused our seal to be affixed to the present letter. Given at St.-Gilles on the Thursday before the feast of St. Mary Magdalene, in the year of Our Lord 1291.[87]

In 1266 the archbishop of Rouen directed a Norman squire, who had contracted a clandestine marriage in defiance of his command, to undertake a long and circuitous pilgrimage, first to the shrines of Peter and Paul at Rome, then on to that of St. Nicholas at Bari, returning via the well-known pilgrimage site of St.-Gilles in Provence. This would be a trip of well over 2000 miles. On his return, the squire should bring to the archbishop "letters testifying that all these things had been properly done."[88]

Pilgrimage could be imposed by secular courts as well as by churchmen.[89] In the Franco-Flemish town of Douai, for example, it became commonplace in the later Middle Ages. In February 1253 the urban authorities there ruled, as part of a judgment on Huet Boinebroke, that "he must go to Our Lady of Rocamadour . . . by

[83] Peter Damian, *Epistola* 151 (4, p. 1).

[84] *The Inquisition at Albi 1299–1300*, pp. 253–55.

[85] *Registrum Hamonis Hethe diocesis roffensis* 1, pp. 467–68.

[86] Rode, *Consuetudines et observantiae monasteriorum sancti Mathiae et sancti Maximini Treverensium*, p. 169.

[87] Ganshof, "Pèlerinages expiatoires," p. 395 n. 21.

[88] *The Register of Eudes of Rouen*, p. 623.

[89] A thorough case-study is Van Cauwenbergh, *Les pélerinages expiatoires et judiciaires dans le droit communal de la Belgique au moyen âge*.

mid-August."[90] Over ninety years later, in 1354, the aldermen (*échevins*) of Douai ordered another townsman to undertake a pilgrimage to Our Lady of Chartres as a punishment for the "outrageous words" he had spoken to them.[91] Dozens of other examples could be cited.[92] It was frequently the case in the Middle Ages that punishments could be commuted, that is, redeemed for a cash payment, and this principle came to be applied to penitential pilgrimage. As a result, scales of payments were drawn up, specifying how much the redemption payment was for specific pilgrimage sites—the more distant the shrine, the higher the payment to secure exemption from the journey. A list of this type survives from Douai from around the year 1400. It includes 42 sites, a large number of them Marian shrines, and the tariff for redemption ranges from 40 *livres* for the distant south Italian shrine of Bari, to a mere 12 *sous* for such nearby pilgrimage sites as Notre-Dame of Bapaume and St. Druon in Sebourg, neither of them more than a day's journey distant.[93] Just as the pilgrim journey shades off into tourism in one direction, so, in the form of the penitential pilgrimage, it can be seen as a form of punishment, even as a tool of secular justice.

The Shrines of Medieval Christendom

The hagiographer who wrote the Life of St. Martin of Leon (d. 1203) describes the pilgrimages that Martin undertook early in life, perhaps devising a purely imaginary itinerary to illustrate the saint's assiduous pilgrim spirit: Martin starts with a trip to Santiago, then "through the other churches of the saints . . . imploring God's mercy through the merits and prayers of the saints"; he comes to Rome, where he spends Lent in penance, passing a night in vigil before the altar in St. Peter's, and subsequently receiving communion and a blessing from Pope Urban (who has to be Urban III, 1185–87, for the chronological indications to harmonize); after Rome he visits the shrines of St. Michael at Monte Gargano and St. Nicholas at Bari before going on to the Holy Land, where he spends a long time "in the sites of the birth and passion of our Lord Jesus Christ"; next on his itinerary is Constantinople, where "he adored most devoutly the relics of the blessed apostles, martyrs, confessors and virgins resting there"; indefatigable, he returns slowly via the shrines of St. Denis and St. Martin in France, Thomas Becket in England, and St. Patrick in Ireland, and is on his way to St. Giles, St. Sernin, and St. Antony in southern France when diverted by events.[94]

[90] Espinas, *La vie urbaine de Douai au Moyen Age* 3, p. 321.

[91] Ibid. 4, p. 359.

[92] For example, ibid. 4, pp. 580–85; and comments at 1, pp. 758–62.

[93] Ibid. 4, pp. 753–55; examples of such tariffs from other towns in Van Cauwenbergh, *Les pélerinages expiatoires et judiciaires dans le droit communal de la Belgique au moyen âge*, pp. 222–36.

[94] Luke of Tuy, *Vita sancti Martini* 4–7, cols. 13–14; there is a facsimile of the Leon manuscript of the text in *Santo Martino de Leon*, ed. Viñayo.

Birgit of Sweden, who died in 1373, was another saint renowned as a pilgrim. During her canonization proceedings the frequent pilgrimages she had undertaken were brought up to illustrate her sanctity. The destinations specifically mentioned were the shrines of St. James at Santiago, the Three Kings at Cologne, the garments of the Virgin Mary at Aachen, St. Olav's tomb at Trondheim in Norway, the Provençal shrines of Mary Magdalene at St.-Maximin and Martha at Tarascon, the shrines of the Apostles Andrew, Matthew, and Thomas in the kingdom of Naples, St. Nicholas at Bari, the archangel Michael at Monte Gargano, the four doctors of the Roman Church, Augustine, Ambrose, Gregory, and Jerome, Francis at Assisi, and, not least, Jerusalem itself.[95] Some of these were the great public shrines of Christendom, while others, like Olav of Norway, reflected more particular and personal choices. Since Birgit lived for many years in Italy, the number of Italian shrines is not surprising, but she also visited several of the most important pilgrimage destinations north of the Alps, like Santiago and Cologne, though she never made the crossing to Canterbury to pray at Becket's shrine, as Martin of Leon had done.

As the itineraries of Martin and Birgit show, there was agreement on which were the chief pilgrimage shrines of Christendom, but these were surrounded by a penumbra of other local holy places. This network of nearby pilgrimage sites is well illustrated by the will of Alice Cooke of Horstead, in which she asked that pilgrimages be undertaken for the benefit of her soul to nine different sites in Norfolk: Our Lady at Reepham; the Holy Spirit (perhaps at Elsing); St. Parnell, Stratton; St. Leonard without Norwich; St. Wandred, Bixley; St. Margaret, Horstead; Our Lady of Pity, Horstead; St. John's head at Trimingham; and the Holy Rood at Crostwight.[96] None of these places was more than 20 kilometres (12 miles) from Horstead, so these "pilgrimages" involved less than a day's walk. It was also possible for the devout to combine pilgrimage to the great shrines with a devotion to these lesser sanctuaries. During the canonization hearings into the sanctity of Yves Hélory in 1330, one of his servants declared that he had been on pilgrimage to Rome, twice to Santiago, then to "the Seven Saints of Brittany."[97] These seven were the reputed founders of Christianity in the region, and a pilgrimage to all their shrines would involve a circular tour of Brittany, visiting St.-Pol-de-Léon, Tréguier (St. Tudwal), St.-Brieuc, St.-Malo, Dol (St. Samson), Vannes (St. Patern), and Quimper (St. Corentinus).

The division of shrines into greater and lesser took precise form under the Inquisition. The tireless inquisitor Bernard Gui, explaining the penalties that could be inflicted on heretics, defined four "major" pilgrimage sites—Rome, Santiago, Canterbury, and Cologne—and then listed twenty "minor" pilgrimages, most of

[95] *Acta et processus canonizacionis Beate Birgitte*, pp. 14, 309, 579; the shrines of the Apostles Andrew, Matthew, and Thomas were at Amalfi, Salerno, and Ortona, respectively; those of Augustine, Ambrose, Gregory, and Jerome at Pavia, Milan, and (both Gregory and Jerome) Rome.

[96] Hart, "The Shrines and Pilgrimages of the County of Norfolk," p. 277 (who suggests Elsing but without his grounds); most of these places appear on the map of pilgrimage sites in Norfolk in Marks, *Image and Devotion in Late Medieval England*, p. 282, maps 10–11.

[97] *Processus de vita et miraculis sancti Yvonis*, p. 58; cf. AASS Maii 4 (1685), pp. 547–48.

them to shrines in the south of France (see map 3). Since he was writing in Toulouse, "major" and "minor" referred to the length of the journey as well as the standing of the shrine: the major shrines are all more than 500 miles from Toulouse.[98]

Bernard Gui's "major" shrines are limited to western Christendom. Neither Jerusalem nor Constantinople is included in his list, although both cities were drawing Christian pilgrims throughout the medieval period. Christian pilgrimage indeed began in the Holy Land, and the Church of the Holy Sepulchre in Jerusalem continued to be an ultimate goal for thousands—the empty tomb that was even more precious than the tombs that housed the bodies of the saints. Constantinople, starting late and with no accumulated resources of martyr relics, rose to be one of the greatest sacred repositories in Christendom, with a famous collection of Passion relics, numerous relics and miraculous images of the Virgin Mary, and remains of the apostles and other major saints. Pilgrims to the imperial city, like those to Jerusalem or Rome, had a whole range of holy sites to see during their visit. Antony of Novgorod, who came to Constantinople in 1200, visited seventy-six shrines in the city and twenty-one in the suburbs, while, later in the Middle Ages, during the fourteenth and early fifteenth centuries, there is evidence of groups of Russian pilgrims being shown around the holy sites of Constantinople by guides.[99]

Of Gui's major pilgrimage destinations, Rome was the oldest and most revered.[100] The city drew especially large crowds in Jubilee years, when a plenary indulgence, a full release from the temporal punishment of sin, was granted to those who came to the city and visited the shrines of Peter and Paul. The first of these was in 1300 and the crowds were so dense that traffic regulations had to be imposed on the bridge leading to the Vatican, with one stream on the north side going towards the shrine, while the south side was reserved for those returning.[101] The original intention was that this Jubilee should be repeated every hundred years, but it came to be celebrated more frequently (in 1350, 1390, 1423, 1450, 1475, and every twenty-five years subsequently).[102]

But crowds of pilgrims came to Rome every year, and a literature grew up to guide them round the sites. From the twelfth century, this not only led them from shrine

[98]Bernard Gui, *Practica inquisitionis heretice pravitatis* 2. 3; 3. 13, 45, pp. 37–39, 94, 97–98, 166. The minor shrines are the Marian shrines at Rocamadour, Le Puy, Vauvert, Montpellier, and Serignan, St.-Guilhem-le-Désert, St. Peter of Montmajour (Arles), St. Martha of Tarascon, St. Mary Magdalene at St.-Maximin, St. Antony of Vienne, St. Martial and St. Leonard in Limoges, St. Denis, St. Louis at St.-Denis or Paris, St. Mary of Chartres, St. Severinus in Bordeaux, St. Mary de Soulac, St. Foy at Conques, St. Paul of Narbonne, and St. Vincent of Castres; one version of the list also includes St. Dominic in Bologna (Gui was a Dominican), another St. Gilles.

[99]Majeska, "Russian Pilgrims in Constantinople."

[100]Birch, *Pilgrimage to Rome*; *Romei e giubilei.*

[101]Dante, *Inferno* 18. 28–33.

[102]*La storia dei giubilei* 1–2; three important papal rulings on the frequency of Jubilees are in *Extravagantes communes* 5. 9. 1, 2, 4, cols. 1303–8 (Boniface VIII, *Antiquorum habet fida relatio*, 22 Feb. 1300, Po. 24917; Clement VI, *Unigenitus Dei filius,* 27 Jan. 1343; Sixtus IV, *Quemadmodum*, 29 Aug. 1473).

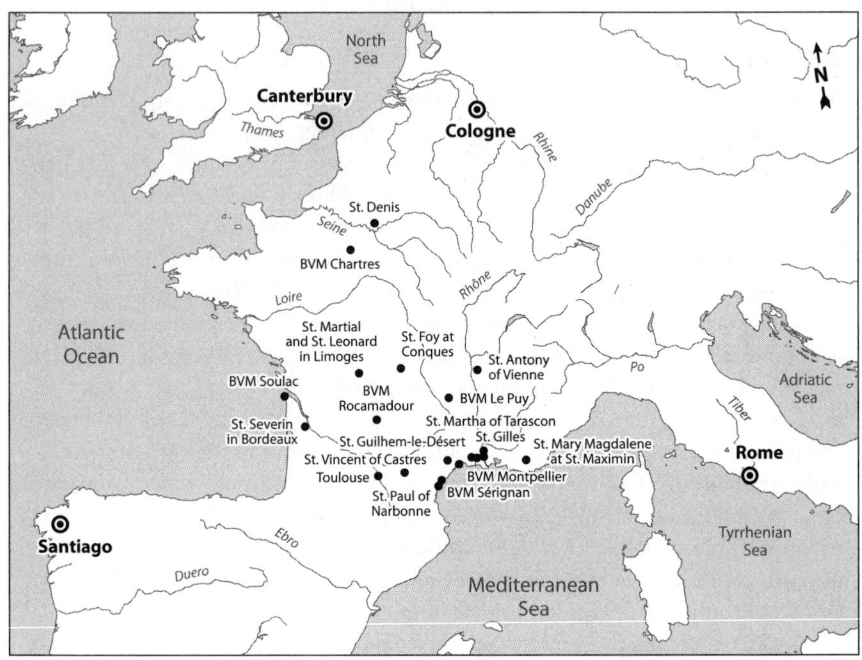

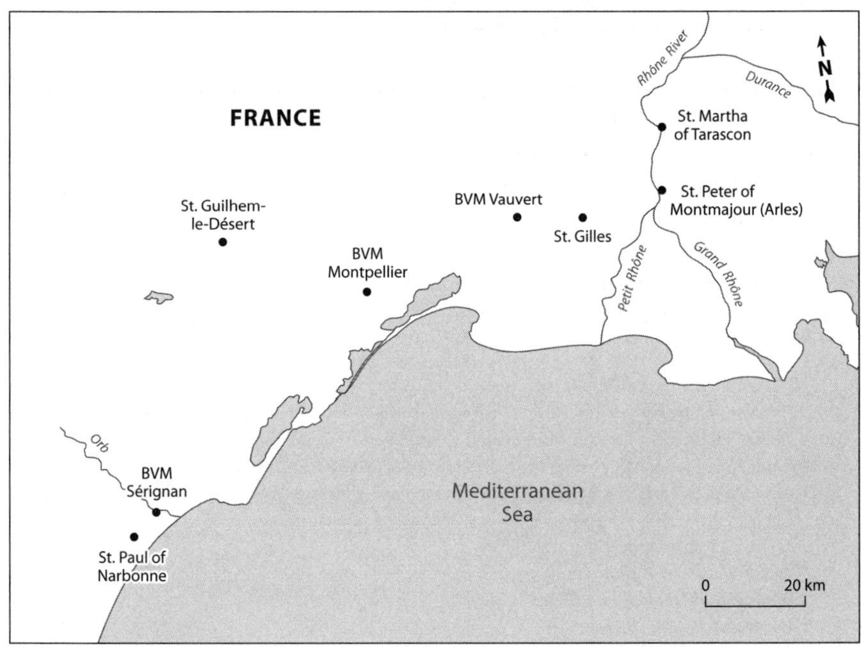

Map 3.

Bernard Gui's major and minor shrines. "BVM" marks Marian shrines.

to shrine but also specified the level of indulgences to be gained at each, usually stated as so many hundreds or thousands of years—a thousand years at the church of St. Cosmas and St. Damian, a hundred years at St. Cecilia in Trastevere, and so on (although the different guides are inconsistent in their figures). These guides were available in the vernacular languages—German, English and so on—and they were printed in large numbers from the end of the fifteenth century.[103] The latest technology, as well as a careful system of quantification of spiritual benefit, was being enlisted in the service of the cult of the saints.

Santiago de Compostella, one of the most famous shrines of Christendom, was almost as far west as one could go, adjacent to Finisterre—"Land's End." This site was associated with the apostle James. From the late Roman period churchmen had often attempted to make a link between their own church, wherever it might be, and Jesus' apostles, claiming that one of the apostles had been the first missionary in their area, or had died there, or, at least, had their bones brought to the site. The most famous, and most credible, of such links was that between Peter and Paul and Rome, but there were many other apostolic claims: John and Ephesus, Mark and Alexandria (and later Venice), Denis and Paris, Martial and Limoges (see the discussion on p. 172). One of the most successful of all these apostolic pedigrees was that associating St. James with Spain (figure 10.2). The crucial development here was the supposed discovery of the saint's bones in north-west Spain in the ninth century.

Later legends associated the unearthing of St. James's tomb in Galicia with bishop Theodemir of Iria, who died in 847, and this is not implausible. Writing in the middle of the ninth century, the monk Usuard of St.-Germain recorded St. James's feast-day on 25 July, adding, "His most holy bones were translated from Jerusalem to Spain, and interred in its most distant region, where they are venerated with the greatest reverence by that people."[104] By the later part of that century his cult had the support of kings. Alfonso III (866–910) regarded St. James as his lord and patron and made grants to his church at Compostella "so that you might grant us victory over our enemies," and in 899 a grand new church was dedicated there, in the presence of the king and numerous bishops and counts.[105] The first recorded foreign pilgrim to Santiago was Gottschalk, bishop of Le Puy, in 950. He travelled "for the sake of prayer . . . going humbly to beg God's mercy and the aid of St. James the Apostle." He also used the opportunity of his visit to Spain to acquire a copy of Ildefonsus of Toledo's treatise on the perpetual virginity of Mary, a very appropriate choice for a bishop from a see with an important Marian shrine of its own.[106]

Pilgrimage to St. James (Santiago) became so common that it generated its own terminology. Just as a pilgrim going to Rome might be termed a "Rome-seeker"

[103] *The Stacions of Rome*, p. 1, line 4; Miedema, *Die römischen Kirchen im Spätmittelalter nach den "Indulgentiae ecclesiarum urbis Romae"*; eadem, ed., *Rompilgerführer in Spätmittelalter und Früher Neuzeit*.

[104] Usuard, *Martyrologium*, p. 272 (PL 124: 295).

[105] *Tumbo A de la Catedral de Santiago*, nos. 14, 18, pp. 66–67, 71–74 (25 July 893, 6 May 899).

[106] Vázquez de Parga et al., *Las peregrinaciones a Santiago* 1, pp. 41–42; the manuscript he acquired is now BnF, lat. 2855.

10.2. Shrine of St. James, Santiago. © 2013. Photo Spectrum/Heritage Images/Scala, Florence.

(*Romipeta*), so a pilgrim to Santiago could be called a "James-seeker" (*Iacobipeta*).[107] The current huge cathedral began to be constructed around 1075. In 1120 the pope raised Compostella to the status of an archbishopric "on account of the greater reverence for St. James the Apostle, whose glorious body adorns your church."[108] The expansion of the cult between the ninth and the twelfth century is celebrated in the *Historia compostellana*, a work dedicated to the exploits of Diego Gelmírez, bishop and then archbishop of Santiago (1100–1140). An especially revealing passage describes the reactions of a group of Muslim envoys on a diplomatic mission in 1121.[109] As they approached Galicia, "they saw very many Christian pilgrims coming to and going from Santiago for the sake of prayer," and they asked their Spanish guide and interpreter, "Who is this, whom the Christian multitude visit with such devotion?" They apparently noted that many of the pilgrims came from beyond the Pyrenees, and said it was hard for them even to continue their journey because of the crowds.

[107] For example, *Vita Bonae virginis* 2 (21), p. 151.
[108] *Historia compostellana* 2. 16. 2, p. 254.
[109] *Historia compostellana* 2. 50, pp. 307–12.

Their guide explained that this was St. James the Apostle, and that he was revered by "France, England, Italy, Germany and all the lands of the Christians, especially Spain." When they finally arrived at Santiago, the envoys were amazed at the size and beauty of the cathedral church, confessing that, "we have seen nothing to be compared with this, on either side of our sea (that is, the Mediterranean)," and acknowledging the saint's glory. Their Christian guide explained the miraculous cures that St. James performed, giving sight to the blind, mobility to the lame, health to lepers and others, and freedom to captives: "on this account such a great crowd visits his body." Some days later, one of the Muslim envoys experienced this healing power himself, for, being afflicted with a suppurating abscess, he entrusted a candle to a pious widow, who offered it at St. James's shrine and prayed for the Muslim, who was quickly restored to health. The envoys were convinced of James's powers: "rightly is he sought out by Christians from both sides of the Pyrenees for the sake of prayer, rightly venerated by such a multitude of Christians with such devotion, rightly called patron and protector by the Christians!"

The highly partisan story clearly serves to glorify the cult of St. James by showing that even unbelievers were impressed by it (they admit that "their Muhammad cannot do such things"!), but the picture of a popular cult with numerous pilgrims from beyond the Pyrenees seems to be accurate. The flow of foreign pilgrims continued during later centuries. Evidence suggests that Santiago was by far the most popular foreign pilgrimage destination for Scandinavian pilgrims in the later Middle Ages and the names of more than 300 English pilgrims who visited Santiago in the fourteenth century are known.[110] Some of those who had made the journey to Galicia evidently treasured their memories and sought some lasting form to express their experience, as at Assisi, where there was a fraternity of those who had visited St. James's shrine. Its members engaged in charitable works, and in 1422 there is record in the town of a "new hospital of St. James of Galicia, built by the fraternity of men who had visited his church."[111] In this Umbrian town, which was itself a great focus of pilgrimage, the journey to Santiago has thus created both a bond between some of the townsmen and a new memorial to the name of St. James. In the same period the fraternity of St. James at Paris ruled that, if a pregnant woman went to Compostella, she and her baby could be admitted to the confraternity when they returned.[112] A visit to St. James's shrine, even in the womb, counted for something.

Canterbury, although a latecomer, made a determined and highly successful bid to enter the top rank of pilgrimage sites. The monk responsible for recording Becket's miracles mentions that the future glory of the saint's shrine had been predicted in a prophecy: "O Canterbury, how sweet and delightful you will be in future! For behold the day will come when people will flood to her, just as they do at present

[110] Krötzl, *Pilger, Mirakel und Alltag*, pp. 386–87; Storrs, *Jacobean Pilgrims from England to St James of Compostella*, pp. 161–68.

[111] Cenci, ed., *Documentazione di vita assisana* 1, p. 428.

[112] Péricard-Méa, "Les femmes et le pèlerinage," p. 32.

to St.-Gilles or Santiago or Rome or Jerusalem."[113] This citation makes it clear who were the competitors to beat. The inclusion of Canterbury in Bernard Gui's list of four major pilgrimage sites shows how successfully it climbed into the highest rank. Already by 1220, the date of Becket's Translation, the shrine was receiving the highest level of offerings ever recorded for an English shrine: £700, at a time when the revenue accounted for at the royal exchequer was about £12,700 per annum.[114]

Throughout the thirteenth, fourteenth, and fifteenth centuries, and on into the sixteenth, there was a constant stream of visitors to Becket's shrine. The Canterbury monks even elaborated a series of Jubilees, just like Rome; indeed the date of the Translation in 1220 was chosen to fit the biblical definition of a Jubilee.[115] Foreign visitors were common, like the Bohemian nobleman Leo of Rozmital, who came to Canterbury in the middle of the fifteenth century. "The monastery there," he wrote, "is of such elegance that you will scarcely find its like in any Christian province." He went in to visit the shrine: "it is cast from pure gold and adorned with jewels, enriched with such magnificent offerings that I do not know its equal. For the tomb has been generously enriched by many kings, princes, wealthy merchants and other pious men." Leo was shown all the church's relics, which he carefully lists, starting with Becket's head.[116]

Chaucer's *Canterbury Tales* are a permanent literary reminder of the central place that Becket's shrine played in later medieval England, drawing pilgrims of all backgrounds for a variety of reasons. The General Prologue to the *Tales* describes a group of pilgrims assembling at an inn in Southwark, on the southern end of London Bridge, before they set out to travel the 100 kilometres (sixty miles) to the shrine of St. Thomas Becket at Canterbury. Chaucer gives little vignettes of twenty-seven of these pilgrims, and refers to two others later in the *Tales*. They range in class from a knight and his squire to a cook and a ploughman. The Church is well represented among them, with a monk, friar, parson, summoner, and pardoner, and there are three women, a prioress, a nun, and the Wife of Bath, a much-married widow who had already been on pilgrimage to Jerusalem, Rome, and Santiago. Although the journey to Canterbury is the frame for the tales that are told, there is little in the work that is specifically to do with this pious undertaking and any other diverse travelling group would have served the author's purpose. Nevertheless, the *Canterbury Tales* vividly convey the social diversity of pilgrimage and the opportunities for sociability it offered.

Cologne began its rise to prominence as a pilgrimage destination because of an event which occurred in 1164, just six years before Becket's murder, namely, the arrival in the city of the relics of the Three Magi or Three Kings, captured when the emperor Frederick Barbarossa overcame Milan (in the fifteenth century an attempt

[113] Benedict of Peterborough, *Miracula sancti Thomae* 1. 6, p. 35.

[114] Nilson, *Cathedral Shrines of Medieval England*, p. 149.

[115] Foreville, *Le jubilé de saint Thomas Becket*.

[116] Stanley, *Historical Memorials of Canterbury*, pp. 264–65; cf. *The Travels of Leo of Rozmital*, pp. 43–44, 50–51.

was made to recover them by the Milanese, who clearly saw them as their Elgin Marbles).[117] An early eyewitness account described the three bodies of the kings as exceptionally well preserved through embalming, so that their skin and hair were intact; one of them appeared about 15, one 30, and one 60 (pictorial representations of the Three Kings frequently portray them as young, adult, and aged).[118] The reputation of the shrine spread quickly. In the 1180s the famous knight and tournament champion William Marshal "wished to go on pilgrimage to the Three Kings at Cologne," which he did, in the company of the Flemish baron Jacques d'Avesnes.[119] The most spectacular surviving monument of the cult of the Three Kings in Cologne is the imposing golden reliquary in the cathedral (earlier, pp. 271–72). This was made in the late twelfth and early thirteenth century and is covered with biblical figures, including of course the Three Kings, offering their gifts to a crowned and enthroned Virgin and Child. Behind the Kings, without a crown, is the figure of Otto IV, who had been elected king at Cologne in 1198 and had offered three golden crowns to the shrine in 1200.[120]

In the following centuries pilgrims came to Cologne from as far away as Scotland, Spain and Hungary. Edward III of England visited the shrine and made offerings there in 1338; a century later Philip the Good, duke of Burgundy, offered a golden lamp at the shrine; members of the royal dynasties of Denmark, Cyprus, and Portugal are found there in the fourteenth and fifteenth centuries; while the Hapsburg rulers regularly came to venerate the Kings after their coronation at nearby Aachen.[121]

Cologne's supply of saintly bones was further increased by the discovery of the remains of St. Ursula and her eleven thousand virgins. Ursula was reputedly a British princess martyred at Cologne by the Huns. There are traces of a cult from the eighth or ninth centuries, and a church dedicated to her was located on the site of a former Roman cemetery at the edge of the city. In the twelfth century bones began to be turned up here in large numbers. They were identified as those of Ursula's companions by means of inscriptions and through the visions of the nun Elizabeth of Schönau. By the end of the Middle Ages St. Ursula's was full of bust reliquaries and bones of the Eleven Thousand Virgins, and they are displayed there to this day, in the Golden Chamber.[122] Cologne has not ceased to be a magnet for pilgrims.

Logistics

The resemblance between medieval pilgrimage and the modern tourist industry is more than simply a comic parallelism. There are deep functional similarities, involving getting people to where they want to go, ensuring that they want to go

[117] Hofmann, *Die Heiligen Drei Könige*, p. 338.
[118] Robert of Torigni, *Chronica*, p. 220 (s.a. 1164).
[119] *History of William Marshal*, lines 6176–92 (1, p. 314).
[120] *Annales sancti Trudperti*, p. 292 (s.a. 1199).
[121] Hofmann, *Die Heiligen Drei Könige*, pp. 133–35, 142.
[122] Montgomery, *St. Ursula and the Eleven Thousand Virgins of Cologne*.

to the right places, turning their practical needs into a source of profit, and satisfying their psychological impulses, such as the desire to tread in the footsteps of the famous and to boast about one's travel to the stay-at-homes.

Pilgrims were of very varied social status, from kings to beggars, and their experience of the practicalities of pilgrimage would vary accordingly. Louis VII of France (1137–80) is an example of a keen royal pilgrim. In 1148 he was in Jerusalem "to pray and fulfil his pilgrimage," an incident in what historians label the Second Crusade, and the king visited Santiago "for the sake of prayer" in 1154, Mont-St.-Michel in 1158, and the shrine of Thomas Becket in 1179, when, "for love and honour of God and St. Thomas" he gave the monks the gift of 100 barrels of wine annually, an endowment later known as "St. Thomas's wine."[123] A few years before Louis visited Santiago, someone of very much humbler status, Botilda, wife of the cook of the monastery of Norwich, had also been there. She also made her way to St.-Gilles in Provence on the trip.[124]

Pilgrimage was an activity of spring and summer. In 1153 the bishop of Cambrai undertook a pilgrimage to Santiago, departing in the fourth week of Lent (which would have been 25–31 March) and returning on St. John's Day, 24 June.[125] "In wintertime," it was acknowledged, "few pilgrims visit the threshold of St. James, fearing the difficulty of the journey and the harshness of winter."[126] This is amply supported by analysis of the safe-conducts granted by the royal chancery of Aragon to pilgrims going to Santiago in the years 1378–1422. Of 133 such grants, 69, that is, over half, were issued in March, April, or May.[127] Chaucer famously wrote that it was after the April showers that "Thanne longen folk to goon on pilgrimages," while the rules for the provision for pilgrims drawn up by the monastery of Montserrat in Aragon c. 1330 mention the pressure on their resources "when many Rome-farers (*romipete*) flood by in summer," actually terming this season "the time of Rome-faring (*tempus romipetagii*)."[128] In Canterbury, at the end of the Middle Ages, offerings at the site of Becket's martyrdom were almost four times higher in spring and summer than in winter.[129]

Pilgrimages could be long and dangerous and it was sensible to prepare for the worst, like the Catalan lady Richell, who drew up her will in spring 1067 before setting out on a pilgrimage to Our Lady of Le Puy and Saint Foy of Conques: "I fear

[123] William of Tyre, *Chronicon* 16. 29 (2, p. 757); Robert of Torigni, *Chronica*, pp. 182, 283, 320; see Graboïs, "Louis VII pèlerin"; on "St Thomas' wine," see Foreville, "Charles d'Orléans et le 'Vin de Saint Thomas.'"

[124] Thomas of Monmouth, *Vita sancti Willelmi Norwicensis* 2. 6, 4. 10, pp. 78, 178.

[125] Lambert of Wattrelos, *Annales Cameracenses*, p. 525.

[126] *Historia compostellana* 3. 14. 3, p. 442.

[127] Vázquez de Parga et al., *Las peregrinaciones a Santiago* 3, pp. 29–32, app. no. 17 (one of these 134 documents is not dated precisely).

[128] Geoffrey Chaucer, *Canterbury Tales*, General Prologue, line 12, p. 23; Ribas i Calaf, *Annals de Montserrat*, appendix 4, p. 110.

[129] Nilson, *Cathedral Shrines of Medieval England*, pp. 116–17.

that my death might come upon me suddenly," she wrote.[130] An Italian pilgrim of the late twelfth century, "hastening to the threshold of St. James" (that is, Santiago), also thought it prudent to draw up his last will and testament before he left.[131] In 1397, Valentino di Guidarello of Foligno drew up his will, as he explained, because he wished to visit the shrine of St. James in Galicia and "feared the unknown dangers of human fragility that no one can predict"; he wanted, he said, to avoid any difficulty concerning his property after his death.[132] In the absence of travel insurance, setting one's affairs in order and providing for prayers for one's soul made especially good sense. It was also usually necessary for pilgrims, like other travellers, to have permission from their superiors before they departed on their journey. Many letters granting this authorization survive from the English royal archives.

All medieval travel had to be by foot, by horse or by water. There was special virtue in undertaking pilgrimage on foot rather than on horseback, as in the case of St. Birgit of Sweden, who showed her devotion to St. Olav of Norway when

> she went on foot for thirty days from the kingdom of Sweden to the kingdom of Norway, where the holy body of St. Olav is buried, to visit it, although she had with her several horses on which she could have ridden.[133]

Whether travelling on foot or by horse, water crossings represented a particular difficulty, and provision of bridges and ferries was a recognized charitable activity. Queen Margaret of Scotland (d. 1093), herself later recognized as a saint, established a free ferry for pilgrims who wished to cross the Firth of Forth on their way to the important shrine at St. Andrews:

> Since religious devotion brought crowds of people from all sides to the church of St. Andrew, she had shelters constructed on both shores of the sea that divides Lothian from Scotia, so that, after the effort of their journey, pilgrims and the poor might take their rest there, finding everything that was necessary for refreshment of the body . . . she also provided ships to take them across, coming and going, and nothing was ever charged to them as a fare for their journey.[134]

These sites are known as North and South Queensferry to this day.

A sea journey might involve less muscular effort but presented its own difficulties. A Middle English poem gives a lively and vivid description of the miseries suffered by pilgrims going by sea from "Sandwich or Winchelsea or Bristol or where that it be" to the shrine of St. James at Compostella. Their route would take them across the Bay of Biscay, famous for its storms. No sooner are they at sea when "their hearts

[130] *Cartulario de Sant Cugat del Vallés* 2, pp. 321–22, no. 656.

[131] *Romei e Giubilei*, p. 284, no. 6 (a document from the Archivio di Stato, Florence).

[132] Sensi, "Il pellegrinaggio a Santiago," p. 1265, no. 6.

[133] *Acta et processus canonizacionis Beate Birgitte*, p. 14.

[134] Turgot, *Vita sanctae Margaretae Scotorum reginae* 9, p. 247.

begin to fail," while the sailors rush around them at their business, observing of the pilgrims that "some are likely to cough and groan ere it be full midnight."[135]

Accommodation was obviously a major daily concern for pilgrims. Monasteries on the route might extend hospitality, especially to wealthy or noble pilgrims. The English landowner Ansgot of Burwell was so pleased with the "great charity and love" he was shown by the monks of Sauve Majeure near Bordeaux on the return leg of his pilgrimage to Santiago that he founded a priory for them on his Lincolnshire lands.[136] Monastic charity was supplemented by hospitals or hostels. Throughout the medieval period, but particularly from the eleventh century onwards, hundreds of these were constructed throughout Europe.[137] The description as "hospitals or hostels" is necessary, since few of these foundations offered only medical care, some were designed for the long-term sick or infirm, and others specifically provided only short-term accommodation for the poor or travellers, including pilgrims. When Erik the Good of Denmark (1095–1103) founded "a hospital for the poor and pilgrims," this could have been a combination of almshouses for permanent residents and free lodgings for travellers (not only pilgrims).[138]

If pilgrims were lucky enough to find a bed, they could not always expect to have it to themselves. A donation to a hostel in Mellid, near Lugo on the road to Santiago, refers to the twenty-four beds in the hostel, each for two persons, while an early-sixteenth-century carving, now in Klagenfurt in Austria, shows three pilgrims sharing a bed.[139] Like bridge-building, the provision of hostels for pilgrims was a pious work. The eighth-century Lombard queen Ansa was praised on her tomb for providing "wide roofs" for western pilgrims visiting the shrines of St. Peter at Rome and St. Michael at Monte Gargano.[140] And these hostels or hospitals could also offer a last service for pilgrims, by burying them when they died. In 1168 the bishop of Calahorra allowed the lady Isabel to construct an oratory and cemetery at the hospital she had built in the town of Azofra in the Rioja on the route to Santiago. He underlined, however, that the oratory was solely for the pilgrims and, similarly the graveyard was "for the burial of pilgrims only," and the parish church of Azofra otherwise retained all its rights.[141] French or other pilgrims who never quite made it to the shrine of St. James, or who died on their return journey, could find a last resting place in this little Riojan town.

Such charitable foundations were important, but much travel and accommodation was commercial. There was profit to be made from pilgrims. As early as the third

[135] *Oxford Book of Medieval English Verse*, no. 236, pp. 500–503.

[136] *Calendar of Documents Preserved in France*, p. 448, no. 1239; Vázquez de Parga et al., *Las peregrinaciones a Santiago* 1, p. 51.

[137] Schmugge, "Die Anfänge des organisierten Pilgerverkehrs im Mittelalter."

[138] *Historia sancti Kanuti ducis et martyris* 1, p. 189.

[139] Vázquez de Parga et al., *Las peregrinaciones a Santiago* 1, p. 326; *Wallfahrt kennt keine Grenzen*, p. 133, fig. 51 (from the Landesmuseum für Kärnten).

[140] *Epitaphium Ansae reginae*, p. 192.

[141] Vázquez de Parga et al., *Las peregrinaciones a Santiago* 3, p. 60, no. 54.

quarter of the fourth century, enterprising Egyptians were making money by hiring out camels to those visiting the desert site where St. Antony had lived.[142] At the foot of the hill on which the shrine and basilica of St. Simeon Stylites were built, there arose what has been called a "pilgrimage boomtown," providing accommodation, food and drink, guides, and souvenirs.[143] The entrepreneurs in this trade often had a bad reputation for fleecing pilgrims or even worse: "the innkeeper sits in ambush for pilgrim guests."[144] Stories of innkeepers who raised false charges against their customers, or even killed them, circulated widely. In the Codex Calixtinus, a twelfth-century pilgrimage compilation from Santiago, there is a long, sometimes rambling, but always heartfelt denunciation of the tricks and deceits of innkeepers and others who prey on pilgrims. They give them good wine to taste but then sell them much worse wine, or even cider; the food they sell is often days old; they use trick measures, which look much bigger outside than they really are within; they get their guests drunk, then rob them; they constantly overcharge them and swindle them when exchanging money; they sell them sub-standard candles; in short, "every wickedness and every deceit is in great abundance along the pilgrimage routes."[145]

Some of the more serious dangers of travel along the pilgrim routes are evoked in a document of bishop Sancho of Pamplona, when founding a hostel for travellers at the pass of Roncesvalles, a major transit point for pilgrims to Santiago. He noted that the local people had told him that "many thousands of travellers had died there, some suffocated by the whirling snows, many eaten alive by attacking wolves."[146] In the rough, wild country south of Oviedo, a hostel was established "so that pilgrims and others travelling through that place may escape danger to their property and their bodies, because we know that many people have often encountered robbers and brigands and wicked men in that place."[147]

Less dramatic, but more constant, were language problems. There are several surviving bilingual phrasebooks made for pilgrims to the Holy Land, and sometimes there are references to specific interpreters brought on pilgrimage. For instance, Bishop William of Orkney, who had studied in Paris and thus knew French as well as Latin, was asked by Earl Rognvald to accompany him on his pilgrimage to the Holy Land (1151–53) as an interpreter.[148] And when a high-born Irishman, a relative of the king of Connacht, came to Becket's shrine at Canterbury in the 1170s, he brought with him "a monk as interpreter."[149]

[142] Jerome, *Vita Hilarionis* 20. 12, pp. 268–70 (PL 23: 44–45); this must refer to the period 356–71.

[143] Vikan, *Early Byzantine Pilgrimage Art*, pp. 9–10.

[144] *Hospes in insidiis sedet hospitibus peregrinis*: John of Salisbury, *Entheticus in dogmate philosophorum*, line 1535, p. 205.

[145] *In sanctorum itineribus: Liber sancti Jacobi: Codex Calixtinus* 1. 17, pp. 160–71 (from *Veneranda dies*, a sermon ascribed to pope Calixtus).

[146] Vázquez de Parga et al., *Las peregrinaciones a Santiago* 3, p. 57, no. 51.

[147] Ibid., p. 63, no. 57.

[148] *Orkneyinga Saga* 85, p. 161.

[149] William of Canterbury, *Miracula sancti Thomae* 6. 19, p. 431; he is described as "Theodorici regis cognatus," possibly a reference to Toirdelbach Ua Conchobair (d. 1156).

Female pilgrims faced particular problems.[150] Women were more vulnerable on the roads. In 747, St. Boniface wrote to the archbishop of Canterbury urging him to discourage English women from going on pilgrimage to Rome. Very few of them, he claimed, retained their integrity on the journey, and almost every city on the pilgrim route had its English prostitute or loose woman.[151] When Margery Kempe, an indefatigable pilgrim, was abandoned by her companions in Venice on their return from the Holy Land, she asked a fellow-countryman to travel with her to Rome, but he was at first reluctant, because, he said, "I fear that my enemies will rob me, and perhaps take you away from me and defile your body."[152] And such fears were not without foundation. One French noblewoman was kidnapped while on pilgrimage and taken to the municipal brothel in Dijon.[153]

But female pilgrims also faced doubt about their motives. Pilgrims were meant to be sober and pious. Clearly they did not always attain this ideal, and it was female pilgrimage in particular that was viewed with most suspicion. One motive for pilgrimage, wrote a crusty fourteenth-century critic, was "the desire of married women who like to wander about" (a contemporary English translation renders this alliteratively as the "likynge and wille that wyves have to wende about").[154] The Knight of La Tour Landry, writing a guide to the conduct of young women at the same period, insisted that "one should not go on holy journeys for some silly pleasure," and told a salutary tale about pilgrims to the shrine of Our Lady of Rocamadour. Aristocratic women who had dyed their hair were quite unable to enter the church until they had cut off their coloured tresses. These gaudy tokens were displayed inside, presumably alongside the ex-votos of cured pilgrims.[155] The "riot, revelling and ribaldry" that characterized pilgrimage was still the target of criticism in the sixteenth century.[156]

One female pilgrim about whom we are unusually well-informed was a princess. In the spring of 1317 Mary, sister of King Edward II, undertook a journey of pilgrimage across southern England. Mary was a nun at the great Benedictine nunnery of Amesbury, but she travelled with the servants and companions suitable for a royal lady. Within the course of two months she visited the image of the Virgin Mary at Caversham; the great pilgrim centre of Canterbury; England's most ancient shrine at St. Albans; and, once again on her return journey, Caversham. An account roll survives, itemising her outgoings on the trip.[157] These included cash offerings at the shrines: five shillings at the image of the Virgin Mary at Caversham on the outward trip, along with three shillings for the relics in the chapel there, plus six pence for

[150] Morrison, *Women Pilgrims in Late Medieval England*; Dor and Henneau, eds., *Femmes et pèlerinages*; Craig, *Wandering Women and Holy Matrons*.

[151] Boniface, *Epistulae* 78, p. 252.

[152] *The Book of Margery Kempe* 1. 30, p. 77.

[153] Rossiaud, *Medieval Prostitution*, p. 33.

[154] Ranulph Higden, *Polychronicon* 7. 44 (8, pp. 326–27, with Trevisa's translation).

[155] *Le Livre du Chevalier De La Tour Landry* 34, 53, pp. 79, 112.

[156] Thomas More, *A Dialogue Concerning Heresies* 2. 10, p. 226 (modernized).

[157] London, Kew, The National Archives, E 101/377/2.

an offering to the image by Mary's companion Isabella of Lancaster, who also gave three pence to the relics; a large sum of twenty-six shillings and six pence in offerings at Christchurch and St. Augustine's, Canterbury; at St. Albans five shillings at the high altar, three shillings at the shrine of St. Alban, and another three at the shrine of St. Amphibalus; on the return journey another three shillings at Caversham, plus six pence from Isabella of Lancaster. The distances involved in this pilgrimage were not great: Canterbury is about 200 kilometres (125 miles) from Amesbury, St. Albans about 105 kilometres (65 miles) from Canterbury. And there were distractions on the way: a large amount was spent on exotic spices, and one of the expenses listed in Lady Mary's accounts is for her gambling debts. The Knight of La Tour Landry would have disapproved.

Pilgrim Guides and Pilgrim Badges

Pilgrimage generated its own literature, in the form of travel guides and descriptions of holy sites. The earliest dates from 333, and gives travelling instructions from Bordeaux to the Holy Land, as well as detailed lists of what to see when you are there, from "Mount Carmel, where Elijah made his sacrifice" to the Dead Sea, where, "if a man enters it to swim, the water tips him up."[158] Later in the same century the lady traveller Egeria left an account of her tour of biblical locations, including trips to the Burning Bush, Mount Nebo (from which Moses saw the Promised Land) and the site of Abraham's house, along with a very detailed description of the church services celebrated at Jerusalem.[159] These early visitors showed considerable interest in Old Testament sites as well as New Testament ones, and are not particularly concerned with tombs, shrines, or relics.

Over the following centuries a large number of travel guides were dedicated to both the Holy Land and Rome.[160] Texts describing Rome showed particular interest in the many shrines of the saints to be found there, one of the city's defining features. A seventh-century composition, *The Holy Places of the Martyrs*, traces an itinerary around the cemeteries where the saints' remains were located:

> In the southern part of the city, on the via Ostiense, the apostle Paul rests in the body, and Timothy, bishop and martyr, whom the Book of Silvester records, sleeps in the same place, and, in front of the basilica, is an oratory of the martyr Stephen, and there is a stone there which was used in the stoning of Stephen, placed on the altar.[161]

[158] *Itinerarium Burdigalense.*

[159] Egeria, *Itinerarium Egeriae.*

[160] See, for example, *Codice topografico della Città di Roma* 3, pp. 3–65 (*Mirabilia urbis Romae*); Külze, *Peregrinatio graeca in Terram Sanctam*; *Pilgrimage to Jerusalem and the Holy Land, 1187–1291.*

[161] *De locis sanctis martyrum*, pp. 108–9.

The best known pilgrim guide from the medieval period is nowadays often referred to simply by that title, *The Pilgrim's Guide*. It forms the fifth and final book of the Codex Calixtinus, the compilation of texts about St. James and Compostella put together for French pilgrims around 1140.[162] There is plenty of practical travel advice in it, about good and bad rivers, what to eat, the wickedness of ferrymen and toll-collectors, and generally unflattering observations on the different people the pilgrim would encounter. Gascons are "chatterboxes, long-winded, mocking, lustful, drunken, prodigal eaters, poorly dressed and wasters of treasure, but accustomed to war and extremely hospitable to the poor"; the Navarrese copulate with animals and even put chastity-belts on their livestock to stop others having access to them; the Galicians, although "more like our French race than the other uncivilized Spanish peoples," are bad-tempered and litigious.

The *Guide* is naturally alert to the condition of the roads and bridges, and gratefully records the names of those who repaired them, with the pious prayer, "May their souls and those of their helpers rest in eternal peace!" If pilgrimage brought spiritual benefits, so too did smoothing the progress of pilgrims. And the route to the shrine at Santiago offered the chance to visit other shrines too. The *Guide* lists many saints in France along the various "feeder" routes that led to the Pyrenees: St. Giles in Provence, St. Foy at Conques, St. Sernin at Toulouse, St. Leonard in the Limousin, St. Martin, St. Hilary, the head of John the Baptist at St.-Jean-d'Angély, and others. The Guide culminates in a description of the church at Santiago and the shrine of St. James, concluding with a plea that "pilgrims to St. James, rich or poor, are to be received properly and cared for with diligence."

Guides to the route to Santiago continued to be produced throughout the Middle Ages. In 1495 there appeared in print a rhymed German route-planner, authored by the friar Hermann König of Vach.[163] He described an "Upper Route" from Switzerland, through the south of France, crossing the Pyrenees at Roncesvalles, and a "Lower Route," from Aachen, via Paris and Bordeaux, the two routes converging at Burgos before passing westwards across Castile. He gives clear instructions about the route, advises that pilgrims should be careful with their money, and goes into some detail about the hostels along the route, sometimes straining to find a rhyme for *spitall*, the German for "hostel."

Pilgrims undertook a difficult and sometimes dangerous journey, in pursuit of a religious goal. Travel to the more distant sites might well be a once-in-a-lifetime experience. They wanted tangible mementos as well as memories and spiritual benefits. Hence there arose an important industry, the production of pilgrim tokens and badges.[164] From early times pilgrims brought back little flasks (ampullae) containing oil or water from the holy sites they had visited. These were sometimes decorated

[162] *The Pilgrim's Guide to Santiago*.

[163] Hermann König, *Das Wallfahrtsbuch des Hermannus Kunig*.

[164] There is a large and growing literature: Spencer, *Pilgrim Souvenirs and Secular Badges*; *Beyond Pilgrim Souvenirs and Secular Badges*; Haasis-Berner, *Pilgerzeichen des Hochmittelalters*; *Das Zeichen am Hut im Mittelalter. Europäische Reisemarkierungen*.

with images of the saint or the shrine.[165] Amongst the most common examples are ampullae from the shrine of St. Menas, showing him between two camels.[166]

Some pilgrimage destinations offered natural objects as souvenirs instead of, or as well as, ampullae. Those visiting the Holy Land brought back a palm as a sign of their journey, which is why they were often called "palmers," while the shrine of St. James in Spain was especially associated with the symbol of the scallop shell. A carving from the monastery of Santo Domingo de Silos, dating to around 1100, shows Christ as a pilgrim, carrying a shoulder bag with a scallop shell—the symbol of Santiago de Compostella—on it. These shells were sold in the courtyard outside the church of Santiago.[167] They might retain some miraculous powers as well as being a souvenir. In 1106 a knight in southern Italy, who was suffering from a swollen throat, expressed his hope in them: "If I could find one of the shells that pilgrims are accustomed to bring back from St. James, and touch my swollen throat with it, it would be healed immediately." So it happened, and the knight set off to Santiago to give thanks.[168] In the twelfth century a new kind of pilgrim souvenir came into existence—the metal badge or token. Pilgrims now brought back from Santiago not only real scallop shells but also scallops made from lead. Similarly, the Marian shrine at Rocamadour produced leaden images of the Virgin Mary.[169]

England's most important shrine after 1170, that of Thomas Becket at Canterbury, offered ampullae containing water, supposedly mixed with a drop of Becket's blood, and these were sometimes the conduit of miraculous healing. Guernes (Garnier) of Pont-Ste.-Maxence, a clerk from the Ile-de-France, writing a French verse *Life of Thomas Becket* in the early 1170s, mentions the ampullae that pilgrims carried away from Canterbury, comparing them with the lead tokens and other souvenirs from other shrines: "One carries back a palm from Jerusalem / and from Rocamadour a Mary cast in lead, / from St. James a scallop shell cast in lead; / now God has given St. Thomas this ampulla / which is cherished and honoured by everyone."[170] Later in the Middle Ages, Becket's shrine offered metal tokens as well as ampullae. Fourteenth-century badges from Canterbury are in various forms: some are of the saint's head, others show him travelling by boat or on horseback, or depict the martyrdom itself. Made of tin or an alloy of tin and lead, in size they are usually 6 to 9 centimetres (2 ⅓ to 3 ½ inches) across, and provided with pins and clasps for fastening to clothing. A few are smaller, such as the tin-lead circular badge with

[165] Vikan, *Early Byzantine Pilgrimage Art*; idem, "Byzantine Pilgrims' Art."

[166] Papaconstantinou, *Le culte des saints en Egypte*, pp. 146–54, 459–62.

[167] *The Pilgrim's Guide to Santiago* 2, p. 72.

[168] *Liber sancti Jacobi: Codex Calixtinus* 2. 12, pp. 273–74.

[169] For a good general discussion with many illustrated examples, see Köster, "Mittelalterliche Pilgerzeichen von Notre-Dame de Rocamadour."

[170] Guernes de Pont-Ste.-Maxence, *La vie de Saint Thomas*, lines 5896–5900 (1, p. 334); the edition by Walberg, pp. 181–82, reads "cross" (*cruiz*) for "palm" (*palme*).

Thomas's head and the inscription "Thomas's head" (*caput Thome*), only 2.4 centimetres across (just under an inch).[171]

Badges and tokens were worn on bags, hats, and other clothing. The pilgrim who is a character in the late-fourteenth-century English poem *Piers Plowman* is described as having "hundreds of ampullas on his hat."[172] Such pilgrims are also depicted on the St. Anne altarpiece of around 1500 from the Carmelite church in Frankfurt (figure 10.1). The production and sale of pilgrim badges became a profitable business, which was often the cause for dispute between secular badge-makers and local ecclesiastics, or between those wishing to enforce their monopoly and interlopers. The archbishops of Santiago sought to regulate the "scallop-shell-makers" of Compostella, while the latter were concerned to prohibit the production of "counterfeit badges."[173] The canons of St. Peter's in Rome had rights over the income from "the leaden or tin tokens bearing the images of the apostles Peter and Paul that are worn by those visiting their shrines, as an indication of their devotion and proof that they have completed their journey."[174] One of the most remarkable examples of a dispute over pilgrim badges involved the struggle between the merchants of Le Puy and the Hospital of St. Mary of Le Puy, which was granted a monopoly in 1210 and fought for it over the course of two centuries, winning a successful revindication in 1439.[175] Production of pilgrim badges was usually from moulds, which allowed a swift multiplication of images. Some of these survive, like a late-fourteenth-century example for casting tokens of Thomas Becket, made of stone, and 9.6 centimetres by 8.4 centimetres (approximately 3 ¾ inches by 3 ⅓ inches) in dimension (figure 10.3).[176]

An inventive manufacturer of pilgrim badges, like Olivier Sellier, who produced such badges for pilgrims coming to the shrine of Charles of Blois at Guingamp in Brittany, would also make wax ex-votos for sale to those who were miraculously healed. He had used as much as 500 pounds of wax on figures of men, women, heads, eyes, legs, feet, arms, hands, birds, and horses.[177] The production of pilgrim badges points to the industrial future: manufacture of cheap consumer items through a quick repetitive process. There is an especially direct link to the invention of printing, for, before producing moveable type, Gutenberg had made special pilgrim tokens with reflecting mirrors for the periodic display of the Marian relics at Aachen.[178]

Pilgrimage was an important aspect of the cult of the saints, but it was also tied to other elements of Christianity, notably the desire to see the Holy Land and the scenes of Jesus' life, and the idea that human existence on earth was an exile from the true heavenly homeland. Pilgrimage as allegory for the human life was a natural

[171] *Age of Chivalry*, pp. 221–22, nos. 54–61.
[172] William Langland, *Piers Plowman*, pp. 248 (Z 5. 162; B 5. 520; A 6. 8; C 7. 164).
[173] Vázquez de Parga et al., *Las peregrinaciones a Santiago de Compostela* 1, pp. 132–34.
[174] Innocent III, *Die Register Innocenz' III* 1, pp. 272–73.
[175] See Cohen, "In Haec Signa: The Pilgrim-Badge Trade in Southern France."
[176] *Age of Chivalry*, p. 396, no. 451.
[177] *Monuments du procès de canonisation du Bienheureux Charles de Blois*, pp. 395–98 (witness 181).
[178] Koster, "Gütenbergs Strassburger Aachenspiegel-Unternehmen von 1438/1440."

10.3. Pilgrim-badge mould for casting tokens of Thomas Becket, made in England, stone, fourteenth century. London, British Museum. © The Trustees of the British Museum.

development. "Do you not know that the life of man on earth is a pilgrimage?," asked Peter of Blois in the twelfth century, while *The Pilgrimage of Human Life* is the title of an extremely successful long poem by the fourteenth-century French Cistercian Guillaume de Deguileville. It survives in many manuscripts and was translated into numerous languages, including English, in a version probably by John Lydgate. Guillaume's poem is addressed to "those who undertake pilgrimage through this wild world."[179] For the ancient Romans to be a *peregrinus* was something to lament, the pitiable homeless wanderer representing the opposite of the citizen, with his rooted and cherished status. For many Christian thinkers, it was a state to be embraced.

[179] Peter of Blois, *Epistola* 170, col. 466; Guillaume de Deguileville, *Le pèlerinage de la vie humaine*, lines 29–30, p. 2.

CHAPTER 11

Dedications and Naming

Dedication of Churches and Altars

The first Christians did not meet in specially sanctified buildings but in houses belonging to members of their community. It was not the building but the congregation (Greek *ekklēsia*) that formed "the church." Later, there is some evidence, during the periods of peace from persecution, of places especially reserved for services, but it was in the fourth century that the situation changed fundamentally and for good, with large buildings in every city permanently set aside for Christian worship. Eusebius writes of "festal consecrations in the towns" after the end of the persecutions.[1] These buildings were often called "houses of the Lord" (*kyriaka* in Greek, the most likely origin for the English word "church" and its equivalents in Germanic and Slavonic languages).[2] At first the only churches to bear the name of a particular saint were those erected over the martyrs' tombs. St. Peter's in Rome was the church of St. Peter because it housed his body. Soon, however, the practice of associating a church with a saint underwent a radical development. In Egypt, the first evidence for churches dedicated to a saint dates to the middle of the fifth century, but within a hundred years it was a common custom.[3] Eventually it became a well-nigh universal practice for a church to have a patron saint after whom it was named: "the ancient house of the Lord finally became the house of a saint."[4]

A crucial part of this development was the introduction of relics into almost all churches. This removed the distinction between the martyr churches above the graves of the saints and the churches housing the ordinary congregations in the cities and villages. In the process the Christian altar, originally a table for the Lord's Supper, assumed some of the character of a grave or tomb: holy bones and the Eucharist were now linked. When St. Ambrose moved the bodies of the martyrs Protasius and

[1] Eusebius, *Historia ecclesiastica* 10. 3. 1 (3, p. 80).

[2] OED, s.v. "church."

[3] Papaconstantinou, *Le culte des saints en Egypte*, p. 308.

[4] *Les Ordines Romani du haut Moyen Âge* 4, p. 377. On dedications in general, see Binns, *Dedications of Monastic Houses*, pp. 1–58; for an exemplary regional study, Orme, *English Church Dedications*; there is bibliography for the Holy Roman Empire in Flachenecker, "Researching *Patrocinia* in German-speaking Lands"; a collective volume, *Mises en scène et mémoires de la consécration de l'église dans l'occident medieval*, has a useful bibliography at pp. 365–80.

Gervasius into his newly constructed church in Milan in the late fourth century, he placed them beneath the altar, so that "the triumphal victims should have their place where Christ is offered in sacrifice."[5] But the association of altar and martyr had been made long before, in the Book of Revelation, where St. John says, "I saw under the altar the souls of them that were slain for the word of God" (Revelations 6:9). It became a standard custom for relics to be placed under or inside an altar when it was consecrated. To take a concrete example, on 7 May 482, when the bishop of Jerusalem consecrated a church in the monastery where St. Euthymius had lived in the Judaean desert, he placed under the altar relics of the Cilician martyrs Tarachus, Probus, and Andronicus.[6]

Relics were usually placed in a hollow space within the altar, sometimes known as a "grave" (*sepulchrum*). The writings of Gregory of Tours offer many instances. He describes the wooden church at Thiers in the Auvergne, which had, within its altar, a silver reliquary containing stones stained with the blood of the martyr Symphorian.[7] In the case of another church, he tells how on one occasion, when an altar had been constructed there with a little space prepared in it to receive the relics, the bishop found that the box containing the relics was too large to fit; miraculously, at his prayers and the prayers of the holy deacon who had raised the altar, the space enlarged and the reliquary shrank to fit.[8] It was the task of the bishop to provide relics for the altars of new churches, as Gregory of Tours himself did in the case of "the church recently constructed in the village of Pressigny, which was without relics of the saints."[9] Surviving altars from Gregory's time have relic spaces of such dimensions as 27 centimetres wide by 16 centimetres deep or 16 centimetres wide by 15 centimetres deep (10 ½ by 6 ¼ or 6 ¼ by 5 ¾ inches).[10]

Inscriptions sometimes record the deposition of relics. There are numerous examples from early medieval Spain: "The relics of the saints, namely John the Baptist, Eulalia, Justus, Rufinus and Felix martyrs. This church was dedicated by bishop Pimenius on 25 May, in the (Spanish) era 686 [= AD 648]"—this from the old Roman city of Salpensa, south-east of Seville; "In the name of the Lord. Here were enclosed the relics of saints Stephen, Servandus, Germanus, Justus and Rufinus martyrs on 15 January in the era 712 [= AD 674], in the seventh year of bishop Theodoracis"—this from Vejer de la Frontera, south of Cadiz.[11]

The Second Council of Nicaea (787) emphasized the importance of the practice of depositing relics in a church at the time of its consecration, and condemned any

[5] Ambrose, *Epistularum liber decimus*, *Epistula* 77 (22). 13, p. 134 (PL 16: 1021).

[6] Cyril of Scythopolis, *Vita Euthymii* 44, p. 66 (PG 114: 700–701).

[7] Gregory of Tours, *Gloria martyrum* 51, p. 524 (repr., 1969, p. 74).

[8] Gregory of Tours, *Liber vitae patrum* 15. 1, p. 721 (repr., 1969, p. 271).

[9] Ibid., 8. 11, p. 700 (repr., 1969, p. 250); Pressigny is either Le Grand-Pressigny or Le Petit-Pressigny, Indre-et-Loire.

[10] Beaujard, *Le culte des saints en Gaule*, p. 372.

[11] García Rodríguez, *El culto de los santos en la España romana y visigoda*, pp. 450–51.

bishop who failed to do so.[12] Even so, the practice was general rather than universal, and relics were not essential for the dedication of a church or altar. In England the Council of Chelsea of 816 ruled that the bishop should place in the church he was dedicating a box containing the consecrated Eucharist and relics, but that if relics were not available the Eucharist alone sufficed.[13] The thirteenth-century liturgical writer William Durandus made the same point, that the Eucharist alone could be an acceptable substitute for relics when dedicating an altar.[14] And there are even forms of service for a dedication without relics.[15]

Nevertheless, a Christian church usually contained relics, and these were often numerous. The relationship between the relics in the church and the patron saint after whom it was named was a complex one. Relics could determine the dedication of a church. Around the year 400 bishop Gaudentius of Brescia, dedicating a basilica in which he had placed relics of John the Baptist, Andrew, Thomas, and Luke, as well as the remains of six later martyrs, along with portions of the Forty Martyrs of Sebaste, concluded his sermon by saying, "So we have these forty, and the aforementioned ten, gathered together from various lands, whence we decree that this basilica, dedicated to their merits, should be called 'The Assembly of Saints' [*Concilium sanctorum*]."[16] This is a very unusual dedication, and was in fact soon abandoned, but the point is rather that Gaudentius sees the dedication of the church reflecting the relics within it. Some centuries later, Willibrord, missionary to the Frisians in the late seventh century, brought with him relics of the saints, so that "when he founded churches among that people, he might have to hand relics of the saints to place in them, and, when he had deposited them, he might dedicate each place in honour of him whose they were."[17] The Carolingian nobleman Einhard, after building a church on his estate in the Main valley, pondered "in the name and honour of which saint or martyr it ought to be dedicated."[18] Hearing that martyr relics could be obtained in Rome, he sent a mission there and eventually acquired the remains of Marcellinus and Peter. Hrabanus Maurus, abbot of Fulda in the ninth century, founded many churches, both for his dependent priories and in other places, and, "collecting relics of the saints from far and wide, he had those churches consecrated in their name and honour."[19] Here "the name" derives from the imported relics. In cases such as these, there is a close association between the relics in the church and the name it bore.

But churches could be dedicated to saints whose physical remains were thousands of miles away, and of whose relics they possessed not a fragment, and altars too some-

[12] *Conciliorum oecumenicorum generaliumque decreta* 1, pp. 327–28 (cl. 7).

[13] *Councils and Ecclesiastical Documents*, ed. Haddan and Stubbs 3, p. 580.

[14] William Durandus, *Rationale divinorum officiorum* 1. 7. 23 (140, p. 90); idem, *Pontificale* 2. 2. 3, p. 456.

[15] Binns, *Dedications of Monastic Houses*, pp. 13–14.

[16] Gaudentius of Brescia, *Tractatus* 17, p. 150 (PL 20: 970).

[17] Bede, *Historia ecclesiastica* 5. 11, p. 484.

[18] Einhard, *Translatio et miracula sanctorum Marcellini et Petri* 1. 1, p. 240.

[19] Rudolf of Fulda, *Miracula sanctorum in ecclesias Fuldenses translatorum* 1, p. 330.

times do not contain relics of the saints to whom they are dedicated.[20] Beginning in Ephesus in the fifth century, churches were even dedicated to the Virgin Mary, who, having been taken up bodily into heaven, was generally thought to have left no bones on earth. The possibility of dedications to a saint that were independent of possession of physical remains enormously expanded the range of that saint's activities. It could be claimed that miracles would take place not only where the saint's bones were buried, but "everywhere in the world where a church or an oratory or even an altar is dedicated to their name."[21]

It was not only the patron saint of the church who was honoured there, for inside the church there would often be altars dedicated to other saints or images of them. There was thus a small saintly network available for worshippers. In 1498 a survey was made of the churches of the Order of Santiago in the diocese of Badajoz, and it demonstrates this multiplicity of cult objects very clearly.[22] At Almendralejo, the church was dedicated to the Virgin Mary and possessed an image of her, but it also had an altar dedicated to St. Silvester and another dedicated to St. Bartholomew, with a wooden image of that saint. The church of Calamonte was likewise dedicated to the Virgin, and had an image of her, but also altars dedicated to St. Catherine (Catalina) and St. Blaise, each represented in a wall painting. At Montemolin there was a church of St. James containing an altar dedicated to him; it also housed a sculptured image of the Virgin Mary, an altar of St. Mary with a sculptured image of the Virgin and Child, an altar of St. Michael, images of the Virgin and St. John standing beside the crucifix, an altar of St. Catherine with a painting of the saint and an altar of St. Gregory, also with a painting. A worshipper entering such a church would be coming into a world of images and altars, each providing a focus for prayer and veneration. It would be possible to have a favourite saint or go to different saints for different purposes.

A study of the relics in the altars in the church of St. Stephen at Dijon shows some of the complexities.[23] Several altars were constructed or reconstructed in the twelfth and early thirteenth centuries, the high altar being consecrated in 1141 after a destructive fire four years earlier. Of twelve altars, five were dedicated to particular saints: Stephen (the patron of the church), the Virgin Mary, Peter, Andrew and John the Evangelist. John's altar was in a crypt below that of the Virgin Mary, "so that he should be the foundation and support of that work, whom Christ on the cross made guardian of his mother." The altars contained around ten different relics each, although the high altar had more than twenty-three, and these were in glass and marble containers. Most were corporeal relics, and the early martyrs were well

[20] Beaujard, *Le culte des saints en Gaule*, p. 256; Binns, *Dedications of Monastic Houses*, p. 14.

[21] Nec solum signis mirandis ossa eius pullulant de illo sepulture sue loco sed ubique terrarum ubi ecclesia vel oratorium aut etiam altare attitulatur nomini suo tot et talia micant magnalia: Jocelin of Furness, *Vita Helene*, Gotha, Forschungsbibliothek Memb. I 81, fol. 212 (the emendations by Harbus, *Helena of Britain*, p. 177, are not necessary).

[22] Méndez Venegas, "Relación hagionímica de la Orden de Santiago."

[23] Durnecker, "Consécrations d'autels et dépôts de reliques. L'exemple de Saint-Étienne de Dijon."

represented. In this case the altars did contain relics of the saints to whom they were dedicated, although, as we have seen, this was not a universal feature at this period.

Relics placed in altars could be chosen thematically, as in the case of an altar "in honour of the holy virgins" in St. Maximin, Trier, which contained relics of saints Felicity, Agnes, Cecilia, Lucy, Walgisga, Modesta, Brigid, Agatha, Helen, and Aldegundis.[24] Of these ten virgin saints, five were early martyrs, one was the mother of the emperor Constantine (and hence unlikely to be technically a virgin), one was an early Irish abbess, two were Merovingian abbesses, and of the deeply obscure Walgisga nothing can be said. They thus form a wide chronological and geographical sample of the category "virgin saint." Less comprehensive, but still clearly thematic, was the altar established by bishop Baldwin of Paderborn in his cathedral church in 1357. This was dedicated to the Virgin Mary and three ruler-saints: Charlemagne, the emperor Henry II, and Oswald, king and martyr.[25]

The ceremony for dedicating a church was fairly similar in East and West and its basic outline remained relatively unchanged between the earliest liturgical evidence in the eighth and ninth centuries and the end of the Middle Ages. At its heart lay the sanctification of the building by the bishop through the sprinkling of holy water, the anointing of the altar, and prayers and blessings. It was also usually assumed that relics would be placed in the church being dedicated. There are early texts titled "pronouncement when the relics of the holy martyrs are to be deposited and order how a church should be dedicated" and "order how relics are deposited in the holy Roman Church"; later, and more elaborate, descriptions of the rituals of dedication and deposition in the texts of liturgical writers; and also illustrations, such as those in the Metz Pontifical, produced in the years 1303–16 and now in the Fitzwilliam Museum in Cambridge, which has numerous pictures showing the dedication of a church, with relics being brought in procession and a vigil kept before them in a tent.[26] In the thirteenth century, William Durandus specified that the container holding the relics should also have within it, besides the customary three particles of incense,

> A little leather parchment written in big letters, stating whose relics are enclosed there, and the saint in whose honour and name that church and altar are dedicated, the name of the consecrator and the indulgence he granted for the anniversary of the dedication, and also the year, month and day when it was dedicated.[27]

[24] *Fundationes et dedicationes ecclesiarum*, pp. 967, 1271.

[25] Hengst, "Die Altäre und Benefizien des Paderborner Domes," p. 238.

[26] *Les Ordines Romani du haut Moyen Âge* 4, pp. 337–39 (Ordo XLI), 395–402 (Ordo XLII); William Durandus the elder, *Pontificale* 2. 2, p. 455–78; the Metz Pontifical is Cambridge, Fitzwilliam Museum MS 298, with the dedication ceremony on fols. 1–62; there is a (mostly monochrome) facsimile edition: *The Metz Pontifical*. For Byzantine ceremonial: *L'eucologio Barberini gr. 336*, caps. 150–56, pp. 159–74. There is a bibliography of English sources in Orme, *English Church Dedications*, p. 5 n. 19.

[27] William Durandus the elder, *Pontificale* 2. 2. 3–4, p. 456.

William Durandus obviously expects that a church will have a patron saint, but it was not a legal requirement, and it is significant that the *Golden Legend*, which is contemporary with William Durandus, and devotes a very long final chapter to the subject of "The Dedication of a Church," has nothing to say about a patron saint.[28] Nevertheless, it was generally assumed that a church would have a saint to whom it was dedicated, and it was even decreed that every church should have an image of this saint (see later, pp. 484–85). The anniversary of the dedication of the church and the feast-day of the saint to whom it was dedicated were rarely identical, and both were usually celebrated. At the abbey of St.-Germain-des-Prés outside Paris the feast of the dedication of the church was 21 April, the feast of its patron, St. Germain (Germanus) himself, 28 May (with a further Translation feast on 25 July).[29] Dedication feasts were often recorded in liturgical Kalendars, and give clues as to the Kalendar's place of origin. And they were occasionally changed. In 1375 the bishop of Roskilde allowed the clergy of St. Mary's church in Copenhagen to transfer the feast of the dedication of their church from 14 September to the Sunday after Corpus Christi for (unspecified) "legitimate and reasonable causes," granting an indulgence of forty days for the occasion.[30] Another example, from Cornwall, is cited earlier (p. 128).

It thus seems that the bishop's permission was required to change the date of the feast-day of the dedication, but there were no legal implications in a church's dedication to a particular saint and it did not need to be specified in grants or other formal documents. Usually it was quite adequate to identify a church not by its patron saint but simply by its location. Most villages would have only one church, and the name of the place would be a sufficient indicator. However, in the larger settlements, with many churches, this would not be enough, and then the dedication could be a useful additional label, although if there were more than one church with the same dedication, then a further identifier would be needed. Hence the City of London had its St. Mildred Bread Street and St. Mildred Poultry, named both by saint and street.

Since the dedication of a church was not a legal fact about that church, it could be changed easily, without any official requirement or need for notification—it was not like a modern person changing his or her name through public authorization. Hence changes in dedication were common, in the Middle Ages and subsequently, and modern dedications are not a reliable guide to the medieval pattern.[31] A striking example of multiple, variable dedications is provided by the monastic church of Silos

[28] Jacobus de Voragine, *Legenda aurea* 178 (2, pp. 1283–98).

[29] BnF, lat. 12043 (Diurnale Guillermi abbatis, 1399), fols. 2v, 3, 4.

[30] *Kjøbenhavns Diplomatarium* 1, p. 92, no. 74.

[31] For a short but pithy (and sympathetic) discussion of the problems of establishing pre-Reformation dedications in England, see Northeast, "Moving the Signposts: Changes in the Dedications of Suffolk Churches after the Reformation"; Orme, *English Church Dedications*, p. 37, points out the stability of dedications of parish churches in Devon from at least the twelfth century to the Reformation; for many examples from the diocese of Leon, López Santos, *Influjo de la vida cristiana en los nombres de pueblos españoles*, pp. 140–54 ("Cambio de titulares").

in Castile, which, in the space of less than four months in 1076, received two grants, one from the famous warrior Rodrigo Díaz, known as El Cid, and his wife Jimena, one from the king, Alfonso VI.[32] In the first, the grant is to made to

> the house of St. Sebastian and his companions and St. Mary the Virgin and the holy apostles Peter and Paul and St. Andrew the apostle and St. Martin, bishop and confessor of Christ, and also St. Millán the priest and St. Philip the apostle.

The king's grant is to

> the lords, our glorious and, after God, most powerful patrons, St. Dominic the confessor of Christ and abbot, and St. Martin the bishop, and also the venerable martyrs Sebastian and Fabian whose relics lie enclosed in this place of St. Dominic.

The monastery was in the process of changing its primary patronage from the martyr St. Sebastian to its recently deceased saintly abbot, Dominic (it is now known as Santo Domingo de Silos), but there are also a number of other saints invoked in these grants. Only Sebastian and Martin are common to both lists, but there was never any doubt about the church that was the recipient.

The church of Coldingham in southern Scotland was originally dedicated to the Virgin Mary; in the early twelfth century, after it was granted to the monks of Durham, who prided themselves on possession of the incorrupt body of St. Cuthbert, he was added to the dedication; and later in that century, when the relics of the Anglo-Saxon saint Æbbe were found and brought to the church of Coldingham (now a dependent priory of Durham), she too became part of the dedication of the church. Hence, by the thirteenth century, pious donations to the priory could be made "to God and the blessed Mary and St. Cuthbert and St. Æbbe and the monks of Durham serving God at Coldingham."[33] It is a process that exemplifies two important ways that dedications could be shaped: possession by a superior institution that had its own dedication (Cuthbert in the case of Durham) and discovery ("invention") of new relics (of Æbbe).

Silos and Coldingham are cases of gradual and complex changes and variations that do not appear to have been the product of any particular moment of choice or decision. A more conscious, and indeed vehement, process is suggested by report of how Simon, the rector of West Tarring in Sussex in the time of Henry III (1216–72), built a new chancel to his church and dedicated it "in honour of St. Thomas the martyr, archbishop, and turned out (*expulsit*) St. Nicholas, who had previously been patron."[34] In this instance, the new saint kicked out the old, rather than joining him.

[32] *Documentación del monasterio de Santo Domingo de Silos (954–1254)*, no. 18, p. 22; no. 19, p. 24.

[33] *The Miracles of St Æbbe of Coldingham and St Margaret of Scotland*, pp. xv–xvi, xxii; Raine, ed., *The History and Antiquities of North Durham*, app., pp. 14, 28–30, 46, nos. 64, 125–27, 133–34, 196.

[34] Salzman, "Some Sussex Miracles," p. 70, citing Oxford, Magdalene College, Sele Deeds, Durrington 15.

Thomas Becket was renowned for his intransigence. Another kind of change that occurs particularly in the later Middle Ages and in regions with many local saints, is the addition of a common, universal saint to more obscure one. There are at least twelve examples in Cornwall. In the thirteenth century, for example, the church at Morwenstow added the instantly recognizable John the Baptist to the native but purely local St. Morwenna.[35]

Mapping the geographical distribution of dedications of churches and altars is one of the ways of establishing the scope and range of a saint's cult.[36] At one extreme, churches dedicated to the Virgin Mary could be found throughout Christendom, in their thousands, while, at the other, there is a church dedicated to St. Modwenna in one place only (Burton upon Trent). Most saints, naturally, were somewhere in the intermediate range, and can be classed as local, regional or supra-regional. For instance, mapping the churches and altars dedicated to St. Remigius or Remi, along with his images and relics, produces a clear pattern, with a dense cluster around his primary cult centre at Rheims, which then thins out in all directions.[37] The vast majority of dedications are within 250 kilometres (155 miles) of Rheims. The cult also exhibits a limited correlation with language boundaries, since the decrease in density of dedications is rather less sharp in France than in German-speaking regions. When combined with other types of evidence, such as mentions in Kalendars and the copying of hagiography, this map establishes Remigius as an important regional saint, with a homeland in northern France but with recognition well beyond that area.

A map of the cult of the Three Kings shows an understandably dense cluster of chapels and altars around Cologne (their cult is rather too late to have had much impact on the dedication of parish churches), and a fairly heavy distribution up the Rhine as far as Switzerland. Northwestern Italy around Milan also had many altars and chapels, but these are mainly post-Reformation rather than indications of medieval veneration. The distribution of altars and chapels east of Cologne, into Germany and central Europe, is quite significant, but they dry up almost at once to the west, so France and Britain have only a handful.[38]

Another approach to the subject is to take a given area (often a diocese) and create an inventory of all the dedications within it. A study of over 160 churches in the eastern part of the diocese of Genoa in the period from the tenth to the thirteenth century revealed an unsurprising dominance of the Virgin Mary, with approximately 16 per cent of all dedications, followed by St. Martin (10 per cent), Michael and Peter (each 7 per cent), Lawrence (6 per cent), Margaret and John the Baptist (each 5 per cent), and Andrew (3 per cent). All remaining dedications were below 3 per cent, representing four cases or fewer. Some of these poorly represented saints were, nevertheless, significant for the locality, such as Ambrose, bishop of Milan, with four

[35] Orme, *English Church Dedications*, p. 39.

[36] For instance, the maps in Jones, *Saints in the Landscape*, pp. 163–76.

[37] *Grosser Historischer Weltatlas 2: Mittelalter*, p. 68 ("Die Verehrung des Hl. Remigius").

[38] Hofmann, *Die Heiligen Drei Könige*, fold-out map at end.

dedications, or Columbanus, whose shrine at Bobbio lay inland from Genoa and who had three dedications.[39] A comparable study of the dedications of the 1,337 churches recorded in the diocese of Burgos in the years 800–1230 found eighty-three saints mentioned, with numbers of dedications varying from 217, in the case of the Virgin Mary, to 1. These single cases were fairly numerous—sixteen in all—and involved several early martyrs, some with Spanish origins, like Claudius of Leon, and saints with important cults elsewhere, like St. Isidore, as well as obscure local figures. After Mary, Martin (with 108 dedications), Peter (91), John (82), and Michael (64) head the list.[40]

A comparison of the town churches of Rome and London in the late Middle Ages reveals another example of regional variation. A list of Roman churches with their dedications, which was drawn up around 1300, has 381 entries.[41] Saints with more than ten dedications are as follows:

Mary 73
Salvator 34
Nicholas 23
Lawrence 21
Andrew 19
Stephen 15
John 13
Blaise 11

The City of London had 97 historic parishes within the walls.[42] The most common dedications, with more than three instances, are:

Mary 14
All Hallows (that is, All Saints) 8
Michael 7
Martin 5
Benet (Benedict) 4
Peter 4
Margaret 4

A glance shows that, apart from the shared predominance of the Virgin Mary, there is no overlap in these most popular dedications. Apostles and early martyrs dominate the Roman pattern, while the London sample is highly eclectic—"All Saints," an archangel, two early medieval confessor-saints, a famous Apostle and a legendary female martyr. However, all the popular Roman saints, except for Blaise, did have at

[39] Moggia, "Il culto dei santi nel medioevo."

[40] García de Cortázar et al., "Hagionimia de iglesias y monasterios en la diócesis de Burgos."

[41] *Codice topografico della Città di Roma* 3, pp. 271–90, from Paris, Arsenal 525; for early dedications, see Jost, *Die Patrozinien der Kirchen der Stadt Rom.*

[42] They are listed in *The City of London* (The British Atlas of Historic Towns 3), pp. 63–99, "Gazetteer," and mapped there on the final map, "The Parishes."

least one church dedication in London, while the most popular London saints were also represented in Rome. What one sees, therefore, is a strong regional coloration but not wholly distinct cultural worlds.

Simple movement of people could explain some patterns of saintly dedications. When Hunfried, archbishop of Magdeburg (1024–51), had a crypt built in his cathedral church and dedicated it to St. Kilian, the explanation for his choice of saint is not difficult, for he had previously been a canon of Würzburg, a church which was dedicated to Kilian, "his former patron."[43] His promotion from a Franconian canon to a Saxon archbishop had brought with it a new dedication to Kilian on the banks of the Elbe. A similar explanation lies behind the altar of St. Saba (Sabas) in the monastery of Bury St. Edmunds, which was constructed by Abbot Anselm (1121–48), who had been abbot of St. Saba in Rome.[44]

But the large-scale and long-term patterns cannot be explained simply by such individual links and contacts. There were regional differences that suggest differing traditions of sainthood, or even differing types of society. Its large number of local saints, whose cults might be quite unknown beyond the region, distinguished the Celtic world. Of the ancient dedications in Wales, 55 per cent are to Celtic saints.[45] In Cornwall there are 133 ancient churches dedicated to Celtic saints, mostly to different individuals.[46] And the parting of the ways between western and eastern Christendom was also reflected in some aspects of the dedication patterns. As discussed earlier, dedications to Old Testament figures were a feature of eastern rather than western churches, while Peter, a dominant figure in many parts of the West, had only a handful of churches in Constantinople, most of them in partnership with Paul.[47]

In western Europe in the early Middle Ages, dedications to Peter, prince of the apostles, and to the first great confessor-saint, Martin, were common, sometimes even outstripping those to the Virgin Mary. Of the 71 known dedications from England in the period 597–800, 20 are to Peter (with another 6 to Peter and Paul jointly), 19 to Mary.[48] The 26 Petrine dedications thus constitute over a third of the total. On the continent Martin was equally significant. When the diocese of Würzburg was founded in 742, it was endowed with 26 churches. Exactly half of these were dedicated to St. Martin, while the patrons of the remaining thirteen were Mary, John the Baptist and St. Remigius or Remi (three cases each); Peter (two cases); and Michael the archangel and Andrew (a single case each).[49]

Mary was the special saint of Constantinople from early times. There were more than 120 churches dedicated to the Virgin Mary in Constantinople and its

[43] *Gesta archiepiscopurm Magdeburgensium*, p. 398.
[44] *The Customary of the Benedictine Abbey of Bury St Edmunds*, p. 116.
[45] Yates, "The Distribution and Proportion of Celtic and non-Celtic Dedications in Wales."
[46] Orme, *English Church Dedications*, p. 15.
[47] Janin, *La géographie ecclésiastique de l'Empire byzantin*, pp. 397–401.
[48] Orme, *English Church Dedications*, p. 17 (Levison's figures for 597–800 tabulated).
[49] *Diplomata Ludowici Germanici, etc.*, no. 41, pp. 54–55.

European suburbs, far outstripping any other dedication.[50] In the West, Mary was important in the early Middle Ages, but, as just noted, not predominant. This was a position she did obtain over the course of the Middle Ages. New Marian feasts have been discussed earlier (pp. 154–57), and the burst of enthusiasm for Marian miracle stories and Marian shrines is another indicator. The persistent rise of the Virgin Mary throughout the medieval period is also exemplified by the decision of the Cistercians, the most important new monastic Order of the twelfth century, to dedicate all their churches to her. Just as they sought to create new international forms of organization, transcending the older Benedictine models of local rootedness, so they chose a universal rather than any local saint as their patron. Sometimes Cistercian monasteries did add an additional saint to the Virgin Mary in their dedication, as in the case of Frauenthal in the diocese of Würzburg, founded by local aristocrats in 1232 "in honour of God, the blessed Mary and the holy martyrs Kilian and his companions."[51] Kilian, as just mentioned, was the patron of the diocese. A more complex situation is found in the case of the Cistercian house of Revesby in Lincolnshire, founded in 1143. A contemporary Cistercian source explains that

> the abbey has two names, for it is called "St. Lawrence's" because in the village where the abbey was built there was a church once dedicated to St. Lawrence, which still stands; and the other designation comes from the village, which is called Revesby, whence the abbey is also called by this name.[52]

This suggests that "St. Lawrence's" is to be understood as a name for the abbey, like "Revesby," and not as a dedication. So when the abbot describes himself on the monastic seal as "abbot of St. Lawrence," or when grants are made "to God and St. Mary and the monks of St. Lawrence," it is this locative sense that is meant rather than a secondary dedication.[53] What it does show, however, is that saints could give their names to places.

Place Names

The cult of the saints had a marked impact on place names.[54] Some well-known places owe their names to the saints venerated there, even if few now remember them. Visitors to St.-Tropez are unlikely to think of the martyr St. Torpes, whose

[50] Janin, *La géographie ecclésiastique de l'Empire byzantin*, pp. 156–244.

[51] *Wirtembergische Urkundenbuch* 3, no. 818, p. 313.

[52] Walter Daniel, *Vita Ailredi* 20, p. 28.

[53] Binns, *Dedications of Monastic Houses*, pp. 159–60; Owen, "Some Revesby Charters." In his *Mappa Mundi*, p. 429, Gervase of Canterbury simply records "Revesbi, Sanctae Mariae."

[54] López Santos, *Influjo de la vida cristiana en los nombres de pueblos españoles*; Bach, *Deutsche Namenkunde* 2/1, pp. 327, 335, 338, 367–68; 2/2, pp. 185–91; Dubois and Lemaitre, *Sources et méthodes de l'hagiographie médiévale*, pp. 191–210, "Les saints dans la toponymie."

church is recorded in the town in 1055.[55] And the influence of the saints on place names continued well after the Reformation in those parts of the world occupied by Catholics, as St. Louis (Missouri), San Diego, and Santiago de Chile bear witness. The building of thousands of churches dedicated to named saints provided a simple way of identifying a locality by reference to the patron saint of that church, and towns and cities with famous shrines often came to be referred to by the saint's name rather than an earlier place name.[56] The hills north, south, east, and west of Fulda in central Germany each had a church with a different dedication, and are still known today as Frauenberg, Johannesberg, Petersberg, and Andreasberg from their churches of the Virgin Mary (*Frau*—"Our Lady"), John, Peter, and Andrew.[57] Towns in Britain such as St. Andrews, St. Davids and St. Albans take their names from the saints whose chief shrines they contained. Sankt Pölten in Austria derives its name from St. Hippolytus, the patron saint of the monastery founded there in the eighth or ninth century. A process of gradual erosion led from "Hippolytus" to "Pölten." Exactly the same process produced the place name Ippollitts in Hertfordshire, where the local chapel (and later church) was dedicated to St. Hippolytus. Throughout the Christian world saints could lend their names to sites associated with them.

Some place names derived from the saints can be found in the Middle East and may date from the early centuries of saintly cult. Saints were often referred to in Aramaic or Syriac by the honorific terms *Mar* or *Mor*, meaning "lord," giving rise to place names like Mar Mikha'il (St. Michaels), on the coast road south of Beirut, while the Egyptian honorific *Abba* or *Apa* is found in the place name Abu Qir (Aboukir), derived from "Kyros," with reference to St. Cyrus, the martyr venerated at the site. In Merovingian France, too, a saint was usually known as "Lord"—*dominus* or *domnus* in Latin, shortened to *dam* or *dom*—and this practice gave rise to such place names as Dammartin or Dommartin (from Saint Martin), Dampierre or Dompierre (from Saint Peter) and Domremy (the birthplace of Joan of Arc) from St. Remy or Remigius. Dompierre in the department of Nord is recorded as "the village of Lord/Saint Peter" in 1176.[58] Martin and Peter were popular saints and these names are therefore fairly frequent, but the less well-known saints are also represented: the place name Domfront, single examples of which occur in Maine, Normandy and Picardy, recalls St. Front, the legendary first bishop of Périgueux. Such names in Dam- or Dom- occur mainly in northern and eastern France, and seem to have been formed in the early Middle Ages, being superseded by the form "Saint X." Hundreds of French places have names of this later type, from St.-Aaron (Côtes-du-Nord) to St.-Zacharie (Var), with some of high frequency, such as St.-André, St.-Denis,

[55] Dauzat and Rostaing, *Dictionnaire étymologique des noms de lieux en France*, p. 630: *ecclesia sancti Torpetis*.

[56] "A dozen wills mention a church by location alone for every will that refers to its dedication": Orme, *English Church Dedications*, p. 29.

[57] Zimmermann, "Patrozinienwahl und Frömmigkeitswandel im Mittelalter," 20, pp. 56–57.

[58] *Villa Domni Petri*; for this and the following, Dauzat and Rostaing, *Dictionnaire étymologique des noms de lieux en France*, pp. 237–39, 249, 449–50, 582–638.

St.-Etienne, St.-Georges, St.-Jean, St.-Laurent, St.-Martin, and St.-Pierre (male saints are more common in place names than female saints).

Even though it appears that most people identified their local church by the place it was situated rather than by its patronal saint, the saint might distinguish a place from other locations with the same name. The saint's name could be used as a distinguishing suffix, applied especially to place names that were common and otherwise hard to distinguish. Thus the French name Le Mesnil, which means "peasant house and holding" and understandably occurs quite frequently, is differentiated by such forms as Le Mesnil-St.-Denis, Le Mesnil-St.-Firmin, Le Mesnil-St.-Georges, and so on. Occasionally, by a curious process of accretion, such suffixes could even be applied to places which already drew their names from saints: in the Haut-Sâone there are two villages called Dampvalley after St. Valley (Valerius), distinguished by the suffixes Dampvalley-lès-Colombe ("with the dovecots") and Dampvalley-St.-Pancras. In this last case, where the name literally means "St. Valley St. Pancras," the suffix St.-Pancras" indicates the dedication of the nearby priory that owned the village. In England, just as in France, dedications were used to differentiate places with the same name, as, for instance, in the case of Hinton St. Mary and Hinton St. George in south-west England, about twenty miles apart and both bearing a common name, Hinton, meaning "high township." Hinton St. George is first recorded with the distinguishing suffix in 1246, and its parish church is indeed dedicated to St. George, while Hinton St. Mary seems to be so called because it belonged to St. Mary's Shaftesbury.[59] A very curious case of a saintly suffix, where the original meaning of the place name as a saint's name was so deeply forgotten that the saint was added to it again, occurs in the settlement in Lugo in Galicia called San Jorge de Santiorjo, which is equivalent to "St. George of St. George."[60]

Apart from the form "Lord X" or "St. X," there are other types of place name that contain a saint's name. Boston, meaning "Botolph's stone," takes its name from the early Anglo-Saxon saint, Botolph or Botwulf, and the "stone" may be a reference to a stone church founded by or dedicated to him.[61] The English word "stow" has, alongside more general meanings, the sense of "holy place," and is often found followed by a saint's name, as in Bridestowe (Devon), Edwinstowe (Nottinghamshire), and Felixstowe (Suffolk), commemorating the holy places dedicated to St. Brigid, St. Edwin and St. Felix respectively.[62] The English referred to the great French monastery of Fleury, where the bones of St. Benedict supposedly lay, as "Saint Benedict's stow."[63] And there are place names that point only to the saints generally, rather than to specific individuals. The Irish places Skreen in County Meath and Skreen in

[59] *Close Rolls of the Reign of Henry III 1242–1247*, p. 480; "Hynton Mare" occurs in a grant of 1545: *Letters and Papers, Foreign and Domestic, of the Reign of Henry VIII* 20/1, no. 465 (17), p. 210.

[60] López Santos, *Influjo de la vida cristiana en los nombres de pueblos españoles*, p. 50.

[61] Ekwall, *The Concise Oxford Dictionary of Place Names*, p. 54.

[62] Ibid., pp. 64, 161, 177 and, on "Stow" as an element, 448.

[63] Ælfric, *Lives of Saints* 2, p. 314 (no. 32).

County Sligo both derive their names from the Irish scrín, meaning "shrine."[64] The name Mechtern on the outskirts of Cologne developed from "by the martyrs" (*ad martyres*).[65]

If there is good early evidence, it is possible to see the name of a settlement before it was influenced by the local patron saint. Thus, in the region of the eastern Pyrenees, *Acuciano* (attested in 872 and derived from a Roman personal name) became Sant Esteve (St. Stephen) by 988; *Pla de Corts* (976) was elaborated into Sant Joan Pla de Corts by 1189; *Lotas* (840, "muddy place") into Sant Miquel de Llotes by 1395; and, most ominously, a place called simply "The Gallows" in the ninth century is now Sant Pere dels Forcats (*furcae* is the Latin for gallows, *forca* the modern Catalan).[66]

The emergence of a place name derived from a saint is traceable in detail in the case of Bury St. Edmunds in East Anglia. It takes its name from the Anglo-Saxon king murdered by Vikings in 869. According to the earliest account of his life and death, written over a century later, Edmund's relics were eventually translated to a wooden church in Bedric's worth (*Beadericesworth*), this name meaning "Bedric's *worth* or homestead," and this place name is confirmed by a royal charter of 945, which was issued for "the monastery which is sited in the place called 'at Bedric's *worth*.'"[67] A will from the period 962–91 makes a grant "to St. Edmund's sanctuary at Bedric's *worth*."[68] But by 1022–34 land granted to the abbey can be simply donated "to St. Edmundsbury."[69] In Domesday Book (1087) the abbey's estates are described as "the land of St. Edmund" and the saint is recorded as the tenant: "St. Edmund holds Saxham," "St. Edmund holds Somerton," "St. Edmund has full jurisdiction," and so on. The town of Bury St. Edmunds is described in the following phrase: "the town where lies buried the king and glorious martyr St. Edmund."[70] The name Bedricsworth eventually disappeared from view, eclipsed by the fact that the settlement was now the home of an important saint.

Saintly naming showed regional patterns, both in the selection of saints and in the style of naming. Thus the saints of Merovingian Aquitaine (about fifty in

[64] Bourke, ed., *Studies in the Cult of Saint Columba*, p. 139.

[65] The etymology is recorded as early as the tenth century: Monstratur autem usque hodie in loco, ubi sanctus Gereon trucidatus est, sanguinis ipsius spectaculum et ipse locus, Ad Martyres, ab incolis acceptum servat vocabulum: *Passio Gereonis* 1. 14, p. 38.

[66] Guiter, "Eglises et toponymie sur les Pyrénées Orientales," pp. 14–15; the modern French names are St.-Estève, St.-Jean-Pla-de-Corts, St.-Michel-de-Llotes and St.-Pierre-dels-Forcats; all are in the Pyrénées-Orientales.

[67] Abbo of Fleury, *Passio sancti Eadmundi* 13, p. 82; *aet Baederices wired*: Sawyer, *Anglo-Saxon Charters*, no. 507.

[68] *Into sanctæ Eadmundes stowe to Bydericeswyrthe*: Sawyer, *Anglo-Saxon Charters*, no. 1494.

[69] *Into seynt Eadmundes biri*: ibid., no. 1537.

[70] *Domesday Book* 2, fols. 356–72.

number) had places named after them, but virtually all were within the boundaries of Aquitaine.[71] The Celtic lands showed a particularly distinctive pattern, with a variety of place name elements linked to the saints and a very high number of purely local saints. In the Brittonic areas, such as Brittany, Cornwall, and Wales, place names beginning with Lan- or Llan- usually indicate a church dedicated to, or associated with, a particular saint. In Cornwall, a quarter of the parish churches have (or had) names with the element *lann*, many of them compounded with the name of a saint, such as Landewednack, "church of St. Winwaloe," or Lanhydrock, "church of St. Hydroc," although sometimes the modern name has reverted to the more usual English form: the place recorded as Langoron in 1201 is now St. Goran.[72] In Wales the form is usually Llan-, so Llanbadarn means "the church of St. Padarn," Llanilltud "the church of St. Illtud," and so on. There is also the Welsh place name element *merthyr*, which comes from the Latin *martyres* or *martyrium*, signifying a place with relics (not necessarily of a martyr). Merthyr Tydfil in south Wales, for instance, means "the place with relics of St. Tudful."[73] In the Gaelic areas, the first element Kil- is common in these types of name: Kilbride is "the church of St. Brigid," Kilpatrick "the church of St. Patrick." Brigid and Patrick are well-known saints, but what is especially noteworthy about most of these Celtic saints is that they are so numerous and so limited in the extent of their cult.

Saints thus left an imprint on place names. Oddly enough, the reverse process sometimes occurred, for, in a few extraordinary cases, entirely imaginary "saints" were generated by place names. In the Pyrenees, the Roman landlord Quinterenus imprinted his name on his estate, Quinterenacu ("Quinterenus's place"), which, by a process of phonetic change, had become Centernaco by the ninth century. Since the initial "C" was soft, the development into Sent Arnach (attested in 1319) is understandable, as is the natural assumption that there must be a Saint Arnach after whom the place is named.[74] The name of the little settlement Santa Leciña in Aragon suggests a female saint, Leciña, but in fact derives from the Latin for "forest pasture with holm oaks (*saltus* + *ilicina*)."[75] In Cornwall, the place name Kenwyn, probably meaning "White Ridge," had, by the fourteenth century, stimulated the birth of a St. Kenwyn, venerated as the patron of the local church.[76]

[71] Higounet, "Les saints mérovingiens d'Aquitaine dans la toponymie."

[72] Padel, "Local Saints and Place-Names in Cornwall," p. 307: Orme, *English Church Dedications*, pp. 92, 93, 84.

[73] Sharpe, "Martyrs and Local Saints in Late Antique Britain," pp. 141–44.

[74] Guiter, "Eglises et toponymie sur les Pyrénées Orientales," p. 16; the French name is St.-Arnac (Pyrénées-Orientales).

[75] López Santos, *Influjo de la vida cristiana en los nombres de pueblos españoles*, p. 75.

[76] Orme, *English Church Dedications*, pp. 40, 89–90; Bach, *Deutsche Namenkunde* 2/2, p. 541, for comparable German examples.

Personal Names

At the canonization hearings into Werner of Bacharach in 1428–29, one of the witnesses said that his grandfather, uncle, cousin, and brother had all been named Werner "in honour of that saint."[77] The cult of the saints left a deep mark on the practice of the naming of people.[78] This was something that developed over time. The first Christians simply bore the names that were common in their own societies—mainly Hebrew, like John and Matthew, or Greek, like Timothy. As the religion spread, one finds Christians with Syriac names, Latin names, Coptic names, and so on. There seems to have been no unwillingness to perpetuate names which contained references to the pagan gods, so there are early Christians called Dionysius (from the god Dionysus), Apollinaris (from Apollo), and Isidore (from Isis). A neutral common ground could be found in the generic "god" names: Theodore meant "gift of god" but did not specify which one.

Eventually, explicitly Christian names appeared. Although many names which can be labelled "Christian" in late antiquity relate not to individual saints but to general theological beliefs, such as Anastasius and Anastasia (from the Greek for "resurrection") or Athanasius ("deathless"), the naming of children after the saints was also a Christian practice even before the time of Constantine. Dionysius, bishop of Alexandria (c. 247–64), although himself having a pagan name, provides one of the earliest observations on the practice:

> I consider that there have been many people with the same name as John the apostle, who, because of the love, admiration and esteem they had for him, and wishing to be loved by the Lord like him, were glad to bear the same name, just as many children of believers are named Paul and Peter.[79]

The popularity of these apostolic names, John, Peter, and Paul, was to be one of the most enduring, and ever strengthening, features of Christian naming practice.

Bishop Dionysius explains the adoption of the names of the apostles by the love and admiration that believers have for them, but also hints that there might be some benefit from bearing those names—"wishing to be loved by the Lord like him." This idea, that a good choice of name could bring divine favour, was developed further. The Syrian bishop Theodoret of Cyrrhus, writing in the first half of the fourth century, noted that it was customary to give children the names of martyrs, "thus assuring them of a firm protection."[80] Some decades later, in the 390s, John Chrysostom urged believers to abandon the practice of giving their children the names of family members but instead to name them after "the just, the martyrs, the bishops, the apostles." "Call them Peter," he urged, "call them John, call them after some other saint."

[77] *Processus Bacheracensis de vita, martyrio et miraculis beati Wernheri* 5. 41, p. 725.
[78] Mitterauer, *Ahnen und Heilige.*
[79] Eusebius, *Historia ecclesiastica* 7. 25. 14 (2, p. 207).
[80] Theodoret of Cyrrhus, *Graecorum affectionum curatio* 8. 67 (2, p. 334).

To give preference to saints over ancestors in this way would be "a great help for us and our children."[81] To name a child after a saint created a permanent special bond between them. It was a long-lasting custom. A thousand years later, at the end of the fifteenth century, the Scottish theologian John Ireland advised believers to seek out as intercessors "the soul of Jesus, the blessed mother of God . . . thy good angel, the saint that thou art named after."[82]

Sometimes the choice of a saint's name is explained. One motive was acknowledgment of help in conceiving the child in the first place. George, the author of the *Life of Theodore of Sykeon*, was born after Theodore had blessed his parents, and Theodore himself named the boy George, giving him the name of the saint to whom he had a special devotion; subsequently George's parents had another son, whom, this time, they named after their benefactor, Theodore.[83] St. Nicholas of Tolentino was born after his parents had prayed to St. Nicholas of Bari, who told them in a vision, "a son will be born to you and will be called Nicholas, so that he, who is to be born into the world by my help, should bear my name."[84] The Princess of Galilee, living in Cyprus after the fall of the crusader states, was childless for the first fourteen years of her marriage, but then, hearing of the miracles of St. Peter Martyr, "poured out prayers to him, promising, that if he obtained a son for her from the Lord, she would give him his name." So it turned out.[85] Or the promise might be made at a later and more desperate stage, during a difficult childbirth, as in the case of a woman of Cividale, who had always mocked the local devotion to St. Benevenuta, but, encouraged by a pious widow, now invoked her:

> O blessed virgin Benevenuta, pay no attention to my faults but, considering all the grace that God gave you in this life, help me in my need, and, if you free me through your merits, I will always be especially devoted to you and bring a candle to your tomb to burn there in your honour and I will name the creature I bring forth with your name.[86]

There might be more than one motive for choosing a name. In 1240 a daughter was born to the king and queen of England, who was named Margaret, the first in the royal family to be so called. The contemporary chronicler, Matthew Paris, suggests two reasons for the choice: "Queen Eleanor brought forth a daughter for the king. She was given the name Margaret, which is the name of her aunt, that is, the queen of France, and because in the labours of childbirth she invoked St. Margaret."[87] By her choice of name, queen Eleanor could give both her sister and the helpful saint a

[81] John Chrysostom, *De inani gloria* 47–50, pp. 144–48.

[82] John Ireland, "Of Penance and Confession," p. 47 (spelling modernized).

[83] *Vita Theodori Syceotae* 170, p. 160.

[84] *Il processo per la canonizzazione di S. Nicola da Tolentino*, p. 18.

[85] Ambrogio Taegio, *Vita sancti Petri martyris* 8. 63, pp. 705–6. This is probably the wife of Balian of Ibelin (d. 1316).

[86] *Vita devotissimæ Benevenutæ de Foro-Julii* 122, p. 183.

[87] Matthew Paris, *Chronica majora* 4, p. 48.

compliment. Similarly multiple motives can be found in the account written in Florence in 1443 by a father of his newborn child, Peter John:

> He was baptized on 28 March and given the name Peter in honour of St. Peter Martyr, to whom my wife had made a vow to give his name . . . the second name I had given to him, John, is in honour of St. John the Evangelist, because of the devotion I bear him, but also to bring back in a sense John our brother.[88]

Here we find a vow to an Italian Dominican saint, a special devotion to John the Evangelist (patron saint of Florence) and the memorialization of a deceased uncle, not to mention the novel habit of bearing two forenames, just beginning here in northern Italy in the late Middle Ages and otherwise very rare in the medieval period.

The way a saint's name could spread, and the tensions sometimes involved, are illustrated by a few stories from the posthumous Miracles of St. Francis. In one instance a judge's wife from Tivoli had given birth to six daughters but no son. "Unwilling to persist in tillage whose fruit was so displeasing," she separated from her husband. Eventually her confessor prevailed upon her to try again: "she should beg a son from St. Francis, to whom she would give the name of Francis." The woman then gave birth to twin boys, Francis and Blaise (the choice of this second name is not explained). Another story concerns a man called Matthew of Tolentino, who had named his daughter Francisca but, annoyed that the friars had moved their convent from the town, renamed her with the female form of his own name, Matthaea. The girl fell ill to the point of death and was only restored to health when her father gave her back her original name. On another occasion a woman from Pisa wanted to call her son Francis after the saint, but her mother-in-law scoffed at this name "as if it were for peasants" and wanted the child to be called Henry after a relative. Again, the child became desperately ill and recovered only when "adorned with the name of Francis."[89]

Francis, in fact, provides the ideal case study for the diffusion of a saint's name, since, although the saint was not the first person to bear this name, it was rare before his time, and it is highly likely that people called Francis in the thirteenth century and later are named after him.[90] Francis was canonized in 1228, and it is possible to trace the spread of his name in the following generations. In Monselice, south of Padua, there was not a single person called Francis in 1250, but there were 17 in 1300, when it was the seventh most common male name.[91] Elsewhere it seems to have been the fourteenth century that saw his name become widespread. Lists from the town of Salon in south-west Provence show no man called Francis in 1304 but seven with this name in 1354, while the name became one of the most popular in

[88] Klapisch–Zuber, "Le nom 'refait,' " p. 83.

[89] Thomas of Celano, *Tractatus de miraculis beati Francisci* 12. 99, 104–5, pp. 306, 308.

[90] For discussion of the name before the impact of the saint, Bihl, "De nomine S. Francisci."

[91] Rippe, "L'onomastique dans la Vénétie du XIII siècle," pp. 274, 276, 283.

the Tuscan countryside between 1300 and 1371.[92] Amongst candidates for office in Florence in the period 1450–1500 it is the most common name.[93] A curious case of the name "piggy-backing" occurred at the end of the Middle Ages, when a child born at Paola in southern Italy, after his parents had prayed to St. Francis, was called Francis in his honour; this child himself grew up to be a saint (St. Francis of Paola, canonized in 1519) and was much revered by the French royal family. In 1518 the French queen prayed to St. Francis of Paola for a male child and "a very beautiful one" was born; she christened the baby Francis in honour of the saint (although the fact that she was the wife of Francis I might also have been relevant). A child named in honour of a saint who was named in honour of a saint shows how naming trends could ramify.[94]

In the Gaelic world a particular form of naming developed, in which the term "Mael" or "Gille" was prefixed to the saint's name. "Gille" means "servant" (as in the modern term "gillie" for an attendant on a Highland shoot), and "Mael" means "cropped one," that is, someone who has been shorn to indicate dedication to the saint as master. So Gilla Phátraic means "servant of St. Patrick" and Máel Coluim "cropped one of St. Columba": they correspond to the modern surname Gilpatrick and the modern forename Malcolm. Four Scottish kings of the tenth, eleventh, and twelfth centuries bore the name Malcolm. The counterpart to "Gille" and "Mael" in the Brittonic speaking regions was *gwas* or *gos* ("vassal"), which is found prefixed to saints of various origins, not only British (Gwas-Dewi, Gwas-Cadoc) but also Gaelic (Gwas-Patric, that is, Gospatrick) and English (Gwas-Cuthbert).[95] The charters of William the Lion, king of Scots (1165–1214), mention men called Gilchrist, Gillandreas, Gillebride ("servant of Brigid"), Gillecolm (an equivalent of Malcolm), Gillemichel, Gillemor ("servant of Mary"), Gillepatric; Malcolm, Malise ("cropped one of Jesus"), Malmur, Malpatric; as well as Gospatrick or Cospatrick, which was the preferred name in the line of the earls of Dunbar.[96] Names of this "Gille" and "Mael" type are a rough equivalent of the ancient Greek and Roman names formed from the name of a pagan god, such as Dionysius ("follower of Dionysus"), Apollinaris ("follower of Apollo"), but did not develop other than in the Celtic world. There are occasional references to people in other regions who have been dubbed "man and little slave of St. Dunstan" or "man of St. Æbbe" because of their special relationship with the saint, but these are nicknames rather then baptismal or given names.[97]

[92] Rutkowska-Plachcinska, "Les prénoms bourgeois dans le sud de France," pp. 10–11; Ronciére, "Orientations pastorales du clergé, fin XIIe–XIVe siècle: le témoinage de l'onomastique toscane," pp. 61–62.

[93] Herlihy, "Tuscan Names, 1200–1530," p. 575.

[94] *Libellus de vita et miraculis sancti Francisci de Paula* 1. 2, p. 107; *Sancti Francisci Paulani canonizatio*, p. 217; the Dauphin Francis died in 1536, before his father, so never became king.

[95] Edmonds, "Personal Names and the Cult of Patrick in Eleventh-century Strathclyde and Northumbria," esp. 42–51.

[96] *Acts of William I, King of Scots, 1165–1214*, index, snn.

[97] *Vita et miracula sancte Ebbe virginis*, p. 26; Osbern of Canterbury, *Vita et miracula sancti Dunstani*, miracula 9, p. 135.

A child might be named for the saint on whose day it was born, as Thomas Aquinas noted.[98] One Bohemian chronicler of the later Middle Ages indeed claimed that this was an old general practice among the Czechs: "they gave to their children the names of the saints on whose days they were born into this world."[99] Even if this were not the case, individuals might still feel a sense of association with the saints who shared their name. Some late Byzantine authors wrote Lives of their name saint.[100] In the West, in the late Middle Ages, wealthy patrons commissioned paintings in which they are shown under the protection of a name-saint. An altarpiece painted by Hans Memling for the merchant prince Willem Moreel and his wife Barbara, shows them kneeling before St. William and St. Barbara.[101] Anne of Brittany, queen of France (d. 1514), is depicted in her Book of Hours in prayer with female saints behind her, including St. Anne.[102] Since the queen was not born on St. Anne's day, the link is through the name, not the date.

Another link between saint and namesake, even if the child had not been named for the saint on whose day it was born, could be a special feeling for the saint's day. Today many Catholic and Orthodox Christians (and even some Protestants) celebrate a "name day," that is, the feast-day of the saint whose name they bear. It is not easy to find evidence of this custom before the sixteenth century. However, an isolated instance that seems to indicate a particular concern for the name day can be found in the case of Anne of Bohemia, queen of Richard II of England, who, it was noted, "had a special devotion to St. Anne because she herself was called Anne."[103] A monastic chronicler recording her death in 1394 claims (wrongly) that she was buried on St. Anne's day, and comments, "this queen had petitioned the pope that her (St. Anne's) feast-day should be celebrated more solemnly in the English church."[104] Although the chronicler is wrong about the day of her burial, he might be right about

[98] Thomas Aquinas, *Summa Theologiae* III q. 37 a. 2 co. (52, p. 146).

[99] Peter of Zittau, *Chronicon Aulae Regiae* 6, p. 12.

[100] Talbot, "Old Wine in New Bottles," p. 25; Frazier, *Possible Lives: Authors and Saints in Renaissance Italy*, p. 36.

[101] Now in the Groeninge Museum, Bruges. Most commentators on the painting describe the saint behind Willem Morel as "St. William of Maleval," see for example Corti, *L'opera completa di Memling*, table XVIII; Vos, *Hans Memling: The Complete Works*, p. 238, no. 63. There is considerable confusion about this figure, who seems to be a blend of William de Gellone, William, duke of Aquitaine, and William, founder of the Gugliemites, but the identification of the saint depicted by Memling as *a* St. William is rendered certain by the very similar iconography in a depiction of a saint explicitly identified as "St. William" in a contemporary Netherlandish manuscript: BL, Harley 3828, fols. 19v (miniature), 20 (invocation of "beati Willermi confessoris"). The miniature is reproduced in Rudy, "An Illustrated Mid-Fifteenth-Century Primer," p. 87, fig. 22. The same iconography appears in the saint on the banner of the armourers' guild in fifteenth-century Ghent, reproduced in BS 7, cols. 469–70, and there identified as William de Gellone (cf. BS 7, cols. 467–70, 479–80).

[102] BnF, lat. 9474, fol. 3; reproduced in *Kings, Queens and Courtiers: Art in Early Renaissance France*, fig. 38, p. 101.

[103] Knighton, *Chronicon*, p. 548.

[104] *Historia vitae et regni Ricardi secondi*, p. 134; for the actual date of her burial see *The Westminster Chronicle 1381–1394*, p. 520 and n.

her request to the pope, since there is another piece of evidence that could well relate to this. In the summer of 1381 Pope Urban VI wrote to the English bishops, explaining that recently some English petitioners had informed the pope that the people of England had a special devotion to St. Anne, and had asked him to command that the English bishops and people should celebrate her feast-day "solemnly and devoutly." Urban was happy to agree, and instructed the bishops to celebrate the feast and command their flocks to do so also. This letter was then incorporated in a mandate of William de Courtenay, archbishop of Canterbury, commanding the bishops subject to him to celebrate the feast.[105] It is probably significant that the pope's letter was written at exactly the time that the negotiations for the match between King Richard and Anne of Bohemia were being concluded. Urban himself had a strong interest in creating ties between the English crown and Anne's family, since they were both amongst his leading supporters against the rival pope in Avignon, and it is not impossible that the elevation of the feast of the bride's name-saint was a ritual courtesy associated with the more practical negotiations about dowries and alliances. Archbishop Courtenay himself officiated at queen Anne's coronation in January 1382.

The saints also sometimes had a part to play when an individual adopted a new name. The later seventh century saw several cases of the adoption of new or additional names of a Christian and Roman nature by leading Anglo-Saxons. The West Saxon king Caedwalla went to Rome in 689, was baptized by the pope, and received the name Peter. He died only ten days later and was buried in St. Peter's, close to the saint whose name he had been given.[106] Willibrord, the Anglo-Saxon missionary to the Frisians, was ordained bishop by the pope, and simultaneously given the name Clement, on St. Clement's eve 695. In a passage written in his own hand, he calls himself "Clement Willibrord."[107] The English singing master brought from Kent to Northumbria by bishop Wilfrid in the later seventh century was "Aeddi, with the second name Stephen."[108] In these three instances, the added name is that of a Christian martyr, and in at least two of them it marked a change of religious status (baptism, ordination).

Although it was by no means a universal practice, there are examples of the custom of adopting a new name when making profession as a monk. After the Byzantine emperor Michael I was deposed in 813, he and his two sons became monks, changing their names from Michael, Nicetas, and Theophylact to Athanasius, Igna-

[105] *Concilia magnae Britanniae et Hiberniae* 3, p. 178, printed from Courtenay's Register in Lambeth Palace Library, fol. 38. Courtenay's letter is dated 18 May 1383, so almost two years after Urban's, but he had only succeeded to the archbishopric (on the murder of his predecessor) on 30 July 1381 and received the pallium in May 1382. Urban's letter is dated to June "in the fourth year of our pontificate," and, since he was elected and enthroned in April 1378, this must be 1381. The date is given variously: Pfaff, *New Liturgical Feasts in Later Medieval England*, p. 2; Saul, *Richard II*, p. 324; Scase, "St. Anne and the Education of the Virgin," p. 83.

[106] Bede, *Historia ecclesiastica* 5. 7, pp. 468–72.

[107] *The Calendar of St Willibrord*, p. 13; Bede, *Historia ecclesiastica* 5. 11, p. 486.

[108] Ibid., 4. 2, p. 334.

tius, and Eustratius.[109] St. Cyril the Phileote (d. 1110) had been called Cyriacus before he became a monk, and his brother Michael adopted the name Matthew when he entered the monastic life.[110] In these cases the significance of the new names is not clear, but sometimes the new name was certainly that of a saint. Bartholomew of Farne, a twelfth-century hermit-saint, was given the name Bartholomew, replacing his earlier secular name, when he entered a monastery, "so that he should be a co-inheritor in heaven of him whose name he shared on earth."[111] As is made explicit from this wording, he was being given the same name as St. Bartholomew the apostle. A slightly later contemporary, named Henry, became Augustine when he entered the Augustinian Order, hence presumably taking the name of the fifth-century saint who had given his name to the Order.[112]

Although it is sometimes said that the first pope to adopt a new name on election was John II (533–35), who had previously been called Mercurius (an unmistakably pagan name, derived from the god Mercury), both the *Liber pontificalis* and the evidence of inscriptions make it clear that Mercurius was in fact his second or surname (*cognomen*): both before and after election he was John Mercurius.[113] The custom of popes assuming a new name at election begins only in the tenth century. Thereafter it is standard. Often this meant Germanic names being replaced with Latin ones, as in the case of Bruno of Egisheim who became Leo IX, or Lothario da Segni who became Innocent III, but even those with impeccable biblical or Latinate names adopted new ones on their election: James Pantaleon became Urban IV, Benedict Caetani became Boniface VIII, Bartholomew Prignano became Urban VI. Papal names were chosen from a restricted repertoire: the seventy-nine popes and antipopes between 1000 and 1400 had a total of only twenty-six different names, some of them, like Benedict, Clement, Gregory, and Innocent, being held by six or more bearers. It may be that the holders associated these names with the saints who bore them, but it is more likely that they looked back to earlier papal incumbents.

Sometimes one can identify a tension, or a hesitation, between a saint's name and a significant family name. According to the *Heimskringla*, the son of king Olof of Sweden (d. 1022), born on the eve of St. James's day, was baptized James, but the Swedish nobles insisted he take instead the ancient royal name of Anund, which was

[109] Pratsch, *Der hagiographische Topos*, pp. 126–27 ("Namensänderungen"), with other examples; *Prosopographie der mittelbyzantinischen Zeit* 1, nos. 2666, 4989, 8336, for sources.

[110] Nicholas Kataskepenos, *Vita Cyrilli Phileotis* 21. 1, 22. 2, pp. 104, 107. De Meester, *De monachico statu iuxta disciplinam Byzantinam*, p. 374, asserts that, as in these cases, newly professed monks often took a new name beginning with the same letter as their former one, as does the *Oxford Dictionary of Byzantium* 2, p. 1436, s.v. "names"; another example would be Abraham, who became Athanasius, founder of Athonite monasticism in the tenth century: Athanasius of Panagiou, *Vita prima Athanasii Athonitae* 23, p. 13.

[111] Geoffrey of Durham, *Vita Bartholomaei Farnensis* 3, p. 296.

[112] Innocent III, *Selected Letters of Pope Innocent III Concerning England*, no. 27, p. 83 (*Epistola* 9. 136).

[113] *Liber pontificalis* 1, p. 285: Iohannes qui et Mercurius; ibid., n. 1: papa N Iohanne cognomento Mercurio.

the name he ruled under.[114] In a very similar way, the son of Alfonso I of Portugal, who was born on St. Martin's day (11 November), 1154, "was, on that account, given the baptismal name Martin; later he was called Sancho." He did indeed succeed his father as Sancho I (1185–1211), taking a name important in his illustrious grandmother's dynasty rather than that of the great saint.[115]

One of the most interesting developments in the study of saints and names in the late twentieth century has been the detailed exploration of the way that saints' names became more common in the later Middle Ages, displacing to some extent the earlier local vernacular name repertoires.[116] The names of biblical saints, like John, James, Peter and Mary, and the great universal martyr-saints, like Catherine and Margaret, as well as a select few of the confessors, such as Antony and Nicholas, came to predominate. Alongside this change, went two other developments: the reduction in the variety of names used and the adoption of hereditary family surnames. These processes were not uniform, but they were clear, and sometimes fairly dramatic, producing a European naming pattern in 1500 radically different from that of 1100.

A chronicler in Genoa noticed the rise of saints' names amongst the ruling class of his city. Writing at the very beginning of the fifteenth century, he observed, "The custom of men's names has changed for the better, for if you look at what the ancient leaders were called, you find the name of scarcely any saint."[117] His perception was entirely accurate. A study comparing three lists of Genoese male citizens in the mid-twelfth, mid-thirteenth, and mid-fourteenth centuries shows the eclipse of the Germanic names that predominate in the first list (the most common names then are William, borne by 15.7 per cent of the citizens, Obert 4.8 per cent, Ansald by 4.1 per cent) and the rise of the names of the universal saints (in the latest list the most common names are John, borne by 9.7 per cent, Antony 8.6 per cent, and Nicholas 8.2 per cent).[118]

The change can be seen among the ruling dynasties, even though they were traditional and conservative in their name choices, since their claims resided in their ancestry. In most parts of western Europe in the early Middle Ages kings bore Germanic names, part of the heritage of the barbarian conquests of the fourth and fifth centuries. Rulers of the Franks, Anglo-Saxons, Lombards, and Christian Spaniards held to the ancestral name-hoard, whatever phonological mutations it might undergo (Chlodowech became Louis and Ludwig, Adalfuns became Alfonso). But in

[114]Snorri Sturluson, *Heimskringla*, "Saint Olav's Saga," 88, 94, pp. 332, 348.

[115]*Annales domni Alfonsi Portugallensium regis*, p. 158; for discussion see Thoma, *Namensänderungen in Herrscherfamilien des mittelalterlichen Europa*, pp. 121–22.

[116]See the studies published under the general title *Genèse médiévale de l'anthroponymie moderne*; Littger, *Studien zum Auftreten der Heiligennamen im Rheinland*; Mitterauer, *Ahnen und Heilige*, chapter 7; Martínez Sopena, ed., *Antroponimia y sociedad: sistemas de identificación hispano-cristianos en los siglos IX a XIII* (16 statistical regional studies showing the rise of the two-part name, that is, baptismal name and patronymic); Wilson, *The Means of Naming: A Social and Cultural History of Personal Naming in Western Europe*, chapter 6; summary comment in Bartlett, *The Making of Europe*, pp. 270–80.

[117]Stella, *Annales Genuenses*, p. 57.

[118]Kedar, "Noms de saints et mentalité populaire à Gênes," p. 433.

the course of the eleventh and twelfth centuries, new, non-Germanic names slowly made their appearance amongst these royal dynasties. The first king of France to bear such a name was Philip I, born 1052; the first king of England Stephen, born around 1092; the first king of Germany Philip of Swabia, born 1177. It is not a simple task to interpret the meaning of the choice of these new names. Philip was an apostle, but also the father of Alexander the Great. The mother of Philip I of France was a Russian princess who bore the name Anna, a biblical name not common in the West at this time, and perhaps this is relevant to the choice of a name for her son. Stephen of England was the son of Stephen-Henry, count of Blois, who had been christened Henry but taken the supplementary name Stephen, perhaps after his deceased uncle, the first in the dynasty to bear a non-Germanic name.[119] Such doublets of a traditional noble Germanic name and a Christian name were not unknown amongst the nobles of France and Lorraine at this time.[120]

A classic example of the slow spread of biblical names is the rise of the name "John." In origin a Hebrew name, it was borne by two of the most important biblical saints, John the Baptist and John the Evangelist, the reputed author of both the fourth Gospel and the Book of Revelation. St. John's day (24 June) was the old summer solstice, and was celebrated as Midsummer with memorable rituals and bonfires. Crucifixion scenes showed John the Evangelist alongside the Virgin Mary at the foot of the cross. The name John was not unknown in the early Middle Ages, but its geographical scope was limited. In western Europe there was a distinction between the Germanic names of the north and east and the Latin/Romance names of the south and west, complicated though this was by the presence of ruling dynasties of Germanic origin in Spain and Italy (and hence such Germanic names as Ferdinand in Spain).[121] The name John was taken up in the Latin region far earlier than in the Germanic. In Mediterranean Europe, John was a familiar name from late antiquity onwards. It was, for example, the most common papal name in the early Middle Ages, when, as mentioned, popes did not change their given names (the first bearer John I held office 523–26), and it was extremely common in the Byzantine Empire. Of the seventy-eight men who are mentioned in Procopius's *Secret History* of the mid-sixth century, ten (12.8 per cent) bear the name John, while in eleventh-century Byzantine sources it is by far the most popular name.[122] In general, the Byzantine name repertoire was marked by an earlier and more extensive imprint of biblical and saintly names, as table 11.1 shows.

The situation in non-Mediterranean Europe is quite different. Here, while the name John is not unknown in the early Middle Ages, it is rare. There are a handful of cases from Anglo-Saxon England (the only well known bearer is St. John of Beverley, bishop of York, who died in 721), and there are not many more from the Frankish

[119] LoPrete, *Adela of Blois*, p. 42 and n. 84.

[120] Parisse, "La conscience chrétienne des nobles aux XIe et XIIe siècles," pp. 261–63.

[121] On which, see Piel and Kremer, *Hispano-gotisches Namenbuch*.

[122] Patlagean, "Les débuts d'une aristocratie byzantine et le témoinage de l'historiographie: système des noms et liens de parenté aux IXe–Xe siècles," p. 25; Prosopography of the Byzantine World website.

TABLE 11.1
Most Common Byzantine Names, 1025–1102

John	929
Michael	534
Constantine	524
Leo	374
Basil	343
Theodore	342
Nicholas	329
George	305
Nicetas	228
Nikephoros	210
Stephen	156
Gregory	142
Peter	108
Demetrius	107
Mary	106

Source: Prosopography of the Byzantine World website: names with more than 100 instances.

realm.[123] Between the eleventh and the thirteenth centuries this all changed. The trend can be illustrated by the first appearance of a king named John: England 1199; Scotland 1292; France 1316; Castile 1379; Portugal 1385. And in the population as a whole the tendency was stronger. Between 1066 and 1207 the percentage of Winchester burgesses with biblical, Greek, or Latin names rises from 2.6 to 31.3, with John, which is not represented at all at the earlier date, making up 5 per cent of the total by the early thirteenth century.[124] Among a group of serfs freed in the Sens region of France in 1257, the names John, Stephen, and Peter predominated, borne by more than a quarter of the total.[125] By the later Middle Ages the distinction between Mediterranean and non-Mediterranean Europe had been eroded. In the year 1427 the most common name among male heads of household in Florence was John, comprising 8 per cent of the total.[126] Its predominance in Bavaria at this period was

[123] Prosopography of Anglo-Saxon England (PASE) database; Morlet, *Les noms de personne sur le territoire de l'ancienne Gaule* 2, pp. 65–66.

[124] Biddle, ed., *Winchester in the Early Middle Ages*, pp. 185, 187.

[125] Jordan, *From Servitude to Freedom: Manumission in the Sénonais*, pp. 92–96.

[126] Herlihy, "Tuscan Names, 1200–1530," p. 564.

even greater. More than a quarter of males there were Johannes or Hans, while biblical and saints' names had also conquered the repertoire of Bavarian female names: Anne was borne by 21 per cent, Margaret by 17 per cent, Barbara by 16 per cent, and Elizabeth by 15 per cent.[127] The story of the rise of the name "John" in western Europe can be paralleled by its female equivalent, Johanna or Joan.

The trend was general and widespread. In the county of Nice, the Germanic names that had predominated in the thirteenth century, such as William, Raymond, and Bertrand, ceded their place to Peter, John, and James by the fifteenth.[128] The most common names amongst the town councillors of Dresden in the fourteenth century were John (borne by over 30 per cent), Nicholas (almost 24 per cent), and Peter (more than 15 per cent), these three thus making up over two thirds of the total.[129] Lesser saints were not always completely eclipsed by the universal saints, but might keep their heads up to a degree. In the town of St.-Léonard-de-Noblat, 16 kilometres (10 miles) east of Limoges, and site of an important shrine to St. Leonard, over 40 per cent of males in the late fourteenth and early fifteenth century bore the names John or Peter, but a sizeable proportion (7.3 to 11.3 per cent at different times) were called Leonard, and this proportion actually rose to 15.2 per cent in the 1460s and 1470s, pushing Peter into third place.[130] Leonard's cult was quite widespread, in fact, and in its heartland the name was a common choice.

By the end of the Middle Ages, names like John, Peter, James, and Stephen for men, and Anne, Barbara, Catherine, and Margaret for women, that is, names of biblical saints or celebrated female martyrs, had ceased to be rare or regional and had become the common stock of Christian naming. Many women also bore feminized versions of male saints' names. The twenty-eight nuns of the nunnery of San Lorenzo of Panisperna in Rome in 1379 were named Agnes, Angela (two cases), Antonia, Augustina, Catherine, Clare, Constance, Francisca (two cases), Gemma, Isabella (three cases), Jacoba (two cases), Johanna, Laurencia, Leonarda, Lucia, Marmenia, Mathea, Pace, Paula, Philippa, Sabella, Thomassa, and Victoria.[131] This is an exemplary selection of saints' names, many of them biblical, with a dash of Franciscan preferences; almost half of them are female versions of male names.

The shift towards biblical and saints' names does not seem to have been part of a conscious policy on the part of the ecclesiastical authorities, although there are cases of higher clergy recommending these names, such as John Chrysostom, or Antoninus, archbishop of Florence (1446–59), who condemned the choice of "pagan names" such as Lancelot, or shortened forms or nonsense names: "care should be taken to impose the name of a male or female saint," he insisted.[132]

[127] Sargent, "Saints' Cults and Naming Patterns in Bavaria," p. 682.

[128] Compan, *Étude d'anthroponymie provençale* 1, pp. 327–28.

[129] Fleischer, "Die Namen der Dresdener Ratsmitglieder bis 1500."

[130] Perouas et al., *Léonard, Marie, Jean et les autres. Les prénoms en Limousin*, p. 56.

[131] *Acta et processus canonizacionis Beate Birgitte*, p. 31.

[132] Herlihy, "Tuscan Names, 1200–1530," p. 576, citing Antoninus, *Summa theologica* (Verona, 1740), 2, col. 645.

To give one's children the names of the saints was a way of expressing cultural identity. If the practice was abandoned, part of one's distinctive religious character was lost. This is clear from the so-called Apocalypse of Samuel of Kalamoun, a lament by an Egyptian Christian about the cultural impact of the Arab conquest on his country (the text has been dated to the eighth, ninth and tenth centuries). He bewails the loss of the Coptic language and also the replacement of the names of the native saints with Arabic names. He is dismayed by his fellow countrymen who "name their children after their [the Arabs'] names and abandon the names of the angels and prophets and apostles and martyrs."[133]

Needless to say, the naming pattern of Christian Europe in 1500 cannot be explained simply by the adoption of saints' names over the previous centuries. There are popular names like William, which are not associated with an important saint, while the fact that a name is in origin an imported saintly name, like John, might not have any necessary weight in its actual choice by an individual family—it might simply be a compliment to rich Uncle Hans. And the concentration of name choice into a much smaller repertoire of names, and the, surely connected, development of hereditary surnames, are not logically dependent on the rise of saints' names. Nevertheless, there had been a slow revolution in the name choices of the European population, a change that resulted in a deep imprint of the saints on their linguistic culture.

[133] Iskander, "Islamization in Medieval Egypt," p. 225.

CHAPTER 12

Images of the Saints

The Image in Early Christianity

The most easily perceptible heritage of the medieval cult of the saints is the vast body of images that have survived, from many periods and places, and in many media: frescoes, panel-paintings, manuscript illuminations, sculptures and carvings, woodcuts, and more. But this was not an original feature of the cult. Christianity arose in a world with sharply contrasting traditions about the representation of the divine. The tap-root of the new religion was Judaism, which had a strict prohibition against making "any graven image or any likeness of any thing that is in heaven above, or that is in the earth beneath, or that is in the water under the earth" (Exodus 20:4; Deuteronomy 5:8), and the Hebrew Bible records the history of the long struggle to keep Israel free of the contagion of idol-worship. But the Greek and Roman world, in which Christianity swam like a fish in the sea, had an exuberant tradition of making images and likenesses of all those things, including the gods themselves.

The Old Testament ban applied to two things: *pesel* and *temunah* in Hebrew. The words used in the standard Greek and Latin translations of the Bible are, for the first term, Greek *eidolon*, which means "image" or "idol," and Latin *sculptile*, "a carved or sculptured image," and, for the second, *homoioma* and *similitudo*, both meaning "likeness." A prohibition on creating idols or graven images is obviously less restrictive than a ban on making any likeness. Some early Christian exegetes suggested that *eidolon* referred to an image of a non-existent creature, such as the jackal-headed gods of Egyptian religion, while *homoioma* meant an image of a thing that does exist—sun and moon, men and animals.[1] The target of the Commandment was obviously idol-worship, but, taken literally, it could be read as a prohibition on any representational image.

Hostility to representational images can be more or less general: a complete ban; a ban solely on images of the deity or of prophetic founders like Muhammad; a ban on images (either of the deity or in general) only in places of worship; a ban solely on reverence being paid to images. The early Christian polemical onslaught on the

[1] Theodoret of Cyrrhus, *Quaestio in Exodum* 38, and Procopius of Gaza, *Epitome of Catena on the Octateuch*, ed. Thümmel, *Die Frühgeschichte der ostkirchlichen Bilderlehre*, pp. 316–17 (nos. 53–54), with German translation at p. 85.

cult of images of the pagan gods was fierce and unequivocal, but it left the question of whether a Christian religious image could be allowed. An explicit Christian statement on the illegitimacy of depicting the divine is found in the 320s or 330s in a letter written by Eusebius, one of the leading bishops of the Roman Empire, to Constantina (or Constantia), sister of Constantine the Great.[2] The imperial lady had requested a picture of Christ. The bishop was troubled. Constantina obviously could not be asking for a picture of God, but there were problems also with depicting Jesus Christ on earth. During the Transfiguration even his close disciples had been unable to bear the glory of his appearance. "Who," asked Eusebius, "could trace the shining, flashing splendours of such worth and glory in dead and soulless colours and lines?" He goes on to refer to the pagan practice of creating idols of the gods; Constantina surely understands "that such things are not right for us." A picture of Jesus contravenes the Ten Commandments. Has Constantina overlooked the passage in which God prohibits the making of any likeness (*homoioma*)? "Such things are banned and banished from churches throughout the world." Eusebius himself had confiscated paintings of Paul and Jesus.

But it was Constantina's impulses, not Eusebius's arguments, that were to triumph. Christian imagery can be found in a funerary context, in the Roman catacombs, from around the year 200, and the third century sees images in churches. Pictures of biblical scenes are to be found on the walls of the church at Dura Europos in Syria, the only known pre-Constantinian church, and if, in the early years of the fourth century, the Council of Elvira in southern Spain had to rule that "there ought not to be pictures in church, lest what is venerated and adored be painted on walls," then it is fairly certain that the same practice was in existence in that region.[3] Once Christian representational imagery had come into existence, it was only a short time before images of the saints were produced. Since the saints were not simply early heroes of Christianity but also active intercessors, these images focussed devotion rather than just being mimetic or memorial. One of the earliest references to the practice of making and revering images of the saints is found in the Apocryphal Acts of the apostle John, which date to the later second or third century. They contain a story in which one of John's devotees at Ephesus secretly commissions a portrait of the saint, which he then sets up in his bed-chamber, surrounded with garlands, lamps and altars. When John discovers this, he exhorts the man to paint with the colours of the virtues rather than waste time on this "dead image of the dead."[4] Thus, from this early period, there survives both a vivid description of private devotion to a saint's image and a critique of such a practice based on the greater importance of moral

[2] Eusebius, *Epistola ad Constantiam Augustam* (PG 20: 1545–49); also in *Die ikonoklastische Synode von Hiereia 754*, pp. 91–112 (by Annette von Stockhausen, with German tr.). The traditional attribution of the letter to Eusebius of Caesarea has been questioned but also convincingly defended: Gero, "The True Image of Christ: Eusebius' Letter to Constantia Reconsidered."

[3] Placuit picturas in ecclesia esse non debere ne quod colitur et adoratur in parietibus depingatur: *Concilios visigóticos e hispano–romanos*, p. 8 (cl. 36).

[4] *Acta Iohannis* 26–29 (1, pp. 177–81).

and spiritual values. Both the practice and the critique were to have a long history in Christianity.[5]

In the fourth century, with the official acceptance of Christianity, evidence multiplies for images of the saints, in the form both of individual paintings in private possession and of public images in church. The depiction of St. Paul confiscated by bishop Eusebius is an example, and he also reports that he had seen "images of the apostles Paul and Peter, and of Christ himself, preserved in coloured pictures."[6] Later in the fourth century images of Paul and Peter alongside Christ could be found "in many places."[7] The shrine of St. Theodore at Euchaïta in the Pontus c. 380 was decorated with paintings depicting "the brave deeds of the martyr," along with wooden carvings in the shape of living creatures and an image of "the human form of Christ."[8] By the 390s images of Jesus, the prophets and the apostles could be found on walls, hangings and mosaics in many churches.[9] At the end of the century the poet Prudentius refers to a painted depiction of the martyrdom of St. Cassian on or near his tomb. He was assured that "that image records the history which has been handed down in books."[10] There was an image of St. Martin in the baptistery at Sulpicius Severus's foundation at *Primuliacum* in southern Gaul.[11]

As is clear from Prudentius's remark, images of the saints in church brought home their stories to worshippers. In the 420s the shrine of St. Stephen at Uzalis in north Africa possessed a painting, in wax on cloth, of the saint driving off a dragon with the sign of the cross, while, nearby in Hippo, Augustine was able to point to a picture of the stoning of Stephen while giving a sermon on the saint.[12] He may have thought that "those who seek Christ and his apostles not in holy books but in painted walls" would naturally fall into error, but this did not stop him using such visual aids in his preaching.[13] Indeed, one defence of Christian religious imagery was based on its value in teaching and spreading knowledge of the faith. It was a commonplace amongst the literate clergy that images were "the books of the illiterate." As early as 380 Gregory of Nyssa spoke of the religious paintings at a shrine as "a speaking book."[14]

A dramatic clash between the old views and the new practices occurred in southern Gaul in the late sixth century. In October of the year 600 Pope Gregory the Great wrote to bishop Serenus of Marseilles about the iconoclasm that the rigorous

[5] For stimulating general reflections on the Christian image, see Freedberg, *The Power of Images*; Belting, *Likeness and Presence: A History of the Image Before the Era of Art*.

[6] Eusebius, *Historia ecclesiastica* 7. 18. 4 (2, p. 192).

[7] Augustine, *De consensu evangelistarum* 1. 10, p. 15 (PL 34: 1049).

[8] Gregory of Nyssa, *De sancto Theodoro*, p. 63 (PG 46: 737).

[9] Epiphanius of Salamis, *Letter to the Emperor Theodosius*, ed. Thümmel, *Die Frühgeschichte der ostkirchlichen Bilderlehre*, pp. 300–302 (no. 37), with German translation at pp. 67–68.

[10] Prudentius, *Peristefanon* 9, lines 9–20, p. 326.

[11] Paulinus of Nola, *Epistula* 32. 3, pp. 277–78.

[12] *Miracula sancti Stephani* 2. 4, p. 344 (PL 41: 851); Augustine, *Sermo* 316: 5 (PL 38: 1434).

[13] Augustine, *De consensu evangelistarum* 1. 10, p. 16 (PL 34: 1049).

[14] Gregory of Nyssa, *De sancto Theodoro*, p. 63 (PG 46: 737).

bishop had been engaged in: "Burning with thoughtless zeal, you have been smashing images of the saints, with the alleged reason that they should not be worshipped." Gregory points out that no other priest engages in such destructive behaviour, and asks if Serenus thinks only he is wise and holy. Moreover, "it is one thing to worship a picture, another thing to learn from the story depicted what one should worship. What the literate learn from reading, pictures convey to the illiterate."[15] Gregory thus relies for his defence of holy images both on the fact that the practice is widespread and ancient, and on the didactic value of such images. The pope almost casually says that adoration and instruction are different things, but Serenus's fears about worship of images were not groundless. By the time of Gregory's letter the churches of Gaul possessed images of Christ to which miraculous powers were ascribed, and a few surviving icons of the Virgin and child in Rome may date from this period or shortly thereafter.[16] The wonder-working image was to be a common feature of the cult of the saints throughout the Middle Ages and beyond.

A text that reveals some of the doubts and difficulties raised by the veneration of images comes from the pen of John, archbishop of Thessalonica in the first half of the seventh century.[17] It is in the form of a debate between a pagan and a Christian. The pagan claims that his worship of idols is no more a veneration of the mere physical material than is Christian veneration of images of God and the saints: "we do not worship these, but the incorporeal forces revered by means of them." The Christian responds that Christians make images of men who have actually lived—the saints—and of God as he was incarnate in human form—"we do not invent anything, as you do." "What about angels?" asks the pagan; they are invisible and incorporeal, but Christians venerate images of them. This is just like "the worship we accord to our gods through their statues." Here the Christian launches into a short bout of angelology. Angels are not entirely incorporeal; they are limited as to place; and they have often appeared in human form. The debate is presumably fictional, but it does show that Christian leaders thought pictorial representation of the holy required justification, and that the line between icon and idol had to be emphasized and spelled out. The pagan is given some good lines. Subsequent developments were to show that doubts among Christians about the legitimacy of picturing the divine were strong and enduring.

[15]Gregory I, *Registrum epistolarum* 11. 10 (2, pp. 873–76); cf. ibid. 9. 209 (2, p. 768) of the previous year. For a searching examination of the letters, Chazelle, "Pictures, Books and the Illiterate: Pope Gregory I's Letters to Serenus of Marseilles."

[16]Gregory of Tours, *Gloria martyrum* 21–22, p. 501 (repr., 1969, p. 51); Wolf, "Cult Images of the Virgin in Medieval Rome."

[17]Mansi 13, cols. 164–65; Thümmel, *Die Frühgeschichte der ostkirchlichen Bilderlehre*, pp. 327–28, no. 64. The text was cited at the Second Council of Nicaea in 787. John's dates are uncertain, but the more recent consensus places him in the period 600–620.

Byzantine Iconoclasm

The most ferocious conflict over holy images during the medieval period took place in the Byzantine empire between 726 and 843.[18] In those years the state swung from one extreme position to another and patriarchs were dismissed and replaced, while a large polemical literature was produced on both sides. Two periods of iconoclasm (726–87 and 815–43) were separated by an intervening restoration of the veneration of icons, a position finally and definitely asserted in 843.

Much of the debate was focussed on images of Christ, but images of the Virgin Mary, of other saints and of the angels were also objects of controversy. In the sixth and seventh centuries images of the saints could commonly be found in private hands and were also being venerated in churches. Around 600, one Byzantine military man, when posted away from Constantinople, carried an icon in his baggage "for his personal security," while a pious woman in the city had images of Cosmas and Damian painted on the walls of her house, even obtaining a miraculous cure by drinking some of the plaster from these images in a glass of water.[19] Icons could be carried into battle.[20] Bishop Julian of Atramytion (modern Edremit in western Turkey), in the first half of the sixth century, refers to "the paintings we revere in the sanctuaries."[21] The assault on images was thus aimed at a widespread and deeply felt religious practice.

According to the *Short History* of Nikephoros, probably written in the 780s, it was the emperor Leo III (717–41) who initiated Byzantine iconoclasm. Interpreting the volcanic explosion of Thera (Santorini) in 726 as an expression of "divine wrath" against the veneration of "holy images," Leo determined on their removal, and dismissed the patriarch Germanus when he was uncooperative.[22] Leo's opponents in the West reported that "the emperor decreed there should be no images of any saint or martyr or angel, for he asserted that all these things were accursed." They accused him of organizing bonfires of icons in the middle of Constantinople, and punishing by execution or mutilation any who resisted.[23] Leo's son and successor, Constantine V

[18] There is an enormous bibliography. Some general titles are Gero, *Byzantine Iconoclasm during the Reign of Leo III*; idem, *Byzantine Iconoclasm during the Reign of Constantine V*; Bryer and Herrin, eds., *Iconoclasm*; Brubaker and Haldon, *Byzantium in the Iconoclast Era (c. 680–850): The Sources*; idem, *Byzantium in the Iconoclast Era*. It should be noted that 726 is only one possible date for the beginning of the controversy.

[19] *Miracula Cosmae et Damiani* 13, 15, pp. 132, 137–38; as with all apparently pre-iconoclastic references to images, doubt has been expressed about the date, for example, Kitzinger, "The Cult of Images in the Age before Iconoclasm," p. 148: "There is no conclusive evidence that these Miracles were written before the outbreak of the [iconoclastic] Controversy."

[20] See the example of Heraclius, earlier, p. 322.

[21] Thümmel, *Die Frühgeschichte der ostkirchlichen Bilderlehre*, pp. 320–21, no. 58, with German translation at pp. 103–5; PG 99: 1537; for the problems in translating this phrase, Thümmel, p. 104 n. 196, and Kitzinger, "The Cult of Images in the Age before Iconoclasm," pp. 94–95 n. 33.

[22] Nikephoros of Constantinople, *Breviarium historicum* 59–60, 62, pp. 128–31.

[23] *Liber Pontificalis* 1, pp. 404, 409.

(741–76), continued and intensified his father's policies. In 754 the Council of Hiereia condemned icons, including those of the saints.[24] The saints were alive in heaven; who would wish to depict them "through a dead and hateful craft"?[25] The iconoclast bishops at the Council cited the prohibition from the Ten Commandments, alongside other biblical passages and excerpts from the Fathers, including Eusebius's letter to Constantina.

The Council of Hiereia was attended by 338 bishops but by no representatives of the pope or the eastern patriarchates (and the patriarchate of Constantinople was vacant at the time, whence the label "the headless council" used by opponents of iconoclasm). So, although iconoclasm within the Byzantine empire had the backing of the emperor, it was rejected outside the empire, and by many within it too. After the death of Constantine V and of his son Leo IV (775–80), power came into the hands of Leo's widow Irene, acting first as regent, eventually as empress in her own right, and she reversed the policy of her predecessors. At the Second Council of Nicaea in 787 it was asserted that paintings or mosaics of Christ, Mary, the angels and the saints could be set up in churches, on walls, on panels, in houses and streets, and reverence and honour paid to them: "whoever venerates an image, venerates the being depicted in the image."[26]

This did not, however, settle the matter, and the conflict over images was renewed early in the ninth century. The emperor Leo V (813–20), pondering the defeats that the Christians had suffered at the hands of their non-Christian enemies, concluded that the reason lay in "the veneration of images, nothing else."[27] He reverted to an iconoclast policy, and in 815, just like his predecessor Leo III, dismissed an uncooperative patriarch. That same year he summoned a council to Hagia Sophia to endorse the decrees of the iconoclast Council of Hiereia. A hostile source describes the subsequent reign of terror: "everywhere he cast down and burned the icons of the churches and smashed holy vessels that had images; he cut out the tongues of those who dared to say anything."[28] Iconoclasm remained official policy under the two subsequent emperors. Curiously enough, the second restoration of icons, like the first, was initiated by an empress-regent, in this case Theodora, widow of the emperor Theophilus, who had died in 842. After the pro-iconoclast patriarch had been deposed, icons were restored for good in 843, on the first Sunday of Lent, a day still celebrated in the Eastern Church as "The Triumph of Orthodoxy."

Our understanding of iconoclasm is complicated by the nature of the surviving sources. There are very few extant icons from the period before iconoclasm, except those from Greek Christian sites outside the Byzantine empire, notably the monastery of St. Catherine in Sinai. This lack might be explained by large-scale destruction

[24] *Die ikonoklastische Synode von Hiereia 754*.

[25] *Die ikonoklastische Synode von Hiereia 754*, p. 48 (Mansi 13, col. 276).

[26] *Conciliorum oecumenicorum decreta*, pp. 135–36 (*Horos*).

[27] *Historia de Leone Bardae Armenii filio*, p. 349.

[28] Ibid., p. 361.

during the iconoclast period, although there are other explanations. And because of the eventual triumph of the champions of icons, the literature produced by the iconoclasts has almost entirely perished, except in the form of excerpts quoted by their opponents in the course of refuting them. There is thus a curious and piquant symmetry between the surviving evidence for the iconoclasts and their opponents. If we assume that the destruction caused by the iconoclasts was significant, then they have permanently obscured the early history of icons, just as the supporters of icons tried to wipe the record clean of the arguments of the iconoclasts.

Perhaps because of these difficulties in the source material, Byzantine iconoclasm is a subject that seems to bring out strongly sceptical and revisionist tendencies in historians. It has been suggested both that icon veneration was not so important in the period before iconoclasm, and that iconoclasm itself was not so violent or sustained, as earlier scholarship believed. Some argue that iconoclasm started later, was more intermittent and had less official backing than the traditional accounts assert.[29] It is not necessary to address these issues in detail here. It clearly is the case that depiction of the saints and veneration of their images were controversial issues in the eighth and ninth centuries, and that victory eventually went to the pro-icon party. Thereafter the icon had a special place in the eastern Church. While images of the saints were not unimportant in the West, and became increasingly significant in the later Middle Ages (a subject discussed later), the icon was ubiquitous in the East and was incorporated in a systematic way into church lay-out, liturgy, and devotional practice.

The physical obliteration of sacred images was one of the most dramatic policies pursued by the iconoclasts, and one that caused the most outrage amongst their opponents. Although, as mentioned, there has been a tendency amongst scholars to play down the amount of destruction, there remains a sufficient body of evidence to attest to the reality of the removal or whitewashing of images. In the late 720s Bishop Thomas of Claudiopolis (modern Bolu, Turkey) was reported to have ordered the "destruction (or deposition) of images" in his diocese.[30] In the 760s the iconoclast patriarch Niketas scraped off the mosaics and plastered over the paintings of images of the saints in his patriarchal buildings at Constantinople.[31] Iconoclasts are depicted whitewashing images of Christ in the Khludov Psalter, produced soon

[29] For example, Schreiner, "Der byzantinische Bilderstreit"; Brubaker, "Icons before Iconoclasm?," p. 1253: "there is little evidence for a 'cult of sacred images' in pre-iconoclast Byzantium"; Noble, *Images, Iconoclasm, and the Carolingians*, p. 48: "We must be skeptical of what the sources say about the iconoclasts"; ibid., p. 109: "there were only a few brief periods of active hostility to images." Sometimes, however, the case for later legendary elaboration may be right: see the discussion of the supposed destruction of the Chalke icon by Leo III in Brubaker and Haldon, *Byzantium in the Iconoclast Era*, pp. 128–35.

[30] Letter of Germanus, Thümmel, *Die Frühgeschichte der ostkirchlichen Bilderlehre*, p. 379, line 30 (Mansi 13, col. 108; PG 98: 165); the term used is *kathairesis*.

[31] Nikephoros of Constantinople, *Breviarium historicum* 86, pp. 160–62 (if this work dates to the 780s, as suggested by the editor, p. 12, it is quite close in time to these events); cf. Theophanes, *Chronographia*, s.a. 6259, p. 443.

after the restoration of icons in 843. One illustration juxtaposes an iconoclast patriarch engaged in this activity with one of Christ's tormentors offering vinegar to him on the cross.[32] The parallel between the iconoclasts and this New Testament scene had already been drawn in the previous century in a tract condemning the iconoclast emperor Constantine V.[33]

The defenders of images (sometimes labelled iconophiles or iconodules) developed their own extensive arguments.[34] The earliest material is found in some letters of Germanus, patriarch of Constantinople (715–30), who had to deal with two bishops in Anatolia whose consciences were troubled by the veneration of holy images.[35] One of them was that Thomas of Claudiopolis, who went so far as to remove all icons. Germanus warned against "innovations" of this nature, which disturbed "long established custom"; "whole cities" are being upset, he writes. In his letters on the issue he defends the kissing of icons, and the lighting of lamps and the burning of incense before them. When we revere images of the saints in this way, we are not giving them divine worship but honouring the brave deeds of the saints and holding them up as models and examples. Pictures of the saints can stir us up, just as reading or hearing their deeds can, and the fact that many of these icons perform miracles, such as curing the sick or exuding myrrh, shows that they have divine approval. Those who criticise holy images are giving ammunition to the Jews and the Muslims, who will be delighted to see Christians decry the tradition of holy images. One of Germanus's arguments in favour of icons is that the emperor himself has caused images of the apostles and prophets to be raised in front of the imperial palace. This sits rather uneasily with the reputation that Leo III acquired as the fount and origin of iconoclasm.

During the first period of iconoclasm the most loquacious iconophile theorist was not in fact an inhabitant of the Byzantine empire but a Greek Christian living in the Islamic caliphate, John of Damascus. His writings include extensive discussion of the question of the veneration of images, and he was so prominent as a champion of icons that he was the target of a quadruple excommunication by the iconoclast Council of Hiereia, whose delegates chose to use his Arabic family name as an additional indication of contempt: "Mansur, the ill-named and Saracen-minded."[36] In the later iconoclast period the two main champions of icon-veneration were the

[32] Moscow, State Historical Museum, MS 129, fols. 23v, 67; these images have been reproduced in many places; there is a complete facsimile: *Salterio griego Jlúdov*.

[33] *Adversus Constantinum Caballinum* 17, cols. 333–36.

[34] Pelikan, *The Christian Tradition: A History of the Development of Doctrine 2: The Spirit of Eastern Christendom*, pp. 91–145 ("Images of the Invisible"); Parry, *Depicting the Word: Byzantine Iconophile Thought*.

[35] Mansi 13, cols. 100–105, 108–28; PG 98, 156–87; Thümmel, *Die Frühgeschichte der ostkirchlichen Bilderlehre*, pp. 374–87, nos. 80–82, with German translation at pp. 155–70; the letters are discussed by Brubaker and Haldon, *Byzantium in the Iconoclast Era*, pp. 94–105, who follow the argument that the letter to Thomas of Claudiopolis dates to after Germanus's deposition in 730.

[36] *Die ikonoklastische Synode von Hiereia 754*, p. 68 (Mansi 13, col. 356).

abbot Theodore of Studios (d. 826) and Nikephoros, the patriarch deposed in 815. Both suffered exile for their beliefs, and used this enforced leisure to write polemical works.

A great deal of the polemical literature produced by the party in favour of icon veneration consists of abstract and sometimes abstruse discussion of the nature of Christ and the significance of pictorial representation. John of Damascus, Theodore of Studios, and the patriarch Nikephoros had to deal with the awkward question of the Old Testament prohibition and they tried hard to keep a firm distinction between icon veneration and the practices of idolatrous pagans. They recognized that icons did not have a firm scriptural basis, but reasoned that the Church could create its own traditions and rituals. They stressed the exemplary and commemorative function of images, as well as their educational value for the illiterate. And they continually besmirched their opponents by comparing them with the image-hating Jews and Muslims.

The dossier of iconoclastic argument is thinner, but, despite the gaps in the evidence, it is possible to grasp something of this point of view. The iconoclast version of history saw Christ freeing humanity from the demon-inspired and ruinous worship of idols; then the spread of the faith under the guidance of the apostles, the Fathers, and the first six general councils (of 325–681); but, with the development of icon-veneration, came the devil's counter-attack—"unnoticed, he revived idolatry under the cloak of Christianity."[37] A letter of the iconoclast emperors Michael II and Theophilus dating to 824 gives details of what they found objectionable in the cult of icons. They provide a long list of the abuses of image veneration: burning lights and incense before the images, singing hymns before them, adoring them and asking them favours; wrapping them in cloth and having them receive children from the font; arranging to have the hair cut from the head of infants or new monks fall onto the images; scraping the paint from the images, mixing it with wine, and giving it to communicants after Mass; placing the consecrated host in the hands of an image, so that communicants receive it from the image; using icons as altars in private houses.[38] For them, all these actions were superstitious and magical. In the case of some of these practices, such as the employment of an icon as a godparent, there is independent corroboration from sources favourable to icons.[39]

Byzantine iconoclasm is associated primarily with opposition to the cult of images, but the iconophiles did sometimes accuse the iconoclasts of disdaining the cult of the saints in general.[40] The Council of Nicaea of 787, which restored icons, condemned anyone who rejected "the gospel book, the figure of the cross, the painted

[37] Ibid., p. 32 (Mansi 13, cols. 216–17, 221).

[38] *Concilia aevi Karolini* 1/2, no. 44A, pp. 478–79.

[39] Theodore of Studios, *Epistula* 17 (1, pp. 48–49) (PG 99: 961).

[40] For examples of such charges, *Adversus Constantinum Caballinum* 21, col. 337; Theophanes, *Chronographia*, s.a. 6218, p. 406.

image, the holy relic of a martyr," thus associating hostility to relics and to images.[41] The deposed patriarch Nikephoros accused Constantine V of having the relics of the saints burned, but this charge is in a work written more than forty years after the emperor's death, and no substantiated cases of mistreatment of relics can be found.[42] The iconoclast Council of Hiereia itself formally condemned anyone who did not accept prayer to the saints and the role of the saints as intercessors.[43] The charge appears to be simply defamation.

Since the restoration of icons in 843, the icon has continued to be one of the defining features of the Eastern Church.[44] Orthodox worship concentrates in a special way on these images of the Virgin Mary, Bible scenes or the saints, which can be found in houses as well as churches. Reverence for icons spread with eastern Christianity into Russia after the tenth century, and to this day it is a marked feature of the Russian church. After the Russian prince Jaroslav had constructed a church in honour of St. Boris and St. Gleb, he commanded "that the saints be painted on an icon, so that the faithful, entering the church and seeing their image depicted, as if seeing the saints themselves, would with faith and love bow down to them and kiss their image."[45] An inventory of the Russian monastery of St. Pantalemon on Mount Athos in 1142 lists ninety icons.[46] Approximately 3,000 kilometres (1,800 miles) to the north of Athos, the artists of late-medieval Novgorod created their own school of icon-painting. These images of Mary, George, Elijah, and other saints which confront the viewer or worshipper attest the central role the image has played in the cult of the saints in the Orthodox Church.

Images in the Medieval West

Media

The iconoclastic controversy reverberated in Carolingian western Europe as well as in Byzantium.[47] The reception in the west of the decrees of the Council of Nicaea of 787, which papal representatives attended, was complex and unharmonious, partly because of problems of translation between Greek and Latin, partly because of misunderstandings between the pope and Charlemagne. The proceedings of the Council circulated in western Europe in a highly misleading Latin version. Charlemagne and his bishops sponsored a riposte. Images, they argued, should not be put on the same level as relics of the saints, which are either parts of the body of holy men or

[41] *Conciliorum oecumenicorum decreta*, p. 137 (*Horos*).

[42] Nikephoros of Constantinople, *Antirrhetici tres adversus Constantinum* 2. 4, col. 341; Wortley, "Iconoclasm and Leipsanoclasm."

[43] *Die ikonoklastische Synode von Hiereia 754*, p. 64 (Mansi 13, col. 348).

[44] See for example Maguire, *The Icons of Their Bodies: Saints and Their Images in Byzantium*.

[45] Nestor, *Lesson on the Life and Murder of the Blessed Passion-Sufferers Boris and Gleb*, p. 22.

[46] Lazarev, *The Russian Icon*, p. 32.

[47] See the monumental study by Noble, *Images, Iconoclasm, and the Carolingians*.

things that had been in contact with them.[48] They stressed the contrast between eastern and western practice:

> We venerate the saints in their bodies or rather the remnants of their bodies, or even in their clothing, according to the traditions of our fathers, but they deem that they get great profit in their faith when they worship (painted) walls and panels.[49]

This sharp divide between veneration of relics and veneration of images was certainly overdrawn: the west had its images, the east its relics. The dispute arose from misunderstandings, compounded with lurking political differences. Pope Hadrian I made a reasoned plea, "So why should we not revere the saints, the servants of God, and make images of them in their memory, lest they be consigned to oblivion?"[50]

Angry reactions to the veneration of images continued later in the Carolingian period. When the Spanish cleric Claudius took up his position as bishop of Turin, around 816, he found "all the basilicas full of images." He immediately began to destroy them, but this raised a storm of opposition, and his adversaries were so incensed that, "if the Lord had not helped me, they would have swallowed me alive." This does not appear to have prevented some rational debate going on. Claudius says that his opponents, the defenders of images, argued that they do not regard the image itself as having any divine quality, but that they revere it to honour the one whose likeness it is. He will have none of this: "if those who abandon the worship of demons revere images of the saints, they have not abandoned idols but simply changed their names." He would not make an exception even for images of the cross: "God commanded us to bear our cross, not to worship it."[51] Claudius's contemporary Agobard of Lyons was also intransigent. He recommended crushing images of the saints into pieces, and commented that the saints themselves would approve of this (perhaps his words imply these images were sculptures rather than paintings).[52]

Whatever the heat of Carolingian debate about images, as soon as there is reasonably abundant evidence in western Europe, it is clear that images of the saints were everywhere. Some were wall paintings, others statues, yet others impressions in metal or wax. Three-dimensional representations were a direct affront to the Old Testament commandment against "graven images" and their disturbing impact can be judged by the condemnations expressed by the northern French cleric Bernard of Angers when he encountered (almost life-size) statues of the saints in the south of

[48] *Opus Caroli regis contra synodum* 3. 24, pp. 448–52 (cf. p. 334).

[49] Ibid., 3. 16, p. 411.

[50] Hadrian I, *Epistola ad Constantinum et Irenem*, col. 1232.

[51] Claudius of Turin, *Epistola* 12, pp. 610–13; cf. Agobard of Lyons, *De picturis et imaginibus* 19, p. 168.

[52] Agobard of Lyons, *De picturis et imaginibus* 23, p. 172. Claudius of Turin and Agobard of Lyons employ some identical phrasing, and there has been some discussion about whether Agobard depended on Claudius or vice versa: O'Brien, "Locating Authorities in Carolingian Debates on Image Veneration," who argues strongly for Claudius's dependency on Agobard.

France for the first time, around the year 1013.[53] He describes the practice, which was clearly unfamiliar to him, in the following words:

> It is an age-old tradition and ancient custom in the whole region of the Auvergne and Rouergue and Toulouse, as also in the surrounding lands, that everyone, if possible, makes a statue of his saint in gold or silver or some other metal, and places in it the head of the saint or a significant part of the body.

When Bernard came across a golden statue of St. Gerald of Aurillac on the altar of the abbey church at Aurillac, which was carved in such a life-like fashion that the local peasantry thought it was staring back at them, he initially adopted the superior tone of a northern French intellectual. Turning to his friend Bernerius, and speaking in Latin to avoid angering the local laity, he said, "What do you make of this idol, brother? Would Jupiter or Mars think themselves unworthy of such a statue?" He explains his thinking at this time. The only permissible three-dimensional image, in his view, was the crucifix; the saints should be commemorated only in writing or in wall-paintings. A few days later Bernard and Bernerius arrived at Conques, where they found crowds invoking St. Foy before her statue. Again Bernard was struck by the foolishness of these proceedings, "judging it absurd and far from the bounds of reason that so many rational beings should invoke an object that could not speak or feel." He exchanged a supercilious sideways glance with his friend and likened the statue of St. Foy to an idol of Venus or Diana.

But Bernard's opinions underwent a complete transformation. Miracles of healing proved the power of the image; miracles of punishment showed that those who mocked it were made to suffer. Bernard heard the story of a cleric called Odalricus, who prided himself on his learning, and who had spoken disrespectfully of the statue. That night St. Foy herself appeared to him, demanding, "You wicked wretch, why did you dare to criticize my image?" She then beat him with her rod so fiercely that he died the following day, after recounting the experience. Bernard concluded that "the image of St. Foy ought not be destroyed or criticized," and went on to chronicle the saint's miracles. Remarkably, the image of St. Foy survives to this day (figure 12.1). It stands 85 centimetres (almost 3 feet) high, rich with gold and jewels, enthroned in majesty. This complex object is a composite of items from many centuries and cultures: the golden face is late Roman (an imperial statue and a parade helmet have both been suggested as its origin), into which glass eyes have been set; the throne and probably the crown were added in the late tenth century; gems and classical cameos were embedded in the statue through the centuries; and restoration was undertaken in the sixteenth century.[54]

[53] Bernard of Angers, *Liber miraculorum sancte Fidis* 1. 13, pp. 112–14; see the comments of Remensnyder, "Un problème de cultures ou de culture? La statue-reliquaire et les *joca* de sainte Foy," pp. 351–68.

[54] The most detailed physical analysis is by Taralon and Taralon-Carlini, "La Majesté d'or de Sainte Foy de Conques."

12.1. Image of St. Foy, Conques. © 2013. De Agostini Picture Library/Scala, Florence.

Bernard of Angers singles out the south of France for its "age-old tradition" of statues of the saint, and Agobard and Claudius had been outraged by the situation in their dioceses of Lyons and Turin, but such statues could also be found in other regions at this time.[55] The Golden Madonna of Essen, a figure 74 centimetres (29 inches) high and made of a wooden core covered with gold leaf, is generally dated to c. 980. At this same period, the abbey of Cluny in Burgundy had a statue-reliquary of its patron, St. Peter. In the early 990s, after a dispute over tithes between Cluny and the bishop of Riez, the bishop came to the church and surrendered his claim "in the presence of the precious relics of the saints that are contained in the image of St. Peter."[56] The fact that "the image" contained relics shows that it was a statue rather then a painting or embroidery. It was carried in procession on Palm Sunday and might be taken out on other occasions.[57] There is mention of a golden image of the archangel Michael at St.-Martial, Limoges, c. 1000.[58] By the middle of the eleventh century the church of Coventry in the English Midlands had an image of the Virgin, which was decorated with a necklace of precious gems.[59] And many wooden carvings of the enthroned figure of the Virgin Mary survive from the eleventh and twelfth centuries, some of them with cavities designed to hold relics.[60]

Sculptured images of the saints are thus certainly in evidence from the tenth century, and probably existed earlier. Later in the Middle Ages, over the course of the eleventh to sixteenth centuries, they became ubiquitous. Entering a church, worshippers could expect to see carved figures of the saints (sometimes with real clothes).[61] There would also be images in other media: wall-paintings, panel paintings, stained glass, textiles. And there were other images of saints on fonts, on capitals of columns, and on the reliquaries already discussed.

One of the most widespread images in a church would be that of the saint to whom the church was dedicated, and such images were sometimes even required. In Anglo-Saxon England, for example, conciliar legislation commanded that there be paintings of the saints to whom the church or altar was dedicated.[62] In 1287 the diocese of Exeter ruled that every parish church should have its "image of the Virgin Mary and of the saint of that place."[63] At the Council of Trier in 1310 it was ordained that

[55] Hubert and Hubert, "Piété chrétienne ou paganisme? Les statues-reliquaires de l'Europe carolingienne."

[56] *Recueil des chartes de l'abbaye de Cluny* 3, p. 101, no. 1866.

[57] *Consuetudines Cluniacensium antiquiores*, p. 64; Ulric of Cluny, *Antiquiores consuetudines Cluniacensis monasterii* 3. 15, col. 759.

[58] Ademar of Chabannes, *Chronicon* 3. 44, p. 164.

[59] William of Malmesbury, *Gesta pontificum Anglorum* 4. 175, pp. 470–72.

[60] Forsyth, *The Throne of Wisdom*.

[61] A few examples in Orme, *English Church Dedications*, p. 7.

[62] *Councils and Ecclesiastical Documents*, ed. Haddan and Stubbs, 3, p. 580 (Council of Chelsea, 816).

[63] *Councils and Synods with Other Documents Relating to the English Church 2 (1205–1313)* 2, p. 1006 (Statutes of Exeter II, 1287).

> in every church, either in front of, or behind, or above the altar, there should be an image or sculpture or writing or picture expressly designating and manifesting to any onlooker the saint in whose merit and honour that altar is constructed.[64]

This provision of appropriate images can sometimes be traced in more detail, as in the case of a bequest made in 1317 by a pious lady from Tolentino in the Italian Marche, who left money to the Augustinian friars in the town for "a panel in which should be depicted the story of St. Augustine"; at this time their church was dedicated to Augustine (it is now San Nicola).[65]

Pictures of saints, whatever their medium, could be of two basic kinds: a single image, often staring back at the worshipper, or a figure in narrative action (although the types were sometimes combined, as in the so-called narrative icon). The former might stimulate the impression of a personal relationship between saint and worshipper, the latter might draw people into a story, like the paintings in Tolentino, just mentioned. The most extensive array of saints' images of the first, iconic, type is that in the cathedral of Monreale, built by William II, king of Sicily (1166–89), where a total of 174 saints are represented in mosaic—72 full-length, 93 in medallions, 6 in bust, plus 3 in narrative scenes.[66] They have labels in Latin (except for two stylite saints, Daniel and Simeon, who are labelled in Greek) and are a mixture of western and eastern saints—the artists worked in a Byzantine tradition and are likely to have been Greek. Anyone in Monreale cathedral—king, monk, or lay person—would be able to contemplate dozens of holy figures, each named, looking directly back.

Narrative scenes came in various forms. The great bronze doors of Gniezno cathedral, cast in the second half of the twelfth century, show the life of St. Adalbert (d. 997). The doors are large (about 328 centimetres by 84 centimetres [10 ¾ feet by 2 ¾ feet]), and have eighteen scenes of the life of Adalbert—being made a bishop, preaching to the pagan Prussians, being cut down, being enshrined.[67] Scenes from the life of St. Wenceslas decorate the stairwell of the Great Tower at Charles IV's Karlstein castle in Bohemia.[68] And large panel paintings or wall paintings depicting stories of the saints were commonly found in churches.

Another public place where images of the saints were visible was in church windows. Stained glass offered pictures and stories, usually without words. Some had the saints as subjects. A rare surviving example of a series of stained glass windows depicting saintly miracles can be found in Canterbury Cathedral. Here, in the Trinity Chapel, an eastern extension of the cathedral that was built to provide a new and magnificent setting for the shrine of St. Thomas Becket, are the so-called Becket

[64] Mansi 25, cols. 265–66 (c. 69).

[65] Lett, *Un procès de canonisation au Moyen Âge*, p. 55, citing the thesis of Ezzio Ruggeri.

[66] Brodbeck, *Les saints de la Cathédrale de Monreale.*

[67] Mohnhaupt, "Typologisch strukturierte Heiligenzyklen. Die Adalbertsvita der Gnesener Bronzetür," with bibliography at p. 367 n. 8.

[68] *Gothic Mural Painting in Bohemia and Moravia*, pp. 114–16.

Windows.[69] Seven large windows (averaging 6.5 metres high by 1.85 metres wide, approximately 21 by 6 feet) depict Becket's posthumous miracles, many of them corresponding to the written records kept at the shrine in the 1170s. They contain crowded narratives—one window has thirty-three different scenes—and show the pilgrims suffering, at the tomb and being cured. The scenes are labelled, although the lettering is now often illegible, and named individuals are identified. The windows are thus a visual equivalent of a Miracle Book kept at a shrine.

The Franciscans provide a somewhat poignant example of the saints in stained glass. They were originally committed to extremes of poverty and humility, and their history is marked by recurrent attempts to respect or restore these ideals. This had it impact in the world of images, and in 1260 they ruled that no Franciscan church should have images in stained glass, except those of the crucifix, the Virgin Mary, St. John and the two great Franciscan saints of the thirteenth century, Francis himself and Antony of Padua.[70] St. Francis and St. Antony of Padua were thus exempt from the general rules about depiction. They were too famous not to be drawn.

In the later medieval West, the elaboration of visual imagery around the altar provided an important space for the representation of the saints.[71] From the early twelfth century, pictures and sculptures in front of, on top of, and behind, the altar became more common, more elaborate and larger in scale, eventually producing the vast and complex altarpieces of the fifteenth century and beyond. Panels behind or on top of an altar presented large, visible surfaces, which naturally invited ornamentation and decoration, and they became one of the most important spaces for religious painting and sculpture. Diego Gelmírez, archbishop of Santiago, is recorded as constructing "a precious and finely worked panel behind the altar of St. James" in his cathedral church around the year 1135.[72] The court ordinances of James III of Majorca, which were issued in 1337, prescribe that his chapel should possess "a beautiful silver altarpiece, with images." One reason for these images in the king's chapel, as so often, was to edify and instruct the illiterate in the congregation, "for it is agreed that pictures, and such like, are the letters of the simple."[73] By the end of the Middle Ages some altarpieces had developed into monumental structures, more like a wall than a panel.

The relation between the subject painted on an altarpiece and the altar itself was not always simple.[74] During the rebuilding of Siena cathedral in the first half of the fourteenth century, the relics of the city's four patron saints (Crescentius, Savinus, Ansanus, and Victorinus) were moved from the crypt to four altars in the body of

[69] Caviness, *The Windows of Christ Church Cathedral, Canterbury*, pp. 175–214, pls. XIII–XV, 111–60.

[70] *Constitutiones generales Ordinis Fratrum Minorum . . . in Capitulo generali apud Narbonam* 3. 18, p. 48.

[71] Williamson, "Altarpieces, Liturgy, and Devotion."

[72] *Historia Compostellana* 3. 44, p. 502.

[73] *Leges palatinae* 7. 12, fol. 68v (AASS Junii 3: lxxii).

[74] For comment of exemplary clarity, see Humfrey, *The Altarpiece in Renaissance Florence*, pp. 62–70.

the church. Each was given a newly commissioned altarpiece. The only one that survives complete is Simone Martini's *Annunciation* for the altar of St. Ansanus, but it is known that all four showed scenes from the life of the Virgin Mary.[75] This single undertaking thus illustrates three distinct things: the elevation of the saints from a less public to a more public place; the creation of altarpieces, an active process in this period; and the predominance, even for these patron saints, of the Virgin Mary, who cast her mantle over them.

A common shape for an altarpiece was a diptych or triptych, that is, a two-leaved or three-leaved hinged tablet of metal, ivory or wood. The illustrations would usually be on both the inner and outer sides, so a triptych might have six different surfaces for pictures, only two or three of which would have been visible to an observer at any one time. A common arrangement of a composite altarpiece of this type was for a large image of the Virgin Mary to be flanked or surrounded by saints. A characteristic example is that painted by the Sienese artist Meo da Siena around 1320 for the abbey church of Santa Maria di Valdiponte at Montelabate near Perugia.[76] It measures 233 by 242 centimetres (92 by 95 inches), so it would have risen up behind the altar well over the height of a man. Its central image is a Virgin and Child, with two prophets and Christ above. Along the bottom, on a much smaller scale, are the twelve apostles. To the (viewer's) right of the Virgin and Child are depictions of John the Evangelist and the local saint, Emiliano, to the left Peter and Gregory. Above these saints are smaller images of saints Martha and Catherine, Antony Abbot and Benedict, two figures now missing, and Agnes and Mary Magdalene. The whole thus presented to its congregation of monks a total of twenty-four saints, including the great founding figures of the Church and the monastic movement, as well as a local saint. Four of the saints are female, two of them biblical, two early martyrs. The altarpiece offered a rich cast of holy characters, varied in type and ranging over the depths of time, whom the monks of Santa Maria di Valdiponte could revere, invoke, identify with, or dream about. (See plate 8.)

The loss of many paintings from the Middle Ages leaves only an incomplete record of what must have once existed. The situation with textiles is yet more acute. A whole world of elaborate and colourful images has more or less disappeared. Records sometimes reveal what has been lost. For instance, the abbey of St. Antony in the Viennois possessed a large tapestry with 200 scenes from the life of St. Antony of Egypt. It does not survive but there are two manuscript copies from the fifteenth century, now in Malta and Florence.[77] In the same century the treasures of the cathedral church of Glasgow included a large tapestry depicting the life of St. Kentigern, the patron saint of the diocese, although this is only known because it is recorded in an inventory.[78] Surviving fragments of textiles showing narrative scenes of the saints

[75] Ploeg, *Art, Architecture and Liturgy: Siena Cathedral in the Middle Ages*, pp. 109–10.

[76] Now in the Galleria nazionale dell'Umbria in Perugia.

[77] *A Picture Book of the Life of Saint Anthony the Abbot* describes the Malta manuscript and reproduces its illustrations (pp. 7–8 on the tapestry).

[78] *Registrum episcopatus Glasguensis* 2, p. 334.

include an altar cloth now in Brunswick with six images from the Passion of St. Margaret of Antioch and tapestries in Tournai depicting the Lives of the local saints Piat and Eleutherius, which are amongst the most extensive surviving set of textile illustrations with saintly subjects.[79]

Although they would be small and extremely schematic, images of the saints on coins would be more familiar than any others. Coins were the only mass-produced objects for most of the Middle Ages (in the early thirteenth century two English mints were putting out about four million pennies per year) and saints were not uncommonly represented on them. For example, the Přemyslid rulers of Bohemia introduced the figure of St. Wenceslas on the reverse of their coins early in the eleventh century, and he remained there until the extinction of the dynasty two centuries later, his iconography becoming fixed as a warrior figure, with banner and shield. This is also how he appears on the reverse of their seals, which survive from the twelfth century. The saint on the reverse of the coin or seal matches and reinforces the duke or king on the obverse.[80] In the later Middle Ages several of the Stewart kings of Scots had St. Andrew depicted on their gold coinage.[81]

Some of the best preserved images from the Middle Ages are those in the parchment books. Parchment is durable, and a closed book keeps the pictures from the destructive effect of light (and other things). Saints were depicted in parchment in various ways. Sometimes they make a discreet appearance, peeking out from the illuminated initials, as in an early-twelfth-century manuscript from Cîteaux, containing saints' Lives, in which fourteen saints are illustrated in initials.[82] Alternatively, they might be given a full page or most of it. The Menologion of Basil II (976–1025), the surviving volume of which covers the year from September to February, dedicates a page to each saint's day or great feast, each with an illustration.[83] It contains 430 miniatures in all. And, from the tenth century onwards, there survive illustrated saints' Lives, with narrative sequences, either interspersed in the text of the Life or grouped in a separate section in the volume.[84]

The oldest surviving illustrated saints' Lives are in a volume produced at Fulda in the late tenth century; the Life of Kilian in this volume is illustrated with eleven pictures, the Life of Margaret with ten.[85] The prayers with which the volume concludes

[79] Städtisches Museum, Brunswick, B Nr. 56; Weigert, *Weaving Sacred Stories: French Choir Tapestries and the Performance of Clerical Identity*; *Saints de choeurs. Tapisseries du Moyen Age et de la Renaissance.*

[80] Wolverton, *Hastening Toward Prague*, pp. 165–85.

[81] Stewart, *The Scottish Coinage*, pp. 37, 48, 49, 71, pls. V (70, 73), VII (89, 90), X (137, 138); the kings concerned are Robert III (1390–1406), James II (1437–60), and James IV (1488–1513).

[82] Załuska, *L'enluminure et le Scriptorium de Cîteaux au XIIe siècle* (MS Dijon 641).

[83] BAV, Vat. gr. 1613; there is a monochrome facsimile edition from 1907: *Il menologio di Basilio II*; for the text, *Menologium Basilianum*, PG 117: 19–614; a colour facsimile was published in 2005, *El "Menologio" de Basilio II Emperador de Bizancio*, but it is rare; see the accompanying volume of essays, *El "Menologio de Basilio II": Città del Vaticano, Biblioteca Apostolica Vaticana, Vat. Gr. 1613: libro de estudios.*

[84] Wormald, "Some Illustrated Manuscripts of the Lives of the Saints"; Abou-El-Haj, *The Medieval Cult of Saints*, with a helpful chart on pp. 140–43; Hahn, *Portrayed on the Heart.*

[85] Hanover, Niedersächsische Landesbibliothek, MS I 189; there is a facsimile edition: *Passio Kiliani.*

are written for a woman or women, and, although the book is a de luxe product in some sense, generous in its use of purple and gold, it is relatively small—thirty-eight folios measuring 15 by 20.6 centimetres (about 6 by 8 inches)—and it might have been made for a high-born and pious lady rather than for any liturgical or communal use. From the eleventh century, examples of illustrated saints' Lives increase in number. St. Cuthbert's Life was the subject of a full programme of illustrations twice in a century. The first was produced at the beginning of the twelfth century, the second at its end, both, in all likelihood, in Durham, where Cuthbert lay enshrined.[86] The earlier manuscript has fifty-five drawings throughout the text, the later manuscript forty-five full-page miniatures (others have been lost). Produced in the same place and accompanying the same text (an expanded version of Bede's prose Life of St. Cuthbert), the two sets of illustrations are, nevertheless, in quite contrasting styles. The earlier pictures are coloured line-drawings without frames, of a type common in Anglo-Saxon illustrated books, while the later series are in full, deep colour and set in thick rectangular frames. Narrative action has been replaced with an iconic quality suited to reverence and contemplation; the opening image of the later volume indeed depicts a monk kissing the feet of a standing and luxuriously vested Cuthbert.

From the later Middle Ages there is a great treasury of illustration in hagiographical and liturgical books. A few examples can be mentioned. A manuscript of William of St.-Pathus's *Life and Miracles of St. Louis*, made in the 1330s, has ninety-two images, each of which occupies about a third of the page.[87] Each image has a coloured and decorated rectangular frame, although the actions sometimes encroach upon it, as in the vigorous depiction of the battle of Mansura, where a Muslim scimitar and a French knight's sword break out of the picture space. The backgrounds are abstract rather than realistic, with various geometrical designs that show up Louis's golden halo in contrast. The pictures of the posthumous miracles often show the sufferer kneeling before an image of St. Louis, with crown, sceptre and halo, and depict many of the details of healing cult, including the candles the length of the sufferer, shaped into a coil, and the ex-votos hanging by the shrine. The book has certainly been a French royal possession since 1373 and may well have always been one.[88]

Another royally commissioned manuscript, and one of the most spectacular illustrated works inspired by the cult of the saints, is the so-called Hungarian Angevin Legendary. The bulk of this book is now in the Vatican Library, with scattered leaves in five other places.[89] In its original state, it may have consisted of as many as

[86] The two manuscripts are Oxford, University College MS 165, and BL, Add. 39943 (Yates Thompson 26); see Baker, "Medieval Illustrations of Bede's Life of St. Cuthbert"; Marner, *St Cuthbert*; Lawrence-Mathers, *Manuscripts in Northumbria in the Eleventh and Twelfth Centuries*, pp. 89–108.

[87] BN fr. 5716; see Chung-Apley, "The Illustrated *Vie et miracles de saint Louis*."

[88] Delisle, *Recherches sur la librairie de Charles V* 1, p. 319 (no. XCV); 2, p. 154* (no. 938).

[89] BAV, Vat. lat. 8541; there is a facsimile edition: *Heiligenleben: Ungarisches Legendarium Cod. Vat. lat. 8541*; see also Török, "Neue Folii aus dem 'Ungarischen Anjou–Legendarium'"; there are brief discussions in Szakács, "Le culte des saints à la cour et le Légendaire des Anjou-Hongrie," and Klaniczay, *Holy Rulers and Blessed Princesses*, pp. 356–62.

200 painted pages, each containing four pictures (549 miniatures survive). It was made around the same time as the illustrated *Life and Miracles of St. Louis*, and for a branch of the same family, descendants of St. Louis's brother, Charles of Anjou, who had established themselves by force in Italy and by force backed by hereditary claims in Hungary. The Angevin rulers of Hungary thus had strong links both with France and Italy, and the Legendary was produced by Italian painters for their court. The book contains virtually no text, other than some short Latin captions, and must have relied on the viewer being fairly familiar with the stories it shows. These have as their subject the main universal saints, such as the apostles, Mary Magdalene, Benedict, and George, along with some distinctively Hungarian saints, like Ladislas, the Hungarian king who died in 1095. The incidents and scenes represented are often in the elaborate and apocryphal forms that were common in the later Middle Ages, and correspond to tales from the popular contemporary collection, the *Golden Legend*. For instance, St. Hilary of Poitiers is shown refuting a heretical (and imaginary) Pope Leo, who dies immediately, just as in the *Golden Legend* (even if the author expresses some reservations about the story).[90] The pictures in the Hungarian Angevin Legendary are lively, richly coloured and set against gold backgrounds; they constitute a striking monument to the opulent visual culture surrounding the saints that could be found in the courts of later medieval Europe. (See plate 9.)

Depicting the Saints

In the thirteenth century the Franciscan chronicler Salimbene noted that "No one should anywhere be depicted as a saint in painting unless his or her canonization has been made public by the Church."[91] The implication is obviously that saints were depicted in a distinctive way. One of the simplest and most general methods of indicating sanctity was the halo, the golden ring or circle around the head.[92] This was one attribute that all saints had. The Christian halo was borrowed from the nimbus, the radiating crown with which the rulers of the late Roman Empire were depicted, and Christians used it at first only for images of Christ, but it then spread to other holy figures. After it developed this new, more general use, a method was devised to show Christ's halo in a way different from others, with an internal cross. Around 1200 the bishop and liturgical writer Sicard of Cremona explained, "Christ's halo is distinguished from the halo of the saints by the shape of a cross."[93] With the elaboration of rules of perspective, Renaissance artists were able to show the halo from any angle. It often hovered above the saint's head at a slight, rather jaunty, slant.

There were significant variations in the shape of the halo. A square or rectangular halo signified a person still alive.[94] It was given in early medieval Rome to living or

[90] BAV, Vat. lat. 8541, fol. 102; Jacobus de Voragine, *Legenda aurea* 17 (1, p. 147).

[91] Salimbene, *Cronica*, p. 502.

[92] See, in general, Collinet-Guérin, *Histoire du nimbe*.

[93] Sicard of Cremona, *Mitralis de officiis* 1. 12, p. 50 (PL 213:43).

[94] Ladner, "The So-called Square Nimbus."

recently deceased popes or donors. John the Deacon, writing in the ninth century, describes a depiction of Pope Gregory I which had "around the head, not a round halo, but a shape like a panel, which is the mark of a living person."[95] In the Codex Benedictus there is a striking image of abbot Desiderius of Monte Cassino bowing before St. Benedict, the former with square, the latter with round halo.[96] The opening page of a late-eleventh-century Life of St. Agericus includes a depiction of the saint, with a circular halo, and a depiction of the author, probably abbot Stephen of St.-Airy, with a very distinct square halo.[97] Another variant of the halo occurs between the fourteenth and sixteenth centuries in some Spanish paintings, which show St. Joseph with a polygonal halo, either with straight or scalloped edges. The same design is occasionally also used in late medieval Spain for the Three Kings, Abraham, and John the Baptist, all holy figures who died before Christ (as, presumably, did St. Joseph).[98]

By the end of the Middle Ages there are indications in Italy that canonized and non-canonized saints were sometimes distinguished by the kinds of halo they wore, with the non-canonized being shown with rays (or, occasionally, with a polygonal halo) rather than a full circular halo.[99] The practice began around 1330 but was far from systematically observed. A good clear example is provided by the panels painted by Fra Angelico for the predella of the altar of San Domenico, Fiesole, in the 1420s (the predella is the base on which the altarpiece stands).[100] (See plate 10.) The panels measure 32 by 244 centimetres (12 ⅔ by 96 inches). The central panel shows the risen Christ surrounded by angels. On either side is a panel depicting numerous saints, while at the far right and far left are two smaller panels, each showing a group of Dominicans, eighteen on the left, nineteen on the right. The saints in the inner panels (including the canonized Dominicans among them) all have fully circular haloes, while, of the thirty-seven Dominicans on the outer panels, all, except two kneeling tertiaries, are shown with rays. This is why they are often labelled "blessed of the Order." Although this term invokes a distinction that only became systematic much later, it is clear that Fra Angelico was making a clear division between the canonized and uncanonized by this visual means. There are other unambiguous examples, like the painting of the Blessed Gabriel Ferretti by Carlo Crivelli, painted around 1489 and depicting Gabriel kneeling as the Virgin and Child appear to him in a vision. His halo consists of rays emanating from his head.[101] Although the papacy approved the cult of Gabriel as a "blessed" in the eighteenth century, he

[95] John the Deacon, *Vita Gregorii magni* 4. 83, col. 231.

[96] BAV, Vat. lat. 1202, fol. 2; *The Codex Benedictus: An Eleventh-century Lectionary from Monte Cassino*.

[97] *Ornamenta ecclesiae* 1, pp. 234–35, item B 34 (Verdun, Bibliothèque municipale MS 8).

[98] Schulze, "Vieleckige Nimben in der spanischen Malerei."

[99] Bisogni, "Raggi e aureole ossia la distinzione della santità."

[100] National Gallery, London: NG663. 1–5; see Gordon, *The Fifteenth Century. Italian Paintings* 1, pp. 2–25.

[101] National Gallery, London: NG668.

has never been canonized. In his little treatise on canonization Troilus de Malvitiis noted the distinction between the two kinds of halo, and it was also recognized by one of the witnesses in the canonization hearings for Catherine of Siena, early in the fifteenth century, who had seen pictures of Catherine "with rays or a circlet of rays around her head, just as blessed persons who are not yet canonized are customarily depicted," although he had to admit that he had often seen uncanonized people depicted with the full halo.[102] This slippage and uncertainty was characteristic. The Florentine writer Franco Sacchetti bemoaned the way that an image of an uncanonized saint with rays and labelled "blessed" could easily slide into becoming an image with a full halo, labelled "saint."[103] And, even in the sixteenth century, there are cases of an argument being made for canonization because the candidate had been depicted "with a halo, as saints are customarily depicted."[104]

Beyond this general visual feature of sanctity, there arose the question of identifying any individual saint. When people encountered an image of a saint, in the public space of a church or on the page of an illustrated book, the picture or sculpture might be identified by a written inscription, but this, of course, relied on the ability of worshippers to read. More universal was some kind of visual cue, perhaps in the way the saint was depicted, or perhaps in some associated object, or both: an old man with a key was St. Peter, a young girl with a lamb St. Agnes. These attributes, as they are usually called, became a standard feature of depictions of the saints.[105] As early as 540 there is a reference to the church of St. Stephen in Gaza having representations of Stephen and John the Baptist, "each with his customary symbols."[106] And, already in the same period, St. Menas is customarily depicted with two camels. These can be seen on the ampullae that pilgrims brought home from his shrine in Egypt and on ivory panels of the sixth century.[107]

These identifying features could be generic, since saints were often grouped into categories, as discussed earlier, so it would be possible to recognize a martyr-saint from his or her palm, a bishop-saint from his vestments, or a hermit-saint from his rough clothing. This is why scholars today can refer to "a portrait of a bishop-saint," and so on, even when uncertain of the identity of the individual. It was also common to show martyrs with the instruments of their martyrdom, so that Catherine bears the wheel prepared for her torture, Bartholomew the knife used to flay him, and Stephen, also distinguished by being dressed as a deacon, a stone.[108] Saints might also

[102] Troilus de Malvitiis, *Opusculum de canonizatione sanctorum*, fol. a3; *Il processo Castellano*, p. 28.

[103] Sacchetti, Letter XI, p. 494.

[104] *Acta ex processu Gerardi tinctorii* 3. 22, p. 774.

[105] Kaftal, *Iconography of the Saints in Italian Painting*; Réau, *Iconographie de l'art chrétien* 3; *Lexicon der christlichen Ikonographie* 1, s.v. "Attribute," 5–8: *Ikonographie der Heiligen*; Rochelle, *Post-biblical Saints Art Index*; Schurr, *Die Ikonographie der Heiligen*.

[106] *Synēthē symbola*: Choricius of Gaza, *Laudatio Marciani* 2. 38, p. 38.

[107] Papaconstantinou, *Le culte des saints en Egypte*, pp. 146–54, 459–62.

[108] There is a brief exposition of these conventions in William Durandus, *Rationale divinorum officiorum* 1. 3. 11–16 (140, pp. 39–40).

be depicted with something indicating the special help they offered: St. Leonard, famous for freeing prisoners, is shown with a broken chain and lock in late medieval images. These attributes changed and developed over time, and might show regional variation. For example, the tradition that St. Christopher had a dog's head was gradually marginalized by the portrayal of him carrying the infant Christ.

The conventions governing how saints were depicted can be deduced from the surviving images but are also sometimes made explicit, something especially clear when both the contract with the artist and the painting survive, as in the case of Bennozo Gozzoli's *Virgin and Child Enthroned Among Angels and Saints*, now in the National Gallery in London. This was painted in accordance with the terms of a contract agreed in 1461 between the artist and the Florentine guild that commissioned it. Every saint in it was specified: John the Baptist, St. Zenobius, and St. Jerome on the Virgin's right, St. Peter, St. Dominic, and St. Francis on her left. John and Jerome are to be depicted "in their customary costume," and Zenobius, an early bishop of Florence, in pontifical vestments.[109]

Saints who appeared in visions were often recognized because they resembled their painted images. Examples can be found in the Greek East very early. Cosmas and Damian appeared to St. Theodore of Sykeon looking "just as they did in the icon" that hung in the room.[110] The Miracles of Artemios mention a child who recognized St. Artemios because he looked like the icon in his church.[111] St. Demetrius appeared repeatedly "in the form in which he is painted in icons."[112] There are examples in the West too: when St. Servatius appeared in a vision to Giselbert, duke of Lotharingia (d. 939), the duke recognized the saint "from the image made of gold that was in his sanctuary"; an eleventh-century monk "saw in a vision St. Michael the archangel, whose appearance he had got to know, instructed by pictures"; and there is mention, at this same period, of a vision of St. Peter, "dressed in Hebrew clothes, as he is everywhere seen in pictures."[113]

Sometimes there are cases where the worshipper does not, as in the foregoing examples, recognize the saint from a picture that he or she has already seen, but, rather, realizes who a saintly figure is only when encountering the image later. For instance, when Ariulf, the pagan Lombard duke of Spoleto, was fighting against the Byzantines, he was amazed to find a bold warrior, unknown to him, who defended him with his shield against any attack. Later, after the battle, entering the church of St. Savinus in Spoleto, he saw a picture of the saint and immediately recognized him

[109] Cited by Hope, "Altarpieces and the Requirements of Patrons," p. 566 n. 13, from L. Tanfani Centofanti, *Notizie di artisti tratte dai documenti pisani* (Pisa, 1897), p. 84.

[110] *Vita Theodori Syceotae* 39, p. 34.

[111] *Miracula sancti Artemii* 34, p. 180.

[112] *Miracula sancti Demetrii* 1. 8, 10, 15, pp. 102, 115, 162.

[113] Iocundus, *Translatio sancti Servatii* 41, p. 105; for Iocundus, see Boeren, *Jocundus. Biographe de saint Servais*, with an edition of the *vita*; Desiderius of Monte Cassino, *Dialogi de miraculis sancti Benedicti* 2. 6, p. 1130; Peter Damian, *Disputatio de variis apparationibus et miraculis* 4, col. 588.

as the man who had fought at his side in the battle.[114] A similar sequence of events is implied in the witness statement in the canonization process of Dorothea of Montau in 1404, which describes how Dorothea "appeared to the witness in such clothing as she is depicted wearing in the church of Marienwerder," even though the witness "did not know her previously nor had he seen her image nor, at that time, had he heard anything about her sanctity."[115] Recognition of the similarity with the painted or carved image must have been subsequent to the vision.

Despite some long-term continuities in depictions of saints, changes could be made to update them, as, rather remarkably, in the Niederwildungen altarpiece of 1403, where one of the apostles at Pentecost is wearing glasses.[116] A telling case of such "modernization" is evident from a comparison of two cycles of illustrations for the Life and Miracles of Edmund King and Martyr, one made around 1130, now in the Pierpont Morgan Library in New York, the other produced in the 1430s, three centuries later, and now housed in the British Library.[117] These two sets of images present strong contrasts in both style and imagery. The twelfth-century manuscript has 32 full-page images prefaced to the text, the fifteenth-century one 120 illustrations, 2 of these, in the prologue, being full-page, but all the rest occupying about a third or half of a page and scattered throughout the text at appropriate points. The earlier images are in the bold, slightly exaggerated style of the English Romanesque, with elongated figures, bright colours and imaginative use of geometrical forms and divisions of the page. Three centuries later, the crowded narrative scenes of the later work have a completely different visual impact, with carefully modelled features and more naturalistic composition. What is also striking is the way that both works depict physical features—clothing, armour, ships, and buildings—as they found them in their own world. There is no sense of anachronism here. The twelfth-century pictures show mounted knights, with the arms and armour of the Norman period, Viking ships with dragon heads like those on the Bayeux Tapestry and churches with the round arches and twin towers to be found in the cathedrals or abbeys of the time. In the later manuscript the ships are of fifteenth-century design, the ladies wear high-horned headdresses, many of the men have the cropped hairstyle familiar from images of Henry V, while one outdoor scene (fol. 65) shows a windmill, something not introduced into England until the late twelfth century, long after Edmund's day, and later, too, than the Pierpont Morgan book. Most remarkably, the Vikings have been made exotic by being given the elaborate turbans and scimitars usually the attributes of Mongols or Muslims. Since the earlier and the later works illustrate many of the same incidents, it is possible to set side-by-side their two pictorial versions of an identical textual account, as in Edmund's posthumous appearance to Sweyn of

[114] Paul the Deacon, *Historia Langobardorum* 4. 16, pp. 151–52.

[115] *Die Akten des Kanonisationsprozesses Dorotheas von Montau*, p. 397.

[116] Corley, *Conrad von Soest*, fig. 136, pls. XVIII–XIX.

[117] Pierpont Morgan M. 736 (images on-line); BL, Harley 2278; there is a facsimile of the London manuscript: *The Life of St Edmund King and Martyr: A Facsimile*. For discussion of the former, McLachlan, *The Scriptorium of Bury St. Edmunds*, pp. 74–119, 330–32; Hahn, *Portrayed on the Heart*, pp. 216–54.

Denmark, whom he kills with a spear. The Pierpont Morgan version has a crowned figure in a decorated surcoat thrusting a long spear, while the version from the 1430s shows Edmund in the full plate armour of its own time, complete with visored helmet and a tabard bearing his coat-of-arms, the three crowns. Edmund's cult could make the transition to the world of windmills, plate-armour and heraldry with no apparent strain.

Images and Devotion

It is hard to explore the personal and emotional effects of images of the saints in the past, although occasionally there are explicit testimonies. The sixth-century lawyer and historian Agathias wrote the following inscription for an image of the archangel Michael:

> It was bold to depict in wax the invisible chief of the angels, who is bodiless in form, but it is not without its reward, since by looking at the image a mortal man will be able to direct his soul towards a more powerful imagination: no longer does he have a wavering reverence, but, having inscribed the image within himself, he fears him as if he were present. The eyes stir up the deep senses, and craftsmanship knows how to convey by colours the prayer of the heart.[118]

Amid this complex poetical language, the thought stands out that contemplating the image of the saint—presumably a painting in wax—can lead to a powerful internalization that makes the saint "present." Pictures place things before our eyes "as if seen in the present," echoed the liturgist William Durandus, which is why, he explained, we show more reverence in church to images and to pictures than to books.[119]

There was, however, a countervailing argument, repeatedly expressed, that pictures were, in fact, just a substitute for books. One twelfth-century ecclesiastic wrote of "the revered images of the saints, which the simple populace and god-fearing folk, who are to be praised for their rough piety, use rather like books, and which arouse the less educated to devotion in place of reading."[120] The language here ("simple populace," "rough piety," "less educated") is thoroughly condescending: images are a substitute, offered to the uneducated in place of the written word to which the educated elite have access. But, despite its condescension, it was a view that allowed the leaders of the Church, both East and West, to endorse the use of holy images. "An image is a means of remembrance, and what a book is to those familiar with letters, an image is to the illiterate," wrote John of Damascus.[121] Pope Gregory the Great thought that

[118] *Anthologia Graeca* 1. 34 (1, pp. 20–22).

[119] William Durandus, *Rationale divinorum officiorum* 1. 3. 4 (140, p. 36).

[120] Venerabiles quoque sanctorum imagines, quibus simplex populus et plebs Dei cultrix pia ruditate commendabilis, quasi pro libris utitur, que vice lectionis simpliciores ad devotionem excitant: William of Tyre, *Chronicon* 6. 23 (1, p. 339).

[121] John of Damascus, *De imaginibus oratio* 1. 17, p. 93 (PG 94: 1248).

wall-paintings in churches enabled the illiterate "at least to read, through seeing on the walls, what they are unable to read in books."[122]

So these varied voices build up a range of possibilities of how images might have their effects: illiterate people being instructed by wall-paintings, illiterate people roused to devotion by pictures, highly literate people understanding the way an image of a saint can reach the depths of the imagination. Thomas Aquinas recognized these diverse effects when he wrote that there were three reasons that the Church permitted images:

> to instruct the illiterate, who learn from them as if they were books; so that the mystery of the incarnation and the example of the saints may be brought to mind more often, being represented before our eyes every day; thirdly, to stir up the feeling of devotion, which is aroused more powerfully be seeing than by hearing.[123]

The way that an image could form the focus for prayer and devotion is illustrated in a story from the Miracles of St. Dominic of Sora.[124] Dominic was a reforming Italian abbot, who died in 1031, and was at once venerated as a saint. A wealthy man, who had a son with a withered arm and leg, determined to seek out Dominic's help, and so, on the saint's feast-day, he ordered his servants to prepare a banquet for the poor and needy, and then set out with the boy to a church dedicated to Dominic. (There is no mention of the tomb, so this cannot be Dominic's shrine at Sora, southeast of Rome.) Here,

> he placed himself before an image of Dominic, gazing at it with the eyes of his body while he directed the eyes of his mind to him whose image had been made in his memory. He did not cease importuning him for his son's health, with his heart, with his mouth, and with many sighs drawn from the depth of his soul. Meanwhile the boy begged his father to lift him up onto his shoulders, saying that he wished to kiss some part of the image that he was contemplating. When the boy had been lifted onto his father's shoulders, he tried to stretch out both arms to embrace the image . . . he embraced the image with both arms, then, drawing the embrace yet tighter, he kissed the lower part of the image.

Here the image is the focus of intense inner attention on the part of the worshipper. It can also be embraced, so is either a statue or a fairly solid panel painting. And it clearly provided a cult centre quite separate from the physical remains of the saint.

A particular variant of the saintly image is one in which the worshipper is shown alongside the saint. Such images occur in frescoes, mosaics, panel paintings and il-

[122] Gregory I, *Registrum epistularum* 9. 209 (2, p. 768).

[123] Thomas Aquinas, *Super Sententiis* 3 d. 9 q. 1 a. 2 qc. 2 ad 3, p. 294.

[124] *Vita et miracula sancti Dominic Sorani*, miracle 25, pp. 68–69; for discussion of the text, see, in addition to the editor's comments, Howe, *Church Reform and Social Change in Eleventh-Century Italy: Dominic of Sora and His Patrons*, pp. 163–78.

luminated manuscripts, and usually represent the patron or owner revering, or being presented to, the saint, and hence enable them to picture themselves with their saint. Usually the worshipper is depicted smaller, often much smaller, than the saint. Images of this type were a long-established tradition, in both East and West. The so-called Bible of Leo, for example, which was produced in Constantinople in the first half of the tenth century, opens with coloured paintings of the high official Leo kneeling and presenting the book to the Virgin Mary, and the abbot Makar and the monastic founder Constantine (Leo's brother) prostrate before St. Nicholas.[125] A twelfth-century bronze-gilt reliquary from northern Germany, which contained relics of the emperor Henry II (canonized in 1146), depicts the emperor saint enthroned, while to his right a smaller figure, labelled "Weiland the monk," kneels and offers him the reliquary, unmistakable because of its quatrefoil shape. Weiland is presumably the craftsman who made the reliquary and it is noteworthy that he bears the name of a smith famous in Germanic legend.[126] The painting above the tomb of Francesco Dandolo, Doge of Venice, which dates to around 1339, shows the Doge being presented by his name-saint, Francis of Assisi, to the Virgin and Child, while his wife Elizabeth is presented by her name-saint.[127]

Developments in pictorial techniques in the later Middle Ages, such as advances in portraiture, the application of perspective and the invention of painting in oils, made it possible to depict saint and worshipper together in highly realized and naturalistic scenes, clearly occupying the same space. Great men might commission such images for public display. The Rolin Madonna, for example, a masterpiece by Jan Van Eyck, portrays the powerful churchman and politician Nicholas Rolin kneeling in a chapel, contemplating the Virgin and Child in front of him. All the figures are lifelike and of the same scale, and an open arcade behind them shows a fifteenth-century city and river scene.[128] Similarly, Van Eyck's *Madonna with Canon van der Paele*, of 1436, shows the donor, Canon van der Paele, kneeling and holding his spectacles, being presented to the Virgin and Child by St. George, his name-saint, all set in a convincingly depicted ecclesiastical interior.[129] The canon's surplice just touches Mary's robe; the carpet beneath her throne extends its geometrical patterns towards the viewer; the figure of St. Donatian, opposite St. George, could be any splendidly vested late medieval bishop (he has no halo). The hieratic quality of some of the earlier images of donor and saint has here been modulated by an intense realism.

[125] BAV, Reg. gr. 1, fols. 2v, 3; there is a facsimile: *Die Bibel des Patricius Leo*; see Spatharakis, *The Portrait in Byzantine Illuminated Manuscripts*, pp. 7–14.

[126] Louvre OA 49; Lasko, *Ars Sacra*, p. 212, with full-page colour plate at ill. 291; *Treasures of Heaven: Saints, Relics, and Devotion in Medieval Europe*, p. 83, no. 39.

[127] The tomb is in the chapter house of Santa Maria Gloriosa dei Frari in Venice; see Roberts, "Donor Portraits in Late Medieval Venice," pp. 72–74.

[128] The painting is now in the Louvre; see the discussion in Gelfand and Gibson, "Surrogate Selves: The *Rolin Madonna* and the Late-Medieval Devotional Portrait."

[129] Now in the Groeninge Museum, Bruges.

Van Eyck's influence can be seen in the *Virgin of the Councillors*, a painting by the Valencian artist Luis Dalmau, which has a group of donors kneeling before the Virgin and backed by locally appropriate saints. The donors are the five executive councillors of Barcelona, and the contract between them and Luis Dalmau, drawn up in 1443, survives, as well as the painting itself. The painting was to be set up in the chapel of the Barcelona City Hall and it measures 270 by 275 centimetres or about 9 feet high and wide, although it now lacks its base, which was also painted. Three councillors kneel on one side, two on the other. The contract specifies that they were to be depicted "just as they are in life," and stipulates the colours of their robes. Behind one group stands St. Eulalia, "the patron and special advocate of the city," behind the other is St. Andrew, on whose feast-day (30 November) the councillors of Barcelona entered office.[130] The painting witnesses to both the civic and individual pride of the councillors, but it is a pride carefully subordinated to the saints, whom they revere and who protect them.

Yet more striking are images where the donor and saints are introduced into biblical scenes, such as the triptych of Jan Crabbe by Hans Memling, dating to the late 1460s, which shows the patron, Jan Crabbe, abbot of the Cistercian monastery of The Dunes, present at the crucifixion.[131] He kneels in prayer close to the grieving Mary Magdalene, who embraces the cross. Behind him stand John the Baptist (his name-saint) and St. Bernard (the most important saint of his Order), while, behind the Magdalene, John the Evangelist comforts the Virgin Mary. On the outer wings kneel two lay people, an elderly woman and a younger man, who have been interpreted as relatives of abbot Jan, each of them backed by a standing saint (probably St. Anne and St. William of Maleval).[132] The whole scene is integrated by being set in the same detailed landscape, which runs right across the background, with a late medieval townscape in the distance.

There is evidence to suggest that there was a multiplication of images and a proliferation of new media over the course of the Middle Ages. This meant that images of the saints were more widespread, in many different settings.[133] For instance, the ceremony of canonization as described in a treatise of 1488 mentions for the first time that "an image of the person to be canonized" was displayed in St. Peter's.[134] This trend towards an increased role for images can be seen to imply a decreased role for relics. One scholar writing of the late Middle Ages talks of "the triumph of the image over the relic," and the point can even be put as sharply as in the following dichotomy: "Where early medieval devotion to the saints was focused on

[130] Sobré, *Behind the Altar Table: The Development of the Painted Retable in Spain*, pp. 288–97.

[131] Different sections are in the Museo Civico, Vicenza, the Pierpont Morgan Library, New York, and the Groeninge Museum, Bruges.

[132] On him, see note on p. 463, earlier.

[133] For two exemplary studies devoted to particular regions, see Higgitt, *"Imageis maid with mennis hand": Saints, Images, Belief and Identity in Later Medieval Scotland*, and Marks, *Image and Devotion in Late Medieval England.*

[134] Patrizi Piccolomini, *Caeremoniale romanum* 1. 6. 6 (1, p. 121).

their relics, late medieval devotion focused on images."[135] Relics were expected to be unique—one head, no more than two hands, and so on (despite conflicting claims and multiple bodies)—but images were essentially non-unique. In their essence they were reproducible. This meant they could spread a cult in a way totally divorced from bodily remains, free from the limits on the movements of corpses and parts of corpses. The cult of Enrico or Rigo of Bolzano, which was centred in the place of his death, Treviso, attained a wide geographical dissemination through images in this manner: "at Rome and Perugia and those areas the image of this praiseworthy man was painted in many places, and throngs of people came to those images and God performed many miracles."[136]

As images of the saints became more widespread, more people could gain access to, or even own, images of the saints, and hence images entered the private world as well as the public space in a way they had not done before. There is increasing evidence for the presence in private houses of relatively small panel paintings with devotional subjects.[137] These could be the focus of prayer. This is an observation about practices current in the middle of the thirteenth century:

> It is the custom of noble Roman ladies, whether widows or married, especially those whose wealth is in the service of their distinguished position and whom Christ fills with his love, to have little rooms or some private space in their homes suitable for prayer. Here they have a painted image depicting the saint whom they specially venerate.[138]

This was a new and powerful function of the image: a painting of a favourite saint to which you could retire, to reflect upon the nature of the pictured person and reap the harvest of private conversation with your heavenly patron. One of the early signs of a new cult was the appearance of devotional images of the saint in people's houses. Within a year of the death of Bernardino of Siena on 20 May 1444, pictures or sculptures of the saint were to be found in rooms in private houses, much to the dismay of the bishop of Naples, who thought such practices were wrong prior to official canonization.[139]

It is in the Books of Hours and private prayer books of the later Middle Ages that one finds some of the most striking devotional images of the period.[140] These books, usually small but costly, contain prayers, psalms, and other devotional texts for private lay use. Commissioned by or for very high status individuals, they are often lavishly illustrated with biblical scenes, depictions of church services, and

[135] Wirth, "Image et relique dans le cristianisme occidental," p. 332; Duffy, *The Stripping of the Altars*, p. 167.

[136] Peter, bishop of Treviso, *Vita Henrici Baucenensis* 2. 19, p. 374.

[137] Schmidt, *Painted Piety: Panel Paintings for Personal Devotion in Tuscany*.

[138] Thomas de Celano, *Tractatus de miraculis beat Francisci* 2. 8, pp. 275–76.

[139] *Il processo di canonizzazione di Bernardino da Siena*, pp. 57*–58*.

[140] Wieck, *Time Sanctified: The Book of Hours*; idem, *Painted Prayers: The Book of Hours in Medieval and Renaissance Art*; Reinburg, *French Books of Hours*.

pictures of the saints. The standard components of Books of Hours were a Kalendar; Gospel readings; the Hours of the Virgin; the Hours of the Cross; the Hours of the Holy Spirit; the Penitential Psalms; the Marian prayers *Obescro te* and *O intemerata*; a Litany; and the Office of the Dead. They often also contained additional prayers addressed to Mary and the saints (Suffrages), which might be illustrated.

A manuscript now in the British Library provides a good example of just how rich a crop of saints' images such private prayer books could offer.[141] It consists of forty-one folios (a few leaves are now missing) and measures 23.5 by 17 centimetres (9 ¼ by 6 ⅔ inches), so it would be comfortable enough to hold in the hand. There are thirty-nine virtually full-page paintings of saints, with a Low German prayer following each one, usually in rhyme. It has been dated variously to the 1420s and to c. 1450. One suggestion is that it was made for the Burgundian princess Mary of Cleves and, although this has been disputed, it is clear that the book was owned by a high-born woman from the area where French and German culture overlapped in the lands around the lower Rhine. The prayers are in the dialect of Cologne and the selection of saints mixes Cologne saints like Gereon and French saints like Vigor of Bayeux. The book is not organized according to the liturgical year, and seems to be a prayer book with a selection of saints made especially for this owner. The prayers are in the form of direct addresses to the saints ("O St. Leonard, God's friend," and so on) and the images could form a visual focus for devotion while they were uttered.

Books of Hours sometimes include pictures of the owner of the book in prayer, like the tiny image in the Suffrages from a fragment of a French Book of Hours dating to around 1500, now in Boston.[142] It shows a richly dressed lady kneeling before a draped box on which lies an open book, perhaps intended to represent the book that contains the image (whether the book depicted in the painting contains another image of the book, and so on, is a dizzying issue). Behind her are carved or sculpted figures standing in niches, presumably saints, so perhaps she is a wealthy lady in a private chapel. No individual identifiable saint is depicted on this page, but there are two other images in the book, of a man and a woman, and a woman alone, kneeling before saints.[143] Pictures like this of worshippers at prayer sometimes show them before images of the saints rather than the actual saints themselves, as in the elaborate painting in the Psalter-Hours of Yolande of Soissons, which shows Yolande in prayer (with her dog) before an image of the Virgin and Child upon an altar.[144]

It is unquestionable that there survive many more images of the saints, in book illustrations, wall paintings and panel paintings, from the later Middle Ages than from earlier centuries, but one might wonder whether this simply means that such later material is more likely to be preserved. Is there really a multiplication of images in the later Middle Ages or is this an illusion produced by the differential ravages of

[141] BL, Egerton MS 859; see Panofsky, *Early Netherlandish Painting* 1, p. 106; Gorissen, "Ein illuminiertes kölner Gebetbuch."

[142] Gardner Museum, 3, fol. 25v.

[143] Ibid., fols. 19, 22.

[144] New York, Pierpont Morgan Library, M. 729, fol. 232v.

time? Something that might incline us to see this apparent proliferation as a real one, is the fact that there were real technical developments at this time that made it easier to multiply images, namely the arrival of paper and the wood block print. If the pressure to supply images was great enough to generate new media, then it makes sense to see the later medieval centuries as a genuine age of the image.

The availability of paper pictures of saints is clear from the following advice:

> If you cannot read, then take a picture of paper where Mary and Elizabeth are depicted as they meet each other, you buy it for a penny. Look at it and think how happy they had been, and of good things. . . . Then do them reverence, kiss the image on the paper, bow in front of the image, kneel before it.[145]

The advice here combines two things: the exhortation to see the historical event in one's mind's eye, vividly realizing the characters and emotions, and the instructions on formal veneration of a cult object.

Paper spread from the thirteenth century onwards, reaching northern Europe in the fourteenth. It was the early fifteenth century that saw the birth of a new medium, dependent upon paper, capable of depicting the saints. The woodcut was a print made by the impression on a sheet of paper of a carved and inked block of wood. Because it was a printing process, hundreds of identical images could be produced in a short period. Cheap images of the saints were now available, to be placed in their houses by devout individuals or to be hung up in public in large numbers on appropriate occasions, such as processions. The woodcut of the "Madonna of the Fire" (*Madonna del Fuoco*), which was shown in the cathedral at Forlì from 1428, was so-called because it had survived the fire that destroyed the house of the schoolteacher who had it hanging on his wall.[146] In this period the feast-day of Catherine of Siena might be celebrated not only by decorating the church with flowers and branches, but also by hanging up her image on sheets of paper, an image "that was easily reproducible."[147] Just like mass-produced pilgrim badges (earlier, pp. 440–42), these "easily reproducible" woodcuts of saints show new artisanal techniques, developed in the urban workshops of the later Middle Ages, being enlisted in the service of the cult of the saints and to the profit of their makers.

Images were not only a focus of devotion, but also powerful instruments of miracle-working.[148] In the later Middle Ages there was an increase in the number of miraculous images of the Virgin Mary. Some had existed from early times. There was a miraculous icon of the Virgin at the church of the Hodegetria in Constantinople from early in the Middle Ages, and the image of the Virgin in Santa Maria Maggiore in Rome was supposedly taken on procession by Pope Gregory the Great

[145] Clemen, *Die Volksfrömmigkeit des ausgehenden Mittelalters*, p. 14, citing Johann Geiler von Kaiserberg (d. 1510) without exact reference.

[146] Cobianchi, "The Use of Woodcuts in Fifteenth-century Italy," p. 50.

[147] *De facili multiplicablis: Il processo Castellano*, p. 93.

[148] *The Miraculous Image in the Late Middle Ages and Renaissance.*

to avert a plague.[149] These miraculous images of Mary were sometimes reputedly painted "by no human hand," sometimes by the Apostle Luke (he was eventually credited with thirteen versions).[150] But from around 1300 until the Reformation these wonder-working images of Mary multiplied (see earlier, p. 161): Pilar, Guadalupe, Częstochowa, Walsingham, all over Europe new and important shrines, associated with images, sprang to life. The painting of the Virgin Mary at Impruneta, a little distance from Florence, was brought in procession to the city in times of need, especially when rain was required, but also for other crises, such as plague or war; the first recorded procession took place in the middle years of the fourteenth century.[151]

Alongside the veneration of miraculous images by worshippers in a church or a procession, there are also cases of more intimate contact, when sufferers applied images to an afflicted part of the body to obtain a cure. A nun in Ascoli, in the Italian Marche, who was troubled by a growth in one of her arm bones, conceived the idea of applying to it a picture of St. Peter Martyr: "As soon as she attached the image, with care and devotion, that bone, which had caused her such great suffering, returned to its normal place and shape."[152] In the late 1380s the Duchess of Bourbon, during a prolonged and painful delivery, placed an image of St. Peter of Luxemburg on her belly, and "at once her pains disappeared and she gave birth without grief to a very beautiful daughter."[153] A cloth painted with the image of San Gennaro, from the church of Ischia near Naples, raised to life a widow's son after she had covered him with it, "placing the face of the picture on his face, its eyes on his eyes, its mouth on his mouth, its palms on his palms and its feet on his feet." She knew that the prophet Elisha had revived a boy by lying on him in this way.[154]

There is a strange and sad indication of the ubiquity of saintly images in Christian private devotion at the end of the Middle Ages. When the Spanish Inquisition was undertaking its campaign against converts from Judaism who nevertheless continued Jewish practices in private, its officials regarded the possession of images of saints in the home as an important sign of sincere conversion. It is an issue that recurs in the case of Marina González from 1494. The arraignment against her claimed that one proof of the falseness of her Christianity was "she did not have in her house the image or picture of any saint, male or female." The lawyer representing her denied this charge: "As for the charge concerning images, she had not given up having them, but had images of St. Catherine and the Cross of St. Antony that she had from girlhood, on a cloth opposite the living room, where she prayed." He put a question about this

[149] Vassilake, ed., *Images of the Mother of God: Perceptions of the Theotokos in Byzantium*, index s.v. "Virgin: Hodegetria"; Jacobus de Voragine, *Legenda aurea* 46 (1, pp. 289–90).

[150] *Bacci, Il pennello dell'Evangelista. Storia delle immagini sacre attribute a san Luca.*

[151] Trexler, "Florentine Religious Experience: The Sacred Image," pp. 11–21; Bacci, *Pro remedio animae: immagini sacre e pratiche devozionali in Italia centrale*, pp. 48–53.

[152] Ambrogio Taegio, *Vita sancti Petri martyris* 9. 71, p. 708.

[153] *Processus de vita et miraculis beati Petri de Luxemburgo* 2. 5. 202, p. 579.

[154] *Miracula sancti Januarii* 11, p. 886 (cf. ibid., p. 785, from "*Menæa Græca*").

to the witnesses: "if they know that Marina González prayed with great devotion to the Cross of St. Antony and to the images of St. Catherine and other saints that she had." Although one of the witnesses claimed that he had not seen in her house "an image of a saint, male or female, nor a cross, nor any sign of a Christian," Marina's lawyer, in his summing up, called this witness a liar, and reasserted that "she had images of the saints and the Cross of St. Antony," "for devotion." Marina's fate was miserable. After being tortured by simulated drowning ("waterboarding"), she went on hunger strike in prison, and was eventually handed over to the secular authorities for execution.[155] The uncertainty about her possession of saintly images is unlikely to have been a determining piece of evidence, but it was certainly seen as casting doubt on the genuineness of her Christianity: the truly Christian home would have pictures of the saints.

[155] *Records of the Trials of the Spanish Inquisition in Ciudad Real* 2, pp. 8–41, citations at pp. 12, 14, 16, 22, 29.

CHAPTER 13

The Literature of Sanctity

Types of Hagiography

For more than a thousand years, hagiography, that is, writing about the saints and their miraculous powers, was one of the main branches of European literature.[1] Even after the great disruption of the Protestant Reformation, it continued to be an important part of the cultural world of Catholic and Orthodox Europe. In the Middle Ages such literature was vast in volume and variety. The standard handbook on medieval Latin hagiography, which is far from complete, lists more than 9,000 individual works.[2] It is a literature that has not always received proper scholarly attention, firstly because it was for long under the shadow of confessional controversy, with Protestants regarding it as papistical and childish, and secondly because a narrow definition of "literature" excluded it from the consideration of literary scholars and their canon of texts to be studied. As late as 1994 a scholar in this field could write, "As a consequence of a bias of literary historians in favour of 'high' literature, the legends [saints' Lives] have normally not received much attention in surveys of medieval vernacular literature."[3] In recent generations, however, interest in hagiography has developed to a remarkable degree, with societies and journals dedicated to it and a general recognition of its importance and value as literature, as a source for social history and as a window into medieval mentalities.

The earliest literature devoted specifically to post-biblical Christian saints consisted of accounts of the trials and sufferings of the martyrs (known as "Passions," from the Latin for "suffering"). Some of these seem to be based almost word-for-word on the exchanges between the Roman magistrate and the martyr in the court-

[1]The classic studies are Delehaye, *Cinq leçons sur la méthode hagiographique*; idem, *Les légendes hagiographiques*; Aigrain, *L'Hagiographie*; more recent guides include Berschin, *Biographie und Epochenstil im lateinischen Mittelalter*; Sigal, "Le travail des hagiographes aux XIe et XIIe siècles"; Dubois and Lemaitre, *Sources et méthodes de l'hagiographie médiévale*; von der Nahmer, *Die lateinische Heiligenvita*; *Hagiographies*; Grégoire, *Manuale di agiologia*; Boesch Gajano, "L'agiografia"; *Gregorio Magno e l'agiografia fra IV e VII secolo*; Monaci Castagno, *L'agiografia cristiana antica*; for Byzantium, see Ehrhard, *Überlieferung und Bestand der hagiographischen und homiletischen Literatur der griechischen Kirche*; *The Ashgate Research Companion to Byzantine Hagiography*.

[2]BHL.

[3]Görlach, "Middle English Legends, 1220–1530," p. 432.

room, while others offer more discursive narratives. Over the years scholars have devoted a great deal of attention to separating the more historically credible from the rest. Eventually, after the triumph of Christianity in the fourth century, the genre of martyrdom accounts took wing, and purely legendary and fantastical Passions of the martyrs were composed, even if, on occasion, the martyr who was the subject was indeed a real historical person.[4] Some of the best known saints, such as George, Christopher, and Lucy, are of this type—genuine martyrs whose names are attested in early sources but whose stories are later elaborations.

The literature of sanctity continually diversified. Its many genres include, alongside the Passions of the martyrs, the Lives of the confessor saints. These often contain accounts of posthumous miracles, but free-standing miracle collections, or Miracle Books, some produced at the shrine itself, are also numerous. Then there are accounts of the discoveries and translations of saints' bodies; some of these became popular texts and were much copied, notably those of Gervasius and Protasius, Stephen, Benedict, Nicholas, and Mary Magdalene. Collected Lives, in the form of Legendaries and related genres, became a dominant form in the later Middle Ages, while there were always sermons, poems and occasional pieces on the subject of the saints and their wonderful deeds.

The distinction between Passions of the martyrs and Lives of confessor saints was traditional and deeply entrenched. It is neatly exemplified by the activities of Burchard, librarian of the monastery of the Michelsberg in Bamberg in the mid-twelfth century. His predecessor had collected numerous little booklets containing Lives and Passions of the saints, but Burchard considered these inconvenient and too easily stolen, so he had them bound in four big volumes: "Passions of the saints in two volumes; Lives of the saints in two volumes." His tidying up must have involved a decision on each text: did it belong with the Passions or with the Lives?[5] The balance between Passions and Lives can be explored by a survey undertaken of two of the great collections of such material. In the Bibliothèque nationale in Paris and the Bibliothèque royale de Belgique there are 1,083 hagiographical texts dating to the period prior to 1200: Passions of the martyrs account for 53.5 per cent of them, followed by 24.8 per cent for Lives and 21.8 per cent for miscellaneous items such as accounts of translations, miracles and sermons on the saints.[6] So, in this huge and important corpus of medieval hagiographical material, stories of the martyrs clearly predominate.

Just as there was a body of thought that regarded martyrs as the highest class of saint, so their Passions might be considered the most prestigious kind of hagiography. The sixth-century monastic leader Cassiodorus, writing his guidance for monks in the 550s, recommended the assiduous reading of saints' Lives of all kinds, making

[4] Aigrain, *L'Hagiographie*, pp. 140–55.

[5] Dengler-Schreiber, *Scriptorium und Bibliothek des Klosters Michelsberg*, pp. 62, 184, 186, 196.

[6] Heinzelmann, *Translationsberichte*, pp. 45–46.

a special point that a confessor provided just as important an example as a martyr or virgin:

> not only are crowns bestowed through bloody contest or virginity of the flesh, but also all those who, with God's help, conquer the vices of their body and believe rightly receive the palm of holy reward.[7]

His point is quite clear, that reading the Lives of confessors is as valuable as reading the Passions of martyrs and the Lives of virgins, and the suspicion naturally arises that he only needed to make this point because some people preferred tales of "bloody contest" to the less spectacular, even if exemplary, Lives of confessors.

Hagiographic literature soon found a place in Christian public worship. It was especially natural that, on the day that the anniversary of a martyr was celebrated, there should be readings from the accounts of his or her sufferings.[8] The Third Council of Carthage, held in 397, made this explicit: "It is permitted to read out the Passions of the martyrs when their annual commemorations are celebrated."[9] Augustine of Hippo was one of the bishops present at this assembly, and he has left a series of sermons on the theme of the martyrs, and it is often clear from what he says in these that they followed a reading of the martyr's Passion.[10] Evidence for this practice in other parts of the Christian world is later. It appears in the sixth century in Gaul, where Bishop Caesarius of Arles (503–42) was kind enough to allow those members of his congregation with bad feet to sit "when very long Passions are being read out."[11] Gregory of Tours remembered attending as a child a Mass in honour of St. Polycarp, where his Passion was read out, in the settlement of Riom in the Auvergne.[12] The earliest explicit evidence from Spain comes in the following century. Braulio, bishop of Zaragoza (631–51), explains in the preface to his Life of St. Emiliano, that "I have written a short little book about the life of the saint, so that it can be read as quickly as possible in the Mass celebrated for him."[13] While it is possible that hagiographic readings had been part of church services in Gaul and Spain for a long time before this clear evidence, the situation in Rome is different. Here the absence of the custom as a general norm is attested explicitly, and its introduction is attributed to Pope Hadrian I (772–95): "Until the time of Hadrian, the Passions or Deeds of the saints were read out only in those churches dedicated to that saint."[14] Evidence for the practice in Byzantium comes at about this same time. The Life of St. Stephen the

[7] Cassiodorus, *Institutiones* 1. 32. 4, pp. 80–81 (PL 70: 1147).

[8] For the following, see De Gaiffier, "La lecture des actes des martyrs dans la prière liturgique"; idem, "La lecture des passions des martyrs à Rome"; Saxer, *Morts, martyrs, reliques*, pp. 200–208, 315–21; Martimort, *Les lectures liturgiques et leurs livres*, pp. 97–102.

[9] *Concilia Africae, a. 345–a. 525*, pp. 43, 186, 265, 306; cf. p. 21.

[10] Augustine, *Sermones* 273–340, PL 38: 1247–1484; see, for example, cols. 1249, 1426.

[11] Caesarius of Arles, *Sermo* 78 (3, p. 238); the sermon was also commonly attributed to Augustine: *Sermo* 300 (PL 39: 2319).

[12] Gregory of Tours, *Gloria martyrum* 85, pp. 545–46 (repr., 1969, pp. 95–96).

[13] Braulio, *Vita Emiliani*, col. 701.

[14] *Les Ordines Romani du haut Moyen Âge* 2, pp. 465–66 (Ordo XII).

Younger, who died in 764 or 765, tells of his pious upbringing, including regular attendance at the vigils of the saints, where, unlike the rest of the congregation, he would remain standing during the readings, listening intently to "the martyr Passion or the Life or the teachings of the Fathers."[15]

By 800, then, it was normal Christian custom to read out from hagiographic literature during services on saints' days. The author of the Life of Bernard of Tiron explained in his preface the great benefits of this public reading of hagiographic texts:

> When we recite such writings on the feast-days of the saints, we pay due praise to God, we foster the memory of the saints, we fill the minds of the faithful with profitable edification and we offer the honour of veneration that is due to the saints.[16]

But hagiography was read out in many milieux other than church services. In monasteries it could be heard in the monks' Chapter House and dining room, not to mention individual private reading.[17] The Chapter was the daily meeting of monks or canons, and involved not only discussion of business but also reading of texts, including hagiographic texts, or at least announcements of saints' days. Abbot Peter of Celle, writing in the twelfth century, refers to "the little book that is read in the Chapter about the feast-days of the saints and about the commemoration of our departed brethren."[18] Sometimes the manuscripts themselves make clear in what circumstances they were read, like the fourteenth-century collection of French Lives produced for the nuns of Campsey in Suffolk, which bears the inscription "for reading aloud during dinner."[19] Similarly, a copy of the *Golden Legend* is listed among the "dining room books" in a fifteenth-century Dutch catalogue.[20] Texts are sometimes divided into "readings." As well as his Major Legend of St. Francis, Bonaventure produced a Minor Legend for liturgical use, which is divided into sections for reading during services commemorating the saint.

Not all hagiographic manuscripts were grand objects, designed for public reading in church or cloister. The great palaeographer Bernhard Bischoff identified a substantial number of manuscripts containing saints' Lives that show clear evidence of having been folded in half (or even in four), presumably to be stuffed into a pocket or bag. Their average dimensions are 23.3 by 16.6 centimetres (about 9 ½ by 6 ½ inches), so the folded size would be quite convenient to take on a journey or simply to carry to a private spot for quiet reading. An example is a leaflet of 7 folios containing the Passion of St. Maurice and his companions, which was written in

[15] Stephen the Deacon, *Vita Stephani Junioris* 8, p. 97 (PG 100: 1081).

[16] Geoffrey Grossus, *Vita Bernardi Tironiensis*, prologue, p. 223.

[17] Philippart, *Les légendiers latins*, pp. 112–22; De Gaiffier, "A propos des légendiers latins," pp. 65–68 on reading in the refectory.

[18] Peter of Celle, *Epistola* 142, p. 524.

[19] *De lire a mengier*: BL, Add. 70513 (formerly Welbeck Abbey I C I), fol. 265v; for a detailed individual case-study, see Gremont, "*Lectiones ad prandium* à l'abbaye de Fécamp."

[20] *Libri refectorales*: Dolbeau, "Notes sur l'organisation interne des légendiers latins," p. 24 n. 11.

southern Germany in the late tenth century. It is 26.5 by 19.0 centimetres (about 10 ½ by 7 ½ inches) and shows signs of having been folded twice, so producing a little packet quite as convenient as a modern paperback.[21] A survey of the hagiographic booklets in the Bibliothèque nationale in Paris found that 12 per cent (38 of 314) were folded in this way.[22] One ingenious method of carrying a saint's Life is shown by a French Life of St. Margaret, written in the year 1491, and made up of a roll of six leaves sewn end to end, contained in a cylindrical leather case 10.5 centimetres (just over 4 inches) long and 4.6 centimetres (about 1 ¾ inches) in diameter.[23] The case shows scenes from St. Margaret's Life. Smaller than some pepper-grinders, it could easily have been carried about the person.

Hagiography was written in many languages and literary forms. The Greek and Latin texts of the ancient world were supplemented during the Middle Ages by a large and lively hagiographic literature in the vernacular (later, pp. 578ff.). And the length, form and structure of hagiography were extraordinarily diverse. Much was in verse, including one of the earliest collections of narratives about the saints, Prudentius's *Peristephanon* (or *Peristefanon*). This contains fourteen poems about martyr-saints, many of them from Prudentius's homeland of Spain.[24] Prudentius was not an ecclesiastic but a lawyer and high-ranking official of the later Roman empire, who, at some point, as he approached sixty, determined that his "sinful soul should shed its folly" and that he should turn his poetic talents to praise of God and the saints, and to battle against heresy and paganism.[25] His *Psychomachia*, a poem on the battle of the virtues and the vices, was highly influential throughout the Middle Ages.[26]

He opens the *Peristephanon* with a poem dedicated to the martyrs Emetherius and Celedonius of Calahorra, which was in all likelihood Prudentius's own home town:

> The names of the two martyrs are written in heaven in golden letters that Christ inscribed there; he inscribed the same words on earth in letters of blood. With this garland the happy land of the Ebro is renowned throughout the world. In the eyes of God this place seemed worthy to hold their bones.[27]

In these two brief verses he highlights the way the martyrs are simultaneously receiving their reward in heaven and yet still adorning and glorifying the place of their martyrdom on earth. The company of the saints in the court of heaven was united yet diverse, and every place that housed the bones of a martyr could feel that it had a special and particular patron.

[21] Bischoff, "Über gefaltene Handschriften"; the manuscript is Einsiedeln 256 (461) (ibid., p. 95).

[22] Poulin, "Les *libelli* dans l'édition hagiographique," pp. 30 and 34.

[23] New York, Pierpont Morgan Library, M. 1092.

[24] Prudentius, *Peristefanon*; see Roberts, *Poetry and the Cult of the Martyrs: The Liber Peristephanon of Prudentius.*

[25] Prudentius, *Praefatio.*

[26] Prudentius, *Psychomachia.*

[27] Prudentius, *Peristefanon* 1, lines 1–5, p. 251.

This sense of the support offered by the martyr-patron is even sharper in the poems of Prudentius's contemporary, Paulinus of Nola. His early life was not dissimilar to Prudentius's—landed property, high-level education, political office—but Paulinus then made a much more decisive break than Prudentius, disposing of his estates, becoming a priest and eventually bishop of Nola in southern Italy. Here the local martyr-saint was Felix, and Paulinus entered into a deep relationship with his "reverend father, eternal patron, sustainer," as he called him.[28] From 395 Paulinus wrote each year, as "the yearly debt of the tongue," a poem for Felix's feast-day.[29] In some of these "birthday poems" he gives an account of Felix's life and martyrdom, in others he describes the scene on his feast-day. Felix's feast-day (*natalis*), he writes, is dearer to him that his own birthday (*natalis*).[30]

The poems of Prudentius and Paulinus stand at the head of a long tradition of Christian verse celebration of the saints. Alexander of Ashby, who wrote verses for seventy-two feast-days from Andrew (30 November) to Catherine (25 November), explained why he chose the verse form:

> In this little work I have employed the brevity of verse, so that the weakness of memory might be helped more powerfully by it. For this is the special usefulness of poetry, that in its succinctness memory has a great support. I have myself learned this by experience, for when I strive to imprint something more deeply in my memory, I can retain it by no easier method than if I treat it in one or more verses.[31]

Alexander's claim is that metrical form helps memorization, and it is certainly the case that knowing the expectations of stress or length in a line reduces the number of possibilities of what the next word might be.

There are some examples of twin prose and verse Lives by the same author, perhaps to show off literary dexterity.[32] Bede wrote both a prose and a verse Life of St. Cuthbert, while Thiofrid, abbot of Echternach (d. 1110), composed a two-part Life of St. Willibrord, founder of his monastery.[33] Bede's two Lives were composed independently at different times, but Thiofrid's pendant pair was consciously a so-called twin work (*opus geminum*), although the saint has to become "Wilbrord" in the verse part in order to fit the scansion.[34] The ninth-century Fulda monk, Bruno Candidus, wrote such a work about Eigil, an earlier abbot of his monastery, some

[28] Paulinus of Nola, *Carmen* 21, lines 344–45, p. 169; see the penetrating comments of Brown, *The Cult of the Saints*, pp. 53–60.

[29] Paulinus of Nola, *Carmen* 15, lines 1–2, p. 51.

[30] Ibid., lines 2–3, p. 51.

[31] Alexander of Ashby, *Liber festivalis*, prologue, p. 155.

[32] On this form see the editor's comments in Alcuin, *The Bishops, Kings, and Saints of York*, pp. lxxviii–lxxxviii.

[33] Bede, *Vita sancti Cuthberti*; Bede, *Vita sancti Cuthberti metrica*; Thiofrid of Echternach, *Vita sancti Willibrordi*.

[34] There is one exception: Ac Willibrordi monuit nomen recitari, Thiofrid of Echternach, *Vita sancti Willibrordi, vita metrica* 4, line 68, p. 498.

twenty years after Eigil's death (which occurred in 822).[35] He had composed, he wrote, two books on the life of abbot Eigil, one in prose and one in verse: "which I have requested should be bound together, so that one of them should support the other in the narration of events."[36] Such "twin works" had, according to Hrabanus Maurus, two advantages: they stopped the reader becoming bored and, "if someone should not understand something in one part, he should quickly see that it is expounded more fully in the other."[37]

Reasons for Writing

Writing in the 1090s, Faricius, the Italian-born future abbot of Abingdon, advanced three reasons for writing saints' Lives:

> So that God, who suffers the pains that the faithful endure in their bodies for him, should be praised in his majesty.
> So that the saints, who have suffered such sweat, fasting, vigils and opprobrium and suffering, either spontaneously or inflicted by enemies, may be celebrated most gloriously by subsequent generations of believers.
> So that we, their feeble successors, by reading or hearing their most victorious exploits, by raising the eyes of our mind, might follow their innocent footsteps.[38]

So, to simplify Faricius's elaborate prose, saints' Lives are written to praise God, to celebrate the saints and to provide an example.

It was an absolute commonplace of hagiographic literature that saints provided examples to be followed: "the individual Passions of saints are nothing other than lessons in the Christian life."[39] As early as the first recorded case of martyr cult, that of Polycarp in the mid-second century, the purpose of celebrating the anniversary of the saint's death is not only as "a memorial for those who have already fought the contest" but also "for the training and preparation of those who will do so one day" (earlier, p. 4). Celebrating the saint's day thus combines honouring Polycarp with training Christians to face the kind of martyrdom he had already suffered. Recollecting his courage will fortify believers for their own future trials. Hagiography formed part of the spiritual diet of monks for similar reasons. Cassiodorus exhorted monks to read the Lives of the Fathers and the Passions of the martyrs constantly, "so that holy imitation should stir you up and lead you to the heavenly kingdom."[40]

[35] Bruno Candidus, *Vita Eigilis abbatis Fuldensis*.

[36] Ibid., 1. preface, p. 223.

[37] Hrabanus Maurus, *In honorem sancte crucis*, p. 225.

[38] Faricius, *Vita sancti Aldhelmi*, preface, p. 98.

[39] *Sanctorum singule passiones nihil aliud sunt quam instructiones Christianitatis vite*: *Passio sancti Phoce*, fol. 228; for general discussion of the issue, Vauchez, "Saints admirables et saints imitables."

[40] Cassiodorus, *Institutiones* 1. 32. 4, p. 80 (PL 70:1147).

In one of his sermons St. Augustine acknowledges that ordinary Christians might find the idea of imitating God or Jesus a daunting one: "what similarity is there between me and Christ?," they could reasonably ask. This is why the martyrs were especially important, in offering more approachable models for imitation.

> The martyrs have constructed for us a highway, sweeping away all the excuses of weakness and unbelief. It was to be built from solid stones on which we might safely walk, and they made it with their blood and their confessions of faith. . . . Who would be ashamed to say, "I am not equal to God"? Clearly not equal. "I am not equal to Christ." Unequal even to the mortal Christ. Peter was what you are. Paul was what you are. The apostles and prophets were what you are. If you are reluctant to imitate the Lord, imitate your fellow servant.[41]

Even a heroic martyr was like us in substance: "he did not have flesh of another kind than ours."[42]

But, despite this ever-repeated invocation of the exemplary function of hagiography, in practice saints were more often seen as powerful patrons to be prayed to rather than models to be emulated, as wonder-workers rather than as examples. There is a big difference between the awe-struck approach to a mighty source of supernatural aid and the attempt to model oneself on a virtuous man or woman. Even hagiographers who used the terminology of example might also stress the great gap between devotee and saint. In the *Dialogues* of Gregory the Great, an interlocutor suggests there are two things to be gained from "the examples of the fathers." They can stir up in the listener a love of the life to come, but also, if the hearer "thinks he is something," he will be brought back to earth by considering how much better they were.[43] Jacques de Vitry, marvelling at Mary of Oignies's ascetic practices, commented prudently, "Let us imitate her virtues; but her miraculous deeds we cannot imitate, without some special gift."[44]

But there is one class of person that really did take saints as a model: the saints themselves. The seventh-century saint Hadelin supposedly moved from his native Aquitaine to the missionary lands around the Meuse inspired by the examples of the early bishops of Trier, saints Agricius, Maximinus, and Paulinus—"the saint wished to be their imitator."[45] Adalhard of Corbie was "a most famous imitator of St. Augustine, like one following his footsteps."[46] The restless English merchant Godric, hearing of the miracles performed by St. Cuthbert when he lived as a hermit on the remote Farne Island, was himself stirred by desire for the solitary life.[47] St. Hugh of

[41] Augustine, *Sermo* 325 (PL 38: 1448).

[42] Augustine, *Sermo* 273 (PL 38: 1252).

[43] Gregory I, *Dialogi* 1. Prol. 9 (2, p. 16).

[44] Ejus virtutes imitemur; opera vero virtutum ejus, sine privato privilegio imitari non possumus: Jacques de Vitry, *Vita Mariae Oigniacensis* 1. 1. 2, p. 639.

[45] *Vita sancti Hadelini* 1. 2, p. 373.

[46] Paschasius Radbertus, *Vita sancti Adalhardi Corbeiensis abbatis* 14, col. 1516.

[47] Reginald of Durham, *Libellus de vita et miraculis sancti Godrici heremitae de Finchale* 5, pp. 31–32.

Lincoln was "a devoted imitator" and "special emulator" of St. Martin.[48] In these cases, hagiography, which must be the source of information about these long-dead saints, led to aspirations to imitate them. The most graphic account of a saint inspired by hagiography is in the story of John Colombini (d. 1367), founder of the Congregation of Jesuati. He was a prominent merchant of Siena, married with children, holder of civic offices and with a keen eye for profit. One day he came home to dinner, but it was not ready, and, to calm him down while he waited, his wife gave him a book of saints' Lives to read. At once he was struck by the story of Mary of Egypt, the worldly woman who had repented. His life changed at this point and he turned to poverty and chastity, before founding his Order shortly before his death.[49]

Apart from the depiction of a wonderful or exemplary figure, clergy and monks could use hagiographic writing to express their claims to property and status. This could be done in more or less direct ways. Accounts of the terrible punishments that befell anyone who infringed the rights and property of the saint—that is, the church—had an explicitly deterrent purpose (see pp. 404ff., earlier), but a less blatant tactic was to embed a claim in a narrative about the founding saint. For instance, Theodore of Sykeon's Life asserts that the emperor had granted his monastery immunity from the control of the local bishop.[50] And this kind of claim in the form of a narrative is also found in the twelfth-century *Life of St. Kentigern*, which says that the pope promised the saint that "he should be subject to no bishop." This is totally incredible as an account of events in seventh-century Scotland, where Kentigern lived, but can be understood easily as a contemporary claim about the standing of the church of Glasgow, of which Kentigern was patron.[51] And, as mentioned earlier (p. 32), the hagiography of St. Patrick was intended, in large part, to assert the supremacy of the church of Armagh.

But such specific proprietorial concerns form only a small part in the overall picture of writing about the saints. Hagiography was a record of supernatural power and was itself a vehicle of such power. At the end of the Life of St. Margaret the virgin martyr, the saint utters a prayer to God:

> that whoever reads the book of my deeds or hears my Passion, from that hour let their sins be wiped away . . . and whoever reads or carries the little book of this Passion, from that time let no sins be imputed to them . . . and whoever builds a church in my name, or writes my Passion, or buys it from the profit of just labour, let them be filled with the Holy Spirit.[52]

[48] Adam of Eynsham, *Magna vita sancti Hugonis* 1. 7; 5. 17 (1, p. 24; 2, p. 199).

[49] *Vita beati Johannis Colombini*, p. 567; Rossi, *Vita beati Johannis Colombini* 2. 13–19, p. 356.

[50] *Vita Theodori Syceotae* 82, p. 72.

[51] *Ut nulli episcopi esset subiectus*: Jocelin of Furness, *Vita Kentigerni* 33, p. 219.

[52] *Vita sancte Margarete virginis et martyris*, p. 140 (p. 46 for the Middle English; also in *Seinte Margarete*, p. 78).

God is happy to grant Margaret's requests, so the physical book of her Passion then has power against sin and brings spiritual benefit for anyone reading it, carrying it, writing it or buying it.

The Hagiographers

Hagiography was sometimes written by learned and powerful men, like Athanasius, bishop of Alexandria, author of the classic Life of St. Antony, or Gregory of Tours, bishop and historian as well as author of dozens of hagiographic pieces, but much was produced by obscure or anonymous writers in the service of their local saint. Sixty per cent of the Latin hagiographic works of the early Middle Ages are anonymous.[53] In most cases, it is plausible to posit that the authors were monks or clergy of a church associated with the saint in question. The contemporary Life of the sixth-century bishop of Le Mans, Domnolus, for example, was clearly written by a cleric of Le Mans, since he mentions "an estate belonging to *our* church."[54] The author of the Life of Gertrude of Nivelles was a monk, since he writes "I and another brother," and he was closely associated with Gertrude's nunnery, since he was summoned to comfort the nuns on Gertrude's death in the 659.[55] From indications such as these it is possible to learn something even of anonymous authors.

Hagiographers often wrote in their prefaces that the work had been imposed on them by the order of superiors. This may well have been the case, but it also meant that they avoided the charge of presumption in taking up their pens to record the wonderful deeds of such spiritual heroes. The author of a Life of St. Carileph wrote, "We have not undertaken this work through our own presumption but at the command of the holy bishops who head the Church."[56] Writing a Life of St. Wolfhelm of Brauweiler early in the twelfth century, the monk Conrad of Brauweiler explained that he did so at the urging of his abbot and a neighbouring abbot. "But, most distinguished fathers," he asked,

> what have you enjoined us to do? Neither is my knowledge sufficient, nor does my literary skill suffice. But there is such authority in your command that, although we shake at what you demand, we consider it wrong to deny you.[57]

Sometimes hagiographic writing arose naturally from the position that a monk or cleric held. Those in charge of the shrine would wish to record the miracles that occurred there and might even have a special charge to do so. The huge collection of Becket's miracles was begun by the Canterbury monk, Benedict, "at the will and command of the brethren," and, then, in June 1172, a year and a half after the

[53] Schulenburg, *Forgetful of their Sex*, p. 31.
[54] *Vita Domnoli episcopi Cenomanensis* 2. 13, p. 609.
[55] *Vita sanctae Geretrudis* 7, p. 464.
[56] *Vita Carilefi presbyteri*, prologue, 3, p. 90.
[57] Conrad of Brauweiler, *Vita Wolfhelmi abbatis Brunwilarensis*, prologue, 1, p. 181.

martyrdom, because the task was too great for one man, he was joined by the monk William, "commanded by the common decree" of the monks in Chapter.[58]

Even when not officially charged with the duty, certain individuals would be known for their hagiographic activity. The author of the *Miracles of St. Erkenwald* describes the cure of a Frenchman visiting London and the excited crowd turning up at St. Paul's cathedral, where the saint was enshrined: "it was reported to the clergy, the bells rang out, clergy and people rejoiced together . . . to me, who was present, was enjoined the task of writing an account of the miracle."[59] It is unlikely that the choice in this case was random; here was the man who was known to be keeping such a record.

On other occasions it is clear that hagiographic writers had been formally commissioned to undertake their work by members of another community, for a saint with whom they might have had no prior connection. Goscelin of St.-Bertin, a Flemish monk who settled in England in the second half of the eleventh century, produced at least a dozen hagiographical works (some works are attributed to him plausibly but not certainly), and these were written chiefly for monasteries that gave him shelter and support. For example, while staying at the abbey of Ramsey under abbot Herbert de Losinga (1087–91), he wrote a new version of the Life and Miracles of St. Ivo, a local saint, "at the request of the whole body of monks."[60] Later he was at St. Augustine's abbey, Canterbury, where he wrote at length on the local saints, especially Augustine, "apostle of the English," whose translation in 1091, along with the other saints in the abbey, he described in detail.[61] Subsequent generations praised his achievements as a hagiographer: "he was second to none since Bede in praising the saints of England—happy the tongue, that served so many saints!"[62] Goscelin was something like an itinerant hagiographer.

Such commissioned hagiography is the target of some mocking words by Eadmer, a monk not of St. Augustine's but of its rival, Christchurch Canterbury. He refers scathingly to the claims of the monks of Glastonbury to possess the body of St. Dunstan, one of the most important saints of Christchurch, and the weakness of their fabrications: "Why did you not consult some man from overseas?," he asks sarcastically. "They have great experience and knowledge and are well able to invent many things, so that you could pay a price for them to put together some plausible lie for you, on such a great matter."[63] It could be Goscelin seen through a hostile lens.

Professional writers, who could be invited to produce hagiography to order, can sometimes be found. Working in the thirteenth century, the poet Henry of

[58] Benedict of Peterborough, *Miracula sancti Thomae*, prologue, p. 26; William of Canterbury, *Miracula sancti Thomae* 1, preface, p. 138; Koopmans, *Wonderful to Relate*, pp. 145–48.

[59] Arcoid, *Miracula sancti Erkenwaldi* 7, p. 140.

[60] Goscelin of St.-Bertin, *Vita et miracula sancti Yvonis episcopi Persae*, prologue, 1, PL 155, col. 81.

[61] Sharpe, *A Handlist of the Latin Writers*, pp. 151–54, lists his works.

[62] William of Malmesbury, *Gesta regum Anglorum* 4. 342, p. 592.

[63] Eadmer, *Epistola ad Glastonienses*, p. 415 (PL 159: 803); see Sharpe, "Eadmer's Letter to the Monks of Glastonbury."

Avranches specialized in producing verse adaptations of hagiographic works for paying patrons. His name suggests he was from Normandy but he worked in Germany, Italy and, for the longest time, England. His verse Life of St. Francis was addressed to Pope Gregory IX (1227–41). He wrote poems on English saints, both famous, like Thomas Becket, and less well-known, like St. Fremund, and received payments of money and wine from the English royal Exchequer from 1242–63, sometimes for specific pieces of work, like the verse Lives of St. George and St. Edward the Confessor for which he was paid in 1254.[64]

Henry of Avranches received 10 marks of silver for his two Lives of George and Edward. All hagiographers expected rewards. These might be concrete, in the form of payments like those received by Henry, but they might be prayers (which they would doubtless also have considered a material reward). Also, "the martyr written about" would be expected to reward "his writer."[65] Hagiographers hoped that the saint they glorified would be grateful to them. "For this little service," wrote Gonzalo de Berceo, author of a Castilian verse Life of St. Dominic of Silos, "I well believe that my lord St. Dominic will request something from my lord Christ for me."[66]

The kind of hagiographer a society produced was clearly influenced by the kind of society it was. An educated lay official like Constantine Akropolites (d. 1324), author of 29 works on saints, was more likely in the urban, highly literate world of Byzantium.[67] And some of the big, long-term developments of the Middle Ages left their mark on writing about the saints. From the twelfth century the elaboration of papal canonization influenced hagiography. Lives and Miracle Books might now be written to help obtain canonization or in response to it. Thomas of Celano's *First Life of St. Francis* was commissioned by Pope Gregory IX immediately prior to Francis's canonization in the summer of 1228.[68] The Life of Thomas Helye of Biville, a Norman priest who died in 1257, was written by a certain Clement in the middle of attempts to have Thomas canonized. He actually incorporated into his text the results of a papally mandated inquiry into Thomas's miracles (although, in the event, Thomas never was canonized).[69] The Carthusians engaged in a flurry of hagiographical activity in 1515–16 amidst efforts to have their founder, St. Bruno, canonized.[70]

The rise of the friars in the same period also had its impact. Although they were committed to the full-time religious life, just as monks were, the friars were not tied to any one particular religious house, and hence their hagiography was less bound to place, to the local saints of a given community. It was their Order that formed the framework of their hagiographic activity. The standard Life of Francis was by Bonaventure, head of the Order but not a native or friar of Assisi, while the first

[64] Rigg, *A History of Anglo-Latin Literature*, pp. 179–93.

[65] William of Canterbury, *Miracula sancti Thomae* 1, preface, p. 139.

[66] Gonzalo de Berceo, *Vida de Santo Domingo de Silos* 758, p. 449.

[67] Alice-Mary Talbot, "Hagiography in Late Byzantium," pp. 177–79.

[68] Thomas of Celano, *Vita prima sancti Francisci* prologue, 1, p. 3.

[69] Clement, *Vita et miracula beati Thomæ Heliæ*.

[70] Collins, *Reforming Saints: Saints' Lives and Their Authors in Germany, 1470–1530*, pp. 80–81.

hagiographic narrative about St. Dominic was by Jordan of Saxony, Dominic's successor as head of his Order, a German who had no local ties with the saint, and his work was addressed generally to "all the brethren."[71] It is true that there were many Franciscan saints with purely local cults, especially in Italy, and their hagiography often has an element of civic pride. The Life of the Poor Clare, Helen Enselmini of Padua, for example, written by Sicco Polentone in the fifteenth century, begins with an encomium of the city of Padua.[72] However, in general, the hagiography of the friars is less the voice of a particular religious community than is the case with earlier monastic Lives and Miracle Books. This is also reflected in the friars' taste for collective hagiographies (discussed later).

The relationship between the hagiographer and the saint he wrote about varied from the emotional and intense to the purely professional. At one extreme there were paid writers like Henry of Avranches, at the other there were cases like Thomas of Monmouth, a monk of Norwich who was the chief protagonist of St. William of Norwich, the boy supposedly martyred by the Jews. Thomas is not known to have written anything other than the Life and Miracles of St. William, he wrote obsessively over decades about the saint, his miracles and the respect that should be shown him, and reported that St. William, appearing in a vision, referred to Thomas as "my secretary."[73]

Female hagiographers were, as might be expected, rare, but not unknown (almost all Lives of female saints were written by men). Byzantium seems to have produced only two: in the sixth century, Sergia, head of the nunnery in Constantinople founded by St. Olympias (d. 408), wrote an account of the translation of the foundress's relics, and, six centuries later, the high-born Theodora Raoulaina (d. 1300), composed a Life of the ninth-century brothers and victims of iconoclasm, Theodore and Theophanes Graptoi.[74] In the West, the nun Baudonivia wrote the second book of the Life of Radegund soon after 600, supplementing the version already composed by Venantius Fortunatus at the request of the nuns of her convent at Poitiers, which Radegund had founded.[75] Baudonivia is depicted in a manuscript of the later eleventh century from Poitiers, at work with a stylus in one hand and wax tablets in the other, an unusual early picture of an identifiable female writer.[76]

At the end of the eighth century, almost two centuries after Baudonivia, a nun at the convent of Heidenheim in southern Germany wrote Lives of St. Winnebald and St. Willibald, two English brothers active in missionary work in the region.

[71] Jordan of Saxony, *Libellus de principiis Ordinis Praedicatorum* 1, p. 25.

[72] Polentone, *Vita et visiones beatae Helenae (Enselmini)* 1–2, pp. 512–13.

[73] Thomas of Monmouth, *Vita sancti Willelmi Norwicensis* 4. 9, p. 175 (the context makes it quite clear that "secretary," not "sacrist" is meant).

[74] BHG 1376 and BHG 1793: *Holy Women of Byzantium*, p. xiv; Talbot, "Old Wine in New Bottles," pp. 20–21, on Raoulaina.

[75] Baudonivia, *Vita sanctae Radegundis*.

[76] Poitiers, Bibliothèque municipale 250, fol. 43v; it is reproduced in various places, for example, Abou-El-Haj, *The Medieval Cult of Saints*, fig. 10; Schulenburg, *Forgetful of Their Sex*, pl. 3.

The Life of Willibald was written while its subject was still alive and is a travelogue rather than a hagiography, giving a detailed account of Willibald's journeys derived from his own lips, but the Life of Winnebald is a more conventional saint's Life, which terms Winnebald a "confessor" and "athlete of Christ," mentions posthumous miracles and culminates in an account of the translation of his body in 777.[77] The nun who wrote these Lives concealed her name in a code in the text, and this was not cracked until 1931: "I, an English woman named Hugeburc, wrote these things."[78]

Hugeburc stands at the head of a long, if never abundant, stream of female hagiographers active in Germany. In the tenth century the Saxon nun Hroswitha of Gandersheim wrote of the saints in Latin plays and poems. Her six dramas are modelled on Terence but with more uplifting themes than his. She has employed Terentian form and style, she says, which he used "to record the foul affairs of lascivious women," "to celebrate the praiseworthy chastity of holy virgins."[79] The dramas deal with saints or groups of saints, few of them famous (Gallicanus; Agape, Chionia, and Irene; John the Apostle; Abraham and Maria; Thais; and Fides, Spes, and Caritas), while the subjects of her poems are, along with the Virgin Mary and the Ascension of Christ, Gengulph, Pelagius, Theophilus, Basil, Denis, and Agnes. The dramas do show an interest in female figures, including repentant prostitutes, but the poems are chiefly about male saints. Other female hagiographers were at work in Germany around this time too. It has been suggested the author of the earliest Life of Matilda, wife of Henry I of Germany, which was written in the 970s, was a nun.[80]

Writing soon after 1056 (she refers to the recent death of the emperor Henry III in that year), Bertha, an aristocratic nun of Vilich, near Bonn, wrote a Life of Adelheid, first abbess of the house.[81] In her dedicatory preface to archbishop Anno of Cologne she makes an extravagant display of humility, calling herself "that poor vile sinner, unworthy to be termed his handmaid" and lamenting her rustic style. Contemporaries were more appreciative: "Bertha was conspicuous for her great knowledge of letters," wrote a German monk of a subsequent generation. "She wrote a Life of St. Adelheid, first abbess of Vilich, in a most satisfactorily elegant style, and left a fruitful heritage of piety and learning in that place."[82] In the following century a more celebrated aristocratic nun, at a nunnery 100 kilometres (60 miles) up the Rhine, penned some hagiographic works amongst her large output. Hildegard of Bingen is known for her visions, her songs and her letters, but she also produced two Lives of saints, dealing with Disibod and Rupert, the patrons of the two

[77] Hugeburc, *Vita Willibaldi episcopi Eichstetensis*; *Vita Wynnebaldi abbatis Heidenheimensis*.

[78] "Ego una Saxonica nomine Hugeburc ordinando hec scribebam": MGH, SS 15/1, p. 106 n. (y); the code was cracked by Bischoff, "Wer ist die Nonne von Heidenheim?"; see also Gottschaller, *Hugeburc von Heidenheim*; Klüppel, "Die Germania (750–950)," pp. 168–70.

[79] Hrotsvit, *Opera omnia*, p. 132 (bk. 2, pref.).

[80] Corbet, *Les saints ottoniens*, p. 120; *Vita Mathildis reginae antiquior*, pp. 11–12 (editorial introduction).

[81] Bertha of Vilich, *Vita Adelheidis abbatissae Vilicensis*.

[82] Conrad of Brauweiler, *Vita Wolfhelmi abbatis Brunwilarensis* 25, p. 190.

communities she lived in (Disibodenberg and Rupertsberg).[83] Her visionary powers were useful in acquiring knowledge of these figures of the distant past. At the beginning of her account of Rupert, who supposedly lived in the time of Charlemagne, she explains her method: "Just as the living light showed me and taught me in true vision, so I speak of him."

Female hagiographers can be found in other countries. Around 1280 Agnes d'Harcourt wrote the Life of Isabella, sister of St. Louis and Charles of Anjou, at the request of the latter.[84] Agnes was abbess of the nunnery of Longchamp, a house of Poor Clares which Isabella had founded, and came from a noble Norman family. Two of her uncles, canon lawyers in royal service, founded the College d'Harcourt for Norman students at Paris. Agnes wrote in French rather than Latin, and emphasized Isabella's royal descent, citing St. Louis as one of her sources of information. Isabelle's piety involved humility, devotion to church services and the Bible, charity to the poor, flagellation till she bled, and the foundation of Longchamp. Agnes describes the opening of Isabelle's tomb after nine days, reports how the dead saint "appeared as if she were sleeping," mentions the distribution of relics (mainly items of her clothing), and concludes with the account of forty of the saint's miracles.

The Life

Hagiography and Biography

There is a big question about the relationship between the saint's life, meaning everything that happened to that person between birth and death, and the saint's Life, meaning a written account that sets out the various reasons why that person should be regarded as a saint. The Life does indeed often start with a saint's birth or childhood and almost invariably ends with his or her death, but in between those more or less fixed markers there is considerable room for variation in structure and subject, and certainly no requirement for a unilinear chronological narrative: saints did not have "a career."[85] This is why Lives often lack chronological indicators and why they are sometimes organized thematically or by association, introducing stories with phrases such as "a similar incident occurred." As a result, some Lives are very close to being collections of anecdotes. As Alain Boureau has pointed out in relation to the *Golden Legend*, which was the most successful collection of saints' Lives made in the Middle Ages, "the hagiographic account presents itself as an assemblage of distinct narrative moments, without significant connections."[86] This observation is true of most saints' Lives. What gives the saint's Life its coherence is not its structure but its

[83] Hildegard of Bingen, *Vita sancti Dysibodi episcopi*; eadem, *Vita sancti Rupperti confessoris*.

[84] Agnès d'Harcourt, *La vie de la bienheureuse Isabelle de France*; see Allirot, "Isabelle de France, sœur de saint Louis"; Field, *Isabelle of France*.

[85] Charles-Edwards, *Early Christian Ireland*, p. 350.

[86] Boureau, *La légende dorée*, p. 213.

purpose. Every hagiographic work is "an exercise in persuasion," and its purpose was to persuade the reader that its subject was a saint.[87]

It is a commonplace of current scholarship that hagiography is not biography "in the modern sense" (although this "modern sense" is not usually defined with any precision).[88] Not all scholars agree with this, however. Walter Berschin, for example, asserted that "the overlap shared by biography and hagiography was greater than is today commonly assumed."[89] Often it is possible to know no more about a saint than is contained in the hagiographical works dedicated to him or her. In such cases the attempt to extract from them some biographical information about a person who lived long ago is not pointless; but there is no distinction between such an attempt and the analysis of the Life of the saint, seen as a piece of writing with its own set of religious and social assumptions. The saint is only seen through the writing about the saint as saint. In these instances, which form the majority of cases, there can be no lifting of the veil; it is a veil that is created by the fact that, by the time people in the present can have any kind of encounter with the long dead person, that dead person has already been conceptualized as a saint, with all the implications. Yet there are other cases where the amount of evidence that survives gives some information about the person before this took place. There are plenty of sources that describe the life of Thomas Becket, archbishop of Canterbury, before his murder in 1170 made him a martyr, and comparison between these strictly contemporary sources and the hagiography produced after 1170 can highlight the literary process whereby someone became a saint.[90]

It has been argued that "all saints are, more or less, constructed figures."[91] And, indeed, to be recognized as a saint removes some of the traces of human individuality. In the case of the martyr-saint Agnes, we can be fairly certain that she was a real person, because of the good early evidence, including mention in the first martyr list of 354.[92] By this date there was already a large basilica over her tomb on the Via Nomentana north-east of Rome.[93] In the fifth century a Passion was composed, later attributed to St. Ambrose.[94] This largely fantastic account mentions attempts at sexual humiliation of the young girl and her execution (by a sword after an unsuccessful attempt to burn her). In the first half of the seventh century Pope Honorius I commissioned an enormous mosaic of the saint, standing between images of himself

[87] Kleinberg, "Proving Sanctity," p. 185.

[88] To cite only one example: "the primary function of works like I Celano was not to provide a biography of Francis in the modern sense of that term, but rather to explain Francis's significance to a particular community": Burr, *The Spiritual Franciscans*, p. 349 n. 2.

[89] Berschin, "Biography," p. 607; cf. his comments in *Biographie und Epochenstil* 1, pp. 17–19.

[90] Jansen, *Wo ist Thomas Becket? Der ermordete Heilige zwischen Erinnerung und Erzählung*; Staunton, *Thomas Becket and His Biographers*.

[91] "Tous les saints, plus ou moins, font figure de saints construits": Delooz, *Sociologie et canonisations*, pp. 7–8.

[92] *Liber Pontificalis* 1, pp. 11–12; *Codice topografico della Città di Roma* 2, pp. 1–28.

[93] Brandenburg, *Ancient Churches of Rome*, pp. 69–70.

[94] Pseudo-Ambrose, *Passio sanctae Agnetis*.

and his great predecessor Gregory the Great.[95] Agnes is dressed in imperial costume, a halo around her head, and the symbols of her execution, fire and a sword, at her feet; she gazes out at worshippers in the direct, authoritarian manner of the famous mosaics of the emperor Justinian and the empress Theodora at Ravenna. Thus, although there was a real young woman, perhaps a frightened teenager, who faced the brutal force of the Roman state, and was killed to the roars of a hostile and gratified crowd, almost all trace of this girl has been lost by the time she became the hieratic figure in the mosaic.

Consequently, it is a misunderstanding to think that a comprehensive survey of sanctity would look like a vast collective biography. Whereas a dictionary of medieval queens or medieval popes can be based on a reasonably well defined category, since most queens or popes attained relatively clear public and official recognition by contemporaries, a dictionary of medieval saints cannot. Hence a great collective enterprise like the Italian *Bibliotheca sanctorum*, published in fourteen volumes between 1961 and 1987, while being an extremely valuable work of reference, might give a false impression. The standardized format of the entries obscures the reality: a vast diversity, from entirely fictional characters to well known figures recorded by contemporaries, from angels to spelling mistakes, from figures with universal cult to those unknown beyond their town. The category of "saint" into which they are all poured has a flattening effect, diminishing these contrasts and differences.

The existence of a saintly model that transcended the individuality of particular saints was recognized in the medieval period. In the preface to his *Life of the Fathers*, Gregory of Tours explains why he has chosen this singular form—*Life*—rather than the plural *Lives*. "It is manifest," he claims, "that it is better to say *Life of the Fathers* rather than *Lives*, since, although there may be diversity of merit and power, one life of the body nourishes them all in the world."[96] The things the saints had in common were more significant than the things that gave them individual identity. It was hence possible to write the Life of a holy man without any specific knowledge, since it was clear what it meant to be a holy man. Agnellus of Ravenna, writing his serial biographies of the bishops of his church in the ninth century, admitted that he had been able to find out "nothing certain" about some of the prelates of the past. But, in order to make his work complete, he had nevertheless "composed a Life of them." He justified this invention by the presumption of their sanctity: "I do not believe I lied, since they were prayerful, chaste, and charitable, and obtained the souls of men for God."[97]

One consequence of the existence of such a view was the ready application of details of one saint's life to another. Medieval writers were much more thorough and shameless borrowers of other writers' words than is customary today. This seems to have been considered a tribute rather than a theft. Hagiographers were especially

[95] Brandenburg, *Ancient Churches of Rome*, pp. 244–45.

[96] Gregory of Tours, *Liber vitae patrum*, preface, p. 662 (repr., 1969, p. 212).

[97] Agnellus of Ravenna, *Liber pontificalis ecclesiae Ravennatis* 32, p. 297.

liable to plunder phrases or whole passages from earlier authors. Felix, the author of a Life of the English hermit Guthlac, written probably in the 730s, drew freely on the Lives of earlier saints who had spent time as hermits: Antony, Paul the Hermit, and Martin from among the early heroes of the Church, and, from nearer his own time, Fursey and Cuthbert. When Felix addresses the king of the East Angles in his preface, "Since you have required of me that I should write to you about St. Guthlac's way of life, how it began, and what happened before his holy vows, and what kind of end his life had," he has borrowed his words from the Latin translation of Athanasius's *Life of Antony*: "So, since you have required of me that I should write to you about St. Antony's way of life, since you wish to learn how it began, and who he was before his holy vows, and what kind of end his life had."[98] There is no harm here, and the echo of the Life of the great desert saint is entirely appropriate. However, it is a slightly different situation when Guthlac's death is described in exactly the same words that Bede had used to describe Cuthbert's: "he fortified himself with communion of the body and blood of Christ, and, raising his eyes to heaven and spreading his hands on high, he sent forth his soul to the joys of perpetual exaltation" (Bede has "of the heavenly kingdom").[99] It is impossible to tell whether Guthlac's end was indeed exactly like Cuthbert's, or if this is simply literary borrowing to cover Felix's ignorance. The plot is thickened by the fact that Bede had borrowed much of his wording from Gregory the Great's Life of St. Benedict.[100]

Sometimes a whole Life was borrowed, with a simple change of name to apply it to a different saint.[101] One such Life, plagiarized wholesale from another Life, is the Passion of St. Honorina, a virgin martyr revered in Normandy from the ninth century. The account of her martyrdom is simply that of St. Dorothea with the names changed.[102] Similarly, the accounts of St. Genulf and St. Winard, both martyr-saints with limited cults in France, are identical except for the names:

> In the time of the emperor Decius, the persecution of Christians raged so fiercely in the city of Rome that, by command of this emperor, almost all who confessed Christ were compelled to sacrifice to idols or perish in various tortures. In those days there was a most Christian man called Genitus . . . they called their son, dear to God, Genulf.[103]

> In the time of the emperor Decius, the persecution of Christians raged so fiercely in the city of Rome that almost all who confessed Christ were

[98] Felix, *Vita sancti Guthlaci*, prologue, p. 62; Evagrius, *Vita beati Antonii abbatis, auctore Sancto Athanasio*, preface, col. 126.

[99] Felix, *Vita sancti Guthlaci* 50, p. 158; Bede, *Vita sancti Cuthberti* 39, p. 284.

[100] Gregory I, *Dialogi* 2. 37 (2, p. 244).

[101] Delehaye, *Les légendes hagiographiques*, pp. 87–100; De Gaiffier, "Les 'doublets' en hagiographie latine."

[102] *Acta sanctae Dorotheae virginis*; BHL 3981; De Gaiffier, "Les 'doublets' en hagiographie latine," p. 264.

[103] *Vita Genulfi*, p. 792.

> compelled by this wicked emperor to sacrifice to idols or perish in various tortures. In those days there was a most Christian man called Genitus . . . they called their son, dear to God, by the name of Winard.[104]

These are extreme examples of hagiographic borrowing, and no one would deny that it would be eccentric to call the Life of Winard "a biography." But not all hagiographers worked like this. Some did indeed create a wholly fictional confection, spun from commonplaces, borrowed passages and their own invention, but others pieced together evidence of a saint from earlier generations, transmitted orally or in writing, while yet others wrote about people they had known long and well. And it is excessively scrupulous to deny the label "biography" to long and detailed accounts by people who knew the saint personally. Some writers might even begin their work before the saint was dead. Sulpicius Severus sought out St. Martin before he wrote his Life of the saint, which was finished before Martin's death in 397. Eadmer, who was chaplain to St. Anselm, archbishop of Canterbury, and his self-appointed biographer, made preparatory notes for a Life during Anselm's lifetime. Anselm commanded Eadmer to destroy what he had written about him, since he considered himself unworthy to be the subject of literary commemoration, but Eadmer circumvented this command by copying out his text onto other pages and then destroying the originals, which, Eadmer confesses, "perhaps was not free of the sin of disobedience" (one might dispense with that "perhaps").[105] It was not uncommon, in the case of hagiographers who knew their subject personally, for this knowledge to be concentrated in the later years of the saint's life. Adam of Eynsham, for example, who wrote a full and lengthy Life of St. Hugh of Lincoln, was Hugh's chaplain only for the last three years of the saint's life, and had to rely on Hugh's own reminiscences to build up a picture of his earlier life.[106]

The confessional provided special entry into the saint's mind, and confessors were sometimes willing to reveal what they heard. Raymond of Capua, who was both confessor to Catherine of Siena and author of her Life, tells how, when the saint was a girl, her mother was looking out for a husband for her, and advised her to wash her face more often and do her hair, to make her more attractive to possible suitors. Catherine was at first opposed, but her much loved older sister, who was herself already married, eventually persuaded her to pay attention to her appearance. In later life, recollecting this lapse when confessing to Raymond of Capua, Catherine would sob and cry, decrying her failing as a mortal sin. Raymond would try to persuade her this was not so, and ascertained that she had not done this out of desire to please men; indeed, she always hurried away when her father's apprentices were present, and never stared out the window to glimpse passers-by. But, lamented Catherine, it was a sign that she had loved her sister more than God, and Raymond should not excuse her sins. This difficult period in Catherine's childhood had eventually been

[104] *Vita Vinardi*, pp. 668–69.

[105] Eadmer, *Vita Anselmi* 2. 72, pp. 149–51.

[106] Adam of Eynsham, *Magna vita sancti Hugonis*.

concluded when her sister, "who had induced these vanities," died in childbirth, and Catherine then shaved off all her hair, but this incident from her girlhood remained an unresolved concern for her.

Raymond justifies his breach of the confessional explicitly. "I know," he asserts, "that, after she flew up to heaven, it is allowed to me to reveal things that redound to her praise, even though they were secret at the time." And the stories he recounts are by no means all conventional tales told about any saint. His account actually reveals something of the life of an Italian business family of the fourteenth century, and the discordant ideals of feminine seclusion and feminine attractiveness it might harbour. Catherine, admiring her married sister, keeping away from the window, and torn by guilt, emerges vividly through the layers of narrative.[107] Hagiographic writing includes lively and particular prose of this kind, as well as the commonplaces and borrowings found in some other Lives.

Organizing the Narrative

Hagiographers sometimes express the difficulty of their task. Muirchú, composing his *Life of Patrick* in the later seventh century, borrowed the opening words of Luke's Gospel to evoke those who had tried and failed to produce such a Life:

> "Many have tried to organize this narrative according to what has been handed down to them from their fathers and from those who were, from the beginning, ministers of the word," but, on account of the very great difficulty of the work of narration and the diverse opinions and frequent doubts of many people, they never arrived at the one and certain path of historical truth.[108]

Muirchú pictures himself setting out in a feeble boat on an uncharted and dangerous hagiographic ocean:

> I have brought the childish rowing boat of my meagre intellect down into the perilous deep ocean of sacred narrative, where huge mounds of waves swell up wildly among the sharpest rocks, implanted in unfamiliar waters.

Hagiographers attempted to resolve the problem confronting Muirchú—"organizing the narrative"—in a variety of ways. Saints' Lives were by no means always organized in chronological order. The author of the Life of Agnes of Bohemia, the thirteenth-century holy princess and nun, states this explicitly in the prologue: "in the course of this narrative I have not always described events according the order of time."[109] He has instead grouped his material thematically, in thirteen books:

1. Her origins and behaviour as a child.

[107] Raymond of Capua, *Vita Catharinae Senensis* 41–47, pp. 60–68 (AASS Aprilis 3, pp. 863–65).

[108] Muirchú, *Vita sancti Patricii*, prologue, p. 62.

[109] *Vita illustrissime uirginis sororis Agnetis ordinis Sancte Clare de Praga*, prologue, ed. Seton, p. 62; ed. Vyskočil, p. 100.

2. The holy life she led after her parents' death when living with her brother.
3. How she entered the Order of the holy virgin Clare.
4. Her great humility and obedience.
5. Her holy and sincere poverty.
6. Her harsh mortification of the flesh.
7. Her zeal for prayer and her amazing devotion to the sacrament of the altar.
8. Her most fervent love for the cross of Christ.
9. Her great charity towards her sisters and those in trouble.
10. The revelations divinely granted to her.
11. Her death and the things that happened on that occasion.
12. The burial of her holy body.
13. The miracles performed by the divine power.

Clearly there is an overarching narrative from birth to death (and beyond), but the bulk of the Life is structured around her saintly virtues—humility, asceticism, devotion to prayer, and so on.

Bonaventure, writing his official Life of Francis, also adopted a less than strictly chronological approach:

> In order to avoid confusion, I have not always composed the narrative following chronological order, but instead I have made the effort to keep to a more appropriate structure, according to whether it seemed more fitting to treat together different things that happened at the same time or similar things that happened at different times.[110]

Raymond of Capua's long Life of Catherine of Siena is organized in three parts: part one deals with the saint's family origin and childhood, and the events before she began a public life, part two with her way of life and spiritual gifts, including miracles performed in her lifetime, and part three with her death and posthumous miracles.[111]

BIRTH AND CHILDHOOD

The typical saint's Life does begin at the beginning: "Antony was Egyptian by race, with well-born parents"; "Martin was born in the town of Sabaria in Pannonia, but was brought up in Italy at Pavia, with parents who were not low according to the dignity of the word"; "there was a man of venerable life, Benedict by name and grace . . . born from a free family in the district of Nursia."[112] These brisk characterizations give a name, a place, and a rough indication of social class. Sometimes this is all there is in the way of background, but, on occasion, there is a good deal more. In Wales and Ireland, societies where long genealogies were especially prized, there are works dedi-

[110] Bonaventura, *Legenda maior sancti Francisci*, prologue, p. 559.

[111] Raymond of Capua, *Vita Catharinae Senensis*.

[112] Athanasius, *Vita Antonii* 1. 1, p. 130; Sulpicius Severus, *Vita sancti Martini* 2. 1 (1, p. 254); Gregory I, *Dialogi* 2. Prol. (2, p. 126).

cated to describing the family descent of the saints.[113] One genealogy of St. Brigid goes back twenty-five generations.[114] These elaborate lists of ancestors are not likely to be a factual record but instead reflect dynastic claims and the horizons of the local churches.

A common opening statement in saints' Lives is that the saint was of noble descent but "nobler" in behaviour, virtue, or piety. Adalhard of Corbie was "noble according to the flesh but nobler in his behaviour," Margaret of Hungary "noble in her stock but nobler in her behaviour," and Elzear of Sabran "illustrious and noble in his stock but more illustrious and more noble in his saintliness."[115] Although it is a small change, it is revealing that a slightly later writer, reworking a Life of Ubaldus, a twelfth-century bishop of Gubbio, augments the original text, which says "St. Ubaldus came from noble stock," by the phrase "noble indeed by family, but he was nobler in his integrity of life."[116] It is as if any mention of the nobility of a saintly subject automatically generated this pious platitude. Hagiographers wanted their subjects to be of good family but also to stress that there were even more desirable qualities.

Another common convention is the mother's premonitory dream.[117] When Columbanus's mother was pregnant with the saint, she dreamed that a bright sun shone forth from her body, casting its beams throughout the entire world. Wise men told her that this signified she would give birth to someone of outstanding talents, who would work for his own salvation and that of others.[118] The mother of Yves Hélory supposedly told one of her friends that Yves was going to be a saint, something attested by dreams that she had had.[119] Queen Constanza, the mother of Agnes of Bohemia, also had a dream during her pregnancy. She dreamed she entered a chamber where all her royal robes were kept, but among them was a simple grey tunic with a cord of the kind worn by nuns of the Order of Poor Clares. Wondering who had put this rough garment amongst her gorgeous clothes, she heard a voice: "Do not be amazed, for the child you are bearing will wear such garments and will be a light to all Bohemia!"[120]

Sometimes the dreams needed a little encouraging interpretation. The mother of St. Leoba, who had long been childless, dreamed that she had a church bell in her bosom, which rang when she took it out. Her old nurse explained to her that she was going to have a baby girl, who should be vowed to God's service. As soon as

[113] *Vitae sanctorum Britanniae et genealogiae*; *Corpus genealogiarum sanctorum Hiberniae.*

[114] Ibid., p. 3.

[115] Paschasius Radbertus, *Vita sancti Adalhardi Corbeiensis abbatis* 15, col. 1516; Garinus, *Vita Margaritae Hungaricae* 1. 1, p. 900; *Vita sancti Elzearii de Sabrano* 1. 1, pp. 576–77.

[116] Jordanus, *Vita sancti Ubaldi Eugubini pontificis* 2. 1, p. 47; Tebaldus, *Vita sancti Ubaldi Eugubini pontificis* 1. 1, p. 630; on this saints, see Brufani and Menestò, eds., *Nel segno del santo protettore.*

[117] Examples are assembled in Lanzoni, "Il sogno presago della madre incinta."

[118] Jonas, *Vita Columbani* 1. 2, p. 154.

[119] *Processus de vita et miraculis sancti Yvonis*, p. 12.

[120] *Vita illustrissime uirginis sororis Agnetis ordinis Sancte Clare de Praga* 1, ed. Seton, p. 64; ed. Vyskočil, pp. 101–2.

the mother made this vow, she conceived.[121] St. Bernard's mother, pregnant with the saint, was disturbed when she dreamed that she was carrying a barking puppy in her womb. Consulting a pious man about this, she was reassured to have his view:

> Don't be afraid; all is well. You will be the mother of a fine puppy, a guardian of God's house, who will bark loudly on its behalf against the enemies of the faith. For he will be a remarkable preacher and, like a good dog, thanks to his healing tongue, he will heal many diseases of many souls.[122]

It must have been even more worrying when the pregnant mother of Vincent Ferrer heard barking coming from her womb, but she too was reassured. Her cousin the bishop of Valencia explained that this meant "she was going to give birth to a child who would in future be a most fervent, learned, and holy preacher of the Gospel of Christ."[123]

Occasionally a Life gave little or no information about the saint's childhood. This could lead later authors to attempt to fill the gap, either by rewriting the Life with a childhood sequence added at the beginning or by writing a short independent piece on the subject. An important English example is St. Cuthbert (d. 687). Although three Lives of Cuthbert were written within forty years of his death, two of them by the great historian Bede, they gave no information about his family or place of origin and contained only one, very generalized, story about his boyhood. Cuthbert's relics eventually came to rest in the great Benedictine monastery of Durham, where, in the twelfth century, one of the monks set about remedying this omission. The treatise *On the Origins of St. Cuthbert* begins with a preface explaining that the author had come across some writings "that set forth saint Cuthbert's birth in Ireland and his royal and noble descent," and that this account had been corroborated by an Irish bishop, who "revealed to us many other things which we had previously known nothing about," including the name of Cuthbert's father and mother and the city of his birth.[124] What had happened was clearly the plundering of an earlier Life of an Irish saint to provide the missing biographical details.

Sometimes the saint's childhood was presented as a time of precocious seriousness, with the child portrayed as a "child-old man" (*puer senex*). St. Benedict had "the heart of an old man" even in childhood.[125] The young Antoninus, later to be archbishop of Florence, was also of this type: "for already at that time there was an

[121] Rudolf of Fulda, *Vita Leobae abbatissae Biscofesheimensis* 6, p. 124.

[122] *Vita prima sancti Bernardi* 1. 1. 2, cols. 227–28.

[123] Ranzano, *Vita sancti Vincentii Ferrerii* 1. 3, p. 485.

[124] *Libellus de ortu sancti Cuthberti* (from York Minster MS XVI I 12); the case for the authorship of Reginald of Durham (or Coldingham) is advanced by Sharpe, "Were the Irish Annals Known to a Twelfth-Century Northumbrian Writer?"; other discussions include Dodds, "The Little Book of the Birth of St. Cuthbert"; Grosjean, "The Alleged Irish Origin of St. Cuthbert"; Clancy, "Magpie Hagiography in Twelfth-century Scotland: The Case of *Libellus de nativitate Sancti Cuthberti*."

[125] Gregory I, *Dialogi* 2, prologue (2, p. 126).

early old age and immense gravity in his manners, speech and physical bearing."[126] As a boy, St. Odilo of Cluny combined innocence and maturity:

> In his childhood he took pleasure in humility, chastity, innocence and purity, and, as far as his age allowed, he engaged in works of mercy. He surpassed all of his contemporaries in wisdom and good behaviour, so that he was considered by everyone, not a boy, but an old man, in his maturity even if not in age.[127]

The attitude to games can be an important issue. The only story that Bede transmitted about Cuthbert's early years relates how, when he joined a group of children playing, a three-year-old reproached him: "he began to berate him with the firmness of an old man, urging him not to indulge in fun and games but to subject both his mind and his body to the same steady firmness."[128] Here it is the prim infant rather than the saint who is the "child-old man." A depiction of this scene in an illustrated version of the Life of Cuthbert provides some rare evidence about children's games in the medieval period.[129] As a child St. Malachy of Armagh was "a boy in years but an old man in his behaviour." He was never restless with his teachers, never avoided discipline, never bored with reading and never keen on games, "which that age usually regards as sweet and natural."[130] But games were not always seen as a frivolous diversion. Theodore of Sykeon, growing up in a small Anatolian town in the 530s, combined a severe refusal to utter or hear swearing or blasphemy with the ability to beat his companions in all their "childhood games."[131] And, as a child, Elizabeth of Thuringia promised so many *Ave Maria*s and genuflections if she won at games.[132]

THE QUESTION OF MARRIAGE

The Life can envisage either supportive or obstructive families. A smooth preparation for sainthood is depicted in the Life of Gerard of Anjou: "he was born of free parents and raised by their diligent care, reborn in holy baptism and given to religious teachers to be imbued with ecclesiastical learning and letters."[133] But on many occasions there was a clash between the aspirations of the young saint and the intentions of his or her family. When Rainier dell'Acqua, the only son of a prosperous family in Pisa, began weeping uncontrollably in repentance of his sins, his parents thought he had gone mad and considered locking him up.[134]

[126] Castiglione, *Vita Antonini archiepiscopi Florentini* 1, p. 314.

[127] Iotsald of St.-Claude, *Vita sancti Odilonis* 1, pp. 147–48.

[128] Bede, *Vita sancti Cuthberti* 1, p. 156.

[129] Oxford, University College, MS 165, fol. 8.

[130] Bernard of Clairvaux, *Vita sancti Malachiae* 1. 1, p. 310.

[131] *Vita Theodori Syceotae* 5, p. 5.

[132] *Libellus de dictis quatuor ancillarum*, p. 112.

[133] *Vita sancti Girardi confessoris* 1. 2, p. 494.

[134] Benincasa, *Vita sancti Rainerii confessoris* 16, pp. 428–29; analyzed in detail in Barbero, *Un santo in famiglia*, pp. 224–28.

Nowhere was this clash of values sharper than in the issue of marriage.[135] Many saints, certainly the majority, were unmarried; many were virgins; some were virgins even though married, for celibate marriage is sometimes a possible choice, as in the case of several of the royal female saints already discussed (Etheldreda, Salome, Cunigunda of Germany and Cunigunda of Poland). Both male and female saints sometimes had to fight to maintain their desire to live without sex or marriage. One of the earliest pieces of hagiography in the French language, the *Life of St. Alexis*, begins with the well-born Alexis fleeing from his bride and his homeland on his wedding night.[136] Similarly, when the parents of the ninth-century Greek saint Gregory the Decapolitan had already summoned the witnesses for their son's marriage contract, and then unwisely sent him to obtain some things for the wedding, he used the opportunity to slip away and seek out holy men and solitude.[137] The brothers of St. Thomas Aquinas were opposed to his entry into the Dominican Order and sought to do all they could to reverse his decision to join, even holding him captive and tempting him with "a very beautiful girl, adorned with the attire of a courtesan, who, by look, by touch, by little games and in every way she could, enticed him to sin."[138] Needless to say, Thomas, who had already accepted divine wisdom as his bride, resisted successfully.

A particularly harsh family dispute is described in the Life of the Hainault saint, Oda (d. 1158). When her parents learned of her desire to preserve her virginity and become a nun, they "were troubled and disturbed by this, and grieved greatly; taking counsel with their friends and relatives, they decided to hamper the vow of chastity with the shackles of marriage." A nice young man was found, and a wedding day named. On the day, the house was decorated with pictures and hangings and a festive crowd assembled, all in their best clothes. The bridegroom replied happily when the priest asked him if he would take Oda as his lawful wedded wife. When it came to Oda's turn, however, she said nothing. Some attributed this to arrogance, others to maidenly modesty, and a married woman in the congregation spoke to her kindly, advising her to answer when the priest asked. Oda replied to her that she could not take the young man or anyone else as her husband, since she was vowed to another, "from whose embraces I can never be separated, by love of another, by gifts, or by the threats and blows of my parents." Publicly shamed, the bridegroom galloped off in indignation, while Oda fled from her muttering relatives into the family home, found a sword and cut off her own nose, "to deform the beauty of her attractive form." Eventually, she was allowed to become a Premonstratensian nun.[139]

[135] Glasser, "Marriage in Medieval Hagiography."

[136] *La Vie de Saint Alexis*, lines 56–80, p. 3.

[137] *Vita Gregorii Decapolitae* 3, p. 64.

[138] William de Tocco, *Ystoria sancti Thome de Aquino* 11, p. 112 (AASS Martii 1, p. 661).

[139] Philip of Harvengt, *Vita beatae Odae virginis*, cols. 1362–69.

She was virtually a martyr in the eyes of her hagiographer, but a disobedient and wilful daughter in the eyes of her parents.

In the case of lay saints, especially high-born ones, family pressure to marry could be intense. For kings, marriage might even be presented as a duty, since, as the advisers of St. Ethelbert argued, "it was not fitting for a king to be without children" (earlier, p. 220). Royal female saints also faced pressure to marry, since they were valuable commodities in the world of international diplomacy. Isabella of France, St. Louis's sister, resisted the highest suitors: "She was entreated by her relatives to marry the son of the Holy Roman Emperor, but she never agreed to any physical marriage because she had chosen Our Lord Jesus Christ as her eternal bridegroom."[140] But there are several famous cases of married female saints from royal or noble families: Margaret of Scotland in the eleventh century, Elizabeth of Thuringia in the thirteenth, Birgit of Sweden in the fourteenth. All had children, and, in the case of Margaret, her hagiographer makes a point of stressing how important it was to her, "that they should be brought up with all care and should be taught good behaviour."[141] One of Birgit's daughters, Catherine, herself became a saint. It was clearly not impossible to be married, bear children, and be a saint; it was just rare.

The narrative of a saint's life was deeply shaped by whether the saint's family was supportive or obstructive, and whether marriage and sex were difficulties or sublimely ignored. The life of some saints is a natural progression from saintly child to saintly adult to saintly death, but others face more intense conflict and starker choices. The Latin word *conversio* does not mean "conversion" in the narrow modern sense of turning from one religion (or none) to another, but dedication to the monastic life. This is a critical moment in the lives of many saints. One of the fullest and most psychologically complex accounts of a conversion, a "turning" towards a religious life, is found in the Life of St. Francis by Thomas of Celano, who presents a wealthy, frivolous, and impressionable young man completely transformed by illness (see earlier, p. 66). The small group of prostitute saints, like Thais and Mary of Egypt, obviously needed to convert.[142] The most celebrated of these was Mary Magdalene, who, "just as she was resplendent in wealth and beauty, so all the more she abandoned her body to pleasure." (One theory was that she did this on the rebound, after being jilted by John the Evangelist.) Her life was sharply divided between the time before and after her conversion.[143]

THE SAINT'S DEATH

Though there were many styles of sanctity and many different roles that saints could take—martyrs, bishops, abbots, hermits, monks and nuns, lay people, royalty—what

[140] Agnès d'Harcourt, *Vie d'Isabelle de France* 7, p. 54.

[141] Turgot, *Vita sanctae Margaretae Scotorum reginae* 5, p. 240.

[142] Ward, *Harlots of the Desert*; Karras, "Holy Harlots."

[143] Jacobus de Voragine, *Legenda aurea* 92 (1, pp. 628–29, 640–41).

they all faced in common, like us, was death. And this was a special focus of the hagiographers, who might well devote large parts of the Life to the saint's death.[144]

Nihil est certius morte et nihil incertius hora mortis—"nothing is more certain than death and nothing less certain that the hour of death." This sombre claim was a common phrase in medieval wills. In a world where it was thought that your state on the death-bed determined your fate for eternity, it was naturally desirable to have foreknowledge of the date of one's death. This was one of the special gifts given to devotees of St. Oswald: for every year that they celebrated his feast, they received a day's forewarning of their death.[145] Saints were often given such foreknowledge. St. Antony of Egypt went to bid farewell to his followers, "forewarned by providence about his end."[146] After Stephen, bishop of Apt, fell ill in 1046, he turned to the surrounding clergy and "indicated that the day of his departure was near," something he was informed of "through the spirit of foreknowledge."[147] St. Berard, a twelfth-century bishop of Marsi, "learned by divine revelation that the end of this life was approaching," knowledge that impelled him to yet more active reforming work in his diocese. Summoning an assembly of his clergy and flock, he announced his forthcoming death, taking the opportunity to excommunicate some of the more notorious sinners. Then, "as the day of the saint's death drew near, just as the saint had predicted the year and time of his death, so he predicted the day of his death."[148] Two years before his death, Elzear of Sabran, who was a secular count, told his wife that he would not live long after he had cleared all the debt on his lordships, and so it turned out.[149]

Death-bed scenes were an essential part of the Life. Almost all were public. Some were serene, with the saint receiving communion and passing away peacefully, surrounded by admiring followers. Others emphasized the saint's sufferings, perhaps stressing the point by mentioning Christ's Passion, or having the saint listen to the Gospel account of the Passion, as in the case of St. Liebert of Cambrai (d. 1076), where the explicit reason is "so that the sufferings of the Lord's Passion, which he bore for our salvation, should be recited to the one leaving this world, and the spirits of demons be repelled by the winnowing fan of such great reading."[150] It is a bold and energetic image to see the Passion story as a great fan swatting devils aside around the dying man.

[144]Boglioni, "La scène de la mort dans les premières hagiographies latines"; Platelle, "La mort précieuse"; for a particular group, Heuclin, "L'ermite et la mort durant le haut Moyen Age"; Lauwers, "La mort et le corps des saints"; Sigal, "La mort des saints dans les Vies et les procès de canonisation du Midi de la France."

[145]Gervase of Tilbury, *Otia Imperialia* 2. 17, p. 432.

[146]Athanasius, *Vita Antonii* 89. 1, p. 362.

[147]*Vita sancti Stephani episcopi Aptensis* 18, p. 314.

[148]*Vita Berardi Marsorum episcopi* 13–14, pp. 133–34.

[149]*Vita sancti Elzearii de Sabrano* 14. 68, p. 592.

[150]Rodulfus of Cambrai, *Vita domni Lietberti ecclesiae Cameracensis episcopi* 64, p. 865.

Thomas of Celano deals with the death and burial of St. Francis in Book Two of his *First Life*. He introduces the theme immediately after describing the stigmata, perhaps seeing the reception of those miraculous signs as the crescendo of Francis's life. "According to the laws of nature," he writes, "and the mode of the human condition, it is necessary that the outer man decay from day to day." He then describes the saint's numerous ailments, especially his eye problems. The remedies sound as invasive as the diseases: cauterization, blood-letting, plasters, and eye-drops. By the time Francis entered Assisi for the last time he was vomiting blood and in constant pain; he admitted that martyrdom would be less painful than his current state. After having St. John's account of the Passion read to him, Francis died.[151]

A similar long period of suffering preceded the death of St. Cunigunda of Cracow (d. 1292):

> When, because of her merits, the remunerator of all wished to repay her devotion with eternal rewards, so that his servant should not be deprived of her daily pay, he first visited her with a grave illness. For she was stricken with a very grave illness on the feast-day of St. Matthew the Evangelist (21 September) and burdened with various pains. From that day until the feast-day of St. James (25 July) she lay in bed, and the tongue cannot recount nor human sense express how great her agonies were and how patiently and devoutly she bore them.[152]

But a painful death could also raise doubts about the sufferer's sanctity. When archbishop Anno of Cologne died in 1075, there were those who advanced his claim to be a saint, but others who argued quite the contrary:

> Consider the end of this man, to whom you presume to attribute sanctity. A violent pain in the feet sent his soul unhappily on its way. It would certainly be very cruel for a man of any goodness to be consumed by divine punishment in this way. That he did not live a good life is proved by this punishment, and by the horrible death he died.[153]

In a less combative way some of those who gathered around the death-bed of the saintly John, abbot of Gorze, who suffered over several days, asked, "how could the great Creator allow such a faithful servant to be distressed so cruelly at his death?"[154] There were answers to these questions. As the Bible says, "whom the Lord loveth he chasteneth, and scourgeth every son he receiveth" (Hebrews 12:6).[155] Earthly suffering could be a kind of spiritual testing and strengthening, and was, in any case, nothing in comparison to the heavenly rewards to be won: "when we are considering

[151] Thomas of Celano, *Vita prima sancti Francisci* 2. 4, 5, 7, 8, pp. 75, 79, 81–83, 85.

[152] *Vita et miracula sanctae Kyngae ducissae Cracoviensis* 63, p. 726.

[153] *Vita Annonis* 3. 25, p. 513.

[154] John of St. Arnulf, *Vita Iohannis abbatis Gorziensis*, preface, p. 42 (MGH, SS 4, p. 337).

[155] *Vita Annonis* 3. 25, p. 513.

the elect, who are on their way to eternal life, what kind of objection is it, that they sometimes have painful deaths?"[156]

Since some people were recognized as saints while alive, there was obviously an anxious period of waiting for the saint to die and make the crucial transition to the new state. The dead saint was a precious commodity and so an object of competition and rivalry. Hence the hovering around dying holy men and women, attempts to procure their bodies at the point of death, and the somewhat gruesome practice of taking relics from the corpse before burial. Ideally the saint should die in his or her home town. When the dying Francis arrived in Assisi in 1226, the local populace was delighted: "the whole multitude of the people were hoping that the saint of God was about to die and this was the cause of such great exultation."[157] But such convenient expirations could not be guaranteed. The saintly Syrian hermit Marcian discovered that several people were building funeral oratories for him, hoping eventually to have his body in these shrines, but he outwitted them by arranging to have his body buried in an unidentified place, known only to a few trusted disciples.[158] When it was thought (wrongly) that another Syrian holy man, James of Cyrrestica, who lived outside the town of Cyrrhus, was about to die, crowds gathered from the surrounding countryside "to carry off the body," but the citizens of Cyrrhus sent an armed force to assert their rights and brought the saint into town on a litter.[159] There could be rivalry between a saint's place of birth and place of death. According to Fortunatus's Life of Severinus, bishop of Bordeaux, the saint was originally from Trier, and when he died he was buried by his faithful clergy of Bordeaux in a secret crypt, "fearing lest the citizens of Trier should steal the saint for themselves."[160] On one occasion in the seventh century, a dispute over the destination of a saint's body was decided by two innocent children, who raised the bier and took it off "at the Saviour's command."[161]

Several of the conventional features of the saint's burial are to be found in the account of the end of William Fermat, a Norman hermit of the eleventh century.[162] His body was immediately the target of violent contention among three neighbouring communities, Domfront, Mayenne and Mortain, but, "at the command of Robert, count of Mortain, the clergy, along with an innumerable number of the populace, brought the venerable body to Mortain," the men of Domfront and Mayenne going away empty handed. The victorious party placed in it a stone sarcophagus that, until then, no one had been able to lift, but now proved easy to transport. Some said the saint had predicted where he should be buried in the church at Mortain. His body

[156] John of St. Arnulf, *Vita Iohannis abbatis Gorziensis*, preface, p. 42 (MGH, SS 4, p. 338).

[157] Thomas of Celano, *Vita prima sancti Francisci* 2. 7. 105, p. 82.

[158] Theodoret of Cyrrhus, *Historia Religiosa* 3. 18 (1, pp. 280–84); cf. ibid. 21. 30 (2, p. 114).

[159] Ibid. 21. 9 (2, p. 82).

[160] Venantius Fortunatus, *Vita Severini episcopi Burdegalensis* 5, p. 222 (the textual tradition has alternatives to Trier).

[161] *Virtutes Fursei abbatis Latiniacensis* 19, pp. 446–47.

[162] Stephen of Rennes, *Vita Guillelmi Firmati* 4. 27–28, p. 340.

gave off "the fragrance of the most sweet smell," and soon his tomb was the scene of miracles:

> Hearing was given to the deaf, sight to the blind, dexterity to the lame, cure to those possessed by demons, health to the sick and purification to the leprous; many, at the invocation of his name and by God's help, were freed from prison and released from chains.

The dispute over the body, the miraculous tractability of the coffin, the prophecy about the place of burial, the odour of sanctity and, of course, the miracles, recur in scores of accounts of saintly interments.

A perplexing, but also illuminating, situation that sometimes arises in hagiographic accounts is the apparent existence of two (or more) bodies of a single saint. This seems to have been a particular feature of the Celtic lands. For instance, when the Welsh saint Teilo died, there was a conflict among the three churches with which he had been associated—Penally, Llandeilo and Llandaff—over who should have the body. The clergy of the three places agreed that the case should be left in the hands of Jesus Christ, who would indicate "by an evident sign to which of them the holy body of the saint should more worthily be committed." On the morning after this had been agreed they were amazed to find three, completely identical, bodies of St. Teilo. They went off happily to their churches and buried their body (the author of this account, a cleric of Llandaff, cannot resist adding that Llandaff was most famous for the miracles that happened at Teilo's tomb).[163]

One way that inventive hagiographers could explain the apparent existence of two or three sites claiming a saint's body in this way was the theory of mass delusion. When St. Modwenna (also known as Darerca and Moninna) died, the Irish, Scots, and English quarrelled over who should possess her body, but eventually all thought they possessed it.[164] Possibly such stories originate either in two or more separate saints being identified, or in one saint being wrongly regarded as several. Sometimes the two bodies are only apparent and one of them disappears. The seventh-century Irish hagiographer Muirchú writes of "bitter contention" over the body of St. Patrick between, on one side, the O'Neills and the men of Airthir, on the other, the Ulaid. Airthir was the kingdom in which Armagh was situated, while the Ulaid controlled Dún Lethglaisse, where, as even Armagh polemicists recognized, Patrick's body lay (it is now Downpatrick). This dispute between the kingdoms of Ulster over the saint's body "came to war." The O'Neills and the men of Airthir invaded the kingdom of the Ulaid and reached the site where Patrick's body lay. There, "they were misled by a fortunate delusion" and thought they had found "the holy body"; on their way back, however, it disappeared.[165]

[163] *Vita sancti Teliavi*, pp. 116–17.

[164] Conchubranus, *Vita sanctae Monennae* 3. 11, p. 236; Geoffrey of Burton, *Vita sancte Modvenne virginis* 40, pp. 168–74.

[165] Muirchú, *Vita sancti Patricii* II. 13 (11)–14 (12), pp. 120–22.

Having died, the saint went to heaven. There were conventions about the way the soul carried to heaven was described. Brightness and lightness are common. Fire and light ascending to heaven often accompanied the deaths of holy men and women. Watching the flocks on the cold hills of southern Scotland one night, Cuthbert "saw the darkness of the long night broken by a light pouring from heaven, in which choirs of the heavenly host came to earth and, snatching up a soul of extraordinary brightness, returned to their home above without delay."[166] What he had seen was the soul of St. Aidan being carried to heaven. Francis's soul ascended "like a kind of star, as big as the moon, but with the brightness of the sun, carried up on a white cloud."[167] When St. Peter of Morone (Celestine V) died in 1296, he appeared to one of his disciples, Robert of Salle, "in the gleaming white stole of immortality and with a serene countenance." Robert was confused, since he assumed that Peter was alive and still in the strict confinement imposed by Pope Boniface VIII, who had replaced him. "Father," he asked, "has the pope agreed to let you travel here?" "The king has commanded this," replied Peter. "And where are you going, Father?" asked Robert. "My dearest son," said Peter, "I have to climb a great mountain, for this is the king's wish." Suddenly coming out of the ecstatic trance into which he had fallen, Robert looked up and saw Peter ascending through the clouds. Four days later he received the news of Peter's death.[168]

Sometimes there is a strong (and rather charming) recognition of the way that artistic conventions influenced these supernatural visions. After William of Æbelholt died in 1203, he was seen in a vision going up to heaven, clothed in a white stole:

> And, just as in the pictures that record the Lord's ascension—he is painted having been received into the clouds with only his feet visible—so this saint had been received into the white clouds and only his feet and the tips of his clothes could be seen.[169]

Most dead humans smell disgusting. But dead saints, like William Fermat, just mentioned, do not: "holy flesh declares itself most evidently through its wonderful smell."[170] When St. Sualo, a hermit who had settled in the diocese of Eichstätt in the eighth century, was exhumed fifty years after his death, "such a great and indescribable vapour, with a wonderful smell, suddenly rushed out, that the whole church was filled with the sweetest scent."[171] And after the tomb of St. Stephen was opened early in the fifth century the smell was so wonderful that those present imagined

[166] Bede, *Vita sancti Cuthberti* 4, pp. 164–66.

[167] Thomas of Celano, *Vita prima sancti Francisci* 2. 8, p. 86.

[168] *Vita Roberti Salentini* 1. 16, p. 498.

[169] *Vita et miracula sancti Willelmi abbatis Ebelholtensis* 29, pp. 341–42.

[170] Thiofrid of Echternach, *Flores epytaphii sanctorum* 1. 5, p. 21; see Roch, *L'intelligence d'un sens*, esp. part two, chapter 1 (pp. 105–57), "La mort parfumée des saints," and part two, chapter 4 (pp. 249–328), "La fragrance des corps saints"; despite its title, Albert, *Odeurs de sainteté*, has only one page on this topic.

[171] Ermanric, *Sermo de vita sancti Sualonis* 10, p. 162.

they were in paradise.[172] The body of the dead saint might smell of lilies, roses, and incense.[173] It might smell so fragrant, "that you would think it had been anointed with sweet unguent" (as indeed it might have been).[174] The odour of sanctity was naturally a subject of interest to the commissioners in canonization processes. During the examination of a witness in the hearings into the sanctity of Vincent Ferrer, the archpriest of Vannes in Brittany (where Vincent was buried) explained that he had participated in his funeral, which had taken place on the Friday following the saint's death on the Wednesday. He was then asked, "if, on account of the distance of time that had elapsed between his death and his burial, he had noticed any offensive smell as he carried the body."[175] He had not.

The Martyrdom of the Virgin Saint

A particular form of saintly death has provoked a large amount of attention. Martyrdom accounts ("Passions") inevitably describe physical violence. Certain high-status Christians, like Cyprian, bishop of Carthage, were given mercifully quick and simple execution by beheading, but many others were subject to torture, which was a normal part of the judicial process in the Roman Empire, or were executed in the heat and horror of the amphitheatre by being burned alive or thrown to wild animals. These tortures are described both in the historical and in the legendary accounts of martyrdom, and the cruelties are sometimes elaborated to an extraordinary degree, raising the question whether there might be some attempt to give readers a sadomasochistic gratification, especially in the detailed descriptions of violence to women.

In its original version, the *Golden Legend*, the most popular collection of saints' Lives of the later Middle Ages, devotes thirteen chapters to virgin martyrs of the Roman period. They are, in calendrical order, Lucy, Anastasia, Agnes, Agatha, Juliana, "A Virgin of Antioch," Margaret, Christina, Euphemia, Justina, Daria (she occurs in the entry for Crisantus), Cecilia, and Catherine.[176] The standard narrative contains the following elements. A girl, in her teens, is either a Christian in a non-Christian family, or is converted in the course of the narrative. She is usually sought in marriage and refuses, or occasionally, like Cecilia, enters a non-consummated marriage. Her religious insubordination and her refusal to marry face a fierce reaction from her own family. Lucy is denounced by her fiancé, Anastasia is imprisoned by the husband with whom she had not slept, Juliana is punished and handed over to the authorities by her father. St. Christina was originally (despite her name)

[172] *Revelatio Sancti Stephani* 45, p. 215.

[173] *Vita beatae Helenae Ungarae*, p. 275.

[174] Jerome, *Vita Hilarionis* 32. 7, p. 296 (PL 23: 52).

[175] *Procès de la canonisation de Saint Vincent Ferrier*, p. 7.

[176] Jacobus de Voragine, *Legenda aurea* 4, 7, 24, 39, 43, 60, 89, 94, 134, 138, 153, 165, 168 (1, pp. 49–52, 75–77, 169–73, 256–61, 267–69, 415–20, 616–20, 646–49; 2, pp. 951–54, 971–76, 1071–72, 1180–87, 1205–15); Faith, Hope, and Charity, and Apollonia were soon added, ibid., 1, pp. 308, 444–45; Justina's story, although it ends in martyrdom, is of a completely different type from the others.

dedicated to the service of the pagan gods, but rejected them. Her father is both incensed and confused: "if you worship three gods, why not also worship others?," he asks. Obviously not convinced by her affirmation of Trinitarian doctrine, he orders her to be stripped and beaten by twelve men, then thrust into prison. Her distraught mother comes to her begging, "My daughter Christina, light of my eyes, have mercy on me!" Christina rejects her mother as strongly as her father had rejected her: "Who are you calling your daughter?," she asks. Her father then has her brought before the judge.

Hostile Roman officials play a major role in these accounts, as persecutors, interlocutors and sometimes as aspiring husbands or would-be rapists. They have the title governor, prefect or judge. Only in the case of Catherine is the emperor himself involved. They question the girl, demand that she sacrifice to the gods and prescribe the punishments when she does not. These punishments involve the elaborate application of pain. Juliana is stretched on a wheel until her bones break and the marrow comes out, then plunged into hot lead. Margaret is strung up and beaten, first with rods and then with instruments with iron teeth, until her bones are laid bare. Later she is burned with flaming torches, "as far as her inmost parts," and then thrust into a vat of cold water. Euphemia is placed on a fiery wheel, hung by the hair, crushed between stones, thrown to the beasts. Cecilia is placed in boiling water.

This menu of tortures became a standard feature of the literary imagination. In Shakespeare's *Winter's Tale* the faithful Paulina says to the maddened king Leontes:

What studied torments, tyrant, hast for me?
What wheels? racks? fires? what flaying? boiling?
In leads or oils? what old or newer torture
Must I receive . . . ?[177]

The virgin martyrs embrace their tortures. "I delight in these pains," says Agatha, "like one who hears good news or sees someone they have long desired to see." They can even turn them into occasions for defiance. When Christina's flesh is mangled, in the presence of the father who has brought her to the court, she takes lumps of it and throws them at him, saying, "Take this, you tyrant, and eat the flesh you gave birth to." The virgins are indeed distinguished by their stubborn defiance and strident tone. Agatha tells her pagan persecutor, "Your words are foolish and empty and pollute the air. Wretched man, without sense or intellect, why do you want me to worship stones?" Margaret calls her judge "an impudent dog." Cecilia is actually asked by the judge, "Where did you get such presumption in your replies?"

Sexual humiliation is one of the cruelties inflicted on them. Christina, her head shaved, is led naked through the city to the temple of Apollo. Catherine is stripped naked, beaten with scorpions, and thrust into a dark prison. The judge seeks to rape Euphemia. In this menu of sexual assault, the breasts are a particular target. The judge orders one of Agatha's breasts to be tortured and twisted and then cut off, but

[177] Act 3, scene 2.

it is miraculously restored at night by St. Peter. She is later rolled naked on hot tiles. Christina's breasts are cut off and then "milk flowed like blood." In the story of Catherine, the queen Catherine converts has her breasts cut off before she is executed.

Sometimes the virgins are condemned to a brothel, an especially public and demeaning form of sexual humiliation. In all cases in which this punishment is imposed, however, the saints are preserved from defilement. The unnamed virgin of Antioch is told that she will either sacrifice to the pagan gods or be sent to a brothel. She is indeed sent there, but is saved by the unlikely figure of a soldier, who changes clothes with her to enable her to escape unnoticed. Agnes is told by the prefect: "Chose one of two things: either sacrifice to the goddess Vesta, along with the virgins, if virginity is so pleasing to you, or be a whore among the prostitutes." When she refuses to sacrifice, she is stripped and led naked to the brothel, but her hair miraculously grows to cover her and an angel protects her in the brothel. Daria, a Vestal Virgin who had converted to Christianity, is sent to the brothel, but is guarded there by a lion that has escaped from the amphitheatre.

Especially cruel are the sentences on Euphemia and Lucy. The judge dealing with Euphemia orders his official "to summon all the wanton young men to her, to have sex with her until she dies from exhaustion." Likewise, Lucy is condemned to be taken away by the pimps and made available for any man, until she is dead. Her response is heroic:

> The body is not polluted unless the mind consents. For if you have me violated against my will, my crown of chastity will be doubled. My body is ready for any torture. What are you waiting for? Son of the devil, get on with whatever punishments you desire to inflict!

The handing over of the virgin to a brothel was such a regular narrative feature that it even occurs in oddly inappropriate forms, as in the tale of Agatha, who is handed over to "the prostitute Aphrodisia and her nine daughters of the same wickedness," in order to get her to change her mind about her faith. This is not a punishment, nor is Agatha condemned to be a prostitute, and it is a very implausible way of getting her to renounce Christ. The formula is so imbedded that the author of this account fails to notice how poorly it supports the verisimilitude of the story.

It is clear that these narratives, even in the case of martyrs whose historical existence is almost certain, are fantastic tales. The supernatural support that the saints receive is dramatic in the extreme. Lucy cannot be dragged off to the brothel even by yoked oxen; Catherine is fed in prison with heavenly food for twelve days, Anastasia for two months; sudden earthquakes free the suffering saints; Juliana defeats a demon and drags him around on a chain, before tossing him into a latrine. The fire that is meant to torture Christina kills 1500 people, while, when the ingenious wheels that have been designed to torment Catherine are broken by an angel, four thousand pagans are killed. Christina spends five days in a fiery furnace, singing and walking about. The saints also engage in informative conversations with demons. One explains to St. Margaret how Solomon enclosed an infinite multitude of demons in a vessel but, after the king's death, men broke it in the search for treasure and the demons escaped.

The *Golden Legend* supplies a conveniently assembled and manageable sample of such accounts of the torture of virgin martyrs, but the genre can be found far and wide, from the manuscripts copied out in the Frankish monasteries of the eighth century to the vernacular versions of the very end of the Middle Ages. There are hundreds of copies of these texts. They can be found in the East as well as in the West, as becomes clear if one compares the accounts of virgin martyrs in the tenth-century Byzantine collection of Symeon Metaphrastes with those in the *Golden Legend*. Many of the same patterns (and some of the same saints) appear: the confrontation with the Roman judge, the defiant tone of the martyrs, and, emphatically, the horrific and elaborate tortures.[178] In the Greek accounts Juliana is tied and beaten, hung up by her hair, red-hot irons are placed on her arm-pits and sides, and attempts are made to put her in a fiery furnace and boiling cauldron; Euphemia is tied and beaten, crushed by wheels, cast into a burning fiery furnace, thrown to fierce marine creatures and to lions and bears; Charitina has her hair shaved, red-hot coals placed upon her head, then vinegar poured on it, has hot irons attached to her breasts, is thrown into the sea with a stone around her neck, tied naked to a wheel with chopping blades, has her hands and feet chopped off and her teeth pulled out.[179] The assault on the female breast is found in the Greek as in the Latin tales. As in the later Latin version, the empress in the story of Catherine has her breasts cut off; Barbara has her breasts cut off with a knife and is ordered to be beaten naked through the land, although God covers her with a miraculous robe; Pistis (Faith), daughter of Sophia (Wisdom), has her breasts cut off.[180] And, although condemnation to the brothel does not occur in any of the texts in Symeon Metaphrastes's collection, it can be found in other Greek accounts of virgin-martyrs.[181]

Throughout Christendom, from the early Middle Ages to the Renaissance, one strand of hagiography thus described the torture and sexual humiliation of innocent young women. It is without doubt that women were subjected to sexual humiliation and torment in reality during the persecution of Christians under the Roman empire. Perpetua and Felicity, for example, were exposed naked in a net in the arena at Carthage.[182] But the medieval stories of virgin martyrs are not historical reports—they are fictions. It is quite reasonable to ask why certain features were included in a fiction, and scholars studying these texts have remarked on the attractions of "sex,

[178] On Symeon Metaphrastes in general, see Høgel, *Symeon Metaphrastes: Rewriting and Canonization*.

[179] Symeon Metaphrastes, *Martyrium sanctae Julianae martyris*; idem, *Martyrium sanctae Euphemiae*; idem, *Martyrium sanctae Charitinae*.

[180] Symeon Metaphrastes, *Martyrium sanctae et magnae martyris Aecaterinae*, col. 297; idem, *Certamen sanctae et gloriosae magnae martyris Christi Barbarae*, col. 313; idem, *Martyrium sanctarum mulierum Sophiae et ejus filiarum Fidei, Spei et Charitatis*, col. 505.

[181] For example, *Martirium sanctae virginis martyris Agnetis*, p. 357; *Martirium sanctae Luciae virginis*, p. 62.

[182] *Passio sanctarum Perpetuae et Felicitatis*, p. 128.

violence and sexual violence" that seem implicit in them.[183] "Hagiography," some argue, "affords a sanctioned space in which eroticism can flourish and in which male voyeurism becomes licit."[184] "Sadism," it has been said, "contributes significantly to the success of this genre. . . . The eroticism grows out of the torment."[185]

The idea behind these suggestions is that depictions of sexual violence against women either can be or must be satisfying a male urge or feeding a male fantasy. Such a position is not intrinsically absurd, but it is necessary to consider alternative explanations. It is not a safe assumption that all descriptions of female suffering and humiliation address male erotic desire. There are other possible meanings to such scenes. And this is true, even when explicit forms of sexual voyeurism can be found, as in the story of Anastasia, whose judge "tore off her dress and made that beauty, which should be revered even by angels, stand totally naked, uncovered and unclothed, the more to shame the virgin, who was unaccustomed to crowds and the gaze of men."[186] Here there is no question of the motive—to have a naked young girl shown to crowds of men—but this is part of the logic of the story, and not necessarily a source of a clandestine thrill for the audience (although that cannot be ruled out).

Moreover, in a genre (hagiography) and an ideology (Christianity) that treasured virginity, a threat to virginity was especially wicked, and the threat to the virgin martyrs' sexual integrity has to be sexual in nature. Some of these accounts of the sufferings of virgin martyrs are found in works that are actually addressed to virgins. The story of the unnamed virgin of Antioch found in the *Golden Legend* comes originally from Ambrose's treatise *On Virgins*, which was addressed to his sister, herself a consecrated virgin.[187] When Aelred of Rievaulx, another brother full of advice, was encouraging his sister to live a withdrawn and virginal life and resist temptations, he urged her "think of the blessed Agnes . . . who turned a brothel into a place of prayer."[188] The Middle English version of the Life of St. Margaret was directed, as is stated in the prologue, "particularly to maidens." It contains all the standard repertoire of sexual humiliation: faced with Margaret's defiance, the Roman governor commands, "Strip her stark naked and hang her up high and beat her bare body with biting rods," and later has Margaret's "fine flesh" torn with iron hooks and her "snow-white skin" scorched and blackened with burning candles.[189] If the address to maidens is taken seriously, then it is young women who are being asked to contemplate these assaults on the virgin body—assaults that are successfully, indeed triumphantly, resisted. So, accounts of virgin martyrs, especially if addressed

[183] Winstead, *Virgin Martyrs*, p. 12.

[184] Gravdal, *Ravishing Maidens: Writing Rape in Medieval French Literature*, p. 24.

[185] Heffernan, *Sacred Biography*, pp. 276, 282.

[186] Symeon Metaphrastes, *Vita et conversatio et martyrium Anastasiae Romanae*, cols. 1300–1301.

[187] Ambrose, *De virginibus* 2. 4. 22–33, pp. 236–56.

[188] Aelred of Rievaulx, *De institutione inclusarum* 16, p. 652.

[189] *Seinte Margarete*, pp. 44, 52, 54, 74.

to young women, could be "designed to reveal the ideological force of virginity."[190] Some feminist scholars are prepared to argue that "To identify these texts as forms of pornography is reductive and simplistic," and that they are better seen as vindications of "voluntary self-sacrifice and the power that can be bestowed and shared through suffering."[191]

Although male martyrs as well as female martyrs are subjected to horrifying tortures in the hagiography of martyr saints, and therefore the excruciating suffering is common to both sexes, the men are not sexually humiliated (although one can imagine ways that they could be). Their nakedness is not one of their torments, as it is for the shamed virgins. When these martyr stories begin to be illustrated in the later Middle Ages, in illuminated manuscripts, panel paintings and other media, this difference is made explicit in a new way. Images of men stretched on racks or flayed alive contrast with half-naked women having their breasts sliced off. It is no surprise that modern viewers often imagine that pictures of this latter type might have an erotic or sexual significance.

It is difficult enough to identify the sexual tastes of people one knows; those of people hundreds of years ago are even harder to fathom. A rare piece of explicit evidence about the erotic potential of depictions of the saints comes from an early Protestant tract, in which one of the characters recalls, "I often had wicked thoughts when looking at the images of female saints on the altar." He compares the style of these saintly images with that of contemporary prostitutes: "No whore can dress or adorn herself in such a glamorous or shameless way, as they now fashion the mother of God, St. Barbara, Catherine, and other saints."[192] This is an erotic reaction very far from that hypothesised by scholars discussing the tortures of the virgin martyrs, for, although two of the saints mentioned are indeed virgin martyrs, the arousal is prompted by the elegant and beautifully attired figures of Barbara and Catherine in late medieval paintings or carvings. Nevertheless, it is an important contemporary comment about the possibility of erotic response to female saints.

In the absence of comparable evidence about the responses of readers (or hearers and viewers) to the tortures of the virgin martyrs, it is entirely speculative to say that this literature appealed to a taste for sexual sadism. Such a claim rests on our knowledge of the existence in the modern world of pornography that involves violence and abuse, and a well documented audience for this material, whose reactions and tastes are known. We may postulate that there were people of similar make-up in the medieval period, but we may believe, instead, that psychosexual types vary over time, rather than being part of an unchanging human nature. And, it must be said, modern pornography of this type occupies a well-charted social and commercial world that has nothing in common with the one that produced the stories of virgin

[190] Wogan-Browne, "Saints' Lives and the Female Reader," p. 321.

[191] Lewis, "'Lete me suffre': Reading the Torture of St. Margaret of Antioch," pp. 70, 82; see also the measured discussion in Mills, *Suspended Animation: Pain, Pleasure and Punishment in Medieval Culture*, pp. 106–44.

[192] *Gesprechbiechlin neüw Karsthans*, p. 428 (the tract dates to 1521; the authorship is not certain).

martyrs. They were written and copied by monks and nuns, often in collections that contained dozens of stories of saints of a quite different type, and were read seriously by devout women. Their condemnation by moderns as pornography, as also their vindication as assertions of the power of young women, has to be an ultimately unresolvable matter.

Rewriting Saints' Lives

Since some saints have been venerated for a thousand years and more, it is not surprising that their images and literary contours have been revised, retouched, and, on occasion, completely transformed over the centuries. A saint can have a different nature at different times and places and for different groups—St. George, for example, only acquired his dragon in the course of the early Middle Ages, and only developed his "English" side in the late Middle Ages. The rewriting of a saint's Life is the clearest example of such remodelling.[193] When a new author took up the pen, the window opened on new vistas—stylistic, ideological, even in the basic shape of the narrative. Rewriting, in a genre as extensive and long-lived as hagiography, can obviously take many forms: omission; addition; rewording; restructuring; new framing elements (sometimes called "hypotext"), such as prologues and headings. A prose Life could be turned into a verse Life or vice versa, and, of course, there were translations from one language into another.

Hagiographical rewriting was especially dynamic among the ecclesiastics of the Carolingian period (c. 750–900), who disparaged the style of the hagiographic works written in the preceding Merovingian period, and whose rewriting and recopying of the earlier texts was so extensive that scarcely any examples of Merovingian hagiography survive in manuscripts from the Merovingian period itself.[194] The Life of St. Riquier by the great scholar Alcuin provides an example of such revision. During a visit to the monastery of Centula (St.-Riquier) in the year 800, Alcuin recalled, "Abbot Angilbert had prayed that I rewrite in a more cultivated way a little book about the life of the most holy confessor Riquier which had been composed in a more simple style."[195] Alcuin's rewriting involved expansion, addition of biblical quotations, and a general flattening and smoothing of the earlier version. For instance, the Irish missionaries who convert Riquier are, in the earlier version, attacked

[193]Talbot, "Old Wine in New Bottles"; Goullet and Heinzelmann, ed., *La réécriture hagiographique dans l'Occident médiéval*; Goullet, *Écriture et réécriture hagiographiques*; Goullet et al., *L'hagiographie mérovingienne à travers ses réécritures*.

[194]Rare exceptions are the *Vita Wandregisili* (BHL 8804) in the eighth-century manuscript BnF, lat. 18315, and the *Passio Agaunensium martyrum* (BHL 5737) in the seventh-century BnF, lat. 9550, fols. 81v–86v; there is also the eighth-century Legendary in Munich, Staatsbibliothek, Clm 3514 ("Codex Velseri"), which contains the *Passio sancti Iuliani martyris* (BHL 4540; pp. 273–77) and the *Vita sancti Medardi episcopi* (BHL 5864; pp. 232–39); see Fouracre and Gerberding, *Late Merovingian France*, p. 64 and n. 138; Goullet et al., *L'hagiographie mérovingienne à travers ses réécritures*, pp. 12, 219.

[195]Alcuin, *Epistola* 306, p. 465 *(Vita Richarii*, prefatory letter) (also MGH, SRM 4, p. 389).

by the local peasantry because they are taken for wicked spirits (*dusi*) who will carry off their harvest; in Alcuin's version, there is no mention of this, and the peasants are motivated simply by "insolence." Both Alcuin and the earlier version describe a baby miraculously saved from a dangerous fall landing "like a little bird," but the early version describes how the child's worried mother ran up and found him "on a mound of earth which they call a molehill." In Alcuin, she finds him simply "on the ground."[196] Wicked spirits and molehills are not essential props to Riquier's sanctity, but they do add colour and individuality. It was evidently a colour and an individuality that Carolingian taste might find quaint or redundant.

Another energetic reviser of saints' Lives was the eleventh-century Bavarian monk, Otloh of St. Emmeram. In the preface to his Life of Boniface, the great saint of Fulda, where Otloh was at the time of writing, he explains the impulse behind this composition:

> My brethren of Fulda, I have striven to meet your requests, as far as the small stock of my knowledge allows. For you requested that I should make clearer and more comprehensible the Life of our holy father Boniface, which had been written long ago in the distinguished and elegant style of saint Willibald, but which was in some places so obscure to weak intellects that it was hard to see what exactly it was saying.[197]

Otloh also mentions, with modest and proper pride, the use he has made of Boniface's Letters, which were not available to the earlier hagiographer but which he has dug out through his own researches.[198] He inserts the texts of some of these letters into the Life at appropriate points (an epistolary technique of which there are other examples in hagiography).[199]

In another of his hagiographical writings, Otloh describes how he had constructed his own Life of St. Nicholas:

> Except for one chapter at the end, everything else I have collected from two little books, one which can be found in many places, the other which was brought to us by an unknown person, who said that he had acquired it in distant regions, adjoining Greece. In this I found many things that were not in the other, although expressed in a very crude style. I have attempted to compose one book from these two, adding nothing of my own, just omitting superfluous material from both, and correcting what was ungrammatical in

[196] *Vita Richarii . . . primigenia* 2, 5, pp. 445, 447; Alcuin, *Vita Richarii* 2, 10, pp. 110, 122 (the editor also prints the earlier life, from Krusch's edition, at pp. 14–26) (MGH, SRM 4, pp. 390, 395); see also Veyrard-Cosme, "Alcuin et la réécriture hagiographique."

[197] Otloh of St. Emmeram, *Vita Bonifacii*, prologue, p. 111.

[198] Ibid., p. 113.

[199] Notably the augmented version of the Becket Quadrilogus: Duggan, *Thomas Becket: A Textual History of His Letters*, pp. 205–23, 278–84.

> the new one. Where they agreed, I have followed one of them, where they differed, I have chosen what seemed best to me.[200]

Otloh thus had access to a version of Nicholas's Life newly acquired from the East as well as the standard version readily available in Germany, and he worked by combining the two texts, following his own preference when they disagreed, and revising the style of the newly acquired version according to the grammatical conventions of his own time and place.

Of all the attempts to rewrite saints' Lives, one of the most extensive and successful was that undertaken by the Byzantine official Symeon Metaphrastes in the tenth century.[201] His name reflects his triumph—it means "Symeon the Rewriter." He took 148 earlier Lives and Passions and revised them, often making their style more "correct" and Attic (the most prestigious Greek dialect). His collection became a standard source for hagiographic readings and survives in more than seven hundred manuscripts. Stylistic revision of earlier Lives continued to be an activity of some Byzantine writers down to the extinction of their state. In the Palaeologan period (1261–1453) more than 160 hagiographical works were produced, the bulk of them being reworkings of Lives of earlier saints.[202] Their authors were "literati, not monks," like the important official Constantine Akropolites, who earned the soubriquet "the new Metaphrastes" from his activity as a reviser and rewriter. Some of his works were partly inspired by personal experience. In his encomium of St. Theodosia, a ninth-century iconophile martyr, he remarks, "I will not pass over the wonder that the saint did for me," and recounts how she cured him of a serious leg injury that had been inflicted by a horse, so well that he could walk as if he were twenty again.[203] Most of his hagiography was intended to be read out on the feast-day of the saint, often in the church that held their relics. The impulse behind this late Byzantine rewriting was partly literary, the constant urge to have works in the approved style, and partly a response to the disruption during the Latin occupation of Constantinople (1204–61), which had left gaps in the hagiographical record.

In the West an earlier, and more severe, disruption in the hagiographical record was associated with the Viking raids. For example, when Orderic Vitalis, monk of the Norman monastery of St.-Évroul in the early twelfth century, was attempting to piece together the story of the life of its founding father, who had lived more than four centuries earlier, he had to have recourse to what he learned "not from written sources but from what I have been told by my elders." Such oral tradition was especially important because of the destruction of many earlier written materials:

[200] Otloh of St. Emmeram, *Vita sancti Nicolai*, prologue, pp. 408–9 (from Clm 14419, fols. 20v–21).

[201] Høgel, *Symeon Metaphrastes: Rewriting and Canonization*.

[202] For the following, Talbot, "Old Wine in New Bottles"; eadem, "Hagiography in Late Byzantium."

[203] Constantine Akropolites, *Sermo in sanctam martyrem Theodosiam* 41–43, pp. 138–39 (PG 140: 932–33).

> In the great storms that raged so horribly in the time of the Danes, writings of our forebears perished in fire, along with churches and buildings. . . . When the books perish, the deeds of the men of old fall into oblivion.[204]

For Orderic, the doings of the saintly Évroul lay on the other side of the fiery veil of Viking savagery, and had to be reconstructed carefully, drawing on whatever sources might be at hand.

Political and military upheaval of this type could clearly create the need for some kind of recuperation, a recovery or replacement of the hagiographic record. But, more usually, rewriting was a response to cultural change within the writer's society. For instance, the new technical scholastic terminology that arose in the twelfth century, as universities were born and Aristotle's works were translated into Latin, sometimes left an imprint on hagiographic rewriting. An author of the later twelfth century could pride himself on rewriting a Life from a century earlier "in a scholastic style," complacently telling his readers that they should not "look for the words, the order or the substance of the old and now virtually outdated version," and then peppering his prose with semi-technical terms.[205] Renaissance humanism had a similar effect. The humanists of the fifteenth and early sixteenth centuries may have had a supercilious attitude to much of the medieval past, but this did not prevent their producing saints' Lives, sometimes new and sometimes revisions of earlier texts.[206] They viewed the accumulated stock of medieval hagiography with deep distaste. "These writings are so foolish," wrote the Florentine canon Antonio degli Agli around 1450, "so uncouth, careless, feeble, and, so to speak, childish, that senile old women and men would scarcely hear and believe them." Having thus managed to censure hagiography as both childish and senile, he points out the effects such pitiful writings might have on the sceptical and secular: "they would mock, not only them, but also the simplicity of Christians, who believe and accept such foolish and childish stories."[207] He himself undertook to write an account of the early martyrs which was serious and accurate. Similarly, the great humanist scholar Alberti himself revised the Life of St. Potitus in a more elegant style.[208]

One fairly drastic transformation is the shift from verse to prose, or prose to verse.[209] Rewriting verse as prose was less common than vice versa, but could be undertaken, as in the case of the prose reworking of Prudentius's Passion of Cassian of Imola, rewritten "in ordinary language, so that what is contained in books should also be recounted to the people and what is known to the ears of learned doctors

[204] Orderic Vitalis, *Historia ecclesiastica* 6. 9 (3, pp. 282–84).

[205] Gerald of Wales, *Vita sancti Davidis archiepiscopi Menevensis*, prologue, p. 377; Bartlett," Rewriting Saints' Lives."

[206] Frazier, *Possible Lives: Authors and Saints in Renaissance Italy*; Collins, *Reforming Saints: Saints' Lives and Their Authors in Germany, 1470–1530.*

[207] Webb, "Sanctity and History: Antonio Agli and Humanist Hagiography," p. 300.

[208] Alberti, *Vita sancti Potiti*; the rewriting is discussed in the editorial introduction on pp. 31–41.

[209] See especially the discussion in Goullet, *Écriture et réécriture hagiographiques*, pp. 151–63.

should not be unknown to all the faithful."[210] Here, the assumption is that (Latin) verse is harder for most people than prose. Yet most transpositions were from prose to verse. Sometimes versification resulted in expansion, as when a ninth-century author, producing a poetic version of Venantius Fortunatus's Life of Germanus of Paris, turned the earlier writer's simple phrase, "he was brought up and instructed in good behaviour," into "as the young man was educated, he grew in good behaviour, being a cultivator of the virtues and a lover of the Church." Here there is not just a redundancy of synonyms, but also, by the addition of "the Church," a greater explicitness.[211] For someone who knew Latin, it is not clear that the poem would be harder than the prose version.

Henry of Avranches, mentioned earlier (pp. 514–15), who wrote a series of saints' Lives in verse, took Thomas of Celano's *First Life of Francis* as the source for his own *Versified Legend of St. Francis*.[212] In 2,585 hexameters, he gave a classical veneer to Thomas's unpretentious prose account of the actions and virtues of this charismatic saint. Henry's opening words, "I will sing the deeds of the holy leader, who first found the way to conquer monsters" echoes the opening lines of Virgil's *Aeneid*: "I sing of arms, and the man who first came to Italy from the shores of Troy." Henry then refers to the heroes of antiquity:

> What did Julius do that was worth remembering, or Alexander, compared with Francis? Julius defeated the enemy, Alexander the world, but Francis conquered both. Not only did Francis conquer the world and the enemy but also himself, conqueror and conquered in the same battle.

A standard medieval term for the devil was "the enemy," so there is a little word-play here: Julius Caesar conquered the Gauls and Pompey, Francis conquered Satan and his satellites, "the monsters" of the opening line. Henry then draws a pen-portrait of Assisi: "the ancient town of Assisi, which stretches towards the valley of Spoleto and clings to the steep height of olive-bearing rock, its roofs in serried ranks from high to low." All Thomas of Celano has is "the city of Assisi, which is situated at the edge of the valley of Spoleto."[213] Even more inflated is Francis's speech before the Sultan of Egypt.[214] Thomas of Celano deals with Francis's encounter with the Sultan in half-a-dozen sentences, but Henry seizes the opportunity to put into his mouth a learned and sometimes abstract defence of the Christian faith. Francis here "proves

[210] *Passio Cassiani*, fol. 157v; see Goullet, *Écriture et réécriture hagiographiques*, pp. 300–301.

[211] "Moribus honestis altus et institutus est": Venantius Fortunatus, *Vita sancti Germani episcopi Parisiensis* 3, p. 373; "Moribus honestis crescit institutus iuvenis, / Virtutum cultor existens, amator ecclesiae": *Rhythmus de vita et miraculis sancti Germani episcopi Parisiensis* 3. 15, p. 125.

[212] Henry of Avranches, *Legenda sancti Francisci versificata*. For summary of the text, Rigg, *A History of Anglo-Latin Literature*, pp. 184–85; for brief but cogent comments on the changes Henry made to Thomas' text, *Francis of Assisi: Early Documents* 1, pp. 425–26.

[213] Henry of Avranches, *Legenda sancti Francisci versificata* 1, lines 1–2, 11–15, 28–31, pp. 407–8; Thomas of Celano, *Vita prima sancti Francisci* 1. 1, p. 5.

[214] Thomas of Celano, *Vita prima sancti Francisci* 1. 20, pp. 43–44; Henry of Avranches, *Legenda sancti Francisci versificata* 8, lines 134–80, pp. 460–61; see Tolan, *Saint Francis and the Sultan*, pp. 54–92.

himself a philosopher" and he "syllogizes" rather than preaches, as he demonstrates that God is the first cause and proves to the Muslims (rather unnecessarily) that God is one. He summarizes the story of redemption, from the fall of Lucifer to the coming of Christ, and explains how "Christ's living flesh" is present simultaneously in all churches. "As he taught the articles of faith" writes Henry, "with his eloquent tongue, he moved the philosophers and the king, and no one dared harm him." The shift from Thomas of Celano's prose to Henry of Avranches's verse, accompanied by the more elaborate rhetoric, the classical allusions and the introduction of more than eighty citations of or allusions to Ovid has imprinted on the work an ostentatious literary style and a classical tone quite different from the original.

An example of multiple rewritings, over a period of 450 years, in verse and prose and in three languages, is provided by the Life of Edward the Confessor.[215] A Life, more historical than hagiographical, was written immediately after the king's death in 1066. In the 1130s, when a cult was developing at Westminster, where Edward was buried, Osbert of Clare, prior of Westminster, built on the foundation of this earlier work to produce a truly hagiographical Life, complete with miracles. Osbert undertook this task as part of a campaign to have Edward officially canonized, and, although this did not happen at this time, a later attempt was successful, and in 1161 Edward became the first papally canonized English saint. As a result, a new Life was commissioned from the great Cistercian writer Aelred of Rievaulx. Aelred's Life was the well-spring from which eight later versions flowed: a French poem very soon afterwards, written by a nun of Barking, which was then reworked in prose in the thirteenth century; a Latin verse version and Matthew Paris's French verse version, both also in the thirteenth century; and then, in the fifteenth century, two Latin versions, one of them in verse and dedicated to king Henry VI, and one in prose, and two English versions, one in verse and one in prose, this last being incorporated into Caxton's printed *Golden Legende*. We thus go from the last days of Anglo-Saxon England to the world of print, with a grand total of ten rewritings and reworkings. A similar story could be told of many works of hagiography.

Legendaries

The Genre

One of the most important hagiographic genres is that of the Legendary, a collection of Lives of the saints.[216] The tradition of collective biographies, which grouped together the stories of men or women who, in one sense or another, might be seen

[215] Pezzini, *The Translation of Religious Texts in the Middle Ages*, chapter 14 (pp. 333–72), "The Genealogy and Posterity of Aelred of Rievaulx's *Vita sancti Edwardi regis et confessoris*."

[216] Poncelet, "Le légendier de Pierre Calo," pp. 5–44; Levison, "Conspectus codicum hagiographicorum"; Philippart, *Les légendiers latins*; Dolbeau, "Notes sur l'organisation interne des légendiers latins." The term "Legendary" is used in this book for collections of accounts of both martyrs and confessors.

as comparable, was an ancient one. In the first century BC Cornelius Nepos wrote "Of famous men," which does not survive, and "Of excellent commanders of foreign nations," which does; Plutarch's Parallel Lives, arranged in pairs of Greek and Roman subjects, was produced around the year AD; a generation later there appeared Suetonius's Twelve Caesars, the only collective biography by this author (who wrote several) to survive in its entirety; and both Philostratus (third century) and Eunapius (fourth century) wrote Lives of the Sophists. In addition to this secular Greco-Roman tradition, the Hebrew Bible (Old Testament) and Greek New Testament contain biographical or semi-biographical material, sometimes of a collective nature. The Acts of the Apostles, tracing the deeds of Jesus' followers, first with its main focus on Peter, then on Paul, is of this type. Building on these precedents and examples, Christians of the fifth and sixth centuries created collective biographies for many of the apostles. An especially widespread text was the so-called Pseudo-Abdias, probably written in Gaul in the sixth century.[217] In the ninth century the text was being copied in Germany: a manuscript, perhaps from Regensburg, contains accounts of Peter, Paul, James the Less, Philip, Andrew, James the Great, John the Evangelist, Thomas, Bartholomew, Matthew, and Simon and Jude.[218] Pseudo-Abdias probably lies behind Cynewulf's Old English poem on the apostles, which is roughly contemporary with the Regensburg manuscript.[219]

Given this background, the attempt to bring together materials about post-apostolic saints was to be expected, and occurs soon after the emergence of the first Lives of confessor saints in the fourth century (on which see earlier, on p. 18). The earliest strand of this anthologizing urge involved collective accounts of the heroic ascetics of the deserts of Egypt and the Near East. The so-called *History of the Monks in Egypt* was written in Greek in 394, and soon translated into Latin. In this same tradition Palladius's *Lausiac History* of c. 420 contains seventy-one short chapters, each dedicated to one of the ascetic men or women who lived heroic lives in the deserts. These texts, often in expanded and conflated forms, were to be a central feature of monastic reading throughout the rest of the Middle Ages.[220]

The demand for Legendaries can be traced in the early centuries of the Middle Ages. Pope Gregory the Great, writing in 598 in response to a request for collection of deeds of the martyrs, explained that the church of Rome possessed a martyrology that enabled it to celebrate the martyrs' feast-days, but this gave only the name, day and place of death. He knew of no collection of Passions or Lives, other than that in Eusebius, who had composed a History of the Church and an account of the Martyrs

[217] *Codex apocryphus Novi Testamenti* 2, pp. 388–742.

[218] Dublin, Trinity College 737 (olim G. 4. 16), fols. 9–126v; described by Colker, *Trinity College Library Dublin: Descriptive Catalogue* 2, pp. 1169–73; with *Supplement One*, p. 213, for the Regensburg connection.

[219] Cross, "Cynewulf's Traditions about the Apostles in *Fates of the Apostles*," which uses the Trinity College manuscript of Pseudo-Abdias.

[220] *Historia monachorum in Aegypto*; Palladius, *Historia Lausiaca*; the most comprehensive version of the Latin is the *Vitae patrum sive historiae eremiticae libri decem*.

of Palestine in the fourth century.[221] Early in the seventh century the bishop of Paris undertook "to gather together the deeds of the holy martyrs" and solicited copies of texts from his clerical colleagues. For this enterprise he was praised as equal to Eusebius.[222] Such evidence shows that in this period collective hagiography was attractive but hard to find. This need was to be met fully and conclusively.

Both Pope Gregory and his contemporary and namesake, Gregory of Tours, made a contribution to the genre of collective hagiography, the former in his *Dialogues*, which discuss the holy men of Italy, the latter in *The Glory of the Martyrs*, *The Life of the Fathers*, and *The Glory of the Confessors* (earlier, pp. 35ff. and 45ff.). Soon these single-authored compendia were to be joined by Legendaries in the strict sense, anthologies of saint' Lives of diverse origins. The oldest surviving manuscript of a Legendary, which is now in the Staatsbibliothek in Munich, was written in a French monastery in the eighth century and originally contained 30 hagiographic pieces, all except one being Passions of early Christian martyrs (the exception is the Life of St. Medard, bishop of Noyon, who died in the mid-sixth century).[223] The Legendary is arranged according to the calendar (with some, perhaps only apparent, exceptions) and could have provided material for recitation to the monastic community during mealtimes, as was certainly later the practice.

From the ninth and tenth centuries onwards, the number of surviving Legendaries multiplies. In Byzantium, the tenth and early eleventh centuries saw the creation of several important collective hagiographical texts: the Synaxarion of Constantinople, consisting of abridged accounts of the saints and intended to provide liturgical readings; the collection of rewritten Lives by Symeon Metaphrastes; and the Menologion of Basil II. In their different ways these texts represent ambitious anthologies and mark a watershed in Byzantine hagiography.[224] In the West a collection of fifty-two saints' Passions was written at the Spanish monastery of San Pedro de Cardeña in the tenth century, containing martyrdom accounts from all over the early Christian world, but especially from Spain: Leocadia from Toledo, Eulalia and Cucufas from Barcelona, Emetherius and Celedonius of Calahorra, and so on. It is a large book, 37 by 28 centimetres (about 14 ½ inches by 11), and was originally 260 folios, before it was expanded by the addition of accounts of some of the Spanish Christians killed in Muslim Cordoba in the ninth century.[225] In England, Ælfric of Eynsham, writing in the 990s, recommended that, among other "holy books," a priest should possess a "passional," that is, a collection of accounts of saints.[226] Although it is improbable that every priest would possess such a book, it is clear that some collections existed in numerous manuscript copies and had a fairly wide regional distribu-

[221] Gregory I, *Registrum epistularum* 8. 28 (2, p. 549).

[222] Warnecarius, *Epistolae aevi Merowingici collectae* 14, pp. 456–57.

[223] Munich, Bayerische Staatsbibliothek, Clm 3514 ("Codex Velseri").

[224] Efthymiadis, "Hagiography from the 'Dark Age' to the Age of Symeon Metaphrastes," pp. 129–30.

[225] BL, Add. 25600; edited in *Pasionario hispánico (siglos VII–XI)* 2.

[226] *Councils and Synods with Other Documents Relating to the English Church* 1, part I, pp. 206–7 (cl. 51).

tion. For example, there is a Cistercian Legendary that was used in some twenty monasteries in north-eastern France and survives in forty manuscripts, mostly dating to the late twelfth and early thirteenth centuries.[227] Some of the Legendaries of the later Middle Ages were of great size and scope. The French Cistercian Legendary just mentioned had 432 texts dealing with 340 feast-days. There is a surviving complete set in six volumes, which average 47 centimetres high and 33 centimetres wide (18 ½ by 13 inches).[228] And, although not all the volumes have survived, the Legendary from the Saxon monastery of Böddeken must, in its complete form, have had 900 Lives.[229]

In the case of the more extensive Legendaries it was not always easy for a collector of saints' Lives to arrange his material, and we find a somewhat apologetic note in one ninth-century anthology:

> In this volume are contained the passions and deeds of various saints, which we have not been able to arrange in proper order, since we entered them into the volume as we found them in various places and at various times.[230]

But most authors of legendaries did better than this. Standard ways of organizing were either according to the calendar or thematically—apostles, martyrs, confessors, and so on. But other kinds of categorization can also be found.

Some collections consisted of female saints only. One tenth-century manuscript, probably from the monastery of Echternach, is made up of the Lives of eight female saints, all bar one (Brigid) being early martyrs.[231] Centuries later, there is a fifteenth-century collection of Lives of female saints in French, with twenty-eight entries, starting with the Virgin Mary and Mary Magdalene. Elizabeth of Thuringia is the only saint in this collection who lived after 800, so it is inspired by a historical rather than contemporary interest.[232] In the 1440s the English friar Osbern Bokenham produced thirteen Lives of female saints, most of them of early virgin martyrs, and many commissioned by female patrons. These Lives were then copied into a single volume, which was given to a nunnery.[233] In late medieval Byzantium also a few collections of Lives of female saints were produced.[234]

Legendaries might also contain saints from one region or one people only. An early example is Gregory the Great's *Dialogues*, of which the full and proper title is *Four Books on the Miracles of the Italian Fathers*.[235] Around about 1200 the monks of Gloucester put together a volume titled *The Life of the Welsh Saints*. The singular

[227] Rochais, *Un légendier cistercien de la fin du XIIe siècle*.

[228] Ibid. 1, p. 49 (BnF, lat. 16732–37).

[229] Moretus "De magno Legendario Bodecensi."

[230] Cited by Levison, "Conspectus codicum hagiographicorum," p. 530, from a manuscript now in Rome, Biblioteca Nazionale, Farfa 29, fol. 6.

[231] BnF, lat. 10862.

[232] BL, Add. 41179.

[233] Bokenham, *Legendys of Hooly Wummen*.

[234] Ehrhard, *Überlieferung und Bestand der hagiographischen und homiletischen Literatur der griechischen Kirche* 3/2, pp. 906–15.

[235] *Libri quatuor de miraculis patrum italicorum*: Gregory I, *Dialogi* (2, p. 10).

"Life" might have been deliberate (compare the comments of Gregory of Tours on p. 520, earlier), and the collection was certainly designed "to provide some record of the Celtic saints of Wales."[236] At the end of the fourteenth century a large compilation of the Lives of Irish saints was made, which, in its original shape, must have contained about 230 folios.[237] The Lives are in Latin, some of them translated from Irish, and represent saints from most parts of the country. There are some indications that it might have been put together in the part of Ireland settled by the English, rather than in the areas dominated by the native Irish, but these settlers could still identify with the native saints. The tireless anthologizer Jean Gielemans (d. 1487) collected hagiographical material from his own region of Brabant with a proudly patriotic purpose: it would serve "the edification of the people of Brabant" to read of "the deeds of the saints, male and female, who have sprung up in Brabant from the beginning, as if in God's Paradise."[238]

A principle of organization that is very common in modern times is alphabetical order. Although there are instances of the use of alphabetical order in the ancient world, and the large tenth-century Byzantine encyclopaedia known as the *Suda* is also alphabetically arranged, it was only in the twelfth and thirteenth centuries that the needs of preachers and academics made this kind of system anything other than a rarity.[239] One of the first genres to which it was applied with any degree of regularity was the so-called Distinctions, that is, systematically arranged lists of biblical and theological terms, with their various symbolical meanings. Alphabetization was then applied to concordances, subject indexes, and other kinds of text, with Albertus Magnus using it in his book on animals, although apologizing that this kind of categorization is "not truly philosophical."[240] Alphabetical order was never common for Legendaries but there are examples. For instance, one was produced by the Spanish Franciscan Juan Gil de Zamora (d. c. 1318). In his preface he explains that the volume contains abbreviated versions of saints' Lives for the benefit of "our brethren . . . since when they go out preaching they cannot carry with them a great load of books." The entries are in alphabetical order partly "so that they may be found the more easily."[241] Some of Juan Gil's principles of alphabetization are interesting (under "H" we find

[236] BL, Cotton Vespasian A XIV; the collection is on fols. 12v–105v, and the title on fol. 12v reads "Incipiunt capitula in vita sanctorum Walensium"; many of the Lives are printed in *Vitae sanctorum Britanniae et genealogiae*; the comment is by Hughes, "British Museum Manuscript Vespasian A XIV," pp. 199–200.

[237] *Vitae sanctorum Hiberniae e Codice olim Salmanticensi*; Sharpe, *Medieval Irish Saints' Lives*, pp. 228–46.

[238] Hazebrouck-Souche, *Spiritualité, sainteté et patriotisme. Glorification du Brabant dans l'oeuvre hagiographique de Jean Gielemans*, p. 60 n. 146, citing the *Agyolgus Brabantinorum*.

[239] Daly, *Contributions to a History of Alphabetization in Antiquity and the Middle Ages*; Rouse and Rouse, *Preachers, Florilegia and Sermons*, pp. 1–90.

[240] Albertus Magnus, *De animalibus* 23. 1 (2, p. 1430); Rouse and Rouse, *Preachers, Florilegia and Sermons*, p. 35.

[241] Fratres nostri . . . quia cum ad predicandum exeant tantum honus librorum secum defferre non possunt; secundum ordinem alphabeti . . . ut facilius inveniantur: BL, Add. 41070, fol. 1; the preface is

"Hisidore of Seville" and "Helizabeth of Thuringia," under "X," "Christopher") but there is no doubt of their usefulness as a finding aid, with even the occasional cross-reference ("Fillip and James—look under P"). John of Tynemouth's *Sanctilogium*, which was produced in the middle of the fourteenth century, contains the Lives of 156 British saints in calendrical order, but, at some point in the century after its composition, it was reorganized in alphabetical order.[242] The fifteenth-century London lawyer Robert Bale then made a summary of this alphabetical version, *The Alphabet of the Saints of England*.[243] And amongst the most successful of the Legendaries of the early days of print is a work alphabetically organized, Boninus Mombritius's *Sanctuarium*, printed in Milan in 1477 (it has been called "the last medieval legendary").[244]

Even less common than alphabetical arrangement is chronological arrangement. An example of a Legendary arranged in this way is Bernard of Brihuega's collection of martyrs' Passions, put together at the request of Alfonso X of Castile (1252–84) and his queen Beatrice. Bernard explains that "everything that is told in order is listened to more readily and committed more easily to memory." He wishes "to put the earlier first and the later afterwards," but notes that it is sometimes difficult to find out exactly when the martyrs lived (and died). A great help is any indication of which emperor they suffered under, so Bernard appended to his work a catalogue of the emperors, from the time of Tiberius, "when Stephen the first martyr was stoned," to the time of Constantine: "Once each emperor has been assigned to his proper time, and when one knows which emperors killed which martyrs, it follows that one will know which martyrs were earlier and which later."[245] A later successor in the enterprise of producing chronologically arranged collections of saints' Lives was the Italian humanist Antonio degli Agli. His *Lives and Deeds of the Saints*, in ten books, is dedicated to Pope Nicholas V (1447–55) and contains 228 entries, most of them "ordered according to the times," which means, in virtually all cases, emperor's reigns, just as with Bernard of Brihuega.[246]

---

edited by Dolbeau, "Les prologues des légendiers latins," pp. 391–92, and the contents analyzed in Pérez-Embid Wamba, *Hagiología y sociedad en la España medieval*, pp. 307–15.

[242] The calendrically ordered text is BL, Cotton Tiberius E I, from St. Albans; the reordered version is in BL, Cotton Otho D IX (s. xv); Oxford, Bodleian Library, Tanner 15 (AD 1499) from Christ Church, Canterbury; and York Minster XVI. G. 23, fols. 109–192v (AD 1454) from York (described in Ker and Piper, *Medieval Manuscripts in British Libraries* 4, pp. 705–6). The reordered work was printed by Wynkyn de Worde in the *Nova legenda Anglie* of 1516 and edited from the Cottonian and Bodleian manuscripts in 1901: *Nova legenda Anglie*.

[243] *Alphabetum sanctorum Angliae*: Dublin, Trinity College, MS 509, pp. 272–86; the title is as given in Bale, *Scriptorum illustrium Maioris Brytanniae* 2, p. 65.

[244] Mombritius, *Sanctuarium*; Frazier, *Possible Lives: Authors and Saints in Renaissance Italy*, p. 101.

[245] Díaz y Díaz, "La obra de Bernardo de Brihuega," p. 152; Pérez-Embid Wamba, *Hagiología y sociedad en la España medieval*, pp. 255–302, citations at pp. 257, 259; Bernardo's work consists of five volumes in all, Salamanca, Biblioteca Universitaria 2537–41.

[246] Frazier, *Possible Lives: Authors and Saints in Renaissance Italy*, pp. 73–74, 333–34. Another example of chronological organization is Antoninus of Florence's monastic Lives in BAV, Vat. lat. 9209, fols. 51v–154v (olim 96v–199v), of 1484, titled *Vitae patrum sanctorum Egipti et aliquorum aliorum*

In the later Middle Ages collections of stories about holy members of the religious Orders were popular reading among their fellow monks, friars, and nuns. In fourteenth-century Germany there came into existence books that have been christened "Sisters' Books" (*Schwesternbücher*) by modern scholars.[247] These were anthologies of anecdotes about the lives and wonderful experiences of the nuns of a particular convent. They were especially common among the south German Dominican nuns, and a typical short narration is as follows: "A sister called Anne of Constance went to the image of Our Lady holding our Lord in her arms, and took the child's foot in her hand with great reverence. The foot became flesh and blood in her hand."[248] The circulation among the nuns of such stories of wonders centred upon Mary and the Christ child would stimulate and confirm that Christocentric and Eucharistic piety so typical of the later medieval centuries.

But the stories were also tied to an individual religious house, so they also embodied local pride. A curious example of these strong local attachments, expressed in this case in a male rather than a female house, comes from the Cistercian monastery of Himmerode, in the diocese of Trier, in the fifteenth century.[249] Here a monk went through the huge collection of miracle stories that had been assembled two centuries earlier by Caesarius of Heisterbach in his *Dialogue of Miracles*, and excerpted all those that had to do with his own monastery of Himmerode (which was the mother-house of Heisterbach). He explains his goals:

> For a long time I have been moved by manifold desires to compile into one little work the lives and deeds of our holy fathers, that is, the monks and lay brothers of this monastery, which are assembled here and there in various places and sections of the Dialogue of Caesarius of Heisterbach of blessed memory.

At last, with the encouragement of the prior and some of his fellow-monks, he had completed this task, so that the simpler brethren, who might find Caesarius's compendium daunting, could read "the deeds of our holy fathers," and be inspired by their example. The great pool of exemplary stories that Caesarius had laboriously collected so long ago had thus been canalized into a stream of local significance, a kind of "Brothers' Book" parallel to the contemporary "Sisters' Books," if not so current.

Dominican Anthologies

The rise of the friars in the early thirteenth century had a deep effect on hagiography, not only through the generation of new Lives of their own saints, propounding new

---

abbreviata per fratrum Antoninum archiepiscopum Florentinum: cited by Dolbeau, "Notes sur l'organisation interne des légendiers latins," pp. 13, 25 n. 24.

[247] Discussed in Barow-Vassilevitch, *Ich schwime in der gotheit als ein adeler in dem lufft!*

[248] *Das Katharinentaler Schwesternbuch*, p. 109.

[249] BL, Add. 21616: *Vitae siue gesta sanctorum et venerabilium patrum monasterii in Hemmenrode* (1459).

images of sanctity, but also through their impact on the genre of Legendaries. The friars, in particular the Dominicans, had a special use for saints' Lives. The official name of the Dominicans is "The Order of Preachers" and their role as active evangelists amongst ordinary lay people made them deeply interested in good stories and memorable anecdotes with which they could enliven their sermons. The Lives of the saints offered a treasury of such material, and, quite soon after the foundation of the Order, inventive Dominicans began to produce anthologies of abbreviated saints' Lives, organized according to the liturgical calendar and suitable for use by preachers.

These anthologies were not just for use within the Order. Jean de Mailly, a French Dominican, who composed the first version of his *Abbreviation of the Deeds and Miracles of the Saints* in the late 1220s, explained his purpose in the preface:

> Since many priests do not have Passions and Lives of the saints, and because of their office they ought not to be ignorant of them or be silent about them, in order to arouse the devotion of the faithful towards the saints, we have narrated briefly the lives especially of those who are recorded in Kalendars, so that the shortness of this little book will not generate weariness and that lack of books will not be an excuse for parish priests. If anyone should not find the Life of his patron here, it should not be hard for him if he should seek it in its entirety elsewhere.[250]

Twenty years after Jean wrote these words his example was followed by another Dominican, from the friary of Trent in the South Tyrol.[251] Bartholomew of Trent, whose collection has 355 chapters, most of them dedicated to individual saints, explains in his preface, "I have striven to compile in one volume the lives, behaviour and deeds of the saints, which are scattered through various volumes." He admits that he is interested "especially in those familiar to the Order I profess and the country I live in," that is, Dominicans and Italy, respectively. And he is explicit about the purpose of his collection: "so that the holy Order of Preachers, and others, should have swiftly to hand something about the saints to propound to listeners."[252]

Rather unusually for a collector of saints' Lives, Bartholomew introduces several passages of first-person reminiscence into his text. Discussing one of the Marian feast-days, he writes, "I was often present at this feast-day in the church of Novacella, where I was brought up as a boy"; when writing of the translation of St. Dominic's body in 1233, he notes "at which I myself was present"; and he gives a lively account of his fever and delirium at Benevento in 1243.[253] Bartholomew's life was not without incident. He was involved in the dramatic dispute between the popes and the

[250] Jean de Mailly, *Abbreviatio in gestis et miraculis sanctorum*, cited by Perrot, *Le passionnaire français au Moyen Age*, p. 9; there is no modern edition of the Latin, but a French translation was published in 1947: Jean de Mailly, *Abrégé des gestes et miracles des saints*.

[251] Bartholomew of Trent, *Liber epilogorum in gesta sanctorum*.

[252] Ibid., prologue, p. 3.

[253] Ibid., 275, 177, 270, pp. 250, 128, 241 (Novacella or Neustift is just north of Brixen).

Holy Roman Emperor, Frederick II, which raged in the 1240s, at the time he was composing his work. Although he enthused about Frederick's victories in 1241 in a letter he wrote that year, this did not prevent Pope Innocent IV from choosing him to carry peace proposals to the emperor in 1243. Things evidently did not work out. In 1245 Pope Innocent issued sentence of deposition against the emperor, and in 1248 he wrote an enigmatic but ominous letter to the Prior Provincial of Lombardy, the head of the Italian Dominicans, expressing concern for the salvation of the soul of brother Bartholomew, revoking the privileges he had been granted and instructing the Prior "to subject him to the correction and discipline of the Order, dealing with him as seems fitting to you for the salvation of his soul."[254]

We do not know the eventual fate of brother Bartholomew, but his collection became one of the sources for the most successful book of the Middle Ages. This was the most widely disseminated of all anthologies of saints' Lives, the so-called *Golden Legend*, produced in the 1260s (and subsequently revised and reworked) by the Dominican Jacobus de Voragine (Voragine is Varazze, near Genoa).[255] The organization of Jacobus's work is complicated by a historical theory. Following earlier authors, he describes parallels between the course of the Church year and the course of human history.[256] He distinguishes four ages: the "age of deviation," from Adam to Moses; "the age of renewal" from Moses to Christ; "the age of reconciliation" under Christ; and "the age of pilgrimage," which is our present life. These have their parallels in the time between Septuagesima (the third Sunday before Lent) and Easter; the season of Advent, culminating in Christmas; Easter to Pentecost; and the time between the Octave of Pentecost and Advent. Not fitting very easily into this scheme, the time between Christmas and Septuagesima is partly to be paired with the age of reconciliation and partly with the age of pilgrimage, the division between them coming at the Octave of Epiphany:

Advent	Age of renewal
Christmas to Octave of Epiphany	Age of reconciliation
Octave of Epiphany to Septuagemisa	Age of pilgrimage
Septuagemisa to Easter	Age of deviation
Easter to Pentecost	Age of reconciliation
Octave of Pentecost to Advent	Age of pilgrimage

[254] Ibid., pp. XXII–XXV.

[255] Jacobus de Voragine, *Legenda aurea*; for analysis, Boureau, *La légende dorée*; Reames, *The Legenda aurea: A Reexamination of Its Paradoxical History*; Dunn-Lardeau, ed., *Legenda aurea*; Fleith, *Studien zur Uberlieferungsgeschichte der lateinischen Legenda Aurea*; Fleith and Morenzoni, eds., *De la sainteté a l'hagiographie: genèse et usage de la Légende dorée*; *La Légende dorée*, ed. Boureau, pp. XV–XLVIII; Le Goff, *À la recherche du temps sacré: Jacques de Voragine et la Légende dorée.*

[256] Jacobus de Voragine, *Legenda aurea*, prologue (1, pp. 3–5); John Beleth, *Summa de ecclesiasticis officiis* 55–56, pp. 96–103.

The feast-days of the Church year can then be assigned to these various seasons, beginning with Advent. There are 178 chapters in the final version of the *Golden Legend* to come from Jacobus's pen, the vast majority of them dedicated to a single saint, but with some devoted to feasts such as Christmas, the Annunciation and Septuagemisa, and one for the dedication of a church. Very few recent saints are included: two from the twelfth century (Bernard and Thomas Becket) and four from the thirteenth (Dominic, Francis, Elizabeth of Thuringia, and Peter Martyr). As has been pointed out, the selection of saints in Legendaries always remained "masculine and archaic."[257]

Jacobus was a compiler, and his sources can often be tracked down. For instance, in his chapter on John the Evangelist, he tells how "St. Edmund, king of England" had a special devotion to the saint and could deny no request made in his name. One day a pilgrim begged him for alms in the name of St. John and the king, "in the absence of his chamberlain," having nothing else to offer, gave him the ring from his finger. Some time later an English knight overseas encountered the same pilgrim, who gave him the ring to return to the king, with the message, "He to whom, and for love of whom, you gave this ring, returns it to you," clearly showing that the pilgrim was St. John in disguise.[258] Jacobus has taken this story, virtually word for word, from his fellow Dominican Bartholomew of Trent, whose collection of saints' Lives had been produced less than twenty years before Jacobus first began his work.[259] Bartholomew's immediate source has not been identified, but the ultimate origin of the story is clear, although it is associated not with "St. Edmund, king of England" but with Edward the Confessor, the king of England who died in 1066 and was the first English saint to be officially canonized. Following the canonization (in 1161) there was a grand translation ceremony in Westminster Abbey in 1163, and it is probably for this occasion that the Cistercian writer, Aelred of Rievaulx, wrote a Life of Edward. In this he tells how Edward had an especial devotion to St. John, how a pilgrim asked him for alms and how, because his treasurer was not present at that moment, he gave him his own ring. Later two English pilgrims in the Holy Land encounter a venerable old man who identifies himself as St. John and gives them the ring to return to the king, praising his chastity and intimating that he would die within six months "and with me will follow the Lamb."[260]

A story about Edward the Confessor, originally emphasizing his chastity (which was "a special privilege" he shared with St. John), had thus migrated to Italy, and become attached to King Edmund instead—Edmund was an English royal saint

[257] Philippart, *Les légendiers latins*, p. 43.

[258] Jacobus de Voragine, *Legenda aurea* 9 (1, p. 96).

[259] Bartholomew of Trent, *Liber epilogorum in gesta sanctorum* 19, p. 38.

[260] Aelred of Rievaulx, *Vita sancti Edwardi regis et confessoris*, cols. 769–70; see also Marzella, "L'anello del re e il 'paradiso' dell'evangelista: genesi di un episodio della '*Vita sancti Edwardi regis et confessoris*' di Ælredo di Rievaulx"; I am grateful to Dr. Marzella for an advance copy of this illuminating article.

who was much better known in Italy than Edward.[261] The function of the tale had also been inverted, from an anecdote about St. John designed to elevate Edward, to an incident in John's story, in which the king's role is secondary. Every narrative component in the *Golden Legend* could be pursued in this way, leading to a vast and intricate system of springs and tributaries, often channelled through Dominican predecessors like Bartholomew or the encyclopaedist Vincent of Beauvais.

Once gathered in this way Jacobus's anthology had an amazing success. A thousand manuscripts survive from the later Middle Ages, a number that dwarfs any other medieval work. It was translated into all the main vernaculars, sometimes in many versions. For instance, it was rendered into German eight times and Dutch twice in the later Middle Ages. The most widely diffused of these translations, the so-called Alsace Golden Legend, survives in thirty-six manuscripts.[262] The *Golden Legend* was a goldmine for any cleric or friar preparing a sermon.[263] It is very telling that, in the Dominican library at Florence, the *Golden Legend* was shelved with the sermon collections.[264] When William Caxton sat down to make his English translation of the *Golden Legend* in the early 1480s, he had in front of him a Latin version, a French version, and an earlier English version, "whiche varyed in many and dyvers places." He synthesized and reordered the three earlier works to produce his own, which was printed on his press in Westminster in 1483. He almost lagged during the course of making the translation but was encouraged by the earl of Arundel, whose promise of a "buck in summer and a doe in winter" for the rest of his life bucked him up.[265] It was one of the largest and most ambitious products to come from Caxton's press. Stories about the saints are amongst the richest and most treasured literary inheritances of the Middle Ages, and the *Golden Legend* is the preeminent collection of such stories.

But although the *Golden Legend* was the most successful Dominican compilation by far, it was not the last. In the generation following Jacobus de Voragine there was Bernard Gui's *Saintly Mirror* of the 1320s, which was organized both thematically and calendrically. He explains its construction in his preface.[266] The work is in four parts, "lest the quantity be too much for one volume." Part one deals with the feasts of Jesus, beginning with Advent, the feasts of the Virgin Mary, the Cross, angels, All Saints, All Souls, and the feast of the dedication of the church. Part two deals with John the Baptist, and, in liturgical order, the apostles, starting with Peter

[261] For his veneration in Siena and Lucca, see Ploeg, *Art, Architecture, and Liturgy: Siena Cathedral in the Middle Ages*, pp. 149, 158.

[262] Williams-Krapp, *Deutschen und niederländischen Legendare des Mittelalters*, p. 13; *Die Elsässische Legenda Aurea*.

[263] Delcorno, "La Legenda aurea dallo scrittoio al pulpito," has a detailed analysis of the use of particular chapters of the *Golden Legend* in sermons, including some by Jacobus de Voragine himself.

[264] Orlandi, *La biblioteca di S. Maria Novella in Firenze*, pp. 53 (no. 503), 54 (no. 528) (catalogue of 1489); some other saints' Lives were also shelved in this section.

[265] Caxton, *Golden Legende*, preface.

[266] Bernard Gui, *Speculum sanctorale*, preface; see Dubreil-Arcin, *Vies de saints, légendes de soi: L'écriture hagiographique dominicaine*.

and Paul, and including the evangelists Luke and Mark (who were not among the twelve apostles). This part concludes with Lives of the seventy-two apostles whom Christ had sent out according to Luke's Gospel, although Bernard Gui has to admit limitations here: he has included material about "the deeds of those I was able to find, because I was not able to have at hand the deeds of all of them." He says that the missing Lives could be written at the end of this section if and when they turn up. Part three of his work deals with the martyrs, beginning with Stephen, whose feast was 26 December, and continuing through the year, while part four is dedicated to confessor-saints, beginning with Silvester (31 December). He recommends that part three and part four each have their own volume, although the first two parts could conveniently be contained in one. There are indeed surviving manuscripts containing individual Parts.[267] Bernard Gui sums up the whole purpose of these Legendaries pithily: "Nothing prepares an easier entrance for understanding than brevity that is not obscure."[268]

Not long after Bernard Gui composed his collection, another Dominican undertook a similarly ambitious project. This was Peter Calo, a native of Chioggia on the Venetian lagoon. The most complete exemplar of his Legendary is in Venice today, and consists of 1,173 folios covering 862 saints and feast-days. The average length per item is thus 1⅓ folios, and meets Bernard Gui's requirement for "brevity."[269] Peter Calo's death in 1348, a year when half the population of Europe died, marked no break in the production, copying and adaptation of Legendaries. The great Dominican collections, to which one might add Vincent of Beauvais's *Mirror of History*, since it contains hundreds of saints' Lives, were standard features of late medieval libraries, while new Legendaries were written by non-Dominican authors, like that of another Venetian, Peter Natalis, which, as he himself says, he began on 11 June 1369 and, working "without a break," finished on 26 May 1372.[270] It is a useful piece of evidence about how long these mammoth compilations might take to complete.

In a sense Legendaries continue to the present day, since the anthology is a natural form for discussing hundreds or thousands of individual saints. Butler's *Lives of the Saints*, compiled by the English Catholic priest Alban Butler and first published in four volumes in the 1750s, has been a first point of reference in English ever since. Even the *Bibliotheca sanctorum*, the great scholarly enterprise produced in Italy in the 1960s, although organized in alphabetical rather than calendar order, continues the tradition of another Italian product, the *Golden Legend*. The huge and miscellaneous assemblage of saints to be found in the bigger legendaries expresses one aspect of the cult of the saints very well. Just as medieval paintings of the court of heaven show apostles, early martyrs, medieval bishops and recent friars, and include men

[267] Bernard Gui, *Scripta de sancto Dominico*, pp. 195–200, lists manuscripts of part four alone; for examples of manuscripts with parts one and two, part two alone, part three alone, and parts three and four, Dubreil-Arcin, *Vies de saints, légendes de soi: L'écriture hagiographique dominicaine*, p. 431.

[268] Bernard Gui, *Speculum sanctorale*, preface, p. 421.

[269] Poncelet, "Le légendier de Pierre Calo," pp. 44–116.

[270] Ibid., p. 35.

and women from all over Christendom, so the Legendary embodied the community of saints, that diverse but united host of Christian spiritual heroes drawn from across the lands and the centuries.

Miracle Books

In the words of one Byzantine hagiographer, to attempt to recount the miracles of the saints is like trying to measure the Atlantic Ocean.[271] Stories of saintly miracles certainly number in the thousands and perhaps the tens of thousands. In the 175 years prior to the Reformation, more than 12,000 miracles were recorded in Bavaria alone.[272] The Miracle Book of St. Bernardino of Siena, which was put together in the decade after the saint's death in 1444, has some 2,500 accounts.[273] There is discussion earlier (pp. 333ff.) of the nature of the miracles that saints supposedly performed, both before and after death. Here the focus is upon the literary forms in which miracles were narrated and recorded, upon the genre not the events.[274]

Saints' Lives recounted miracles, sometimes many of them, which the saint performed during his or her lifetime, but, quite early, stories of posthumous miracles were appended to the Life or recorded in a separate work. The first example of a free-standing collection of posthumous miracles seems to be that of St. Stephen from the 420s, and, not long afterwards, a collection of more than forty miracles of St. Thecla was put together at her shrine in Anatolia (earlier, pp. 22, 24). Thereafter, Byzantine miracle collections can be found in every century down to the extinction of the state in 1453.[275] In the West, Gregory of Tours collected hundreds of stories of posthumous miracles in the late sixth century, and he had numerous successors throughout the Middle Ages.

Both the free-standing Miracle Book and the collection of posthumous miracles appended to a Life continued to be common literary forms throughout the Middle Ages. The relative weighting of Life and Miracles in the composite works could vary in the extreme. Raymond of Capua devotes only 3 per cent or so of his Life of Catherine of Siena to her posthumous miracles, although he apologizes that "because of my aging memory, I cannot recollect the details of all the others."[276] By contrast, the *Passion and Miracles of St. Olav*, associated with archbishop Eysteinn (Øystein) of

[271] *Miracula Cosmae et Damiani* 26, p. 167.

[272] Sargent, "Miracle Books," p. 458.

[273] Jansen, "Un exemple de sainteté thaumaturgique."

[274] For an exemplary study of these accounts as stories, see Koopmans, *Wonderful to Relate*; a more schematic approach is taken by Andrić, *The Miracles of St John Capistran*, pp. 225–80; see also Haubfleisch, *Miracula post mortem*.

[275] Efthymiadis, "Greek Byzantine Collections of Miracles."

[276] Raymond of Capua, *Vita Catharinae Senensis* 378–94, pp. 530–44 (AASS Aprilis 3, pp. 948–51).

Nidaros (1161–88), divides roughly into 14 per cent on Olav's life (and death) and 86 per cent on the miracles.[277]

Miracle collections vary enormously in length. The longest contain hundreds of accounts, and there are plenty of miracle collections of forty or fifty tales, while sometimes a short piece recounts a single miracle, like the cure of a visiting Irish pilgrim by the ancient patron saint of Narni in Umbria, St. Juvenal, recorded in 1233.[278] The longer collections sometimes fill an entire volume. A good example is Reginald of Durham's *Miracles of Cuthbert*, for the original manuscript of the work survives, still in the library of the cathedral priory of Durham where it was written.[279] It is almost certainly an autograph manuscript in Reginald's own hand. It is a small book, 15 by 10.7 centimetres (less than 6 inches high and just over 4 inches wide), consisting of 166 folios. It must have been written over several years, since it is dedicated to Aelred of Rievaulx, who died in 1167, while its final pages describe events during the Scots invasions of 1173–74.[280] The handwriting is remarkably uniform throughout the text, although there are numerous marginal additions, chiefly words or phrases clarifying or amplifying something in the text, as the author revised his own work.

Reginald's book is dedicated to just one subject, Cuthbert's miracles, and is the work of one hand. But such clear examples of unitary and extensive composition, with an identifiable author and unambiguous date, are far from being the rule for Miracle Books. More common are anonymous works, while many medieval Miracle Books are serial compositions, often written by several authors in succession. The Miracles of St. Foy were composed over decades, the Miracles of St. Benedict over centuries.[281] Sometimes the break between authors is fairly clear, when a new pen is taken up with words such as those in the *Passion and Miracles of St. Olav*:

> After reading through what has been entrusted to us by antiquity about the life and miracles of St. Olav, we, who are illumined by his new miracles, deem it proper to commit to writing, for the memory of future generations, the deeds done to his glory which we have ourselves seen or have been proved by the testimony of truthful men.[282]

In the manuscript, a heading in red marks the break.[283] Clearly, any generalization about Miracle Books needs to take into account multiple authorship.

[277] *Passio et miracula Beati Olavi.*

[278] *Miraculum sancti Iuvenalis anno mccxxxiii patratum.*

[279] Mynors, *Durham Cathedral Manuscripts*, p. 73, no. 123, describing Durham, Cathedral Library, Hunter 101.

[280] It has been suggested that the collection was composed in two stages, the first 111 chapters in 1165–66, the reminder in 1172–74: Tudor, "The Cult of St Cuthbert in the Twelfth Century," p. 449.

[281] Bernard of Angers, *Liber miraculorum sancte Fidis*; *Miracula sancti Benedicti.*

[282] *Passio et miracula Beati Olavi*, p. 104.

[283] Oxford, Corpus Christi College 209, fol. 81 (consulted on-line).

Collections of miracle accounts are often found in manuscripts along with other kinds of works, hagiographic and not, and these assemblages of different compositions can sometimes reveal the interests of their compilers and copyists. The mixture of Lives, miracle accounts and other hagiographic texts that is a common feature of books produced in medieval ecclesiastical communities can be illustrated by a volume from the eleventh century, now in the Vatican Library.[284] It belonged to the Benedictine abbey of Notre-Dame de Luçon in the Vendée (north-western France) and contains 106 folios:

Fols. 1–8: Translation of St. Benedict
Fols. 8–43v: Miracles of St. Benedict
Fols. 43v–50v: Sermon for St. Benedict's feast-day
Fols. 50v–82v: Life of St. Maurus
Fols. 82v–84: Life of St. Scholastica
Fols. 84–106v: Miracles of St. Maurus

Benedict, Maurus, and Scholastica form a closely knit group of saints. Benedict was the great sixth-century monastic founder, Maurus his most important disciple and Scholastica his sister. Although they were Italian in origin, it was claimed that the bones of all three came to rest in France, so they were of obvious interest for French Benedictine monks. The texts in the volume explain how Benedict's relics were brought to France, recount some of his miracles during the upheavals of the Viking raids, describe St. Maurus's monastic activities in his monastery of Glanfeuil (now St.-Maur-de-Glanfeuil), the subsequent decline and restoration of Glanfeuil and especially St. Maurus's miraculous punishment of the local aristocrats who mistreated the monks. It would have made a gratifying anthology for the monks of Luçon.

The energy devoted to recording miracles was not an unvarying constant. At the monastery of Mont-St.-Michel, to judge by surviving accounts, the monks showed only an intermittent interest in the miraculous events that took place in their abbey or through invocation of their saint. Three fifteenth-century manuscripts contain reports of miracles from the preceding centuries, most of them appearing in more than one of the volumes.[285] These records break down chronologically, as shown in table 13.1.

One might be equally impressed at the length of this record and struck by its enormous discontinuities. Monks of Mont-St.-Michel were recording miracles for five centuries (and nor did they stop in the fifteenth century) but they also apparently either failed to record or failed to witness any for periods of a century or more.

[284] BAV, Cod. Reg. 456; the texts it contains are: BHL 1117; 1123; PL 133: 721–29; BHL 5772–73; 7514; 5775.

[285] Bouet, "Les formes de dévotion des pèlerins qui se rendent au Mont Saint-Michel" (there is a slight discrepancy between text and table regarding the fifteenth-century miracles [pp. 67, 83]). The manuscripts are Avranches, Bibliothèque muncipale, 211, 212 and 213, described in *Catalogue général des manuscrits des bibliothèques publiques de France, Départements* 10: *Avranches*, etc., pp. 94–100.

Table 13.1
Miracles Recorded at Mont-St.-Michel

Prior to 1000	4 miracles
1010–50	6 miracles
1146	1 miracle
1263–70	3 miracles
1333	18 miracles
1388–89	3 miracles
1445–57	4 miracles

Miracle stories could be gathered in various ways. One of the simplest was to keep a book at the shrine, which was usually the responsibility of a particular monk or cleric, although, very remarkably, Robert of Cricklade, was asked to write up his own cure, and his account incorporated verbatim in the Miracle Book.[286] After Becket's miracles had been recited publicly in the Canterbury chapter, they were written down in "a big book."[287] In the first half of the fifteenth century, the church at Vannes kept a book for recording the miracles which took place at the tomb of Vincent Ferrer.[288] When miracles were recorded in a book at the shrine in this way, this shrine-book (or a fair copy of it) was usually the unique example of the collection, although additional manuscript copies were sometimes made, especially in the case of cults with wide appeal and dissemination. The miracles of Thomas Becket recorded by Benedict of Canterbury, for example, survive in seventeen complete and eight partial copies.[289]

The record of shrine miracles might also be displayed publicly. There are examples of miracles being recorded, in the vernacular, on sheets of parchment that were then attached to the wall of the church where the shrine was housed, as was the case in St. Lewinna's church in Sussex in the eleventh century.[290] Any literate lay person could then read these public statements, and read them out to others. Three large wooden panels, suspended at the shrine of the child-saint Werner of Bacharach, were covered with texts, one describing his miracles, one announcing the indulgences that pilgrims would receive and one, in the vernacular, containing an account of his death.[291]

[286] Benedict of Peterborough, *Miracula sancti Thomae* 2. 52, p. 101.

[287] William fitz Stephen, *Vita sancti Thomae Cantuariensis* 155, p. 151.

[288] *Procès de la canonisation de Saint Vincent Ferrier*, pp. 7–8.

[289] Koopmans, *Wonderful to Relate*, p. 129.

[290] Drogo, *Translatio sancte Lewinnae* 1. 6, p. 784; see Blair, "A Saint for Every Minster?," p. 479 n. 69; idem, "A Handlist of Anglo-Saxon Saints," p. 543.

[291] *Processus Bacheracensis de vita, martyrio et miraculis beati Wernheri* 1. 5, 8. 65, pp. 715–16, 731.

But Miracle Books could be put together in other ways. An assiduous monk might browse earlier accounts and talk to his fellows. Sometimes an outsider showed an interest, like Bernard of Angers, who initiated the substantial Miracle Book of St. Foy, and began his work by visiting the shrine, talking to eye-witnesses of miracles and making notes on loose sheets of parchment, which he then later wrote up into a fair copy.[292] Sometimes a concerted group effort was made to collect miracles. In 1255 the Dominicans put out a general call for information about miracles of their two canonized saints, Dominic and Peter Martyr:

> Brethren who know, or get to know in future, any miracles of St. Dominic or St. Peter that are not written down, should write to the prior of Bologna about those relating to St. Dominic and to the prior of Milan about those relating to St. Peter, and they should have them recorded in writing as a perpetual memorial.[293]

On another occasion the bishop and civic authorities of an Italian town commissioned a small group of lawyers and notaries to enquire into the local saint's miracles and make a written record of them.[294]

While most miracle collections, especially those produced at a particular shrine, reflected local interests and horizons, there were also miracle collections that did not come from one place. The Miracles of the Virgin Mary, first assembled in England in the early twelfth century and expanded and elaborated over the years, form a classic example of such an anthology of miracles from diverse times and places. And there were also collections of miracles of more than one saint, like the *Dialogue of the Deeds of Holy Franciscans*, which was composed in the 1240s at the command of the Minister General of the Order, and contained accounts of the miracles of nineteen of the first generation of friars. It was based partly on information from papal canonization hearings and partly on oral accounts from fellow friars.[295]

The authors who devoted their efforts to recording the miracles of a saint or saints had no reason to believe that their task would ever be finished. A saint might begin to work miracles but there was no reason why he or she should stop. A shrine-book would be left open for further entries, even if they never came, and all authors of Miracle Books pictured a future of further miracles. Since these books were envisaged as being continually updated, they often have no explicit ending but simply stop at the point where recording in fact ended. This is why many Miracle Books have clear, sometimes elaborate, prefaces and prologues but much less often a conclusion, epilogue, or even a simple indication that the work has ended.

Shrine-books are likely to record miracles in chronological order, but collections made in other ways, or those based on shrine-books but rewritten and reorganized,

[292] Bernard of Angers, *Liber miraculorum sancte Fidis* 1. preface (epistola), 7, pp. 74–75, 98–99.

[293] *Acta capitulorum generalium ordinis praedicatorum* 1, pp. 76–77.

[294] Peter, bishop of Treviso, *Vita Henrici Baucenensis* 2. 21, p. 374.

[295] *Dialogus de gestis sanctorum Fratrum Minorum*, prologue, pp. 2–3.

may have no apparent principle of organization. Some authors are even quite explicit that it does not matter in what order you recount miracles:

> The rest of the wonders and miracles that the Lord worked through them for the salvation of men will be described just as they come to my mind, since I consider it irrelevant in what order they are narrated, for in telling them one should give more weight to "what" and "why" than to "when" something was done.[296]

This principle explains why some composite collections of miracles are so hard to date and show little sign of consecutive order.

Gilbert Dagron, who edited the fifth-century *Miracles of St. Thecla*, commented on the repetitive and chronologically disjointed nature of the text.[297] He analyzed some of the "unimaginative" techniques of literary transition which the author employed to pass from one miracle to the next:

> Association by subject matter: "because we have mentioned eyes," "because a siege has been mentioned"
> Association by mood or tone: proceeding to relate "a more fearful" miracle
> Transition through invocation of memory and oblivion: "let us not pass over," "who can forget . . . ?"
> Simple metaphors of motion: "one must go on"

Such issues of literary construction were a permanent feature of a genre characterized by its paratactic nature, that is, by being an assemblage of similar units not organized by clear principles of subordination or connection. Authors of miracle accounts do not always seek to avoid the charge of recounting one damned thing after another, but devices such as those mentioned by Dagron do give some literary articulation to many Miracle Books. This can involve something as simple as a reference to the passage of time ("shortly after this," "on another occasion") or, as Dagron observed, comparison with a previous miracle ("a not dissimilar miracle").

Some monks thought that, when it came to miracle accounts, "a simple and unpolished style seems more suitable for recitation to the people," but, although miracles can be recorded in a dry, brief and formulaic way, there are many examples of Miracle Books written by learned and eloquent writers, willing to offer a full and colourful narrative of many pages.[298] A good example of the latter, more expansive kind, is provided by the collection of posthumous miracles of St. Cuthbert produced

[296] Einhard, *Translatio et miracula sanctorum Marcellini et Petri* 3. 4, p. 249.

[297] *Miracula Theclae*, editorial introduction, pp. 152–53.

[298] Implex et minus polita locutio . . . ad recitandum in populao aptior videbatur: Alcuin, *Epistola* 306, p. 465 (*Vita Richarii*, prefatory letter) (also in MGH, SRM 4, p. 389); see the comments of Van Uytfanghe, "The Consciousness of a Linguistic Dichotomy (Latin-Romance) in Carolingian Gaul," pp. 120–22.

by Reginald of Durham.[299] Reginald's book on St. Cuthbert is, in essence, a collection of 129 miracle stories, some of them dating back to earlier centuries but the majority from his own lifetime. The average length of these tales is over 700 words, so the longer of them have a real chance to develop narrative momentum and variety. Reginald's technique is to begin each chapter with a general and elevated passage, before embarking on his tale, which is often introduced with a clearly defined narrative marker: "There is a village called Norham"; "In the year of the incarnation 1165"; "There was a certain young man, Ernaldus by name."[300] The stories are presented as illustrations of the points in the general passage that precedes them. Thus, for instance, chapter 29 of the work begins, "St. Cuthbert, who has mercy on all who are pitiable and unfortunate, gives judgment and justice. He does judgment on those who persecute him and on the wicked, brings justice to those who are dutiful and devout." This very general point is then exemplified by a story set in the reign of king Stephen (1135–54), when a Norwegian fleet raided the Northumbrian coast and, in defiance of promises given to the hermits on Farne Island, slaughtered their sheep for food and took their timber to repair the ships. As soon as the raiders broke their word in this way, the fountain of St. Cuthbert on the island dried up; the moment they sailed away, the fountain burst forth again.[301]

Writers of Miracle Books were aware that one of their chief tasks was to convince. They were recounting amazing stories and needed to ensure they carried their readers or hearers with them. One tactic was to stress your own lack of credulity and insist that you were as probing and sceptical as any reader. An author could outflank doubters and sceptics by being even more demanding in his examination of the truth about miracles. As one collector of Becket's miracles put it,

> on account of other people, and especially because of the disparagement of the ill-willed, it is not without value to raise doubts about the individual details. We raise doubts, so that others might not be doubtful; in examining the truth, we have shown ourselves unyielding and, as it were, unconvinced.[302]

"Nothing should be written of him or his miracles," wrote another contemporary of Becket, "unless it is the purest truth, examined, cleansed and sieved seven times."[303]

One thing that could build up the impression of verisimilitude was specific detail, especially names and dates. If enough detailed identification were provided, the plausibility of the miracle increased. The anonymous author of the *Miracles of Thecla* explains that he will reassure his readers of the truth of his accounts by giving the

[299] Reginald of Durham, *Libellus de admirandis beati Cuthberti virtutibus*; see Ward, *Miracles and the Medieval Mind*, pp. 62–66; Tudor, "The Cult of St Cuthbert in the Twelfth Century"; Crumplin, "Rewriting History in the Cult of St Cuthbert," chapter 5, apps. 1 and 4; eadem, "Modernizing St Cuthbert."

[300] Reginald of Durham, *Libellus de admirandis beati Cuthberti virtutibus* 73, 82, 113, pp. 149, 173, 254.

[301] Reginald of Durham, *Libellus de admirandis beati Cuthberti virtutibus* 29, pp. 65–66.

[302] Benedict of Peterborough, *Miracula sancti Thomae* 1. 9, pp. 39–40.

[303] Peter of Celle, *Epistola* 142, p. 522.

names of persons and places involved.[304] Desiderius of Monte Cassino, recounting the miracles that took place in and around Monte Cassino, promises, "In order to remove any trace of doubt for the readers, in every case I add the persons who related it to me."[305] Gregory of Tours actually apologizes for not always having the names of those cured at Martin's tomb.[306] This kind of forensic detail blossomed in papal canonization proceedings, when the techniques of the court-room were literally brought to bear on the case for sanctity, but the question of evidence, the citation of names and dates and witnesses, and the language of proof, had long been part of the rhetoric of the Miracle Books.

Vivid narration can help build up the credibility of a miracle account. Just as a successful play or film is one during which the audience forgets this is a play or film and enters into the imaginary world being presented, so an absorbing tale can spin a world that is hard *not* to believe. The story of Thomas of Eldersfield in the Miracles of St. Wulfstan is such a tale and has drawn some attention.[307] Thomas was embroiled in a brawl with George, the husband of his former lover, and, after George had brought the matter to court, the two were sentenced to fight it out in a duel. Thomas invoked the saintly bishop of Worcester, Wulfstan, to help him, but was nevertheless defeated. As an act of mercy he was reprieved from hanging, but condemned to have his eyes and testicles torn out, a task that was done by George's friends and relatives. Afterwards the local lads kicked the testicles among the watching girls. Eventually, when the fun was over, everyone went home, leaving Thomas half-dead. A kindly woman tended him, and, nine days after the duel, on the Feast of the Assumption, the Virgin Mary and St. Wulfstan appeared to him in a vision. When the bandages were removed from his eyes, he found he could see, and, moreover, his testicles were restored. A visiting bishop, doubtful of the story, came to look for himself and even had his chaplain touch Thomas's testicles to make sure. "So," concludes the author of the story,

> let there be glory and praise to God for ever, who has deigned to work such great miracles in the church of Worcester, through the merits of his glorious mother, the ever-virgin Mary, and of St. Wulfstan and the other saints resting there.

Accounts like these are marked by the large amount of information that is, in a sense, "irrelevant" to the miracle. In order to demonstrate Wulfstan's posthumous miraculous power, there was no need to discuss many of the topics that crop up in this narrative: Thomas's social background, as a free-born but not wealthy man who had made his way through service to one of the king's great officials, or his escape after the assault by jumping over the fence that separated the road from the growing crops,

[304] *Miraculae Theclae* prologue, p. 284.

[305] Desiderius of Monte Cassino, *Dialogi de miraculis sancti Benedicti,* prologue, p. 1117.

[306] Gregory of Tours, *De virtutibus sancti Martini* 3. 45, p. 543 (repr., 1969, p. 193).

[307] *Miracula sanctissimi Wlstani* 2. 16, pp. 168–75; *Pleas of the Crown for the County of Gloucester . . . 1221*, no. 87, pp. 21–22, 141–42; Hyams, "The Strange Case of Thomas of Eldersfield."

or the image of his testicles being used as footballs. All this strong realization and visualization, memorable vignettes of social history that they are, perhaps make the miracle itself more plausible.

A similar strong realization of the narrative is effected by the use of direct speech, a literary technique notable in many miracle accounts. Medieval authors knew, both from the traditions of classical rhetoric and from the everyday experience of telling stories, that good dialogue could give life and clarity to a story. Much of this had to be made up, but there was generally no objection to such invention.

One of the miracles of Thomas Becket illustrates the point. A peasant named Ailward, who, like Thomas of Eldersfield, had been blinded and castrated as punishment for a crime, implored the saint's help. One night, while he was sleeping in the house of a kindly man who had given him shelter, St. Thomas appeared to him,

> saying, "Good man, are you asleep? Wake up, for tomorrow you are to keep vigil with a light at the altar of St. Mary. Behold, Thomas has come to you, and you will recover your sight." Then, at sunrise, the housemaid said, "I saw in a dream, Ailward, that you had recovered your sight." He replied, "This is possible for the Lord, just as all things are possible."

As the day drew on Ailward was able to see a sunbeam shining on the wall.

> He exclaimed, "God be praised! I see." His host was amazed at hearing this and said, "What is it? You are raving." And he placed his hand in front of Ailward's eyes and said, "Do you see what I am doing?" He answered, "I see a hand moving."[308]

All of this could either have been narrated without such speech, or have been rendered into indirect speech. But the direct address of the saint, the (quite unnecessary) maid with her dream, and her use of Ailward's name, and the brief but dramatic exchange between Ailward and the householder mean that this passage verges on a play-script.

Some exchanges are even more like a script, and this resemblance can be underlined by setting them out as such. The following dialogue took place between the powerful Merovingian noble Erchinoald and Leutsinda his wife, who resented the outlay her husband had been making in honour of the recently deceased St. Fursey:[309]

> Leutsinda said to her husband: "So! You are leaving me and my sons and daughters forsaken, without money or property, handing over all our things into the hands of someone we do not know and about whose origin we are ignorant."
>
> Erchinoald said to her: "Leutsinda, my sweetest one, do not say such things."

[308] William of Canterbury, *Miracula sancti Thomae* 2. 3, p. 158 (the miracle is depicted in one of the "Becket windows" in Canterbury cathedral).

[309] *Virtutes Fursei abbatis Latiniacensis* 20, p. 447.

Leutsinda replied: "If you carry on as you have begun, you can put me out of you life!"

Erchinoald said: "Don't blather, Leutsinda, because if you don't control your anger, I will no longer be responsible for you and you will lose all the pleasant things I have brought you."

Leutsinda replied: "I wish I had never had that wedding day that has now brought me such reproach!"

Erchinoald said: "My dearest, if you knew how much good has come to us, from the day he became known to us, you would never carry on like this. Know for sure, if his anger is turned against you, you and yours will be lost."

Laughingly Leutsinda said: "Listen everyone! What harm can a man who has been rotting for thirty days do to me?"

The answer is, he could make her blind.

There were saint-plays in the later Middle Ages, but clearly the dramatic dialogue was inherent in hagiographical narrative long before then.

Three Examples

A brief look at three miracle collections from the twelfth and thirteenth centuries will bring out both the fundamental common features of the genre and the variations any individual example might exhibit. The collections in question are those of St. Æbbe from Coldingham in southern Scotland, St. Zoilus from Carrión in Castile, and St. Gunther from Brevnov in Bohemia.[310] These were all saints of strictly local reputation and the number of miracles recorded is relatively modest: forty-three, twenty-one, and thirty-nine, respectively. The authors are anonymous but can be presumed to have been Benedictine monks of the monasteries which housed the shrines of the three saints.

The miracles of St. Æbbe were recorded at the end of the twelfth century by the monks of the priory of Coldingham, who claimed to have found the remains of this Anglo-Saxon abbess at some point earlier in the century. The actual impetus to the revival of the cult, however, was not this discovery, but the building of an oratory to the saint by a local layman. This was the original focus of the miracles, and it may be significant that the beneficiaries of Æbbe's grace were more likely to be young, poor and female than is the case with most cults—ordinary lay people initiated the cult and continued to sustain it. Of the forty-three miracles recorded all but one are healing miracles, dealing with the usual ailments like paralysis, dumbness, and blindness. The solitary non-healing miracle concerns some sceptical women who were miraculously unable to see water drawn from St. Æbbe's well.

[310] *Vita et miracula sancte Ebbe virginis*, pp. 30–66; *Miracula gloriosissimi martyris beati Zoyli*; *Miracula beati Guntheri*. On Zoilus, see Henriet, "Un hagiographe au travail: Raoul et la reécriture du dossier de Zoile de Carrión." On Gunther, see Lang, "Gunther der Eremit in Geschichte, Sage und Kult."

At some point in the same century a record was made of a group of twenty-one miracles attributed to St. Zoilus, an early Cordoban martyr whose relics had been translated to the monastery named after him in Carrión in Castile. Some of these are of the common healing type—a cripple cured, sight restored to the blind. Almost a quarter (five) record expulsion of demons, with one vivid description of a possessed woman "imitating the lowing of herds, the barking of dogs, and the song of birds."[311] But the most striking feature of the collection is the importance of punishment miracles, especially those directed against disrespect for the saint's feast-day. A peasant woman from Villalcázar refused to interrupt her ordinary routine work of spinning on the saint's day, despite the warnings of a helpful neighbour; she lost the use of her right hand. On another occasion a smith continued working on the feast-day of Zoilus's translation—something that would, from the noise, have been immediately obvious to his neighbours, who asked him if he did not fear the saint's anger; the smith responded with mockery but then immediately, while working with the red-hot sickles he was making, pierced his own hand. Peasants harvesting their crops or bringing in the hay on the saint's feast-day (27 June), or even simply baking bread, faced similar expressions of the saint's disfavour. Zoilus protected his property as well as his day. Animals that grazed on the monastery's crops dropped dead, as was discovered by the servants of a neighbouring knight, who ended up with four of his horses as dog-food, and a sceptical Jew, whose mule "fell dead on the spot, struck by Saint Zoilus." A third of the recorded miracles deal with punishment of sceptics. This small Spanish collection thus seems marked by an effort to establish the saint's credentials.

A combination of traits that were common to the whole of Latin Europe with a modest but unmistakable regional coloration can be found if we turn to the account of the miracles of St. Gunther at his shrine in the Benedictine monastery of Brevnov in Bohemia. Gunther (d. 1045) was a monk of Niederaltaich, who had retired to the thick woods between Bavaria and Bohemia to live as a hermit. On his death, his body was brought to Brevnov, where it became the centre of a healing cult. Records of thirty-nine miracles survive, and those that can be dated fall in the period 1243–63. Twenty-two of the beneficiaries are male, seventeen female, and this ratio of 56:44 is not far out of line with the general ratio in such records of 61:39.[312] The kinds of miracle reported are fairly typical, with the most common ailments cured being some form of crippling (*contractus* is the Latin term used to describe the sufferer), blindness, demonic possession, and deafness or dumbness. The shrine in Brevnov was thus a thaumaturgic centre of a type found throughout Europe.

As with all miracle accounts, the familiar and uniform surface is sometimes varied with unusual incidents or moments. Particularly striking is the report of what

[311] *Miracula gloriosissimi martyris beati Zoyli* 13, p. 516, perhaps inspired by Gregory I, *Dialogi* 3. 4. 2 (2, p. 270).

[312] For example, Finucane, *Miracles and Pilgrims*, p. 143; Sigal, *L'homme et le miracle*, p. 300.

befell a servant of the abbot sometime in the 1240s.[313] While he was lying ill he was approached by two demons. One was in the form of a married woman with whom the servant had had a secret affair. The other was in the form of her husband. While the demon in the form of the woman embraced the sick servant fondly, the demon in the form her husband threatened to kill him with a big stick. The servant was saved only by invoking St. Gunther, who appeared and drove off the demons. The thankful man promised to fast for two days before St. Gunther's feast-day for the rest of his life. "This," comments the author of the account, who knew the man, "he has fulfilled faithfully to this day."

This is a very unusual miracle, but its oddity has nothing specifically Bohemian about it (except perhaps in the English usage where a "Bohemian" is "one who leads a free, vagabond, or irregular life"). However, there are some other features of these miracles that do reflect the situation in Bohemia, notably the international and multi-ethnic nature of the cult following. The very first miracle recorded concerns a Hungarian nobleman, while we can also find a man from Niederaltaich, a Bavarian merchant and a Thuringian nobleman. Moreover, these accounts reveal the ethnic diversity within Bohemia as well as visits by travellers from outside. Names of those who came to the shrine are sometimes ethnically neutral or ambiguous (Johannes, Barbara) but more often suggest a linguistic affiliation, as with Bertold, son of the burgess Ulric and his wife Margaret, or Drahomila of Benesov, the former suggesting a German cultural ambience, the latter a Czech. The likelihood that Bertold and Ulric belonged to the German-speaking stratum of the Bohemian urban population is reinforced by the names of their companions: Frederick, Gottfried, Henry, and (another) Ulric. A yet more explicit reference in the account of Bertold's cure is the report of a crowd of "more than two hundred people, German and Bohemian, who had come together from various regions for the feast-day of St. Wenceslas."[314] The co-existence of two or more peoples (*gentes*) in one kingdom or principality in this way was not uncommon in the Middle Ages.

There are clearly differences among the three collections. The Spanish author shows a strand of anti-semitism that is not present in the other two texts, and also seems to represent an embattled cult, which required constant miraculous chastisement in order to maintain proper levels of veneration. The text from Bohemia reflects the ethnic diversity of that region in the High Middle Ages, while Æbbe's miracles show a local cult of humble folk. But more obvious are the basic features the texts have in common: small collections of miracle accounts of the twelfth or thirteenth centuries, produced by Benedictine monks to commemorate a saint whose body they possessed. Formal features are also common, since the episodic nature of the material means that the basic literary unit is a short, self-contained narrative. The authors all devote between 100 and 200 words to each miracle, with the Brevnov monk the most loquacious. The amount of detail given varies, but usually includes a

[313] *Miracula beati Guntheri* 1. 10, p. 1077.
[314] Ibid., 2. 30, p. 1083.

brief characterization of the person involved, such as "a poor little girl" or "a certain Bavarian who was in Brevnov at that time," and sometimes mentions personal names and place of origin. Pilgrims from distant parts obviously reflected well on the cult, and hence the author from Carrión lays special emphasis on a woman who came to Zoilus's shrine from as far away as Normandy: "it was not only among us that the fame of the blessed martyr grew, but it also flew across the Alps, swam across the seas and penetrated the islands." There is variation in the amount of attention paid to chronology. The author of the miracles of Zoilus gives no dates at all, the author of those of Æbbe records only that the oratory, which was the initial centre of the cult, was built in 1188, while the Brevnov collection begins to give precise dates some way into the text, perhaps because a new author had taken up the pen: the first such date is 2 September 1248 and the last miracle in the collection describes a cure "on the feast-day of St. Severinus the bishop [23 October] at the third hour in the year of grace 1263." What is of central concern to all three writers is the miraculous incident, and, when describing this, their language is usually of greater precision and the incidental detail richer than elsewhere. In the case of cures, the major category, the authors describe symptoms, duration of illness, and the process of cure, while the monk of Carrión is eloquent on the subject of the punishments inflicted on those who doubt St. Zoilus:

> A certain peasant, scorning the observance of the feast of the holy martyr Zoilus, promptly set out to collect his crops, but while he was harvesting he was punished by the divine power, for his hands were monstrously distorted and he was forced to stop work.

It is highly likely, if not verifiable in detail, that Benedictine monks of this period, be they in Scotland, Spain or Bohemia, would have a common cultural ground in the language of Psalter and liturgy, as well as the practical Latin of law and administration, and the lithe and effective narrative language the three authors employ is not marked by strong national or regional variation. In the improbable event of an encounter, they could have communicated easily and, despite the contrasts between the three saints they served—an early martyr, an Anglo-Saxon abbess and an eleventh-century German hermit—they would certainly have understood the purpose and goal of the others' writing: to chronicle the miraculous interventions of their saint, as a pious duty and as a record and instrument of their saintly reputation.

Sermons

The saints were celebrated in church services on their feast-days, and it was natural that, if the service included a sermon, the subject of that sermon would be the saint concerned. From the fourth century written versions of such sermons survive, notably from the Greek fathers like Gregory of Nyssa, whose panegyrics on St. Stephen, Theodore the Recruit, and the Forty Martyrs of Sebaste were delivered to commemorate and honour the saints on their feast-days and usually at their shrines.[315] Augustine has left more than a hundred sermons that he preached on saint's days or in honour of the saints.[316] Some of these saints were great biblical figures like John the Baptist, Peter and Paul, or Stephen, others were revered martyr-saints of north Africa, like Cyprian, and Perpetua and Felicity. Augustine rejoiced that the feast-days of the martyrs were celebrated with such enthusiasm: "now in this land, in this life, in homes, in the fields, in the cities of the world, behold the fervent praise of the martyrs!"[317] The saints provided "an example to be imitated by us"; that is why "these feast-days have been instituted in Christ's Church."[318] These exemplary figures demonstrated the clean, fast movement of the Christian hero: "the martyrs put down here and laid aside here all the baggage of the profit of this world, and ran along the road that leads to life, like soldiers ready for action."[319]

Augustine had a special devotion to the local saints, especially Cyprian, whom he names in his writings 589 times.[320] He invokes the martyr-bishop on his feast-day:

> When he was alive, he ruled the church of Carthage; now he is dead, he brings it honour. There he exerted the office of bishop, there he consummated his martyrdom . . . and it is much sweeter to drink Christ's blood in that place on Cyprian's feast-day, because Cyprian's blood was poured out so devotedly for the name of Christ[321]

The tradition of preaching a sermon on a saint's feast-day continued throughout the Middle Ages. In the early centuries, sermons in Latin would be addressed to a monastic or clerical community. A good example is Alcuin's sermon for St. Willibrord's day, which is appended to the Life of the saint that he wrote and is dedicated to the abbot of Echternach, where Willibrord's body lay.[322] Alcuin begins with a general point that, while the saints are celebrated throughout Christendom, it is natural that there is special devotion to those whose bones are near: "they are honoured more familiarly by a special veneration on the part of their own fellow-citizens." He gives many examples: Peter and Paul in Rome, Ambrose in Milan, the Theban Legion in Agaunum (St.-Maurice-en-Valais), Hilary in Poitiers, Martin in Tours (even though it is a city with "pitiful walls"), Denis and Germanus in Paris, and Remigius in Rheims. Then, turning to a direct address to the monks of Echternach, he says, "Beloved brethren, let us rejoice in the Lord, who has granted to us such a teacher of how

[315] Gregory of Nyssa, *De sancto Theodoro*; *In sanctum Stephanum I–II*; *In XL martyres Ia–Ib*; *In XL martyres II*.

[316] Augustine, *Sermones* 273–340 (PL 38: 1247–1484); Augustine, *Sermons on the Saints* (containing many sermons not printed in PL).

[317] Augustine, *Sermo* 312 (PL 38: 1422).

[318] Augustine, "Sermons inédits de S. Augustin pour des fêtes des saints," p. 74; idem, *Sermo* 325 (PL 38: 1447).

[319] Augustine, *Sermo* 326 (PL 38: 1449).

[320] Yates, "Augustine's Appropriation of Cyprian the Martyr-Bishop against the Pelagians," p. 122.

[321] Augustine, *Sermo* 310 (PL 38: 1413).

[322] Alcuin, *Vita Willibrordi: Homilia*.

to live, an instructor in justice, and the author of our unity"; he refers directly to the feast-day on which the sermon is being preached: "let all the people rejoice with us, who have assembled today for the feast-day of the most holy father." He tells how Willibrord abandoned his native land (which was something that Alcuin himself had done), mentions his preaching amongst the pagans and his willingness to suffer martyrdom (although he had not actually done so). He then addresses the saint himself: "O most blessed priest of Christ, do not abandon us, as we labour on earth, but continue helping us with your prayers from heaven." He persists in this direct speech to the saint, before turning again to his "dearest brethren" and stressing how Willibrord provides an example of how to spurn earthly things and strive for heaven. Although it is a literary construction, this sermon has all the feel of a speech that could have been given, with its direct address to listeners, its careful modulations and its effective brevity.

At the end of the twelfth century Martin of Leon wrote sermons for several saints, including St. Isidore (two for the feast of the translation, one for the feast-day of the death), John the Baptist, the Assumption and Nativity of the Virgin Mary, the Holy Cross, St. Michael, and All Saints; the average length of these sermons is 2,250 words, representing a spoken time (if they were spoken) of about a quarter of an hour.[323] They are packed with biblical citation and allusion. For instance, at the opening of the second sermon on the Translation of St. Isidore we read:

> The envoy of the highest king, that is, "the angel" which the Lord sent "round about them that fear him" (Ps. 33:8; 34:7), one of those who "always see the face of the Father, who is in heaven" (Matt. 18:10), announced by a happy rumour in the court of the highest emperor, who "commands the winds and sea" (Matt. 8:26), that a house of St. Isidore, once archbishop of Seville, should be prepared, or rather restored, within the walls of the city of Leon.[324]

This is a high style to describe the translation of the relics of St. Isidore of Seville.

Some saints were the subjects of many sermons throughout the medieval period in many different countries. A study of Latin sermons on Thomas Becket prior to 1400 produced an inventory of 184 sermons, preached by secular clergy, monks and Franciscan and Dominican friars, in Canterbury, Oxford, Chichester, Paris, Rome, Avignon, and Coimbra, as well as dozens of unknown locations.[325] Eventually, it became a common practice for preachers to produce two series of sermons, one for Sundays and the moveable feasts based on Easter (the *temporale*), another for the feast-days of the saints, which were fixed (the *sanctorale*). A highly successful sermon sequence for the *sanctorale* is Jordan of Quedlinburg's *Sermons on the Saints*, or *Opus Dan*, which survives in sixty-five manuscripts and six early printed editions.[326]

[323] Martin of Leon, *Sermones de sanctis*.

[324] Ibid., col. 55.

[325] Roberts, *Thomas Becket in the Medieval Latin Preaching Tradition*.

[326] Saak, "*Quilibet Christianus*: Saints and Society in the Sermons of Jordan of Quedlinburg," p. 319 n. 11; I have used Jordan of Quedlinburg, *Sermones de sanctis (Opus Dan)* (Strassburg, 1484).

Jordan was a member of the Order of Augustinian Hermits, an Order of friars, and was active in the middle decades of the fourteenth century. When he wrote his *Opus Dan*, he had already completed a sermon sequence on the *temporale* and in his preface to the later work he plays elaborately with the conceit that the first series was "the fountain Jor" and this second series "the fountain Dan," which join to make the name Jordan, which he hopes will be as fruitful for readers as the river Jordan. His collection contains 271 sermons, including some for classes of saint (virgins, confessors, and so on) and a few miscellaneous ones ("to monks and friars," "concerning students"). The main sequence (sermons 2–214) runs from Andrew (30 November) to Catherine (25 November), with many cases of several sermons for the same saint. The printed edition has a subject index arranged alphabetically, so it would be easy to find discussion of "angels," "conversion" or "faith," as well as clarification of "locusts, what they are." The saints represented in Jordan's collection are in no way unusual, although, as a member of an Augustinian Order, he does give special attention to "our glorious father Augustine," celebrating his translation as well as his feast-day, and comparing him to the sun for his clarity and influence.[327]

Jordan begins each sermon with a quotation from the Bible and then elaborates it, citing from the Gloss (the standard Bible commentary), from other parts of scripture, and from the Church Fathers, especially Augustine. He has the typical high scholastic taste for making lists, and this sometimes gets out of hand. For instance, in his sermon for St. Cecilia's day, he starts by citing a verse from the Song of Songs—"the king hath brought me into his chambers"—and then comments that, "In these words three things are touched on that concern St. Cecilia."[328] The first of these is "the nobility of the rational mind." For the mind to be raised to union with God, he goes on, three things are necessary: complete contempt for earthly status, fervent reaching of the desire towards God, and inner perfection of divine inflowing. After commenting on each of these, Jordan turns to the second main heading of his sermon, which is Cecilia's perpetual involvement in godly speech and discourse. To achieve such familiarity with the divine, Jordan says, three things are necessary: chastity, peace of mind, and love of God. There are eight levels of chastity, two of them common to all the chaste, and six others. These are all listed before Jordan turns to the third and final section of his sermon, and then winds up with a recollection of the image of the chambers from the Song of Songs. Without a visible diagram, it is possible that hearers might become a little confused about where exactly they were in this forest of headings and sub-headings.

Another well-regarded example of the genre, *Sermons on the Saints*, is the collection produced by the charismatic Catalan preacher Vincent Ferrer (d. 1419), which also became popular in the age of print (there are many editions from 1487 onwards).[329] He gives sermons for sixty-five saint's days or feasts throughout the year,

[327] Sermo 185.
[328] Sermo 206; the passage is Song of Songs 1:4.
[329] Vincent Ferrer, *Sermones de sanctis*.

running, as customary, from Andrew (30 November) to Catherine (25 November), although, since he gives more than one sermon for some of these, the total number of sermons is seventy-eight. The prominence given to St. Dominic, whose Octave is celebrated with four sermons, and the presence of the Dominican saints Thomas Aquinas and Peter Martyr are explained by the fact that Vincent Ferrer was himself a Dominican, but the selection of saints is otherwise not distinctive or personal. It includes the great saints of the New Testament and the most widely revered early martyrs. Apart from the Dominicans, the only saints of a period later than 604 (the death of Gregory the Great) are Thomas Becket and Francis. Francis was universally known, but Vincent's sermon on Becket has to explain that there are three saints named Thomas (the Apostle, Becket, and Aquinas), and that one of them "was archbishop of the city of Canterbury in England," and that his hearers "should not think that these three are one and the same Thomas."[330]

Like Jordan of Quedlinburg, Vincent is fond of lists. "In the story of St. Mark," he says, "I have found three great good things that he had."[331] These three are "conversion to the truth, perfection of humility, and holy devotion." Mark had been converted from Judaism by Peter's preaching, and Peter had advanced five arguments: about the Trinity, the Incarnation, the Passion, the duration of the law of Moses, and the time of the Messiah. Vincent Ferrer was an experienced polemicist against the Jews, and knew what were the main points at issue, and the debate between Peter and Mark in this sermon surely echoes that between Vincent and his actual Jewish hearers. Mark's humility was shown by the fact that he cut off his own thumb in order to make himself ineligible for the priesthood, since he did not deem himself worthy of such a high office—he only became bishop of Alexandria after St. Peter had miraculously restored it. And Mark's third great quality, holy devotion, explains Vincent, means giving glory to God in all things. He gives an example:

> If you make your son a priest so that he can live comfortably in peace, this shows lack of holy devotion; you should make your son a priest so that he can pray for you and so that God should be praised and glorified by him. Similarly if you make your son a monk or friar, so that he should become an abbot or a master of theology or a bishop.

At the end of Vincent's sermon he manages to get Mark's relics to Venice, but the thrust of his words is not narrative but theological and moral. Refuting the Jews and probing the motives of those planning their sons' future in the Church are more powerful driving forces in the sermon than telling the story of the saint.

Vincent can become fairly abstract but he is also a master of concrete images, as is well illustrated in his sermon on St. Antony's day.[332] His scriptural text is from Wisdom 10:12—"In a sore conflict she gave him the victory"—an apt verse for Antony,

[330] Ibid., fol. 18v.

[331] Ibid., fols. 57v–59 for the following.

[332] Ibid., fols. 27–29.

the great ascetic pioneer of the Egyptian desert. But he generalizes the lesson at once: "Sensory experience makes clear that the present life is nothing but a field of battle, both as regards the body and as regards the soul." Turning first to the body, he employs elementary science to explain and a memorable simile to drive home the point:

> The moment human beings are born, from the day of birth to the end, they are in a battle, for the four qualities within the body are continually fighting—hot with cold and dry with wet; until they finally kill the person, they are always at war, corrupting, changing, diminishing and opposing each other, as if there were in the belly four snakes biting and fighting each other.

These qualities are enemies within our body. Turning to the soul, Vincent evokes the picture of a noble maiden in the countryside, who is attacked by three armed men, one with a drawn sword, one with a crossbow and one with a lance. In these battles of the body and the soul, God gave to St. Antony the victory: he defeated "the world that comes up in front with a drawn sword; the flesh that comes up on the right with a drawn crossbow; and the devil who comes from the left shaking his spear." There is much more in the sermon, but enough has been said to convey its blending of difference kinds of discourse, its strong pictorial quality and its agile ability to circle back to its nominal subject.

Latin sermons were accessible only to the Latin literate, mainly clergy and monks, although a gifted preacher could, of course, translate them spontaneously. But in the later Middle Ages, vernacular sermons were being written down. John Mirk's *Festial* is an example in English.[333] This sermon collection, which deals with saints' days and other church feasts, was based on the *Golden Legend* but expanded and elaborated its source, for instance by adding saints of local significance like Wenefrid, who was revered in Shropshire where Mirk was writing. Mirk begins his sermons, "Good men and women," speaking directly to the audience, and mentioning the current feast-day. On St. Andrew's day, "you shall come to church to serve God, and worship the holy apostle for the special virtues that he had: one, for his high holiness of living, another for the great miracles he did, the third for the great passion he suffered." Mirk has an easy, conversational style:

> Christian men and women, such a day shall be St. Wenefrid's day. . . . Wherefore you that have devotion to this holy saint, come that day to the church to worship God and this holy maiden and martyr. Then how she suffered martyrdom you shall now hear. For though some know it, there are many that know it not; and though a good tale be twice told, it is the better to learn and for to understand.

Mirk's *Festial* had enormous success. It has indeed been called "the most widely read English sermon cycle in the fifteenth century," as well as "the most frequently printed

[333] Mirk, *Festial*.

English text before the Reformation."[334] Use of the vernacular, and the technical innovation of printing, ensured that parishioners could hear more about the saints than ever before, just at the time that the cult of the saints was to suffer its most violent and dramatic assault.

The Literature of Canonization Proceedings

There is a sense in which the vast bulk of written material produced during the course of a canonization hearing can hardly be classified as "literature." It had no single author, was created over years or decades, and served legal and bureaucratic purposes. Yet, on the other hand, it was shaped by well-defined common expectations, and its formal features can be recognized at once. So, although the texts that were generated by the canonization process are different from the Lives and miracle collections written by a single author, they can reasonably be regarded as a textual genre.

The ground-breaking work on medieval canonization is André Vauchez's analysis of seventy-one canonization proceedings from the period 1198–1432. His extensive bibliography lists his sources under the following headings: investigative processes at the diocesan level and local inquests; canonization processes ordered by the papacy; texts relating to the curial phase of the canonization process; hagiographic texts, that is, Lives and miracles collections (which were often included in canonization dossiers). The culminating document was the canonization bull, although, by the logic of things, this is rarely found in the dossiers produced by the canonization hearings.[335]

Collections of documents relevant to a saint's canonization might be gathered in different times and places, with their content varying, as well as what they were copied with and bound with. For example, the documents relating to the canonization process of Birgit of Sweden, produced in the years 1373–80 (with a few added miracles from 1387–88), which were published in the early twentieth century, are found primarily in three manuscripts:

Stockholm, Royal Library, A 14, written by one scribe in Italy in the late fourteenth century, but then brought to Vadstena, the Swedish monastery Birgit founded; it consists of 253 paper folios.[336]

BAV, Ottobonianus lat. 90; a late-fourteenth-century book of 133 parchment folios; palaeographical evidence suggests this book was put together by a team of thirteen scribes.

BL, Harley 612, a mid-fifteenth-century book from the Bridgettine abbey of Syon at Isleworth near London; it has 302 parchment folios.

[334] Powell, "Mirk, John."

[335] There is a collection of such bulls in *Codex constitutionum quas summi pontifices ediderunt in solemni canonizatione sanctorum*, although many have, of course, been re-edited subsequently.

[336] There is a facsimile: *Acta et processus canonizationis Sanctae Birgittae. Codex Holmiensis A 14.*

There is a large amount of documentation in these manuscripts, gathered from various stages of the canonization process. The most extensive text is the record of the twenty-four witnesses who gave their testimony in Rome between July 1379 and February 1380, but there are shorter records of witness testimony given at various times and places: Spoleto, 1373; Naples, 1376; Vadstena, 1377; and so on, as well as letters from the bishop of Linköping reporting further miracles. The articles of inquiry, which guided the interrogations, are included in the texts more than once. There is also a complete text of a Life of Birgit; letters from the king of Sweden, and many bishops, urging the canonization; and all the long-winded and legalistic documents relating to the authorization of the inquiries and the rights of parties to be represented by proxy. The modern edition runs to over 600 pages.[337]

The first two manuscripts appear to have been compiled in Italy as part of the canonization process itself. Neither of them has anything referring to the successful outcome of the process in 1391. Initially conceived of as working tools for the cardinals and others involved in the decision about Birgit's sanctity, in later generations they could provide edifying general reading, for the nuns and monks of Vadstena and perhaps the higher clergy of Rome, into whose hands the Ottobonianus manuscript came. The English book is different. It was written many years after Birgit's canonization by Thomas Colyngbourn for the Bridgettine abbey of Syon, which had been founded by Henry V in 1415. It contains, alongside the material relating to the canonization of Birgit, Birgit's *Revelations*, and various other texts, including the Life of Birgit's saintly daughter Catherine. It is thus an anthology of material of particular interest to Birgit's own Order, not a document from the process of canonization itself, the outcome of which was of course known to Thomas Colyngbourn.

Comparable to the Stockholm and Rome manuscripts is the large collection of material relating to the canonization of Thomas de Cantilupe, bishop of Hereford, now in the Vatican Library.[338] Here we have a mass of documentation assembled in one volume. It consists of 319 folios and contains transcripts of letters, forms of oaths, the articles of inquiry, testimony of witnesses, references to a subsidiary inquiry into Thomas's excommunication, and a final summary. The bulk of the material concerns proceedings of 1307, but some of the letters copied into the volume are earlier, such as those from Pope Clement V initiating the inquiry (1306), those from the English bishops urging Thomas's claims to sanctity (1294, 1299, 1305), and even one from Pope Innocent IV (1243–54) granting Thomas the right of non-residence during his time as a law student. It is a working document, and the names of the notaries who made the record are included, along with their distinctive authenticating marks. Dozens of fat volumes of this type are scattered throughout the libraries of Europe.

[337] *Acta et processus canonizacionis Beate Birgitte*; see also Nyberg, "The Canonization Process of St. Birgita of Sweden"; Hess, *Heilige machen im spätmittelalterlichen Ostseeraum*, pp. 103–73.

[338] BAV, Vat. lat. 4015.

Sometimes canonization proceedings became a source for a hagiographic Life. In the prologue to his *Life of St. Louis*, William of St.-Pathus explained that his account was dependent on the canonization hearings undertaken at St.-Denis in 1282–83. He had been able to obtain copies of these hearings from Paris and Rome through the good offices of John, bishop of Lisieux, the special proctor charged with furthering the canonization, and John of Antioch, papal penitentiary. William recognized that his own role as confessor to Margaret, Louis's widow, and Blanche, their daughter, played a part in the willingness of these high clergy to share such valuable records.[339] Another instance of a Life based, at least in part, on canonization records is the Life of Nicholas of Tolentino by Peter of Monterubbiano, who, however, occasionally improved his source, writing that Nicholas had encouraged a woman to pray, not to St. Blaise, as in the testimony at the canonization inquest, but to St. Augustine, the patron of the Order of Augustinian Hermits, to which both Nicholas and Peter belonged.[340]

These records of the canonization process were generated by the most complex and bureaucratic legal system in late medieval Europe. Over a thousand years earlier the fate of the martyrs had been recorded in trial reports. There is a curious symmetry to the fact that the both the earliest texts to be inspired by the cult of the saints and the latest are legal documents.

Vernacular Hagiography

One of the most dramatic forms of hagiographic rewriting was translation into another language. This began early, with the interplay of Greek and Latin, not to mention languages further east and south, such as Coptic, Syriac, Armenian, Georgian, and many others. In the early Middle Ages, hagiography went easily from Greek into Latin and Latin into Greek. Southern Italy, which was mainly Greek-speaking, formed an important region of cultural contact, while Rome itself housed Greek-speaking monks. Many of the popes were themselves Greek-speaking, down to the time of Pope Zacharias (741–52), a native of Calabria.

Translation of Greek hagiography into Latin began under the later Roman empire and occurred throughout the early medieval period.[341] In the sixth century, Dionysius Exiguus, famous for devising the system of counting years from the birth of Christ (AD), translated several works from Greek into Latin, including a Life of Pachomius, a formative figure in the history of Christian monasticism, and an account

[339] Guillaume de St.-Pathus, *Vie de saint Louis*, prologue, pp. 3–5.

[340] *Il processo per la canonizzazione di S. Nicola da Tolentino*, pp. 126, 237, 244; Peter of Monterubbiano, *Vita et miracula Nicolai Tolentinatis* 4. 36, p. 653; Lett, *Un procès de canonisation au Moyen Âge*, p. 28.

[341] Siegmund, *Die Überlieferung der griechischen christlichen Literatur in der lateinischen Kirche*, pp. 195–277 ("Hagiographische Literatur").

of the discovery of the head of John the Baptist, for reading on his feast-day.[342] An important translator of a later century was Anastasius Bibliothecarius ("the Librarian"), a powerful Italian ecclesiastic, who made an unsuccessful bid for the papacy in 855, but recovered from this to become a leading adviser of successive popes for twenty years, from 858 until his own death c. 878. He was fluent in Greek and one of his main literary activities was translating from Greek into Latin. In the preface to one of his earliest translations, the Life of John the Almsgiver by Leontius of Naples, Anastasius explains that he is undertaking this task "so that such a great man should be useful and profitable not only to those who have mastery of the Greek language but also to those of Latin speech." He has not attempted to follow Greek word order and has translated "not word for word but sense for sense." He does not wish "the Latin world to grieve at being deprived of this great salt, by which Greece rejoices to be so well flavoured."[343] He went on to produce a total of nine hagiographical translations, as well as other versions from the Greek, notably of the acts of the last two ecumenical councils of 787 and 869.[344] The task of transmitting Greek hagiography to the Latin world was taken up after Anastasius's death by several translators working in Naples. One of the most influential of the works produced here was John the Deacon's version of the Life of St. Nicholas, which spread quickly and was an important instrument in Nicholas's progress to becoming one of the most important saints in the Latin West, as he was in the East.[345] Translations from the Greek in the early medieval period could thus have a significant influence on the cult of the saints in the Latin West. Translation in the other direction, from Latin into Greek, also took place, but on a smaller scale.[346] Most of these texts concerned early martyrs of Rome and other parts of the West, such as Perpetua and Felicity, with a few dedicated to leading confessor-saints, like Ambrose and Benedict, this last translated by Zacharias, the last Greek-speaking pope.[347]

In the Greek world the languages of the educated and the mass of the population were different in style and character, but they were the same language. Hagiographic works were frequently recast in a higher style, but they did not need translation to be accessible to the bulk of the population. In the medieval Latin West the situation was not the same. Although the earliest western hagiography, such as the *Passion of Perpetua and Felicity* and the *Life of Martin*, was written in a world where Latin was the ordinary language of many people, over the course of time these texts became impenetrable to the bulk of the population as the ordinary languages and the Latin of the churchmen or lawyers diverged. In many regions, where Germanic or Celtic

[342] Dionysius Exiguus, *Vita sancti Pachomii abbatis Tabennensis*; idem, *De inventione capitis sancti Joannis Baptistae*.

[343] Anastasius Bibliothecarius, *Epistola* 1.

[344] See Neil, *Seventh-century Popes and Martyrs: The Political Hagiography of Anastasius Bibliothecarius*.

[345] John the Deacon, *Vita beati Nicolai episcopi* (also ed. Mombritius, *Sanctuarium* 2, fols. 161v–168).

[346] Lequeux, "Latin Hagiographical Literature Translated into Greek."

[347] *Passio sanctarum Perpetuae et Felicitatis* (BHG 1482); there are four Greek versions of Lives of Ambrose (BHG 67–70); for the Life of Benedict, see earlier, p. 46.

or Slavic languages were spoken, the Latin used by the monks, the clergy, and the highly educated would always have been incomprehensible to most people, but even in the areas of Romance tongue people eventually had to be taught Latin, just as in the other parts of Catholic Europe. Monks and clergy could read Latin hagiography, or should have been able to do so, but there was for some time no hagiography written in the vernacular, the ordinary language of the people. Over the course of the centuries this changed, as hagiography was translated from Latin into the vernacular and eventually composed in it. By the end of the Middle Ages the diverse languages of western and central Europe had a rich hagiographical literature of their own.

Two non-Mediterranean cultures that employed the vernacular remarkably early were the Irish and the Anglo-Saxon, both of them producing texts in their own languages by the seventh century. Amongst these vernacular texts were hagiographical writings.[348] An Old Irish version of the Life of Brigid was produced in the eighth or ninth century, although it retained a great deal of Latin throughout, sometimes in the form of complete sentences, sometimes as a mere word in a sentence otherwise in Irish.[349] The Tripartite Life of Patrick and the Life of Adomnán, abbot of Iona, are slightly later, probably from the tenth century, both of them presenting fierce saints who denounce or endorse kings and condemn or sanction their lineages. Adomnán, for example, predicts the death of the High King, Congal mac Fergusa, and announces that no king will be descended from him.[350] Irish vernacular hagiography continued to be written throughout the Middle Ages, totalling fifty or so Lives overall.[351]

Old English, like Irish, produced a remarkably early and extensive vernacular literature. Hagiographic works in Old English include the Old English Martyrology of the ninth century and Ælfric's saints' Lives of the late tenth century. The Old English Martyrology, which survives (incomplete) in five manuscripts, provides short passages on more than 200 saints.[352] Most are early martyrs, some of whom are given only a few sentences, while others are of particular interest to English listeners, such as Gregory the Great, "our foster-father," Etheldreda of Ely or Cuthbert. Two Irish saints (or saints important in Ireland), Patrick and Columba, have entries (as doubtless Brigid would have had, but the section covering her feast-day of 1 February is missing). There is some description of the saint's origins and nature—Mark was St. Peter's godson, Christopher had a dog's head—and the occasional intrusion of a Teutonic note, as when the Roman martyrs Protus and Hyacinth refuse to worship an idol of Thor. It is the earliest surviving narrative martyrology in the vernacular.

[348] Herbert, "Latin and Vernacular Hagiography of Ireland"; Cross, "English Vernacular Saints' Lives before 1000 A.D."; Whatley, "Late Old English Hagiography."

[349] *Bethu Brigte.*

[350] *Betha Phatraic*; *Betha Adamnáin*, at pp. 52–55 (c. 10); Herbert, *Iona, Kells, and Derry*, pp. 151–79.

[351] Sharpe, *Medieval Irish Saints' Lives*, p. 6.

[352] *The Old English Martyrology.*

In the 990s Ælfric produced Old English homilies for fifty-four saints, in three series.[353] One collection was commissioned by the powerful and learned English nobleman Æthelweard while Ælfric was a monk at Cerne, a monastery patronized by Æthelweard and his son.[354] Æthelweard was even able to persuade him to translate an account of St. Thomas the apostle despite Ælfric's own doubts about its authenticity.[355] Ælfric writes that the first two series deal with the saints that the English "venerate with feast-days," and the third with those that "not the people but the monks revere in their services."[356] But, although these are saints that the English venerate, they are not usually English saints. Indeed, of the fifty-four saints for whom Ælfric supplies a homily, only six are English (including the pre-Saxon Alban).[357] However, this does not mean that Ælfric does not have a special regard for England. Etheldreda is "an English maiden," and, anachronistically but tellingly, the persecution of Diocletian reaches "to England."[358]

These accounts by Ælfric are based on Latin originals. As he himself says, "We say nothing new in this composition, because it has been written long ago in books in Latin."[359] In the case of his homily for St. Benedict the source is Book Two of the *Dialogues* of Gregory the Great, which was entirely devoted to Benedict. Although there already was an Old English translation of this text, made a hundred years earlier during the reign of king Alfred, Ælfric did not use this but made his own version, drastically condensing Gregory's text for his own purposes, omitting names and superfluous details, but adding occasional clarifications for his English audience: he gives a sum in pounds and pence, rather than gold coins, and explains that in Benedict's country they use oil "as we do butter."[360]

Ælfric was an important channel through which Latin hagiography poured into the vernacular culture of late Anglo-Saxon England, and his works were read and copied in the eleventh and twelfth centuries until linguistic and cultural change made their language no longer comprehensible. The Norman Conquest of England had, as one of its consequences, a curious reversal of the direction of translation. After 1066, when many monks and leading ecclesiastics were more familiar with French and Latin than with Old English, translations were made into those languages from English. This atypical direction of translation, from vernacular into Latin, included some hagiographical examples. For example, William of Malmesbury undertook a

[353] *Ælfric's Catholic Homilies. The First Series*; *Ælfric's Catholic Homilies. The Second Series*; Ælfric, *Lives of Saints*; *Ælfric's Catholic Homilies: Introduction, Commentary and Glossary.*

[354] Ælfric, *Lives of Saints* 1, preface, p. 4.

[355] Ælfric, *Lives of Saints* 2, pp. 398–400 (no. 36); Ælfric, *Catholic Homilies. The Second Series*, pp. 297–98.

[356] Ælfric, *Lives of Saints* 1, preface, p. 2.

[357] Lapidge, "Ælfric's Sanctorale"; Whatley, "Late Old English Hagiography," pp. 460–82.

[358] Ælfric, *Lives of Saints* 1, pp. 414 (no. 19), 432 (no. 20); cf. earlier, p. 229.

[359] Ibid., p. 4.

[360] Gretsch, *Ælfric and the Cult of Saints*, p. 147 (see her whole discusssion, pp. 127–56); the earlier version of Gregory's *Dialogi* is by Wærferth of Worcester: *Bischofs Wærferth von Worcester Übersetzung der Dialoge Gregors des Grossen.*

Latin version of the Life of Wulfstan of Worcester, which had been written in English by the Worcester monk Coleman, while his namesake, William of St. Albans, said that his Latin Life of St. Alban and St. Amphibalus was translated from "a book composed in the English language."[361]

The earliest hagiographic writing in German is the Old High German *Song of St. George* (*Georgslied*), perhaps written at the monastery of St. George on the Reichenau island in Lake Constance.[362] It is about 60 lines long, but is incomplete. This is George before the dragon. The saint is "a famous count" who withstands torture for his faith and has miraculous powers. The script, language and spelling of the *Song of St. George* are difficult and uncertain. The scribe of this work himself found the novelty of his task daunting, for the text breaks off with his name and a note of despair: "I cannot do it! Wisolf." Wisolf was struggling with this text, in all probability, around 900. By 1100 hagiography in German had a more confident tone. The *Song of Anno* (*Annolied*) of that time tells of St. Anno, archbishop of Cologne (1056–75), setting his story in a wide panorama of universal and German history. It begins with the invocation of ancient heroic tales: "We have heard songs of old things, how brave heroes fought and strong castles were cast down, how loving friendships were shattered and powerful kings fell."[363] Now, the poet says, it is time to turn to consider "how we ourselves must end." Quickly sketching in history from the Creation to the Redemption, he narrows his focus to Cologne, clearly his main interest, which God has blessed with "so many saints," Anno amongst them. The poem then veers off again, to describe the origin of political power in human society, the sequence of empires and, in a dense and knotted section, the ancestry of the various German peoples. Returning to the subject of Cologne, we learn that seven of the archbishops of Cologne are saints, to whom Anno is now added. Anno's virtues and tribulations are described, as well as the miracles that occurred at his tomb after his death.

The story of hagiography in the Romance languages is more complicated, since it is often hard to tell when everyday spoken Latin can reasonably first be called French, Spanish or Italian, but it seems that this change had happened by the eleventh century at the latest, for Theobald of Vernon, a canon of Rouen cathedral in the middle of the that century, won a reputation as a translator of hagiography: "he translated the deeds of many saints from the Latin and reforged them gracefully enough into everyday language." He was noted for "the ringing rhythm" of these songs.[364] None of Theobald's works has come down to the present day but, not long after his time, a surviving piece of French verse was produced on the Life of Alexis.

[361] William of Malmesbury, *Vita Wulfstani, epistola*, pp. 8–10; William of St. Albans, *Acta sanctorum Albani, Amphibali et sociorum*, preface, p. 149. The truth of William's statement has been doubted: McLeod, "Alban and Amphibal," p. 409.

[362] *Althochdeutsche Literatur*, ed. Schlosser, pp. 242–46.

[363] *Annolied*.

[364] *Inventio et miracula sancti Vulfrani* 65, p. 76.

From this time on, the turn of the eleventh and twelfth centuries, as literature in the vernacular languages gained in prestige and currency, there was a flood of translations of hagiographic works from Latin into all the tongues of Europe. Almost 300 saints or groups of saints are the subject of Lives written in Middle English, while an inventory of medieval hagiographic writing in French and Provençal contains 228 items (and this figure does not include the Legendaries).[365] As mentioned earlier (p. 81) there are more than 1,100 late-medieval manuscripts containing hagiography in Italian. From 1200 a hagiographic literature in Old Norse flourished in Iceland and Norway, eventually forming a corpus that treated of more than a hundred saints or groups of saints, both native and international.[366] The Life of St. Francis, along with other Franciscan materials, was translated into Hungarian around 1370, and hagiography in the Polish vernacular makes a modest beginning at about the same time.[367]

From the thirteenth century numerous Legendaries were also produced in western vernaculars. There are about a hundred Legendaries in French prose.[368] The earliest was created around 1250 and contained translations of martyr passions. An Anglo-Norman version was composed in England. The so-called *South English Legendary* is a collection of saints' Lives in English verse. More than forty manuscripts of the work survive, the earliest from the later thirteenth century.[369] The most recent saint in the collection is St. Edmund of Abingdon (d. 1240): "In England he was born, in the town of Abingdon. / Glad might the mother be, that bore such a son!" The German Passional of the later Middle Ages was based mainly on the *Golden Legend*, but was rearranged thematically: Jesus; the Apostles; other saints (this last book circulated independently). Around 1460 the German Cistercian nun Regula composed *The Book of Holy Virgins and Women*, in German, containing fifty-seven accounts of saintly women, for her fellow nuns in Lichtental near Baden-Baden.[370]

Vernacular hagiography, like vernacular literature in general, could penetrate more deeply into society than works written in Latin, although it paid the price of having a much more restricted geographical range. A Latin Life could be read by monks and clergy from Scotland to Sicily and from Portugal to Poland, but vernacular works travelled outside their language area only through translation. Cogitosus's Life of St. Brigid was copied in monastic and clerical communities throughout Latin Christendom, but the Irish Life of Brigid survives in one fifteenth-century

[365] D'Evelyn and Foster, "Saints' Legends"; Brunel-Lobrichon et al., "L'hagiographie de langue française," pp. 327–58.

[366] Le Breton-Filippusdóttir, "Hagiographie vernaculaire d'Island et de Norvège," p. 419.

[367] Klaniczay and Madas, "La Hongrie," p. 141; Dunin-Wąsowicz, "Hagiographie polonaise entre XIe et XVIe siècle," pp. 193–94.

[368] Perrot, *Le passionnaire français au Moyen Age*; see also Meyer, "Légendes hagiographiques en français."

[369] *The South English Legendary*.

[370] Williams-Krapp, *Deutschen und niederländischen Legendare des Mittelalters*, pp. 30, 50–51, 363–65.

manuscript. This pattern of distribution is clear even from the present location of manuscripts of Lives in Latin and the vernacular. For example, the vast majority of hagiographic texts in Old Norse are to be found in Scandinavian libraries, with a few outliers in England; none are housed in continental libraries. There are a dozen versions of the Life of St. Margaret in Old English and Middle English, surviving in about eighty manuscripts; all of these are in Britain—mostly in Oxford, Cambridge, or London—except for three wanderers that have found their way to Tokyo and New Haven.[371] In contrast, the Latin Life of Margaret on which many of these versions were based survives in more than a hundred manuscripts, to be found in libraries throughout western Europe, from London to Naples.

But, whatever its geographical limitations, this new literature—writing about the saints in the ordinary everyday language—reached a far greater audience that the Latin of the clergy and monks. Sometimes it is possible to know the exact target audience for a piece of vernacular hagiography, as in the case of the Portuguese version of the Life of St. Eligius (Eloi), which was produced for the goldsmiths of Lisbon in the fifteenth century, Eligius himself having been a worker in precious metals.[372] Here a group of urban craftsman would be able to hear the Life of an appropriate patron in their own language. Medieval writers also often linked the vernacular, everyday language with women. Dante explains such an association. "The first person who began to write as a poet in the vernacular," he says, "was moved to do so because he wanted to make his words understood by a lady who found it difficult to understand verse in Latin."[373] Despite the remarkable record of nuns writing hagiography in Latin (earlier, pp. 516ff.), there does seem to have been some basis for this view. Lay people, urban populations, women—the vernacular literature of sanctity had a new, and far larger, audience.

If Latin hagiography was part of the world of clerical and monastic culture, then vernacular hagiography had its links with the contrasting world of the minstrels and lay performers. This is especially true of work in verse, where the rhyme and accented rhythm of hagiographic poems were often the same as those of vernacular epic or romance. For instance, most French verse hagiography is in octosyllabic rhyming couplets, the same form employed in the romances: of the twenty-five French verse hagiographies composed in England in the twelfth and thirteenth centuries, twenty-one were in octosyllables.[374] Wandering musicians might take the saints as the subject of their song. An English confessor's handbook of the early thirteenth century, distinguishing various types of entertainer and jester, and decrying most as reprehensible, notes that, nevertheless, "there are others who are called minstrels, who sing of the exploits of princes and the lives of the saints and bring comfort to men in their

[371] Clayton and Magennis, *The Old English Lives of St Margaret*; D'Evelyn and Foster "Saints' Legends," pp. 606–8; Index of Middle English Verse (on-line).

[372] Mattoso, "Le Portugal de 950 à 1550," p. 94.

[373] Dante Alighieri, *La vita nuova* 25, pp. 174–75.

[374] Laurent, *Plaire et édifier: les récits hagiographiques composés en Angleterre aux XIIe et XIIIe siècles*, pp. 581–89.

illnesses and troubles."[375] The author of the *Life of St. Andrew* in French verse is a repentant minstrel: "I have often treated of love," he writes, "of great joy and sorrow, of vanity and folly, of mockery, laughter and levity. . . . When I was young, I did these things and turned my mind to them, of which I repent and wish to refrain, for such things are contrary to God."[376] But, although he is loudly proclaiming a change in his themes, he did not need to alter his language or style.

One of the most important hagiographers writing in Castilian in the thirteenth century was Gonzalo de Berceo. His works include verse Lives of the Spanish saints Millán (Emiliano) and Dominic of Silos, as well as shorter works on St. Lawrence and St. Oria (Auria), and a collection of Miracles of the Virgin Mary in 911 quatrains. He expresses his desire to write in the vernacular on several occasions: "I want to make a poem in the clear romance tongue in which people are accustomed to speak with their neighbours"; "I want to make the Passion of our lord St. Lawrence in the romance tongue, so that everyone can know it."[377] Gonzalo employs a rhyming quatrain of four lines, each of fourteen syllables with a caesura (Spanish alexandrines), which is the same form as the Castilian Book of Alexander, of the first half of the thirteenth century, and in several places he refers to himself as a "minstrel" of the saints.[378] Just as the lay minstrels sang of the epic deeds of the heroes of antiquity, so Gonzalo, a learned cleric as well as a gifted poet in the vernacular, sang of the epic deeds of the saints.

In the central and later centuries of the Middle Ages, the French language had an especial cultural prestige (Dante considered writing in French before deciding on Tuscan). As a consequence, translations from and into French were particularly common. Even Lives of Welsh saints were translated into French. Those of Teilo and David, in French prose, are found in a manuscript now in the British Library, with the author of the former (who may also have written the latter) giving his name, William des Nes, and the date, 1325.[379] In England, where French had been imposed as a ruling class language in 1066, it remained the idiom of power and prestige for centuries, even if it soon ceased being a mother tongue. At Barking, the great nunnery east of London, one or two of the nuns composed saints' Lives in French in the late twelfth century. One of them was certainly the nun Clemence of Barking, who names herself in the *Life of St. Catherine* that she translated into French: "I who have translated her Life am called Clemence by name; I am nun of Barking."[380] There is

[375] Thomas of Chobham, *Summa confessorum* 6. 4. 2, pp. 291–92.

[376] *La Vie Saint Andrier l'Apostle*, lines 5–14, p. 437.

[377] Gonzalo de Berceo, *Vida de Santo Domingo de Silos* 2, p. 259; idem, *Martirio de San Lorenzo* 1, p. 463.

[378] Gonzalo de Berceo, *Vida de Santo Domingo de Silos* 289, 775, 776, pp. 331, 453.

[379] La vie de saint Thelyan translee de latin en francois que Mestre Guillaume des Nes translate lan mil iii^{c} et xxv le iour de saint Michiel archange: BL, Add. 17275, fol. 199v; the Life of Teilo is on fols. 195v–199v, that of David on fols. 199v–201v.

[380] Jo ki sa vie ai translatee, / Par nun sui Clemence numee. / De Berkinge sui nunain: Clemence of Barking, *Vie de sainte Catherine*, lines 2689–91, p. 85; on Clemence, see Legge, *Anglo-Norman Literature*, pp. 66–72; Wogan-Browne, *Saints' Lives and Women's Literary Culture*, pp. 227–45.

also a French *Life of Edward the Confessor*, based on that by the famous Cistercian writer Aelred of Rievaulx.[381] All we know about the author of this translation is that she was a nun of Barking (she explicitly declines to give her name).[382] Whether we wish to posit two nuns of Barking translating saints' lives into French at the same period or would prefer to have just one, Clemence, who for some reason is less forthcoming about her identity in the *Life of Edward* than in the *Life of Catherine*, is really a matter of taste. These Lives are translated from Latin, which shows that the author or authors were literate in Latin, but not composed in it. The nun of Barking who wrote the Life of Edward the Confessor apologizes for the quality of her French: "I know the faulty French of England," she says.[383] This is early evidence of a self-consciousness about the French of England that has clear hints of an inferiority complex.

At the end of the Middle Ages hagiography continued to move from one language to another. Sometimes there was translation from one vernacular to another. For instance, legendaries were translated from Castilian to Portuguese.[384] Renaissance humanists revived the practice of translating Greek hagiography into Latin.[385] But the main direction continued to be from Latin into the vernacular. In the long tradition of the convention of authorial modesty, translators sometimes emphasized their inadequacy for the task in hand. In the 1440s, the English friar Osbern Bokenham was translating Lives of female saints from Latin into English: "diverse legends, which my rudeness / From Latin had turned into our language, / Of holy women." He recounts his deficiencies with great energy: "My little experience in rhyming's art / . . . the dullness / Of my wit . . ." and asks God only to give him ability "That I may translate in words plain / Into our language out of Latin."[386] Whether he was sincere or not, Bokenham's modesty should not disguise the fact that, by the time he wrote, a whole new literature had come into existence—hagiography "in words plain."

[381] *La Vie d'Edouard le Confesseur*; see Wogan-Browne, *Saints' Lives and Women's Literary Culture*, pp. 249–56; Aelred of Rievaulx, *Vita sancti Edwardi regis et confessoris*.

[382] En Berkinges en l'abeïe / Fu translatee ceste vie, / Pur amur Saint Edward la fist / Une ancele al dulz Jhesu Crist. / Mais sun num n'i vult dire a ore: *La Vie d'Edouard le Confesseur*, lines 5304–8, p. 273.

[383] Un faus franceis sai d'Angleterre: *La Vie d'Edouard le Confesseur*, line 7, p. 109. The nun was perhaps too modest about her French, for the editor of the Life concludes his linguistic analysis of the poem with the judgment, "En conclusion, nous pouvons dire que la langue de notre poème est remarquablement pure" (p. 102).

[384] Mattoso, "Le Portugal de 950 à 1550," p. 91.

[385] Frazier, *Possible Lives: Authors and Saints in Renaissance Italy*, p. 23.

[386] Bokenham, *Legendys of Hooly Wummen*, lines 5038–40, 5078–80, 5252–53, pp. 138, 139, 144.

CHAPTER 14

Doubt and Dissent

Early Polemics

From the earliest days of Christianity, Christians lived alongside non-Christians, who might be deeply unconvinced of the sanctity of their saints and the legitimacy of their veneration. Augustine had to defend martyr cult against pagan critics, who saw in it simply a variant of their own polytheism (see later, pp. 610ff.). Jewish and Muslim attitudes echoed this point. Writing a polemical treatise around 1200, Alan of Lille felt the need to justify Christians against the charges raised against them by Muslims and Jews. As well as criticizing the practice of having images in churches, these opponents also claimed "that we have made many gods, since we worship the saints, such as Peter and Paul." Alan advanced the standard defence of images, partly from Old Testament precedent (the images of the cherubim), and partly by distinguishing the veneration paid to images from that paid to God, a distinction also central to his defence of the cult of the saints. Christians reverenced the saints with *dulia*, a kind of worship appropriate to human beings, but not with *latria*, due to God alone.[1] Jews and Muslims often accused medieval Christians of idolatry and polytheism, and some intellectual ingenuity was needed to rebut the charges.

But criticism did not come only from those of other religions. At all times there have been sceptical voices about the saints and their miracles within the Christian community. These dissentient views are of various kinds. Some people regarded the cult of the saints as either an irrelevance or as a pernicious diversion of spiritual energy: love of God and love of one's fellow man were the heart of the matter, and hence, for both mystics and moral reformers, entreaties addressed to the holy dead, and the adornment and veneration of their tombs, were likely to be regarded as a wasteful loss of direction. But there were other voices raised against the saints that had a quite different tone. These expressed, not a principled dissent, but a visceral cynicism. The stories of the saints, in the eyes of these folk, were ridiculous, and probably cooked up by monks and priests eager for wealth and status. Such disrespect did not require elaborate discussion. The man who lowered his breeches and

[1] Alanus de Insulis, *Contra paganos* (*De fide catholica* 4) 11–12, pp. 343–46 (PL 210: 427–28).

broke wind in the direction of a saint's shrine as it was carried in procession was expressing a view, even if not arguing a position.[2]

Augustine was aware that pagans might see no real distinction between worship of the old gods and the new saints. But his fellow Christians might also feel something of the same, and react with horror to the new developments. One of the most sustained attacks on the cult of relics, viewed as just old paganism creeping back, came from an author named Vigilantius, writing around the year 400.[3] His treatise is known only from the passages quoted in St. Jerome's characteristically unrestrained and sarcastic rebuttal, but a picture of his views can be built up, nevertheless.

Vigilantius certainly opposed the veneration of relics: "we see a virtually pagan rite introduced into churches on the pretext of religion . . . and everywhere they kiss and adore some kind of dust, wrapped in a little container of precious cloth."[4] His objections are both theological and ritual. Since he does not believe that the dead can pray for the living, he denies the intercessory power of the saints, while he also decries the practice of lighting candles and keeping night vigils at their shrines.[5] Jerome clearly feels a little vulnerable on the issue of candles and vigils. He recognizes that the pagans too burn candles before the images of the gods, but says there is no harm in simple layfolk and pious women doing the same before the shrines of the saints—"they receive their reward according to their faith"—and that the notorious opportunity for sexual misbehaviour that nocturnal vigils offered should not lead to condemnation of the practice if engaged in devoutly.[6] Vigilantius also "argues against the signs and miracles that are performed in the churches of the martyrs."[7] The critique of relic-cult in Vigilantius's work is linked to several other positions. He opposes the celibacy of the clergy (and is subjected to particularly coarse abuse on this topic by Jerome) and sees no particular virtue in the monastic life. "If all men cloistered themselves," he supposedly argued, "and lived alone, who will fill the churches? Who will win over secular people? Who will be able to call sinners to virtue?"[8] Finally, he opposed the practice of sending alms to the Christian communities of the Holy Land.[9]

Vigilantius thus rejected the cult of relics, with its attendant rituals and miracles; the idea that the clergy should be set apart by sexual renunciation; monasticism; and the special place of the Holy Land. In retrospect he must appear as someone swimming against the tide, as the deep currents of the fourth century swept in miraculous relics, a sanctified priesthood, heroic asceticism and pilgrimage. Yet the anger

[2] William of Malmesbury, *Gesta pontificum Anglorum* 5. 275, p. 656.

[3] Jerome, *Contra Vigilantium* (PL 23: 339–52).

[4] Ibid., 4, p. 11 (PL 23: 342–43).

[5] Ibid., 6, 7, 9, pp. 13–15, 16–18, 20–21 (PL 23: 344, 345, 347).

[6] Ibid., 7, 9, pp. 16–18, 20–21 (PL 23: 345–46, 347–48).

[7] Ibid., 10, p. 21 (PL 23: 348).

[8] Ibid., 2, 15, pp. 7–8, 27–29 (PL 23: 340–41, 351).

[9] Ibid., 13, pp. 24–26 (PL 23: 349–50).

behind Jerome's response, even given his usual levels of resentment, suggests that Vigilantius's position was viewed as a real challenge. Nor was Vigilantius entirely alone. "Alas!" says the choleric Church Father, "he is said to have bishops as fellows in his crime."[10] What was happening around the year 400, and is revealed in the controversy between Vigilantius and Jerome, was a final decision on the trajectory of Christianity for the next thousand years. Jerome won.

Some of these issues recur in Byzantium early in the Middle Ages. The iconoclastic crisis that began in 726 has been discussed earlier, with its arguments about images of the saints. But, in the period leading up to that outbreak, more radical views were also expressed in Byzantium. There were even those who did not believe that the souls of the saints could appear on earth, and who, like Vigilantius, thought saintly intercession impossible. An important piece of evidence for such unorthodox views is (as in the case of Vigilantius and Jerome, and so often in medieval circumstances) an orthodox attempt to rebut them, in this case the treatise *On the State of Souls after Death*, written by a priest of Constantinople, Eustratius, around 600.[11] Eustratius explains the belief he is opposing, prior to refuting it:

> After departure from this life and the withdrawal of souls from the body, the souls remain inactive, whether they are saintly or otherwise; even if the souls of the saints appear to some people, they do not appear in their own substance and being, as these people claim, but give the appearance of the souls of the saints in action by assuming a certain divine power; but they are in a certain place and are never able to manifest themselves to anyone in this life after the departure from the body.[12]

Nicholas Constas, analyzing Eustratius's text, points out that his arguments demonstrate the existence of controversy about the very possibility of saintly intercession at the time he wrote, in the late sixth century:

> critical voices denied that the souls of the dead could involve themselves in the affairs of the living, or intercede on their behalf in heaven, or be affected by the intentions and activities of the church on earth . . . they nullified the cult of the saints and the efficacy of relics.[13]

Eustratius cites the Bible, the Fathers and the Lives of the saints to prove that his opponents' views are false.[14] The souls of the departed do appear in this life, "sent

[10] Ibid., 2, p. 7 (PL 23: 340).

[11] Eustratius of Constantinople, *De statu animarum*; see discussion in Krausmüller, "God or Angels as Impersonators of Saints"; Constas, "An Apology for the Cult of the Saints in Late Antiquity"; Dal Santo, "The God-Protected Empire? Scepticism towards the Cult of Saints in Early Byzantium"; idem, *Debating the Saints' Cults in the Age of Gregory the Great*.

[12] Eustratius, *De statu animarum*, lines 52–60, p. 5.

[13] Constas, "An Apology for the Cult of the Saints in Late Antiquity," p. 271.

[14] Eustratius, *De statu animarum*, editorial introduction, pp. 121–39.

out to help many," and "it is clear that those who come to the relics of the saints receive healing from them, if God wills it." The saints are intercessors, and "to act as an intercessor is a form of action not inaction."[15] The echo of the argument between Vigilantius and Jerome is clear.

A particular target of the sceptics attacked by Eustratius was the apparent bodily appearances of the saints. "How," they demanded (talking apparently of the warrior saints, like George), "could the souls of the saints, which are separated from their bodies" appear to believers dressed in full armour or on horseback?[16] According to Eustratius, his opponents believed that saints did not in fact appear in reality but only "by assuming a certain divine power." One even more radical, and surprising, attempt to come to terms with the unacceptable physicality of the saints was to assert that the saints could not actually appear in visible form, and that such apparent forms were actually angels.[17] This view turns up in Byzantine discussions throughout the seventh and eighth centuries. It is perhaps to be seen as a reaction against a tradition in which saints had been so very physical: Thecla with her fiery chariot, her willingness to embrace female followers, her love of literature; Cosmas and Damian, pretending to be bath-attendants, and rustling up nasty-tasting medicines; or Artemios, a saint who specialized in treating hernias and was thus constantly inspecting and handling testicles.[18]

An isolated instance of this kind of angelic impersonation also occurs in the West. A blind man called Alberic, who had taken up residence alongside the church of St. Marcellinus in Seligenstadt in the late 820s, had a nocturnal vision of a venerable man dressed in white. The visionary form asked Alberic if he knew who he was. Without hesitation, Alberic identified him as St. Marcellinus, but got an unexpected reply: "It is not as you think, but I am the archangel Gabriel, and I have taken on the person and form of Marcellinus." God had committed to the archangel charge of all matters concerning Marcellinus and his fellow martyr Peter.[19] However unusual these events might seem, the theory of angelic impersonation was an attempt to deal with a difficult problem. If the saints were in heaven, how could they be on earth? And if they were to resume their bodies at the Last Judgment, how could they appear in bodily form in the present?

Scepticism of this kind was based on doubts about the reality of saintly appearances, but hostility towards saints' cults on the part of some Christians was stimulated by the way that they shifted the focus of veneration away from the centres of communal worship and toward the grave. In the middle years of the fourth century, one assembly of Catholic bishops had to rule, "If anyone decries the assemblies and services at the martyrs' tombs, he should be anathemized."[20] Clearly someone was

[15] Ibid., lines 126, 379–81, 399–400, pp. 7, 17, 18.

[16] Ibid., lines 2006–8, p. 83.

[17] Krausmüller, "God or Angels as Impersonators of Saints."

[18] Earlier, pp. 25, 42; *Miracula sancti Artemii.*

[19] Einhard, *Translatio et miracula sanctorum Marcellini et Petri* 3. 13, p. 253.

[20] *Discipline générale antique 1/ii: Les canons des synodes particuliers*, p. 97 (Council of Gangres, cl. 20).

decrying them. A particularly heartfelt protest of this kind comes in a document from Coptic Egypt. It states its case without reservation:

> The Catholic Church, which God ransomed with his own blood does not need the honour of the martyrs; rather the places of the martyrs should be under the power of the Catholic Church. . . . Just as the sun does not need the light of a lamp, so the Church does not need the bodies of the martyrs.

The text condemns the practice of naming churches after saints—"the name of Christ is enough to honour the church"—and the construction of buildings at the site of the martyrs' tombs, a custom, the author alleges, that echoes pre-Christian Egyptian usage.[21] The tension between the gatherings of the Christian community for shared Eucharist within the city and the new shrines in the cemeteries outside could hardly be more forcefully expressed.

Western Heretics

As discussed earlier (pp. 480–81), the Byzantine controversy about sacred images in the eighth and ninth centuries had echoes in the Carolingian world, as western popes, princes, and bishops responded to eastern debates, even if not always with full understanding of them. The discussion centred primarily upon images, but sometimes extended to other facets of the cult of the saints. Claudius of Turin, that determined critic of image worship, also had reservations about pilgrimages to Rome, and, at one point, seems to have expressed a general doubt about the value of saintly intercession: "let no one trust in the merit or intercession of the saints, for, unless they have the same faith, justice and truth that they have, and through which they are pleasing to God, they will not be able to be saved."[22] But such views were extremely uncommon at this time. It was only with the new millennium that critical voices became stronger.

The heretical movements that arose in western Europe in the eleventh century and grew to great proportions in later centuries, prompting a counter-attack on the part of the Church with crusade and inquisition, were generally not receptive to the cult of the saints. Reservations about the saints can be found amongst the very earliest heretics recorded in the medieval West, those who were arrested and interrogated at Orleans in 1022 and Arras in 1025. The former group supposedly "considered it pointless to invoke the holy martyrs and confessors."[23] The latter were more cautious, considering that "there was no special gift of power in the confessor saints and

[21] "Canons of Basil," cl. 31, 33, pp. 248–51; they may have originally been composed in Syria: *The Coptic Encyclopedia* 2, p. 459, s.v. "Canons of Saint Basil" (René-Georges Coquin).

[22] Claudius of Turin, *Epistola* 12, p. 613.

[23] Sanctos martyres atque confessores implorare pro nihilo ducebant: *Gesta synodi Aurelianensis*, p. 537.

that no-one should be venerated except the apostles and martyrs."[24] Such doubts about intercession recur amongst the reported views of twelfth-century dissenters. In 1143–44 Eberwin of Steinfeld reported to St. Bernard on heretics in Cologne, "They put no reliance on the intercession of the saints," and they also denied purgatory and hence prayers for the dead.[25] Soon afterwards, in 1145, Bernard undertook a preaching campaign against heretics in the south of France. These dissenters supposedly "mocked prayers and offerings for the dead, invocation of saints . . . pilgrimages by the faithful . . . solemn feast-days."[26] The heretics, Bernard wrote, "laugh at us for baptizing infants, for praying for the dead, for asking the saints for help."[27] Repeatedly, heretics linked prayer for the dead and prayer to the saints. Both involved contact between the living and the invisible. Both involved intercession. Denying the possibility of one perhaps made it more likely that one would reject the other.

This rejection of the intercessory power of the saints, and of the corollary idea that they should be venerated, was viewed by orthodox writers of the time as one of the defining beliefs of the Cathars, the dualist heretics concentrated in southern France and northern Italy.[28] Alexander Nequam wrote of the Cathars, "They suggest that the bodies of the saints are not worthy of veneration and seek to persuade people that no honour should be paid to the relics of the saints."[29] His contemporary, the Cistercian chronicler Ralph of Coggeshall, reported that, "they assert that there should be no prayers for the dead and no requests for the intercession of the saints."[30] Underlying these views were the Cathars' parallel assumptions that the living cannot help the dead and the dead cannot help the living. Since the saints do not pray for us, it is futile to invoke them. "The prayers of the saints do nothing for the living," they reportedly asserted, and "the saints who are now sleeping with Christ do not pray for us."[31] Some Cathars thought that the saints were not yet in glory but "in a certain place," a phrase recalling the views of Eustratius's adversaries.[32] Others denied that the saints had performed miracles and denounced veneration of images as idolatry.[33]

[24] Nullum in sanctis confessoribus donum virtutis spectare, praeter apostolos et martyres neminem debere venerari: *Acta synodi Atrebatensis* 1, 11, cols. 1271 (with date erroneously given as 1035), 1301–3.

[25] In suffragiis sanctorum non confidunt: in Bernard of Clairvaux, *Sermones in Canticum Canticorum 51–68*, p. 422 (PL 182: 679).

[26] Ridebantur orationes oblationesque pro mortuis, sanctorum invocationes, . . . fidelium peregrinationes, . . . dierum solemnium vacationes: *Vita prima sancti Bernardi* 3. 6, col. 313.

[27] Irrident nos, quod baptizamus infantes; quod oramus pro mortuis; quod sanctorum suffragia postulamus: Bernard of Clairvaux, *Sermones in Canticum Canticorum* 66. 9, p. 354 (PL 183: 1098).

[28] d'Alatri, "Culto dei santi ed eretici in Italia."

[29] Innuunt etiam corpora sanctorum non esse digna veneratione sed et reliquiis sanctorum honorem exhibendum non esse persuadere intendunt: Alexander Nequam, *Speculum speculationum* 1. 2. 6, p. 21.

[30] Astruunt non orandum pro mortuis, non sanctorum suffragia expetenda: Ralph of Coggeshall, *Chronicon Anglicanum*, p. 124.

[31] Alanus de Insulis, *De fide catholica* 1. 72, col. 373; Bonacursus, *Manifestatio haeresis Catharorum*, p. 210 (not in the version in PL 204).

[32] Ranieri Sacconi, *De Catharis et Pauperibus de Lugduno*, p. 77.

[33] Salvo Burci, *Liber suprastella*, p. 18; Döllinger, *Beiträge zur Sektengeschichte des Mittelalters* 2, p. 40; *Le Registre d'Inquisition de Jacques Fournier* 2, pp. 54, 420 (127b, 205a).

The other main heretical movement of the high Middle Ages, the Waldensians, shared Cathar doubts about the veneration of the saints. In his comprehensive inquisitorial handbook of the early fourteenth century, the inquisitor Bernard Gui reports the heretical views of various sects. According to him, the Waldensians assert that supposed miracles done by the saints are false, and that the saints in heaven do not hear the prayers addressed to them, nor pay any attention to the veneration that is offered to them. Since the saints do not pray for us, there is no need to beg their intercession. "Because of this," adds Gui, "they despise the solemnities that we celebrate in reverence of the saints . . . and work on feast-days, if they can do so without danger." He adds, however, that this is a secret doctrine of the Waldensian elite rather than a belief held by the large body of followers, and that some of them do believe in the observance of Sundays and feasts of the Virgin Mary and apostles.[34] It is certain that there was some diversity of belief amongst heretical groups, but rejection of prayer to the saints occurs so commonly as a charge against Waldensians that it is hard to believe it was an esoteric part of their teaching.[35]

The Cathars and Waldensians not only held general views about the cult of the saints, but also often expressed opinions about particular saints. Cathars, with their dualist beliefs, regarded this world as the creation of the bad God, whom they regularly identified as the God of the Old Testament. Hence it is understandable that they thought that the prophets of the Old Testament were "wicked and damned," some of them adding John the Baptist to this list.[36] Similarly, since the Catholic Church was the Church of the bad God, its great champions, the Fathers Ambrose, Augustine, Jerome and Gregory, were also damned.[37] It is clear from the questions that the inquisitors put to the Waldensians that other individual saints were also the subject of controversy: "Do you believe that St. Martin is saved and that his soul is in the kingdom of heaven?"[38] This was obviously a diagnostic test.

This question about St. Martin was only the culmination of a long list of similarly diagnostic interrogations covering a whole range of activities associated with the cults of the saints:

> Do you know the *Ave Maria*? Do you know any pious prayer addressed to any particular saint? If you know it, say it. Do you believe that the Virgin Mary and the other saints know our miseries and pray for us? Who is the patron saint of your parish? When is their feast-day celebrated? Do you celebrate that

[34] Bernard Gui, *Practica inquisitionis heretice pravitatis* 5. 2. 4, p. 248. Much of the wording is identical to that in the treatise attributed to David of Augsburg.

[35] Stephen de Bourbon, *Tractatus de diversis materiis praedicabilibus* 4. 7. 343, p. 297; Döllinger, *Beiträge zur Sektengeschichte des Mittelalters* 2, pp. 300, 305, 306, 345; *Quellen zur böhmischen Inquisition im vierzehnten Jahrhundert*, p. 321.

[36] Döllinger, *Beiträge zur Sektengeschichte des Mittelalters* 2, pp. 34, 285; Salvo Burci, *Liber suprastella*, pp. 83–91; *Le Registre d'Inquisition de Jacques Fournier* 1, p. 282 (52a).

[37] Bonacursus, *Manifestatio haeresis Catharorum*, pp. 208–9 (PL 204: 777).

[38] Döllinger, *Beiträge zur Sektengeschichte des Mittelalters* 2, p. 334; the text is from clm 1339, not 339 as stated; cf. p. 321.

> feast? What kind of saint are they? Angel, martyr, confessor? Apostle, virgin, widow? Have you kissed relics of the saints? Have you visited the shrines of saints to obtain indulgences? Have you been to Rome?[39]

This staccato quiz was designed to shake out and trap anyone who had tried to ignore or disregard saintly cult.

It is not surprising that the heretics had a particular animus against the individual saints who were their persecutors. Notable among them were St. Dominic, founder of the Dominican Order, which was deeply involved in running the Inquisition, and St. Peter Martyr, a Dominican inquisitor murdered by heretics in 1252. A charge brought against a critic caught up in the Inquisitors' dragnet in Bologna in 1299 was that he had said that the Dominicans "had made some Peter Martyr a saint, although he was not a saint, and he scorned this Peter Martyr."[40] One of the diagnostic questions asked of Italian Cathars by the inquisitors was, "Whether St. Dominic and St. Peter Martyr are saints?"[41] When serious opposition to the activities of the Inquisition and the Dominicans occurred in the heretical stronghold of Albi in 1302, a symbolic manifestation of this hostility was the destruction of the images of St. Dominic and St. Peter Martyr that had been placed on one of the city gates.[42] At the end of the fourteenth century, inquisitors were turning up heretics in Piedmont who believed that "St. Peter Martyr was a bad man and a sinner and he is not a saint and he is damned in hell because he persecuted Christ's servants."[43]

The later Middle Ages saw an increase in the range and depth of lay devotion. This often involved an intense commitment to the cult of the saints, in such forms as new pilgrimage sites or confraternities dedicated to a saint, but it also saw a rise in critical and hostile views. One group of dissidents who expressed strong and sometimes colourful opinions about the cult of the saints were the so-called Lollards, who were active in England from the late fourteenth century until they were subsumed in the Protestant Reformation.[44] Inspired to some degree by the teachings of the Oxford theologian John Wycliffe (d. 1384), these anti-clerical reformers disseminated the Bible in the vernacular, criticized images and pilgrimages, and viewed the wealth and power of the contemporary Church as a deviation from true Christianity. Lollard beliefs reportedly included the view

> that the feasts of the saints, such as Stephen, Lawrence, Margaret, Catherine and the other saints, should not be observed or celebrated, because no one

[39] Döllinger, *Beiträge zur Sektengeschichte des Mittelalters* 2, pp. 333–34 (shortened); the text is from clm 1339, not 339 as stated.

[40] *Acta S. Officii Bononie ab anno 1291 usque ad annum 1310* 1, pp. 234, 256–57.

[41] Döllinger, *Beiträge zur Sektengeschichte des Mittelalters* 2, p. 319 (Codex Casanatense H 111 34).

[42] Bernard Gui, *De fundatione et prioribus conventuum provinciarum Tolosanæ et Provinciæ Ordinis Praedicatorum*, p. 203.

[43] Merlo, *Eretici e inquisitori nella società piemontese*, p. 40.

[44] Aston, "Lollards and Images"; Hudson, *The Premature Reformation*, pp. 301–9, 311–13.

> knows whether they are damned or not, nor should any belief be placed in the canonization and approval of the saints by the Roman curia.[45]

This constituted a direct challenge to the late medieval cult of the saints.

Some doubts about the veneration of saints were indeed expressed by Wycliffe. Like the heretics arrested at Arras in 1025, he made a distinction between "apostles, martyrs and saints of the early church" and "modern saints"; he argued that papal canonization was certainly not a guarantee of sanctity, for the Church may make a mistake in canonizing someone, and many of those "modern saints" have been canonized "because of their family connections, or through payments and gifts"; Christ should be the focus of Christian worship, not the "multiplicity of saints"; indeed, "every saint would pray for us more effectively if his or her cult were abandoned and we loved our Jesus more."[46] He also attacked "the unruly and greedy cult around relics"; he thought it wrong that recently canonized saints, in their "tombs adorned with gold and precious stones," should be more honoured than the apostles and early saints; "Christ's law and scripture" showed that there are more useful occupations than "going on pilgrimage, venerating relics and amassing money."[47]

The Lollards were not all theologians, and their views about religious practices could be expressed in an earthier way than was possible in Wycliffe's Oxford Latin. On one occasion, a hostile chronicler reports, two Lollards chopped up a wooden statue of St. Catherine to cook their dinner, joking that "this holy image will certainly be holy firewood for us." "They hate images," the chronicler notes, "and call them idols." He adds that they refer to the miraculous image of the Virgin at Walsingham as "the witch of Walsingham."[48] "The Lady of Falsingham" was another mocking title they bestowed on her.[49] Lollards nursed a particular resentment of Thomas Becket, England's most famous saint, claiming he "was a false traitor and damned in hell."[50]

Costly images and pilgrimages were two targets of the Lollard critique and, indeed, opposition to these things was taken to be characteristic of their outlook, for repentant Lollards had to promise to reverence the images of the saints and not to despise pilgrimage.[51] Their criticism of pilgrimage was based partly on the grounds that many pilgrims went away more for a kind of holiday than for pious purposes: "commonly such pilgrimages be maintaining of lechery, of gluttony, of drunkenness"; "no pilgrimage ought to be performed or made, for all pilgrimages serve for nothing but only to give goods to priests who are too wealthy and to deck out barmaids

[45] Knighton, *Chronicon*, p. 436.

[46] Wycliffe, *Tractatus de ecclesia* 2, pp. 44–46.

[47] Ibid., 19, p. 465.

[48] Knighton, *Chronicon*, p. 296.

[49] *Heresy Trials in the Diocese of Norwich*, p. 148.

[50] David, "Lollards, Reformers and St. Thomas of Canterbury," p. 5 (alleged statement of Margery Backster, 1429).

[51] Aston, "Lollards and Images," p. 143.

and make innkeepers proud."[52] The revelry of pilgrims, with their songs, bells and bagpipes, makes such a ruckus as if a king were coming to town.[53] But pilgrimages are also a waste of money which could be better spent helping the poor. The same is true of elaborate gilded images. People have ornate crucifixes but allow "poor men, brought with Christ's precious blood, to be by them naked, hungry, thirsty.... Dear Lord! What alms is it to paint gaily dead stones and rotten stocks with such alms that is poor men's good and livelihood and suffer poor men perish for hunger."[54]

So, support for the poor was better than expenditure on these ostentatious aspects of the cult of the saints. But the Lollards' ultimate ground for rejection of prayer to the saints was that it was unnecessary, since God himself could be approached directly: "all prayer ought to be made only to God, and to no other saints, for it is doubtful if there be any such saints in heaven as these Mass-singers approve and command to be honoured and prayed to here on earth."[55] Or, more succinctly, "What need is it to go to the feet, when we may go to the head?"[56] This viewpoint, that the cult of the saints intruded an unnecessary layer between worshippers and their God, fits with the generally anti-ritual and anti-clerical position of most heretical movements. Orthodox inquisitors had to insist, in opposing these views, that we should "put our trust and hope of help in all the saints of heaven as means and mediators that may bring us to heaven."[57]

Sceptics and Scoffers

Alongside the serious and principled objections against the cult of the saints that were raised by these heretics, there was also a bubbling broth of mockery, disrespect, doubt, disbelief, disdain, and derision. This rich world of more anarchic and impulsive reactions was often expressed in gestures and colourful language. The best source of information about these sceptics and scoffers is—only apparently paradoxically—the hagiographical literature devoted to glorifying the saints. Since one of the things that powerful saints could do, in life or after it, was convince doubters and punish those who derided them, records of their triumphs as avengers necessarily described the insults and disregard to which they were subject.[58] For instance, the shameless woman who lifted her skirt to show her backside to the missionary saints Paternus

[52] Hudson, ed., *Selections from English Wycliffite Writings*, pp. 86 (treatise on images, modernized), 36 (confession of Hawisia Moone, 1430, modernized).

[53] Hudson, ed., *Two Wycliffite Texts*, p. 64 (William Thorpe, 1407).

[54] Hudson, ed., *Selections from English Wycliffite Writings*, pp. 83, 85 (treatise on images, modernized).

[55] Ibid., p. 36 (confession of Hawisia Moone, 1430, modernized).

[56] Foxe, *Acts and Monuments* 4, p. 229 (the words of Agnes Ward, Lincoln diocese, 1521).

[57] *The Register of Thomas Spofford, Bishop of Hereford*, p. 154 (abjuration of John Woodhulle, 1433, modernized).

[58] Sigal, *L'homme et le miracle*, pp. 210–16; Goodich, *Miracles and Wonders*, pp. 47–68 ("'Popular' Voices of Doubt"); Golinelli, *Il medioevo degli increduli* (with useful bibliography).

and Scubilio was punished by ulcerous sores, but the miraculous punishment can be told only because there is the prior record of the derisive gesture.[59]

Frequently, scorn was directed not to the saints and their miracles in general but to a living individual with a reputation for saintliness. Geneviève is now the patron saint of Paris, but her Life describes how at one point the citizens of Paris wanted to stone her or drown her, blaming her as a "pseudo-prophet," because she had persuaded their wives that they should not seek to hide their property in the face of a barbarian attack, but should instead respond with prayer and fasting.[60] After St. Godric of Finchale had set up his hermitage garden on land that had been the common pasture of the local peasants, they (understandably) objected, and trampled the garden down with their animals, laughing at him and launching coarse insults.[61] In both cases, of course, the saint is vindicated; these incidents are recorded in their hagiography. Saints had to face such trials and tribulations and it was recognized by the author of the Life of Geneviève that, "all men have not faith, but the Lord is faithful, who shall stablish you and keep you from evil" (2 Thessalonians 2:2–3). Perhaps these incidents really did occur, rather than being uplifting parables, and in both cases were stirred up by resentment against poseurs who were seen as disruptive hypocrites, who put their own self-regarding piety before the practical needs of practical people.

Some also found the transition from living acquaintance to dead saint unconvincing. If they had known the saint during his or her lifetime, they might recognize their humanity but not their sanctity: "it was not good to call someone a saint whom, not long before, they had seen just like other mortals, subject to the passions of this life, being hungry and thirsty, eating and drinking."[62] A tailor who had been reprimanded for working on a saint's day expressed similar feelings. He was unconvinced by the saints: "They were certainly mortals, brought up rich but in nature just like me, and after the course of this life they were placed with their fathers like the rest; I do not worship or revere them, for death has taken away both their power to help and their ability to harm."[63]

A cavalier disregard could be expressed concerning dead saints, as in the case of the Swedish noble who vigorously disparaged St. Birgit when her relics were brought back to Sweden in 1374: "What do I care about that old woman and her relics? If I had a horse worth forty marks I wouldn't care anything at all for her!"[64] Such defiance was invariably punished. During the Scots' invasions of England in 1173 and 1174, northern troops mustered at Durham to resist them. Many of the soldiers commended themselves to the protection of St. Cuthbert, dismounting and

[59] *Vita Paterni* 1. 4, p. 427; this is an elaborated version of Venantius Fortunatus's Life, which has the same incident in different words: *Vita sancti Paterni* 6. 18, p. 34.

[60] *Vita Genovefae virginis Parisiensis* 12–13, pp. 219–20.

[61] Reginald of Durham, *Libellus de vita et miraculis sancti Godrici heremitae de Finchale* 26, pp. 74–75.

[62] *Miracula Galterii abbatis Sancti Martini*, p. 212 (AASS Aprilis 1: 767).

[63] *Miracula Rictrudis* 2. 3. 34, p. 106; Sigal, *L'homme et le miracle*, pp. 213–14.

[64] *Acta et processus canonizacionis Beate Birgitte*, pp. 109, 147.

ungirding their swords before entering his church, but one proud knight disdained to follow their example and indeed spurred his horse right up to the threshold of the church. "We have known so many churches of the saints," he spouted, "and the names of saints more outstanding than the name of St. Cuthbert, whose churches we have approached up to the threshold on horseback." As might be expected, his horse immediately threw him into the mud and he had to be helped to Cuthbert's shrine to beg mercy.[65] Another disrespectful military man received a more drastic punishment in an incident in Umbria. Outside the church of St. Ubaldus at Gubbio were two ancient elms, which, according to legend, had grown from the ox-goads of the carters who had transported the saint's body there. When, during the incessant wars of late medieval Italy, the place was garrisoned, a soldier used one of the elms for target practice, and, when the custodian of the place urged him, "Brother, do not shoot at these trees, for they stand here in memory of the saint," he gave him an insulting answer and continued to shoot. A terrible pain struck his arm, and, within an hour, he was dead.[66]

Other recurrent figures in hagiographic writing are those who did not believe in miracles. In the 1270s one sceptic expressed his opinions of the miraculous cures supposedly taking place at the tomb of the great canon lawyer Raymond of Peña-forte: "whoever is blind stays blind, and whoever is deaf stays deaf, and he who comes to his tomb lame goes away lame."[67] Even the great formative works of hagiography encountered scepticism. Sulpicius Severus had scarcely completed his *Life of St. Martin* before he was being accused of lying. "I shudder to say what I recently heard," reported his helpful friend Postumianus, "that some wretch was saying that you were a great liar in that book of yours."[68] Doubts about the wonders that Sulpicius Severus had recorded continued through the centuries: almost two hundred years after Martin's death, Gregory of Tours reported with disgust that "someone, filled, as I believe, with a wicked spirit," had maintained that some of the miracles in the Life of Martin were impossible.[69]

An attitude that is frequently ascribed to mockers and sceptics is a deep cynicism about the motives of those who were promoting a saint's cult. For instance, when the women who were spinning in the square at Utrecht saw a crowd going into the Dominican church to honour St. Peter Martyr, one of them supposedly commented, "See how these Preachers have found a new method to enrich themselves; in order to amass money and build big palaces, they have now found a new martyr!"[70] The Franciscans could be tarred with the same brush. When the cult of St. Louis of Toulouse was beginning to flourish at his tomb in the Franciscan convent at Marseilles, one

[65] Reginald of Durham, *Libellus de admirandis beati Cuthberti virtutibus* 127, pp. 272–73.

[66] *De sancto Ubaldo episcopo*; the incident is dated to 1482–1508 by the reference to Duke Guido (Guidobaldo da Montefeltro).

[67] BAV, Vat. lat. 6059, fol. 45.

[68] Sulpicius Severus, *Dialogi* 1. 26. 4, p. 208.

[69] Gregory of Tours, *De virtutibus sancti Martini* 2. 32, p. 620 (repr., 1969, p. 170).

[70] Ambrogio Taegio, *Vita sancti Petri martyris* 8. 60, p. 705.

of the local women expressed her scorn: "The Friars Minor have begun to treat him as a saint quickly, so that they can increase their profit from the offering of candles and donations."[71] Similarly, the Italian chronicler Salimbene observed that new cults were encouraged not only by the desire of the sick to be cured, but also by the appeal of novelties and by the ambition and greed of the clergy. He tells a story of a clove of garlic being passed off as the little toe of a saint.[72]

Sceptics thought that many so-called miracles were fraudulent, manipulated by cunning clergy. The lamps that burned before the body of St. Maximinus in Trier reputedly moved miraculously of their own accord, but one disrespectful visitor, with the revealing name Rusticus ("peasant"), said, on seeing this, "O, you deceivers! You say that St. Maximinus does this, and you do it yourselves by some trick."[73] One Franciscan friar said that he had difficulty believing in miracles, because "there had been many frauds about the working of miracles for the sake of gain," and he told the story of what had happened after the death of the saintly Friar Geoffrey of Oxford. A man had come to the friars and said he could make them rich if they wished. When asked how, the man explained that friar Geoffrey had a saintly reputation and that, if a few miracles happened at his tomb, then that would bring in a great income to the friars. When the friar asked how miracles could take place, unless God ordained it, the man had a ready answer: he had twenty-four men at his command who produced miracles whenever he wished and he had sent them to many places in England to produce miracles for a profit.[74]

These miracle fakers could, if detected, have the result of sowing doubt in people's minds about any report of a miracle. Wolfhere, the hagiographer of St. Godehard of Hildesheim, reports exactly this situation in the 1050s.[75] He describes certain "people of deceptive mind" who travelled from shrine to shrine, claiming to be blind or mute or incapacitated; they would then throw themselves about and punch the air, saying that they were cured and hoping to receive alms from the onlookers. "When they were caught red-handed in such trickery," says Wolfhere, "even the genuine miracles of the saints were dragged down into perilous disbelief by this deceit." People who experienced real miracles of healing were now thought to be lying, "not only by unbelievers but also by the faithful." Wolfhere goes on to relate only miracles of St. Godehard that were "certainly true," but he has already thrown light on a world of trickery and scepticism.

The fact that the cult of the saints was, in essence, the veneration of dead bodies, was also, for some people, the grounds for doubt and derision. When the relics of St. Bibianus (or Vivianus) were being taken in joyous procession to the abbey of Figeac in Aquitaine, a peasant woman, seeing the crowds and hearing the hymns, ran to her husband, who was working in the fields and urged him, "Take a short

[71] John de Orta, *Vita sancti Ludovici episcopi Tolosani* 66, p. 374 (AASS Augusti 3: 821).

[72] Salimbene, *Cronica*, pp. 502–3.

[73] *Vita sancti Maximini*, p. 24.

[74] BAV, Vat. lat. 4015, fols. 46–46v; Vauchez, *Sainthood*, p. 556.

[75] Wolfhere, *Vita sancti Godehardi episcopi posterior* 34, p. 216.

break, darling." His response to her suggestion that they go to see the relics "with the greatest devotion," was brusque: "Get back quickly to your business, since what you see are perhaps the bones of some dead person, which have been collected together and which foolish opinion venerates."[76] Relics were, indeed, "the bones of some dead person," but to say so in this way was to express distance and contempt.

The claim that a saint's body had been preserved incorrupt could also face scepticism. When the body of St. Olav of Norway was disinterred in 1031, a year after his death, and found supposedly incorrupt, the hostile Alfífa (Aelfgifu), member of a rival dynasty, commented sarcastically, "Mighty little do bodies decompose when buried in sand. It would not be the case if he had lain in earth." In this instance the issue was eventually decided by a form of trial by fire, although even this did not silence Alfífa's objections.[77] What is worth comment here is the naturalistic and materialistic nature of her objection: the state of the body is to be explained by how it was buried, not by its sanctity. In 1432 a Franciscan friar staying at Monticiano near Siena had the bad taste to assert publicly that the local saint, Antony, who had been a member of a different mendicant Order, the Augustinian Hermits, and was revered as incorrupt, "had a stinking body and was in no way worthy of veneration."[78] It is unlikely he would have advanced this view about a fellow-Franciscan.

But the stinking body was not only a stumbling block to faith. It could be regarded as an irrelevance to true religion. A woman in Prussia, when urged to visit the tomb of the saintly Dorothea of Montau, responded, "And how can a foul and stinking body help me? I wish to put my trust in my Lord Jesus Christ."[79] Here we are seeing not a robust and materialist irreligiously but a more austere and demanding, we might say a more puritanical, religiosity. While many people knew that corpses decayed and would not believe that they nevertheless maintained a special supernatural power, this woman was saying, instead, that only Jesus saves. As the German mystic, Meister Eckhart, had asked, "People, what is it that you are seeking in dead bones?"[80] The Protestant Reformation legitimized both attitudes. Hatred of the priests and their pretensions and their rituals, a general anti-sacramentalism for which there is much evidence in the Middle Ages, could ally with a principled critique of the medieval theology of intercession. The woman who put her trust only in Jesus might, in terms of temperament and conviction, be far from the surly peasant deriding "the bones of some dead person," but they were pushing in the same direction.

Lay satire of the late Middle Ages could convey an elaborately ironical attitude toward the cult of the saints, as so imaginatively expressed in the first story in Boccaccio's *Decameron* of the early 1350s. The main character is a figure nicknamed Ciappelletto, from Prato outside Florence, who is a perjurer, trouble-maker, mur-

[76] *Translatio et miracula sancti Viviani*, p. 261.

[77] Snorri Sturluson, *Heimskringla*, "St Olaf's Saga," 244, p. 528.

[78] *Vita et miracula Antonii Ordinis Eremitarum Augustini*, p. 834.

[79] *Miracula beatae Dorotheæ* 5. 21, p. 566.

[80] *Deutsche Mystiker des 14 Jhts.* 2, p. 599 (Meister Eckhart, *Spruch* 8).

derer, blasphemer, homosexual, robber, drunkard, and gambler. While on business in Burgundy, where he is not known, and staying in the house of two Florentine money-lenders there, he falls seriously ill. His hosts are troubled: it would be discreditable to throw him out; but he is so wicked that he would be unlikely to confess to a priest, and, if he died unconfessed, he would not be given Christian burial; and, even if he did confess, his sins were so great that no priest would absolve him, and again he would be thrown into a ditch when dead. The money-lenders fear this would be the excuse for the local people, who hated them, to riot and plunder their property. Ciappelletto, who has overheard their debate and knows he is dying, reassures them that he will not let this dire situation arise, and tells them to bring him the holiest friar they can find, which they do.

The dialogue that follows between the scoundrel and the unsuspecting friar is a masterpiece of comic effrontery. Ciappelletto acknowledges that he has not been to confession that week because of his illness; admits that he has always been a virgin; repents that after his regular weekly fast, he sometimes drank water with great appetite; confesses that he has given way to the sin of anger when he sees how young men nowadays do not go to church but haunt taverns. Increasingly impressed by his saintliness, the venerable friar asks if he wishes to be buried in the friars' church, which Ciappelletto agrees to, out of respect for their Order. After receiving the viaticum and extreme unction, he dies. The money-lenders, who have eavesdropped on this outrageously mendacious deathbed scene, send for the friars, and the brother who received Ciappelletto's confession persuades his prior to receive the body in solemn procession, in the hope of miracles. The following day the people assemble and the friar preaches on the dead man's virtues, his virginity and his devotion. Ciappelletto is at once regarded as a saint: the crowd kiss his body and take his clothes as relics, and after his interment in the church, light candles, say prayers and hang wax ex-votos at his tomb. He is now "St. Ciappelletto."

The story is meant to be comic. The gullibility of the friar, and of the ordinary people, is depicted with cool mockery. The completely amoral Ciappelletto is shown in control of events. He decides on this final piece of blasphemous irreligiosity because, as he says, he has affronted God so often and so deeply that one last outrage will not bother him. What the tale assumes is that a saint's cult can be completely spurious, a creation of fraud and credulity. And that doubt could extend to any cult—who knew whether the bones within the shrine were not in fact those of a bold impostor? It is not surprising that copies of the *Decameron* were supposedly amongst the things burned in the "Bonfire of the Vanities" organized by the puritan friar Savonarola in 1497.[81]

[81] *La vita del beato Ieronimo Savonarola* (formerly attributed to Pacifico Burlamacchi) 40, p. 130.

CHAPTER 14

Policing the Saints

For a book "originally written in the form of a thesis for the degree of Bachelor of Divinity," Eric Kemp's *Canonization and Authority in the Western Church*, published in 1948, has proved of remarkably enduring value, and one of the reasons for its permanent importance is the insight so pithily conveyed in its title: canonization was an aspect of authority. This is true even when one extends the concept of "canonization" beyond the specific form of papal canonization as found in the later medieval centuries. The right to recognize sanctity enhanced the status and power of its possessor and, from the earliest days, ecclesiastical authorities sought to control and manage all aspects of the cult of the saints, as in the parallel case of pilgrimage, where, it has been observed, "the hierarchy was in favour of the interest shown in holy places, but it sought to channel it, or at least keep it under control."[82]

One of the earliest pieces of ecclesiastical legislation about the cult of the saints comes from the Council of Carthage in 401:

> No credence shall be given to any martyr's shrine, unless the body or relics are there, or the origin is attested by a trustworthy tradition of the neighbourhood or in a *Passion*. The altars that are being set up everywhere on the basis of the dreams or empty, so-called, revelations of certain men, are to be utterly condemned.[83]

This ruling suggests a world of pullulating activity, threatening, in the eyes of the Catholic establishment, to lapse into religious anarchy. Individual dreams and visions were, in the eyes of these authorities, no basis for a saintly cult.

This decree, hammered out by a council of embattled bishops in North Africa in the first years of the fifth century, was to have an important part in the long history of ecclesiastical attempts to control the cult of the saints. Its influence is clear in the legislation issued during the reign of Charlemagne four hundred years later. In the so-called *Admonitio generalis* of 789 the monarch ordered that "The spurious names of martyrs and the memorials of uncertain saints should not be venerated."[84] One of the canons of the Council of Frankfurt, held five years later, is: "No new saints shall be revered or invoked nor shrines to them raised by the roadside, but they only are to be venerated in church who are set apart by the authority of *Passions* or by merit of life."[85] These rulings were transmitted to the canon law collections of the eleventh and twelfth centuries, and hence became a standard part of the legal training of the higher clergy.[86] Their assumption was that bishops would have the last word. The same assumption can be found in more local legislation, like that of the Council of

[82] Maraval, *Lieux saints et pèlerinages d'Orient*, p. 47.

[83] *Concilia Africae, a. 345–a. 525*, pp. 204–5.

[84] *Capitularia regum Francorum* 1, no. 22, p. 56 (*Admonitio generalis*, cl. 42).

[85] *Concilia aevi Karolini* 1/1, p. 170, no. 19, cl. 42.

[86] Burchard, *Decretum* 3. 54, col. 683; Ivo of Chartres, *Decretum* 3. 57, col. 210; Gratian, *Decretum* 3 (de consecratione) 1. 26, cols. 1300–1301.

Westminster of 1102: "Let no one, through unheard-of boldness, treat as holy any bodies of the dead, or springs, or other things (as we have known has happened), without permission of the bishop."[87]

A new note of papal aggrandizement comes in during the late twelfth and early thirteenth century. The papal letter *Audivimus*, of 1171–72 (discussed more fully earlier, pp. 58–59), ruled about a supposed saint, "you may not revere him as a saint without the permission of the Roman Church," while at the Fourth Lateran Council of 1215 a canon was issued that stated unequivocally, "No one should presume to venerate in public newly discovered relics unless they have first been given the approval of the Roman pontiff."[88] The Papal Decretals of 1234, the first official codification of western canon law, incorporated both *Audivimus* and the ruling of the Fourth Lateran Council.[89] The Greek Church never developed an equivalent to papal canonization, largely because it had no pope, but recognition by the "Great Church," that is, Hagia Sophia in Constantinople, meant, in a society dominated so much by its capital as Byzantium, something like official acknowledgement.

As always, it was one thing to declare the law, another to enforce it. The bishops of the early Middle Ages fought hard to maintain their authority over the cult of the saints. It has been pointed out that translations of martyrs' bodies into the new urban churches of the late antique period not only integrated martyr cult and communal Eucharistic worship, but also ensured that martyr cult would "remain safely under clerical control."[90] St. Martin, bishop of Tours in the late fourth century, confronted just the problem described in the canon of the Council of Carthage, that of a dubious shrine. Outside the city there was a tomb. Local tradition said it was a martyr-grave, and earlier bishops had placed an altar there. Martin had his doubts and asked the older clergy about the name of the martyr, since "ancestral memory had handed down nothing certain." Eventually he went to the spot itself, and prayed to God to reveal who the occupant of the grave was. A shadowy figure emerged from the grave. I am no martyr, he confessed, but a brigand. Martin ordered the altar destroyed, and "so freed the people from the error of that superstition."[91]

More threatening yet than such misguided local cults were the disputes over sanctity that arose from schisms and parties within the Christian community. From its early days, Christianity was marked by factions and disputes. Paul's epistles are full of warnings against schism, while the First Epistle of Clement of c. 96 refers to "jealousy and malice, strife and sedition" among the Christians of Corinth.[92] The emperor Julian was of the opinion "that no beasts are as dangerous to man as most Christians are to each other in their savagery."[93] These differences sometimes resulted

[87] *Councils and Synods with Other Documents Relating to the English Church* 1, part II, p. 678 (cl. 27).

[88] *Conciliorum oecumenicorum decreta*, p. 263 (cl. 62).

[89] *Decretales Gregorii IX*, 3. 45. 1, *Audivimus*, 3. 45. 2, *Quum ex eo*, col. 650.

[90] Markus, *The End of Ancient Christianity*, p. 145.

[91] Sulpicius Severus, *Vita sancti Martini* 11 (1, p. 276).

[92] Clement of Rome, *Epistola ad Corinthios* 3, p. 102.

[93] Ammianus Marcellinus, *Res gestae* 22. 5 (3, p. 99).

in long-term and widespread divisions. Movements such as the Christian Gnosticism of the second and third centuries, or the Arianism of the fourth and subsequent centuries, represented genuine and serious alternatives to the tradition that called itself catholic and orthodox. Even groups of more limited geographical range, such as the Donatists of north Africa in the fourth and fifth centuries, could produce rival hierarchies, with their own bishops, congregations and churches, sometimes next door to the Catholics. And these "heretical" bodies, as their opponents termed them, viewed themselves as the true Church, and might have their own saints and martyrs.

The Donatists, in particular, laid claim to the Christian tradition of martyrdom, since they split from their fellow Christians because they were unwilling to have dealings with anyone who had compromised under persecution. They denounced those who had handed over Christian scriptures when the Roman authorities demanded them, and would not accept their ordinations as legitimate. For well over two centuries, these rigorists lived alongside the Catholics in north Africa. Their opponents charged them with extreme practices, such as encouraging suicide, and with reverencing those who killed themselves as martyrs. A council at Carthage, which was held in the 340s, denied such people "the name of martyrs," while Augustine berated those who recovered the bodies of these suicides, carefully preserved their blood and venerated their tombs.[94]

The first people to be executed for heresy by the Roman state were the Spanish bishop Priscillian and four followers, who were put to death in 385. A martyr cult sprang up at once:

> His adherents, who had previously honoured him as a saint, afterwards began to venerate him as a martyr. The bodies of those executed were brought back to Spain and their funerals were celebrated with great ceremony. It was even regarded as highly devout to swear by Priscillian.[95]

Orthodox churchmen referred to "the false martyrdoms of the Priscillianists," but for Priscillian's followers they were simply saints and martyrs.[96] Such disputes over "false martyrs" found an echo in the canons of the Council in Trullo, held in the imperial palace in Constantinople in 692, which condemned "martyrologies that have been falsely concocted by enemies of the truth" and ordered them to be burned.[97] It was a fundamental aspect of ecclesiastical authority to be able to determine who was a saint and who not.

No one truly knows who is saved and who is damned, so the question naturally arose of whether all the people that the Church said were saints really were saints. And, conversely, perhaps some ordinary Christian, unrecognized by the authorities,

[94] *Concilia Africae, a. 345–a. 525*, p. 4; Augustine, *Sermones post Maurinos reperti*, p. 539 (Sermones e codice Guelferbytano 28. 5).

[95] Sulpicius Severus, *Chronica* 2. 51. 4, p. 346 (PL 20: 158).

[96] Augustine, *Contra mendacium* 5. 9, p. 481 (PL 40: 524); Chadwick, *Priscillian*, p. 237.

[97] *Conciliorum oecumenicorum generaliumque decreta* 1, p. 271 (canon 63). Treated briefly by Herren, "Book Burning as Purification," pp. 215–16.

might be one of the blessed in heaven, whose prayers could help those on earth. This was even acknowledged by Pope Innocent IV: "we do not deny that anyone is allowed to offer prayers to any dead person whom he believed to be a good man, asking him to intercede with him before God."[98] Whether a papal decision on canonization might be wrong, was a disputed issue. Some theologians argued that "it is not possible for the Church to make a mistake in such matters," but others thought it quite possible.[99] But there was clearly the fear that, unless the firm hand of the papacy were in control, things might run riot, and then "the uneducated and ignorant populace and the unlettered crowd, deceived by various frauds or perhaps by diabolical trickery, might venerate someone as a saint who is not a saint."[100]

Sometimes the authorities decided on the repression of a cult. The simplest way to do this was to put guards around the tomb, as happened in the case of some of the "political martyrs" of late medieval England (earlier, p. 182). Another example of politically inspired repression can be found in the case of Charles of Blois. Charles was killed in battle in 1364 during a prolonged civil war between rival claimants to the duchy of Brittany, Charles being backed by the king of France, and his enemy by the king of England. Charles's cult was clearly seen to have political implications, for some years after his death it was reported that his image in the Franciscan church at Dinant had been covered with whitewash "at the command of the present duke of Brittany at the suggestion of the English." When this image supposedly bled real blood, the wondering bystanders were upbraided by some of the English present, who served the victorious duke, Charles's rival: "false peasants, you believe he is a saint but you lie, wicked peasants, by St. George he is not a saint!"[101]

The creation of the Inquisition in the thirteenth century gave the ecclesiastical authorities a new and powerful weapon to police saintly cult.[102] Sometimes even light-hearted banter might land someone in trouble, as in the case of the southern French miller William "of the Mill." When some women came to his mill and wished "that God and St. Martin would give good milling," William replied, "I am St. William and will do the milling." This not very witty remark brought William before the Inquisition.[103]

[98] Non negamus quoniam cuilibet liceat alicui defuncto quem credebat bonum virum porrigere preces ut pro eo intercedat ad Deum: Innocent IV, *Apparatus super V libros decretalium*, ad X. 3. 45. 1, *Audivimus*; followed by Hostiensis, *Lectura siue Apparatus super quinque libris Decretalium*, ad X. 3. 45. 1, *Audivimus*.

[99] Ecclesia in talibus errare non potest: Thomas Aquinas, *Quodlibet* 9, q. 8 s. c. 1, p. 493; see Schenk, *Die Unfehlbarkeit des Papstes in der Heiligsprechung*.

[100] Pellegrini, "La sainteté au XVe siècle," p. 324, citing Archivio di Stato de l'Aquila, MS S108, fol. 12v (from the time of Eugenius IV).

[101] *Monuments du procès de canonisation du Bienheureux Charles de Blois*, p. 283 (witness 119); see the discussion in Héry, "Le culte de Charles de Blois: résistances et réticences."

[102] Several examples are analyzed in Peterson, "Contested Sanctity: Disputed Saints, Inquisitors, and Communal Identity in Northern Italy."

[103] BnF, Collection Languedoc Doat 21, fol. 227v (1241, Beaucaire, Lauzerte [Tarn-et-Garonne]).

Since the ecclesiastical authorities insisted that they should make the ultimate decision about who was a saint and who was not, they were especially alarmed when faced with sustained opposition on this point. A particularly acute crisis of this kind developed in the south of France in the early fourteenth century.[104] The Franciscan Order was riven by controversy about how far the friars had diverged from the intentions of their founder, St. Francis. Some held that Franciscans were committed to owning no property and living a life of uncompromising poverty, others that various accommodations were quite legitimate. This issue of principle rapidly became entangled with the issue of authority. If the leaders of the Order, or, even more awkwardly, the pope himself, delivered rulings on these matters, were all the friars bound to obey, even against their conscience? Conflict and controversy eventually turned to violence. In the spring of 1318 four radical Franciscans were burned at the stake. In the following years repression continued, aimed both at the recalcitrant friars (the "Spiritual Franciscans") and their lay supporters—the Beguins as they are termed (distinct from the"beguines" mentioned earlier, p. 72). Inquisition records reveal a clandestine network of resistance in the south of France at this time, and one aspect of this resistance was the veneration of the executed friars and Beguins as saints.

A large number of Beguins, both men and women, were burned at Lunel, 8 kilometres (13 miles) east of Montpellier, in autumn 1321. The authorities were clearly not vigilant enough to prevent sympathisers descending on the scene next day in the pursuit of relics of the dead. Martin of Saint Antony later confessed that he and others "came to the place where they were burned and several of them were still almost intact." They broke up the body of Esclaramonde Durban, one of the executed heretics, in order to place the remains in a sack, and Martin himself took her heart or kidney (perhaps indistinguishable by this point). He chose Esclaramonde because of her goodness, and kept the body organ at home, where visitors would reverence it and sometimes request to be given it or part of it, although Martin always refused these requests.[105]

The charred fragments of the Beguins of Lunel began to circulate in the region. Two brothers of Esclaramonde Durban, who had been present at her execution, received some of her bones and flesh, which they kept in their houses. One of them, Bernard, said he did this "out of the love and affection which he had towards his sister," while the other, Raymond, claimed "that he had hoped his sister and the others of her sect who had been condemned and burned might at some time be deemed good people."[106] Fragments of the martyred Beguins were being shown in a sack in a hostelry in Montpellier.[107]

[104] Manselli, *Spirituels et Béguins du Midi*; Burr, *The Spiritual Franciscans*; Elliott, *Proving Woman: Female Spirituality and Inquisitional Culture*, pp. 173–77; Burnham, *So Great a Light, So Great a Smoke: The Beguin Heretics of Languedoc*.

[105] BnF, Collection Languedoc Doat 28, fols. 16–16v.

[106] Ibid., fols. 12–12v, 27–27vv.

[107] Ibid., fol. 15.

When word arrived that the inquisitors were seeking out people who kept relics of the Beguins, some of them panicked. Jacoba Amorosia, who had been given the jaw-bone of a woman burned at Lunel, hastily threw it into a pig-sty.[108] One man, Berengar Rocha, gave an interesting explanation to the Inquisition why he had disposed of the relic he had possessed.

> When he was on the way back from Lunel, a certain man gave him a piece of the flesh of those who were burned in Lunel, and he accepted it out of the devotion that he had at that time towards the heretics, on account of their holy life and conduct . . . he placed that piece of flesh in a pomegranate rind on a table in his house, and kept it for two or three months. When he had heard from others that it could not decay, he looked at the piece of flesh after that time and, seeing that it had rotted, he threw it into a field outside his house.[109]

Berengar's explanation is partly designed to exonerate himself, but also reveals the existence of a strong general assumption that holy relics were immune from the usual process of bodily decay.

Several suspects questioned by the Inquisition asserted that either they themselves or people they had spoken with regarded the executed Beguins as saints and martyrs.[110] One of the women burned at Lunel, Astruga of Lodève, was being termed "Saint Astruga."[111] The testimony of the renegade priest, Bernard Peirotas, is exceptionally illuminating on this point.[112] He had seen and venerated Esclaramonde's heart, and he believed that she and the other Beguins and friars who had been executed were victims of a malicious persecution by the religious orders. He had attended the burning of some Beguins at Béziers in January 1322. Next day some people brought to him remains of those executed, which he placed in a sack, treating them "reverently like the relics of holy martyrs." He also saw the clothes of the burned Beguins, which some devotees had purchased from the executioner. Because he was a priest, Bernard could go further in his devotion than others. He had said an Office of the Martyrs for those executed, and also a special commemoration for them. When talking about them, he had termed them "martyrs and saints," and had seen at Béziers "a parchment book in which were written all the names of the Beguins who had been burned" (such lists survive).[113] He had seen a letter exhorting their supporters to go to Lunel to see "the soldiers or martyrs fighting the good fight." This is exactly how the Christian cult of the saints had begun a thousand years earlier. In

[108] Ibid., fol. 13v. The reading *maxilla* ("jaw-bone") is more likely than *mamilla* ("breast").

[109] Ibid., fols. 14v–15.

[110] For example, ibid., fol. 14.

[111] Ibid., fol. 20v.

[112] Ibid., fols. 21–27.

[113] Puig i Oliver, "Notes sobre el manuscript del *Directorium Inquisitorum* de Nicolau Eimeric conservat a la Biblioteca de l'Escorial," pp. 538–39; Burnham, *So Great a Light, So Great a Smoke: The Beguin Heretics of Languedoc*, p. 82 n. 94. The practice of keeping such martyrologies is condemned by Eymerich, *Directorium inquisitorum* 2. q. 15, p. 284.

fact the Inquisitors explicitly condemned the Beguins' claim that their martyrs "were of no less merit in the eyes of God than St. Lawrence and St. Vincent."[114]

Many of the Spiritual Franciscans and Beguins of southern France were inspired by the ideas of Peter John Olivi, a Franciscan theologian of an earlier generation, whose tomb at Narbonne became a focus for their activities, as well as a healing shrine of the traditional kind. They regarded him as "an uncanonized saint."[115] Pope John XXII, the most vigorous enemy of the Spiritual Franciscans and Beguins, gave instructions that his body should be removed and the cult suppressed. According to one account

> The lord pope John had the bones of brother Peter John exhumed and had everything, the wax images as well as the cloths that the simple people had brought to his tomb, burned publicly at Narbonne. But others say that, although the bones were exhumed, they were not burned with everything else, but were taken to Avignon and thrown into the Rhone at night.[116]

Whether the eventual fate of Olivi's bones was fire or water, there is no doubt that the history of the suppression of the Spirituals and Beguins shows how determined the ecclesiastical authorities were that the lines they drew between heretics and saints should be enforced. Heretical relics, heretical liturgy and heretical shrines had to be wiped out.

[114] Bernard Gui, *Practica inquisitionis heretice pravitatis* 5. 4, p. 270; Eymerich, *Directorium inquisitorum* 2. q. 15, p. 283.

[115] Bernard Gui, *Practica inquisitionis heretice pravitatis* 5. 4, p. 272; cf. BnF, Collection Languedoc Doat 28, fols. 190v, 194, 205, 236v, 237v, 241, 242.

[116] Eymerich, *Directorium inquisitorum* 2. q. 26, comment. 51, p. 313; Bernard Gui says Olivi's body was removed and hidden away in 1318 and there are various opinions about where it is, *Practica inquisitionis heretice pravitatis* 5. 4. 12, p. 287; Angelo Clareno says that it was burned "as people say (*ut fertur*)," *Expositio regulae fratrum minorum*, epilogue, pp. 233–34; see Burr, *The Spiritual Franciscans*, pp. 211–12.

CHAPTER 15

Reflections

Saints and Gods

Saints were human beings, and this implies two things they were not: they were not immortals, like the gods of ancient Greece and Rome, and so they shared humanity and mortality with the human mortals who prayed to them; and they were not purely natural forces, like the trees and springs and mountains revered by many pre-Christian and non-Christian worshippers.

That the saint was a human being like us had some fundamental consequences. Every saint had a life-story here on earth, with parents, family, a local community, and all the incidents that a purely secular biography also offers. Moreover, there was the possibility, or even probability, of there being living saints amongst us now. Although there is a sense in which sainthood is a retrospective judgment, applied only to the dead (like the ancient saying, "Call no man happy until he is dead"), logic demands that some living people must be heading for sainthood, and identifying them was a natural interest for sufferers seeking miraculous cures or for communities alert for prestigious patrons. This dynamic did not operate in the same way in the case of gods or holy springs. Yet there were also similarities.

The heart of the Christian cult of the saints was the invocation of powerful invisible beings, human in form. Described in this way, is there anything to distinguish such cult from the devotion shown to the gods of Greece and Rome, or, for that matter, to anthropomorphic deities anywhere? There are real resemblances. The ancient gods, like the saints, had their shrines, to which one could go to seek assistance or advice with appropriate rituals, and their annual festivals; they might appear in dreams or visions, to give instructions; they could provide help in battle; and they had demands to make of worshippers as well as aid to offer. Like the saints, the gods were numerous, and often provided special patronage either for a city or state, or for a particular group—Athena was the patron goddess of Athens, Artemis Agrotera the patron goddess of hunters.

Similarities between deities and saints are particularly strong in the case of the cult of the pagan heroes, rather than that of the Olympian gods, since the heroes were human beings and had tombs here on earth. Heroes were either the offspring of gods and humans, or they were humans deified after death (or both). Crucially, unlike Zeus, Athena, and the like, they had lived on earth as humans, had undergone death, and had an earthly tomb, like Christian saints. Their tombs were often inside the city, unlike the tombs of ordinary people (although many hero-shrines were in fact cenotaphs, without human remains).[1]

A good example of the way an honoured human could become a hero is the case of the Spartan general Brasidas. After he was killed in the defence of Amphipolis in 422 BC, he was buried in the city, in front of the marketplace. The men of Amphipolis put an enclosure around his tomb and, every year thereafter, made sacrifices and offerings to him, and honoured him with games.[2] The special tomb and the annual commemoration are common points of hero cult and saintly cult. Likewise, reading Plutarch's account of how the cult of the hero Theseus had begun in Athens, it is hard not to be reminded of the hundreds of discoveries and translations of relics that took place in medieval Christendom. One impetus for the Athenians to honour the long-dead Theseus as a hero was his appearance on their side at the battle of Marathon, fought against the Persians in 490 BC. They were also advised by an oracle from the priestess of Pythian Apollo "to raise up the bones of Theseus, to put them in a place of honour and guard them." It took them some time to locate the bones, which were buried in an Aegean island, but eventually, guided by an eagle, they found them and brought them back in honour to Athens. "And now," says Plutarch, "he lies in the middle of the city," receiving a great sacrifice annually.[3]

Pagans themselves from the earliest days expressed the idea that the cult of the saints was simply an equivalent to the worship of the gods. The very first martyr account mentions the fear that Christians might worship the martyrs in the same way they did Christ. After Polycarp's execution, there was an attempt to prevent the Christians obtaining his remains, "lest," it was argued, "abandoning the crucified one, they begin to worship this man."[4] Similarly, during the Diocletianic persecution, some martyrs were exhumed and thrown into the sea, in order to prevent people worshipping them in their tombs and treating them as gods.[5] From the pagan perspective, there was nothing unlikely in this strange sect, which already worshipped one executed criminal, from taking up others.

Christians had to confront the pagan claim that their cult of the martyrs was simply the worship of another set of gods. Augustine mentions "those who consider that the pagans worshipped the gods in temples, while we worship the dead in their tombs," and he tried to clarify the difference between the cult of the Christian martyrs and the cult of pagan gods. "We do not regard the martyrs as gods," he wrote, and, while he recognized that both Greco-Roman paganism and the Christian martyr-cult of his own day had shrines, priests and altars, he insisted that martyr churches were built as memorials to dead men, not as temples to gods, and that the Christian altar was not the site of sacrifices to the martyrs but of sacrifice to God

[1] There is a summary of the main features of hero-cult in Ekroth, "The Cult of Heroes."

[2] Thucydides, *Peloponnesian War* 5. 11.

[3] Plutarch, *Theseus* 35–36.

[4] *Passio Polycarpi* 17, p. 14.

[5] Eusebius, *Historia ecclesiastica* 8. 6. 6 (3, p. 13).

(that is, the Eucharist).[6] Cyril of Alexandria, writing around 435, reiterated this point: "We do not say that the holy martyrs are gods nor have we been accustomed to revere them with divine worship [*latreutikōs*] but only relatively and with honour [*timetikōs*]."[7] The first term derives from *latria*, originally meaning "servitude," the latter from *timê*, meaning "honour."

Even so, the evident parallel between martyr cult and the cult of pagan gods and deified heroes was taken up by sceptics and anti-clerical thinkers of modern times as a stick to beat the Christians. In his *Natural History of Religion* (section X) the great Enlightenment philosopher David Hume argued, in a rather partisan way,

> The heroes in paganism correspond exactly to the saints in popery and holy dervises (that is, dervishes) in Mahometanism. The place of Hercules, Theseus, Hector, Romulus, is now supplied by Dominic, Francis, Anthony, and Benedict. Instead of the destruction of monsters, the subduing of tyrants, the defence of our native country; whippings and fastings, cowardice and humility, abject submission and slavish obedience, are become the means of obtaining celestial honours among mankind.

Hume's bold claim that the ancient heroes "correspond exactly" to Catholic saints is somewhat diluted by his next point, that the qualities the two groups exhibit are quite different: valour and patriotism have been replaced by self-mortification and abasement. Hume's words suggest he would have agreed with Nietzsche's view of Christianity as a "slave morality" (*Sklavenmoral*), but he hovers somewhat in his desire to denigrate Christian cult both by equating it with its pagan predecessor and by stressing its far less admirable values.

The issue was important, too, during the French Third Republic in the debates between anticlericals and supporters of ecclesiastical power. A book published in Paris in 1907, with the fighting title *The Saints Successors to the Gods*, started with the forthright statement, "the cult of the martyrs and the saints is of pagan origin."[8] This was only one of numerous publications attempting to denigrate, or at least relativize, the cult of the saints by painting it as merely a Christianized version of the worship of the old gods. More, and massive, ammunition was provided for the French anticlericals by the appearance in 1908 of the French translation of Ernst Lucius's posthumous volume on the origins of the cult of the saints, published originally in German.[9] Lucius's viewpoint is well expressed in some of the book's sub-headings: "the cult of the saints as Christian hero-cult"; "the healing martyrs as heirs of the

[6] Augustine, *De civitate dei* 22. 10; 8. 26 (1, p. 246; 2, p. 828).

[7] Cyril of Alexandria, *Contra Julianum* 6, col. 812; further discussion in Maraval, *Lieux saints et pèlerinages d'Orient*, pp. 145–48.

[8] Saintyves, *Les saints successeurs des dieux*, p. 2; Saintyves was the pseudonym of the French folklorist and publisher Émile Nourry; the book bears the imprint Émile Nourry! Numerous publications of this press were placed on the Index.

[9] Lucius, *Die Anfänge des Heiligenkults in der christlichen Kirche*; Lucius, *Les origines du culte des saints dans l'Eglise chrétienne*.

pagan healing gods"; "Mary as heiress of the ancient deities." The tradition of Hume and the anticlerical writers is not dead. Lucius is cited with approval in a publication of 1997 that has as the subject of one of its chapters, "the reception by the church of pagan acts and practices along with pagan converts."[10]

One of the protagonists in this debate, on the moderate Catholic side, was the Jesuit Hippolyte Delehaye (1859–1941), a founding father of the modern study of the cult of the saints. Delehaye was willing freely to admit the numerous parallels between the cult of the ancient heroes and the cult of the Christian saints, indeed amassing a large number of examples before concluding:

> When one has demonstrated among the Greeks a cult which, in all its details, recalls that of the saints, with its tombs, translations, inventions, visions and dubious or forged relics, what further parallels could one demand, in order to establish that the cult of the saints is nothing but a pagan survival?[11]

He immediately goes on, however, to insist that the cult of the saints derived not from the cult of the heroes but from the cult of the martyrs. While acknowledging, even stressing, resemblances between heroes and saints, Delehaye denied any dependence.[12]

It is indeed important to distinguish the question of actual continuity from that of functional similarity. Proving the direct descent of a holy figure, a site or a practice is a different matter from pointing to general features of a cult that look alike. Continuity of site is the simplest issue, for there are well-attested cases of shrines to Christian saints replacing temples to pagan gods, often as a conscious policy.[13] The relics of St. Cyrus and St. John, for example, were brought to the temple of Isis at Menouthis, which continued as a pilgrimage centre, now with Christian saints rather than a pagan goddess at its heart.[14] Gregory the Great instructed the missionaries to the Anglo-Saxons to preserve the pagan temples, removing the idols and consecrating them with holy water, altars, and relics.[15] But such instances do not, of course, support the critical Enlightenment or anti-clerical view that the cult of the saints was simply pagan cult in new clothing, since it was entirely apparent to Christian contemporaries that this was a triumphant replacement of the old (and to their mind, false) with the new (and to their mind, true). A poignant example is the church of St. Gereon in Cologne, where excavation revealed, in the foundations of one of the pillars, the broken fragments of an altar to Isis, "she of the countless names (*myrionymo*)." In a hollow in the surface of the altar were the ashes of the

[10] MacMullen, *Christianity and Paganism in the Fourth to Eighth Centuries*, title of chapter 4.

[11] Delehaye, *Les légendes hagiographiques*, p. 156.

[12] On Delehaye, see Joassart, "*Hippolyte Delehaye*"; for general context, Müller, *Gemeinschaft und Verehrung der Heiligen: geschichtliche-systematische Grundlegung der Hagiologie*, pp. 168–78.

[13] For example, Maraval, *Lieux saints et pèlerinages d'Orient*, pp. 53–55.

[14] Fernández Marcos, *Los Thaumata de Sofronio: Contribución al estudio de la incubatio cristiana*, pp. 13–19.

[15] Bede, *Historia ecclesiastica* 1. 30, p. 106.

last sacrifice.[16] Gereon had indeed replaced Isis, but by overthrowing her, not by a clandestine substitution.

The cases of actual continuity between a pagan god and a Christian saint are few and uncertain. It is, in any case, unclear what "continuity" would mean. Apart from continuity of cult site, it could refer to the name, to the attributes or to some aspects of cult, for example, the date of the festival or feast-day. Efforts were made by writers like Ernst Lucius to show that "the martyrs who received the highest veneration were those that people had endowed with properties and capacities stemming from the inheritance of an ancient deity."[17] In Delehaye's ironic formulation the anticlerical proponents of continuity were trying "to show that some famous saint was nothing but a god in disguise, a refugee from the pantheon dressed in second-hand Christian clothes."[18]

A fascinating story that does deal with the issue is found among the miracles of Cosmas and Damian, and involves the identification of the saints with the pagan gods Castor and Pollux.[19] According to this account the pagan population of Constantinople, hearing of the miraculous cures at the Cosmidion, "invoked the glorious servants of Christ, Cosmas, and Damian, under the names of Castor and Pollux." A pagan, suffering from a severe disease, came to the shrine, thinking he was appealing to those gods. Cosmas and Damian ignored him. Eventually they gave him their attention: "Is it to us that you have come, friend? Do you refer to us as Castor and Pollux?" Once the saints have identified themselves, the suppliant promises to convert, and is immediately cured. It is worth noting the seamless transition here, from supernatural healing by twins deemed to be sons of Zeus, to supernatural healing by twins deemed to be early Christian saints. It is undoubtedly a case of Christian saints with certain features taking on the role of gods with the same features, but it is something carefully recorded by a hagiographer who sees nothing here that will undermine faith in the saints.

Outside the Greco-Roman world there is a saint who has often been seen simply as a version (in some sense) of a pagan deity. This is Brigid of Ireland. The identification of saint and goddess relies partly on an entry in *Cormac's Glossary*, of the early tenth century, which, under the heading "Brigid," reads "a poetess, daughter of the Dagda . . . the goddess whom poets adored."[20] It is also certain that the Celtic tribe of the Brigantes, who lived in what is now northern England, revered a goddess called Brigantia. Philologists agree that the names Brigid and Brigantia both derive from a word for "high" but this does not establish very much. Since there is an early Life of Brigid that describes her in purely human terms (see earlier, pp. 33–35), it

[16] Gerkan, "St. Gereon in Köln," p. 215; the last use can be dated by a coin of 346 found in the ashes; the columns were probably those of a mausoleum, later incorporated into the church: *Topographie chrétienne des cités de la Gaule* 12: *Province ecclésiastique de Cologne*, p. 54.

[17] Lucius, *Die Anfänge des Heiligenkults in der christlichen Kirche*, p. 202.

[18] Delehaye, *Les origines du culte des martyrs*, p. 405.

[19] *Miracula Cosmae et Damiani* 9, pp. 113–17.

[20] *Sanas Chormaic. Cormac's Glossary*, p. 23.

might be the case that a woman and a goddess had the same name. Alternatively, the saint may have acquired some "goddess-like" features—by the twelfth century, at latest, a perpetual fire burned at her mother church at Kildare, tended exclusively by women.[21] It has been argued of her later hagiographers, who elaborated this side of Brigid's image, that, "They were not transforming a goddess into a saint. They were casting a saint as a goddess."[22]

The attempt to link individual saints to pagan predecessors is of limited value, partly because so many cults can, in fact, be traced back to known historical individuals, partly because the concept of continuity itself is unclear. What is certain, is that there are large general similarities between the Christian cult of the saints and the cult of the gods, both in the ancient world and elsewhere. It is hard to look at a picture of Isis suckling her baby, the infant Horus, without thinking of the Virgin Mary and the Christ child, or to see Anubis weighing the souls of the dead and not ponder the similarities with the archangel Michael doing the same job (figure 15.1). And these similarities are not accidental: the former assumes that God (or a god) has a mother, the latter that people are judged—weighed in the balance—after death. These are the common beliefs of the two different religions, so common that an archaeologist coming across an unlabelled image of the Virgin Mary in Egypt might have trouble distinguishing it from an image of Isis.[23]

The functional equivalences between polytheistic pagan religion and the cult of the saints were many: the existence of numerous local patrons, who could be invoked at a shrine; the miracles of healing and punishment; the annual festivities. The ex-votos in the form of wax or metal body parts at the shrine of a Christian saint would not surprise devotees of the old gods. The Etruscans and Romans gave ex-votos of pottery and marble in the shape of intestines, rib-cages and human torsos open to reveal the entrails.[24] Excavation has discovered almost 200 wooden votive objects in the form of various body parts at a Celtic shrine at the source of the river Seine, dedicated to the goddess Sequana.[25] Ex-votos in the Greek temples also included painted panels, sometimes showing the family that had commissioned them, as in the rare surviving painting dedicated to the nymphs of Pitsa (near Corinth) and dated to around 530 BC.[26] A parishioner whisked from a church in Renaissance Italy to a temple in ancient Greece would quickly deduce what kind of building he was in (and the opposite is also true).

If we believe the accounts of the past, one thing that the saints did, and did for tens of thousands of sufferers, was to cure illness. If you are desperately sick or think you are dying, what could be more welcome than an invisible friend with the power

[21] Gerald of Wales, *Topographia hibernica* 2. 34–36, pp. 120–21.

[22] Bitel, "St. Brigit of Ireland."

[23] Tran Tam Tinh, *Isis Lactans*; Mathews and Muller, "Isis and Mary in Early Icons."

[24] Tabanelli, *Gli ex-voto poliviscerali etruschi e romani*.

[25] Deyts, *Les bois sculptés des sources de la Seine*.

[26] Muthmann, *Mutter und Quelle. Studien zur Quellenverehrung in Altertum und Mittelalter*, pp. 95–96 and pl. 14.1; Van Straten, "Gifts for the Gods," pp. 83–84.

15.1. Limestone figure of Isis suckling Horus (Harpocrates), Ptolomeie, h. 35 cm. London, British Museum. © The Trustees of the British Museum.

to heal you? The search for healing has, historically, led to the temples of the gods and the shrines of the saints as much as to the doctors and hospitals—and often still does. Some Greek and Roman gods had a reputation for healing, most notably Asclepius. Statues of Asclepius represent him as a bearded man, often with his symbol, a snake. Indeed, when the Romans were suffering from a plague in the third century BC, they sent to Greece for Asclepius, whose spirit was brought back by ship in the form of a snake.[27] A snake entwined around a staff is still a symbol of the medical profession. Reports of seventy cures and other miraculous events are recorded on inscriptions at the shrine of Asclepius at Epidaurus in Greece.[28] There are cases of cures of blindness, paralysis, even baldness, and several suppliants came to pray for children. There are also occasional punishment miracles, like the story of the fishmonger who promised a tenth of his profits to Asclepius but failed to pay and saw his fish struck by lightning and burned up. The usual practice is for the worshipper to sleep at the shrine, and then to be cured during sleep, often experiencing a dream or vision in which the god appeared. The Christians saw Asclepius as a particular rival to their own healing cults. One late Roman bishop, praising the miracles of the martyr Phocas, exulted, "End your work, places of healing! Be venerated no more, Asclepius!"[29]

The early Christians were not blind to the similarities between aspects of pagan cult and their own. Justin Martyr noted that Christ's healing miracles were very like those attributed to Asclepius.[30] And Christians were familiar with the ex-votos of pagan cult. Gregory of Tours mentions a pagan shrine near Cologne in the first half of the sixth century, where "the local barbarians" would come to make offerings, engage in ritual feasting, and present to images of the gods wooden carvings of the parts of the body that they hoped would be healed.[31] Christians had various ways of explaining pagan cult and its apparent resemblances to their own religion. There was the demonic theory: the cult of the gods and goddesses was really the worship of demons and the similarities between Christian and pagan cult could be explained by the devil mimicking true religion.[32] Then there was euhemerism, the theory that some pagan gods were simply men, who had benefitted mankind and thus been revered as gods. Augustine often speaks in this vein.[33] He also believed that crowd psychology explained the apparent movements of pagan idols:

> Who can doubt that idols lack feeling? Yet when they are placed in shrines, and held in high honour, and attended by worshippers who pray and offer sacrifice, they impress weak minds with the similitude of living limbs and senses, so that they seem to be alive and to breathe; especially from the insistent veneration of the multitude, by which such cult is paid to them.[34]

Lactantius gave systematic treatment to the origin of pagan religion. Foolish men, he writes, had treated natural forces, like the sun and the moon and the elements, as gods, and had them personified them, calling fire Vulcan, the sea Neptune, and so on, and then attributed to them all the vile emotions of humans—lust, greed and

[27] Livy, *Ab urbe condita*, 10. 47. 6–7, *periocha* 11.
[28] LiDonnici, *The Epidaurian Miracle Inscriptions*.
[29] Asterius of Amasea, Homily 9. 13, p. 127.
[30] Justin, *Apologia* 22. 6, pp. 136–38.
[31] Gregory of Tours, *Liber vitae patrum* 6. 2, p. 681 (repr., 1969, p. 231).
[32] For example, Firmicus Maternus, *De errore*.
[33] For example, *Sermo* 273 (PL 38: 1249).
[34] Augustine, *Epistolae* 102. 3. 18, p. 19 (PL 33: 377).

violence. "These," he says to the pagans, "are the religions that were handed down to you from your ancestors and that you seek to defend with such determination."[35]

But, whatever their theory of religion, Christian apologists did not seek to disguise the way that the saints had replaced the gods. "The Lord," writes Theodoret, in his refutation of the pagans, "has introduced his own dead in place of your gods"—"saints successors of the gods" indeed![36] They even spoke the language of functionalism: one late Roman bishop claimed that one saint could "fulfil all the functions of the many gods" of the pagans.[37]

But some aspects of the old religion had no parallel in the new: there was no place for blood sacrifice or institutional divination in Christianity.[38] While Christianity took up the idea of sacrifice, and indeed made it cosmic, and had a central ritual that involved drinking blood, it set its face against animal sacrifice. In this, it was like rabbinical Judaism rather then Temple Judaism, like Buddhism rather than Hinduism. Islam does have a "festival of sacrifice," *Eid al-Adha*, in which large numbers of animals are slaughtered, although they are not conceived of as being offered to God but to family, friends and the poor. The rejection of blood sacrifice by Christians meant that the offerings that were a central part of the cult of the saints were, typically, coins or candles, and never slaughtered animals. Some medieval thinkers had an elaborate theory that blood sacrifice was a kind of training of humanity, preparing it to receive Christianity: "It was by God's marvellous dispensation that this common opinion of all mankind, placing the hope of salvation in the cult of sacrifice, prepared the way for the future dispensation."[39] The principle of sacrifice was right, but the need for animal blood had passed.

The second aspect of the old religion that was not reflected in the cult of the saints was the practice of institutional divination, that is, regular and routine methods of consulting the deity about an issue, a course of action or a dilemma. The methods available to the Greeks and Romans for this purpose were numerous: oracles at Delphi and elsewhere, inspired seers, divination from natural signs (such as the flight of birds and the entrails of sacrificed animals). It is possible that the cult of the saints could have fulfilled this function. In fact, in sixth-century Egypt it did. Worshippers came to the shrines of the saints bearing two sheets of papyrus, one with a positive, one with a negative command, and followed the instructions of the one that was returned to them. Questions were usually specific: "O God of St. Philoxenus our guardian, if you command that Anoup be brought into your hospital, show your power and let this sheet come out." One suppliant asked if he should become a banker, a pregnant woman wondered if she should stay in the house where she was living with her mother.[40] All this evidence shows the way that the cult of the

[35] Lactantius, *Divinae institutiones* 2. 6 (1, pp. 138–40) (PL 6: 284–85).

[36] Theodoret of Cyrrhus, *Graecorum affectionum curatio* 8. 69 (2, p. 335).

[37] *Energeias pleroi*: Asterius of Amasea, Homily 9. 13, p. 127.

[38] A topic discussed in Bartlett, "Reflections on Paganism and Christianity in Medieval Europe."

[39] Baldwin of Ford, *Tractatus de sacramento altaris* 1, p. 90.

[40] Papaconstantinou, *Le culte des saints en Egypte*, pp. 336–39.

saints could have developed but did not. In virtually all parts of Christendom and in virtually all periods, such routine divination was not part of accepted practice. One could pray to the saints, but one could not demand an oracle. Medieval Christianity had no specific institutional provision for supplying the oracular. As a consequence unofficial divinatory practices flourished, to fill this gasp. Christians might appeal to dreams or visions to vindicate a course of action, but this was charismatic and unpredictable rather than regular. Hence, with the possible exception of the Celtic world, prophetic authority in the Middle Ages was either illicit or visionary, not institutionalized. "Divination is a sin," wrote Thomas Aquinas, "whereby someone usurps for himself or herself knowledge of future things that pertains properly to God." The Old Testament may, he admitted, have specified some divinatory procedures, but "there is in the new law nothing ordained to gain prior knowledge of future temporal events."[41]

The cult of the saints thus had many similarities with the pagan cults that surrounded it in its early days, but cannot be sensibly viewed as a simple adaptation of them, and fulfilled only some of the same functions.

Saints and Nature

There are strange features of the natural world: places where water springs from the ground, high places that seem to go up to the sky, even beautiful and numinous woods. These were the focal point of veneration in many times and places. Seneca lists the sites that might evoke religious awe and become the scene of worship: a secluded grove with tall and ancient trees; a deep cave in the mountains; the source of a great river, suddenly flowing from the hidden depths of the earth; hot springs; and deep lakes.[42]

Holy wells and other sacred water sources are found in many cultures. There were probably close to a thousand holy wells and springs in ancient Gaul.[43] The Greeks and Romans were familiar with nymphaea, shrines dedicated to the water nymphs and often located in caves or grottoes, or artificial equivalents, although they were also found in urban settings. One of Horace's most celebrated odes (3. 13) was addressed to the spring of Bandusia, promising a sacrifice: "O fountain of Bandusia, brighter than glass. Tomorrow I will give you a kid . . . its red blood will colour your cold waters." Many temples were situated on high spots, and Mount Olympus was viewed as the home of the gods, while worship often took place in sacred groves, which were protected by special laws.[44] One definition of a grove was "a multitude of trees, with religious practices."[45]

[41] Thomas Aquinas, *Summa Theologiae* IIa–IIae q. 95. 1–2 (40, pp. 36–42).

[42] Seneca, *Ad Lucilium epistulae morales* 4. 41. 3.

[43] Rousselle, *Croire et guérir: la foi en Gaule dans l'Antiquité tardive*, p. 31.

[44] For example, *Inscriptiones Latinae Liberae Rei Publicae* 2, pp. 3–5, nos. 505–6 (Lex Luci Spoletina).

[45] Lucus est arborum multitudo cum religione: Servius, *In Aeneidem* 1. 310, p. 163.

Writing around AD 200, the Christian convert Clement of Alexandria claimed, "the prophetic streams are now dead," but he was a little premature.[46] The cult of these natural objects continued deep into the Middle Ages, officially in the unconverted regions of northern and eastern Europe, unofficially almost everywhere. The Saxons had their holy oak, the Irminsul. In the eleventh century the pagan Prussians refused to let Christians approach their groves and springs, fearing that they would be polluted.[47] Springs, trees, mountains were part of the indigenous polytheistic religions of Europe and the Mediterranean.

Christianity was not a religion that prized the sacredness of nature. In his celebrated book on the origins of the cult of the saints, Peter Brown pointed out the way that the rise of the cult resulted in "a natural world made passive by being shorn of the power of the gods."[48] The Christian definition of a grove was not "trees plus religion," but "a cluster of trees that blocks out the light of the sun."[49] The assault on holy springs and trees was a central plank of the Christian platform.[50] It continued throughout the medieval period (and beyond). St. Martin, destroying the holy trees of Gaul, argued "there is nothing religious in a tree trunk."[51] In the sixth century a reforming bishop in southern France sought to stop the local people making offerings at a sacred lake, with the phrase (probably borrowed from Martin's) that "there is no religion in a pond."[52] He was eventually successful and the offerings were then brought instead to a nearby church he had founded. In the early eleventh century the monk Raoul Glaber expressed the view that one of the most notable of the errors into which humans might fall was veneration of springs and trees by the sick.[53] The Council of Westminster of 1102 prohibited unlicensed reverence not only of dead bodies but also of fountains; later in the century Hugh, bishop of Lincoln, had "a bitter struggle" to stop the veneration of springs at Berkhamstead in Hertfordshire, High Wycombe in Buckinghamshire and other places.[54]

Such unofficial devotions continued throughout the medieval period. In the middle of the fifteenth century the bishop of St.-Papoul in southern France was deeply disturbed by a healing spring that suddenly sprang into life in his diocese.[55] He thought the matter serious enough to call in the Inquisition. The bishop was

[46] Clement of Alexandria, *Protrepticus* 2. 11, p. 19.

[47] Adam of Bremen, *Gesta Hammaburgensis ecclesiae pontificum* 4. 18, p. 456.

[48] Brown, *The Cult of the Saints*, p. 124.

[49] Isidore of Seville, *Etymologiae* 17. 6 (PL 82: 606).

[50] Some of the following examples are cited in Bartlett, "Reflections on Paganism and Christianity in Medieval Europe."

[51] *Nihil esse religionis in stipite*: Sulpicius Severus, *Vita sancti Martini* 13. 1 (1, p. 280); a phrase repeated in *Vita sancti Ottonis episcopi Babenbergensis (Vita Prieflingensis)* 3. 11, p. 186.

[52] *Nulla est enim religio in stagnum*: Gregory of Tours, *Gloria confessorum* 2, pp. 749–50 (repr., 1969, pp. 299–300).

[53] Rodulfus Glaber, *Historiarum libri quinque* 4. 3. 8, p. 184.

[54] *Councils and Synods with Other Documents Relating to the English Church* 1, part II, p. 678 (cl. 27); Adam of Eynsham, *Magna vita sancti Hugonis* 5. 17 (2, p. 201).

[55] Montagnes, "La répression des sacralités populaires en Languedoc au xv siècle."

particularly concerned because the spring was not associated with any saint. When prohibiting the "uneducated crowd" from paying "vain and superstitious devotions" to the spring, he made some general points about the powers of nature and the powers of the saints: "Miraculous healing is granted by God's power through the merits and prayers of the saints, and is not simply attributable to an irrational and inanimate created being"; "if a spring or some other inanimate body provides any help in healing, this is in respect to the saints, who suffered martyrdom there or did some service dear to God in that inanimate place." Nature had no innate powers to help or heal, he was arguing: it was only when a landscape was imprinted with the virtue of the saints that it could become sacral.

But even the association of a spring with a saint was not always enough to sacralize it. When a foreign abbot came to the holy well of St. Ives in eastern England and drank from it, he was rebuked by one of his own monks:

> It is not right for a wise and devout man to countenance the foolishness and superstition of peasants, who are deceived by pagan error into worshipping water or the bones of some dead people, which the fantastical demonic marvels seduce them into believing to be the proven relics of saints.[56]

This rigorist not only doubted the authenticity of the relics but saw the veneration of water as a superstitious habit of the ignorant rural population. Heretics too might put reverence for natural objects and the cult of the saints in the same category, as superstitious practices. When they saw springs and trees being venerated, this encouraged their own doubts about the powers of the saints.[57]

The debate about the religion of open spaces was vigorous. When some people objected that the supposed miracles occurring at the spring of St. Agilus or St. Aile in northern France were the work not of God but of demons, since the miraculous cures occurred "in a wild and remote place where there is neither divine worship nor the shrine of a saint," the author championing the miracles countered, "it does not seem to me that a charge should be raised against a place because it is in the open country, since the Lord has deigned to distinguish many remote places with wonders."[58] But one problem with "remote places" is that they are harder to supervise. A church that has been consecrated by a bishop and is served by monks or clergy contains the holy within its walls and is under clerical control.

Building a church over a sacred well was indeed one way to harness its sacrality to Christian purposes. The fountain in Lucania dedicated to the water deity Leucothea (the "white goddess") was converted to a baptistery; it is now called San Giovanni in Fonte—St. John in the Spring—taking the name of the Baptist as natural for a site of holy water.[59] And there are other cases of saints being used to replace earlier

[56] *Miracula sancti Yvonis episcopi Persae*, pp. lxxi–lxxii.

[57] *Quellen zur Geschichte der Waldenser*, pp. 97–98 (the Passau Anonymous).

[58] *Miracula sancti Agili* (BHL 149) 2. 3. 20–21, p. 594.

[59] Cassiodorus, *Variae* 8. 33, pp. 340–42; Spanu, "*Fons vivus*. Culti delle acque e santuari cristiani tra tarda antichità e alto medioevo," pp. 1069–71, pls. XXXI–XXXII.

pagan natural sacral sites as part of a conscious policy. Bishop Wigbert of Merseburg (1004–9), for example, sought to wean his Slav parishioners away from their sacred trees in this way:

> By diligent preaching he recalled his flock from the empty superstition of their error and uprooted the grove called *Zutibure* [*swiety bor*, "holy grove"] which the local inhabitants honoured as a god and which, from ancient times, had never been violated, constructing there a church dedicated to the holy martyr Romanus.[60]

The pagan worshippers of Greece and Rome and of medieval eastern and northern Europe had their public and communal ceremonies and sites, but they could also approach the holy in the shade of a grove of tall trees or down the steps leading to underground caves and pools. For medieval Christians, the official sacred place was the indoor and man-made space of the church. And within their churches, the most holy spots were the altars, which contained relics and might display them, and the shrines of the saints. Human remains within a consecrated building, not trees or pools, evoked awe and reverence.

But, despite all this evidence for saints as opponents of and substitutes for the holy springs, the saints left their deepest mark on the landscape through their association with wells and springs. Thousands of springs and fountains bore (and bear) the names of saints, usually with some explanatory story, like that relating to the early British saint Decuman, martyred in Devon, who, after decapitation, carried his own head "to that spring of purest water, in which he used to wash his head, and which is still today called 'St. Decuman's fountain,' in memory and reverence of him."[61] It is possible to see this impregnation of the landscape with the traces of the saints as a Christianization, but also as a sign of the resilience and deep psychological roots of veneration of the forces of nature.

Saints and the Dead

The evidence is strong that the Christian cult of the saints has its roots in ancient mortuary practice rather than in the cult of the gods.[62] The treatment of the holy Christian dead only gradually differentiated itself from the rites and ceremonies conducted at the tombs of ordinary family members, be they Christian or pagan.[63] The earliest focus of the cult of the saints was the martyr's tomb, located in a cemetery outside the walls of the ancient city and surrounded by the tombs of ordinary believers (and pagans). An annual gathering at the tomb, with prayers and "offerings,"

[60] Thietmar of Merseburg, *Chronicon* 6. 37, p. 282.

[61] *Vita sancti Decumani*, p. 265.

[62] Classically, Saxer, *Morts, martyrs, reliques*.

[63] Saxer, *Morts, martyrs, reliques*; Volp, *Tod und Ritual in den christlichen Gemeinde der Antike*; vigorously reasserted by MacMullen, "Christian Ancestor Worship in Rome."

is attested in Christian communities at least from 200, when Tertullian, writing in north Africa, records that "we make offerings for the dead, for their anniversary, on that day of the year," and, addressing a young Christian widow about the honours she pays her dead husband, mentions that "you pray for his spirit, for which you render annual offerings."[64] Like the pagans, Christians might commemorate their dead by feasting at the tomb, and scenes of banqueting are common in the Christian catacombs.[65] The third-century *Didascalia* urges believers to "pray and offer for those who are asleep" and mentions the Eucharist at gravesites.[66] Augustine's mother, Monica, bringing her picnic to the saint's shrine (earlier, p. 14), represents this old common custom, shared by family dead and the holy dead.

The birth of the Christian cult of the saints is marked by the gradual divergence between this treatment of the ordinary Christian dead and treatment of the saints. This epochal divergence is symbolized in Augustine's comment: "we pray *for* our dead but *to* the martyrs." Augustine is here making a sharp distinction between the ordinary dead, for whom Christians pray, and the martyrs, who do not need the prayers of the living and are, indeed, their advocates. "We pray for the other faithful departed," he wrote, "but we do not pray for the martyrs; for they left this life so perfect that they do not need our help but we need theirs."[67] It was indeed "an insult" to pray *for* the martyrs.[68] Although they had died, they were not like the other dead. This is why Peter Brown called the saints "The Very Special Dead."[69]

Since the cult of the saints was directed neither immediately to immortal gods nor to natural objects, such as the springs and trees revered in many pagan religions, but to dead human beings, ancient Christianity saw a convergence of the site of ordinary communal worship and the site of relics, that is, the bones of the holy dead. This happened either by the construction of churches above the tombs of the martyrs, or by the removal of relics into churches. Both were taking place by the middle of the fourth century. This at once meant a new relationship between the holy and the dead. While the ancient Greeks and Romans (and subsequently the Muslims) sought to separate the living and the dead, to differentiate cemeteries and areas of residence, Christians intermingled them. Moving the remains of the dead into city churches broke the ancient taboo demarcating the places of the living and the dead, and disregarded deeply felt legal and moral prohibitions both on the disturbance of human remains and on the presence of the dead in the city. It was a development that marked off Christianity sharply from pagan and Jewish religions, which knew the difference between a place of worship and a cemetery, and regarded the cult of

[64] Tertullian, *De corona* 3. 3, p. 1043; *De exhortatione castitatis* 11. 1, p. 1031 (PL 2: 79, 926).

[65] Nicolai et al., *The Christian Catacombs of Rome*, pp. 109–12.

[66] *The Didascalia Apostolorum in Syriac* 26, vol. 180 (Eng. tr.), pp. 243–44.

[67] Pro aliis fidelibus defunctis oratur, pro martyribus non oratur: tam enim perfecti exierunt, ut non sint suscepti nostri, sed advocati: Augustine, *Sermo* 285 (PL 38: 1295).

[68] Augustine, *Sermo* 159 (PL 38: 868); a point reiterated in medieval canon law: *Decretales Gregorii IX,* 3. 41. 6, *Quum Marthae*, col. 639.

[69] Brown, *The Cult of the Saints,* title of chapter four.

corporeal relics as ghoulish. Even in the late Roman period, imperial law emphasized that bodies should be placed outside the city, so that "they should preserve the sanctity of the dwellings of the inhabitants," that is, so that they should not pollute them by their presence.[70] In the cities of late antique and early medieval Europe, many aspects of ancient public life disappeared, while the bones of the saints provided new centres for community ceremony: as baths went out, the dead came in.

The radical pagan emperor Julian the Apostate reproached the Christians for this distasteful intimacy with the dead: "You have filled everywhere with tombs and sepulchres . . . why do you haunt the sepulchres?"[71] His contemporary Eunapius describes the activities of Christian monks with equal scorn:

> Collecting together the bones and skulls of those who had been condemned for many crimes, whom the city courts had punished, they proclaimed them gods, haunted their graves and supposed that they were better by defiling themselves at their tombs. They called them martyrs and messengers of a sort and ambassadors for what they requested of the gods.

Eunapius lamented that the doleful prophecy of the pagan philosopher Antoninus had been fulfilled: the line between temple and tomb had disappeared.[72]

There is evidence that early Christians too did not always find the new regime natural or easy. The injunction of the *Didascalia*, "do you approach without restraint to those who rest, and you shall not declare (them) unclean," must be directed to those who were uneasy about approaching the dead.[73] The Christians of late-fourth-century Syria still needed reminding, "the bones of the dead cannot pollute the human soul," while, at the same period, in emphasizing the extraordinary charisma of the relics of a saint, Gregory of Nyssa had also to concede that most people found corpses "disgusting" and regarded it as unlucky even to walk past a grave.[74]

Later, in the eight century, John of Damascus recognized the revolutionary changes in attitudes to death and the dead body that Christianity had brought. In the time of the Old Law, he wrote,

> the Temple was not erected in the name of men. Nor was the death of righteous men celebrated as a festival but was mourned, and anyone who had been in contact with a corpse, even of Moses himself, was deemed unclean. But now the commemorations of the saints are celebrated as festivals.[75]

This breach between the two distinct worlds of living worshippers and dead bodies was a target in early Islamic critique of Christian practice. The *hadith*, which

[70] *Codex Theodosianus* 9. 17. 6 (381*)*, p. 465.

[71] Julian, *Contra Galileos* 335C, 339E, pp. 414, 416.

[72] Eunapius, *Vitae sophistarum*, p. 424.

[73] *The Didascalia Apostolorum in Syriac* 26, vol. 180 (Eng. tr.), p. 244.

[74] *Constitutiones apostolorum* 6. 27. 8 (2, pp. 380–82); Gregory of Nyssa, *De sancto Theodoro*, p. 62 (PG 46: 737).

[75] John of Damascus, *De imaginibus oratio* 1. 21, pp. 108–9 (PG 94: 1253).

are sayings attributed to the prophet Muhammad but recorded generations after his death, include some that express aversion to the practice of mingling the dead with the place of worship: "May Allah curse the Jews and Christians for they built the places of worship at the graves of their Prophets," and, talking of the Ethiopian Christians and throwing in a condemnation of holy images, "If any religious man dies amongst those people they would build a place of worship at his grave and make these pictures in it. They will be the worst creature in the sight of Allah on the Day of Resurrection."[76] "You bury your dead in your places of prayer, which God ordered you to keep pure," is the charge in correspondence attributed to Caliph Umar II (717–20) but probably from late-ninth-century Syria.[77] It was a charge well known enough for a thirteenth-century English chronicler to put in the mouth of the Sultan of Egypt: "you Christians," he says, "who revere the bones of the dead."[78] Despite such comments, however, a cult of the holy dead did develop in medieval Islam (see the following).

So saints were human. But they were, in the main, dead humans, and this raised acute questions about two intertwined issues: their location, and their relation to their physical body. The cult of the saints was focussed upon their physical remains and had its origin in commemorative rituals at the tombs of the martyrs. Even when the cult had elaborated and multiplied to the astonishing extent it attained over the course of the Middle Ages, corporeal relics, that is, body parts, still retained this centrality. The simplest conception was that saints were present at their burial place, and many visions of saints involve their coming out of or returning to their tomb. A demon once boasted that he could not be ejected from the body of the woman he had possessed since the saint who had been invoked, Isidore, was currently away from his shrine, which was in in Leon, and "busy freeing captives in the land of the Moors."[79] If Isidore was off in the Muslim world, he could not then be in his shrine. Yet, in some other sense, the saint was in heaven. Nor, moreover, did the servants of a saint wish to circumscribe his or her power by limiting it to the tomb, but often asserted that it could be effective anywhere. Gregory the Great even claimed that saints did more remarkable miracles in places where their body did *not* lie buried, in order to reassure the doubtful of their presence.[80] Where then was the saint—in the tomb or reliquary, in heaven, everywhere?

In the debate between Jerome and Vigilantius, discussed earlier, the question of the location of the dead saints was at issue. "You say," protests Jerome, "that the souls of the apostles and martyrs are in the bosom of Abraham, or in the place of rest, or under the altar of God, nor can they leave their tombs and be present where they wish." He dismisses this notion. The saints are with God, God is everywhere,

[76] *Sahih Bukhari* 1. 8. 427 and 419 (cf. 426, 428) (on-line); also, with different translation, in Meri, *The Cult of Saints among Muslims and Jews in Medieval Syria*, pp. 131–32, as cited by Ibn Tamīya.

[77] Gaudeul, "The Correspondence between Leo and Umar," p. 149.

[78] Matthew Paris, *Chronica majora* 5, p. 342.

[79] *Historia translationis sancti Isidori* 6. 5, p. 177.

[80] Gregory I, *Dialogi* 2. 38. 3 (2, p. 246).

therefore the saints are everywhere. And it would be a disgrace if one admitted that demons could range around the world, but that the souls of the martyrs were under some kind of house arrest.[81] It was an issue that was raised in a particularly clear form by the practice of burial *ad sanctos*, that is, close to the saints, something that was valued from an early date. Gregory of Nyssa placed the bodies of his parents alongside the relics of the Forty Martyrs, so that at the Last Judgment they might be resurrected with these powerful patrons.[82] Maximus of Turin believed that, "If we rest with the holy martyrs, we escape the shades of hell, if not by our own merits at least by holiness of association."[83]

But there were voices that disagreed with this highly physical interpretation of burial *ad sanctos*. St. Augustine wrote, "When somebody is buried close to the shrines of the martyrs, there is only this benefit to the dead person, namely, that anyone praying for him and entrusting him to the patronage of the martyrs, has the strength of feeling in his prayer increased."[84] Archbishop Julian of Toledo, writing in the seventh century, repeated Augustine's point and elaborated it, explaining the effect of such a privileged location on the person praying for a departed loved one in the following way:

> Thus, when he considers within himself where the body of his loved one is buried, and the place dedicated to the revered martyr comes into his mind, a strong feeling of remembrance and prayer will entrust the beloved soul to that same martyr.[85]

Julian is making the point that the value of being buried near to a saint is entirely to do with the psychology of the living: they are stirred to more intense prayer for the dead. The link is associative and subjective, not literally physical.[86]

Debate and perplexity about where the saints were also ties in with the common assertion that the whole of a saint was in the smallest fragment of his or her relics. The complications arose from the fact that saints were corporeal—they had (or were) bodies—but their power was meant to be everywhere. At the end of the fourteenth century the Italian writer Sacchetti deplored the faddish way the Italians of his day would first run to one image of the Madonna, then switch to another, and another, as rumours of miracles swirled around them: "as if the Virgin had more power to bestow grace in one place than in another!"[87] It was a general assumption

[81] Jerome, *Adversus Vigilantium* 6, pp. 13–14 (PL 23: 344).

[82] On p. 15, earlier.

[83] *Consortii sanctitate*: Maximus of Turin, *Sermo* 12, p. 42.

[84] Augustine, *De cura pro mortuis gerenda* 18. 22, p. 659 (PL 40: 610); see the comments in Yasin, *Saints and Church Spaces in the Late Antique Mediterranean*, pp. 212–22.

[85] Julian of Toledo, *Prognosticon futuri saeculi* 1. 20, p. 38 (PL 96: 474).

[86] Twentieth-century commentators sometimes characterized the literally physical view as "magical": Kötting, *Der frühchristliche Reliquienkult und die Bestattung im Kirchengebäude*, p. 26 ("eines magischen Sicherheitsgefühls"); García Rodríguez, *El culto de los santos en la España romana y visigoda*, p. 360 ("una efficacia 'quasi' mágica").

[87] Sacchetti, Letter XI, p. 497.

that saints did have "more power to bestow grace in one place than in another," even if clergy and theologians might have reasons to stress the omnipresence of the saints. These enigmas about the location of supernatural beings were not limited to Christian sainthood. The Homeric gods manifested themselves in certain places, but did this mean they were then not elsewhere? And in what sense was the Temple in Jerusalem "the House of the Lord"?

At one level, these were philosophical questions about the relationship of spirit and body, and form part of a gamut of such issues that the philosopher-theologians of the Middle Ages tried to deal with. When they asked if many angels could be in the same spot at once or debated the nature of Christ's presence in the Eucharist, it was this spirit-body conundrum they were grappling with. Hagiographic writers rarely addressed the issue with the theoretical generality of the theologians, but there is no doubt that the question formed a constant theme in their thinking and often provoked explicit argumentation or, at the least, a bold assertion of paradox like the inscription at the tomb of St. Martin: "Here lies interred bishop Martin of holy memory; his soul is in the hand of God but he is wholly present here, manifest in gracious miracles of every kind."[88]

In the *Confessions* Augustine describes how, before his conversion, he used to worry away at the problem of God's substance: was the deity a physical body, and how did he relate to the physical universe? Did he penetrate it, or was he coterminous with it? The issue was how literal, physical, corporeal, God was.[89] The breakthrough for Augustine, that allowed his conversion, was the realization that God was spirit. But, late in life, despite not previously being interested in saints and relics, he embraced the cult of relics with enthusiasm—he had gone back to that idea of the physicality of the supernatural that had troubled him as a young man.

Tomb-shrines in Judaism and Islam

A cult of the holy dead is shaped by the different ways of dealing with dead bodies that different cultures follow. A cult centred on the tombs of the holy dead, or on their enshrined physical remains, presupposes a particular way of disposing of the dead. The "Abrahamic" religions—Judaism, Christianity, and Islam—all insist (or have traditionally insisted) on burial as the only proper way to dispose of the dead; they are inhumation religions. Because of this, and in contrast to the religions that scatter the ashes of their dead or have them consumed by animals or relatives, there is always a site for the dead body of a Jew, Christian or Muslim. There is somewhere to go. The existence of this local habitation and a name was one of the strengths of the cult of the saints, although it also led to the centuries-long discussion of the

[88] PL 74: 673. The text is recorded in several manuscripts, one of the oldest of which appears to be an early ninth-century collection of Martiniana from Tours, BnF, lat. 5325 (fol. 134).

[89] Augustine, *Confessiones* 7. 1, pp. 92–93.

power of saint at and away from tomb. Cremation did not actually mean that there could be no cult of the dead saint. The earliest recorded martyr cult, that of Polycarp, focussed on his ashes, since he was burned alive, while the Forty Martyrs of Sebaste were likewise burned, and their ashes provided a rich store of relics. But the usual focus of Christian saintly cult was the body buried in the tomb.

Although the three religions shared the practice of inhumation, one thing that distinguished the Christian cult of the saints from its Jewish and Muslim equivalents was the fragmentation and circulation of body parts. Human remains were moved, broken up, and dispersed. Sometimes dozens of churches claimed part of a saint's body. Such a division of the holy figure was extremely unusual in Judaism and Islam, and Jews and Muslims might indeed regard reverence for fragmentary human remains as grotesque. The head of Hussein, the martyred grandson of the prophet Muhammad, was revered separately from the rest of his body, the former coming eventually to Cairo, the latter enshrined in Karbala, but this was a consequence of his decapitation at death, not of a subsequent translation.

There is clear evidence of a cult of holy tombs in both Judaism and Islam. By the time of Jesus, the Holy Land was covered with the tombs of Jewish patriarchs and prophets.[90] A Jewish writer in tenth-century Jerusalem criticized the practice of visiting tomb-shrines that some of his fellow Jews undertook, and, in doing so, had to describe it:

> How can I be silent while certain idolatrous practices are rampant among Israel? They pass the night among tombstones. They make requests of the dead. They light candles upon the graves of the righteous ones and burn incense before them in order to cure a host of illnesses. They make pilgrimage to the tombs of these dead saints and make votive offerings to them.[91]

Pilgrimage to the Temple in Jerusalem had been an obligation upon Jews until its destruction in AD 70, but veneration of the tombs of the holy dead, and, in particular, "making requests" of them, had no scriptural authority and could thus be condemned as "idolatrous" in this way. It was, nevertheless, a common custom amongst the Jews of the Middle East. Particularly important shrine-tombs were those of the prophet Ezekiel in Iraq, the prophet Samuel near Jerusalem and the rabbis of Galilee. At these places perpetual lights burned, offerings were made and vows undertaken. Some of them attracted Muslim as well as Jewish pilgrims.[92]

There are approximate equivalents to Christian saints in Islam, in the"friends of God (*awliyā'*)." These included companions of the prophet, martyrs, mystics, and ascetics, and, amongst the Shi'ites, imams. And, despite some hostile views about tomb-shrines ascribed to the prophet Muhammad, there were shrines of the holy

[90] Jeremias, *Heiligengräber in Jesu Umwelt*; Klauser, "Christlicher Märtyrerkult, heidnischer Heroenkult und spätjüdische Heiligenverehrung."

[91] Meri, *The Cult of Saints among Muslims and Jews in Medieval Syria*, pp. 220–21 (shortened).

[92] Ibid., pp. 214–50.

dead in Islam, just as there were in Christendom. The graves of the biblical prophets, the family and companions of Muhammad, Muslim martyrs, Sufi mystics, and pious teachers and rulers, all might become the focus of devotion. On occasion these shrines were actually inside mosques.

These tomb-shrines became the goal of pilgrims. Muslims distinguished the obligatory pilgrimage to Mecca (the *Hajj*) from pious pilgrimages to shrines (*ziyāra*), the former being a duty for all Muslims, the latter a custom that was sometimes controversial. One of the great centres of *ziyāra* was the cemetery of al-Qarāfa on the edge of Cairo, where dozens of tomb-shrines attracted pilgrims. In 1083 an observer wrote of al-Qarāfa:

> This is also one of the wonders of the world for the tombs it contains of prophets, of the kindred of Muhammad, of his Companions, of the followers of the Companions, of learned men and ascetics, and of saintly men renowned for their miracles and of wonderful report.[93]

Proximity to the tombs of the saints brought special grace and favour, as is shown, for example, in the case of Sayyida Nafīsa (d. 824), a descendant of the prophet Muhammad renowned for her piety. She was buried in her own house in Egypt, and the thirteenth-century encyclopaedist Ibn Khallikān said of her, "the spot on which her house stood is now occupied by her mausoleum. . . . This tomb has a great reputation, experience having shown that prayers said near it are answered."[94] Pilgrims came with hopes of many kinds:

> Of the graves they expect release from debt, their daily bread, here sterile women pray for children, here they make their vows and offerings of oil and other gifts in the belief that through these they will be delivered from their difficulties and brought into better circumstances.[95]

Muslim shrine-tombs might be marked by impressive built structures, a characteristic form being the domed mausoleum, and could be given resources and institutional continuity through permanent endowments. Some had mosques and seminaries attached. Just as in Christendom, pilgrim guide-books were produced in Islam to explain the sights to keen pilgrims. One such work, written in Syria late in the twelfth century, mentions holy sites ranging from Cordoba in the west to Samarkand in the east, although the author admits he had not actually visited Spain and expressed some doubts about his Spanish informants. While he refers to such obvious tourist highlights as the Pyramids and the Dome of the Rock (under Crusader control at the time he visited), his main attention is on holy tombs, of all different periods: "At Hebron, the grotto with the tombs of Abraham, Isaac and Jacob"; "The

[93] Williams, "The Cult of 'Alid Saints in the Fatimid Monuments of Cairo. Part II: The Mausolea," p. 40, citing ibn Jubayr.

[94] Ibid., p. 40.

[95] Goldziher, "Veneration of Saints in Islam," p. 321, citing al-Maqrīzī.

city of Basra. There, the tomb of Talha, Companion of the Messenger of God"; "In the cemetery of Mosul, the tomb of Sheikh al-Ma'afa ibn Imran."[96]

Some of the practices at tomb-shrines are described by a fourteenth-century Islamic scholar: "praying to tombs, circumambulating them, kissing them, touching them, rubbing their cheeks in their soil, worshipping their patrons, seeking aid from them, requesting from them aid, sustenance, health, fulfilling debts, dispelling worries, seeking aid against misfortunes or distress."[97] Dust from the tombs of the saints had healing powers, just as in the Christian cult of the saints.[98] There was a special celebration of Muslim saints on their "birthdays" (*mawālid*), a word that, like its Christian counterpart, sometimes referred to the day of their death.

The predominance of male saints was even more marked in Islam than in Christianity. Of 316 saints mentioned in Moroccan hagiographical documents of the eleventh and twelfth centuries, only 6 were women.[99] This tiny proportion (not even 2 per cent) compares with a figure of around 10 per cent in contemporary Christendom (see earlier, pp. 145ff.), even though this period was in fact a low point for Christian female saints. And, if one compares the miracles performed by Muslim and Christian saints in their lifetimes, it appears broadly true that Islamic saints were more likely to prophesy the future, more likely to engage in spectacular physical miracles, such as walking on water or covering vast distances in an instant, and slightly less likely to heal, than their Christian counterparts.[100]

A flourishing cult of the saints, both Muslim and Jewish, both living and dead, continued in Morocco until the twentieth century. One study analyzed the cults of 652 Jewish saints in that country, many of them with Muslim as well as Jewish devotees.[101] Favoured sites for the tomb-shrines of these holy dead included caves, mountains, springs and trees; some saints were in fact known by such names as "Master of the Green Palm Tree" and "Master of the Fig Tree."[102] They were sites of healing and pilgrimage. Once a year, on the anniversary of the death of a Jewish saint, the devotees would make their way to the tomb—the local Muslims often providing transport animals for hire, just as the Egyptians had done for pilgrims in the fourth century—and pray, chant, dance, light candles, and slaughter animals.[103] As in the case of Muslim saints, the Jewish saints of modern Morocco were overwhelmingly male: less than 4 per cent were women.[104] And these saints ranged in time from those

[96] al-Harawī, *Guide des lieux de pèlerinage.*

[97] Meri, *The Cult of Saints among Muslims and Jews in Medieval Syria*, p. 25, citing Ibn Qayyim al-Jawzīya.

[98] For example, Taylor, *In the Vicinity of the Righteous: Ziyāra and the Veneration of Muslim Saints in Late Medieval Egypt*, pp. 53–54.

[99] Cornell, *Realm of the Saint: Power and Authority in Moroccan Sufism*, p. 321 n. 42.

[100] Ibid., p. 115; Taylor, *In the Vicinity of the Righteous: Ziyāra and the Veneration of Muslim Saints in Late Medieval Egypt*, pp. 130–63.

[101] Ben-Ami, *Culte des saints et pèlerinages judéo-musulmans au Maroc.*

[102] Ibid., p. 39.

[103] Ibid., pp. 63–64.

[104] Ibid., p. 11.

who had supposedly come to Morocco during the period of the first Temple (before 586 BC) to people who died in the 1950s and were known personally to their devotees.[105] In the early part of the twentieth century the tomb of Rabbi Hananiah Ha-Cohen in Marrakesh was a regular gathering spot for young people on a Saturday night, since, as one of them explained, "in those days there were no films or theatre."[106]

Despite all the evidence for the cult of the holy dead among Jews and Muslims, it never became an essential and fully accepted part of community religion in the way that it did in medieval Christendom. The communal worship of synagogue and mosque remained the heart of Judaism and Islam, partly because the dead were never integrated with these places of worship to the extent that occurred in the Christian church. Moreover, like some Christians, many Muslims and Jews regarded the cult of the saints as a perversion of their own religion, a contamination by the polytheistic impulse and a detestable recrudescence of paganism. Hence voices decrying the tomb-shrines, the petitionary prayer and the rituals at the grave, rejecting them with a violence that was as strong as any Calvinist's, could be heard, especially in Islam. The purist critic Ibn Taymīya (1263–1328) viewed this whole network of practices as a corruption of Islam: "In the golden age of Islam there were not any shrines on tombs. . . . That is against the religion of Muslims."[107] He thought the purpose of visiting tombs was to pray for the dead, not to seek their intercession: "the living does not have need for the dead by making a request of him or seeking his intercession. But rather, the dead derives benefit from the living."[108] This distinction between praying *to* the dead and praying *for* the dead is exactly the Christian distinction between the cult of saints and prayer on behalf of the ordinary deceased. Ibn Taymīya's views continue to be powerful in some version of modern Islam, such as the so-called Wahhabi or Salifist branches, ascribed to by the Saudis, who destroyed tomb-shrines in the holy places of Mecca and Medina, both when they took temporary control of them in the early nineteenth century and, more permanently, in the twentieth. When Islamic militants seized control of Timbuktu in 2012, one of their first actions was to take pickaxes to the shrines.

Saints and Ancestors

Writing in 1988, Michel Lauwers suggested a parallel between the cult of the saints and the cult of ancestors, found in many societies: "Isn't medieval sanctity, after all, very close to the ancestor cult of traditional societies . . . rather as if the saint had the

[105] Ibid., pp. 216, 199.

[106] Ibid., p. 179.

[107] Meri, *The Cult of Saints among Muslims and Jews in Medieval Syria*, pp. 273–74; for more on this critic, Taylor, *In the Vicinity of the Righteous: Ziyāra and the Veneration of Muslim Saints in Late Medieval Egypt*, pp. 168–94.

[108] Meri, *The Cult of Saints among Muslims and Jews in Medieval Syria*, p. 131.

status of an ancestor?"[109] Regardless of what one makes of the concept of "traditional societies," the parallel is worth consideration, although it is sometimes hard to make a distinction between simple reverence for the ancestral dead and a cult. Respect for one's ancestors and rites of memorialization might come close to worship: lighting lights, offering food or flowers, honouring images of the dead. Perhaps a distinguishing feature of ancestor cult—or ancestor worship as it is sometimes called—is that it involves the veneration of dead ancestors who are believed still to have powers to help or harm.

Egyptians were renowned for the attention they paid to the dead: mummification; special instructions for the afterlife inserted into the shroud or coffin; grave goods; monuments, for the powerful; even endowed mortuary priests, fulfilling the same functions as the chantry priests of later medieval Europe.[110] Yet it seems that pagan Egyptians were concerned more with helping the dead than with seeking help from them. The funerary texts have an insistent anxious tone: "I will possess my body for ever, for I will not become corrupt, I will not decay, I will not be putrid, I will not become worms."[111] Those who made such prayers were unlikely to be prayed to. However, in the early days of Egyptian Christianity there are hints of the prospect of a saintly cult as ancestor cult, suggesting a different path that the cult of the holy dead could have taken. Some Egyptians kept their mummified dead in their homes. They did this with the martyrs too. St. Antony condemned the practice and even went to the length of arranging a secret burial for himself so that he would not be treated in this way.[112] Yet one can imagine a world in which the practice that Antony condemned would have established itself. Revering the mummified dead in a private house would have produced a quite different kind of cult from that which did emerge, the veneration of the remains of the holy dead in the public space of the communal churches.

The Romans had images of their ancestors in their homes as well as shrines for the household deities (the Lares and Penates). The masks of the ancestors were carried in family funerals. Yet the strongly patriarchal tone of upper-class Roman family life did not express itself in a vigorous cult of divinized ancestors. Although, according to Cicero, the shades of the dead "have their rights" and should be regarded as divine, and Ovid says that the "ancestral spirits" should be placated by small gifts at the tomb, the tone is cool and almost patronizing.[113] Expressing public pride in one's ancestors is not the same as treating them as powerful gods.

[109] "La sainteté médiévale n'est-elle pas, en définitive, fort proche de l' 'ancestralité' des sociétés traditionelles? . . . Un peu comme si le saint accédait au statut d' 'ancêtre.' ": Lauwers, "La mort et le corps des saints," pp. 49–50.

[110] Frankfurt, *Ancient Egyptian Religion*, pp. 94–95.

[111] *Journey through the Afterlife: Ancient Egyptian Book of the Dead*, p. 161.

[112] Athanasius, *Vita Antonii* 90–91, pp. 364–70; see the comments of Baumeister, "Vorchristliche Bestattungssitten und die Entstehung des Märtyrerkultes in Ägypten."

[113] Cicero, *De legibus* 2. 22; Ovid, *Fasti* 2, lines 533–34.

The Chinese are often regarded as the most devout followers of ancestor-cult. The soul of the deceased ancestor is believed to be located in the soul tablet, a wooden board inscribed with his or her name, which is kept in the house, in a special hall in large houses, or in the ancestral temple in the case of clan founders. Ritual practices include a meal in which the dead are believed to share, the lighting of candles, and the burning of incense. In addition to rituals at the ancestral shrine in the house, annual banquets take place at the tombs. Since the middle of the twentieth century, soul tablets are often accompanied by photographs.

An ancestor cult with some resemblances to the Christian cult of the saints can be found in the Incan Empire. The Incas mummified their rulers and kept the mummies either in the Temple of the Sun at Cuzco or in the houses of the segment of the dynasty that descended from the ruler in question. Mummification is a way of keeping the dead present, and these mummified ancestors were participants in life. They were brought out on ceremonial occasions, carried shoulder high on a kind of bier, just as reliquaries were, and offered food and drink. The mummies might review the troops or give answers to questions.[114] When we read of the different branches of the Inca royal family bringing the mummified bodies of their ancestors out, to meet each other, it is hard to deny that some of the same dynamics are at work that we encounter in the assemblies of the eleventh-century Peace of God, when reliquary-images of the saints were brought together in public assemblies. In each case there are human remains that express the corporate identity of the different groups who have come together and symbolize their common purpose. The difference is that the mummies really were the ancestors of the Inca dynastic clans but the saints were associated with their devotees in more diverse and indirect ways.

Amongst Christians there was pride in having a saint in the family. The kings of England valued their connection to Edward the Confessor, the kings of France emphasized their descent from St. Louis, and the family of Elizabeth of Thuringia advertized their relationship to the saint. Some families even had a record of producing saints, like the ducal dynasty of Andechs-Meran, which produced thirty-two saints in the period 1150–1500.[115] But, in general, saints were not the property of a family. They might be associated with an Order, a city or a guild, but they were rarely their exclusive possession. Christians could turn to any of the sainted dead. So, while there are some cases of Christian saintliness running in families, and evidence for family pride in being related to a saint, the quality of saintliness itself is not hereditary. Christianity, with its virgin founder and, in many times and places, its celibate priesthood, set family and holiness in opposition. Other religions did not do this. Temple Judaism had a hereditary priesthood, and Islam has always valued descent from the prophet, or, in Shia Islam, from imams. This does not mean that Judaism

[114] Cobo, *Inca Religion and Customs*, pp. 39–43, 250–55; Vega, *Comentarios reales* 6. 5 (Mexico City, 1990), pp. 225–26.

[115] Vauchez, *Sainthood*, p. 180.

and Islam have an "ancestor cult," but it does mean the hereditary or family element in their sainthood has been stronger than in Christianity.

Christians did pay attention to their ancestors (and to other relatives), but in a cult of the dead separate from the cult of the saints. This involved prayers for the dead, a complex imaginary geography of the afterlife, chantry chapels, effigies, and many other forms of commemoration. It is an open question whether the amount of effort put into the commemoration of the (non-saintly) dead, and the investment of resources it represented, was greater than that devoted to the cult of the saints.

Comparisons and Conclusions

The Christian cult of the saints has some unique features, but also some that are shared with other religions in other times and place. The first Christian saints were martyrs, executed for their faith, and there are figures in other religious traditions who are referred to as "martyrs" in English-language treatments, although there are often important differences from the martyrs of Christianity. The Jewish tradition of martyrdom could look back to the time of the Maccabees in the second century BC, when many Jews were killed during the attempt of the Seleucid dynasty to supress the Jewish religion. In the Middle Ages, Jewish communities kept lists of the victims of anti-Jewish pogroms in Germany, and they were commemorated in prayers on the Sabbath.[116] The massacres of 1096 at the time of the First Crusade were marked by their scale and by the fact that many German Jews did not wait to be killed by Christians who were offering "conversion or death," but took their own lives after killing the other members of their family, and this desperate measure was to be repeated during attacks on the Jews later in the Middle Ages. Both in the case of murder and suicide, Jewish martyrdom ("sanctification of the name of the Lord," as it is termed in Hebrew) involved non-resistance. In this, it resembled Christian martyrdom. In contrast to Christian cult, however, there was no specific ritual treatment of the grave of a martyr.

The equivalent in Arabic for "martyr" is *shahid*, which literally means "witness," just as "martyr" does. Islamic martyrs often die fighting. This is rarely the case for Christian martyrs, whose original models were those who suffered at the hands of the state without offering physical resistance. As discussed earlier, martyrs who fell in battle were a special category of Christian saint, and not a numerous one. Martyrdom has a special place in Shi'a Islam, because its foundational event, which is celebrated annually with enormous emotion and public display, is the martyrdom of Hussein, grandson of the prophet, in 680 at the battle of Karbala. The story of that day is recounted in history and poetry, and commemorated on its anniversary, the day of Ashura, with processions, sermons and mourning rituals, sometimes including

[116] *Das Martyrologium des Nürnberger Memorbuches.*

self-flagellation. In modern times "martyrdom" has been enormously important in militant Islam, marking those who die in armed struggle.

The parallels between Christian, Jewish, and Muslim martyrdom exist, but are outweighed by the differences. Christian martyrdom is distinguished by its centrality to the concept of Christian sainthood—it is, indeed, its origin—and is marked off from Jewish martyrdom by the importance it attaches to individual martyr cults, with all the associated rituals, and from Muslim martyrdom by its almost exclusively passive character. The differences stem partly from the social and political differences between the religious communities—as a persecuted minority Jews were more likely to suffer without resistance than to die as religious warriors—and partly from their different religious ideals—Christianity started with a sacrificial death not, like Judaism and Islam, with the formation of a new community with laws and armies.

As discussed in the opening section of this book, the age of Christian saints did not end with the age of martyrs, and the fourth century saw the creation of a new kind of saint, the confessor, a heroic Christian who had nevertheless not died for his or her faith. Central to this new, and non-bloody, kind of sanctity was asceticism, a rigorous life-long programme of self-denial and taming of bodily instincts. Sexual renunciation, fasting, sleep deprivation, and self-inflicted pain and discomfort were part of the ascetic's armour, designed to deny both the flesh and the devil, and to win the reward of heavenly bliss. Whatever other features Christian sanctity might have, this was always one of its strongest and most continuous characteristics and it did indeed go back to the root of the religion, for, in contrast to the other Abrahamic faiths, Judaism and Islam, the founder of Christianity had not married, held property or governed a community, but had instead launched a revivalist movement which preached repentance and had as its counsel of perfection the abandonment of worldly wealth. Sexual renunciation and poverty could be an element of Jewish or Muslim sanctity, but had nothing like the central role they played in Christian sainthood.

Christian saints attained their exalted status and their recognition in society not by taking the ordinary values of that society to a higher degree, but by inverting them. They rejected family, sexual pleasure, and wealth, things that most people desire, and took up a life of self-denial and poverty. This was part of their striving for holiness. Abjection and deprivation did not automatically convey spiritual status. They had to be chosen. To be poor was a misfortune; to embrace poverty was a virtue. Curiously, once the extraordinary state of sanctity had been obtained, the saint was now able to help ordinary people with ordinary needs: to heal their children or bring them children, to free them from unjust (or even from just) captivity, to bring good weather.

In their radical asceticism Christian saints are closer to the holy men of Hinduism and Buddhism than to those of Judaism or Islam. The Hindu holy man (*sadhu*) renounces sex and property and lives the life of a wandering beggar, like the first Franciscan friars. While Jewish and Muslim saints were sometimes praised for their abstinence, many were married, possessed property, and might have positions of authority and leadership. This was also true of some Christian saints, but the most important components of Christian sanctity were virginity, or at least celibacy, self-mortification and renunciation of property. It is not a coincidence that monasticism has flourished most strongly in Christianity and Buddhism, both of them with powerful ideals of asceticism.

Some of the ritual practices found in the Christian cult of the saints are also important parts of other religions. The kindling of artificial light, for example, seems to be one very widespread way of marking out a place as sacred or set-apart. Amongst the instructions God gave for the making of the Ark of the Covenant were detailed specifications for a seven-armed lamp or menorah (Exodus 25:31–40). An account of a pagan philosopher visiting the shrine of Apollo at Daphne in 362 describes him "lighting some candles, as is customary."[117] The cult of the tomb-shrines of Judaism, discussed earlier, involved lighting candles on the tomb. Ritualized food-sharing at shrines is also common in several religions. In the fourth century, as Christians came to accept the lighting of candles at the martyrs' tombs, but to reject the idea of ritual food-sharing in those same locations, they were sorting out which cult practices they were to adopt and where to draw lines between their own cults and those of other religions.

Some practices have been highly controversial. The role of the image in religious practice, for example, was a field of dispute not only between religious traditions but also within them. Medieval Christianity came to embrace the sacred image as a major part of its devotional rituals—two-dimensional only in the East (after a traumatic conflict), both two- and three-dimensional in the West. These two branches of Christendom placed anthropomorphic images at the heart of their devotional rituals. Few things marked a sharper gulf from Judaism and Islam, which regarded this aspect of Christianity as alien and hateful. Christians found themselves in a delicate position because their own faith had started as vehemently opposed to idolatry. Its defining heroes, the martyrs, were those who had refused to sacrifice to images of the gods, images that were essential elements of the polytheistic paganism of Greece and Rome. In their defence of the practice of image-veneration Christians often seem more ingenious than convincing, suggesting that they felt the strength of the arguments of Jews and Muslims. It has indeed sometimes been suggested that the attack on holy images during the period of Byzantine iconoclasm was influenced by the uncompromisingly hostile attitude to such images in Islam. If the Muslims, who rejected images, had conquered half or more of the Byzantine Empire, perhaps the Byzantines should also reject them to regain God's favour. Whether this theory is true or not, the fissure between Christendom and Islam was also one between two traditions about images. Part of the process of converting Hagia Sophia to a mosque after the Turkish conquest of 1453 was the plastering over of the mosaics of Christ and the saints.

[117] Ammianus Marcellinus, *Res gestae* 22. 13. 3 (3, p. 129).

Other religions, far from Europe, also had a central place for holy images in human form. Hindu gods and goddesses are represented both in human and animal shapes, and the statue of the Buddha is the focus of Buddhist temples. In this respect medieval Christianity came to align itself with the polytheistic religions of Asia and the ancient world rather than with the other Abrahamic religions.

Holy relics are found in many cultures other than that of the Christian Middle Ages.[118] Buddhists revere the relics of the Buddha and other Buddhist saints. These relics are usually their cremated remains, although body parts, such as the tooth of the Buddha revered in Sri Lanka, and contact relics (bowls, robes, and so on) are also not uncommon. The transmission of these relics was recorded in texts of the same type as the medieval western translation account. Buddhist relics are often enshrined in a *stupa*, a structure in the form of a dome or rounded tower, of which there are thousands in the lands where Buddhism is important. These might be permanently endowed. A case from Siam is recorded in an inscription of 1168, which mentions the gift of land and other goods "for the upkeep of an enshrined corporal relic of the Buddha."[119] If not cremated, the body of a sage might remain incorrupt for centuries, and, in China, Zen (Ch'an) masters were often mummified and their bodies kept in temples as objects of veneration.[120] The parallels between Christian and Buddhist practice are so striking that one western scholar, studying the custom of worshippers' remains being placed in *stupas* around a central *stupa* with its relic, has even used the phrase "burial *ad sanctos*" to describe it.[121]

The Christian cult of the saints, as it emerged in the late Roman world and developed throughout the medieval centuries, was wide and deep. People of all social ranks and levels of education were involved. And this widespread participation was shaped, orchestrated, and sometimes suppressed by direction and regulation on the part of the authorities. Sketching in the origins of any saintly cult, Pierre-André Sigal distinguished two phases: "At the beginning, popular piety . . . [then] the religious communities take over."[122] As he suggests, a successful cult required two essential components: considerable support from local lay people, who chose to regard a tomb in their region as a centre of healing power; and the approval of an ecclesiastical establishment, that is, a big church and the community of monks or clergy attached to it. Without the former one might have a saint who was purely nominal, whose name was recited or whose tomb was given some special honours within the church, but was otherwise ignored; without the latter crowds might sometimes gather but there would be no public liturgical commemoration, and no pens put to work to ensure a permanent memory of the saint. Both the ubiquity and the official embrace

[118] Borgeaud and Volokhine, eds., *Les objets de la mémoire: pour une approche comparatiste des reliques et de leur culte.*

[119] Wyatt, "Relics, Oaths, and Politics in Thirteenth-century Siam," p. 12.

[120] Sharf, "The Idolization of Enlightenment: On the Mummification of Ch'an Masters in Medieval China."

[121] Schopen, "Burial *Ad Sanctos* and the Physical Presence of Buddha in Early Indian Buddhism."

[122] Sigal, *L'homme et le miracle*, pp. 167, 172.

made Christian saintly cult different from that in its kindred religions, for neither Judaism nor Islam made the saintly tomb quite so dominant in religious practice, nor did they have anything like the centralized ecclesiastical institutions of medieval Christendom, so the saints' cults that sprang up at Jewish or Muslim tombs were not subject to the same scrutiny, by bishop or pope, as Christian cults.

One striking thing about the Christian cult of the saints is how adaptable and malleable it has been. It arose in the cities of the ancient Greek and Roman world but spread in its early centuries deep into the deserts of Egypt and the Middle East and then westwards to the cool, wet landscapes of Gaul and Britain, reaching the Atlantic coasts of Ireland, a country never subdued by Rome, in the fifth century. It has remained a central part of Christian worship and devotion ever since, in the monasteries of Germany and Greece, the trading towns of the Italian Renaissance, the baroque churches of Austria and Mexico, in Russia, Armenia and Georgia, in the industrial cities of modern France, and the Catholic and Orthodox congregations of North America. It is only the Protestants of Europe and their overseas descendants who have ever really turned their backs on the saints. This wide appeal can be explained partly because the cult of the saints met needs, in particular the need for the hope of a cure in a sick and suffering world without effective medicine, but it also suffused the imagination of worshippers. The stories of the saints and their bright images were concrete embodiments of these invisible patrons. And the stories and the images meant that the fame and name of a saint could be universal, spreading far beyond the revered tomb that formed the original focus of a cult. Yet that local identity was never lost: people went to Rome to visit the apostles Peter and Paul because that was where they were, even if their pictures and statues could be found everywhere and their tale was told in every church. Just as the saints were both universal and local, so they were present but also transcended time, and they were often imagined as a glorious company in heaven, apostles rubbing shoulders with medieval bishops, virgin martyrs with saintly queens. They have shaped the lives and imaginations of millions, and still do.

GLOSSARY

Asceticism — Denial of pleasure and comfort for religious motives.

Apse — A semi-circular or polygonal recess at the east end of a church.

Beguines — Pious women who lived in communities without taking vows, often supporting themselves by handicrafts.

Confessor — A saint who is not a martyr.

Ex-voto — An offering to a saint made in pursuance of a vow, sometimes in an appropriate shape, such as a model body part for a cure or a model ship for salvation from shipwreck.

Feast/feast-day — The annual commemoration of a saint, or of some important event in Christian history.

Hagiography — Writing about the saints—Passions, Lives, miracle accounts, accounts of translations.

Indulgence — Release from the temporal punishment of sin granted by an ecclesiastical authority (often in the form of so many days of purgatorial punishment).

Inventio/invention — The finding of a saint's remains, often after a visionary revelation.

Kalendar — A list of saints' feast-days, beginning on 1 January, usually with a page for each month and indications of the level of solemnity of the feast. Often prefixed to Psalters and liturgical books.

Legendary — A collection of saints' Lives.

Martyrology — A list of saints (originally martyrs, but subsequently including confessors) according to the calendar of the year, with notes of their origin and fate.

Mendicants — Friars (literally "beggars").

Octave — A subsidiary feast-day celebrated a week after the main festival.

Passion — An account of the trial and suffering of a martyr, especially during the persecutions in the time of the Roman Empire.

Relics — Literally, "remains." The body, or parts of the body, of a saint ("corporeal relics") or items that had been in contact with the saint or the saint's tomb ("contact relics").

Synaxarion — In the Greek Church, a collection of readings from saints' Lives for the feast-days of the saints organized according to the calendar year.

Translation — Ritual relocation of a saint's relics. This might involve transportation over many miles, from one place to another, but could also simply entail removal from one part of a church to another.

BIBLIOGRAPHY OF WORKS CITED

Abbreviations

AASS	Acta sanctorum (68 vols. to date, Antwerp, Brussels, and so on, 1643–)
AASSOSB	*Acta sanctorum ordinis sancti Benedicti*, ed. Jean Mabillon (9 vols., Paris, 1668–1701; 2nd ed., Venice, 1733–40)
AB	*Analecta Bollandiana*
AQ	Ausgewählte Quellen zur deutschen Geschichte des Mittelalters (Darmstadt)
ASV	Archivum Secretum Vaticanum
BAV	Biblioteca Apostolica Vaticana
BHG	*Bibliotheca Hagiographica Graeca* (cited by item number)
BHL	*Bibliotheca Hagiographica Latina* (cited by item number)
BL	British Library
BnF	Bibliothèque nationale de France
BS	*Bibliotheca sanctorum*
CC	Corpus Christianorum (Turnhout)
CCCM	Corpus Christianorum, Continuatio Medievalis (Turnhout)
CCSG	Corpus Christianorum, Series Graeca (Turnhout)
CCSL	Corpus Christianorum, Series Latina (Turnhout)
CSEL	Corpus Scriptorum Ecclesiasticorum Latinorum (Vienna)
EETS	Early English Text Society
o.s.	original series
Mansi	Mansi, Giovanni Domenico, ed., *Sacrorum conciliorum nova et amplissima collectio*
MGH	Monumenta Germaniae Historica
AA	Auctores antiquissimi
DD	Diplomata
SRG	Scriptores rerum Germanicarum in usum scholarum
SRM	Scriptores rerum Merovingicarum
SS	Scriptores (in folio)
MOPH	Monumenta Ordinis Fratrum Praedicatorum historica (Rome)
OED	*Oxford English Dictionary*
OMT	Oxford Medieval Texts
PG	Patrologia cursus completus, series graeca, ed. J.-P. Migne (162 vols., Paris, 1857–66) (cited by column numbers)

PL	Patrologiae cursus completus, series latina, ed. J.-P. Migne (221 vols., Paris, 1844–64) (cited by column numbers)
Po.	Potthast, *Regesta pontificum Romanorum* (cited by item number)
RS	Rerum Britannicarum Medii Aevi Scriptores ("Rolls Series") (London)
SC	Sources chrétiennes (Paris)
Settimane di Studio	Settimane di Studio del Centro Italiano di Studi sull'Alto Medioevo
SH	Subsidia hagiographica (Brussels)

Manuscripts

Albi, Médiathèque municipale Pierre Almaric d'Albi
Ms. 5 (olim Bibliothèque municipale 150) (Kalendar) (consulted on-line)
Cambridge, Corpus Christi College (consulted on-line)
44 (English Pontifical; 11th century)
79 (English Pontifical; 15th century)
161 (English collection of saints' Lives; c. 1200)
540 (southern French Book of Hours; late 14th century)
Dublin, Trinity College
82 (Irish Carmelite Missal; later 15th century)
86 (Irish Carmelite Breviary; later 15th century)
89 (Italian Franciscan Breviary; late 14th or 15th century)
509 (Robert Bale's *Alphabetum sanctorum Angliae*; 15th century)
737 (German pseudo-Abdias; 9th century)
Durham, Cathedral Library
Hunter 101 (Reginald of Durham; c. 1170)
Exeter, Cathedral Library
3508 (Psalter; 13th century)
3518 (martyrology; 12th century)
Geneva, Bibliothèque de Genève
lat. 33 (French Book of Hours; late 15th century) (consulted on-line)
Gotha, Forschungsbibliothek
Memb. I 81 (English Legendary; 14th century) (consulted on microfilm)
Laon, Bibliothèque municipale
254 (Breviary; 14th century) (consulted on-line)
London, BL
Add. 4836 (French Book of Hours; 15th century)
Add. 10788 (Italian liturgical handbook; 15th century)
Add. 17275 (saints' Lives in French; 14th century)
Add. 17354 (Dutch Book of Hours; 15th century)
Add. 21616 (*Vitae siue gesta sanctorum et venerabilium patrum monasterii in Hemmenrode*; 1459)
Add. 21926 ("Grandison Psalter"; late 13th century)
Add. 25600 (Spanish Legendary; 10th century)
Add. 41070 (Juan Gil de Zamora's Legendary; c. 1300)
Add. 41179 (Lives of female saints in French; 15th century)

Add. 46203 (Cistercian Missal; late 12th century)
Add. 70513 (French saints' Lives; 14th century)
Add. 59616 ("Customary of the Shrine of St. Thomas Becket"; 1428)
C. 18. E. 2. (118): "Iste reliquie ostenduntur in ecclesia Tungrensi"
Cotton Otho D IX (*Nova legenda Anglie*; 15th century)
Cotton Tiberius E I (John of Tynemouth's *Sanctilogium*; later 14th century)
Cotton Vespasian A XIV (Welsh saints' Lives; late 12th century)
Egerton MS 859 (prayer book made in Cologne; 15th century)
Egerton MS 3763 (prayer book of Arnulf II of Milan; 998–1018)
Harley 4664 (Coldingham Breviary; late 13th century)
Lansdowne 451 (English Pontifical; 15th century)

London, Kew, The National Archives
E 101/377/2 (account roll of Mary, sister of King Edward II; 1317)
SC 8/246/12267 (licence for pilgrimage; 1350)

Munich, Bayerische Staatsbibliothek
Clm 3514 ("Codex Velseri"; Legendary; 8th century)
Clm 14569 (Kalendar; 11th century)

New York, Pierpont Morgan Library (images on-line)
M. 44 (northern French Psalter; c. 1175)
M. 75 (French Breviary; 1350–74)
M. 729 (Psalter-Hours of Yolande de Soissons; late 13th century)

Oxford, Bodleian Library
Tanner 15 (Nova legenda Anglie; 1499)

Oxford, Corpus Christi College
209 (Passio et miracula beati Olavi) (consulted on-line)

Paris, BnF
Collection Languedoc Doat 21 (Inquisitorial records; 17th-century transcript of 13th-century documents)
Collection Languedoc Doat 28 (Inquisitorial records; 17th-century transcript of early-14th-century documents)
lat. 7299 (Kalendar; late 10th century)
lat. 9474 (Hours of Anne of Brittany; c. 1500)
lat. 9550 (miscellaneous; 7th century)
lat. 10862 (Lives of female saints; 10th century)
lat. 12043 (Diurnale Guillermi abbatis; 1399)
lat. 17626 (saints' Lives; 10th century)
lat. 18315 (*Vita Wandregisili*; 8th century)
nouv. acq. lat. 311 (Geoffroy de Courlon, *Libellus super reliquiis*; late 13th century)

Philadelphia, Free Library
MS Lewis E 185 (Lewis Psalter; 13th century) (consulted on-line)

St. Gallen, Stiftsbibliothek
Cod. Sang. 453 (Chapter book; 12th century) (consulted on-line)
Cod. Sang. 566 (Kalendar; 9th century) (consulted on-line)

Vatican City
ASV
Reg. Vat. 12 (Register of Honorius III; 1222–24)
Reg. Vat. 13 (Register of Honorius III; 1224–27)

Reg. Vat. 18 (Register of Gregory IX; 1235–38)
Reg. Vat. 44 (Register of Nicholas IV; 1288–92)
Riti, Processus 2929 (Clare of Montefalco)
BAV
Cod. Reg. 456 (Hagiography of Benedict et al.; 11th century)
Vat. lat. 1122 (John of Jentzenstein [Jenstein], *Miracula beate Marie visitacionis*; late 14th century)
Vat. lat. 4015 (canonization process of Thomas de Cantilupe; 1307)
Vat. lat. 6059 (canonization hearings of Raymond of Peñaforte; 16th-century transcripts)
Vat. lat. 8541 (Hungarian Angevin Legendary; mid-14th century)
York Minster
XVI. G. 23 (*Nova legenda Anglie*; 1454)

Printed Primary Sources

Abbo, *Bella Parisiacae urbis*, ed. Paul von Winterfeld, MGH, *Poetae latini aevi carolini* 4/1 (Berlin, 1899), pp. 72–122.

Abbo of Fleury, *Passio sancti Eadmundi* (BHL 2392), ed. Michael Winterbottom, *Three Lives of English Saints* (Toronto, 1972), pp. 67–87.

Abraham of Ephesus, *Oratio in Annuntiationem beatissimae Mariae virginis* (BHG 1136h), ed. Martin Jugie, *Patrologia Orientalis* 16 (1922), pp. 442–47.

Accounts of the Lord High Treasurer of Scotland 4: *1507–13*, ed. James Balfour Paul (Edinburgh, 1902).

Acta apostolorum apocrypha, ed. R. A. Lipsius and M. Bonnet (2 vols. in 3, Leipzig, 1891–1903).

Acta capitulorum generalium ordinis praedicatorum 1 *(1220–1303)*, ed. Benedictus Maria Reichert (MOPH 3, 1898).

Acta capitulorum generalium ordinis praedicatorum 2 *(1304–1378)*, ed. Benedictus Maria Reichert (MOPH 4, 1899).

Acta et miracula Bernardi confessoris (BHL 1202), AASS Octobris 6 (1794), pp. 631–32.

Acta et processus canonizacionis Beate Birgitte, ed. Isak Collijn (Uppsala, 1924–31).

Acta et processus canonizationis Sanctae Birgittae. Codex Holmiensis A 14 (Handskrifter från Sveriges medeltid utgivna i ljustryck 1; Stockholm, 1920 [facsimile, with an introduction by Isak Collijn]).

Acta ex processu Gerardi tinctorii, AASS Iunii 1 (1695), pp. 768–76.

Acta Iohannis, ed. Eric Junod and Jean-Daniel Kaestliper (2 vols., CC, Series Apocryphorum 1–2, 1983).

Acta Maximiliani (BHL 5813), ed. Musurillo, *Acts of the Christian Martyrs*, pp. 244–48.

Acta Pauli et Theclae (BHG 1710), ed. Richard Adelbert Lipsius and Maximilien Bonnet, *Acta apostolorum apocrypha* (2 vols. in 3, Leipzig, 1891–1903) 1, pp. 235–72 (English transl. *The Apocryphal New Testament*, pp. 272–81).

Acta proconsularia sancti Cypriani (BHL 2037), ed. Musurillo, *Acts of the Christian Martyrs*, pp. 168–74.

Acta sanctae Dorotheae virginis (BHL 2323), AASS Februrarii 1 (1658), pp. 773–76.

Acta S. Officii Bononie ab anno 1291 usque ad annum 1310, ed. Lorenzo Paolini and Raniero Orioli (3 vols., Fonti per la storia d'Italia 106, 1982–84).

Acta synodi Atrebatensis, PL 142, cols. 1271–1312.
Acta translationis corporis sancti Isidori (BHL 4488), ed. Francisco Santos Coco, *Historia Silense* (Madrid, 1921), pp. 93–99 (PL 81: 39–43).
Acts of the Parliaments of Scotland 1, ed. Thomas Thomson and Cosmo Innes (Edinburgh, 1844).
Acts of William I, King of Scots, 1165–1214, ed. Geoffrey Barrow (Regesta regum Scottorum 2, Edinburgh, 1971).
Actus beati Francisci et sociorum eius (BHL 3119b–d), ed. Paul Sabatier (Paris, 1902).
Adam of Bremen, *Gesta Hammaburgensis ecclesiae pontificum*, ed. Werner Trillmich, *Quellen des 9. und 11. Jahrhunderts zur Geschichte der Hamburgischen Kirche und des Reiches* (AQ 11, Darmstadt, 1961), pp. 135–503.
Adam of Eynsham, *Magna vita sancti Hugonis: The Life of Hugh of Lincoln*, ed. Decima Douie and D. Hugh Farmer (2 vols., London, 1961–62; repr. OMT, 1985).
Ademar of Chabannes, *Chronicon*, ed. P. Bourgain (CCCM 129, 1999).
———, *Epistola de Apostolatu Martialis* (BHL 5584), PL 141, cols. 89–112.
Ado of Vienne, *Martyrologium*, ed. Jacques Dubois and Geneviève Renaud, *Le martyrologe d'Adon* (Paris, 1984).
Adomnán, *Life of St Columba*, tr. Richard Sharpe (London, 1995).
———, *Vita Columbae*, ed. Alan Orr Anderson and Marjorie Ogilvie Anderson, *Life of Columba* (rev. ed., OMT, 1991).
Adso of Montier-en-Der, *Vita sancti Mansueti primi Leucorum urbis pontificis* (BHL 5209–10), PL 137, cols. 619–44.
Adversus Constantinum Caballinum, PG 95, cols. 309–44.
Ælfric, *Catholic Homilies: The First Series*, ed. Peter Clemoes (EETS Supplementary Series 17, 1997).
———, *Catholic Homilies: The Second Series*, ed. Malcolm Godden (EETS Supplementary Series 5, 1979).
———, *Lives of Saints*, ed. Walter W. Skeat (4 vols. in 2, EETS o.s. 76, 82, 94, 114, 1881–1900 [Ælfric's Homilies, Third Series]).
Ælfric's Catholic Homilies: Introduction, Commentary and Glossary, ed. Malcolm Godden (EETS Supplementary Series 18, 2000).
Aelred of Rievaulx, *De institutione inclusarum*, ed. A. Hoste and C. H. Talbot, *Opera ascetica Aelredi Rievallensis* (CCCM 1, 1971), pp. 637–82.
———, *De sanctis ecclesiae Haugustaldensis*, ed. James Raine, *The Priory of Hexham* (2 vols., Surtees Society 44, 46, 1864–65) 1, pp. 172–203.
———, *De spiritali amicitia*, ed. A. Hoste, *Aelredi Rievallensis opera omnia* 1*: opera ascetica* (CCCM 1, 1971), pp. 287–350.
———, *Relatio de Standardo*, ed. Richard Howlett, *Chronicles of the Reigns of Stephen, Henry II and Richard I* (4 vols., RS, 1884–89) 3, pp. 179–99.
———, *Vita sancti Edwardi regis et confessoris* (BHL 2423), PL 195, cols. 737–90.
Agnellus of Ravenna, *Liber pontificalis ecclesiae Ravennatis*, ed. Oswald Holder-Egger, MGH, *Scriptores rerum Langobardicarum et Italicarum saec. VI–IX* (Hanover, 1878), pp. 278–391.
Agnès d'Harcourt, *La vie de la bienheureuse Isabelle de France*, ed. Sean L. Field, *The Writings of Agnes of Harcourt* (Notre Dame, 2003), pp. 52–92.
Agobard of Lyons, *De grandine et tonitruis*, ed. L. van Acker, *Agobardi Lugdunensis opera omnia* (CCCM 52, 1981), pp. 1–15.

Agobard of Lyons, *De picturis et imaginibus*, ed. L. van Acker, *Agobardi Lugdunensis opera omnia* (CCCM 52, 1981), pp. 149–81.

Aimoin of St.-Germain-des-Prés, *De translatione sanctorum martyrum Georgii monachi, Aurelii et Nathaliae* (BHL 3409), PL 115, cols. 939–48.

Akropolites, Constantine, *Sermo in sanctam martyrem Theodosiam* (BHG 1774), ed. Sofia Kotzabassi, *Das hagiographische Dossier der heiligen Theodosia von Konstantinopel: Einleitung, Edition und Kommentar* (Byzantinisches Archiv 21, Berlin, 2009), pp. 123–40.

Akropolites, George, *The History*, tr. Ruth Macrides (Oxford, 2007).

Die Akten des Kanonisationsprozesses Dorotheas von Montau von 1394 bis 1521, ed. Richard Stachnik (Cologne and Vienna, 1978).

Alanus de Insulis, *Contra paganos (De fide catholica 4)*, ed. Marie-Thérèse d'Alverny, *Islam et chrétiens de Midi (XIIe–XIVe s.)* (Cahiers de Fanjeaux 18, 1983), pp. 301–50.

———, *De fide catholica*, PL 210, cols. 305–430.

Albert Suerbeer, *Historia canonizationis et translationis sancti Edmundi archiepiscopi et confessoris*, ed. Edmund Martene and Ursin Durand, *Thesaurus novus anecdotorum* 3 (Paris, 1717), pp. 1831–74.

Alberti, Leon Battista, *Vita sancti Potiti* (BHL 6912d), ed. Cecil Grayson, *Opuscoli inediti* (Florence, 1954), pp. 63–88.

Albertus Magnus, *De animalibus*, ed. Hermann Stadler (2 vols., Beiträge zur Geschichte der Philosophie des Mittelalaters 15–16, Münster, 1916–20).

———, *Summa theologica*, ed. A. Borgnet, *Opera omnia* 32 (Paris, 1895).

Alcuin, *The Bishops, Kings, and Saints of York*, ed. Peter Godman (OMT, 1982).

———, *Epistolae*, ed. Ernst Dümmler, MGH, *Epistolae* 4 *(Karolini aevi* 2*)* (Berlin, 1895).

———, *Vita Richarii* (BHL 7223), ed. Christiane Veyrard-Cosme, *L'oeuvre hagiographique en prose d'Alcuin: Vitae Willibrordi, Vedasti, Richarii* (Florence, 2003), pp. 109–37.

———, *Vita Willibrordi: Homilia* (BHL 8937), ed. Wilhelm Levison, MGH, SRM 7 (Hanover and Leipzig, 1920), pp. 138–41.

Alexander Nequam (Neckham), *Speculum speculationum*, ed. R. M. Thomson (Oxford, 1988).

Alexander of Ashby, *Liber festivalis*, ed. Greti Dinkova-Bruun, *Alexandri Essebiensis opera poetica* (CCCM 188A, 2004), pp. 151–270.

Alexander of Hales, *Glossa in quatuor libros Sententiarum Petri Lombardi* (4 vols., Quaracchi, 1951–57).

Alpert of Metz, *De diversitate temporum*, ed. Hans van Rij and Anna Sapir Abulafia (Amsterdam, 1980).

The Alsfeld Passion Play: Text and Translation, ed. Larry E. West (Lewiston, NY, 1997).

Althochdeutsche Literatur: ausgewählte Texte mit Übertragungen, ed. Horst Dieter Schlosser (Frankfurt am Main, 1989).

Amalarius of Metz, *Liber officialis*, ed. J. M. Hanssens, *Amalarii episcopi opera liturgica omnia* (3 vols., Studi e testi 138–40, Vatican City, 1948–50), 2.

Ambrose, *De virginibus*, ed. Peter Dückers (Fontes christiani, Turnhout, 2009).

———, *Epistularum liber decimus*, ed. Michaela Zelzer, *Sancti Ambrosii opera* 10 (CSEL 82/3, 1982).

Ammianus Marcellinus, *Res gestae*, ed. Edouard Galletier et al., *Histoires* (6 vols. in 7, Paris, 1968–99).

Amulo of Lyons, *Epistolae*, ed. Ernst Dümmler, MGH, *Epistolae* 5 (*Karolini aevi* 3) (Berlin, 1899), pp. 361–78.

Analecta hymnica medii aevi, ed. Guido Maria Dreves and Clemens Blume (55 vols., Leipzig, 1886–1922, plus indexes, 2 vols. in 3, Bern, 1978).

Anastasius Bibliothecarius, *Epistola* 1, ed. E. Perels and G. Laehr, MGH, *Epistolae* 7 (*Karolini aevi* 5) (Berlin, 1928), pp. 395–98.

Anastasius of Sinai, *Quaestiones et responsiones*, ed. Marcel Richard and Joseph Munitiz (CCSG 59, 2006).

Anastasius of Sinai (attrib.), *Quaestiones et responsiones*, PG 89, cols. 311–824.

Ancrene Wisse, ed. Bella Millett (EETS o.s. 325, 2005).

Andrew of Crete, *Orationes in nativitatem sanctissimae Deiparae I–IV*, PG 97, cols. 805–81.

Angelo Clareno, *Expositio regulae fratrum minorum*, ed. Livarius Oliger (Quaracchi, 1912).

Angilbert, *De ecclesia Centulensi libellus*, ed. Georg Waitz, MGH, SS 15 (Hanover, 1887), pp. 173–79.

Anglo-Saxon Chronicle, ed. Charles Plummer and John Earle, *Two of the Saxon Chronicles Parallel* (2 vols., Oxford, 1892–99 [vol. 1 text]).

Anglo-Saxon Litanies of the Saints, ed. Michael Lapidge (Henry Bradshaw Society 106, 1991).

Angsar, *Miracula Willehadi* (BHL 8899), AASS Novembris 3 (1910), pp. 847–51.

Annales Bertiniani, ed. Georg Waitz, SRG (Hanover, 1883).

Annales Corbeienses maiores, ed. Franz-Josef Schmale, *Die größeren Annalen von Corvey* (Münster, 1996).

Annales domni Alfonsi Portugallensium regis, ed. Monica Blöcker-Walter, *Alfons I. von Portugal: Studien zu Geschichte und Sage des Begründers der portugiesischen Unabhängigkeit* (Zürich, 1966), pp. 151–61.

Annales Fuldenses, ed. Friedrich Kurze, SRG (Hanover, 1891).

Annales Magdaburgenses, ed. Georg Heinrich Pertz, MGH, SS 16 (Hanover, 1859), pp. 105–96.

Annales Quedlinburgenses, ed. Martina Giese, MGH, SRG (Hanover, 2004).

Annales sancti Trudperti, ed. Georg Heinrich Pertz, MGH, SS 17 (Hanover, 1861), pp. 285–94.

Annalista Saxo, ed. Georg Waitz, MGH, SS 6 (Hanover, 1844), pp. 553–777.

Annals of Ulster, ed. Seán Mac Airt and Gearóid Mac Niocaill (Dublin, 1983).

Annolied, ed. Max Roediger, MGH, *Deutsche Chroniken* 1 (Hanover, 1895), pp. 115–32.

The Anonimalle Chronicle 1307 to 1334, ed. Wendy Childs and John Taylor (Yorkshire Archaeological Soc., Record Ser. 147, 1991 for 1987).

Anso, *Vita Ursmari episcopi et abbatis Lobbiensis* (BHL 8416), ed. Wilhelm Levison, MGH, SRM 6 (Hanover and Leipzig, 1913), pp. 453–61.

Anthologia Graeca, ed. W. R. Paton, *The Greek Anthology* (5 vols., London and New York, 1916–18).

The Antient Kalendars and Inventories of the Treasury of His Majesty's Exchequer, ed. Francis Palgrave (3 vols., London, 1836).

Antonini Placentini Itinerarium, ed. P. Geyer, *Itineraria et alia geographica* (CC 175, 1965), pp. 127–74.

The Apocryphal New Testament, ed. Montague Rhodes James (Oxford, 1924).

Arcoid, *Miracula sancti Erkenwaldi* (BHL 2601), ed. E. Gordon Whatley, *The Saint of London: The Life and Miracles of St. Erkenwald* (Binghamton, 1989), pp. 100–164.

Arnold of St. Emmeram, *Libri de sancto Emmerammo* (BHL 2541) (extracts), ed. Georg Waitz, MGH, SS 4 (Hanover, 1841), pp. 543–74.

Asterius of Amasea, *Homilies I–XIV*, ed. C. Datema (Leiden, 1970).

Athanasius, *Vita Antonii*, ed. G.J.M. Bartelink (SC 400, 1994).
Athanasius of Panagiou, *Vita prima Athanasii Athonitae* (BHG 187), ed. Jacques Noret, *Vitae duae antiquae Sancti Athanasii Athonitae* (CCSG 9, 1981), pp. 1–124.
Audacht Morainn, ed. Fergus Kelly (Dublin, 1976).
Augustine, *Confessiones*, ed. Martin Skutella and Lucas Verheijen (CCSL 27, 1981).
———, *Contra mendacium*, ed. Joseph Zycha, *De fide et symbolo, etc.* (CSEL 41, 1900), pp. 467–528.
———, *De civitate dei*, ed. Bernhard Dombart and Alphonse Kalb (2 vols., CCSL 47–48, 1955).
———, *De consensu evangelistarum*, ed. Franz Weihrich (CSEL 43, 1904).
———, *De cura pro mortuis gerenda*, ed. Joseph Zycha, *De fide et symbolo, etc.* (CSEL 41, 1900), pp. 619–60.
———, *De diversis quaestionibus octoginta tribus*, ed. Almut Mutzenbecher (CCSL 44A, 1975).
———, *De opere monachorum*, ed. Joseph Zycha, *De fide et symbolo, etc.* (CSEL 41, 1900), pp. 529–96.
———, *De peccatorum meritis et remissione*, ed. Carl Urba and Josef Zycha (CSEL 60, 1913), pp. 1–151.
———, *De vera religione* ed. K.-D. Daur, *De doctrina christiana. De vera religione* (CCSL 32, 1962), pp. 187–260.
———, *Enarrationes in Psalmos* (1–50), ed. Eligius Dekkers and Iohannes Fraipont (CCSL 38, 1956).
———, *Epistulae LVI–C*, ed. K. D. Daur (CCSL 31A, 2005).
———, *Epistulae CI–CXXXIX*, ed. K. D. Daur (CCSL 31B, 2009).
———, *In Johannis Evangelium tractatus CXXIV*, ed. Radbod Willems (CCSL 36, 1954).
———, "Nouveaux sermons de S. Augustin. IV–VII. 'De martyribus,'" ed. C. Lambot, *Revue Bénédictine* 50 (1938), pp. 3–25.
———, *Sermones*, PL 38–39.
———, *Sermones post Maurinos reperti*, ed. Germain Morin, *Miscellanea Agostiniana* 1 (Rome, 1930).
———, "Sermons inédits de S. Augustin pour des fêtes des saints," ed. C. Lambot, *Revue Bénédictine* 59 (1949), pp. 55–81.
———, *Sermons on the Saints*, tr. Edmund Hill, *The Works of St. Augustine: A Translation for the Twenty-first Century* III/8–9 (New York, 1994).
"B.," *Vita sancti Dunstani* (BHL 2342), ed. Michael Winterbottom and Michael Lapidge, *The Early Lives of St. Dunstan* (OMT, 2012), pp. 3–108.
Baldwin of Ford, *Tractatus de sacramento altaris*, ed. J. Morson (2 vols., SC 93–94, 1963).
Bale, John, *Scriptorum illustrium Maioris Brytanniae, quam nunc Angliam et Scotiam vocant: catalogus* (2 vols. in 1, Basel, 1557–59).
Bartholomew of Trent, *Liber epilogorum in gesta sanctorum*, ed. Emore Paoli (Florence, 2001).
Basil of Caesarea, *Homilia XVIII in Gordium martyrem* (BHG 703), PG 31, cols. 489–508.
———, *Homilia XIX in sanctos quadraginta martyres* (BHG 1205), PG 31, cols. 508–26.
———, *Homilia XXIII in Mamantem martyrem* (BHG 1020), PG 31, cols. 589–600.
Baudonivia, *Vita sanctae Radegundis* (BHL 7049), ed. Bruno Krusch, MGH, SRM 2 (Hanover, 1888), pp. 377–95.
Bede, *Chronica maiora*, ed. Theodor Mommsen, *Chronica minora saec. IV. V. VI. VII.* 3 (MGH, AA 13, Berlin, 1898), pp. 223–327.

———, *Historia abbatum* (BHL 8968), ed. Charles Plummer, *Venerabilis Baedae opera historica* (2 vols., Oxford, 1896) 1, pp. 364–87.

———, *Historia ecclesiastica gentis Anglorum: Ecclesiastical History of the English People*, ed. Bertram Colgrave and R.A.B. Mynors (OMT, 1969).

———, *Martyrologium*, ed. Jacques Dubois and Geneviève Renaud, *Édition pratique des martyrologes de Bède, de l'anonyme lyonnais et de Florus* (Paris, 1976).

———, *Vita sancti Cuthberti* (BHL 2021), ed. Bertram Colgrave, *Two Lives of Cuthbert* (Cambridge, 1940), pp. 142–306.

———, *Vita sancti Cuthberti metrica* (BHL 2020), ed. Werner Jaeger (Leipzig, 1935).

Benedict of Peterborough, *Miracula sancti Thomae*, ed. J. C. Robertson, *Materials for the History of Thomas Becket* (7 vols., RS, 1875–85) 2, pp. 21–281.

Beneš Krabice of Weitmile, *Cronica ecclesiae Pragensis*, ed. Josef Emler, *Fontes rerum Bohemicarum* 4 (Prague, 1884), pp. 459–548.

Benincasa, *Vita sancti Rainerii confessoris* (BHL 7084), AASS Iunii 3 (1701), pp. 423–66.

Bernard Gui, *De fundatione et prioribus conventuum provinciarum Tolosanæ et Provinciæ Ordinis Praedicatorum*, ed. P. A. Amargier (MOPH 24, 1961).

———, *Practica inquisitionis heretice pravitatis*, ed. C. Douais (Paris, 1886).

———, *Scripta de sancto Dominico*, ed. Simon Tugwell (MOPH 27, 1998).

———, *Speculum sanctorale, preface*, ed. Léopold Delisle, *"Notice sur les manuscrits de Bernard Gui," Notices et extraits des manuscrits de la Bibliothèque Nationale* 27 (1879), pp. 169–455, at pp. 421–24.

Bernard of Angers, *Liber miraculorum sancte Fidis*, ed. Luca Robertini (Spoleto, 1994).

Bernard of Clairvaux, *Epistolae*, ed. Jean Leclerq and Henri-Marie Rochais, *Sancti Bernardi opera* (8 vols., Rome, 1957–78) 7–8.

———, *Sermones in Canticum Canticorum* 51–68, ed. Jean Leclercq et al., *Sermons sur le Cantique* 4 (SC 472, 2003).

———, *Vita sancti Malachiae* (BHL 5188), ed. Jean Leclerq et al., *Sancti Bernardi Opera* (8 vols., Rome, 1957–78) 3, pp. 295–378.

Berno of Reichenau, *Qualiter adventus Domini celebretur*, PL 142, cols. 1079–86.

Bernold of Constance (or St. Blasien), *Micrologus de ecclesiasticis observationibus*, PL 151, cols. 973–1022.

Beroul, *Tristan*, ed. Philippe Walter, *Tristan et Iseut* (Paris, 1989), pp. 21–229.

Bertha of Vilich, *Vita Adelheidis abbatissae Vilicensis* (BHL 67), ed. Oswald Holder-Egger, MGH, SS 15/2 (Hanover, 1888), pp. 755–63.

Betha Adamnáin: The Irish Life of Adamnán, ed. Máire Herbert and Pádraig Ó Riain (London, 1988).

Betha Colum Cille, ed. Máire Herbert, *Iona, Kells and Derry*, cols. 180–202.

Betha Phatraic, ed. Whitley Stokes, *The Tripartite Life of Patrick* (2 vols., RS, 1887).

Bethu Brigte, ed. Donncha Ó hAodha (Dublin, 1978).

Die Bibel des Patricius Leo: Codex Reginensis Graecus I B (Codices e Vaticanis selecti 75, Zurich, 1988).

Bokenham, Osbern, *Legendys of Hooly Wummen*, ed. Mary S. Serjeantson (EETS, o.s. 206, 1938 for 1936).

Bonacursus, *Manifestatio haeresis Catharorum*, ed. Raoul Manselli, "Per la storia dell'eresia nel secolo XII," *Bulletino dell'istituto storico per il medio evo* 67 (1955), pp. 189–264 (text pp. 206–11).

Bonaventure, *In tertium librum Sententiarum*, *Opera omnia* (10 vols., Quaracchi, 1882–1902), 3.

———, *Legenda maior S. Francisci*, *Analecta Franciscana* 10 (1926–41), pp. 555–652.

———, *Legenda minor S. Francisci*, ibid., pp. 655–78.

Boniface, *Epistulae*, ed. Reinhold Rau (AQ 4b, 1968).

Boniface VIII, *Sermones et bulla de canonisatione sancti Ludovici*, *Recueil des historiens des Gaules et de la France* 23 (Paris, 1894), pp. 148–60.

The Book of Margery Kempe, ed. Sanford Brown Meech (EETS o.s. 212, 1940).

The Book of St Gilbert, ed. Raymonde Foreville and Gillian Keir (OMT, 1987).

Bower, Walter, *Scotichronicon*, ed. Donald Watt et al. (9 vols., Aberdeen and Edinburgh, 1987–98).

Braulio, *Vita Emiliani* (BHL 100), PL 80, cols. 699–714.

Breviarium ad usum insignis ecclesiae Sarum 3 (*Sanctorale*), ed. Francis Procter and Christopher Wordsworth (Cambridge, 1886).

Bridgwater Borough Archives, 1200–1377, ed. Thomas Bruce Dilks (Somerset Record Soc. 48, 1933).

Bruno Candidus, *Vita Eigilis abbatis Fuldensis* (BHL 2440–41), ed. Georg Waitz, MGH, SS 15/1 (Hanover, 1887), pp. 221–33 (Book 1); ed. Ernst Dümmler, MGH, Poetae Latini Aevi Carolini 2 (Berlin, 1884), pp. 94–117 (Book 2).

Bruno of Querfurt, *Passio sancti Adalberti* (BHL 38), ed. Lorenz Weinrich, *Heiligenleben zur deutsch-slawischen Geschichte* (AQ 23, 2005), pp. 70–116.

The Brut or The Chronicles of England, ed. Friedrich W. D. Brie (2 parts, EETS, original series 131 and 136, 1906–8).

Bullarium diplomatum et privilegiorum sanctorum romanorum pontificum Taurinensis editio 4 (1859).

Bullarium Equestris Ordinis Sancti Iacobi de Spatha (Madrid, 1719).

Burchard of Worms, *Decretum*, PL 140, cols. 537–1058.

Caesarius of Arles, *Sermones*, ed. Marie-José Delage, *Sermons au peuple* (SC 175, 243, 330, 1971–86).

Caesarius of Heisterbach, *Dialogus miraculorum*, ed. J. Strange (2 vols. and index, Cologne, 1851–57).

———, *Libri miraculorum*, ed. Alfons Hilka, *Die Wundergeschichten des Caesarius von Heisterbach* 3 (Bonn, 1937), pp. 1–222.

———, *Sermo de translatione beate Elyzabeth*, ed. Alfons Hilka, ibid., pp. 381–90.

———, *Vita, passio et miracula sancti Engelberti* (BHL 2546–48), ed. Fritz Zschaeck, ibid., pp. 223–328.

———, *Vita sancte Elyzabeth lantgravie* (BHL 2494), ed. Alfons Huyskens, ibid., pp. 344–81.

Calendar of Documents Preserved in France Illustrative of the History of Great Britain and Ireland 1: *A.D. 918–1206*, ed. J. H. Round (London, 1899).

The Calendar of St Willibrord from MS Paris Lat. 10837, ed. H. A. Wilson (Henry Bradshaw Society 55, 1918).

Calendar of the Close Rolls, Edward IV 2 (London, 1953).

Le calendrier palestino-géorgien du Sinaiticus 34 (Xe siècle), ed. Gérard Garitte (SH 30, 1958).

Calvin, Jean, *Traité des reliques*, ed. Francis M. Higman, *Three French Treatises* (London, 1970), pp. 47–97.

Die Canones Theodori, ed. Paul Willem Finsterwalde (Weimar, 1929).
Canonici Wissegradensis continuatio Cosmae, ed. Josef Emler, *Fontes rerum Bohemicarum* 2/1 (Prague, 1874), pp. 203–37.
"The Canonization of St Hugh of Lincoln," ed. Hugh Farmer, *Lincolnshire Archaeological and Architectural Society Reports and Papers*, n.s. 6 (1956), pp. 86–117.
The Canonization of St Osmund, ed. A. R. Malden (Wiltshire Record Soc., 1901).
"Canons of Basil," tr. Wilhelm Riedel, *Die Kirchenrechtsquellen des Patriarchats Alexandrien* (Leipzig, 1900), pp. 231–83.
Cantigas de Santa Maria, ed. Walter Mettmann (2 vols., Vigo, 1981).
Capitularia regum Francorum 1, ed. Alfred Boretius, MGH (Hanover, 1883).
Capitularia regum Francorum 2, ed. Alfred Boretius and Victor Krause, MGH (Hanover, 1897).
Carmen in victoriam Pisanorum, ed. H.E.J. Cowdrey, "The Mahdia Campaign of 1087," *English Historical Review* 92 (1977), pp. 1–29 (text at 23–29).
Cartulaire de l'abbaye de Conques en Rouergue, ed. Gustave Desjardins (Paris, 1879).
Cartulario de Sant Cugat del Vallés, ed. José Rius Serra (3 vols., Barcelona, 1945–47).
Cassiodorus, *Institutiones*, ed. R.A.B. Mynors (Oxford, 1937).
———, *Variae*, ed. A. J. Fridh (CCSL 96, 1973).
Castiglione, Francesco da, *Vita Antonini archiepiscopi Florentini* (BHL 577), AASS Maii 1 (1680), pp. 313–25.
Caxton, William, *Golden Legende* (Westminster, 1483).
Cenci, Cesare, ed., *Documentazione di vita assisana* 1300–1550 (3 vols., Grottaferrata, 1974–76).
Chanson de Roland, ed. F. Whitehead (Oxford, 1942).
Chartae latinae antiquiores: Facsimile-Edition of the Latin Charters prior to the Ninth Century 18: *France VI*, ed. Hartmut Atsma et al. (Zurich, 1985).
Chartae latinae antiquiores: Facsimile-Edition of the Latin Charters prior to the Ninth Century 29: *Italy X*, ed. Jan-Olof Tjäder et al. (Zurich, 1993).
Chaucer, Geoffrey, *Canterbury Tales, General Prologue*, ed. Larry D. Benson, *The Riverside Chaucer* (Boston, 1987), pp. 23–36.
Choricius of Gaza, *Laudatio Marciani*, ed. Richard Foerster, *Choricii Gazaei opera* (Leipzig, 1929).
Christian, *Vita et passio sancti Wenceslai et sancte Ludmile* (BHL 8825), ed. Jaroslav Ludvíkovsky, *Kristiánova Legenda* (Prague, 1978).
Chronica Adefonsi imperatoris, ed. Antonio Maya Sánchez, *Chronica hispana saeculi XII. Pars* 1 (CCCM 71, 1990), pp. 109–248.
Chronica de Mailros, ed. Joseph Stevenson (Bannatyne Club 49, 1835).
Chronica Minor Minoritae Erphordensis, Continuatio I, Monumenta Erphesfurtensia Saec. XII. XIII. XIV., ed. Oswald Holder-Egger, MGH, SRG (Hanover and Leipzig, 1899), pp. 671–85.
Chronica Monasterii Casinensis, ed. Hartmut Hoffmann, MGH, SS 34 (Hanover, 1980).
Chronica Monasterii Sancti Michaelis Clusini, ed. Gerhard Schwartz and Elisabeth Abegg, MGH, SS 32/2 (Leipzig, 1934), pp. 959–70.
Chronica XXIV Generalium Ordinis Minorum (Analecta Franciscana 3, 1897).
Chronicon Besuensis abbatiae, ed. E. Bougaud and J. Garnier, *Chronique de l'abbaye de Saint-Bénigne de Dijon suivie de la chronique de Saint-Pierre de Bèze* (Dijon, 1875), pp. 231–503.

Chronicon de Lanercost, 1201–1346, ed. Joseph Stevenson (Bannatyne Club 65 and Maitland Club 46, Edinburgh, 1839).
Chronicon paschale, PG 92, cols. 67–1028.
Chronicon Sancti Huberti Andaginensis, ed. L. C. Bethmann and Wilhelm Wattenbach, MGH, SS 8 (Hanover, 1848), pp. 565–630.
Chronicon Sancti Michaelis in pago Virdunensi, ed. André Lesort, *Chroniques et chartes de l'abbaye de Saint-Mihiel* (*Mettensia* 6, 1909–12), pp. 1–38.
Chronicon Sancti Petri Vivi Senonensis, ed. Robert-Henri Bautier and Monique Gilles, *Chronique de Saint-Pierre-le-Vif de Sens, dite de Clarius* (Paris, 1979).
Chronique de l'abbaye de Signy, ed. Léopold Delisle, *Bibliothèque de l'Ecole des Chartes* 55 (1894), pp. 644–60.
Circumvectio Taurini episcopi (BHL 7996), AASS Augusti 2 (1735), pp. 650–56.
Claudius of Turin, *Epistolae*, ed. Ernst Dümmler, MGH, *Epistolae* 4 (*Karolini aevi* 2) (Berlin, 1895), pp. 586–613.
Clemence of Barking, *Vie de sainte Catherine*, ed. William Macbain, *Life of St Catherine* (Anglo-Norman Text Society 18, 1964).
Clement, *Vita et miracula beati Thomæ Heliæ* (BHL 8252–53), ed. Léopold Delisle, *Vie du bienheureux Thomas Hélie de Biville* (Cherbourg, 1860 [AASS Octobris 8: 606–18]).
Clement of Alexandria, *Protrepticus*, ed. Miroslav Marcovich (Leiden, 1995).
Clement of Rome, *Epistola ad Corinthios*, ed. Annie Jaubert (SC 167; rev. ed., 2000).
Close Rolls of the Reign of Henry III 1242–1247 (London, 1916).
Cobo, Bernabé, *Inca Religion and Customs*, ed. Roland Hamilton (Austin, 1990).
Codex apocryphus Novi Testamenti, ed. Johann Albert Fabricius (2nd ed., 3 vols., Hamburg, 1719).
Le codex arménien Jérusalem 121, ed. Athanase Renoux (Patrologia Orientalis 35/1, pp. 1–215 [introduction], 36/2, pp. 139–388 [text with introduction], 1969–71).
The Codex Benedictus: An Eleventh-century Lectionary from Monte Cassino, ed. Paul Meyvaert (facsimile edition, with commentary, 2 vols., Codices e Vaticanis selecti 50, New York, 1981–82).
Codex constitutionum quas summi pontifices ediderunt in solemni canonizatione sanctorum, ed. Giusto Fontanini (Rome, 1729).
Codex Iustinianus, ed. Paul Krueger (Berlin, 1877).
Codex Theodosianus, ed. Theodor Mommsen and Paul Meyer, *Theodosiani libri XVI cvm Constitutionibus Sirmondianis et Leges novellae ad Theodosianum pertinentes* (2 vols., Berlin, 1905), 1/2.
Codice topografico della Città di Roma, ed. R. Valentini and G. Zuchetti (4 vols., Fonti per la Storia d'Italia 81, 88, 90–91, 1940–53).
Cogitosus, *Vita sanctae Brigitae* (BHL 1457), AASS Februarii 1 (1658), pp. 135–42.
Columbanus, *Epistolae*, ed. G.S.M. Walker, *Sancti Columbani Opera* (Dublin, 1957), pp. 2–56.
Commynes, Philippe de, *Mémoires*, ed. Joël Blanchard (2 vols., Geneva, 2007 [vol. 1 text]).
Comnena, Anna, *Alexiad*, ed. Bernard Leib (3 vols., Paris, 1937–45).
Conchubranus, *Vita sanctae Monennae* (BHL 2096), ed. Mario Esposito, *Proceedings of the Royal Academy of Ireland* 28C (1910), pp. 202–51.
Concilia aevi Karolini 1/1, ed. Albert Werminghoff, MGH, *Concilia* 2/1 (Hanover and Leipzig, 1906).

Concilia aevi Karolini 1/2, ed. Albert Werminghoff, MGH, *Concilia* 2/2 (Hanover and Leipzig, 1908).

Concilia Africae, a. 345–a. 525, ed. Charles Munier (CCSL 149, 1974).

Concilia magnae Britanniae et Hiberniae, ed. David Wilkins (4 vols., London, 1737).

Conciliorum oecumenicorum decreta, ed. Giuseppe Alberigo et al. (3rd ed., Bologna, 1973).

Conciliorum oecumenicorum generaliumque decreta 1, ed. Giuseppe Alberigo (CC, 2006).

Concilios visigóticos et hispano-romanos, ed. José Vives (Barcelona and Madrid, 1963).

Conrad of Brauweiler, *Vita Wolfhelmi abbatis Brunwilarensis* (BHL 8987), ed. Roger Wilmans, MGH, SS 12 (Hanover, 1856), pp. 181–95.

Conrad of Eberbach, *Exordium magnum Cisterciense*, ed. Bruno Griesser (CCCM 138, 1994).

Conrad of Marburg, *Epistola de vita beate Elyzabet* (BHL 2490), *Quellenstudien zur Geschichte der heiligen Elisabeth*, pp. 155–60.

Constantine Porphyrogenitus, *De administrando imperio*, ed. G. Moravcsik (2nd. ed., Washington, DC, 1967).

Constituti Comunis Senarum, ed. Lodovico Zdekauer, *Il constituto del comune di Siena dell'anno 1262* (Milan, 1897).

Constitutiones apostolorum, ed. Marcel Metzger (3 vols., SC 320, 329, 336, 1985–87).

Constitutiones et acta publica imperatorum et regum 1, ed. Ludwig Weiland (MGH, Hanover, 1893).

Constitutiones et acta publica imperatorum et regum 2, ed. Ludwig Weiland (MGH, Hanover, 1896).

Constitutiones generales Ordinis Fratrum Minorum . . . in Capitulo generali apud Narbonam, ed. Michael Bihl, *Archivum Franciscanum Historicum* 34 (1941), pp. 13–94, 284–358.

Consuetudines Cluniacensium antiquiores, ed. Kassius Hallinger (Corpus consuetudinum monasticorum 7/2, Siegburg, 1983).

Continuatio Reginonis, ed. Friedrich Kurze, *Reginonis abbatis Prumiensis Chronicon cum continuatione Treverensi* (MGH, SRG, Hanover, 1890), pp. 154–79.

Li coronemenz Looïs, ed. Ernest Langlois, *Le couronnement de Louis: chanson de geste du XIIe siècle* (2nd ed., Paris, 1968).

Corpus genealogiarum sanctorum Hiberniae, ed. Pádraig Ó Riain (Dublin, 1985).

Corpus Iuris Civilis 3: *Novellae*, ed. Rudolf Schoell and Wilhelm Kroll (10th ed., Berlin, 1972).

Cosmas of Prague, *Chronica Boemorum*, ed. Berthold Bretholz (MGH, SRG, n.s., Berlin, 1923).

Councils and Ecclesiastical Documents Relating to Great Britain and Ireland, ed. Arthur West Haddan and William Stubbs (3 vols. in 4, Oxford, 1869–78).

Councils and Synods with Other Documents Relating to the English Church 1 *(871–1204)*, ed. D. Whitelock et al. (2 vols., Oxford, 1981).

Councils and Synods with Other Documents Relating to the English Church 2 *(1205–1313)*, ed. F. M. Powicke and C. R. Cheney (2 vols., Oxford, 1964).

Les coutumes de Saint-Gilles, ed. E. Bligny-Bondurand (Paris, 1915).

Cranmer, Thomas, *Miscellaneous Writings and Letters*, ed. John Edmund Cox (Parker Society, 1846).

Crespin, Jean, *Acta Martyrum, eorum videlicet, qui hoc seculo in Gallia, Germania, Anglia, Flandria, Italia, constans dederunt nomen Euangelio, idque sanguine suo obsignarunt: ab Wicleffo & Husso ad hunc vsque diem* (Geneva, 1556).

———, *Recueil de plusieurs personnes qui ont constamment enduré la mort pour le Nom de nostre Seigneur Iesus-Christ* (Geneva, 1554).

Cromwell, Thomas, *Life and Letters of Thomas Cromwell*, ed. Roger Bigelow Merriman (2 vols., Oxford, 1902).

Cronica sancti Petri Erfordensis moderna, *Monumenta erphesfurtensia saec. XII. XIII. XIV.*, ed. Oswald Holder-Egger, MGH, SRG (Hanover and Leipzig, 1899), pp. 117–369.

Curia Regis Rolls 1 (London, 1922).

The Customary of the Benedictine Abbey of Bury St Edmunds in Suffolk, ed. Antonia Gransden (Henry Bradshaw Society 99, 1973).

Cyprian of Carthage, *Ad Fortunatam*, ed. Robert Weber (CCSL 3, 1972), pp. 181–216.

———, *De lapsis*, ed. Maurice Bévenot (CCSL 3, 1972), pp. 217–42.

———, *Epistularium*, ed. G. F. Diercks (3 vols., CCSL 3B–D, 1994–99).

Cyril of Alexandria, *Contra Julianum*, PG 76, cols. 490–1064.

Cyril of Jerusalem, *Catacheses mystagogicae*, ed. A. Piédagnel, *Catéchèses mystagogiques* (SC 126, 1966).

Cyril of Scythopolis, *Vita Euthymii* (BHG 647–48), ed. Eduard Schwartz, *Kyrillos von Skythopolis* (Texte und Untersuchungen zur Geschichte der Altchristlichen Literatur 49/2, 1939), pp. 5–85.

———, *Vita Sabae* (BHG 1608), ibid., pp. 85–200.

———, *Vita Theodosii* (BHG 1777), ibid., pp. 235–41.

Damaso e i martiri di Roma (Vatican City, 1985).

Dante Alighieri, *La vita nuova*, ed. Domenico de Robertis, *Opere minori* 1/1 (Milan and Naples, 1984), pp. 3–247.

De apparitione sancti Michaelis (BHL 5948), ed. Georg Waitz, MGH, *Scriptores rerum Langobardicarum et Italicarum* (Hanover, 1878), pp. 541–42.

De apparitione sancti Michaelis (BHL 5951), PL 96, cols. 1389–94.

Decrees of the Ecumenical Councils, ed. Norman P. Tanner (2 vols., London, 1990).

Decretales Gregorii IX, ed. Emil Friedberg, *Corpus iuris canonici* 2 (Leipzig, 1881), cols. 1–928.

Decretum Gelasianum de libris recipiendis et non recipiendis, ed. Ernst von Dobschütz (Texte und Untersuchungen zur Geschichte der altchristlichen Literatur 38/4, 1912).

Delaborde, H.-François, "Le procès du chef de Saint Denis en 1410," *Mémoires de la Société de l'histoire de Paris et de l'Ile-de-France* 11 (1884), pp. 297–409.

De locis sanctis martyrum, ed. R. Valentini and G. Zuchetti, *Codice topografico della Città di Roma* (4 vols., Fonti per la Storia d'Italia 81, 88, 90–91, 1940–53), 2, pp. 101–31.

Depositions and Other Ecclesiastical Proceedings from the Courts of Durham from 1311 to the Reign of Elizabeth (Surtees Society 21, 1845).

De revelatione capitis beati Joannis Baptistae tractatus (BHL 4293–97), AASS Iunii 4 (1707), pp. 757–61; PL 4: 931–38.

De reversione beati Martini a Burgundia (BHL 5653), PL 133, cols. 815–38.

De sancto Ubaldo episcopo, AASS Maii 7 (1688), p. 785.

Desiderius of Monte Cassino, *Dialogi de miraculis sancti Benedicti* (BHL 1141), ed. Gerhard Schwartz and Adolf Hofmeister, MGH, SS 30/2 (Leipzig, 1934), pp. 1111–51.

Deutsche Mystiker des vierzehnten Jahrhunderts 2, ed. Franz Pfeiffer (Leipzig, 1857).

De virtutibus quae facta sunt post discessum beate Geretrudis abbatisse (BHL 3495), ed. Bruno Krusch, MGH, SRM 2 (Hanover, 1888), pp. 464–71.

Dialogus de gestis sanctorum Fratrum Minorum, ed. Ferdinand M. Delorme (Quaracchi, 1923).

The Didascalia Apostolorum in Syriac, ed. Arthur Vööbus (Scriptores Syri 175–76, 179–80, Louvain, 1979).

Didymus of Alexandria, *De trinitate (2. 1–7)*, ed. Ingrid Seiler (Meisenheim am Glan, 1975).

Diehl, Ernst, *Inscriptiones latinae Christianae veteres* (3 vols., Berlin, 1925–31).

Dionysius Exiguus, *De inventione capitis sancti Joannis Baptistae* (BHL 4290–91), PL 67, cols. 417–23.

———, *Vita sancti Pachomii abbatis Tabennensis* (BHL 6410), ed. H. Van Cranenburgh, *La vie latine de Saint Pachôme* (SH 46, 1969).

Diplomata Friderici I. 1, ed. Heinrich Appelt (MGH, DD, Hanover, 1975).

Diplomata Ludowici Germanici, Karlomanni, Ludowici iunioris, ed. Paul Kehr (MGH, DD, Berlin, 1934).

Diplomata regum Burgundiae e stirpe Rudolfina, ed. Theodor Schieffer (MGH, DD, Munich, 1977).

Diplomatarium Danicum 4/7 *(1399–1400)*, ed. Aage Andersen et al. (Copenhagen, 2000).

Discipline générale antique 1/ii: *Les canons des synodes particuliers*, ed. Périclès-Pierre Joannou (Grottaferrata, 1962).

Documentación del monasterio de Santo Domingo de Silos (954–1254), ed. Miguel C. Vivancos Gómez (Burgos, 1988).

Documents Illustrative of the Social and Economic History of the Danelaw, ed. F. M. Stenton (London, 1920).

Documents sur l'ancienne province de Languedoc, ed. C. Douais (2 vols., Paris and Toulouse, 1901–4).

Döllinger, Ignaz von, *Beiträge zur Sektengeschichte des Mittelalters* 2: *Dokumente vornehmlich zur Geschichte der Valdesier und Katharer* (Munich, 1890).

Domesday Book, ed. Abraham Farley (2 vols., London, 1783; supplementary vol. ed. H. Ellis, 1816).

Die Dresdener Bilderhandschrift des Sachsenspiegels, ed. Karl von Amira (Leipzig, 1902–26).

Drogo, *Liber miraculorum sancti Winnoci* (BHL 8956), AASS Novembris 3 (1910), pp. 275–84.

———, *Translatio sancte Lewinnae* (BHL 4902), ed. Oswald Holder-Egger, MGH, SS 15/2 (Hanover, 1888), pp. 782–89 (excerpts).

Durham Liber Vitae, ed. David Rollason and Lynda Rollason (3 vols., London, 2007).

The Durham Ritual, ed. T. J. Brown (Early English Manuscripts in Facsimile 16, Copenhagen, 1969).

Dye zaigung des hochlobwirdigen hailigthums der Stifft kirchen aller hailigen zu Wittenburg (Wittenberg, 1509).

Eadmer, *Epistola ad Glastonienses*, ed. William Stubbs, *Memorials of Saint Dunstan* (RS, 1874), pp. 412–22.

———, *Historia novorum*, ed. Martin Rule (RS, 1884).

———, *Vita Anselmi*, ed. R. W. Southern, *The Life of St Anselm* (Nelson's Medieval Texts, 1962, reprint OMT, 1972).

Early Charters of the Cathedral Church of St Paul, London, ed. Marion Gibbs (Camden, 3rd ser., 58, 1939).

Early Sources of Scottish History 500 to 1286, ed. A. O. Anderson (2 vols., Edinburgh, 1922).

Eberhard of Fürstenfeld, *Exordium et miracula sancti Leonhardi in Inchenhofen* (BHL 4879d), AASS Novembris 3 (1910), pp. 184–204.

Egeria, *Itinerarium Egeriae*, ed. E. Franceschini and R. Weber, *Itineraria et alia geographica* (CCSL 175, 1965), pp. 27–90.

Einhard, *Translatio et miracula sanctorum Marcellini et Petri* (BHL 5233), ed. Georg Waitz, MGH, SS 15/1 (Hanover, 1887), pp. 238–64.

Ekkehard of Aura, *Chronica*, ed. Georg Waitz, MGH, SS 6 (Hanover, 1844), pp. 1–267.

Die "Elsässische Legenda Aurea," 1: *Das Normalcopus*, ed. Ulla Williams and Werner Williams-Krapp (Tübingen, 1980); 2: *Das Sondergut*, ed. Konrad Kunze (Tübingen, 1983).

English Benedictine Libraries: The Shorter Catalogues, ed. Richard Sharpe et al. (Corpus of British Medieval Library Catalogues 4, London, 1994).

English Episcopal Acta 10: *Bath and Wells 1061–1205*, ed. Frances Ramsay (Oxford, 1995).

Ephraem the Syrian, *Carmina Nisibena*, ed. Edmund Beck, *Des Heiligen Ephraem des Syrers Carmina Nisibena* (Corpus scriptorum christianorum orientalium 218–19, 240–41 = Scriptores Syri 92–93, 102–3, Louvain, 1961–63).

Epitaphium Ansae reginae, ed. Ludwig Bethmann and Georg Waitz, MGH, *Scriptores rerum Langobardicarum et Italicarum saec. VI–IX* (Hanover, 1878), pp. 191–92.

Epitaphium Bosonis regis, ed. Karl Strecker, MGH, *Poetae latini aevi carolini* 4/2–3 (Berlin, 1923), pp. 1027–28.

Erasmus, *Colloquia familiaria*, ed. L.-E. Halkin et al., *Erasmi opera omnia* 1/3 (Amsterdam, 1972).

Erchanbert of Freising, *Epistolae variorum* 23, ed. Ernst Dümmler, MGH, *Epistolae* 5 (*Karolini aevi* 3) (Berlin, 1899), p. 338.

Ermanric, *Sermo de vita sancti Sualonis* (BHL 7925), ed. Oswald Holder-Egger, MGH, SS 15/1 (Hanover, 1887), pp. 151–63.

Ermentarius, *De translationibus et miraculis sancti Filiberti* (BHL 6808–9), ed. René Poupardin, *Monuments de l'histoire des abbayes de Saint-Philibert* (Paris, 1905), pp. 19–70.

Ernoul, *Chronique d'Ernoul et de Bernard le Trésorier*, ed. L. De Mas Latrie (Paris, 1871).

L'eucologio Barberini gr. 336 (ff. 1–263), ed. Stefano Parenti and Elena Velkovska (Rome, 1995).

Eugenius III, *Epistolae et privilegia*, PL 180, cols. 1013–1606.

Eugenius of Toledo, *Epistulae*, ed. Friedrich Vollmer, MGH, AA 14 (Berlin, 1905), pp. 283–90.

Eugippus, *Vita Severini* (BHL 7655–57), ed. Philippe Régerat (SC 374, 1991).

Eulogius, *Memoriale sanctorum*, ed. Juan Gil, *Corpus scriptorum Muzarabicorum* (2 vols., Madrid, 1973), 2, pp. 363–459.

Eunapius, *Vitae sophistarum*, ed. Wilmer C. Wright (Cambridge, MA, 1921).

Eusebius of Caesarea, *Demonstratio evangelica*, ed. Ivar A. Heikel (Die Griechischen christlichen Schriftsteller der ersten drei Jahrhunderte 23 [Eusebius 6], Leipzig, 1913).

———, *Epistola ad Constantiam Augustam*, ed. Thümmel, *Die Frühgeschichte der ostkirchlichen Bilderlehre*, pp. 282–84 (no. 13).

———, *Historia ecclesiastica*, ed. Gustave Bardy (4 vols., SC 31, 41, 55, 73, 1952–87).

———, *Vita Constantini*, ed. Friedhelm Winkelmann (Die Griechischen Christlichen Schriftsteller 7/1 [Eusebius 1/1], Berlin, 1975).

Eustratius of Constantinople, *De statu animarum post mortem*, ed. Peter Van Deun (CCSG, 60, 2006).

Evagrius, *Historia ecclestiastica I–III*, ed. J. Bidez and L. Parmentier, *Histoire ecclésiastique* (SC 542, 2011).

———, *Vita beati Antonii abbatis, auctore Sancto Athanasio* (BHL 609), PL 73, cols. 125–70.

Exchequer Rolls of Scotland 5: *1437–54*, ed. George Burnett (Edinburgh, 1882).

Extravagantes communes, ed. Emil Friedberg, *Corpus iuris canonici* 2 (Leipzig, 1881), cols. 1237–1312.

Exuviae sacrae Constantinopolitanae, ed. Paul Riant (2 vols., Geneva, 1877–78).

Eymerich, Nicholas, *Directorium inquisitorum* (Rome, 1587).

Fabric Rolls of York Minster, ed. James Raine (Surtees Soc. 35, 1859).

Faricius, *Vita sancti Aldhelmi* (BHL 256), ed. Michael Winterbottom, *Journal of Medieval Latin* 15 (2005), pp. 93–147.

Feet of Fines of the Ninth Year of the Reign of King Richard I (Pipe Roll Soc. 23, 1898).

Felix, *Vita sancti Guthlaci* (BHL 3723), ed. Bertram Colgrave, *Life of Saint Guthlac* (Cambridge, 1956).

Festa apostolorum, AASS Novembris 2/2 (1931), pp. 2–3.

Firmicus Maternus, *De errore*, ed. Robert Turcan (Paris, 1982).

Fita, Fidel, "El templo del Pilar y san Braulio de Zaragoza: Documentos anteriores al siglo XVI," *Boletín de la Real Academia de la Historia* 44 (1904), pp. 425–61.

Flavius Anselmus, *Vita Berengarii (*BHL 1181–82*)*, AASS Maii 6 (1688), pp. 448–49.

Flete, John, *The History of Westminster Abbey*, ed. J. Armitage Robinson (Cambridge, 1909).

Flores historiarum, ed. Henry Richards Luard (3 vols., RS, 1890).

Folcard, *Vita sancti Iohannis episcopi Eboracensis* (BHL 4339), ed. James Raine, *The Historians of the Church of York and Its Archbishops* (3 vols., RS, 1879–94) 1, pp. 239–60.

Folcwin, *Gesta abbatum sancti Bertini Sithiensium*, ed. Oswald Holder-Egger, MGH, SS 13 (Hanover, 1881), pp. 607–35.

Fontes liturgiae Carmelitanae, ed. Paschalis Kallenberg (Rome, 1962).

Fontes Vitae S. Thomas Aquinatis, ed. D. Prümmer and M.-H. Laurent (Documents inédits publiés par la Revue Thomiste, 6 fasc., 1912–37).

Fonzo, Lorenzo di, "L'Anonimo Perugino tra le fonti francescane del secolo XIII. Rapporti letterari e testo critico," *Miscellanea francescana* 72 (1972), pp. 117–483.

Formulae Salicae Bignonianae, ed. Karl Zeumer, MGH, *Formulae Merowingici et Karolini aevi* (Hanover, 1886), pp. 227–38.

Fouracre, Paul, and Richard A. Gerberding, eds., *Late Merovingian France: History and Hagiography 640–720* (Manchester, 1996).

Foxe, John, *The Acts and Monuments of John Foxe,* ed. Stephen Reed Cattley (8 vols., London, 1837–41).

Francis of Assisi: Early Documents, ed. Regis J. Armstrong et al. (3 vols. and index, New York, 1999–2002).

Fundationes et dedicationes ecclesiarum, ed. Oswald Holder-Egger, MGH, SS 15/2 (Hanover, 1888), pp. 960–1125, 1269–88.

Galbert of Bruges, *De multro . . . Karoli comitis Flandriarum*, ed. Jeff Rider, *Histoire du meurtre de Charles le Bon* (CCCM 131, 1994).

Garinus, *Vita Margaritae Hungaricae (Legenda minor)* (BHL 5332), AASS Ianuarii 2 (1643), pp. 900–906.

Gaudentius of Brescia, *Tractatus*, ed. Ambrosius Glueck (CSEL 68, 1936).

Gautier de Coinci, *Les miracles de Nostre Dame*, ed. V. Frédéric Koenig (4 vols., Geneva, 1955–70).

Geoffrey de Villehardouin, *La conquête de Constantinople*, ed. Edmond Faral (2nd. ed., 2 vols., Paris, 1961).

Geoffrey Grossus, *Vita Bernardi Tironiensis* (BHL 1251), AASS Aprilis 2 (1675), pp. 222–55.

Geoffrey le Baker, *Chronicon*, ed. E. Maunde Thompson (Oxford, 1889).

Geoffrey of Burton, *Vita sancte Modvenne virginis* (BHL 2097), ed. Robert Bartlett, *Life and Miracles of St Modwenna* (OMT, 2002).

Geoffrey of Coldingham, "De statu ecclesiae Dunelmensis," in *Historiae Dunelmensis scriptores tres*, ed. J. Raine (Surtees Soc. 9, 1839), pp. 3–31.

Geoffrey of Durham, *Vita Bartholomaei Farnensis* (BHL 1015), ed. Thomas Arnold, *Symeonis monachi opera omnia* (2 vols., RS, 1882–85) 1, pp. 295–325.

Geoffroy de Courlon, *Chronique de l'abbaye de Saint-Pierre-le-Vif de Sens*, ed. M. G. Julliot (Sens, 1876).

———, *Le livre des reliques de l'abbaye de Saint-Pierre-le-Vif de Sens*, ed. Gustave Julliot and Maurice Prou (Sens, 1887).

George of Pisidia, *Heraclias*, ed. Agostino Pertusi, *Giorgio di Pisidia. Poemi I: panegirici epici* (Studia Patristica et Byzantina 7, Ettal, 1959), pp. 240–61.

Gerald of Wales (Giraldus Cambrensis), *De principis instructione*, ed. J. S. Brewer et al., *Opera* (8 vols., RS, 1861–91) 8.

———, *Gemma ecclesiastica*, ibid., 2.

———, *Itinerarium Kambriae*, ibid., 6, pp. 1–152.

———, *Topographia hibernica*, ibid., 5, pp. 1–204.

———, *Vita Galfridi archiepiscopi Eboracensis*, ibid., 4, pp. 355–431.

———, *Vita sancti Davidis archiepiscopi Menevensis* (BHL 2111), ibid., 3, pp. 375–404.

———, *Vita sancti Hugonis Lincolniensis episcopi* (BHL 4020), ibid., 7, pp. 81–147.

———, *Vita sancti Remigii episcopi Lincolniensis* (BHL 7146–47), ibid., 7, pp. 1–80.

Gerard de Fracheto, *Vitae fratrum Ordinis Praedicatorum*, ed. Benedictus Maria Reichert (MOPH 1, 1896).

Gerhard, *Vita et miracula sancti Oudalrici episcopi Augustani* (BHL 8359), ed. Georg Waitz, MGH, SS 4 (Hanover, 1841), pp. 377–425.

Germanus of Constantinople, *In praesentationem sanctae Deiparae* 1–2, PG 98, cols. 292–320.

Gervase of Canterbury, *Chronica*, ed. William Stubbs, *The Historical Works of Gervase of Canterbury* (2 vols., RS, 1879–80), 1.

———, *Mappa mundi*, ibid., 2, pp. 414–49.

Gervase of Tilbury, *Otia Imperialia*, ed. S. E. Banks and J. W. Binns (OMT, 2002).

Gesprechbiechlin neüw Karsthans, ed. H. Demmer, *Martin Bucers deutsche Schriften* 1: *Frühschriften 1520–1524*, ed. Robert Stupperich (Gütersloh, 1960), pp. 406–44.

Gesta abbatum Trudonensium, ed. Rudolf Köpke, MGH, SS 10 (Hanover, 1852), pp. 213–448.

Gesta archiepiscoporum Magdeburgensium, ed. Wilhelm Schum, MGH, SS 14 (Hanover, 1883), pp. 361–486.

Gesta episcoporum Halberstadensium, ed. Ludwig Weiland, MGH, SS 23 (Hanover, 1874), pp. 73–123.

Gesta episcoporum Viridunensium, ed. Georg Waitz, MGH, SS 4 (Hanover, 1841), pp. 36–51.
Gesta Francorum, ed. Rosalind Hill (Nelsons Medieval Texts, 1962).
Gesta Henrici quinti, ed. Frank Taylor and John S. Roskell (OMT, 1975).
Gesta pontificum Autissiodorensium, ed. Michael Sot et al., *Les gestes des évêques d'Auxerre* (3 vols., Paris, 2002–9).
Gesta sanctorum patrum Fontanellensis coenobii, ed. F. Lohier and J. Laporte (Société de l'histoire de Normandie, Rouen, 1936).
Gesta synodi Aurelianensis, *Recueil des historiens des Gaules et de la France* 10 (2nd ed., Paris, 1874), pp. 536–39.
Gilbert of Limerick, *De statu ecclesie*, PL 159, cols. 997–1004.
Glanvill, *The Treatise on the Laws and Customs of England Commonly Called Glanvill*, ed. G.D.H. Hall (London, 1965; rev. ed., 1993).
Gonzalo de Berceo, *Martirio de San Lorenzo*, ed. Pompilio Tesauro, *Obra completa* (Madrid, 1992), pp. 455–89.
———, *Vida de Santo Domingo de Silos*, ed. Aldo Ruffinatto, *Obra completa* (Madrid, 1992), pp. 251–453.
Gonzo, *Miracula sancti Gengulphi* (BHL 3330), AASS Maii 2 (1680), pp. 648–55.
Goscelin of St.-Bertin, *Historia translationis sancti Augustini episcopi* (BHL 781), PL 155: 13–46.
———, *Liber confortarius*, ed. C. H. Talbot, *Analecta monastica* 3 (*Studia Anselmiana* 37,1955), pp. 1–117.
———, *Vita et miracula sancti Yvonis episcopi Persae* (BHL 4622), PL 155, cols. 81–89, plus *Chronicon abbatiae Ramesiensis*, ed. W. Dunn Macray (RS, 1886), pp. lix–lxxv.
———, *Vita sanctae Wulfhildae* (BHL 8736b,d), ed. Marvin L. Colker, "Texts of Jocelyn of Canterbury Which Relate to the History of Barking Abbey," *Studia monastica* 7 (1965), pp. 383–460, text at pp. 418–34.
Gottfried von Strassburg, *Tristan*, ed. Peter Ganz and Reinhold Bechstein (2 vols., Wiesbaden, 1978).
Gratian, *Decretum*, ed. Emil Friedberg (*Corpus iuris canonici* 1, Leipzig, 1879).
The Great Roll of the Pipe for the Twenty-fifth Year of the Reign of King Henry II (Pipe Roll Soc. 28, 1907).
The Gregorian Sacramentary under Charles the Great, ed. H. A. Wilson (Henry Bradshaw Soc. 49, 1915).
Gregory I, *Dialogi*, ed. Adalbert de Vogüé (3 vols., SC 251, 260, 265, 1978–80).
———, *Homiliae in Evangelia*, ed. Raymond Étaix et al., *Homélies sur l'Évangile* (2 vols., SC 485, 522, 2005–8).
———, *Moralia in Iob*, ed. Marc Adriaen (3 vols., CCSL 143, 1979–85).
———, *Registrum epistularum*, ed. Dag Norberg (2 vols., CCSL 140–140A, 1982).
———, *Vita Benedicti*, tr. Zacharias (BHG 27), ed. Gianpaolo Rigotti, *Gregorio Magno, Vita di san Benedetto, versione greca di papa Zaccaria* (Alessandria, 2001).
Gregory of Nazianzus, *De vita sua* (II.1.11), PG 37, cols. 1029–1166.
———, *Oratio* 33, *contra Arianos*, ed. Claudio Moreschini (SC 318, 1985), pp. 156–96.
Gregory of Nyssa, *De sancto Theodoro* (BHG 1760), ed. John P. Cavarnos, *Gregorii Nysseni opera* 10/1 (Leiden, 1990), pp. 59–71.
———, *Epistulae*, ed. Pierre Maraval, *Lettres* (SC 363, 1990).

———, *In Basilium fratrem* (BHG 244), ed. Otto Lendle, *Gregorii Nysseni opera* 10/1 (Leiden, 1990), pp. 107–34.
———, *In sanctum Stephanum I–II* (BHG 1654–55), ed. Otto Lendle, ibid., pp. 73–105.
———, *In XL martyres Ia–Ib* (BHG 1206–7), ed. Otto Lendle, ibid., pp. 135–56.
———, *In XL martyres II* (BHG 1208), ed. Otto Lendle, ibid., pp. 157–69.
Gregory of Tours, *De passione et virtutuibus sancti Iuliani*, ed. Bruno Krusch (MGH, SRM 1/ii, Hanover, 1885), pp. 562–84 (repr. 1969, pp. 112–34).
———, *De virtutibus sancti Martini*, ibid., pp. 584–661 (repr. 1969, pp. 134–211).
———, *Gloria confessorum*, ibid., pp. 744–820 (repr. 1969, pp. 294–370).
———, *Gloria martyrum*, ibid., pp. 484–561 (repr. 1969, pp. 34–111).
———, *Glory of the Confessors*, tr. Raymond Van Dam (Liverpool, 1988).
———, *Glory of the Martyrs*, tr. Raymond Van Dam (Liverpool, 1988).
———, *Liber vitae patrum*, ed. Bruno Krusch, MGH, SRM 1/ii (Hanover, 1885), pp. 661–744 (repr. 1969, pp. 211–94).
———, *Libri historiarum X*, ed. Bruno Krusch and Wilhelm Levison (MGH, SRM 1/i, Hanover, 1937–51).
———, *Life of the Fathers*, tr. Edward James (2nd ed., Liverpool, 1991).
Gregory VII, *Registrum*, ed. Erich Caspar, MGH, *Epistolae selectae* 2 (2 parts, Berlin, 1920–23).
Grimaldus, *Vita Dominici Siliensis* (BHL 2238), ed. Vitalino Valcárcel (Logroño, 1982).
Guernes de Pont-Ste.-Maxence, *La vie de Saint Thomas*, ed. Jacques T. E. Thomas (2 vols., Louvain and Paris, 2002).
———, *La vie de Saint Thomas*, ed. Emmanuel Walberg (Paris, 1971).
Guibert de Nogent, *De sanctis et eorum pigneribus*, ed. R.B.C. Huygens, *Quo ordine sermo fieri debeat; De bucella iudae data et de veritate dominici corporis; De sanctis et eorum pigneribus* (CCCM 127, 1993), pp. 79–175.
———, *Dei gesta per Francos*, ed. R.B.C. Huygens (CCCM 127A, 1996).
Guillaume de Deguileville, *Le pèlerinage de la vie humaine*, ed. J. J. Stürzinger (London, 1893).
Guillaume de St.-Pathus, *Vie de saint Louis*, ed. H.-François Delaborde (Paris, 1899).
Gunther of Pairis, *Hystoria Constantinopolitana*, ed. Peter Orth (Hildesheim and Zurich, 1994).
Hadrian I, *Epistola ad Constantinum et Irenem*, PL 96, cols. 1215–34.
Haimo of Halberstadt (recte of Auxerre), *In Epistolam ad Ephesios*, PL 117, cols. 699–734.
Haito of Basel, *Capitula*, ed. Peter Brommer, MGH, *Capitula episcoporum* 1 (Hanover, 1984), pp. 203–19.
Harawi: ʻAlī ibn Abī Bakr al-Harawī, *Guide des lieux de pèlerinage*, tr. Janine Sourdel-Thomine (Damascus, 1957).
Hariulf, *Chronicon Centulense*, ed. Ferdinand Lot, *Chronique de l'abbaye de Saint-Riquier* (Paris, 1894).
———, *Vita sancti Arnulfi episcopi Suessionensis* (BHL 704), PL 174, cols. 1371–1438.
Die Heidelberger Bilderhandschrift des Sachsenspiegels, ed. Walter Koschorreck (Frankfurt, 1971).
Die Heiligen Englands, ed. Felix Liebermann (Hanover, 1889).
Heiligenleben: Ungarisches Legendarium Cod. Vat. lat. 8541 (Codices e Vaticanis selecti 78, Zürich, 1990).

Heiric of Auxerre, *Miracula sancti Germani episcopi Antissiodorensis* (BHL 3462), PL 124, cols. 1207–70.

Helbig, Herbert, and Lorenz Weinrich, eds., *Urkunden und erzählende Quellen zur deutschen Ostsiedlung im Mittelalter* (AQ 26, 2 vols., Darmstadt, 1968–70).

Helgaud, *Epitoma vite regis Rotberti pii*, ed. Robert-Henri Bautier and Gillette Labory (Paris, 1965).

Henrici VI Angliae regis miracula postuma (BHL 3816r), ed. Paul Grosjean (SH 22, 1935).

Henry of Avranches, *Legenda sancti Francisci versificata*, *Analecta Franciscana* 10 (Quaracchi, 1926–41), pp. 405–521.

Herbord, *Dialogus de vita et operibus beati Ottonis Babenbergensis episcopi* (BHL 6397), ed. Lorenz Weinrich, *Heiligenleben zur deutsch-slawischen Geschichte* (AQ 23, 2005), pp. 282–493.

Heresy Trials in the Diocese of Norwich, 1420–31, ed. Norman Tanner (Camden fourth series 20, 1977).

Hermann of Laon, *De miraculis sanctae Mariae Laudunensis* (BHL 5398), PL 156, cols. 961–1020.

Hermann the Archdeacon, *Liber de miraculis sancti Edmundi* (BHL 2395–96), ed. Thomas Arnold, *Memorials of St Edmund's Abbey* (3 vols., Rolls Series, 1890), 1, pp. 26–92.

Hessisches Urkundenbuch 1.1, ed. Arthur Wyss (Leipzig, 1879).

Hilary of Arles, *Vita Honorati* (BHL 3975), ed. Marie-Denise Valentin (SC 235, 1977).

Hilary of Poitiers, *Contra Constantium*, ed. A. Rocher (SC 334, 1987).

Hildegard of Bingen, *Vita sancti Dysibodi episcopi* (BHL 2204), ed. and tr. Hugh Feiss and Christopher P. Evans, *Two Hagiographies: Vita sancti Rupperti confessoris, Vita sancti Dysibodi episcopi* (Dallas Medieval Texts and Translations 11, Paris and Louvain, 2010), pp. 86–156.

———, *Vita sancti Rupperti confessoris* (BHL 7388), ibid., pp. 44–84.

Hilduin of St.-Denis, *Epistolae variorum* 20, ed. Ernst Dümmler, MGH, *Epistolae* 5 (*Karolini aevi* 3) (Berlin, 1899), pp. 327–35.

———, *Passio sanctissimi Dionysii* (BHL 2175), PL 106, cols. 23–50.

Hillinus, *Miracula sancti Foillani* (BHL 3078), AASS Octobris 13 (1883), pp. 417–26.

Hincmar of Rheims, *Vita Remigii episcopi Remensis* (BHL 7152–63), ed. Bruno Krusch, MGH, SRM 3 (Hanover, 1896), pp. 239–341.

Hippolytus, *Traditio apostolica*, ed. Bernard Botte (2nd ed., SC 11 bis, 1984).

Histoire des ducs de Normandie et des rois d'Angleterre, ed. Francisque Michel (Société de l'Histoire de France 18, 1840).

Historia canonizationis et translationis sancti Bernwardi episcopi (BHL 1259), AASS Octobris 11 (1864), pp. 1024–34.

Historia compostellana, ed. Emma Falque Rey (CCCM 70, 1988).

Historia de Leone Bardae Armenii filio, ed. Immanuel Bekker, *Leonis Grammatici Chronographia* (Bonn, 1842), pp. 335–62.

Historia de Sancto Cuthberto, ed. Ted Johnson South (Cambridge, 2002).

Historia Ecclesie Abbendonensis: The History of the Church of Abingdon, ed. John Hudson (2 vols., OMT, 2002–7).

Historia institutionis (communis festi Basilii Magni, Gregorii Theologi et Johannis Chrysostomi) (BHG 746y), PG 29, cols. CCCXC–CCCXCIII.

Historia inventionis corporis et miraculorum sancti Goslini (BHL 3623), AASS Februarii 2 (1658), pp. 632–38.
Historia miraculorum sancti Ursmari in circumlatione per Flandriam (BHL 8425), AASS Aprilis 2 (1675), pp. 573–78.
Historia monachorum in Aegypto, ed. André-Jean Festugière (SH 53, 1971).
The Historians of the Church of York and Its Archbishops, ed. James Raine (3 vols., RS, 1879–94).
Historia Norwegie, ed. Inger Ekrem and Lars Boje Mortensen (Copenhagen, 2003).
Historia sancti Kanuti ducis et martyris (BHL 1554), ed. M. G. Gertz, *Vitae sanctorum Danorum* (Copenhagen, 1908–12), pp. 189–200.
Historia Silense, ed. Justo Perez de Urbel and Atilano Gonzalez Ruiz-Zorrilla (Madrid, 1959).
Historia translationis sancti Isidori (BHL 4491), ed. Juan A. Estévez Sola, *Chronica hispana saeculi XIII* (CCCM 73, 1997), pp. 143–79.
Historia translationis sancti Vedasti Bellovacum dein Atrebatvm (BHL 8516–17), AASS Februarii 1 (1658), pp. 806–12.
Historia translationum sancti Mamantis (BHL 5199), AASS Augusti 3 (1737), pp. 440–46.
Historia vitae et regni Ricardi secondi, ed. George B. Stow (Philadelphia, 1977).
A Historie of the Estate of Scotland from July 1558 to April 1560, ed. David Laing, *The Miscellany of the Wodrow Society* 1 (Edinburgh, 1844), pp. 49–85.
History of William Marshal, ed. A. J. Holden (3 vols., Anglo-Norman Texts Society, occasional publications series 4–6, 2002–6).
Holy Women of Byzantium: Ten Saints' Lives in English Translation, ed. Alice-Mary Talbot (Washington, DC, 1996).
Die "Honorantie civitatis Papie": Transkription, Edition, Kommentar, ed. Carlrichard Brühl and Cinzio Violante (Cologne, 1983).
Honorius Augustodunensis, *Elucidarium*, PL 172, cols. 1109–76.
———, *Gemma animae*, PL 172, cols. 541–738.
———, *Sacramentarium*, PL 172, cols. 737–814.
———, *Speculum ecclesiae*, PL 172, cols. 813–1108.
Hostiensis (Henry de Segusio), *Lectura siue Apparatus super quinque libris Decretalium* (2 vols., Strassburg, 1512).
———, *Summa super titulis decretalium* (Venice, 1490).
Hrabanus Maurus, *Carmina*, ed. Ernst Dümmler, MGH, *Poetae latini aevi Carolini* 2 (Berlin, 1884), pp. 154–258.
———, *In honorem sancte crucis*, ed. Michel Perrin (CCCM 100, 1997).
———, *Martyrologium*, ed. John McCulloh (CCCM 44, 1979).
Hrotsvit, *Opera omnia*, ed. Walter Berschin (Munich, 2001).
Huber, Werner T., ed., *Bruder Klaus: Niklaus von Flüe in den Zeugnissen seiner Zeitgenossen* (Zurich, 1996).
Hudson, Anne, ed., *Selections from English Wycliffite Writings* (Cambridge, 1978).
———, *Two Wycliffite Texts: The Sermon of William Taylor 1406. The Testimony of William Thorpe 1407* (EETS, o.s. 301, 1993).
Hugeburc, *Vita Willibaldi episcopi Eichstetensis* (BHL 8931), ed. Oswald Holder-Egger, MGH, SS 15/1 (Hanover, 1887), pp. 86–106.
———, *Vita Wynnebaldi abbatis Heidenheimensis* (BHL 8996), ed. Oswald Holder-Egger, MGH, SS 15/1 (Hanover, 1887), pp. 106–17.

Hugh of Flavigny, *Chronicon*, ed. Georg Heinrich Pertz, MGH, SS 8 (Hanover, 1848), pp. 288–502.

Hugo Pictavinus, *Historia Vezeliacensis*, ed. R.B.C. Huygens, *Monumenta Vizeliacensia* (CCSL 42, 1976), pp. 395–607.

Hydatius, *Continuatio chronicorum Hieronymianorum*, ed. Theodor Mommsen, MGH, AA, *Chronica minora saec. IV. V. VI. VII.* 2 (Berlin, 1894), pp. 13–36.

Die ikonoklastische Synode von Hiereia 754: Einleitung, Text, Übersetzung und Kommentar ihres Horos, ed. Torsten Krannich et al. (Tübingen, 2002).

Innocent III, *Die Register Innocenz' III*, ed. Othmar Hageneder et al. (Rome and Vienna, 1964–).

———, *Selected Letters of Pope Innocent III concerning England*, ed. C. R. Cheney and W. H. Semple (Edinburgh and London, 1953).

Innocent IV, *Apparatus super V libros decretalium* (Venice, 1491).

Inquisitio de vita et miraculis Laurentii Sublacensis (BHL 4792), ed. Willibald Gnandt, *Vita S. Cleridonæ virginis, B. Laurentii anachoretæ, nec non et servi Dei Hippoliti Pugnetti monachi* (Innsbruck, 1902), pp. 67–99.

The Inquisition at Albi 1299–1300, ed. Georgene W. Davis (New York, 1948).

Inscriptiones Christianae urbis Romae septimo saeculo antiquiores, n.s. 1, ed. A. Silvagni (Rome, 1922).

———, n.s. 10, ed. Danilo Mazzoleni and Carlo Carletti (Vatican City, 1992).

Inscriptiones Latinae Liberae Rei Publicae, ed. Attilio Degrassi (2 vols., Florence, 1963–65).

Insignis liber de poenitentia et tentationibus religiosorum, PL 213, cols. 863–904.

Inventio et miracula sancti Vulfranni (BHL 8740), ed. J. Laporte, *Mélanges publiés par la Société de l'Histoire de Normandie* 14 (Rouen, 1938), pp. 21–83.

Inventio sanctae Cordulae virginis et martyris (BHL 1951), AASS Octobris 9 (1858), pp. 580–84.

Iocundus, *Translatio sancti Servatii* (BHL 7626–32), ed. Rudolf Köpke, MGH, SS 12 (Hanover, 1856), pp. 85–126.

Iohannis Euchaitorum Metropolitae quae in codice Vaticano graeco 676 supersunt, ed. Johannes Bollig and Paul de Lagarde (Abhandlungen der Königlichen Gesellschaft der Wissenschaften zu Göttingen 32, 1882).

Iotsald of St.-Claude, *Vita sancti Odilonis* (BHL 6281), ed. Johannes Staub, MGH, SRG (Hanover, 1999).

Ireland, John, *Of Penance and Confession*, ed. W. A. Craigie, *The Asloan Manuscript* (2 vols., Scottish Texts Society, n.s. 14, 16, 1923–25), pp. 1–80.

Isidore of Seville, *Etymologiae*, ed. W. M. Lindsay (2 vols., Oxford, 1911, unpaginated).

Itinerarium Burdigalense, ed. P. Geyer and O. Cuntz, *Itineraria et alia geographica* (CCSL 175, 1965), pp. 1–26.

Itinerarium peregrinorum et gesta regis Ricardi, ed. William Stubbs, *Chronicles and Memorials of the Reign of Richard I* 1 (RS, 1864).

Ivo of Chartres, *Decretum*, PL 161, cols. 47–1344.

Jacobus de Voragine, *Legenda aurea*, ed. Giovanni Paolo Maggioni (2nd ed., 2 vols. [paginated continuously], Florence, 1998).

Jacques de Vitry, *Epistulae*, ed. R.B.C. Huygens, *Lettres de Jacques de Vitry* (Leiden, 1960).

———, *Vita Mariae Oigniacensis* (BHL 5516), AASS Iunii 4 (1707), pp. 636–66.

James, Montague R., "Two Lives of Ethelbert, King and Martyr," *English Historical Review* 32 (1917), pp. 214–44.

Jan Długosz, *Vita et miracula Stanislai episcopi Cracoviensis* (BHL 7839–41), AASS Maii 2 (1680), pp. 202–75.
Jean de Joinville, *Vie de saint Louis*, ed. Jacques Monfrin (Paris, 1995).
Jean de Mailly, *Abrégé des gestes et miracles des saints*, ed. A. Dondaine (Paris, 1947).
Jerome, *Adversus Vigilantium*, ed. J.-L. Feiertag (CCSL 79C, 2005).
———, *Chronicon*, ed. Rudolf Helm, *Die Chronik des Hieronymus* (Die griechischen christlichen Schriftsteller der ersten drei Jahrhunderte 47: Eusebius Werke 7/1, 1913).
———, *Commentariorum in Matheum libri IV*, ed. D. Hurst and M. Adriaen (CCSL 77, 1969).
———, *Epistulae*, ed. Jérôme Labourt, *Saint Jérôme. Lettres* (8 vols., Paris, 1949–63).
———, *In Hiezechielem*, ed. François Glorie, *S. Hieronymi presbyteri opera* 1/4 (CCSL 75, 1964).
———, *Vita beati Pauli monachi Thebaei* (BHL 6596), ed. Edgardo M. Morales, *Trois vies de Moines* (SC 508, 2007), pp. 144–82.
———, *Vita Hilarionis* (BHL 3879), ed. Edgardo M. Morales, *Trois vies de Moines* (SC 508, 2007), pp. 212–98.
Jocelin of Furness, *Vita Patricii* (BHL 6513), AASS Martii 2 (1668), pp. 540–80.
———, *Vita sancti Kentigerni* (BHL 4646), ed. A. P. Forbes, *Lives of St Ninian and St Kentigern* (Edinburgh, 1874), pp. 159–242.
———, *Vita sancti Walthenis abbatis* (BHL 8783), AASS, Augusti 1 (Antwerp, 1733), pp. 248–76.
Johannes Andreae, *Novella Commentaria in quinque Decretalium libros* (Venice, 1489).
John Beleth, *Summa de ecclesiasticis officiis*, ed. Heribert Douteil (2 vols., CCCM 41–41A, 1976 [text in 41A]).
John Chrysostom, *De inani gloria*, ed. Anne-Marie Malingrey (SC 188, 1972).
———, *De sancto Babyla*, ed. Margaret A. Schatkin, *Discours sur Babylas* (SC 362, 1990).
———, *Homilia de sanctis martyribus* (BHG 1186), PG 50, cols. 645–54.
———, *Homilia in martyrem Pelagiam* (BHG 1477), PG 50, cols. 579–84.
———, *Homilia in sanctos martyres* (BHG 1188), PG 50, cols. 705–12.
———, *In epistulam I ad Corinthios*, PG 61, cols. 9–382.
———, *Oratio in sanctas Bernicen et Prosdocen*, PG 50, cols. 629–40.
John de Orta, *Vita sancti Ludovici episcopi Tolosani* (BHL 5055), *Processus canonizationis et legendae variae Sancti Ludovici O.F.M., episcopi Tolosani* (Analecta Franciscana 7, 1951), pp. 335–80.
John Malalas, *Chronographia*, ed. Johannes Thurn (Berlin and New York, 2000).
John Moscus, *Pratum spirituale*, PG 87/3, cols. 2851–3112.
John of Avranches, *De officiis ecclesiasticis*, ed. R. Delamare (Paris, 1923).
John of Damascus, *De imaginibus oratio* 1, ed. Bonifatius Kotter, *Contra imaginum calumniatores orationes tres* (Die Schriften des Johannes von Damaskos 3, Berlin, 1975).
———, *Laudatio sanctae martyris Barbarae* (BHG 217), ed. Bonifatius Kotter, *Die Schriften des Johannes von Damaskos* 5 (Berlin and New York, 1988), pp. 247–78.
John of Salisbury, *Entheticus in dogmate philosophorum*, ed. Jan Van Laarhoven, *Entheticus maior and minor* (3 vols., Studien und Texte zur Geistesgeschichte des Mittelalters 17, Leiden, 1987), 1, pp. 105–227.
John of St. Arnulf, *Vita Iohannis abbatis Gorziensis* (BHL 4396), ed. Michel Parisse, *La vie de Jean, abbé de Gorze* (Paris, 1999).
John of Worcester, *Chronicle* 2, ed. R. R. Darlington and P. McGurk (OMT, 1995).

John the Deacon, *Vita beati Nicolai episcopi* (BHL 6104–13), ed. Pasquale Corsi, "La 'Vita' di san Nicola e un codice della versione di Giovanni diacono," *Nicolaus. Rivista di teologia ecumenico-patristica* 7 (1979), pp. 361–80.

———, *Vita Gregorii magni* (BHL 3641), PL 75, cols. 59–242.

Jonas, *Vita Columbani* (BHL 1898), ed. Bruno Krusch, MGH, SRG (Hanover and Leipzig, 1905).

Jordan of Quedlinburg, *Sermones de sanctis (Opus Dan)* (Strassburg, 1484).

Jordan of Saxony, *Libellus de principiis Ordinis Praedicatorum*, ed. Heribert Christian Scheeben, (MOPH 16, 1935), pp. 3–88.

Jordanus, *Vita sancti Ubaldi Eugubini pontificis* (BHL 8354t), ed. Angelo M. Fanucci, *Vita di S. Ubaldo* (2nd ed., Gubbio, 1992).

Journal d'un bourgeois de Paris, ed. Colette Beaune (Paris, 1989).

Julian, *Contra Galileos*, ed. Wilmer C. Wright, *The Works of the Emperor Julian* (3 vols., Cambridge, MA, 1913–23), 3, pp. 311–427.

Julian of Toledo, *Historia Wambae*, ed. Wilhelm Levison, MGH, SRM 5 (Hanover and Leipzig, 1910), pp. 501–26.

———, *Prognosticon futuri saeculi*, ed. J. N. Hillgarth, *Opera sancti Iuliani Toletanae sedis episcopi. Pars I* (CCSL 115, 1976), pp. 11–126.

Justin, *Apologia*, ed. Dennis Minns and Paul Parvis (Oxford, 2009).

Kallistos, Nikephoros, *Historia Ecclesiastica*, PG 145, cols. 557–1332; PG 146; PG 147, cols. 9–448.

Das Katharinentaler Schwesternbuch, ed. Ruth Meyer (Tübingen, 1995).

Kjøbenhavns Diplomatarium 1, ed. Oluf Nielsen (Copenhagen, 1872).

Knighton, Henry, *Chronicon*, ed. G. H. Martin, *Knighton's Chronicle* 1337–1396 (OMT, 1995).

Ködiz von Salfeld, Friedrich, *Das Leben des heiligen Ludwig*, ed. Heinrich Rückert (Leipzig, 1851).

König, Hermann, *Das Wallfahrtsbuch des Hermannus Kunig von Vach und die Pilgerreisen der Deutschen nach Santiago de Compostela*, ed. Konrad Haebler (Strassburg, 1899).

Die Konstitutionen Friedrichs II. für das Königreich Sizilien, ed. Wolfgang Stürner, MGH, *Constitutiones et acta publica imperatorum et regum 2, supplementum* (Hanover, 1996).

Lactantius, *Divinae institutiones*, ed. Eberhard Heck and Antonie Wlosok (4 vols., Munich, Leipzig, 2005–11).

Lambert of Wattrelos, *Annales Cameracenses*, ed. Georg Heinrich Pertz, MGH, SS 16 (Hanover, 1859), pp. 509–54.

Lanfranc, *Decreta Lanfranci monachis Cantuariensibus transmissa*, ed. David Knowles, *The Monastic Constitutions of Lanfranc* (London, 1951).

Langland, William, *Piers Plowman*, ed. A.V.C. Schmidt (2nd ed., 2 vols., Kalamazoo, 2011 [text vol. 1]).

Lateinische Osterfeiern und Osterspiele 8, ed. Walther Lipphardt (Berlin, 1990).

Lawrence of Durham, *Hypognosticon*, ed. Susanne Daub, *Gottes Heilplan–verdichtet: Edition des Hypognosticon des Laurentius Dunelmensis* (Erlangen and Jena, 2002).

The Laws of the Medieval Kingdom of Hungary 1, ed. Janos M. Bak et al. (Bakersfield, CA, 1989).

Das Leben der heiligen Elisabeth, ed. Max Rieger (Stuttgart, 1868).

Legenda sancti Emerici ducis (BHL 2528), ed. Emma Bartoniek, *Scriptores Rerum Hungaricarum* 2 (Budapest, 1938), pp. 441–60.

Legenda sanctorum martirum quinque fratrum minorum (BHL 1170), *Portugaliae Monumenta Historica, Scriptores* 1/1 (Lisbon, 1856), pp. 113–16.

La Légende dorée, ed. Alain Boureau (Paris, 2004).

Leges palatinae (facs. ed., Bloomington, IN, 1994).

Lepine, David, and Nicholas Orme, eds., *Death and Memory in Medieval Exeter* (Devon and Cornwall Record Society, n.s. 47, 2003).

Letaldus of Micy, *Miracula sancti Maximini* (BHL 5820), PL 137, cols. 795–824.

Letters and Papers, Foreign and Domestic, of the Reign of Henry VIII 13/2 (London, 1893).

Letters and Papers, Foreign and Domestic, of the Reign of Henry VIII 20/1 (London, 1905).

Lex Frisionum, ed. Karl August Eckhardt and Albrecht Eckhardt (MGH, Fontes Iuris Germanici Antiqui in usum scholarum separatim editi 12, Hanover, 1982).

Libellus de dictis quatuor ancillarum (BHL 2493m), *Quellenstudien zur Geschichte der heiligen Elisabeth*, pp. 112–40.

Libellus de ortu sancti Cuthberti (BHL 2026), ed. J. Raine, *Miscellanea biographica* (Surtees Soc. 8, 1838), pp. 63–87.

Libellus de vita et miraculis sancti Francisci de Paula, AASS Aprilis 1 (1675), pp. 106–20.

Liber cartarum prioratus sancti Andree in Scotia, ed. Thomas Thomson (Bannatyne Club, Edinburgh, 1841).

Il "Liber" della beata Angela da Foligno, ed. Enrico Menestò, 1: *transcrizione del ms. 342 della Biblioteca Communale di Assisi*, ed. Francesco Verderosa (Spoleto, 2009).

Liber Eliensis, ed. E. O. Blake (Camden, 3rd ser., 92, 1962).

Liber historiae Francorum, ed. Bruno Krusch, MGH, SRM 2 (Hanover, 1888), pp. 215–328.

Le liber mozarabicus sacramentorum, ed. Marius Férotin (Paris, 1912).

Le liber ordinum en usage dans l'église wisigothique et mozarabe d'Espagne, ed. Marius Férotin (Paris, 1904).

Le Liber Pontificalis, ed. Louis Duchesne (rev. ed., 3 vols., Paris, 1955–57).

Liber sacramentorum Augustodunensis, ed. Odilo Heiming (CCSL 159b, 1984).

Liber sacramentorum Romanae Aeclesiae ordinis anni circuli, ed. Leo Cunibert Mohlberg (Rome, 1960).

Liber sancti Jacobi: Codex Calixtinus, ed. Walter Muir Whitehill (Santiago de Compostela, 1944).

Liber sancti Thome de Aberbrothoc, ed. Cosmo Innes (2 vols., Bannatyne Club, Edinburgh, 1848–56).

Liber sextus, ed. Emil Friedberg, *Corpus iuris canonici* 2 (Leipzig, 1881), cols. 929–1124.

Libro de Alexandre, ed. Francisco Marcos Marín (on-line edition).

LiDonnici, Lynn R., *The Epidaurian Miracle Inscriptions: Text, Translation, and Commentary* (Atlanta, 1995).

Liebermann, Felix, ed., *Die Gesetze der Angelsachsen* (3 vols., Halle, 1898–1916).

The Life of Christina of Markyate, ed. C. H. Talbot (rev. ed., OMT, 1987).

The Life of St Edmund King and Martyr: A Facsimile (BL, Harley 2278) (London, 2004).

Lindsay, David, *Ane Satyre of the Thrie Estaits* (Edinburgh, 1602).

Little, A. G., "Decrees of the General Chapters of the Friars Minor, 1260 to 1282," *English Historical Review* 13 (1898), pp. 703–8.

Liudprand of Cremona, *Antapodosis*, ed. Albert Bauer and Reinhold Rau, *Quellen zur Geschichte der sächsischen Kaiserzeit* (AQ 8, rev. ed., Darmstadt, 1977), pp. 244–494.

Le Livre du Chevalier De La Tour Landry pour l'enseignement de ses filles, ed. Anatole de Montaiglon (Paris, 1854).

Loewenfeld, Samuel, ed., *Epistolae pontificum romanorum ineditae* (Leipzig, 1885).
Luke of Tuy, *Vita sancti Martini* (BHL 5600), PL 208, cols. 9–24.
Luther, Martin, *An den christlichen Adel deutscher Nation*, *D. Martin Luthers Werke* 6 (Weimar, 1888), pp. 381–469.
———, *Predigten des Jahres 1522*, *D. Martin Luthers Werke* 10/3 (Weimar, 1905).
———, *Widder den newen Abgott*, *D. Martin Luthers Werke* 15 (Weimar, 1899), pp. 183–98.
Mansi, Giovanni Domenico, ed., *Sacrorum conciliorum nova et amplissima collectio* (31 vols., Florence, 1759–98).
Marcellinus Comes, *Chronicon*, ed. Theodor Mommsen, MGH, AA 11, *Chronica minora saec. IV. V. VI. VII* (Berlin, 1894), pp. 37–108.
Marculf, *Formulae*, ed. Karl Zeumer, MGH, *Formulae Merowingici et Karolini aevi* (Hanover, 1886), pp. 32–106.
Marianus Scotus, *Chronicon*, ed. Georg Waitz, MGH, SS 5 (Hanover, 1844), pp. 481–562.
Martène, Edmond, and Ursin Durand, ed., *Thesaurus novus anecdotorum* (5 vols., Paris, 1717).
Martin of Leon, *Sermones de sanctis* (incl. BHL 4485, 4492–93), PL 209, cols. 9–62.
Martirium sanctae Luciae virginis (BHG 995), ed. Giuseppe Rossi Taibbi, *Martirio di santa Lucia. Vita di santa Marina* (Palermo, 1959), pp. 49–70.
Martirium sanctae virginis martyris Agnetis (BHG 45), ed. Pio Franchi de' Cavalieri, *Scritti agiografici* 1 (Studi e testi 221, 1962), pp. 355–60.
Martyrium Ricardi archiepiscopi (BHL 7217), ed. James Raine, *The Historians of the Church of York and Its Archbishops* (3 vols., RS, 1879–94), 2, pp. 306–11.
Das Martyrologium des Nürnberger Memorbuches, ed. Siegmund Salfeld (Berlin, 1898).
Martyrologium Hieronymianum, ed. Henri Quentin, AASS Novembris 2/2 (1931).
Martyrologium Romanum, AASS Decembris, *Propylaeum* (1940).
Mary and the Fathers of the Church: The Blessed Virgin Mary in Patristic Thought, ed. Luigi Gambero (Eng. tr., San Francisco, 1999).
Mary in the Middle Ages: The Blessed Virgin Mary in the Thought of Medieval Latin Theologians, ed. Luigi Gambero (Eng. tr., San Francisco, 2003).
Materials for the History of Thomas Becket, ed. J. C. Robertson (7 vols., RS, 1875–85).
Matthew Paris, *Chronica majora*, ed. Henry R. Luard (7 vols., RS, 1872–84).
Mattioti, Giovanni, *Vita di S. Francesca Romana*, ed. Mariano Armellini (Rome, 1882).
Maximus of Turin, *Sermones*, ed. Almut Mutzenbecher (CCSL 23, 1962).
Memorials of the Church of SS. Peter and Wilfrid Ripon 3 (Surtees Soc. 81, 1888 for 1886).
El "Menologio" de Basilio II Emperador de Bizancio (Vat. gr. 1613) (Codices e Vaticanis selecti 64.1, Vatican City, 2005).
Il menologio di Basilio II (Cod. Vaticano greco 1613) (2 vols., Codices e vaticanis selecti 8, Turin, 1907).
Menologium Basilianum, PG 117, cols. 19–614.
Methodius, *Symposium*, ed. Herbert Musurillo, *Le banquet* (SC 95, 1963).
The Metz Pontifical, ed. E. S. Dewick (Roxburghe Club 138, 1902).
Miedema, Nine Robijntje, ed., *Rompilgerführer in Spätmittelalter und Früher Neuzeit: Die "Indulgentiae ecclesiarium urbis Romae" (deutsch/niederländisch). Edition und Kommentar* (Tübingen, 2003).
Milo, *Vita Amandi episcopi*, ed. Bruno Krusch, MGH, SRM 5 (Hanover and Leipzig, 1910), pp. 450–83.

The Miracles of Our Lady of Rocamadour: Analysis and Translation, ed. Marcus Bull (Woodbridge, 1999).

The Miracles of St Æbbe of Coldingham and St Margaret of Scotland, ed. Robert Bartlett (OMT, 2003).

Miracula Adelheidis reginae (BHL 65), ed. Herbert Paulhart, *Die Lebensbeschreibung der Kaiserin Adelheid von Abt Odilo von Cluny* (Mitteilungen des Instituts für Österreichische Geschichtsforschung. Ergänzungsband 20: Festschrift zur Jahrtausendfeier der Kaiserkrönung Ottos des Grossen 2, 1962), pp. 45–54.

Miracula Amelbergae virginis (BHL 325), AASS Julii 3 (1723), pp. 105–12.

Miracula beatae Dorotheae (BHL 2333), AASS Octobris 13 (1883), pp. 560–67.

Miracula beatae Marie virginis in Carnotensi ecclesia facta (BHL 5389), ed. Antoine Thomas, "Les miracles de Notre-Dame de Chartres," *Bibliothèque de l'École des Chartes* 42 (1881), pp. 505–50.

Miracula beati Domitiani (BHL 2248), AASS Februarii 1 (1658), pp. 703–4.

Miracula beati Guntheri (BHL 3715–17), AASS Octobris 4 (1780), pp. 1074–84.

Miracula Cosmae et Damiani (BHG 385–91), ed. Ludwig Deubner, *Kosmas und Damian: Texte und Einleitung* (Leipzig and Berlin, 1907), pp. 97–206.

Miracula Deiparae ad Fontem (BHG 1072), AASS Novembris 3 (1910), pp. 878–89.

Miracula Eutropii episcopi Santonensis (BHL 2787), AASS Aprilis 3 (1675), pp. 736–44.

Miracula ex processu canonizationis Thomae de Cantilupe, AASS Octobris 1 (1765), pp. 610–705.

Miracula Galterii abbatis Sancti Martini (BHL 8797), ed. J. Depoin, *Cartulaire de l'abbaye de St.-Martin de Pontoise* (Pontoise, 1895), pp. 202–14.

Miracula gloriosissimi martyris beati Zoyli (BHL 9025), ed. Henrique Florez, *España sagrada* 10 (3rd ed., Madrid, 1792), pp. 508–20.

Miracula Marculphi anno MCI facta Peronæ in Picardia (BHL 5270), AASS Maii 7 (1688), pp. 533–39.

Miracula Nynie Episcopi (BHL 6240b), ed. Winifred W. MacQueen, *Transactions of the Dumfriesshire and Galloway Natural History and Antiquarian Society* 38 (1959–60), pp. 21–57.

Miracula Nynie Episcopi (BHL 6240b), ed. Karl Strecker, MGH, *Poetae latini aevi Karolini* 4/2–3 (Berlin, 1923), pp. 943–62.

Miracula Rictrudis (BHL 7252), AASS Maii 3 (1680), pp. 89–118.

Miracula Rudesindi (BHL 7358), ed. Manuel C. Díaz y Díaz et al., *Ordoño de Celanova, Vida y milagros de san Rosendo* (La Coruña, 1990).

Miracula sanctae Bertiliæ (BHL 1289), AASS Ianuarii 1 (1643), pp. 1115–19.

Miracula sanctae Genovefae post mortem (BHL 3342), AASS Ianuarii 1 (1643), pp. 147–51.

Miracula sancte Elyzabet (BHL 2491), *Quellenstudien zur Geschichte der heiligen Elisabeth*, pp. 161–236.

Miracula sancte Elyzabet anno 1235 comprobata (Ordo I) (BHL 2491d), *Quellenstudien zur Geschichte der heiligen Elisabeth*, pp. 243–62.

Miracula sancte Margarite Scotorum regine, *The Miracles of St Æbbe of Coldingham and St Margaret of Scotland*, pp. 70–144.

Miracula sancti Agili (BHL 149), AASS Augusti 6 (1743), pp. 587–97.

Miracula sancti Agrippini (BHL 174–7), AASS Novembris 4 (1925), pp. 122–28.

Miracula sancti Aigulphi (BHL 196), AASS Septembris 1 (1746), pp. 758–63.

Miracula sancti Artemii (BHG 173), ed. Virgil S. Crisafulli and John W. Nesbitt, *The Miracles of St. Artemios* (Leiden, 1996).
Miracula sancti Bavonis (BHL 1054), AASS Octobris 1 (1765), pp. 293–303.
Miracula sancti Benedicti (BHL 1123–9), ed. E. de Certain, *Miracles de S. Benôit* (Société de l'histoire de France 96, 1858).
Miracula sancti Columbani (BHL 1904), ed. H. Bresslau, MGH, SS 30/2 (Leipzig, 1934), pp. 997–1015.
Miracula sancti Demetrii (BHG 499–528), ed. Paul Lemerle, *Les plus anciens receuils des miracles de Saint Démétrius et la pénétration des Slaves dans les Balkans* 1 (Paris, 1979).
Miracula sancti Eugenii Broniensia (BHL 2689), ed. D. Misonne, "Les miracles de Saint Eugène à Brogne," *Revue Bénédictine* 76 (1966), pp. 231–91.
Miracula sancti Faronis (BHL 2830), AASS Octobris 12 (1867), pp. 616–19.
Miracula sancti Girardi monachi Andegavensis (BHL 3549), AASS Novembris 2/1 (1894), pp. 502–9.
Miracula sancti Heinrici (BHL 3815) (excerpts), ed. Georg Waitz, MGH, SS 4 (Hanover, 1841), pp. 814–16.
Miracula sancti Januarii (BHL 4138), AASS Septembris 6 (1757), pp. 884–87.
Miracula sancti Martialis anno 1388 patrata (BHL 5581), ed. Francis Arbellot, AB 1 (1885), pp. 411–46 (also ed. Jean-Loup Lemaitre, "Les miracles de saint Martial accomplis lors de l'ostention de 1388," *Bulletin de la société archéologique et historique du Limousin* 102 [1975], pp. 67–139).
Miracula sancti Petroci (BHL 6640d), ed. Paul Grosjean, *"Vie et miracles de S. Petroc,"* AB 74 (1956), pp. 171–74.
Miracula sancti Severi martyris (BHL 7687, 7690), AASS Novembris 1 (1887), pp. 233–35.
Miracula sancti Sigismondi martyris, per ipsum in sanctam Pragensem ecclesiam manifeste demonstrata (BHL 7720), *Catalogus codicum hagiographicorum latinorum antiquorum saeculo XVI qui asservantur in Bibliotheca Nationali Parisiensi* (4 vols., Brussels, 1889–93) 3, pp. 462–69.
Miracula sancti Stephani (BHL 7860–61), ed. Jean Meyers, *Les miracles de saint Étienne* (Turnhout, 2006), pp. 263–354.
Miracula sancti Thomae de Aquino (without BHL no.), AASS Martii 1 (1668), pp. 723–24.
Miracula sancti Veroli (BHL 8547), AASS Iunii 3 (1701), pp. 382–88.
Miracula sancti Yvonis episcopi Persae (BHL 4623), ed. W. Dunn Macray, *Chronicon abbatiae Ramesiensis* (RS, 1886), pp. lxxv–lxxxiv.
Miracula sanctissimi Wlstani (BHL 8758), ed. R. R. Darlington, *William of Malmesbury, Vita Wulfstani* (Camden, 3rd ser., 40, 1928), pp. 115–80.
Miracula sanctorum martyrum Claudii, Luperci et Victori in translatione (BHL 1834), AASS Octobris 13 (1883), pp. 294–96.
Miracula Simonis de Montfort (BHL 7760), ed. James Orchard Halliwell, *The Chronicle of William de Rishanger of the Barons' Wars: The Miracles of Simon de Montfort* (Camden Society 15, 1840), pp. 67–110.
Miracula Simonis Tudertini (without BHL no.), AASS Aprilis 2 (1675), pp. 819–31.
Miracula Theclae (BHG 1718), ed. Gilbert Dagron, *Vie et miracles de Sainte Thècle* (SH 62, 1978), pp. 284–412 (Eng. tr. *Miracle Tales from Byzantium*, ed. Alice-Mary Talbot and Scott Fitzgerald Johnson (Cambridge, MA, 2012), pp. 3–183).
Miracula varia Cunegundi imperatricis (BHL 2005), AASS Martii 1 (1668), pp. 278–80.

Miracula varia sancti Vulfranni (BHL 8741), AASS Martii 3 (1668), pp. 150–61.

Miraculum sancti Iuvenalis anno mccxxxiii patratum (BHL 4616), AASS Maii 1 (1680), p. 394.

Mirk, John, *Festial*, ed. Susan Powell (2 vols., EETS o.s. 334–35, 2009–11).

Mombritius, Boninus, *Sanctuarium* (2 vols., Milan, 1477?; repr. with supplementary material, Paris, 1910).

The Monastic Breviary of Hyde Abbey, Winchester, ed. J.B.L. Tolhurst (6 vols., Henry Bradshaw Society 69–71, 76, 78, 80, 1932–42).

Monti, Gennaro M., "Il testo e la storia esterna delle assisse normanne," in *Lo stato normanno svevo: lineamenti e ricerche* (Trani, 1945), pp. 83–184.

Monumenta Boica 8 (Munich, 1767).

Monumenta Juridica: The Black Book of the Admiralty 1, ed. Travers Twiss (RS, 1871).

Monumenta necrologica monasterii sancti Petri Salisburgensis, ed. Sigismund Herzberg-Fränkel, MGH, *Necrologia Germaniae* 2 (Berlin, 1904).

Monuments de l'histoire des abbayes de Saint-Philibert, ed. René Poupardin (Paris, 1905).

Monuments du procès de canonisation du Bienheureux Charles de Blois, duc de Bretagne, 1320–1364, ed. François Plaine and A. de Serent (St.-Brieuc, 1921).

More, Thomas, *A Dialogue Concerning Heresies*, ed. Thomas M. C. Lawler et al., *The Complete Works of St. Thomas More* 6/1 (New Haven, 1981).

Mueller, Joan, ed., *Clare's Letters to Agnes: Texts and Sources* (New York, 2001).

Muirchú, *Vita sancti Patricii* (BHL 6497), ed. Ludwig Bieler, *Patrician Texts in the Book of Armagh* (Dublin, 1979), pp. 62–122.

Musurillo, Herbert, ed., *The Acts of the Christian Martyrs* (Oxford, 1972).

Narratio de miraculo a Michaele Archangelo patrato (BHG 1282), ed. Max Bonnet (Paris, 1890).

Nestor, *Lesson on the Life and Murder of the Blessed Passion-Sufferers Boris and Gleb*, tr. Paul Hollingsworth, *The Hagiography of Kievan Rus'* (Cambridge, MA, 1992), pp. 3–32.

Nestoriana. Die Fragmente des Nestorius, ed. Friedrich Loofs (Halle, 1905).

Nicetas of Remesiana, *De symbolo*, ed. A. E. Burn (Cambridge, 1905).

Nicholas IV, *Les Régistres de Nicolas IV*, ed. Ernest Langlois (Paris, 1888–1905).

Nicholas Kataskepenos, *Vita Cyrilli Phileotis* (BHG 468), ed. Étienne Sargologos, *La vie de Saint Cyrille le Philéote, moine byzantin (+1110)* (SH 39, 1964).

Nicholas of Fara, *Vita clarissimi viri fratris Joannis de Capistrano* (BHL 4360), AASS Octobris 10 (1861), pp. 439–83.

Nikephoros of Constantinople, *Antirrhetici tres adversus Constantinum*, PG 100, cols. 205–534.

———, *Breviarium historicum*, ed. Cyril Mango, *Nikephoros of Constantinople: Short History* (Washington, DC, 1990).

Notes et documents de l'histoire de Saint Vincent Ferrier, ed. (H.) Fages (Louvain and Paris, 1905).

Notitia de locis sanctorum apostolorum (BHL 648), AASS Novembris 2/2 (1931), p. 2.

Notker Balbulus, *Gesta Karoli magni imperatoris*, ed. Hans F. Haefele, MGH, SRG, n. s. 12 (Berlin, 1959).

Notker of Hautvilliers, *De translatione sanctae Helenae imperatricis* (BHL 3787), AASS Augusti 3 (1737), pp. 603–4, 607–11, 645.

Nova legenda Anglie, ed. Carl Horstman (2 vols., Oxford, 1901).

Odilo of Cluny, *Epitaphium domne Adalheide auguste* (BHL 63), ed. Herbert Paulhart, *Die Lebensbeschreibung der Kaiserin Adelheid von Abt Odilo von Cluny* (Mitteilungen des Instituts für Österreichische Geschichtsforschung. Ergänzungsband 20: Festschrift zur Jahrtausendfeier der Kaiserkrönung Ottos des Grossen 2, 1962), pp. 27–45.

———, *Vita beati Maioli abbatis* (BHL 5182–83), PL 142, cols. 943–62.

Odo of Cluny, *Vita sancti Geraldi Auriliacensis* (BHL 3411), ed. Anne-Marie Bultot-Verleysen (SH 89, 2009).

The Officium and Miracula of Richard Rolle of Hampole, ed. Reginald Maxwell Wooley (London, 1919).

Der Oldenburger Sachsenspiegel, ed. Ruth Schmidt-Wiegand (Graz, 1995).

The Old English Martyrology, ed. Günter Kotzor, *Das altenglische Martyrologium* (2 vols., Abhandlungen der Bayerischen Akademie der Wissenschaften 88/1 and 88/2, Munich, 1981).

The Old French Evangile de l'enfance, ed. Maureen Boulton (Toronto, 1984).

Optatus of Milevis, *De schismate Donatistarum*, ed. Mirelle Labrousse, *Traité contre les donatistes* (2 vols., SC 412–13, 1995–96).

Opus Caroli regis contra synodum (Libri Carolini), ed. Ann Freeman, MGH, *Concilia* 2, *supplementum* 1 (Hanover, 1998).

El Oracional Visigótico, ed. José Vives (Barcelona, 1946).

Oratio ad probandas reliquias, PL 71, cols. 1185–86.

Orderic Vitalis, *Historia ecclesiastica: The Ecclesiastical History*, ed. Marjorie Chibnall (6 vols., OMT, 1968–80).

Les Ordines Romani du haut Moyen Âge, ed. Michel Andrieu (5 vols., Spicilegium sacrum Lovaniense 11, 23–24, 28–29, 1931–61).

Origen, *Contra Celsum*, ed. Marcel Borret (5 vols., SC 132, 136, 147, 150, 227, 1967–76).

The Origins of Christianity in Bohemia: Sources and Commentary, tr. Marvin Kantor (Evanston, 1990).

Orkneyinga Saga, tr. Hermann Pálsson and Paul Edwards, *Orkneyinga Saga: The History of the Earls of Orkney* (London, 1978; repr., Harmondsworth, 1981).

Osbern of Canterbury, *Vita et miracula sancti Dunstani* (BHL 2344–45), ed. William Stubbs, *Memorials of Saint Dunstan* (RS, 1874), pp. 69–161.

Otloh of St. Emmeram, *Vita Bonifacii* (BHL 1403), ed. Wilhelm Levison, *Vitae Sancti Bonifatii Archiepiscopi Moguntini* (MGH, SRG, Hanover and Leipzig, 1905), pp. 111–217.

———, *Vita sancti Nicolai* (BHL 6126), ed. Wilhelm Wattenbach, "Aus Handschriften," *Neues Archiv* 10 (1885), pp. 408–9 (prologue and last chapter only).

Pachymeres, George, *Romaike historia*, ed. Albert Failler, *Relations historiques* (5 vols., Paris, 1984–2000).

Palladius, *Historia Lausiaca*, ed. G.J.M. Bartelink, *La storia lausiaca* (Milan, 1974).

Pantaleon Diaconus, *Encomium in maximum et gloriosissimum Michaelem* (BHG 1289), PG 98, cols. 1259–66.

Paschasius Radbertus, *De corpore et sanguine Domini*, ed. Beda Paulus (CCCM 16, 1969).

———, *Epitaphium Arsenii (Vita Walae)* (BHL 8761), PL 120, cols. 1559–1650.

———, *Vita sancti Adalhardi Corbeiensis abbatis* (BHL 58), PL 120, cols. 1507–82.

Pasionario hispánico (siglos VII–XI), ed. Angel Fábrega Grau (2 vols., Monumenta Hispaniae Sacra, Serie Litúrgica 6, Madrid, 1953–55).

Passio Cassiani (BHL 1626), ed. Mombritius, *Sanctuarium* 1, fols. 157v–158.

Passio et miracula Beati Olavi (BHL 6322–24), ed. Frederick Metcalfe (Oxford, 1881).
Passio Gereonis (attrib. Helinand) (BHL 3446), AASS Octobris 5 (1786), pp. 36–42.
Passio Kiliani, Ps. Theotimus, Passio Margaretae, orationes (Codices selecti phototypice impressi 83, Graz, 1988, with a commentary volume by Cynthia Hahn).
Passio Leudegarii I (BHL 4849b), ed. Bruno Krusch, MGH, SRM 5 (Hanover and Leipzig, 1910), pp. 282–322.
Passio Polycarpi (BHG 1556–60), ed. Musurillo, *Acts of the Christian Martyrs*, pp. 2–20.
Passio sanctarum Perpetuae et Felicitatis (BHG 1482), ed. Cornelius Van Beek (Nimwegen, 1936), pp. 5–53 (odd pages).
Passio sanctarum Perpetuae et Felicitatis (BHL 6633), ed. Musurillo, *Acts of the Christian Martyrs*, pp. 106–30 (ed. Jacqueline Amat, SC 417, 1996).
Passio sancti Eadwardi regis et martyris (BHL 2418), ed. Christine E. Fell, *Edward King and Martyr* (Leeds, 1971).
Passio sancti Kanuti regis et martiris (BHL 1550), ed. M. G. Gertz, *Vitae sanctorum Danorum* (Copenhagen, 1908–12), pp. 62–71.
Passio sancti Phoce (BHL 6838), ed. Mombritius, *Sanctuarium* 2, fols. 228–31.
Passio sancti Sigismundi regis (BHL 7717), ed. Bruno Krusch, MGH, SRM 2 (Hanover, 1881), pp. 329–40.
Passio sanctorum Mariani et Iacobi (BHL 131), ed. Musurillo, *Acts of the Christian Martyrs*, pp. 194–212.
Passio sanctorum martyrum Fructuosi episcopi, Auguri et Eulogi diaconorum (BHL 3196), ed. Musurillo, *Acts of the Christian Martyrs*, pp. 176–84.
Passio sanctorum Montani et Lucii (BHL 6009), ed. Musurillo, *Acts of the Christian Martyrs*, pp. 214–38.
Patrick, *Confessio and Epistola*, ed. Ludwig Bieler, *Libri epistolarum sancti Patricii episcopi* (2 vols., Dublin, 1952), 1, pp. 56–102; ed. A.B.E. Hood, *St. Patrick: His Writings and Muirchu's Life* (London and Chichester, 1978), pp. 23–38.
Patrizi Piccolomini, Agostino, *Caeremoniale romanum*, ed. Marc Dykmans, *L'oeuvre de Patrizi Piccolomini: ou le cérémonial papal de la première Renaissance* (2 vols., Studi e testi 293–94, 1980–82).
Paulinus, *Vita Ambrosii* (BHL 377), ed. A.A.R. Bastiaensen, *Vita di Cipriano. Vita di Ambrogio. Vita di Agostino* (Vite dei santi 3, 4th ed., Milan, 1997), pp. 51–125.
Paulinus of Nola, *Carmina*, ed. Wilhelm von Hartel (CSEL 30, 2nd ed., 1999).
———, *Epistulae*, ed. Wilhelm von Hartel (CSEL 29, 2nd ed., 1999).
Paul the Deacon, *Epistolae variorum* 13, ed. Ernst Dümmler, MGH, *Epistolae* 4 (*Karolini aevi* 2) (Berlin, 1895), pp. 509–14.
———, *Historia Langobardorum*, ed. Georg Waitz (SRG, Hanover, 1878).
Pelayo of Oviedo, *Historia de arcae sanctae translatione*, ed. Manuel Risco, *España Sagrada* 37 (Madrid, 1789), pp. 352–58 (app. 15).
Peter Abelard, *Historia calamitatum*, ed. Jacques Monfrin (Paris, 1959).
Peter, bishop of Treviso, *Vita Henrici Baucenensis* (BHL 3807), AASS Iunii 2 (1698), pp. 371–75.
Peter Comestor, *Historia scholastica*, PL 198, cols. 1053–1644.
Peter Damian, *Disputatio de variis apparationibus et miraculis*, PL 145, cols. 584–89.
———, *Epistolae*, ed. Kurt Reindel, *Die Briefe des Petrus Damiani* (4 vols., MGH, Die Briefe der deutschen Kaiserzeit 4, Munich, 1983–93).
Peter of Blois, *Epistolae*, PL 207, cols. 1–560.

Peter of Celle, *Epistolae*, ed. Julian Haseldine, *The Letters of Peter of Celle* (OMT, 2001).
Peter of Dusburg, *Chronica terre Prussie*, ed. Klaus Scholz and Dieter Wojtecki (AQ 25, Darmstadt, 1984).
Peter of Monterubbiano, *Vita et miracula Nicolai Tolentinatis* (BHL 6230), AASS Septembris 3 (1750), pp. 644–64.
Peter of Zittau, *Chronicon Aulae Regiae*, ed. Josef Emler, *Fontes Rerum Bohemicarum* 4 (Prague, 1884), pp. 1–337.
Peter the Deacon, *Historica relatio de corpore sancti Benedicti* (BHL 1142), AASS Martii 3 (1668), pp. 288–97.
Peter the Deacon, *Vita, translatio et miracula sancti Martini abbatis* (BHL 5604), AASS Octobris 10 (1861), pp. 835–40.
Peter Tudebode, *Historia de Hierosolymitano itinere*, ed. John Hugh Hill and Laurita L. Hill (Paris, 1977).
Petrus Andreas de Castaneis, *Vita Andreae Corsini* (BHL 445), AASS Ianuarii 2 (1643), pp. 1064–73.
Petrus Chrysologus, *Collectio sermonum*, ed. Alexander Olivar (3 vols., CCSL 24, 24A and 24B, 1975–82).
Philip of Clairvaux, *Vita Elizabeth Sanctimonialis in Erkenrode* (BHL 2484), *Catalogus Codicum Hagiographicorum Bibliothecae Regiae Bruxellensis* 1 (SH 1, 1886), pp. 362–78.
Philip of Harvengt, *Vita beatae Odae virginis* (BHL 6262), PL 203, cols. 1359–74.
Philippe de Mézières' Campaign for the Feast of Mary's Presentation, ed. William E. Coleman (Toronto, 1981).
Philippus Presbyter (Pseudo-Jerome), *Commentarii in librum Iob*, PL 26, cols. 619–802.
Philo of Alexandria, *De vita Mosis*, ed. Roger Arnaldez et al. (Les oeuvres de Philon d'Alexandrie 22, Paris, 1967).
A Picture Book of the Life of Saint Anthony the Abbot, ed. Rose Graham (Roxburghe Club, 1937).
Pierre de Vaux, *Vie de sainte Colette*, ed. Ubald d'Alençon, *Les vies de sainte Colette Boylet de Corbie* (Paris, 1911), pp. 3–201.
Pierre des Vaux-de-Cernay, *Historia Albigensis*, ed. Pascal Guébin and Ernest Lyon (3 vols., Société de l'histoire de France 412, 422, 442, 1926–39).
Pilgrimage to Jerusalem and the Holy Land, 1187–1291, ed. Denys Pringle (Aldershot, 2012).
The Pilgrim's Guide to Santiago de Compostella: Critical Edition, ed. Alison Stones et al. (2 vols., London, 1998).
Pleas of the Crown for the County of Gloucester . . . 1221, ed. F. W. Maitland (London, 1884).
Plummer, Charles, *Vitae sanctorum Hiberniae* (2 vols., Oxford, 1910).
Polentone, Sicco, *Vita et visiones beatae Helenae (Enselmini)* (BHL 3792), AASS Novembris 2/1 (1894), pp. 512–17.
Polo, Marco, *Le devisement du monde*, ed. Philippe Ménard (6 vols., Geneva, 2001–9).
Le Pontifical romano-germanique du dixième siècle, ed. Cyrille Vogel and Reinhard Elze (3 vols., Studi e Testi 226–27, 266, Rome, 1963–72).
Potthast, August, ed., *Regesta pontificum Romanorum (1198–1304)* (2 vols., Berlin, 1874–75).
The Prayer Book of Aedeluald the Bishop, Commonly Called the Book of Cerne, ed. A. B. Kuypers (Cambridge, 1902).
Prima acta sancti Blasii (BHL 1370), AASS Februarii 1 (1658), pp. 336–39.

Procès de condamnation de Jeanne d'Arc, ed. Pierre Tisset (Société de l'histoire de France 466, 477, 479, 1960–71).

Procès de la canonisation de Saint Vincent Ferrier (BHL 8656b,c,d), ed. (H.) Fages (Paris and Louvain, 1904).

I processi inediti per Francesca Bussa dei Ponziani (Santa Francesca Romana) 1440–1453, ed. Placido Tommaso Lugato (Studi e Testi 120, Vatican City, 1945).

Il processo Castellano (BHL 1707), ed. Marie-Hyacinthe Laurent (Fontes vitae sanctae Catharinae Senensis historicae 9, Milan, 1942).

Il processo di canonizzazione di Bernardino da Siena (1445–1450), ed. Letizia Pellegrini, *Analecta Franciscana* 16 (n.s. 4, 2009).

Il processo per la canonizzazione di S. Nicola da Tolentino, ed. Nicola Occhioni (Rome, 1984).

Processus apostolici beatae Joannis Boni, AASS Octobris 9 (1858), pp. 771–885.

Processus Bacheracensis de vita, martyrio et miraculis beati Wernheri, AASS Aprilis 2 (1675), pp. 714–34.

Processus canonizationis beati Ambrosii Massani, AASS Novembris 4 (1925), pp. 571–608.

Processus canonizationis sancti Ludovici episcopi Tolosani, *Analecta Franciscana* 7 (1951), pp. 1–254.

Processus de vita et miraculis B. Petri de Luxemburgo, AASS Julii 1 (Antwerp, 1719), pp. 527–607.

Processus de vita et miraculis sancti Yvonis (BHL 4625), ed. A. de La Borderie et al., *Monuments originaux de l'histoire de S. Yves* (St.-Brieuc, 1887), pp. 1–299.

Processus informativus pro canonizatione Mariæ de Maillye (BHL 5514), AASS Martii 3 (1668), pp. 747–65.

Proclus of Constantinople, Homily 1, "On the Holy Virgin Theotokos," ed. Nicholas Constas, *Proclus of Constantinople and the Cult of the Virgin in Late Antiquity* (Leiden, 2003), pp. 136–56.

Prosper, *Epitoma Chronicon*, ed. Theodor Mommsen, *Chronica minora saec. IV. V. VI. VII.* 1, MGH, AA 9 (Berlin, 1892), pp. 341–485.

Protevangelium Jacobi, ed. Ronald F. Hock, *The Infancy Gospels of James and Thomas* (Santa Rosa, CA, 1995), pp. 31–81.

Prudentius, *Peristefanon*, ed. Maurice P. Cunningham, *Aurelii Prudentii Clementis carmina* (CCSL 126, 1966), pp. 251–389.

———, *Praefatio*, ibid., pp. 1–2.

———, *Psychomachia*, ibid., pp. 149–81.

Psellos, Michael, *Chronographia*, ed. Émile Renauld (2 vols., Paris, 1926).

Pseudo-Ambrose, *Passio sanctae Agnetis* (BHL 156), PL 17, cols. 735–42.

Pseudo-Cyprianus, *De XII abusivis saeculi*, ed. Siegmund Hellmann (Texte und Untersuchungen zur Geschichte der Altchristlichen Literatur 34/1, Leipzig, 1909).

Pseudo-Kodinos, *Traité des offices*, ed. Jean Verpeaux (Paris, 1966).

Pseudo-Matthaei Evangelium, ed. Jan Gijsel, *Libri de Nativitate Mariae* 1 (CC, Series Apocryphorum 9, 1997).

Qualiter caput beate Barbare processu temporis in Pomeraniam pervenit (BHL 930), *Scriptores rerum Prussicarum* 2, ed. Max Töppen (Leipzig, 1863), pp. 399–408.

Queenship and Sanctity: The Lives of Mathilda and the Epitaph of Adelheid, tr. Sean Gilsdorf (Washington, DC, 2004).

Quellen zur böhmischen Inquisition im vierzehnten Jahrhundert, ed. Alexander Patschovsky (MGH, Quellen zur Geistesgeschichte des Mittelalters, Weimar, 1979).

Quellen zur Geschichte der Kölner Laienbruderschaften vom 12. Jahrhundert bis 1562/3, ed. Klaus Militzer (4 vols., Düsseldorf, 1997–2000).
Quellen zur Geschichte der Waldenser, ed. Alexander Patschovsky and Kurt-Victor Selge (Gütersloh, 1973).
Quellenstudien zur Geschichte der heiligen Elisabeth, ed. Albert Huyskens (Marburg, 1908).
Quodvultdeus, *Liber promissionum*, ed. René Braun, *Livre des promesses* (2 vols., SC 101–2, 1964).
Quoniam historiae (Life of Homobonus), ed. Daniele Piazzi, *Omobono di Cremona: biografie dal XIII al XVI secolo* (Cremona, 1991), pp. 50–54.
Radbod of Utrecht, *Libellus de miraculo sancti Martini* (BHL 5656), ed. Oswald Holder-Egger, MGH, SS 15/2 (Hanover, 1888), pp. 1239–44.
Raine, James, ed., *The History and Antiquities of North Durham* (London, 1852).
Rainer, *Miracula sancti Gisleni* (BHL 3556), ed. Oswald Holder-Egger, MGH, SS 15/2 (Hanover, 1888), pp. 579–85 (excerpts).
Ralph Bocking, *Vita sancti Ricardi episcopi Cycestrensis* (BHL 7209), ed. David Jones, *Saint Richard of Chichester: The Sources for His Life* (Sussex Record Soc. 79, 1995 for 1993), pp. 83–159.
Ralph of Coggeshall, *Chronicon Anglicanum*, ed. Joseph Stevenson (RS, 1875).
Ranieri Sacconi, *De Catharis et Pauperibus de Lugduno*, ed. A. Dondaine, *Un traité néo-manichéen du XIIIe siècle: Le Liber de duobus principiis* (Rome, 1939), pp. 64–78.
Ranulph Higden, *Polychronicon*, ed. Churchill Babington and Joseph Rawson Lumby (9 vols., RS, 1865–86).
Ranzano, Pietro, *Vita sancti Vincentii Ferrerii* (BHL 8658), AASS Aprilis 1 (1675), pp. 482–512.
Rather of Verona, *Translatio sancti Metronis* (BHL 5942), ed. Petrus L. D. Reid, *Ratherii Veronensis opera minora* (CCCM 46, 1976), pp. 9–29.
Raymond of Capua, *Vita Catharinae Senensis* (BHL 1702), AASS Aprilis 3 (1675), pp. 853–959, ed. Jörg Jungmayr, *Die Legenda Maior (Vita Catharinae Senensis) des Raimund von Capua* (2 vols., Berlin, 2004 [vol. 1 text]).
Records of the Trials of the Spanish Inquisition in Ciudad Real, ed. Haim Beinart (4 vols., Jerusalem, 1974–85).
Recueil des actes de Charles II le Chauve, roi de France, ed. Arthur Giry et al. (3 vols., Paris, 1943–55).
Recueil des actes de Charles III le Simple, roi de France, ed. Philippe Lauer (Paris, 1940–49).
Recueil des actes de Henri II, roi d'Angleterre et duc de Normandie, concernant les provinces françaises et les affaires de France, ed. Léopold Delisle and Élie Berger (3 vols., Paris, 1916–27).
Recueil des chartes de l'abbaye de Cluny, ed. Auguste Bernard and Alexandre Bruel (6 vols., Paris, 1876–1903).
Regesta de Fernando II, ed. Julio Gonzalez (Madrid, 1943).
Regesta Honorii Papae III, ed. P. Pressutti (2 vols., Rome, 1888–95).
Regesta regum anglo-normannorum, ed. H.W.C. Davis et al. (4 vols., Oxford, 1913–69).
Reginald of Durham, *Libellus de admirandis beati Cuthberti virtutibus* (BHL 2032), ed. James Raine (Surtees Soc. 1, 1835).
———, *Libellus de vita et miraculis sancti Godrici heremitae de Finchale* (BHL 3596), ed. Joseph Stevenson (Surtees Soc. 20, 1845).

———, *Vita sancti Oswaldi regis et martyris*, ed. Thomas Arnold, *Symeonis monachi opera omnia* (2 vols., RS, 1882–85) 1, pp. 326–85.

The Register of Edmund Lacy, Bishop of Exeter, 1420–1455, ed. G. R. Dunstan (5 vols., Canterbury and York Society 60–62, 64, 66, 1963–72).

The Register of Eudes of Rouen, ed. Jeremiah F. O'Sullivan, tr. Sydney M. Brown (New York, 1964).

The Register of Henry Chichele, Archbishop of Canterbury, 1414–1443, ed. E. F. Jacob (4 vols., Canterbury and York Society 42, 45, 46, 47, 1938–47).

The Register of John Morton, Archbishop of Canterbury, 1486–1500, ed. Christopher Harper-Bill (3 vols., Canterbury and York Soc. 75, 78, 89, 1987–2000).

The Register of Thomas Spofford, Bishop of Hereford (1422–1448), ed. Arthur Thomas Bannister (Canterbury and York Soc. 22, 1917).

The Registers of Roger Martival, Bishop of Salisbury, 1315–1330 2, ed. C. R. Elrington (Canterbury and York Society 57, 1963).

Le Registre d'Inquisition de Jacques Fournier, évêque de Pamiers (1318–1325), ed. Jean Duvernoy (3 vols., Toulouse, 1965).

Registrum episcopatus aberdonensis (2 vols., Edinburgh, 1845).

Registrum episcopatus Glasguensis, ed. Cosmo Innes (2 vols., Bannatyne and Maitland Clubs, Edinburgh, 1843).

Registrum Hamonis Hethe diocesis roffensis, A.D. 1319–1352, ed. Charles Johnson (2 vols., Canterbury and York Soc. 48–49, 1948).

Regula Benedicti, ed. Bruce L. Venarde (Cambridge, MA, 2011).

Relatio miraculorum quæ facta sunt meritis beati Rainerii (BHL 7086), AASS Novembris 1 (1887), pp. 391–402.

Revelatio Sancti Stephani (BHL 7850–53), ed. S. Vanderlinden, *Revue des Études Byzantines* 4 (1946), pp. 178–217.

Rhalles, Georgios Alexandros, and Michael Potles, *Syntagma tōn theion kai hierōn kanonōn tōn te hagiōn kai paneuphēmōn Apostolōn* (6 vols., Athens, 1852–59).

Rhygyfarch, *Vita sancti David* (BHL 2107), ed. Richard Sharpe and John Reuben Davies, in *St David of Wales: Cult, Church and Nation*, ed. J. Wyn Evans and Jonathan M. Wooding (Woodbridge, 2007), pp. 107–54.

Rhythmus de vita et miraculis sancti Germani episcopi Parisiensis (BHL 3470–71), ed. Paul von Winterfeld, MGH, *Poetae latini aevi carolini* 4/1 (Berlin, 1899), pp. 124–32.

Richard of Cirencester, *Speculum historiale*, ed. John E. B. Mayor (2 vols., RS, 1863–69).

Richard of Hexham, *Historia*, ed. Richard Howlett, *Chronicles of the Reigns of Stephen, Henry II and Richard I* (4 vols., RS, 1884–89), 3, pp. 137–78.

Richard of San Germano, *Chronica (Ryccardi de Sancto Germano notarii Chronica)*, ed. Carlo Alberto Garufi (Rerum Italicarum Scriptores 7/ii, Bologna, 1938).

Richer of Senones, *Gesta Senoniensis ecclesiae*, ed. Georg Waitz, MGH, SS 25 (Hanover, 1880), pp. 249–345.

Rigord, *Gesta Philippi Augusti*, ed. Elisabeth Carpentier et al., *Histoire de Philippe Auguste* (Paris, 2006).

Rimbert, *Vita Anskarii* (BHL 544), ed. Werner Trillmich, *Quellen des 9. und 11. Jahrhunderts zur Geschichte der Hamburgischen Kirche und des Reiches* (AQ 11, Darmstadt, 1961), pp. 1–133.

Robert of Clari, *La conquête de Constantinople*, ed. Philippe Lauer (Paris, 1924).

Robert of St.-Marianus of Auxerre, *Chronicon*, ed. Oswald Holder-Egger, MGH, SS 26 (Hanover, 1882), pp. 219–76.

Robert of Tawton, *De reliquiarum furto*, ed. Paul Grosjean, "Vie et Miracles de S. Petroc," AB 74 (1956), pp. 131–88 (at 174–88).

Robert of Torigni, *Chronica*, ed. Richard Howlett, *Chronicles of the Reigns of Stephen, Henry II and Richard I* (4 vols., RS, 1882–89) 4.

Robert the Monk, *Historia Iherosolimitana*, *Recueil des historiens des croisades* (16 vols., Paris, 1841–1906), *Historiens Occidentaux* 3, cols. 717–882.

Rode, Johannes, *Consuetudines et observantiae monasteriorum sancti Mathiae et sancti Maximini Treverensium*, ed. Peter Becker (Corpus consuetudinum monasticarum 5, Siegburg, 1968).

Rodulfus Glaber, *Historiarum libri quinque*, ed. John France, *Opera* (OMT, 1989).

Rodulfus of Cambrai, *Vita domni Lietberti ecclesiae Cameracensis episcopi* (BHL 4929), ed. Adolf Hofmeister, MGH, SS 30/2 (Leipzig, 1934), pp. 840–66.

Roger of Howden, *Chronica*, ed. William Stubbs (4 vols., RS, 1868–71).

Rossi, Joannes Baptista, *Vita beati Johannis Colombini*, AASS Julii 7 (1731), pp. 354–98.

Rostang of Cluny, *Translatio capitis sancti Clementis Cluniacum* (BHL 1853), *Exuviae sacrae Constantinopolitanae* 1, cols. 127–40 (PL 209, cols. 905–14).

Rudolf and Meginhard of Fulda, *Translatio sancti Alexandri* (BHL 283), ed. Bruno Krusch, "Die Übertragung des H. Alexander von Rom nach Wildeshausen," *Nachrichten der Gesellschaft der Wissenschaften zu Göttingen, phil.-hist. Klasse* (1933), pp. 405–36.

Rudolf of Fulda, *Miracula sanctorum in ecclesias Fuldenses translatorum*, ed. Georg Waitz, MGH, SS 15/1 (Hanover, 1887), pp. 328–41.

———, *Vita Leobae abbatissae Biscofesheimensis* (BHL 4845), ed. Georg Waitz, MGH, SS 15/1 (Hanover, 1887), pp. 118–31.

Sacchetti, Franco, *Il libro delle Rime con le lettere. La battaglia delle belle donne*, ed. David Puccini (Turin, 2007).

Sachsenspiegel: Die Wolfenbütteler Bilderhandschrift, ed. Ruth Schmidt-Wiegand (Berlin, 1993).

Sachsenspiegel: Landrecht and Lehnrecht, ed. Karl August Eckhardt (MGH, Fontes Iuris Germanici Antiqui, n.s. 1, 2 vols., Göttingen, 1955–56).

Sächsische Weltchronik, ed. Ludwig Weiland, MGH, *Deutsche Chroniken* 2 (Hanover, 1877), pp. 1–279.

Le sacramentaire grégorien: ses principales formes d'après les plus anciens manuscrits, ed. Jean Deshusses (2nd ed., 3 vols., Fribourg, 1979–82).

Sahih Bukhari (on-line).

Saint Thècle, Saints Côme et Damien, Saints Cyr et Jean (extraits), Saint Georges, ed. A.-J. Festugière (Paris, 1971).

Salimbene de Adam, *Cronica*, ed. Oswald Holder-Egger, MGH, SS 32 (Hanover and Leipzig, 1905–13).

Salterio di Santa Elisabetta. Facsimile, ed. Claudio Barberi (facs. with commentary vol., Cividale del Friuli, 2002).

Salterio griego Jlúdov (ms. gr. 129, Museo Histórico del Estado, Moscú) (2 vols., Madrid, 2007 [not seen]).

Salvo Burci, *Liber suprastella*, ed. Caterina Bruschi (Rome, 2002).

Sanas Chormaic: Cormac's Glossary, tr. John O'Donovan (Calcutta, 1868).

Sancti Francisci Paulani canonizatio, AASS Aprilis 1 (1675), pp. 216–18.

Santo Martino de Leon, ed. Antonio Viñayo (Leon, 1984).

Saxo Grammaticus, *Gesta Danorum*, ed. Karsten Friis-Jensen (2 vols., Copenhagen, 2005).

Seinte Margarete, in *Medieval English Prose for Women*, ed. Bella Millett and Jocelyn Wogan-Browne (Oxford, 1990), pp. 44–85.

Sermo de adventu sanctorum Wandregisili, Ansberti et Vulframni in Blandinium (BHL 8810), ed. N.-N. Huyghebaert, *Une translation de reliques à Gand en 944: Le Sermo de adventu sanctorum Wandregisili, Ansberti et Vulframni in Blandinium* (Brussels, 1978).

Sermo de capitis Johannis Baptistae inventionibus (BHG 841), PL 67, cols. 434–46.

Serpi, Dimas, *Vita Saluatoris de Horta*, AASS Martii 2 (1668), pp. 668–91.

Servius, *In Aeneidem I–II*, ed. E. K. Rand et al., *Commentaria in Vergilii carmina* 2 (Lancaster, PA, 1946).

Sicard of Cremona, *Mitralis de officiis*, ed. Gábor Sarbak and Lorenz Weinrich (CCCM 228, 2008).

Sidonius Apollinaris, *Epistulae (I–V)*, ed. André Loyen (Paris, 1970).

Las siete partidas (Real Academia de la Historia, 3 vols., Madrid, 1807).

Sigebert of Gembloux, *Chronica*, ed. Ludwig Bethmann, MGH, SS 6 (Hanover, 1844), pp. 268–374.

———, *Chronica: Auctarium Hasnoniense*, ed. Ludwig Bethmann (MGH, SS 6, Hanover, 1844), pp. 441–42.

———, *Vita Deoderici episcopi Mettensis* (BHL 8055), ed. Georg Heinrich Pertz, MGH, SS 4 (Hanover, 1841), pp. 461–83.

———, *Vita sancti Maclovii sive Machutii episcopi* (BHL 5119), PL 160, cols. 729–46.

———, *Vita Wicberti* (BHL 8882), PL 160, cols. 661–76.

Simund de Freine, *Vie de saint Georges*, ed. John E. Matzke, *Les oeuvres de Simund de Freine* (Paris, 1909), pp. 61–117.

Snorri Sturluson, *Heimskringla*, tr. Lee M. Hollander (Austin, 1964).

Sophronius of Jerusalem, *Miracula Cyri et Ioannis* (BHG 478–479a), ed. Natalio Fernández Marcos, *Los Thaumata de Sofronio: Contribución al estudio de la incubatio cristiana* (Madrid, 1975), pp. 241–400.

Sources of the Modern Roman Liturgy: The Ordinals by Haymo of Faversham and related documents, ed. S.J.P. Van Dijk (2 vols., Leiden, 1963).

The South English Legendary, ed. Charlotte D'Evelyn and Anna J. Mill (3 vols., EETS, o.s. 235–36, 244, 1956–59).

Sozomen, *Historia ecclesiastica*, ed. Joseph Bidez and Günther Hansen (4 vols., SC 306, 418, 495, 516, 1983–2008).

"S. Pierre Célestin et ses premiers biographes," AB 16 (1897), pp. 365–487.

The Stacions of Rome, ed. Frederick J. Furnivall (EETS, o.s. 25, 1867).

Statuta capitulorum generalium ordinis Cisterciensis, ed. Josephus-Maria Canivez (8 vols., Louvain, 1933–41).

Statuta et Consuetudines Ecclesiæ Cathedralis Beatæ Mariæ Virginis Sarisberiensis: Statutes and Customs of the Cathedral Church of the Blessed Virgin Mary of Salisbury, ed. Christopher Wordsworth and Douglas Macleane (London, 1915).

Die Statuten des deutschen Ordens nach den altesten Handschriften, ed. Max Perlbach (Halle, 1890).

Statutes of Lincoln Cathedral, ed. Henry Bradshaw and Christopher Wordsworth (2 vols. in 3, Cambridge, 1892–97).

The Statutes Ordained by Richard Duke of Gloucester for the College of Middleham, ed. James Raine, *Archaeological Journal* 14 (1857), pp. 160–70.

Statuti di Bologna dell'anno 1288, ed. Gina Fasoli and Pietro Sella (2 vols., Studi e testi 73, 85, Vatican City, 1937–39).

Stella, Giorgio, and Giovanni Stella, *Georgii et Iohannis Stellae Annales Genuenses*, ed. Giovanna Petti Balbi (Rerum italicarum scriptores, n.s. 17/2, 1975).

Stephen de Bourbon, *Tractatus de diversis materiis praedicabilibus*, ed. A. Lecoy de la Marche, *Anecdotes historiques, légendes et apologues tirés du receuil inédit d'Etienne de Bourbon* (Société de l'Histoire de la France 185, 1877).

Stephen of Rennes, *Vita Guillelmi Firmati* (BHL 8914), AASS Aprilis 3 (1675), pp. 334–41.

Stephen of Ripon (Eddius Stephanus), *Vita Wilfridi episcopi* (BHL 8889), ed. Bertram Colgrave (Cambridge, 1927).

Stephen the Deacon, *Vita Stephani Junioris* (BHG 1666), ed. Marie-France Auzépy, *La vie d'Etienne le Jeune* (Aldershot, 1997).

Stubbs, William, ed., *Select Charters* (9th ed., Oxford, 1913).

Suger, *Gesta Suggerii abbatis (De rebus in administratione sua gestis)*, ed. Françoise Gasparri, *Suger: Oeuvres* (2 vols., Paris, 1996–2001), 1, pp. 54–154.

———, *Scriptum consecrationis ecclesiae sancti Dionysii (Libellus de consecratione ecclesiae sancti Dionysii)*, ed. Françoise Gasparri, *Suger: Oeuvres* (2 vols., Paris, 1996–2001), 1, pp. 2–52.

———, *Vita Ludovici Grossi regis*, ed. Henri Waquet (Paris, 1929).

Sulpicius Severus, *Chronica*, ed. Ghislaine de Senneville-Grave (SC 441, 1999).

———, *Dialogi*, ed. Jacques Fontaine, *Gallus: dialogues sur les "vertus" de saint Martin* (SC 510, 2006).

———, *Vita sancti Martini* (BHL 5610), ed. Jacques Fontaine (3 vols., SC 133–35, 1967–69).

Summarium processuum impressum Antonini archiepiscopi Florentini, AASS Maii 1 (1680), pp. 335–51.

Symeon Metaphrastes, *Certamen sanctae et gloriosae magnae martyris Christi Barbarae* (BHG 216), PG 116, cols. 301–16.

———, *Martyrium sanctae Charitinae* (BHG 300), PG 115, cols. 997–1005.

———, *Martyrium sanctae et magnae martyris Aecaterinae* (BHG 32), PG 116, cols. 276–301.

———, *Martyrium sanctae Euphemiae* (BHG 620), ed. François Halkin, *Euphémie de Chalcédonie* (SH 41, 1965), pp. 145–61 (PG 115, cols. 713–32).

———, *Martyrium sanctae Julianae martyris* (BHG 963), PG 114, cols. 1437–52.

———, *Martyrium sanctarum mulierum Sophiae et ejus filiarum Fidei, Spei et Charitatis* (BHG 1638), PG 115, cols. 497–513.

———, *Vita et conversatio et martyrium Anastasiae Romanae* (BHG 77), PG 115, cols. 1293–1308.

Symeon of Durham, *Libellus de exordio atque procursu istius hoc est Dunhelmensis ecclesie*, ed. David Rollason (OMT, 2000).

Symeon of Durham (attrib.), *De miraculis et translationibus sancti Cuthberti* (BHL 2029), ed. Thomas Arnold, *Symeonis monachi opera omnia* (2 vols., RS, 1882–85), 1, pp. 229–61; 2, pp. 333–62.

Le Synaxaire arménien de Ter Israël, ed. G. Bayan (Patrologia orientalis 21, 1930).

Synaxarium Ecclesiae Constantinopolitanae, ed. Hippoltye Delehaye, AASS Novembris *Propylaeum* (1902).

Synaxarium et miracula sancti Isaiae prophetae (BHG 958d and f), ed. Hippolyte Delehaye, AB 42 (1924), pp. 257–65.

Synodicon Hispanum 4: Ciudad Rodrigo, Salamanca y Zamora, ed. Antonio García y García et al. (Madrid, 1987).

Synodicon Hispanum 6: Avila y Segovia, ed. Antonio García y García et al. (Madrid, 1993).

The Syriac Chronicle Known as That of Zachariah of Mitylene, ed. F. J. Hamilton and E. W. Brooks (London, 1899).

The Syriac Life of St Symeon Stylites, tr. Robert Doran, *The Lives of Symeon Stylites* (Kalamazoo, 1992), pp. 101–98.

Syrische Lebensbeschreibung des hl. Symeon, ed. Hans Lietzmann, *Das Leben des heiligen Symeon Stylites* (Texte und Untersuchungen zur Geschichte der Altchristlichen Literatur 32/4, Leipzig, 1908), pp. 80–187.

Taegio, Ambrogio, *Vita sancti Petri martyris* (BHL 6723), AASS Aprilis 3 (1675), pp. 686–719.

Tafel, G.L.F., and G. M. Thomas, eds., *Urkunden zur älteren Handels- und Staatsgeschichte der Republik Venedig* (3 vols., Fontes rerum austriacarum II, 12–14, Vienna, 1856–57).

Tebaldus, *Vita sancti Ubaldi Eugubini pontificis* (BHL 8357), AASS Maii 3 (1680), pp. 630–37.

Tertullian, *Apologeticum*, ed. E. Dekkers, *Tertulliani opera* 1 (CCSL 1, 1954), pp. 77–171.

———, *De baptismo*, ed. J.G.P. Borleffs, *Tertulliani opera* 1 (CCSL 1, 1954), pp. 275–95.

———, *De corona*, ed. E. Kroymann, *Tertulliani opera* 2 (CCSL 2, 1954), pp. 1037–65.

———, *De exhortatione castitatis*, ed. E. Kroymann, *Tertulliani opera* 2 (CCSL 2, 1954), pp. 1013–35.

Testaments de l'officialité de Besançon, 1265–1500, ed. Ulysse Robert (2 vols., Paris, 1902–7).

Thangmar, *Vita Bernwardi (*BHL 1253*)*, ed. Georg Heinrich Pertz, MGH*,* SS 4 (Hanover, 1841), pp. 754–82.

Theobald of Bèze, *Acta, Translationes et Miracula sancti Prudentii Martyris* (BHL 6979), AASS Octobris 3 (1770), pp. 348–78.

Theodore of Studios, *Epistulae*, ed. Georgios Fatouros (2 vols., Berlin, 1992).

Theodoret of Cyrrhus, *Graecorum affectionum curatio*, ed. Pierre Canivet, *Thérapeutique des maladies helléniques* (rev. ed., 2 vols., SC 57, 2001–2).

———, *Historia Religiosa*, ed. Pierre Canivet and Alice Leroy-Molinghen, *Histoire des moines de Syrie* (2 vols., SC 234, 257, 1977–79).

———, *Interpretatio Epistolae ad Colossenses*, PG 82, cols. 591–628.

Theodulf of Orleans, *Carmina*, ed. Ernst Dümmler, MGH, *Poetae latini aevi Carolini* (Berlin, 1881), pp. 437–581.

Theophanes, *The Chronicle of Theophanes the Confessor*, tr. Cyril Mango and Roger Scott (Oxford, 1997).

———, *Chronographia*, ed. C. de Boor (2 vols., Leipzig, 1883–85 [text vol. 1]).

Thesaurus palaeohibernicus: A Collection of Old-Irish Glosses, Scholia, Prose, and Verse, ed. Whitley Stokes and John Strachan (2 vols., Cambridge, 1901–3).

Thietmar of Merseburg, *Chronicon*, ed. Werner Trillmich (AQ 9, Darmstadt, 1957).

Thiofrid of Echternach, *Flores epytaphii sanctorum*, ed. Michele Camillo Ferrari (CCCM 133, 1996).

———, *Vita sancti Willibrordi* (BHL 8940–41), AASS Novembris 3 (1910), pp. 459–500.
Thomas Aquinas, *Quaestiones disputatae de potentia*, ed. Roberto Busa, *Opera omnia* (7 vols., Stuttgart-Bad Cannstatt, 1980) 3, pp. 186–269.
———, *Quodlibeta*, ed. Roberto Busa, *Opera omnia* (7 vols., Stuttgart-Bad Cannstatt, 1980) 3, pp. 438–501.
———, *Summa Theologiae*, ed. Thomas Gilby et al. (60 vols., London, 1964–76).
———, *Super Sententiis*, ed. Roberto Busa, *Opera omnia* (7 vols., Stuttgart-Bad Cannstatt, 1980) 1.
Thomas of Celano, *Tractatus de miraculis beati Francisci*, *Analecta Franciscana* 10 (Quaracchi, 1926–41), pp. 269–331.
———, *Vita prima sancti Francisci* (BHL 3096), *Analecta Franciscana* 10 (Quaracchi, 1926–41), pp. 1–117.
———, *Vita sanctae Clarae* (BHL 1815), ed. Giovanni Boccali, *Legenda latina sanctae Clarae virginis* (Assisi, 2001).
———, *Vita secunda sancti Francisci* (BHL 3105), *Analecta Franciscana* 10 (Quaracchi, 1926–41), pp. 129–260.
Thomas of Chobham, *Summa confessorum*, ed. F. Broomfield (Analecta mediaevalia Namurcensia 25, Louvain and Paris, 1968).
Thomas of Eccleston, *De adventu fratrum minorum in Angliam*, ed. A. G. Little (2nd ed., Manchester, 1951).
Thomas of Monmouth, *Vita sancti Willelmi Norwicensis* (BHL 8926), ed. Augustus Jessopp and Montague Rhodes James, *The Life and Miracles of St William of Norwich* (Cambridge, 1896).
Thomas Tuscus, *Gesta imperatorum et pontificum*, ed. Ernst Ehrenfeuchter, MGH, SS 22 (Hanover, 1872), pp. 483–528.
Three Eleventh-century Anglo-Latin Saints' Lives: Vita S. Birini, Vita et miracula S. Kenelmi and Vita S. Rumwoldi, ed. Rosalind C. Love (OMT, 1995).
Thümmel, Hans Georg, *Die Frühgeschichte der ostkirchlichen Bilderlehre: Texte und Untersuchungen zur Zeit vor dem Bilderstreit* (Berlin, 1992).
Tírechán, *Collectanea de sancto Patricii* (BHL 6496), ed. Ludwig Bieler, *Patrician Texts in the Book of Armagh* (Dublin, 1979), pp. 124–62.
Tomellus, *Historia monasterii Hasnoniensis*, ed. Oswald Holder-Egger, MGH, SS 14 (Hanover, 1883), pp. 147–60.
Translatio altera sanctae Fidis (BHL 2939–40), AASS Octobris 3 (1770), pp. 294–300.
Translatio capitis sancti Martini (BHL 5664), *Cat. Paris* 2, cols. 567–72.
Translatio Chrysanti et Dariae (BHL 1793), ed. Oswald Holder-Egger, MGH, SS 15/1 (Hanover, 1887), pp. 374–76 (excerpts).
Translatio cum miraculis beati Guthlaci anachorite (BHL 3729), ed. Carl Horstman, *Nova legenda Anglie* (2 vols., Oxford, 1901) 2, pp. 719–27.
Translatio et miracula sancti Firmini Flaviniacensibus (BHL 3018–19), ed. Oswald Holder-Egger, MGH, SS 15/2 (Hanover, 1888), pp. 803–11.
Translatio et miracula sancti Viviani (BHL 1327–28), AB 8 (1889), pp. 256–77.
Translatio miraculosa ecclesie beate virginis Marie de Loreto (BHL 5400) (Rome, c. 1486).
Translatio prima sancti Bavonis (BHL 1055), ed. Maurice Coens, "Translations et miracles de saint Bavon au XIe siècle," AB 86 (1968), pp. 39–66, at pp. 52–55.
Translatio sancti Annonis archiepiscopi (BHL 512), ed. Rudolf Köpke, MGH, SS 11 (Hanover, 1854), pp. 514–18.

Translatio sancti Auctoris episcopi Trevirensis (BHL 748), AASS Augusti 4 (1739), pp. 48–52.
Translatio sancti Liborii (BHL 4913), ed. Alfred Cohausz, *Erconrads Translatio sancti Liborii* (Paderborn, 1966), pp. 48–111.
Translatio sancti Marci (BHL 5283–84), ed. Nelson Mc Cleary, "Note storiche ed archeologiche sul testo della 'Translatio Sancti Marci,'" *Memorie storiche forogiuliesi* 27–29 (1931–1933), pp. 238–64.
Translatio sancti Viti martyris (BHL 8718), ed. Irene Schmale-Ott (Münster in Westfalen, 1979).
Translatio sancti Wlstani (BHL 8760e), ed. R. R. Darlington, *William of Malmesbury, Vita Wulfstani* (Camden, 3rd. ser., 40, 1928), pp. 180–8.
Translatio secunda sancti Bavonis (BHL 1057), ed. Maurice Coens "Translations et miracles de saint Bavon au XIe siècle," AB 86 (1968), pp. 39–66, at pp. 55–60.
Translationes reliquiarum corporis sancti Apollinaris a Ravenna in Gorinchem (BHL 632), AASS Julii 5 (1727), pp. 378–85.
Translationis sanctorum Wandregisili et Ansberti quae supersunt (BHL 8809t), ed. Oswald Holder-Egger, MGH, SS 30/2 (Leipzig, 1934), pp. 815–20.
The Travels of Leo of Rozmital, tr. Malcolm Letts (Hakluyt Soc., 2nd ser, 108, 1957 for 1955).
Triumphus sancti Lamberti de castro Bullonio (BHL 4690), ed. Wilhelm Arndt, MGH, SS 20 (Hanover, 1868), pp. 497–511.
Triumphus sancti Remacli de Malmundariensi coenobio (BHL 7140–41), ed. Wilhelm Wattenbach, MGH, SS 11 (Hanover, 1854), pp. 433–61.
Troilus de Malvitiis, *Opusculum de canonizatione sanctorum* (Bologna, 1487).
Tudor Royal Proclamations 1, ed. Paul L. Hughes and James F. Larkin (New Haven, 1964).
Tumbo A de la Catedral de Santiago, ed. Manuel Lucas Alvarez (Santiago, 1998).
Turgot, *Vita sanctae Margaretae Scotorum reginae* (BHL 5325), ed. James Raine, *Symeonis Dunelmensis opera et collectanea* 1, ed. J. Hodgson Hinde (Surtees Society 51, 1868), pp. 234–54.
Ubertino da Casale, *Declaratio contra falsitates datas per fratrem Raymundum*, ed. Franz Ehrle, *Archiv für Litteratur- und Kirchengeschichte des Mittelalters* 3 (Berlin, 1887), pp. 162–95.
Ulric of Cluny, *Antiquiores consuetudines Cluniacensis monasterii*, PL 149, cols. 635–778.
Ursio of Hautmont, *Acta Marcelli papae* (BHL 5237), AASS Ianuarii 2 (1643), pp. 9–14.
Usuard, *Martyrologium*, ed. Jacques Dubois, *Le Martyrologe d'Usuard* (SH 40, 1965).
Valor ecclesiasticus (6 vols., Record Commission, London, 1810–34).
Vega, Garcilaso de la, *Comentarios reales* (Mexico City, 1990).
Venantius Fortunatus, *Carmina*, ed. Marc Reydellet (3 vols., Paris, 1994–2004).
———, *Vita sanctae Radegundis* (BHL 7048), ed. Bruno Krusch, MGH, SRM 2 (Hanover, 1888), pp. 364–77.
———, *Vita sancti Germani episcopi Parisiensis* (BHL 3468), ed. Bruno Krusch, MGH, SRM 7 (Hanover and Leipzig, 1920), pp. 372–418.
———, *Vita sancti Paterni* (BHL 6477), ed. Bruno Krusch, MGH, AA 4/2 (Berlin, 1885), pp. 33–37.
———, *Vita Severini episcopi Burdegalensis* (BHL 7652), ed. Wilhelm Levison, MGH, SRM 7 (Hanover and Leipzig, 1920), pp. 219–24.
Verba seniorum (BHL 6527–31), PL 73, cols. 851–1062.

Verus, *Vita Eutropii* (BHL 2782), ed. P. Varin, *Bulletin du Comité historique des monuments écrits de l'histoire de France: Histoire, sciences, lettres* 1 (1849), pp. 52–64.
Victor of Vita, *Historia persecutionis Africanae provinciae*, ed. Karl Halm, MGH, AA 3/1 (Berlin, 1878).
Victorinus de Poetovio (Ptuj), *In Apocalypsin*, ed. M. Dulaey (SC 423, 1997).
Victricius of Rouen, *De laude sanctorum*, ed. R. Demeulenaer, *Foebadi Aginnensis Liber contra Arrianos, etc.* (CCSL 64, 1985), pp. 53–93.
Vida e miracles de sancta Flor, ed. Clovis Brunel, AB 64 (1946), pp. 5–49.
La Vie d'Edouard le Confesseur, ed. Östen Södergård (Uppsala, 1948).
La Vie de Saint Alexis, ed. C. Storey (rev. ed., Oxford, 1968).
La Vie Saint Andrier l'Apostle, ed. A. T. Baker, "The Passion of Saint Andrew," *The Modern Language Review* 11 (1916), pp. 420–49.
La Vie seinte Osith, virge e martire, ed. D. W. Russell, *Papers on Language and Literature* 41 (2005), pp. 339–445.
Vigneulles, Philippe de, *Mémoires*, ed. Heinrich Michelant, *Gedenkbuch des Metzer Bürgers Philippe von Vigneulles aus den Jahren 1471 bis 1522* (Bibliothek des litterarischen Vereins in Stuttgart 24, 1852).
Villani, Matteo, *Cronica*, ed. Francesco Gherardi Dragomanni (2 vols., Florence, 1846).
Vincent, *Vita (major) sancti Stanislai Cracoviensis episcopi* (BHL 7833–35), ed. Wojciech Ketrzynski, *Monumenta Poloniae historica* 4 (Lwów, 1884), pp. 362–438.
Vincent Ferrer, *Sermones de sanctis*, ed. Simon Berthier (Lyons, 1539), fols. 1–148v.
———, *Sermons* 3, ed. Gret Schib (Barcelona, 1975).
Vincent of Beauvais, *Speculum historiale* (Douai, 1624).
Virtutes Fursei abbatis Latiniacensis (BHL 3213), ed. Bruno Krusch, MGH, SRM 4 (Hanover, 1902), pp. 440–49.
Vita Ædwardi regis (BHL 2421), ed. Frank Barlow (2nd ed., OMT, 1992).
Vita Aegidii abbatis (BHL 93), AASS Septembris 1 (1746), pp. 299–303.
Vita altera Chounradi episcopi Constantiensis (BHL 1918), ed. Georg Heinrich Pertz, MGH, SS 4 (Hanover, 1841), pp. 436–45.
Vita altera sancti Pachomii (BHG 1400), ed. François Halkin, *Sancti Pachomii Vitae Graecae* (SH 19, 1932), pp. 166–271.
Vita Andreae de Galleranis (BHL 450), AASS Martii 3 (1668), pp. 52–57.
Vita Annonis archepiscopi Coloniensis (BHL 507), ed. Rudolf Köpke, MGH, SS 11 (Hanover, 1854), pp. 462–518.
Vita Aventini (BHL 877), AASS Februarii 1 (1658), pp. 476–77.
Vita beatae Helenae Ungarae (BHL 3790m), AASS Novembris 4 (1925), pp. 272–76.
Vita beate Hedwigis (maior legenda) (BHL 3766), ed. Wolfgang Braunfels, *Der Hedwigs-Codex von* 1353*: Sammlung Ludwig* (2 vols., Berlin, 1972) 2, pp. 71–155.
Vita beati Giraldi de Salis (BHL 3547), AASS Octobris 10 (1861), pp. 254–66.
Vita beati Johannis Colombini (BHL 4384), ed. G. D. Mansi, *Stephani Baluzii Miscellanea novo ordine digesta* (4 vols., Lucca, 1761–64) 4, pp. 566–71.
Vita Berardi Marsorum episcopi (BHL 1176), AASS Novembris 2/1 (1894), pp. 128–35.
Vita Bertilae abbatissae Calensis (BHL 1287), ed. Wilhelm Levison, MGH, SRM 6 (Hanover and Leipzig, 1913), pp. 95–109.
Vita Bonae virginis (BHL 1389), AASS Maii 7 (1688), pp. 145–63.
Vita Caesarii episcopi Arelatensis (BHL 1508–9), ed. Germanus Morin, *Sancti Caesarii Aretalensis opera varia* (Maredsous, 1942), pp. 291–345.

Vita Carilefi presbyteri (BHL 1570), AASS Julii 1 (1719), pp. 90–99.

La vita del beato Ieronimo Savonarola, ed. Piero Ginori Conti (Florence, 1937).

Vita der Mathilde von Canossa (Codices e Vaticanis selecti 62, Zürich, 1984, with edition and German translation).

Vita devotissimæ Benevenutæ de Foro-Julii (BHL 1149), AASS Octobris 13 (1883), pp. 152–85.

Vita divi Hieronymi (BHL 3870), PL 22, cols. 201–14.

Vita Domnoli episcopi Cenomanensis (BHL 2273), AASS Maii 3 (1680), pp. 606–10.

Vitae Baldomeri epitome (BHL 899), AASS Februarii 3 (1658), pp. 683–84.

Vita Eliae Spelæote (BHG 581), AASS Septembris 3 (1750), pp. 843–88.

Vita Eligii episcopi Noviomagensis (BHL 2474), ed. Bruno Krusch, MGH, SRM 4 (Hanover and Leipzig, 1902), pp. 663–741.

Vita Elisabethae reginae Portugalliae, AASS Julii 2 (1721), pp. 173–213.

Vitae patrum sive historiae eremiticae libri decem, PL 73–74.

Vitae sanctorum Britanniae et genealogiae, ed. A. W. Wade-Evans (Cardiff, 1944).

Vitae sanctorum Hiberniae e Codice olim Salmanticensi, ed. W. W. Heist (SH 25, 1965).

Vita et miracula Antonii Ordinis Eremitarum Augustini (BHL 586), AASS Aprilis 3 (1675), pp. 832–34.

Vita et miracula Austrigisili episcopi Biturigi (BHL 826, 841), ed. Bruno Krusch, MGH, SRM 4 (Hanover and Leipzig, 1902), pp. 191–208.

Vita et miracula Isidori agricolae (BHL 4494), ed. Fidel Fita, "Madrid desde el año 1235 hasta el de 1275. Ilustraciones y textos de la vida de San Isidro por Juan Diácono," *Boletin de la Real Academia de la Historia* 9 (1886), pp. 102–52.

Vita et miracula sanctae Kyngae ducissae Cracoviensis (BHL 4666–67), ed. Wojciech Kętrzyński, *Monumenta Poloniae historica* 4 (Lwów, 1884), pp. 682–744.

Vita et miracula sancte Ebbe virginis (BHL 2357b), *The Miracles of St Æbbe of Coldingham and St Margaret of Scotland*, pp. 2–66.

Vita et miracula sancti Dominic Sorani (BHL 2242, 2244), ed. François Dolbeau, "Le dossier de saint Dominique de Sora d'Albéric du Mont-Cassin à Jacques de Voragine," *Mélanges de l'Ecole française de Rome. Moyen-Age* 102 (1990), pp. 17–78, at pp. 34–78.

Vita et miracula sancti Fiacrii (BHL 2916), ed. Jacques Dubois, *Un sanctuaire monastique au Moyen Age: Saint-Fiacre-en-Brie* (Geneva, 1976), pp. 67–71, 75–134.

Vita et miracula sancti Martini episcopi (BHG 1181), ed. François Halkin, "Légende grecque de saint Martin, évêque de Tours," *Rivista di Studi bizantini e neoellenici* n.s. 20–21 (1983–84), pp. 69–91.

Vita et miracula sancti Willelmi abbatis Ebelholtensis (BHL 8908), ed. M. G. Gertz, *Vitae sanctorum Danorum* (Copenhagen, 1908–12), pp. 300–69.

Vita et passio sancti Adalberti (BHL 37), ed. Lorenz Weinrich, *Heiligenleben zur deutsch-slawischen Geschichte* (AQ 23, 2005), pp. 28–68.

Vita Euthymii Sardensis (BHG 2145), ed. Jean Gouillard, "La vie d'Euthyme de Sardes (+831), une oeuvre du patriarche Méthode," *Travaux et mémoires* 10 (1987), pp. 1–101.

Vita Fulgentii (BHL 3208), PL 65, cols. 117–50.

Vita Gebehardi episcopi Constantiensis (BHL 3292), ed. Wilhelm Wattenbach, MGH, SS 10 (Hanover, 1852), pp. 582–94.

Vita Genovefae virginis Parisiensis (BHL 3335), ed. Bruno Krusch, MGH, SRM 3 (Hanover, 1896), pp. 204–38.

Vita Genulfi (BHL 3352), AASS Octobris 12 (1867), pp. 792–94.

Vita Gertrudis ab Oosten, Beghinae Delphis (BHL 3505), AASS Ianuarii 1 (1648), pp. 349–53.

Vita Gregorii Decapolitae (BHG 711), ed. Georgios Makris, *Ignatios Diakonos und die Vita des Hl. Gregorios Dekapolites* (Stuttgart and Leipzig, 1997).

Vita illustrissime uirginis sororis Agnetis ordinis Sancte Clare de Praga (BHL 154bc), ed. Walter W. Seton, *Some New Sources for the Life of Blessed Agnes of Bohemia* (London, 1915), pp. 61–150; ed. Jan Kapistrán Vyskočil, *Legenda blahoslavené Anežky* (Prague, 1932), pp. 99–135.

Vita Iulii et Iuliani (BHL 4558), AASS Ianuarii 2 (1643), pp. 1101–4.

Vita Iuvenalis episcopus Narniensis (BHL 4614), AASS Maii 1 (1680), pp. 387–90.

Vita Joannis Ciritae (without BHL no.), PL 188, cols. 1661–70.

Vita Johannis Bassandi (BHL 4336), AASS Augusti 5 (1741), pp. 875–92.

Vita Leonorii episcopi et confessoris (BHL 4881), AASS Julii 1 (1719), pp. 121–24.

Vita Marculphi abbatis I (BHL 5266), AASS Maii 1 (1680), pp. 71–75.

Vita Marculphi abbatis II (BHL 5267), AASS Maii 1 (1680), pp. 75–79.

Vita Margaritae Fontanae (without BHL no.), AASS Septembris 4 (1753), pp. 135–39.

Vita Mathildis reginae antiquior (BHL 5683), ed. Bernd Schütte, *Die Lebensbeschreibungen der Königin Mathilde* (MGH, SRG 66, Hanover, 1994), pp. 107–42.

Vita Mathildis reginae posterior (BHL 5684), ibid., pp. 143–202.

Vita Niconis (BHG 1366–67), ed. Denis F. Sullivan, *The Life of St Nikon* (Brookline, MA, 1987).

Vita Norberti (BHL 6248), ed. Hatto Kallfelz, *Lebensbeschreibungen einiger Bischöfe des 10.–12. Jahrhunderts* (AQ 22, 1973), pp. 452–540.

Vita Odiliae abbatissae Hohenburgensis (BHL 6271), ed. Wilhelm Levison, MGH, SRM 6 (Hanover and Leipzig, 1913), pp. 37–50.

Vita Paterni (BHL 6477), AASS Aprilis 2 (1675), pp. 427–30.

Vita Petri Heremiae (BHL 6713), AASS Martii 1 (1668), pp. 294–97.

Vita prima sanctae Brigidae (BHL 1455), AASS Februarii I (1658), pp. 118–35.

Vita prima sancti Bernardi (BHL 1217–20), PL 185, cols. 225–368.

Vita Raymundi Palmarii, AASS Julii 6 (1729), pp. 644–57.

Vita Richarii . . . primigenia (BHL 7245), ed. Bruno Krusch, MGH, SRM 7 (Hanover and Leipzig, 1920), pp. 438–53.

Vita Rigoberti episcopi Remensis (BHL 7253), ed. Wilhelm Levison, MGH, SRM 7 (Hanover and Leipzig, 1920), pp. 58–78.

Vita Roberti Salentini (BHL 7271), AASS Julii 4 (1725), pp. 495–509.

Vita sanctae Balthildis (BHL 905), ed. Bruno Krusch, MGH, SRM 2 (Hanover, 1888), pp. 482–508.

Vita sanctae Chrothildis (BHL 1785), ed. Bruno Krusch, MGH, SRM 2 (Hanover, 1888), pp. 341–48.

Vita sanctae Darercae seu Moninnae abbatissae (BHL 2095), *Vitae sanctorum Hiberniae e Codice olim Salmanticensi*, pp. 83–95.

Vita sanctae Euphrosynae (BHG 627), AASS Novembris 3 (1910), pp. 861–77.

Vita sanctae Geretrudis (BHL 3490), ed. Bruno Krusch, MGH, SRM 2 (Hanover, 1888), pp. 453–64.

Vita sanctae Zitae virginis (BHL 9019–20), AASS Aprilis 3 (1675), pp. 499–510.

Vita sancte Margarete virginis et martyris (BHL 5303), ed. Frances M. Mack, *Seinte Marherete* (EETS, o.s. 193, 1934), pp. 127–42.

Vita sancti Arnulfi (BHL 689–92), ed. Bruno Krusch, MGH, SRM 2 (Hanover, 1888), pp. 432–46.

Vita sancti Arnulfi episcopi Suessonensis (BHL 704), AASSOSB 6/2, cols. 505–55.

Vita sancti Ciarani de Saigir (BHL 4657), ed. Charles Plummer, *Vitae sanctorum Hiberniae* (2 vols., Oxford, 1910) 1, pp. 217–33.

Vita sancti Cuthberti auctore anonymo (BHL 2019), ed. Bertram Colgrave, *Two Lives of Cuthbert* (Cambridge, 1940), pp. 60–138.

Vita sancti Danielis stylitae (BHG 489), ed. Hippolyte Delehaye, *Les saints stylites* (SH 14, 1923), pp. 1–94.

Vita sancti Decumani (BHL 2118), ed. Carl Horstman, *Nova legenda Anglie* (2 vols., Oxford, 1901) 1, pp. 263–65.

Vita sancti Elzearii de Sabrano (BHL 2523), AASS Septembris 7 (1760), cols. 576–93.

Vita sancti Erkenwaldi (BHL 2600), ed. E. Gordon Whatley, *The Saint of London: The Life and Miracles of St. Erkenwald* (Binghamton, 1989), pp. 86–96.

Vita sancti Frontonis episcopi Petragoricensis (BHL 3184–85), AASS Octobris 11, pp. 407–14.

Vita sancti Girardi confessoris (BHL 3548), AASS Novembris 2/1 (1894), pp. 493–501.

Vita sancti Hadelini (BHL 3733), AASS Februarii 1 (1658), pp. 372–76.

Vita sancti Launomari (BHL 4733), AASSOSB 1, cols. 335–38.

Vita sancti Mariani (BHL 5523), AASS Aprilis 2 (1675), p. 760.

Vita sancti Marii solitarii (BHL 5542), AASS Iunii 2 (1698), pp. 115–26.

Vita sancti Maximini (BHL 5822), AASS Maii 7 (1688), pp. 21–24.

Vita sancti Meginrati (BHL 5878), ed. Oswald Holder-Egger, MGH, SS 15/1 (Hanover, 1887), pp. 444–48.

Vita sancti Ottonis episcopi Babenbergensis (Vita Prieflingensis) (BHL 6394), ed. Lorenz Weinrich, *Heiligenleben zur deutsch-slawischen Geschichte* (AQ 23, 2005), pp. 119–91.

Vita sancti Parthenii (BHG 1422), PG 114, cols. 1347–66.

Vita sancti Pauli Iunioris in monte Latro (BHG 1474), ed. Hippolyte Delehaye, AB 11 (1892), pp. 5–74, 136–82.

Vita sancti Paulini Trevirensis (BHL 6562–63), AASS Augusti 6 (1743), pp. 676–79.

Vita sancti Stephani episcopi Aptensis (BHL 7896), AASS Novembris 3 (1910), pp. 311–14.

Vita sancti Teliavi (BHL 7997), ed. J. G. Evans and J. Rhys, *Liber Landavensis: The Text of the Book of Llan Dâv* (Oxford, 1893), pp. 97–117.

Vita secunda sancti Patricii (BHL 6504), ed. Ludwig Bieler, *Four Latin Lives of Saint Patrick* (Dublin, 1971), pp. 47–97.

Vita Theclae (BHG 1717), ed. Gilbert Dagron, *Vie et miracles de Sainte Thècle* (SH 62, 1978), pp. 167–283.

Vita Theodori Syceotae (BHG 1748), ed. André-Jean Festugière, *Vie de Théodore de Sykéon* (2 vols., SH 48, 1970 [text vol. 1; partial Eng. tr. Elizabeth Dawes and Norman H. Baynes, *Three Byzantine Saints*, Oxford, 1948, pp. 85–192]).

Vita venerabilis Lukardis (BHL 5064), AB 18 (1899), pp. 305–67.

Vita Vinardi (BHL 8948), AASS Octobris 5 (1786), pp. 668–70.

Vitalis, *Vita sancti Bertrandi episcopi Convenensis* (BHL 1304), AASS Octobris 7 (1845), pp. 1173–84.

Wærferth of Worcester, *Bischofs Wærferth von Worcester Übersetzung der Dialoge Gregors des Grossen*, ed. Hans Hecht (2 vols., Leipzig and Hamburg, 1900–1907).

Walafrid Strabo, *De exordiis et incrementis quarundam in observationibus ecclesiasticis rerum*, ed. Alfred Boretius and Victor Krause, MGH, *Capitularia regum Francorum* 2 (Hanover, 1897), pp. 473–516.

———, *Versus de beati Blaithmaic vita et fine*, ed. Ernst Dümmler, MGH, *Poetae latini aevi carolini* 2 (Berlin, 1884), pp. 297–301.

———, *Vita Galli* (BHL 3247–49), ed. Bruno Krusch, MGH, SRM 4 (Hanover and Leipzig, 1902), pp. 280–337.

Waleran of Naumburg, *Miraculum de Bohemundo* (BHL 4874), AASS Novembris 3 (1910), pp. 160–68.

Walsingham, Thomas, *Historia Anglicana*, ed. Henry Thomas Riley (2 vols., RS, 1863–64).

Walter Daniel, *Vita Ailredi* (BHL 2644 as), ed. Maurice Powicke, *The Life of Ailred of Rievaulx* (London and Edinburgh, 1950; repr. OMT, 1978).

Walter of Coventry, *Memoriale*, ed. William Stubbs (2 vols., RS, 1872–73).

Walther of Therouanne, *Vita Karoli comitis Flandriae*, ed. Rudolf Köpke, MGH, SS 12 (Hanover, 1856), pp. 531–61.

Walther von der Vogelweide, *Werke: Gesamtausgabe* (1. *Spruchlyrik*; 2. *Liedlyrik*), ed. Günther Schweikle (Stuttgart, 1994–98).

Warnecarius, *Epistolae aevi Merowingici collectae* 14, ed. W. Gundlach, MGH, *Epistolae* 3 (*Merowingici et Karolini aevi* 1) (Berlin, 1892), pp. 456–57.

Webb, Diana, ed., *Saints and Cities in Medieval Italy* (Manchester, 2007).

West, J. R., ed., *St Benet of Holme, 1020–1210* (2 vols., Norfolk Record Soc. 2–3, 1932).

The Westminster Chronicle 1381–1394, ed. L. C. Hector and Barbara Harvey (OMT, 1982).

Widukind of Corvey, *Res gestae saxonicae*, ed. Albert Bauer and Reinhold Rau, *Quellen zur Geschichte der sächsischen Kaiserzeit* (AQ 8, rev. ed., Darmstadt, 1977), pp. 1–183.

Wied, Hermann von, *Einfaltigs bedencken, etc.* (Bonn, 1543).

———, *Simplex ac pia deliberatio, etc.* (Bonn, 1545).

William de Tocco, *Ystoria sancti Thome de Aquino* (BHL 8153), ed. Claire Le Brun-Gouanvic, *Ystoria sancti Thome de Aquino de Guillaume de Tocco (1323). Édition critique, introduction et notes* (Toronto, 1996).

William Durandus the Elder, *Pontificale*, ed. Michel Andrieu, *Le pontificale romain au Moyen Âge* 3: *Le pontificale de Guillaume Durand* (Studi e testi 88, Vatican City, 1940).

———, *Rationale divinorum officiorum*, ed. A. Davril and T. M. Thibodeau (3 vols., CCCM 140, 140A, 140B, 1995–2000).

William fitz Stephen, *Vita sancti Thomae Cantuariensis* (BHL 8176), ed. J. C. Robertson, *Materials for the History of Thomas Becket* (7 vols., RS, 1875–85) 3, pp. 1–154.

William of Æbelholt, *Tractatus de revelatione capitis et corporis beate Genovefe* (BHL 3346), ed. M. G. Gertz, *Vitae sanctorum Danorum* (Copenhagen, 1908–12), pp. 378–82.

William of Andres, *Chronica Andrensis*, ed. Johannes Heller, MGH, SS 24 (Hanover, 1879), pp. 684–773.

William of Auxerre, *Summa de officiis ecclesiasticis*, ed. Franz Fischer (electronic edition, Inauguraldissertation zur Erlangung der Doktorwürde der Philosophischen Fakultät der Universität zu Köln, Cologne, 2007).

William of Canterbury, *Miracula sancti Thomae* (BHL 8185), ed. J. C. Robertson, *Materials for the History of Thomas Becket* (7 vols., RS, 1875–85) 1, pp. 137–546.

William of Chartres, *Vita et miracula sancti Ludovici regis Francorum* (BHL 5036), AASS Augusti 5 (1741), pp. 559–68.

William of Malmesbury, *Gesta pontificum Anglorum*, ed. Michael Winterbottom (2 vols., OMT, 2007 [text vol. 1]).

———, *Gesta regum Anglorum*, ed. R.A.B. Mynors et al. (2 vols., OMT, 1998–99 [text vol. 1]).

———, *Vita Wulfstani* (BHL 8756), ed. M. Winterbottom and R. M. Thomson, *Saints' Lives: Lives of SS. Wulfstan, Dunstan, Patrick, Benignus and Indract* (OMT, 2002), pp. 1–155.

William of Nangis, *Gesta Philippi tertii regis Franciae*, ed. P.C.F. Daunou, *Recueil des historiens des Gaules et de la France* 20 (Paris, 1840), pp. 466–539.

———, *Gesta sancti Ludovici* (BHL 5037), ed. P.C.F. Daunou, *Recueil des historiens des Gaules et de la France* 20 (Paris, 1840), pp. 309–465.

William of Poitiers, *Gesta Guillelmi ducis Normannorum*, ed. R.H.C. Davis and Marjorie Chibnall (OMT, 1998).

William of St. Albans, *Acta sanctorum Albani, Amphibali et sociorum* (BHL 213), AASS Iunii 4 (1707), pp. 149–59.

William of Tyre, *Chronicon*, ed. R.B.C. Huygens (2 vols, CCCM 63–63A, 1986).

Willibald, *Vita Bonifatii* (BHL 1400), ed. Reinhold Rau, *Bonifatii epistulae. Willibaldi Vita Bonifatii* (AQ 4b, Darmstadt, 1968), pp. 454–524.

Wills and Inventories from the Registers of the Commissary of Bury St Edmund's and the Archdeacon of Sudbury, ed. Samuel Tymms (Camden Soc. [o.s.] 49, 1850).

Wirtembergische Urkundenbuch 3 (Stuttgart, 1871).

Wolf, Kenneth Baxter, ed., *The Life and Afterlife of St. Elizabeth of Hungary: Testimony from Her Canonization Hearings* (Oxford, 2010).

Wolfhere, *Vita sancti Godehardi episcopi posterior* (BHL 3582), ed. Georg Heinrich Pertz, MGH, SS 11 (Hanover, 1854), pp. 196–218.

Wormald, Francis, ed., *English Benedictine Kalendars after A.D. 1100* (2 vols., Henry Bradshaw Soc. 77, 81, 1939–46).

Wycliffe, John, *Tractatus de ecclesia*, ed. Johann Loserth (Wyclif Soc., London, 1886).

Secondary Literature

Abou-El-Haj, Barbara, *The Medieval Cult of Saints: Formations and Transformations* (Cambridge, 1994).

Agapitos, Panagiotis A., "Teachers, Pupils and Imperial Power in Eleventh-Century Byzantium," in *Pedagogy and Power: Rhetorics of Classical Learning*, ed. Yun Lee Too and Niall Livingstone (Cambridge, 1998), pp. 170–91.

Age of Chivalry: Art in Plantagenet England, 1200–1400, ed. Jonathan Alexander and Paul Binski (London, 1987).

Aigrain, René, *L'Hagiographie: ses sources, ses méthodes, son histoire* (Paris, 1953).

Aitchison, Briony, "Holy Cow!: The Miraculous Cures of Animals in Late Medieval England," *European Review of History* 16 (2009), pp. 875–92.

Al-Andalus: The Art of Islamic Spain, ed. Jerrilynn D. Dodds (New York, 1992).

Albert, Jean-Pierre, *Odeurs de sainteté: la mythologie chrétienne des aromates* (Paris, 1990).

Alexander, Dominic, *Saints and Animals in the Middle Ages* (Woodbridge, 2008).

Allirot, Anne-Hélène, "Isabelle de France, sœur de saint Louis: la vierge savante (une étude de la Vie d'Isabelle de France écrite par Agnès d'Harcourt)," *Médiévales* 48 (2005), pp. 55–98.

L'Altare d'Oro di Sant' Ambrogio, ed. Carlo Capponi (Milan, 1996).

Anderson, M. O., *Kings and Kingship in Early Scotland* (Edinburgh and London, 1973).

Andrić, Stanko, *The Miracles of St John Capistran* (Budapest, 1999).

Angenendt, Arnold, "Corpus Incorruptum: Eine Leitidee der mittelalterliche Reliquienverehrung," *Saeculum* 24 (1991), pp. 320–48 (repr. in Angenendt, *Die Gegenwart von Heiligen und Reliquien*, ed. Hubertus Lutterbach [Münster, 2010], pp. 109–43).

———, *Heilige und Reliquien. Die Geschichte ihres Kultes vom frühen Christentum bis zur Gegenwart* (Munich, 1994).

Anglo-Norman Dictionary, ed. Louise Stone and William Rothwell (London, 1977–92).

Anti, Elisa, *Santi e animali nell'Italia Padana (secoli IV–XII)* (Bologna, 1998).

Antoine, Élisabeth, "Images de miracles. Le témoinage des ex-voto peints en Italie centrale (XIVe–XVIe siècles)," in *Miracle et karāma*, pp. 353–74.

Antonsson, Haki, "Saints and Relics in Early Christian Scandinavia," *Mediaeval Scandinavia* 15 (2005), pp. 51–80.

Antonsson, Haki, and Ildar H. Garipzanov, ed., *Saints and Their Lives on the Periphery: Veneration of Saints in Scandinavia and Eastern Europe (c. 1000–1200)* (Turnhout, 2010).

Archéologie et architecture d'un site monastique: Ve–XXe siècles: 10 ans de recherche à l'abbaye Saint-Germain d'Auxerre, ed. Christian Sapin (2000).

Aronow, Gail, "A Description of the Altars in Siena Cathedral in the 1420s," in *Sienese Altar-pieces 1215–1460*, ed. Henk Van Os (2 vols., Groningen, 1988–90), 2, pp. 225–42.

The Art of Medieval Spain: A.D. 500–1200, ed. John P. O'Neill (New York, 1994).

Ash, Marinell, and Dauvit Broun, "The Adoption of St Andrew as Patron Saint of Scotland," in *Medieval Art and Architecture in the Diocese of St Andrews*, ed. John Higgitt (British Archaeological Association, 1994), pp. 16–24.

The Ashgate Research Companion to Byzantine Hagiography, ed. Stephanos Efthymiadis (Farnham, 2011).

Ashley, Kathleen, and Pamela Sheingorn, ed., *Interpreting Cultural Symbols: Saint Anne in Late Medieval Society* (Athens, GA, 1990).

Aston, Margaret, *England's Iconoclasts* 1: *Laws against Images* (Oxford, 1988).

———, "Lollards and Images," in *Lollards and Reformers: Images and Literacy in Late Mediaeval Religion* (London, 1984), pp. 135–92.

Avner, Rina, "The Initial Traditions of the Theotokos at the Kathisma: Earliest Celebrations and the Calendar," in *The Cult of the Mother of God in Byzantium*, ed. Leslie Brubaker and Mary B. Cunningham (Farnham, 2011), pp. 9–29.

Azevedo, Pedro A. d', "Inquiração de 1336 sobre os milagres da Rainha D. Isabel," *Boletim da segunda classe. Academia Real das Sciencias de Lisboa* 3 (1910), pp. 294–303.

Bacci, Michele, *Il pennello dell'Evangelista. Storia delle immagini sacre attribute a san Luca* (Pisa, 1998).

———, *Pro remedio animae: immagini sacre e pratiche devozionali in Italia centrale (secoli XIII e XIV)* (Pisa, 2000).

Bach, Adolf, *Deutsche Namenkunde* (3 vols. in 5, Heidelberg, 1952–56).

Bachrach, David S., *Religion and the Conduct of War, c. 300–c. 1215* (Woodbridge, 2003).

Bainbridge, Virginia R., *Gilds in the Medieval Countryside: Social and Religious Change in Cambridgeshire, c. 1350–1558* (Woodbridge, 1996).

Baker, Malcolm, "Medieval Illustrations of Bede's Life of St. Cuthbert," *Journal of the Warburg and Courtauld Institutes* 41 (1978), pp. 16–49.

Barbero, Alessandro, *Un santo in famiglia: vocazione religiosa e resistenze sociali nell'agiografia latina medievale* (Turin, 1991).

Barchard, David, "Sykeon Rediscovered? A Site at Kiliseler Near Beypazarı," *Anatolian Studies* 53 (2003), pp. 175–79.

Barlow, Frank, *Edward the Confessor* (London, 1970).

Barow-Vassilevitch, Daria, *Ich schwime in der gotheit als ein adeler in dem lufft!: Heiligkeitsmuster in der Vitenliteratur des 13. und 14. Jahrhunderts* (Göppingen, 2005).

Bartlett, Robert, *England under the Norman and Angevin Kings 1075–1225* (Oxford, 2000).

———, *The Making of Europe: Conquest, Colonization and Cultural Change 950–1350* (Harmondsworth and Princeton, 1993).

———, "Reflections on Paganism and Christianity in Medieval Europe," *Proceedings of the British Academy* 101 (1998 Lectures and Memoirs) (1998), pp. 55–76.

———, "Rewriting Saints' Lives: The Case of Gerald of Wales," *Speculum* 58 (1983), pp. 598–613.

Bartolomei Romagnoli, Alessandra, ed., *Francesca Romana: La santa, il monastero e la città alla fine del Medioevo* (Florence, 2009).

Battiscombe, C. F., ed., *The Relics of Saint Cuthbert* (Oxford, 1956).

Baumeister, Theofried, "Vorchristliche Bestattungssitten und die Entstehung des Märtyrerkultes in Ägypten," *Römische Quartalschrift für christliche Altertumskunde und Kirchengeschichte* 69 (1974), pp. 1–6.

Bäumer, Suitbert, "Der Micrologus ein Werk Bernold's von Konstanz," *Neues Archiv* 18 (1893), pp. 429–46.

Bautier, Anne-Marie, "Typologie des ex-votos mentionnés dans les textes antérieurs à 1200," in *La piété populaire au moyen âge. Actes du 99e Congrès national des Sociétés savantes* 1 *[= Section de philologie et d'histoire jusqu'à 1610]* (Paris 1977, 1977), pp. 237–84.

Beaujard, Brigitte, *Le culte des saints en Gaule: les premiers temps, d'Hilaire de Poitiers à la fin du VIe siècle* (Paris, 2000).

Becher, Matthias, *Eid und Herrschaft: Untersuchungen zum Herrscherethos Karls des Grossen* (Sigmaringen, 1993).

Belli D'Elia, Pina, *La Basilica di S. Nicola a Bari: un monumento nel tempo* (Galatina, 1985).

———, "Pellegrini e pellegrinaggi nella testimonianza delle imagini," in *Pellegrinaggi e santuari di San Michele nell'Occidente medievale/Pèlerinages et sanctuaires de Saint-Michel dans l'Occident médiéval: atti del secondo convegno internazionale dedicato all'Arcangelo Michele, atti del XVI Convegno Sacrense (Sacra di San Michele, 26–29 settembre 2007)*, ed. Giampietro Casiraghi and Giuseppe Sergi (Bari, 2009), pp. 441–75.

Belting, Hans, *Likeness and Presence. A History of the Image Before the Era of Art* (Eng. tr., Chicago, 1994).

Ben-Ami, Issachar, *Culte des saints et pèlerinages judéo-musulmans au Maroc* (abbreviated French tr., Paris, 1990).

Bengtson, Jonathan, "St. George and the Formation of English Nationalism," *Journal of Medieval and Early Modern Studies* 27 (1997), pp. 317–40.

Berend, Nora, ed., *Christianization and the Rise of Christian Monarchy: Scandinavia, Central Europe and Rus' c. 900–1200* (Cambridge, 2007).

Berschin, Walter, *Biographie und Epochenstil im lateinischen Mittelalter* (4 vols. in 5, Stuttgart, 1986–2004).

———, "Biography," in *Medieval Latin: An Introduction and Bibliographical Guide*, ed. F.A.C. Mantello and A .G. Rigg (Washington, DC, 1996), pp. 607–17.
Bertelsmeier-Kierst, Christa, ed., *Elisabeth von Thüringen und die neue Frömmigkeit in Europa* (Frankfurt am Main, 2008).
Bertrand, Paul, "Authentiques de reliques: authentiques ou reliques?," *Le Moyen Age* 112 (2006), pp. 363–74.
Bethell, Denis, "The Lives of St. Osyth of Essex and St. Osyth of Aylesbury," AB 88 (1970), pp. 75–127.
Beyond Pilgrim Souvenirs and Secular Badges: Essays in Honour of Brian Spencer, ed. Sarah Blick (Oxford, 2007).
Biblioteca agiografica italiana, ed. Jacques Dalarun et al. (3 vols., Florence, 2003).
Bibliotheca Hagiographica Graeca, ed. François Halkin (3rd ed., 3 vols., SH 8a, 1957; *Novum Auctarium*, SH 65, 1984).
Bibliotheca Hagiographica Latina (2 vols., SH 6, 1898–1901; *Novum Supplementum*, ed. H. Fros [SH 70, 1986]).
Bibliotheca sanctorum (14 vols., Rome, 1961–87).
Bibliotheca sanctorum orientalium (2 vols., Rome, 1998–99).
Biddle, Martin, ed., *Winchester in the Early Middle Ages* (Oxford, 1976).
Bihl, Michael, "De nomine S. Francisci," *Archivum Franciscanum Historicum* 19 (1926), pp. 469–529.
Binns, Alison, *Dedications of Monastic Houses in England and Wales*, 1066–1216 (Woodbridge, 1989).
Binski, Paul, *Becket's Crown: Art and Imagination in Gothic England 1170–1300* (New Haven, 2004).
———, *Westminster Abbey and the Plantagenets: Kingship and the Representation of Power, 1200–1400* (London, 1995).
Birch, Debra, *Pilgrimage to Rome in the Middle Ages* (Woodbridge, 1998).
Birch, Walter de Gray, *History of Scottish Seals from the eleventh to the seventeenth century* (2 vols., Stirling and London, 1905–7).
Birkett, Helen, *The Saints' Lives of Jocelin of Furness: Hagiography, Patronage and Ecclesiastical Politics* (Woodbridge, 2010).
Bischoff, Bernhard, "Über gefaltene Handschriften, vornehmlich hagiographischen Inhalts," in *Mittelalterliche Studien* 1 (Stuttgart, 1966), pp. 93–100.
———, "Wer ist die Nonne von Heidenheim?," *Studien und Mitteilungen zur Geschichte des Benediktinerordens und seiner Zweige* 49 (Neue Folge, 18) (1931), pp. 387–88.
Bisconti, Fabrizio, "Le origini del pellegrinaggio petriano e il culto dei martiri romani," in *Romei e Giubilei. Il pellegrinaggio medievale a San Pietro (350–1350)*, ed. Mario D'Onofrio (Milan, 1999), pp. 35–42.
Bisconti, Fabrizio, and Danilo Mazzoleni, *Alle origini del culto dei martiri: testimonianze nell'archeologia cristiana* (Rome, 2005).
Bisogni, Fabio, "Raggi e aureole ossia la distinzione della santità," in *Con l'occhio e col lume. Atti del corso seminariale di studi su S. Caterina da Siena*, ed. Luigi Trenti and Bente Klange Addabbo (Siena, 1999), pp. 349–51.
Bitel, Lisa M., "St. Brigit of Ireland: From Virgin Saint to Fertility Goddess" (on-line).
Bitton-Ashkelony, Bruria, *Encountering the Sacred: The Debate on Christian Pilgrimage in Late Antiquity* (Berkeley, 2005).

Blair, John, "A Handlist of Anglo-Saxon Saints," in *Local Saints and Local Churches*, ed. Thacker and Sharpe, pp. 495–565.

———, "A Saint for Every Minster? Local Cults in Anglo-Saxon England," in *Local Saints and Local Churches*, ed. Thacker and Sharpe, pp. 455–94.

Bledniak, Sonia, "L'hagiographie imprimée: oeuvres en français, 1476–1550," in *Hagiographies* 1, pp. 359–405.

Blickle, Peter, André Holenstein, Heinrich Richard Schmidt, and Franz-Josef Sladeczek, eds., *Macht und Ohnmacht der Bilder: reformatorischer Bildersturm im Kontext der europäischen Geschichte* (Historische Zeitschrift, Beihefte, Neue Folge 33, 2002).

Blume, D., and M. Werner, eds., *Elisabeth von Thüringen—eine europäische Heilige* (2 vols., Katalog und Aufsätze, Petersberg, 2007).

Boeren, P. C., *Jocundus. Biographe de saint Servais* (The Hague, 1972).

Boesch Gajano, Sofia, "La 'Bibliotheca sanctorum.' Problemi di agiografia medievale," *Rivista di storia della Chiesa in Italia* 26 (1972), pp. 139–53.

———, "L'agiografia," in *Morfologie sociali e culturali in Europa fra tarda antichità e alto medioevo* (Settimane di Studio 45, 2 vols., 1998) 2, pp. 797–843.

———, *Gregorio Magno: Alle origini del Medioevo* (Rome, 2004).

Boglioni, Pierre, "La scène de la mort dans les premières hagiographies latines," in *Le sentiment de la mort au Moyen Age* (Montreal, 1979), pp. 183–210.

Borgeaud, Philippe, and Youri Volokhine, eds., *Les objets de la mémoire: pour une approche comparatiste des reliques et de leur culte* (Bern, 2005).

Borst, Arno, "Patron Saints in Medieval Society," in *Medieval Worlds: Barbarians, Heretics and Artists in the Middle Ages* (Eng. tr., Cambridge, 1991), pp. 125–44.

Böse, Kristin, *Gemalte Heiligkeit: Bilderzählungen neuer Heiliger in der italienischen Kunst des 14. und 15. Jahrhunderts* (Petersberg, 2008).

Bouchard, Constance, "Episcopal *Gesta* and the Creation of a Useful Past in Ninth-Century Auxerre," *Speculum* 84 (2009), pp. 1–35.

Bouet, Pierre, "Les formes de dévotion des pèlerins qui se rendent au Mont Saint-Michel," in *Pellegrinaggi e santuari di San Michele nell'Occidente medievale/Pèlerinages et sanctuaires de Saint-Michel dans l'Occident médiéval: atti del secondo convegno internazionale dedicato all'Arcangelo Michele, atti del XVI Convegno Sacrense (Sacra di San Michele, 26–29 settembre* 2007*)*, ed. Giampietro Casiraghi and Giuseppe Sergi (Bari, 2009), pp. 67–84.

Boulton, D'Arcy Jonathan Dacre, *The Knights of the Crown: The Monarchical Orders of Knighthood in Later Medieval Europe 1325–1520* (Woodbridge, 1987).

Bourdua, Louise, "Entombing the Founder St. Augustine of Hippo," in *Art and the Augustinian Order in Early Renaissance Italy*, ed. Louise Bourdua and Anne Dunlop (Aldershot, 2007), pp. 29–50.

Boureau, Alain, *La légende dorée: le système narratif de Jacques de Voragine* (Paris, 1984).

Bourke, Cormac, ed., *Studies in the Cult of Saint Columba* (Dublin, 1997).

Bozóky, Edina, "La politique des reliques des premiers comtes de Flandre (fin du IXe–fin du XIe siècle)," in *Les reliques: objets, cultes, symboles*, ed. Edina Bozóky and Anne-Marie Helvétius (Turnhout, 1999), pp. 271–92.

———, *La politique des reliques de Constantine à Saint Louis* (Paris, 2006).

Bozóky, Edina, and Anne-Marie Helvétius, eds., *Les reliques: objets, cultes, symboles* (Turnhout, 1999).

Brakke, David, *Athanasius and the Politics of Asceticism* (Oxford, 1995).

Brand, Benjamin, "The Vigils of Medieval Tuscany," *Plainsong and Medieval Music* 17 (2008), pp. 23–54.
Brandenburg, Hugo, *Ancient Churches of Rome from the Fourth to the Seventh Century* (Eng. tr., Turnhout, 2005).
Branner, Robert, "The Sainte-Chapelle and the Capella Regis in the Thirteenth Century," *Gesta* 10 (1971), pp. 19–22.
Braulik, Georg, "Verweigert die Westkirche den Heiligen des Alten Testaments die liturgische Verehrung?," *Theologie und Philosophie* 82 (2007), pp. 1–20.
Braun, Joseph, *Die Reliquiare des christlichen Kultes und ihre Entwicklung* (Freiburg im Breisgau, 1940).
Bray, Dorothy Ann, *A List of Motifs in the Lives of the Early Irish Saints* (Helsinki, 1992).
Breatnach, Caoimhín, "The Significance of the Orthography of Irish Proper Names in the Codex Salmanticensis," *Eriu* 55 (2005), pp. 85–101.
Bredekamp, Horst, and Frank Seehausen, "Das Reliquiar als Staatsform. Das Reliquiar Isidors von Sevilla und der Beginn der Hofkunst in Léon," in *Reliquiare im Mittelalter*, ed. Bruno Reudenbach and Gia Toussaint (Berlin, 2005), pp. 137–64.
Bredero, Adriaan H., *Bernard of Clairvaux: Between Cult and History* (Eng. tr., Edinburgh, 1996).
Bresslau, Harry, *Handbuch der Urkundenlehre für Deutschland und Italien* (2nd ed., 2 vols., Leipzig, 1912–31).
Brodbeck, Sulamith, *Les saints de la Cathédrale de Monreale en Sicilie: iconographie, hagiographie et pouvoir royal à la fin du XIIe siècle* (Rome, 2010).
Brooke, Rosalind B., *The Image of St Francis: Responses to Sainthood in the Thirteenth Century* (Cambridge, 2006).
Broun, Dauvit, and Thomas Owen Clancy, eds., *Spes Scotorum: Hope of Scots. Saint Columba, Iona and Scotland* (Edinburgh, 1999).
Browe, Peter, *Die eucharistischen Wunder des Mittelalters* (Breslau, 1938).
Brown, Andrew, *Civic Ceremony and Religion in Medieval Bruges c. 1300–1520* (Cambridge, 2011).
Brown, Peter, *Augustine of Hippo: A Biography* (London and Berkeley, 1967).
———, *The Cult of the Saints: Its Rise and Function in Latin Christianity* (Chicago, 1981).
———, "Enjoying the Saints in Late Antiquity," *Early Medieval Europe* 9 (2000), pp. 1–24.
———, "The Rise and Function of the Holy Man," *Journal of Roman Studies* 61 (1971), pp. 80–101.
Brubaker, Leslie, "Icons before Iconoclasm?," in *Morfologie sociali e culturali in europa fra tarda antichità e alto medioevo* (2 vols., Settimane di Studio 45, 1998), 2, pp. 1215–54.
Brubaker, Leslie, and John Haldon, *Byzantium in the Iconoclast Era c. 680–850* (Cambridge, 2011).
———, *Byzantium in the Iconoclast Era (c. 680–850): The Sources: An Annotated Survey* (Aldershot, 2001).
Brufani, Stefano, and Enrico Menestò, eds., *Nel segno del santo protettore: Ubaldo, vescovo, taumaturgo, santo* (2nd ed., Spoleto, 1992).
Brundage, James A., "Cruce Signari: The Rite for Taking the Cross in England," *Traditio* 22 (1966), pp. 289–310.
Brunel-Lobrichon, G., A.-F. Leurquin-Labie, and M. Thiry-Stassin, "L'hagiographie de langue française sur le Continent, IXe–XVe siècle," in *Hagiographies* 2, pp. 291–371.
Bryer, Anthony, and Judith Herrin, eds., *Iconoclasm* (Birmingham, 1977).

Burnham, Louisa, *So Great a Light, So Great a Smoke: The Beguin Heretics of Languedoc* (Ithaca, NY, 2008).

Burr, David, *The Spiritual Franciscans: From Protest to Persecution in the Century after Saint Francis* (University Park, PA, 2001).

Bynum, Caroline Walker, "Seeing and Beyond: The Mass of St. Gregory in the Fifteenth Century," in *The Mind's Eye: Art and Theological Argument in the Middle Ages*, ed. Jeffrey F. Hamburger and Anne-Marie Bouché (Princeton, 2006), pp. 208–40.

———, *Wonderful Blood: Theology and Practice in Late Medieval Northern Germany and Beyond* (Philadelphia, 2007).

Bynum, Caroline Walker, and Paula Gerson, eds., *Body-Part Reliquaries* (*Gesta* 36.1, special issue, 1997).

Cabrol, F., "L'annonce des fêtes," *Dictionnaire d'archéologie chrétienne et de liturgie* 1/2 (Paris, 1907), cols. 2230–41.

Caciola, Nancy, *Discerning Spirits: Divine and Demonic Possession in the Middle Ages* (Ithaca, NY, 2003).

Cameron, Averil, "The Theotokos in Sixth-Century Constantinople," *Journal of Theological Studies* 29 (1978), pp. 79–108.

Cárdenas, Livia, *Friedrich der Weise und das Wittenberger Heiltumsbuch* (Berlin, 2002).

Carletti, Carlo, "I graffiti sull'affresco di san Luca nel Cimiterio di Commodilla: Addenda et corrigenda," *Rendiconti della Pontificia Accademia Romana di Archeologia* 57 (1984–58), pp. 129–43.

Caroli, Martina, "Bringing Saints to Cities and Monasteries: 'Translationes' in the Making of a Sacred Geography (9th–10th Centuries)," in *Towns and Their Territories between Late Antiquity and the Early Middle Ages*, ed. G. P. Brogiolo et al. (Leiden, 2000), pp. 259–74.

———, "Dalla reliquia all'immagine: percorsi nell'area ravennate," in *Santuari cristiani d'Italia: committenze e fruizione tra Medioevo e età moderna*, ed. Mario Tosti (Rome, 2003), pp. 45–69.

Carr, Annemarie Weyl, "Icons and the Object of Pilgrimage in Middle Byzantine Constantinople," *Dumbarton Oaks Papers* 56 (2002), pp. 75–92.

Cartron, Isabelle, *Les pérégrinations de Saint-Philibert: genèse d'un réseau monastique dans la société carolingienne* (Rennes, 2009).

Catalogue général des manuscrits des bibliothèques publiques de France, Départements 10*: Avranches, etc.* (Paris, 1889).

Catalogus codicum hagiographicorum latinorum antiquorum saeculo XVI qui asservantur in Bibliotheca Nationali Parisiensi (4 vols., SH 2, 1889–93).

Caudron, Simone, "Les châsses reliquaires de Thomas Becket émaillées à Limoges: Leur géographie historique," *Bulletin de la Société archéologique et historique du Limousin* 121 (1993), pp. 55–83.

Caviness, Madeline Harrison, *The Windows of Christ Church Cathedral, Canterbury* (Corpus vitrearum medii aevi: Great Britain 2, London, 1981).

Chadwick, Henry, *Priscillian of Avila: The Occult and the Charismatic in the Early Church* (Oxford, 1976).

Chadwick, Nora K., *The Age of the Saints in the Early Celtic Church* (Oxford, 1961).

Chaney, William A., *The Cult of Kingship in Anglo-Saxon England: The Transition from Paganism to Christianity* (Manchester, 1970).

Charanis, Peter, "The Monk as an Element of Byzantine Society," *Dumbarton Oaks Papers* 25 (1971), pp. 61–84.

Charles-Edwards, T. M., "Brigit (439/452–524/526)," in *Oxford Dictionary of National Biography* (60 vols. plus indices, Oxford, 2004), 7, pp. 650–54.
———, *Early Christian Ireland* (Cambridge, 2000).
Chavasse, Antoine, *Le sacramentaire gélasien (Vaticanus Reginensis 316)* (Paris, 1958).
Chave-Mahir, Florence, *L'exorcisme des possédés dans l'Église d'Occident (Xe–XIVe siècle)* (Turnhout, 2011).
Chazelle, Celia M., "Pictures, Books and the Illiterate: Pope Gregory I's Letters to Serenus of Marseilles," *Word and Image* 6 (1990), pp. 138–53.
Cheney, C. R., *A Handbook of Dates for Students of British History* (rev. ed., London, 2000).
———, "Rules for the Observance of Feast-Days in Medieval England," *Bulletin of the Institute of Historical Research* 34 (1961), pp. 117–47.
Chevalier, Ulysse, *Repertorium hymnologicum* (6 vols., Louvain, 1892–1920).
Chibnall, Marjorie, "The Translation of the Relics of St. Nicholas and Norman Historical Tradition," in *Piety, Power and History in Medieval England and Normandy* (Aldershot, 2000), pp. 33–41 (Essay III).
Christin, Olivier, *Une révolution symbolique: l'iconoclasme huguenot et la reconstruction catholique* (Paris, 1991).
Chung-Apley, Jane Geein, "The Illustrated Vie et miracles de saint Louis of Guillaume de Saint-Pathus (Paris, B.N., MS. Fr. 5716)" (Ph. D. thesis, University of Michigan, 1998).
Ciappelli, Giovanni, "Edificazione e politica nella nascita (tardiva) di un culto. La Vita di S. Andrea Corsini," in *Tra edificazione e piacere della lettura: le vite dei santi in età medievale*, ed. Antonella Degl'Innocenti and Fulvio Ferrari (Trent, 1998), pp. 31–52.
Ciarrochi, Arnoldo, and Ermanno Mori, *Le tavolette votive italiane* (Udine, 1960).
Cioffari, Gerardo, *Storia della Basilica di S. Nicola di Bari* 1*: l'epoca normanno sveva* (Bari, 1984).
Ciresi, Lisa Victoria, "Of Offerings and Kings: The Shrine of the Three Kings of Cologne and the Aachen Karlschrein and Marienschrein in Coronation Ritual," in *Reliquiare im Mittelalter*, ed. Bruno Reudenbach and Gia Toussaint (Berlin, 2005), pp. 165–85.
The City of London, ed. Mary Lobel (The British Atlas of Historic Towns 3, 1989).
Clanchy, Michael, *Abelard: A Medieval Life* (Oxford, 1997).
Clancy, Thomas Owen, "Magpie Hagiography in Twelfth-century Scotland: The Case of *Libellus de nativitate Sancti Cuthberti*," in *Celtic Hagiography and Saints' Cults*, ed. Jane Cartwright (Cardiff, 2003), pp. 216–31.
———, "Scottish Saints and National Identities in the Early Middle Ages," in *Local Saints and Local Churches*, ed. Thacker and Sharpe, pp. 397–421.
Clayton, Mary, *The Apocryphal Gospels of Mary in Anglo-Saxon England* (Cambridge, 1998).
———, *The Cult of the Virgin Mary in Anglo-Saxon England* (Cambridge, 1990).
Clayton, Mary, and Hugh Magennis, *The Old English Lives of St Margaret* (Cambridge, 1994).
Clemen, Otto, *Die Volksfrömmigkeit des ausgehenden Mittelalters* (Dresden and Leipzig, 1937).
Clemoes, Peter, *The Cult of St Oswald on the Continent* (Jarrow lecture for 1983, Jarrow, 1984).
Cobianchi, Roberto, "The Use of Woodcuts in Fifteenth-century Italy," *Print Quarterly* 23 (2006), pp. 47–54.
Coens, Maurice, "Anciennes litanies des saints," in *Recueil des études bollandiennes* (SH 37, 1963), pp. 129–322.

———, "Catalogus codicum hagiographicorum latinorum archivi historici civitatis Coloniensis," AB 61 (1943), pp. 140–201.

Cohen, Esther, "In Haec Signa: The Pilgrim-Badge Trade in Southern France," *Journal of Medieval History* 2 (1976), pp. 193–214.

Cole, Penny J., *The Preaching of the Crusades to the Holy Land, 1095–1270* (Cambridge, Mass., 1991).

Colker, Marvin L., *Trinity College Library Dublin: Descriptive Catalogue of the Mediaeval and Renaissance Latin Manuscripts* (2 vols., Aldershot, 1991, with *Supplement One* [Dublin, 2008]).

Collinet-Guérin, Marthe, *Histoire du nimbe: des origines aux temps modernes* (Paris, 1961).

Collins, David J., *Reforming Saints: Saints' Lives and Their Authors in Germany, 1470–1530* (Oxford, 2007).

Commentarius historicus de beato Andrea Hispellate, AASS Iunii 1 (1695), pp. 364–70.

Compan, André, *Étude d'anthroponymie provençale: les noms de personne dans le comté de Nice aux XIIIe, XIVe et XVe siècles* (2 vols., Lille, 1976).

Comte, Marie-Christine, *Les reliquaires du Proche-Orient et de Chypre à la période protobyzantine (IVe –VIIIe siècles)* (Turnhout, 2012).

Congregatio de causis sanctorum, *Index ac status causarum* (Vatican City, 1999).

Conner, Patrick W., *Anglo-Saxon Exeter: A Tenth-century Cultural History* (Woodbridge, 1993).

Constable, Giles, "Opposition to Pilgrimage in the Middle Ages," *Studia Gratiana* 19 (1976), pp. 123–46 (repr. in his *Religious Life and Thought (11th–12th centuries)* [London, 1979], item 4, with same pagination).

Constas, Nicholas, "An Apology for the Cult of the Saints in Late Antiquity: Eustratius Presbyter of Constantinople, On the State of Souls after Death (CPG 7522)," *Journal of Early Christian Studies* 10/2 (2002), pp. 267–85.

Cook, William, "Fraternal and Lay Images of St. Francis in the Thirteenth Century," in *Popes, Teachers, and Canon law in the Middle Ages*, ed. James Ross Sweeney and Stanley Chodorow (Ithaca, NY, 1989), pp. 263–89.

The Coptic Encyclopedia, ed. Aziz S. Atiya (8 vols., New York, 1991).

Corbet, Patrick, *Les saints ottoniens: sainteté dynastique, sainteté royale et sainteté feminine autour de l'an mil* (Francia, Beiheft 15, Sigmaringen, 1986).

Corley, Brigitte, *Conrad von Soest: Painter among Merchant Princes* (London, 1996).

———, *Painting and Patronage in Cologne 1300–1500* (Turnhout, 2000).

Cormack, Margaret Jean, *The Saints in Iceland: Their Veneration from the Conversion to* 1400 (SH 78, 1994).

Cornell, Vincent J., *Realm of the Saint: Power and Authority in Moroccan Sufism* (Austin, 1998).

Corpus Nummorum Italicorum 4 (Rome, 1913).

Corti, Maria, *L'opera completa di Memling* (Milan, 1969).

Coué, Stephanie, *Hagiographie im Kontext: Schreibanlass und Funktion von Bischofsviten aus dem 11. und vom Anfang des 12. Jahrhunderts* (Berlin, 1997).

Coulton, G. G., *Medieval Panorama* (Cambridge, 1938).

Cowdrey, H.E.J., "The Peace and Truce of God in the Eleventh Century," *Past and Present* 46 (1970), pp. 42–67.

Craig, Leigh Ann, *Wandering Women and Holy Matrons: Women as Pilgrims in the Later Middle Ages* (Leiden, 2009).

Cronyn, J. M., and C. V. Horie, "The Anglo-Saxon Coffin: Further Investigations," in *St Cuthbert, His Cult and Community to AD 1200*, ed. Gerald Bonner et al. (Woodbridge, 1989), pp. 247–85.

———, *St. Cuthbert's Coffin: The History, Technology, and Conservation* (Durham, 1985).

Crook, John, *The Architectural Setting of the Cult of the Saints in the Early Christian West, c. 300–c. 1200* (Oxford, 2000).

———, *English Medieval Shrines* (Woodbridge, 2011).

Cross, James E., "English Vernacular Saints' Lives before 1000 A. D.," in *Hagiographies* 2, pp. 413–27.

———, "Cynewulf's Traditions about the Apostles in Fates of the Apostles," *Anglo-Saxon England* 8 (1979), pp. 163–75.

Crossley, Paul, "The Politics of Presentation: The Architecture of Charles IV of Bohemia," in *Courts and Regions in Medieval Europe*, ed. Sarah Rees Jones et al. (York, 2000), pp. 99–172.

Crouch, David J. F., *Piety, Fraternity, and Power: Religious Gilds in Late Medieval Yorkshire, 1389–1547* (Woodbridge, 2000).

Crumplin, Sally, "Modernizing St. Cuthbert: Reginald of Durham's Miracle Collection," in *Signs, Wonders, Miracles: Representations of Divine Power in the Life of the Church*, ed. Kate Cooper and Jeremy Gregory (Studies in Church History 41, 2005), pp. 179–91.

———, "Rewriting History in the Cult of St. Cuthbert from the Ninth to the Twelfth Centuries" (unpublished Ph. D. thesis, St. Andrews, 2005).

Cubitt, Catherine, "Sites and Sanctity: Revisiting the Cult of Murdered and Martyred Anglo-Saxon Royal Saints," *Early Medieval Europe* 9 (2000), pp. 53–83.

Culte et pèlerinages à Saint Michel en Occident: les trois monts dédiés à l'archange, ed. Pierre Bouet et al. (Rome, 2003).

Culto e santuari di san Michele nell'Europa medievale, ed. Pierre Bouet et al. (Bari, 2007).

Dalarun, Jacques, *La sainte et la cité: Micheline de Pesaro (+1356), tertiaire franciscaine* (Rome, 1992).

d'Alatri, Mariano, "Culto dei santi ed eretici in Italia nei secoli XII e XIII," *Collectanea franciscana* 45 (1975), pp. 86–104.

Dal Santo, Matthew *Debating the Saints' Cults in the Age of Gregory the Great* (Oxford, 2012).

———, "The God-Protected Empire? Scepticism towards the Cult of Saints in Early Byzantium," in *An Age of Saints? Power, Conflict, and Dissent in Early Medieval Christianity*, ed. Peter Sarris et al. (Leiden, 2011), pp. 129–49.

Daly, Lloyd W., *Contributions to a History of Alphabetization in Antiquity and the Middle Ages* (Brussels, 1967).

Dassmann, Ernst, *Sündenvergebung durch Taufe, Busse und Martyrerfürbitte in den Zeugnissen frühchristlicher Frömmigkeit und Kunst* (Münster, 1973).

Dauzat, A., and C. Rostaing, *Dictionnaire étymologique des noms de lieux en France* (2nd ed., Paris, 1983).

David, J. F., "Lollards, Reformers and St. Thomas of Canterbury," *University of Birmingham Historical Journal* 9 (1963–64), pp. 1–15.

Davis, Stephen J., *The Cult of St Thecla: A Tradition of Women's Piety in Late Antiquity* (Oxford, 2001).

d'Avray, David, "Popular and Elite Religion: Feastdays and Preaching," in *Elite and Popular Religion*, ed. Kate Cooper and Jeremy Gregory (Studies in Church History 42, 2006), pp. 162–79.

De Farcy, L., "L'ancien trésor de la cathédrale d'Angers (1)," *Revue de l'art chrétien* 30 (1880), pp. 185–208.
De Gaiffier, Baudouin, "A propos des légendiers latins," AB 97 (1979), pp. 57–68.
———, "La lecture des actes des martyrs dans la prière liturgique en Occident," AB 72 (1954), pp. 134–66.
———, "La lecture des passions des martyrs à Rome avant le IXe. siècle," AB 87 (1969), pp. 63–78.
———, "Les 'doublets' en hagiographie latine," AB 96 (1978), pp. 261–69.
———, "Les reliques de l'abbaye de San Millán de la Cogolla au XIIIe siècle," AB 53 (1935), pp. 90–100.
———, "Les revendications de biens dans quelques documents hagiographiques du XIe. siècle," AB 50 (1932), pp. 123–38.
Delcorno, Carlo, "La Legenda aurea dallo scrittoio al pulpito," in *Exemplum e letteratura* (Bologna, 1989), pp. 79–101.
Delcorno Branca, Daniela, "Un camaldolese alla festa di S. Giovanni: La processione del Battista descritta da Agostino di Portico," *Lettere Italiane* 55 (2003), pp. 3–25.
Delehaye, Hippolyte, *Cinq leçons sur la méthode hagiographique* (SH 21, 1934).
———, *Les légendes hagiographiques* (4th ed., SH 18, 1955).
———, *Les origines du culte des martyrs* (2nd ed., SH 20, 1933).
———, *Les saints stylites* (SH 14, 1923).
———, *Sanctus: Essai sur le culte des saints dans l'antiquité* (SH 17, 1927).
Delisle, Léopold, *Recherches sur la librairie de Charles V, roi de France, 1337–1380* (2 vols., Paris, 1907).
Delooz, Pierre, *Sociologie et canonisations* (Liège, 1969).
De Meester, Placido, *De monachico statu iuxta disciplinam Byzantinam* (Vatican City, 1942).
Demm, Eberhard, "Zur Rolle des Wunders in der Heiligkeitskonzeption des Mittelalters," *Archiv für Kulturgeschichte* 57 (1975), pp. 300–344.
Demus, Otto, *Romanesque Mural Painting* (London, 1970).
Dengler-Schreiber, Karin, *Scriptorium und Bibliothek des Klosters Michelsberg in Bamberg* (Graz, 1979).
Der Nersessian, Sirarpie, *L'Illustration des psautiers grecs du Moyen Age* 2 (Paris, 1970).
Deuffic, Jean-Luc, ed., *Reliques et sainteté dans l'espace médiéval* (Pecia 8–11, St.-Denis, 2006).
D'Evelyn, Charlotte, and Frances A. Foster, "Saints' Legends," in *A Manual of the Writings in Middle English* 1050–1500, 2, ed. J. Burke Severs (New Haven, 1970), pp. 561–635.
De Vooght, D. P., "Les miracles dans la vies de saint Augustin," *Recherches de théologie ancienne et médiévale* 11 (1939), pp. 5–16.
Dewez, Léon, and Albert van Iterson, "La lactation de saint Bernard: légende et iconographie," *Cîteaux in de Nederlanden* 7 (1956), pp. 165–89.
Deyts, Simone, *Les bois sculptés des sources de la Seine* (Paris, 1983).
Díaz y Díaz, M. C., "La obra de Bernardo de Brihuega, colaborador de Alfonso X," in *Strenae: Estudios de filología e historia dedicados al Profesor Manuel García Blanco* (Acta Salmanticensia: Filosofía y Letras 16, 1962), pp. 145–61.
Dickinson, J. C., *The Shrine of Our Lady of Walsingham* (Cambridge, 1956).
Doble, Gilbert H., *Some Remarks on the Exeter Martyrology (Exeter Chapter MSS. 3518)* (Bristol, 1933).

Dodds, Madeleine Hope, "The Little Book of the Birth of St. Cuthbert," *Archaeologia Aeliana* 4th ser., 6 (1929), pp. 52–94.

Doelle, Ferdinand, "De institutione festi SS. Stigmatum," *Archivum Franciscanum Historicum* 3 (1910), pp. 169–70.

Dolbeau, François, "Notes sur l'organisation interne des légendiers latins," in *Hagiographie, cultures et sociétés, IVe–XIIe siècles: Actes du colloque organisé à Nanterre et à Paris 12–5 mai 1979* (Paris, 1981), pp. 11–29.

———, "Les prologues des légendiers latins," in *Les prologues médiévaux*, ed. Jacquelin Harnesse (Turnhout, 2000), pp. 345–93.

———, "Un vol de reliques dans le diocèse de Reims au milieu du XIe siècle," *Revue Bénédictine* 91 (1981), pp. 172–84.

Dor, Juliette, and Marie-Elisabeth Henneau, eds., *Femmes et pèlerinages* (Compostela Group of Universities, 2007).

Dörfler-Dierken, Angelika, *Die Verehrung der heiligen Anna in Spätmittelalter und früher Neuzeit* (Göttingen, 1992).

Downey, Glanville, "The Shrines of St. Babylas at Antioch and Daphne," in *Antioch-on-the-Orontes* 2, ed. Richard Stillwell (Princeton, 1938), pp. 45–48.

Dubois, Jacques, and Jean-Loup Lemaitre, *Sources et méthodes de l'hagiographie médiévale* (Paris, 1993).

Dubreil-Arcin, Agnès, *Vies de saints, légendes de soi: L'écriture hagiographique dominicaine jusqu'au Speculum sanctorale de Bernard Gui († 1331)* (Turnhout, 2011).

Duffy, Eamon, *The Stripping of the Altars: Traditional Religion in England, c. 1400–c. 1580* (New Haven, 1992).

Duggan, Anne, *Thomas Becket: A Textual History of His Letters* (Oxford, 1980).

Dunin-Wąsowicz, Teresa, "Hagiographie polonaise entre XIe et XVIe siècle," in *Hagiographies* 3, pp. 179–202.

Dunn-Lardeau, Brenda, ed., *Legenda aurea: sept siècles de diffusion* (Montreal, 1986).

Du Plessis, Toussaint, *Histoire de l'église de Meaux* (2 vols., Paris, 1731).

Dupreux, Cécile, "La lactation de saint Bernard de Clairvaux. Genèse et évolution d'une image," in *L'image et la production du sacré*, ed. Françoise Dunand et al. (Paris, 1991), pp. 165–93.

Durnecker, Laurent, "Consécrations d'autels et dépôts de reliques. L'exemple de Saint-Étienne de Dijon du XIe au début du XIIIe s.," in *Mises en scène et mémoires de la consécration de l'église dans l'occident medieval*, ed. Didier Méhu (Turnhout, 2007), pp. 189–216.

———, "Les reliques de St.-Etienne de Dijon du XIe au XVe s.," in *Reliques et sainteté dans l'espace médiéval*, ed. Jean-Luc Deuffic (Pecia 8–11, St.-Denis, 2006), pp. 439–56.

Duval, Yvette, *Auprès des saints corps et âme: l'inhumation "ad sanctos" dans la chrétienté d'Orient et d'Occident du IIIe au VIIe siècle* (Paris, 1988).

———, *Loca sanctorum Africae: le culte des martyrs en Afrique du IVe au VIIe siècle* (2 vols., Collection de l'Ecole Française de Rome 58, 1982).

Eales, Richard, "The Political Setting of the Becket Translation of 1220," in *Martyrs and Martyrologies*, ed. Diana Wood (Studies in Church History 30, 1993), pp. 127–39.

Edmonds, Fiona, "Personal Names and the Cult of Patrick in Eleventh-century Strathclyde and Northumbria," in *Saints' Cults in the Celtic World*, ed. Steve Boardman et al. (Woodbridge, 2009), pp. 42–65.

Efthymiadis, Stephanos, "Greek Byzantine Collections of Miracles: A Chronological and Bibliographical Survey," *Symbolae Osloenses* 74 (1999), pp. 195–211.

———, "Hagiography from the 'Dark Age' to the Age of Symeon Metaphrastes (Eight–Tenth Centuries)," in *The Ashgate Research Companion to Byzantine Hagiography* 1: *Periods and Places*, ed. Stephanos Efthymiadis (Farnham, 2011), pp. 95–142.

———, "Late Byzantine Collections of Miracles and Their Implications," in *The Heroes of the Orthodox Church: The New Saints, 8th–16th c.*, ed. Eleonora Kountoura-Galake (Athens, 2004), pp. 239–250, reprinted with same pagination in Efthymiadis, *Hagiography in Byzantium* (Farnham and Burlington, VT, 2011), item XVI.

Ehrhard, Albert, *Überlieferung und Bestand der hagiographischen und homiletischen Literatur der griechischen Kirche* (3 vols. in 4, Leipzig, 1936–52).

Eire, Carlos M. N., *War against the Idols: The Reformation of Worship from Erasmus to Calvin* (Cambridge, 1986).

Ekroth, Gunnel, "The Cult of Heroes," in *Heroes: Mortals and Myths in Ancient Greece*, ed. Sabine Albersmeier (New Haven, 2009), pp. 120–43.

Ekwall, Eilert, *The Concise Oxford Dictionary of Place Names* (4th ed., Oxford, 1960).

Elliott, Dyan, *Proving Woman: Female Spirituality and Inquisitional Culture in the Later Middle Ages* (Princeton, 2004).

Elm, Kaspar, "Augustinus canonicus–Augustinus hermita: A Quattrocento Cause Célèbre," in *Christianity and the Renaissance: Image and Religious Imagination in the Quattrocento*, ed. Timothy Verdon and John Henderson (Syracuse, NY, 1990), pp. 83–107.

Enamels of Limoges 1100–1350 (New York, 1996).

Enciclopedia cattolica (12 vols., Vatican City, 1948–54).

Encyclopedia of Medieval Pilgrimage, ed. Larissa J. Taylor et al. (Leiden, 2010).

Erb, Rainer, ed., *Die Legende vom Ritualmord: zur Geschichte der Blutbeschuldigung gegen Juden* (Berlin, 1993).

Espinas, Georges, *La vie urbaine de Douai au Moyen Age* (4 vols., Paris, 1913).

Ewig, Eugen, *Spätantikes und fränkisches Gallien: gesammelte Schriften (1952–1973)* (2 vols., Munich, 1976).

Fajt, Jiří, ed., *Court Chapels of the High and Late Middle Ages and Their Artistic Decoration* (Prague, 2003).

———, *Magister Theodoricus, Court Painter to Emperor Charles IV: The Pictorial Decoration of the Shrines at Karlstejn Castle* (Prague, 1998).

Falk, Brigitta, "Bildnisreliquiare. Zur Entstehung und Entwicklung der metallenen Kopf-, Büsten- und Halbfigurenreliquiare im Mittelalter," *Aachener Kunstblätter* 59 (1992/3), pp. 99–238.

Farmer, David Hugh, *The Oxford Dictionary of Saints* (5th ed., Oxford, 2003).

Farmer, Sharon, *Communities of Saint Martin: Legend and Ritual in Medieval Tours* (Ithaca, NY, 1991).

Fenelli, Laura, *Il tau, il fuoco, il maiale. I canonici regolari di Sant'Antonio abate tra assistenza e devozione* (Spoleto, 2006).

Fernández Conde, Francisco Javier, *El libro de los testamentos de la catedral de Oviedo* (Rome, 1971).

Fernández Marcos, Natalio, *Los Thaumata de Sofronio: Contribución al estudio de la incubatio cristiana* (Madrid, 1975).

Field, Sean L., *Isabelle of France: Capetian Sanctity and Franciscan Identity in the Thirteenth Century* (Notre Dame, 2006).

Finucane, Ronald, *Contested Canonizations: The Last Medieval Saints, 1482–1523* (Washington, DC, 2011).

———, *Miracles and Pilgrims: Popular Beliefs in Medieval England* (London, 1977; reiss., Basingstoke, 1995).

———, *The Rescue of the Innocents: Endangered Children in Medieval Miracles* (Basingstoke, 1997).

Fischer, Hans, *Katalog der Handschriften der Universitätsbibliothek Erlangen* 1: *Die Lateinischen Pergamenthandschriften* (Erlangen, 1928).

Flachenecker, Helmut, "Researching *Patrocinia* in German-speaking Lands," in *Saints of Europe: Studies towards a Survey of Cults and Culture*, ed. Graham Jones (Donington, 2003), pp. 74–91.

Flavey, Kathleen C., "The Italian Saint Play: The Example of Perugia," in *The Saint Play in Medieval Europe*, ed. Clifford Davidson (Kalmazoo, 1986), pp. 181–204.

Fleischer, Wolfgang, "Die Namen der Dresdener Ratsmitglieder bis 1500," *Beiträge zur Namenforschung* 12 (1961), pp. 44–87.

Fleith, Barbara, *Studien zur Uberlieferungsgeschichte der lateinischen Legenda Aurea* (SH 72, Brussels, 1991).

Fleith, Barbara, and Martina Backes, "Eine Heilige für alle? Zur Funktion von Elisabethlegenden in Text und Bild im französischsprachigen Raum," in *Elisabeth von Thüringen und die neue Frömmigkeit in Europa*, ed. Christa Bertelsmeier-Kierst (Frankfurt am Main, 2008), pp. 251–74.

Fleith, Barbara, and Franco Morenzoni, eds., *De la sainteté a l'hagiographie: genèse et usage de la Légende dorée* (Geneva, 2001).

Fletcher, Richard, *Saint James's Catapult: The Life and Times of Diego Gelmírez of Santiago de Compostela* (Oxford, 1984).

Flynn, Maureen, *Sacred Charity: Confraternities and Social Welfare in Spain, 1400–1700* (Basingstoke, 1988).

Folz, Robert, *Les saintes reines du Moyen Age en Occident* (SH 76, 1992).

———, *Les saints rois du moyen âge en Occident (VIe–XIIIe s.)* (SH 68, 1984).

Les fonctions des saints dans le monde occidental (IIIe–XIIIe siècle) (Collection de l'École Française de Rome 149, 1991).

Foreville, Raymonde, "Charles d'Orléans et le 'Vin de Saint Thomas,'" in *Thomas Becket dans la tradition historique et hagiographique* (London, 1981), pp. 22–32 (no. XII).

———, *Le jubilé de saint Thomas Becket: du XIIIe au XVe siècle (1220–1470): étude et documents* (Paris, 1958).

———, "Les 'Miracula S. Thomae Cantuarensis,'" in *Thomas Becket dans la tradition historique et hagiographique* (London, 1981), pp. 443–68 (no. VII).

Forsyth, Ilene H., *The Throne of Wisdom: Wood Sculptures of the Madonna in Romanesque France* (Princeton, 1972).

Fouracre, Paul, "Merovingian History and Merovingian Hagiography," *Past and Present* 127 (1990), pp. 3–38.

Franconia sacra: Meisterwerke kirchlicher Kunst des Mittelalters in Franken (Würzburg, 1952).

Frankfurt, Henri, *Ancient Egyptian Religion* (New York, 1948).

Frazier, Alison Knowles, *Possible Lives: Authors and Saints in Renaissance Italy* (New York, 2005).

Freedberg, David, *The Power of Images: Studies in the History and Theory of Response* (Chicago, 1989).

Fröjmark, Anders, "The Canonization Process of Brynolf Algotsson," in *Procès de canonisation au Moyen Age*, ed. Klaniczay, pp. 87–100.

Frugoni, Chiara, *Francesco e l'invenzione delle stimmate* (Turin, 1993).

Gaier, Claude, "Le rôle militaire des reliques et de l'étendard de saint Lambert dans la principauté de Liège," *Le Moyen Âge* 72 (1966), pp. 235–50.

Galletti, Anna Imelda, " 'Infirmitas' e terapia sacra in una città medievale (Orvieto, 1240)," *La Ricerca Folklorica* 8 (1983), pp. 17–34.

Ganshof, F. L., "Charlemagne's Use of the Oath," in *The Carolingians and the Frankish Monarchy* (London, 1971), pp. 111–24.

———, "Pèlerinages expiatoires flamands à Saint-Gilles pendant le XIVe siècle," *Annales du Midi* 78 (1966), pp. 391–407.

Ganz, David, and Walter Goffart, "Charters Earlier than 800 from French Collections," *Speculum* 65 (1990), pp. 906–32.

Gaposchkin, M. Cecilia, *The Making of Saint Louis: Kingship, Sanctity, and Crusade in the Later Middle Ages* (Ithaca, NY, 2008).

García de Cortázar, José Ángel, Elisa Álvarez Llopis, and Carmen Díez Herrera, "Hagionimia de iglesias y monasterios en la diócesis de Burgos en los siglos IX a XIII," *Edad Media* 10 (2009), pp. 183–98.

García de la Borbolla, Angeles "Hagiografía de frontera. Los santos como defensores de un espacio a partir de los relatos hagiográficos peninsulares (siglos XII–XIII)", in *Frontiers in the Middle Ages*, ed. O. Merisalo (Louvain-la-Neuve, 2006), pp. 675–92.

García Rodríguez, Carmen, *El culto de los santos en la España romana y visigoda* (Madrid, 1966).

Gardner, Julian, "Pope Nicholas IV and the Decoration of Santa Maria Maggiore," *Zeitschrift für Kunstgeschichte* 36 (1973), pp. 1–50.

Garms, Jörg, "Gräber von Heiligen und Seligen," in *Skulptur und Grabmal des Spätmittelalters in Rom und Italien*, ed. Jörg Garms and Angiola Maria Romanini (Vienna, 1990), pp. 83–105.

Garrison, F., "A propos des pèlerins et de leur condition juridique," in *Etudes d'histoire du droit canonique dediées à Gabriel Le Bras* (2 vols., Paris, 1965), pp. 1165–89.

Gaudeul, Jean-Marie, "The Correspondence between Leo and Umar: Umar's Letter Rediscovered?," *Islamochristiana* 10 (1984), pp. 109–57.

Geary, Patrick, *Furta sacra: Thefts of Relics in the Central Middle Ages* (2nd ed., Princeton, 1990).

———, "La coercition des saints dans la pratique religeuse médiévale," in *La culture populaire au moyen âge*, ed. Pierre Boglioni (Montreal, 1979), pp. 146–61 (reprinted in his *Living with the Dead* [Ithaca, NY, 1994], pp. 116–24, in English translation).

———, "L'humiliation des saints," *Annales, E.S.C.* 34 (1979), pp. 27–42 (reprinted in *Saints and Their Cults: Studies in Religious Sociology, Folklore and History*, ed. Stephen Wilson [Cambridge, 1983], pp. 123–140, in English translation, and in his *Living with the Dead in the Middle Ages* [Ithaca, NY, 1994], pp. 95–115).

———, "Sacred Commodities: The Circulation of Medieval Relics," in *The Social Life of Things*, ed. Arjun Appadurai (New York, 1986), pp. 169–91.

Geddes, Janes, *The St Albans Psalter* (London, 2005).

Gelfand, Laura D., and Walter S. Gibson, "Surrogate Selves: The Rolin Madonna and the Late-Medieval Devotional Portrait," *Simiolus: Netherlands Quarterly for the History of Art* 29 (2002), pp. 119–38.

Genèse médiévale de l'anthroponymie moderne (6 vols., Tours, 1989–2008).

Gerkan, Armin von, "St. Gereon in Köln," *Germania* 29 (1951), pp. 215–18.
Gero, Stephen, *Byzantine Iconoclasm during the Reign of Constantine V, with Particular Attention to the Oriental Sources* (Louvain, 1977).
———, *Byzantine Iconoclasm during the Reign of Leo III, with Particular Attention to the Oriental Sources* (Louvain, 1973).
———, "The True Image of Christ: Eusebius' Letter to Constantia Reconsidered," *Journal of Theological Studies* 32 (1981), pp. 460–70.
Ghirardacci, Cherubino, *Della historia di Bologna. Parte seconda* (Bologna, 1654).
Gibb, Andrew J., "Pilgrims and Prostitutes: Costume and Identity Construction in Twelfth-Century Liturgical Drama," *Comparative Drama* 42 (2008), pp. 359–84.
Gijsel, Jan, *Die unmittelbare Textüberlieferung des sog. Pseudo-Matthäus* (Brussels, 1981).
Giordano, Oronzo, "Sociologia e patologia del miracolo in Gregorio di Tours," *Helikon (Rivista di tradizione e cultura classica dell'Università di Messina)* 18–19 (1978–9), pp. 161–209.
Girault, Pierre-Gilles, "La châsse et les reliques de saint Gilles au Moyen Age," in *Reliques et sainteté dans l'espace médiéval*, ed. Jean-Luc Deuffic (Pecia 8–11, St.-Denis, 2006), pp. 179–204.
Giunta, Diega, "The Iconography of Catherine of Siena's Stigmata," in *A Companion to Catherine of Siena*, ed. Carolyn Muessig et al. (Leiden, 2012), pp. 259–94.
———, "La questione delle stimmate alle origini della iconografia cateriniana e la fortuna del tema nel corso dei secoli," in *Con l'occhio e col lume. Atti del corso seminariale di studi su S. Caterina da Siena*, ed. Luigi Trenti and Bente Klange Addabbo (Siena, 1999), pp. 319–47.
Glacken, Clarence J., *Traces on the Rhodian Shore: Nature and Culture in Western Thought from Ancient Times to the End of the Eighteenth Century* (Berkeley, 1967).
Glasser, Marc, "Marriage in Medieval Hagiography," *Studies in Medieval and Renaissance History* n.s. 4 (1981), pp. 3–34.
The Glory of Byzantium: Art and Culture of the Middle Byzantine Era, A.D. 843–1261, ed. Helen C. Evans and William D. Wixom (New York, 1997).
Godefroy, Jean, "L'histoire du Prieuré de Saint-Ayoul de Provins et le récit des miracles du saint," *Revue Mabillon* 27 (1937), pp. 94–107; 28 (1938), pp. 29–48, 84–98, 112–25.
Goetz, Hans-Werner, "Heiligenkult und Geschlecht. Geschlechtsspezifisches Wunderwirken in frühmittelalterlichen Mirakelberichten," in *Frauen-Beziehungsgeflechte im Mittelalter (Das Mittelalter 1/2)*, ed. Hedwig Röckelein and Hans-Werner Goetz (1996), pp. 89–111.
———, "Wunderberichte im 9. Jahrhundert. Ein Beitrag zum literarischen Genus der frühmittelalterlichen Mirakelsammlungen," in *Mirakel im Mittelalter: Konzeptionen, Erscheinungsformen, Deutungen*, ed. Martin Heinzelmann et al. (Stuttgart, 2002), pp. 180–226.
Goffart, Walter, *The Narrators of Barbarian History (A.D. 550–800): Jordanes, Gregory of Tours, Bede, and Paul the Deacon* (Princeton, 1988).
Golding, Brian, "The Hermit and the Hunter," in *The Cloister and the World: Essays in Medieval History in Honour of Barbara Harvey*, ed. John Blair and Brian Golding (Oxford, 1996), pp. 95–117.
Goldziher, Ignaz, "Veneration of Saints in Islam," in *Muslim Studies* 2, ed. S. M. Stern (Eng. tr., London, 1971), pp. 255–341.
Golinelli, Paolo, *Città e culto dei santi nel medioevo italiano* (Bologna, 1991).
———, *Il medioevo degli increduli: miscredenti, beffatori, anticlericali* (Milan, 2009).

Gonthier, Dominique, and Claire Le Bas, "Analyse socio-économique de quelques recueils de miracles dans la Normandie du XIe au XIIIe siècle," *Annales de Normandie* 24 (1974), pp. 3–36.

Good, Jonathan, *The Cult of St George in Medieval England* (Woodbridge, 2009).

Goodich, Michael, *Lives and Miracles of the Saints: Studies in Medieval Latin Hagiography* (Aldershot, 2004).

———, *Miracles and Wonders: The Development of the Concept of Miracle, 1150–1350* (Aldershot, 2007).

———, *Violence and Miracle in the Fourteenth Century* (Chicago, 1995).

———, *Vita perfecta: The Ideal of Sainthood in the Thirteenth Century* (Stuttgart, 1982).

Gordon, Dillian, *The Fifteenth Century. Italian Paintings* 1 (National Gallery Catalogues, 2003).

Gorissen, Friedrich, "Ein illuminiertes kölner Gebetbuch aus der Mitte des 15. Jahrhunderts (London, Brit. Mus. Egerton 859)," *Wallraf-Richartz-Jahrbuch* 30 (1968), pp. 129–84.

Görlach, Manfred, "Middle English Legends, 1220–1530," in *Hagiographies* 1, pp. 429–85.

Gothic Mural Painting in Bohemia and Moravia, 1300–1378 (London, 1964).

Gottschaller, Eva, *Hugeburc von Heidenheim: philologische Untersuchungen zu den Heiligenbiographien einer Nonne des achten Jahrhunderts* (Munich, 1973).

Goullet, Monique, *Écriture et réécriture hagiographiques: essai sur les réécritures de Vies de saints dans l'Occident latin médiéval (VIIIe–XIIIe s.)* (Turnhout, 2005).

Goullet, Monique, and Martin Heinzelmann, eds., *La réécriture hagiographique dans l'Occident médiéval: transformations formelles et idéologiques* (Ostfildern, 2003).

Goullet, Monique, Martin Heinzelmann, and Christiane Veyrard-Cosme, eds., *L'hagiographie mérovingienne à travers ses réécritures* (Beihefte zu Francia 71, 2010).

Grabmann, Martin, "Hagiographische Texte in einer Handschrift des kirchenhistorischen Seminars der Universität Muenchen," *Archivum Fratrum Praedicatorum* 19 (1949), pp. 379–82.

Graboïs, Aryeh, "Louis VII pèlerin," *Revue d'histoire de l'Eglise en France* 74 (1988), pp. 5–22.

Graus, František, "Der Heilige als Schlachtenhelfer-Zur Nationalisierung einer Wundererzählung in der mittelalterlichen Chronistik," in *Festschrift für Helmut Beumann zum 65. Geburtstag*, ed. Kurt-Ulrich Jäschke and Reinhard Wenskus (Sigmaringen, 1977), pp. 330–48.

———, "Die Gewalt bei den Anfängen des Feudalismus und die 'Gefangenenbefreiungen' der merowingischen Hagiographie," *Jahrbuch für Wirtschaftsgeschichte* (1961, part 1), pp. 61–156.

———, *Volk, Herrscher und Heiliger im Reich der Merowinger: Studien zur Hagiographie der Merowingerzeit* (Prague, 1965).

Gravdal, Kathryn, *Ravishing Maidens: Writing Rape in Medieval French Literature* (Philadelphia, 1991).

Graviers, Jean des, "L'expression 'dominicae resurrectionis dies' dans les oeuvres de Grégoire de Tours," *Ephemerides liturgicae* 48 (1934), pp. 289–300.

Gray, H. L., "Incomes from Land in England in 1436," *English Historical Review* 49 (1934), pp. 607–39.

Grégoire, Réginald, *Manuale di agiologia: introduzione alla letteratura agiografica* (2nd ed., Fabriano, 1996).

Gregorio Magno e l'agiografia fra IV e VII secolo, ed. Antonio Degl'Innocenti et al. (Florence, 2007).

Gremont, Denis-Bernard, "Lectiones ad prandium à l'abbaye de Fécamp au XIIIe siècle," *Cahiers Leopold Delisle* 20 (1971, 2nd semestre), pp. 1–41.

Gretsch, Mechthild, *Ælfric and the Cult of Saints in Late Anglo-Saxon England* (Cambridge, 2005).

Grimaldi, Floriano, *La chiesa di Santa Maria di Loreto nei documentia des seculi XII–XV* (Ancona, 1984).

———, *La historia della Chiesa di Santa Maria de Loreto* (Loreto, 1993).

Grimme, Ernst Günther, *Hans von Reutlingen: "golsmit zo aach"* (Aachen, 1999).

Grosjean, Paul, "The Alleged Irish Origin of St. Cuthbert," in *The Relics of Saint Cuthbert*, ed. C. F. Battiscombe (Oxford, 1956), pp. 144–54.

Grosser Historischer Weltatlas 2: Mittelalter (Bayerische Schulbuch-Verlag, rev. ed., Munich, 1979).

Grotefend, Hermann, *Zeitrechnung des deutschen Mittelalters und der Neuzeit* (2 vols., Hanover, 1891–98).

Grotowski, Piotr Ł., *Arms and Armour of the Warrior Saints: Tradition and Innovation in Byzantine Iconography (843–1261)* (Leiden, 2010).

Guillot, Olivier, "Les saints des peuples et des nations," in *Santi e demoni nell'alto medioevo occidentale* (2 vols., Settimane di Studio 36, 1989) 1, pp. 205–51.

Guiter, Henri, "Églises et toponymie sur les Pyrénées Orientales," in *Espaces religieux et communautés méridionaux: Actes du 64e congrès de la Fédération historique du Languedoc méditerranéen et du Roussillon, Villeneuve-lès-Avignon, 15–17 mai 1992* (Montpellier, 1994), pp. 11–17.

Gunn, Victoria A., "Bede and the Martyrdom of St. Oswald," in *Martyrs and Martyrologies*, ed. Diana Wood (Studies in Church History 30, 1993), pp. 57–66.

Haarländer, Stephanie, *Vitae episcoporum. Eine Quellengattung zwischen Hagiographie und Historiographie, untersucht an Lebensbeschreibungen von Bischöfen des Regnum Teutonicum im Zeitalter der Ottonen und Salier* (Stuttgart, 2000).

Haasis-Berner, Andreas, *Pilgerzeichen des Hochmittelalters* (Veröffentlichungen zur Volkskunde und Kulturgeschichte 94, Würzburg, 2003).

Haenens, Albert d', *Les invasions normandes en Belgique au IXe siècle* (Louvain, 1967).

Hagiographies: Histoire internationale de la littérature hagiographique latine et vernaculaire en Occident des origines à 1550, ed. Guy Philippart (5 vols. to date, CC, 1994–).

Hahn, Cynthia, *Portrayed on the Heart: Narrative Effect in Pictorial Lives of the Saints from the Tenth through the Thirteenth Century* (Berkeley, 2001).

Hall, Ursula, *St Andrew and Scotland* (St. Andrews, 1994).

Hallenbeck, Jan T., *The Transferral of the Relics of St. Augustine of Hippo from Sardinia to Pavia in the Early Middle Ages* (Lewiston, NY, 2000).

Hamann, Richard, *Die Abteikirche von St. Gilles und ihre künstlerische Nachfolge* (3 vols., Berlin, 1955).

Harbison, Peter, *The High Crosses of Ireland: An Iconographical and Photographic Survey* (3 vols., Bonn, 1992).

Harbus, Antonina, *Helena of Britain in Medieval Legend* (Cambridge, 2002).

Harris, Julie A., "Muslim Ivories in Christian Hands: The Leire Casket in Context," *Art History* 18 (1995), pp. 213–21.

Hart, Richard, "The Shrines and Pilgrimages of the County of Norfolk," *Norfolk Archaeology* 6 (1864), pp. 277–94.

Harvey, Barbara, "Work and 'Festa Ferianda' in Medieval England," *Journal of Ecclesiastical History* 23 (1972), pp. 289–308.

Hazebrouck-Souche, Véronique, *Spiritualité, sainteté et patriotisme. Glorification du Brabant dans l'oeuvre hagiographique de Jean Gielemans (1427–1487)* (Turnhout, 2007).

Head, Thomas, "The Genesis of the Ordeal of Relics by Fire in Ottonian Germany: An Alternative Form of 'Canonization,'" in *Procès de canonisation au Moyen Age*, ed. Klaniczay, pp. 19–37.

———, *Hagiography and the Cult of the Saints: The Diocese of Orleans, 800–1200* (Cambridge, 1990).

———, "'I Vow Myself to Be Your Servant': An Eleventh-Century Pilgrim, His Chronicler, and His Saint," *Historical Reflections/Réflexions Historiques* 11 (1984), pp. 215–251.

———, "Saints, Heretics, and Fire: Finding Meaning through the Ordeal," in *Monks and Nuns, Saints and Outcasts*, ed. Sharon Farmer and Barbara Rosenwein (Ithaca, NY, 2000), pp. 220–38.

Heffernan, Thomas J., "'God hathe schewed forr him many grete miracules': Political Canonization and the Miracula of Simon de Montfort," in *Art and Context in Late Medieval English Narrative: Essays in Honor of Robert Worth Frank, Jr.*, ed. Robert R. Edwards (Cambridge, 1994), pp. 177–91.

———, *Sacred Biography: Saints and Their Biographers in the Middle Ages* (New York and Oxford, 1988).

Hegel, Eduard, *Das mittelalterliche Pfarrsystem und seine kirchliche Infrastruktur in Köln um 1500* (Geschichtlicher Atlas der Rheinlande IX.1, Cologne, 1992).

Heinzelmann, Martin, *Translationsberichte und andere Quellen des Reliquienkultes* (Turnhout, 1979).

———, "Une source de base de la littérature hagiographique latine: le recueil de miracles," in *Hagiographie, cultures et sociétés IVe–XIIe siècles* (Paris, 1981), pp. 235–59.

Heinzelmann, Martin, and Jean-Claude Poulin, *Les vies anciennes de Saint Geneviève de Paris* (Paris, 1986).

Héliot, Pierre, and Marie-Laure Chastang, "Quêtes et voyages des reliques au profit des églises françaises du Moyen Age," *Revue d'histoire ecclésiastique* 59 (1964), pp. 783–822; 60 (1965), pp. 5–32.

Hen, Yitzhak, *Culture and Religion in Merovingian Gaul A.D. 481–751* (Leiden, 1995).

Hengst, Karl, "Die Altäre und Benefizien des Paderborner Domes und anliegender Kapellen von 777–1550," in *Felix Paderae civitas. Der heilige Liborius 836–1986*, ed. Hans Jürgen Brandt and Karl Hengst (Paderborn, 1986), pp. 214–65.

Hennig, John, "The Meaning of All the Saints," *Medieval Studies* 10 (1948), pp. 147–61.

Henriet, Patrick, "*Rex, lex, plebs.* Les miracles d'Isidore de Séville à León (XIe–XIIIe siècles)," in *Mirakel im Mittelalter: Konzeptionen, Erscheinungsformen, Deutungen*, ed. Martin Heinzelmann et al. (Stuttgart, 2002), pp. 334–50.

———, "Un hagiographe au travail: Raoul et la reécriture du dossier de Zoile de Carrión (années 1130)," in *La réécriture hagiographique dans l'Occident médiéval*, ed. Goullet and Heinzelmann, pp. 251–83.

Herbers, Klaus, "Politik und Heiligenverehrung auf der Iberischen Halbinsel. Die Entwicklung des 'politischen Jakobus,'" in *Politik und Heiligenverehrung im Hochmittelalter*, ed. Jürgen Petersohn (Vorträge und Forschungen 42, Sigmaringen, 1994), pp. 177–275.

Herbert, Máire, "Hagiography and Holy Bodies: Observations on Corporeal Relics in Pre-Viking Ireland," in *L'Irlanda e gli irlandesi nell'alto Medioevo* (Settimane di Studio 57, Spoleto, 2010), pp. 239–57.

———, *Iona, Kells, and Derry: The History and Hagiography of the Monastic familia of Columba* (Oxford, 1988).

———, "Latin and Vernacular Hagiography of Ireland from the Origins to the Sixteenth Century," in *Hagiographies* 3, pp. 327–60.

Herlihy, David, "Did Women Have a Renaissance? A Reconsideration," *Medievalia et Humanistica* 13 (1985), pp. 1–22 (repr. in his *Women, Family, and Society in Medieval Europe: Historical Essays,* 1978–1991 [Providence, 1995], pp. 33–56).

———, "Tuscan Names, 1200–1530," *Renaissance Quarterly* 41 (1988), pp. 561–82.

Herren, Judith, "Book Burning as Purification," in *Transformations of Late Antiquity. Essays for Peter Brown*, ed. Philip Rousseau and Manolis Papoutsakis (Farnham, 2009), pp. 205–22.

Herrick, Samantha Kahn, "Studying Apostolic Hagiography: The Case of Fronto of Périgueux, Disciple of Christ," *Speculum* 85 (2010), pp. 235–70.

Herrmann-Mascard, Nicole, *Les reliques des saints: Formation coutumière d'un droit* (Paris, 1975).

Héry, Laurent, "Le culte de Charles de Blois: résistances et réticences," *Annales de Bretagne* 103/2 (1996), pp. 39–56.

Hess, Cordelia, *Heilige machen im spätmittelalterlichen Ostseeraum: die Kanonisationsprozesse von Birgitta von Schweden, Nikolaus von Linköping und Dorothea von Montau* (Berlin, 2008).

Heuclin, Jean, "L'ermite et la mort durant le haut Moyen Age," *Revue du Nord* 68 (1986), pp. 153–68.

Higgitt, John, *"Imageis maid with mennis hand": Saints, Images, Belief and Identity in Later Medieval Scotland* (Whithorn, 2003).

Higounet, Charles, "Les saints mérovingiens d'Aquitaine dans la toponymie," in *Paysages et villages neufs du Moyen Age* (Bordeaux, 1975), pp. 67–75.

The History of Parliament: The House of Commons 1386–1421, ed. J. S. Roskell et al. (4 vols., Stroud, 1993).

Hlaváček, Ivan, "Die heimischen und lokalen Heiligen in den urkundlichen Datierungen Böhmens des Hoch- und Spätmittelalters (einige Sondierungen)," in *Fonctions sociales et politiques du culte des saints dans les sociétés de rite grec et latin au Moyen Age et à l'époque moderne. Approche comparative*, ed. Marek Derwich and Michel Dmitrev (Wrocław, 1999), pp. 237–46.

Hodges, Richard, *Light in the Dark Ages: The Rise and Fall of San Vincenzo al Volturno* (London, 1997).

Hoffmann, Erich, *Die heiligen Könige bei den Angelsachsen und den skandinavistischen Völkern* (Neumünster, 1975).

Hoffmann, Hartmut, *Gottesfriede und Treuga Dei* (MGH, Schriften, Stuttgart, 1964).

Hofmann, Hans, *Die Heiligen Drei Könige: zur Heiligenverehrung im kirchlichen, gesellschaftlichen und politischen Leben des Mittelalters* (Bonn, 1975).

Hofmeister, Philipp, *Die christlichen Eidesformen: eine liturgie- und rechtsgeschichtliche Untersuchung* (Munich, 1957).

Høgel, Christian, *Symeon Metaphrastes: Rewriting and Canonization* (Copenhagen, 2002).

Holum, Kenneth G., and Gary Vikan, "The Trier Ivory, *Adventus* Ceremonial, and the Relics of St. Stephen," *Dumbarton Oaks Papers* 33 (1979), pp. 113–33.

Hope, Charles, "Altarpieces and the Requirements of Patrons," in *Christianity and the Renaissance: Image and Religious Imagination in the Quattrocento*, ed. Timothy Verdon and John Henderson (Syracuse, NY, 1990), pp. 535–71.

Horníčková, Kateřina, "Memory, Politics, and Holy Relics: Catholic Tactics amidst the Bohemian Reformation," *Bohemian Reformation and Religious Practice* 8 (2011), pp. 135–44.

Hoving, Thomas P. F., "The Face of St. Juliana: The Transformation of a Fourteenth Century Reliquary," *Metropolitan Museum of Art Bulletin* n.s. 21 (1962–63), pp. 173–81.

Howard-Johnston, James, and Paul Antony Hayward, eds., *The Cult of Saints in Late Antiquity and the Middle Ages: Essays on the Contribution of Peter Brown* (Oxford, 1999).

Howe, John, *Church Reform and Social Change in Eleventh-Century Italy: Dominic of Sora and His Patrons* (Philadelphia, 1997).

———, "The Hagiography of Saint-Wandrille (Fontenelle)," in *L'hagiographie du haut moyen age en Gaule du nord: manuscrits, textes et centres de production*, ed. Martin Heinzelmann (Beihefte zu Francia 52, 2001), pp. 127–92.

———, "Saintly Statistics," *Catholic Historical Review* 70 (1984), pp. 74–82.

Hsia, R. Po-chia, *Trent 1475: Stories of a Ritual Murder Trial* (New Haven, 1992).

Hubert, Jean, and Marie-Clotilde Hubert, "Piété chrétienne ou paganisme? Les statues-reliquaires de l'Europe carolingienne," in *Cristianizzazione ed organizzazione ecclesiastica delle campagne nell'alto medioevo: espansione e resistenze* (Settimane di Studio 28, 2 vols., 1982), 1, pp. 235–68.

Hudson, Anne, *The Premature Reformation: Wycliffite Texts and Lollard History* (Oxford, 1988).

Hughes, Kathleen, "British Museum Manuscript Vespasian A XIV ('Vitae Sanctorum Wallensium'): Its Purpose and Provenance," in *Studies in the Early British Church*, ed. Nora K. Chadwick (Cambridge, 1958), pp. 183–200.

———, "The Changing Theory and Practice of Irish Pilgrimage," *Journal of Ecclesiastical History* 11 (1960), pp. 143–51.

Humfrey, Peter, *The Altarpiece in Renaissance Florence* (New York and London, 1993).

Hummel, Edelhard, *The Concept of Martyrdom according to St. Cyprian* (Washington, DC, 1946).

Hunt, E. D., *Holy Land Pilgrimage in the Later Roman Empire AD 312–460* (Oxford, 1982).

Hunt, R. W., *The Schools and the Cloister: The Life and Writings of Alexander Nequam* (Oxford, 1984).

Hussey, Joan, "The Canons of John Mauropous," *Journal of Roman Studies* 37 (1947), pp. 70–73.

Hyams, Paul, "The Strange Case of Thomas of Eldersfield," *History Today* 36 (1986), pp. 9–15.

Insley, John, "Anglo-Saxons in Rome: The Evidence of the Names," in *Nomen et Fraternitas: Festschrift for Dieter Geuenich on His 65th Birthday*, ed. Uwe Ludwig and Thomas Schilp (Berlin and New York, 2008), pp. 107–13.

Iskander, John, "Islamization in Medieval Egypt: the Copto-Arabic 'Apocalypse of Samuel' as a Source for the Social and Religious History of Medieval Copts," *Medieval Encounters* 4 (1998), pp. 219–27.

Jaffé, Philip, *Regesta pontificum romanorum . . . ad annum . . . 1198* (rev. ed., 2 vols., Leipzig, 1885–88).

Jancey, Meryl, ed., *St Thomas Cantilupe, Bishop of Hereford: Essays in His Honour* (Hereford, 1982).

Janin, Raymond, *La géographie ecclésiastique de l'Empire byzantin: Première partie, Le siège de Constantinople et le patriarcat oecuménique. Tome III, Les églises et les monastères* (2nd ed., Paris, 1969).

Janini, José, and José Serrano, *Manuscritos litúrgicos de la Biblioteca Nacional* (Madrid, 1969).

Jankulak, Karen, *The Medieval Cult of St Petroc* (Woodbridge, 2000).

Jansen, Annemiek, "The Development of the St. Oswald Legends on the Continent," in *Oswald: Northumbrian King to European Saint*, ed. Clare Stancliffe and Eric Cambridge (Stamford, 1995), pp. 230–40.

Jansen, Philippe, "Un exemple de sainteté thaumaturgique à la fin du Moyen Âge: les miracles de St. Bernardine de Sienne," *Mélanges de l'Ecole française de Rome. Moyen Age* 96 (1984), pp. 129–51.

Jansen, Stefanie, *Wo ist Thomas Becket? Der ermordete Heilige zwischen Erinnerung und Erzählung* (Husum, 2002).

Jenal, Georg, *Erzbischof Anno II. von Köln (1056–1075) und sein politisches Wirken. Ein Beitrag zur Geschichte des Reichs- und Territorialpolitik im 11. Jahrhundert* (2 vols., Stuttgart, 1974–75).

Jeremias, Joachim, *Heiligengräber in Jesu Umwelt* (Göttingen, 1958).

Joassart, Bernard, "Hippolyte Delehaye (1859–1941): Un bollandiste au temps de la crise moderniste," in *Sanctity and Secularity during the Modernist Period*, ed. L. Barmann and C.J.T. Talar (SH 79, 1999), pp. 1–45.

Johnson, Richard Freeman, *Saint Michael the Archangel in Medieval English Legend* (Woodbridge, 2005).

Johnson, Scott Fitzgerald, *The Life and Miracles of Thekla: A Literary Study* (Washington, DC, 2006).

Jolly, Karen Louise, "Prayers from the Field: Practical Protection and Demonic Defense in Anglo-Saxon England," *Traditio* 61 (2006), pp. 95–147.

Jones, Graham, *Saints in the Landscape* (Stroud, 2007).

Jordan, William C., *From Servitude to Freedom: Manumission in the Sénonais in the Thirteenth Century* (Philadelphia, 1986).

Jørgensen, Torstein, and Gastone Saletnich, *Letters to the Pope: Norwegian Relations to the Holy See in the Late Middle Ages* (Stavanger, 1999).

Jost, Michael F. P., *Die Patrozinien der Kirchen der Stadt Rom vom Anfang bis in das 10. Jahrhundert* (Horrea 3, Neuried, 2000).

Journey through the Afterlife: Ancient Egyptian Book of the Dead, ed. John H. Taylor (London, 2010).

Jung, Jacqueline E., "From Jericho to Jerusalem: The Violent Transformation of Archbishop Engelbert of Cologne," in *Last Things: Death and the Apocalypse in the Middle Ages*, ed. Caroline Walker Bynum and Paul Freedman (Philadelphia, 2000), pp. 60–82.

Junghans, Martina, *Die Armreliquiare in Deutschland vom 11. bis zur Mitte des 13. Jahrhunderts* (PhD Dissertation, Rheinische Friedrich-Wilhelms-Universität, Bonn, 2002).

Justice, Steven, "Did the Middle Ages Believe in their Miracles?," *Representations* 103 (2008), pp. 1–29.

Kaftal, George, *Iconography of the Saints in Italian Painting from Its Beginnings to the Early XVIth Century* (4 vols., Florence, 1952–85).

Kaiser, Reinhold, "Quêtes itinérantes avec des reliques pour financer la construction des églises (XIe–XIIe siècles)," *Le Moyen Age: Revue d'histoire et de philologie* 101:2 (1995), pp. 205–225.

Karras, Ruth Mazo, "Holy Harlots: Prostitute Saints in Medieval Legend," *Journal of the History of Sexuality* 1 (1990), pp. 3–32.

Kauffmann, C. M., *Romanesque Manuscripts, 1066–1190* (A Survey of Manuscripts Illuminated in the British Isles 3, London, 1975).

Kedar, Benjamin Z., "Noms de saints et mentalité populaire à Gênes au XIVe siècle," *Le Moyen Age* 73 (1967), pp. 431–46.

Kellner, K. A. Heinrich, *Heortologie: oder die geschichtliche Entwicklung des Kirchjahres und der Heiligenfeste von den ältesten Zeiten bis zur Gegenwart* (3rd ed., Freiburg im Breisgau, 1911).

Kelly, Fergus, *A Guide to Early Irish Law* (Dublin, 1988).

Kemp, Eric W., *Canonization and Authority in the Western Church* (London, 1948).

Kennedy, V. L., *The Saints of the Canon of the Mass* (2nd ed., Vatican City, 1963).

Ker, N. R., *Medieval Manuscripts in British Libraries* 2: *Abbotsford-Keele* (Oxford, 1977).

Ker, N. R., and A. J. Piper, *Medieval Manuscripts in British Libraries* 4 (Oxford, 1992).

Kieckhefer, Richard, *Unquiet Souls: Fourteenth-Century Saints and Their Religious Milieu* (Chicago, 1984).

Kings, Queens and Courtiers: Art in Early Renaissance France, ed. Martha Wolff (Art Institute of Chicago, 2011).

Kirk, James, "Iconoclasm and Reform," *Records of the Scottish Church History Society* 24 [1990–92]), pp. 366–83.

Kishpaugh, Mary Jerome, *The Feast of the Presentation of the Virgin Mary in the Temple: An Historical and Literary Study* (Washington, DC, 1941).

Kitzinger, Ernst, "The Cult of Images in the Age before Iconoclasm," *Dumbarton Oaks Papers* 8 (1954), pp. 83–150.

Klaniczay, Gábor, "Dreams and Visions in Medieval Miracle Accounts," in *Ritual Healing: Magic, Ritual and Medical Therapy from Antiquity until the Early Modern Period*, ed. Ildikó Csepregi and Charles Burnett (Micrologus Library 48, Florence, 2012), pp. 147–70.

———, *Holy Rulers and Blessed Princesses: Dynastic Cults in Medieval Central Europe* (Eng. tr., Cambridge, 2002).

———, "Miracoli di punizione e maleficia," in *Miracoli: dai segni alla storia*, ed. Sofia Boesch Gajano and Marilena Modica (Rome, 1999), pp. 109–35.

Klaniczay, G., and E. Madas, "La Hongrie," in *Hagiographies* 2 (1996), pp. 103–60.

Klapisch-Zuber, Christiane, "Le nom 'refait,'" *L'Homme* 20 (1980), pp. 77–104.

Klauser, Theodor, "Christlicher Märtyrerkult, heidnischer Heroenkult und spätjüdische Heiligenverehrung," in *Gesammelte Arbeiten zur Liturgiegeschichte, Kirchengeschichte und christlichen Archäologie* (Münster, 1974), pp. 221–29.

———, "Festankündigung," in *Reallexikon für Antike und Christentum* 7 (Stuttgart, 1969), cols. 767–85.

Klein, Holger A., "Eastern Objects and Western Desires: Relics and Reliquaries between Byzantium and the West," *Dumbarton Oaks Papers* 58 (2004), pp. 283–314.

Kleinberg, Aviad M., *Prophets in Their Own Country: Living Saints and the Making of Sainthood in the Late Middle Ages* (Chicago, 1992).

———, "Proving Sanctity: Selection and Authentication of Saints in the Later Middle Ages," *Viator* 20 (1989), pp. 183–205.

Kleine, Uta, *Gesta, fama, scripta: Rheinische Mirakel des Hochmittelalters zwischen Geschichtsdeutung, Erzählung und sozialer Praxis* (Stuttgart, 2007).

Kleinschmidt, Beda, *Die heilige Anna: ihre Verehrung in Geschichte, Kunst und Volkstum* (Düsseldorf, 1930).

Klingender, Francis, *Animals in Art and Thought to the End of the Middle Ages*, ed. Evelyn Antal and John Harthan (London, 1971).

Klüppel, Theodor, "Die Germania (750–950)," in *Hagiographies* 2, pp. 161–209.

Kolia-Dermitzaki, Athina, "The Execution of the Forty-two Martyrs of Amorion: Proposing an Interpretation," *Al-Masaq* 14 (2002), pp. 141–62.

Kolmer, Lothar, *Promissorische Eide im Mittelalter* (Regensburg, 1989).

Koopmans, Rachel, "The Conclusion of Christina of Markyate's Vita," *Journal of Ecclesiastical History* 51 (2000), pp. 663–97.

———, *Wonderful to Relate: Miracle Stories and Miracle Collecting in High Medieval England* (Philadelphia, 2011).

Koster, Kurt, "Gütenbergs Strassburger Aachenspiegel-Unternehmen von 1438/1440," *Gutenberg-Jahrbuch* 58 (1983), pp. 24–44.

Köster, Kurt, "Mittelalterliche Pilgerzeichen von Notre-Dame de Rocamadour," in *Pilgerzeichen und Pilgermuscheln von mittelalterlichen Santiagostraßen* (Ausgrabungen in Schleswig: Berichte und Studien 2, Neumünster, 1983), pp. 43–88.

Kötting, Bernhard, *Der frühchristliche Reliquienkult und die Bestattung im Kirchengebäude* (Cologne and Opladen, 1965).

———, *Peregrinatio religiosa: Wallfahrten in der Antike und das Pilgerwesen in der alten Kirche* (Münster, 1950).

Kovács, Eva, "Le chef de Saint Maurice a la cathedrale de Vienne (France)," *Cahiers de civilisation médiévale* 7 (1964), pp. 19–26.

Koziol, Geoffrey, "Monks, Feuds, and the Making of Peace in Eleventh-Century Flanders," in *The Peace of God: Social Violence and Religious Response*, ed. Thomas Head and Richard Landes (Ithaca, NY, 1992), pp. 239–59.

Kracht, Hans-Joachim, and Jakob Torsy, *Reliquiarium Coloniense* (Siegburg, 2003).

Krafft, Otfried, *Papsturkunde und Heiligsprechung: die päpstlichen Kanonisationen vom Mittelalter bis zur Reformation: ein Handbuch* (Cologne, 2005).

Krausmüller, Dirk, "God or Angels as Impersonators of Saints: A Belief and Its Contexts in the 'Refutation' of Eustratius of Constantinople and in the Writings of Anastasius of Sinai," *Gouden Hoorn/Golden Horn* 6/2 (1998–99) (on-line journal).

Kretzenbacher, Leopold, *Die Seelenwaage: Zur religiösen Idee vom Jenseitsgericht auf der Schicksalswaage in Hochreligion, Bildkunst und Volksglaube* (Klagenfurt, 1958).

Krötzl, Christian, "*Fama sanctitatis:* Die Akten der spätmittelalterlichen Kanonisationsprozesse als Quelle zu Kommunikation und Informationsvermittlung in der mittelalterlichen Gesellschaft," in *Procès de canonisation au Moyen Age*, ed. Klaniczay, pp. 223–44.

———, "Miracles au tombeau—miracles à distance. Approches typologiques," in *Miracle et karāma*, pp. 557–76.

———, *Pilger, Mirakel und Alltag: Formen des Verhaltens im skandinavischen Mittelalter (12.–15.Jht.)* (Helsinki, 1994).

Krüger, Astrid, *Litanei-Handschriften der Karolingerzeit* (MGH, Hilfsmittel 24, Hanover, 2007).

Krüger, Klaus, "Elisabeth von Thüringen und Maria Magdalena. Reliquien als Geburtshelfer im späten Mittelalter," *Zeitschrift des Vereins für Thüringische Geschichte* 54 (2000), pp. 75–108.

Küch, Friedrich, "Zur Geschichte der Reliquien der Heiligen Elisabeth," *Zeitschrift für Kirchengeschichte* 45 (N.F. 8) (1927), pp. 198–215.

Kühne, Hartmut, *Ostensio Reliquiarum: Untersuchungen über Entstehung, Ausbreitung, Gestalt und Funktion der Heiltumsweisungen im Römisch-deutschen Regnum* (Berlin, 2000).

Külze, Andreas, *Peregrinatio graeca in Terram Sanctam: Studien zu Pilgerführern und Reisebeschreibungen über Syrien, Palästina und den Sinai aus byzantinischer und metabyzantinischer Zeit* (Frankfurt, 1994).

Kuttner, Stephan, "La réserve papale du droit de canonisation," *Revue historique de droit français et étranger*, 4th ser., 17 (1938), pp. 172–228 (repr. in *The History of Ideas and Doctrines of Canon Law in the Middle Ages* [London, 1980] with same pagination).

Ladner, Gerhart B., "The So-called Square Nimbus," in *Images and Ideas in the Middle Ages: Selected Studies in History and Art* (2 vols., Rome, 1983), 2, pp. 115–66.

Landes, Richard, *Relics, Apocalypse, and the Deceits of History: Ademar of Chabannes, 989–1034* (Cambridge, MA, 1995).

Landes, Richard, and Thomas Head, eds., *The Peace of God: Social Violence and Religious Response around the Year 1000* (Ithaca, NY, 1992).

Lang, Gotthard, "Gunther der Eremit in Geschichte, Sage und Kult," *Studien und Mitteilungen zur Geschichte des Benediktinerordens und seiner Zweige* 59 (1941/2), pp. 1–83.

Langmuir, Gavin, "Thomas of Monmouth: Detector of Ritual Murder," *Speculum* 59 (1984), pp. 820–46 (also in his *History, Religion and Antisemitism* [Berkeley, 1990]).

Lanzoni, Francesco, "Il sogno presago della madre incinta nella letteratura medievale e antica," AB 45 (1927), pp. 225–61.

Lapidge, Michael, "Ælfric's Sanctorale," in *Holy Men and Holy Women: Old English Prose Saints' Lives and Their Contexts*, ed. Paul E. Szarmach (Albany, NY, 1996), pp. 115–29.

———, "A New Hiberno-Latin Hymn on St Martin," *Celtica* 21 (1990), pp. 240–51.

Laporte, Jean-Pierre, *Le trésor des saints de Chelles* (Chelles, 1988).

Lappin, Anthony, *The Medieval Cult of Saint Dominic of Silos* (Leeds, 2002).

Lapsley, Gaillard T., *The County Palatine of Durham* (Cambridge, MA, 1900).

Lasko, Peter, *Ars Sacra, 800–1200* (2nd ed., New Haven, 1994).

Lauer, Rolf, *Der Schrein der Heiligen Drei Könige* (Cologne, 2006).

Laurent, Françoise, *Plaire et édifier: les récits hagiographiques composés en Angleterre aux XIIe et XIIIe siècles* (Paris, 1998).

Lauwers, Michel, "La mort et le corps des saints: La scène de la mort dans les vitae du haut Moyen Age," *Le Moyen Age* 94 (1988), pp. 21–50.

Lawrence, C. H., *The Life of St Edmund by Matthew Paris* (Stroud, 1996).

Lawrence-Mathers, Anne, *Manuscripts in Northumbria in the Eleventh and Twelfth Centuries* (Woodbridge, 2003).

Lazarev, Viktor Nikitich, *The Russian Icon from Its Origins to the Sixteenth Century* (Eng. tr., Collegeville, MN, 1997).

Le Breton-Filippusdóttir, Steinunn, "Hagiographie vernaculaire d'Island et de Norvège," in *Hagiographies* 3, pp. 361–451.

Leclercq, Jean, "Saint Antoine dans la tradition monastique médiévale," *Studia Anselmiana* 38 (1956), pp. 229–47.

Lefort, Louis, "La chasse aux reliques des martyrs en Egypte au IVe. siècle," *La Nouvelle Clio* 6 (1954), pp. 225–30.

Legge, M. Dominica, *Anglo-Norman Literature and Its Background* (Oxford, 1963).

Legner, Anton, *Kölner Heilige und Heiligtümer: ein Jahrtausend europäischer Reliquienkultur* (Cologne, 2003).

———, *Reliquien in Kunst und Kult zwischen Antike und Aufklärung* (Darmstadt, 1995).

Le Goff, Jacques, *À la recherche du temps sacré: Jacques de Voragine et la Légende dorée* (Paris, 2011).

Leisibach, Josef, *Die liturgischen Handschriften des Kapitelsarchiv in Sitten* (Iter Helveticum 3, Freiburg, 1979).

Lemeneva, Elena, "The Borders and Borderlines of Sainthood: On the Stigmata of St. Catherine of Siena," *Annual of Medieval Studies at Central European University* 6 (2000), pp. 193–202.

Lepelley, Claude, "Les réticences de saint Augustin face aux légendes hagiographiques d'après la lettre Divjak 29*," in *Transformations of Late Antiquity: Essays for Peter Brown*, ed. Philip Rousseau and Manolis Papoutsakis (Farnham, 2009), pp. 147–58.

Lequeux, Xavier, "Latin Hagiographical Literature Translated into Greek," in *The Ashgate Research Companion to Byzantine Hagiography* 1: *Periods and Places*, ed. Stephanos Efthymiadis (Farnham, 2011), pp. 385–99.

Lermen, Birgit, and Dieter Wynands, *Die Aachenfahrt in Geschichte und Literatur* (Aachen, 1986).

Leroquais, Victor, *Les bréviaires manuscrits des bibliothèques publiques de France* (6 vols., Paris, 1934).

———, *Les psautiers manuscrits des bibliothèques publiques de France* (2 vols., plus vol. of plates, Mâcon, 1940–41).

Lerou, Sandrine, "L'usage des reliques du Christ par les empereurs aux XIe et XIIe siècles: le saint bois et les saints pierres," in *Byzance et les reliques du Christ*, ed. Jannic Durand and Bernard Flusin (Paris, 2004), pp. 159–82.

Leroy, Beatrice, "La mort et la vie chrétienne en Navarre au XIVe siècle (Etude de testaments de la seconde moitié du XIVe siècle)," *Scripta Theologica* 16 (1984), pp. 485–97.

Lett, Didier, *Un procès de canonisation au Moyen Âge: essai d'histoire sociale: Nicolas de Tolentino, 1325* (Paris, 2008).

Levison, Wilhelm, "Conspectus codicum hagiographicorum," in MGH, SRM 7 (Hanover, 1920), pp. 529–706.

Lewis, Katherine J., *The Cult of St Katherine of Alexandria in Late Medieval England* (Woodbridge, 2000).

———, " 'Lete me suffre': Reading the Torture of St. Margaret of Antioch in Late Medieval England," in *Medieval Women: Texts and Contexts in Late Medieval Britain. Essays for Felicity Riddy*, ed. Jocelyn Wogan-Browne et al. (Turnhout, 2000), pp. 69–82.

Lexicon der christliche Ikonographie, ed. Wolfgang Braunfels (8 vols., Rome, 1968–76).

Lexikon der antiken christlichen Literatur, ed. Siegmar Döpp and Wilhlem Geerlings (Freiburg, 1998).

Lexikon des Mittelalters (9 vols., Munich, 1977–99).

Leyser, Conrad, "The Temptations of Cult: Roman Martyr Piety in the Age of Gregory the Great," *Early Medieval Europe* 9 (2000), pp. 289–307.

Lifshitz, Felice, "The Migration of Neustrian Relics in the Viking Age: The Myth of Voluntary Exodus, the Reality of Coercion and Theft," *Early Medieval Europe* 4 (1995), pp. 175–92.

Lightbown, Ronald W., *Mediaeval European Jewellery* (London, 1992).

Line, Philip, *Kingship and State Formation in Sweden, 1130–1290* (Leiden, 2006).

Linehan, Peter, "The Beginnings of Santa María de Guadalupe and the Direction of Fourteenth-Century Castile," *Journal of Ecclesiastical History* 36 (1985), pp. 284–304.

Littger, Klaus Walter, *Studien zum Auftreten der Heiligennamen im Rheinland* (Munich, 1975).

Little, Lester, *Benedictine Maledictions: Liturgical Cursing in Romanesque France* (Ithaca, NY, 1993).

Local Maps and Plans from Medieval England, ed. R. A. Skelton and P.D.A. Harvey (Oxford, 1986).

Local Saints and Local Churches in the Early Medieval West, ed. Alan Thacker and Richard Sharpe (Oxford, 2002).

Lomax, Derek, *La Orden de Santiago (1170–1275)* (Madrid, 1965).

Loomis, C. Grant, *White Magic: An Introduction to the Folklore of Christian Legend* (Cambridge, MA, 1948).

López Santos, Luis, *Influjo de la vida cristiana en los nombres de pueblos españoles* (Leon, 1952).

LoPrete, Kimberly A., *Adela of Blois: Countess and Lord (c. 1067–1137)* (Dublin, 2007).

Lorcin, Marie-Thérèse, "Le temps chez les humbles: passé, présent et futur dans les testaments foréziens (1300–1450)," *Revue historique* 279 (1988), pp. 313–36.

Lotter, Friedrich, "Heiliger und Gehenkter: Zur Todesstrafe in hagiographischen Episodenerzählungen des Mittelalters," in *Ecclesia et Regnum: Beiträge zur Geschichte von Kirche, Recht und Staat im Mittelalter. Festschrift für Franz-Josef Schmale*, ed. Dieter Berg and Hans-Werner Goetz (Bochum, 1989), pp. 1–19.

Lübeck, Konrad, "Die Reliquienerwerbungen des Abtes Rabanus Maurus," in *Fuldaer Studien* (3 vols., Fulda, 1949–51), 2, pp. 113–32.

Lucas, A. T., "The Social Role of Relics and Reliquaries in Ancient Ireland," *Journal of the Royal Society of Antiquaries of Ireland* 116 (1986), pp. 5–37.

Lucius, Ernst, *Die Anfänge des Heiligenkults in der christlichen Kirche* (Tübingen, 1904).

———, *Les origines du culte des saints dans l'Eglise chrétienne* (Paris, 1908).

Luscombe, David, "Denis the Pseudo-Areopagite in the Middle Ages from Hilduin to Lorenzo Valla," in *Fälschungen im Mittelalter* (MGH Schriften 33, 6 vols., 1988–90), 1, pp. 133–52.

MacCormack, Sabine, *Tradition and Ceremony in Late Antiquity* (Berkeley, 1981).

Machilek, Franz, "Privatfrömmigkeit und Staatsfrömmigkeit," in *Karl IV.: Staatsmann und Mäzen*, ed. Ferdinand Seibt (Munich, 1978), pp. 87–101.

MacMullen, Ramsay, "Christian Ancestor Worship in Rome," *Journal of Biblical Literature* 129 (2010), pp. 597–613.

———, *Christianity and Paganism in the Fourth to Eighth Centuries* (New Haven, 1997).

Macrides, R. J., "Justice under Manuel Komnenos: Four Novels on Court Business and Murder," in *Fontes Minores* 6 (*Forschungen zur byzantinischen Rechtsgeschichte* 11), ed. Dieter Simon (Frankfurt, 1984), pp. 99–204, reprinted with same pagination in Macrides, *Kinship and Justice in Byzantium, 11th–15th centuries* (Aldershot, 1999), item IX.

Maddicott, J. R., "Follower, Leader, Pilgrim, Saint: Robert de Vere, Earl of Oxford, at the Shrine of Simon de Montfort, 1273," *English Historical Review* 99 (1994), pp. 641–53.
Maguire, Henry, *The Icons of Their Bodies: Saints and Their Images in Byzantium* (Princeton, 1996).
Majeska, George, "Russian Pilgrims in Constantinople," *Dumbarton Oaks Papers* 56 (2002), pp. 93–108.
Mallardo, Domenico, "L'incubazione nella cristianità medievale napoletana," AB 67 (1949), pp. 465–98.
Mango, Cyril, "On the Cult of Saints Cosmas and Damian at Constantinople," in *Thymiama ste mneme tes Laskarinas Mpoura* (Athens, 1994), pp. 189–92.
———, "Constantinople as Theotokoupolis," in *Mother of God: Representations of the Virgin in Byzantine Art*, ed. Maria Vassilaki (Milan, 2000), pp. 17–25.
Maniura, Robert, *Pilgrimage to Images in the Fifteenth Century: The Origins of the Cult of Our Lady of Częstochowa* (Woodbridge, 2004).
Manselli, Raoul, *Spirituels et Béguins du Midi* (French tr., Toulouse, 1989).
Maraval, Pierre, *Lieux saints et pèlerinages d'Orient: histoire et géographie des origines à la conquête arabe* (Paris, 1985).
Marienlexikon, ed. Remigus Bäumer and Leo Scheffczyk (6 vols., St. Ottilien, 1988–94).
Marks, Richard, *Image and Devotion in Late Medieval England* (Stroud, 2004).
Markus, R. A., "How on Earth Could Places Become Holy? Origins of the Christian Idea of Holy Places," *Journal of Early Christian Studies* 2 (1994), pp. 257–71.
———, *The End of Ancient Christianity* (Cambridge, 1990).
Marner, Dominic, *St Cuthbert: His Life and Cult in Medieval Durham* (London, 2000).
Marrou, Henri, "Les saints de l'ancien testament au martyrologe romain," in *Mémorial J. Chaine* (Lyons, 1950), pp. 281–90.
Martimort, A. G., *Les lectures liturgiques et leurs livres* (Typologie des sources du Moyen Age occidental 64, Turnhout, 1992).
Martínez Sopena, Pascual, ed., *Antroponimia y sociedad: sistemas de identificación hispano-cristianos en los siglos IX a XIII* (Santiago, 1995).
Marzella, Francesco, "L'anello del re e il 'paradiso' dell'evangelista: genesi di un episodio della 'Vita sancti Edwardi regis et confessoris' di Ælredo di Rievaulx," *Hagiographica* 18 (2011), pp. 217–62.
Mathews, Thomas F., and Norman Muller, "Isis and Mary in Early Icons," in *Images of the Mother of God: Perceptions of the Theotokos in Byzantium*, ed. Maria Vassilaki (Farnham, 2005), pp. 3–12.
Mattoso, José, "Le Portugal de 950 à 1550," in *Hagiographies* 2, pp. 83–102.
Matzke, John E., "Contributions to the History of the Legend of Saint George," *Proceedings of the Modern Languages Association* 18 (1903), pp. 99–171.
McCleery, Iona, "Isabel of Aragon (d. 1336), Model Queen or Model Saint?," *Journal of Ecclesiastical History* 57 (2006), pp. 668–92.
McCormick, Michael, *Eternal Victory: Triumphal Rulership in Late Antiquity, Byzantium and the Early Medieval West* (Cambridge, 1986).
McCready, William D., *Signs of Sanctity: Miracles in the Thought of Gregory the Great* (Toronto, 1989).
McCulloh, John M., "The Cult of Relics in the Letters and Dialogues of Pope Gregory the Great: A Lexicographical Study," *Traditio* 32 (1976), pp. 145–84.

McLachlan, Elizabeth Parker, *The Scriptorium of Bury St. Edmunds in the Twelfth Century* (New York, 1986).

McLeod, W., "Alban and Amphibal: Some Extant Lives and a Lost Life," *Mediaeval Studies* 42 (1980), pp. 407–30.

Medieval Reliquary Shrines and Precious Metalwork, ed. Kilian Anheuser and Christine Werner (London, 2006).

Meisterwerke aus Elfenbein der Staatlichen Museen zu Berlin (Berlin and Brunswick, 1999).

Meloni, Pier Lorenzo, "Mobilità di devozione nell'Umbria medievale: due liste di pellegrini," in *Chiesa e società dal secolo IV ai nostri giorni. Studi storici in onore del P. Ilarino da Milano* 1 (Rome, 1979), pp. 327–59.

Méndez Venegas, Eladio, "Relación hagionímica de la Orden de Santiago," in *Memoria Ecclesiae* 3: *Iglesia y cultura en las edades media y moderna: Santoral hispano-mozárabe en España* (Oviedo, 1992), pp. 181–201.

Menestò, Enrico, ed., *Il beato Andrea Caccioli da Spello* (Spoleto, 1997).

El "Menologio de Basilio II": Città del Vaticano, Biblioteca Apostolica Vaticana, Vat. Gr. 1613: libro de estudios con ocasión de la edición facsímil, ed. Francesco d'Aiuto (Vatican City, 2008).

Meri, Josef W., *The Cult of Saints among Muslims and Jews in Medieval Syria* (Oxford, 2002).

Merlo, Grado G., *Eretici e inquisitori nella società piemontese del trecento* (Turin, 1977).

Meyer, Paul, "Légendes hagiographiques en français," *Histoire littéraire de la France* 33 (1906), pp. 328–458.

Michalski, Sergiusz, *The Reformation and the Visual Arts: The Protestant Image Question in Western and Eastern Europe* (Eng. tr., London, 1993).

Michel, Paul-Henri, *Les fresques de Tavant* (Paris, 1944).

Miedema, Nine Robijntje, *Die römischen Kirchen im Spätmittelalter nach den "Indulgentiae ecclesiarum urbis Romae"* (Tübingen, 2001).

Millénaire monastique du Mont-Saint-Michel 3: *Culte de saint Michel et pèlerinage au Mont*, ed. Marcel Baudot (Paris, 1971).

Mills, Robert, *Suspended Animation: Pain, Pleasure, and Punishment in Medieval Culture* (London, 2005).

Mimouni, Simon C., *Dormition et assomption de Marie: Histoire des traditions anciennes* (Paris, 1995).

Miracle et karāma: Hagiographies médiévales comparées, ed. Denise Aigle (Turnhout, 2000).

Miracles, prodiges et merveilles au Moyen Age (Paris, 1995).

The Miraculous Image in the Late Middle Ages and Renaissance, ed. Erik Thunø and Gerhard Wolf (Rome, 2004).

Mirakel im Mittelalter: Konzeptionen, Erscheinungsformen, Deutungen, ed. Martin Heinzelmann et al. (Stuttgart, 2002).

Mises en scène et mémoires de la consécration de l'église dans l'occident medieval, ed. Didier Méhu (Turnhout, 2007).

Mitchell, Stephen, *Anatolia. Land, Men and Gods in Asia Minor* 2: *The Rise of the Church* (Oxford, 1993).

Mitterauer, Michael, *Ahnen und Heilige: Namengebung in der europäischen Geschichte* (Munich, 1993).

Moggia, Carlo, "Il culto dei santi nel medioevo: Alcune considerazioni quantitative e tipologiche sulle dedicazioni pievane e parocchiali nella arcidiocesi genovese di levante (secoli X–XIII)," *Mélanges de l'Ecole Française de Rome. Moyen Age* 117 (2005), pp. 305–21.

Mohnhaupt, Bernd, "Typologisch strukturierte Heiligenzyklen. Die Adalbertsvita der Gnesener Bronzetür," in *Hagiographie und Kunst. Der Heiligenkult in Schrift, Bild und Architektur*, ed. Gottfried Kerscher (Berlin, 1993), pp. 357–68.

Monaci Castagno, Adele, "Il vescovo, l'abate e l'eremita: tipologia della santità nel Liber Vitae Patrum di Gregorio di Tours," *Augustinianum* 24 (1984), pp. 235–64.

———, *L'agiografia cristiana antica* (Brescia, 2010).

Möncke, Gisela, "Der Gute Konrad von Weissensee. Eine unbekannte Heiligenvita aus dem Jahr 1508," *Gutenberg-Jahrbuch* 81 (2006), pp. 276–82.

Montagnes, B., "La répression des sacralités populaires en Languedoc au xv siècle," *Archivum Fratrum Praedicatorum* 52 (1982), pp. 155–85.

Montaner Frutos, Alberto, "Sobre el étimo de rome(r)o 'peregrino' y su parentela románica," *Romance Philology* 63 (2009), pp. 155–82.

Montgomery, Scott B., *St Ursula and the Eleven Thousand Virgins of Cologne: Relics, Reliquaries and the Visual Culture of Group Sanctity in Late Medieval Europe* (Bern, 2009).

Moorhead, John, *Ambrose: Church and Society in the Late Roman World* (London, 1999).

Moorman, J.R.H., *A History of the Franciscan Order* (Oxford, 1968).

Moretus, H., "De magno Legendario Bodecensi," AB 27 (1908), pp. 257–358.

Morlet, Marie Thérèse, *Les noms de personne sur le territoire de l'ancienne Gaule du VIe au XIIe siècle* (3 vols., Paris, 1968–85).

Morris, Colin, "Martyrs on the Field of Battle before and during the First Crusade," in *Martyrs and Martyrologies*, ed. Diana Wood (Studies in Church History 30, 1993), pp. 93–104.

Morrison, Susan Signe, *Women Pilgrims in Late Medieval England: Private Piety as Public Performance* (London and New York, 2000).

Moskowitz, Anita Fiderer, *Nicola Pisano's Arca di San Domenico and its Legacy* (University Park, PA, 1994).

Mostert, Marco, *The Library of Fleury: A Provisional List of Manuscripts* (Hilversum, 1989).

Moule, C.D.F., "The Vocabulary of Miracle," in *Miracles*, ed. Moule (London, 1965), pp. 235–38.

Moulet, Benjamin, *Évêques, pouvoir et société à Byzance (VIIIe–XIe siècle)* (Paris, 2011).

Muir, Lynette R., "The Saint Play in Medieval France," in *The Saint Play in Medieval Europe*, ed. Clifford Davidson (Kalmazoo, 1986), pp. 123–80.

Müller, Gerhard Ludwig, *Gemeinschaft und Verehrung der Heiligen: geschichtliche-systematische Grundlegung der Hagiologie* (Freiburg im Breisgau, 1986).

Muthmann, Friedrich, *Mutter und Quelle. Studien zur Quellenverehrung in Altertum und Mittelalter* (Basel, 1975).

Mynors, R.A.B., *Durham Cathedral Manuscripts* (Oxford, 1939).

Nahmer, Dieter von der, *Die lateinische Heiligenvita: eine Einführung in die lateinische Hagiographie* (Darmstadt, 1994).

Naphy, W. G., "Baptisms, Church Riots and Social Unrest in Calvin's Geneva," *Sixteenth Century Journal* 26 (1995), pp. 87–97.

Neil, Bronwen, *Seventh-century Popes and Martyrs: The Political Hagiography of Anastasius Bibliothecarius* (Turnhout, 2006).

Nelson, Janet, "Royal Saints and Early Medieval Kingship," in *Sanctity and Secularity: The Church and the World*, ed. Derek Baker (Studies in Church History 10, 1973), pp. 39–44 (repr. in her *Politics and Ritual in Early Medieval Europe* [London, 1986], pp. 69–74).

Newman, J. H., "The Benedictine Schools," in *Historical Sketches* 2 (London, 1873), pp. 433–87 (originally in *Atlantis*, Jan. 1859).

Nicolai, Vincenzo Fiocchi, Fabrizio Bisconti, and Danilo Mazzoleni, *The Christian Catacombs of Rome: History, Decoration, Inscriptions* (Regensburg, 1999).

Nieri, Antonio, "Culto dei santi dell'antico testamento," in *Culto dei santi a Venezia*, ed. Silvio Tramontin et al. (Venice, 1965), pp. 155–80.

Nilles, Nicolaus, *Kalendarium manuale utriusque ecclesiae orientalis et occidentalis* (2nd ed., 2 vols., Innsbruck, 1896–97).

Nilson, Ben, *Cathedral Shrines of Medieval England* (Woodbridge, 1998).

Nixon, Virginia, *Mary's Mother: Saint Anne in Late Medieval Europe* (University Park, PA, 2004).

Njus, Jesse, "The Politics of Mysticism: Elisabeth of Spalbeek in Context," *Church History* 77 (2008), pp. 285–317.

Noble, Thomas F. X., *Images, Iconoclasm, and the Carolingians* (Philadelphia, 2009).

Noga-Banai, Galit, *The Trophies of the Martyrs: An Art Historical Study of Early Christian Silver Reliquaries* (Oxford, 2008).

Northeast, Peter, "Moving the Signposts: Changes in the Dedications of Suffolk Churches after the Reformation," in *East Anglian Studies*, ed. Adam Longcroft and Richard Joby (Norwich, 1995), pp. 201–5.

Norton, Christopher, "Richard Scrope and York Minster," in *Richard Scrope: Archbishop, Rebel, Martyr*, ed. P.J.P. Goldberg (Donington, 2007), pp. 138–213.

Nyberg, Tore, "The Canonization Process of St. Birgita of Sweden," in *Procès de canonisation au Moyen Age*, ed. Klanizcay, pp. 67–85.

O'Brien, Joshua M., "Locating Authorities in Carolingian Debates on Image Veneration: The Case of Agobard of Lyon's *De Picturis et Imaginibus*," *Journal of Theological Studies* 62 (2011), pp. 176–201.

Ó Carragáin, Éamonn, *Ritual and the Rood: Liturgical Images and the Old English Poems of the Dream of the Rood Tradition* (London, 2005).

Offenstadt, Nicholas, *Faire la paix au Moyen Age: discours et gestes de paix pendant la Guerre de Cent Ans* (Paris, 2007).

Ó Floinn, Raghnall, *Irish Shrines and Reliquaries of the Middle Ages* (Dublin, 1994).

Ogden, Dunbar H., *The Staging of Drama in the Medieval Church* (Newark, DE, 2003).

Oikonomidès, Nicholas, *Documents et études sur les institutions de Byzance* (London, 1976).

Ó Mara, Róisín, "Die heilige Brigid und ihr Kult im Salzburger Land," in *Virgil von Salzburg, Missionar und Gelehrter*, ed. Heinz Dopsch and Roswitha Juffinger (Salzburg, 1985), pp. 381–83.

O'Rahilly, Thomas F., *The Two Patricks* (Dublin, 1942).

Ó Riain, Pádraig, *A Dictionary of Irish Saints* (Dublin, 2011).

Ó Riain-Raedel, Dagmar, "Edith, Judith, Matilda: The Role of Royal Ladies in the Propagation of the Continental Cult," in *Oswald: Northumbrian King to European Saint*, ed. Clare Stancliffe and Eric Cambridge (Stamford, 1995), pp. 210–29.

Orlandi, Stefano, *La biblioteca di S. Maria Novella in Firenze dal sec. XIV al sec. XIX* (Florence, 1952).

Orme, Nicholas, *English Church Dedications: With a Survey of Cornwall and Devon* (Exeter, 1996).

Ornamenta Ecclesiae: Kunst und Künstler der Romanik, ed. Anton Legner (3 vols., Cologne, 1985).

Orselli, Alba Maria, *L'idea e il culto del santo patrono cittadino nella letteratura latina cristiana* (Bologna, 1965).

Ortenberg, Veronica, "Archbishop Sigeric's Journey to Rome in 990," *Anglo-Saxon England* 19 (1990), pp. 197–246.

Owen, Dorothy M., "Some Revesby Charters of the Soke of Bolingbroke," in *A Medieval Miscellany for Doris Mary Stenton*, ed. Patricia M. Barnes and Cecil F. Slade (Publications of the Pipe Roll Society n.s. 36, 1962), pp. 221–34.

Oxford Book of Medieval English Verse, ed. Celia and Kenneth Sisam (Oxford, 1970).

Oxford Dictionary of Byzantium (3 vols., Oxford, 1991).

Pächt, Otto, C. R. Dodwell, and Francis Wormald, *The St Albans Psalter* (London, 1960).

Paciocco, Roberto, *Canonizzazioni e culto dei santi nella christianitas (1198–1302)* (Assisi, 2006).

Padel, O. J., "Local Saints and Place-names in Cornwall," in *Local Saints and Local Churches*, ed. Thacker and Sharpe, pp. 303–60.

La Pala d'Oro, ed. H. R. Hahnloser and R. Polacco (Venice, 1994).

Panofsky, Erwin, *Early Netherlandish Painting: Its Origins and Character* (2 vols., Cambridge, MA, 1953).

Papa, Giovanni, *Le cause di canonizzazione nel primo periodo della Congregazione dei Riti: 1588–1634* (Rome, 2001).

Papaconstantinou, Arietta, *Le culte des saints en Egypte des Byzantins aux Abbassides* (Paris, 2001).

Parisse, Michel, "La conscience chrétienne des nobles aux XIe et XIIe siècles," in *La cristianità dei secoli XI e XII in occidente: coscienza e strutture di una società* (Miscellanea del Centro di Studi Medioevali 10, Milan, 1983), pp. 259–80.

Parry, Kenneth, *Depicting the Word: Byzantine Iconophile Thought of the Eighth and Ninth Centuries* (Leiden, 1996).

Patlagean, Evelyne, "Les débuts d'une aristocratie byzantine et le témoinage de l'historiographie: système des noms et liens de parenté aux IXe–Xe siècles," in *The Byzantine Aristocracy IX to XIII Centuries*, ed. Michael Angold (British Archaeological Reports, International Series 221, 1984), pp. 23–43.

Patriotische Heilige: Beiträge zur Konstruktion religiöser und politischer Identitäten in der Vormoderne, ed. Dieter R. Bauer et al. (Stuttgart, 2007).

A Patristic Greek Lexicon. ed. G.W.H. Lampe (Oxford, 1961).

Peers, Glenn, *Subtle Bodies: Representing Angels in Byzantium* (Berkeley, 2001).

Le Pèlerinage (Cahiers de Fanjeaux 15, Toulouse, 1980).

Pelikan, Jaroslav, *The Christian Tradition: A History of the Development of Doctrine* 2: *The Spirit of Eastern Christendom, 600–1700* (Chicago, 1974).

Pellegrinaggi e santuari di San Michele nell'Occidente medievale/Pèlerinages et sanctuaires de Saint-Michel dans l'Occident médiéval: atti del secondo convegno internazionale dedicato all'Arcangelo Michele, atti del XVI Convegno Sacrense (Sacra di San Michele, 26–29 settembre 2007), ed. Giampietro Casiraghi and Giuseppe Sergi (Bari, 2009).

Pellegrini, Letizia, "La sainteté au XVe siècle entre procès et droit canonique: avant et après Bernardin de Sienne," in *Procès de canonisation au Moyen Age*, ed. Klanizcay, pp. 309–26.

———, "*Negotium imperfectum*: il processo per la canonizzazione di Ambrogio da Massa (O. M., Orvieto 1240)," *Società e storia* 17 (1994), pp. 253–78.

Peña, Ignace, Pascal Castellana, and Romuald Fernández, *Les stylites syriens* (Milan, 1975).

Pérez-Embid Wamba, Javier, *Hagiología y sociedad en la España medieval: Castilla y León (siglos XI–XIII)* (Huelva, 2002).

Péricard-Méa, Denise, "Les femmes et le pèlerinage," in *Femmes et pèlerinages*, ed. Juliette Dor and Marie-Elisabeth Henneau (Compostela Group of Universities, 2007), pp. 25–46.

Perouas, Louis, Bernadette Barriere, Jean Boutier, Jean-Claude Peyronnet, and Jean Tricard, *Léonard, Marie, Jean et les autres. Les prénoms en Limousin depuis un millénaire* (Paris, 1984).

Perrot, Jean-Pierre, *Le passionnaire français au Moyen Age* (Geneva, 1992).

Petersohn, Jürgen, "Apostolus Pomeranorum. Studien zur Geschichte und Bedeutung des Apostelepithetons Bischof Ottos I. von Bamberg," *Historisches Jahrbuch* 86 (1966), pp. 257–94.

———, "Die Litterae Papst Innocenz' III. zur Heiligsprechung der Kaiserin Kunigunde (1200)," *Jahrbuch für fränkische Landesforschung* 37 (1977), pp. 1–25.

Petersohn, Jürgen, ed., *Politik und Heiligenverehrung im Hochmittelalter* (Vorträge und Forschungen 42, Sigmaringen, 1994).

Peterson, Janine L., "Contested Sanctity: Disputed Saints, Inquisitors, and Communal Identity in Northern Italy, 1250–1400" (PhD Dissertation, Indiana University, 2006).

Peyer, Hans Conrad, *Stadt und Stadtpatron im mittelalterlichen Italien* (Zurich, 1955).

Pezzini, Domenico, *The Translation of Religious Texts in the Middle Ages: Tracts and Rules, Hymns and Saints' Lives* (Bern, 2008).

Pfaff, Richard W., *The Liturgy in Medieval England. A History* (Cambridge, 2009).

———, *New Liturgical Feasts in Later Medieval England* (Oxford, 1970).

Philippart, Guy, *Les légendiers latins et autres manuscrits hagiographiques* (Typologie des sources du Moyen Age occidental 24–25, Turnhout, 1977).

Picard, Jean-Charles, *Le souvenir des évêques: sépultures, listes épiscopales et culte des évêques en Italie du Nord des origines au Xe siècle* (Bibliothèque des Ecoles françaises d'Athènes et de Rome 268, Rome, 1988).

Piel, Joseph M., and Dieter Kremer, *Hispano-gotisches Namenbuch: der Niederschlag des Westgotischen in den alten und heutigen Personen– und Ortsnamen der Iberischen Halbinsel* (Heidelberg, 1976).

Pietri, Charles, "L'évolution du culte des saints aux premiers siècles chrétiens: Du témoin à l'intercesseur," in *Les fonctions des saints dans le monde occidental*, pp. 15–36.

Pietri, Luce, *La ville de Tours du IVe au VIe siècle: naissance d'une cité chrétienne* (Rome, 1983).

Pietschmann, Klaus, "Ablauf und Dimensionen der Heiligsprechung des Antoninus von Florenz (1523). Kanonisationspraxis im politischen und religiösen Umbruch," *Quellen und Forschungen aus italienischen Archiven und Bibliotheken* 78 (1998), pp. 388–463.

"Pilgrimage in the Byzantine Empire," ed. Alice-Mary Talbot, *Dumbarton Oaks Papers* 56 (2002), pp. 59–241.

Pinder-Wilson, R. H., and C.N.L. Brooke, "The Reliquary of St. Petroc and the Ivories of Norman Sicily," *Archaeologia* 104 (1973), pp. 261–306.

Piroyansky, Danna, *Martyrs in the Making: Political Martyrdom in Late Medieval England* (Basingstoke, 2008).

Platelle, H., "La mort précieuse. La mort des moines d'après quelques sources des Pays-Bas du Sud," *Revue Mabillon* 60 (1982), pp. 151–74.

Ploeg, Kees van der, *Art, Architecture and Liturgy: Siena Cathedral in the Middle Ages* (Groningen, 1993).

Polc, Iaroslaus, *De origine festi visitationis B. M. V.* (Rome, 1967).

Pollock, Frederick, and Frederic William Maitland, *The History of English Law before the Time of Edward I* (2nd ed., 2 vols., Cambridge, 1898; reiss. 1968).

Poncelet, Albert, "Catalogus codicum hagiographicorum latinorum bibliothecarum Neapolitanarum," AB 30 (1911), pp. 137–251.

———, "Le légendier de Pierre Calo," AB 29 (1910), pp. 5–116.

Potter, G. R., ed., *Huldrych Zwingli* (London, 1978).

Potts, Cassandra, "When the Saints Go Marching: Religious Connections and the Political Culture of Early Normandy," in *Anglo-Norman Political Culture and the Twelfth-century Renaissance*, ed. Charles Warren Hollister (Woodbridge, 1997), pp. 17–31.

Poulin, Joseph-Claude, "Les *libelli* dans l'édition hagiographique avant le XIIe siècle," in *Livrets, collections et textes: études sur la tradition hagiographique latine*, ed. Martin Heinzelmann (Beihefte der Francia 63, 2006), pp. 15–193.

———, *L'hagiographie bretonne du haut Moyen Âge: répertoire raisonné* (Ostfildern, 2009).

Powell, Susan, "Mirk, John (fl. c. 1382–c. 1414)," in *Oxford Dictionary of National Biography* (60 vols. plus indices, Oxford, 2004) 38, pp. 368–69.

Pratsch, Thomas, *Der hagiographische Topos. Griechische Heiligenviten in mittelbyzantinischer Zeit* (Berlin and New York, 2005).

Procès de canonisation au Moyen Age: Aspects juridiques et religieux / Medieval Canonization Processes: Legal and Religious Aspects, ed. Gábor Klaniczay (Rome, 2004).

Prosopographie der mittelbyzantinischen Zeit, Abteilung I: 641–867 (6 vols., Berlin, 1998–2002).

Prothero, George Walter, *The Life of Simon de Montfort, Earl of Leicester* (London, 1877).

Proud, Joanna, "Collections of Saints' Lives in the Thirteenth and Fourteenth Centuries: Interpreting the Manuscript Evidence," in *Lives in Print: Biography and the Book Trade from the Middle Ages to the 21st Century*, ed. Robin Myers et al. (London, 2002), pp. 1–21.

Prudlo, Donald, *The Martyred Inquisitor: The Life and Cult of Peter of Verona* (Aldershot, 2008).

Puig i Oliver, Jaume de, "Notes sobre el manuscript del *Directorium Inquisitorum* de Nicolau Eimeric conservat a la Biblioteca de l'Escorial (ms. N. I. 18)," *Arxiu de Textos Catalans Antics* 19 (2000), pp. 527–60.

Quentin, Henri, *Les martyrologes historiques du Moyen Age* (Paris, 1908).

Radford, U. M., "The Wax Images Found in Exeter Cathedral," *Antiquaries Journal* 29 (1949), pp. 164–68, with pls. XIX–XXI.

Rapp, Claudia, *Holy Bishops in Late Antiquity* (Berkeley, 2005).

Rauer, Christine, *Beowulf and the Dragon: Parallels and Analogues* (Cambridge, 2000).

Reames, Sherry, *The Legenda Aurea: A Reexamination of Its Paradoxical History* (Madison, WI, 1985).

Réau, Louis, *Iconographie de l'art chrétien* 3: *Iconographie des saints* (3 vols., Paris, 1958–59).

Reclams Lexikon der Heiligen und der biblischen Gestalten: Legende und Darstellung in der bildenden Kunst, ed. Hiltgart L. Keller (Stuttgart, 1968).

Reinburg, Virginia, *French Books of Hours: Making an Archive of Prayer, c. 1400–1600* (New York, 2012).

Remensnyder, Amy G., "Un problème de cultures ou de culture? La statue-reliquaire et les joca de sainte Foy de Conques dans le Liber Miraculorum de Bernard d'Angers," *Cahiers de civilisation médiévale* 33 (1990), pp. 351–79.

Reudenbach, Bruno, "Visualizing Holy Bodies: Observations on Body-Part Reliquaries," in *Romanesque Art and Thought in the Twelfth Century: Essays in Honor of Walter Cahn*, ed. Colum Hourihane (Princeton, 2008), pp. 95–106.

Ribas i Calaf, Benet, *Annals de Montserrat (1258–1485)*, ed. Francesc Xavier Altés i Aguiló (Barcelona, 1997).

Richards, Jeffrey, *Consul of God: The Life and Times of Gregory the Great* (London, 1980).

Richter, Michael, *Sprache und Gesellschaft im Mittelalter* (Stuttgart, 1979).

Rico Camps, Daniel, "A Shrine in Its Setting: San Vicente de Ávila," in *Decorations for the Holy Dead: Visual Embellishment on Tombs and Shrines of Saints*, ed. Stephen Lamia and Elizabeth Valdez del Alamo (Turnhout, 2002), pp. 57–76.

Ridyard, Susan J., *The Royal Saints of Anglo-Saxon England: A Study of the West Saxon and East Anglian Cults* (Cambridge, 1988).

Rigg, A. G., *A History of Anglo-Latin Literature 1066–1422* (Cambridge, 1992).

Riley-Smith, Jonathan, "Death on the First Crusade," in *The End of Strife*, ed. D. M. Loades (Edinburgh, 1984), pp. 14–31.

———, *The First Crusade and the Idea of Crusading* (London, 1985).

Rippe, Gérard, "L'onomastique dans la Vénétie du XIII siècle: l'exemple de Monselice," in *Les cadastres anciens des villes et leur traitement par l'informatique*, ed. J.-L. Biget et al. (Rome, 1989), pp. 269–85.

Rivière, Baron de, "Deux calendriers liturgiques de l'église cathédrale d'Albi," *Bulletin de la Société archéologique du Midi de la France* (1895–96), pp. 70–82.

Roberts, Angela Marisol, "Donor Portraits in Late Medieval Venice c. 1280–1413" (PhD Thesis, Queen's University, Kingston, Ontario, 2007).

Roberts, Michael John, *Poetry and the Cult of the Martyrs: The Liber Peristephanon of Prudentius* (Ann Arbor, 1993).

Roberts, Phyllis B., *Thomas Becket in the Medieval Latin Preaching Tradition* (Steenbrugge, 1992).

Rocacher, Jean, *Rocamadour et son pèlerinage: etude historique et archéologique* (2 vols., Toulouse, 1979).

Roch, Martin, *L'intelligence d'un sens: Odeurs miraculeuses et odorat dans l'Occident du haut Moyen Âge (Ve–VIIIe siècles)* (Turnhout, 2009).

Rochais, H.-M., *Un légendier cistercien de la fin du XIIe siècle: le "Liber de Nataliciis" et de quelques grands légendiers des XIIe et XIIIe siècles* (2 vols., Documentation Cistercienne 15, Rochefort, 1975).

Rochelle, Mercedes, *Post-biblical Saints Art Index* (Jefferson, NC, 1994).

Röckelein, Hedwig, *Reliquientranslationen nach Sachsen im 9. Jahrundert: über Kommunikation, Mobilität und Öffentlichkeit im Frühmittelalter* (Stuttgart, 2002).

Rodgers, Edith C., *Discussion of Holidays in the Later Middle Ages* (New York, 1940).

Rohland, Johannes Peter, *Der Erzengel Michael, Arzt und Feldherr: zwei Aspekte des vor- und frühbyzantinischen Michaelskultes* (Leiden, 1977).

Roisin, Simone, *L'hagiographie Cistercienne dans le diocèse de Liège au XIIIe. siècle* (Louvain and Brussels, 1947).

Rollason, David, "Lists of Saints' Resting-Places in Anglo-Saxon England," *Anglo-Saxon England* 7 (1978), pp. 61–93.

———, "The Miracles of St Benedict: A Window on Early Medieval France," in *Studies in Medieval History presented to R.H.C. Davis*, ed. Henry Mayr-Harting and R. I. Moore (London, 1985), pp. 73–90.

———, *Saints and Relics in Anglo-Saxon England* (Oxford, 1989).

———, "The Wanderings of St Cuthbert," in *Cuthbert: Saint and Patron*, ed. Rollason (Durham, 1987), pp. 45–59.

Rollier-Hanselmann, Juliette, "D'Auxerre à Cluny: technique de la peinture murale entre le VIIIe et le XIIe s. en Bourgogne," *Cahiers de civilisation médiévale* 40 (1997), pp. 57–90.

Romei e giubilei. Il pellegrinaggio medievale a San Pietro (350–1350), ed. Mario D'Onofrio (Milan, 1999).

Ronciére, Charles de la, "Orientations pastorales du clergé, fin XIIe–XIVe siècle: le témoinage de l'onomastique toscane," *Comptes Rendus de l'Académie des Inscriptions et Belles-Lettres* (1983), pp. 43–65.

Rosada, Maurizio, "'Sigillum Sancti Marci.' Bolle e sigilli di Venezia," in *Il sigillo nella storia e nella cultura. Mostra documentaria*, ed. Stefania Ricci (Rome, 1985), pp. 109–48.

Rosenberg, Marc, "Ersten Zellenschmelz nördlich der Alpen," *Jahrbuch der Königlich Preussischen Kunstsammlungen* 39 (1918), pp. 1–50.

Rossiaud, Jacques, *Medieval Prostitution* (Eng. tr., Oxford, 1988).

Rouche, Michel, "Miracles, maladies et psychologie de la foi a l'époque carolingienne en France," in *Hagiographie, cultures et sociétés, IVe–XIIe siècles: Actes du colloque organisé à Nanterre et à Paris 12–5 mai 1979* (Paris, 1981), pp. 319–37.

Rouse, Mary A., and Richard H. Rouse, "The Goldsmith and the Peacocks: Jean de la Mote in the Household of Simon de Lille, 1340," *Viator* 28 (1997), pp. 283–303.

Rouse, Richard H., and Mary A. Rouse, *Preachers, Florilegia and Sermons: Studies on the Manipulus florum of Thomas of Ireland* (Toronto, 1979).

Rousselle, Aline, *Croire et guérir: la foi en Gaule dans l'Antiquité tardive* (Paris, 1990).

Rowland Jr., Robert J., "The Sojourn of the Body of St. Augustine in Sardinia," in *Augustine in Iconography: History and Legend*, ed. Joseph C. Schnaubelt and Frederick Van Fleteren (New York, 1999), pp. 189–98.

Rubin, Miri, "Choosing Death? Experiences of Martyrdom in Late Medieval Europe," in *Martyrs and Martyrologies*, ed. Diana Wood (Studies in Church History 30, 1993), pp. 153–83.

———, *Corpus Christi: The Eucharist in Late Medieval Culture* (Cambridge, 1992).

———, *Mother of God: A History of the Vigin Mary* (London, 2009).

Rück, Peter, "Zur Verbreitung der Festdatierung im 13. Jahrhundert in Urkunden aus dem Gebiet der Schweiz," *Archiv für Diplomatik* 38 (1992), pp. 145–92.

Rudy, Kathryn M., "An Illustrated Mid-Fifteenth-Century Primer for a Flemish Girl: British Library, Harley MS 3828," *Journal of the Warburg and Courtauld Institutes* 69 (2006), pp. 51–94.

Rushforth, Rebecca, *Saints in English Kalendars before A.D. 1100* (Henry Bradshaw Society 117, 2008 for 2005).

Russo, Daniel, *Saint Jérôme en Italie: étude d'iconographie et de spiritualité (XIIIe–XVe siècle)* (Paris and Rome, 1987).

Rutkowska-Plachcinska, Anna, "Les prénoms bourgeois dans le sud de France aux XIIIe et XIVe siècles," *Acta Poloniae Historica* 49 (1984), pp. 5–42.

Saak, E. L., "Quilibet Christianus: Saints and Society in the Sermons of Jordan of Quedlinburg, OESA," in *Models of Holiness in Medieval Sermons* (Turnhout, 1996), pp. 317–38.

Sachse, Franz, *Das Aufkommen der Datierungen nach dem Festkalender in Urkunden der Reichskanzlei und der deutschen Erzbistümer. Ein Beitrag zur Chronologie des Mittelalters* (Erlangen, 1904).

Saints de choeurs. Tapisseries du Moyen Age et de la Renaissance (Milan, 2004).

Saintyves, P., *Les saints successeurs des dieux* (Paris, 1907).

Salin, Édouard, *La civilisation mérovingienne d'après les sépultures, les textes et le laboratoire* (4 vols., Paris, 1949–59).

Salter, David, *Holy and Noble Beasts: Encounters with Animals in Medieval Literature* (Woodbridge, 2001).

Saltman, Avrom, *Theobald, Archbishop of Canterbury* (London, 1956).

Salzman, L. F., "Some Sussex Miracles," *Sussex Archaeological Collections* 66 (1925), pp. 62–82.

Sánchez Ameijeiras, Rocío, "Imagery and Interactivity: Ritual Transaction at the Saint's Tomb," in *Decorations for the Holy Dead: Visual Embellishment on Tombs and Shrines of Saints*, ed. Stephen Lamia and Elizabeth Valdez del Alamo (Turnhout, 2002), pp. 21–38.

Sanctity in the North: Saints Lives and Cults in Medieval Scandinavia, ed. Thomas A. DuBois (Toronto, 2008).

Sankt Elisabeth: Fürstin, Dienerin, Heilige (Sigmaringen, 1981).

Santi e demoni nell'alto medioevo occidentale (secoli V–XI) (2 vols., Settimane di Studio 36, Spoleto, 1989).

Sargent, Steven D., "Miracle Books and Pilgrimage Shrines in Late Medieval Bavaria," *Historical Reflections/Réflexions historiques* 13 (1986), pp. 455–71.

———, "Saints' Cults and Naming Patterns in Bavaria, 1400–1600," *Catholic Historical Review* 76 (1990), pp. 673–96.

Saul, Nigel, *Richard II* (New Haven and London, 1997).

Sawyer, Birgit, *The Viking-Age Rune-Stones* (Oxford, 2000).

Sawyer, P. H., *Anglo-Saxon Charters: An Annotated List and Bibliography* (London, 1968).

Saxer, Victor, *Morts, martyrs, reliques en Afrique chrétienne aux premiers siècles* (Paris, 1980).

Scase, Wendy, "St. Anne and the Education of the Virgin: Literary and Artistic Traditions and Their Implications," in *England in the Fourteenth Century*, ed. Nicholas Rogers (Stamford, 1993), pp. 81–96.

Schaab, Meinrad, "Eide und andere Treuegelöbnisse in Territorien und Gemeinden Südwestdeutschlands zwischen Spätmittelalter und Dreißigjährigem Krieg," in *Glaube und Eid: Treueformeln, Glaubensbekenntnisse und Sozialdisziplinierung zwischen Mittelalter und Neuzeit*, ed. Paolo Prodi (Munich, 1993), pp. 11–30.

Scheller, R. W., *Die Seelenwägung und das Kelchwunder Kaiser Heinrichs II* (Koninklijke Nederlandse Akademie van Wetenschappen, 1997).

Schenk, Max, *Die Unfehlbarkeit des Papstes in der Heiligsprechung* (Freiburg, 1965).

Schimmelpfennig, Bernhard, *Die Zeremonienbücher der römischen Kurie im Mittelalter* (Tübingen, 1973).

Schmid, Wolfgang, "Vom Rheinland nach Böhmen. Studien zur Reliquienpolitik Kaiser Karls IV," in *Die Goldene Bulle: Politik–Wahrnehmung–Rezeption*, ed. Ulrike Hohensee et al. (2 vols., Berlin-Brandenburgische Akademie der Wissenschaften: Berichte und Abhandlungen, Sonderband 12, 2009) 1, pp. 431–64.

Schmidt, Victor M., *Painted Piety: Panel Paintings for Personal Devotion in Tuscany, 1250–1400* (Florence, 2005).

Schmitt, Jean-Claude, *Le saint lévrier. Guinefort, guérisseur d'enfants depuis le xiiie siècle* (2nd ed., Paris, 2004).

Schmugge, Ludwig, "Die Anfänge des organisierten Pilgerverkehrs im Mittelalter," *Quellen und Forschungen aus italienischen Archiven und Bibliotheken* 64 (1984), pp. 1–83.

Schopen, Gregory, "Burial *Ad Sanctos* and the Physical Presence of Buddha in Early Indian Buddhism: A Study in the Archaeology of Religions," in *Bones, Stones, and Buddhist Monks: Collected Papers on the Archaeology, Epigraphy, and Texts of Monastic Buddhism in India* (Honolulu, 1997), pp. 114–47.

Schreiner, Klaus, "'Peregrinatio laudabilis' und 'peregrinatio vituperabilis.' Zur religiösen Ambivalenz des Wallens und Laufens in der Frömmigkeitstheologie des späten Mittelalters," in *Wallfahrt und Alltag in Mittelalter und früher Neuzeit*, pp. 133–63.

Schreiner, Peter, "Der byzantinische Bilderstreit: kritische Analyse der zeitgenössischen Meinungen und das Urteil der Nachwelt bis heute," in *Bisanzio, Rome e l'Italia nell'alto medioevo* (2 vols., Settimane di Studio 34, 1988), pp. 319–427.

Schulenburg, Jane Tibbetts, *Forgetful of Their Sex: Female Sanctity and Society, 500–1100* (Chicago, 1998).

———, "Sexism and the Celestial Gynecaeum from 500 to 1200," *Journal of Medieval History* 4 (1978), pp. 117–33.

Schulze, Wilhelm A., "Vieleckige Nimben in der spanischen Malerei," *Das Münster* 40 (1987), pp. 51–53.

Schurr, Eva, *Die Ikonographie der Heiligen: Eine Entwicklungsgeschichte ihrer Attribute von den Anfängen bis zum achten Jahrhundert* (Detelbach, 1997).

Scribner, R. W., *Popular Culture and Popular Movements in Reformation Germany* (London, 1987).

Sensi, Mario, "Il pellegrinaggio a Santiago attraverso i testamenti dei pellegrini italiani," in *Santuari, pellegrini, eremiti nell'Italia centrale* (3 vols. and index, Spoleto, 2003), 2, pp. 1227–1324.

———, "Mondo rurale e micro santuari per la terapia degli animali," ibid., 3, pp. 1437–54.

———, "Pellegrinaggi votivi e vicari alla fine del Medioevo, l'esempio umbro," ibid., 1, pp. 65–166.

Shalem, Avinoam, *Islam Christianized: Islamic Portable Objects in the Medieval Church Treasuries of the Latin West* (rev. ed., Frankfurt, 1998).

Sharf, Robert H., "The Idolization of Enlightenment: On the Mummification of Ch'an Masters in Medieval China," *History of Religions* 32 (1992), pp. 1–31.

Sharpe, Richard, "Eadmer's Letter to the Monks of Glastonbury Concerning St. Dunstan's Disputed Remains," in *The Archaeology and History of Glastonbury Abbey: Essays in Honour of the Ninetieth Birthday of C. A. Ralegh Radford*, ed. Lesley Abrams and James P. Carley (Woodbridge, 1991), pp. 205–15.

———, *A Handlist of the Latin Writers of Great Britain and Ireland before* 1540 (Turnhout, 1997).

———, "Martyrs and Local Saints in Late Antique Britain," in *Local Saints and Local Churches*, ed. Thacker and Sharpe, pp. 75–154.

———, *Medieval Irish Saints' Lives* (Oxford, 1991).

———, "Were the Irish Annals Known to a Twelfth-century Northumbrian Writer?," *Peritia* 2 (1983), pp. 137–39.

Shoemaker, Stephen J., *Ancient Traditions of the Virgin Mary's Dormition and Assumption* (Oxford, 2002).

Siegmund, Albert, *Die Überlieferung der griechischen christlichen Literatur in der lateinischen Kirche bis zum zwölften Jahrhundert* (Munich-Pasing, 1949).

Sigal, Pierre-André, "La mort des saints dans les Vies et les procès de canonisation du Midi de la France," in *La Mort et l'au-delà en France méridionale (XIIe–XVe siècle)*, ed. Jean-Louis Biget (Cahiers de Fanjeaux 33, 1998), pp. 17–40.

———, "La possession démoniaque dans la région de Florence au XVe siècle d'apres les miracles de saint Jean Gualbert," in *Histoire et société: mélanges offerts à Georges Duby* (4 vols., Aix-en-Provence, 1992) 3, pp. 101–12.

———, "Le déroulement des translations de reliques, principalement dans les régions entre Loire et Rhin aux XIe et XIIe siècles," in *Les Reliques. Objets, cultes, symboles*, ed. Edina Bozóky and Anne-Marie Helvétius (Turnhout, 1999), pp. 213–27.

———, *Les marcheurs de Dieu: pèlerinages et pèlerins au Moyen Age* (Paris, 1974).

———, "Les voyages de reliques aux XIe et XIIe siècles," in *Voyage, quête, pèlerinage dans la littérature et la civilisation médiévales* (Aix-en-Provence and Paris, 1976), pp. 75–104.

———, "Le travail des hagiographes aux XIe et XIIe siècles: sources d'information et méthodes de rédaction," *Francia* 15 (1987), pp. 149–82.

———, "L'ex-voto au Moyen-Age dans les regions du Nord-Ouest de la Mediterranee (XIIe–XVe siecles)," *Provence historique* 33 (1983), pp. 13–31.

———, *L'homme et le miracle dans la France médiévale: XIe.–XIIe. siècles* (Paris, 1985).

———, "Maladie, pèlerinage et guérison au XIIe. siècle: les miracles de saint Gibrien à Reims," *Annales* 24/6 (1969), pp. 1522–39.

———, "Un aspect du culte des saints: le châtiment divin aux XIe. et XIIe. siècles d'après la littérature hagiographique du Midi de la France," in *La religion populaire en Languedoc du XIIIe siècle à la moitié du XIVe siècle* (Cahiers de Fanjeaux 11, 1976), pp. 39–59.

Signori, Gabriela, *Wunder* (Frankfurt, 2007).

Smith, Caroline, "Martyrdom and Crusading in the Thirteenth Century: Remembering the Dead of Louis IX's Crusades," *Al-Masaq* 15 (2003), pp. 189–96.

Smith, Julia, "The Problem of Female Sanctity in Carolingian Europe c. 780–920," *Past and Present* 146 (1995), pp. 3–37.

———, "Women at the Tomb: Access to Relic Shrines in the Early Middle Ages," in *The World of Gregory of Tours*, ed. Kathleen Mitchell and Ian Wood (Leiden, 2002), pp. 163–80.

Sobré, Judith Berg, *Behind the Altar Table: The Development of the Painted Retable in Spain,* 1350–1500 (Columbia, MO, 1989).

Sot, Michel, *Gesta episcoporum, gesta abbatum* (Typologie des sources du Moyen Âge occidental 37, Turnhout, 1981).

Southern, R. W., "The English Origins of the 'Miracles of the Virgin,'" *Mediaeval and Renaissance Studies* 4 (1958), pp. 176–216.

Spanu, Pier Giorgio, "*Fons vivus.* Culti delle acque e santuari cristiani tra tarda antichità e alto medioevo," in *L'acqua nei secoli altomedievali* (2 vols., Settimane di Studio 55, 2008), 2, pp. 1029–77, with pls. I–XXXVI.

Spatharakis, Iohannis, *The Portrait in Byzantine Illuminated Manuscripts* (Leiden, 1976).
Spencer, Brian, *Pilgrim Souvenirs and Secular Badges* (Medieval Finds from Excavations in London 7) (London, 1998).
Spiegel, Gabrielle, "The Cult of Saint Denis and Capetian Kingship," *Journal of Medieval History* 1 (1975), pp. 43–69; repr. in Stephen Wilson, ed., *Saints and Their Cults* (Cambridge, 1983), pp. 141–68, and in Spiegel, *The Past as Text* (Baltimore, 1997), pp. 138–62.
Stahl, Alan, *Zecca: The Mint of Venice in the Middle Ages* (Baltimore, 2000).
Stancliffe, Clare, "Red, White and Blue Martyrdom," in *Ireland in Early Medieval Europe: Studies in Memory of Kathleen Hughes*, ed. Dorothy Whitelock et al. (Cambridge, 1982), pp. 21–46.
Stanley, Arthur Penrhyn, *Historical Memorials of Canterbury* (London, 1906).
Staunton, Michael, *Thomas Becket and His Biographers* (Woodbridge, 2006).
Stenton, F. M., "St. Benet of Holme and the Norman Conquest," *English Historical Review* 37 (1922), pp. 225–35.
Stewart, Ian Halley, *The Scottish Coinage* (rev. ed., London, 1967).
Stieglecker, Roland, *Die Renaissance eines Heiligen: Sebastian Brant und Onuphrius eremita* (Wiesbaden, 2001).
Stone, Lawrence, "The Revival of Narrative: Reflections on a New Old History," *Past and Present* 85 (1979), pp. 3–24.
La storia dei giubilei (4 vols., Rome, 1997–2000).
Storrs, Constance Mary, *Jacobean Pilgrims from England to St James of Compostella: From the Early Twelfth to the Late Fifteenth Century* (London, 1998).
Sullivan, Karen, "I do not name to you the voice of St. Michael": The Identification of Joan of Arc's Voices," in *Fresh Verdicts on Joan of Arc*, ed. Bonnie Wheeler and Charles T. Wood (New York and London, 1999), pp. 85–111.
Summerson, Henry, "George (d. c. 303?)," in *Oxford Dictionary of National Biography* (60 vols. plus indices, Oxford, 2004) 21, pp. 775–92.
Sumption, Jonathan, *Pilgrimage: An Image of Medieval Religion* (London, 1975).
Sutton, Anne F., and Livia Visser-Fuchs, *The Hours of Richard III* (Stroud, 1990).
Szakács, Bela Z., "Le culte des saints à la cour et le Légendaire des Anjou-Hongrie," in *L'Europe des Anjou: aventure des princes angevins du XIIIe au XVe siècle* (Paris, 2001), pp. 194–201.
Tabanelli, Mario, *Gli ex-voto poliviscerali etruschi e romani: storia, ritrovamenti, interpretazione* (Florence, 1962).
Talbot, Alice-Mary, "The Anonymous Miracula of the Pege Shrine in Constantinople," *Palaeoslavica* 10.2 (*Essays Presented to Ihor Ševčenko*) (2002), pp. 222–28.
———, "Hagiography in Late Byzantium (1204–1453)," in *The Ashgate Research Companion to Byzantine Hagiography*, ed. Stephanos Efthymiadis (Farnham, 2011), pp. 173–95.
———, "Old Wine in New Bottles: The Rewriting of Saints' Lives in the Palaeologan Period," in *The Twilight of Byzantium: Aspects of Cultural and Religious History in the Late Byzantine Empire*, ed. Slobodan Ćurčić and Doula Mouriki (Princeton, 1991), pp. 15–26.
———, "Pilgrimage to Healing Shrines: The Evidence of Miracle Accounts," *Dumbarton Oaks Papers* 56 (2002), pp. 153–73.
———, "Two Accounts of Miracles at the Pege Shrine in Constantinople," in *Mélanges Gilbert Dagron* (Travaux et Mémoires 14, 2002), pp. 605–15.

Tamburr, Karl, *The Harrowing of Hell in Medieval England* (Cambridge, 2007).

Taralon, Jean, and Dominique Taralon-Carlini, "La Majesté d'or de Sainte Foy de Conques," *Bulletin Monumental* 155 (1997), pp. 11–58.

Taylor, A. J., "Edward I and the Shrine of St. Thomas of Canterbury," *Journal of the British Archaeological Association* 132 (1979), pp. 22–28.

Taylor, Christopher S., *In the Vicinity of the Righteous: Ziyāra and the Veneration of Muslim Saints in Late Medieval Egypt* (Leiden, 1999).

Terian, Abraham, *Patriotism and Piety in Armenian Christianity: The Early Panegyrics on Saint Gregory* (Crestwood, NY, 2005).

Terpstra, Nicholas, *Lay Confraternities and Civic Religion in Renaissance Bologna* (Cambridge, 1995).

El tesoro visigodo de Guarrazar, ed. Alicia Perea (Madrid, 2001).

Thacker, Alan, "Bede and His Martyrology," in *Listen, O Isles, unto Me. Studies in Medieval Word and Image in Honour of Jennifer O'Reilly*, ed. Elizabeth Mullins and Diamuid Scully (Cork, 2011), pp. 126–41, 350–53.

———, "*Membra Disjecta*: The Division of the Body and the Diffusion of the Cult," in *Oswald: Northumbrian King to European Saint*, ed. Clare Stancliffe and Eric Cambridge (Stamford, 1995), pp. 97–127.

———, "*Peculiaris patronus noster*: The Saint as Patron of the State in the Early Middle Ages," in *The Medieval State: Essays Presented to James Campbell*, ed. J. R. Maddicott and D. M. Palliser (London, 2000), pp. 1–24.

———, "Rome of the Martyrs: Saints, Cults and Relics, Fourth to Seventh Centuries," in *Roma felix: Formation and Reflections of Medieval Rome*, ed. Éamonn Ó Carragain and Carol Neuman de Vegvar (Aldershot, 2007), pp. 13–49.

Thoma, Gertrud, *Namensänderungen in Herrscherfamilien des mittelalterlichen Europa* (Munich, 1985).

Thomas, I. G., "The Cult of Saints' Relics in Medieval England" (PhD Thesis, University of London, 1975).

Tolan, John, *Saint Francis and the Sultan: The Curious History of a Christian-Muslim Encounter* (Oxford, 2009).

Tomei, Alessandro, *Iacobus Torriti pictor: una vicenda figurativa del tardo Duecento romano* (Rome, 1990).

Topographie chrétienne des cités de la Gaule 12: *Province ecclésiastique de Cologne*, ed. Nancy Gauthier (Tours, 2002).

Török, Gyöngyi, "Neue Folii aus dem 'Ungarischen Anjou-Legendarium,'" *Zeitschrift für Kunstgeschichte* 55 (1992), pp. 565–77.

Torra, Alberto, "El arca de Sant Cugat: notas hagiográficas y documentales," *Anuario de estudios medievales* 23 (1993), pp. 543–61.

Toynbee, Margaret, *St Louis of Toulouse and the Process of Canonization in the Fourteenth Century* (Manchester, 1929).

Tran Tam Tinh, V., *Isis Lactans: Corpus des monuments greco-romains d'Isis allaitant Harpocrate* (Leiden, 1973).

Treasures of Early Irish Art (New York, 1977).

Treasures of Heaven: Saints, Relics and Devotion in Medieval Europe (New Haven, 2010).

Le trésor de la Sainte-Chapelle, ed. Jannic Durand and Marie-Pierre Laffitte (Paris, 2001).

Trexler, Richard, "Florentine Religious Experience: The Sacred Image," *Studies in the Renaissance* 19 (1972), pp. 7–41.

———, *Public Life in Renaissance Florence* (Ithaca, NY, 1980).
Trombetta, Pierre-Jean, "L'ex-voto au Moyen-Age. Un phénomène sous-estimé," in *Religion and Belief in Medieval Europe: Papers of the "Medieval Europe Brugge 1997" Conference* 4, ed. Guy De Boe and Frans Verhaeghe (Zellik, 1997), pp. 255–64.
Tudor, Victoria, "The Cult of St Cuthbert in the Twelfth Century: The Evidence of Reginald of Durham," in *St Cuthbert, His Cult and Community to AD 1200*, ed. Gerald Bonner et al. (Woodbridge, 1989), pp. 447–67.
———, "The Misogyny of St Cuthbert," *Archaeologia Aeliana* 5th ser., 12 (1984), pp. 157–67.
Turner, D. H., "The Customary of the Shrine of St Thomas Becket," *Canterbury Cathedral Chronicle* 70 (1976), pp. 16–22.
Tyerman, C. J., "Were There Any Crusades in the Twelfth Century?," *English Historical Review* 110 (1995), pp. 553–77.
Ullmann, Walter, "*Romanus Pontifex indubitanter efficitur sanctus*: *Dictatus Papae* 23 in Retrospect and Prospect," *Studi Gregoriani* 6 (1959/61), pp. 229–64.
Valente, Claire, "Simon de Montfort, Earl of Leicester, and the Utility of Sanctity in Thirteenth-Century England," *Journal of Medieval History* 21 (1995), pp. 27–49.
Van Cauwenbergh, Etienne, *Les pélerinages expiatoires et judiciaires dans le droit communal de la Belgique au moyen âge* (Louvain, 1922).
Van Dam, Raymond, *Saints and Their Miracles in Late Antique Gaul* (Princeton, 1993).
Van Esbroek, Michel, "La lettre de l'empereur Justinien sur l'Annociation et la Noël en 561," AB 86 (1968), pp. 351–71.
Van Herwaarden, Jan, "Obligatory Pilgrimages and the Cult of Santiago de Compostela in the Netherlands in the Middle Ages," in *Between Saint James and Erasmus: Studies in Late-Medieval Religious Life: Devotions and Pilgrimages in the Netherlands* (Leiden, 2003), pp. 379–412.
Van Houts, Elisabeth, "Historiography and Hagiography at St-Wandrille: The 'Inventio et Miracula Sancti Uulfranni,'" *Anglo-Norman Studies* 12 (1989), pp. 233–51.
Van Landschoot, Anne, "La translation des reliques de saint Vit de l'abbaye de Saint-Denis à celle de Corvey en 836," *Revue belge de philologie et d'histoire* 74 (1996), pp. 593–632.
Van Os, Henk, *Der Weg zum Himmel: Reliquienverehrung im Mittelalter* (Regensburg, 2001).
Van Straten, F. T., "Gifts for the Gods," in *Faith, Hope and Worship. Aspects of Religious Mentality in the Ancient World*, ed. H. S. Versnel (Leiden, 1981), pp. 65–151.
Van Uytfanghe, Marc, "The Consciousness of a Linguistic Dichotomy (Latin-Romance) in Carolingian Gaul: The Contradictions of the Sources and Their Interpretation," in *Latin and the Romance Languages in the Early Middle Ages*, ed. Roger Wright (London, 1991), pp. 114–29.
———, "La controverse biblique et patristique autour du miracle, et ses répercussions sur l'hagiographie dans l'Antiquité tardive et le haut Moyen Âge latin," in *Hagiographie, cultures et sociétés, IVe–XIIe siècles: Actes du colloque organisé à Nanterre et à Paris 12–5 mai* 1979 (Paris, 1981), pp. 205–33.
Vasella, Oskar, "Flüe, Niklaus von," in *Neue Deutsche Biographie* 5 (Berlin, 1961), p. 260.
Vassilaki, Maria, ed., *Images of the Mother of God: Perceptions of the Theotokos in Byzantium* (Aldershot, 2005).
Vauchez, André, *La sainteté en Occident aux derniers siècles du moyen âge* (Rome, 1981); Eng. tr. *Sainthood in the Late Middle Ages* (Cambridge, 1997).

———, "Saints admirables et saints imitables: les fonctions de l'hagiographie ont-elles changé aux derniers siècles du Moyen Age?," in *Les fonctions des saints dans le monde occidental (IIIe–XIIIe siècle)* (Rome, 1991), pp. 161–72.

———, "The Stigmata of St. Francis and Its Medieval Detractors," *Greyfriars Review* 13 (1999), pp. 61–89 (translated from *Mélanges de l'Ecole française de Rome* 80 [1968], pp. 596–625).

Vázquez de Parga, Luis, José María Lacarra, and Juan Uría Ríu, *Las peregrinaciones a Santiago de Compostela* (3 vols., Madrid, 1948–49).

Verzone, Paolo, "Les églises du haut Moyen Age et le culte des anges," in *L'art mosan*, ed. Pierre Francastel (Paris, 1953), pp. 71–80.

Veyrard-Cosme, Christiane, "Alcuin et la réécriture hagiographique: d'un programme avoué d'*emendatio* à son actualisation," in *La réécriture hagiographique dans l'Occident médiéval: transformations formelles et idéologiques*, ed. Monique Goullet and Martin Heinzelmann (Ostfildern, 2003), pp. 71–86.

Vidas, Marina, "Elizabeth of Bosnia, Queen of Hungary, and the Tomb-Shrine of St. Simeon in Zadar: Power and Relics in Fourteenth-Century Dalmatia," *Studies in Iconography* 29 (2008), pp. 136–75.

Vies des saints et des bienheureux, ed. Jules Baudot and Léon Chaussin and (from vol. 4) Les RR. PP. Bénédictins de Paris (13 vols., Paris, 1935–59).

Vikan, Gary, "Byzantine Pilgrims' Art," in *Heaven on Earth: Art and the Church in Byzantium*, ed. Linda Safran (University Park, PA, 1998), pp. 229–66.

———, *Early Byzantine Pilgrimage Art* (2nd ed., Washington, DC, 2010).

Vio, Gastone, *Le scuole piccole nella Venezia dei dogi* (Vicenza, 2004).

Vocino, Giorgia, "Le traslazioni di reliquie in età carolingia (fine VIII–IX secolo): uno studio comparativo," *Rivista di storia e letteratura religiosa* 44 (2008), pp. 207–55.

Vogtherr, Thomas, *Der König und der Heilige: Heinrich IV., der heilige Remaclus und die Mönche des Doppelklosters Stablo-Malmedy* (Munich, 1990).

Volkmar, Christoph, *Die Heiligenerhebung Bennos von Meißen (1523/24)* (Münster, 2002).

Volp, Ulrich, *Tod und Ritual in den christlichen Gemeinde der Antike* (Leiden, 2002).

Vos, Dirk de, *Hans Memling: The Complete Works* (London, 1994).

Wacht, Manfred, "Inkubation," in *Reallexikon für Antike und Christentum* 18 (Stuttgart, 1998), cols. 179–265.

Wagner, Anne, "Collection de reliques et pouvoir épiscopal au Xe siècle: L'exemple de l'évêque Thierry 1er de Metz," *Revue d'histoire de l'Eglise de France* 83 (1997), pp. 317–41.

Walker, P.W.L., *Holy City, Holy Places?: Christian Attitudes to Jerusalem and the Holy Land in the Fourth Century* (Oxford, 1989).

Walker, Rose, *Views of Transition: Liturgy and Illumination in Medieval Spain* (London, 1998).

Walker, Simon, "Political Saints in Later Medieval England," in *The McFarlane Legacy: Studies in Late Medieval Politics and Society*, ed. R. H. Britnell and A. J. Pollard (Stroud, 1995), pp. 77–106 (reprinted in Walker, *Political Culture in Late Medieval England*, ed. Mike Braddick [Manchester, 2006], pp. 198–222).

Wallach, Luitpold, *Alcuin and Charlemagne: Studies in Carolingian History and Literature* (Ithaca, NY, 1959).

Wallfahrten in der europäischen Kultur/ Pilgrimage in European Culture. Tagungsband Příbram, 26.–29. Mai 2004 / Proceedings of the Symposium Příbram, May 26th–29th 2004, ed. Daniel Doležal and Hartmut Kühne (Frankfurt am Main, 2006).

Wallfahrt kennt keine Grenzen, ed. Lenz Kriss-Rettenbeck and Gerda Möhler (Munich, 1984).

Wallfahrt und Alltag in Mittelalter und früher Neuzeit (Österreichische Akademie der Wissenschaften, Philosophisch-Historische Klasse, Sitzungsberichte 592, Vienna, 1992).

Walter, Christopher, *The Warrior Saints in Byzantine Art and Tradition* (Aldershot, 2003).

Ward, Benedicta, *Harlots of the Desert: A Study of Repentance in Early Monastic Sources* (Kalamazoo, 1987).

———, *Miracles and the Medieval Mind: Theory, Record and Event 1000–1215* (Aldershot and Philadelphia, 1982).

Warner, Marina, *Alone of All Her Sex* (London, 1976).

Warr, Cordelia, "Hermits, Habits and History—The Dress of the Augustinian Hermits," in *Art and the Augustinian Order in Early Renaissance Italy*, ed. Louise Bourdua and Anne Dunlop (Aldershot, 2007), pp. 17–28.

———, "Visualizing Stigmata: Stigmatic Saints and Crises of Representation in Late Medieval and Early Modern Italy," in *Saints and Sanctity*, ed. Peter Clarke and Tony Claydon (Studies in Church History 47, 2011), pp. 228–47.

Wasyliw, Patricia Healy, *Martyrdom, Murder, and Magic: Child Saints and Their Cults in Medieval Europe* (New York, 1996).

Webb, Diana, *Medieval European Pilgrimage, c. 700–c. 1500* (New York, 2002).

———, *Patrons and Defenders: The Saints in the Italian City-states* (London, 1996).

———, "Sanctity and History: Antonio Agli and Humanist Hagiography," in *Florence and Italy: Renaissance Studies in Honour of Nicolai Rubinstein*, ed. Peter Denley and Caroline Elam (London, 1988), pp. 297–308.

Weigert, Laura, *Weaving Sacred Stories: French Choir Tapestries and the Performance of Clerical Identity* (Ithaca, NY, 2004).

Weilandt, Gerhard, "Heiligen-Konjunktur: Reliquienpräsentation, Reliquienverehrung und wirtschaftliche Situation an der Nürnberger Lorenzkirche im Spätmittelalter," in *Von Goldenen Gebeinen: Wirtschaft und Reliquie im Mittelalter*, ed. Markus Mayr (Innsbruck, 2001), pp. 186–220.

Weinstein, Donald, and Rudolph M. Bell, *Saints and Society: The Two Worlds of Western Christendom, 1000–1700* (Chicago, 1982).

Wenz-Haubfleisch, Annegret, *Miracula post mortem: Studien zum Quellenwert hochmittelalterlicher Mirakelsammlungen vornehmlich des ostfränkisch-deutschen Reiches* (Siegburg, 1998).

West, C.M.A., "Unauthorised Miracles in Mid-Ninth-Century Dijon and the Carolingian Church Reforms," *Journal of Medieval History* 36 (2010), pp. 295–311.

Westlake, H. F., *The Parish Guilds of Mediaeval England* (London, 1919).

Wetzstein, Thomas, *Heilige vor Gericht. Das Kanonisationsverfahren im europäischen Spätmittelalter* (Cologne, 2004).

———, "*Virtus morum et virtus signorum*? Zur Bedeutung der Mirakel in den Kanonisationsprozessen des 15. Jahrhunderts," in *Mirakel im Mittelalter: Konzeptionen, Erscheinungsformen, Deutungen*, ed. Martin Heinzelmann et al. (Stuttgart, 2002), pp. 351–76.

Whatley, E. G., "Late Old English Hagiography, ca. 950–1150," in *Hagiographies* 2, pp. 429–99.

Wickham, Chris, *Framing the Early Middle Ages: Europe and the Mediterranean, 400–800* (Oxford, 2005).

Wieck, Roger S., *Painted Prayers: The Book of Hours in Medieval and Renaissance Art* (New York, 1997).

———, *Time Sanctified: The Book of Hours in Medieval Art and Life* (New York, 1988).

Wiegand, Theodor, *Milet: Ergebnisse der Ausgrabungen und Untersuchungen* 3/1: *Der Latmos* (Berlin, 1913).

Williams, Caroline, "The Cult of 'Alid Saints in the Fatimid Monuments of Cairo. Part II: The Mausolea," *Muqarnas* 3 (1985), pp. 39–60.

Williams-Krapp, Werner, *Deutschen und niederländischen Legendare des Mittelalters: Studien zu ihrer Überlieferungs-, Text- und Wirkungsgeschichte* (Tübingen, 1986).

Williamson, Beth, "Altarpieces, Liturgy, and Devotion," *Speculum* 79 (2004), pp. 341–406.

Wilson, Stephen, *The Means of Naming: A Social and Cultural History of Personal Naming in Western Europe* (London, 1998).

Winstead, Karen A., *Virgin Martyrs: Legends of Sainthood in Late Medieval England* (Ithaca, NY, 1997).

Wirth, Jean, "Image et relique dans le cristianisme occidental," in *Les objets de la mémoire* (Bern, 2005), pp. 325–42.

Wittekind, Susanne, "Caput et corpus. Die Bedeutung der Sockel von Kopfreliquiaren," in *Reliquiare im Mittelalter*, ed. Bruno Reudenbach and Gia Toussaint (Berlin, 2005), pp. 107–35.

Wittmer-Butsch, Maria, and Constanze Rendtel, *Miracula: Wunderheilungen im Mittelalter: eine historisch-psychologische Annäherung* (Cologne, 2003).

Wogan-Browne, Jocelyn, "Saints' Lives and the Female Reader," *Forum for Modern Language Studies* 27 (1991), pp. 314–32.

———, *Saints' Lives and Women's Literary Culture c. 1150–1300: Virginity and Its Authorizations* (Oxford, 2001).

Wolf, Gerhard, "Cult Images of the Virgin in Medieval Rome," in *Images of the Mother of God: Perceptions of the Theotokos in Byzantium*, ed. Maria Vassilaki (Aldershot, 2005), pp. 23–49.

Wolf, Gunther, "Die Kanonisationsbulle von 993 für den Hl. Oudalrich von Augsburg und Vergleichbares," *Zeitschrift der Savigny-Stiftung für Rechtsgeschichte (Kanonistische Abteilung)* 122 (2005), pp. 742–57.

Wolf, Kenneth Baxter, *Christian Martyrs in Muslim Spain* (Cambridge, 1988).

———, "The Life and Afterlife of San Isidro Labrador," in *Church, State, Vellum and Stone: Essays on Medieval Spain in Honor of John Williams*, ed. Julie Harris and Therese Martin (Leiden, 2005), pp. 131–43.

Wolverton, Lisa, *Hastening toward Prague: Power and Society in the Medieval Czech Lands* (Philadelphia, 2001).

Wormald, Francis, "Some Illustrated Manuscripts of the Lives of the Saints," *Bulletin of the John Rylands Library* 35 (1952/3), pp. 248–66.

Wortley, John, "The Earliest Relic-Importations to Constantinople," in *Studies on the Cult of Relics in Byzantium up to 1204* (Farnham, 2009), pp. 207–25 (item IV).

———, "Iconoclasm and Leipsanoclasm: Leo III, Constantine V and the Relics," *Byzantinische Forschungen* 8 (1982), pp. 253–79 (reprinted in *Studies on the Cult of Relics in Byzantium up to 1204* [Farnham, 2009], item VII).

Wünsch, Thomas, "Der Heilige Bischof: Zur politischen Dimension von Heiligkeit im Mittealter und ihrem Wandel," *Archiv für Kulturgeschichte* 82 (2000), pp. 261–302.

Wyatt, David K., "Relics, Oaths and Politics in Thirteenth-century Siam," *Journal of Southeast Asian Studies* 32 (2001), pp. 3–66.

Yarrow, Simon, *Saints and Their Communities: Miracle Stories in Twelfth-century England* (Oxford, 2006).

Yasin, Ann Marie, *Saints and Church Spaces in the Late Antique Mediterranean: Architecture, Cult, and Community* (Cambridge, 2009).

Yates, Jonathan, "Augustine's Appropriation of Cyprian the Martyr-Bishop against the Pelagians," in *More than a Memory: The Discourse of Martyrdom and the Construction of Christian Identity in the History of Christianity*, ed. Johan Leemans (Louvain, 2005), pp. 119–35.

Yates, W. N., "The Distribution and Proportion of Celtic and non-Celtic Dedications in Wales," *Journal of the Historical Society of the Church in Wales* 23 (1973), pp. 5–17.

Yeoman, Peter A., "Saint Margaret's Shrine at Dunfermline Abbey," in *Royal Dunfermline*, ed. Richard Fawcett (Edinburgh, 2005), pp. 79–88.

Young, Karl, *The Drama of the Medieval Church* (2 vols., Oxford, 1933).

Załuska, Yolanta, *L'enluminure et le Scriptorium de Cîteaux au XIIe siècle* (Cîteaux, 1989).

Zanetti, Ugo, "Fêtes des anges dans les calendriers et synaxaires orientaux," in *Culto e insediamenti micaelici nell'Italia meridionale fra tardo antichità e medioevo*, ed. Carlo Carletti and Giorgio Otranto (Bari, 1994), pp. 323–49.

Zatta, Jane Dick, "The 'Vie Seinte Osith': Hagiography and Politics in Anglo-Norman England," *Papers on Language and Literature* 41 (2005), pp. 306–38 (originally published in *Studies in Philology* 96 [1999], pp. 367–93).

Das Zeichen am Hut im Mittelalter. Europäische Reisemarkierungen. Symposion in memoriam Kurt Köster (1912–1986) und Katalog der Pilgerzeichen im Kunstgewerbemuseum und im Museum für Byzantinische Kunst der Staatlichen Museen zu Berlin, ed. Hartmut Kühne et al. (Europäische Wallfahrtsstudien 4, Frankfurt am Main, 2008).

Zender, M., and J. Fellenberg gen. Reinold, "Reliquientranslationen zwischen 600 und 1200," in *Atlas zur Kirchengeschichte*, ed. Hubert Jedin et al. (2nd ed., Freiburg, 1987), pp. 24*–25*, map 28.

Zettler, Alfons, "Die politischen Dimensionen des Markuskults im hochmittelalterlichen Venedig," in *Politik und Heiligenverehrung im Hochmittelalter*, ed. Jürgen Petersohn (Vorträge und Forschungen 42, Sigmaringen, 1994), pp. 541–71.

Ziegler, Joseph, "Practitioners and Saints: Medical Men in Canonization Processes in the Thirteenth to Fifteenth Centuries," *Social History of Medicine* 12 (1999), pp. 191–225.

Zimmermann, Gerd, "Die Cyriakus-Schlacht bei Kitzingen (8.8.1266) in Tradition und Forschung," *Jahrbuch für Fränkischen Landesforschung* 27 (1967), pp. 417–25.

———, "Patrozinienwahl und Frömmigkeitswandel im Mittelalter, dargestellt an Beispielen aus dem alten Bistum Würzburg," *Würzburger Diözesangeschichtsblätter* 20 (1958), pp. 24–126; 21 (1959), pp. 5–124.

Zimmermann, Michel, "Aux origines de la Catalogne féodale: les serments non datés du règne de Ramon Berenguer Ier," in *La Formació i expansió del feudalisme Català*, ed. Jaume Portella i Comas (Girona, 1986), pp. 109–49.

Zocca, Elena, *Dai "santi" al "santo." Un percorso storico-linguistico intorno all'idea di santità (Africa romana, secc. II–V)* (Verba seniorum, n.s. 13, Rome, 2003).

Zoepf, Ludwig, *Das Heiligen-Leben im 10 Jht.* (Leipzig and Berlin, 1908).

Zwierlein-Diehl, Erika, *Die Gemmen und Kameen des Dreikönigenschreines* (Studien zum Kölner Dom 5, Cologne, 1998).

INDEX

Page numbers of sustained discussions are in bold. Saints are indexed under their proper names, but churches and places dedicated to saints are indexed under the abbreviations or words for *saint* in the languages used in the countries discussed in the book.